D0208628

ALMANACS OF AMERICAN WARS

# WORLD WAR II ALMANAC

## VOLUME II

Keith D. Dickson

Facts On File

*An imprint of Infobase Publishing*

**World War II Almanac**

Facts On File, Inc.
An imprint of Infobase Publishing
132 West 31st Street
New York NY 10001

**Library of Congress Cataloging-in-Publication Data**

Dickson, Keith D.
   World War II almanac / Keith D. Dickson.
      p. cm. — (Almanacs of American wars)
   Includes bibliographical references and index.
   ISBN 13: 978-0-8160-6297-3 (hc : alk. paper)
   1. World War, 1939–1945—Almanacs. 2. World War, 1939–1945—Chronology. 3. Almanacs, American. I. Title. II. Title: World War Two almanac. III. Title: World War 2 almanac.
   D731.D53 2008
   940.540973'03—dc22    2007011207

Facts On File books are available at special discounts when purchased in bulk quantities for businesses, associations, institutions, or sales promotions. Please call our Special Sales Department in New York at (212) 967-8800 or (800) 322-8755.

You can find Facts On File on the World Wide Web at http://www.factsonfile.com

Text design by Erika K. Arroyo
Cover design by Pehrsson Design/Salvatore Luongo

Printed in the United States of America

VB Hermitage 10 9 8 7 6 5 4 3 2 1

This book is printed on acid-free paper and contains 30 percent postconsumer recycled content.

# CONTENTS

## VOLUME I

## VOLUME II

# ≡ August 8, 1944– November 19, 1945

## Chronology of Key Events *continued*

## August 8

**CBI:** In China, Japanese forces capture Hengyang after a seven-week battle. Although unable to stop the Japanese offensive, American air power is able to slow down the speed of the enemy advance.

The fall of the city opens the Allied airbases at Lingling and Kweilin to Japanese attack; they are the next objectives of the enemy offensive.

Fourteenth Air Force P-40s attack trucks and barges near Hengyang.

**ETO:** The VIII Corps clears the Brittany Peninsula of German forces except for port cities, of which only a few are deemed essential to the Allied operation in France.

There exists an opportunity for Allied forces to trap major German combat units between Falaise and Argentan. Eisenhower, Bradley, and Montgomery, seeing the possibilities offered by the German counterattack at Mortain, issue plans to subordinates. General Bradley directs Third Army to shift its advance to the northeast, to Alençon, and prepare to attack toward Argentan in the rear of German forces and link with Canadian forces encircling from the north and headed for Argentan. First Army is to continue its drive along the Vire-Mortain-Domfront line. The 2nd and 3rd Armored Divisions move to cut off the attacking German forces at Ger and Domfront. The Third Army captures LeMans and advances to cut supply lines at Alençon near Falaise. XX Corps elements reach the Loire River.

The First Airborne Army is formed under the command of Lieutenant General Lewis H. Brereton. The army is composed of the XVIII Airborne Corps (the 82nd, 101st, and 17th Airborne Divisions), commanded by Major General Matthew B. Ridgway, the British 1st and 6th Airborne Divisions, the IX Troop Carrier Command, and two Royal Air Force troop carrier groups.

In support of Frantic operations 78 B-17s with 55 P-51 Mustangs as escort fly from airfields in Soviet Ukraine to attack airfields in Romania en route to bases in Italy. Eighth Air Force sends 681 B-17s and 414 B-24 Liberators escorted by 365 P-47 Thunderbolts and P-51 Mustangs to attack V-weapon sites in the Pas-de-Calais area and railroad bridges and airfields in France. Eight bombers are lost and 438 are damaged. Aircrews report one confirmed kill. Aircrew losses are 18 killed, 24 wounded, and 44 missing. Fighter pilots report four confirmed kills and one probable. Five fighters are lost and the pilots are reported missing.

P-51s escort RAF Coastal Command Beaufighters (two-seat long-range maritime strike aircraft) on a convoy strike in Norway. Three P-51s are lost and three damaged. One pilot is wounded and three are reported missing.

Over 170 P-38 Lightnings, P-47 Thunderbolts, and P-51 Mustangs conduct fighter-bomber attacks on rail lines. Four fighters are lost and three are damaged. Five pilots are reported missing.

During the night five B-17s drop leaflets over France.

Lieutenant General Hoyt S. Vandenberg is designated as commander of the Ninth Air Force.

Ninth Air Force A-20 Havocs and B-26 Marauders attack bridges, a radar site, and fly ground support missions. P-47 and P-38 fighters fly armed reconnaissance missions.

German submarine *U-667* torpedoes a U.S. freighter in a convoy in the English Channel; the freighter is abandoned by the crew and sunk with a second torpedo.

**ITALY:** Twelfth Air Force B-25 Mitchells and B-26 Marauders attack rail lines and bridges in the Po and Rhône Valleys. A-20 Havocs attack logistics storage areas. P-47 Thunderbolts attack convoys and bridges.

**PACIFIC:** U.S. submarine *Sterlet* torpedoes and sinks a Japanese auxiliary submarine chaser near Chichi Jima.

**CENTRAL PACIFIC:** Seventh Air Force B-25 Mitchells from the Marshalls bomb Ponape Island and B-24 Liberators bomb Truk.

Destroyers USS *Gansevoort* and *Bancroft* and land-based Marine Corps aircraft from Majuro attack Japanese positions on Maloelap Atoll.

**CENTRAL PACIFIC, GUAM:** The 305th and 307th Infantry Regiments of the 77th Infantry Division capture Mount Santa Rosa, supported by a flanking attack by the 306th Infantry.

Seventh Air Force B-25 Mitchells from Saipan bomb Japanese defenses.

**NEW GUINEA:** FEAF B-24 Liberators bomb targets near Manokwari. A-20 Havocs bomb a radio station near Hollandia. B-24 Liberators bomb Yap Island and airfields on Halmahera Island.

## August 9

**CBI:** Tenth Air Force receives the 426th Night Fighter Squadron. The squadron, equipped with P-61 Black Widow night fighters, arrives at Madhaiganj, India, from the United States.

In China, Fourteenth Air Force B-25 Mitchells bomb targets near Hengyang. P-40s and P-51 Mustangs attack trucks, gun positions, and Japanese troops around Hengyang and Siangtan and destroy a pontoon bridge near Changsha.

**ETO:** The XV Corps (5th Armored Division, French 2nd Armored Division, 79th and 90th Infantry Divisions) of Third Army attacks toward Alençon, advancing toward the rear of German forces at Mortain.

Eighth Air Force sends 577 B-17s and 247 B-24 Liberators, escorted by 570 P-38 Lightnings, P-47 Thunderbolts, and P-51 Mustangs, to attack aircraft production and tank production facilities in southeast Germany. Weather conditions force most of the bombers to abort the mission or strike targets of opportunity. Eighteen bombers are lost and 381 are damaged. Aircrews report one confirmed kill. Aircrew losses are two killed, 20 wounded, and 153 missing. Fighter pilots report 39 confirmed kills in the air and 24 on the ground. Three fighters are lost and seven are damaged. Three pilots are reported missing.

More than 110 P-47s escorted by 40 P-51 Mustangs conduct fighter-bomber attacks on German communication targets in France.

B-17s escorted by 16 P-38s fly a Micro H radar (micro H was a combo of two earlier radar targeting systems used to guide bombers to targets) pathfinder test mission against Aubigny airfield in France.

During the night six B-17s drop leaflets over the Netherlands and France.

Ninth Air Force sends nearly 400 A-20 Havocs and B-26 Marauders to attack ammunition storage sites and railroad bridges. P-47 and P-38 fighters fly armed reconnaissance missions.

Captain Darrell R. Lindsey leads a formation of 30 B-26 Marauders of the 394th Bomber Group, Ninth Air Force, to destroy the L'lsle Adam railroad bridge over the Seine River. The bridge is a critical target as it is one of the few crossing points left that will allow German forces to escape to safety as Allied armored divisions race to cut off the enemy's path of retreat. The bridge is heavily defended with antiaircraft guns. As Lindsey begins his bombing run, his B-26's right engine bursts into flames from antiaircraft fire. Without hesitation, Lindsey returns to the formation and presses the attack even as the right wing of his aircraft is covered in flames. Lindsey drops his bombs on target and then gives the order for the crew to bail out and brings the aircraft to a lower altitude. Just as the last crewman exits the aircraft, the bomber explodes and crashes. For his superb skill as a pilot and his cool courage in the face of certain death, Captain Lindsey will receive the Medal of Honor.

**MEDITERRANEAN:** The Dragoon invasion force leaves Naples, Italy, for southern France with 151,000 men and 19,400 vehicles.

Fifteenth Air Force sends more than 300 B-17s and B-24 Liberators escorted by P-38 Lightnings and P-51 Mustangs to attack an aircraft assembly plant, airfields, and an oil refinery in Hungary and a marshaling yard and oil refinery in Yugoslavia.

**ITALY:** Twelfth Air Force B-25 Mitchells and B-26 Marauders attack airfields and rail lines. A-20 Havocs bomb targets along the coastal road from Nice, France, to Genoa, Italy. P-47 Thunderbolts attack railroad bridges.

**SOUTHWEST PACIFIC AREA:** U.S. submarine *Seawolf* lands men and supplies on Palawan in the Philippines.

**PACIFIC:** President Roosevelt aboard the destroyer USS *Cummings* visits the Puget Sound Navy Yard.

U.S. submarine *Barbel* torpedoes and sinks two cargo ships in the Ryukyus.

**NEW GUINEA:** FEAF A-20 Havocs, P-39 Airacobras, and P-40s attack troops, shipping, and logistics sites. B-24s bomb Yap and targets at Boela on Ceram and Ambon Islands in the Moluccas.

## August 10

**ALEUTIANS:** Eleventh Air Force B-25 Mitchells on a shipping sweep attack two Japanese patrol boats off Shimushu Island in the Kuriles. Aircrews report one boat sunk and the other damaged.

**CBI:** Because it is no longer combat effective, the 5307th Composite Unit (Provisional), known as Merrill's Marauders, is disbanded. The unit has suffered 2,394 casualties (sick, killed, wounded, and missing) during the campaign.

The Fourteenth Air Force reports that since its operations against Japanese ground forces in China began on May 26 over 100 Japanese aircraft have been destroyed, along with nearly 600 trucks, 1,000 small boats used for supply, and 100 bridges. During this same period three U.S. aircraft have been lost in combat.

In China, Fourteenth Air Force P-40s strafe Taiyuan airfield. Pilots report more than 20 Japanese aircraft destroyed on the ground. Other P-40s attack trucks at Siangtan and Changsha.

**ETO:** The VII Corps, supported by IX Tactical Air Force, halts the German counterattack at Mortain.

The 5th Infantry Division captures Nantes. The XX Corps captures Angers in support of XV Corps.

Eighth Air Force sends 175 B-24 Liberators escorted by 249 P-51 Mustangs to attack fuel dumps and bridges near Paris. One B-24 is lost and 20 are damaged. Aircrew losses are one wounded and one missing. Fighter pilots report eight confirmed kills. Three fighters are lost; three pilots are reported missing.

A total of 583 P-38 Lightnings and P-51s attack rail targets in France. Fighter pilots report 19 confirmed kills. Two P-38s and four P-51s are lost.

During the night one B-17 drops leaflets over Brest, France.

The B-24s of the 856th, 857th, 858th, and 859th Bombardment Squadrons (Heavy) of the 492nd Bombardment Group (Heavy) are tasked to support Carpetbagger operations.

Ninth Air Force sends 200 A-20 Havocs and B-26 Marauders to attack railroad bridges near Paris. P-47 and P-38 fighters fly armed reconnaissance missions near Paris and Amiens.

**MEDITERRANEAN:** Fifteenth Air Force sends more than 450 B-17s and B-24 Liberators escorted by P-38 Lightnings and P-51 Mustangs to attack oil refineries at Ploeşti, Romania.

**ITALY:** General Sir Harold R. L. G. Alexander holds a conference with his commanders to map out future operations of the Allied ground forces in Italy. The Anvil-Dragoon operation has drawn down much of the combat strength of Fifth Army, leaving the British Eighth Army with the preponderance of forces. Alexander proposes an offensive along the eastern coast of Italy, with Eighth Army to break the German line and drive into the broad open plains and outflank the Gothic Line. General Mark Clark's Fifth Army will gain operational control of the British XIII Corps to conduct supporting attacks toward Pistoia in order to hold the Germans in place five days after the Eighth Army begins its attack. The attack is named Operation Olive and is scheduled for August 25.

Twelfth Air Force P-47 Thunderbolts attack gun positions on the southern coast of France in preparation for Dragoon.

**SOUTHWEST PACIFIC AREA:** U.S. submarine *Guitarro* attacks a Japanese convoy off the northwest coast of Luzon, sinking a merchant tanker.

**PACIFIC:** During the night Twentieth Air Force sends 24 B-29 Superfortresses from Chengtu, China, to bomb the city of Nagasaki, Japan. Aircrews report one confirmed fighter kill, the first for the B-29. Another 31 B-29 Superfortresses staging through China Bay on Ceylon bomb oil refineries at Palembang, Sumatra, and mine the Moesi River. This 3,900-mile single-stage combat flight is the longest by B-29s during the war.

U.S. submarine *Bowfin* torpedoes and sinks a cargo ship in the Ryukyus.

**CENTRAL PACIFIC:** Seventh Air Force B-24 Liberators flying from Saipan make the first attack on Iwo Jima Island in the Volcano Islands. P-47 Thunderbolts from Saipan attack Japanese fighters still resisting on Tinian. B-24s from Kwajalein bomb Wotje Atoll.

**CENTRAL PACIFIC, GUAM:** Army and marine units eliminate the last Japanese tanks and organized units in the northern tip of the island. Major General Roy S. Geiger declares Guam secured. Lieutenant General Alexander A. Vandegrift and Admiral Nimitz arrive to establish their headquarters. The battle for Guam cost the United States over 1,700 dead and 5,900 wounded.

**NEW GUINEA:** The last Japanese forces resisting near the Driniumor River are eliminated. Those who have not been killed have retreated toward Wewak. The 43rd Infantry Division takes over the Driniumor-Aitape defenses. The Japanese have lost over 8,800 men in 30 days of near continuous combat. American losses stand at 597 killed, 1,691 wounded, and 85 missing.

FEAF B-25 Mitchells, A-20s, and P-38 Lightnings attack targets around Geelvink Bay. P-39 Airacobras, P-38 Lightnings, P-40s, and P-47 Thunderbolts attack Japanese positions between Aitape and Wewak.

At Noemfoor, the last defenders are encountered at Hill 380 and eliminated by elements of the 503rd Parachute Infantry. The battle for the island costs the Americans 65 killed and 343 wounded. Over 2,000 Japanese are killed.

U.S. submarine *Cod* torpedoes and sinks a Japanese auxiliary submarine chaser south of Celebes Island.

## August 11

**ALEUTIANS:** Eleventh Air Force B-25 Mitchells sink a Japanese guardboat east of Paramushiru, Kuriles.

## August 11

**CBI:** Tenth Air Force P-40s attack a Japanese headquarters at Bhamo.

In China, Fourteenth Air Force sends 23 B-24 Liberators to bomb Changsha. Another 16 B-25s bomb Hengyang, and more than 40 P-51 Mustangs and P-40s bomb bridges, villages, logistics storage facilities, vehicles, and troop assembly areas near Hengyang.

A cargo vessel is damaged by a mine laid by Twentieth Air Force B-29s near Palembang, Sumatra.

**ETO:** The 30th Infantry Division recaptures Mortain. The failed German counterattack at Mortain leaves German forces nearly surrounded on three sides by Allied divisions.

Eighth Air Force sends 408 B-17s and 406 B-24 Liberators escorted by 365 P-38 Lightnings and P-51 Mustangs to attack transportation targets, fuels storage sites, and airfields in France. Five bombers are lost and 188 are damaged. Aircrew losses are three killed, eight wounded, and 28 missing. One P-51 is lost and one P-51 is damaged. One pilot is wounded and one is reported missing.

A total of 28 B-24s fly in support of Carpetbagger operations. During the night six B-17s drop leaflets over France.

Ninth Air Force A-20 Havocs and B-26 Marauders attack bridges and an ammunition storage area. P-47 and P-38 fighters fly armed reconnaissance missions over northern France.

**ITALY:** Twelfth Air Force B-25 Mitchells, B-26 Marauders, and P-47 Thunderbolts strike gun positions along the French and Italian coasts as the Dragoon invasion force departs Naples for France.

**PACIFIC:** U.S. submarine *Tang* attacks a Japanese convoy off southern Honshu, sinking a merchant cargo ship.

**CENTRAL PACIFIC:** Seventh Air Force B-25 Mitchells from Makin Island bomb Ponape Island.

**CENTRAL PACIFIC, GUAM:** The day after the island is declared secured, the 306th Infantry Regiment assaults the command post of General Obata on Mount Mataguac. This will be the pattern of action on Guam until the end of the war. Although almost 11,000 Japanese soldiers have been killed, an estimated 10,000 still live in the hills and jungle. American troops will encounter Japanese throughout the next year, and another 8,500 will be killed in skirmishes. For years after the war, gaunt Japanese soldiers will continue to emerge from the thickets, unable to believe that Japan has surrendered.

**NEW GUINEA:** FEAF A-20 Havocs attack shipping, barges, and a radar station along the coast of Geelvink Bay. A-20s attack a Japanese headquarters near Sawar. P-39 Airacobras attack troops, logistics sites, and barges.

U.S. submarine *Cod* torpedoes and sinks a Japanese cargo ship south of Celebes Island.

## August 12

**ALEUTIANS:** Eleventh Air Force sends four B-24 Liberators to attack shipping in Higashi Banjo Strait and buildings and a runway on Suribachi in the Kurile Islands. Aircrews report three confirmed kills and 13 probables.

**CBI:** In China, Fourteenth Air Force B-25 Mitchells bomb the railyards at Hengyang. P-51 Mustangs and P-40s attack targets of opportunity around the area.

**ETO:** The XV Corps of Third Army captures Alençon. Patton orders an attack toward Argentan. The 5th Armored Division approaches Argentan; the French 2nd Armored Division is at Ecouche.

Eighth Air Force sends 301 B-17s and 276 B-24 Liberators, escorted by 386 P-47 Thunderbolts and P-51 Mustangs, to attack airfields and marshaling yards in eastern France. Three bombers are lost and 76 are damaged. Aircrew losses are 19 killed, eight wounded, and 32 missing. Fighter pilots report one confirmed kill. Three P-51s are lost, and the three pilots are reported missing.

Nearly 500 P-38 Lightnings, P-47s, and P-51s attack transportation targets in the Paris and Brussels areas. Fighter pilots report five confirmed kills in the air and 13 on the ground. Thirteen fighters are lost, and the pilots are reported missing.

More than 200 P-47s and P-51s attack transportation targets in northeast France. Two P-51s are lost and three are damaged. The pilots are reported missing.

During the night six B-17s drop leaflets over France. A total of 72 B-17s and 62 P-51 Mustangs supporting Frantic operations depart Fifteenth Air Force bases in Italy, and most bomb an airfield in southern France before landing in Britain.

Ninth Air Force sends A-20 Havocs and B-26 Marauders to attack fuel storage sites and roads in the Argentan area. P-47 and P-38 fighters fly armed reconnaissance missions and support ground forces.

**MEDITERRANEAN:** Fifteenth Air Force sends more than 300 B-17s and B-24 Liberators escorted by P-51 Mustangs to attack German positions around Toulon and Marseille, France, and Genoa, Italy, in preparation for Operation Dragoon.

**ITALY:** Twelfth Air Force B-25 Mitchells and B-26 Marauders along with A-20 Havocs and P-47 Thunderbolts attack defensive positions north of the Arno River.

**SOUTHWEST PACIFIC AREA:** U.S. submarine *Puffer* attacks a Japanese convoy off Mindoro, sinking a tanker and damaging another tanker.

**PACIFIC:** President Roosevelt departs Puget Sound to return to Washington.

U.S. submarine *Pompon* attacks a Japanese convoy in the Sea of Okhotsk, damaging a cargo ship east of Sakhalin Island.

**CENTRAL PACIFIC:** Seventh Air Force B-24 Liberators from Saipan bomb shipping, the seaplane base, and the airfield at Chichi Jima Island in the Bonin Islands. B-25 Mitchells from the Gilbert Islands bomb Nauru Island. B-24s from the Marshall Islands bomb Truk.

**NEW GUINEA:** FEAF A-20 Havocs P-39 Airacobras, and P-47 Thunderbolts attack Japanese troops and targets of opportunity in the Sarmi area.

The B-24 Liberators of the 321st and 400th Bombardment Squadrons (Heavy) of the 90th Bombardment Group (Heavy) redeploy to Biak Island.

## August 13

**ALEUTIANS:** Eleventh Air Force sends six B-25 Mitchells to fly a shipping sweep over the Kurile Islands. Aircrews report one Japanese fighter shot down.

**CBI:** In China, Fourteenth Air Force sends more than 30 B-25 Mitchells to bomb Hengyang, and Pailochi airfield as well as shipping. Aircrews report three cargo ships sunk. P-40s and P-51 Mustangs attack trucks, bridges, railyards, and Japanese troops near Hengyang. P-40s and P-38 Lightnings attack Tengchung.

**ETO:** German forces begin to withdraw from their exposed position near Mortain. The XV Corps of Third Army reaches Argentan and holds against heavy German assaults. General Bradley orders Patton to stop his advance beyond Argentan to allow British forces to advance. This is the boundary line between the British and American army groups. He is also concerned by Ultra intercepts that indicate the Germans intend to counterattack Bradley's widely spread forces. The Germans begin a general withdrawal to the Seine River as Field Marshal Montgomery's 21st Army Group attacks southward. The boundary leaves a gap through which several German divisions escape.

A total of 37 P-47 Thunderbolts discover 800 to 1,000 enemy vehicles of all types in the pocket west of Argentan. In just one hour, the P-47s make continuous attacks until they are out of ammunition. They report nearly 500 vehicles destroyed. One pilot even drops his belly tank on a group of 12 trucks and reports that all were burning. The XIX TAC P-47s have destroyed or damaged more than 1,000 vehicles, 45 tanks and armored vehicles, and 12 locomotives. Inside the pocket they also report destroying 10 German strongpoints.

Eighth Air Force sends 798 B-17s and 466 B-24 Liberators escorted by 131 P-51 Mustangs to support ground forces and attack coastal batteries and transportation targets between Le Havre and Paris. Twelve bombers are lost and 485 are damaged. Aircrew casualties are three killed, 12 wounded, and 113 missing.

One Aphrodite B-17 carrying a 2,000-pound bomb load is launched against Le Havre. The bomber misses its target, and an RAF Mosquito fighter-bomber accompanying the bomber is destroyed in the explosion.

Over 800 P-38 Lightnings, P-47 Thunderbolts, and P-51s fly fighter-bomber missions against transportation targets along the Seine River. A total of 13 fighters are lost and five are damaged. One pilot is killed, one wounded, and 13 are missing.

Two B-17s fly a Micro H radar test mission over France.

A total of 36 B-24s fly in support of Carpetbagger operations. During the night six B-17s drop leaflets over Belgium, France, and the Netherlands.

Ninth Air Force sends nearly 600 A-20 Havocs and B-26 Marauders to attack fuel storage sites, roads, ammunition storage areas, and troop positions to hold the enemy in the Falaise pocket. P-47 and P-38 fighters support ground forces and fly armed reconnaissance missions.

**Mediterranean:** Fifteenth Air Force sends 424 B-24 Liberators and 136 B-17s attack gun positions and bridges in southern France.

During the night Twelfth Air Force A-20 Havocs attack targets along the Monaco-Toulon road.

**Italy:** Twelfth Air Force B-25 Mitchells and B-26 Marauders attack coastal defense guns around Marseilles. A-20 Havocs attack ammunition storage areas in the Arno River Valley.

**Southwest Pacific Area:** U.S. submarine *Bluegill* attacks a Japanese convoy off Mindanao near Davao Gulf, and sinks a submarine chaser, an auxiliary submarine chaser, and a transport.

**Pacific:** U.S. submarine *Barbel* torpedoes and sinks a Japanese auxiliary in the Ryukyus.

U.S. submarine *Tambor* torpedoes and sinks a Japanese cargo ship in the Sea of Okhotsk.

**New Guinea:** FEAF B-24 Liberators bomb bivouacs and supply dumps at Manokwari. P-47 Thunderbolts and P-39 Airacobras support ground forces at Sarmi.

U.S. submarine *Cod* attacks a Japanese landing ship east of Celebes Island in the Banda Sea, but cannot complete the attack after being engaged by the landing ship with accurate and heavy fire.

U.S. submarine *Flier* is sunk by a mine near North Borneo.

## August 14

**CBI:** In China, Fourteenth Air Force P-40s and P-51 Mustangs bomb the railyards, river shipping, and troop areas at Hengyang.

**ETO:** General Bradley orders Lieutenant General George S. Patton Jr.'s Third Army to disrupt the retreat of German forces by attacking eastward. The XV Corps moves in response to the orders, headed for Dreux.

Eighth Air Force sends B-17s and B-24 Liberators escorted by 388 P-47 Thunderbolts and P-51 Mustangs to attack engine production facilities, airfields, an oil production facility, bridges, and rail lines along the French-German border. Two B-17s are lost and 285 bombers are damaged. Aircrew casualties are 10 wounded and 18 missing. Fighter pilots report 18 confirmed kills. One P-51 is lost. The pilot is reported missing.

Over 130 P-38s and P-47s fly fighter-bomber missions in the Paris area. Fighter pilots report three confirmed kills. One P-38 and two P-47s are lost and three fighters are damaged. Two pilots are reported missing.

A total of 37 B-24s fly in support of Carpetbagger operations. One B-24 is lost. During the night six B-17s drop leaflets over France.

Ninth Air Force sends A-20 Havocs and B-26 Marauders to attack railroad bridges and rail targets to delay the German retreat across France. P-47 and P-38 fighters support ground forces and actually take the surrender of some German troops near Carrouges who had experienced more than enough of American air power over the past few weeks. The soldiers wave white flags and march down the road toward American lines shepherded by the fighters.

**MEDITERRANEAN:** Vice Admiral H. Kent Hewitt's Western Task Force conducts demonstrations to divert German attention from the main landing beaches.

Fifteenth Air Force sends more than 500 B-17s and B-24 Liberators escorted by 145 P-38 Lightnings and P-51 Mustangs to attack German positions in Toulon, France, and Genoa, Italy.

**ITALY:** Twelfth Air Force B-25 Mitchells and B-26 Marauders attack coastal defenses in the Toulon-Nice area. P-47 Thunderbolts attack radar sites, convoys, bridges, and roads along the coast in support of Dragoon. A-20 Havocs attack fuel storage areas in the Po River valley.

**SOUTHWEST PACIFIC AREA:** A Japanese cargo ship is sunk off Takao, Formosa, by a mine airdropped by Fourteenth Air Force B-24 Liberators.

**PACIFIC:** U.S. submarine *Croaker* torpedoes and sinks a Japanese gunboat southwest of Inchon, Korea.

**CENTRAL PACIFIC:** The Seventh Air Force is reorganized. The VII Bomber Command includes the B-24s of the 11th, 30th, and 494th Bombardment Groups (Heavy) and the B-25s of the 41st Bombardment Group (Medium). The VII Fighter Command includes the 15th, 21st (in Hawaii), and 318th Fighter Groups and the 6th Night Fighter Squadron. The headquarters of VII Bomber Command moves from Kwajalein Atoll to Saipan.

Saipan-based B-24 Liberators bomb Iwo Jima Island. B-25 Mitchells from the Marshall Islands bomb Ponape Island and B-24 Liberators bomb Wotje Atoll.

**CENTRAL PACIFIC, TINIAN:** The 4th Marine Division reembarks. The 2nd Marine Division will garrison Saipan and Tinian. The marines have suffered nearly 2,000 casualties to secure Tinian and have killed an estimated 5,000 of the enemy and captured 400 prisoners.

**NEW GUINEA:** FEAF A-20 Havocs, P-47 Thunderbolts, P-38 Lightnings, and P-40s attack targets near Wewak along with Royal Australian Air Force (RAAF) aircraft.

B-25 Mitchells and B-24 Liberators attack Ternate Island in the Moluccas and targets throughout the Halmahera Islands.

U.S. submarine *Cod* torpedoes and sinks a Japanese landing ship east of Celebes Island in the Banda Sea.

U.S. submarine *Ray* attacks a Japanese convoy, sinking a cargo ship and damaging another off Borneo.

### August 15

**CBI:** Tenth Air Force P-51 Mustangs, P-47 Thunderbolts, P-40s, and A-36 Intruder (Apache) fighter-bombers attack the Bhamo area, Lashio airfield, and rail targets between Naba and Hopin.

In China, Fourteenth Air Force P-40s attack Lungling and Tengchung. Nearly 100 P-40s and P-51 Mustangs attack troops, horses, trucks, river shipping, artillery, and logistics storage sites near Hengyang and Changsha.

In French Indochina, four P-40s attack coastal shipping.

**ETO:** The XX Corps of Third Army (7th Armored Division and the 5th Infantry Division) reaches Chartres.

Eighth Air Force sends 517 B-17s and 417 B-24 Liberators escorted by 293 P-38 Lightnings and P-51 Mustangs to attack airfields in the Netherlands, Germany, and Belgium. Sixteen bombers are lost and 103 are damaged. Aircrews report 13 confirmed kills and three probables. Aircrew casualties are seven killed, nine wounded, and 140 missing. Fighter pilots report 14 confirmed kills in the air and seven on the ground. Five fighters are lost and five are damaged. One pilot is wounded, and five are reported missing.

More than 30 P-47 Thunderbolts conduct dive-bombing and skip-bombing attacks on a locomotive repair shop and locomotives in the marshaling yard at Braine-le-Comtes. One P-47 is lost and four are damaged. Four pilots are reported missing.

A total of 12 B-24s fly in support of Carpetbagger operations.

Ninth Air Force sends more than 300 A-20 Havocs and B-26 Marauders to attack fuel storage sites and ammunition storage areas. P-47 and P-38 fighters support ground forces and fly armed reconnaissance missions.

**Mediterranean: Operation Dragoon.** Vice Admiral H. Kent Hewitt, Naval Commander Western Task Force and Commander Eighth Fleet, directs the landing.

The invasion of southern France begins at 0430 with the 1st Provisional Troop Carrier Division's 416 C-47s and 25 gliders delivering the 1st Airborne Task Force with 9,000 paratroopers and glider infantry to designated drop zones. Only 283 men are injured in the initial jump and glider landings, a remarkably low rate. The 1st Special Service Force conducts a raid on Iles d'Hyères to clear the approaches for the amphibious forces. Beginning at 0800, the 3rd Infantry Division and 45th Infantry Division land with little opposition. The 45th later links up with the paratroopers as planned. The 36th Infantry Division lands on a mined beach and encounters heavy fire from German positions. By midday there are 86,500 men on the beachhead, protected by Allied air cover, which suppresses German defenses and allows the invasion force to move inland quickly. Over 2,000 prisoners are captured on the first day.

Fifteenth Air Force sends more than 250 B-17s and B-24 Liberators escorted by P-38 Lightnings and P-51 Mustangs to attack Cannes and Toulon, France, and bridges over the Rhône River. P-51 Mustangs escort C-47s carrying the paratroopers of the 1st Airborne Task Force.

Sergeant James P. Connor leads an infantry platoon of the 7th Infantry Regiment, 3rd Infantry Division. Landing on Red Beach with his platoon, Sergeant Connor's mission is to capture Cape Cavalaire, which overlooks the landing beaches. Although seriously wounded in the neck by a mine that killed his platoon lieutenant, Sergeant Connor refuses medical aid and takes charge of the platoon as it crosses the beach in the face of a heavy mortar barrage. Wounded again, he refuses to be evacuated and encourages the demoralized survivors of the platoon to continue the assault toward a group of strongly fortified buildings. He is wounded again and unable to move, but continues to support and encourage the dozen or so men left standing. Because of his inspiring example, this small group is able to overwhelm the strongpoint and accomplish the mission. For his determined leadership and inspirational courage in the face of overwhelming odds, Sergeant Connor will receive the Medal of Honor.

**ITALY:** During the night Twelfth Air Force A-20 Havocs bomb airfields near the Rhône River. A-20 Havocs, B-25 Mitchells, B-26 Marauders, P-38 Lightnings, and P-47 Thunderbolts support the Dragoon landings, attacking defenses near the beaches, troop concentrations, and gun positions. Later the bombers and fighters attack roads and bridges leading into the beachhead. The headquarters of the 64th Fighter Wing redeploys from Italy to St. Tropez, France.

**NEW GUINEA:** FEAF P-39 Airacobras dive-bomb antiaircraft positions at Wewak. B-24 Liberators bomb the airfield on Halmahera Island.

Fifth Air Force B-24 Liberators attack a Japanese convoy and sink a cargo ship in the Banda Sea.

## August 16

**CBI:** Tenth Air Force P-51 Mustangs attack airfields at Lashio. P-40s and P-51s attack Japanese positions near Pinbaw. P-47 Thunderbolts and P-51s attack targets of opportunity near Bhamo.

**ETO:** Over 100,000 German soldiers are now contained in a 20-mile-by-20-mile pocket at Falaise. In the Third Army area, XV Corps (5th Armored Division and the 79th Infantry Division) captures Dreux. The XII Corps (the 4th Armored Division and the 35th Infantry Division) reaches Orléans.

Eighth Air Force sends 659 B-17s escorted by 412 P-47 Thunderbolts and P-51 Mustangs to attack aircraft and oil production facilities in central Germany. Sixteen bombers are lost and 323 damaged. Aircrews report six confirmed kills and four probables. Aircrew casualties are four killed, 12 wounded, and 149 missing. Fighter pilots report 20 confirmed kills and one probable. Two fighters are lost and one is damaged. The two pilots are reported missing.

Another attack is made against aircraft production facilities, airfields, and oil production facilities in Germany by 431 B-24 Liberators, escorted by 156 P-47 Thunderbolts and P-51 Mustangs and 42 P-38 Lightnings. Seven bombers are lost and 182 are damaged. One P-51 is lost. Fighter pilots report 12 confirmed kills. Five bomber crewmen are wounded and 66 are reported missing.

During the night eight B-17s drop leaflets over France.

Ninth Air Force sends more than 100 A-20 Havocs and B-26 Marauders to attack ammunition storage sites and railroad bridges, and a marshaling yard. P-47 and P-38 fighters support ground forces and fly armed reconnaissance missions.

**MEDITERRANEAN:** Task Force Butler is formed under the command of Brigadier General Frederick B. Butler with one infantry battalion, a cavalry reconnaissance squadron, an artillery battalion, a tank battalion, and a tank destroyer battalion to exploit gains and advance toward Grenoble and Montélimar in an attempt to trap and destroy the German Nineteenth Army as it retreats north through the Rhône Valley and into Germany. The 3rd Infantry Division advances north on Route 17 in pursuit of the retreating enemy.

Fifteenth Air Force sends 89 B-24 Liberators to bomb a chemical production plant at Friedrichshafen, Germany. Over France, 108 B-17s support Operation Dragoon by attacking railroad bridges. P-51 Mustangs escort C-47s airdropping supplies on the beachhead.

Twelfth Air Force B-25 Mitchells and B-26 Marauders attack bridges on the Rhône River. A-20 Havocs attack ammunition storage sites and German positions on the beachhead.

**PACIFIC:** U.S. submarine *Croaker* torpedoes and sinks a Japanese auxiliary minesweeper west of Korea.

**CENTRAL PACIFIC:** Seventh Air Force B-24 Liberators from Saipan bomb Chichi Jima Island in the Bonin Islands. B-24s from the Marshall Islands bomb Truk.

**ADMIRALTIES:** The C-47s of the 13th Troop Carrier Squadron of the 403rd Troop Carrier Group redeploy from Espiritu Santo Island in the New Hebrides Islands to Los Negros Island.

**NEW GUINEA:** FEAF P-39 Airacobras hit troops and positions around Manokwari.

## August 17

**CBI:** Fourteenth Air Force B-25 Mitchells, P-40s, P-51 Mustangs, and P-38 Lightnings attack the road and airfield near Hengyang.

In French Indochina P-40s attack shipping in the Haiphong area.

**ETO:** St-Malo falls to the 83rd Infantry Division of Middleton's VIII Corps.

German forces begin to break as Allied forces form a pocket around them at Falaise-Argentan. The Third Army, led by the XII and XX Corps and supported by XV Corps, pushes toward Paris to cut the German line of retreat at the Paris-Orléans Gap between the Loire and Seine Rivers.

Eighth Air Force sends 397 P-38 Lightnings and P-47 Thunderbolts to attack targets around Paris and Brussels. Fighter pilots report three confirmed kills. One P-47 is damaged. Over 300 P-51 Mustangs attack communications targets. Seven fighters are lost and four are damaged. One pilot is wounded and seven pilots are reported missing.

A total of 33 B-24 Liberators fly in support of Carpetbagger operations during the night.

Ninth Air Force sends more than 400 A-20 Havocs and B-26 Marauders to attack road and rail bridges, and a marshaling yard. P-47 and P-38 fighters attack German forces near St-Malo.

Staff Sergeant Stanley Bender of E Company, 7th Infantry Regiment, 3rd Infantry Division, faces heavy enemy fire from a German machine gun near La Lande, France. Bender climbs on a knocked-out tank and looks for the source of the fire. Ignoring the bullets that pass by him, Staff Sergeant Bender locates the German position and orders two squads to provide covering fire. He then jumps off the tank and leads his men from another squad down an irrigation ditch. He then moves off alone to locate the rear of the enemy position, again in full view of the Germans, who continue to send a high volume of fire in his direction. Attacking the first machine gun position, he eliminates the defenders and advances toward the second machine gun position about 25 yards away. As bullets strike around him and hand grenades explode close by, Bender continues forward and dispatches the second position. Signaling an advance, Staff Sergeant Bender kills the last defenders to secure the position. Inspired by his display of courage, his soldiers continue the attack, capturing 26 German soldiers and taking three bridges over the Maravenne River. For his great courage and determined actions in the face of enemy fire, Staff Sergeant Bender will receive the Medal of Honor.

**MEDITERRANEAN:** The French II Corps lands in southern France. At this point 12,000 vehicles, 46,000 tons of supplies, and 86,000 men have landed on the beaches. The Allies have captured 7,845 prisoners.

Fifteenth Air Force sends 53 B-17s and B-24 Liberators escorted by P-38 Lightnings and P-51 Mustangs to attack the airfield at Nish in Yugoslavia. Another 250 B-24 Liberators escorted by P-51 Mustangs bomb oil refineries near Ploeşti, Romania.

Twelfth Air Force A-20 Havocs, A-36 Intruder (Apache) fighter-bombers, P-51 Mustangs, and P-40s attack rail cars, bridges, airfields, and roads in southern France in support of invasion forces.

**PACIFIC:** U.S. submarine *Croaker* torpedoes and sinks a Japanese merchant cargo ship off the west coast of Korea.

**CENTRAL PACIFIC:** Seventh Air Force B-24 Liberators from Saipan bomb Iwo Jima Island in the Volcano Islands. B-25 Mitchells from Makin bomb Ponape Island.

**NEW GUINEA:** At the Vogelkop Peninsula, the airfield constructed on Middelburg Island is operational.

FEAF P-40s, supporting ground forces, attack remnants of Japanese defenders on Biak Island. A-20 Havocs and P-38 Lightnings attack targets around Manokwari. B-25 Mitchells sink a transport vessel off Halmahera Island. B-24 Liberators bomb airfields on Ambon and Ceram Islands in the Moluccas.

The headquarters of the 5th Bombardment Group (Heavy) redeploys from Los Negros Island in the Admiralties to Wakde Island. The P-38 Lightnings of the 68th Fighter Squadron, 347th Fighter Group, redeploy from Bougainville Island to Middelburg Island.

**August 18**

**CBI:** Tenth Air Force P-47 Thunderbolts and P-51 Mustangs destroy a road bridge and Japanese positions near Bhamo. P-47 Thunderbolts attack Lashio airfield.

**ETO:** The Third Army's XV Corps moves to seize crossings on the Seine River and trap German forces still holding south of the river. The 2nd Infantry Division and the 29th Infantry Division are sent to Brittany to support VIII Corps as it initiates an attack on the port of Brest.

Eighth Air Force sends more than 500 B-17s and more than 250 B-24 Liberators escorted by nearly 140 P-51 Mustangs and 100 P-38 Lightnings to attack airfields, bridges, fuel storage areas, and industrial targets in France and Belgium. Only two bombers are lost and over 100 are damaged. Aircrew casualties are six killed, eight wounded, and 21 missing. Fighter pilots report two confirmed kills on the ground. Four fighters are lost and two are damaged. Four pilots are reported missing.

During the night seven B-17s drop leaflets over France.

Ninth Air Force sends nearly 100 A-20 Havocs and B-26 Marauders to attack fuel storage sites, railroad bridges, and roads to impede the retreat of German forces. P-47 and P-38 fighters support ground forces near Argentan and attack German forces assembling near the Seine River.

**MEDITERRANEAN:** Fifteenth Air Force sends 370 B-17s and B-24 Liberators to bomb oil refineries near Ploeşti, Romania.

Twelfth Air Force B-25 Mitchells and B-26 Marauders attack coastal guns near Toulon. A-20 Havocs, A-36 Intruder (Apache) fighter-bombers, and P-51 Mustangs attack rail lines and rail cars. The headquarters of the XII Tactical Air Command redeploys from Italy to France.

**SOUTHWEST PACIFIC AREA:** U.S. submarine *Hardhead* torpedoes and sinks the Japanese light cruiser *Natori* east of Samar Island, in the Philippines.

USS *Rasher* and USS *Redfish* discover a Japanese convoy off the west coast of Luzon. The *Rasher* sinks an escort carrier, a transport, a cargo ship, and an oiler and damages a transport. The *Redfish* damages a merchant tanker.

U.S. submarine *Ray* torpedoes and sinks a Japanese merchant tanker at the southern end of Palawan.

**CBI:** Fourteenth Air Force P-40s and P-51 Mustangs attack river shipping, troops, and ground transportation near Hengyang.

**ETO:** The 90th Infantry Division of V Corps, U.S. First Army, meets elements of the Canadian First Army to close the Falaise-Argentan Pocket at Chambois, capturing 50,000 prisoners and 5,000 armored vehicles. The First Army's XIX Corps (2nd Armored Division, the 28th and 30th Infantry Divisions) moves north to support the left flank of Third Army's XV Corps. The 79th Infantry Division of the XV Corps, Third Army, crosses the Seine River while the 5th Armored Division moves to block crossing sites German forces may use. Major General Manton S. Eddy takes command of XII Corps from Major General Gilbert R. Cook.

French Forces of the Interior, a paramilitary resistance group, battle German troops in Paris, seizing government buildings. Bradley's 12th Army Group is given the task of moving north to the Seine River to block the German retreat.

The Ninth Air Force's 50th and 53rd Troop Carrier Wings redeploy from Italy, where they were supporting Dragoon and return to Britain. P-47 Thunderbolts and P-38 Lightnings attack German assembly areas near the Seine River.

**MEDITERRANEAN:** Task Force Butler advances toward Grenoble to trap retreating German forces in the Rhône valley. The 36th Infantry Division follows Butler's task force as the 3rd and 45th Infantry Divisions advance north. Since the invasion on August 15, Seventh Army has captured 16,500 prisoners and suffered about 5,000 casualties. German air elements in southern France redeploy, giving the Allies total command of the air.

Fifteenth Air Force sends 65 B-17s escorted by 125 P-51 Mustangs to bomb the oil refineries at Ploeşti, Romania. This is the last time the Fifteenth Air Force will attack the Ploeşti oil refinery.

Twelfth Air Force B-25 Mitchells and B-26 Marauders attack rail and road traffic and bridges in southern France. A-20 Havocs, A-36 Intruder (Apache) fighter-bombers, P-51 Mustangs, and P-40s attack German positions in support of Task Force Butler.

Battleship *Nevada* and French battleship *Lorraine,* with heavy cruiser *Augusta* and escorted by four destroyers, conduct a reconnaissance in force off Toulon and bombard the harbor.

**ITALY:** Private Masato Nakae of the 100th Infantry Battalion is attacking German infantry near Pisa, Italy, when his Thompson submachine gun is damaged by a shell fragment. Private Nakae quickly picks up an M-1 rifle and fires rifle grenades at the Germans. Nakae throws six grenades to disrupt an attack on his position and forces them to retreat. During a mortar bombardment that follows Private Nakae is wounded. Despite his injuries, he continues to fight as the Germans attack again. His heroic defense against superior enemy forces will win him the Medal of Honor.

**SOUTHWEST PACIFIC AREA:** USS *Bluefish* torpedoes and sinks a fast fleet tanker/seaplane carrier and damages a hospital ship off the west coast of Luzon in a second day of attacks on this convoy.

U.S. submarine *Spadefish* torpedoes and sinks a Japanese landing craft repair ship west of Luzon.

**CENTRAL PACIFIC:** Seventh Air Force P-47 Thunderbolts from Saipan drop incendiaries on Japanese holdouts on Tinian Island.

**NEW GUINEA:** FEAF P-39 Airacobras bomb and strafe Japanese positions along the western coast of Geelvink Bay. Other P-39s attack Japanese positions near Wewak. A-20 Havocs support ground forces near Sarmi.

The B-24 Liberators of the 72nd Bombardment Squadron (Heavy), 5th Bombardment Group (Heavy), redeploy from Momote airfield on Los Negros Island to Wakde Island.

U.S. submarine *Redfin* lays mines off Sarawak, Borneo.

## August 20

**CBI:** The P-47 Thunderbolts from the 88th Fighter Squadron of the 80th Fighter Group redeploy from Myitkyina and return to Shingbwiyang.

In China, Fourteenth Air Force B-25 Mitchells and P-40s attack buildings, a pontoon bridge, and river transport near Hengyang.

Fourteenth Air Force B-24 Liberators sink a Japanese army tanker near Hong Kong.

**ATLANTIC:** Navy TBM Avengers and FM-2 Wildcat fighters from escort carrier USS *Bogue* sink German submarine *U-1229* in the North Atlantic.

**ETO:** The XX Corps reaches Fontainebleau. The 79th Infantry Division of the XV Corps establishes a bridgehead on the Seine River.

Ninth Air Force sends 61 B-26 Marauders to attack German assembly areas near the Seine River. The B-26s of the 584th and 585th Bombardment Squadrons (Medium), 394th Bombardment Group (Medium), redeploy from England to France.

**MEDITERRANEAN:** Fifteenth Air Force sends more than 460 B-17s and B-24 Liberators escorted by P-38 Lightnings and P-51 Mustangs to attack an airfield and marshaling yard in Hungary and oil refineries in Czechoslovakia and Poland.

In France, Twelfth Air Force B-26 Marauders A-36 Intruder (Apache) fighter-bombers, P-51 Mustangs, and P-40s attack coastal defense installations at Toulon. B-25 Mitchells attack bridges and airfields along the Rhône River. A-20 Havocs support ground forces.

**PACIFIC:** Twentieth Air Force sends 61 B-29 Superfortresses from Chengtu, China, to bomb the Imperial Iron and Steel Works at Yawata, Japan. During the night another 10 B-29s attack the same target. Fourteen B-29s are lost—one to antiaircraft fire, one by air-to-air bombing, and a Japanese fighter deliberately rams one Superfortress. Aircrews report 17 confirmed kills.

**CENTRAL PACIFIC:** Seventh Air Force B-24 Liberators from Saipan bomb Yap. B-24s from the Marshalls bomb Truk.

**NEW GUINEA:** Lieutenant General Krueger establishes the Morotai Task Force, composed of Headquarters XI Corps, the 31st Infantry Division, and the 126th Infantry Regiment, 32nd Infantry Division. The 6th Infantry Division, with two regimental combat teams, is the task force reserve at Sansapor. Major General Charles P. Hall is the task force commander with 57,000 men of all services. The task force is to land on the southern coast of Morotai Island and capture Doroeba airfield. Naval Task Force 77, commanded by Rear Admiral Daniel E. Barbey, will be composed of six escort carriers and 10 destroyer escorts and accompanied by a covering force of two heavy cruisers, three light cruisers, and 10 destroyers.

FEAF P-39 Airacobras attack Japanese shipping off Manokwari and P-40s attack gun positions, buildings, and logistics storage sites. B-24 Liberators bomb targets on Halmahera Island.

The B-24s of the 23rd and 31st Bombardment Squadrons (Heavy), 5th Bombardment Group (Heavy), redeploy from Momote airfield on Los Negros Island in the Admiralties to Wakde Island.

### August 21

**CARIBBEAN:** Sixth Air Force redeploys the B-24 Liberators of the 74th Bombardment Squadron, VI Bomber Command, from Rio Hato, Panama, to the Galápagos Islands.

**CBI:** The headquarters of the 1st Combat Cargo Group and the C-47s of the 1st Combat Cargo Squadron arrive at Sylhet, India, from the United States. The squadron will fly its first mission in early September.

In China, Fourteenth Air Force B-25 Mitchells bomb Hengyang airfield. P-51 Mustangs and P-40s attack river transports and road traffic around Tenchung, Hengyang, Tungting Lake, and Changsha.

U.S. submarine *Muskallunge* attacks a Japanese convoy, sinking an army transport off Cam Ranh Bay, French Indochina.

**ATLANTIC:** The Dumbarton Oaks conference, which lays the foundation for the establishment of a new global security organization, is held in Washington, D.C. The organization will be a representative body, without a security or police force. The members will contribute forces as necessary to keep the peace. The conference issues a set of guidelines for the organization of the United Nations, a Secretariat, and an International Court of Justice. Also recommended is a Security Council of five permanent members (United States, Great Britain, China, USSR, and France) and six non-permanent member nations, which would have executive powers over the General Assembly of member nations. The USSR desires absolute veto power in the Security Council, even for disputes where it is one of the nations involved in a dispute. The United States holds the view that veto power would be exercised only in extraordinary circumstances to preserve the peace. The USSR sees the veto power as a means of protecting its interests. The USSR also seeks 16 seats in the General Assembly, one for each of the nominally independent member states of the Soviet Union.

**MEDITERRANEAN:** Task Force Butler moves into blocking positions in the Rhône Valley near Montélimar.

Fifteenth Air Force sends more than 200 B-24 Liberators escorted by P-51 Mustangs to attack airfields in Yugoslavia and Hungary.

Twelfth Air Force A-36 Intruder (Apache) fighter-bombers and P-51 Mustangs attack communication sites, gun positions, and roads in southern France.

**ITALY:** Twelfth Air Force B-25 Mitchells, B-26 Marauders, and A-20 Havocs attack roads and bridges in the Po River valley. P-47 Thunderbolts attack rail cars and vehicles.

**SOUTHWEST PACIFIC AREA:** USS *Guitarro, Haddo, Harder,* and *Ray* attack a Japanese convoy off Mindoro. Three cargo ships and two tankers are sunk.

Navy PB4Y Privateers damage a cargo vessel in Davao harbor.

**CENTRAL PACIFIC:** Seventh Air Force B-24 Liberators from Saipan bomb Yap. B-25 Mitchells from Makin Island bomb Nauru Island.

Navy PB4Y Privateers damage a Japanese guardboat and a small cargo vessel northwest of Marcus Island.

**NEW GUINEA:** FEAF A-20 Havocs, P-47 Thunderbolts, P-38 Lightnings, and P-40s attack logistics storage areas near Manokwari and Sarmi.

## August 22
**CBI:** In China, Tenth Air Force P-51 Mustangs and P-47 Thunderbolts attack Japanese positions around Tengchung in support of Chinese ground forces. In Burma, P-47 Thunderbolts strafe targets near Bhamo.

U.S. submarine *Pintado* attacks a Japanese convoy, sinking a merchant tanker southeast of Shanghai.

**ETO:** The XX Corps of Third Army reaches the Seine River. The leaders of the Resistance in Paris appeal to the Allies for help. General Charles de Gaulle presses General Eisenhower to provide forces, arguing that there will be no battle for the city and that the French Forces of the Interior have provided great assistance to the Allied advance. Eisenhower decides to initiate the pre-planned employment of the French 2nd Armored Division under Major General Jacques P. LeClerc and the U.S. 4th Infantry Division.

The German Seventh and Fifth Panzer armies cease to exist. The remnants retreat across the Seine River, heading for the German border and safety. France is now open to the uncontested advance of the Allied forces.

Ninth Air Force P-47 Thunderbolts and P-38 Lightnings support ground forces and fly armed reconnaissance missions.

**MEDITERRANEAN:** The 36th Infantry Division enters Grenoble while Task Force Butler establishes road blocks north of Montélimar, reinforced by elements of the 36th Infantry Division. German forces attempt to break through the American defenses and the 36th Infantry Division is pushed back. The units of the division are short on ammunition.

Fifteenth Air Force sends 39 B-24 Liberators to bomb the oil refinery near Vienna, Austria. Over 50 German fighters attack the bombers and shoot down one B-24. Aircrews report 13 confirmed kills. B-17s bomb oil refineries at Odertal, Germany.

**ITALY:** Twelfth Air Force B-26 Marauders and A-20 Havocs attack bridges and convoys in the Po River valley.

**SOUTHWEST PACIFIC AREA:** USS *Haddo* and *Harder* sink three Japanese escort vessels at the entrance to Manila Bay.

U.S. submarine *Spadefish* attacks a Japanese convoy and damages a tanker in Luzon Strait.

**PACIFIC:** U.S. submarine *Bowfin* attacks a Japanese convoy, sinking a cargo ship in the Ryukyus.

U.S. submarine *Tang* torpedoes and sinks a Japanese cargo ship off Honshu, Japan.

**CENTRAL PACIFIC:** Seventh Air Force B-24 Liberators from Saipan bomb Yap. B-24s from Kwajalein bomb Mille Atoll.

**NEW GUINEA:** FEAF A-20 Havocs and P-39 Airacobras attack Japanese positions around Manokwari. P-47 Thunderbolts, P-38 Lightnings, and P-40s attack targets near Wewak.

The B-24 Liberators of the 370th, 371st, 372nd, and 424th Bombardment Squadrons (Heavy) of the 307th Bombardment Group (Heavy) redeploy from Los Negros Island in the Admiralty Islands to Wakde Island.

## August 23

**CBI:** Tenth Air Force P-47 Thunderbolts attack Japanese forces and logistics bases located along the Burma Road from Wanling to Lungling.

In China, Fourteenth Air Force B-25 Mitchells, P-40s, and P-51 Mustangs attack Japanese positions and vehicles near Hengyang.

**ETO:** The V Corps (4th Infantry Division and 2nd French Armored Division) advances toward Paris.

Eighth Air Force P-47 Thunderbolts bomb and strafe rail transportation in northeast France.

During the night six B-17s drop leaflets over France and Belgium.

Ninth Air Force sends P-47 and P-38 fighters to support ground forces and attack German assembly areas on the Seine River.

German submarine *U-989* torpedoes and damages a U.S. freighter on the way to Utah beach.

**Mediterranean:** The French II Corps captures the heights above Toulon. Six airfields are established in southern France for the XII Tactical Air Force. Three U.S. fighter groups will redeploy to these airfields.

Romania surrenders to Soviet forces.

Fifteenth Air Force sends more than 400 B-17s and B-24 Liberators escorted by P-38 Lightnings and P-51 Mustangs to bomb the oil refinery and aircraft production facilities at Vienna, Austria. Over 60 German fighters attack the bombers and shoot down nine B-24s. Aircrews report 29 confirmed kills.

Twelfth Air Force A-20 Havocs, A-36 Intruder (Apache) fighter-bombers, P-51 Mustangs, and P-40s support ground forces in southern France.

**Italy:** Twelfth Air Force B-25 Mitchells and B-26 Marauders attack rail and road traffic and bridges along the Arno River. A-20 Havocs and P-47 Thunderbolts support ground forces in southern France.

**Southwest Pacific Area:** U.S. submarine *Haddo* torpedoes and sinks a destroyer off Luzon.

**Pacific:** U.S. submarine *Tang* attacks a Japanese convoy off Honshu, sinking a cargo ship.

**Central Pacific:** Seventh Air Force B-25 Mitchells from the Gilbert Islands attack Ponape Island. B-24 Liberators from Saipan bomb Yap and Iwo Jima.

Seventh Air Force B-24 Liberators sink a Japanese auxiliary submarine chaser near Chichi Jima.

**New Guinea:** FEAF B-25 Mitchells, A-20 Havocs, and P-38 Lightnings attack barge locations and troop positions around Wewak.

B-24 Liberators bomb Halmahera Island.

## August 24

**CBI:** In China, Fourteenth Air Force B-25 Mitchells and P-40s attack towns, river and road traffic, and rail lines around Hengyang.

**ETO:** The French 2nd Armored Division advances toward Paris.

Eighth Air Force sends more than 800 B-17s and nearly 500 B-24 Liberators, escorted by over 600 P-38 Lightnings, P-47 Thunderbolts, and P-51 Mustangs, to attack aircraft production facilities, oil refineries, and airfields in Germany. A total of 27 bombers are lost and over 500 are damaged. Aircrews report 10 confirmed kills and three probables. Aircrew casualties are four killed, 45 wounded, and 247 missing. Fighter pilots report 10 confirmed kills in the air and 14 confirmed kills on the ground. Four fighters are lost and three are damaged. Three pilots are reported missing.

During the night one B-17 drops leaflets over Brest, France.

Ninth Air Force P-47 and P-38 fighters support ground forces and attack pontoon bridges over the Seine River as German forces continue to retreat.

**MEDITERRANEAN:** The French II Corps occupies Toulon. The 1st Airborne Task Force captures Cannes.

Fifteenth Air Force sends more than 500 B-17s and B-24 Liberators escorted by P-38 Lightnings and P-51 Mustangs to bomb oil refineries in Czechoslovakia, airfields in Yugoslavia and Hungary, and railroad bridges in Italy. Aircrews and fighter pilots report 40 confirmed kills.

Twelfth Air Force A-20 Havocs attack convoys in the Rhône River valley. B-26 Marauders attack gun positions near Marseille, France. A-20 Havocs and P-47 Thunderbolts attack German forces in southern France in support of the Seventh Army.

**SOUTHWEST PACIFIC AREA:** A Japanese coastal patrol vessel sinks U.S. submarine *Harder* off the west coast of Luzon.

U.S. submarine *Ronquil* attacks a Japanese convoy off Formosa, sinking two cargo ships.

U.S. submarine *Sailfish* attacks a Japanese convoy in Luzon Strait, sinking a transport.

**PACIFIC:** The headquarters of Twentieth Air Force's 73rd Bombardment Wing (Very Heavy) arrives in the Mariana Islands with B-29 Superfortresses. The wing commander is Brigadier General Emmett O'Donnell, Jr.

U.S. submarine *Seal* sinks a cargo ship off the southeast coast of Hokkaido, Japan.

**CENTRAL PACIFIC:** Seventh Air Force B-24 Liberators from the Marshalls bomb Truk. B-25 Mitchells bomb Nauru Island.

**NEW GUINEA:** The headquarters of the 307th Bombardment Group (Heavy) redeploys from Los Negros Island in the Admiralties to Wakde Island. P-47 Thunderbolts of the 340th and 341st Fighter Squadrons of the 348th Fighter Group redeploy from Wakde Island to Noemfoor Island. FEAF B-24 Liberators bomb an airfield on Halmahera Island. B-25 Mitchells bomb shipping in the Celebes.

## August 25

**CBI:** Tenth Air Force P-47 Thunderbolts destroy a bridge near Bhamo.

Fourteenth Air Force B-24 Liberators bomb the Kowloon docks in Hong Kong. P-51 Mustangs and P-40s attack targets near Hengyang.

**ETO:** The V Corps enters the city of Paris. Major General Jacques P. LeClerc's French 2nd Armored Division and the U.S. 4th Infantry Division enter Paris. LeClerc takes the surrender of 10,000 German soldiers in the name of the Provisional Government of France. The First Army's XIX Corps, commanded by Major General Charles H. Corlett, reaches Elbeuf, closing a large portion of the Seine River to the Germans as an escape route. Patton's Third Army has control of four crossing sites on the Seine River.

Bradley orders the 12th Army Group to cross the Seine River and attack northeast to support Montgomery's 21st Army Group, which General Eisenhower has designated as the main effort. The XX Corps (7th Armored Division and 90th Infantry Division) will capture Rheims and the XII Corps (4th Armored Division and 35th and 80th Infantry Divisions) of Third Army will capture Châlons.

Leading elements of the Third Army are 140 miles beyond Paris and 60 miles from the German border. Resistance is negligible. Fuel supplies now have to be transported overland from both the port of Cherbourg and the Normandy beaches to reach the extended forces. There is not enough capacity to haul the thousands of tons of fuel needed to continue the advance.

Eighth Air Force sends more than 700 B-17s and 400 B-24 Liberators escorted by 569 P-47 Thunderbolts and P-51 Mustangs to bomb liquid oxygen and ammonia production facilities in Belgium and France, the Peenemünde Experimental Station, aircraft component plants, airfields, and synthetic oil production facilities. Eighteen bombers are lost and over 300 are damaged. Aircrew casualties are one killed, 24 wounded, and 173 missing. Fighter pilots report 11 confirmed kills and two probables in the air and 40 confirmed kills on the ground. Seven fighters are lost.

Another 10 B-24 Liberators escorted by P-47s fly an Azon glide bomb mission to Moerdijke in the Netherlands. Aircrews report no damage to the target.

B-24s escorted by P-38s and P-51s attack targets in Belgium, and 24 of the 69 bombers are damaged and four crewmen are wounded.

One C-47 flies a Carpetbagger mission during the night. During the night six B-17s drop leaflets over France and Belgium.

Ninth Air Force sends 240 A-20 Havocs and B-26 Marauders to attack German positions near Brest. P-47 and P-38 fighters support ground forces and attack German bridges over the Seine River. Fighter pilots report using napalm bombs to attack the suspected headquarters of Field Marshal Walter Model, the commander in chief of German forces on the west front.

The headquarters of the 394th Bombardment Group (Medium) redeploys to France from England.

Private Harold A. Garman is assigned to Company B, 5th Medical Battalion, 5th Infantry Division, and is engaged in moving casualties delivered by boats from a bridgehead on the Seine River near Montereau, France. German machine guns begin firing on a boatload of wounded as it crosses the river. Private Garman dives into the water to rescue the wounded and steers the boat while still under heavy fire to the shore. Garman's courageous deed and devotion to duty will win him the Congressional Medal of Honor.

**MEDITERRANEAN:** German forces break through the 36th Infantry Division lines near Grenoble, opening an escape route for the Nineteenth Army.

Operation Olive begins in Italy. The British Eighth Army begins an attack along a 17-mile front on the Adriatic coast. Although the British make some progress initially, the offensive stalls by early September.

Fifteenth Air Force sends more than 300 B-17s and B-24 Liberators escorted by P-38 Lightnings and P-51 Mustangs to bomb airfields and aircraft production facilities in Czechoslovakia.

Twelfth Air Force B-25 Mitchells and B-26 Marauders attack bridges over the Rhône River.

**ITALY:** Operation Olive begins. The British Eighth Army launches a two corps attack on the eastern coast of Italy. Mark Clark's Fifth Army is to launch supporting attacks within five days.

A-20 Havocs and P-47 Thunderbolts attack convoys, gun positions, bridges, and roads north of the Arno River.

The headquarters of the 27th Fighter Group and the P-47s of the 522nd, 523rd, and 524th Fighter Squadrons redeploy from Corsica to southern France. The headquarters of the 79th Fighter Group also redeploys from Corsica to southern France.

**SOUTHWEST PACIFIC AREA:** U.S. submarine *Picuda* attacks a Japanese convoy and sinks a destroyer and merchant tanker north of Luzon. U.S. submarine *Redfish* follows with an attack on the same convoy, damaging a cargo ship.

**PACIFIC:** U.S. submarine *Tang* torpedoes and sinks a Japanese merchant tanker off Honshu, Japan.

**CENTRAL PACIFIC:** Seventh Air Force B-24 Liberators from Saipan bomb Iwo Jima. B-25 Mitchells from the Gilberts bomb Ponape Island.

**NEW GUINEA:** B-24 Liberators bomb the Palau Islands. B-25 Mitchells attack shipping in the Celebes and report sinking one cargo ship.

The B-24s and B-17s of the 394th Bombardment Squadron (Heavy), 5th Bombardment Group (Heavy), redeploy from Los Negros Island in the Admiralties to Wake Island. B-25 Mitchells of the 822nd Bombardment Squadron (Medium) of the 38th Bombardment Group (Medium) redeploy from Nadzab to Biak Island.

## August 26

**ALEUTIANS:** Eleventh Air Force B-24 Liberators bomb Paramushiru Island in the Kuriles on an early morning raid. B-25 Mitchells attack and sink a patrol boat. A B-25 is damaged. Other B-24s bomb targets on Kashiwabara and on Otomari Cape.

**CBI:** The Mars Task Force is activated under the command of Brigadier General Thomas S. Arms. The task force is composed of a new unit named the 5332nd Brigade (Provisional), the 475th Infantry Regiment (the remnants of the Marauders and New Galahad), the 124th Cavalry Regiment (the last U.S. Army unit actually to have horses, but now converted to infantry), and the 1st Chinese Separate Regiment (a unit that never actually served). Supporting the infantry are the 612th and the 613th Field Artillery Battalions with 75 millimeter pack howitzers.

**ETO:** German aircraft bomb Paris as more than 2,000 German soldiers continue to fight in the city. General Charles de Gaulle makes his official entry into Paris. German forces have been pushed against the left bank of the Seine River between Elbeuf and Le Havre.

German forces are using barges to ferry nearly 27,000 troops across the Seine River. The Germans have suffered a significant defeat. At least 20 infantry divisions have been destroyed and another 12 severely depleted. The Allies have captured 200,000 soldiers and another 200,000 are casualties. Another 1,300 tanks, 20,000 vehicles, 500 assault guns, and 1,500 pieces of artillery have been either captured or destroyed. The German air force has lost over 2,300 aircraft in combat and another 1,100 destroyed on the ground.

Eighth Air Force sends more than 300 B-17s escorted by P-51 Mustangs to attack German defenses at Brest. Seven B-17s are damaged and one P-51 is lost. Aircrew casualties are 18 killed.

On other attacks, over 250 B-17s and 300 B-24 Liberators, escorted by over 360 P-38 Lightnings, P-51 Mustangs, and P-47 Thunderbolts, bomb oil refineries, chemical works, fuel storage areas, marshaling yards, and airfields. Ten bombers are lost and 144 are damaged. Aircrew casualties are two killed, eight wounded, and 96 missing. Fighter pilots report one confirmed kill on the ground. Three fighters are lost and one is damaged. Three pilots are reported missing.

Over 380 P-47s and P-51s attack transport targets in Belgium, France, and Germany. Fighter pilots report one confirmed kill. Two P-47s and seven P-51s are lost and 15 fighters are damaged. One pilot is reported wounded and eight are reported missing.

During the night six B-17s drop leaflets over France and Belgium.

Ninth Air Force sends A-20 Havocs and B-26 Marauders to attack fuel storage sites. P-47 and P-38 fighters support ground forces and attack German troops at the Seine and Loire Rivers.

The First Allied Airborne Army takes operational control of the IX Troop Carrier Command from Ninth Air Force. The headquarters of the 323rd Bombardment Group (Medium) and the B-26 Marauders of the 453rd, 454th, 455th, and 456th Bombardment Squadrons (Medium) redeploy from England to France.

Three motor torpedo boats prevent an attempt to reinforce the German garrison at Le Havre. Two German artillery ferries are sunk.

**MEDITERRANEAN:** Allied naval forces enter Toulon harbor after exchanging fire with coastal batteries.

Fifteenth Air Force B-24 Liberators bomb German troops and barracks at Bucharest, Romania.

Twelfth Air Force B-25s and B-26 Marauders bomb gun positions near Marseille, France.

**ITALY:** Twelfth Air Force A-20 Havocs and P-47 Thunderbolts attack rail lines, bridges, and roads in northern Italy and southern France.

**SOUTHWEST PACIFIC AREA:** U.S. submarine *Guitarro* attacks a Japanese convoy, sinking a merchant tanker, damaging another, and forcing another tanker to run aground west of Panay Island in the Philippines.

U.S. submarine *Stingray* lands men and supplies on Luzon.

**PACIFIC:** Navy PV-1 Mariner patrol bombers sink a Japanese vessel between Odomari and Onnekotan Islands, Kuriles.

**CENTRAL PACIFIC:** Seventh Air Force B-24 Liberators from Saipan bomb Iwo Jima.

**NEW GUINEA:** FEAF A-20 Havocs attack Japanese positions near Sarmi. P-38 Lightnings, P-40s, and P-47 Thunderbolts attack targets near Wewak. P-39 Airacobras maintain patrols over Geelvink Bay. B-24 Liberators bomb the airfield on Peleliu in the Palaus.

The headquarters of the 348th Fighter Group moves from Wakde Island to Noemfoor. B-25 Mitchells of the 823rd Bombardment Squadron (Medium), 38th Bombardment Group (Medium), redeploy from Nadzab to Biak Island.

## August 27

**ALEUTIANS:** Eleventh Air Force sends five B-24 Liberators on a bombing and photoreconnaissance mission over Paramushiru Island. Four B-25 Mitchells conduct a shipping sweep around the Kurile Islands. Aircrews report damaging one picket boat and sinking another.

**CBI:** In China, Fourteenth Air Force B-25 Mitchells bomb Hengyang, Tien Ho, White Cloud, and Pailochi airfields.

**ETO:** General Eisenhower and General Bradley enter Paris. The city is placed under the control of General Pierre Koenig, who had been commander of the French Forces of the Interior. With the success of Dragoon and the collapse of German forces on the Normandy front, Eisenhower decides to continue the pursuit, cross the Rhine, and reach the Ruhr. Eisenhower continues to hold to the broad-front strategic approach where the Allied armies advance together and can be mutually supporting, rather than a series of deep, unsupported thrusts on a narrow axis of advance. The VII Corps (3rd Armored Division and 9th Infantry Division) crosses the Seine River.

Eighth Air Force sends more than 1,000 B-17s and B-24 Liberators, escorted by over 500 P-38 Lightnings, P-51 Mustangs, and P-47 Thunderbolts, to bomb marshaling yards, docks, and transportation targets in northern Germany and France. Three bombers are lost and 75 are damaged. Aircrew casualties are one killed, five wounded, and 19 missing. Fighter pilots report one confirmed kill in the air and one confirmed kill on the ground. Ten fighters are lost and 11 are damaged. One pilot is reported killed, and 10 pilots are reported missing.

Over 300 P-47s fly fighter-bomber missions against transportation targets in France. Fighter pilots report 14 confirmed kills on the ground. One P-47 is lost, and the pilot is reported missing.

During the night six B-17s drop leaflets over France and the Netherlands.

Ninth Air Force sends A-20 Havocs and B-26 Marauders to attack German defenses near Rouen. P-47 fighters engage German fighters, and pilots report 11 confirmed kills in the air and five on the ground. Six P-47s are lost.

**MEDITERRANEAN:** The 36th Infantry Division restores its lines after the German attack, but the bulk of the German army has escaped the trap. Montélimar is captured, bringing organized German resistance to an end south of a line from Grenoble to Bordeaux. A total of 42,000 German prisoners have been captured since the landings on August 15.

Fifteenth Air Force sends more than 500 B-17s and B-24 Liberators escorted by P-38 Lightnings and P-51 Mustangs to attack oil refineries in Germany and transportation targets in northern Italy.

Twelfth Air Force B-26 Marauders and B-25 Mitchells bomb gun positions near Marseille, France.

**ITALY:** Twelfth Air Force B-25 Mitchells and B-26 Marauders attack bridges. A-20 Havocs attack ammunition storage sites. A-20 Havocs and P-47 Thunderbolts attack bridges and roads north of the Arno River.

**Central Pacific:** Seventh Air Force B-24 Liberators from Saipan bomb Iwo Jima.
**New Guinea:** The B-25 Mitchells of the 75th Bombardment Squadron (Medium)
42nd Bombardment Group (Medium) redeploy to Hollandia.

## August 28

**Aleutians:** Eleventh Air Force B-25 Mitchells sink an auxiliary submarine chaser
near the Paramushiru Straits in the Kuriles.
**CBI:** The Fourteenth Air Force takes operational control of the 311th Fighter Group
from Tenth Air Force. The Group's three squadrons, the 528th, 529th, and 530th,
are equipped with P-51 Mustangs and will be stationed at Chengtu. B-25 Mitchells
bomb Tien Ho, White Cloud, Hankow, and Pailochi airfields. Other B-25s attack
river and road transportation from Hengyang to Puchi.
**ETO:** The XII Corps captures Châlons.

Eighth Air Force sends more than 800 P-38 Lightnings, P-47 Thunderbolts, and
P-51 Mustangs to attack rail lines in the Netherlands, Belgium, France, and Germany. Fighter pilots report 19 confirmed kills and one probable kill in the air and
11 confirmed kills on the ground. A total of 20 fighters are lost and 19 are damaged.
Twenty pilots are reported missing.

During the night six B-17s drop leaflets over France and the Netherlands.

Ninth Air Force sends A-20 Havocs and B-26 Marauders to attack fuel storage
sites, railroad bridges, and a marshaling yard. P-47 and P-38 fighters attack airfields,
escort C-47s transporting wounded, and fly armed reconnaissance missions.
**Mediterranean:** The city of Marseille surrenders to French forces. The port can
be made available to resupply Allied forces in the ETO. The 3rd Infantry Division
attacks German delaying forces near Montélimar. The 36th and 45th Infantry Divisions capture Livron. Remnants of the German Nineteenth Army escape north to
join Army Group B, reorganizing in northern France. The Seventh Army has captured 15,000 prisoners and 4,000 vehicles but is unable to pursue the retreating Germans. The army is at the limit of a 450-mile-long supply line and cannot advance
any farther. The Americans have suffered 2,700 casualties, the French 4,000.

Twelfth Air Force B-25 Mitchells bomb railroad bridges near Lyon, France. A-20
Havocs attack ammunition storage facilities, and A-36 Intruder (Apache) fighter-
bombers attack vehicles in the Rhône River valley.

Fifteenth Air Force sends more than 300 B-17s and B-24 Liberators escorted
by P-38 Lightnings and P-51 Mustangs to bomb an oil refinery in Austria and oil
refineries and a marshaling yard in Hungary.

German submarine *U-859* torpedoes and sinks a U.S. freighter in the Gulf of
Aden.
**Italy:** Twelfth Air Force A-20 Havocs attack targets along the Po River valley. P-47
Thunderbolts attack roads and bridges north of the Arno River.
**Central Pacific:** Seventh Air Force B-25 Mitchells from the Gilbert Islands bomb
Ponape Island. B-24 Liberators from Saipan bomb Iwo Jima. B-24s from the Mar-
shalls bomb Truk.
**New Guinea:** FEAF B-24 Liberators bomb the airfield on Koror Island in the
Palaus.

## August 29

**CBI:** The Japanese 11th Army with seven divisions attacks along the rail line from Hengyang to Canton as part of an effort to open a land transportation corridor from northern China to Indochina. From there, the army intends to turn toward Kweilin and Liuchow to capture the Fourteenth Air Force's airfields and eliminate attacks on shipping and B-29 attacks on the Japanese homeland. The Japanese intend to force China to capitulate.

In Burma, Tenth Air Force B-25 Mitchells, P-51 Mustangs, and P-47 Thunderbolts attack bridges.

In China, Fourteenth Air Force B-24 Liberators, escorted by 45 fighters, bomb the Yoyang railroad yards. B-25 Mitchells bomb Pailochi, White Cloud, Tien Ho, and Hankow airfields and convoys near Hengyang and Hankow. P-40s attack trucks and a storage area near Changsha. P-40s claim eight Japanese fighters shot down.

A detachment of B-25s of the 491st Bombardment Squadron (Medium), 341st Bombardment Group (Medium), is sent from Yankai to Liuchow.

**ETO:** The 28th Infantry Division marches through Paris. XX Corps captures Rheims. VII Corps crosses the Aisne River. XIX Corps (2nd Armored Division and the 30th and 79th Infantry Divisions) crosses the Seine River. Elements of the Third Army capture crossings over the Meuse River. After learning from Bradley that he will not be receiving his army's allocation of 140,000 gallons of fuel due to other priorities, Lieutenant General George S. Patton, Jr. records his reaction in his diary: "it was a terrible mistake to halt even at the Meuse . . . there were no Germans ahead of us except those we were actually fighting."

Eighth Air Force P-38 Lightnings and P-47 Thunderbolts attack rail lines, marshaling yards, airfields, bridges, and highways in France, Belgium, and Germany. Fighter pilots report 20 confirmed kills on the ground. Three P-47s are lost and eight are damaged. Three pilots are reported missing.

Ninth Air Force redeploys the B-26 Marauders of the 586th Bombardment Squadron (Medium), 394th Bombardment Group (Medium), from England to France.

Sergeant John J. McVeigh of H Company, 23rd Infantry Regiment, 2nd Infantry Division, faces a German counterattack near Brest, France. Taking a hasty defensive position along a hedge, the Americans are pushed back, leaving a heavy machine-gun section exposed. Sergeant McVeigh stands up in front of the Germans and directs his squad's rifle fire into the enemy. He then charges the Germans with nothing but a combat knife to defend the machine-gun position. In the hand-to-hand struggle, Sergeant McVeigh is killed. McVeigh's squad and the machine-gun section are able to break the German assault. For his indomitable spirit and courage under fire in the face of certain death, Sergeant McVeigh will receive the Medal of Honor.

**MEDITERRANEAN:** Fifteenth Air Force sends more than 500 B-17s and B-24 Liberators escorted by P-38 Lightnings and P-51 Mustangs to attack targets in the Po River valley, oil refineries in Hungary, and railroad bridges in Czechoslovakia and Yugoslavia.

Twelfth Air Force P-47 Thunderbolts attack convoys in France. Fighter pilots report 100 vehicles destroyed. In France, P-51 Mustangs and P-40s attack targets in the Rhône valley.

Marine detachments from the heavy cruiser USS *Augusta* and light cruiser USS *Philadelphia* accept the surrender of the German garrisons on two islands in Marseille harbor.

**ITALY:** Twelfth Air Force B-25 Mitchells and B-26 Marauders attack bridges. A-20 Havocs attack fuel storage areas. P-47 Thunderbolts attack bridges and roads and conduct ground support missions in the Arno River valley.

Fifteenth Air Force P-38 Lightnings with Droopsnoot attack bridges in northern Italy near Latisana.

P-47s of the 316th Fighter Squadron 324th Fighter Group redeploy from Corsica to France.

**PACIFIC:** Major General Curtis E. LeMay takes command of the Twentieth Air Force's XX Bomber Command at Kharagpur, India.

**CENTRAL PACIFIC:** Seventh Air Force B-24 Liberators from Saipan bomb Iwo Jima. B-25 Mitchells from the Gilberts bomb Nauru Island.

**NEW GUINEA:** FEAF B-24 Liberators bomb Koror, Malakal, and Arakabesan Islands. P-38 Lightnings attack a seaplane base at Halong in the Celebes.

C-47s of the 22nd Troop Carrier Squadron, 374th Troop Carrier Group, redeploy from Australia to Finschhafen. Thirteenth Air Force B-24s of the 868th Bombardment Squadron (Heavy) redeploy from Los Negros Island in the Admiralties to Noemfoor Island. This squadron relies on radar for low-level night bombing attacks on shipping instead of identifying the target visually.

U.S. submarine *Jack* torpedoes and sinks a Japanese minesweeper and a cargo ship off the north end of Celebes Island.

A U.S. Navy PBY Catalina sinks a Japanese vessel at the entrance to Ambon Bay, Ceram Island.

## August 30

**CBI:** In China, Fourteenth Air Force B-25 Mitchells bomb the airfields at Hengyang, Pailochi, and Hankow as the Japanese bring up additional reinforcements. P-40s and P-51 Mustangs bomb road and rail junctions, bridges, vehicles, troops, town areas, and various targets of opportunity near Changsha, Hengshan, and Hengyang.

**ATLANTIC:** German submarine *U-482* torpedoes and sinks a U.S. tanker in convoy CU 36 (New York to United Kingdom) off the coast of Scotland.

**ETO:** The XX Corps captures Verdun. Third Army is notified that no additional fuel is available.

The 3rd Armored Division captures Laon. The 80th Infantry Division captures Châlons-sur-Marne. Eighth Air Force sends more than 700 B-17s and nearly 150 B-24 Liberators escorted by P-51 Mustangs to attack the U-boat base and shipyards at Kiel and V-weapon sites at Pas-de-Calais. A total of 159 bombers are damaged. The B-17s and B-24s attacking the V-weapon sites use H2X radar to assist the timing of bomb release. No bomber or fighter losses are reported.

During the night six B-17s drop leaflets over Belgium and France.

Ninth Air Force sends 75 A-20 Havocs and B-26 Marauders to attack fuel storage sites and gun positions.

B-26s of the 596th Bombardment Squadron (Medium) redeploy from England to France.

**MEDITERRANEAN:** The 1st Airborne Task Force captures Nice.

Soviet forces capture Ploeşti oil refinery. With the fall of Romania, 1,100 U.S. air crewmen of the Fifteenth Air Force who were held as prisoners of war are freed.

Fifteenth Air Force sends more than 100 B-17s and B-24 Liberators escorted by P-38 Lightnings and P-51 Mustangs to attack rail bridges in Yugoslavia. P-51 Mustangs strafe the Kecskemét, Hungary, and Oradea, Romania, airfields.

In France, Twelfth Air Force A-36 Intruder (Apache) fighter-bombers attack convoys and rail lines in the Rhône valley.

**ITALY:** Twelfth Air Force A-20 Havocs and P-47 Thunderbolts attack road and rail lines in the Po Valley.

**SOUTHWEST PACIFIC AREA:** U.S. submarine *Narwhal* lands men and supplies on east coast of Luzon.

**CENTRAL PACIFIC:** Seventh Air Force B-24 Liberators from Saipan bomb Yap. B-24s from Kwajalein bomb Mille Atoll.

**NEW GUINEA:** FEAF P-39 Airacobras attack along the coast of Geelvink Bay. B-24 Liberators bomb Koror and Malakal Islands. P-38 Lightnings bomb oil tanks, barracks, and antiaircraft positions on Ceram Island.

## August 31

**CBI:** There are 20 air groups and a total of 149,014 men in-theater.

**ATLANTIC:** There are 24 ground combat divisions in the continental United States preparing for deployment at this time.

In China, Fourteenth Air Force B-25 Mitchells attack the airfields at Tien Ho, White Cloud, and Hengyang. P-51 Mustangs and P-40s attack trucks, logistics sites, river transport, bridges, and troop concentrations near Changsha, Hengyang, and Nanyo.

**ETO:** The V Corps (5th Armored Division and the 4th and 28th Infantry Divisions) crosses the Seine River.

At this time there are 34 American ground combat divisions in the theater and 103 air groups, a total of 2,053,417 men.

A total of 37 B-24s and C-47s fly in support of Carpetbagger operations. During the night six B-17s drop leaflets over France.

Ninth Air Force sends nearly 100 B-26 Marauders and A-20 Havocs to bomb an ammunition storage site and gun positions.

B-26s of the 587th Bombardment Squadron (Medium), 394th Bombardment Group (Medium), and the 597th, 598th, and 599th Bombardment Squadrons (Medium) of the 397th Bombardment Group (Medium) redeploy from England to France.

**MEDITERRANEAN:** At this time in the Mediterranean theater there are six American ground combat divisions in-theater and 46 air groups, a total of 712,915 men. The French II Corps moves north of VI Corps to reach Patton's Third Army.

Fifteenth Air Force sends 38 B-17s to begin evacuating American POWs from Bucharest, Romania, to Italy (Operation Reunion). The bombers will complete the mission on September 3.

P-51 Mustangs strafe airfields in Romania and Hungary. Pilots report at least 150 confirmed kills on the ground.

In southern France, Twelfth Air Force A-20 Havocs and P-47 Thunderbolts attack convoys, roads, and rail lines as Seventh Army advances north.

**ITALY:** German forces begin a withdrawal from the Arno River defensive line in response to Eighth Army's attack on the east coast of Italy (Operation Olive). The U.S. IV Corps with the 1st Armored Division and the 370th RCT of the 92nd Infantry Division advances northeast of Pisa with the mission of capturing Monte Pisano and the city of Lucca. The 92nd Infantry Division is an all-black unit led by white officers.

Twelfth Air Force B-25 Mitchells and B-26 Marauders attack railroad bridges in the Po River valley. A-20 Havocs also attack targets in the Po Valley and attack bridges, and roads in the Arno valley.

**SOUTHWEST PACIFIC AREA:** The Vogelkop operation is completed. U.S. casualties between April and August in SWPA total 9,500, with an estimated 110,000 Japanese casualties. Over 30,000 Japanese soldiers are isolated in New Guinea, and over 96,000 Japanese soldiers and sailors are trapped at Rabaul. The Far Eastern Air Force (FEAF) has 2,629 first-line combat aircraft and 633 transport aircraft.

General MacArthur's headquarters issues instructions to Lieutenant General Walter Krueger's Sixth Army to be ready for operations to seize airfields on Mindanao Island, gain control of Leyte, the Surigao Strait, and the island of Samar in the Philippines. The operation is set for mid-November or December.

In Luzon Strait USS *Barb* torpedoes and sinks an auxiliary minesweeper and a cargo ship. USS *Queenfish* torpedoes and sinks an army tanker and damages another tanker. USS *Sealion* torpedoes and sinks a minelayer. U.S. submarine *Redfish* lands supplies and evacuates personnel from Palawan Island.

**PACIFIC:** At this time there are 21 American ground combat divisions, 11 separate regiments, and five marine divisions in-theater. There are also 35 air groups. The total strength of U.S. forces in the Pacific is 1,102, 422.

TG 38.4 (Rear Admiral Ralph E. Davison) attacks Iwo Jima and Chichi Jima. F4F Hellcats from USS *Franklin* sink an auxiliary minesweeper and cargo ship off Iwo Jima.

## September 1

**ALEUTIANS:** During the night Eleventh Air Force sends one B-24 on a raid on Paramushiru Island in the Kuriles. Later, a B-25 aircrew reports sinking a vessel off the coast of Paramushiru.

**CBI:** Tenth Air Force P-47 Thunderbolts attack Bhamo and strafe river boats.

In China, Fourteenth Air Force B-24 Liberator aircrews report sinking a small cargo ship in Formosa Strait. P-40s and P-51 Mustangs attack bridges, roads, shipping, airfields, troops, and other targets of opportunity near Hengyang and Changning. The 528th Fighter Squadron of the 311th Fighter Group deploys a detachment of P-51 Mustangs from Shwangliu to operate from airfields at Hanchung and Lianshan.

**ATLANTIC:** A U.S. Coast Guard cutter locates a German weather ship off Greenland, and the ship is scuttled by her crew to avoid capture. German submarine *U-703* attacks the cutter, but ice prevents a hit.

**ETO:** As commander of SHAEF, General Eisenhower takes operational control of both the U.S. and British Army Groups from General Montgomery and establishes headquarters at Versailles. Montgomery takes command of the 21st Army Group and General Bradley continues as commander of the 12th Army Group. The 12th Army Group is composed of three armies: the First under Lieutenant General Hodges, the Third under Lieutenant General Patton, and the Ninth under Lieutenant General Simpson. Allied supply lines now stretch 600 to 900 miles from the beaches at Normandy and the port of Cherbourg to the front lines. Truck transport becomes the primary means of supplying forces.

The XX Corps of Third Army crosses the Meuse River. Third Army halts to bring up supplies. The 3rd Armored Division makes a 30-mile advance past Laon.

Eighth Air Force sends 12 B-24 Liberators with Azon-equipped bombs and escorted by 15 P-51 Mustangs to attack the Ravenstein railroad bridge in the Netherlands. Nearly 1,000 B-17s and B-24 Liberators escorted by over 500 P-38 Lightnings and P-51s are sent against targets in Germany and France, but the mission is recalled due to bad weather over the targets. Eight bombers are damaged. Aircrew casualties are 30 killed and two are wounded. Three fighters are lost and two are damaged. Two pilots are reported missing.

Over 250 P-47 Thunderbolts attack rail lines in France. Fighter pilots report five confirmed kills on the ground. Three fighters are lost and 29 are damaged. Three pilots are reported missing.

A total of 31 B-24s fly in support of Carpetbagger operations.

U.S. Strategic Air Forces in Europe (USSTAF) takes administrative control of Ninth Air Force's IX Troop Carrier Command. First Allied Airborne Army retains operational control.

Ninth Air Force sends B-26 Marauders to attack gun positions and defenses in Brest. P-47 and P-38 fighters support ground forces and fly armed reconnaissance missions near Amiens, Cambrai, Rheims, and Verdun.

The B-26s of the 556th, 557th, 558th and 559th Bombardment Squadrons (Medium), 387th Bombardment Group (Medium), redeploy from England to France.

**MEDITERRANEAN:** The 45th Infantry Division is unable to hold German forces as they battle to escape along the Lyon-Geneva highway.

Fifteenth Air Force sends nearly 500 B-17s and B-24 Liberators escorted by P-38 Lightnings and P-51 Mustangs to attack railroad bridges and marshaling yards in Yugoslavia and Hungary.

**ITALY:** Twelfth Air Force B-25 Mitchells bomb road and rail bridges near Venice. A-20 Havocs attack gun positions and targets of opportunity in the Po River valley. A-20 Havocs and P-47 Thunderbolts attack troop concentrations, gun positions, rail lines, bridges, logistics storage areas, and highways north of Florence.

**SOUTHWEST PACIFIC AREA:** Over 50 FEAF B-24 Liberators bomb airfields on Mindanao Island in the Philippines.

U.S. submarine *Narwhal* lands men and supplies on east coast of Luzon.

U.S. submarine *Tunny* is damaged in an air attack in Luzon Strait and is forced to terminate her patrol.

**PACIFIC:** Naval Operating Base, Saipan, is established.

Heavy cruiser USS *New Orleans,* light cruiser *Biloxi,* and four destroyers from TG 38.4, bombard Japanese positions on Iwo Jima and Chichi Jima. U.S. submarine *Pilotfish* torpedoes and sinks a Japanese auxiliary vessel near Chichi Jima.

**CENTRAL PACIFIC:** Seventh Air Force B-24 Liberators from the Marshalls bomb Truk.

**NEW GUINEA:** Brigadier General Donald J. Myers arrives at Wakde with the 123rd RCT, 33rd Infantry Division, to relieve the 31st Infantry Division and assume control of the Sarmi-Maffin Bay area.

## September 2

**CBI:** Tenth Air Force B-25 Mitchells bomb Japanese activity along the Burma Road near Wanling. More than 20 B-24 Liberators fly fuel to Kunming, China.

In China, Fourteenth Air Force B-25 Mitchells bomb the Hengyang airfield and P-40s attack gun positions, troop concentrations, and river transports near Hengyang and Changning.

**ATLANTIC:** JCS issues orders for a combined SWPA-Central Pacific attack on Leyte, set for December 20. As a preliminary to the Leyte invasion, MacArthur will capture Morotai Island, while Nimitz will attack the Palau Islands. The JCS avoids providing any instructions on the next objectives of the theater commanders. Nevertheless, the JCS orders plans drawn up for offensive operations against both Formosa and Luzon.

**ETO:** The XIX Corps arrives at the border of Belgium south of Tournai. The German harbor batteries at St-Malo surrender, almost two weeks after the garrison in the city had surrendered.

Eighth Air Force sends P-47 Thunderbolts to attack road and rail targets in Belgium. Nine fighters are damaged.

Two C-47s fly in support of Carpetbagger operations in France.

Ninth Air Force P-47s and P-38s support ground forces and fly armed reconnaissance missions.

**MEDITERRANEAN:** Fifteenth Air Force sends nearly 400 B-24 Liberators escorted by over 175 P-38 Lightnings and P-51 Mustangs to bomb marshaling yards and road and rail bridges in Yugoslavia.

In France, Twelfth Air Force P-51 Mustangs and P-40s attack rail lines near Lyon.

**ITALY:** The U.S. 442nd Regimental Combat Team is dispatched to southern France.

Fifteenth Air Force establishes the headquarters for the XV Fighter Command (Provisional) with operational control of the 306th Fighter Wing and the seven fighter groups. Three of the squadrons have P-38 Lightnings and four have P-51 Mustangs.

Twelfth Air Force B-25 Mitchells, A-20 Havocs, and P-47 Thunderbolts attack bridges in the Po River valley.

**Southwest Pacific Area:** FEAF sends more than 50 B-24 Liberators to bomb logistics storage areas, troop locations, shipyards, and airfields on Mindanao in the Philippines.

**Pacific:** U.S. submarine *Guardfish* torpedoes and sinks a Japanese cargo ship north of Chichi Jima.

U.S. submarine *Finback* is conducting a lifeguard mission in support of the air attack on Chichi Jima. The submarine is to rescue any downed pilots. One flyer is rescued—Lieutenant (j.g.) George H. W. Bush. Bush's two other crewmembers do not survive. Bush later becomes the 41st president of the United States.

**Central Pacific:** Seventh Air Force B-25 Mitchells from the Marshalls bomb Ponape Island and Nauru Island.

**New Guinea:** FEAF B-24 Liberators bomb Koror Island in the Palaus.

## September 3

**CBI:** In Burma, Tenth Air Force B-25 Mitchell aircrews report damaging a bridge at Indaw.

In China, Fourteenth Air Force B-25 Mitchells attack supply convoys supporting the Japanese Eleventh Army. B-24 Liberators bomb the Nanking marshaling yards. B-25 Mitchell aircrews report destroying at least 45 trucks and damage nearly 100 others near Hengyang and Tungting Lake. Over 100 P-40s, P-51 Mustangs, and P-38 Lightnings attack troops, rail lines, and bridges near Hengyang and Changning.

**ETO:** First Army reports that German forces have been cleared out within its zone of advance. The 1st Infantry Division of VII Corps assists in blocking the retreat of nearly 20 German divisions of the German Seventh Army, now nothing more than disorganized remnants. Prisoners captured near Mons are estimated at 25,000.

Nearly 400 B-17s escorted by P-51 Mustangs make a bombing run on 16 gun batteries and defensive positions at Brest. Two B-17s are lost and 13 are damaged. Aircrew casualties are 16 missing. Another 345 B-17s with P-51 escort are sent against a synthetic oil production facility in northern Germany. One B-17 is lost and 103 are damaged. Fighter pilots report seven confirmed kills. One P-51 is lost and two are damaged. The pilot is reported as missing.

Over 100 P-47 Thunderbolts attack transportation targets in Belgium and Germany. One P-47 is lost and 19 are damaged. One pilot is reported wounded and one is reported missing.

During the night, a total of 40 B-24s and four C-47s fly in support of Carpet-bagger operations.

Ninth Air Force A-20 Havocs and B-26 Marauders attack German gun positions and defenses at Brest. P-47 and P-38 fighters support ground forces and fly armed reconnaissance missions.

**Mediterranean:** The 177th Cavalry Reconnaissance Squadron blocks the road at Bourgen-Bresse, but the unit takes heavy losses as the Germans fight to hold the Belfort Gap to allow remaining elements to retreat to safety.

The French II Corps liberates Lyon. The VI Corps attacks German forces defending Belfort.

Fifteenth Air Force sends more than 300 B-17s and B-24 Liberators escorted by P-38 Lightnings and P-51 Mustangs to bomb lines of communication in Hungary and Yugoslavia and slow the retreat of German troops as they are pressed hard by advancing Soviet forces.

In southern France, Twelfth Air Force P-51 Mustangs and P-47 Thunderbolts attack convoys, bridges, and roads as the Germans abandon Lyon in front of the advancing Seventh Army.

**ITALY:** Operation Olive is stalled by heavy rains and flooding. The Eighth Army has suffered 8,000 casualties since August 25 and has failed to break through the Gothic Line.

Twelfth Air Force B-25 Mitchells and B-26 Marauders attack rail and road bridges in the Po River valley. A-20 Havocs and P-47 Thunderbolts attack rail cars and vehicles near Turin.

**PACIFIC:** Naval Task Group 12.5, commanded by Rear Admiral Allen E. Smith, with the small carrier USS *Monterey,* three heavy cruisers, and three destroyers, bombard Wake Island.

**CENTRAL PACIFIC:** Seventh Air Force B-24 Liberators from Saipan bomb Iwo Jima.

**NEW GUINEA:** At Cape Opmarai, the newly constructed airfield torn out of the jungle is operational.

Headquarters XIII Bomber Command redeploys from Los Negros Island in the Admiralties to Wakde Island.

## September 4

**CBI:** The Japanese capture Lingling, eliminating another Fourteenth Air Force air base. General Chennault, seriously limited by a lack of fuel and ammunition, is hard-pressed to slow the enemy advance. Stilwell is reluctant to provide additional support, believing that only Chiang Kai-shek can save the situation by reorganizing his forces and committing to American direction. Chiang believes Stilwell is sacrificing China in favor of Burma and sends messages to President Roosevelt demanding that Stilwell be recalled.

Tenth Air Force sends 24 B-24 Liberators to fly 32,000 gallons of fuel to Kunming, China. In Burma, P-47 Thunderbolts attack Bhamo.

Fourteenth Air Force B-25 Mitchells, with P-51 Mustangs flying escort bomb Lingling. Aircrews report numerous enemy casualties.

**ATLANTIC:** Admiral Ernest J. King (COMINCH) requests a decision from other members of the JCS on whether Formosa or Luzon would be the next objective of the offensive. King argues for Formosa, viewing it as the most rapid approach to cut off the vital Japanese supply line from the East Indies and Indochina. Formosa also provides U.S. air forces access to the coast of China to establish airfields for the strategic bombing of the Japanese home islands.

**ETO:** The First Army's VII Corps attacks toward Namur and captures the city. V Corps crosses the Meuse River.

During the night Private First Class Gino J. Merli's company, in the 18th Infantry Regiment, 1st Infantry Division, is overrun by a superior German force near Sars la Bruyere, Belgium. Merli fights in his position until German troops kill or capture most of his comrades. Feigning death, Merli waits until the enemy withdraws, then holds his position throughout the night, fighting back and disrupting the enemy's assault. When the area is retaken the next day, American troops find Merli still at his position. Around him are the bodies of more than 50 enemy soldiers. For his courage and dedication in the face of overwhelming odds, Private First Class Gino J. Merli will receive the Medal of Honor.

**MEDITERRANEAN:** Twelfth Air Force's 85th Bombardment Squadron (Light), 47th Bombardment Group (Light), redeploys the squadron's A-20 Havocs from Corsica to southern France.

**ITALY:** Fifteenth Air Force sends nearly 400 B-17s and B-24 Liberators escorted by P-38 Lightnings and P-51 Mustangs to attack submarines in Genoa harbor and lines of communication in northern Italy. Twelfth Air Force B-25 Mitchells and B-26 Marauders attack rail and road bridges in the Po River valley. A-20 Havocs bomb vehicles near Turin and Milan.

**PACIFIC:** U.S. submarine *Bowfin* torpedoes and sinks a Japanese guardboat northeast of the Bonin Islands.

**CENTRAL PACIFIC:** Seventh Air Force B-24 Liberators from Kwajalein bomb Wotje Atoll.

### September 5

**CBI:** Tenth Air Force sends eight B-25 Mitchells to bomb targets at Indaw, while 21 B-24 Liberators fly fuel to Kunming, China.

Fourteenth Air Force B-25 Mitchells bomb Hengyang airfield.

**ETO:** Ninth Army becomes operational under the command of Lieutenant General William H. Simpson. The army is composed of the 6th Armored Division and the 2nd, 8th, 29th, and 83rd Infantry Divisions. Simpson takes operational control of VIII Corps and is given the mission to reduce German strongholds on the peninsula while protecting the flank of the Third Army. The VII Corps of First Army crosses the Meuse River and meets limited but organized resistance for the first time in weeks. The Third Army's XII Corps crosses the Moselle River north of Nancy. The XX Corps crosses the river north and south of Metz.

Eighth Air Force sends more than 500 B-17s escorted by over 300 P-51 Mustangs to attack the aircraft engine production facility at Stuttgart and the synthetic oil plant at Ludwigshafen. Over 200 B-24 Liberators bomb the Karlsruhe marshaling yard. Six bombers are lost and 354 are damaged. Aircrew casualties are three killed, 16 wounded, and 58 missing. Fighter pilots report 19 confirmed kills in the air and 14 confirmed kills on the ground. Three P-51s are lost and seven are damaged. Three pilots are reported missing.

More than 140 B-17s escorted by P-51s make a visual bombing run on gun positions and fortifications at Brest. Two B-17s are lost and one is damaged. Aircrew losses are 18 missing.

Over 200 P-38 Lightnings and P-47 Thunderbolts attack transportation targets in western Germany. Fighter pilots report 62 confirmed kills on the ground. Four P-47s are lost and 12 are damaged. The pilots are reported missing. Other P-38s and P-47s attack airfields near Hanau and Giessen in Germany. Pilots report two confirmed kills in the air and 66 on the ground. Four fighters are lost and five are damaged. Four pilots are reported missing.

A total of 46 B-24s and two C-47s fly in support of Carpetbagger operations. One bomber is lost. During the night seven B-17s drop leaflets over Belgium, the Netherlands, and Germany.

Ninth Air Force sends 300 A-20 Havocs and B-26 Marauders to attack German defensive positions near Brest and a coastal battery. P-47 fighters also attack gun positions at Brest and P-38s attack ground targets in support of ground forces.

**MEDITERRANEAN:** Fifteenth Air Force sends more than 400 B-17s and B-24 Liberators escorted by P-38 Lightnings and P-51 Mustangs to attack transportation targets and lines of communication in Hungary and northern Italy. Twelfth Air Force P-47 Thunderbolts fly ground support missions for the Seventh Army in the Rhône River valley.

Off the invasion beaches of southern France, a French and a U.S. destroyer locate and eliminate three German manned torpedoes and capture the crews.

**ITALY:** The U.S. IV Corps occupies Monte Pisano and the city of Lucca. The Germans defend Pistoia, which blocks Route 64, the road north to Bologna.

Twelfth Air Force B-25 Mitchells and B-26 Marauders attack rail and road traffic in the Po River valley. A-20 Havocs attack ammunition storage sites. P-47 Thunderbolts attack German defensive positions along the Gothic Line.

A-20 Havocs of the 84th and 86th Bombardment Squadrons (Light), 47th Bombardment Group (Light), redeploy from Corsica to France.

**PACIFIC:** U.S. submarine *Albacore* sinks Japanese cargo ship south of Kyushu, Japan.

**CENTRAL PACIFIC:** Seventh Air Force B-24 Liberators from Saipan bomb Iwo Jima. B-25 Mitchells from the Gilberts bomb Nauru and Ponape Islands.

**NEW GUINEA:** FEAF B-24 Liberators bomb the airfield on Peleliu Island and airfields on Celebes Island. A-20 Havocs attack Halmahera Island in the Moluccas.

B-25 Mitchells of the 405th Bombardment Squadron (Medium), 38th Bombardment Group (Medium), redeploy from Nadzab to Biak Island. The Fifth Air Force's 547th Night Fighter Squadron with P-38 Lightnings and P-61 Black Widow night fighters arrives at Oro Bay from the United States.

## September 6

**CBI:** Tenth Air Force sends 24 B-24 Liberators to fly about 34,000 gallons of fuel to Kunming, China. Fourteenth Air Force sends 20 B-25 Mitchells to bomb transportation targets near Lingling and Hengyang airfield. P-40s and P-51 Mustangs attack marshaling yards, troop areas, trucks, river transports, and ammunition storage sites.

**ETO:** The 5th Armored Division of V Corps captures Sedan and advances into the Ardennes Forest. Eighth Air Force sends more than 200 P-38 Lightnings and P-47 Thunderbolts to attack rail and road movement near Rotterdam in the Netherlands and in the Aachen and Koblenz areas in Germany. One P-38 and three P-47s are shot down and 12 fighters are damaged. The four pilots are reported missing. The logistics pinch for ground forces in France becomes serious enough that 70 B-24 Liberators begin flying supplies to forward airfields in France.

Ninth Air Force B-26 Marauders and A-20 Havocs attack gun positions and fortifications at Brest, and a coastal battery. P-47 Thunderbolts also attack the defenses at Brest and attack an ammunition storage site, and P-38 fighters fly cover for ground units.

**MEDITERRANEAN:** Fifteenth Air Force sends more than 500 B-17s and B-24 Liberators escorted by P-38 Lightnings and P-51 Mustangs to attack marshaling yards in Romania, Yugoslavia, and Hungary.

**ITALY:** During the night Twelfth Air Force A-20 Havocs attack targets of opportunity near Milan.

**SOUTHWEST PACIFIC AREA:** FEAF B-24 Liberators and B-25 Mitchells bomb airfields and port facilities in the Philippines.

**PACIFIC:** The headquarters of Twentieth Air Force's 498th Bombardment Group (Very Heavy) arrives at Saipan from the United States.

**CENTRAL PACIFIC:** Seventh Air Force B-24 Liberators from Saipan bomb Iwo Jima. B-24s from the Marshalls bomb Truk.

Vice Admiral Marc A. Mitscher's Task Force 58 (with three task groups: TG 38.1, TG 38.2, TG 38.3) begins operations against the western Carolines. The small carrier USS *Independence* has an air group aboard that is specially trained for night operations.

Two U.S. destroyers bombard gun positions on Aguijan Island in the Marianas.

U.S. submarine *Albacore* torpedoes and sinks a Japanese auxiliary minesweeper off Shikoku, Japan. U.S. submarine *Hake* torpedoes and damages a Japanese destroyer east of the Ryukyus.

**NEW GUINEA:** FEAF B-25 Mitchells bomb targets on Halmahera and Morotai Islands. A-20 Havocs also attack targets on Halmahera Island. A-20s, B-25 Mitchells, and P-40s attack airfields, barges, and logistics sites.

P-47 Thunderbolts of the 69th, 310th, and 311th Fighter Squadrons, 58th Fighter Group, redeploy from Saidor to Noemfoor Island. The B-25s of the 71st Bombardment Squadron (Medium), 38th Bombardment Group (Medium), redeploy from Nadzab to Biak Island.

## September 7

**ALEUTIANS:** Eleventh Air Force B-25 Mitchells attack a small fishing fleet between Paramushiru and Onnekotan (Onekutan) Islands in the Kuriles.

**CBI:** Tenth Air Force sends 22 B-24 Liberators to fly fuel to Kunming, China.

Fourteenth Air Force sends 24 B-25 Mitchells to bomb targets at Kiyang, Lingling, and Yoyang. Other B-25s bomb Tien Ho and White Cloud airfields at Canton. P-40s and P-51 Mustangs attack troops, rail lines and rail cars, river shipping, logistics storage facilities, and bridges.

In French Indochina, four P-38 Lightnings attack targets of opportunity near Hanoi.

**ATLANTIC:** The JCS planners support Admiral King's reasoning that Formosa should be the objective for the next offensive in the Pacific. March 1, 1945, is set as the target date for Operation Causeway.

**ETO:** Ninth Air Force P-47 Thunderbolts and P-38s provide air cover and ground support for the 8th and 29th Infantry Divisions.

**MEDITERRANEAN:** The 3rd Infantry Division captures Besançon and the 45th Infantry Division presses retreating German forces.

Twelfth Air Force redeploys the headquarters of the 47th Bombardment Group (Light) and the A-20 Havocs of the 97th Bombardment Squadron (Light) from Corsica to France.

Technician Fifth Grade Robert D. Maxwell and three other men of the 7th Infantry Regiment, 3rd Infantry Division, are surprised by a platoon-size German raiding force approaching the battalion command post near Besançon, France. Carrying only .45-caliber automatic pistols, the four soldiers defend the battalion observation post against overwhelming fire. When a German hand grenade lands in the midst of the group, Maxwell throws himself on it. For his courage in defending the battalion command post and his selfless act of sacrifice to save the lives of others, Technician Fifth Grade Maxwell will receive the Medal of Honor.

**ITALY:** General Mark Clark notes in his diary, "The fate of the Fifth Army is tied up with that of the Eighth Army." Clark prepares the U.S. II Corps to attack north up Route 65 and drive German forces from the Futa Pass and the Il Giogo Pass and break the Gothic Line.

**SOUTHWEST PACIFIC AREA:** U.S. submarine *Paddle* torpedoes and sinks a Japanese transport, which is carrying 750 American prisoners of war. *Paddle* also damages a tanker off the coast of Mindanao.

**PACIFIC:** Twentieth Air Force begins deploying elements of the 873rd, 874th, and 875th Bombardment Squadrons (Very Heavy) of the 498th Bombardment Group (Very Heavy) to Saipan from the United States. The squadrons' first missions are scheduled for late October.

Carrier aircraft from Admiral William F. Halsey's Third Fleet begin widespread attacks on Yap and the Palau Islands, as well as Mindanao in the Philippines. Aircraft and shipping are the primary targets. The intent is to limit Japanese reinforcement of the Philippines and reduce the air threat to a U.S. invasion force headed for the Philippines.

**CENTRAL PACIFIC:** Seventh Air Force B-24 Liberators using radar-guided bombing techniques attack Iwo Jima.

Carrier aircraft from Naval Task Groups 38.1, 38.2, and 38.3 attack Japanese positions throughout the Palau Islands. Three light cruisers, screened by four destroyers, under command of Rear Admiral F. E. M. Whiting, bombard Peleliu, Angaur, and Ngesebus. A heavy cruiser, a light cruiser, and four destroyers bombard Yap. Aircraft from Naval Task Group TG 38.4 (Rear Admiral Ralph E. Davison) attack targets on Yap and Ulithi.

**NEW GUINEA:** FEAF A-20 Havocs, P-47 Thunderbolts, P-38 Lightnings, and P-40s attack airfields at Wewak and Manokwari.

B-24 Liberators bomb Celebes Island and B-25 Mitchells and P-38 Lightnings attack Halmahera Island. A-20 Havocs bomb Boela airfield on Ceram Island.

### September 8

**CBI:** Tenth Air Force sends 23 B-24 Liberators to fly fuel to Kunming, China.

The Japanese Eleventh Army occupies Lingling airfield after the Fourteenth Air Force abandons it.

Fourteenth Air Force sends three B-24 Liberators to attack shipping near Hong Kong. Aircrews report sinking a Japanese destroyer. In China, B-25 Mitchells attack bridges near Kiyang and attack troop concentrations, rail lines, and roads near Hengyang and Lingling. Over 100 P-40s and P-51 Mustangs escort the bombers and fly sweeps over the area.

In French Indochina 18 B-24 Liberators bomb bridges at Hue, Duc Tho, and Quang Tri. Aircrews report destroying the main bridge at Quang Tri.

During the night Japanese bombers attack the headquarters, logistics base, and parked B-29s at Hsinching airfield near Chengtu. One bomber and a C-46 are damaged; two soldiers are wounded.

**ETO:** VII Corps captures Liège. The Ninth Army conducts a three-division attack on Brest, supported by artillery and air bombardment. The first attack fails.

Eighth Air Force sends more than 700 B-17s to bomb the Ludwigshafen oil refinery and an oil storage depot at Kassel in Germany. Over 300 B-24 Liberators bomb the marshaling yard at Karlsruhe, Germany. The B-17s are escorted by over 200 P-51 Mustangs; the B-24s escorted by nearly 100 P-51s. A total of 10 bombers are lost and 412 are damaged. Aircrew casualties are 18 killed, 27 wounded, and 83 missing. Fighter pilots report only one P-51 damaged.

More than 100 P-38 Lightnings cross the Rhine River to strafe and bomb rail lines in Germany. Fighter pilots report seven confirmed kills on the ground. Nearly 200 P-47 Thunderbolts and P-51s strafe targets along the Rhine River valley. One P-47 and one P-51 are lost and 13 fighters are damaged. One pilot is wounded and two are reported missing.

One C-47 supports Carpetbagger operations in France.

A total of 110 B-24s fly supplies to forward airfields to support the ground forces.

During the night seven B-17s drop leaflets over the Netherlands, Germany, and France.

Ninth Air Force P-47 and P-38 fighters support the 2nd, 5th, 8th, and 29th Infantry Divisions in the XX Corps area.

The headquarters and troop carrier squadrons of the 439th and the 441st Troop Carrier Groups redeploy C-47s from England to France.

Private First Class Ernest W. Prussman is a squad leader in the 13th Infantry Regiment, 8th Infantry Division. As elements of his battalion come under heavy mortar and machine-gun fire from the hedgerows near the town of Les Coates in Brittany, PFC Prussman leads his men to attack the German position. As he vaults a hedgerow, Prussman encounters and disarms two German soldiers. Approaching the next hedgerow, Prussman's squad destroys a machine-gun position and captures

A V-2 being readied for launch  *(German Museum, Munich)*

two enemy soldiers. As Prussman leads his men toward a third position, he is shot and mortally wounded, but not before he flings a grenade at his enemy, killing him. Prussman's initiative, leadership, and courage under fire will win him the Medal of Honor.

The first V-2 rocket is fired from a location in the Netherlands toward England. It lands in southwest London, killing or injuring 20 civilians. The rocket is over 46 feet long, carries a 2,150-pound warhead, and is powered by alcohol and liquid oxygen. Able to travel at speeds reaching 3,600 miles per hour, it has a maximum range of 200 miles. Mobile and easily hidden, the V-2 will prove to be a powerful but largely ineffective weapon. Between September 8 and March 27, 1945, an average of about five V-2s will be launched at London every day, causing about 2,700 casualties. In all, 3,000 V-2s will be launched—1,250 at England and 1,750 at Antwerp.

**MEDITERRANEAN:** Fifteenth Air Force sends 354 B-17s and B-24 Liberators escorted by P-38 Lightnings to bomb railroad bridges and marshaling yards in Yugoslavia. P-51 Mustangs attack the airfield at Ecka in Yugoslavia. Pilots report 58 enemy aircraft destroyed on the ground. One P-51 and one pilot are lost. Over Landza airfield in Yugoslavia, P-51s destroy 18 German aircraft on the ground.

Twelfth Air Force P-47 Thunderbolts attack a convoy near Strasbourg.

**ITALY:** Twelfth Air Force P-47 Thunderbolts attack vehicles, bridges, and German positions in the Po River valley.

**SOUTHWEST PACIFIC AREA:** U.S. submarine *Bashaw* torpedoes and sinks a Japanese transport off Mindanao.

U.S. submarine *Spadefish* torpedoes and sinks a Japanese transport and three cargo ships off northeast Taiwan.

**PACIFIC:** The JCS lays out a strategic direction for operations in the Pacific. The invasion of Leyte in the Philippines will begin by December 20, be carried out by MacArthur's SWPA forces, and be supported by Admiral Nimitz's naval forces. Nimitz's POA planners will prepare options for an attack on either Luzon beginning February 20 or Formosa on March 1. MacArthur's forces are to concentrate on reducing the Japanese air threat over Luzon to support both offensive options being prepared. This air offensive will be coordinated with Twentieth Air Force and with the air commander in CBI.

Accompanied by the commander of the XX Bomber Command, Major General Curtis E. LeMay, Twentieth Air Force sends 90 B-29 Superfortresses from the base at Chengtu, China, to bomb the Showa Steel Works at Anshan. All but 11 bombers hit the primary target. The initial targets of Twentieth Air Force, as determined by the Joint Chiefs of Staff in Washington, are targets supporting Japanese steel production.

U.S. submarine *Seal* damages Japanese destroyer *Namikaze* off Hokkaido, Japan.

**CENTRAL PACIFIC:** Seventh Air Force B-24 Liberators from Saipan bomb Iwo Jima. B-25 Mitchells from the Gilberts bomb Ponape Island. B-24s from Kwajalein bomb Wotje Atoll.

Seventh Air Force B-24 Liberators bomb shipping off Chichi Jima, damaging two cargo vessels.

**NEW GUINEA:** FEAF P-39 Airacobras strafe targets along the coast near Wewak. P-47 Thunderbolts, P-38 Lightnings, and P-40s attack targets of opportunity.

B-24 Liberators bomb Langoan airfield, Celebes Island. B-25 Mitchells bomb Halmahera Island.

The A-20 Havocs of the 673rd and 674th Bombardment Squadrons (Light), 417th Bombardment Group (Light), redeploy from Saidor to Noemfoor Island.

## September 9

**ALEUTIANS:** Eleventh Air Force sends three B-24 Liberators on a nighttime raid on Kashiwabara, on Paramushiru Island in the Kuriles.

**CBI:** Tenth Air Force sends 17 B-24 Liberators to fly fuel to Kunming, China. B-25 Mitchells bomb a Japanese headquarters at Manwing.

In China, Fourteenth Air Force sends 24 B-25 Mitchells to bomb river transport and troop assembly areas around Kiyang, Lingling, and Lingkwantien. Aircrews report that the bridge at Lingling is heavily damaged. B-24s bomb cargo ships in the South China Sea. Aircrews report four ships sunk or heavily damaged.

The 322nd Troop Carrier Squadron is activated at Kunming, China. The squadron, under operational control of Fourteenth Air Force, is equipped with C-47s.

**ETO:** The XIX Corps enters Holland.

General Eisenhower informs the CCS that he intends to maintain his original strategic approach for the offensive against Germany, making two simultaneous thrusts into the Ruhr. At this time, however, due to limits on the availability of logistic support for both axes of attack, he will give priority of logistics support to Allied forces under General Montgomery in the north.

Eighth Air Force sends more than 800 B-17s escorted by nearly 300 P-51 Mustangs to attack the marshaling yard at Mannheim and an armaments production facility at Düsseldorf. Another 337 B-24 Liberators escorted by 128 P-51s bomb the marshaling yard at Mainz. Eleven B-17s and three B-24s are lost, and a total of over 450 bombers are damaged. Aircrew casualties are seven killed, 13 wounded, and 150 missing. One P-51 is lost.

B-17s with P-51 escort fly Operation Grassy, dropping supplies to members of the French Resistance.

A total of 40 B-24s and C-47s fly in support of Carpetbagger operations. During the night seven B-17s drop leaflets over Belgium, France, and Germany.

P-47 fighters attack targets in northeastern Germany. Pilots report one confirmed kill and one probable in the air and one confirmed kill and one probable on the ground. Nearly 200 P-47s and P-51s bomb and strafe shipping along the coast between Germany and the Netherlands and attack rail and road traffic near Frankfurt am Main. Fighter pilots report 13 confirmed kills. Eight fighters are lost and 16 damaged. One pilot is wounded, and seven others are reported missing.

Ninth Air Force sends P-47s and P-38s to support VIII Corps near Brest and the 2nd, 5th, and 8th Infantry Divisions of XX Corps, Third Army, near Metz.

**MEDITERRANEAN:** The 83rd Infantry Division captures about 20,000 German soldiers who surrender in southwest France.

**ITALY:** Twelfth Air Force B-26 Marauders attack rail bridges in the Po River valley. B-25 Mitchells bomb troop assembly areas and logistics sites. A-20 Havocs and P-47 Thunderbolts attack rail lines, convoys, and rail cars.

**SOUTHWEST PACIFIC AREA:** Naval Task Force 38 begins strikes against Japanese targets on Mindanao. Carrier aircraft sink a transport in the Sulu Sea west of Mindanao and two transports and a cargo ship east of Mindanao. Two light cruisers and four destroyers under Rear Admiral Laurance T. DuBose, supported by aircraft from the small carrier USS *Langley,* attack a coastal convoy on the west coast of Mindanao.

U.S. submarine *Queenfish* torpedoes and sinks a transport and passenger-cargo ship and damages a torpedo boat northwest of Luzon.

**PACIFIC:** U.S. submarine *Bang* torpedoes and sinks a Japanese transport and cargo ship north of the Bonin Islands.

U.S. submarine *Seal* torpedoes and sinks a Japanese cargo ship in the Sea of Okhotsk.

**CENTRAL PACIFIC:** During the night, Seventh Air Force B-25 Mitchells from the Gilbert Islands bomb Nauru Island. One B-24 from Saipan on a snooper mission (non-visual radar-guided bombing) attacks Iwo Jima.

**NEW GUINEA:** FEAF P-38 Lightnings and A-20 Havocs attack airfields in the Molucca Islands. B-24 Liberators bomb an airfield on Celebes Island and on Halmahera Island.

The headquarters of the 417th Bombardment Group (Light) moves from Saidor to Noemfoor Island.

## September 10

**CBI:** Tenth Air Force sends 23 B-24 Liberators to fly fuel to Kunming, China.

In China, Fourteenth Air Force sends 45 B-25 Mitchells to bomb the towns of Kutkai, Tunganhsien, Lingling, and Tunghsiangchiao. Aircrews report hitting a fuel storage area near Lingling. More than 100 P-40s and P-51 Mustangs attack bridges, railroads, logistics storage facilities, rail and road traffic, airfields, and river transport.

**ATLANTIC:** W. Averell Harriman, ambassador to the Soviet Union, reports on changing attitudes of the Soviet leadership in recent weeks. Harriman believes that the American emphasis on cooperation and friendship may be misunderstood as weakness by the Soviet leadership. "Unless we take issue with the present policy there is every indication the Soviet Union will become a world bully wherever their interests are involved."

**ETO:** The XV Corps (French 2nd Armored Division and the U.S. 79th Infantry Division) moves to guard the Third Army's right flank as it advances westward. The 5th Armored Division of V Corps liberates Luxembourg City. The VII Corps artillery begins bombarding German territory. As Allied Expeditionary Force commander, General Eisenhower sees the capture of the port of Antwerp in the Netherlands as essential. As the largest port in Europe, it can support the logistics requirements of the Allied armies. Eisenhower also wants to clear the coastline of V-weapon sites and seize airfields. He also wants to destroy the bulk of the remaining, organized German forces west of the Rhine River. Montgomery argues for "one powerful full-blooded thrust across the Rhine and into the heart of Germany, backed by the whole of the resources of the Allied Armies." This offensive will be the decisive blow that ends the war for the European theater. Montgomery is unhappy with Eisenhower's broad-front strategy, believing that it spreads Allied power too thinly, not allowing for a concentration of forces sufficient to overwhelm German defenses. He stresses his plan for an attack in the 21st Army Group area that will cross the Rhine River quickly and break into the open terrain beyond and capture the undefended Ruhr from the rear. Therefore, Field Marshal Montgomery's 21st Army Group is directed to be the main effort and will conduct its offensive operation in Holland. This means that the majority of logistics support will be directed to Montgomery, leaving Bradley's 12th Army Group with minimal support.

Field Marshal Montgomery lays out a proposal to open a corridor 65 miles deep into Holland using airborne forces and the British Second Army. The airborne units will seize the bridges at Eindhoven, Grave, Nijmegen, and Arnhem. The XXX Corps will then send armored spearheads into Germany.

Eighth Air Force sends more than 750 B-17s escorted by over 350 P-47 Thunderbolts and P-51 Mustangs to attack a tank factory at Nürnberg, an aircraft components facility at Furth, a motor vehicle facility at Gaggenau, and a jet-propulsion component production facility and an engine factory. Another 388 B-24 Liberators escorted by 153 P-38 Lightnings and P-51s attack the marshaling yards at Ulm and Heilbronn. A total of seven bombers are lost and 387 are damaged. Aircrew casualties are one killed, 18 wounded, and 65 missing. Fighter pilots report two confirmed kills in the air and one probable, and 67 confirmed kills on the ground. Five fighters are lost and nine are damaged. One pilot is wounded, and five pilots are reported missing.

P-47 Thunderbolts strafe airfields and ground and rail traffic in a sweep over Cologne, Frankfurt am Main, and Kassel. Pilots report 10 confirmed kills on the ground. Eight P-47s are lost and five are damaged. The eight pilots are reported missing.

A total of 35 B-24s and C-47s fly in support of Carpetbagger operations.

During the night six B-17s drop leaflets over France, the Netherlands, and Germany.

Ninth Air Force sends more than 300 A-20 Havocs and B-26 Marauders to attack German defensive positions and ammunition storage areas, and a railroad bridge over the Moselle River. P-47 and P-38 fighters support ground forces of Third Army in the Metz-Nancy area.

The headquarters of Naval Forces France is established in Paris, commanded by Vice Admiral Alan G. Kirk.

**MEDITERRANEAN:** The French II Corps liberates Dijon. The VI Corps captures Besançon.

Fifteenth Air Force sends more than 300 B-17s and B-24 Liberators escorted by P-38 Lightnings and P-51 Mustangs to attack depots, oil refineries, and industrial targets near Vienna. In Italy, another 88 B-24s escorted by P-38 Lightnings and P-51 Mustangs bomb the port of Trieste. In France, 45 B-24s escorted by P-51s fly supplies to the Seventh Army at Lyon.

Twelfth Air Force A-20 Havocs attack communication support targets and P-47 Thunderbolts attack rail lines.

**ITALY:** The Fifth Army launches attacks directed at Il Giogo Pass in support of Operation Olive. Ultra intercepts have indicated that German forces have been diverted from the Fifth Army front to stop Eighth Army's offensive.

The 34th and 91st Infantry Divisions of the U.S. II Corps advance up Route 65. The 91st Division, commanded by Major General William C. Livesay, will attack Il Giogo Pass. The 34th Division will conduct a holding attack on the Futa Pass. The 85th Infantry Division will follow in support. The U.S. IV Corps will follow withdrawing German forces on the coast and capture Pistoia.

Twelfth Air Force B-25 Mitchells and B-26 Marauders attack rail bridges in the Po River valley and ammunition storage sites. A-20 Havocs and P-47 Thunderbolts attack German defensive positions along the Gothic Line.

**SOUTHWEST PACIFIC AREA:** Carrier aircraft from Naval Task Force 38 attack shipping and airfields on Mindanao. Pilots report a cargo ship sunk off Mindanao.

**PACIFIC:** U.S. submarine *Sunfish* torpedoes and sinks a Japanese merchant tanker west of Kyushu, Japan.

**CENTRAL PACIFIC:** Seventh Air Force B-24 Liberators from Saipan bomb Iwo Jima and shipping off the island. B-24 Liberators from Eniwetok bomb Truk.

**NEW GUINEA:** FEAF A-20 Havocs, P-47 Thunderbolts, P-38 Lightnings, and P-40s attack airfields in western New Guinea. A-20 Havocs, B-25 Mitchells, and P-38 Lightnings attack targets on Buru Island and Ceram Island. B-24 Liberators bomb airfields on Celebes Island and on Halmahera Island.

### September 11

**ALEUTIANS:** Eleventh Air Force sends four B-25 Mitchells on a shipping search. Aircrews report sinking a small craft off Shimushu Island in the Kuriles.

**CBI:** Tenth Air Force sends 23 B-24 Liberators to fly fuel to Kunming, China.

P-47 Thunderbolts attack roads and Japanese troops and vehicles near Bhamo. In China, P-47s also attack assembly areas and road traffic near Tengchung and Lungling.

Fourteenth Air Force sends B-24 Liberators to bomb logistics storage sites near Manling. B-25 Mitchells bomb Tunganhsien and Lingling. P-40s attack trucks traveling the Burma Road. P-40s and P-51 Mustangs attack river shipping, rail lines, troop assembly areas, and logistics sites near Canton and the area around Tungting Lake.

**ETO:** The French 1st Armored Division links with the French 2nd Armored Division near Sombernon. The V Corps represents the first American forces to cross into German territory and approach the West Wall or Siegfried Line, as the Allies call it, a series of fortifications and obstacles emplaced between the border of France and Germany. Construction began in 1936 but was halted early in the war. Although obsolete, the concrete defensive positions are located on terrain that enhances their effectiveness, and are sufficiently strong to both delay Allied forces and provide a rallying point for retreating German forces to reorganize into a coherent defense.

The XIX Corps crosses the Meuse River. First Army reports that only 850 tanks of its authorized strength of 1,010 are combat capable. The 3rd Armored Division has only 75 tanks combat capable, of its authorized strength of 232 tanks.

After weeks of delay, Stalin finally gives permission for the Western Allies to begin airdropping supplies to Polish fighters under siege by German forces in Warsaw.

Eighth Air Force sends 735 B-17s escorted by over 500 P-51 Mustangs and P-47 Thunderbolts to attack synthetic oil plants and refineries in Germany. Another 396 B-24 Liberators escorted by 164 P-38 Lightnings and P-51s attack oil refineries, an engine production facility, and logistics storage areas. The German Luftwaffe counters with over 500 aircraft attacking the formations. A total of 39 bombers are lost and 386 damaged. Aircrews report 17 confirmed kills and 25 probables. Aircrew casualties are five killed, 38 wounded, and 375 missing. Fighter pilots report 115 confirmed kills and seven probables in the air and 42 confirmed kills on the ground. Seventeen fighters are lost, and 26 are damaged. A total of 21 pilots are reported missing.

As part of this attack, 75 B-17s and 64 P-51s are flying a mission in support of Operation Frantic. The bombers hit their primary target at Chemnitz and proceed to airfields in Soviet Ukraine.

A total of 38 B-24s fly in support of Carpetbagger operations. During the night six B-17s drop leaflets over France and Germany.

Ninth Air Force sends over 350 A-20 Havocs and B-26 Marauders to attack German defensive positions in the Metz area in support of Third Army. P-47 and P-38 fighters support ground forces near Brest.

The headquarters of the 440th Troop Carrier Group redeploys from England to France.

**MEDITERRANEAN:** Fifteenth Air Force sends 54 B-24 Liberators to fly supplies to Seventh Army in France.

**ITALY:** Twelfth Air Force B-26 Marauders attack German positions at the Il Giogo Pass and at the Futa Pass. B-25 Mitchells attack logistics sites and bridges. A-20 Havocs and P-47 Thunderbolts attack gun positions, convoys, logistics sites, bridges, and roads.

The P-47s of the 65th and 66th Fighter Squadrons, 57th Fighter Group, redeploy from Corsica to Ombrone, Italy.

**PACIFIC:** Admiral Nimitz advises Lieutenant General Holland M. Smith, commanding general of Fleet Marine Force Pacific, to retain the 2nd and 3rd Marine Divisions in the Marianas as a reserve for future landings against the island of Formosa and as the main units for the attack on Iwo Jima.

U.S. submarine *Albacore* torpedoes and sinks a Japanese auxiliary submarine chaser off Kyushu, Japan. U.S. submarine *Finback* torpedoes and sinks two Japanese cargo ships north of Chichi Jima.

**CENTRAL PACIFIC:** Seventh Air Force B-24 Liberators from Saipan bomb Iwo Jima and attack shipping targets off Chichi Jima Island.

A U.S. destroyer bombards logistics storage areas on Aguijan Island, Marianas.

Seventh Air Force B-24 Liberators bomb Iwo Jima. Aircrews report damaging a Japanese cargo vessel.

**NEW GUINEA:** FEAF A-20 Havocs, P-47 Thunderbolts, P-38 Lightnings, and P-40s attack airfields in western New Guinea. P-38 Lightnings attack airfields on Buru Island and oil storage facilities on Ceram Island. B-25 Mitchells bomb airfields on Celebes Island and B-24 Liberators, A-20 Havocs, and B-25s bomb airfields on Halmahera Island.

U.S. submarine *Pargo* torpedoes and sinks a Japanese auxiliary netlayer in the Java Sea southwest of Celebes Island.

## September 12

**CARIBBEAN:** German submarine *U-518* torpedoes and damages a U.S. freighter off Key West, Florida.

**CBI:** Tenth Air Force sends 25 B-24 Liberators to fly fuel to Kunming, China. P-47 Thunderbolts attack command and control targets at Bhamo, while other P-47s attack Japanese vehicles and logistics sites on the Burma Road.

In China, Fourteenth Air Force sends 10 B-25 Mitchells and six P-40s to attack Japanese positions at Lungling. P-51 Mustangs and P-40s attack targets near Lingling and Hengyang.

The 74th Fighter Squadron of the 23rd Fighter Group redeploys P-40s and P-51s from Kweilin and Liuchow to Luliang.

U.S. submarine *Growler* torpedoes and sinks a Japanese destroyer in the South China Sea and an escort vessel south of Hong Kong. U.S. submarine *Pampanito* torpedoes and sinks a passenger-cargo ship and a tanker off Hainan Island.

**ATLANTIC: Octagon Conference Begins.** President Roosevelt, Prime Minister Churchill, and their military chiefs of staff convene in the last of their mid-war conferences. They agree on British and American occupation zones in Germany. Roosevelt and Churchill initial the Morgenthau Plan for postwar German de-industrialization. Decisions on the Pacific war include ordering Admiral Mountbatten to drive the Japanese from Burma as soon as possible, starting no later than March 15, 1945, and including an amphibious invasion (Operation Dracula) and a drive to reopen the Burma Road to China. The American invasion of Leyte is approved, as are plans for the British fleet and the RAF to support the final campaigns against Japan, which include an invasion of the Japanese mainland on Kyushu (Operation Olympic) to establish a base of operations for the final attack on Honshu and Tokyo (Operation Coronet). Operational control of Seventh Army will pass from General Wilson to General Eisenhower on September 15. The direction of strategic bombing in Europe will return to control of the CCS from General Eisenhower, who directed it in support of Overlord. The CCS approves Eisenhower's strategic approach for the defeat of Germany, focusing on the Ruhr, with the main effort coming from the north.

**ETO:** First Army's VII Corps, commanded by Major General J. Lawton Collins, advances toward Aachen with the 1st Infantry Division and elements of the 3rd Armored Division. The infantry will flank Aachen while the tanks advance toward the Roer River. The 9th Infantry Division is given the task of sweeping the Hürtgen Forest. Collins's units are quickly stopped before the obstacles and pillboxes of the Siegfried Line.

Eighth Air Force sends 647 B-17s, escorted by 474 P-51 Mustangs and P-47 Thunderbolts, to attack oil refineries in Germany. Nearly 300 B-17s use radar-equipped pathfinders to bomb the primary targets. Another 241 B-24 Liberators also use pathfinders and are escorted by 105 P-38 Lightnings, P-47s, and P-51s to attack industrial targets and transportation targets. The German Luftwaffe sends nearly 450 fighters against the formations. A total of 35 bombers are lost and 309 are damaged. Aircrews report 27 confirmed kills and 14 probables. Aircrew casualties are 10 killed, 21 wounded, and 317 missing. Fighter pilots report 54 confirmed kills and seven probables in the air and 21 confirmed kills on the ground. Twelve fighters are lost and two damaged. Twelve pilots are reported missing.

A total of 36 B-24s and C-47s fly in support of Carpetbagger operations. During the night seven B-17s drop leaflets over the Netherlands, France, and Germany.

Ninth Air Force sends A-20 Havocs and B-26 Marauders to attack German defensive positions on the Siegfried Line and at Nancy in support of Third Army.

Second Lieutenant Raymond Zussman commands two tanks in the 756th Tank Battalion, attached to an infantry company near Noroy le Bourg, France. Approaching the town on foot in advance of the tanks and infantry, Second Lieutenant Zussman captures several German soldiers and locates a number of defensive positions. As the defenders begin engaging his first tank, Zussman calmly directs fire on the targets. Walking alongside the tank, he enters the town and directs the tank fire on several houses, forcing 20 soldiers to surrender. Going forward alone, he is fired on by German troops in another house. Ignoring the fire, he directs the tank to fire on the position, forcing the surrender of another 15 soldiers. Minutes later, he walks on alone and returns with another 30 prisoners. For his conspicuous acts of bravery and calm courage under fire, Second Lieutenant Zussman will win the Medal of Honor.

**MEDITERRANEAN:** Elements of Major General LeClerc's 2nd Armored Division, from Third Army, meet the French II Corps of the Seventh Army at Dijon near Châtillon-sur-Seine.

Fifteenth Air Force sends more than 300 B-17s and B-24 Liberators escorted by P-38 Lightnings and P-51 Mustangs to attack airfields, engine assembly plants, and a jet aircraft production facility near Munich, Germany.

Over 50 B-24s fly supplies to Seventh Army in southern France.

**ITALY:** The 91st and 85th Infantry Divisions of II Corps attack Il Giogo Pass, Monticelli Ridge, and Monte Altuzzo. The British Eighth Army resumes the Operation Olive offensive.

The 363rd Infantry Regiment of the 91st Infantry Division is stopped before Il Giogo Pass by difficult terrain and heavy enemy fire on Montecelli Ridge. Montecelli Ridge is one of the best-prepared defensive positions on the exceptionally well prepared Gothic Line. The ridge holds a series of nearly invisible concrete positions, protected by barbed wire barriers 25 feet deep and wide minefields laid along all of the lower approaches to the ridge.

Twelfth Air Force B-25 Mitchells attack rail bridges in the Po River valley. B-26 Marauders bomb German defensive positions. A-20 Havocs and P-47 Thunderbolts attack convoys, troops, bridges, antiaircraft positions, and roads.

The headquarters of the 57th Fighter Group and the P-47s of the 64th Fighter Squadron redeploy from Corsica to Ombrone airfield in Italy.

Brigadier General Benjamin W. Chidlaw takes command of XII Fighter Command.

**SOUTHWEST PACIFIC AREA:** Naval Task Force 38 attacks airfields on Cebu Island, Philippines. Carrier aircraft attack Japanese shipping throughout the area around Cebu, sinking a gunboat, a motor torpedo boat, three auxiliary submarine chasers, an auxiliary netlayer, two auxiliary minesweepers, two guardboats, two transports, six cargo ships, a merchant tanker, and three transports. One minesweeper is damaged.

Admiral William F. Halsey, commander of the Third Fleet, receives reports from Filipinos that Leyte has only a small force of Japanese infantry on the island. This information, combined with the lack of any appreciable response to the American air attack, prompts Halsey to recommend that offensive operations against Yap be cancelled in favor of an attack on Leyte.

U.S. submarine *Sealion* torpedoes and sinks a Japanese transport and passenger-cargo ship in the South China Sea, east of Hainan Island. The passenger-cargo ship carries 1,300 Allied prisoners of war. Three days later USS *Pampanito* and USS *Sealion* will rescue 127 British and Australian POWs who survived.

**PACIFIC:** U.S. submarine *Pipefish* torpedoes and sinks a Japanese auxiliary vessel off Shikoku, Japan.

**CENTRAL PACIFIC:** Seventh Air Force B-25 Mitchells from the Gilberts bomb Nauru Island.

U.S. light minelayers ships begin clearing mines in the shoals between Angaur and Peleliu Islands.

**CENTRAL PACIFIC, PELELIU:** Rear Admiral Jesse Oldendorf, commanding the Fire Support Group with eight cruisers, 12 destroyers, seven minesweepers, 15 rocket-firing landing craft, and six submarines, begins preparatory fire on Peleliu. Three aircraft carriers and five escort carriers also support the naval bombardment with SBD Dauntless dive-bombers and Hellcat fighters all attacking carefully selected pre-invasion targets.

**NEW GUINEA:** FEAF A-20 Havocs and B-25 Mitchells attack airfields in western New Guinea. P-38 Lightnings attack airfields on Buru Island, and P-47 Thunderbolts attack facilities on Ceram Island. B-24 Liberators bomb airfields on Celebes Island, and B-24s and B-25s bomb airfields on Halmahera Island and radar facilities on Morotai Island.

U.S. submarine *Redfin* makes an unsuccessful attack on a Japanese cargo vessel in the Makassar Strait and escapes a depth-charge attack.

### September 13

**CBI:** Tenth Air Force P-47 Thunderbolts strafe targets of opportunity on the Irrawaddy River.

Fourteenth Air Force B-24s attack cargo ships off the Pescadores Islands near Formosa. Aircrews report three ships sunk.

U.S. submarine *Sunfish* torpedoes and sinks a cargo ship and damages another in the East China Sea off Shanghai.

**ETO:** General Dwight Eisenhower informs Field Marshal Montgomery that his 21st Army Group will receive an additional 1,000 tons of supplies per day as the main effort. Reinforced by the First Allied Airborne Army and part of the 12th Army Group, his mission is to secure a bridgehead across the Rhine River in Holland and advance on the flank of German forces now occupying the defenses of the West Wall (or Siegfried Line) and capture the port of Antwerp. Bradley's 12th Army Group is to conduct limited attacks to draw German forces away from the main attack. The operation is called Market Garden.

The First Army's VII Corps uses the 1st Infantry Division to attempt to encircle Aachen from the south while XIX Corps moved on Aachen from the north. A task force of the 3rd Armored Division of VII Corps is able to advance about two miles before being stopped by mud and German defenses.

Eighth Air Force sends 673 B-17s, escorted by over 300 P-47 Thunderbolts and P-51 Mustangs, and 342 B-24 Liberators, escorted by 99 P-38 Lightnings and P-51s, to attack oil refineries, ammunition storage depots, and targets of opportunity in Germany. Fifteen bombers are lost and 413 are damaged. Aircrews report one confirmed kill. Aircrew casualties are five killed, 13 wounded, and 143 missing. Fighter pilots report 33 confirmed kills in the air and 20 confirmed kills on the ground. Eight fighters are lost, and the pilots are reported missing.

Eleven B-24 Liberators escorted by 15 P-51s are sent to bomb the oil refinery at Hemminstedt, Germany, using Azon bombs.

During the night eight B-17s drop leaflets over the Netherlands, Belgium, and Germany.

The 73 B-17s from Operation Frantic escorted by 63 P-51 Mustangs depart from airfields in the Soviet Ukraine and bomb industrial targets at Diosgyor, Hungary, en route to Fifteenth Air Force airfields in Italy.

Ninth Air Force sends P-47 and P-38 fighters to support ground forces at Brest and in the Nancy-Metz area and fly armed reconnaissance missions over the lower Rhine River valley as XIX Tactical Air Command initiates an effort to cut rail lines west and east of the Rhine River.

The C-47s of the 95th, 97th, and 98th Troop Carrier Squadrons of the 440th Troop Carrier Group redeploy from England to France.

**MEDITERRANEAN:** The VI Corps captures Vesoul, blocking the last avenue of escape for the German Nineteenth Army.

Fifteenth Air Force sends more than 300 B-17s and B-24 Liberators escorted by P-38 Lightnings and P-51 Mustangs to attack an oil refineries in Germany and Poland and a marshaling yard in Czechoslovakia.

**ITALY:** Two battalions of the 363rd Infantry Regiment attack Montecelli Ridge after a heavy artillery bombardment.

Twelfth Air Force B-25 Mitchells and B-26 Marauders attack German defensive positions north of Florence. A-20 Havocs and P-47 Thunderbolts attack rail lines, rail cars, and bridges.

**SOUTHWEST PACIFIC AREA:** Naval Task Groups 38.2 (Rear Admiral Gerald F. Bogan), 38.1 (Vice Admiral John S. McCain), and 38.3 (Rear Admiral Frederick C. Sherman) attack targets on Cebu, Negros, and Legaspi Islands in the Philippines.

**CENTRAL PACIFIC, PELELIU:** Admiral Jesse Oldendorf calls off the prelanding bombardment, reporting that all targets assigned have been hit and destroyed. Oldendorf's force has fired 2,350 16-inch and 14-inch rounds from ships, and 1,800 500-pound bombs have been dropped on the island.

**NEW GUINEA:** FEAF A-20 Havocs, P-38 Lightnings, P-47 Thunderbolts, and B-25 Mitchells attack airfields in western New Guinea.

B-24 Liberators and B-25s bomb airfields on Morotai Island.

Thirteenth Air Force headquarters redeploys from Los Negros Island in the Admiralties to Hollandia.

Fifth Air Force A-20 Havocs sink a cargo ship off southeastern Ceram Island.

## September 14

**ALEUTIANS:** Eleventh Air Force sends three B-24 Liberators on a night raid against shipping and the airfield on Paramushiru Island in the Kuriles.

**CBI:** General Joseph Stilwell flies from Burma to Kweilin to assess the situation. Chinese troops are nearly incapable of any sustained resistance. The Chinese Y Force captures Tengchung after more than two months of bitter fighting.

Tenth Air Force sends four B-25 Mitchells to drop booby-trapped fragmentation bombs on Bhamo.

Fourteenth Air Force P-40s and P-51 Mustangs attack river shipping, troop compounds, logistics storage depots, and buildings near Lungling and other areas south of Tungting Lake.

The headquarters of the 23rd Fighter Group redeploys from Liuchow to Luliang, and the B-24s of the 373rd Bombardment Squadron (Heavy) of the 308th Bombardment Group (Heavy) also redeploy to Luliang.

**ETO:** First Army reaches its limit of advance. Without sufficient supplies, it can advance no farther. The VII Corps reaches the German border near Aachen. The V Corps holds a 50-mile front within Germany. The XXIX Tactical Air Force is activated under Ninth Air Force to provide direct support to Ninth Army. SHAEF air strength in-theater is now 4,700 fighters and 6,000 bombers.

General Eisenhower sends a letter to Army Chief of Staff General George C. Marshall informing him of SHAEF's plan to make an all-out attempt to reach the Rhine River, but cautions that, despite unexpected rapid advances, the possibility of a rapid advance to Berlin is not practical.

The 47th Infantry Regiment of the 9th Infantry Division attacks near the Hürtgen Forest to protect the 3rd Armored Division as it reaches the Vicht River. The area is heavily wooded with tall trees that cut out the sun, steep hills, and deep streambeds. Although German forces in the area are weak and of low quality, they take advantage of every support the terrain offers and occupy the fortifications of the West Wall, protected by minefields, barbed wire, and concrete pillboxes that provide interlocking fire.

The U.S. Third and Seventh Armies link, establishing a solid line of Allied forces from Antwerp to Switzerland.

Eighth Air Force sends two Aphrodite explosives-laden B-17s to crash into the oil refinery at Hemminstedt, Germany, but the aircraft miss the target.

Ninth Air Force sends over 100 B-26 Marauders and A-30s to attack German fortifications at Brest. P-47 and P-38 fighters fly armed reconnaissance missions. The headquarters of the XXIX Tactical Air Command (Provisional), under the command of Brigadier General Richard E. Nugent, is activated to support the U.S. Ninth Army, which will be subordinate to General Omar Bradley's Twelfth Army Group.

Sergeant Joseph J. Sadowski is a tank commander with the 37th Tank Battalion, 4th Armored Division. He is part of Combat Command A and is approaching the town of Valhey, France, when German antitank guns begin to fire on the Americans. Sergeant Sadowski's tank is hit and knocked out. Sadowski orders the crew to abandon the tank and take cover near a building. Everyone escapes but one man. Sadowski, braving a hail of fire, returns to the tank to rescue his comrade. While attempting to pry open the hatch, he is killed by enemy fire. For his inspirational courage and willingness to risk his own life to save the life of a fellow soldier, Sergeant Sadowski will receive the Medal of Honor.

**ITALY:** Twelfth Air Force B-26 Marauders and B-25 Mitchells attack German defensive positions at Il Giogo Pass and Monte Altuzzo. A-20 Havocs and P-47 Thunderbolts attack road and rail lines in the Po River valley.

Second Lieutenant Thomas W. Wigle takes over as leader of the 3rd Platoon of K Company, 135th Infantry Regiment, 34th Infantry Division, after it has failed in two attacks on a fortified position on Monte Frassino. He leads the third attack; in the face of intense fire, he covers his men with rifle fire as they cross a series of stone walls. Approaching the three houses that are the center of the German defensive position, he attacks alone, supported by a base of fire from his platoon. He bursts into the house and, firing his M-1 carbine, drives out the defenders, then chases them and enters the second house and finally herds most of the defenders into the cellar of the third house. He is mortally wounded as his men join him. The Americans capture the position and 36 prisoners as a result of Wigle's heroic actions. He will receive the Medal of Honor.

**SOUTHWEST PACIFIC AREA:** Naval Task Groups 38.2 (Rear Admiral Gerald F. Bogan) and 38.3 (Rear Admiral Frederick C. Sherman) attack targets on Panay and Negros Islands. Carrier aircraft damage a motor torpedo boat. Naval TG 38.1 (Vice Admiral John S. McCain), steaming to support landings on Morotai, attacks targets on Mindanao. SB2C Helldivers sink a fast transport in Davao Gulf. Destroyers *Farenholt, McCalla,* and *Grayson* bombard a suspected Japanese radar installation at mouth of Davao Gulf.

**CENTRAL PACIFIC:** Seventh Air Force B-24 Liberators from Saipan bomb Iwo Jima. B-25 Mitchells from the Gilberts bomb Ponape Island. B-24s from Eniwetok bomb Truk.

**NEW GUINEA:** FEAF A-20 Havocs, P-38 Lightnings, P-47 Thunderbolts, and B-25 Mitchells attack airfields in western New Guinea and on the Vogelkop Peninsula.

B-25 Mitchells bomb airfields on Celebes Island and B-24 Liberators bomb airfields on Halmahera Island.

The B-25s of the 69th Bombardment Squadron (Medium), 42nd Bombardment Group (Medium), redeploy from Hollandia to Sansapor.

## September 15

**CBI:** A Combat Cargo Task Force is formed within Eastern Air Command, under Brigadier General Frederick W. Evans, to support the British Fourteenth Army's offensive into southern Burma.

Tenth Air Force sends 13 B-24 Liberators to fly fuel to Liuchow, China. P-47 Thunderbolts bomb Kutkai and sweep the river near Bhamo. Other P-47s attack targets on the Burma Road.

In China, Fourteenth Air Force sends 19 B-24 Liberators to bomb a military storage area at Hengyang.

The headquarters of the 68th Composite Wing redeploys from Kweilin to Liuchow.

**ATLANTIC:** At the Octagon conference, acting on a message from Third Fleet commander, Admiral William F. Halsey, the JCS cancels orders for an invasion of Mindanao and orders an attack on Leyte. Halsey has reported that Japanese air cover in the Philippines is very weak and recommends that the Leyte invasion begin in October rather than November. The JCS informs Nimitz that he is to cancel the Palaus invasion and move to Leyte as well. Nimitz argues that the island of Peleliu is essential as a forward base for operations against Leyte. As a result of Halsey's information, the Leyte invasion is moved up from December 20 to October 20. Nimitz will transfer operational control of the 7th and 96th Infantry Divisions to SWPA to form the XIV Corps. Admiral Nimitz is directed to bypass the island of Yap.

Roosevelt and Churchill approve the Morgenthau Plan. Henry Morgenthau is the U.S. secretary of the treasury, and his ideas have gained increasing influence in the administration over the past year. Morgenthau believes the War Department's plan for postwar occupation of Germany is too gentle. His plan divides Germany permanently into two sections, north and south, and dismantles completely her industrial capacity, reducing the states to basic subsistence agriculture. There will be no aid or support to Germany whatsoever. The Soviet Union will get most of Germany's dismantled industry as reparations. Although the plan is strongly opposed by many advisers, it remains the unofficial Allied plan until the Potsdam Conference in August 1945. The Morgenthau Plan, coupled with the demand for unconditional surrender, is a propaganda coup for Hitler. Germany's defeat meant the complete destruction of the nation and the subjugation of the German people. Despite wavering faith in Hitler, German national morale rallies.

President Roosevelt relents in his insistence on U.S. forces occupying northwest Germany after the war. He agrees to U.S. forces occupying southwest Germany and the division of Berlin into zones of occupation.

**ETO:** Operation Dragoon has succeeded in clearing German forces from southern France. Operational control of the Dragoon forces passes from the Mediterranean theater to General Eisenhower in the European theater. The French First Army under General de Lattre de Tassigny and the U.S. Seventh Army under Lieutenant General Alexander E. Patch are designated as the 6th Army Group under the command of Lieutenant General Jacob L. Devers. Each army group is assigned its own tactical air force to provide direct support to its ground forces. General Montgomery has the Second Tactical Air Force, General Bradley has the Ninth Tactical Air Force, and General Devers has the First Tactical Air Force.

Although under operational control of SHAEF, the commander of the Mediterranean theater is still responsible for logistics support.

SHAEF returns operational control of the Allied Strategic Air Forces to the Combined Chiefs of Staff. The U.S. Strategic Air Forces commander, General Carl Spaatz, has operational control of the Eighth Air Force and Fifteenth Air Force and administrative control of the U.S. Tactical Air Force in Europe.

The XII Corps captures Nancy. At this point, the battle for France has cost the German armed forces about 500,000 men. About 200,000 men are trapped by the Ninth Army in the coastal ports of Brittany and battle casualties are estimated at 300,000. The Fifth Panzer Army and the Seventh Army have ceased to exist.

In the First Army area, Combat Command B of the 3rd Armored Division passes through the West Wall (or Siegfried Line). The 1st Infantry Division occupies positions overlooking Aachen. The 39th Infantry Regiment of the 9th Infantry Division attacks near Lammersdorf.

Eighth Air Force reorganizes to support three bombardment divisions. One fighter wing of VIII Fighter Command will support each bombardment division.

The 1st Bombardment Division is supported by the 67th Fighter Wing (the 20th, 352nd, 356th, 359th, and 364th Fighter Groups); the 2nd Bombardment Division is supported by the 65th Fighter Wing (the 4th, 56th, 355th, 361st, and 479th Fighter Groups); and the 3rd Bombardment Division is supported by the 66th Fighter Wing (the 55th, 78th, 339th, 353rd, and 357th Fighter Groups).

Ninth Air Force P-47 Thunderbolts and P-38 Lightnings of the IX Tactical Air Command support First Army, and the fighters of the XIX Tactical Air Command support Third Army.

**MEDITERRANEAN:** Lieutenant General Joseph T. McNary is appointed as the Deputy Supreme Allied Commander Mediterranean to replace Lieutenant General Jacob L. Devers, now commander of the 6th Army Group in the ETO.

Fifteenth Air Force sends 276 B-17s and B-24 Liberators escorted by P-38 Lightnings and P-51 Mustangs to bomb airfields and a submarine base in Greece.

**ITALY:** One company of the 363rd Infantry Regiment occupies the crest of Montecelli Ridge and holds for four days against repeated German counterattacks. The company loses 14 killed and 126 wounded and is reduced to 50 men.

The headquarters of XII Fighter Command assumes operational control over the headquarters of the 87th Fighter Wing, the 47th Bombardment Group (Light, with A-20 Havocs), and the 57th and 86th Fighter Groups (P-47s) from XII Tactical Air Command. Ninth Air Force takes operational control of XII Tactical Air Command now that Seventh Army has joined with General Eisenhower's forces as part of the ETO.

The P-47s of the 347th Fighter Squadron of the 350th Fighter Group redeploy from Sardinia to Tarquinia.

**SOUTHWEST PACIFIC AREA:** General MacArthur's headquarters notifies Sixth Army that the Mindanao operation is cancelled and confirms October 20 as the new date for the Leyte operation. The XXIV Corps (7th and 96th Infantry Divisions), under the operational control of Admiral Nimitz, will shift to General MacArthur to replace XIV Corps (24th and 37th Infantry Divisions). The 24th Infantry Division will move to X Corps (1st Cavalry Division), replacing the 40th Infantry Division. The 40th and the 37th Infantry Divisions have to be replaced because they cannot leave New Britain in time to meet the October 20 date for the landing.

The JCS designates General MacArthur as the supreme commander of land, sea, and air forces. One problem facing MacArthur is the lack of land-based air to support the invasion. Leyte is 500 miles from the nearest fighter base. He will have to rely on naval aviation to isolate the enemy on Leyte and interdict supply lines and reinforcements.

U.S. submarine *Guavina* torpedoes and sinks a Japanese fast transport south of Mindanao.

**CENTRAL PACIFIC, PELELIU: Operation Stalemate II.** As Naval Task Group 32.5, commanded by Rear Admiral Jesse B. Oldendorf, provides gunfire support, the 1st Marine Division lands a first wave of 5,000 men on the beaches at Peleliu preceded by amphibious tractors mounting 75 millimeter guns to suppress enemy positions.

An example of a Japanese pillbox on Peleliu. Originally covered with vegetation, it was nearly invisible. Firing ports oriented along natural lines of advance put marines within optimum killing range. These positions could be destroyed only by a direct assault.

Major General William H. Rupertus, the division commander, has told his subordinates that he expects a "rough but fast" operation lasting two or three days. The marines are facing about 10,900 Japanese troops occupying a complex of deep caves, bunkers, pillboxes, and a tunnel system that has largely been untouched by the naval and air bombardment at an area known as Umurbrogol. From these heights, the Japanese can observe the beaches and direct fire on the marines. The 1st Marine Regiment, commanded by Colonel Lewis B. "Chesty" Puller, immediately encounters a heavy crossfire from beach defenses untouched by naval bombardment. Many amphibious tractors carrying the radio sets for the regiment are destroyed by Japanese mortar fire. Captain George Hunt of Company K, 3rd Battalion, 1st Marines, captures the Point, an outcropping of rock on the left flank of the landing beach. There is no contact with Puller's regiment for several critical hours as the marines struggle against machine gun and artillery fire as they attempt to press forward.

The 7th Marine Regiment moves to the southeast to secure the division's right flank. Marines are stopped by strong Japanese resistance. Major General Rupertus commits his reserve, the 1st Battalion, 7th Marines, to shore up the 1st Marine Regiment, which has suffered heavy casualties. The 5th Marine Regiment also takes heavy fire on the landing beaches and moves inland toward the airfield with difficulty. Due to heavy Japanese resistance, none of the division's objectives are reached. A total of 30 M4A1 Sherman tanks land and occupy defensive positions. During the night 500 Japanese troops with tanks attack the defensive lines of the 5th Marines. The attack is rapidly halted by American tanks and antitank guns. The 7th Marines stops a determined counterattack with the support of naval gunfire. Captain Hunt's small force of about 40 men holds the Point against determined Japanese counterattacks through the night. By morning only 18 marines are able to fight, and the bodies of more than 400 Japanese soldiers lie around them.

First Lieutenant Carlton R. Rouh, 1st Battalion, 5th Marines, examines an apparently cleared dugout position before permitting his men to use it as an 81 millimeter mortar observation post. As First Lieutenant Rouh examines the position, he is shot by a Japanese soldier inside the pillbox. While he is being given first aid a Japanese grenade lands close to the two marines assisting him. Rouh pushes the men to one side and uses his own body to block the explosion. His exceptional spirit of loyalty and self-sacrifice will win him the Medal of Honor.

**NEW GUINEA: Operation Trade Wind.** Naval Task Force 77 (Rear Admiral Daniel E. Barbey) commands this operation. Task Group 77.2 (Rear Admiral Russell S. Berkey), with two heavy cruisers, three light cruisers, and 10 destroyers, and Task Group 77.1 (Rear Admiral Thomas L. Sprague), with six escort carriers and eight destroyer escorts, provide support for the landing.

Marines of the 1st Marine Division occupy fighting positions on Peleliu Island, September 15, 1944.

The 155th and 167th RCTs of the 31st Infantry Division land at Morotai Island preceded by naval gunfire and an air bombardment by B-24 Liberators, A-20 Havocs, and P-47 Thunderbolts. A coral reef prevents a beach landing, forcing the troops to wade in about 100 yards. Fortunately, the landing is uncontested. General MacArthur joins the 124th RCT on the beach. The abandoned airfield on the island is deemed to be unsuitable. The engineers locate another suitable site on the southern coast. Because of the impassable coral reef, another beachhead is established.

FEAF P-39 Airacobras bomb Manokwari airfield.

Fifth Air Force A-20 Havocs bomb Japanese shipping off the southeast coast of Ceram. Pilots report sinking two fishing vessels.

## September 16
**ALEUTIANS:** Eleventh Air Force sends three B-24 Liberators to bomb Kataoka naval base on Shimushu Island.

**CBI:** Tenth Air Force sends 19 B-24 Liberators to fly fuel to Kunming, China.

In China, Fourteenth Air Force sends 20 B-24 Liberators to bomb Hengyang. Over 100 P-40s and P-51 Mustangs attack targets of opportunity near Lungling and around Changsha and Lingling.

**ATLANTIC: The Octagon Conference Ends.** The unconditional surrender of the Axis powers is reaffirmed, and Roosevelt remains uncomfortable with on not having any U.S. ground forces occupying southwest Germany. The U.S. will use its airpower in Europe while the USSR and Great Britain contribute the majority of the ground forces for occupation duties. The British fleet will join Nimitz's naval forces after the defeat of Germany. On the future of the Pacific, the Allies agree to place the Pacific islands given to Japan after World War I under a mandate from the League of Nations (the Marshalls among them) under the control of an international trusteeship. The United States is far less amenable to returning colonies or territories lost to the Japanese. No territories will be returned without previous approval from the United States.

**ETO:** An element of the German Nineteenth Army, blocked from reaching Germany by the conjunction of the Seventh and Third Armies, and continuously harassed by the XIX Tactical Air Force and French Forces of the Interior, surrenders 20,000 soldiers and civilians to Ninth Army. The VI Corps reaches Lure and Luxeuil-les-Bains, which mark main avenues of approach into Germany. Supply shortages prevent any further advances.

In the First Army area, the 47th and 60th Infantry Regiments of the 9th Infantry Division encounter strong German fortifications in the Hürtgen Forest.

Eighth Air Force sends 178 P-47 Thunderbolts and 149 P-51 Mustangs to bomb and strafe targets in northern Germany and an airfield near Kaiserslautern. Fighter pilots report six confirmed kills on the ground. One P-51 is lost and 10 damaged. The pilot is reported missing.

A total of 32 B-24s and C-47s fly in support of Carpetbagger operations. One B-24 is lost. During the night seven B-17s drop leaflets over Germany, France, and the Netherlands.

Ninth Air Force sends more than 150 A-20 Havocs and B-26 Marauders to attack road and rail targets in the Netherlands. P-47 and P-38 fighters support ground forces in stopping German counterattacks against the XII and XV Corps of Patton's Third Army.

Ninth Air Force redesignates Headquarters IX Bomber Command as the 9th Bombardment Division (Medium).

**ITALY:** Twelfth Air Force B-25 Mitchells and B-26 Marauders attack fuel storage areas and logistics depots and German defensive positions. A-20 Havocs and P-47 Thunderbolts attack German defenses along the Fifth Army's front lines.

The P-47s of the 526th Fighter Squadron, 86th Fighter Group, redeploy from Corsica to Grosseto, Italy.

**SOUTHWEST PACIFIC AREA:** U.S. submarines *Picuda* and *Redfish,* operating south of Formosa, torpedo and sink a cargo ship and a fleet tanker, respectively.

**PACIFIC:** Nimitz requests that his subordinate service commanders reexamine plans for Operation Causeway (the invasion of Formosa), given the directive from the JCS to speed up the invasion of Leyte.

U.S. submarine *Sea Devil* torpedoes and sinks Japanese submarine *I-364* off Honshu, Japan.

**CENTRAL PACIFIC:** Seventh Air Force sends 17 B-24 Liberators from Saipan to bomb Iwo Jima.

**CENTRAL PACIFIC, PELELIU:** The 5th Marines moves past the airfield, while the 14-inch guns of the battleship USS *Mississippi* destroy a complex of blockhouses holding up the advance of the 1st Marines. Major General William H. Rupertus presses the 1st and 5th Marines to keep up the momentum of the attack and open more maneuver room in the center of the island and clear the enemy from the division's right flank. The 1st Marines, reinforced by a battalion of the 7th Marines, is ordered to capture Umurbrogol. With temperatures averaging 105°F, the marines are slowed by a lack of water. When marines do receive water, it is contaminated with oil and useless to drink. At Umurbrogol the 1st Marines encounter a landscape that defies description. A coral mass 50 to 300 feet high juts out of the sand, covered in jungle foliage. Hidden in its crevices, valleys, cliffs, and ridges are innumerable caves, tunnels, and firing positions that are designed to trap and kill as many American troops as possible. There is no military logic to this defense. The Japanese soldiers intend to die, but will force the Americans to come to them.

**NEW GUINEA:** FEAF A-20 Havocs, P-38 Lightnings, P-47 Thunderbolts, and B-25 Mitchells attack airfields in western New Guinea.

B-24 Liberators bomb logistics sites on Celebes Island. B-25 Mitchells and B-24s bomb Buru Island, Ambon Island, Haroekoe Island, and Amboina Island.

The headquarters of the 42nd Bombardment Group (Medium) redeploys from Hollandia to Sansapor.

Motor torpedo boats begin operating from Morotai Island to attack Japanese barge traffic and stop any attempts to attack Morotai from Halmahera.

Lieutenant Arthur M. Preston, commander of Torpedo Boat Squadron 33, volunteers to rescue a downed pilot in Wasile Bay, Halmahera Island. He takes two PT boats 60 miles through heavily mined waters. Enemy coastal guns fire on the PT boats as they attempt to enter the bay. Turned back several times, Preston is able to reach the pilot covered by a smokescreen laid by friendly aircraft. With the Japanese guns firing from only 150 yards away, Preston calmly brings the pilot on board and escapes, but also succeeds in sinking a small cargo ship with his 40 millimeter guns. Lieutenant Preston's courageous actions to save the downed flier in the face of certain destruction will win him the Medal of Honor.

## September 17

**CBI:** Tenth Air Force sends 16 B-24 Liberators to fly fuel to Liuchow, China. P-47 Thunderbolts attack Bhamo.

Fourteenth Air Force sends 15 B-25 Mitchells escorted by eight P-51 Mustangs to bomb Japanese-controlled airfields. Another 29 B-24 Liberators bomb Changsha. P-51 Mustangs and P-40s attack strongpoints, river shipping, rail lines, gun positions, and vehicles near Changsha, Lingling, and Hengshan.

U.S. submarine *Barb* torpedoes and sinks a Japanese escort carrier and tanker in the South China Sea southeast of Hong Kong. USS *Barb* and USS *Queenfish* rescue 32 British and Australian prisoners of war, survivors of the September 12 attack on their transport ship by USS *Sealion.*

**ETO: Operation Market Garden.** During the day, Eighth Air Force sends more than 500 P-38 Lightnings, P-47 Thunderbolts, and P-51 Mustangs to escort the cargo aircraft of the First Allied Airborne Army, carrying about 20,000 paratroopers and glider infantry of the 82nd Airborne and 101st Airborne Divisions to drop zones in Holland. The 82nd is to capture bridges at Nijmegen and Grave, while the 101st is to capture bridges at Vegel and Son north of Eindhoven. The American paratroopers will open the way for the XXX Corps of the British Second Army to drive north and link with the British 1st Airborne Division, which is to seize the bridges at Arnhem. The British divisions will then cross the Rhine River to outflank the Siegfried Line defenses and reach the Ruhr—General Eisenhower's operational objective for the destruction of German forces.

Shortly after recovering from the surprise, the Germans are able to isolate the British 1st Airborne and prevent units from capturing the bridges across the Rhine. The 82nd is able to capture the Maas bridge at Grave but fails to capture the Nijmegen bridge; the 101st captures all but the Son bridge. The British tanks, advancing on a narrow highway corridor, make extremely slow progress against German defenses.

Fighters precede the airborne troops, attacking antiaircraft positions and German troop positions and warding off about 30 German fighters. Pilots report seven confirmed kills in the air and one on the ground. Thirteen fighters are lost and 52 damaged. Two pilots are wounded, and 11 are reported missing. Nearly 900 B-17s are escorted by about 140 P-51 Mustangs to attack antiaircraft positions and airfields in the Netherlands in support of the airborne landings. Two B-17s are lost and 120 are damaged. Aircrew casualties are nine killed, six wounded, and 15 missing. One P-51 is lost and the pilot is reported missing.

An Operation Frantic mission is completed with the return of 70 B-17s and 57 P-51s to Britain from Fifteenth Air Force airfields in Italy.

American paratroopers over the Netherlands in the first phase of operation Market Garden, September 17, 1944

Ninth Air Force sends P-47 and P-38 fighters of the XIX Tactical Air Command to support VIII Corps in Brest; IX Tactical Air Command P-38 Lightnings and P-47 Thunderbolts fly armed reconnaissance missions and provide support to the 4th and 2nd Infantry Divisions and the 5th Armored Division.

Sergeant Harold O. Messerschmidt, a squad leader in L Company, 30th Infantry Regiment, 3rd Infantry Division, is defending a hill near Radden, France. A German attack against his position leaves Sergeant Messerschmidt the only man standing. Although wounded and holding a weapon without ammunition, Messerschmidt continues to fight, keeping the enemy from taking the position until reinforcements arrive. Sergeant Messerschmidt is killed in hand-to-hand combat. For his courageous stand against overwhelming odds, Sergeant Messerschmidt will receive the Medal of Honor.

**MEDITERRANEAN:** Fifteenth Air Force sends more than 400 B-17s and B-24 Liberators escorted by P-38 Lightnings and P-51 Mustangs to attack oil refineries and marshaling yards near Budapest, Hungary.

**ITALY:** The 339th Infantry Regiment of the 85th Infantry Division captures Monte Verucca; the 337th Infantry Regiment captures Monte Pratone. German forces are forced to abandon Futa Pass. The IV Corps has lost 2,731 men since September 10.

Twelfth Air Force B-25 Mitchells and B-26 Marauders attack rail and road traffic and bridges in the Po River valley. A-20 Havocs and P-47 Thunderbolts attack convoys, bridges, and roads in support of the Fifth Army attack.

The headquarters of the 86th Fighter Group and the P-47s of the 527th Fighter Squadron redeploy from Corsica to Grosseto, Italy.

**SOUTHWEST PACIFIC AREA:** FEAF B-25 Mitchells bomb Buayoan airfield on Mindanao Island in the Philippines.

**PACIFIC:** Twentieth Air Force elements of the headquarters of the 497th Bombardment Group (Very Heavy) and the 869th, 870th, and 871st Bombardment Squadrons (Very Heavy) arrive at Saipan from the United States. The B-29 Superfortresses will be ready to fly bombing missions against the Japanese home islands by the end of October.

**CENTRAL PACIFIC:** Seventh Air Force sends one B-24 on a snooper bombing mission from Saipan against Iwo Jima. B-25 Mitchells from the Gilberts bomb Nauru Island.

Naval Task Group 32.1 (Rear Admiral William H. P. Blandy) lands the 81st Infantry Division on Angaur, Palaus, supported by carrier aircraft and naval gunfire.

**CENTRAL PACIFIC, PELELIU:** The 2nd Battalion 1st Marines captures Hill 200, but comes under heavy fire from the Japanese holding the adjacent Hill 210. Puller asks for reinforcements, having lost one-third of his regiment since the landing. About 1,236 men are now casualties. The 1st Marines has encountered the first Japanese defensive line of hidden caves and mutually supported firing positions that make every open space a death trap. The Japanese remain hidden and cannot be detected.

The 81st Infantry Division lands at Angaur, also in the Palua Islands. Major General Paul J. Mueller commands the division in this operation. The 321st and 322nd Infantry Regiments attack the island from different directions. The 52nd, 154th, and 306th Engineers and the 710th Tank Battalion support the infantry.

**NEW GUINEA:** FEAF P-47 Thunderbolts and P-40s attack airfields on an island south of the Vogelkop Peninsula. B-25 Mitchells and P-39 Airacobras attack targets on Amboina and Ceram Islands. B-24 Liberators, B-25s, and P-38 Lightnings attack Langoan airfield on Celebes Island.

### September 18

**CBI:** Tenth Air Force sends 18 B-24 Liberators to fly fuel to Liuchow, China.

In China, Fourteenth Air Force sends 30 B-25 Mitchells to attack fuel storage areas at Lingling, Taohsien, and Chuanhsien. B-24 Liberators attack shipping in the Formosa Strait. Aircrews report one cargo ship sunk. Over 100 P-40s and P-51 Mustangs attack troops, trucks, tanks, shipping, and other targets of opportunity.

A detachment of P-51s from the 529th Fighter Squadron, 311th Fighter Group, begins operating from Hsian.

**ETO: Operation Market Garden.** The British XXX Corps breaks through stubborn German defenses to reach Eindhoven. British armored forces from XXX Corps link with the 101st Airborne at Grave. The 101st Airborne attacks German positions from the north to clear the town. The 82nd Airborne has not captured the Nijmegen bridge.

German forces conduct a strong counterattack against the Third Army near Luneville to restore their defensive line along the Moselle River.

Eighth Air Force sends more than 200 B-24 Liberators escorted by over 500 P-38 Lightnings, P-47 Thunderbolts, and P-51 Mustangs to drop supplies to the paratroopers of the First Allied Airborne Army in Holland. Seven B-24s are lost and 160 damaged. Aircrew casualties are one killed, 26 wounded, and 61 missing. The fighters also escort C-47s of the First Allied Airborne Army to drop reinforcements near Arnhem. P-51s, P-47s, and P-38s attack road and rail lines and antiaircraft positions. Over 100 German fighters oppose the sweep. Pilots report 29 confirmed kills in the air. A total of 20 fighters are lost, and 55 are damaged. One pilot is killed, and 20 pilots are reported missing.

Brest, a major Atlantic U-boat base with a garrison of 30,000 men, surrenders to U.S. forces. The port has been thoroughly destroyed by German forces before the surrender. The responsibility for watching the German garrisons trapped at Lorient, St-Nazaire, and Quiberon Bay is turned over to Free French Forces.

In the First Army area, the 60th Infantry Regiment of the 9th Infantry Division gains the ridge beyond Monschau. American forces in First Army are not equipped to attack the fortifications of the Siegfried Line, nor are they in sufficient strength to mount effective attacks.

Operation Frantic continues with over 100 B-17s escorted by 137 P-51s dropping 1,248 containers of supplies to beleaguered Polish fighters in Warsaw. One B-17 is lost, and seven are damaged. Two fighters are lost. Pilots report four confirmed kills in the air and three on the ground. Two pilots are reported missing. After the drop, 64 P-51s continue escorting the B-17s to airfields in the Soviet Ukraine.

During the night eight B-17s drop leaflets over France, Germany, and the Netherlands.

Ninth Air Force P-47 Thunderbolts and P-38 Lightnings support the VIII Corps at Brest.

Ninth Air Force redeploys the headquarters of the 409th Bombardment Group (Light) and the A-20 Havocs of the 640th, 641st, 642nd, and 643rd Bombardment Squadrons (Light) from England to France. The headquarters of the 9th Bombardment Division (Medium) redeploys from England to Chartres, France.

At Best, Holland, a platoon of H Company, 502nd Parachute Infantry Regiment, 101st Airborne Division, makes an attack to capture a bridge across the Wilhelmina Canal. When the platoon is cut off and surrounded, Private First Class Joe E. Mann sets out to locate the enemy. Moving close to a German 88 millimeter gun, he destroys it and engages the enemy, even though wounded four times. Although heavily bandaged, Mann insists on pulling his turn at guard duty during the night. At dawn, the Germans make a counterattack. Warning his comrades, Mann throws himself on a grenade. His courage and dedication above and beyond the call of duty will win him the Medal of Honor.

**MEDITERRANEAN:** Fifteenth Air Force sends more than 460 B-17s and B-24 Liberators escorted by P-38 Lightnings and P-51 Mustangs to attack marshaling yards and railroad bridges in Hungary and railroad bridges in Yugoslavia.

**ITALY:** The 363rd Infantry Regiment of the 91st Infantry Division captures Il Giogo Pass and Monticelli Ridge. The 338th Infantry Regiment of the 85th Infantry Division captures Monte Altuzzo. American casualties for six days of combat are 2,730. General Mark Clark decides to attack along the two highways leading to Bologna. The 34th, 91st, and 85th Infantry Divisions will attack on Route 65, the quickest and most direct way to Bologna. He also decides to send the 88th Infantry Division with Combat Command A of the 1st Armored Division on the road to Imola to exploit the boundary between the Fourteenth and Tenth German armies.

Twelfth Air Force B-25 Mitchells support the British Eighth Army at Rimini. B-26 Marauders and P-47 Thunderbolts attack rail and road traffic and bridges in the Po Valley.

The P-47s of the 525th Fighter Squadron, 86th Fighter Group, redeploy from Corsica to Grosseto, Italy.

**SOUTHWEST PACIFIC AREA:** FEAF B-24 Liberators bomb oil storage areas near Davao on Mindanao Island in the Philippines.

U.S. submarine *Flasher* torpedoes and sinks a Japanese auxiliary gunboat off Manila Bay.

**PACIFIC:** The headquarters of Twentieth Air Force's 499th and 500th Bombardment Groups (Very Heavy) arrive at Saipan from the United States.

U.S. submarine *Pipefish* torpedoes and damages a Japanese army transport off Honshu, Japan. U.S. submarine *Thresher* torpedoes and sinks a cargo ship in the Yellow Sea.

**CENTRAL PACIFIC:** Seventh Air Force sends 28 B-24 Liberators from Eniwetok to bomb Truk. B-25 Mitchells from the Gilberts bomb Ponape Island.

**CENTRAL PACIFIC, PELELIU:** In the Umurbrogol, the Japanese counterattack the marines on Hill 200. The 1st Marines attempt to retake the lost position. The 1st Marine Division commander, General William Rupertus, refuses to consider using the army's 81st Infantry Division in what he considers a purely marine fight. The 1st Battalion and 3rd Battalion of the 7th Marines control the east road and the causeway on the island and capture the Japanese defenses on Ngarmoked Island after a two-day fight against heavily fortified caves.

Private First Class Charles H. Roan is part of the attack by 2nd Battalion, 7th Marines, on one of the innumerable coral outcroppings that make up the battlefield of Peleliu. Roan and his squad are partly cut off from their company during the fighting and are quickly attacked by Japanese troops in a cave above and behind them. Private First Class Roan and four other marines seek cover from the shower of grenades landing in their midst. Roan is wounded by one grenade explosion, then, seeing that another grenade is nearby, he shields his comrades with his own body and takes the blast. Private First Class Roan's courage and personal sacrifice is worthy of receiving the Medal of Honor.

Private First Class Arthur J. Jackson, 3rd Battalion, 7th Marine Regiment, is a rifleman facing flanking fire from Japanese troops concealed in strongly fortified positions at Peleliu. Jackson moves forward and charges one of the enemy positions holding 35 Japanese soldiers. He fires into the opening and throws white phosphorus grenades and explosive charges into the pillbox, eliminating the position. As Japanese fire from the other positions hits around him, Private Jackson attacks two other smaller positions and then moves through the area destroying a total of 12 pillboxes and killing at least 50 Japanese soldiers. For his extraordinary valor in facing a determined enemy and certain death, Private First Class Jackson will win the Medal of Honor.

**NEW GUINEA:** At Morotai Island, American troops encounter no enemy forces. Elements of the 126th Infantry land at Cape Coerongoe and Cape Sopi to establish radar facilities.

FEAF A-20 Havocs, B-25 Mitchells, P-39 Airacobras, P-38 Lightnings, P-40s, and P-47 Thunderbolts attack the island south of the Vogelkop Peninsula and Manokwari.

The headquarters of the 310th Bombardment Wing (Medium) redeploys from Hollandia to Morotai Island. The B-24 Liberators of the 371st Bombardment Squadron (Heavy), 307th Bombardment Group (Heavy), redeploy from Wakde Island to Noemfoor Island.

B-25 Mitchells bomb Langoan airfield on Celebes Island.

## September 19

**CBI:** President Roosevelt urges Chiang Kai-shek to place General Stilwell in command of all Chinese ground forces, including the Communists, to meet the crisis caused by the Japanese *Ichigo* offensive in China. President Roosevelt writes a stern letter to Chiang Kai-shek: "I have urged time and again . . . that you take drastic action. . . . Now when you have not yet placed General Stilwell in command of all forces in China, we are faced with the loss of a critical area in east China. . . ."

Fourteenth Air Force sends 28 B-25 Mitchells to bomb Lingling, Chuanhsien, and Shanhsien. Over 150 P-40s and P-51 Mustangs attack bridges, railroads, troops, and rail and road traffic around Tungting Lake and from the Yangtze River area to the South China Sea.

**ETO:** In Operation Market Garden, the British armored units are held up before Nijmegen as German troops arrive in strength to prevent the bridge from being captured.

Over 170 P-51 Mustangs supporting the First Allied Airborne Army in Holland encounter over 100 German fighters. Pilots report 23 confirmed kills and four probables. Six P-51s are lost and three are damaged. One pilot is killed and six are reported missing.

In the First Army area, the 39th Infantry Regiment of the 9th Infantry Division attacks Hill 554 near Lammersdorf in the Hürtgen Forest. This hill controls the main road to Schmidt. The 60th Infantry Regiment of the 9th Infantry Division attacks to capture the town of Hürtgen.

The VIII Corps captures Brest.

Eighth Air Force sends 796 B-17s escorted by 240 P-47 Thunderbolts and P-51 Mustangs to attack marshaling yards in western Germany. Weather prevents most of the bombers from hitting the primary target. Most attack targets of opportunity including bridges and rail lines. Seven bombers are lost and 281 are damaged. Aircrew casualties are six wounded and 56 missing. Fighter pilots report three confirmed kills. One P-47 is lost and the pilot is reported missing.

An Operation Frantic mission sends 100 B-17s and 61 P-51 Mustangs from airfields in Soviet Ukraine to bomb the marshaling yard at Szolnok, Hungary, en route to Fifteenth Air Force airfields in Italy.

Ninth Air Force sends B-26 Marauders to attack marshaling yards and slow German reinforcements to Aachen. P-47 Thunderbolts and P-38 Lightnings of the IX Tactical Air Command support V Corps in stopping a German counterattack near Wallendorf. Fighters support paratroopers in Holland as part of Operation Market Garden. XIX Tactical Air Command P-47 and P-38 fighters escort A-20 Havocs and B-26s and support ground forces in Holland and at Brest and Nancy in France.

The headquarters of the 391st Bombardment Group (Medium) redeploys from England to France.

**MEDITERRANEAN:** Fifteenth Air Force sends 96 B-24 Liberators escorted by P-38 Lightnings to attack rail bridges in Yugoslavia.

**ITALY:** Twelfth Air Force A-20 Havocs and P-47 Thunderbolts attack German defensive positions, bridges, and roads.

**SOUTHWEST PACIFIC AREA:** U.S. submarine *Bang* attacks Japanese shipping off east coast of Formosa, sinking a tanker and damaging a coastal patrol craft.

**PACIFIC:** Twentieth Air Force deploys elements of the 881st, 882nd, and 883rd Bombardment Squadrons (Very Heavy), 500th Bombardment Group (Very Heavy), to Saipan from the United States. The squadrons' first missions are scheduled for mid-November.

U.S. submarine *Scabbardfish* torpedoes and damages a Japanese submarine tender northwest of Okinawa. U.S. submarine *Shad* torpedoes and sinks a coast defense ship off Honshu, Japan.

**CENTRAL PACIFIC:** Seventh Air Force sends 29 B-24 Liberators from Saipan to attack shipping at Chichi Jima Island. Aircrews report a landing ship and a small cargo vessel damaged.

B-24 Liberators on snooper and armed reconnaissance missions bomb Iwo Jima.

**CENTRAL PACIFIC, PELELIU:** The 7th Marines control the area identified as Purple Beach on the east side of the island. Once secured, it becomes the primary logistics support site.

Hill 100 is a ridge near Horseshoe Valley in the Umurbrogol. The 1st Marines attack to capture the hill, but as soon as they do, they discover the Japanese occupy positions all around, above, and even below them in caves and tunnels. Exposed to a murderous fire during the day, then attacked at night by infiltrators, the marines hold Hill 100, but fewer than 10 are still capable of fighting. The hill has to be abandoned. In four days of combat the 1st Marine Regiment has lost 1,500 men.

The 1st Marines reinforced by the 2nd Battalion of the 7th Marines is stopped before a chain of hills named the Five Sisters. Captain Everett P. Pope commands C Company, 1st Battalion, 1st Marines. Pope's company attacks and holds a steep coral mound named Hill 100. Although his company has taken heavy casualties and is quickly surrounded and trapped by Japanese forces, Captain Pope rallies the dozen survivors and organizes a defense. Throughout the night, the Japanese attack again and again to regain the critical hill, but each time they are driven off by Pope's men. By daylight only eight marines are still standing; without the means to hold their ground any longer, they are ordered to withdraw. Captain Pope's courage under fire and his inspiring leadership in the face of overwhelming odds will win him the Medal of Honor.

**NEW GUINEA:** FEAF B-24 Liberators, B-25 Mitchells, and P-38 Lightnings attack shipping, fuel storage sites, and port facilities in the Celebes.

The headquarters of the 8th Fighter Group and the P-38s of the 36th Fighter Squadron redeploy to Morotai Island. The headquarters of the 347th Fighter Group and the P-38s of the 339th Fighter Squadron redeploy to Middleburg Island.

U.S. submarine *Redfin* sinks Japanese fishing vessel east of Celebes Island.

## September 20

**CBI:** In China, Fourteenth Air Force sends 27 B-25 Mitchells to bomb Lingling, Chuanhsien, Chuanhsien, and Kiyang. Over 100 P-51 Mustangs and P-40s attack troops, horses, trucks, and river shipping near Chuanhsien, Lingling, Kiyang, and Changsha.

**ETO:** In Operation Market Garden, the 505th Parachute Infantry Regiment attacks through Nijmegen to capture the south end of the bridge. The 504th Parachute Infantry Regiment, with a company of the 307th Engineers, crosses the Waal River, using British assault boats in full view of the enemy. The assault troops suffer heavy casualties, but at the end of the day the paratroopers secure the area and open the bridge to British tanks.

The First Army begins the battle for Aachen.

The VI Corps of Seventh Army begins crossing the Moselle River. The 36th Infantry Division crosses near Eloyes and meets heavy German fire. The division takes heavy casualties but captures the town. The 3rd Infantry Division crosses at Rupt.

Eighth Air Force sends nearly 700 P-38 Lightnings, P-47 Thunderbolts, and P-51 Mustangs to support the First Allied Airborne Army in Arnhem and Nijmegen. Two fighters are shot down by antiaircraft fire and nine are damaged.

Ninth Air Force sends B-26 Marauders to attack marshaling yards to prevent German reinforcements from reaching Aachen. P-47 and P-38 fighters of the IX Tactical Air Command support V and VIII Corps near the Dutch-German border, and P-38 Lightnings and P-47s of the XIX Tactical Air Command support XV and XX Corps near Nancy.

**MEDITERRANEAN:** Fifteenth Air Force sends more than 500 B-17s and B-24 Liberators escorted by P-38 Lightnings and P-51 Mustangs to attack marshaling yards, oil refineries, and airfields in Czechoslovakia and railroad bridges near Budapest, Hungary.

**ITALY:** The headquarters of XII Fighter Command takes operational control of the P-47s of the 27th and 79th Fighter Groups. The command's mission is to support Fifth Army.

**SOUTHWEST PACIFIC AREA:** FEAF B-24 Liberators attack Japanese shipping off Formosa, damaging three cargo vessels.

**CENTRAL PACIFIC:** The 81st Infantry Division, with artillery support from the 316th, 317th, 318th, and 906th Field Artillery Battalions, breaks the Japanese defenses at Angaur Island. About 1,400 Japanese troops defend the island. The 321st Infantry Regiment is made available to Major General Roy S. Geiger for employment at Peleliu.

Seventh Air Force B-24 Liberators from the Marshall Islands attack Jaluit Atoll and B-25 Mitchells from Makin bomb Nauru Island.

The 322nd Infantry Regiment supported by tanks meets strong Japanese resistance from a defensive position on Angaur Island known as the Bowl. This begins a nine-day battle to eliminate the enemy position.

**CENTRAL PACIFIC, PELELIU:** The 7th Marines attacks south into the Umurbrogol. The area left under Japanese control has been compressed into a pocket 950 yards long and 450 yards wide. The terrain here is a jumble of cliffs, sinkholes, tall, knife-like ridges, and crevasses. Any sizable force entering the canyons or valleys is subjected to heavy fire from all directions. If ridgelines are occupied, the next higher ridgeline or hilltop sweeps the area with rifle and machine-gun fire. At night, the Japanese attack from their caves and tunnels to drive the Americans off any position they still held during the day.

**NEW GUINEA:** FEAF P-47 Thunderbolts, P-38 Lightnings, and P-40s attack antiaircraft positions and logistics sites at Moemi and Ransiki airfields.

B-24 Liberators, A-20 Havocs, and P-47 Thunderbolts attack Halmahera Island. B-24s, B-25 Mitchells, A-20s, and P-38 Lightnings conduct day and night raids on airfields on Ceram Island, Buru Island, Amboina Island, and a town on Timor Island.

The B-25s of the 75th Bombardment Squadron (Medium), 42nd Bombardment Group (Medium), redeploy from Hollandia to Sansapor. P-38s of the 80th Fighter Squadron 8th Fighter Group redeploy to Morotai Island. The B-24s of the 370th and 372nd Bombardment Squadrons (Heavy), 307th Bombardment Group (Heavy), redeploy from Wakde Island to Noemfoor Island.

## September 21

**CBI:** Tenth Air Force sends 21 B-24 Liberators to fly fuel to Kunming, China.

In China, Fourteenth Air Force sends 27 B-25 Mitchells to bomb Kiyang, Yungming, and Lingling. P-40s and P-51 Mustangs attack river shipping, troops, horses, and logistics sites near Kiyang.

**ETO:** The 45th Infantry Division of the VI Corps, Seventh Army, crosses the Moselle River near Épinal. The 180th Infantry Regiment meets heavy resistance before the city.

Eighth Air Force sends 90 P-47 Thunderbolts and P-51 Mustangs to conduct escort ground support missions for First Allied Airborne Army C-47s dropping supplies and paratroopers of the Polish 1st Brigade near Driel in Holland. Nearly 50 German fighters attack the Americans. Fighter pilots report 20 confirmed kills. Three fighters are lost and three damaged. Three pilots are reported missing.

Over 300 B-17s escorted by 73 P-38 Lightnings and P-51 Mustangs bomb the synthetic oil plant at Ludwigshafen and the marshaling yard at Mainz. A total of 106 B-17s are damaged. Aircrew casualties are two wounded. One P-51 is lost, and the pilot is reported missing. Nearly 180 B-24 Liberators bomb the marshaling yard at Koblenz escorted by 44 P-51s. Two B-24s are lost and 86 damaged. Aircrew casualties are 15 killed, three wounded, and 18 missing.

Ninth Air Force sends 79 A-20 Havocs and B-26 Marauders to attack marshaling yards in Germany. The P-47 and P-38 fighters of the IX Tactical Air Command support the V Corps at Wallendorf.

The A-20 Havocs of the 670th Bombardment Squadron (Light), 416th Bombardment Group (Light), redeploy from England to France.

Private John R. Towle is a bazooka gunner in C Company, 504th Parachute Infantry Regiment, 82nd Airborne Division, near Oosterhout, Holland. His company is in a defensive position at the Nijmegen bridgehead when about 100 German infantry, two tanks, and a personnel carrier attack. Private Towle takes the initiative to stop the tanks himself. He exposes himself to enemy fire in order to reach an exposed dike roadbed where he can best engage the enemy. He fires on the tanks; although they take only superficial damage, they retreat. Towle then fires into a house and kills a group of German troops occupying it as a strongpoint. Going back for more bazooka rounds, Private Towle then moves forward again to attack the personnel carrier. As he prepares to fire, a mortar round explodes nearby, killing him. Private Towle's exceptional devotion to duty and courage in the face of danger will win him the Medal of Honor.

**MEDITERRANEAN:** Fifteenth Air Force sends more than 300 B-17s and B-24 Liberators escorted by P-38 Lightnings and P-51 Mustangs to attack marshaling yards and bridges in Hungary and road and rail lines in Yugoslavia. Two C-47s escorted by eight P-51s evacuate Fifteenth Air Force former prisoners of war from Yugoslavia to Italy.

**ITALY:** The 88th Infantry Division, commanded by Major General Paul W. Kendall, moves the 350th and 349th Infantry Regiments toward Imola to outflank German forces facing the attacking British Eighth Army.

**SOUTHWEST PACIFIC AREA:** Based on the approval of the JCS for the invasion of Leyte on October 20, SWPA headquarters orders Sixth Army to seize and secure Dinagat and Homonhon Islands as a preliminary action to bringing a landing force into Leyte Gulf. Upon landing, Krueger's Sixth Army will have 60 days to defeat enemy forces and establish airbases necessary for future operations. The Eighth Army (to be established on September 25 under Lieutenant General Robert L. Eichelberger) will take over all former Sixth Army missions in New Guinea, New Britain, the Admiralties, and Morotai. The Australian First Army will take the combat missions of XIV Corps in the Solomons and Sixth Army in New Guinea. General Kenney's Fear East Air Force will attack targets on Mindanao and in the Netherlands East Indies from bases in New Guinea and Morotai.

Naval Task Force 38 (Vice Admiral Marc A. Mitscher) carrier aircraft attack Japanese shipping in Manila Bay and Subic Bay, attack Clark Field and Nichols Field, and attack the Cavite Navy Yard. A destroyer, five tankers, two oilers, 16 cargo ships, a coastal defense ship, a passenger-cargo ship, and a cargo vessel are sunk. A Japanese destroyer, two cargo vessels, and two tankers are damaged.

U.S. submarine *Haddo*, while on a lifeguard mission for the air attacks on Luzon, torpedoes and sinks a Japanese surveying ship southwest of Manila. Off the north coast of Luzon, USS *Picuda* torpedoes and sinks a Japanese transport. USS *Redfish* torpedoes and sinks a transport.

**PACIFIC:** U.S. submarine *Searaven* torpedoes and sinks a Japanese army transport off Sakhalin Island.

U.S. submarine *Shad* torpedoes and sinks a Japanese auxiliary minesweeper off Honshu, Japan.

**CENTRAL PACIFIC:** Seventh Air Force B-25 Mitchells from the Gilberts bomb Ponape Island.

**CENTRAL PACIFIC, PELELIU:** The 1st Marines recapture Hills 200 and 210, but an attack to recapture Hill 100 fails. Major General Roy S. Geiger orders Major General William H. Rupertus to pull the 1st Marines out of the line. The Umurbrogol Pocket has nearly destroyed the regiment. The 321st Infantry Regiment of the 81st Division is to arrive as reinforcements. The 1st Marines have by now lost 1,749 men and have captured 10 coral ridges, 22 pillboxes, three blockhouses, 13 antitank guns, and have cleared 144 defended caves. The Umurbrogol has been hardly touched. The 7th Marines attack into the area called the Wildcat Bowl toward Hill 140.

**NEW GUINEA:** FEAF P-39 Airacobras, P-47 Thunderbolts, P-38 Lightnings, and P-40s attack antiaircraft positions and logistics sites at Moemi and Ransiki airfields.

B-24 Liberators bomb Amboina and Celebes Islands. P-38 Lightnings and B-25 Mitchells bomb targets on Celebes Island, an airfield on Buru Island, and a barge off Halmahera Island.

## September 22

**CBI:** Tenth Air Force sends 13 B-24 Liberators to fly fuel to Kunming, China.

In China, Fourteenth Air Force sends 24 B-24 Liberators to bomb Hankow. B-25 Mitchells and P-51 Mustangs attack transportation targets at Hengyang and Yungming. P-40s and P-51 Mustangs attack convoys near Changsha and troops, gun positions, rail lines, bridges, and roads near Chuanhsien, Lingling, Hankow, and Kiyang.

**ATLANTIC:** German submarine *U-979* torpedoes a U.S. Navy storeship off Reykjavik, Iceland.

**ETO:** Allied commanders meet in Versailles to clarify strategy and establish priorities for future operations. It is deemed essential that the 21st Army Group open the port of Antwerp if any major offensive is to take place. Without the port, the Allies are very limited in what they can do. Once Antwerp is taken, the 21st Army Group will take operational control of the U.S. First Army and cross the Rhine River in the north. The 12th Army Group will extend its front northward toward Cologne. The 6th Army Group (the U.S. Seventh Army and the French First Army) will move to occupy Strasbourg and Alsace.

Eighth Air Force sends nearly 80 P-47 Thunderbolts to support the British paratroopers at Arnhem. One P-47 is lost and one is damaged.

Over 450 B-17s and 200 B-24 Liberators escorted by 268 P-51 Mustangs attack vehicle production facilities in western Germany. Three bombers are lost and 107 are damaged. Aircrew casualties are seven killed and 27 missing. One P-51 is lost and the pilot is reported missing. One fighter is damaged.

Over 100 B-24s fly fuel to France to support ground forces as logistics lines are stretched to the breaking point.

A Frantic mission is completed with the arrival of 84 B-17s and 51 P-51s in Britain from airfields in Italy.

**MEDITERRANEAN:** Fifteenth Air Force sends more than 360 B-17s and B-24 Liberators escorted by 270 P-38 Lightnings and P-51 Mustangs to attack an airfield and industrial area of Munich, Germany. Another 76 B-24s bomb the marshaling yard at Larissa, Greece.

Over 60 B-24s fly fuel to France to support ground forces.

**ITALY:** Twelfth Air Force B-25 Mitchells and B-26 Marauders attack rail bridges. A-20 Havocs and P-47 Thunderbolts attack roads and rail bridges as the Germans withdraw from Pistoia.

The headquarters of the 87th Fighter Wing redeploys from Corsica to Italy.

First Lieutenant Orville E. Bloch, E Company, 338th Infantry Regiment, 85th Infantry Division, distinguishes himself through several acts of extraordinary courage when he personally eliminates five German machine-gun positions near Firenzuola, Italy. Attacking the first position, he forces five Germans to surrender. Arming a hand grenade, Lieutenant Bloch then runs toward the next machine-gun position at the corner of a building and eliminates the defenders. Bloch burst into the doorway of the building, firing his carbine from the hip as the German defenders fire furiously in his direction. Bloch wounds three enemy soldiers and forces the other seven to surrender. As another machine gun is put into action at the next corner of the building, Lieutenant Bloch assaults the position, again firing his carbine from his hip as he wounds two and forces another six soldiers to surrender. In this one action Lieutenant Bloch is responsible for capturing 19 German soldiers and clearing a formidable defensive position. For his heroism and determination to overcome all odds, First Lieutenant Bloch will receive the Medal of Honor.

**SOUTHWEST PACIFIC AREA:** Carrier aircraft from Naval Task Force 38 continue attacks on Japanese shipping in the Philippines. A gunboat, two auxiliary submarine chasers, a cargo ship, and three tankers are sunk. An auxiliary submarine chaser and two cargo ships are damaged.

U.S. submarine *Narwhal* lands personnel and supplies on the southwest coast of Mindanao.

**CENTRAL PACIFIC:** Seventh Air Force sends 15 B-24 Liberators from Saipan to bomb Chichi Jima.

B-25 Mitchells from Makin Island bomb Nauru Island.

The 323rd Infantry Regiment of the 81st Infantry Division makes an unopposed landing on the island of Ulithi.

**CENTRAL PACIFIC, PELELIU:** The 1st Marines are relieved after suffering 56 percent casualties. Along with the 2nd Battalion 7th Marines, the unit has lost a total of 1,838 men.

The 321st Infantry Regiment of the 81st Infantry Division lands at Peleliu and is under the operational control of the 1st Marine Division.

**NEW GUINEA:** At Morotai, a battalion of the 167th Infantry Regiment, 31st Infantry Division, repulses a weak Japanese counterattack.

FEAF A-20 Havocs bomb Utarom airfield, while P-39 Airacobras, P-47 Thunderbolts, P-38 Lightnings, and P-40s attack other targets in northwestern New Guinea.

B-24 Liberators bomb Celebes Island; B-24s and B-25 Mitchells bomb Ceram Island, Ambon Island, and the airfield on Haroekoe Island.

U.S. submarine *Lapon* torpedoes and damages a cargo ship west of Celebes Island.

U.S. submarine *Pargo* makes an unsuccessful attack on a Japanese cargo vessel and avoids a destroyer depth-charge attack.

## September 23

**CBI:** Tenth Air Force sends 19 P-47 Thunderbolts to attack bridges from Wanlin to Bhamo to Myitkyina. Aircrews report one bridge destroyed. A total of 21 B-24 Liberators fly fuel to Kunming and Liuchow, China.

In China, Fourteenth Air Force sends 15 B-24 Liberators to attack targets on the Burma Road near Chefang. Other B-24s bomb the docks at Amoy. B-25 Mitchells attack Chuanhsien, Yungming, and Lungling. P-40s and P-51 Mustangs attack Japanese troop concentrations, gun positions, rail lines, bridges, and highways near Chuanhsien, Yungming, and Lingling.

**ATLANTIC:** Due to the continuation of the war in Europe after the failure of Market Garden, logistics assessments by JCS planners confirm that an invasion of Formosa (Operation Causeway) is not possible in 1944. Planning for Causeway was based on the assumption that the war in Europe would be over in December 1944, and both support troops and supplies would be available to support an invasion. Luzon is supportable logistically with resources currently available in the Pacific and can be accomplished in 1944. U.S. forces will most likely isolate and bypass Formosa and turn to the Bonin Islands and the Ryukyus instead for long-range bomber bases, which will support an eventual invasion of Japan.

**ETO:** Eighth Air Force sends more than 500 P-38 Lightnings, P-47 Thunderbolts, and P-51 Mustangs to attack antiaircraft positions and ground targets near Nijmegen, as the paratroopers of the 82nd and 101st Airborne Divisions and the Polish 1st Brigade make an airborne assault to reinforce troops already in combat. Over 150 German fighters attack the Americans. Pilots report 27 confirmed kills and two probables in the air. A total of 14 U.S. fighters are lost and 37 are damaged. One pilot is wounded and 14 others are reported missing.

Over 160 B-24s fly fuel to France to support ground forces.

**MEDITERRANEAN:** Fifteenth Air Force sends 147 B-17s, escorted by 290 P-38 Lightnings and P-51 Mustangs, to attack a synthetic oil refinery in Czechoslovakia and a marshaling yard in Austria.

**ITALY:** Twelfth Air Force B-25 Mitchells and B-26 Marauders attack rail bridges in the Po River valley. A-20 Havocs and P-47 Thunderbolts attack gun positions, and rail and road targets along the Gothic Line.

**SOUTHWEST PACIFIC AREA:** Lieutenant General Walter Krueger's Sixth Army headquarters issues the approved plan for the Leyte landing. Three days before the landings, the 6th Ranger Battalion will occupy Dinagat Island, Homonhon Island, and Suluan Island at the entrance to Leyte Gulf. The X Corps (1st Cavalry Division and 24th Infantry Division, minus the 21st Infantry Regiment, which has been organized as a separate regimental combat team) under command of Major General Franklin C. Sibert will land to capture the city of Tacloban, the airfield at Tacloban, and Palo. The corps is then to control the San Juanico Straits to the east of Leyte Island and advance rapidly through the Leyte Valley to the north coast and capture Capoocan, Barugo, and Cariga on Carigara Bay and destroy Japanese forces in the area. The XXIV Corps (7th and 96th Infantry Divisions, minus the 381st Infantry Regiment, operating as a separate regimental combat team) under the command of Major General John R. Hodge will land at Dulag and attack westward to destroy enemy forces and occupy the Dagami-Burauen area. If necessary, the corps will move south to capture Abuyog and Baybay. The 21st Infantry Regiment and the 6th Ranger Battalion will land at Cabalian Bay on the extreme southern tip of the island, secure the strait between Leyte and Panoan Islands, and attack north to link with XXIV Corps. The X and XXIV Corps will then clear Japanese forces from the Ormoc Valley and the west coast of the island. The 32nd and 77th Infantry Divisions and the 381st RCT will be in reserve, ready to be landed within 24 hours three days after the initial invasion to support the operations of either XXIV Corps or X Corps. Philippine troops are to be placed under Sixth Army's operational control once the U.S. forces are established ashore. Lieutenant General George C. Kenney's Far East Air Force (FEAF) with over 2,500 aircraft will provide no land-based air support. The plan depends on a rapid seizure of Leyte so that Kenney can bring in aircraft to support the ground forces. Air support for the invasion will come from two sources. The first is Vice Admiral Thomas C. Kinkaid's Seventh Fleet, with its light carriers supporting about 500 aircraft. Kinkaid is under the operational control of MacArthur. The other source is Admiral William F. Halsey's Third Fleet, with its fleet carriers and over 1,000 aircraft. Halsey, however, will only be in support of

MacArthur. Still under Nimitz's operational control, Halsey's primary mission is to destroy the Japanese fleet if the opportunity arises, "or could be created," in Nimitz's words. The date of the landing, October 20, is designated as A-day. Leyte Island's defenders are estimated to be about 20,000 men.

**PACIFIC:** Battleship USS *West Virginia* returns to Pearl Harbor and rejoins the Pacific Fleet. The *West Virginia* is the last ship repaired from the December 7, 1941, attack on Pearl Harbor.

U.S. submarine *Apogon* torpedoes and sinks a Japanese guardboat east of Honshu, Japan.

U.S. submarine *Escolar* departs Midway on her first war patrol.

**CENTRAL PACIFIC:** Seventh Air Force sends 15 B-24 Liberators from Saipan to bomb Chichi Jima, Haha Jima, and Ani Jima Islands. A B-24 from Kwajalein Atoll makes a night raid on Wake Island.

Naval Task Group 33.19 (Rear Admiral William H. P. Blandy) lands the 323rd Regimental Combat Team, 81st Infantry Division, on Ulithi Atoll in the Carolines.

**CENTRAL PACIFIC, PELELIU:** The Japanese begin reinforcing Peleliu from Koror and Babelthuap Islands. The army's 321st Infantry Regiment, 81st Infantry Division, is committed to the battle. Major General William H. Rupertus meets with Major General Roy S. Geiger and the III Amphibious Corps staff to lay out a plan to isolate and eliminate Japanese defenses in the Umurbrogol. The 321st Infantry and the 5th Marines are to flank the enemy by moving on the west road while the 7th Marines press from the south. There is an hour-long artillery bombardment of the cliffs near the west road to clear the advance.

**NEW GUINEA:** At Morotai, elements of the 126th Infantry Regiment encounter Japanese troops dug in on Hill 575. An American attack fails to capture the position. That night, the enemy abandons the position.

FEAF P-47 Thunderbolts and P-40s bomb antiaircraft guns at Manokwari, Moemi, and Ransiki airfields.

B-24 Liberators and B-25 Mitchells bomb airfields on Celebes Island. P-47 Thunderbolts attack an airfield on Halmahera Island.

Headquarters, Thirteenth Air Force redeploys from Hollandia to Noemfoor Island. P-47s of the 460th Fighter Squadron, 348th Fighter Group, redeploy from Nadzab to Noemfoor Island.

A Japanese gunboat and transport are damaged by mines laid by U.S. submarine *Bowfin* on January 29 off Balikpapan, Borneo.

## September 24

**ALEUTIANS:** Eleventh Air Force sends eight B-24 Liberators to bomb Kurabu Cape airfield on Paramushiru Island. Twelve Japanese fighters attack and damage two of the bombers. One B-24 is forced to land in the Soviet Union. Aircrews report one confirmed kill.

**CBI:** Tenth Air Force sends 11 B-24 Liberators to fly fuel to Liuchow, China. P-47 Thunderbolts attack bridges and troops near Bhamo.

In China, Fourteenth Air Force sends 26 B-25 Mitchells to bomb White Cloud airfield at Canton.

**ETO:** In Operation Market Garden, the British Second Army arrives at the lower Rhine. Eighth Air Force sends 47 B-24 Liberators to fly fuel to France to support ground forces.

Ninth Air Force sends P-47 and P-38 fighters of the XIX Tactical Air Command to support the 7th Armored Division of the Third Army.

The B-26 Marauders of the 572nd Bombardment Squadron (Medium), 391st Bombardment Group (Medium), redeploy from England to France.

The XII Corps of the Third Army stops a German counterattack at Chateau Salins.

Staff Sergeant Joseph E. Schaefer is a squad leader in the 2nd Platoon of I Company, 18th Infantry Regiment, 1st Infantry Division, defending an important crossroads near Stolberg, Germany. Two German infantry companies, supported by machine guns, launch an early morning attack and overwhelm the defenders, leaving only Staff Sergeant Schaefer's squad still capable of fighting. Moving his men to a nearby house, he puts them into position and then stands by the main entrance, which is the focus of enemy fire on the building. There, using his M-1 rifle, he stops the first assault. He also stops a second attack as the Germans employ grenades and flame throwers against the squad's position. A third assault comes from two directions. Staff Sergeant Schaefer kills the attackers approaching his doorway, then dashes out in full view of the enemy to engage the second attacking force from a hedgerow. As the enemy withdraws, he captures 10 soldiers. As the Americans begin a counterattack, Schaefer advances to retake the lost position, crawling and running in the face of heavy fire, and is able to free a squad of captured American soldiers. For his leadership against overwhelming odds and dedication to duty, Staff Sergeant Schaefer will receive the Medal of Honor.

**MEDITERRANEAN:** Fifteenth Air Force sends more than 360 B-17s and B-24 Liberators escorted by P-38 Lightnings and P-51 Mustangs to bomb airfields, port facilities, and a marshaling yard in Greece.

**ITALY:** Twelfth Air Force P-47 Thunderbolts attack German strongpoints, troop concentrations, and communications targets along the Fifth Army's front.

**SOUTHWEST PACIFIC AREA:** Naval Task Force 38's carrier aircraft sink eight cargo ships and damage an ammunition ship, four cargo ships, a supply ship, an oiler, a tanker, a small cargo ship, a torpedo boat, a minelayer, a submarine chaser, an auxiliary submarine chaser, an auxiliary minesweeper, and a transport. A tanker is sunk in the South China Sea. A supply ship, a cargo ship, and an oiler are damaged.

U.S. submarine *Barbero* bombards a Japanese radar installation on Batag Island off the north coast of Samar in the Philippines.

**CENTRAL PACIFIC:** Seventh Air Force B-24 Liberators from Saipan bomb Chichi Jima. B-25 Mitchells from the Gilberts bomb Nauru and Ponape Islands. B-24s from Kwajalein bomb Truk.

In the Marianas, 16 P-47 Thunderbolts attack antiaircraft positions on Rota Island.

The 323rd Infantry Regiment secures Ulithi Atoll. As the battle for Peleliu rages on, Ulithi Atoll and not Peleliu will become the major naval base for future operations.

**CENTRAL PACIFIC, PELELIU:** Marine fighter aircraft begin operating from the airfield on the island. The 321st Infantry Regiment captures Hill 100 in the Umurbrogol. For the next three days the infantrymen battle the Japanese. Colonel Robert F. Dark, the commander of the regiment, forms mobile task forces of tanks and infantry armed with flamethrowers to dislodge the defenders from their positions. Task Force Neal, commanded by Captain George C. Neal, takes tanks and infantry north, then turns south to support the fight to hold Hill 100.

**NEW GUINEA:** FEAF P-47 Thunderbolts, P-38 Lightnings, and P-40s attack airfields in northwestern New Guinea.

B-24 Liberators and B-25 Mitchells bomb airfields on Ceram Island, Buru Island, and Haroekoe Island. Other B-24s bomb Timor.

## September 25

**CBI:** Generalissimo Chiang Kai-shek responds to President Roosevelt's September 19 letter by attacking General Stilwell personally, refusing under any circumstances to appoint him as commander of Chinese forces, and demands that he be replaced. In effect, the Generalissimo tells the president that the future of Chinese-American relations hangs on whether or not General Stilwell remains as theater commander.

Tenth Air Force sends 19 B-24 Liberators to fly fuel to Kunming, Liuchow, and Yungning in China.

In China, Fourteenth Air Force B-25 Mitchells bomb Mangshih, Kweiyang, and the Hengyang railyards. B-24 Liberators bomb Nanking. Over 100 P-51 Mustangs and P-40s fly armed reconnaissance over the area south of the Yangtze River, attacking bridges, town areas, troop concentrations, and various targets of opportunity.

**ETO:** In Operation Market Garden, the 2,163 survivors of the British 1st Airborne Division withdraw across the Rhine to safety. The paratroopers leave 7,000 of their comrades behind—dead, wounded, missing, or captured. The U.S. 82nd Airborne Division has lost 1,432 men, and the 101st Airborne Division has 2,110 casualties. The failure of Market Garden blemishes Montgomery's standing within Eisenhower's headquarters. He will no longer have the influence he once had. By deciding on a quick thrust over the Rhine River instead of capturing Antwerp, Montgomery's failure has made Eisenhower's logistics problem only worse. The optimism that the war in Europe was near an end is shattered, and a period of stalemate on the front lines now begins.

General Bradley orders First Army to protect the flank of Montgomery's 21st Army Group; when sufficiently resupplied and reinforced, Lieutenant General Courtney H. Hodges's divisions will attack toward the Rhine River and Bonn and Cologne. Lieutenant General George S. Patton, Jr.'s Third Army will hold in place. Lieutenant General William H. Simpson's Ninth Army will occupy the area before the Ardennes Forest when it arrives from Brittany. The 94th Infantry Division is given the task of containing German forces holding ports in Brittany and is under 12th Army Group's operational control.

Eighth Air Force sends nearly 1,000 B-17s escorted by 410 P-38 Lightnings and P-51 Mustangs to attack the Ludwigshafen oil facility and marshaling yard and Frankfurt am Main industrial area. Five B-17s are lost and 128 damaged. Aircrew casualties are nine wounded and 18 missing. Two fighters are lost and one is damaged. The two pilots are reported missing.

Over 250 B-24 Liberators escorted by 157 P-38 Lightnings, P-47 Thunderbolts, and P-51 Mustangs bomb marshaling yards at Koblenz. Fourteen B-24s are damaged. One P-51 is lost, and the pilot is reported missing.

A total of 176 B-24s fly fuel to France to support the ground forces. One bomber is lost.

Ninth Air Force P-47 and P-38 fighters support ground forces and conduct dive-bombing attacks on rail lines.

The A-20 Havocs of the 668th Bombardment Squadron (Light), 416th Bombardment Group (Light), redeploy from England to France as do the B-26 Marauders of the 449th Bombardment Squadron (Medium), 322nd Bombardment Group (Medium).

**MEDITERRANEAN:** Fifteenth Air Force sends 51 B-24 Liberators escorted by P-38 Lightnings and P-51 Mustangs to attack port facilities in Greece.

Fourteenth Air Force B-24 Liberators sink two German submarines (*U-565* and *U-596*) off Salamis, Greece.

**ITALY:** The 88th Infantry Division captures Castel del Rio.

Twelfth Air Force A-20 Havocs and P-47 Thunderbolts attack road and rail targets, troops, bridges, and ground support forces.

**SOUTHWEST PACIFIC AREA:** U.S. submarine *Nautilus* lands supplies on Cebu.

**PACIFIC:** U.S. submarine *Barbel* torpedoes and sinks a Japanese cargo ship west of the Ryukyu Islands. U.S. submarines *Guardfish* and *Thresher* each torpedo and sink a Japanese cargo ship in the Yellow Sea.

U.S. submarine *Searaven* torpedoes and sinks a small vessel in the Kuriles.

**CENTRAL PACIFIC:** Seventh Air Force B-24 Liberators from Saipan bomb Iwo Jima. During the night B-24s from Kwajalein stage through Eniwetok to bomb Truk. Most miss the primary target and bomb Wake, Param, and Moem Islands.

Seventh Air Force B-24 Liberators from Saipan bomb targets on the Bonin Islands.

**CENTRAL PACIFIC, PELELIU:** The 1st Battalion of the 5th Marines captures the radio station complex; the 3rd Battalion of the 5th Marines then attacks to capture the ridges beyond. The marines now have established a strong position on the north and west sections of the island.

Private First Class John D. New of the 2nd Battalion, 7th Marines, 1st Marine Division, is occupying an observation post with two other marines when he spots a Japanese soldier emerging from a cave in a cliff above them. The soldier tosses a grenade that lands in the midst of the three marines. Private First Class New dives on the grenade and is killed, but he saves the lives of his comrades. For his courage and willingness to sacrifice himself for his comrades, Private First Class New will receive the Medal of Honor.

**NEW GUINEA:** Lieutenant General Walter Krueger's Alamo Force is redesignated as U.S. Sixth Army. The Alamo Force's accomplishments in the New Guinea campaign are impressive. Krueger and his staff have orchestrated and brought to reality General MacArthur's vision, conducting simultaneous and sequential operations effectively coordinating land, air, and naval power in a combination intended to place the Japanese at a disadvantage. American forces have fought a determined enemy who had little choice but to fight and die honorably. The jungles and islands of New Guinea have some of the most forbidding and inhospitable terrain in the world, and yet Americans have defeated the Japanese, recognized experts in this warfare, and then carved, blasted, and dug pathways into the jungle for airfields, depots, and ports that ultimately overwhelmed the enemy and opened the way to the Philippines.

Sixth Army is composed of two corps, I Corps, commanded by Major General Innis P. Swift, and X Corps, commanded by Major General Edwin D. Patrick. General MacArthur also establishes the U.S. Eighth Army, commanded by Lieutenant General Robert L. Eichelberger.

FEAF B-25 Mitchells, A-20 Havocs, and P-40s attack airfields in northwestern New Guinea. A-20s attack logistics storage areas on Halmahera Island. B-24 Liberators bomb Buru Island airfield. B-24s and B-25 Mitchells along with P-38 Lightnings attack airfields on Celebes Island.

## September 26
**ALEUTIANS:** Eleventh Air Force B-24 Liberators use radar-guided bombing to attack Suribachi airfield in the Kurile Islands.
**CBI:** The Japanese Eleventh Army captures the Tanchuck airfield after the Fourteenth Air Force abandons it.

Tenth Air Force sends 19 B-24 Liberators to fly fuel to Liuchow, Yangtong, and Yungning.

In China, Fourteenth Air Force B-25 Mitchells bomb Lungfukwan and Mangshih. P-40s and P-51 Mustangs attack bridges, town areas, troop concentrations, and various targets of opportunity.
**ETO:** A total of 320 P-47 Thunderbolts and P-51 Mustangs from Eighth Air Force and P-38 Lightnings from Ninth Air Force provide ground support to the paratroopers of the First Allied Airborne Army in Holland. Fighter pilots report 32 confirmed kills and one probable. One P-38 is lost and 10 fighters are damaged; the pilot is reported missing. Eighth Air Force sends nearly 700 B-17s escorted by more than 230 P-51 Mustangs to attack the marshaling yard and steel plant at Osnabrück and the marshaling yard at Hamm. One B-17 is lost and three are damaged. Aircrew casualties are two killed, 12 wounded, and 39 missing. Fighter pilots report two confirmed kills. One P-51 is lost and three are damaged; the pilot is reported missing.

A total of 165 B-24s fly fuel to France to resupply the ground forces.

During the night six B-17s and three B-24s drop leaflets over Germany, France, and the Netherlands.

Ninth Air Force sends P-47 and P-38 fighters of the XIX Tactical Air Command to support the Third Army's operations against Metz. The IX Tactical Air Command P-38 Lightnings and P-47s fly armed reconnaissance missions and provide support to the First Army, attacking rail lines across the Rhine River from Bonn.

The A-20 Havocs of the 646th Bombardment Squadron (Light), 410th Bombardment Group (Light), redeploy from England to France.

The headquarters of the U.S. Strategic Air Forces in Europe (USSTAF) redeploys from England to France.

**ITALY:** Twelfth Air Force B-25 Mitchells and B-26 Marauders attack rail and road traffic and bridges in the Po River valley. A-20 Havocs and P-47 Thunderbolts attack convoys, bridges, logistics storage areas, and roads in the Po Valley.

**SOUTHWEST PACIFIC AREA:** A new version of the Musketeer plan is prepared. The original plan was to land on Mindoro as soon as possible after the Leyte landings. The Mindoro operation is scheduled for December 5. MacArthur wants to attack Luzon as soon as possible after the Leyte operation is assured of success. The Joint Chiefs of Staff are uncertain which direction to follow after Leyte—continue to Luzon or bypass Luzon for Formosa.

**PACIFIC:** Twentieth Air Force sends 83 B-29 Superfortresses from Chengtu to bomb Anshan. Nearly all bomb the Showa Steel Works or Dairen, Sinsiang, or targets of opportunity. After the return of the bombers, Japanese aircraft bomb Chengtu and damage five B-29s during the night.

The X Corps commander, Lieutenant General Simon B. Buckner, who is responsible for the land forces for Operation Causeway (the invasion of Formosa) assesses that there are insufficient service and support troops in-theater to make the invasion successful.

U.S. submarine *Thresher* torpedoes and sinks a Japanese cargo ship in the Yellow Sea.

**CENTRAL PACIFIC:** Seventh Air Force B-24 Liberators from the Marshall Islands conduct a night bombing raid on Wake Island. B-25 Mitchells from the Gilbert Islands bomb Nauru Island.

Destroyer escort USS *McCoy Reynolds* sinks Japanese submarine *I-175* northeast of the Palau Islands.

**CENTRAL PACIFIC, PELELIU:** The 321st Infantry Regiment continues to battle to hold Hill 100 and Hill B. The 5th Marines attack into the Umurbrogol to capture the four hills in an area called Hill Row. This area is defended by 1,500 Japanese troops fighting from caves linked by tunnels.

**NEW GUINEA:** FEAF B-24 Liberators and B-25 Mitchells bomb airfields on Ambon Island and Celebes Island.

B-24s of the 31st Bombardment Squadron (Heavy), 5th Bombardment Group (Heavy), redeploy from Wakde Island to Noemfoor Island, and the B-24s of the 424th Bombardment Squadron (Heavy), 307th Bombardment Group (Medium), redeploy from Wakde Island to Noemfoor Island.

U.S. submarine *Pargo* torpedoes and sinks a Japanese minelayer off Borneo.

### September 27

**CBI:** Tenth Air Force P-47 Thunderbolts attack ammunition storage sites, rail bridges, and troop positions in Burma. A total of 10 B-24 Liberators fly fuel to Liuchow and Yungning, China.

In China, Fourteenth Air Force P-40s and P-51 Mustangs attack troop concentrations, gun positions, rail lines, bridges, and roads near Kiyang, Chuanhsien, and Lingling.

**ETO:** The Third Army's XX Corps under Major General Walton H. Walker attacks the city of Metz, one of the most heavily fortified cities in the world. The 11th Infantry Regiment of the 5th Infantry Division, supported by a company of tanks from the 818th Tank Destroyer Battalion, attacks Fort Driant and fails.

Eighth Air Force sends more than 800 B-17s using radar-equipped Pathfinders escorted by more than 400 P-47 Thunderbolts and P-51 Mustangs to attack Ludwigshafen oil refinery and transportation targets. Two B-17s are lost and 308 damaged. Aircrew casualties are six killed, 16 wounded, and 20 missing. Fighter pilots report six confirmed kills. Four fighters are damaged.

Another 315 B-24 Liberators escorted by 207 P-38 Lightnings, P-47 Thunderbolts, and P-51 Mustangs are sent to attack the aircraft production facility at Kassel. Aircrews report five confirmed kills and three probables. A total of 26 B-24s are lost and 47 are damaged. Aircrew casualties are 20 killed, two wounded, and 245 missing. Pilots report 25 confirmed kills in the air and five on the ground. Two P-51s are lost and five fighters are damaged. The pilot is reported missing.

A total of 163 B-24s fly fuel to France to resupply the ground forces.

During the night eight B-17s drop leaflets over Germany, France, and the Netherlands.

Ninth Air Force redeploys the A-20 Havocs of the 644th Bombardment Squadron (Light), 410th Bombardment Group (Light), from England to France.

**ITALY:** Twelfth Air Force A-20 Havocs bomb motor transport in the Po Valley during the night.

P-47 Thunderbolts attack German defenses at Monte Oggioli and attack roads and motor transport, and bomb rail lines between Parma and Piacenza.

The 88th Infantry Division approaches Imola as the 2nd Battalion of the 350th Infantry Regiment captures Monte Battaglia and defends it against heavy counterattacks. II Corps, on Route 65, pushes past Radicosa Pass.

Captain Robert E. Roeder commands G Company, 350th Infantry Regiment, 88th Infantry Division, defending positions on Monte Battaglia. German forces direct several determined counterattacks to recapture the critical terrain. Captain Roeder directs the defense, moving among his men while artillery and rifle fire rain on the company's position. The Germans fail in five attempts, but make a sixth counterattack in the fog using flamethrowers and are able to make a breakthrough. Roeder personally leads the assault to recapture the lost positions and drives the enemy off with heavy casualties. The next morning Roeder is wounded by an artillery shell; after regaining consciousness, he refuses medical treatment and rejoins the battle. Unable to stand, he props himself in a position so that he can be seen by his men, and shouts encouragement as he fires his weapon on advancing German soldiers. He is killed shortly thereafter by another artillery shell. Captain Roeder's valiant defense of a critical position, his dedication to duty, and his spirited leadership will win him the Medal of Honor.

**SOUTHWEST PACIFIC AREA:** U.S. submarine *Bonefish* torpedoes and damages a Japanese oiler southwest of Manila.

USS *Flasher* and USS *Lapon* attack a Japanese convoy in the South China Sea west of Luzon. USS *Flasher* sinks an army transport and damages a tanker; USS

*Lapon* sinks a tanker. U.S. submarine *Narwhal* lands supplies on the north coast of Mindanao, and U.S. submarine *Stingray* lands supplies on the east coast of Luzon.

**PACIFIC:** U.S. submarine *Apogon* torpedoes and sinks a Japanese cargo ship off Shimushir Island, Kuriles. U.S. submarine *Searaven* torpedoes and damages a Japanese destroyer in the Kuriles.

U.S. submarine *Plaice* torpedoes and sinks a Japanese coastal patrol ship west of the Ryukyus.

**CENTRAL PACIFIC:** Seventh Air Force B-24 Liberators from the Marshalls bomb Truk.

At Angaur, the battle for the Bowl continues as the 322nd Infantry Regiment, having turned back a Japanese counterattack, closes in on three sides of the defensive position, using a combination of heavy artillery, tanks, and bulldozers.

**CENTRAL PACIFIC, PELELIU:** The 321st Infantry Regiment clears Japanese positions with tanks and flamethrowers while the 8th Marines bring their 155 millimeter guns to within 180 yards of Amiangal Ridge in the Umurbrogol to destroy Japanese positions. The infantrymen and marines find that they are able to control only the ground they stand on. The Japanese control everything else, even the ground below their feet. The Japanese are able to attack at will from any direction, using interconnected tunnels and multiple, nearly invisible firing positions.

**NEW GUINEA:** FEAF P-40s attack airfields at Ransiki, Kokas, and Warren and bomb shipping around the Vogelkop Peninsula.

B-24 Liberators bomb troops and logistics storage sites on Celebes Island. B-25 Mitchells bomb oil storage tanks on Ceram Island and the airfield on Buru Island.

The B-24s of the 72nd and 394th Bombardment Squadrons (Heavy), 5th Bombardment Group (Heavy), redeploy from Wakde Island to Noemfoor Island. The headquarters of the 35th Fighter Group redeploys to Morotai Island.

A Navy PBY Catalina damages a Japanese cargo ship off Jolo Island in the Celebes Sea.

## September 28

**CBI:** Tenth Air Force sends 26 B-24 Liberators to fly fuel to Liuchow, Yungning, and Kunming, China.

Fourteenth Air Force B-25 Mitchells attack Tien Ho and White Cloud airfields at Canton and river and road traffic around Lingling, Siangtan, and Chuchou. P-40s and P-51 Mustangs attack troop concentrations, gun positions, rail lines, bridges, and roads in southeast China.

**ETO:** The VI Corps of Seventh Army makes rapid progress in the foothills of the Vosges Mountains, but is halted by a combination of heavy rains and strong German resistance along the Meurthe River. The VI Corps halts to rest and refit in preparation for an offensive in October to clear the passages in the Vosges Mountains.

Eighth Air Force sends more than 750 B-17s escorted by over 450 P-38 Lightnings and P-51 Mustangs to attack oil refineries in Germany. Aircrews report 10 confirmed kills and seven probables. A total of 33 B-17s are lost and 383 damaged. Aircrew casualties are four killed, 23 wounded, and 300 missing. Fighter pilots report 26 confirmed kills and one probable in the air and one confirmed kill on the ground. Six fighters are lost and five are damaged. Six pilots are reported missing.

Another 262 B-24 Liberators escorted by 171 P-47 Thunderbolts are sent to bomb the motor production facility at Kassel. One B-24 is lost and 86 are damaged. Aircrew casualties are 10 missing. One P-47 is lost, and three are damaged. The pilot is reported missing.

A total of 194 B-24s fly fuel to France to resupply the ground forces.

During the night six B-17s and four B-24s drop leaflets over Germany, France, and the Netherlands.

Ninth Air Force sends P-47 and P-38 fighters to attack German positions around Arnhem as the British 1st Airborne Division crosses the Rhine to return to friendly lines, thus ending the Market Garden operation.

The headquarters of the 410th Bombardment Group (Light) redeploys from England to France, as do the A-20 Havocs of the 645th and 647th Bombardment Squadrons (Light), 410th Bombardment Group (Light).

**ITALY:** The 350th Infantry Regiment of the 88th Infantry Division holds Monte Battaglia against a strong German counterattack. The U.S. II Corps advances after the Germans withdraw from Radicosa Pass.

**SOUTHWEST PACIFIC AREA:** U.S. submarine *Bonefish* torpedoes and sinks a Japanese merchant tanker in the South China Sea west of Luzon.

**CENTRAL PACIFIC:** Seventh Air Force B-24 Liberators from Saipan bomb naval installations at Chichi Jima.

**CENTRAL PACIFIC, PELELIU:** The 3rd Battalion of the 5th Marines seizes Ngesebus and Kongauru, two small islands north of Peleliu. The marines use tanks to clear out positions defended by about 500 Japanese troops, with the support of naval gunfire (one battleship and 12 cruisers), marine artillery, and marine aircraft.

**NEW GUINEA:** FEAF P-47 Thunderbolts attack Manokwari airfield. B-25 Mitchells and A-20 Havocs attack shipping and the airfield on Celebes Island. P-38 Lightnings attack barges in the Molucca Islands.

Navy PBY Catalinas sink a Japanese cargo ship in the Makassar Straits.

## September 29

**ALEUTIANS:** Eleventh Air Force sends two B-24 Liberators to bomb the Katooka naval base and Kokutan Cape in the Kurile Islands.

**CBI:** Tenth Air Force sends 11 B-25 Mitchells to attack antiaircraft positions and bridges on the Burma Road near Uambkai. Aircrews report the main bridge is damaged and the bypass bridge is destroyed. Eighteen B-24 Liberators fly fuel to Yungning, Liuchow, and Kunming, China.

In China, Fourteenth Air Force sends B-25 Mitchells to bomb Tien Ho and White Cloud airfields at Canton. Nearly 100 P-51 Mustangs, P-40s, and P-38 Lightnings bomb road and rail junctions, bridges, town areas, troop concentrations, and various targets of opportunity south of the Yangtze River.

**ATLANTIC:** Navy PB4Y Privateers sink German submarine *U-863* in the South Atlantic east of Brazil.

German submarine *U-310* torpedoes and damages a U.S. freighter in a convoy in the Barents Sea as it returns to Scotland from the Soviet port of Archangel. The freighter is scuttled by a British destroyer.

**ETO:** Lieutenant General Courtney Hodges, commander of First Army, orders an attack to capture Düren and Cologne. The city of Aachen will have to be controlled for First Army to succeed. The XIX Corps under Major General Charles H. Cortlett will attack to the north; VII Corps under Major General J. Lawton Collins will attack to the south. The V Corps is to flank the Roer and gain a bridgehead over the Rhine River near Cologne. The 9th Infantry Division, given the mission of covering the flank of VII Corps as it attacks near Aachen, has fought in the Hürtgen Forest since September 14. The 39th Infantry Regiment captures Hill 554, but is unable to go any farther. The 60th Infantry Regiment, attacking near Hürtgen for nearly 10 days, battles German counterattacks in the marshy woods.

Operational control of XV Corps (the French 2nd Armored Division and the U.S. 79th Infantry Division) passes from Patton's Third Army to Patch's Seventh Army.

During the night Eighth Air Force sends five B-17s and five B-24s to drop leaflets over Germany, France, and the Netherlands.

Ninth Air Force sends more than 400 A-20 Havocs and B-26 Marauders to attack marshaling yards and rail sidings, antitank defenses, warehouses, and barracks. A total of 1,500 P-47 and P-38 fighters escort the bombers and attack rail lines.

The 452nd Bombardment Squadron (Medium), 322nd Bombardment Group (Medium), moves from Great Saling, England, to the B-26s of the 452nd Bombardment Squadron (Medium), 322nd Bombardment Group (Medium), redeploy from England to France.

**ITALY:** Twelfth Air Force P-47 Thunderbolts attack rail lines south of Milan.

**SOUTHWEST PACIFIC AREA:** U.S. submarine *Narwhal* evacuates 81 Allied POWs from Mindanao who have survived the sinking of their transport by USS *Paddle* on September 7.

**PACIFIC:** B-29 Superfortresses make an initial reconnaissance flight over Okinawa.

U.S. submarine *Skate* torpedoes and sinks a Japanese auxiliary minesweeper and a cargo ship west of the Ryukyus.

**CENTRAL PACIFIC:** Seventh Air Force B-24 Liberators from Saipan bomb Iwo Jima. B-24s from Kwajalein bomb Truk.

**CENTRAL PACIFIC, PELELIU:** The 3rd Battalion 5th Marines reports Ngesebus is secured and turns the island over to the 2nd Battalion of the 321st Infantry Regiment. The marines then move to division reserve. The 7th Marines takes control of the northern end of the Umurbrogol pocket from the 321st Infantry Regiment.

**NEW GUINEA:** FEAF A-20 Havocs and Royal Australian Air Force (RAAF) aircraft attack Utarom airfield.

B-24 Liberators bomb airfields on Celebes Island, Ambon Island, and Haroekoe Island.

### September 30

**CBI:** In Burma, Tenth Air Force sends more than 50 P-47 Thunderbolts to attack a railroad bridge and targets of opportunity along the Burma Road between Mangshih and Lashio.

A total of 18 B-24 Liberators fly fuel to Liuchow, Yungning, and Kunming, China.

In China, Fourteenth Air Force sends 29 B-24 Liberators and 12 B-25 Mitchells to bomb Wuchou, Tien Ho, and White Cloud airfields near Canton. Nearly 100 P-51 Mustangs, P-40s, and P-38 Lightnings attack river shipping, road and rail junctions, bridges, town areas, and troop concentrations south of the Yangtze River.

**ATLANTIC:** Destroyer escort USS *Fessenden* sinks German submarine *U-1062* in the mid-Atlantic.

**ETO:** SHAEF headquarters estimates that since the D-day landings 1 million German soldiers have been killed, captured, or taken prisoner.

Eighth Air Force sends 570 B-17s using radar-equipped Pathfinder bombers escorted by 417 P-47 Thunderbolts and P-51 Mustangs to attack marshaling yards and airfields in western Germany. A total of seven B-17s are lost and 110 are damaged. Aircrew casualties are one killed, five wounded, and 64 missing. One P-51 is damaged.

Another 255 B-24 Liberators, escorted by 170 P-38 Lightnings, P-47 Thunderbolts, and P-51 Mustangs, are sent to bomb the Hamm marshaling yard. One B-24 is lost and 32 are damaged. Aircrew casualties are 10 missing.

A total of 116 B-24s fly fuel to France to resupply the ground forces.

Ninth Air Force sends 14 B-26 Marauders to bomb the Rhine River bridge at Arnhem. P-47 and P-38 fighters attack rail lines and rail cars in western Germany.

The headquarters of the 344th Bombardment Group (Medium) and the B-26s of the 494th 495th, 496th, and 497th Bombardment Squadrons (Medium) redeploy from England to France.

**ITALY:** Twelfth Air Force B-25 Mitchells bomb road and rail bridges in the Po River valley. B-26 Marauders bomb fuel storage areas and bridges. P-47 Thunderbolts of XII Fighter Command attack vehicles, rail lines, roads, and bridges in the Po Valley.

**SOUTHWEST PACIFIC AREA:** U.S. submarine *Nautilus* lands supplies and evacuates personnel from Panay Island in the Philippines.

**CENTRAL PACIFIC:** The headquarters of the 494th Bombardment Group (Heavy) and the B-24 Liberators of the 864th, 865th, 866th, and 867th Bombardment Squadrons (Heavy) deploy from Hawaii to Angaur Island in the Palau Islands. The squadrons' first missions are scheduled for late November.

**CENTRAL PACIFIC, PELELIU:** Major General William H. Rupertus, still wanting the capture of the island to be a marine show, moves the 321st Infantry Regiment to occupy the northern half of the island while two depleted marine regiments are ordered to finish the battle in the Umurbrogol. The 7th Marines battle the Japanese for control of Walt and Boyd Ridges, which dominate the east side of the Umurbrogol Pocket.

**NEW GUINEA:** FEAF A-20 Havocs, P-47 Thunderbolts, and P-40s attack airfields in northwestern New Guinea.

P-38 Lightnings attack targets on Ceram Island, seaplane bases on Celebes Island, and the airfield on Haroekoe Island. B-24 Liberators attack oil storage areas at Balikpapan, Borneo, and the airfield on Celebes Island. B-25 Mitchells attack shipping on Halmahera Island.

B-24s of the 23rd Bombardment Squadron (Heavy) of the 5th Bombardment Group (Heavy) redeploy from Wakde Island to Noemfoor Island.

### October 1

**CBI:** Tenth Air Force P-47 Thunderbolts bomb rail targets throughout northern Burma and sweep the Burma Road area. In China, Fourteenth Air Force sends 18 B-25 Mitchells to bomb Tien Ho and White Cloud airfields near Canton. Over 100 P-51 Mustangs, P-40s, and P-38 Lightnings attack road and rail junctions, bridges, town areas, troop concentrations, and various targets of opportunity south of the Yangtze River and around Mangshih and Hsinganhsien.

**ATLANTIC:** The JCS reports the strength of U.S. land and air forces. In the ETO and the Mediterranean, there are 40 divisions with four more en route. In addition, there are 149 air groups. In the Pacific, there are 47 air groups, 21 army divisions, and six marine divisions.

Vice Admiral Richard S. Edwards is named to the newly created positions of deputy commander in chief, U.S. Fleet, and deputy chief of naval operations.

**ETO:** During the night Eighth Air Force sends nine B-17s to drop leaflets over France, the Netherlands, and Belgium.

B-26 Marauders of the 553rd Bombardment Squadron (Medium) of the 386th Bombardment Group (Medium) and the 573rd, 574th, and 575th Bombardment Squadrons (Medium) of the 391st Bombardment Group (Medium) redeploy from England to France.

**ITALY:** After the 88th Infantry Division has lost over 2,000 men in attempting to reach Imola, General Mark Clark shifts the division toward Route 65 to support the II Corps effort. The II Corps attacks with the 85th and 91st Infantry Divisions, supported by the 6th South African Armored Division, the British 78th Division, and Combat Command B of the U.S. 1st Armored Division. The 34th and 88th Infantry Divisions are to follow the main attack.

The intent is to break through to Bologna and reach the open plains of the Po River valley before the approaching winter weather ends any further offensive action.

Twelfth Air Force B-25 Mitchells and B-26 Marauders attack rail and road traffic, fuel storage areas, industrial targets, and bridges in the Po Valley. XII Fighter Command A-20 Havocs and P-47 Thunderbolts attack a fuel storage area and German defensive positions.

**SOUTHWEST PACIFIC AREA:** U.S. submarine *Cabrilla* torpedoes and sinks two Japanese tankers in the South China Sea, west of Luzon.

**PACIFIC:** U.S. submarine *Snapper* torpedoes and sinks a Japanese coastal minelayer and transport northwest of the Bonins. U.S. submarine *Trepang* torpedoes and sinks a supply ship in the Bonins.

**CENTRAL PACIFIC:** Seventh Air Force B-24 Liberators from Saipan bomb Iwo Jima. B-25 Mitchells from Makin Island bomb Nauru Island. B-24s from Eniwetok bomb Truk.

U.S. destroyer *Bailey* is damaged during a Japanese air attack near Peleliu.

**NEW GUINEA:** FEAF A-20 Havocs and P-38 Lightnings attack Utarom airfield and logistics bases. P-40s attack targets of opportunity; P-47 Thunderbolts and A-20 Havocs attack airfields. B-25 Mitchells and P-38 Lightnings conduct shipping sweeps off Halmahera Island.

B-24 Liberators bomb targets in the Molucca Islands. B-25 Mitchells attack Lembeh Island. P-38 Lightnings attack Ceram and Celebes Islands and shipping off Ambon Island.

The C-47s of the 63rd and 70th Troop Carrier Squadrons of the 403rd Troop Carrier Group redeploy to Biak Island. The 82nd Tactical Reconnaissance Squadron of the 71st Tactical Reconnaissance Group redeploys from Biak Island to Morotai Island with P-40s and F-6 (camera-equipped) Mustangs.

U.S. submarine *Hammerhead* torpedoes and sinks two Japanese ore carriers and a cargo ship north of Borneo.

## October 2

**CBI:** The battle of wills between Chiang Kai-shek and President Roosevelt over General Joseph Stilwell's role in China leads to a definite cooling in U.S.-Chinese relations. Chiang Kai-shek rejects President Roosevelt's proposal to put General Stilwell in command of all Chinese ground forces. In rejecting the president's request Chiang has moved away from U.S. strategic support.

Tenth Air Force sends P-47 Thunderbolts to attack towns and bridges around Bhamo and rail lines in northern Burma.

In China, Fourteenth Air Force sends 16 B-25 Mitchells to bomb Tien Ho and White Cloud airfields near Canton. Over 70 P-40s and P-51 Mustangs attack river traffic and troop areas.

**ATLANTIC:** Admiral Ernest J. King assesses that, because of the continuation of the war in Europe, there will not be sufficient ground forces available in the Pacific theater for the invasion of the island of Formosa. Iwo Jima is considered to be a better target for operations in early 1945 because the island will allow U.S. fighters to escort the B-29 Superfortresses flying from Mariana Islands airfields to strike Japanese cities on the home islands. The capture of Okinawa will also support strategic air operations and cut Japanese air control of the Ryukyu Islands.

**ETO:** First Army's XIX Corps (2nd and 7th Armored Divisions and the 29th and 30th Infantry Divisions) attacks north of Aachen to surround the city and link with VII Corps (3rd Armored Division and the 1st and 9th Infantry Divisions) moving from the south of the city. The V Corps (5th Armored Division and the 4th and 28th Infantry Divisions) is to protect First Army's flank. For the next two weeks XIX Corps will fight German forces in the cold and rain to reach its objective.

Eighth Air Force sends more than 870 B-17s using radar-equipped Pathfinder bombers escorted by 500 P-47 Thunderbolts and P-51 Mustangs to attack production facilities in western Germany. Two B-17s are lost and 273 are damaged. Aircrew casualties are 16 killed, six wounded, and 20 missing. Another 308 B-24 Liberators using Pathfinder and escorted by 212 P-38 Lightnings, P-47 Thunderbolts, and P-51 Mustangs are sent to bomb the marshaling yard at Hamm. Two B-24s are lost and

146 are damaged. Aircrew casualties are one killed and 18 missing. One P-51 is lost and three are damaged. One pilot is killed and another pilot is reported missing.

During the night three B-17s and five B-24s drop leaflets over Germany, France, and the Netherlands.

The Ninth Air Force creates the headquarters, XXIX Tactical Air Command (Provisional). Just like the IX and XIX Tactical Air Commands that provide direct air support to the First and Third Armies, respectively, the XXIX Tactical Air Command will support the Ninth Army.

A-20 Havocs and B-26 Marauders of the 9th Bombardment Division attack German defensive positions. P-38 Lightnings and P-47 Thunderbolts support the First, Third, and Seventh Armies.

The headquarters of the 386th Bombardment Group (Medium) and the B-26s of the 552nd, 554th, and 555th Bombardment Squadrons (Medium) redeploy from England to France.

**MEDITERRANEAN:** The B-24 Liberators of the 885th Bombardment Squadron (Heavy) begin deploying from Maison Blanche, Algeria, to Brindisi, Italy. The squadron's mission is to transport supplies to partisans and drop leaflets in the theater.

**ITALY:** The headquarters of the 27th Fighter Group and the P-47 Thunderbolts of the 522nd, 523rd, and 524th Fighter Squadrons redeploy from Loyettes, France, to Tarquinia, Italy.

**SOUTHWEST PACIFIC AREA:** U.S. submarine *Aspro* torpedoes and sinks a Japanese cargo ship in the South China Sea west of Luzon. U.S. submarine *Pomfret* torpedoes and sinks two Japanese army transports south of Formosa.

**CENTRAL PACIFIC:** Seventh Air Force B-24 Liberators from Saipan bomb Chichi Jima.

**NEW GUINEA:** FEAF P-40s attack vessels off the northwest coast of New Guinea and bomb Otawiri and Ransiki airfields. B-25 Mitchells bomb the airfield on Ambon Island. B-24 Liberators attack Haroekoe Island. P-38 Lightnings attack shipping and targets on Ceram Island and the airfield on Celebes Island. B-25 Mitchells fly a barge sweep off Halmahera Island.

## October 3

**ALEUTIANS:** Eleventh Air Force sends two B-24 Liberators to conduct reconnaissance over Onnekotan, Harumukotan, and Shasukotan Islands in the Kurile Islands. Aircrews report strafing several small vessels.

**CBI:** In China, Fourteenth Air Force sends 23 B-25 Mitchells to attack the Wuchou and Samshui areas, and bomb Tien Ho and White Cloud airfields in Canton. P-51 Mustangs and P-40s attack river transport, roads, town areas, troop concentrations, and various targets of opportunity south of the Yangtze River, focusing on the Hsinganhsien, Pingnam, and Chuanhsien areas.

**ATLANTIC:** Admiral Ernest J. King agrees to recommendations by JCS planners and advocates an offensive directed at Okinawa and Iwo Jima once the invasion of Luzon begins. The JCS issues the directive scheduling the Luzon invasion for December 20, supported by Central Pacific air and naval forces. The directive also states that

Admiral Nimitz will plan for an attack on Iwo Jima on January 20, 1945, followed by an attack to seize one or more islands in the Ryukyus (primarily Okinawa) by March 1, 1945.

**ETO:** The XX Corps of Third Army continues its attack on Metz. This begins a 10-day battle for the city. The 11th Infantry Regiment of the 5th Infantry Division again attacks Fort Driant, and is heavily supported with tanks and engineers in a coordinated assault. For several days German and American soldiers will battle underground for possession of the fort.

Eighth Air Force sends 727 B-17s escorted by 511 P-47 Thunderbolts and P-51 Mustangs to attack airfields and industrial targets in central and southern Germany. Four B-17s are lost and 245 are damaged. Aircrew casualties are two killed, six wounded, and 28 missing. Fighter pilots report two confirmed kills on the ground. Four fighters are lost and one is damaged. Four pilots are reported missing.

Another 338 B-24 Liberators escorted by 188 P-38 Lightnings and P-47 Thunderbolts are sent to bomb transportation targets. A total of 39 B-24s are damaged. Aircrew casualties are two wounded.

During the night four B-17s and six B-24s drop leaflets over Belgium, Germany, France, and the Netherlands.

Ninth Air Force P-38s and P-47 Thunderbolts fly armed reconnaissance over western Germany, attack rail lines across the Rhine River, and support ground forces of the Third Army near Metz, France.

**ITALY:** Twelfth Air Force B-26 Marauders and B-25 Mitchells bomb road and rail bridges and fuel storage depots in the Po River valley. A-20 Havocs and P-47 Thunderbolts of the XII Fighter Command attack fuel storage sites, rail lines, and transportation targets in the Po Valley and support Fifth Army along the front.

**SOUTHWEST PACIFIC AREA:** General MacArthur is notified of the decision to support his Musketeer III plan for the occupation of Luzon. Landing on December 20, he is to establish bases on northern Luzon to support further Allied advances, including Nimitz's attack on the Ryukyu Islands scheduled for March. Plans for Formosa are left inactive until the conclusion of the campaign in the Philippines.

**CENTRAL PACIFIC:** Seventh Air Force B-24 Liberators from Saipan Island attack shipping and bomb the airfield on Iwo Jima.

Destroyer escort USS *Samuel S. Miles* sinks Japanese submarine *I-177* off the Palaus Islands.

U.S. submarine *Thresher* torpedoes and sinks a Japanese guardboat off Marcus Island.

**CENTRAL PACIFIC, PELELIU:** The 7th Marines attack to seize Walt and Boyd Ridges on the east side of the Umurbrogol Pocket. The struggle has gone on for three days with no progress and heavy casualties. The 3rd Battalion 5th Marines attacks into the Horseshoe Valley to capture the hills called the Five Sisters, which overlook Walt and Boyd Ridges. The 3rd Battalion has been reduced to company strength by casualties and is unable to hold the positions taken.

**NEW GUINEA:** FEAF A-20 Havocs, P-47 Thunderbolts, and P-40s attack targets on the Vogelkop Peninsula.

B-24 Liberators bomb oil refineries in Balikpapan, Borneo. B-25 Mitchells attack shipping and the airfields in the Moluccas and on Halmahera Island. B-25s and B-24s attack Ceram and Ambon Islands. P-38 Lightnings attack the seaplane base on Celebes Island and the airfields on Buru Island and Haroekoe Island.

Japanese submarine *RO-41* torpedoes and sinks a U.S. destroyer escort off Morotai. Destroyer escort USS *Richard M. Rowell* accidentally sinks USS *Seawolf* on a mission to land Americans on Samar.

### October 4

**ALEUTIANS:** Eleventh Air Force sends four B-25 Mitchells to bomb shipping off Shimushu Island in the Kurile Islands. The Japanese attack the bombers with about 17 fighters. Aircrews report one confirmed kill.

**CBI:** Tenth Air Force P-47 Thunderbolts damage the approaches to a bridge between Myitkyina and Bhamo.

**ATLANTIC:** The JCS makes the decision to land on Luzon, the main island of the Philippines, and liberate the capital city of Manila. Five divisions will be available to land on Leyte. An attack to seize Iwo Jima is scheduled for January 20, 1945, followed by an attack to capture Okinawa on March 1. Another nine divisions will be available for an attack on Formosa after June 1945.

**ETO:** The Ninth Army's VIII Corps (the 9th Armored Division and the 2nd and 83rd Infantry Divisions) begins occupation of the Ardennes Forest between First and Third Armies.

During the night Eighth Air Force sends four B-17s and five B-24 Liberators to drop leaflets over Germany, France, and the Netherlands.

Ninth Air Force sends P-47 and P-38 fighters of the XIX Tactical Air Command to support Third Army around Metz. The IX Tactical Air Command P-38 Lightnings and P-47s provide support to First Army.

**MEDITERRANEAN:** Fifteenth Air Force sends over 300 B-17s and B-24 Liberators escorted by P-38 Lightnings and P-51 Mustangs to attack the marshaling yard at Munich, Germany.

Nearly 40 P-51 Mustangs strafe airfields in Greece. Another 400 bombers attack rail lines in the Brenner Pass.

**ITALY:** After three days of attacks, the 91st Infantry Division is stalled, having suffered over 1,700 casualties. The 85th Infantry Division now leads the attack up Route 65.

British forces relieve the 350th Infantry Regiment on Mount Battaglia. The 88th Infantry Division has lost over 2,000 men since September 21.

Twelfth Air Force A-20 Havocs and P-47 Thunderbolts attack German defensive positions and communications on the battlefront.

The headquarters of the 79th Fighter Group and the P-47s of the 86th and 87th Fighter Squadrons redeploy from southern France to Iesi.

**SOUTHWEST PACIFIC AREA:** U.S. submarine *Flasher* torpedoes and sinks a Japanese cargo ship in the South China Sea north of Luzon.

Navy PBY Catalinas sink a Japanese cargo ship and two auxiliary sailing vessels near Jolo, in the Philippines.

**CENTRAL PACIFIC:** Seventh Air Force B-24 Liberators from Saipan attack shipping and bomb the airfield at Iwo Jima. B-24s from the Marshalls bomb Truk.

**CENTRAL PACIFIC, PELELIU:** The 7th Marines capture Hill 120 in the Umurbrogol, but are subjected to a severe cross fire, forcing them to retreat.

During the night Private Wesley Phelps of the 3rd Battalion, 7th Marines, 1st Marine Division, defends his position with another marine rifleman against a strong Japanese counterattack. When a grenade lands in the fighting position (foxhole), Private Phelps pushes his fellow marine away and covers the grenade with his own body. Private Phelps's act of courage and self-sacrifice will win him the Medal of Honor.

**NEW GUINEA:** Morotai Island is cleared of the last enemy forces. The newly built airfield at Wama is operational. Morotai is secured at the cost of 30 Americans killed and 85 wounded.

The P-38 Lightnings of the 35th Fighter Squadron, 8th Fighter Group, redeploy to Morotai Island.

B-25 Mitchells bomb Celebes Island. P-40s and B-25s attack airfields on Halmahera Island. A-20 Havocs and B-25s conduct a shipping sweep and bomb Ambon Island and the wharf on Celebes Island.

## October 5

**ALEUTIANS:** Eleventh Air Force sends two B-24 Liberators on a dawn bombing raid against Paramushiru Island.

**CBI:** President Roosevelt replies to Chiang Kai-shek and offers a compromise by proposing to appoint a new adviser while leaving General Stilwell in charge of combat operations in Burma and the direction of the Hump airlift.

Tenth Air Force B-25 Mitchells attack the bridges at Namhkai.

In China, Fourteenth Air Force P-40s and P-51 Mustangs conduct sweeps over southern China and attack river transport, road traffic, bridges, town areas, and troop concentrations.

**ETO:** Eighth Air Force sends more than 700 B-17s using radar-equipped Pathfinder bombers and 360 B-24 Liberators escorted by 675 P-51 Mustangs and P-47 Thunderbolts to attack airfields, industrial production facilities, and rail lines in western and central Germany. Radar assists the timing of bomb release. A total of nine bombers are lost and 357 are damaged. Aircrew casualties are one killed, six wounded, and 71 missing. Fighter pilots report one confirmed kill in the air and 15 on the ground. Four fighters are lost and four are damaged. The four pilots are reported missing.

During the night eight B-17s drop leaflets over Germany, France, and the Netherlands.

Ninth Air Force sends P-47 and P-38 fighters to support XV Corps.

**ITALY:** In the II Corps area, the 91st Infantry Division captures Monghidro and attacks with all three regiments to seize Loiano, preceded by an artillery barrage that drops 30,000 rounds on the German positions. The 362nd Infantry Regiment enters Loiano and repulses an enemy counterattack. The 85th Division, on the 91st Division's right flank, is stopped by German defenses.

Twelfth Air Force A-20 Havocs conduct bombing runs on German positions during the night.

The P-47 Thunderbolts of the 85th Fighter Squadron, 79th Fighter Group, redeploy from southern France to Iesi.

**SOUTHWEST PACIFIC AREA:** U.S. submarine *Cod* torpedoes and sinks a Japanese cargo ship in the South China Sea west of Mindoro.

**PACIFIC:** Admiral Nimitz notifies his subordinate service commanders that Operation Causeway (the invasion of Formosa) is deferred and that planning for the capture of Iwo Jima (Operation Detachment) and capture of islands in the Ryukyus beginning on March 1. The islands are within bombing range of the home islands of Japan and will control the air and sea links to Japan. The islands also afford secure anchorages for the U.S. fleet.

**CENTRAL PACIFIC:** Seventh Air Force B-25 Mitchells from the Gilberts bomb runways and gun positions on Nauru Island. B-24 Liberators from the Marshalls bomb Truk.

**CENTRAL PACIFIC, PELELIU:** The 2nd Battalion, 5th Marines, relieves the 3rd Battalion of the 7th Marines at Umurbrogol. Japanese positions in the Pocket are subjected to air strikes with a new weapon—napalm (jelled gasoline that explodes and burns on impact)—and direct fire from artillery.

**NEW GUINEA:** FEAF A-20 Havocs, B-25 Mitchells, P-39 Airacobras, P-47 Thunderbolts, P-38 Lightnings, and P-40s attack Utarom airfield and other airfields in northwest New Guinea. A-20s attack Japanese positions and logistics storage areas near Sarmi.

B-24 Liberators bomb airfields on Celebes Island. B-25s and P-38 Lightnings bomb the airfield on Celebes Island, the town of Amboina on Ambon Island, and targets of opportunity in the Ambon-Ceram Islands.

## October 6

**CBI:** Tenth Air Force B-25 Mitchells and P-47 Thunderbolts bomb troop concentrations and a bridge.

In China, Fourteenth Air Force sends 12 B-25 Mitchells to bomb targets of opportunity in and around Canton.

**ETO:** In the First Army area, the 39th and 60th Infantry Regiments of the 9th Infantry Division attack toward Schmidt, the key terrain in the Hürtgen Forest. The American infantrymen encounter concrete pillboxes of the West Wall, 20 feet high and 3 to 8 feet thick. Eighth Air Force sends more than 850 B-17s escorted by 540 P-51 Mustangs to attack aircraft production facilities, airfields, and ammunitions storage areas in northern Germany and Berlin. Eighteen B-17s are lost and 269 are damaged. Aircrew casualties are three killed, four wounded, and 163 missing. Fighter pilots report 18 confirmed kills and one probable in the air and 30 confirmed kills on the ground. Four fighters are lost and nine are damaged. The four pilots are reported missing.

Another 406 B-24 Liberators using radar-equipped Pathfinder bombers and escorted by 156 P-47 Thunderbolts are sent to bomb oil production and industrial production facilities in northern Germany. One B-24 is lost and 127 are damaged. Aircrew casualties are one killed, two wounded, and 10 missing. Six P-47s are damaged.

Fighter pilots report one confirmed kill in the air.

During the night four B-17s and six B-24s drop leaflets over Germany, France, and the Netherlands.

Ninth Air Force sends more than 300 A-20 Havocs and B-26 Marauders to attack marshaling yards and ammunition storage areas in Holland and Germany. P-47 and P-38 fighters support the First, Third, and Seventh Armies.

**MEDITERRANEAN:** Fifteenth Air Force P-38 Lightnings and P-51 Mustangs attack airfields in Greece.

**ITALY:** The IV Corps commander, Major General Edward M. Almond, leads a task force composed of the 370th RCT of the 92nd Infantry Division, 2nd Armored Group, with antiaircraft artillery troops converted into infantry, the 751st Tank Battalion, and the 849th Tank Destroyer Battalion. The task force makes a weak attack on Monte Cauala.

**SOUTHWEST PACIFIC AREA:** U.S. submarine *Cabrilla* torpedoes and sinks a tanker and damages a transport off the west coast of Luzon. U.S. submarine *Seahorse* torpedoes and sinks a Japanese coastal patrol boat off Luzon. U.S. submarine *Whale* torpedoes and sinks a Japanese transport and merchant tanker off Luzon.

**PACIFIC:** Twentieth Air Force receives P-61 Black Widow night fighters at Chengtu, China.

**CENTRAL PACIFIC:** Seventh Air Force B-24 Liberators from Saipan bomb Iwo Jima.

One B-24 from Kwajalein bombs a gun battery on Jaluit Atoll.

**NEW GUINEA:** FEAF P-38 Lightnings attack the airfield and shipping at Halmahera Island. B-25 Mitchells and P-38s attack Celebes Island, Ceram Island, Ambon Island, and Buru Island.

## October 7

**CBI:** Fifty-three P-51 Mustangs and P-40s of Fourteenth Air Force, on armed reconnaissance, attack troop concentrations, bridges, river and rail traffic, town areas, and logistics bases.

**ETO:** The XII Corps of Third Army is unable to do more than make limited attacks due to severe shortages of fuel and ammunition. Lieutenant General Patton bitterly complains about fighting three enemies: the Germans, the weather, and time.

Eighth Air Force sends more than 900 B-17s escorted by 557 P-51 Mustangs and P-47 Thunderbolts to attack industrial targets, oil refineries, and airfields in Germany. A total of 36 B-17s are lost and 430 damaged. Aircrews report 11 confirmed kills and 13 probables. Aircrew casualties are four killed, 32 wounded, and 320 missing. Fighter pilots report 29 confirmed kills in the air and one confirmed kill on the ground. Seven fighters are lost and six damaged. Seven pilots are reported missing, and one is wounded.

Another 489 B-24 Liberators escorted by 214 P-51s, P-47s, and P-38 Lightnings are sent to bomb oil refineries, a vehicle production facility, and marshaling yards. Four B-24s are lost and 184 damaged. Aircrew casualties are two killed, six wounded, and 38 missing. Pilots report eight confirmed kills on the ground. Four fighters are lost, and two are damaged. Three pilots are reported missing.

Headquarters Ninth Air Force orders attacks on all bridges, except those over the Rhine River. Over 300 B-26 Marauders and A-20 Havocs attack bridges from

Holland to Germany. P-38 Lightnings and P-47 Thunderbolts attack rail lines, river transport, troop concentrations, and ground support forces.

**MEDITERRANEAN:** Fifteenth Air Force sends more than 350 B-17s and B-24 Liberators escorted by P-38 Lightnings and P-51 Mustangs to bomb oil refineries near Vienna, Austria. Other B-24s and P-51s attack rail transportation in Czechoslovakia and Hungary.

**ITALY:** In heavy rain and fog, the 362nd Infantry Regiment of the 91st Infantry Division attacks Monte Castellari overlooking Route 65.

Twelfth Air Force P-47 Thunderbolts attack German defensive positions along the battlefront.

**SOUTHWEST PACIFIC AREA:** FEAF B-24 Liberators and P-38s attack Zamboanga on Mindanao Island in the Philippines.

U.S. submarine *Cabrilla* torpedoes and sinks a Japanese transport off Vigan, Luzon. U.S. submarine *Cod* torpedoes and damages an oiler in the South China Sea west of Mindoro. U.S. submarine *Hawkbill* torpedoes and damages a cargo ship in the South China Sea, which is later sunk by USS *Baya*. U.S. submarine *Hoe* torpedoes and sinks a Japanese army transport in the South China Sea west of Luzon.

**CENTRAL PACIFIC, PELELIU:** Tanks supported by infantry enter the Horseshoe Valley to destroy cave positions on the Five Sisters in the Umurbrogol Pocket.

**NEW GUINEA:** FEAF P-38 Lightnings and B-25 Mitchells attack airfields and installations in northwestern New Guinea. B-25s bomb Celebes and Ambon Islands, and P-38s attack Halmahera Island and the oil storage area on Ceram Island.

## October 8

**CBI:** Tenth Air Force B-25 Mitchells attack bridges, and P-47 Thunderbolts bomb rail lines in northern Burma.

Fourteenth Air Force P-40s and P-51 Mustangs attack river transport and rail lines.

U.S. submarine *Hoe* torpedoes and sinks a Japanese army transport and damages a coastal patrol ship in the South China Sea east of Hainan.

**ETO:** First Army's VII Corps attacks to encircle Aachen from the south with the 1st Infantry Division. The 18th Infantry Regiment fights to seize Crucifix Hill, one of the key defensive positions around Aachen.

Headquarters Ninth Air Force orders intensive attacks against rail lines in Germany.

Over 300 B-26 Marauders and A-20 Havocs, with fighter escort, attack German strongpoints and bridges between eastern France and western Germany. P-38 Lightnings and P-47 Thunderbolts support the VII, XV, XIX, and XX Corps.

Captain Bobbie E. Brown commands C Company, 18th Infantry Regiment, 1st Infantry Division, and is ordered to attack Crucifix Hill, Aachen, Germany. Brown's leading platoons are stopped by a series of pillboxes and then subjected to artillery fire. Captain Brown moves forward to destroy a pillbox with an explosive charge attached to a long pole. Crawling as close as possible, Brown is able to thrust the armed explosive into the aperture and destroy the pillbox. Taking another explosive charge, he attacks the second pillbox, disregarding the bullets and bomb fragments flying around him. He blasts the second fortification and moves on to the third. He succeeds in destroying it as well, but is wounded. Refusing treatment, he continues to give orders and even goes on an advanced reconnaissance to locate German troops, exposing himself deliberately to draw the Germans' fire. Wounded twice more, Brown is able to deploy his company to repel two counterattacks and eliminate German artillery pieces. He allows himself to be treated only after he is certain his company's position is completely secure. For his example of selfless leadership and great courage in the face of the enemy, Captain Brown will receive the Medal of Honor.

**SOUTHWEST PACIFIC AREA:** U.S. submarine *Becuna* torpedoes and damages a Japanese seaplane carrier in the South China Sea.

**CENTRAL PACIFIC:** Seventh Air Force B-24 Liberators from the Marshalls bomb Wake Island.

**NEW GUINEA:** FEAF A-20 Havocs, B-25 Mitchells, P-38 Lightnings, P-40s, and P-47 Thunderbolts attack airfields, gun positions, troop areas, and logistics storage areas.

B-24 Liberators bomb Ceram Island. P-38 Lightnings attack targets on Halmahera Island and in the Molucca Islands.

## October 9

**CBI:** Generalissimo Chiang Kai-shek rejects President Roosevelt's offer to keep General Stilwell in the theater. He demands that Stilwell be removed.

Tenth Air Force P-47 Thunderbolts attack bridges and B-25 Mitchells attack road bridges near Lashio.

Fourteenth Air Force B-25s bomb river transportation. P-51 Mustangs and P-40s attack river transportation, troops and bridges.

**ETO:** Fort Driant, one of the key defensive positions of the fortress city of Metz, is still in German hands after nearly a week of close combat with the 5th Infantry Division. Admitting failure after losing 500 men, the Americans begin to pull back.

In the First Army area, the 60th and 39th Infantry Regiments of the 9th Infantry Division capture Richeskaul and Wittscheidt west of Schmidt in the Hürtgen Forest.

Eighth Air Force sends more than 1,000 B-17s and B-24 Liberators, escorted by over 600 P-51 Mustangs and 200 P-38 Lightnings and P-47 Thunderbolts from Ninth Air Force, to attack ball-bearing plants at Schweinfurt, marshaling yards at Mainz and Koblenz, and industrial production facilities. One B-24 is lost and 119 bombers are damaged. Aircrew casualties are one killed and 10 missing. Fighter pilots report one confirmed kill in the air and one confirmed kill on the ground. Five fighters are damaged.

During the night two B-24s drop leaflets over the Netherlands.

Ninth Air Force B-26 Marauders and A-20 Havocs attack a rail bridge at Euskirchen, Germany.

**ITALY:** After five days of fighting the 85th Infantry Division has advanced about three miles and has lost 1,400 men. The Germans have laid out strong defenses. Soldiers hold these defensive lines, inflicting maximum casualties, then slip back to the next defensive line to force the Americans into the same attack.

The 362nd Infantry Regiment captures Monte Castellari, forcing the Germans to retreat to Livergnano, the strongest natural defensive barrier on the Gothic Line.

Twelfth Air Force A-20 Havocs and P-47 Thunderbolts attack convoys, bridges, and roads.

**SOUTHWEST PACIFIC AREA:** In the South China Sea, USS *Becuna* torpedoes and damages a tanker and works with USS *Hawkbill* to sink a tanker. USS *Sawfish* torpedoes and sinks a tanker north of Luzon.

**PACIFIC:** Admiral Nimitz sends a directive to Lieutenant General Holland M. Smith, alerting his V Amphibious Corps to prepare plans for the capture of Iwo Jima.

Planning begins for Operation Iceberg, the invasion of Okinawa. Strategic Air Forces of the Pacific Ocean Area are assigned the mission of eliminating the Japanese air threat from the Caroline and Bonin Islands and bombing the airfields on Okinawa and on Kyushu in Japan. Naval air elements will neutralize bypassed Japanese bases and eliminate the Japanese submarine threat. The submarine force will attack Japanese shipping to and from Japan and Formosa. The joint army-navy task force, composed of the U.S. Fifth Fleet, with a naval covering force, an expeditionary force, and expeditionary troops, will combine efforts to capture the objectives. Admiral Richard A. Spruance will command Task Force 50, which includes Vice Admiral Marc A. Mitscher's fast carrier force (Task Force 58) and a British carrier force (Task Force 57). Mitscher's task force will be responsible for eliminating Japanese air strength between Okinawa and the Japanese island of Kyushu. Also under Spruance is Task Force 51, under Vice Admiral Richmond Kelly Turner, who is responsible for the capture of Okinawa and other islands in the Ryukyus. Subordinate to Turner is Task Force 54, the Gunfire and Covering Force, Task Force 52, the Amphibious Support Force with escort carriers, and Task Force 56, the Expeditionary Troops under command of Lieutenant General Simon B. Buckner. Lieutenant General Buckner will command the Tenth Army, composed of the XXIV Corps (commanded by Major General John R. Hodge and including the 7th and 96th Infantry Divisions) and the III Marine Amphibious Corps (commanded by Major General Roy S. Geiger and composed of the 1st and 6th Marine Divisions), as well as the Tactical Air Force Ryukyus under command of Major General Francis P. Mulcahy (USMC) and Naval Force Ryukyus under Rear Admiral C. H. Cobb. General Buckner also has under his operational control the 27th and 77th Infantry Divisions and the 2nd Marine Division as a reserve. The 81st Infantry Division is placed under the operational control of Admiral Nimitz as an area reserve.

Three heavy cruisers and six destroyers of Naval Task Group 30.2 (Rear Admiral Allan E. Smith) conduct a diversionary bombardment of Japanese installations on Marcus Island. Navy PB4Y Privateers from Saipan conduct interdiction patrols in the path of Naval Task Force 58, damaging an auxiliary submarine chaser off Okinawa.

USS *Croaker* torpedoes and sinks a cargo ship west of Kyushu.

**CENTRAL PACIFIC:** Seventh Air Force sends 18 B-24 Liberators from Saipan to bomb Iwo Jima. Another 25 B-25 Mitchells from the Marshalls bomb Truk.

**NEW GUINEA:** FEAF P-40s attack Manokwari. B-25 Mitchells bomb airfields on Halmahera Island. A-20 Havocs, P-38 Lightnings, and P-47 Thunderbolts attack oil storage areas and airfields on Ceram Island, Celebes Island, and Ambon Island.

## October 10

**CBI:** Tenth Air Force P-47 Thunderbolts support British ground forces.

Fourteenth Air Force P-40s and P-51 Mustangs attack roads, bridges, town areas, troop concentrations, and various targets of opportunity.

**MEDITERRANEAN:** Fifteenth Air Force sends more than 170 B-17s and B-24 Liberators escorted by P-38 Lightnings and P-51 Mustangs to attack marshaling yards in northern Italy.

**ITALY:** The II Corps attacks the Livergnano Escarpment, the Germans' most strongly defended position in the entire Apennines. Monte della Formiche is one of the mountains in the center of the Escarpment. The 85th Infantry Division makes the main attack, capturing Monte della Formiche, supported by the 91st and 88th Infantry Divisions making flanking attacks. The 361st Infantry Regiment of the 91st Infantry Division is stopped in front of Livergnano. Twelfth Air Force P-47 Thunderbolts support the attack.

**SOUTHWEST PACIFIC AREA:** U.S. submarine *Lapon* torpedoes and sinks a Japanese army transport in the South China Sea west of Luzon.

**PACIFIC:** Admiral Halsey's Third Fleet begins strikes on targets from the Ryukyus to the Philippines in preparation for the October 20 assault. Task Force 38 has 17 carriers, six fast battleships, 14 cruisers, and 58 destroyers. The main attack is against the airfields on the island of Okinawa, at Naha, Kadena, and Yomitan. Ie Shima Island is also hit. Halsey's F6F Hellcat fighter-bombers, SB2C Helldiver dive-bombers, and TBF Avenger torpedo-bombers destroy 30 cargo ships, 10 transports, a seaplane tender, an escort destroyer, four midget subs, two minesweepers, six patrol boats, and eight antiaircraft boats. The logistics storage depot at Naha is also destroyed. TF-38 will go on to destroy over 600 Japanese navy aircraft in the Philippines and Formosa.

Carrier aircraft from Naval Task Force 38 under Vice Admiral Marc A. Mitscher attack Okinawa and other islands in the Ryukyus. Pilots report sinking a submarine depot ship, a landing ship, a minelayer, an auxiliary submarine chaser, three auxiliary minesweepers, three guardboats, 12 motor torpedo boats, and six cargo ships. Pilots also report damaging a coastal patrol ship, a submarine chaser, a guardboat, and two cargo ships.

U.S. submarine *Barb* torpedoes and sinks a Japanese transport off Kyushu, Japan.

**CENTRAL PACIFIC:** Seventh Air Force sends 14 B-24 Liberators from Saipan to bomb the airfield at Iwo Jima and shipping near the island. Another 12 B-25 Mitchells from Makin bomb runways and antiaircraft positions on Nauru Island.

**New Guinea:** FEAF A-20 Havocs and B-25 Mitchells bomb Utarom airfield. B-24 Liberators escorted by P-47 Thunderbolts and P-38 Lightnings attack oil refineries and the airfield at Balikpapan in Borneo. Aircrews and pilots report 30 confirmed kills. P-47 Thunderbolts attack the airfield on Ambon Island, and P-38 Lightnings and B-25s bomb airfields and other targets on Halmahera Island.

### October 11

**Aleutians:** Eleventh Air Force sends four B-25 Mitchells to attack Japanese installations on Shimushiru and Paramushiru Islands in the Kuriles. Aircrews report three buildings destroyed and two others damaged.

**CBI:** Tenth Air Force P-47 Thunderbolts and B-25 Mitchells attack troop concentrations, gun positions, rail lines, bridges, roads, and logistics sites.

Fourteenth Air Force B-25 Mitchells bomb the bridge near Mangshih. Aircrews report the bridge destroyed.

**ETO:** Eighth Air Force sends 135 B-17s escorted by 135 P-47 Thunderbolts to bomb the Wesseling synthetic oil production facility and the Koblenz marshaling yard. Four B-17s are lost and 61 are damaged. Aircrew casualties are three killed, six wounded, and 38 missing. One P-47 is lost.

During the night nine B-17s and B-24s drop leaflets over Germany, France, and the Netherlands.

Ninth Air Force P-38 Lightnings and P-47 Thunderbolts attack rail lines near Aachen and along the Rhine River. Fighters also support the VII and XIX Corps near Aachen and the XII, XV, and XX Corps around Metz and Saarlautern.

**Mediterranean:** Fifteenth Air Force sends 180 B-17s and B-24 Liberators escorted by P-38 Lightnings and P-51 Mustangs to attack industrial targets near Vienna, Austria, rail bridges in Yugoslavia, and bridges and roads in northern Italy. P-51 Mustangs attack logistics storage depots and rail cars, and destroy 47 aircraft on the ground in Czechoslovakia and Hungary.

**Italy:** In nearly impassable terrain, the 361st and 363rd Infantry Regiments of the 90th Infantry Division make limited gains against strong German defenses.

Twelfth Air Force B-25 Mitchells and B-26 Marauders attack logistics bases and bridges in the Po Valley. A-20 Havocs and P-47 Thunderbolts attack German positions.

**Southwest Pacific Area:** Naval Task Force 78 departs from the Admiralty Islands for Leyte Island, carrying X Corps under the command of Rear Admiral Daniel E. Barbey.

FEAF B-24 Liberators conduct a night raid on airfields on Mindanao Island in the Philippines.

Naval Task Group 38.1 under Vice Admiral John S. McCain and Naval Task Group 38.4 under Rear Admiral Ralph E. Davison attack Japanese airfields and facilities on northern Luzon. Carrier aircraft damage an escort destroyer and a cargo vessel.

U.S. submarine *Tang* torpedoes and sinks two cargo ships in the Formosa Strait.

**Pacific:** U.S. submarine *Trepang* torpedoes and sinks a Japanese landing ship off Honshu, Japan.

**NEW GUINEA:** FEAF P-47 Thunderbolts and A-20 Havocs attack troop concentrations and airfields in New Guinea. A-20 Havocs, P-40s, and P-47 Thunderbolts attack targets on Ambon Island, Celebes Island, Haroekoe Island, and Buru Island. P-38 Lightnings attack an airfield on Halmahera Island.

## October 12
**ALEUTIANS:** Eleventh Air Force B-24 Liberators attack the airfield on Matsuwa-Onnekotan Island and attack shipping targets nearby.
**CBI:** Tenth Air Force P-47 Thunderbolts bomb rail lines, bridges, troops, and logistics sites. B-25 Mitchells attack and destroy a bridge near Lashio.

In China, Fourteenth Air Force B-25s and P-40s attack logistics bases at Chefang and a bridge near Mangshih.
**ETO:** In the First Army area, the 39th Infantry Regiment of the 9th Infantry Division is stopped by German counterattacks as it attempts to advance to Schmidt in the Hürtgen Forest. The 26th Infantry Regiment of the 1st Infantry Division attacks the city of Aachen.

Eighth Air Force sends 290 B-24 Liberators escorted by 210 P-47 Thunderbolts and P-51 Mustangs to bomb the marshaling yard at Osnabrück guided by radar-equipped Pathfinders. Two B-24s are lost and 67 are damaged. Aircrew casualties are 19 missing. Pilots report one confirmed kill and one probable in the air. Another 262 B-17s escorted by 273 P-47 Thunderbolts and P-51 Mustangs are sent to attack aviation production facilities at Bremen. One B-17 is lost and 60 are damaged. Aircrew casualties are seven killed, one wounded, and nine missing. Fighter pilots report 17 confirmed kills and two probables. Five P-51s are lost, and the pilots are reported as missing.

During the night eight B-24s drop leaflets over Germany, France, and the Netherlands. Two bombers are lost.

Ninth Air Force takes operational control and administrative control of headquarters, XII Tactical Air Command, from U.S. Strategic Air Forces in Europe (USSTAF). Nearly 250 B-26 Marauders and A-20 Havocs bomb German positions and rail targets in Germany and the Netherlands. P-47 and P-38 fighters support the VIII, XII, XV, and XX Corps.

Staff Sergeant Jack J. Pendleton of I Company, 120th Infantry Regiment, 30th Infantry Division, is moving through the town of Bardenberg, Germany, when German machine guns begin firing on the infantrymen from a strongpoint at an intersection. Staff Sergeant Pendleton volunteers to lead his squad against the strongpoint after several attempts fail. Moving to within 130 yards of the position, Staff Sergeant Pendleton is wounded. He orders his men to take cover and continues to work his way forward under heavy fire the entire time. He is killed within 10 yards of the position but has sacrificed himself to allow another squad to maneuver and, supported by Pendleton's men, capture the position. For his supreme act of courage and self-sacrifice, Staff Sergeant Pendleton will receive the Medal of Honor.
**MEDITERRANEAN:** Fifteenth Air Force sends 160 P-51 Mustangs to strafe rail lines and Danube River traffic from Vienna, Austria, to Budapest, Hungary.

**ITALY:** Operation Pancake begins. This is a concentrated air attack on Bologna. Fifteenth Air Force sends nearly 700 B-17s and B-24 Liberators with fighter support to attack ammunition and fuel storage areas, troop disposition areas, barracks, vehicle repair shops, and a munitions factory. Twelfth Air Force B-26 Marauders and 117 B-25 Mitchells bomb supply storage areas and troop barracks. A-20 Havocs attack ammunition storage facilities, and P-47 Thunderbolts attack German positions.

**SOUTHWEST PACIFIC AREA:** Carrier aircraft from Naval Task Force 38 (Vice Admiral Marc A. Mitscher) attack airfields, support facilities, and industrial targets on Formosa. Pilots report sinking four transports, six cargo ships, an army ship, and seven merchant tankers. Pilots also report damaging a German ship, a tanker, and four cargo ships west of Formosa. A cargo ship is also reported sunk in Putai harbor, Formosa. The air attacks are intended to clear the skies for Twentieth Air Force B-29s to hit aircraft production facilities, and airfields on Formosa.

U.S. submarine *Ray* torpedoes and sinks a Japanese transport off Mindoro and escapes an attack from escort ships.

**PACIFIC:** Twentieth Air Force inactivates the headquarters of the 58th Bombardment Wing (Very Heavy) and 795th Bombardment Squadron (Very Heavy), 468th Bombardment Group (Very Heavy); the 679th Bombardment Squadron (Very Heavy), 444th Bombardment Group (Very Heavy); the 771st Bombardment Squadron (Very Heavy), 462nd Bombardment Group (Very Heavy). Attacking Japan from bases in India and China is proving far too difficult logistically to support any sustained bombing campaign. Plans are made to redeploy Twentieth Air Force assets elsewhere in the Pacific.

U.S. submarine *Trepang* torpedoes and damages a Japanese destroyer east of Honshu, Japan.

**CENTRAL PACIFIC:** Seventh Air Force B-24 Liberators from Saipan Island bomb the harbor and shipping at Chichi Jima. B-24 Liberators from Kwajalein conduct a night bombing raid on Wake Island.

The first B-29 Superfortress of the Twentieth Air Force, piloted by Brigadier General Haywood S. Hansell, Jr., commander of XXI Bomber Command, arrives on Saipan. A temporary headquarters for the XXI Bomber Command and for the headquarters of the 73rd Bombardment Wing (Very Heavy) is established on the island. Four bomber wings (and their headquarters) are scheduled to deploy to Saipan in the future.

**NEW GUINEA:** FEAF A-20 Havocs, P-38 Lightnings, P-40s, and P-47 Thunderbolts attack targets at Sarmi and Manokwari. A-20 Havocs and P-47 Thunderbolts attack airfields on Ambon Island, Buru Island, Celebes Island, Haroekoe Island, and the town of Boela on Ceram Island. P-38 Lightnings attack targets on Halmahera Island. B-24 Liberators bomb Celebes Island.

## October 13

**ALEUTIANS:** Eleventh Air Force sends four B-25 Mitchells to bomb Kurabu airfield and bomb and strafe buildings on Tomari Cape on Paramushiru Island. Aircrews report several buildings damaged.

**CBI:** U.S. submarine *Bergall* torpedoes and sinks a Japanese merchant tanker off Nha Trang, French Indochina.

**ETO:** The 1st Infantry Division of the VII Corps of First Army begins the battle for the city of Aachen.

Ninth Air Force B-26 Marauders and A-20 Havocs attack bridges in the Netherlands, France, and Germany. P-38 Lightnings and P-47 Thunderbolts support the First, Third, and Seventh Armies.

**MEDITERRANEAN:** Fifteenth Air Force sends more than 650 B-17s and B-24 Liberators escorted by P-38 Lightnings and P-51 Mustangs to attack oil refineries, rail transport repair facilities, and marshaling yards in Austria, Hungary, Czechoslovakia, and Germany. Fighters attack rail lines, airfields, and roads.

**ITALY:** The 361st Infantry Regiment of the 91st Infantry Division moves to flank the German position at Livergnano. Twelfth Air Force P-47 Thunderbolts provide air support.

**SOUTHWEST PACIFIC AREA:** Japanese aircraft attack Naval Task Force 38, hitting the Australian heavy cruiser *Canberra* with an aerial torpedo and damaging carrier USS *Franklin* with a crashed fighter.

**PACIFIC:** Members of the headquarters of V Amphibious Corps move to Pearl Harbor to begin planning for the amphibious assault on Iwo Jima.

**CENTRAL PACIFIC:** Seventh Air Force B-24 Liberators from Saipan bomb Yap. B-24s from the Marshalls bomb Truk. B-25 Mitchells from the Gilberts bomb Nauru Island.

**CENTRAL PACIFIC, PELELIU:** The 3rd Battalion of the 5th Marines begins an attack into the north side of the Umurbrogol Pocket, making advances of 75 yards.

**NEW GUINEA:** Task Force 79 commanded by Vice Admiral Theodore S. Wilkinson leaves Hollandia, carrying the XXIV Corps to Leyte Island. Task Force 78 commanded by Rear Admiral Daniel Barbey.

The Japanese have built up troop strength in the Philippines to about 432,000 men. There are 884 aircraft of all types still available.

FEAF A-20 Havocs and P-47 Thunderbolts attack airfields on Ambon Island, Buru Island, Celebes Island, Haroekoe Island, and the town of Boela on Ceram Island. B-25 Mitchells bomb targets in the Celebes Islands. P-38 Lightnings attack antiaircraft positions on Halmahera Island.

## October 14

**ALEUTIANS:** Eleventh Air Force sends four B-25 Mitchells to bomb and strafe buildings at Otomae Bay in the Kurile Islands.

**ETO:** Eighth Air Force sends more than 1,000 B-17s and B-24 Liberators escorted by 469 P-51 Mustangs and P-47 Thunderbolts to attack marshaling yards in Germany, using radar to assist the timing of bomb release. A total of five bombers are lost and 356 damaged. Aircrew casualties are two killed, eight wounded, and 40 missing. One P-51 is damaged.

Ninth Air Force P-38 Lightnings and P-47s support Third Army.

**MEDITERRANEAN:** Fifteenth Air Force sends 317 B-17s and B-24 Liberators escorted by P-38 Lightnings and P-51 Mustangs to attack oil refineries and marshaling yards in Austria, Hungary, and Czechoslovakia. B-24 Liberators bomb a railroad bridge and marshaling yard in Yugoslavia.

**ITALY:** After four days of air and artillery attacks and infantry assaults, the Germans begin to abandon Livergnano.

Twelfth Air Force A-20 Havocs and P-47 Thunderbolts attack German positions, bridges, roads, logistics sites, and rail lines.

**SOUTHWEST PACIFIC AREA:** Japanese aircraft continue attacks on Naval Task Force 38; the carrier USS *Hancock,* two light cruisers, and two destroyers are damaged. Carrier aircraft damage a coastal minelayer and two auxiliary submarine chasers off Formosa.

U.S. submarine *Bonefish* torpedoes and sinks a Japanese cargo ship in the South China Sea off the west coast of Luzon.

**PACIFIC:** Twentieth Air Force sends 103 B-29 Superfortresses from Chengtu, China, to bomb the Okayama aircraft plant on Formosa in support of MacArthur's invasion of Leyte.

**CENTRAL PACIFIC:** Seventh Air Force redeploys the B-25 Mitchells of the 48th, 396th, and 820th Bombardment Squadrons (Medium) from Makin Island to Wheeler Field, Hawaii.

**NEW GUINEA:** FEAF B-24 Liberators bomb oil refineries and oil production facilities in the Balikpapan, Borneo, area and attack targets on Celebes Island. B-25 Mitchells and P-38 Lightnings attack the airfields on Ambon Island and Haroekoe Island.

U.S. submarine *Angler* torpedoes and sinks a Japanese army transport in the Flores Sea east of Timor. U.S. submarine *Dace* torpedoes and sinks two Japanese merchant tankers and damages a merchant ore carrier off North Borneo.

## October 15

**CBI:** The Allied offensive in Burma is renewed under Vice Admiral Lord Louis Mountbatten. The plan is to advance toward Bhamo and Katha, then move on to control the Burma Road and Lashio. The British Fourteenth Army will continue to press Japanese forces toward the Irrawaddy River and capture Mandalay. The Americans will send three Chinese divisions and the British 36th Division toward Bhamo and Katha to reopen the overland route to China and capture Lashio. The 36th will attack to control the railroad junction at Pinwe.

Tenth Air Force sends 40 P-47 Thunderbolts and 12 B-25 Mitchells to attack roads, troop concentrations, ammunition storage areas, and town areas in support of British forces.

In China, Fourteenth Air Force sends 28 B-24 Liberators, 33 P-51 Mustangs, and 18 P-40s to attack White Cloud airfield in Canton and shipping in the Hong Kong area.

**ETO:** A new SHAEF air staff is created. Allied Expeditionary Air Force headquarters is disbanded. All planning and operations are the responsibility of SHAEF headquarters air staff under Air Chief Marshal Arthur W. Tedder. This arrangement gives SHAEF more direct control over air operations in-theater.

The Allied Air Expeditionary Force chief, Air Marshal Leigh-Mallory, is transferred to the China-Burma-India theater (he is reported missing November 14).

Eighth Air Force sends more than 1,200 B-17s and B-24 Liberators escorted by over 400 P-51s to attack marshaling yards and oil refineries in Germany. A total of eight bombers are lost and 635 are damaged. Aircrew casualties are 17 killed, 22 wounded, and 50 missing. Three P-51s are lost and three are damaged. Three pilots are reported missing.

Nine B-17s are sent on an Aphrodite mission to attack the naval installations on Heligoland Island, Germany. Only two actually make it to the target. Another 23 B-17s fly a cover mission, and 15 P-51s and two P-38 Lightnings escort the entire force. During the night, five B-17s and four B-24 Liberators drop leaflets over the Netherlands, France, and Germany.

Ninth Air Force P-38 Lightnings and P-47 Thunderbolts attack rail lines and support elements of the First, Third, Seventh, and Ninth Armies.

**ITALY:** Twelfth Air Force B-25 Mitchells and B-26 Marauders attack bridges in the Po Valley. A-20 Havocs and P-47 Thunderbolts attack German positions along the battlefront.

The headquarters of the 63rd Fighter Wing redeploys from Corsica to San Pietro, Italy.

**SOUTHWEST PACIFIC AREA:** Rear Admiral Daniel E. Barbey's Task Force 78 links with the rest of his fleet carrying the 1st Cavalry Division from Manus Island. Barbey's Task Force 78 and Vice Admiral Theodore S. Wilkinson's Task Force 79, carrying XXIV Corps, are under the command of Vice Admiral Thomas C. Kinkaid, commander of the Allied Naval Forces of the Southwest Pacific Area and commander of the Seventh Fleet. He also has operational control of Task Force 77, the battleships and cruisers that will provide fire support to the landing force; Rear Admiral Jesse B. Oldendorf commands Task Force 77. The escort carrier group (Task Group 77.4) that will provide air support to the landing forces under Seventh Fleet's direct command is under Rear Admiral Thomas L. Sprague. The Third Fleet carriers, battleships, and cruisers, under command of Admiral Halsey, will provide general support to the landing forces.

Naval Task Group 38.4, under Rear Admiral Ralph E. Davison, is formed to attack Japanese installations near Manila. The carrier *Franklin* is damaged in a Japanese air attack northeast of Luzon.

**CENTRAL PACIFIC:** Seventh Air Force sends 27 B-24 Liberators from Saipan to bomb fuel storage areas, antiaircraft positions, and the airfield on Iwo Jima. B-24s from the Marshalls make a night raid on Wake Island.

**CENTRAL PACIFIC, PELELIU:** The 321st and 323rd Infantry Regiments of the 81st Infantry Division attack into the Umurbrogol Pocket after relieving the last elements of the 3rd Battalion of the 5th Marines. The 1st Marine Division is out of the fight, too depleted to be effective. It will take more than a month and a half to finish off the last Japanese defenders, who forfeit their lives dearly within the Umurbrogol Pocket.

**NEW GUINEA:** FEAF P-47 Thunderbolts attack airfields in New Guinea. A-20 Havocs attack airfields and oil storage areas on Ceram Island. P-38 Lightnings conduct a shipping sweep in the Lesser Sunda Islands and around Halmahera Island and attack the airfield on Ceram Island.

The headquarters of the 38th Bombardment Group (Medium) and the B-25 Mitchells of the 405th and 823rd Bombardment Squadrons (Medium) redeploy from Biak Island to Morotai Island.

### October 16

**ALEUTIANS:** Eleventh Air Force sends seven B-24 Liberators to fly cover for a naval task force.

**CBI:** Tenth Air Force P-47 Thunderbolts attack railroad bridges. B-25 Mitchells, escorted by P-47s, attack the airfield at Shwebo.

Fourteenth Air Force sends eight B-25 Mitchells and 28 B-24 Liberators escorted by 35 P-40s and P-51 Mustangs to attack the Kowloon docks at Hong Kong. Aircrews report three cargo ships and two tankers sunk and five other ships damaged. Eight Japanese fighters attack the formation, and fighter pilots report one confirmed kill. B-24s attack shipping in the South China Sea, Formosa Strait, and the Gulf of Tonkin.

**ETO:** First Army's plan for the capture of Aachen is accomplished as XIX Corps and the VII Corps of the First Army link behind Aachen and repel several German counterattacks. The 18th Infantry Regiment of the 1st Infantry Division and the 119th Infantry Regiment of the 30th Infantry Division play an important role. The 1st Infantry Division continues to battle German defenders in the city.

The 39th and 60th Infantry Regiments of the 9th Infantry Division have been able to advance about 3,000 yards into the Hürtgen Forest after a month of combat. The cost has been 4,500 men killed, wounded, or missing.

**MEDITERRANEAN:** Fifteenth Air Force sends more than 600 B-17s and B-24 Liberators escorted by P-38 Lightnings and P-51 Mustangs to attack industrial targets in Austria and Czechoslovakia.

**ITALY:** The Fifth and the Eighth Armies attack simultaneously in an attempt to break German lines and drive on to Bologna. The 34th Infantry Division with Combat Command A from the 1st Armored Division attacks Monte della Vigna and Monte Belmonte.

The 91st Infantry Divisions supported by elements of the 1st Armored Division also attacks, but makes little progress. The 85th Infantry Division has success but is unable to exploit its gains without reinforcements.

Twelfth Air Force A-20 Havocs and P-47 Thunderbolts attack German defensive positions, roads, and bridges near Monte Belmonte.

**SOUTHWEST PACIFIC AREA:** FEAF P-38 Lightnings attack the harbor, shipping, airfield, and trucks on Cagayan Island in the Philippines.

Japanese torpedo planes damage U.S. light cruiser *Houston* a second time east of Formosa in the Philippines Sea. Carrier aircraft from Task Force 38 sink a torpedo boat and damage an auxiliary vessel in the South China Sea.

**PACIFIC:** Twentieth Air Force sends more than 40 B-29 Superfortresses from Chengtu, China, to bomb the Okayama aircraft production facility and the Heito airfield on Formosa. Some B-29s bomb alternate airfield and harbor targets on Formosa, or bomb Hengyang and several other airfields in China.

U.S. submarine *Besugo* (SS-321) damages Japanese destroyer off Kyushu, Japan.

U.S. submarine *Tilefish* torpedoes and sinks a Japanese guardboat in the Kuriles.

**CENTRAL PACIFIC:** Seventh Air Force B-24 Liberators from the Marshalls bomb Truk.

**NEW GUINEA:** FEAF A-20 Havocs, P-47 Thunderbolts, P-38 Lightnings, and P-40s attack airfields in northwest New Guinea. B-24 Liberators, B-25 Mitchells, and P-38 Lightnings attack the airfields on Boeroe Island, Ceram Island, the town of Amboina on Ambon Island, and shipping in Binnen Bay in the Molucca Islands. B-24s bomb Celebes Island.

The headquarters of the 5th Bombardment Group (Heavy) and the B-24s of the 23rd and 31st Bombardment Squadrons (Heavy) redeploy from Noemfoor Island to Morotai Island.

## October 17

**ALEUTIANS:** Eleventh Air Force sends seven B-24 Liberators to fly cover for a naval task force.

**CBI:** Tenth Air Force P-47 Thunderbolts attack logistics storage areas. B-25 Mitchells bomb airfields and bridges.

In China, Fourteenth Air Force sends 15 B-25 Mitchells, 12 P-40s, and 10 P-51 Mustangs to bomb a logistics storage depot at Tien Ho airfield at Canton.

**ETO:** Eighth Air Force sends more than 1,300 B-17s and B-24 Liberators, led by radar-equipped Pathfinders and escorted by 775 P-51 Mustangs and P-47 Thunderbolts, to attack marshaling yards at Cologne. A total of five bombers are lost and 489 are damaged. Aircrew casualties are three killed, 16 wounded, and 46 missing. One P-51 is lost. The pilot is reported missing.

Ninth Air Force sends 35 B-26 Marauders to attack the rail bridge at Euskirchen in Germany.

**MEDITERRANEAN:** Fifteenth Air Force sends more than 300 B-17s and B-24 Liberators escorted by P-38 Lightnings and P-51 Mustangs to attack the Blechhammer oil refinery in Germany and industrial targets near Vienna.

**ITALY:** Twelfth Air Force A-20 Havocs attack targets in the Po River valley. P-47 Thunderbolts attack rail lines and bridges.

**SOUTHWEST PACIFIC AREA:** Elements of the 6th Ranger Battalion capture the radio station and lighthouse on Suluan Island off Leyte. The Rangers set up navigation lights to guide the transports.

Nearly 60 FEAF B-24 Liberators attack oil storage areas, barracks, and shore targets on Mindanao Island in the Philippines.

Naval Task Group 38.4 under Rear Admiral Ralph E. Davison attacks Japanese installations at Legaspi and Clark Field on Luzon.

**PACIFIC:** Twentieth Air Force sends 10 B-29 Superfortresses from Chengtu, China, to bomb the Einansho air depot on Formosa.

Receiving information of American forces off Leyte, Admiral Toyoda Soemu, Commander in Chief Combined Fleet, orders operation *Sho-1* for defending the Philippines and conducting a decisive naval battle.

**CENTRAL PACIFIC:** Seventh Air Force sends 11 B-24 Liberators from Saipan to bomb shipping off Haha Jima and the town of Okimura in the Bonin Islands. B-25 Mitchells from the Gilberts bomb Nauru Island.

**NEW GUINEA:** FEAF A-20 Havocs, B-25 Mitchells, P-47 Thunderbolts, and P-38 Lightnings attack oil storage areas and airfields at Ceram Island, Ambon Island, and Boeroe Island. B-25 Mitchells and P-38s bomb airfields and shipping at Halmahera Island.

The headquarters of XIII Bomber Command redeploys from Wakde Island to Morotai Island.

## October 18

**ALEUTIANS:** Eleventh Air Force sends four B-25 Mitchells to bomb Kurabu Cape airfield on Paramushiru Island and Suribachi. Aircrews report about 12 Japanese fighters intercepting the bombers. Two fighters are reported shot down.

**CBI:** President Roosevelt recalls General Joseph W. Stilwell from China after Generalissimo Chiang Kai-shek rejects all compromise offers. Major General Albert C. Wedemeyer replaces him. Unlike Stilwell, who reported to both Admiral Lord Louis Mountbatten, the Allied commander for Southeast Asia, and Chiang Kai-shek, Wedemeyer will report only to Chiang as the U.S. commander of the China theater. Stilwell also supervised Lend-Lease to China, but Wedemeyer will have no authority, nor will he be responsible for Chinese forces in Burma. Given this extreme narrowing of duties, Wedemeyer is able to direct his entire attention to Chiang. Far more accommodating than Stilwell, Wedemeyer is helped by welcome news of increased supply tonnage being flown into China. In October, 300 aircraft are bringing in over 35,000 tons of supplies. The increase, however, adds little to the ability of the Fourteenth Air Force to influence events in China.

**ATLANTIC:** The Joint War Plans Committee issues its strategic assessment titled "Operations for the Defeat of Japan." It notes the importance of capturing Iwo Jima to assist in establishing an air and naval blockade of the Japanese home islands and contributing directly to the destruction of Japan's remaining air and naval strength in preparation for an invasion.

**ETO:** General Eisenhower meets with General Omar N. Bradley and Field Marshal Sir Bernard L. Montgomery in Brussels, Belgium, to address Allied operational objectives. All three commanders agree that Allied forces should reach the Rhine River before winter. With Antwerp still unavailable, the armies will have to be supplied through the Normandy beaches and Cherbourg. Eisenhower's objective is the Ruhr. The First and Ninth Armies of Bradley's 12th Army Group will attack toward Aachen and cross the Roer River. First Army will mount the main effort to reach the Rhine south of Cologne. The Ninth Army will support First Army's attack and protect the northern flank. The First Army will give Ninth Army operational control of XIX corps for this task. First Army will receive VIII Corps, and VII Corps will get an additional division. Once across the Roer, the two armies are to attack to the Rhine River in the area between Cologne and Krefeld. The British will clear the Reichswald and cross the Maas River to join with Ninth Army. Third Army is given the lowest priority for support.

Eighth Air Force sends more than 567 B-17s and B-24 Liberators led by radar-equipped Pathfinders and escorted by 565 P-47 Thunderbolts and P-51 Mustangs to attack industrial targets around Cologne. A total of five bombers are lost and 48 damaged. Aircrew casualties are one killed, three wounded, and 45 missing. Five fighters are lost, and the pilots are reported missing.

Ninth Air Force IX Tactical Air Command P-38 and P-47 fighters attack rail lines and support the 1st Infantry Division at Aachen.

Naval Advanced Base La Havre, France, is established.

**ITALY:** The 133rd Infantry Regiment of the 34th Infantry Division fights to seize Monte Belmonte. Twelfth Air Force P-47 Thunderbolts support the attack.

**SOUTHWEST PACIFIC AREA:** Elements of the 6th Ranger Battalion land on Homonhon Island and find it unoccupied. Minesweepers clear channels into Leyte Gulf.

Vice Admiral Jesse B. Oldendorf arrives with the Bombardment and Fire Support Group of Seventh Fleet. This group consists of six battleships, most of which had been the targets at Pearl Harbor on December 7, 1941. Along with the battleships are three heavy cruisers, three light cruisers, and 16 destroyers.

FEAF P-38 Lightnings attack barges, coastal shipping, and vehicles on the coast of Mindanao Island in the Philippines.

Carrier aircraft from Naval Task Groups 38.1 (Vice Admiral John S. McCain) and 38.4 (Rear Admiral Ralph E. Davison) attack Japanese airfields and shipping near Manila. A passenger-cargo ship and two cargo ships are sunk. TG 38.2 (Rear Admiral Gerald F. Bogan) attacks shipping off northern Luzon, sinking an auxiliary submarine chaser, two transports, and three cargo ships.

Aircraft from Seventh Fleet (Vice Admiral Thomas C. Kinkaid) sink seven Japanese ships near Cebu. U.S. submarine *Bluegill* torpedoes and sinks three Japanese cargo ships in the South China Sea. U.S. submarine *Raton* torpedoes and sinks two Japanese cargo ships in the South China Sea southwest of Luzon.

**CENTRAL PACIFIC:** Seventh Air Force B-24 Liberators from Saipan bomb Haha Jima.

**NEW GUINEA:** FEAF B-25 Mitchells, P-47 Thunderbolts, P-38 Lightnings, and P-40s attack targets on the Vogelkop Peninsula. B-25s and P-38s attack airfields on Buru Island and Halmahera Island and attack the town of Amboina on Ambon Island.

The headquarters of 307th Bombardment Group (Heavy) redeploys from Wakde Island to Morotai Island.

The Japanese Imperial Staff issues orders to execute the *Sho-1* plan (*sho* is the word for victory) to defend the Philippines from an American invasion. Japan will concentrate all of her remaining naval and air strength to destroy the landing force. Land forces will destroy the isolated remnants. The plan is highly complex and requires intricate coordination between air, land, and sea commanders. Almost immediately the plan begins to unravel as each commander receives his own instructions and conducts a separate operation.

## October 19

**CBI:** Tenth Air Force P-47 Thunderbolts bomb bridges and support British ground forces.

In China, Fourteenth Air Force sends more than 100 P-51 Mustangs and P-40s on armed reconnaissance from the Tungting Lake area to the Luichow Peninsula. Fighters attack rail lines, gun batteries, bridges, ammunition storage areas, and town areas.

**ETO:** Eighth Air Force sends more than 970 B-17s and B-24 Liberators escorted by over 700 P-51 Mustangs and P-47 Thunderbolts to bomb industrial targets and marshaling yards in western Germany. A total of six bombers are lost and 428 are damaged. Aircrew casualties are seven killed, five wounded, and 59 missing. Two fighters are lost and two are damaged. The two pilots are reported missing.

Ninth Air Force P-38s and P-47s support ground operations in the Third and Seventh Army areas.

**ITALY:** The 85th and 88th Infantry Divisions attack Monte Grande, while the 34th and 91st Infantry Divisions attack Monte Belmonte. The attacks begin in a downpour preceded by a heavy artillery bombardment. Monte Grande is captured, but the attack on Monte Belmonte fails. The 91st Infantry Division makes a limited attack past Livergnano to support the 34th Infantry Division.

Twelfth Air Force redesignates the headquarters of XII Fighter Command as Headquarters, XXII Tactical Air Command.

B-26 Marauders attack rail lines and bridges and lose two bombers to German fighters. Aircrews report two confirmed kills. B-25 Mitchells attack bridges and P-47 Thunderbolts and A-20 Havocs of XXII Tactical Air Command attack German positions in support of ground forces at the Monte Grande area, and attack rail lines and bridges north of the front lines.

**SOUTHWEST PACIFIC AREA:** Seventh Fleet begins the pre-invasion bombardment of Leyte. The Japanese have about 20,000 defenders on the island.

FEAF B-24 Liberators bomb shipping near Sulu and Mindanao Islands and bomb the airfield on Cebu Island.

Carrier aircraft from Naval Task Groups 38.1 (Vice Admiral John S. McCain) and 38.4 (Rear Admiral Ralph E. Davison) attack airfields near Manila and shipping in Manila Bay. Five cargo ships are sunk, and an oiler and a cargo ship are damaged. A U.S. destroyer is damaged by a mine off Leyte; another destroyer is damaged by shore battery fire.

Aircraft from Seventh Fleet (Vice Admiral Thomas C. Kinkaid) sink six Japanese cargo ships at Cebu. U.S. submarine *Narwhal* lands personnel and supplies on Negros Island.

**CENTRAL PACIFIC:** Seventh Air Force B-24 Liberators from Saipan bomb Yap.

**NEW GUINEA:** FEAF A-20 Havocs, P-38 Lightnings, P-47 Thunderbolts, and P-40s attack the airfield at Utarom and others in northwest New Guinea. B-24 Liberators bomb Celebes Island. P-38 Lightnings and P-47 Thunderbolts attack Amboina on Ambon Island and the airfield on Ceram Island.

## October 20

**ETO:** The 1st Infantry Division occupies Aachen after nearly a week of house-to-house fighting.

Ninth Air Force P-38s and P-47s support ground operations in the Third and Seventh Army areas.

Staff Sergeant Robert T. Kuroda of the 442nd Regimental Combat Team encounters enemy fire from a wooded slope near Bruyeres, France. He moves to a position on the crest of a ridge to locate the machine gun. Staff Sergeant Kuroda then moves to within 10 yards of the position and kills the crew. Out of ammunition, Kuroda obtains a Thompson submachine gun and attacks another machine-gun position. He is killed by a sniper shortly thereafter. For his gallant conduct and superb leadership, Staff Sergeant Kuroda will receive the Medal of Honor.

**MEDITERRANEAN:** Fifteenth Air Force sends more than 480 B-17s and B-24 Liberators escorted by P-38 Lightnings and P-51 Mustangs to attack an oil refinery in Czechoslovakia and marshaling yards in Austria and Germany.

**ITALY:** The 133rd and 168th Infantry Regiments of the 34th Infantry Division are ordered to halt and reorganize. The 88th Infantry Division makes a night attack toward Monte Grande overlooking Route 9 and the Po Valley. The division's attack is reinforced by the 337th Infantry Regiment of the 85th Infantry Division. Over 8,400 artillery rounds are fired on enemy positions. The 349th Infantry Regiment initiates the attack in a heavy rain. General Clark has promised Brigadier General Paul W. Kendall a promotion to major general if Monte Grande is captured.

Twelfth Air Force B-25 Mitchells and B-26 Marauders attack rail and road traffic and bridges in the Po Valley. A-20 Havocs and P-47 Thunderbolts of the XXII Tactical Air Command attack German positions at Monte Grande, logistics storage sites, bridges, and roads.

**SOUTHWEST PACIFIC AREA: The Invasion of Leyte—MacArthur Returns.** Seventh Fleet (Vice Admiral Thomas C. Kinkaid), Task Force 78 (Rear Admiral Daniel E. Barbey), and Task Force 79 (Vice Admiral Theodore S. Wilkinson) land four divisions of the Sixth Army (Lieutenant General Walter Krueger) on Leyte.

A four-hour preparatory air and naval bombardment precedes the landing. The Japanese are caught in the midst of changing the location of their main headquarters, causing confusion and a limited response. The 1st Cavalry Division and the two infantry regiments of the 24th Infantry Division of X Corps hold the northern beachhead, having captured Tacloban airfield and Hill 522 in the area of the Palo-Tacloban highway. The 96th and 7th Infantry Divisions of XXIV Corps occupy the southern part of the beachhead. The two corps are separated by about 10 miles. The 21st Infantry RCT lands at Panaon Strait at the southern tip of Leyte.

Japanese air attacks damage the escort carrier USS *Sangamon* and light cruiser USS *Honolulu*. Japanese shore batteries damage a destroyer and an LST (landing ship, tank).

General MacArthur watches the landings from the USS *Nashville* and then arrives onshore in the afternoon, wading 50 yards through the surf to the beach. He is accompanied by Philippine president Sergio Osmeña. MacArthur approaches a portable radio set and speaks into the microphone:

> This is the Voice of Freedom, General MacArthur speaking. People of the Philippines: I have returned! By the grace of Almighty God, our forces stand again upon Philippine soil—soil consecrated in the blood of our two peoples.

FEAF B-24 Liberators bomb Davao on Mindanao Island in the Philippines.

Krueger's Sixth Army has established a beachhead two miles deep and controls the Panaon Strait. The 7th Infantry Division controls Dulag, and the 96th Infantry Division faces Catmon Hill, the highest point on the beachhead.

A Japanese naval strike force under Vice Admiral Takeo Kurita, with five battleships, 12 cruisers, and 15 destroyers receives orders to set out for the Philippines as part of the *Sho* plan. This force is to pass through the San Bernardino Strait and enter Leyte Gulf to attack the invasion fleet and transports. Another, smaller force under Vice Admiral Shoji Nishimura, with two battleships, a cruiser, and four destroyers, is to move to the south through Surigao Strait to enter Leyte Gulf and attack the invasion fleet. The plan is to have the two fleets arrive simultaneously and crush the Americans between their combined forces. Another fleet under Vice Admiral Jisaburo Ozawa with four carriers, three cruisers, and eight destroyers, is to act as a decoy force to lure the U.S. Third Fleet away from its mission of protecting MacArthur's invasion fleet. The Japanese carriers no longer have enough aircraft, or pilots to man them, to be a significant threat. They are to be intentionally sacrificed to achieve a decisive victory. Because the Japanese naval aircraft have been so thoroughly used up in battles with Admiral Halsey's aviators in the weeks before the invasion, none of the three fleets will have air cover and, if discovered, will be entirely vulnerable to American aircraft. Strategically, the Japanese have no other choice. The risks are great, but the loss of the Philippines would be the end of the Japanese sea lifeline to the East Indies and the final blow to the survival of Japan.

**CENTRAL PACIFIC:** Despite Major General William H. Rupertus's protests that his marines are capable of finishing the fight at Peleliu, both Major General Roy S. Geiger and Admiral Chester Nimitz order Rupertus to withdraw his division from the island and turn over the battle to the 81st Infantry Division. When B Company of the 1st Battalion of the 323rd Infantry Regiment relieves the 1st Battalion of the 7th Marines at the Umurbrogol Pocket, B Company's infantrymen are able to replace the marine battalion man-for-man on the line.

Naval Operating Base Guam is established.

**NEW GUINEA:** FEAF B-25 Mitchells bomb the town of Amboina on Ambon Island.

U.S. submarine *Hammerhead* torpedoes and sinks a Japanese transport and a cargo ship off Borneo.

## October 21

**CBI:** Tenth Air Force P-47 Thunderbolts damage bridges in northern Burma and attack Japanese defensive positions in support of British ground forces.

Fourteenth Air Force receives the P-51 Mustangs of the 530th Fighter Squadron, 311th Fighter Group. The squadron redeploys to Kwanghan from Dinjan, India.

**ETO:** As the 1st Infantry Division of VII Corps clears the city of its last defenders, Aachen is the first major German city to surrender to Allied forces. The Americans capture 2,500 prisoners. The First Army has suffered 10,000 casualties in capturing the city since the attacks began on October 2. General Bradley shifts Ninth Army to the far left flank of the 12th Army Group and gives Lieutenant General Simpson operational control of XIX Corps from First Army. First Army's VIII Corps takes responsibility for the Ardennes Forest area. While First Army renews its attack toward Bonn and Cologne, Third Army will attack to reach the Rhine River in the Worms-Mainz area. If possible, both armies are to secure crossings over the river. The First Army commander, Lieutenant General Courtney Hodges, is convinced that the Hürtgen Forest must be cleared of German forces to meet the goals of the offensive to the Rhine. Hodges orders the V Corps, under Major General Leonard T. Gerow, to capture Schmidt. The attack will begin November 1. Major General Gerow selects the 28th Infantry Division, commanded by Major General Norman D. Cota, to attack into the Hürtgen Forest.

Patton orders XX Corps (10th Armored Division and the 90th and 95th Infantry Divisions) to conduct an encirclement of Metz while XII Corps (4th and 6th Armored Divisions and the 35th and 80th Infantry Divisions) will attack northeast.

**MEDITERRANEAN:** Fifteenth Air Force sends more than 100 B-24 Liberators escorted by P-38 Lightnings and P-51 Mustangs to attack marshaling yards in Hungary. Fighters strafe the airfields near the primary targets.

**ITALY:** The 85th and 88th Infantry Divisions attack northeast to occupy the last defensible high ground and capture Monte Castelazzo. The 349th Infantry Regiment of the 88th Division and the 337th Infantry Regiment of the 85th Division make little progress.

Twelfth Air Force B-26 Marauders attack rail bridges. A-20 Havocs and P-47 Thunderbolts of the XXII Tactical Air Command attack bridges and roads.

**SOUTHWEST PACIFIC AREA, LEYTE:** Major General Verne D. Mudge's 1st Cavalry Division captures the city of Tacloban.

The 7th Infantry Division under Major General Archibald V. Arnold attacks to clear Japanese defenses and facilities. The 184th Infantry Regiment of the 7th Infantry Division captures Dulag airfield, and the 32nd Infantry Regiment clears Japanese defensive positions. The 2nd Engineer Special Brigade supports the landing of X Corps.

FEAF B-24 Liberators bomb Cagayan, and B-25 Mitchells bomb Mindanao Island in the Philippines.

Carrier aircraft from Naval Task Group 38.2 (Rear Admiral Gerald F. Bogan) attack shipping and installations on Panay, Cebu, and Negros Islands. An auxiliary minesweeper, an auxiliary submarine chaser, and a tanker are sunk.

Private Harold R. Moon, Jr., of G Company, 34th Infantry Regiment, 24th Infantry Division, is in a defensive position near Pawig. During the night, his company is attacked, and Private Moon is wounded by a high volume of mortar and machine-gun fire directed at his position. Even though the platoon defenses are being overrun, Private Moon holds his ground, firing his weapon and encouraging the survivors of his platoon. Private Moon exposes himself to enemy fire many times to engage threats to the platoon, destroying a light machine gun and directing mortar fire. He fights fearlessly for more than four hours, repulsing several attempts to overwhelm his position. He is killed as he stands up to throw a hand grenade at a Japanese machine-gun position. Clustered around his fox hole are more than 200 dead enemy soldiers. Private Moon's courage and tenacity against overwhelming odds will win him the Medal of Honor.

**CENTRAL PACIFIC:** Seventh Air Force sends 28 B-24 Liberators from Saipan to bomb Iwo Jima. Two B-24s from Guam attack Yap Island. The B-24s of the 26th, 98th, and 431st Bombardment Squadrons (Heavy), 11th Bombardment Group (Heavy), redeploy from Kwajalein Atoll to Guam.

**NEW GUINEA:** FEAF A-20 Havocs, B-25 Mitchells, P-38 Lightnings, P-47 Thunderbolts, and P-40s attack airfields in northwest New Guinea.

P-38 Lightnings and A-20 Havocs attack logistics storage areas on Halmahera Island, the airfield on Ceram Island, and the town of Amboina on Ambon Island.

## October 22

**CBI:** Tenth Air Force P-47 Thunderbolts attack bridges in northern Burma.

In China, Fourteenth Air Force B-25 Mitchells escorted by P-51 Mustangs bomb two railroad bridges at Pingnam. Aircrews report the bridges destroyed.

**ETO:** The VI Corps of Seventh Army attacks Brouvelieures and Bruyères, the key towns blocking the advance through the Vosges Mountains. The 45th Infantry Division attacks from the north and the 36th Infantry Division (with the Japanese-American 442nd Regimental Combat Team attached) attacks from the west and southwest to seize the two towns.

Eighth Air Force sends more than 1,000 B-17s and B-24 Liberators led by radar-equipped Pathfinders and escorted by over 700 P-51 Mustangs and P-47 Thunderbolts to attack industrial targets and transportation targets in western Germany. Two B-17s are lost and 59 bombers damaged. Aircrew casualties are 20 killed, three wounded, and 16 missing. One P-51 is lost and two damaged. The pilot is reported missing.

Eighth Air Force assigns the Carpetbagger group of headquarters, 492nd Bombardment Group (Heavy), and the 856th, 857th, 858th, and 859th Bombardment Squadrons (Heavy) from headquarters of VIII Fighter Command, to the 1st Bombardment Division to operate as a night bombing group. The 856th Bombardment Squadron (Heavy) remains under operational control of Eighth Air Force to support Carpetbagger operations in the Netherlands, Norway, and Denmark.

Ninth Air Force P-38s and P-47s support ground operations in the Third and Seventh Army areas.

**ITALY:** The 85th and 88th Infantry Divisions attack from Monte Grande, but the attack quickly falters.

Twelfth Air Force A-20 Havocs and P-47 Thunderbolts attack rail lines and trains in northern Italy.

**SOUTHWEST PACIFIC AREA:** At about midnight, Vice Admiral Kurita's fleet is spotted by U.S. submarines *Darter* and *Dace*.

FEAF B-25 Mitchells and P-38 Lightnings attack shipping in the Sulu Archipelago, the harbor at Jolo Island, and Zamboanga harbor on Mindanao Island. B-24 Liberators attack airfields on Cebu Island and Mindanao. B-25s attack targets on Samar Island, and B-24s bomb the airfield in the Cagayan Islands.

The headquarters of the 308th Bombardment Wing (Heavy) redeploys from Hollandia to Leyte Island.

Naval Task Force 38 aircraft sink a Japanese auxiliary submarine chaser west of Panay Island.

**PACIFIC:** U.S. submarine *Sea Dog* torpedoes and sinks a Japanese supply ship and a gunboat off Kyushu, Japan.

**CENTRAL PACIFIC:** Seventh Air Force B-24 Liberators from Guam attack Yap, while B-25 Mitchells from Makin bomb Nauru Island.

**NEW GUINEA:** FEAF A-20 Havocs attack Japanese pillboxes and occupied areas near Sawar. B-25 Mitchells attack logistics storage depots in the Molucca Islands. P-38 Lightnings attack the airfields on Celebes Island and Ceram Island.

U.S. submarine *Darter* detects a group of Japanese warships northwest of Borneo, reports their position, and follows.

## October 23

**ALEUTIANS:** In the Kurile Islands, Eleventh Air Force sends three B-24 Liberators to attack Kashiwabara on Paramushiru Island. Another three B-24s bomb Otomari and fly a photoreconnaissance mission over Onnekotan Island. Five B-25 Mitchells bomb the Asahi Bay area.

**CBI:** Tenth Air Force P-47 Thunderbolts attack Japanese troops at Nanhlaing and Kyungyi. B-25 Mitchells attack rail lines and rail cars.

In China, Fourteenth Air Force sends three B-25 Mitchells escorted by seven P-40s to attack a bridge at Lobochai. B-25s and P-51 Mustangs bomb the town area of Menghsu.

**ETO:** During the night Eighth Air Force sends three B-17s and six B-24s to drop leaflets over France and the Netherlands.

**MEDITERRANEAN:** Fifteenth Air Force sends more than 500 B-17s and B-24 Liberators escorted by P-38 Lightnings and P-51 Mustangs to attack the Skoda armament works at Plzen, Czechoslovakia, and marshaling yards and industrial targets in southern Germany.

**SOUTHWEST PACIFIC AREA:** Commander Richard H. O'Kane commands the submarine USS *Tang* and conducts a night surface attack on a Japanese convoy off the Philippine Islands. O'Kane maneuvers his boat to attack three tankers, despite the heavy fire from escort destroyers. He then maneuvers to launch a torpedo at a cargo ship. Surrounded by burning ships, he orders his last two torpedoes fired, and while those hit their marks, *Tang* makes its escape. Commander O'Kane makes a second contact with a large convoy bringing reinforcements to Leyte. Two transports and a tanker are quickly sunk as he engages the ships within 1,000 yards. As Japanese destroyers begin their attack, O'Kane battles the enemy head-on, firing torpedoes. In a freak accident, the *Tang* is hit and sunk by one of its own torpedoes and goes down in 180 feet of water. Commander O'Kane and eight others survive and are taken prisoner. In two days Commander's O'Kane's boat has fired 24 torpedoes, scored 22 hits, and sunk 13 ships. For his extraordinary skill and courage and inspired leadership, Commander O'Kane will win the Medal of Honor.

U.S. submarine *Nautilus* lands personnel and supplies on Luzon; U.S. submarine *Sawfish* torpedoes and sinks a Japanese seaplane carrier west of Luzon.

U.S. submarine *Snook* torpedoes and damages a Japanese merchant tanker in the South China Sea west of Luzon Strait.

**SOUTHWEST PACIFIC AREA, LEYTE:** General MacArthur observes the installment of President Sergio Osmeña as the leader of the legitimate government of the Philippines.

The 5th and 12th Cavalry Regiments of the 1st Cavalry Division move west of Tacloban. The 2nd Cavalry Brigade begins advancing north to clear the San Juanico Strait between Leyte and Samar Islands. The XIV Corps attacks north and west. The 96th Infantry Division attacks past Dulag to capture Catmon Hill.

The Japanese begin reinforcing Leyte. Although Ultra intercepts tip off the Americans, MacArthur's staff believes the ships coming to Leyte are to evacuate troops, not reinforce.

U.S. submarine *Darter* torpedoes and sinks Vice Admiral Kurita's flagship, a cruiser, and heavily damages another heavy cruiser. U.S. submarine *Dace* torpedoes and sinks another heavy cruiser. The damaged cruiser leaves the fleet and returns to Brunei, taking two destroyers with it as escorts. The *Darter* is grounded on a reef; the crew is picked up by *Dace*.

**PACIFIC:** U.S. submarine *Croaker* torpedoes and sinks a Japanese cargo ship in the Yellow Sea off the west coast of Korea.

**CENTRAL PACIFIC:** Seventh Air Force sends eight B-24 Liberators from Guam to bomb Yap.

Destroyer escort USS *Gilligan* bombards Emidj Island, Jaluit Atoll.

**NEW GUINEA:** FEAF A-20 Havocs, P-47 Thunderbolts, and P-40s attack Japanese positions near Sawar.

B-24 Liberators and P-38 Lightnings make shipping sweeps near Celebes Island. B-25 Mitchells, A-20s, and P-38s attack oil storage areas and the airfield on Ceram Island, attack the airfield and town of Amboina on Ambon Island, and attack the airfield on Boeroe Island.

The P-47s of the 39th Fighter Squadron of the 35th Fighter Group redeploy to Morotai Island.

## October 24

**ALEUTIANS:** In the Kurile Islands, Eleventh Air Force sends three B-24 Liberators to bomb Kashiwabara and Kurabu Cape on Paramushiru Island. Two B-25 Mitchells conduct a shipping sweep off Kurabu Cape. Aircrews report one cargo ship damaged and two subchasers hit with machine-gun fire.

**CBI:** The China-Burma-India theater is split into two theaters: China and India-Burma. The headquarters of the Fourteenth Air Force is reassigned from U.S. Army Forces, CBI Theater, to U.S. Forces, China Theater.

Tenth Air Force B-25 Mitchells and P-47 Thunderbolts support British and Chinese ground forces, attacking roads, airfields, and rail lines.

Fourteenth Air Force P-40s, P-51 Mustangs, and P-38 Lightnings attack airfields, logistics storage areas, troops, town areas, and gun positions.

**ITALY:** Over 300 XXII Tactical Air Command P-47 fighters and A-20s attack targets in support of ground forces and attack transportation targets in the Po Valley.

**SOUTHWEST PACIFIC AREA:** Submarine attack group (Task Group 17.15) encounters Japanese shipping in the South China Sea west of Luzon Strait. USS *Drum* torpedoes and sinks a cargo ship; USS *Icefish* torpedoes and sinks a cargo ship; USS *Seadragon* torpedoes and sinks a transport, a cargo ship, and merchant passenger/cargo ship.

Destroyer escort USS *Richard M. Rowell* sinks Japanese submarine *I-54* off Mindanao.

U.S. submarine *Darter* is scuttled after being damaged when it runs aground near Palawan.

U.S. submarine *Shark* is sunk in Luzon Strait.

U.S. submarine *Snook* torpedoes and sinks two cargo ships in the South China Sea.

U.S. submarine *Tang* torpedoes and sinks a Japanese cargo ship in Formosa Strait, and damages a tanker. In a bizarre accident, one of her torpedoes turns and hits *Tang*, sinking the submarine.

U.S. submarine *Nautilus* lands personnel and supplies on Luzon.

**SOUTHWEST PACIFIC AREA, LEYTE:** The 7th Infantry Division drives Japanese defenders back to Burauen. The Japanese resist fiercely, supported by tanks and artillery. The 17th Infantry Regiment, supported by tanks, gains Burauen. The 32nd Infantry Regiment captures Buri airfield.

FEAF B-24 Liberators bomb Buayoan airfield on Mindanao Island, and B-25 Mitchells on armed reconnaissance hit coastal shipping and troops.

The headquarters of the 85th Fighter Wing redeploys from Hollandia to Leyte. The headquarters of the 49th Fighter Group and the P-38 Lightnings of the 7th and 9th Fighter Squadrons redeploy from Biak Island to Tacloban.

Between 150 and 200 Japanese aircraft attack the beachhead at Leyte throughout the day. Nearly 70 aircraft are shot down by antiaircraft fire and fighter aircraft from the escort carriers supporting the landing. The Japanese will continue to attack the beachhead over the next four days.

U.S. submarines *Angler* and *Guitarro* report the position of the Japanese. Vice Admiral Kurita's fleet, now reduced by five ships, enters the Sibuyan Sea. Carrier aircraft from Naval Task Groups 38.2, 38.3, and 38.4 attack Vice Admiral Kurita's Center Force in the Sibuyan Sea. Aircraft from carriers USS *Enterprise, Intrepid,* and *Franklin* and the small carrier USS *Cabot* sink the battleship *Musashi* and damage battleships *Yamato* and *Nagato,* a heavy cruiser, and three destroyers south of Luzon. Aircraft from USS *Franklin* along with aircraft from Naval Task Group 38.4 attack Vice Admiral Nishimura and Vice Admiral Shima's Southern Force in the Sulu Sea, sinking a destroyer off the west coast of Panay. Aircraft from USS *Enterprise* and USS *Franklin* also damage two battleships (*Fuso* and *Yamashiro*). Vice Admiral Ozawa launches carrier aircraft against Halsey's fleet. About 200 Japanese aircraft make an attack on the carriers. American fighters outfly and outfight the inexperienced airmen, destroying at least half of the enemy aircraft (the rest land on Luzon airfields because the pilots are too inexperienced to land on the deck of a carrier). A Japanese dive-bomber attack on TG 38.3 damages the small carrier USS *Princeton* southeast of Luzon, with one 500-pound bomb on the

The USS *Princeton* served in the Pacific from August 1943 until October 24, 1944, when, in the Sibuyan Sea in the Philippines, a single bomb dropped by a Japanese aircraft caused serious damage and led to fires and explosions that caused the ship to sink. The light cruiser USS *Birmingham,* supporting fire fighting operations alongside the carrier, suffered heavy casualties and damage when *Princeton* exploded.

deck causing a great fire inside the ship. The cruiser USS *Birmingham* attempts a rescue and also tries to contain the fire in between alarms of Japanese air and submarine torpedo attack. The fire reaches the *Princeton*'s ammunition storage area and explodes, damaging a light cruiser and three destroyers as the ships work to assist the stricken carrier. The USS *Birmingham,* alongside the carrier at the moment of explosion suffers 229 killed, 426 wounded, and four sailors missing. USS *Princeton* is later scuttled.

Admiral William F. Halsey, Third Fleet commander, orders Vice Admiral Marc A. Mitscher's Naval Task Force 38 to steam north to be ready to meet Vice Admiral Ozawa's Northern Force the following day. Halsey decides to take everything in the Third Fleet with him, including the modern fast battleships that are supposed to be guarding the invasion fleet. Vice Admiral Thomas C. Kinkaid, commander of Seventh Fleet, receives a message from Halsey, but the information is vague, leaving Kinkaid to believe that the battleships of the Third Fleet are still in place. This leaves the San Bernardino Strait open for Kurita's Center Force to reach Leyte Gulf. Kinkaid orders Naval Task Group 77.2 (Rear Admiral Jesse B. Oldendorf) and Naval Task Group 77.3 (Rear Admiral Russell S. Berkey) to prepare to meet the Southern Force as it makes the transit through Surigao Strait to reach Leyte Gulf.

Japanese aircraft damage a destroyer, an LST (landing ship, tank), an LCI (landing craft, infantry), and an oiler east of Leyte. TF 38 aircraft damage a light cruiser and a destroyer at Manila, and sink an ore carrier off Luzon.

As commander of Air Group 15, Commander David McCampbell (USN) attacks a formation of 60 Japanese aircraft, supported by one other fighter, and shoots down nine enemy aircraft, forcing the group to abandon its attack. McCampbell's fearlessness, his superb combat skills, and his willingness to defend the ships of the fleet regardless of the odds, will win him the Medal of Honor.

**PACIFIC:** Admiral Nimitz provides planning outline for Operation Iceberg, the invasion of Okinawa. Admiral Raymond A. Spruance will be overall commander of the operation. The amphibious force commander is Vice Admiral Richmond Kelly Turner.

U.S. submarine *Besugo* torpedoes and damages a Japanese coastal patrol ship off southern Kyushu, Japan. U.S. submarine *Croaker* torpedoes and sinks a Japanese cargo ship and a passenger/cargo ship in the East China Sea. U.S. submarine *Kingfish* torpedoes and sinks a Japanese cargo ship east of Chichi Jima.

**CENTRAL PACIFIC:** Seventh Air Force B-24 Liberators from Guam bomb Yap.

**NEW GUINEA:** FEAF A-20 Havocs, P-47 Thunderbolts, P-38 Lightnings, and P-40s attack targets on the Vogelkop Peninsula.

The B-24 Liberators of the 72nd Bombardment Squadron (Heavy), 5th Bombardment Group (Heavy), redeploy from Noemfoor Island to Morotai Island.

## October 25

**ETO:** The commander of the VI Corps of Seventh Army, Major General Lucien K. Truscott, leaves his command to become commander of Fifth Army in the Mediterranean theater of operations. Major General Edward H. Brooks takes command of VI Corps.

Eighth Air Force sends more than 1,200 B-17s and B-24 Liberators escorted by 475 P-51 Mustangs and P-47 Thunderbolts to attack industrial targets, oil refineries, synthetic oil plants, marshaling yards, and airfields in western Germany, using radar to assist the timing of bomb release. Two B-17s are lost and 198 are damaged. Aircrew casualties are one wounded and 28 missing. One P-51 is lost and one damaged. The pilot is reported missing.

Ninth Air Force P-38 Lightnings and P-47 Thunderbolts attack rail lines in the Saarbrücken area, and support XIX Corps.

**MEDITERRANEAN:** Fifteenth Air Force B-17s bomb an aircraft production facility and a marshaling yard in Austria.

**ITALY:** Twelfth Air Force P-47 Thunderbolts bomb rail lines and rail cars, destroying over 20 locomotives.

**SOUTHWEST PACIFIC AREA: The Battle of Surigao Strait.** Just before midnight Admiral Jesse B. Oldendorf's Naval Task Group 77.2 with battleships and cruisers, supported by Naval Task Group 77.3 (Rear Admiral Russell S. Berkey) and with an Australian heavy cruiser and destroyer and 39 motor torpedo boats forming Naval Task Group 70.1, attacks the Southern Force (Vice Admiral Nishimura and Vice Admiral Shima) as it enters Surigao Strait. Destroyers and patrol torpedo boats catch Vice Admiral Nishimura's fleet in the narrow Surigao Strait. Patrol torpedo boats launch torpedoes followed by three separate coordinated attacks by Destroyer Squadrons 54, 24, and 56. The torpedo attacks slow and disrupt the enemy formation, damaging a light cruiser. One PT boat is lost. Destroyers hit and sink one Japanese destroyer and damage two others. These two destroyers are rapidly sunk by a U.S. light cruiser and destroyer. USS *Albert W. Grant* is hit and damaged by both friendly and enemy gunfire. Japanese battleships *Fuso* and *Yamashiro* are sunk, and a heavy cruiser and destroyer are damaged.

This attack is followed at 0337 by broadsides from the main guns of the Pearl Harbor battleships USS *West Virginia, Pennsylvania, California, Maryland,* and *Tennessee.* Most of Nishimura's fleet is destroyed in a matter of minutes as two Japanese battleships are sunk. Admiral Shima's supporting fleet encounters the survivors and, following a collision between two cruisers, retreats. One destroyer is sunk. The remainder of the fleet is tracked and repeatedly attacked by American aircraft over the next few days.

**SOUTHWEST PACIFIC AREA: The Battle of Leyte Gulf.** Before dawn, Vice Admiral Kurita's fleet enters Leyte Gulf through the San Bernardino Straits untouched. Halsey's entire Third Fleet has moved at top speed northward to engage Vice Admiral Ozawa's carrier decoys. Kurita, however, believes he has found Halsey's carriers. What he has actually spotted is Taffy-3 (Task Unit 77.4.3), under the command of Rear Admiral Clifton F. Sprague and consisting of six light escort carriers, three destroyers, and four destroyer escorts supporting the ground forces on Leyte. Taffy-3 is one of three such light escort groups operating in the gulf. Taffy-3 is all that stands between Kurita and the defenseless invasion ships of MacArthur's landing force.

The Japanese initiate a disorganized attack while Sprague launches aircraft and navigates between rain squalls and destroyer smoke screens to escape the rain of heavy shells from two of the largest battleships in the world, the *Yamato* and the *Nagato.* American fighter and torpedo aircraft, mostly unarmed, make dummy passes at the ships to force them to take evasive action and slow down their pursuit. The three destroyers, the USS *Johnston,* the USS *Hoel,* and the USS *Heerman,* make a determined charge into the midst of the Japanese fleet, launching torpedoes and firing every gun available to buy time for the escort carriers. One Japanese heavy cruiser is damaged, and the *Yamato* is forced out of the battle for a critical time. The *Hoel* is heavily damaged by direct fire and sinks. USS *Samuel B. Roberts* also attacks, disrupting the enemy ships. But Japanese shellfire is too overwhelming as the powerful guns begin to find the range. The escort carrier USS *Gambier Bay* is sunk, the first carrier to be lost to naval gunfire. The USS *Kalinin Bay* is also hit and damaged, but most of the armor-piercing shells fly right through the thin metal skin of the carrier. The *Samuel B. Roberts* takes multiple hits from large-caliber shells and is sunk. The *Johnston* goes down after a second fearless attack, this time on the Japanese destroyer squadron, when it is trapped in a deadly cross fire between the enemy destroyers and the cruisers.

At the point where the Japanese fleet, though crippled, has the Americans ships in its gunsights, Vice Admiral Kurita calls off the attack. Facing nearly constant, punishing attacks from American aircraft, now fully armed with torpedoes and 500-pound armor-piercing bombs, and believing he has sunk several major warships of the Third Fleet, Kurita orders a withdrawal. Of the 32 ships he started with, four battleships, four cruisers, and seven destroyers are left.

After Kurita's fleet moves off, Sprague's carriers are attacked by Japanese aircraft. One rolls in on the USS *St. Lo*, crashing into the escort carrier and sinking it. It is a deliberate suicide attack, turning aircraft into human-guided bombs. This is the first kamikaze attack of the war and adds a shocking new dimension to naval warfare. Faced with near certain defeat, Japanese pilots swear to die rather than face humiliation and dishonor—in the belief that their sacrifices may turn the tide of the war. Other kamikaze attacks follow during the day and damage two other escort carriers, USS *Kalinin Bay* and USS *Kitkun Bay*. The attacks cause heavy damage and casualties.

Japanese kamikazes attack escort carriers of Task Unit 77.4.1 (Rear Admiral Thomas L. Sprague). Escort carriers USS *Suwannee* and USS *Santee* are damaged. Japanese submarine *I-56* torpedoes *Santee* as well.

While Rear Admiral Sprague's sailors fight for their lives, Admiral Halsey engages Ozawa's fleet. Carrier aircraft from Halsey's Third Fleet locate Vice Admiral Ozawa's decoy Northern Force. Aircraft from carriers *Essex* and *Lexington* sink carriers *Zuikaku* and *Chitose* in the Philippine Sea east of Luzon. Another carrier, damaged by air attack from carriers *Lexington* and *Franklin* and the small carrier *Langley*, is sunk by two heavy cruisers and two light cruisers. Aircraft from carriers *Essex*, *Franklin*, *Lexington*, *Enterprise*, and small carrier *San Jacinto* sink the carrier *Zuiho*. Four heavy cruisers and 12 destroyers sink a destroyer. U.S. carrier aircraft damage a total of three battleships, five heavy cruisers, a light cruiser, and a destroyer. Four of the heavy cruisers are so badly damaged that they are scuttled.

Finally stung by a direct inquiry from Admiral Nimitz himself on the location and direction of the fleet, Halsey breaks off contact with Ozawa and moves south. As a result, both Ozawa and Kurita survive, and neither is subjected to the terrible power of Halsey's battleships.

The three separate engagements that make up the Battle of Leyte Gulf have resulted in the end of the Japanese Combined Fleet as an effective fighting force. The Japanese lose a large carrier and three light carriers, three battleships, six heavy cruisers, three light cruisers, and 10 destroyers. The number of ships that are damaged and the number of aircraft lost is significant. American losses are one light carrier, two escort carriers, two destroyers, a destroyer escort, and one patrol torpedo boat. The battleships of Pearl Harbor have their day of glory, doing what they were built to do with crews that have trained many hours for such an opportunity. It is revenge of the highest order. The men of Taffy-3 have fought one of the most remarkable actions in naval warfare. Skill and technology combined with faith and courage have demonstrated the extraordinary fighting capabilities of the American sailor.

Commander Ernest E. Evans, captain of the USS *Johnston*, takes his ship in harm's way against a Japanese battle fleet that includes some of the most powerful warships ever built. Taking aggressive action to move into a position to launch torpedoes, Evans attracts the massive armor-piercing shells from the Japanese battleships as the escort carriers desperately attempt to avoid destruction. After launching torpedoes, Evans continues to fight, supporting other destroyers and destroyer escorts with fire from the ship's five-inch guns, forcing the Japanese ships to maneuver away from the carriers. As the Japanese gunners get the range, the *Johnston*'s steering and power are badly damaged. Evans, undaunted, moves to the rear of the ship to continue to steer, shouting commands through an open hatch to men turning the rudder by hand. The *Johnston* continues to fight until so badly battered the ship can no longer move. It is destroyed and sunk after a furious three-hour battle against impossible odds. Commander Evans dies, having made every possible effort to delay and damage the enemy. His indomitable courage and brilliant professional skill represent one of the greatest moments in U.S. naval history, and he will be recognized with the nation's highest award for valor, the Medal of Honor.

**SOUTHWEST PACIFIC AREA, LEYTE:** The 19th and 34th Infantry Regiments of the 24th Infantry Division expand the beachhead against strong Japanese resistance. The 7th Infantry Division captures San Pablo airfield.

The Japanese land 2,000 reinforcements at Ormoc on Leyte.

**SOUTHWEST PACIFIC AREA:** Over 50 FEAF B-24 Liberators supported by P-38 Lightnings and P-47 Thunderbolts attack naval forces in the Mindanao Sea. Aircrews report sinking a Japanese light cruiser.

The P-38s of the 8th Fighter Squadron, 49th Fighter Group, redeploy from Biak to Tacloban on Leyte Island.

Aircraft from *Essex* and *Lexington* and torpedoes from U.S. submarine *Jallao* sink a light cruiser east of Luzon Strait.

U.S. submarine *Halibut* torpedoes and sinks a Japanese destroyer in the Philippine Sea.

U.S. submarine *Nautilus* lands personnel and supplies on Luzon.

**PACIFIC:** Twentieth Air Force sends 59 B-29 Superfortresses from Chengtu, China, to bomb an aircraft production facility at Omura, Japan, on Kyushu Island. Other B-29s bomb alternate targets and targets of opportunity.

U.S. submarine *Seal* torpedoes and sinks a Japanese transport in the Kuriles.

U.S. submarine *Sterlet* torpedoes and sinks a Japanese merchant tanker in the Bonins.

**CENTRAL PACIFIC:** Seventh Air Force sends 29 B-24 Liberators from Saipan to bomb Iwo Jima. Other B-24s from Saipan and Guam bomb Yap.

The headquarters of the 11th Bombardment Group (Heavy) redeploys from Kwajalein to Guam.

Navy F4U Corsairs sink a Japanese auxiliary submarine chaser north of the Palau Islands.

**NEW GUINEA:** FEAF A-20 Havocs pound supply and fuel storage areas near Sarmi. B-24 Liberators bomb Celebes Island. B-25 Mitchells, A-20 Havocs, and P-38 Lightnings attack targets in the Molucca Islands, Ceram Island, and Haroekoe Island.

## October 26

**ALEUTIANS:** Eleventh Air Force B-24 Liberators bomb installations on Onnekotan Island.

**CBI:** In China, Fourteenth Air Force B-24 Liberators and B-25 Mitchells attack shipping off the Luichow Peninsula.

Major Horace S. Carswell, Jr., is a pilot flying a B-24 Liberator in the 308th Bombardment Group, Fourteenth Air Force, attacking a 12-ship Japanese convoy in the South China Sea. Bringing his bomber down low, he makes a bombing run at 600 feet, but fails to hit his target. He immediately initiates a second low-level bomb run and makes two direct hits on a large tanker. Antiaircraft fire damages Carswell's bomber, knocking out two engines, wounding the copilot, and damaging the steering controls. Carswell is able to turn the stricken bomber toward the coast of China. As the bomber crosses over land, Carswell orders the crew to bail out while he and a crewman without a parachute remain in the bomber and attempt a crash landing. The bomber, with another failed engine, crashes into a mountainside. For his supreme sacrifice and willingness to save his crew, Major Carswell will win the Medal of Honor.

**ETO:** Eighth Air Force sends more than 1,200 B-17s and B-24 Liberators using radar-equipped Pathfinder bombers and escorted by 475 P-47 Thunderbolts and P-51 Mustangs to attack aircraft repair facilities, military vehicle production facilities, and a synthetic oil plant in western Germany. A total of 58 bombers are damaged. Aircrew casualties are 16 killed and two wounded. Fighter pilots report two confirmed kills. One P-51 is lost and one damaged. The pilot is reported missing.

**MEDITERRANEAN:** Fifteenth Air Force B-17s bomb a marshaling yard at Innsbruck, Austria.

**ITALY:** Heavy rains cause flooding, which forces II Corps to reconsolidate in order to maintain connection with its supply lines. The 85th and 88th Infantry Divisions are unable to advance any farther. Rain is so heavy that it has washed out bridges and cut off the main supply lines to forward units. The Fifth Army has reached its limits. There are severe shortages of artillery ammunition. Personnel losses, which have risen to nearly 16,000 men since September 10, have not been replaced. General Mark Clark admits, "Our strength was not enough to get across the final barrier to which the enemy clung."

**SOUTHWEST PACIFIC AREA:** In the Philippines, FEAF B-24 Liberators attack a Japanese naval force off Panay Island. Aircrews report one battleship and two aircraft carriers are hit. P-38 Lightnings attack vehicles near Davao on Mindanao Island. B-25 Mitchells bomb Iligan.

Aircraft from TF 38 planes sink a light cruiser and a destroyer near Mindoro and damage a heavy cruiser and destroyer in the Sibuyan Sea. Aircraft from carriers USS *Hornet* and USS *Wasp* sink a light cruiser south of Mindoro, and aircraft from carrier USS *Hancock* sink a landing ship. Aircraft from Task Unit 77.4.2 sink a destroyer near Panay. Carrier- aircraft sink a merchant tanker in the Sulu Sea.

FEAF B-24 Liberators sink a light cruiser and damage a battleship off Negros Island. Cruisers and destroyers sink a Japanese destroyer off Luzon.

U.S. submarine *Drum* torpedoes and sinks a Japanese transport, a merchant passenger-cargo ship, and a cargo ship north of Luzon. U.S. submarine *Icefish* torpedoes and sinks a Japanese cargo ship west of Luzon Strait. Damaged by a depth-charge attack, the *Icefish* terminates her patrol. U.S. submarine *Rock* torpedoes and sinks a Japanese merchant tanker in the Sulu Sea.

**CENTRAL PACIFIC:** Seventh Air Force B-25 Mitchells from the Gilberts bomb the airfield on Nauru Island.

**NEW GUINEA:** FEAF A-20 Havocs and B-25 Mitchells bomb Utarom. P-40s attack Halmahera Island.

### October 27

**CBI:** Major General Albert C. Wedemeyer is named as Chiang Kai-shek's chief of staff and commander of the China theater. Lieutenant General Daniel I. Sultan, General Stilwell's deputy commander, commands the India-Burma theater. The new American objective is to gain some advantage from the operations in the China theater. The Allied counteroffensive in the India-Burma theater, however, shows promise despite the lack of importance to overall U.S. objectives in the war. General Sultan commands three Chinese divisions (the 38th, the 30th, and the 50th), the British 36th Division, and the U.S. 5332nd Brigade (Provisional), also known as the Mars Task Force. The Mars Task Force is composed of the 124th Cavalry Regiment and the reorganized and refitted Merrill's Marauders, now designated the 475th Infantry Regiment.

General Stilwell departs from China. In his diary he writes, "I was relieved on the arbitrary stand and false statements of Chiang Kai-shek." The relief of Stilwell provides Chiang with a temporary victory, but the U.S. military leadership sours on China and on the commander of the Fourteenth Air Force, General Chennault, who is seen as being too closely associated with the Generalissimo.

The headquarters of Tenth Air Force is reassigned to the new India-Burma theater command.

The Japanese Eleventh Army renews its offensive as Fourteenth Air Force P-51 Mustangs and P-40s attack troops in the Kweilin area, rail traffic near Puchi, and airfields at Siangtan and Changsha.

**ETO:** During the night two B-17s and seven B-24s drop leaflets over Germany, France, and the Netherlands.

**MEDITERRANEAN:** The Supreme Allied Commander, Mediterranean, General Sir Henry Maitland Wilson, orders an end to all offensives. German defenses are too strong and the weather has turned so bad that troops and transportation are hopelessly bogged down. Casualties are not being replaced and supply stockages in-theater are low. Allied casualties total 19,000. The U.S. II Corps has lost 15,000 men since beginning the Operation Olive offensive on September 10, nearly one-third of them in the 88th Infantry Division alone.

**ITALY:** The divisions of the battered U.S. II Corps are rotated out of the line for rest and reorganization. The 366th Separate Infantry Regiment, an all-black unit, and the 758th Light Tank Battalion arrive in Italy. The 366th has been assigned to the Fifteenth Air Force since May 6, 1944, serving as a guard force.

**SOUTHWEST PACIFIC AREA:** In the Philippines FEAF P-38 Lightnings and P-47 Thunderbolts attack shipping off Cebu Island and Mactan Island.

Naval Task Group 38.3 (Rear Admiral Frederick C. Sherman) and Naval Task Group 38.4 (Rear Admiral Ralph E. Davison) attack Japanese shipping and targets around northern Luzon. Carrier aircraft sink a Japanese destroyer north of Panay. Task Force 77 aircraft sink a destroyer off Panay.

The battleship USS *California* is damaged by an air attack off Leyte. A kamikaze hits and damages a U.S. freighter off Leyte.

U.S. submarine *Nautilus* lands men and supplies on east coast of Luzon.

U.S. submarine *Cero* forces a Japanese guardboat aground on Luzon.

U.S. submarine *Bergall* attacks a Japanese convoy and sinks an oiler and a fleet tanker in the Sulu Sea.

**PACIFIC:** U.S. submarine *Kingfish* torpedoes and sinks a Japanese landing ship and a cargo vessel near Iwo Jima.

**CENTRAL PACIFIC:** Seventh Air Force sends two B-24 Liberators from Saipan to bomb Yap.

**NEW GUINEA:** FEAF B-24 Liberators bomb Malili and Palopo on Celebes Island.

## October 28
**ALEUTIANS:** Eleventh Air Force sends eight B-25 Mitchells to fly cover for a naval task force.

**CBI:** In China, Fourteenth Air Force P-40 and P-51 Mustangs strafe villages, troops, and horses near Menghsu and Konghow.

**ETO:** General Eisenhower shifts the main effort from Field Marshal Sir Bernard L. Montgomery's 21st Army Group to General Omar N. Bradley's 12th Army Group. Montgomery is to focus on the capture of Antwerp, the port city essential to supporting future operations. Bradley is to establish a bridgehead over the Rhine River near Cologne. The First Army will make the main attack, with Ninth Army and Third Army in support. The 6th Army Group will also advance to the Rhine River. After the 12th Army Group has secured bridgeheads over the Rhine, the main effort will again shift to the north where Montgomery's 21st Army Group will make the main attack into the Ruhr. This is all in keeping with Eisenhower's broad-front approach—the Allied forces will attack in concert, pressuring the Germans across the entire front until the main effort in the north can strike the decisive blow, followed by a supporting effort from the south to encircle the Ruhr.

Eighth Air Force sends more than 360 B-17s escorted by nearly 200 P-51 Mustangs to attack marshaling yards in Germany. Three B-17s are lost and 140 damaged. Aircrew casualties are 12 wounded and 29 missing. Two P-51 fighters are lost. The pilots are reported missing.

During the night three B-17s and six B-24s drop leaflets over Germany, France, and the Netherlands.

Ninth Air Force sends 45 B-26 Marauders to bomb rail bridges at various locations and the airfield at Euskirchen. P-38 Lightnings and P-47 Thunderbolts support XIX Corps.

Staff Sergeant Lucian Adams of the 30th Infantry Regiment, 3rd Infantry Division, takes action when his company is stopped near St-Die, France, as it attempts to clear the line of supply to a battalion isolated by the enemy. German machine-gun positions cover the approach to the Mortagne Forest, engaging the Americans and causing a number of casualties. Staff Sergeant Adams picks up a Browning

Automatic Rifle and charges forward, firing the weapon from the hip and coming to within a few yards of the German positions. Firing short bursts from the BAR and throwing hand grenades, Staff Sergeant Adams moves through the woods, eliminating three machine guns and killing nine German soldiers. The supply line is reopened, and contact with the isolated battalion is restored. For his singular act of courage, Staff Sergeant Adams will receive the Medal of Honor.

**MEDITERRANEAN:** Fifteenth Air Force B-17s bomb an aircraft production facility at Klagenfurt, Austria. Other B-17s bomb the marshaling yard in Munich.

**ITALY:** Twelfth Air Force, XXII Tactical Air Command, A-20 Havocs and P-47 Thunderbolts attack vehicles and trains north of the front lines.

**SOUTHWEST PACIFIC AREA, LEYTE:** The 96th Infantry Division conducts its first major combat operation in the XXIV Corps area. The 382nd Infantry Regiment captures the Japanese logistics depot at Tabontabon, while the 381st and 383rd Infantry Regiments attack Catmon Hill. The battle for the hill will last three more days.

FEAF B-24 Liberators bomb the airfield on Palawan Island in the Philippines.

The headquarters of the 475th Fighter Group redeploys from Biak to Leyte Island.

Private First Class Leonard C. Brostrom is a rifleman in Company F, 17th Infantry Regiment, 7th Infantry Division. Near Dagami, Leyte, his platoon encounters Japanese in pillboxes, trenches, and spider holes so well camouflaged that they are nearly invisible. As the men in his platoon fall all around him, Private Brostrom locates a pillbox in the center of the Japanese strong point and runs forward with grenades and tosses them through the entrance. Brostrom then faces six soldiers who charge at him from a trench with fixed bayonets. He stops the charge with rifle fire and begins throwing grenades, but is finally wounded and drops to the ground. Although bleeding badly, Brostrom struggles to his feet and throws his remaining grenades with his remaining strength. He dies shortly thereafter as his comrades clear the rest of the enemy strongpoint. Private Brostrom's exceptional courage, his fierce determination, and dedication to duty at the cost of his life will win him the Medal of Honor.

Aircraft from Naval Task Group 38.4 (Rear Admiral Ralph E. Davison) damage a landing ship off Leyte.

Two U.S. destroyers and TBF Avengers from the small carrier USS *Belleau Wood* sink Japanese submarine *I-46*, east of Mindanao.

A kamikaze damages a light cruiser off Leyte. Japanese submarine *I-45* torpedoes and sinks a destroyer escort off Leyte. A destroyer sinks *I-45* shortly thereafter.

**PACIFIC:** Twentieth Air Force, XXI Bomber Command, B-29 Superfortresses from the Marianas conduct their first combat mission. Fourteen B-29s attack submarine pens at Truk.

A reality of war—the drudgery and labor necessary to put men and equipment ashore on a beach is clearly seen as unloading proceeds at Leyte, October 10, 1944. The landing ship tank (LST) has a crew of seven officers and 104 enlisted men, a maximum speed of 12 knots, and can carry 1,600 to 1,900 tons of cargo.

**CENTRAL PACIFIC:** Seventh Air Force B-24 Liberators from Saipan Island bomb Haha Jima. B-24s from Guam bomb Yap.

**NEW GUINEA:** FEAF B-25 Mitchells and P-38 Lightnings attack the town of Amboina on Ambon Island. B-24 Liberators bomb the Wilhelmina Docks on Celebes Island.

## October 29

**ALEUTIANS:** Eleventh Air Force sends four B-25 Mitchells to attack buildings at Tomari Cape on Paramushiru Island. Aircrews report damage to buildings and a cargo ship.

**CBI:** In China, Fourteenth Air Force P-51 Mustangs and P-40s support Chinese ground forces near Lungling and Mangshih. Fighters also attack rail lines between Siaokan and Sinyang, and strafe airfields at Chingmen, Tangyang, and Ichang.

**ETO:** Ninth Air Force sends nearly 170 B-26 Marauders and A-20 Havocs to bomb rail bridges in Germany and the Netherlands. P-47 Thunderbolts and P-38 Lightnings escort bombers attacking rail lines and bridges, and support XIX Corps.

**MEDITERRANEAN:** Fifteenth Air Force sends nearly 700 B-17s and B-24 Liberators escorted by P-38 Lightnings and P-51 Mustangs to attack transportation targets in southern Germany. Most bombers abort the mission due to bad weather, but 35 B-24s hit the marshaling yards at Munich. P-38s attack rail lines and locomotives in Austria.

**ITALY:** Twelfth Air Force A-20 Havocs and P-47 Thunderbolts of the XXII Tactical Air Command attack railroad targets in the Po Valley.

**SOUTHWEST PACIFIC AREA, LEYTE:** The 24th Infantry Division advances 15 miles from Palo facing strong Japanese resistance. The 1st Cavalry clears both sides of San Juanico Strait. The 2nd Battalion of the 32nd Infantry Regiment, 7th Infantry Division, with a reconnaissance troop from the 7th Cavalry, patrols to Abuyog and heads for Ormoc Bay, where the Japanese still are able to land reinforcements and supplies.

A naval operating base is established at Leyte. A naval air station is set up at Samar.

Rear Admiral Gerald F. Bogan's Naval Task Group 38.2 attacks Japanese airfields around Manila and shipping in Manila Bay. Pilots report a heavy cruiser damaged. A kamikaze attack on the fast carriers operating off Leyte damages USS *Intrepid*.

**PACIFIC:** Japanese submarine *I-12* torpedoes and sinks a U.S. freighter in the Pacific between California and Hawaii. The submarine surfaces, shells the sinking ship, and attacks the survivors, killing eight men.

**CENTRAL PACIFIC:** Seventh Air Force sends 19 B-24 Liberators from Saipan to bomb Chichi Jima. B-24s from Guam bomb Yap.

**NEW GUINEA:** FEAF A-20 Havocs and B-25 Mitchells bomb Utarom. P-40s and P-38 Lightnings attack other airfields in northwest New Guinea. B-25 Mitchells and P-38 Lightnings bomb targets on Halmahera Island.

The headquarters of the Thirteenth Air Force redeploys from Noemfoor to Morotai Island.

A Navy PB4Y Privateer patrol bomber sinks a Japanese tanker east of Borneo.

## October 30

**CBI:** Tenth Air Force B-25 Mitchells and P-47 Thunderbolts attack bridges throughout northern Burma.

Fourteenth Air Force sends 13 B-24 Liberators to lay mines in Victoria Harbor, Hong Kong.

**ETO:** Eighth Air Force sends more than 1,200 B-17s and B-24 Liberators escorted by nearly 900 P-47 Thunderbolts and P-51 Mustangs to attack oil refineries, marshaling yards, and oil production facilities in Germany. Two bombers are lost and 49 damaged. Aircrew casualties are one wounded and 21 missing. Six fighters are lost, and the pilots are reported missing.

Of five B-17s sent on an Aphrodite mission against Heligoland Island, Germany, only two reach the target. The bombers are escorted by seven P-47s. Another 26 B-17s, escorted by P-47s, fly cover.

During the night two B-17s and seven B-24s drop leaflets over Germany, France, and the Netherlands.

Private Wilburn K. Ross is a light machine gunner with G Company, 350th Infantry, 3rd Infantry Division. His company makes an attack against a German position near St-Jacques, France, and suffers heavy casualties. The Germans attempt a counterattack to shatter the survivors. But Private Ross sets up his machine gun in front of the line and, fully exposed to enemy fire, stops the assault. He continues to hold off successive German attacks, fighting on alone in his exposed position. Finally out of ammunition, Ross and eight survivors of his company are ordered to pull back. Ross and his comrades receive ammunition just as the Germans begin a final assault. Ross again holds off the enemy, forcing them to retreat. In five continuous hours of combat Private Ross has defended his company's position and killed or wounded at least 58 Germans. For his remarkable act of courage and devotion to duty against overwhelming odds, Private Ross will receive the Medal of Honor.

**MEDITERRANEAN:** During the night Fifteenth Air Force B-24 Liberators bomb a marshaling yard at Klagenfurt, Austria.

**ITALY:** Twelfth Air Force P-47 Thunderbolts and A-20 Havocs of the XXII Tactical Air Command attack targets in the Po Valley.

**SOUTHWEST PACIFIC AREA:** In the 7th Infantry Division area, the 17th Infantry Regiment, reinforced by the 2nd Battalion of the 184th Infantry Regiment, clears Dagami using tanks, flamethrowers, and bayonets.

General Krueger orders the 21st RCT to move from Panaon to rejoin the 24th Infantry Division. A battalion of the 32nd Infantry Division will occupy Panaon.

FEAF B-24 Liberators bomb the airfield on Negros Island in the Philippines. B-25 Mitchells and P-38 Lightnings attack the airfield on Mindanao.

Kamikazes damage the carrier USS *Franklin* and small carrier USS *Belleau Wood* east of Mindanao.

**PACIFIC:** Twentieth Air Force sends eight B-29 Superfortresses from the Marianas to bomb submarine pens at Truk.

U.S. submarine *Salmon* torpedoes and damages a Japanese coastal patrol ship southwest of Kyushu, Japan. As USS *Salmon* and USS *Trigger* coordinate an attack and damage a merchant tanker off Kyushu, the *Salmon* is damaged in a depth-charge attack and must end her patrol.

**CENTRAL PACIFIC:** Seventh Air Force sends eight B-24 Liberators from Guam to bomb Yap. One B-24 from Saipan during the night bombs Iwo Jima on a snooper mission. B-25 Mitchells from Makin Island bomb Nauru Island.

**NEW GUINEA:** FEAF A-20 Havocs and B-25 Mitchells bomb the airfield at Utarom and P-40s attack targets of opportunity. P-38 Lightnings attack the airfield on Borneo. B-24 Liberators bomb the wharf area at Makassar on Celebes Island. P-38 Lightnings attack Piroe on Ceram Island.

Thirteenth Air Force P-38 Lightnings damage a Japanese submarine chaser in the Celebes Sea and sink two merchant tankers off Borneo.

## October 31

**ALEUTIANS:** Eleventh Air Force sends four B-25 Mitchells to bomb buildings at Tomari Cape on Paramushiru Island. Aircrews report damage to burning buildings. Two B-25s are damaged by antiaircraft fire, one severely enough to be forced to make an emergency landing in the Soviet Union.

**CBI:** Major General Albert C. Wedemeyer arrives in Chungking, China, to serve as commander of China theater and chief of staff to Generalissimo Chiang Kai-shek. Wedemeyer has instructions from the Joint Chiefs of Staff to serve as an adviser to Chiang on all matters pertaining to training, equipping, and supporting Chinese forces in their war against the Japanese. Chiang is unwilling to risk the best units of the Nationalist Army in any offensive action and holds them back as protection against the Communist forces operating in northern China. Wedemeyer also has operational control of the Fourteenth Air Force.

During the month of October 35,131 tons of supplies have been flown over the Hump, an amount that is four times the monthly tonnage delivered over the previous year. The Air Transport Command has been flying an average of 18,000 tons a month over the Hump since February, most of it to support the B-29s.

In Burma, Brigadier General John P. Wiley takes command of Mars Task Force after Brigadier General Arms is injured in a vehicle accident.

Tenth Air Force sends more than 60 P-47 Thunderbolts to attack logistics storage areas at Namun, Bhamo, and Nakang.

In China, Fourteenth Air Force sends six P-51 Mustangs to attack shipping at Swatow and Amoy. B-25 Mitchells attack targets of opportunity from Katha to Bhamo along the Irrawaddy River in support of Chinese ground forces.

**ETO:** During the night three B-17s and five B-24s drop leaflets over Germany, France, and the Netherlands.

Ninth Air Force sends P-47 and P-38 fighters of the XII Tactical Air Command to provide support to the Seventh Army near Metz.

**MEDITERRANEAN:** The 885th Bombardment Squadron (Heavy) deploys from Algeria to Brindisi, Italy, with B-17s and B-24 Liberators. This squadron supports partisans and drops leaflets in the Mediterranean theater of operations.

**ITALY:** The JCS agrees to a British proposal to limited actions in the Adriatic to supporting Yugoslav partisans. British planners are unable to provide any suitable recommendation to move forces into Yugoslavia to meet Prime Minister Winston Churchill's timetable. Instead, the focus of action in the Mediterranean will continue to be on German forces in Italy, with Bologna as the objective of Allied offensive operations. The intent is to hold down as many German divisions as possible so that the Germans cannot reinforce against General Eisenhower's offensive, which the Allies believe will be the final drive into Germany that will end the war in Europe.

Twelfth Air Force B-25 Mitchells and B-26 Marauders attack bridges. A-20 Havocs and P-47 Thunderbolts of the XXII Tactical Air Command attack German positions, bridges, and roads in the Po Valley.

**SOUTHWEST PACIFIC AREA:** The 96th Infantry Division captures Catamon Hill on Leyte, clearing pillboxes, bunkers, caves, and trenches.

U.S. submarine *Guitarro* attacks a Japanese convoy and sinks two cargo ships off Luzon.

**PACIFIC:** U.S. submarine *Gabilan* torpedoes and sinks a Japanese oceanographic research vessel off Shikoku, Japan. U.S. submarine *Sterlet* torpedoes and sinks the merchant tanker damaged by USS *Salmon* and USS *Trigger* the previous day.

**CENTRAL PACIFIC:** During the night Seventh Air Force sends a B-24 from Saipan on a snooper mission to bomb Iwo Jima.

**NEW GUINEA:** FEAF P-38 Lightnings and A-20 Havocs attack airfields in northwestern New Guinea. P-47 Thunderbolts and A-20s attack targets on Celebes Island. B-25 Mitchells and P-40s attack targets in the Molucca Islands.

## November 1

**ALEUTIANS:** One Eleventh Air Force B-24 on an armed weather mission bombs Otomari Cape in the Kurile Islands.

**CBI:** Tenth Air Force P-47 Thunderbolts and B-25 Mitchells destroy bridges and rail lines and attack Japanese defenses near Bhamo.

In China, Fourteenth Air Force sends about 70 P-51 Mustangs and P-40s to support Chinese ground forces near Lungling.

**ETO:** The weather in western Europe turns bad, beginning a period of almost daily rain and cold temperatures, which only adds to the misery of Allied fighting forces attacking into the teeth of well-prepared German defenses in a bitter war of attrition.

Eighth Air Force sends more than 300 B-17s and B-24 Liberators, escorted by over 280 P-51 Mustangs and P-47 Thunderbolts, to attack the Hamm marshaling yard, oil production plants near Gelsenkirchen, a marshaling yard at Koblenz, and a bridge at Rudesheim. A total of 56 bombers are damaged. Aircrew casualties are one killed. Fighter pilots report two confirmed kills. Two P-51 fighters are lost, and the pilots are reported missing.

Ninth Air Force sends P-47 and P-38 fighters to attack bridges, roads, and rail lines.

**MEDITERRANEAN:** Fifteenth Air Force sends more than 300 B-17s and B-24 Liberators escorted by P-38 Lightnings and P-51 Mustangs to attack industrial targets and marshaling yards near Vienna.

**ITALY:** Twelfth Air Force A-20 Havocs and P-47 Thunderbolts attack rail lines and bridges, roads and rail cars, in the Po Valley.

**SOUTHWEST PACIFIC AREA:** The 19th and 34th Infantry Regiments of the 24th Infantry Division, after a seven-day-long advance through the Leyte Valley with tanks and supported by three artillery battalions, approach the north coast and their objective, the port of Carigara.

The Japanese reinforce Leyte with 13,000 men from parts of three divisions.

FEAF B-24 Liberators bomb airfields on Cebu Island, Alicante on Negros Island, and a logistics bases at Del Monte on Mindanao Island. P-38 Lightnings follow up the attacks on the airfields. The P-38s destroy about 75 Japanese fighters on the ground and destroy seven more in the air. Three P-38s are lost to antiaircraft fire, but one pilot is able to crash-land his fighter on Leyte. P-47 Thunderbolts attack shipping and coastal targets during a sweep over the Sulu Archipelago.

Kamikazes sink a destroyer and damage three other destroyers in Leyte Gulf. Two other destroyers are damaged by aircraft bombs. U.S. submarine *Atule* attacks a Japanese convoy and sinks a transport in Luzon Strait. U.S. submarine *Blackfin* attacks a Japanese convoy and sinks an auxiliary vessel and transport in Mindoro Strait. U.S. submarine *Ray* torpedoes and sinks a Japanese merchant tanker, then lands personnel and supplies on the west coast of Mindoro.

**CENTRAL PACIFIC:** Seventh Air Force sends eight B-24 Liberators from Guam Island to bomb shipping near Iwo Jima. During the night one B-24 from Saipan on a snooper mission bombs Iwo Jima.

**NEW GUINEA:** FEAF A-20 Havocs and B-25 Mitchells bomb Babo airfield. P-38 Lightnings and B-25s bomb Namlea airfield on Buru Island in the Moluccas.

The B-24s of 394th Bombardment Squadron (Heavy), 5th Bombardment Group (Heavy), redeploy from Noemfoor to Morotai Island.

## November 2

**ALEUTIANS:** Eleventh Air Force sends four B-24 Liberators to bomb Paramushiru and Onnekotan Island in the Kuriles. Four B-25 Mitchells on a photo reconnaissance and offensive sweep bomb targets on Torishima Island. Aircrews report 15 buildings on fire.

**CBI:** Tenth Air Force redeploys its headquarters from New Delhi, India, to Myitkyina.

P-47 Thunderbolts bomb bridges, logistics bases, airfields, and support Chinese and British ground forces. B-25 Mitchells destroy two bridges.

In China, Fourteenth Air Force sends more than 100 P-40s, P-51 Mustangs, and P-38 Lightnings over southern China to attack bridges and industrial facilities, as well as tanks and troop concentrations. Fighters also attack the airfield and rail targets at Gia Lam in French Indochina.

The B-25 Mitchells of the 11th Bombardment Squadron (Medium), 341st Bombardment Group (Medium), redeploy from Yang Tong to Yangkai.

German submarine *U-181* torpedoes and sinks a U.S. tanker in the southern Indian Ocean.

**ETO:** General Omar Bradley gives Lieutenant General Hodges's First Army the task of attacking toward Cologne to establish a bridgehead over the Rhine River, in accordance with Eisenhower's plan laid out on October 28. First Army, in turn, gives Major General Collins's VII Corps the task of making the main attack. However, Hodges requires the Hürtgen Forest to be cleared out to protect the VII Corps flank. The V Corps, commanded by Major General Leonard T. Gerow, is ordered to clear Hürtgen. The VII Corps offensive is intended to begin on November 5, but poor weather prevents air support and the attack is delayed. The battle for Hürtgen Forest begins with an advance by the 28th Infantry Division to capture the town of Schmidt. The division attack stalls before minefields and German fortifications. No gains are made.

Eighth Air Force sends more than 900 B-17s using radar-equipped Pathfinder bombers to mark targets, escorted by nearly 700 P-38 Lightnings, P-51 Mustangs, and P-47 Thunderbolts, to attack synthetic oil installations at Merseburg in central Germany. The bombers encounter over 500 German fighters. Aircrews report 36 confirmed kills and 35 probables. A total of 29 B-17s are lost and 545 are damaged. Aircrew casualties are three killed, 24 wounded, and 370 missing. Fighter pilots report 102 confirmed kills and five probables in the air and 25 confirmed kills on the ground. Fourteen fighters are lost. Five pilots are reported missing.

Nearly 350 B-24 Liberators escorted by 183 P-47s are sent to bomb rail targets at Bielefeld and oil production facilities in Germany. One B-24 is lost and 40 are damaged. Aircrew casualties are one killed, two wounded, and 10 missing. Two P-47s are lost, and the pilots are reported missing.

During the night three B-17s and five B-24s drop leaflets over Germany and the Netherlands.

Ninth Air Force sends 147 B-26 Marauders of the 9th Bombardment Division to attack rail bridges at Mayen, Euskirchen, and Trier. P-47 fighters attack bridges and provide support for ground forces.

First Lieutenant Cecil H. Bolton is the weapons platoon leader of E Company, 413th Infantry Regiment, 104th Infantry Division, covering his company as it crosses the Mark River, Holland, during the night. German machine-gun and mortar fire catches many of the men in midstream. Lieutenant Bolton responds with machine-gun and mortar fire but is unable to locate the German positions. Although wounded badly in the legs by an artillery explosion, Lieutenant Bolton wades into the river to locate the enemy positions, taking a bazooka team with him. Spotting one machine gun in a building, he charges the house and eliminates the position with hand grenades. Taking the bazooka team forward, Bolton eliminates a sniper, then attacks a second German machine-gun position, firing his carbine as the team provides support. Bolton then leads the group forward to an 88 millimeter gun and directs the team in knocking out the gun with bazooka fire. As they return to friendly lines, Bolton is wounded again and unable to walk. He orders the team to abandon him and get away safely, then crawls back to his own lines. First Lieutenant Bolton's inspiring leadership and exceptional heroism will be worthy enough to earn the Medal of Honor.

Second Lieutenant Robert E. Femoyer is the navigator in a B-17 of the 711th Bomber Squadron, 447th Bomber Group, Eighth Air Force, over Merseburg, Germany, when antiaircraft shells damage the aircraft and fragments wound Femoyer. Refusing treatment, he works to bring the bomber back safely. Unable to stand, he insists on being propped up so that he can read the navigation charts. For nearly three hours, Femoyer provides information to return to the airfield without further damage. He dies shortly after being carried from the bomber. For his heroism and self-sacrifice Second Lieutenant Femoyer will receive the Medal of Honor.

**MEDITERRANEAN:** Fifteenth Air Force sends B-17s to bomb an oil refinery and airfield near Klagenfurt, Austria.

**SOUTHWEST PACIFIC AREA:** The 34th Infantry Regiment of the 24th Infantry Division blocks the southern and western approaches to the port of Carigara. The 2nd Cavalry Brigade attacks the city from the east, having advanced against light opposition along the San Juanico Strait. The 24th Infantry Division reports at least 3,000 Japanese killed in clearing the Leyte Valley.

FEAF B-24 Liberators attack a Japanese convoy near Ormoc Bay on Leyte Island. Aircrews report one transport sunk and another damaged. P-38 Lightnings also attack shipping in Ormoc Bay and attack targets on Mindanao Island. B-25 Mitchells bomb airfields on Mindanao.

Japanese aircraft attack airfields at Tacloban, on Leyte.

Thirteenth Air Force B-24 Liberators and P-38 Lightnings attack a convoy unloading reinforcements at Ormoc Bay. One cargo ship is sunk.

U.S. submarine *Pomfret* attacks a Japanese convoy between Formosa and Luzon, sinking a transport and damaging another.

**PACIFIC:** Twentieth Air Force sends 17 B-29 Superfortresses from the Marianas to bomb the submarine pens on Dublon Island at Truk.

**CENTRAL PACIFIC:** Seventh Air Force sends 11 B-24 Liberators from Saipan to bomb Chichi Jima Island.

**NEW GUINEA:** During the night FEAF B-24 Liberators bomb the wharves at Makassar on Celebes Island.

The P-38 Lightnings of the 432nd Fighter Squadron, 475th Fighter Group, redeploy from Biak to Dulag on Leyte Island.

U.S. submarine *Barbero* torpedoes and sinks a Japanese cargo ship in Makassar Strait.

## November 3

**CBI:** Chinese Y Force (also known as the Chinese Expeditionary Force) units capture Lungling, supported by Fourteenth Air Force P-40s, P-51 Mustangs, and P-38 Lightnings.

Tenth Air Force sends 12 B-25 Mitchells, supported by 18 P-47 Thunderbolts, to attack the airfield at Nawnghkio.

**ETO:** In the First Army area the 112th Infantry Regiment of the 28th Infantry Division captures Schmidt in the Hürtgen Forest.

Ninth Air Force sends more than 140 B-26 Marauders and A-20 Havocs to attack a rail overpass at Kaiserslautern and rail bridges. P-47 fighters fly armed reconnaissance, support ground forces, and attack rail lines and bridges.

Senior German generals are briefed on a plan for a winter offensive against the British and Americans. This is a product of Hitler's personal inspiration and is intended initially to break through the lightly defended Ardennes Forest area and reach the Meuse near Liège and Namur, where the logistics support area for the 12th Army Group is located. From there, German forces will push to Antwerp, splitting

British and American forces and occupying the major supply port of the Allies. Three German armies are allocated for this offensive. The attack is intended to take advantage of the bad weather and heavy forest cover to minimize exposure to Allied aircraft. Hitler's generals oppose the plan as far beyond the current capabilities of the forces and seek more reasonable and limited objectives. Hitler dreams of the heady days of 1940, believing he can recreate the master stroke that gave the German army a rapid victory over France and Britain.

**MEDITERRANEAN:** A U.S. destroyer bombards German troop concentrations near French-Italian border.

**ITALY:** Fifteenth Air Force sends 46 B-17s and B-24 Liberators without escort to bomb targets in Austria and Germany. Using cloud cover for protection, the bombers make individual attacks on an ordnance depot and an oil refinery near Vienna, the aircraft production facility at Klagenfurt, Austria, the rail lines near Graz, Austria, and then proceed to bomb the marshaling yard in Munich.

**SOUTHWEST PACIFIC AREA, LEYTE:** Lieutenant General Walter Krueger issues orders to the Sixth Army for the final phase of the Leyte operation. The Ormoc Valley is to be cleared of Japanese forces by a double envelopment. The X Corps moves south into the valley along Highway 2. The XXIV Corps attacks north into the valley from Baybay to Ormoc City, then advances another 12 miles to link with X Corps. The 34th Infantry Regiment of the 24th Infantry Division leads the division out from Carigara to clear the northern coast of Leyte and attack south. The regiment clears enemy positions and occupies Pinamopoan, but heavy rains have washed out the road into the mountains.

FEAF B-25 Mitchells bomb Alicante airfield on Negros Island and P-40s attack a highway and oil storage depot on Leyte Island.

Japanese aircraft attack U.S. shipping and the airfield at Tacloban, Leyte. A kamikaze hits a U.S. freighter carrying troops. Japanese submarine *I-41* torpedoes and damages a light cruiser off Leyte. U.S. submarine *Cero* lands personnel and supplies on the east coast of Luzon. U.S. submarine *Pintado* attacks a small detachment of Japanese warships, sinking a destroyer west of Lingayen Gulf. U.S. submarine *Pomfret* torpedoes and sinks a Japanese cargo ship north of Luzon.

Sergeant Charles E. Mower of A Company, 34th Infantry Regiment, 24th Infantry Division, is an assistant squad leader attacking a strongly defended Japanese position near Capoocan. When the squad leader is killed, Sergeant Mower takes command and leads his men across a stream. During the crossing, Mower is seriously wounded. Ordering the squad to halt and take cover, Mower stands half-submerged in the stream and begins to engage Japanese machine guns and riflemen. As his squad responds by destroying several enemy positions, Mower is killed by Japanese fire while encouraging his men. His courage and determination in the face of certain death and his willingness to make the ultimate sacrifice for his soldiers will win him the Medal of Honor.

**PACIFIC:** Twentieth Air Force sends 49 B-29 Superfortresses from Calcutta, India, to bomb the Malagon railroad yards in Burma.

**CENTRAL PACIFIC:** Seventh Air Force sends 14 B-24 Liberators from Guam to attack shipping at Chichi Jima and Haha Jima Islands.

Japanese aircraft attack airfields on Saipan and Tinian.

**New Guinea:** FEAF A-20 Havocs and B-25 Mitchells bomb Babo airfield and during the night attack targets on Celebes Island and on Halmahera Island, in the Moluccas.

U.S. submarine *Gurnard* attacks a Japanese convoy in the South China Sea and sinks a cargo ship west of Brunei.

## November 4

**Aleutians:** Eleventh Air Force sends six B-24 Liberators to attack the Suribachi and Kurabu facilities and the airfield on Paramushiru Island.

**CBI:** Tenth Air Force sends 17 P-47 Thunderbolts to attack the airfield at Shwebo.

In China, Fourteenth Air Force P-40s, P-51 Mustangs, and P-38 Lightnings attack road traffic near Lungling.

**Atlantic:** Field Marshal Sir John Dill dies in Washington, D.C. He is chief of the British Military Mission in Washington and a member of the Combined Chiefs of Staff, representing the British Chiefs of Staff officially and Prime Minister Churchill unofficially. His close friendship with Chief of Staff George C. Marshall (USA) has been instrumental in smoothing over American and British divergence over strategic issues from 1942 to 1944.

**ETO:** In the Hürtgen Forest, German tanks and infantry drive the 28th Infantry Division back from Schmidt and advance to Kommerscheidt before being stopped.

Eighth Air Force sends more than 770 B-17s and over 340 B-24 Liberators, escorted by over 700 P-51 Mustangs and P-47 Thunderbolts, to attack oil production facilities marshaling yards, and aircraft production facilities in northern Germany. Five bombers are lost and 192 are damaged. Aircrew casualties are one wounded and 46 missing. Three fighters are lost and one is damaged. Three pilots are reported missing.

During the night three B-17s and six B-24s drop leaflets over Germany, France, and the Netherlands.

Ninth Air Force sends 218 B-26 Marauders and A-20 Havocs of the 9th Bombardment Division to attack the Trier ordnance depot and gun positions. P-47 fighters escort the bombers, attack railroads and bridges, and provide support to XIX Corps near Aachen.

**Mediterranean:** Fifteenth Air Force sends more than 700 B-17s and B-24 Liberators escorted by P-38 Lightnings and P-51 Mustangs to attack oil storage areas at Regensburg, the Linz, Austria marshaling yard and benzol plant, the marshaling yards at Munich and Augsburg in Germany, and troop assembly areas in Yugoslavia.

**Italy:** Twelfth Air Force sends more than 200 B-25 Mitchells and B-26 Marauders of the 42nd Bombardment Wing (Medium) to attack railway and road bridges in the Brenner Pass. Over 130 B-25 Mitchells of the 57th Bombardment Wing attack bridges in the Po Valley. A-20 Havocs and P-47 Thunderbolts of the XXII Tactical Air Command attack transportation targets in the Po Valley and German defensive positions south of Bologna.

**Southwest Pacific Area:** In the Philippines FEAF B-24 Liberators bomb Alicante airfield on Negros Island.

U.S. submarines *Bream, Guitarro,* and *Ray* attack a Japanese convoy off western Luzon, sinking a transport. USS *Guitarro* torpedoes a landing ship. U.S. submarine *Sailfish* torpedoes and damages a Japanese destroyer and a landing ship in Luzon Strait.

**CENTRAL PACIFIC:** Seventh Air Force sends 18 B-24 Liberators from Saipan to bomb Iwo Jima.

## November 5

**ALEUTIANS:** Eleventh Air Force B-25 Mitchells fly armed reconnaissance over Shimushu Island and bomb Torishima Island. Four Japanese fighters intercept the four B-25s. Aircrews report one confirmed kill. Three B-24 Liberators bomb Katalka naval base on Shimushu Island. Aircrews report fire damage to buildings and one Japanese fighter shot down of seven that attack the formation.

**CBI:** Tenth Air Force sends 70 P-47 Thunderbolts to attack Lashio airfield and attack Japanese targets on the Burma Road.

**ETO:** The XX Corps establishes bridgeheads over the Saar River at Merzig and Saarlauten.

In the Hürtgen Forest the 109th and 110th Infantry Regiments hold against fierce German counterattacks.

Eighth Air Force sends more than 800 B-17s and 300 B-24 Liberators using H2X radar to spot targets, escorted by over 600 P-47 Thunderbolts and P-51 Mustangs, and attack marshaling yards in western Germany. A total of 12 bombers are lost and 457 are damaged. Aircrew casualties are eight killed, 16 wounded, and over 100 missing. Five fighters are lost and the pilots are reported missing.

During the night three B-17s and seven B-24s drop leaflets over Germany, France, and the Netherlands.

Ninth Air Force sends 160 B-26 Marauders and A-20 Havocs to attack ammunition, ordnance, and logistics bases at Hamburg, Germany. P-47 fighters escort the bombers, attack railroads and bridges, and support V and XIX Corps. P-47s support the 28th Infantry Division in stopping a German counterattack near Kommerscheidt.

**MEDITERRANEAN:** Fifteenth Air Force sends more than 500 B-17s and B-24 Liberators escorted by 139 P-38 Lightnings and 198 P-51 Mustangs to attack the oil refinery near Vienna, Austria. Over 40 B-24 Liberators with fighter escort bomb troop assembly areas in Yugoslavia.

**ITALY:** Twelfth Air Force B-25 Mitchells and B-26 Marauders attack rail and road bridges in the Brenner Pass. A-20 Havocs and P-47 Thunderbolts attack transportation targets in the Po Valley and German defensive positions south of Bologna.

**SOUTHWEST PACIFIC AREA:** In the Philippines FEAF B-24 Liberators and P-40s attack airfields and barges.

The Third Fleet carrier USS *Lexington* is hit by a kamikaze attack east of Luzon.

Vice Admiral John S. McCain, commander of Task Force 38, launches attacks on aircraft, airfields, and shipping on Luzon. Naval Task Group 38.3 attacks warships and auxiliaries in Manila Bay. Carrier aircraft from carriers USS *Lexington* and USS *Essex* and small carrier USS *Langley* sink a heavy cruiser near Corregidor. F4F Hellcats from TG 38.3 sink a patrol boat in Manila Bay. Carrier aircraft from TG 38.1 and 38.3 damage a destroyer, an escort destroyer, a landing ship, and two cargo ships.

**PACIFIC:** Twentieth Air Force sends 53 B-29 Superfortresses from Calcutta, India, to bomb the Singapore naval base in Malaya. Aircrews report heavy destruction to the drydock and a Japanese fleet tanker is damaged. Other B-29s bomb the Pangkalan-brandan refinery on Sumatra.

Another 24 B-29s from the Marianas bomb two airfields on Iwo Jima Island.

**CENTRAL PACIFIC:** Seventh Air Force B-24 Liberators from Guam attack Japanese shipping in the Bonin Islands.

**NEW GUINEA:** FEAF B-25 Mitchells, P-40s, and P-47 Thunderbolts bomb airfields, troop concentrations, and communications targets throughout Halmahera Island. P-40s, P-47s, and A-20 Havocs attack targets on Ceram Island. Almost 50 A-20 Havocs attack Japanese positions at Sarmi.

Ground support elements of the 35th and 36th Fighter Squadrons (P-38 Lightnings) of the 8th Fighter Group redeploy from Morotai Island to Dulag on Leyte Island in the Philippines. The fighters temporarily remain at Morotai.

## November 6

**ALEUTIANS:** Eleventh Air Force sends four B-25 Mitchells to bomb Torishima Island in the Kuriles and are attacked by about 20 Japanese fighters. Aircrews report three confirmed kills and hits on shipping and barges and damage to buildings. One bomber is lost.

**CBI:** Tenth Air Force is assigned to support the India-Burma theater. P-47 Thunderbolts fly combat patrols south of Myitkyina, and eight B-25 Mitchells bomb logistics support sites.

In China, Japanese forces advancing from Canton capture Nanning. Fourteenth Air Force P-40s attack Japanese positions near Mangshih and Lungling.

**ETO:** Major General Leonard T. Gerow, the V Corps commander, orders the 12th Infantry Regiment of the 4th Infantry Division to relieve the 28th Infantry Division and continue the attack toward the town of Hürtgen. The 12th Infantry is outflanked as it tries to advance, and several infantry companies are surrounded in the woods. The regiment will fight for survival for another eight days and will suffer 1,600 casualties.

Eighth Air Force sends more than 1,100 B-17s and B-24 Liberators using radar-guided Pathfinder bombers and escorted by over 700 P-51 Mustangs and P-47 Thunderbolts to attack oil refineries, marshaling yards, and aircraft production facilities. Five bombers are lost and 228 are damaged. Aircrew casualties are three killed, two wounded, and 46 missing. Five fighters are lost and one is damaged. Five pilots are reported missing.

Ninth Air Force, IX Tactical Air Command, P-47 Thunderbolts support ground forces battling in the Hürtgen Forest near Schmidt.

**MEDITERRANEAN:** Fifteenth Air Force sends more than 500 B-17s and B-24 Liberators escorted by P-38 Lightnings and P-51 Mustangs to attack an oil refinery and industrial targets near Vienna, Austria, and a marshaling yard in Yugoslavia.

Destroyer USS *Plunkett* bombards German troop concentrations and pillboxes on the French-Italian border.

**Italy:** Twelfth Air Force B-25 Mitchells and B-26 Marauders attack railroad bridges in the Brenner Pass. A-20 Havocs and P-47 Thunderbolts attack German defensive positions south of Bologna.

**Southwest Pacific Area:** In the Philippines FEAF B-24 Liberators bomb airfields on Cebu and Negros Islands. P-38 Lightnings bomb targets on Leyte and Mindanao Islands.

Carrier aircraft from Vice Admiral John S. McCain's Task Force 38 sink a transport off Luzon. Aircraft from carrier USS *Ticonderoga* (TG 38.3) sink a tanker.

West of Lingayen Gulf three U.S. submarines—*Guitarro, Bream,* and *Raton*—each send a torpedo at a Japanese heavy cruiser and damage it.

**Central Pacific:** Seventh Air Force sends B-24 Liberators from Saipan to bomb shipping at Okimura and Higashi-minato and attack Ani Jima Island. During the night B-24s conduct a snooper (radar-assisted bomb release) mission over the airfields of Iwo Jima.

Seventh Air Force B-24 Liberators from Guam, staging through Saipan, lay 10 mines off Chichi Jima.

**New Guinea:** FEAF B-24 Liberators bomb Malili on Celebes Island. The B-25 Mitchells of the 822nd Bombardment Squadron (Medium) of the 38th Bombardment Group (Medium) redeploy from Biak Island to Morotai Island.

U.S. submarine *Gurnard* lays mines off western Borneo.

## November 7

**CBI:** The Chinese 22nd Division occupies Shwegu. The Japanese Imperial High Command orders the army in Burma to hold southern Burma and abandon any attempt to prevent the Allies from reopening the Burma Road. The army will defend a line about 400 miles north of Rangoon, stretching from Akyab to Mandalay and to Lashio.

In Burma, Tenth Air Force P-47 Thunderbolts hit gun positions, logistics sites, and troops at Bhamo, bomb airfields at Kawlin, Shwebo, and Onbauk, and attack railroad targets of opportunity between Indaw and Shwebo.

In China, Fourteenth Air Force B-25 Mitchells bomb the railyards at Yuncheng. P-51 Mustangs, P-40s, and P-38 Lightnings attack troop concentrations, rail lines, bridges, and highways around Mangshih, Chefang, and Lungling.

**Atlantic:** President Franklin Roosevelt wins an unprecedented fourth term in office, defeating the Republican challenger, Thomas E. Dewey.

**ETO:** Ninth Air Force, IX Tactical Air Command, P-47 Thunderbolts and P-38 Lightnings support the 28th Infantry Division as German counterattacks drive the Americans from Kommerscheidt in the Hürtgen Forest.

**Mediterranean:** Fifteenth Air Force sends more than 500 B-17s and B-24 Liberators escorted by P-38 Lightnings and P-51 Mustangs to attack the oil refinery near Vienna, Austria, troop assembly areas in Yugoslavia, and rail lines in the Brenner Pass.

**Italy:** Twelfth Air Force A-20 Havocs and P-47 Thunderbolts attack German defensive positions south of Bologna.

**Southwest Pacific Area:** The 21st Infantry Regiment of the 24th Infantry Division attacks into the mountains along Highway 2, leading the X Corps advance into the Ormoc Valley on Leyte. The Japanese have built a formidable defensive line among steep hills and high ridges, with log bunkers and fighting positions. The Americans are stopped here, a place they begin calling "Breakneck Ridge." The 24th Infantry Division and the Japanese 1st Division, a unit of experienced combat veterans diverted to Leyte from Manchuria, will fight for two weeks here in a series of grim and exhausting battles.

The 96th Infantry Division fights Japanese defending the low hills west of Dagami.

FEAF B-24 Liberators and P-38 Lightnings attack Fabrica, Alicante, and Bacolod airfields on Negros Island and Opon airfield on Cebu Island in the Philippines. The bombers and fighters also attack communications and logistics targets on Leyte and Mindanao Islands. P-38s and B-25 Mitchells bomb targets near Macajalar Bay and Del Monte airfield on Mindanao.

The staffs of General MacArthur and Admiral Nimitz meet to develop a concept of operations for the invasion of Luzon. Amphibious forces will enter Lingayen Gulf, and the Third Fleet in support will operate north of Luzon.

U.S. submarine *Growler* is sunk off Mindoro by Japanese surface ships.

U.S. submarine *Gunnel* attacks a Japanese convoy off the west coast of Luzon and sinks a torpedo boat. U.S. submarine *Hardhead* torpedoes and sinks a Japanese tanker southwest of Manila. U.S. submarine *Redfin* attacks a Japanese convoy in the South China Sea and sinks a merchant tanker.

**PACIFIC:** U.S. submarine *Albacore* is sunk by a mine off northern Honshu, Japan. U.S. submarine *Queenfish* attacks a Japanese convoy off southern Kyushu, and sinks a cargo ship and an auxiliary submarine chaser. U.S. submarine *Greenling* torpedoes and sinks a Japanese transport and merchant tanker off Honshu, Japan.

U.S. submarine *Sea Fox* sinks Japanese cargo ship south of Kyushu, Japan.

**CENTRAL PACIFIC:** Seventh Air Force B-24 Liberators from Guam bomb Iwo Jima.

**NEW GUINEA:** FEAF B-25 Mitchells and P-38 Lightnings bomb Mandai airfield on Celebes Island and attack shipping and airfields at Ceram Island in the Moluccas. B-24 Liberators bomb Raba estate in the Sunda Islands.

The A-20 Havocs of the 89th Bombardment Squadron (Light), 3rd Bombardment Group (Light), redeploy from Hollandia to Dulag on Leyte Island in the Philippines.

## November 8

**CBI:** Tenth Air Force sends eight B-25 Mitchells to bomb the Bawgyo railroad bridge. Aircrews report the target is destroyed. P-47 Thunderbolts attack roads, troop concentrations, and artillery positions.

Fourteenth Air Force B-25 Mitchells, P-40s, and P-51 Mustangs attack town areas, logistics storage facilities, and various targets of opportunity around Mangshih.

**ETO:** The XII Corps of Third Army attacks on a 30-mile front between Nancy and the Saar River. The attack founders in the rain and mud, but gains a bridgehead over the Moselle River. The XX Corps, attempting to envelop Metz, is slowed by rain and mud and a skillful German defense.

The XIII Corps (7th Armored Division and the 84th and 102nd Infantry Divisions) under Major General Alvin C. Gillen is established under Ninth Army. In the First Army area, VII Corps (the 3rd Armored Division and the 104th, 1st, and 4th Infantry Divisions) is to attack east of Aachen to capture bridges over the Roer River near Düren. The V Corps (the 2nd Armored Division and the 29th and 30th Infantry Divisions) is to protect the flank of VII Corps and attack toward the Roer River at Jülich. The area of attack encompasses the Hürtgen Forest, with heavily wooded hills occupied by a low-quality German infantry, but an infantry occupying all of the most advantageous pieces of terrain and well equipped with mortars and machine guns.

In the Hürtgen Forest the 28th Infantry Division has lost 6,184 men in six days of combat to seize Schmidt. The 112th Infantry Regiment alone has lost 1,500 men killed, wounded, or missing, plus another 544 non-battle casualties, ranging from trench foot, to pneumonia, to combat exhaustion. Trench foot is a problem throughout the American infantry units in the cold and wet conditions of Germany in this autumn of 1944. Soldiers do not have adequate protection for their feet and because units are not moved out of the front lines for weeks at a time, there are few opportunities for changing boots and socks. Over time the feet become swollen and discolored, often leading to incapacitation for several weeks. Sometimes, toes must be amputated.

Eighth Air Force sends more than 670 B-17s and B-24 Liberators, escorted by nearly 800 P-51 Mustangs and P-47 Thunderbolts, to attack the Merseburg oil plants and Rhine marshaling yard. Bad weather causes over half of the bombers to abort the mission. Three B-17s are lost and 23 bombers are damaged. Aircrew casualties are one killed and 27 missing. Fighter pilots report two confirmed kills. A total of 11 fighters are lost, and two are damaged. The eleven pilots are reported missing.

During the night five B-17s and 12 B-24s drop leaflets over Germany, France, and the Netherlands. Two bombers abort the mission.

Ninth Air Force, IX Tactical Air Command, P-47s and P-38s support the 28th Infantry Division at Schmidt as V Corps begins a withdrawal. The XIX Tactical Air Command supports Third Army's attacks on the Metz fortifications.

Technician Fifth Grade Alfred L. Wilson is a medic with the 328th Infantry Regiment, 26th Infantry Division, near Bezange la Petite, France, treating casualties suffered during an artillery bombardment. While assisting the wounded, Technician Fifth Grade Wilson himself is wounded. He refuses treatment and continues to provide aid until he is too weak to stand. He then crawls among his comrades, assisting until loss of blood weakens him to the point where he can only give verbal instructions to untrained soldiers assisting him. He continues in this manner until falling unconscious. For his courage and willingness to sacrifice himself to save the lives of 10 of his comrades, Technician Fifth Grade Wilson will receive the Congressional Medal of Honor.

**MEDITERRANEAN:** Fifteenth Air Force sends 34 B-24 Liberators to bomb troop assembly areas in Yugoslavia.

**ITALY:** The 92nd Infantry Division occupies a six-mile front on the left flank of Fifth Army.

Twelfth Air Force B-25 Mitchells and B-26 Marauders attack railroad bridges and rail lines in the Brenner Pass. A-20 Havocs and P-47 Thunderbolts attack German defensive positions south of Bologna and bridges and rail lines near Parma.

**SOUTHWEST PACIFIC AREA:** FEAF B-24 Liberators bomb Alicante airfield on Negros Island in the Philippines.

A typhoon hits the Philippines. Despite the weather, the 21st Infantry Regiment attacks amid falling trees, torrential rains, and mudslides against the Japanese positions on Breakneck Ridge. The 2nd Battalion of the 19th Infantry captures Japanese positions on Hill 1525.

U.S. submarine *Barbero* attacks a Japanese convoy and sinks a merchant tanker west of Manila. U.S. submarine *Haddo* torpedoes and sinks a Japanese fleet tanker in Mindoro Straits.

The Japanese convoy providing reinforcements to Leyte reaches Ormoc Bay, where Thirteenth Air Force B-25 Mitchells and P-38 Lightnings and four motor torpedo boats attack the convoy. Two escort ships are damaged.

**PACIFIC:** Twentieth Air Force sends 17 B-29 Superfortresses from the Marianas to bomb the airfield on Iwo Jima Island, but cloud cover prevents all but six from hitting the target. Japanese aircraft drop phosphorus bombs on the formations, damaging one B-29. One bomber is forced to crash land in the ocean. It is the first combat loss for the XXI Bomber Command.

U.S. submarine *Queenfish* attacks a Japanese convoy in the East China Sea and sinks a gunboat west of Kyushu, Japan.

**CENTRAL PACIFIC:** Seventh Air Force B-24 Liberators from Saipan bomb shipping at Chichi Jima and Haha Jima Islands and lay 10 mines around Chichi Jima.

**NEW GUINEA:** FEAF B-25 Mitchells and P-38 Lightnings bomb the airfield on Celebes Island and targets on Ceram Island. B-25s attack airfields on Halmahera Island. The P-38s of the 12th Fighter Squadron, 18th Fighter Group, begin operating from Morotai Island.

## November 9

**CBI:** In China, Fourteenth Air Force B-25 Mitchells and P-51 Mustangs attack the Kaifeng railyards. P-40s, P-38 Lightnings, and P-51 Mustangs conduct armed reconnaissance over wide expanses of southern China.

**ETO:** The XX Corps crosses the Moselle River near Thionville, but heavy rains and flooding wash away most of the temporary bridges built.

Antwerp, the largest port in Europe, is captured by Canadian forces after a grueling and bitter fight; it will be several weeks before the port is ready to receive cargo.

Eighth Air Force sends more than 1,000 B-17s and B-24 Liberators escorted by over 700 P-51s to attack transportation targets and German strongpoints near Metz. Four B-17s are lost and 122 bombers damaged. Aircrew casualties are 27 killed, six wounded, and 27 missing. Three fighters are damaged.

Another 139 P-47 Thunderbolts and P-51 Mustangs fly fighter-bomber missions in the Frankfurt-Lannheim area. One P-47 and four P-51 Mustangs are lost. The four pilots are reported missing.

During the night five B-17s and 12 B-24s drop leaflets over Germany, France, and the Netherlands.

Ninth Air Force B-26 Marauders of the 9th Bombardment Division attack road junctions, barracks, artillery parks, logistics storage depots, and repair facilities near the French-German border. The IX Tactical Air Command's fighters fly sweeps over Germany and attack the marshaling yard at Düren. The XXIX Tactical Air Command's P-47 Thunderbolts and P-38 Lightnings support Third Army's attack on Metz.

As the "Lady Jeannette," a B-17 of the 729th Bomber Squadron, 452nd Bombardment Group, reaches the marshaling yards at Saarbrücken, Germany, it is heavily damaged by antiaircraft fire. Three of the aircraft's engines are damaged and on fire, and fire breaks out inside the aircraft from severed fuel lines. Second Lieutenant William E. Metzger, the copilot, agrees with the pilot, First Lieutenant Donald A. Gott, that they will first release bombs on target, then attempt to crash-land the bomber inside friendly lines to save the lives of several severely wounded crewmen. Once inside friendly lines, Second Lieutenant Metzger orders the surviving crewmembers to bail out. With only one working engine, Metzger and Gott attempt to land the aircraft. As it approaches a field at 100 feet, the bomber explodes and crashes, killing everyone. Second Lieutenant Metzger and First Lieutenant Gott will receive the Congressional Medal of Honor for their devotion to duty and willingness to risk their lives for the safety of their aircrew

**ITALY:** Twelfth Air Force A-20 Havocs and P-47 Thunderbolts attack road and rail bridges near Bologna.

**SOUTHWEST PACIFIC AREA, LEYTE:** The 1st Brigade of the 1st Cavalry Division captures Mount Cabungaan and Hill 2926 east of Highway 2.

FEAF P-38 Lightnings attack a convoy off Leyte Island and attack barges and shipping near Ormoc. B-24 Liberators bomb Carolina airfield on Negros Island.

**CENTRAL PACIFIC:** Seventh Air Force B-24 Liberators from Guam attack shipping and antiaircraft positions at Haha Jima Island and strafe Iwo Jima on their return to Guam.

During the night a B-24 conducts a snooper (radar-assisted bomb release) mission on Iwo Jima.

**NEW GUINEA:** FEAF B-25 Mitchells attack airfields and villages on Celebes and Halmahera Islands. A-20 Havocs attack targets on Ceram Island.

The P-38s of the 70th Fighter Squadron, 18th Fighter Group, redeploy from Sansapor, New Guinea, to Morotai Island.

The 408th Bombardment Squadron (Heavy), 22nd Bombardment Group (Heavy), redeploys its B-24 Liberators to Leyte Island along with the P-38s of the 431st Fighter Squadron, 475th Fighter Group, which redeploy from Biak Island to Dulag on Leyte.

### November 10

**CBI:** Tenth Air Force P-47 Thunderbolts attack Japanese concentrations at Bhamo and Indaw, and targets of opportunity along the Irrawaddy River.

In China, the Japanese capture Kweilin after the Fourteenth Air Force abandons the airfield. Fourteenth Air Force P-40s, P-38 Lightnings, and P-51 Mustangs attack rail facilities, roads, troop concentrations, and artillery positions in south China.

**ETO:** Eighth Air Force sends more than 750 B-17s and B-24 Liberators escorted by over 800 P-47 Thunderbolts and P-51 Mustangs to attack airfields near Hanau, Germany. Four bombers are lost and 236 damaged. Aircrew casualties are three killed, 14 wounded, and 38 missing. Fighter pilots report six confirmed kills. No fighters are lost or damaged.

P-47 Thunderbolts attacking communications targets in Germany report two confirmed kills on the ground.

During the night six B-17s and nine B-24s drop leaflets over Germany and the Netherlands. One bomber aborts the mission.

Ninth Air Force's XXIX Tactical Air Command attacks railroads while the P-47 Thunderbolts and P-38 Lightnings of XIX Tactical Air Command escort bombers and support the 80th and 5th Infantry Divisions in their attack on Metz.

**ITALY:** Twelfth Air Force releases elements of the XII Tactical Air Command, including the 324th Fighter Group (314th, 315th, and 316th Fighter Squadrons, with P-47 Thunderbolts) to the European theater of operations to form the First Tactical Air Force (Provisional).

Twelfth Air Force B-25 Mitchells and B-26 Marauders attack rail and road bridges in the Brenner Pass. A-20 Havocs and P-47 Thunderbolts attack rail targets and guns in the Po Valley.

**SOUTHWEST PACIFIC AREA:** In the Philippine Islands FEAF P-38 Lightnings and B-24 Liberators attack Ormoc on Leyte Island. P-38 Lightnings damage a destroyer and a transport. B-25 Mitchells and navy aircraft attack shipping around Ormoc Bay. Aircrews report two destroyers and three transports sunk and one destroyer damaged.

Thirteenth Air Force B-25 Mitchells, P-38 Lightnings, and P-47s attack the Japanese convoy in Ormoc Bay, sinking two cargo ships and damaging a destroyer, a cargo ship, and a coastal patrol boat.

**PACIFIC:** U.S. submarine *Barb* torpedoes and sinks a Japanese transport off eastern Kyushu, Japan.

U.S. submarine *Greenling* torpedoes and sinks a Japanese patrol boat southeast of Honshu.

U.S. submarine *Steelhead* torpedoes and sinks a Japanese repair ship off Honshu, Japan.

**CENTRAL PACIFIC:** Seventh Air Force sends 27 B-24 Liberators from Saipan to bomb Iwo Jima. Six B-24s from Angaur Island bomb Koror Island in the Palaus.

**NEW GUINEA:** FEAF B-25 Mitchells and A-20 Havocs bomb airfields on Ceram Island.

B-24 Liberators of the 19th and 33rd Bombardment Squadrons (Heavy), 22nd Bombardment Group (Heavy), redeploy from the Schouten Islands to Leyte Island. The 460th Fighter Squadron, 348th Fighter Group, redeploys its P-47 Thunderbolts from Noemfoor Island to Tacloban on Leyte. The B-25 Mitchells of the 500th Bombardment Squadron (Medium), 345th Bombardment Group (Medium), redeploy from Biak Island to Dulag on Leyte.

The 371st, 372nd, and 424th Bombardment Squadrons of the 307th Bombardment Group (Heavy) redeploy their B-24 Liberators from Wakde Island to Morotai Island.

An ammunition ship with 3,000 tons of explosives on board explodes in Seeadler Harbor on Manus, Admiralty Islands. Two escort carriers, a destroyer, four destroyer escorts, and a large number of other ships are damaged by the blast.

U.S. submarine *Flounder* sinks German submarine *U-537* in the Java Sea.

## November 11

**CBI:** Tenth Air Force P-47 Thunderbolts attack Japanese positions near Indaw, attacking bridges, Kawlin airfield, and targets of opportunity along the Irrawaddy River.

Japanese forces capture Liuchow after the Fourteenth Air Force abandons the airfield.

Fourteenth Air Force B-25 Mitchells bomb Kweilin airfield in China. P-40s, P-51 Mustangs, and P-38 Lightnings attack targets at Changsha, Lingling, and Hengyang.

**ETO:** The 82nd Airborne Division, under Montgomery's operational control since Market Garden, returns to First Allied Airborne Army. The division has lost an additional 1,682 men fighting in Holland.

Eighth Air Force sends more than 400 B-17s and B-24 Liberators led by Pathfinder radar-guided bombers and escorted by over 350 P-47 Thunderbolts and P-51 Mustangs to attack oil refineries and marshaling yards in Germany. One B-24 is lost and 73 bombers are damaged. Aircrew casualties are eight killed and 10 missing. One P-51 is lost and the pilot is reported missing.

Ninth Air Force sends 190 B-26 Marauders and A-20 Havocs to attack German strongpoints along the West Wall. Fighters from IX Tactical Air Command attack rail lines, escorting bombers and supporting the 28th Infantry Division in the Hürtgen Forest near Schmidt. The fighters of the XIX Tactical Air Command support the XII and XX Corps at Thionville and Metz.

The headquarters of the 320th Bombardment Group and the B-26 Marauders of the 441st, 442nd, 443rd, and 444th Bombardment Squadrons (Medium) redeploy from Corsica to Longvic airfield at Dijon, France, to become part of the First Tactical Air Force (Provisional).

**MEDITERRANEAN:** Fifteenth Air Force sends more than 200 B-17s and B-24 Liberators escorted by P-38 Lightnings and P-51 Mustangs to attack marshaling yards in Germany and Austria, rail lines in Austria, and railroad bridges and airfields in Italy.

**ITALY:** Twelfth Air Force B-25 Mitchells and B-26 Marauders attack rail and road traffic and bridges. A-20 Havocs and P-47 Thunderbolts support ground forces south of Bologna and attack convoys, bridges, and roads.

**SOUTHWEST PACIFIC AREA:** Frustrated by a lack of adequate air support for Sixth Army, General MacArthur requests U.S. Navy carrier aircraft support.

FEAF B-24 Liberators bomb Dumaguete airfield on Negros Island. P-38 Lightnings attack shipping near Leyte Island and targets of opportunity on Mindanao Island.

Carrier aircraft from Rear Admiral Alfred E. Montgomery's Naval Task Group 38.1 and Naval Task Group 38.4, under command of Rear Admiral Ralph E. Davison, attack a Japanese convoy entering Ormoc Bay. Four destroyers, a minesweeper, and four cargo ships are sunk.

**PACIFIC:** Twentieth Air Force sends eight B-29 Superfortresses of the XXI Bomber Command to bomb the Dublon Island submarine pens located on Truk. The bombers are escorted by P-38 Lightnings.

During the night Rear Admiral Allan E. Smith's Naval Task Group 30.2, with three heavy cruisers and five destroyers, bombards Iwo Jima.

U.S. submarine *Queenfish* torpedoes and damages a transport off Kyushu, Japan. U.S. submarine *Scamp* is sunk off Tokyo Bay.

**CENTRAL PACIFIC:** Seventh Air Force sends 29 B-24 Liberators from Guam escorted by P-38 Lightnings to attack the airfields on Iwo Jima.

**NEW GUINEA:** FEAF B-25 Mitchells, P-38 Lightnings, and P-47 Thunderbolts attack shipping at Halmahera Island and attack the airfield on Buru Island. B-24 Liberators and P-38 Lightnings attack Celebes Island.

## November 12

**ALEUTIANS:** Eleventh Air Force sends two B-24 Liberators to fly an armed reconnaissance mission over Onnekotan and Matsuwa Islands.

**CBI:** Tenth Air Force P-47 Thunderbolts support ground forces near Pinwe and Indaw and attack logistics and communications targets near Kawlin. P-47s and B-25 Mitchells attack targets of opportunity during sweeps of the Irrawaddy River.

Fourteenth Air Force P-51 Mustangs and P-40s attack Hengyang airfield as well as river and road transports, artillery, defensive positions, and logistics storage sites around Hengyang, Lingling, and Kweilin.

B-25 Mitchells bomb railroad bridges near Thanh Hoa, French Indochina. Aircrews report one destroyed and two damaged.

**ETO:** The VI Corps (3rd and 36th Infantry Divisions) under the command of Major General Edward H. Brooks and XV Corps (the U.S. 44th, 100th, and 103rd Infantry Divisions and the French 2nd Armored Division) under Major General Wade H. Haislip attack to split the German First and Nineteenth Armies and break into open territory. The 100th Infantry Division leads the attack and makes rapid progress.

Ninth Air Force, IX and XIX Tactical Air Commands, P-47 Thunderbolts and P-38 Lightnings fly patrols and armed reconnaissance along the French-German border.

Eighth Air Force sets the operational tour of duty for fighter pilots at 270 hours.

Private First Class Foster J. Sayers of L Company, 357th Infantry Regiment, 90th Infantry Division, attacks a German position on a hilltop near Thionville, France. As his company moves across an open area to outflank the position, Private First Class Sayers carries his machine gun uphill to within 20 yards of the enemy and begins engaging the Germans to distract them from the American flanking effort. He succeeds in putting heavy and accurate fire on the enemy but is killed by return fire just as his company sweeps the hill to capture the position. For his extraordinary heroism and dedication to duty Private First Class Sayers will receive the Medal of Honor.

**MEDITERRANEAN:** Fifteenth Air Force sends 107 B-24 Liberators to attack bridges, a viaduct, and an airfield in northern Italy.

Destroyer USS *Woolsey* bombards a German howitzer emplacement east of San Remo, Italy.

**ITALY:** Twelfth Air Force A-20 Havocs and P-47 Thunderbolts attack German positions in the northern Apennines and attack rail targets and convoys in the Po Valley.

**SOUTHWEST PACIFIC AREA:** In the Philippines FEAF B-24 Liberators bomb Alicante airfield on Negros Island. P-38 Lightnings attack barges and shipping off Leyte. B-25 Mitchells bomb Daliao and Matina airfields on Mindanao Island.

Kamikazes damage two landing craft repair ships off Leyte. A U.S. freighter is hit by a kamikaze, killing 133 of the 578 troops on board. Another Kamikaze hitting a freighter close by kills 100 of the 557 troops on board. Another freighter carrying troops is hit, killing 21 troops and wounding 41.

U.S. submarine *Redfin* torpedoes and damages a Japanese ship west of Mindoro.

A Navy PB4Y Privateer patrol bomber attacks a Japanese convoy and sinks a cargo ship near Panay.

**PACIFIC:** Twentieth Air Force sends 29 B-29 Superfortresses from Chengtu, China, to bomb Omura, Japan, on Kyushu Island. Because of bad weather over the primary target, some B-29s bomb targets at Nanking, China.

U.S. submarines *Barb* and *Peto* resume attacks against a Japanese convoy in the East China Sea near the Japanese home islands. USS *Barb* torpedoes and sinks a cargo ship and damages another cargo ship. USS *Peto* sinks a cargo ship.

**CENTRAL PACIFIC:** Seventh Air Force sends 29 B-24 Liberators with P-38s from Saipan to bomb the airfield on Iwo Jima. Other B-24s from Angaur Island bomb Koror Island in the Palaus. Seventh Air Force B-24 Liberators lay mines near Haha Jima.

During the night a B-24 conducts a snooper (radar-assisted bomb release) mission on Iwo Jima.

Destroyer USS *Nicholas* sinks Japanese submarine *I-37* south of Yap.

**NEW GUINEA:** FEAF B-24 Liberators, P-40s, and P-47 Thunderbolts attack shipping and airfields at Celebes and Halmahera Islands.

The headquarters of the 345th Bombardment Group (Medium) and the 498th and 499th Bombardment Squadrons (Medium) redeploy from Biak Island to Leyte. The B-25 Mitchells of the two squadrons continue to operate from Biak.

## November 13

**CBI:** Tenth Air Force sends more than 100 P-47 Thunderbolts to attack bridges, troop assembly areas, and logistics storage sites in northern Burma and targets of opportunity along the Irrawaddy River.

**ETO:** UTAH beach ceases operation as an offloading site for supplies to the Allied armies. The truck convoys of the Red Ball Express cease operation after 11 weeks of continuous, 24-hour rotations between the Normandy beaches and the front lines. This nearly impossible effort, borne of the desperate need to maintain forces in the field, has resulted in the delivery of 334,000 tons of supplies to the armies. Although the effort will become legendary, the Red Ball Express is a highly inefficient and inadequate means of resupply.

The 6th Army Group, commanded by Lieutenant General Jacob L. Devers, makes several successful attacks through the Vosges Mountains. The Seventh Army is organized into the VI Corps (the 3rd, 36th, 100th, and 103rd Infantry Divisions) under

Major General Edward H. Brooks and the XV Corps (the French 2nd Armored Division and the 44th and 79th Infantry Divisions). The XV Corps attacks toward Sarrebourg and Strasbourg. The French First Army attacks through the Belfort gap led by the French I Corps. Heavy snow and rain impede the attack.

During the night Eighth Air Force sends four B-17s and eight B-24s to drop leaflets over Germany, France, and the Netherlands.

Staff Sergeant Junior J. Spurrier of G Company, 134th Infantry Regiment, 35th Infantry Division, is attacking the village of Achain, France. Staff Sergeant Spurrier carries a Browning Automatic Rifle and moves to provide support. Throughout the battle, Staff Sergeant Spurrier maintains a steady fire against the German positions in the village. As his Browning Automatic Rifle runs out of ammunition, he uses an M-1 rifle. When that is empty, he uses antitank weapons, a German automatic pistol, and hand grenades, all in the face of heavy enemy fire. For his stubborn persistence and determination in the face of the enemy, Staff Sergeant Spurrier will receive the Medal of Honor.

**MEDITERRANEAN:** During the night Fifteenth Air Force sends 14 B-17s and B-24 Liberators to bomb the oil refinery at Blechhammer, Germany.

**ITALY:** During the night Twelfth Air Force sends A-20 Havocs to bomb ammunition dumps, a pontoon bridge, and targets of opportunity in the Po Valley.

**SOUTHWEST PACIFIC AREA, LEYTE:** The 24th Infantry Division attempts a double envelopment of the Japanese defensive position on Breakneck Ridge. The 2nd Battalion, 19th Infantry, and the 1st Battalion, 34th Infantry, reach Kilay Ridge behind the Japanese main line of resistance. However, heavy rain and thick jungle slow the attack on the ridge, and the units must withdraw. The battle for Kilay Ridge and Breakneck Ridge will continue for nearly two more weeks.

General MacArthur requests Admiral Nimitz to dispatch the Third Fleet carriers to provide air support to ground forces at Leyte.

The 32nd Infantry Division and the 112th Cavalry Regimental Combat Team arrive as reinforcements on Leyte to support X Corps.

FEAF B-24 Liberators bomb the airfield on Negros Island, while P-38 Lightnings attack shipping and other targets of opportunity, including an airfield on Luzon Island. B-25 Mitchells, with P-38s flying escort, bomb an airfield and the town of Zamboanga on Mindanao.

Carrier aircraft from the three carrier task groups (TG 38.1, TG 38.3, and TG 38.4) of TF 38, under temporary command of Rear Admiral Frederick C. Sherman, attack Japanese shipping and port facilities at Manila and in central Luzon. A light cruiser, four destroyers, a fleet tanker, a guardboat, two auxiliary submarine chasers, and 11 cargo ships are sunk, and a destroyer is damaged.

**PACIFIC:** A minesweeper and frigate sink Japanese submarine *I-12* off the U.S. west coast near Los Angeles, California.

U.S. submarine *Seal* torpedoes and sinks a Japanese cargo ship in the Kuriles.

**CENTRAL PACIFIC:** Seventh Air Force sends seven B-24 Liberators from Angaur to bomb oil storage facilities on Malakal Island and attack a bridge between Malakal and Koror Islands in the Palaus.

**New Guinea:** Two waves of 70 FEAF A-20 Havocs attack Pegun Island off New Guinea. P-40s, P-47 Thunderbolts, and A-20s attack Halmahera Island and Ceram Island.

The P-38 Lightnings of the 433rd Fighter Squadron, 475th Fighter Group, redeploy from Biak Island to Leyte. The 501st Bombardment Squadron (Medium), 345th Bombardment Group (Medium), redeploy from Biak Island to Leyte Island, but the squadron's B-25 Mitchells continue to operate from Biak.

### November 14

**CBI:** Tenth Air Force sends 12 B-25 Mitchells to bomb a logistics storage area near Lashio. P-40s and P-47 Thunderbolts attack targets in support of Allied ground forces near Pinwe.

**ETO:** The French First Army led by General de Lattre de Tassigny opens the Belfort Gap and pushes German forces into the high Vosges Mountains.

**Italy:** Twelfth Air Force sends 17 P-47 Thunderbolts to attack rail lines and roads north of the front lines.

**Southwest Pacific Area:** On Leyte, Sixth Army commander Lieutenant General Walter Krueger passes operational control of the 32nd Infantry Division from Sixth Army reserve to X Corps. The 32nd Infantry Division is to replace the 24th Infantry Division, which is battering its way against the Japanese defenses at Breakneck Ridge. The 1st Cavalry Division, reinforced by the 112th Cavalry, fights in the Mount Badian area, in terrain that is covered with thick-forested hills.

FEAF B-24 Liberators, with P-38 Lightnings and P-47 Thunderbolts providing escort, bomb an airfield on Negros Island. P-38s attack vehicles and buildings on Mindanao and Leyte Islands, and attack shipping near Ormoc on Leyte. B-25 Mitchells and P-38s attack airfields on Cebu Island.

Naval Task Force 38 carrier aircraft sink a transport, a merchant tanker, three cargo ships, and damage a transport and a cargo ship. F4F Hellcats from carrier USS *Yorktown* attack a Japanese convoy and sink a merchant tanker and damage a cargo ship.

U.S. submarines *Batfish, Raton,* and *Ray* attack a Japanese convoy off the northwest coast of Luzon. USS *Raton* damages a supply ship and sinks a merchant tanker. USS *Ray* sinks a coastal patrol ship. U.S. submarine *Spadefish* torpedoes and sinks a Japanese cargo ship previously damaged by USS *Barb* south of Mindoro.

**Pacific:** U.S. submarine *Skipjack* torpedoes and damages a Japanese vessel off Shimushiru, Kuriles.

**Central Pacific:** Seventh Air Force sends 22 B-24 Liberators from Saipan and Guam to bomb Woleai Atoll. Aircrews report damage to the airfield and adjacent installations, and setting fire to an oil storage site.

Seventh Air Force B-24 Liberators lay six mines off Ani Jima and Haha Jima.

**New Guinea:** FEAF B-25 Mitchells bomb Pegun Island, supporting an Allied amphibious landing. B-24 Liberators bomb an airfield on Celebes Island.

The 310th Bombardment Wing (Medium) moves from Morotai Island to Leyte; the ground echelon of the 418th Night Fighter Squadron redeploys to Leyte also. The squadron's P-61 Black Widow night fighters remain on Morotai. The B-24s of the 370th Bombardment Squadron (Heavy), 307th Bombardment Group (Heavy), redeploy from Wakde Island to Morotai Island.

U.S. submarine *Jack* attacks a Japanese convoy, sinking a cargo ship and damaging a merchant tanker off southern Java.

### November 15

**CBI:** Tenth Air Force P-47 Thunderbolts bomb rail lines, an airfield, and targets of opportunity during road sweeps in northern Burma.

U.S. submarine *Barbel* attacks a Japanese convoy in the South China Sea east of French Indochina, sinking two transports.

U.S. submarine *Jack* torpedoes and sinks two transports in the South China Sea off the southern coast of French Indochina.

**ETO:** Field Marshal Montgomery's 21st Army Group advances to the Rhine River, controlling an area from the mouth of the river to a distance of 200 miles south.

As the Allied offensives grind on in the heavy woods before the Rhine River, a total of 30 German tank and infantry divisions are being assembled in secrecy in assembly areas west of Cologne to prepare for a major counteroffensive. The plan is to attack through the weakly held American lines in the Ardennes Forest with tanks followed by infantry to capture Antwerp. The capture of the port will sever Allied supply lines and isolate the 21st Army Group in northern Belgium and Holland. Success of this attack depends on surprise and speed. The concept originates with Hitler who had used the Ardennes as the focal point of the German offensive against French and British forces in 1940. As before, the wooded hills provide cover for movement, and the attack launched in bad winter weather will neutralize Allied air power.

During the night six B-17s and six B-24s drop leaflets over Germany, France, and the Netherlands.

The headquarters of XII Tactical Air Command, including the 71st Fighter Wing and the 50th, 358th, and 371st Fighter Groups, is assigned to the First Tactical Air Force (Provisional).

Ninth Air Force P-47 Thunderbolts of the XIX Tactical Air Command provide support to ground forces in XX Corps near Trier and Saarbrücken.

**MEDITERRANEAN:** Fifteenth Air Force sends 80 B-17s and B-24 Liberators to attack a benzol plant at Linz and marshaling yard at Innsbruck, Austria. Bombers also attack troop assembly areas in Yugoslavia.

U.S. destroyer escort collides with an Italian submarine *Luigi Settembrini* west of Gibraltar. The submarine is sunk.

**ITALY:** Headquarters Twelfth Air Force transfers operational control of the headquarters of the 63rd Fighter Wing, the 42nd Bombardment Wing (Medium), the 17th and 320th Bombardment Groups (Medium), and 310th Service Group to the European theater of operations, U.S. Army (ETOUSA).

**SOUTHWEST PACIFIC AREA, LEYTE:** The Sixth Army commander, Lieutenant General Walter Krueger, presents his approved concept for the invasion of Luzon to his subordinate commanders. The Sixth Army is to land and secure beachheads at Lingayen and Damortis, seize the central plains and capture the capital city of Manila, then establish bases for further operations against the Japanese empire.

The Sixth Army is organized into two corps, I Corps under command of Major General Innis P. Swift (6th, 43rd, 32nd, and 33rd Infantry Divisions) and XIV Corps under command of Major General Oscar W. Griswold (40th and 37th Infantry Divisions, the 1st Cavalry Division, and 112th Cavalry RCT). The units in reserve are the 6th Ranger Battalion, the 13th Armored Group, the 25th Infantry Division, and the 158th RCT. Naval forces totaling 850 ships are under command of Vice Admiral Thomas C. Kinkaid and divided into three groups: the Luzon Attack Force (Task Group 77) under Vice Admiral Kinkaid, the San Fabian Task Force (Task Group 78) under Admiral Barbey, and the Lingayen Task Force (Task Group 79) under Admiral Wilkinson. Vice Admiral Kinkaid's task group provides naval and air bombardment of the landing beaches. The Sixth Army will land with two corps abreast with four assault divisions (6th, 43rd, 37th, and 40th Infantry Divisions), and the 25th Infantry Division, the 158th RCT, the 13th Armored Group, and the 6th Ranger Battalion in reserve. The landing, designated as S-day is scheduled for January 9. The XIV Corps will make the main effort to Manila, while I Corps holds Japanese forces in northern Luzon near the Caraballo Mountains. The 158th RCT will reinforce I Corps at San Fabian, and the rest of the Sixth Army reserve forces will be ready to land at S+2.

General MacArthur comes to the recognition that the Japanese have decided to commit a large portion of their combat strength to Leyte.

Elements of the 7th Infantry Division have captured Damulaan, north of Baybay.

FEAF B-24 Liberators, with P-38 Lightnings escorting, bomb an airfield on Negros Island and shipping and targets of opportunity at Mindanao. B-25 Mitchells and P-38s attack Cebu Island and shipping off the coast of Leyte. The headquarters of the 22nd and 43rd Bombardment Groups (Heavy) redeploy from Owi, in the Schouten Islands, to Leyte. The 8th Bombardment Squadron (Light), 3rd Bombardment Group (Light), redeploys from Hollandia to Leyte. The 80th Fighter Squadron, 8th Fighter Group, redeploys from Morotai Island to Leyte. The squadron's P-38s continue to operate from Morotai.

**PACIFIC:** U.S. submarine *Queenfish* attacks a Japanese convoy and sinks a cargo ship-aircraft transport at southern entrance of Tsushima Strait.

U.S. submarine *Saury* torpedoes and damages a Japanese guardboat northwest of the Bonins. U.S. submarines *Sterlet* and *Silversides* torpedo and damage a Japanese guardboat south of Honshu, Japan.

**CENTRAL PACIFIC:** Seventh Air Force B-24 Liberators from Guam attack shipping at Haha Jima and near Chichi Jima.

During the night a B-24 conducts a snooper (radar-assisted bomb release) mission on Iwo Jima.

**NEW GUINEA:** FEAF B-25 Mitchells, P-40s, and P-47 Thunderbolts support the Allied amphibious landings in Mapia Islands off the northwest coast of New Guinea. B-24 Liberators bomb targets on Celebes and Halmahera Islands.

### November 16

**CBI:** The headquarters of the 1st Provisional Tank Group arrives at Myitkyina.

In Burma, Tenth Air Force sends P-47 Thunderbolts to attack troop assembly areas and logistics storage sites at Naungmo, Nawngmoloi, and Lashio. Other P-47s provide support to Allied ground forces near Pinwe.

In China, Fourteenth Air Force sends 23 B-24 Liberators to bomb Changsha.

**ETO:** The First and Ninth Armies begin their attack into the Hürtgen Forest toward the Roer River on a 25-mile front and in a cold rain but are supported by a major air attack on German positions at Eschweiler.

The VII Corps leads the attack with the 104th and the 4th Infantry Divisions added and reinforced by Combat Command reserve of the 5th Armored Division. The 4th Infantry Division is to attack into the Hürtgen Forest to reach the Roer River at Düren. The 16th Infantry Regiment of the 1st Infantry Division attacks toward Hill 232 in the Hürtgen Forest to gain control of the main road leading to Langerwehe and Düren.

The attack is preceded by Operation Queen, the largest air attack in direct support of ground forces in the war. Eighth Air Force sends more than 1,200 B-17s and B-24 Liberators escorted by over 280 P-51 Mustangs to attack German defenses near Aachen, Langerwehe, Eschweiler, and Düren. The air attack is followed by an artillery barrage of 694 guns firing 52,000 artillery rounds into the German positions.

Operation Queen costs the Eighth Air Force a total of 19 bombers damaged. Aircrew casualties are two killed, three wounded, and six missing. One P-51 is lost and four are damaged. One pilot is reported missing.

Ninth Air Force sends 80 B-26 Marauders of the 9th Bombardment Division against German defenses in the Hürtgen Forest. The P-47 fighters of the XIX Tactical Air Command support the XX Corps around Trier and Saarbrücken. Fighters of the IX and XXIX Tactical Air Commands also support the attacks of First and Ninth Armies.

In the Seventh Army area the French I Corps breaks through the Belfort gap.

**MEDITERRANEAN:** Fifteenth Air Force sends more than 500 B-17s and B-24 Liberators escorted by P-38 Lightnings and P-51 Mustangs to attack the Munich marshaling yard and troop assembly areas in Yugoslavia.

**ITALY:** Twelfth Air Force B-25 Mitchells and B-26 Marauders attack rail lines in the Brenner Pass. A-20 Havocs and P-47 Thunderbolts attack German positions in front of the British Eighth Army.

**SOUTHWEST PACIFIC AREA, LEYTE:** The 24th Infantry Division completes the clearing of Japanese forces off Breakneck Ridge. The division is relieved by the 32nd Infantry Division commanded by Major General William H. Gill.

FEAF B-25 Mitchells, B-24 Liberators, P-38 Lightnings and P-47 Thunderbolts attack airfields, harbors, shipping, and targets of opportunity around Mindanao.

**PACIFIC:** U.S. submarine *Scabbardfish* torpedoes and sinks a Japanese transport near Chichi Jima,.

U.S. submarine *Tambor* torpedoes and sinks a Japanese guardboat off Honshu, Japan.

**CENTRAL PACIFIC:** Seventh Air Force sends 12 B-24 Liberators from Saipan to bomb shipping near Chichi Jima. P-38 Lightnings and P-47 Thunderbolts attack Pagan

Island in the Marianas. It is the first combat mission for these P-38s. During the night a B-24 conducts a snooper (radar-assisted bomb release) mission against shipping.

**NEW GUINEA:** FEAF B-24 Liberators, B-25 Mitchells, P-40s, and P-47 Thunderbolts attack airfields on Celebes and Halmahera Islands.

The headquarters of the 3rd Bombardment Group (Light) and 90th Bombardment Squadron (Light) redeploy from Hollandia to Leyte with A-20 Havocs. The headquarters of the 348th Fighter Group also redeploys to Leyte from Noemfoor Island.

### November 17

**ALEUTIANS:** Eleventh Air Force sends four B-24 Liberators to bomb Suribachi airfield on Paramushiru Island. Two Japanese fighters attack the bombers. One B-24 is damaged and forced to land in the Soviet Union.

**CBI:** In Burma, Tenth Air Force B-25 Mitchells bomb bridges at Lashio. Aircrews report destroying one bridge and damaging others. P-47 Thunderbolts hit troop and vehicle assembly areas, logistics storage sites, and provide support to ground forces.

In China, Fourteenth Air Force B-24 Liberators bomb the Kowloon Docks in Hong Kong. P-40s and P-51 Mustangs attack targets of opportunity around Mangshih and Changsha.

U.S. submarine *Gunnel* attacks a Japanese convoy and sinks a torpedo boat and merchant tanker off the coast of French Indochina.

**ETO:** In the Hürtgen Forest, the 8th and 22nd Infantry Regiments of the 4th Infantry Division attack northwest of the town of Hürtgen.

The XX Corps extends its lines around Metz after heavy fighting in very difficult weather conditions.

Ninth Air Force B-26 Marauders support the 104th Infantry Division and the 2nd Armored Division near Aachen and the 4th Infantry Division in the Hürtgen Forest.

First Lieutenant Bernard J. Ray is a platoon leader in F Company, 8th Infantry Regiment, 4th Infantry Division, in the Hürtgen Forest. His company attacks in wet, bitterly cold weather over rough, wooded terrain, encountering minefields and barbed wire covered by machine-gun and rifle fire. As F Company reaches the wire, men begin falling from the heavy enemy fire. First Lieutenant Ray takes demolition charges to blast a path through the wire. As mortar rounds drop closer and closer to his position on the wire, Ray continues to work carefully, fully exposed to enemy fire. He is severely wounded by mortar fire before completing his task. With his last breath, First Lieutenant Ray wires the explosives and sacrifices himself to blast open a gap in the wire. For his acts of courage and supreme sacrifice, First Lieutenant Ray will receive the Medal of Honor.

**MEDITERRANEAN:** Fifteenth Air Force sends more than 600 B-17s and B-24 Liberators escorted by P-38 Lightnings and P-51 Mustangs to attack oil refineries in Germany and Austria and the marshaling yards in Yugoslavia and Hungary.

**ITALY:** Twelfth Air Force B-25 Mitchells and B-26 Marauders attack rail lines and bridges in the Brenner Pass. A-20 Havocs and P-47 Thunderbolts of the XXII Tactical Air Command attack rail lines, rail cars, ammunition and fuel storage sites, and support ground forces.

**SOUTHWEST PACIFIC AREA:** In the Philippines FEAF B-24 Liberators bomb airfields on Luzon and Mindanao Islands.

A kamikaze damages a transport off Leyte. TBM Avengers from escort carrier USS *Anzio* and a destroyer escort sink Japanese submarine *I-26* in the Philippine Sea.

FEAF P-38 Lightnings sink two ships off Samar.

**PACIFIC:** U.S. submarines *Burrfish* and *Ronquil* fight a surface battle with a Japanese guardboat off Honshu, Japan. The guardboat is damaged but scores hits on USS *Burrfish*. U.S. submarine *Picuda* torpedoes and sinks a Japanese landing ship and damages a merchant tanker in the East China Sea. U.S. submarine *Spadefish* torpedoes and sinks a Japanese escort carrier and damages a landing ship in the Yellow Sea. U.S. submarine *Sunfish* torpedoes and damages a Japanese army transport in the Yellow Sea.

**CENTRAL PACIFIC:** Seventh Air Force sends 15 B-24 Liberators from Saipan to attack shipping in the Bonin Islands.

Seventh Air Force B-24 Liberators drop eight mines near Chichi Jima.

A Japanese merchant tanker runs aground near the entrance to Subic Bay.

**NEW GUINEA:** U.S. submarine *Bluegill* is damaged in a depth-charge attack in the Makassar Strait, but remains on patrol.

## November 18

**ALEUTIANS:** Eleventh Air Force sends four B-24 Liberators against shore batteries on Paramushiru Island.

**CBI:** Fourteenth Air Force sends more than 130 P-38 Lightnings, P-51 Mustangs, and P-40s to attack troop concentrations, river transport, rail lines, logistics storage sites, bridges, and highways in a broad sweep over southern China.

U.S. submarine *Pampanito* torpedoes and sinks a Japanese depot ship and merchant cargo ship off Hainan Island.

**ETO:** In the Hürtgen Forest, the 16th Infantry Regiment of the 1st Infantry Division captures Hamich and Hill 232.

The XX Corps of Third Army encircles the fortress city of Metz.

Eighth Air Force sends 47 P-47 Thunderbolts and 355 P-51 Mustangs to conduct sweeps attacking oil storage sites and airfields. The 374 fighters actually involved in the attack are met by 70 German fighters. Fighter pilots report 26 confirmed kills and two probable kills in the air and 69 confirmed kills on the ground. Two P-47s and five P-51s are lost, while two P-51s are damaged. The two pilots are reported missing.

During the night six B-17s and four B-24s drop leaflets over Belgium, France, and the Netherlands.

Ninth Air Force sends more than 300 B-26 Marauders of the 9th Bombardment Division to attack barracks areas, rail bridges, strongpoints in western Germany, and defensive positions in support of ground forces near Aachen.

**MEDITERRANEAN:** Fifteenth Air Force sends more than 600 B-17s and B-24 Liberators escorted by over 300 P-38 Lightnings and P-51 Mustangs to bomb an oil refinery near Vienna, Austria, and airfields in northern Italy.

**ITALY:** Twelfth Air Force B-25 Mitchells and B-26 Marauders attack bridges in northern Italy and southern Yugoslavia. Pilots of the XXII Tactical Air Command report destroying eight locomotives, over 100 rail cars, and about 75 other vehicles.

**SOUTHWEST PACIFIC AREA:** Destroyer escort USS *Lawrence C. Taylor* and TBM Avengers from escort carrier USS *Anzio* sink Japanese submarine *I-41* in the Philippine Sea.

**PACIFIC:** U.S. submarines *Peto, Spadefish,* and *Sunfish* continue attacks on the Japanese convoy in the East China Sea. USS *Peto* sinks two cargo ships. USS *Spadefish* sinks an auxiliary submarine chaser. USS *Sunfish* sinks an army transport.

U.S. submarine *Saury* torpedoes and damages a Japanese cargo ship off southern Honshu, Japan.

**CENTRAL PACIFIC:** Seventh Air Force B-24 Liberators from Saipan and Guam bomb shipping at Chichi Jima and Haha Jima Islands. Seventh Air Force B-24 Liberators lay 12 mines off Haha Jima. B-24s sink an auxiliary sailing vessel off Haha Jima.

**NEW GUINEA:** FEAF B-24 Liberators, with P-38 Lightnings and P-47 Thunderbolts escorting, bomb oil production facilities in Borneo. Other B-24s attack airfields on Celebes, Ceram, and Ambon Islands.

The headquarters of the 58th Fighter Group and the P-47 Thunderbolts of the 310th and 311th Fighter Squadrons redeploy from Noemfoor Island to Leyte.

### November 19

**CBI:** In Burma, Tenth Air Force sends 15 P-47 Thunderbolts to support ground forces at Bhamo and Pinwe.

In China Fourteenth Air Force sends three B-24 Liberators to bomb Samah Bay docks on Hainan Island. P-40s attack troops and river, rail, and road transportation targets near Hankow. Other P-40s, along with P-51 Mustangs and P-38 Lightnings, attack rail facilities, roads, and troop concentrations near Mangshih.

**ETO:** Omaha beach ceases operations as an offloading site for supplies to the Allied armies. The main Allied support bases are now Antwerp, Ghent, Le Havre, Rouen, Cherbourg, and Marseille.

In the Hürtgen Forest, the 26th Infantry Regiment of the 1st Infantry Division attacks toward Langerwehe, but its advance is measured in yards. The 18th Infantry Regiment of the 1st Infantry Division advances past Hill 232.

Ninth Air Force sends more than 450 B-26 Marauders, A-20 Havocs, and A-26 Invaders to bomb storage depots, bridges, road and rail junctions, ordnance depots, and defensive positions along the front lines in Germany. The fighters of the IX, XIX, and XXIX Tactical Air Commands support the VII, XII, XIX, and XX Corps operations near Aachen, the Hürtgen Forest, and Metz.

Soldiers of the 5th Infantry Regiment, 71st Infantry Division, make a cautious entry into a building in Metz, France, November 19, 1944.

Private First Class Francis X. McGraw of H Company, 26th Infantry Regiment, 1st Infantry Division, mans a heavy machine gun near Schevenhutte, Germany, when the Germans make a strong counterattack against his company's defensive position. He employs his weapon to initially halt the attack, then takes his machine gun out of its protected position to bring more accurate fire against the Germans. During the fight, he runs back under fire to retrieve more ammunition for his machine gun. Although wounded, he continues to fight until, finally out of ammunition, he meets the enemy in hand-to-hand combat and is killed. For his extraordinary courage and determination to resist against all odds, Private First Class McGraw will win the Medal of Honor.

**MEDITERRANEAN:** Fifteenth Air Force sends more than 500 B-17s and B-24 Liberators escorted by P-38 Lightnings and P-51 Mustangs to bomb oil refineries and an aircraft production facility in Austria and airfields and marshaling yards in Hungary and Yugoslavia.

**ITALY:** The 366th Separate Infantry Regiment is assigned to Fifth Army.

**SOUTHWEST PACIFIC AREA:** In the Philippines FEAF B-24 Liberators bomb the airfields on Mindanao, Negros, and Leyte Islands. P-47 Thunderbolts attack targets on Mindanao and Leyte.

Carrier aircraft from Naval Task Force 38, commanded by Vice Admiral John S. McCain, attack Japanese shipping off Luzon and airfields. A cargo ship and two escorting submarine chasers are damaged. U.S. submarine *Hake* torpedoes and damages a Japanese light cruiser west of Corregidor. Kamikazes hit three U.S. freighters off Leyte.

**CENTRAL PACIFIC:** Seventh Air Force sends B-24 Liberators from Guam to bomb airfields on Iwo Jima, while 15 other B-24s bomb shipping at Chichi Jima and Haha Jima Islands.

U.S. Destroyer escorts *Conklin* and *McCoy Reynolds* sink Japanese submarine *I-37* west of the Palau Islands.

**NEW GUINEA:** FEAF B-24 Liberators attack targets on Celebes Island. B-25 Mitchells and A-20 Havocs attack airfields and shipping in the Ceram-Ambon-Boeroe Island area.

The headquarters of the 312th Bombardment Group (Light) and the A-20 Havocs of the 386th, 387th, 388th, and 389th Bombardment Squadrons (Light) from Hollandia redeploy to Leyte, along with the B-24s of the 2nd Bombardment Squadron (Heavy), 22nd Bombardment Group (Heavy), and the 403rd Bombardment Squadron (Heavy), 43rd Bombardment Group (Heavy), from the Schouten Islands. The 39th Troop Carrier Squadron of the 317th Troop Carrier Group also redeploys to Leyte from Hollandia.

FEAF B-24 Liberators damage a Japanese transport off Brunei Bay, Borneo.

## November 20

**CBI:** Tenth Air Force P-47 Thunderbolts support ground forces near Pinwe.

Fourteenth Air Force sends eight B-25 Mitchells to attack Japanese barracks at Lashio, Burma.

Fourteenth Air Force B-25 Mitchells sink a Japanese cargo ship in the Yangtze River.

**ETO:** In the Hürtgen Forest, the 8th and 22nd Infantry Regiments are halted by strong German counterattacks near the town of Hürtgen. The regiments have lost 1,500 casualties in about three days.

In the Seventh Army area, the French I Corps reaches the Rhine River and the XV Corps captures Sarrebourg and the Saverne Gap.

Eighth Air Force sends 172 B-17s escorted by over 200 P-47 Thunderbolts and P-51 Mustangs to attack oil production facilities and marshaling yards in Germany. A total of 25 B-17s are damaged.

During the night six B-17s and seven B-24s drop leaflets over Germany, France, and the Netherlands.

Another 310 P-47s and P-51s make fighter-bomber attacks against bridges, rail lines, gun positions, and road traffic in support of ground forces. One P-47 and seven P-51s are lost and one P-51 damaged. The eight pilots are reported missing.

The headquarters of the 17th Bombardment Group (Medium) and the B-26 Marauders of the 34th and 37th Bombardment Squadrons (Medium) redeploy from Corsica to Dijon, France, as part of the First Tactical Air Force (Provisional).

Lieutenant Colonel George L. Mabry, Jr., is commanding the 2nd Battalion, 8th Infantry Regiment, 4th Infantry Division, in the Hürtgen Forest. During an attack his battalion is stopped by minefields and heavy fire. Lieutenant Colonel Mabry moves forward and personally clears a route through the minefield and leads the assault. With the assistance of a few riflemen accompanying him, Mabry clears an obstacle and attacks German defensive positions beyond, capturing three enemy soldiers. Fighting among log bunkers, Mabry takes on a squad of German soldiers in close combat and later captures six more as he leads his battalion to its objective. Lieutenant Colonel Mabry's leadership, courage, and gallantry will win him the Medal of Honor.

**MEDITERRANEAN:** Fifteenth Air Force B-17s and B-24 Liberators bomb industrial targets in Austria, Czechoslovakia, and Yugoslavia.

**SOUTHWEST PACIFIC AREA:** U.S. submarine *Atule* torpedoes and sinks a Japanese minesweeper southwest of Formosa.

U.S. submarine *Gar* lands supplies on the north coast of Mindoro.

**CENTRAL PACIFIC:** A U.S. oiler is sunk by *kaiten* (a manned suicide torpedo) from a Japanese submarine near Ulithi. Japanese aircraft attack three U.S. tankers leaving Ulithi for Eniwetok. One tanker is damaged.

**NEW GUINEA:** FEAF P-38 Lightnings hit targets of opportunity on Celebes Island.

The B-24 Liberators of the 371st Bombardment Squadron (Heavy), 307th Bombardment Group (Heavy), redeploy from Noemfoor Island to Morotai Island. The headquarters of Fifth Air Force redeploys to Leyte along with the A-20 Havocs of the 13th Bombardment Squadron (Light), 3rd Bombardment Group (Light).

### November 21

**ALEUTIANS:** Eleventh Air Force establishes an advance headquarters on Shemya Island. Brigadier General Harry A. Johnson is the deputy commander. A B-24 Liberator airdrops supplies to a stranded B-24 crew forced to land on Kamchatka Island in the Soviet Union on November 17.

**CBI:** Tenth Air Force sends 28 P-47 Thunderbolts to support Allied ground forces in the Pinwe and Bhamo areas.

**ETO:** In the Hürtgen Forest the 121st Infantry Regiment of the 8th Infantry Division attacks toward the town of Hürtgen.

The 44th Infantry Division of VI Corps of the 6th Army Group captures Saarebourg.

Eighth Air Force sends more than 1,200 B-17s and B-24 Liberators using Pathfinder radar-equipped bombers, escorted by over 900 P-51 Mustangs and P-47 Thunderbolts, to attack oil production targets and marshaling yards in Germany. A total of 25 bombers are lost and 574 are damaged. Aircrews report one confirmed kill. Aircrew casualties are 22 killed, 30 wounded, and 283 missing. Fighter pilots report 73 confirmed kills and seven probables in the air and five confirmed kills on the ground. Fifteen fighters are lost, and the pilots are reported missing.

During the night seven B-17s and five B-24s drop leaflets over Germany, France, and the Netherlands.

The B-26 Marauders of the 95th Bombardment Squadron (Medium), 17th Bombardment Group (Medium), redeploy from Corsica to Dijon, France, as part of the First Tactical Air Force (Provisional).

Ninth Air Force B-26 Marauders of the 9th Bombardment Division attack transportation targets and German defenses. P-47 and P-38 fighters escort B-26 Marauders and support the 1st, 8th, and 104th Infantry Divisions fighting in the Hürtgen Forest and the XII and XX Corps in France.

In the Hürtgen Forest, Staff Sergeant John W. Minick of I Company, 121st Infantry Regiment, 8th Infantry Division, volunteers to lead four men to clear barbed wire and locate a path through a minefield to support the battalion's attack. After advancing 300 yards, Minick's group is fired on by a machine gun. Minick orders his men down while he moves to destroy the position, capturing three enemy soldiers. Soon afterward Staff Sergeant Minick comes face to face with about 40 German soldiers. In the short fight he kills 20 and captures 20 more. As the battalion advances, Staff Sergeant Minick again leads the way, assaulting a machine-gun position alone. He is killed when he enters another minefield. For his courage and bravery beyond the call of duty, Staff Sergeant Minick will receive the Medal of Honor.

**MEDITERRANEAN:** Fifteenth Air Force sends more than 25 B-24 Liberators and over 150 P-38 Lightnings to attack troop assembly areas, road and rail traffic, and bridges in Yugoslavia.

**ITALY:** Twelfth Air Force A-20 Havocs attack ammunition storage facilities and P-47 Thunderbolts attack rail lines and bridges and support elements of the Fifth Army south of Bologna.

**SOUTHWEST PACIFIC AREA:** In the Philippines FEAF B-24 Liberators bomb airfields on Mindanao. P-38 Lightnings and P-47 Thunderbolts attack logistics storage areas and troop barges on Leyte.

U.S. submarine *Sealion* attacks a Japanese task force and sinks the battleship *Kongo* and a destroyer near Formosa.

**PACIFIC:** Twentieth Air Force sends 61 B-29 Superfortresses from Chengtu, China, to bomb an aircraft production facility at Omura, Japan, on Kyushu Island. Thirteen B-29s bomb Shanghai, China. Aircrews report 27 Japanese fighters shot down.

Naval Task Force 92, commanded by Rear Admiral John L. McCrea, with two light cruisers and nine destroyers, bombards the Japanese naval air installation on Matsuwa Island in the Kuriles.

U.S. submarine *Flounder* attacks a Japanese convoy in the South China Sea, damaging a cargo ship, which USS *Guavina* sinks shortly thereafter.

U.S. submarine *Scabbardfish* torpedoes and sinks a Japanese ship south of Tokyo.

**CENTRAL PACIFIC:** Seventh Air Force B-24 Liberators from Guam bomb shipping and installations at Chichi Jima and Haha Jima Islands. During the night a B-24 conducts a snooper (radar-assisted bomb release) mission on Iwo Jima.

**NEW GUINEA:** FEAF B-25 Mitchells and B-24 Liberators attack airfields on Celebes Island.

FEAF B-24 Liberators sinks a Japanese ship in Makassar Strait.

## November 22

**CBI:** Tenth Air Force P-47 Thunderbolts support Allied ground forces at Bhamo and Pinwe.

Fourteenth Air Force sends 22 B-24 Liberators to bomb Hankow, while P-51 Mustangs, P-40s, and P-38 Lightnings attack town areas, logistics storage sites, and road and rail traffic in southern China.

**ETO:** In the Hürtgen Forest the 18th Infantry Regiment of the 1st Infantry Division captures Heistern, along the main road to Langerwehe.

The 6th Army Group's First French Army clears the Belfort Gap and reaches the Rhine River. The XX Corps of Third Army occupies Metz, but German troops still hold several forts around the city, including Fort Driant.

The headquarters of the 63rd Fighter Wing redeploys from San Pietro, Italy, to Vittel, France, and the B-26 Marauders of the 432nd Bombardment Squadron (Medium), 17th Bombardment Group (Medium), redeploy from Corsica to Dijon, France, as part of the First Tactical Air Force (Provisional).

**MEDITERRANEAN:** Fifteenth Air Force sends more than 400 B-17s and B-24 Liberators escorted by P-38 Lightnings and P-51 Mustangs to attack marshaling yards at Munich, Germany. Weather prevents nearly half from reaching the primary target. The bombers hit secondary targets, mainly marshaling yards, in Austria and Germany.

**ITALY:** Fifth Army receives the last of its 3,000 replacements. The army is still short 7,000 men.

Twelfth Air Force A-20 Havocs attack rail lines in the Po Valley and P-47 Thunderbolts attack guns, vehicles, and German defensive positions in support of elements of the Fifth Army south of Bologna. Fighters also attack logistics storage areas and pipelines in the rear of German forces.

**SOUTHWEST PACIFIC AREA:** The XXIV Corps takes operational control of the 11th Airborne Division, commanded by Major General Joseph M. Swing, to support its attack north into the Ormoc Valley on Leyte. The 7th Infantry Division has been actively clearing Japanese forces around Burauen, leaving General John R. Hodge with few options. He has only the 32nd Infantry Regiment to employ in the Ormoc Valley and that regiment is locked in an indecisive battle with Japanese forces.

The 11th Airborne Division establishes blocking positions in the mountain passes.

FEAF B-24 Liberators, B-25 Mitchells, P-38 Lightnings, and P-47 Thunderbolts bomb airfields on Negros Island, and bridges, barges, and targets of opportunity on Leyte Island. B-24s also attack an airfield on Mindanao.

U.S. submarine *Besugo* torpedoes and sinks a Japanese landing ship off northern Palawan.

**PACIFIC:** U.S. submarine *Scabbardfish* torpedoes and damages a Japanese escort vessel off Honshu, Japan.

**CENTRAL PACIFIC:** Seventh Air Force sends 22 B-24 Liberators from Saipan, escorted by 22 P-38 Lightnings, to bomb airfields on Moen and Param Islands in the Carolines.

Aircraft from Naval Task Group 38.4 under command of Rear Admiral Ralph E. Davison bomb Japanese airfields on Yap.

**NEW GUINEA:** FEAF B-24 Liberators, P-40s, and P-47 Thunderbolts attack targets on Celebes Island. Other B-24s attack shipping during sweep over Brunei Bay, Borneo.

Japanese aircraft attack the U.S. airfield at Morotai, destroying 15 bombers and damaging 31 other aircraft. The airfields at Morotai have been attacked nearly every day through November. The airfield supports B-24 Liberators and P-47 Thunderbolts of Fifth Air Force.

U.S. submarine *Guavina* torpedoes and sinks a Japanese cargo ship northwest of Borneo.

## November 23

**CBI:** In Burma, Tenth Air Force sends 10 B-25 Mitchells to attack bridges, while P-47 Thunderbolts support ground forces near Pinwe and Bhamo.

Fourteenth Air Force sends 12 B-25 Mitchells to bomb logistics storage sites near Lashio in Burma. B-24 Liberators bomb the Kowloon Docks in Hong Kong.

**ETO:** In the Hürtgen Forest the 8th and 22nd Infantry Regiments of the 4th Infantry Division approach Grosshau.

The French 2nd Armored Division of the French First Army, 6th Army Group, reaches Strasbourg.

Eighth Air Force sends more than 100 B-17s, using radar to assist the timing of bomb release and escorted by more than 70 P-51 Mustangs, to bomb a benzol manufacturing facility and a marshaling yard. One P-51 is lost and one is damaged. The pilot is reported missing.

The headquarters of the 42nd Bombardment Wing (Medium) redeploys from Corsica to Dijon, France, as part of the First Tactical Air Force (Provisional).

German submarine *U-978* torpedoes a U.S. freighter off Barfleur, France.

First Lieutenant Edward A. Silk commands the weapons platoon of E Company, 398th Infantry Regiment, 100th Infantry Division. When his platoon, supporting the battalion attack, encounters a German strongpoint in a farmhouse near St-Pravel, France, First Lieutenant Silk takes action. He runs 100 yards across an open field to reach a low stone wall directly in front of the strongpoint. Firing at the door and windows with his M-1 carbine, he then vaults the wall to charge the farmhouse. Throwing a hand grenade, he destroys a machine-gun position and almost immediately is fired on by a second, hidden machine gun in the woodshed. Without hesitation, Silk charges the position and destroys it with hand grenades. Now out of ammunition, Silk begins throwing rocks through the windows at the Germans inside the farmhouse, ordering them to surrender. Twelve Germans walk out and surrender to the lieutenant. For his exceptional courage and extraordinary act of determination, First Lieutenant Silk will receive the Medal of Honor.

**MEDITERRANEAN:** Fifteenth Air Force sends 81 B-24 Liberators to attack road and rail bridges in Yugoslavia. P-38 Lightnings bomb the marshaling yard and road and rail bridges.

**SOUTHWEST PACIFIC AREA:** On Leyte, the 7th Infantry Division of the XXIV Corps attacks north into the Ormoc Valley and is halted by a strong Japanese counterattack. The 77th Infantry Division is diverted from Guam to land at Leyte and support the 7th Infantry Division attack.

B-24 Liberators bomb an airfield on Mindanao.

A kamikaze damages a U.S. attack transport off Leyte. A U.S. freighter is hit by a torpedo dropped by a Japanese aircraft off Samar Island.

U.S. submarines *Bang* and *Redfish* attack a Japanese convoy in the Formosa Strait. USS *Bang* sinks a cargo ship and a transport. USS *Redfish* sinks a cargo ship.

U.S. submarine *Gar* lands personnel and supplies on the west coast of Luzon.

**PACIFIC:** U.S. submarine *Picuda* attacks a Japanese convoy in Tsushima Strait, sinking two cargo ships.

**CENTRAL PACIFIC:** Seventh Air Force sends 17 B-24 Liberators from Guam to attack shipping at Chichi Jima and Haha Jima Islands.

**NEW GUINEA:** The B-24 Liberators of the 63rd and 64th Bombardment Squadrons (Heavy) of the 43rd Bombardment Group (Heavy) redeploy from the Schouten Islands to Leyte.

### November 24

**CBI:** In Burma, Tenth Air Force P-47 Thunderbolts support ground forces near Pinwe and Bhamo.

Nanning falls to Japanese forces, eliminating nearly all of the Fourteenth and XX Bomber Command airfields in China. The Japanese begin shifting their attacks toward Kunming and Chungking.

Fourteenth Air Force sends B-24 Liberators to bomb warehouses and docks at Hankow, China, and at Haiphong, French Indochina. B-24s also bomb Wanling in Burma.

**ETO:** After three days of attacks against German positions in the Hürtgen Forest, the 121st Infantry Regiment of the 8th Infantry Division begins to come apart. It has lost 600 men to mortar fire, mines, and artillery and has made no gains. Leaders break under the pressure of combat, and soldiers refuse to fight. Colonel Thomas J. Cross takes command of the regiment and prepares to attack the town of Hürtgen again.

The Germans counterattack toward Saarebourg, held by the 44th Infantry Division. Although initially driven back, the division stops the Germans and regains its original positions.

**SOUTHWEST PACIFIC AREA:** On Leyte, the 32nd Infantry Regiment of the 7th Infantry Division counterattacks, supported by tanks and artillery. The 7th Infantry Division is forced to go on the defensive. During the night Japanese troops attack the American artillery, destroying four 105 millimeter guns.

The 32nd Infantry Division captures Limon but makes little progress against strong Japanese defenses.

FEAF B-24 Liberators bomb antiaircraft positions and targets of opportunity around Leyte and Mindanao Islands.

A U.S. submarine chaser and LCI (Landing Craft, Infantry) are damaged by Japanese dive bombers off Leyte.

Thirteenth Air Force P-40s and P-47 Thunderbolts attack ships supporting reinforcement efforts on Leyte. A submarine chaser and three landing ships are sunk.

**PACIFIC:** Twentieth Air Force sends 111 B-29 Superfortresses from the XXI Bomber Command to bomb Tokyo, Japan. Thirty-five B-29s bomb the primary target, the Musashino aircraft plant, and 50 bomb the secondary target, the city and docks. Aircrews report seven enemy fighters shot down. The other bombers either abort en route, or mechanical problems prevent them from dropping bombs. One B-29 is lost off Honshu Island when a Japanese fighter rams it. Another bomber is forced down after running out of fuel.

**CENTRAL PACIFIC:** Seventh Air Force sends two B-24 Liberators from Saipan on a shipping reconnaissance mission; they attack vessels at Haha Jima and Chichi Jima Islands.

**NEW GUINEA:** The B-24 Liberators of the 65th Bombardment Squadron (Heavy), 43rd Bombardment Group (Heavy), redeploy from the Schouten Islands to Leyte.

## November 25

**ALEUTIANS:** Eleventh Air Force sends one B-24 on an armed photo mission and conducts a radar-guided bombing run on Kurabu airfield on Paramushiru Island.

**CBI:** In China, Major General Albert C. Wedemeyer develops a concept that will lead to planning for Operation Alpha, the defense of Kunming in Yunnan Province. Kunming is the terminal for the Hump airlift. Without the airlift, Chinese forces will be unable to stop the Japanese. The plan calls for redeploying Chinese units from the Y Force and Burma to southeastern China. Additional supplies from the Hump airlifts will refit the poor-quality divisions currently defending the area near Kunming, and U.S. advisers will train the units. Wedemeyer's intent is to refit and train 36 Chinese divisions, serving under a single Chinese commander and supported by a Chinese-American staff.

In Burma, Tenth Air Force sends 24 P-47 Thunderbolts to support ground forces near Bhamo, and other P-47s strafe targets of opportunity along the Wuntho-Shwebo rail line.

Fourteenth Air Force sends 12 B-25 Mitchells to bomb storage facilities and village and town areas at Lashio and Wanling in Burma. P-40s, P-51 Mustangs, and P-38 Lightnings attack river and road transportation, rail traffic, troops, buildings, and targets of opportunity in Thailand, Burma, south China, and northern French Indochina.

During the night Fourteenth Air Force B-24 Liberators, conducting a reconnaissance flight over the South China Sea, attack Japanese minesweepers south of Hainan Island,

**ETO:** The 101st Airborne Division, under Montgomery's operational control since Market Garden, returns to the First Allied Airborne Army. The division has suffered an additional 1,912 casualties fighting in Holland.

Seventh Army reports that German resistance in the northern Vosges Mountains has been eliminated.

Eighth Air Force sends more than 1,000 B-17s and B-24 Liberators, escorted by over 900 P-51 Mustangs and P-47 Thunderbolts, to attack the synthetic oil plant at Merseburg and the marshaling yard at Bingen, Germany, using radar to assist the timing of bomb release. Eight B-17s are lost and 244 bombers are damaged. Aircrew casualties are seven killed, six wounded, and 64 missing. Fighter pilots report nine confirmed kills on the ground. Six P-51s are lost and one is damaged. Six pilots are reported missing.

During the night seven B-17s and six B-24s drop leaflets over Germany, France, and the Netherlands.

The 36th Bombardment Squadron (Heavy), VIII Fighter Command, is selected to serve as the screening force to protect Eighth Air Force bombers against German attempts to intercept in-flight communications and as a means of providing early warning and to counter German radar countermeasure efforts.

Ninth Air Force B-26 Marauders of the 9th Bombardment Division attack bridges, roads, and ammunition storage sites in Germany.

**MEDITERRANEAN:** During the night Fifteenth Air Force sends more than 40 B-17s and B-24 Liberators to bomb industrial targets in Austria and the marshaling yards in Munich, Germany.

**ITALY:** General Mark Clark is selected to command Allied ground forces in Italy, now redesignated as the 15th Army Group. General Sir Henry Maitland Wilson takes the place of Sir John Dill as head of the British Military Mission in Washington, D.C. General Dill has died suddenly, forcing changes in the British high command. General Sir Harold R. L. G. Alexander is promoted to field marshal and becomes the Mediterranean theater commander. General Lucian K. Truscott, who had commanded VI Corps in France, takes command of Fifth Army.

Twelfth Air Force P-47 Thunderbolts attack rail lines and bridges.

**SOUTHWEST PACIFIC AREA:** The 511th Parachute Infantry Regiment of the 11th Airborne Division advances west into the mountains from Burauen to link up with the 7th Infantry Division on Leyte. Most of the 7th Infantry Division has assembled on the west coast of Leyte. The 96th Infantry Division, advancing west, encounters entrenched enemy forces.

In the Philippines FEAF P-38 Lightnings and P-47 Thunderbolts attack shipping, airfields, and troop areas around Cebu and Leyte Islands.

Carrier aircraft from Naval Task Groups 38.2 (Rear Admiral Gerald F. Bogan) and 38.3 (Rear Admiral Frederick C. Sherman) attack Japanese shipping off Luzon. Aircraft from carrier USS *Ticonderoga* sink a heavy cruiser. F4F Hellcats, SB2C Helldivers and TBM Avengers from carriers USS *Ticonderoga* and USS *Essex*, along with F4F Hellcats and TBM Avengers from the small carrier USS *Langley*, attack a convoy on the west coast of Luzon and sink a coast defense ship and three landing ships. Aircraft from the carrier USS *Intrepid* sink two fast transports and damage another as well as an escort destroyer. Aircraft from *Essex* and *Langley* sink a cargo ship and damage a cargo ship.

Kamikazes damage carriers USS *Essex*, *Intrepid*, and *Hancock*, and small carrier *Cabot*.

U.S. submarine *Atule* torpedoes and sinks a Japanese cargo ship off Luzon.

U.S. submarine *Hardhead* (SS-365) attacks a Japanese convoy west of Manila and sinks a coastal patrol ship off the Bataan peninsula.

U.S. submarine *Haddo* torpedoes and damages a Japanese escort destroyer off the west coast of Luzon.

U.S. submarine *Pomfret* torpedoes and sinks a Japanese patrol boat and transport in the Luzon Strait.

**CENTRAL PACIFIC:** Seventh Air Force B-24 Liberators from Guam bomb Chichi Jima and Haha Jima.

**NEW GUINEA:** During the night FEAF B-25 Mitchells bomb airfields on Celebes and Halmahera Islands.

Shore battery fire off Halmahera Island sinks a U.S. motor torpedo boat.

U.S. submarine *Cavalla* torpedoes and sinks a Japanese destroyer west of Borneo.

U.S. submarine *Mingo* (SS-261) attacks a Japanese convoy and sinks an army transport in the South China Sea west of Borneo, then survives a depth-charge attack.

## November 26

**CBI:** Tenth Air Force P-47 Thunderbolts provide support to ground forces.

Fourteenth Air Force P-40s, P-51 Mustangs, and P-38 Lightnings attack river, rail, and road traffic at Changsha and Liuchow.

**ETO:** The first ships begin unloading supplies for the Allied armies at the port of Antwerp. General Eisenhower seeks to destroy all German forces west of the Rhine River as an intermediate objective before attempting to cross the river and move into open warfare to encircle the Ruhr.

Eighth Air Force sends more than 1,100 B-17s and B-24 Liberators escorted by over 700 P-51s and P-47 Thunderbolts to attack marshaling yards and oil refineries in western Germany. Over 550 German fighters attack the bombers. A total of 34 bombers are lost and 307 are damaged. Aircrews report 16 confirmed kills and 11 probables. Aircrew casualties are 19 killed, 13 wounded, and 316 missing. Fighter pilots report 112 confirmed kills and two probables. Nine fighters are lost and two are damaged. The nine pilots are reported missing.

During the night eight B-17s and six B-24s drop leaflets over Germany, France, and the Netherlands.

Thirty-six P-51 Mustangs flying a scouting mission over Germany and report five confirmed kills, one probable, and two possibles without any American losses.

Ninth Air Force sends 173 B-26 Marauders and A-20 Havocs to bomb logistics depots and storage areas in Germany. P-47 Thunderbolts and P-38 Lightnings support the 29th Infantry Division and XX and XII Corps.

Private First Class Carl V. Sheridan is a bazooka gunner with K Company, 2nd Battalion, 47th Infantry Regiment, 9th Infantry Division. The company is attacking Frenzenberg Castle in Weisweiler, Germany, but suffers heavy casualties in the approach, leaving only about 35 men able to continue the assault on the castle. At the castle gatehouse, Private First Class Sheridan takes action to eliminate the strongpoint. He advances alone to get a clear shot at the barricaded entrance to the gatehouse, ignoring the rifle fire and exploding grenades, and gets off three shots. As the third rocket destroys the barricade, Private First Class Sheridan pulls out his .45 pistol and leads the attack, shouting, "Come on, let's get them!" As he makes his charge, he is killed by enemy fire. For his extraordinary courage, determination to win victory at all costs, and great skill Private First Class Sheridan will receive the Medal of Honor.

**MEDITERRANEAN:** Fifteenth Air Force sends 39 P-38 Lightnings to fly an offensive sweep over Hungary to attack an airfield as well as road and rail traffic.

**ITALY:** Twelfth Air Force P-47 Thunderbolts support Fifth Army operations south of Bologna and attack rail lines north of the front lines.

**SOUTHWEST PACIFIC AREA:** Japanese transport aircraft land in the surf in the XXIV Corps area. The few survivors carrying demolitions are killed.

FEAF sends more than 40 B-24 Liberators to bomb airfields on Negros, Mindanao, and Cebu Islands. The headquarters of the 22nd Bombardment Group (Heavy) and the B-24 Liberators of the 33rd Bombardment Squadron (Heavy) redeploy from Leyte Island to Angaur Island in the Palaus.

**CENTRAL PACIFIC:** During the night a B-24 on a snooper mission from Guam bombs Iwo Jima. B-24s from Angaur Island bomb Arakabesan Island in the Palaus.

U.S. submarine *Raton* torpedoes and sinks a Japanese ammunition ship north of the Bismarck Archipelago.

**NEW GUINEA:** FEAF B-25 Mitchells, P-40s, and P-38 Lightnings attack targets on Celebes and Halmahera Islands.

U.S. submarine *Pargo* torpedoes and damages a Japanese fleet tanker off Sarawak, Borneo. The submarine is damaged in a depth-charge attack, but remains on patrol.

## November 27

**CBI:** In Burma, Tenth Air Force P-47 Thunderbolts conduct ground support missions near Pinwe.

Fourteenth Air Force sends 17 B-24 Liberators to bomb targets in French Indochina. B-25 Mitchells bomb targets in French Indochina and attack logistics storage areas at Lashio in Burma. A detachment of P-61 Black Widow night fighters from the 426th Night Fighter Squadron begins operating from Hsian, China.

**ETO:** The Seventh Army (12th Armored Division and the 63rd, the 45th, and the 100th Infantry Divisions) of the 6th Army Group attacks north to break the German defenses along the West Wall.

Eighth Air Force sends more than 500 B-17s and B-24 Liberators escorted by over 750 P-51 Mustangs and P-47 Thunderbolts to attack marshaling yards in Germany guided by radar-equipped Pathfinder bombers. A total of 69 bombers are damaged. Aircrew casualties are two wounded. Three fighters are lost, and one is damaged. Three pilots are reported missing.

Four hundred and sixty P-47 Thunderbolts and P-51 Mustangs flying fighter-bomber missions against oil targets in Germany encounter about 750 German fighters. The American fighter pilots report 98 confirmed kills, four probables, and 11 possibles in the air and four confirmed kills and one possible kill on the ground. American losses are two P-47s and 10 P-51s. The pilots are reported missing.

Ninth Air Force P-47 Thunderbolts and P-38 Lightnings support the 104th, 8th, and 1st Infantry Divisions near Hürtgen Forest.

Private Macario Garcia of B Company, 22nd Infantry Regiment, 4th Infantry Division, leads an attack on German positions on a wooded hill near Grosshau, Germany. There is almost no cover for his squad, and the Germans are able to lay down an accurate and heavy volume of fire. Although wounded, Private Garcia continues to fight, crawling forward alone to attack a German position with grenades and rifle fire. He then singlehandedly attacks another position and captures four Germans. After his company has occupied the objective, Private Garcia accepts medical assistance. His heroic action and personal disregard for his own safety will win him the Medal of Honor.

**SOUTHWEST PACIFIC AREA:** On Leyte, after two consecutive nights of attacks near Damulaan, the 7th Infantry Division finally breaks the strength of the Japanese. The Americans count over 500 Japanese dead.

FEAF B-24 Liberators bomb airfields on Negros and Mindanao Islands.

U.S. destroyers bombard Japanese positions at Ormoc Bay on Leyte. Kamikazes sink a U.S. submarine chaser and damage the battleship USS *Colorado* and two light cruisers in Leyte Gulf.

**PACIFIC:** Twentieth Air Force sends 55 B-29 Superfortresses from Calcutta to bomb the Bangsue railroad yards at Bangkok, Thailand. Another 81 Twentieth Air Force B-29s from the Marianas are sent to bomb the Musashino and Nakajima production facilities at Tokyo. The B-29s miss the primary targets and attack the secondary targets in the city and docks, while others attack targets of opportunity. Eleven Japanese aircraft attack Isley Field on Saipan, destroying or damaging several B-29s. Antiaircraft fire and fighters shoot down all but one of the enemy planes.

**CENTRAL PACIFIC:** Seventh Air Force sends 24 B-24 Liberators from Saipan, escorted by 12 P-38 Lightnings, to bomb Iwo Jima. B-24s from Guam conduct a second bombing run. B-24s from Angaur Island bomb an airfield on Mindanao in the Philippines.

Japanese aircraft conduct a raid on the airfield on Saipan and destroy three B-29s and a P-47. Three B-29s, a B-24 Liberator, and a P-47 are damaged.

**CENTRAL PACIFIC, PELELIU:** After nearly a month of fighting in the Umurbrogol Pocket, with the 322nd and 323rd Infantry Regiments using tactics more akin to ancient siege warfare than modern warfare, the Umurbrogol Pocket is eliminated. The Japanese defeat is marked by a few soldiers making an attempt to break through American positions in a night attack. The 81st Infantry Division has lost 542 killed and 2,736 wounded in clearing the Pocket.

Peleliu has cost the Japanese over 10,500 casualties. Only 202 prisoners are captured, and all but 19 of these are Korean laborers and not Japanese soldiers. The last Japanese defenders of Peleliu will not surrender until April 21, 1947, when 26 men emerge from the Umurbrogol tunnels. American casualties for the 1st Marine Division are 6,526 total, with 1,252 killed. The 81st Infantry Division has lost 3,089 men, of which 404 were killed. The total casualty count for the Palau Islands is 9,615 casualties, of which 1,656 are killed. The Palau Islands had been seen in early 1944 as essential to Japan's second line of defense and, lying only 500 miles from Mindanao, were deemed essential objectives for the successful invasion of the Philippines. Now the cost of capturing Peleliu appears far too great for the perceived benefits.

**NEW GUINEA:** FEAF B-25 Mitchells attack the airfields on Buru and Ambon Islands. P-38 Lightnings, P-40s, and P-47 Thunderbolts attack airfields, shipping, and targets of opportunity on Celebes, Halmahera, and Ceram Islands.

## November 28

**CBI:** Tenth Air Force P-47 Thunderbolts support ground forces near Pinwe and Bhamo. The headquarters of the 4th Combat Cargo Group and the 13th Combat Cargo Squadron arrive in India from the United States with C-46 Commandos, a twin-engine heavy-lift cargo aircraft.

**ETO:** Antwerp begins functioning as the main supply base for Allied forces.

Supported by tanks and artillery from Combat Command Reserve of the 5th Armored Division, the 121st Infantry Regiment of the 8th Infantry Division captures the town of Hürtgen and 200 prisoners. The 16th and 18th Infantry Regiments of the 1st Infantry Division capture Langerwehe, opening the road to Düren.

During the night six B-17s and six B-24 Liberators drop leaflets on the Netherlands and Germany. The 845th Bombardment Squadron (Heavy) of the 489th Bombardment Group (Heavy) departs England for the United States. The squadron has been earmarked to transition to B-29 Superfortresses in 1945.

Ninth Air Force P-47 Thunderbolts and P-38 Lightnings support the 1st, 104th, and 8th Infantry Divisions in the Hürtgen Forest.

**ITALY:** General Sir Harold R. L. G. Alexander, supreme commander of Allied forces in the Mediterranean, orders a new offensive for December.

Twelfth Air Force B-25 Mitchells attack rail bridges. A-20 Havocs and P-47 Thunderbolts attack German defensive positions and rail lines.

**SOUTHWEST PACIFIC AREA:** The B-24 Liberators of the 2nd Bombardment Squadron (Heavy), 22nd Bombardment Group (Heavy), redeploy from Leyte Island to Angaur Island in the Palaus.

Four U.S. destroyers sink Japanese submarine *I-46* in Leyte Gulf.

U.S. submarine *Guavina* attacks a Japanese convoy off the southern coast of French Indochina and is driven off by a submarine chaser.

**CENTRAL PACIFIC:** Seventh Air Force B-24 Liberators from Saipan bomb Iwo Jima.

During the night a B-24 conducts a snooper (radar-assisted bomb release) mission on Iwo Jima.

**NEW GUINEA:** FEAF B-24 Liberators, B-25 Mitchells, P-40s, and P-47 Thunderbolts attack targets on Halmahera and Timor Islands.

The P-38 Lightnings of the 35th Fighter Squadron, 8th Fighter Group, redeploy from Morotai Island to Leyte, joining the ground echelon that had departed on November 18.

Thirteenth Air Force B-24 Liberators sink a Japanese merchant tanker off Borneo.

## November 29

**ALEUTIANS:** Eleventh Air Force sends three B-24 Liberators to bomb Kashiwabara on Paramushiru Island.

**CBI:** In Burma, Tenth Air Force sends more than 110 P-47 Thunderbolts to support ground forces near Bhamo and Pinwe and to attack bridges, logistics storage areas, ammunition storage sites, and troops.

Fourteenth Air Force B-25 Mitchells bomb targets in French Indochina and attack Lashio in Burma. P-40s, P-38 Lightnings, and P-51 Mustangs attack targets of opportunity near Chefang, China.

**ETO:** In the Hürtgen Forest, the 26th Infantry Regiment of the 1st Infantry Division attacks Merode, advancing four miles. The advance has cost 4,000 casualties, including 600 losses in the 47th Infantry Regiment of the 9th Infantry Division, attached to the 1st Infantry Division for the attack. Elements of the 8th Infantry Division supported by Combat Command Reserve of the 5th Armored Division attack toward Kleinhau. The 8th Infantry Division has lost 1,247 men, most of them in the 121st Infantry Regiment.

Eighth Air Force sends more than 1,000 B-17s and B-24 Liberators, led by radar-equipped Pathfinder bombers and escorted by over 900 P-51 Mustangs and P-47 Thunderbolts, to attack oil refineries, marshaling yards, and rail viaducts in Germany. One B-24 is lost, and 103 bombers are damaged. Aircrew casualties are three wounded and 10 missing. During the night six B-17s and seven B-24s drop leaflets over Germany, France, and the Netherlands.

The headquarters of the 489th Bombardment Group (Heavy) and the 844th, 846th, and 847th Bombardment Squadrons (Heavy) depart England for the United States to switch to B-29 Superfortresses.

Ninth Air Force sends more than 300 B-26 Marauders and A-20 Havocs to attack German defensive positions. P-47 and P-38 fighters support the 104th Infantry Division as it defends against German counterattacks at Inden and Lammersdorf. Fighters also support the 8th Infantry Division at Hürtgen, and the 7th Armored Division in the XIII Corps attack toward the Roer River.

Staff Sergeant Andrew Miller is a squad leader in G Company, 377th Infantry Regiment, 95th Infantry Division. Over the space of two weeks of combat, Staff Sergeant Miller's extraordinary and heroic actions will win him the Medal of Honor. At

Woippy, France, Miller ignores German machine guns and attacks the positions singlehandedly, forcing the enemy to surrender in one position and destroying the other position with hand grenades. Near Metz, as his squad falters in the face of enemy fire, Miller engages a German machine-gun position with automatic rifle fire and leads the advance. He later leads an attack on a barracks, surprising the enemy and capturing a number of prisoners. When the Germans counterattack, Miller climbs to the roof of the building to fire a bazooka at a German machine gun, ignoring the heavy fire directed at him. At Kerprich Hemmersdorf, Germany, Staff Sergeant Miller leads an attack against the enemy, clearing the way until he is killed.

**ITALY:** Twelfth Air Force P-47 Thunderbolts attack rail lines, rail cars, and vehicles in the Po Valley.

**SOUTHWEST PACIFIC AREA:** In the Philippines FEAF B-24 Liberators, A-20 Havocs, and P-47 Thunderbolts bomb airfields on Mindanao Island.

Kamikazes damage the battleship USS *Maryland* and two destroyers in Leyte Gulf.

U.S. motor torpedo boats attack Japanese shipping in Ormoc Bay, sinking a patrol boat and an auxiliary minelayer. Fifth Air Force B-25 Mitchells and P-47s attack Japanese shipping, sinking a submarine chaser. P-40s and P-47 Thunderbolts sink two cargo ships.

**PACIFIC:** During the night Twentieth Air Force sends 24 B-29 Superfortresses from the Marianas to bomb the docks and industrial targets in Tokyo; two B-29s bomb targets at Yokohama and Numazu.

U.S. submarine *Archerfish* torpedoes and sinks the Japanese carrier *Shinano* off Honshu, Japan. U.S. submarine *Scabbardfish* torpedoes and sinks Japanese submarine *I-365* off Honshu, Japan. U.S. submarine *Spadefish* torpedoes and sinks a Japanese cargo ship off the west coast of Korea.

**CENTRAL PACIFIC:** Seventh Air Force sends 18 B-24 Liberators from Guam to bomb Iwo Jima.

**NEW GUINEA:** FEAF B-24 Liberators, with P-40s, attack the airfield on Celebes Island. B-24s, B-25 Mitchells, and P-47 Thunderbolts attack the airfield on Halmahera Island and attack shipping and other targets of opportunity near Ceram Island, Celebes Island, and northern Borneo.

### November 30

**CBI:** In Burma, Tenth Air Force P-47 Thunderbolts conduct ground attack missions near Bhamo and attack troops, vehicles, and bridges.

The Fourteenth Air Force reports that 36 squadrons are operational, including four heavy bomber squadrons (47 B-24 Liberators), seven medium bomber squadrons (109 B-25 Mitchells), and 22 fighter squadrons (535 P-40s, P-51 Mustangs, P-38 Lightnings).

B-25 Mitchells and P-51 Mustangs attack railroad bridges and buildings in French Indochina. B-25s bomb logistics storage sites and buildings at Lashio and Wanling in Burma. In China, 23 P-38s and P-51s attack targets of opportunity near Chefang.

Japanese air attacks damage the U.S. submarine *Pipefish* in the South China Sea off Hainan. The submarine remains on patrol.

**ETO:** In the Hürtgen Forest, the 22nd Infantry Regiment of the 4th Infantry Division breaks out into the open, flat terrain beyond the woods. Hill 401 is captured with the support of Combat Command A of the 5th Armored Division.

Eighth Air Force sends more than 1,200 B-17s and B-24 Liberators escorted by over 900 P-47 Thunderbolts and P-51 Mustangs to attack oil production facilities and marshaling yards in Germany. A total of 28 B-17s are lost and 522 bombers damaged. Aircrew casualties are 25 killed, 58 wounded, and 395 missing. Fighter pilots report four confirmed kills in the air. Three fighters are lost, and one is damaged. Three pilots are reported missing.

During the night seven B-17s and six B-24s drop leaflets over Germany and the Netherlands.

Ninth Air Force sends 288 B-26 Marauders and A-20 Havocs to attack German defensive positions and strongpoints and a marshaling yard at Zweibrücken. P-47 and P-38 fighters support the 104th Infantry Division of VII Corps at Lammersdorf and Inden in the Hürtgen Forest.

**MEDITERRANEAN:** During the night Fifteenth Air Force sends B-17s to bomb a benzol plant and marshaling yards in Austria, while other B-24s attack the marshaling yards at Munich, Germany.

**ITALY:** Twelfth Air Force B-25 Mitchells and B-26 Marauders attack rail and road traffic and bridges in the Po Valley. A-20 Havocs and P-47 Thunderbolts attack convoys, bridges, rail cars, and roads.

**SOUTHWEST PACIFIC AREA:** The Japanese have been able to land an additional 10,000 troops on Leyte.

The P-38 Lightnings of the 36th and 80th Fighter Squadrons, 8th Fighter Group, operating from Morotai Island return to Leyte. The ground echelon of the 418th Night Fighter Squadron begins redeployment from Leyte Island to Mindoro Island. The squadron's P-61 Black Widow night fighters remain on Morotai Island.

**PACIFIC:** U.S. submarine *Sunfish* torpedoes and sinks a Japanese cargo ship off western Korea.

**CENTRAL PACIFIC:** Seventh Air Force B-24 Liberators from Saipan bomb Iwo Jima. B-24s from Guam bomb Haha Jima. Another 37 B-24s from Angaur Island attack an airfield on Luzon in the Philippines. During the night two B-24s conducts a snooper (radar-assisted bomb release) mission on Iwo Jima, attacking the airfield.

**NEW GUINEA:** FEAF B-24 Liberators attack airfields on Celebes and Halmahera Islands.

The P-47 Thunderbolts of the 340th Fighter Squadron, 348th Fighter Group, redeploy from Noemfoor Island to Leyte.

## December 1

**CBI:** Chinese Y Force (also known as the Chinese Expeditionary Force) units capture Che-fang.

In Burma, Tenth Air Force P-47 Thunderbolts support ground forces near Bhamo.

Fourteenth Air Force B-25 Mitchells bomb logistics storage sites and buildings at Wanling in Burma.

The 14th and 15th Combat Cargo Squadrons of the 4th Combat Cargo Group arrive in India from the United States with C-46 Commando cargo planes. The 427th Night Fighter Squadron redeploys from India to Myitkyina with P-61 Black Widow night fighters.

**ETO:** In the Hürtgen Forest, the 4th Infantry Division is unable to continue the attack and exploit the gains made the previous day. The division has lost 4,053 men in combat and another 2,000 are nonbattle casualties. Since entering the battle for Hürtgen on November 16, the division has advanced three miles.

During the night Eighth Air Force sends seven B-17s and seven B-24s to drop leaflets over Germany, France, and the Netherlands.

Ninth Air Force sends 134 B-26 Marauders and A-20 Havocs to attack German positions along the battle front in Germany. P-47 and P-38 fighters support VII Corps fighting in the Hürtgen Forest and the 8th Infantry Division of V Corps.

**ITALY:** Twelfth Air Force B-25 Mitchells and B-26 Marauders attack rail bridges in the Po Valley. A-20 Havocs and P-47 Thunderbolts of the XXII Tactical Air Command attack road and rail targets.

**SOUTHWEST PACIFIC AREA:** Due to limitations on logistics support and limited air cover available from the airfields on Leyte, General MacArthur delays the landing operation on Mindoro for 10 days. The new date is December 15. Lieutenant General Walter Krueger has formed the Western Visayan Task Force under command of Brigadier General William C. Dunkel, composed of the 19th RCT of the 24th Infantry Division and the 503rd Parachute Infantry Regiment, along with air and naval assets, to conduct the mission. The ground element of the task force is to seize airfields in support of the Luzon amphibious assault.

FEAF B-25 Mitchells attack airfields on Negros Island. B-25s with P-47 support also attack airfields on Cebu Island and Mindanao Islands.

The headquarters of the 3rd Air Commando Group, the 3rd Fighter Squadron (Commando), and 157th, 159th, and 160th Liaison Squadrons (Commando) arrive on Leyte Island from the United States with P-51 Mustangs. The B-24 Liberators of the 408th Bombardment Squadron (Heavy), 22nd Bombardment Group (Heavy), redeploy from Leyte Island to Angaur Island in the Palaus.

**CENTRAL PACIFIC:** Seventh Air Force B-24 Liberators from Saipan and Guam bomb Iwo Jima.

During the night a B-24 conducts a snooper (radar-assisted bomb release) mission on Iwo Jima.

A naval operating base at Kwajalein is established.

**NEW GUINEA:** FEAF B-25s attack targets on Halmahera Island.

The P-47 Thunderbolts of the 342nd Fighter Squadron, 348th Fighter Group, redeploy from Noemfoor Island to Leyte Island.

### December 2

**CBI:** In Burma, Tenth Air Force sends 40 fighter-bombers to support ground forces near Bhamo, and B-25 Mitchells bomb rail targets and bridges in northern Burma.

Fourteenth Air Force P-51 Mustangs, P-40s, and P-38 Lightnings on armed reconnaissance attack troops, horses, vehicles, railroad yards, shipping, and logistics storage areas in southern China and near Lashio in Burma.

**ETO:** Eighth Air Force sends more than 450 B-17s and B-24 Liberators escorted by more than 600 P-51 Mustangs to attack marshaling yards in Germany. Eleven B-24s are lost and four damaged. Aircrews report eight confirmed kills and one probable. Aircrew casualties are two wounded and 102 missing. Fighter pilots report 11 confirmed kills and one probable in the air.

During the night seven B-17s and six B-24s drop leaflets over Germany, France, and the Netherlands.

Ninth Air Force sends more than 200 B-26 Marauders and A-20 Havocs to attack German positions along the battle front in Germany. More than 130 P-47 Thunderbolts and P-51 Mustangs fly fighter sweeps and support the 1st Infantry Division, the 104th Infantry Division, and the 8th Infantry Division

**MEDITERRANEAN:** Fifteenth Air Force sends nearly 500 B-17s and B-24 Liberators to attack oil refineries in Germany and Austria and a marshaling yard in Hungary as well as a road bridge in Czechoslovakia.

**ITALY:** The CCS orders General Alexander to set the priorities for offensive operations. The city of Bologna is still the main objective, but Alexander is cautioned that Allied forces should also ensure the Ravenna-Bologna-La Spezia line is secured.

Twelfth Air Force B-25 Mitchells and B-26 Marauders attack bridges. A-20 Havocs and P-47 Thunderbolts attack airfields, rail cars, and roads. Fighters also support Fifth Army forces south of Bologna.

**SOUTHWEST PACIFIC AREA:** On Leyte the 1st Battalion 34th Infantry Regiment and the 2nd Battalion 19th Infantry Regiment capture the Japanese defensive line at Kilay Ridge. The Japanese lose 900 killed.

FEAF B-24 Liberators bomb airfields on Negros Island and Mindanao Island. FEAF B-24 Liberators and B-25 Mitchells attack targets on Celebes Island. A-20 Havocs, P-38 Lightnings, and P-47 Thunderbolts support ground forces, attack logistics storage areas, and attack communications on Mindanao Island.

The B-24 Liberators of the 19th Bombardment Squadron (Heavy), 22nd Bombardment Group (Heavy), redeploy from Leyte Island to Angaur Island in the Palaus.

Four U.S. destroyers bombard Japanese positions at Palompon and northern Ormoc Bay, at Leyte. During the night another three destroyers enter Ormoc Bay, firing on aircraft, destroyers, and shore batteries. U.S. submarine *Gunnel* lands supplies and evacuates Allied aviators from Palawan.

**PACIFIC:** U.S. submarine *Sea Devil* attacks a Japanese convoy in the East China Sea, sinking a merchant tanker and passenger-cargo ship off Kyushu, Japan.

**CENTRAL PACIFIC:** Seventh Air Force sends 23 B-24 Liberators from Guam to bomb Iwo Jima.

During the night three B-24s from Saipan and Guam conduct a snooper (radar-assisted bomb release) mission on the airfield at Iwo Jima.

**NEW GUINEA:** FEAF B-25 Mitchells bomb the airfield on Buru Island and attack shipping off Ceram Island. B-24 Liberators and B-25s attack targets on Celebes Island.

## December 3

**CBI:** In Burma, Tenth Air Force sends 40 fighter-bombers to support ground forces near Bhamo and B-25 Mitchells to bomb rail targets and bridges in northern Burma.

Fourteenth Air Force P-40s, P-51 Mustangs, and P-47 Thunderbolts attack road and rail junctions, bridges, artillery, town areas, troop concentrations, and various targets of opportunity around Shihhweiyao and from Hengyang to Siangtan and Lingling.

U.S. submarines *Pampanito, Pipefish, Sea Cat,* and *Searaven* attack a Japanese convoy in the South China Sea off the coast of French Indochina. USS *Pipefish* torpedoes and sinks a coastal patrol ship. USS *Pampanito* torpedoes a cargo ship. Both USS *Sea Cat* and USS *Searaven* report torpedoing a tanker.

**ETO:** Ninth Army reaches the Roer River with 10 divisions occupying a 24-mile front, but Bradley worries about the Roer River dams near Schmidt remaining under German control. He believes the Germans can stop any further advance by opening the dams to the south, flooding the river and trapping units on the far side of the Roer. Before any further advances can be made, Bradley decides that the Roer River dams must be captured. This order to the V Corps of First Army initiates another bloody and difficult struggle in the forested hills where the Germans have all the advantages.

The V Corps attacks into the Hürtgen Forest without air support. The bad weather prevents all but a few aircraft from flying. In the Hürtgen Forest, the 28th and 121st Infantry Regiments of the 8th Infantry Division, along with Combat Command B of the 5th Armored Division, capture Brandenberg, a key position on the flank of First Army. About 60 German fighter aircraft make a rare attack on American ground forces near Brandenberg. Antiaircraft platoons in the division account for 19 German aircraft shot down and claim 10 other probables.

Ninth Air Force P-47 Thunderbolts and P-38 Lightnings support the 104th Infantry Division, the 1st Infantry Division, and the 8th Infantry Division, as well as XII Corps.

The Seventh Army's VI Corps attacks north, moving along the Rhine River, while XV Corps attacks toward Bitche.

After Major General William Eagles is wounded, the 45th Infantry Division's new commander is Major General Robert T. Frederick, the former commander of the 1st Special Service Force.

Sergeant Ellis R. Weicht of F Company, 142nd Infantry Regiment, 36th Infantry Division, leads his squad in an attack on the village of St. Hippolyte, France. As the infantrymen clear buildings and move up a winding street, they are engaged by two machine guns from a house about 100 yards away. While the squad takes cover, Sergeant Weicht begins firing on the enemy. He advances under heavy fire until he reaches a house opposite the Germans and destroys the two machine-gun positions. As the squad advances again, two 20 millimeter guns open fire. As the Americans drop artillery on the German position, Sergeant Weicht continues to engage the position and follows up the artillery attack with a one-man assault, eliminating the position. Encountering another position, a road block, Sergeant Weicht moves to the second story of a house and engages the enemy, ignoring the heavy volume of fire directed at him. He continues to fight from this position until killed. For his acts of courage, skill, and leadership, Sergeant Weicht will receive the Medal of Honor.

**MEDITERRANEAN:** Fifteenth Air Force sends 85 B-17s and B-24 Liberators escorted by P-38 Lightnings and P-51 Mustangs to attack industrial production facilities and marshaling yards in Austria. Other B-17s and B-24s airdrop supplies in Yugoslavia.

**ITALY:** Twelfth Air Force P-47 Thunderbolts of the 57th and 350th Fighter Groups support ground forces of the Fifth Army south of Bologna.

**SOUTHWEST PACIFIC AREA:** On Leyte the 1st Cavalry Division attacking south from Carigara clears Japanese defenses and links with the 32nd Infantry Division near Highway 2. Logistics problems are limiting the X Corps advance. Roads are nonexistent or marginal and cease to exist when the rains come, which is often. Supplies reaching the front-line soldiers have to be moved by individuals and small groups over treacherous paths and steep jungle mountainsides.

The 128th Infantry Regiment of the 32nd Infantry Division passes through the 34th Infantry Regiment of the 24th Infantry Division and attacks to clear Japanese positions south of the ridge.

A-20s, P-38 Lightnings, and P-47 Thunderbolts attack logistics sites and airfields on Leyte Island and Masbate Island.

Three U.S. destroyers continue fighting in Ormoc Bay, Leyte. One destroyer is sunk, and two Japanese destroyers are sunk.

**PACIFIC:** Admiral Nimitz requests that the JCS delays the attack on Iwo Jima (Operation Detachment) to February 19 and Okinawa (Operation Iceberg) to April 1. Twentieth Air Force sends 86 B-29 Superfortresses from the Marianas to bomb the Musashino aircraft production facility, docks, and the city of Tokyo. Over the city, 60 B-29s hit the primary target; 15 hit alternate targets. Aircrews report 10 confirmed kills, 11 probable kills, and 18 possible kills. Five B-29s are lost.

**CENTRAL PACIFIC:** Seventh Air Force sends 17 B-24 Liberators from Guam to bomb Iwo Jima.

During the night B-24s conduct a snooper (radar-assisted bomb release) mission on Iwo Jima.

**NEW GUINEA:** FEAF B-24s attack targets on Celebes Island, while B-25 Mitchells bomb airfields on Halmahera Island. A-20 Havocs attack Point Noejew in New Guinea.

## December 4

**CBI:** In Burma, Tenth Air Force sends P-47 Thunderbolts to attack bridges, defensive positions, logistics sites, and troops.

Fourteenth Air Force sends 24 B-25 Mitchells supported by 12 P-40s to attack bridges, buildings, and river, road, and rail traffic at several points in China, French Indochina, and Burma.

**ETO:** Eighth Air Force sends nearly 1,200 B-17s, using Pathfinder radar-equipped bombers and escorted by over 970 P-47 Thunderbolts and P-51 Mustangs, to attack marshaling yards in Germany. Three bombers are lost and 129 damaged. Aircrew casualties are one wounded and 28 missing. Fighter pilots report six confirmed kills on the ground. Three fighters are lost, and the pilots are reported missing.

During the night five B-17s and five B-24s drop leaflets over Germany, France, and the Netherlands.

Ninth Air Force P-47 Thunderbolts support the 1st, 8th, and 104th Infantry Divisions and the XII and XX Corps near the Saar River.

**MEDITERRANEAN:** Fifteenth Air Force sends 26 P-38 Lightnings to bomb a railroad bridge at Zenica in Yugoslavia.

**ITALY:** Twelfth Air Force B-25 Mitchells and B-26 Marauders bomb German defensive positions and attack an ammunition storage site. P-47 Thunderbolts support Fifth Army ground forces south of Bologna. A-20 Havocs attack targets in the Po Valley.

**SOUTHWEST PACIFIC AREA:** On Leyte the 7th Infantry Division continues its advance north in the Ormoc Valley, supported by the novel use of amphibious tanks, which travel at night in the coastal waters and appear ahead of infantry units as they advance the next morning, providing fire support against suspected Japanese positions in the hills alongside the road.

Marine fighter squadrons begin operating on airfields in Leyte.

A U.S. destroyer is damaged in a Japanese air attack off Leyte. U.S. submarine *Flasher* attacks a Japanese convoy southwest of Manila, sinking a destroyer and damaging a merchant tanker. USS *Flasher* escapes a counterattack from escorting ships.

**PACIFIC:** The headquarters of the XXI Bomber Command, Twentieth Air Force, arrives at Harmon Field on Guam from the United States.

**CENTRAL PACIFIC:** During the night two B-24 Liberators conduct a snooper (radar-assisted bomb release) mission on Iwo Jima.

## December 5

**CBI:** In Burma, Tenth Air Force sends P-47 Thunderbolts to support ground forces near Bhamo. Other fighters attack road and rail transportation.

C-47s and C-46s begin Operation Grubworm, a redeployment of the Chinese 14th and 22nd Divisions from Burma to China as part of the Alpha Force to stop a Japanese offensive to capture Kunming in China, a major airfield for the Fourteenth Air Force.

Fourteenth Air Force sends seven B-24 Liberators on sweeps over the Gulf of Tonkin, the South China Sea, and the Formosa Strait. Bombers attack the Kowloon Docks in Hong Kong. Aircrews report damage to a cargo ship.

**ETO:** Third Army encounters German defenses at the West Wall along the west bank of the Saar River.

Eighth Air Force sends nearly 600 B-17s and B-24 Liberators, using Pathfinder radar-equipped bombers and escorted by over 800 P-47 Thunderbolts and P-51 Mustangs, to attack industrial production facilities in Berlin and marshaling yards in Germany. A total of 12 B-17s are lost and 179 bombers damaged. Aircrew casualties are one killed, eight wounded, and 115 missing. Fighter pilots report 90 confirmed kills and seven probables in the air and two possible kills on the ground. A total of 17 P-51 fighters are lost, and two are damaged. All 17 pilots are reported missing.

Six B-24 Liberators fly a screening mission to disrupt German radio intercept equipment and employ radar countermeasures.

During the night four B-17s and eight B-24s drop leaflets over Germany, France, and the Netherlands.

Ninth Air Force sends 172 A-20 Havocs, A-26 Invaders, and B-26 Marauders to attack a marshaling yard, road junction, fuel storage site, and a rail bridge in Germany. P-47 and P-38 fighters escort the bombers and support the 1st, 8th, and 104th Infantry Divisions.

**ITALY:** Twelfth Air Force P-47 Thunderbolts and A-20 Havocs support Fifth Army ground forces south of Bologna.

**SOUTHWEST PACIFIC AREA, LEYTE:** As part of the X Corps attack south in the Ormoc Valley, the 126th and 127th Infantry Regiments of the 32nd Infantry Division meet strong resistance. The 12th Cavalry Regiment captures Hill 2348.

The 7th Infantry Division breaks Japanese defenses at the Palanas River. The 11th Airborne Division attacks from the east.

U.S. submarine *Hake* lands supplies on Panay. An LST (landing ship, tank) and a medium landing ship are damaged in a Japanese air attack off Leyte. Kamikazes damage two destroyers and a cargo ship carrying troops. Over 100 men are killed or injured. Japanese torpedo planes attack a U.S. convoy headed for Leyte. One freighter is torpedoed and abandoned.

Private First Class William A. McWhorter of M Company, 126th Infantry Regiment, 32nd Infantry Division, mans a machine gun in a defensive position when his company comes under attack. A Japanese demolition squad tosses an improvised grenade into the position. McWhorter grabs the grenade and, to protect his assistant gunner, smothers the blast with his body. Private First Class McWhorter's heroism and act of supreme sacrifice will win him the Medal of Honor.

**CENTRAL PACIFIC:** Naval Base, Tinian, is established.

**NEW GUINEA:** FEAF B-24 Liberators bomb airfields on Halmahera Island and targets on northern Borneo while B-25 Mitchells attack targets on Celebes Island.

## December 6

**ALEUTIANS:** Eleventh Air Force sends four B-24 Liberators to bomb Suribachi airfield on Paramushiru Island. Aircrews report damage to the runway and antiaircraft positions. One B-24 is damaged. A B-24 weather airplane is forced to land in the Soviet Union.

**CBI:** The 2nd and 3rd Battalions of the 475th Infantry Regiment of Mars Task Force relieve Chinese forces at Tonkwa. The units of the Chinese 22nd Division begin a redeployment back to China by air at the insistence of Generalissimo Chiang Kai-shek. The 209th and 236th Engineers begin extending the Ledo Road to Bhamo and complete a 1,200-foot pontoon bridge over the Irrawaddy River. The bridge, with a 25-ton capacity, is the third-longest bridge ever built by U.S. Army engineers.

Tenth Air Force P-47 Thunderbolts and B-25 Mitchells bomb bridges and airfields in Burma.

**ETO:** The XII Corps captures Saarbrücken, advancing into the strongest positions of the West Wall. The Third Army in its late autumn battles has taken 29,000 casualties and captured 37,000 prisoners.

In the Hürtgen Forest, German forces make a heavy counterattack on elements of the 8th Infantry Division holding Brandenberg. The 2nd Ranger Battalion is brought in to seize Castle Hill, a key position overlooking Brandenberg. The Rangers capture the objective in a night attack and hold it for two days until relieved. The Rangers take 75 percent casualties.

Eighth Air Force sends more than 800 B-17s and B-24 Liberators using radar to locate targets and, escorted by 800 P-47 Thunderbolts and P-51 Mustangs, to attack oil refineries and marshaling yards in Germany. Four B-17s are lost and 251 bombers are damaged. Aircrew casualties are four wounded and 37 missing. One P-51 fighter is lost and two are damaged. One pilot is reported missing. Twelve B-17s fly a screening mission to disrupt German radio intercept equipment and employ radar countermeasures.

During the night 11 B-17s and B-24s drop leaflets over Germany, France, and the Netherlands.

Ninth Air Force sends 154 A-20 Havocs and B-26 Marauders to bomb German defensive positions along the battle line. P-47 and P-38 fighters escort the bombers and support the V, VII, and XII Corps.

**MEDITERRANEAN:** Fifteenth Air Force sends nearly 300 B-17s and B-24 Liberators escorted by P-38 Lightnings and P-51 Mustangs to attack marshaling yards in Austria, Hungary, Yugoslavia, and Czechoslovakia.

**SOUTHWEST PACIFIC AREA:** On Leyte, the Japanese drop 350 paratroopers near the San Pablo airfield, causing a great deal of confusion and disruption. The intent of the Japanese commander is to use the paratroopers to regain the initiative by eliminating the airfields under American control. The Japanese hold out for four days against an emergency force of rear area troops.

FEAF B-24 Liberators bomb an airfield on Negros Island, while B-25 Mitchells, with P-47 Thunderbolts escorting, bomb airfields on Mindanao Island. P-38 Lightnings covering a convoy off south Leyte Island report several Japanese aircraft shot down.

U.S. submarine *Haddo* torpedoes and damages a Japanese tanker off the west coast of Luzon. U.S. submarines *Segundo, Trepang,* and *Razorback* attack a Japanese convoy near Dalupiri Island as it travels to Manila. USS *Trepang* torpedoes and damages three cargo ships. USS *Segundo* damages three cargo ships as well.

**NEW GUINEA:** FEAF B-24 Liberators attack airfields on Celebes Island. B-25 Mitchells, P-40s, and A-20 Havocs attack airfields on Halmahera Island. A-20s and B-25s bomb Buru Island.

The headquarters of the 417th Bombardment Group (Light) and the A-20s of the 672nd, 673rd, 674th, and the 675th Bombardment Squadrons redeploy from Noemfoor Island to Leyte.

### December 7

**CBI:** In Burma Tenth Air Force sends B-25 Mitchells to bomb bridges while P-47 Thunderbolts support ground forces near Bhamo and attack Japanese troops and logistics sites.

The 16th Combat Cargo Squadron, 4th Combat Cargo Group, arrives in India from the United States with C-46 Commando cargo planes.

Fourteenth Air Force sends eight B-25 Mitchells to attack logistics storage areas near Lashio in Burma. Aircrews of two B-24 Liberators report one cargo vessel sunk in the South China Sea. P-51 Mustang pilots attacking shipping at Hong Kong report sinking a destroyer and a cargo ship. P-51 Mustangs, P-40s, and P-38 Lightnings attack troop concentrations, gun positions, rail lines, logistics storage sites, bridges, and highways in southern China.

**ETO:** General Eisenhower holds a meeting with his senior commanders to establish missions for 1945. Both Montgomery's 21st Army Group and Bradley's 12th Army Group have been struggling in the difficult terrain before the Rhine. After several weeks of fighting, the armies have gained only a few miles. At the small-unit level, gains are measured in yards. The Allied advantage in air power and tanks has been neutralized by both bad weather, which has prevented effective air support to ground forces, and by the nature of the wooded terrain, which limits the use of tanks. Nevertheless, it is agreed that the goal for future operations will be to clear out German forces west of the Rhine River. The Roer River dams are recognized as a priority for the Americans. The Allies plan to launch a new offensive on January 12. In the meantime, Allied forces will make limited attacks, but the majority of the divisions will rest and refit. Field Marshal Montgomery's 21st Army Group will have the priority of effort in the upcoming offensive. Montgomery believes the broad-front strategy Eisenhower continues to promote is wasteful. He argues for a single main thrust (under Montgomery's command) to create the breakthrough.

**MEDITERRANEAN:** Fifteenth Air Force sends 31 B-17s and B-24 Liberators to bomb marshaling yards in Austria.

**ITALY:** Field Marshal Sir Harold R. L. G. Alexander, commander of the 15th Army Group, cancels the planned attack by Fifth Army's II Corps.

Twelfth Air Force A-20 Havocs and P-47 Thunderbolts attack rail lines and bridges.

**SOUTHWEST PACIFIC AREA:** On Leyte the 77th Infantry Division commanded by Major General Andrew D. Bruce arrives to reinforce the XXIV Corps near Ormoc City. Elements of the division advance to Ipil and are stopped by heavy fire. The 77th Division, pressing from the Palanas River, forces the Japanese to retreat. Elements of the 7th Infantry Division seek to link up with the 11th Airborne Division moving against strong Japanese positions west of Burauen.

FEAF B-24 Liberators bomb the airfield and town on Masbate Island and the airfield on Luzon Island.

Rear Admiral Arthur W. Struble's Naval Task Group 78.3 lands elements of the 77th Infantry Division on the eastern shore of Ormoc Bay after a pre-assault naval bombardment. Kamikazes damage two destroyers; one destroyer is scuttled. Two high-speed transports are damaged, and one must be scuttled. Kamikazes also damage an LST and two medium landing ships and sink another medium landing ship.

U.S. submarines *Razorback, Segundo,* and *Trepang* continue attacking the Japanese convoy they hit the previous day. USS *Razorback* torpedoes and sinks a cargo ship damaged the previous day. USS *Trepang* torpedoes and sinks a transport north of Luzon. Two cargo ships torpedoed by USS *Trepang* the previous day finally sink.

Fifth Air Force P-47 Thunderbolts and P-40s and Marine F4U Corsairs attack Japanese shipping in San Isidro Bay, Leyte. Pilots report sinking two escort destroyers, a fast transport, and four cargo ships.

**PACIFIC:** Twentieth Air Force sends 108 B-29 Superfortresses from Chengtu, China, to bomb the Manchuria Airplane Manufacturing Company and an adjacent arsenal at Mukden in Manchuria. Eighty B-29s hit the primary target and the others hit secondary or alternate targets. Aircrews report 10 confirmed kills, 10 probables, and 30 possibles. Seven B-29s are lost.

**CENTRAL PACIFIC:** Japanese aircraft attack the Seventh Air Force airfield on Saipan.

Japanese aircraft attack the airfield on Saipan.

**NEW GUINEA:** FEAF B-25 Mitchells attack airfields on Halmahera Island.

### December 8

**CBI:** The Chinese 22nd Division encounters strong Japanese forces near Tonkwa. The American 475th Infantry occupies positions as the 22nd Division is redeployed to China.

The 1st Tank Battalion of the 1st Provisional Tank Group supports Chinese forces from the 38th Division attacking Japanese defenses at Bhamo. The 2nd and 3rd Battalions of the 475th Infantry Regiment defend Tonkwa against Japanese counterattacks.

Tenth Air Force P-47 Thunderbolts support ground forces near Bhamo and attack targets around Shwebo.

**ETO:** Third Army reports that it has a shortage of 11,000 men in the front-line combat units. Divisions are at half-strength and no replacements are arriving, reflecting a theater-wide shortage of combat troops. Patton begins to strip corps- and army-level support units, converting clerks, cooks, and signalmen into riflemen.

Ninth Air Force P-47 and P-38 fighters support V and VII Corps and XX Corps and XII Corps.

**MEDITERRANEAN:** Fifteenth Air Force sends 24 B-17s and B-24 Liberators to bomb marshaling yards in Austria.

**ITALY:** Twelfth Air Force P-47 Thunderbolts attack trains in the Po Valley. Fighter pilots report four locomotives are destroyed and almost 100 train cars are damaged.

**SOUTHWEST PACIFIC AREA, LEYTE:** Elements of the 1st Cavalry Division capture Wright, the end of the Taft-Wright Highway on Samar. American troops work with Philippine guerrillas to clear the entire highway.

FEAF B-24 Liberators bomb airfields on Cebu and Negros Islands.

Private Elmer E. Fryar of E Company, 511th Parachute Infantry Regiment, 11th Airborne Division, participates in a battalion attack on a Japanese defensive position. The battalion is unable to reach its objective and begins a withdrawal. E Company supports the withdrawal, but the Japanese suddenly launch a counterattack. Observing an enemy platoon moving to outflank his company's position, Private Fryar selects a firing position on high ground to engage the attacking force. He is quickly wounded in the exchange but continues to hold off the enemy. As the company begins its withdrawal, he assists a wounded paratrooper and accompanies his platoon leader, who is also aiding another wounded paratrooper. A Japanese soldier attempts to kill the American officer, but Fryar springs to protect him and is mortally wounded. Fryar uses a grenade to kill the enemy soldier. Fryar's courage under fire and his supreme act of sacrifice for his comrades will win him the Medal of Honor.

Private Ova A. Kelley of A Company, 382nd Infantry Regiment, 96th Infantry Division, sits at the edge of the enemy-held Buri airfield on Leyte. As dawn breaks, the Japanese fire on Kelley's company with rifle and machine-gun fire from entrenchments less than 100 yards distant. After the Americans drop mortar fire on the Japanese positions, Private Kelley takes an armload of hand grenades and attacks the Japanese. His grenade attack is successful in forcing the survivors to retreat. He picks up an M-1 rifle and fires on the retreating Japanese, then picks up an M-1 carbine and continues to fire. By this time his company has pressed the attack, advancing to seize the objective. For his extraordinary courage under fire, Private Kelley will receive the Medal of Honor.

**PACIFIC:** Twentieth Air Force sends 82 B-29 Superfortresses from the Marianas, escorted by Seventh Air Force P-38 Lightnings and 89 B-24 Liberators from Guam and Saipan, to bomb the airfields on Iwo Jima. Navy cruisers also provide naval gunfire support. The intent of the attack is to neutralize Japanese aircraft using Iwo as a base for attacks on Saipan.

Naval Task Group 94.9 (Rear Admiral Allan E. Smith) bombards Iwo Jima.

**NEW GUINEA:** FEAF B-25 Mitchells, P-47 Thunderbolts, and P-40s, along with Royal Australian Air Force (RAAF) aircraft, attack the airfield and other targets on Halmahera Island.

U.S. submarines *Paddle* and *Hammerhead* coordinate an attack on a Japanese convoy and sink a merchant tanker in the South China Sea west of Borneo. USS *Paddle* escapes a depth-charge attack.

## December 9

**CBI:** The 2nd and 3rd Battalions of the 475th Infantry Regiment counterattack Japanese forces at Tonkwa and Mo-hlaing.

Tenth Air Force P-47 Thunderbolts attack bridges, villages and buildings, logistics storage areas, and targets of opportunity.

A Fourteenth Air Force B-24 aircrew reports sinking a cargo ship in the South China Sea. P-51 Mustangs and P-40s attack road and rail junctions, bridges, town areas, troop concentrations, and various targets of opportunity around Kweilin, Liuchow, Lingling, Hengyang, Tuhshan, and Chuchou.

**ETO:** Eighth Air Force sends 413 B-17s escorted by 247 P-47 Thunderbolts and P-51 Mustangs to attack marshaling yards and airfields in western Germany. One B-17 is lost and 67 damaged. Aircrew casualties are three wounded and nine missing. Fighter pilots report one confirmed kill in the air.

During the night four B-17s and seven B-24s drop leaflets over Germany, France, and the Netherlands.

Ninth Air Force sends 254 A-20 Havocs, A-26 Invaders, and B-26 Marauders to bomb German strongpoints, logistics storage sites, and a marshaling yard in western Germany. P-47 and P-38 fighters escort the bombers and support XII and XX Corps.

**MEDITERRANEAN:** Fifteenth Air Force sends 170 B-17s and B-24 Liberators escorted by P-38 Lightnings and P-51 Mustangs to attack industrial production facilities and a marshaling yard in Austria and an oil refinery at Regensburg, Germany, as well as armament production facilities at Plzen, Czechoslovakia.

Two U.S. destroyers bombard German coast artillery positions and troop concentrations along the border between France and Italy.

**PACIFIC:** U.S. submarine *Plaice* damages a Japanese escort destroyer off Kyushu, Japan.

U.S. submarines *Sea Devil* and *Redfish* torpedo and damage the Japanese carrier *Junyo* off Kyushu.

**CENTRAL PACIFIC:** Seventh Air Force B-24 Liberators from Saipan bomb Iwo Jima.

**NEW GUINEA:** FEAF B-24 Liberators bomb a tank farm, a bridge, airfields, and an oil installation at Ambon Island and Ceram Island. B-25 Mitchells attack targets in the Molucca Islands. P-38 Lightnings attack the airfield on Buru Island.

### December 10

**CBI:** The British 36th Division captures Katha. The Japanese prepare to defend along a line about 400 miles north of Rangoon, from Akyab to Mandalay and along the Irrawaddy River to Lashio.

Tenth Air Force P-47 Thunderbolts conduct close support missions near Bhamo. B-25 Mitchells attack logistics storage sites.

Fourteenth Air Force sends 25 B-24 Liberators to bomb the city of Hankow, while three additional B-24s bomb the Samah Bay docks on Hainan Island. P-40s, P-51 Mustangs, and P-38 Lightnings attack vehicles, rail lines, logistics storage sites, bridges, highways, and river transportation around Hochih, Changsha, and Yuncheng.

**ATLANTIC:** German submarine *U-1202* torpedoes and sinks a U.S. freighter off the coast of Wales.

**ETO:** First Army's intelligence section predicts that the German High Command is preparing to launch a major counteroffensive led by tanks south of Aachen.

In the Hürtgen Forest, the 9th and the 104th Infantry Divisions of VII Corps attack toward Düren. The 330th and 331st Infantry Regiments of the 83rd Infantry Division replace the 4th Infantry Division and attack north to push the remaining German defenders from the edge of the forest. Minefields prevent the tanks of the 5th Armored Division from supporting the infantry.

Eighth Air Force sends more than 500 B-17s and B-24 Liberators led by radar-equipped Pathfinder bombers and escorted by nearly 700 P-47 Thunderbolts and P-51 Mustangs to attack marshaling yards in western Germany. A total of 33 bombers are damaged. Aircrew casualties are two killed. Two fighters are lost and one is damaged; the two pilots are reported missing.

Nearly 100 P-51 Mustangs make a fighter sweep and pilots report one possible kill. One P-51 is lost and one is damaged. The pilot is reported missing.

Ninth Air Force sends nearly 130 B-26 Marauders to bomb German defensive positions. P-47 and P-38 fighters escort the bombers and support the 8th, 9th, 83rd, and 104th Infantry Divisions and the 3rd and 5th Armored Divisions.

**MEDITERRANEAN:** Fifteenth Air Force sends more than 550 B-17s and B-24 Liberators escorted by P-38 Lightnings and P-51 Mustangs to attack oil production facilities in Germany.

**ITALY:** Twelfth Air Force B-25 Mitchells and B-26 Marauders attack rail and road targets in the Brenner Pass. A-20 Havocs and P-47 Thunderbolts attack German defensive positions and roads.

**SOUTHWEST PACIFIC AREA, LEYTE:** The 77th Infantry Division clears Japanese defenders from Camp Downes and enters Ormoc City. Over 1,500 Japanese are killed. U.S. casualties are 136 killed, wounded, and missing.

FEAF P-38 Lightnings bomb a port facility on Mindanao.

A kamikaze damages a destroyer off Leyte and an LCT (landing craft, tank) is sunk. A motor torpedo boat is damaged and abandoned.

**CENTRAL PACIFIC:** Seventh Air Force B-24 Liberators from Saipan bomb Iwo Jima.

**NEW GUINEA:** FEAF B-24 Liberators attack tank farms and docks in Borneo. B-25 Mitchells bomb the airfield on Celebes Island and the Molucca Islands.

## December 11

**CBI:** In Burma, Tenth Air Force B-25 Mitchells bomb logistics storage sites, a ferry, and towns. P-47 Thunderbolts support ground forces near Bhamo.

Fourteenth Air Force sends six B-24 Liberators and six B-25 Mitchells escorted by eight P-51 Mustangs to attack targets in French Indochina. P-40s, P-51 Mustangs, and P-47s attack Tien Ho airfield at Canton, China, and Lashio in Burma

**ETO:** Eighth Air Force sends more than 1,500 B-17s and B-24 Liberators escorted by over 800 P-47 Thunderbolts and P-51 Mustangs to attack marshaling yards in western Germany and bridges in south-central Germany. Five bombers are lost and 54 are damaged. Aircrew casualties are two wounded, and 47 missing. Fighter pilots report on a possible kill on the ground. Two P-51s are lost and two are damaged; two pilots are reported missing.

During the night three B-17s and eight B-24s drop leaflets over Germany, France, and the Netherlands.

Ninth Air Force fighters support 3rd Armored Division and the 104th, the 9th and the 83rd Infantry Divisions.

**MEDITERRANEAN:** Fifteenth Air Force sends more than 400 B-17s and B-24 Liberators escorted by P-38 Lightnings and P-51 Mustangs to attack industrial production facilities in Austria.

**ITALY:** Twelfth Air Force B-25 Mitchells and B-26 Marauders attack bridges. A-20 Havocs and P-47 Thunderbolts attack defensive positions, artillery, bridges, and roads.

**SOUTHWEST PACIFIC AREA:** Troops of the 11th Airborne Division and the 149th Infantry Regiment of the 38th Infantry Division are able to eliminate the Japanese paratroopers at San Pablo airfield. Although the Japanese have destroyed several logistics storage sites and a number of aircraft, they have had no appreciable effect on Sixth Army's operations.

FEAF B-24 Liberators bomb the airfield on Cebu Island in the Philippines. B-25 Mitchells, with P-47 Thunderbolts escorting, bomb an airfield on Mindanao Island and P-38 Lightnings and Marine Corps aircraft attack a 13-ship convoy off Leyte Island.

By this date, despite constant attacks on shipping and transports, the Japanese have been able to land more then 34,000 troops at Leyte and deliver another 10,000 tons of supplies.

Kamikazes attack a resupply convoy headed for Ormoc Bay. A destroyer and an LCT (landing craft, tank) are sunk off Leyte. Marine F4U Corsairs attack a Japanese convoy off Leyte, sinking two cargo ships. U.S. submarine *Gar* lands supplies on the west coast of Luzon and picks up intelligence documents.

**PACIFIC:** U.S. submarine *Sea Owl* torpedoes and sinks a Japanese auxiliary submarine chaser in the East China Sea.

**CENTRAL PACIFIC:** Seventh Air Force sends 28 B-24 Liberators from Guam to bomb Iwo Jima. During the night B-24s from Guam and Saipan conduct a snooper (radar-assisted bomb release) mission on Iwo Jima.

**NEW GUINEA:** FEAF B-25 Mitchells, A-20 Havocs, and P-40s attack targets in the Molucca Islands.

FEAF B-25 Mitchells, A-20 Havocs, P-38 Lightnings, and P-40s attack Japanese supply and troop concentrations on the southern shore of Wasile Bay and along the shore north of Halmahera Island. Pilots report one ship sunk.

## December 12

**CBI:** Tenth Air Force sends 11 B-25 Mitchells to bomb logistics storage areas near Lashio. P-47 Thunderbolts attack roads and bridges, a Japanese headquarters. artillery, town areas, troop concentrations, and various targets of opportunity.

Fourteenth Air Force P-40s, P-51 Mustangs, and P-38 Lightnings on armed reconnaissance attack logistics storage sites, rail lines, bridges, and highways in Burma, Thailand, and China.

**ETO:** The 83rd Infantry Division and elements of the 5th Armored Division push northeast of Hürtgen Forest.

The 44th Infantry Division of the VI Corps, Seventh Army, captures Haguenau.

Eighth Air Force sends nearly 900 B-17s and B-24 Liberators, using radar to assist in locating targets and escorted by over 900 P-47 Thunderbolts and P-51 Mustangs, to attack a synthetic oil plant and marshaling yards in western Germany. A total of four bombers are lost and 79 are damaged. Aircrew casualties are 12 killed and 36 missing. Fighter pilots report one possible kill on the ground. Seven fighters are lost and three damaged. Six pilots are reported missing.

B-24 Liberators and B-17s conduct screening missions to jam German radio interception efforts and conduct countermeasures against German radar sites.

During the night seven B-17s and four B-24s drop leaflets over Germany, France, and the Netherlands.

Ninth Air Force sends 90 A-20 Havocs and B-26 Marauders to attack German strongpoints. P-47 and P-38 fighters support the 83rd Infantry Division of the VII Corps, the XII Corps, and the 35th Infantry Division of XX Corps.

**MEDITERRANEAN:** Fifteenth Air Force sends 75 B-17s and B-24 Liberators escorted by P-38 Lightnings and P-51 Mustangs to bomb an oil refinery in Germany and industrial production facilities in Czechoslovakia.

**SOUTHWEST PACIFIC AREA, LEYTE:** After two days of heavy fighting the 17th and 184th Infantry Regiments of the 7th Infantry Division clear Japanese forces from Hill 918 protecting Ormoc Bay.

FEAF B-24 Liberators, with P-47 Thunderbolts and P-38 Lightnings providing escort, bomb the airfield on Negros Island. B-25 Mitchells bomb the airfield on Mindanao.

Marines and Thirteenth Air Force aircraft attack one of the last convoys attempting to provide reinforcements to Japanese forces on Leyte. Another Japanese destroyer and a landing ship are sunk.

Two motor torpedo boats sink a Japanese destroyer off Leyte. A U.S. destroyer is damaged by a kamikaze off Leyte.

**PACIFIC:** The service groups of the 313th Bombardment Wing (Very Heavy), Twentieth Air Force, arrive on Tinian.

**CENTRAL PACIFIC:** Seventh Air Force sends 24 B-24 Liberators from Saipan to bomb Iwo Jima.

During the night B-24s from Saipan and Guam conduct a snooper (radar-assisted bomb release) mission on Iwo Jima.

**NEW GUINEA:** FEAF B-24 Liberators bomb the airfields on Celebes Island and on Ambon-Ceram-Boeroe Islands.

## December 13

**CBI:** Elements of the 1st Provisional Tank Group support the Chinese conducting a siege at Bhamo. The 2nd and 3rd Battalions of the 475th Infantry Regiment stop a Japanese attack near Tonkwa.

Tenth Air Force sends 12 B-25 Mitchells to bomb the logistics storage and personnel area at Mongmit. P-47 Thunderbolts support the 475th Infantry Regiment near Tonkwa and attack logistics sites and vehicles.

Fourteenth Air Force P-51 Mustangs and P-38 Lightnings attack town areas and rail targets in French Indochina and attack a bridge in Thailand. The headquarters of the 341st Bombardment Group (Medium) redeploys from Kunming to Yangkai, China.

U.S. submarine *Bergall* engages a Japanese heavy cruiser in the South China Sea off French Indochina. The submarine damages the cruiser, but the *Bergall* is hit by a dud eight-inch shell and terminates her patrol.

**ETO:** In deep snow, the V Corps of First Army begins its attack to capture the Roer River dams. The 78th and 2nd Infantry Divisions make the attack. This attack will be halted three days later when the German Ardennes offensive begins and Monschau is attacked. The 9th Infantry Division, fighting in the bloody woods from September 13 to October 26, has suffered 3,600 casualties; the 28th Infantry Division, attacking in the same place from October 27 to November 20, has suffered 3,600 casualties; the 4th Infantry Division, from November 6 to December 8, suffers 5,200 casualties. Since November 16 First Army has suffered a total of 21,650 casualties. Ninth Army has lost 10,000 casualties during the same period.

The soldiers of Bradley's 12th Army Group are suffering greatly in the terrible autumn and early winter of 1944. Their suffering will get worse in the next few weeks and months.

The battle for the Hürtgen Forest has lasted from September 14 to December 13. It has cost 24,000 Americans killed, wounded, and missing. Another 9,000 are nonbattle casualties. The gains made for the price paid are reminiscent of the worst leadership on the Western Front in World War I, when generals ordered that objectives be attacked without an understanding of the terrain involved—and then were sidetracked into useless battles of attrition that served no larger purpose. The III Corps under Major General John Millikin captures the last of the Metz forts. The cost of capturing the city far outweighs its usefulness to Third Army. The Americans have given up all their advantages in mobility and firepower to engage in the kind of positional warfare the Germans wished for.

The 103rd and 45th Infantry Divisions of the XV Corps of Seventh Army enter into Germany and encounter the defenses of the West Wall (or Siegfried Line). The 79th Infantry Division and 14th Armored Division advance toward the German border.

Ninth Air Force sends 250 A-20 Havocs, A-26 Invaders, and B-26 Marauders to attack fuel storage sites and German strongpoints. P-47 and P-38 fighters support XX Corps and XII Corps.

**MEDITERRANEAN:** A U.S. destroyer bombards troop concentrations and artillery positions along the French-Italian border.

**SOUTHWEST PACIFIC AREA:** The Western Visayan Task Force en route to Mindoro is attacked by kamikaze aircraft, seriously damaging the *Nashville,* the task force's flagship. On the ship 131 men are killed and 158 wounded. *Nashville* is forced to return to Leyte.

FEAF B-24 Liberators bomb airfields on Negros Island. B-25 Mitchells bomb the airfield on Mindanao Island.

Kamikazes damage a light cruiser and a destroyer near Mindanao.

U.S. submarine *Pintado* torpedoes and sinks a Japanese fast transport and landing ship in the South China Sea near Luzon Strait.

**PACIFIC:** Twentieth Air Force sends 90 B-29 Superfortresses from the Marianas to bomb the Mitsubishi aircraft engine plant at Nagoya, Japan. A total of 71 hit the primary target. Aircrews report considerable damage to the target and report four confirmed kills and one probable kill. Four B-29s are lost.

**CENTRAL PACIFIC:** Seventh Air Force sends 15 B-24 Liberators from Guam to bomb Iwo Jima Island. Three B-24s from Saipan bomb Marcus Island. During the night six B-24s from Saipan and Guam conduct raids against Iwo Jima.

The headquarters of Seventh Air Force arrives at Saipan from Hawaii.

**NEW GUINEA:** FEAF B-25 Mitchells bomb airfields on Haroekoe Island, the Molucca Islands, Ceram Island, Ambon Island, and Buru Island. B-25 Mitchells, P-38 Lightnings, and P-47 Thunderbolts attack shore positions at Galela Bay on Halmahera Island.

### December 14

**CBI:** The 38th Chinese Division captures Bhamo.

Tenth Air Force sends 12 B-25 Mitchells to bomb the logistics storage and troop barracks at Mongmit. P-47 Thunderbolts attack troop concentrations, roads, and logistics areas and support the 475th Infantry Regiment near Tonkwa.

The 1st Fighter Squadron (Commando) with P-51 Mustangs, 2nd Air Commando Group, arrives at Kalaikunda, India, from the United States. The squadron's first missions are scheduled for mid-February 1945.

**ATLANTIC:** Congress establishes the five-star general and flag officer rank.

**ETO:** Ninth Air Force P-38 Lightnings and P-47 Thunderbolts support the 2nd and 99th Infantry Divisions in the Monschau Forest, the 8th Infantry Division near the Bergstein area, the 78th Infantry Division, and XII and XX Corps.

Sergeant Ralph G. Neppel of M Company, 329th Infantry Regiment, 83rd Infantry Division, is leading a machine-gun squad defending an approach to the village of Birgel, Germany, when 20 German troops and a tank approach. As his men engage the infantry at 100 yards, the tank immediately fires at the position, killing or wounding everyone. Sergeant Neppel is blasted 10 yards from his gun and has lost his left leg. Dragging himself back to his machine gun, he kills the German infantrymen and forces the tank to withdraw. Sergeant Neppel's courage and fighting spirit will win him the Medal of Honor.

**ITALY:** Twelfth Air Force A-20 Havocs and P-47 Thunderbolts attack rail lines in the Po Valley and German positions in support of the Fifth Army south of Bologna.

**SOUTHWEST PACIFIC AREA:** On Leyte, the 305th Infantry Regiment of the 77th Infantry Division assaults the last Japanese strongpoint in the Ormoc Valley. Supported by several artillery battalions, tanks, armored bulldozers, and flamethrowers, the infantrymen capture the enemy position. The 32nd Infantry Division advances down Highway 2 from the north in the X Corps area and is met by determined resistance. The infantrymen advance only a short distance past Kilay Ridge.

FEAF B-24 Liberators attack airfields on Negros Island. B-25 Mitchells bomb the airfield on Jolo Island.

U.S. submarine *Blenny* torpedoes and sinks a Japanese coastal patrol ship and a guardboat off Luzon. Aircraft from carrier USS *Hornet* sink a Japanese landing ship off Vigan.

Lieutenant Robert P. Nett commands E Company, 305th Infantry Regiment, 77th Infantry Division. He leads his unit in an attack against an entrenched Japanese battalion near Cognon. Attacking the trench lines, Lieutenant Nett clears the first positions, fighting the enemy hand-to-hand. Wounded three times, he refuses treatment and continues to lead the advance toward the objective. Only when the company has consolidated control of the objective does Lieutenant Nett turn over command and walk unaided to receive medical treatment. For his inspiring leadership and determination to defeat the enemy, Lieutenant Nett will receive the Medal of Honor.

**PACIFIC:** Twentieth Air Force sends 48 B-29 Superfortresses from Calcutta, India, to bomb a railroad bridge at Bangkok, Thailand. A total of 33 hit the primary target. Aircrews report one possible kill. Four B-29s are lost.

**CENTRAL PACIFIC:** Seventh Air Force sends 24 B-24 Liberators from Saipan to bomb Iwo Jima Island. Three B-24s from Saipan bomb Marcus Island. During the night six B-24s from Saipan and Guam conduct a snooper (radar-assisted bomb release) mission against Iwo Jima.

**NEW GUINEA:** FEAF B-25 Mitchells bomb targets on Buru Island.

The 550th Night Fighter Squadron, XIII Fighter Command, arrives at Hollandia, New Guinea, from the United States with P-61 Black Widow night fighters. The squadron's first missions are scheduled for mid-January 1945.

### December 15

**CBI:** The Chinese 38th Division occupies Bhamo after the Japanese abandon the city and withdraw south to Lashio. General Sultan looks to the Mars Task Force (the 5332nd Brigade [Provisional]) to cut the Burma Road and threaten the rear of Japanese forces holding against the Chinese 30th and 38th Divisions.

The 1st Battalion of the 475th Infantry Regiment patrols in the vicinity of Shwegu until relieved by the British 36th Infantry Division.

Tenth Air Force sends 10 B-25 Mitchells to bomb the Hsipaw railroad bridge and others. P-47 Thunderbolts attack bridges and attack Japanese positions along the Namh-Kam-Bhamo road in pursuit of retreating Japanese forces. P-47s attack Lashio airfield.

The 2nd Fighter Squadron (Commando) with P-51 Mustangs, 2nd Air Commando Group, arrives at Kalaikunda, India, from the United States. The squadron's first missions are scheduled for mid-February 1945.

Fourteenth Air Force sends six B-25 Mitchells to bomb logistics sites at Kunlong, China.

**ATLANTIC:** The U.S. Senate approves the promotions of Henry H. Arnold, Dwight D. Eisenhower, Douglas MacArthur, and George C. Marshall to the five-star rank of general of the army and the nominations of William D. Leahy, Ernest J. King, and Chester W. Nimitz as admirals of the fleet.

The headquarters of the Continental Air Force is activated at Bolling Field, Washington, D.C. Its mission is to coordinate the efforts of the First, Second, Third, and Fourth Air Forces and the I Troop Carrier Command. The headquarters is expected to be operational by early May 1945.

**ETO:** The VII Corps of First Army controls the area north of Düren. The V Corps is unable to advance. The Ninth and First Armies report to the 12th Army Group that they have a five-day supply of fuel stocks. The Third Army reports it has a nine-day supply of fuel. The Third Army has drawn up to the German defenses of the West Wall (or Siegfried Line) and has established several bridgeheads over the Saar River.

The Seventh Army of the 6th Army Group advances through German defenses toward Wissembourg along a 22-mile front. Although pushed back, German forces still control the bridgehead over the Rhine River at Colmar. The French First Army is unable to close the salient, now known as the Colmar Pocket. The Germans defend the bridgehead at the Rhine River at Colmar, defeating an attack by the First French Army. Since December 1, Seventh Army has suffered 18,000 casualties and has captured 25,000 prisoners.

General Bradley reports a shortage of 17,000 infantrymen needed to replace combat and noncombat losses in the 12th Army Group.

Eighth Air Force sends more than 670 B-17s, using radar to assist in locating targets and escorted by more than 400 P-47 Thunderbolts and P-51 Mustangs, to attack marshaling yards and armament production facilities in western Germany. One B-17 is lost and 24 damaged. Aircrew casualties are 25 killed and one wounded. Two P-51s are lost, and the pilots are reported missing.

During the night two B-17s drop leaflets over Germany and France.

Ninth Air Force sends 300 A-20 Havocs, A-26 Invaders, and B-26 Marauders to attack fuel storage sites and strongpoints. P-47 and P-38 fighters support the 2nd and 99th Infantry Divisions, the 78th and the 8th Infantry Divisions, and the 5th Armored Division as well as the XX and XII Corps.

Bandleader and Army Air Force major Glenn Miller is lost while flying in a single-engine plane across the English Channel en route to Paris.

Headquarters, Naval Forces Germany, is established at Rosneath, Scotland, under command of Admiral Robert L. Ghormley.

**MEDITERRANEAN:** The death of Field Marshal Sir John Dill requires a new officer to fill the position of chief of the British Military Mission. Supreme Allied Commander Mediterranean, General Sir Henry Maitland Wilson, is selected. Field Marshal Sir Harold R. L. G. Alexander replaces Wilson as the Mediterranean theater commander. General Mark Clark takes command of 15th Army Group, and Major General Lucian K. Truscott becomes Fifth Army commander.

Ultra intercepts indicate a buildup of German forces in front of Fifth Army's IV Corps area, delaying a planned Eighth Army and Fifth Army combined offensive.

Fifteenth Air Force sends more than 300 B-17s and B-24 Liberators escorted by over 250 P-38 Lightnings and P-51 Mustangs to attack marshaling yards in Austria and Germany.

**ITALY:** Twelfth Air Force B-25 Mitchells and B-26 Marauders attack ammunition storage areas, fuel storage areas, and rail bridges. A-20 Havocs and P-47 Thunderbolts attack rail targets and support Fifth Army ground forces south of Bologna.

**SOUTHWEST PACIFIC AREA:** FEAF B-24 Liberators and B-25 Mitchells bomb airfields on Mindanao as the Western Visayan Task Force approaches. The 19th Infantry RCT and the 503rd Parachute Infantry Regiment land on Mindoro after a short naval bombardment. Two LSTs and a destroyer are sunk by kamikazes. San Jose is occupied, and the airfields are in American hands.

B-24s attack targets on Palawan Island. A-20 Havocs and P-47 Thunderbolts attack fuel storage area on Negros Island.

Naval Task Group 78.3, commanded by Rear Admiral Arthur D. Struble, lands ground forces on the southwest coast of Mindoro. Carrier aircraft provide cover for the landing. Kamikazes damage two destroyers, two LSTs, the escort carrier USS *Marcus Island,* and a motor torpedo boat off Mindoro.

U.S. submarine *Hawkbill* torpedoes and sinks a Japanese destroyer west of Luzon.

Carrier aircraft from Task Force 38 sink a Japanese landing ship in the South China Sea off Luzon.

Private First Class Dirk J. Vlug of the 126th Infantry Regiment, 32nd Infantry Division, is occupying a roadblock on the Ormoc Road near Limon when two Japanese tanks advance. Leaving his defensive position, he approaches the tanks with a bazooka and six rounds. Ignoring the fire from the tanks, he fires on the first tank and destroys it. The crew of another tank dismounts and charges toward Private First Class Vlug, who kills one soldier with a pistol. The crewmen retreat and remount the tank but are quickly dispatched by another round from Vlug's bazooka. As three more tanks arrive, Vlug takes a flanking position and hits the first tank; ignoring the fire directed at him, he moves to engage the second tank.

His last two shots destroy the remaining tanks. Private First Class Vlug's heroism and determination in destroying five Japanese tanks singlehandedly will win him the Medal of Honor.

**CENTRAL PACIFIC:** Seventh Air Force sends 13 B-24 Liberators from Guam to bomb Iwo Jima.

During the night a B-24 conducts a snooper (radar-assisted bomb release) mission on Iwo Jima.

**NEW GUINEA:** FEAF B-25 Mitchells attack airfields on Ceram and Ambon Islands. P-40s and P-38s along with B-25s bomb airfields on Boeroe and Halmahera Islands and shipping in the Netherlands East Indies.

## December 16

**CBI:** Tenth Air Force P-47 Thunderbolts support the 475th Infantry Regiment near Tonkwa. Other P-47s attack locomotives, logistics storage areas, buildings, and personnel.

U.S. submarine *Dace* lays mines off French Indochina.

**ETO: The German Ardennes Offensive Begins.** The Germans attack on a 50-mile front in the Ardennes Forest, with 20 divisions supported by 350 aircraft, in an attempt to reverse the course of the war with one final offensive thrust. The offensive depends on the quick capture and control of several critical road junctions: St-Vith, Malmédy, Bastogne, and Houffalize. The badly depleted 4th and 28th Infantry Divisions and the newly arrived 106th Infantry Division, along with the 9th Armored Division of VIII Corps, occupy the area of the attack and are hit with a heavy artillery barrage, followed by infantry assaulting the American lines. Although there is determined resistance in some locations, most of the American troops are scattered. Two infantry regiments of the 106th Infantry are surrounded. The 4th Infantry Division conducts a strong defense. German tanks and infantry break through the boundary between V Corps and VIII Corps and advance six miles. German aircraft drop paratroopers behind American lines to cut the main roads into the Ardennes. Very few of the paratroopers actually make it into the combat area. Many speak English and are dressed like American soldiers, causing an amount of alarm and confusion throughout the battle area far beyond their actual capabilities.

First Lieutenant Charles P. Murray, Jr., of C Company, 30th Infantry Regiment, 3rd Infantry Division, leads a reinforced platoon into contact with a force of 200 Germans attacking American positions on the crest of a ridge near Kaysersberg, France. His radio goes dead after he begins calling adjustments to his initial call for fire. He moves back to his platoon and, taking some rifle grenades, returns to engage the enemy. As the grenades land among the German troops, he receives heavy enemy fire, but continues to fight until the grenades are gone. He then returns to his platoon, takes an automatic rifle and ammunition, and again takes up a position to engage the Germans. His accurate fire breaks up the unit's attack and forces it to retreat. He then advances to his objective with his platoon and captures 10 German soldiers. Although wounded by a grenade, he refuses to be treated until satisfied that his platoon is properly deployed. First Lieutenant Murray's calm and heroic act to disrupt a large enemy unit and protect his men will win him the Medal of Honor.

The German offensive in the Ardennes comes as a complete surprise to General Eisenhower. He believes it to be a serious threat, but General Bradley believes the attack is limited and manageable. Nevertheless, Eisenhower orders Bradley to alert Third Army's 10th Armored Division and Ninth Army's 7th Armored Division to be prepared to move to support First Army.

Eighth Air Force sends 236 B-17s escorted by over 100 P-51 Mustangs to attack rail targets at Stuttgart, Germany. Poor weather prevents all but 81 from hitting the primary target. One B-17 is lost and 10 damaged. Aircrew casualties are three killed and nine missing.

Ninth Air Force P-47 and P-38 fighters support First Army units encountering the leading elements of the German counteroffensive on the Western Front.

When L Company, 393rd Infantry Regiment, 99th Infantry Division, is hit by the artillery barrage that signals the beginning of the Ardennes offensive, Technical Sergeant Vernon McGarity is wounded. He receives first aid but refuses to be evacuated, returning to his squad and leading them in defending their position against a strong German attack. During the battle, McGarity rescues a wounded comrade in an exposed position, ignoring enemy fire. Throughout the night, he keeps his men ready to repulse an attack. The following morning, McGarity's squad faces a tank and infantry attack. Technical Sergeant McGarity personally destroys the lead tank and rescues another wounded American soldier. As the squad runs low on ammunition, McGarity braves heavy fire to find more. When the Germans surround his location and place a machine gun in position to block his squad's retreat, McGarity attacks the Germans and singlehandedly captures the position. When the squad is completely surrounded and has fired its last round of ammunition, the Germans overwhelm the Americans and take them prisoner. For his courage under fire and his inspiring leadership, Technical Sergeant McGarity will win the Medal of Honor.

**MEDITERRANEAN:** Fifteenth Air Force sends more than 600 B-17s and B-24 Liberators escorted by P-38 Lightnings and P-51 Mustangs to attack an oil production facility and armaments production facility in Czechoslovakia and industrial targets and a marshaling yard in Austria.

**ITALY:** Twelfth Air Force A-20 Havocs and P-47 Thunderbolts of the XXII Tactical Air Command attack rail lines and bridges and support Fifth Army ground forces south of Bologna.

**SOUTHWEST PACIFIC AREA:** On Leyte, the 2nd Battalion of the 32nd Infantry Regiment begins moving into the mountains from Ormoc Bay to link up with paratroopers from the 11th Airborne Division making a cross-country advance to clear out the last organized Japanese defenders.

The Third Fleet, providing air support over Luzon, halts operations when a typhoon strikes.

FEAF B-24 Liberators bomb airfields on Mindanao and Palawan Islands.

Carrier aircraft from Task Force 38 sink a cargo ship escorted by a destroyer and sink a submarine chaser in Subic Bay, Luzon. The cargo ship is carrying 1,600 Allied prisoners of war.

**CENTRAL PACIFIC:** During the night Seventh Air Force B-24s from Guam and Saipan conduct snooper (radar-assisted bomb release) missions on Iwo Jima.

U.S. submarine *Finback* attacks a Japanese convoy and sinks a transport near Chichi Jima.

**NEW GUINEA:** FEAF B-25 Mitchells, A-20 Havocs, and P-47 Thunderbolts attack airfields on Ceram Island, and targets of opportunity on north Borneo and around the Vogelkop Peninsula.

## December 17

**CBI:** Tenth Air Force P-47 Thunderbolts support ground forces. The 493rd Bombardment Squadron (Heavy), 7th Bombardment Group (Heavy), sends a detachment of B-24 Liberators from Pandaveswar, India, to Luliang, China, to transport fuel to Suichwan, China.

Fourteenth Air Force sends nine B-24 Liberators to bomb targets at Cam Ranh Bay in French Indochina.

**ETO: The Battle of the Bulge.** German tank and infantry spearheads reach Honsfeld and Losheim and push farther westward. The 99th Infantry Division defending in the Losheim area is steadily being pressed and threatened with destruction. The First Army commander, Lieutenant General Courtney Hodges, decides to defend Elsenborn Ridge in the northwest with elements of the 2nd Infantry Division after the division had been ordered to halt a successful attack and retreat. Combat Command B of the 7th Armored Division arrives to defend St-Vith and collects scattered elements of the 106th Infantry Division.

The members of Battery B of the 285th Field Artillery Observation Battalion are captured, then executed, by German troops at Malmédy. About 125 men are killed or wounded.

The 28th Infantry Division is pushed steadily back and broken into isolated elements. At Clervaux, the 110th Infantry Regiment is overrun. General Eisenhower commits his reserve, the 101st and 82nd Airborne Divisions, into the battle. The units are to arrive under the operational control of the 12th Army Group. Eisenhower orders XVIII Airborne Corps headquarters, commanded by Major General Matthew B. Ridgway, to support First Army. The 4th Infantry Division supported by corps artillery units stops the German advance near Echternach. Operational control of the 1st Infantry Division is transferred from V Corps to VII Corps in order to hold the northern limit of the breakthrough. Combat Command B of the 10th Armored Division moves to Bastogne.

During the night Eighth Air Force sends three B-17s and seven B-24s to drop leaflets over Germany, France, and the Netherlands.

The B-24 Liberators of the 859th Bombardment Squadron (Heavy), 492nd Bombardment Group (Heavy), are detached to Italy. This squadron was supporting Carpetbagger missions.

Ninth Air Force, IX and XIX Tactical Air Commands, sends more than 1,000 P-38 and P-47 fighters to conduct armed reconnaissance missions, defensive patrols, and to attack bridges and gun positions. The fighters support the 8th, 28th, 78th, 99th, and 106th Infantry Divisions, and the 5th Armored Division as German forces begin to press hard against the weak defenses in the Ardennes. Fighters also support the V, VII, VIII, XII, and XX Corps.

Private First Class William A. Soderman is a bazooka gunner in K Company, 9th Infantry Regiment, 2nd Infantry Division, defending a crossroads near Rocherath, Belgium. After a heavy artillery barrage in which his assistant gunner is wounded, Private First Class Soderman hears German tanks approaching. As five tanks approach his position, Soderman waits until he can get the most effective shot. Standing up a few feet in front of the lead tank, he hits and destroys it. Throughout the rest of the night Private First Class Soderman holds his position and engages five more tanks, again standing in full view of the lead tank, firing at point-blank range. He then moves to engage a German infantry platoon with his bazooka. As K Company begins a withdrawal, Private First Class Soderman waits to hold off another tank attack to give the company time to break contact with the enemy. Again Soderman performs his remarkably courageous act, hitting and destroying one tank at close range in full view of the enemy. This time he is seriously wounded and drags himself to American lines. Private First Class Soderman's gallantry and dedication to duty contribute to the survival of his company and slow the German advance in the early hours of the Ardennes offensive. He will receive the Medal of Honor.

**MEDITERRANEAN:** Fifteenth Air Force sends more than 500 B-17s and B-24 Liberators escorted by P-38 Lightnings and P-51 Mustangs to bomb oil refineries and marshaling yards in Germany and Austria. Fighter pilots report 55 confirmed kills.

**ITALY:** Twelfth Air Force A-20 Havocs and P-47 Thunderbolts of the XXII Tactical Air Command attack marshaling yards and rail traffic.

**SOUTHWEST PACIFIC AREA:** In the Philippines FEAF B-24 Liberators and B-25 Mitchells bomb airfields on Negros Island. B-25s and A-20 Havocs attack Japanese positions on Mindanao, and B-24s with P-47 Thunderbolts escorting attack the airfield on Jolo Island.

A kamikaze damages a motor torpedo boat off Mindoro.

**CENTRAL PACIFIC:** Seventh Air Force sends 24 B-24 Liberators from Saipan Island and 26 B-24s from Guam to bomb Iwo Jima. B-24s from Saipan bomb Woleai and Eauriprik Atolls in the Carolines.

During the night B-24s from Saipan and Guam conduct raids on Iwo Jima.

**NEW GUINEA:** FEAF B-24 Liberators and A-20 Havocs attack airfields in Borneo and on Ambon Island.

## December 18

**CBI:** In Burma, after nearly a week of fighting units of the 475th Infantry Regiment around Tonkwa, the Japanese withdraw to reinforce the defense of Mandalay against General Slim's British XIV Corps. During the fighting the 475th has lost 15 killed and 56 wounded. Japanese casualties are estimated at 220.

Tenth Air Force P-47 Thunderbolts and B-25 Mitchells attack bridges in China and Burma. The 427th Night Fighter Squadron at Myitkyina sends P-61 Black Widow night fighters to operate from Kunming, China.

Over 200 Fourteenth Air Force aircraft support 94 Twentieth Air Force B-29s attacking Hankow. Hankow is nearly obliterated, eliminating its use as a Japanese logistics base.

B-25 Mitchells and P-51 Mustangs attack Wuchang. Fighter pilots report 16 confirmed kills in the air and four probables on the ground. One P-51 is lost, and the pilot is reported missing. Six B-25 Mitchells bomb Kunlong escorted by 20 P-51 Mustangs and P-38 Lightnings. The fighters drop napalm on the logistics storage sites after the bombing run.

**ATLANTIC:** The U.S. Supreme Court upholds the wartime relocation of Japanese-Americans, but also says that undeniably loyal Americans of Japanese ancestry cannot be detained.

**ETO: The Battle of the Bulge.** The Germans have opened a 45-mile gap in the Allied lines and are less than four miles from the Meuse River. German forces attacking at a gap in the lines between Malmédy and St-Vith are stopped past Stavelot by a collection of American infantry, engineers, and tank destroyers. The Trois Ponts bridge is destroyed before Germans can use it, blocking the major route to the Meuse River. Combat Command B of the 10th Armored Division arrives in Bastogne. The 101st Airborne, under the temporary command of Brigadier General Anthony McAuliffe, arrives at Bastogne as German forces begin converging on this key town that must be captured if German forces in the southern area of the Bulge are to advance any farther west. German tanks destroy American tanks and infantry attempting to block the roads outside of Bastogne.

The 11th Armored Division and the 17th Airborne Division are ordered to the Meuse—they are the last units SHAEF has available in-theater. Rear echelon and service troops, along with six French infantry battalions, are all rushed to defend the Meuse River line. The 82nd Airborne and the 9th and 30th Infantry Divisions move to support First Army. Elements of the 12th Infantry Regiment of the 4th Infantry Division hold at Berdorf, causing delays in the German timetable.

First Army headquarters retreats from Spa.

German forces reach Stavelot.

Eighth Air Force sends more than 500 B-17s using radar-equipped Pathfinder bombers and escorted by over 250 P-51 Mustangs to attack marshaling yards in western Germany. Heavy cloud cover causes another 358 B-24 Liberators to be recalled. One B-17 is lost and three damaged. Two P-51s are lost. Twenty-two B-17s conduct screening missions to jam German radio interception efforts and conduct countermeasures against German radar sites.

During the night four B-17s and nine B-24s drop leaflets over Germany, France, and the Netherlands.

Another 255 P-47 Thunderbolts and P-51s fly a fighter sweep in western Germany. Fighter pilots report three confirmed kills. One P-47 and one P-51 are lost. The pilots are reported missing.

Ninth Air Force sends more than 160 A-20 Havocs, A-26 Invaders, and B-26 Marauders to attack German defensive positions. P-47 and P-38 fighters support the 2nd, 4th, 28th, and 106th Infantry Divisions and the XII Corps. Fighters also fly armed reconnaissance missions. Pilots report over 40 German aircraft shot down.

**MEDITERRANEAN:** Fifteenth Air Force sends more than 560 B-17s and B-24 Liberators to bomb oil refineries in Germany, Austria, Czechoslovakia, and at Auschwitz, Poland. Bombers also hit marshaling yards in Austria and Hungary.

**ITALY:** Twelfth Air Force A-20 Havocs and P-47 Thunderbolts of the XXII Tactical Air Command attack rail lines and support Fifth Army ground forces south of Bologna.

**SOUTHWEST PACIFIC AREA:** On Leyte, the 77th Infantry Division moves rapidly north toward a linkup with X Corps, capturing Valencia airfield.

The 1st Cavalry Division takes up the attack for the 32nd Division in the X Corps area. Supported by heavy artillery fire, the 12th Cavalry attacks and clears Highway 2.

FEAF A-20 Havocs and P-47 Thunderbolts attack bridges and airfields on Leyte Island. B-25 Mitchells bomb the airfield on Mindanao Island.

Admiral William F. Halsey's Third Fleet encounters a typhoon in the Philippine Sea northeast of Samar. Destroyers USS *Hull, Monaghan,* and *Spence* are sunk. Three destroyer escorts, four small carriers, four escort carriers, a light cruiser, seven destroyers, an oiler, and a fleet tug are damaged. Halsey is nearly relieved after the incident is reported.

A kamikaze damages a motor torpedo boat off Mindoro.

Task Force 38 aircraft sink a cargo ship west of Luzon.

**PACIFIC:** Twentieth Air Force sends 94 B-29 Superfortresses from Chengtu, China, to drop incendiaries on the docks at Hankow, China. Over 200 aircraft of the Fourteenth Air Force support the attack. A total of 84 B-29s hit the primary target. Aircrews report one confirmed kill, three probables, and 13 possibles.

Another 89 B-29 Superfortresses flying out of the Mariana Islands are sent to bomb the Mitsubishi aircraft plant at Nagoya, Japan. A total of 63 hit the primary target. Aircrews report five confirmed kills, 11 probables, and 12 possibles. Four B-29s are lost.

**CENTRAL PACIFIC:** During the night Seventh Air Force sends four B-24 Liberators from Guam and Saipan to conduct snooper (radar-assisted bomb release) missions on Iwo Jima.

**NEW GUINEA:** FEAF A-20 Havocs and P-40s attack seaplane facilities at Sanga Sanga, Borneo, and bomb the airfield on Haroekoe Island.

## December 19

**CBI:** Tenth Air Force B-25 Mitchells and P-47s bomb logistics storage sites, road traffic, bridges, town areas, troop concentrations, and various targets of opportunity in Burma.

Fourteenth Air Force P-51 Mustangs attack shipping targets off Hong Kong. Pilots report sinking two cargo ships. P-40s attack rail cars near Singyang and report destroying two locomotives. P-38 Lightnings bomb the Wanling-Mongyu road in Burma.

U.S. submarine *Redfish* torpedoes and sinks a Japanese carrier *Unryu* in the East China Sea near Shanghai, China. Escort ships damage the *Redfish* with depth charges, forcing her to terminate her patrol.

Fourteenth Air Force P-51 Mustangs attack Japanese shipping at Hong Kong. Pilots report a cargo ship sunk.

**ETO: The Battle of the Bulge.** About 9,000 American soldiers of the 106th Infantry Division, surrounded for three days, surrender to German forces. It is the largest surrender of Americans since Corregidor in 1942. St-Vith and Bastogne are still under American control, but threatened. German forces capture Stoumont, but the 30th Infantry Division reinforced by Combat Command B of the 3rd Armored Division holds the line north of Stoumont and prepares to counterattack. The remainder of the 3rd Armored Division and the 82nd Airborne Division are to block any German advance northwest toward the Meuse River.

Elements of the 28th Infantry Division hold Wiltz. The 2nd and 99th Infantry Divisions hold at Elsenborn Ridge. The 2nd Battalion, 26th Infantry Regiment, of the 1st Infantry Division holds Bütgenbach against six separate tank and infantry assaults. The 1st Battalion of the 501st Parachute Infantry, 101st Airborne, encounters a German column headed toward Bastogne. The Germans are shocked enough by the vigor of the American defense that they delay attacking the town for a day, believing they have encountered a strong armored unit.

General Eisenhower holds a meeting of his senior commanders at Verdun to assess the current situation and map out a plan for a counterattack. Eisenhower intends to limit the German breakthrough by holding Bastogne and Monschau and preventing the enemy from crossing the Meuse River, defending along the line from Namur to Liège. Eisenhower orders Lieutenant General George S. Patton, Jr., to release several of his divisions from Third Army to support the defense of the Bulge. Patton's divisions will be the counterattacking force from the south and units under Montgomery's operational control will counterattack from the north. Patton, who made a contingency plan to deal with a German attack on his army's left flank several days earlier, announces he can have his 4th Armored Division, including the 26th and 80th Infantry Divisions, leading a multidivision attack toward Bastogne in three days. Eisenhower orders the 6th Army Group to cease offensive operations and to defend in place while extending its lines toward Saarlautern in order to allow Third Army to swing forces out of the line and move north. The Allied air forces are ordered to attack German lines of supply west of the Rhine River and marshaling yards east of the Rhine.

Eighth Air Force sends more than 300 B-17s and B-24 Liberators using radar-equipped Pathfinder bombers and escorted by 37 P-47 Thunderbolts to attack road networks, marshaling yards, and troop concentrations in Luxembourg and Germany in an attempt to slow the German attack in the Ardennes. Two B-24s are damaged and three P-47s are damaged. Aircrew casualties are one killed. Fighter pilots report seven confirmed kills; one pilot is wounded.

Ninth Air Force P-47 and P-38 fighters support the 1st, 2nd, 99th, and 106th Infantry Divisions and 7th Armored Division fighting near Malmédy and St-Vith. The fighters also support Twelfth Army troops and the XII Corps near Verdun and St-Avold, France.

The 313th Infantry Regiment, 79th Infantry Division, is engaged in a fight with German troops at the Siegfried Line defenses near Berg, Germany. Technical Sergeant Robert E. Gerstung's heavy machine-gun squad moves forward to support an infantry company making an attack. During an eight-hour battle that sees most of his men killed or wounded, Technical Sergeant Gerstung continues to fight on. When his ammunition runs out, he exposes himself to enemy fire to retrieve more from a disabled tank. When his weapon ceases to function, he moves to another fighting position to man a gun that has had all of its crew killed. A German tank begins firing on him, but Gerstung continues to provide covering fire for the hard-pressed infantrymen, who begin to retreat. Gerstung covers their movement with suppressive fire, walking to the rear with the heavy machine gun cradled in his left arm. Although wounded by a mortar round, Technical Sergeant Gerstung continues to crawl back to safety, carrying the machine gun with him. For his remarkable acts of courage and dedication to duty, Technical Sergeant Gerstung will win the Medal of Honor.

**MEDITERRANEAN:** Fifteenth Air Force sends more than 400 B-17s and B-24 Liberators to bomb oil refineries in Germany, Austria, and Czechoslovakia. Bombers also hit marshaling yards in Austria and Hungary.

**ITALY:** Twelfth Air Force P-47 Thunderbolts attack German gun positions near La Spezia.

**SOUTHWEST PACIFIC AREA:** On Leyte, units of the 1st Cavalry Division capture Lonoy on Highway 2 and flank Japanese positions facing the 32nd Infantry Division. Elements of the 77th Infantry Division meet cavalry patrols near Cananga.

FEAF B-24 Liberators and P-38 Lightnings attack airfields on Luzon Island. B-25 Mitchells bomb an airfield on Negros Island. P-38 Lightnings and P-47 Thunderbolts attack airfields on Leyte.

Navy PB4Y-1 Privateers attack a Japanese convoy in the South China Sea and sink a transport west of Manila.

**PACIFIC:** Twentieth Air Force sends 36 B-29 Superfortresses from the Chengtu, China, area to hit an aircraft plant at Omura, Japan; 17 hit the primary target, and 13 others hit secondary target of Shanghai, China. Another two strike other alternatives; aircrews claim 5-4-12 (five confirmed kills, four probables, and 12 possibles). Two B-29s are lost.

The headquarters of the 505th Bombardment Group (Very Heavy) arrives at Tinian Island, Mariana Islands, from the United States.

**CENTRAL PACIFIC:** Headquarters Seventh Air Force becomes operational on Saipan. Over 50 B-24 Liberators from Guam and Saipan bomb Iwo Jima. Another 14 P-38 Lightnings from Saipan, using three B-29 as navigational escort, strafe airfields on Iwo Jima. During the night B-24s conduct snooper (radar-assisted bomb release) missions on Iwo Jima.

**NEW GUINEA:** FEAF B-25 Mitchells, A-20 Havocs, and P-38 Lightnings attack targets on Celebes Island.

## December 20

**ALEUTIANS:** Eleventh Air Force sends three B-24s on an armed reconnaissance and photoreconnaissance mission over the Kurile Islands, including Kashiwabara, Paramushiru Island, and Katoaka on Shimushu Island. The bombers strafe buildings on Onnekotan Island and bomb Nemo Bay. Another B-24 bombs installations on Onnekotan Island.

**CBI:** In Burma, Tenth Air Force B-25 Mitchells and P-47 Thunderbolts attack troop concentrations, support ground forces, rail lines, logistics storage sites, bridges, and highways. The 492nd Bombardment Squadron (Heavy), 7th Bombardment Group (Heavy), sends a detachment of B-24 Liberators from India to Luliang, China, to ferry fuel to Suichwan, China.

Fourteenth Air Force sends 118 P-51 Mustangs and P-40s to bomb logistics storage sites, road traffic, bridges, town areas, troop concentrations, and various targets of opportunity at Wanling and Lashio in Burma; and Chinchengchiang, Hong Kong, Sinyang, Leiyang, Kweilin, Hengshan, and Hengyang in China. The headquarters of the 1st Combat Cargo Group redeploys from India to Tsuyung, China.

U.S. submarine *Sealion* torpedoes and damages a Japanese supply ship in the South China Sea

**ATLANTIC:** German submarine *U-870* torpedoes and sinks an LST and damages a destroyer escort in the North Atlantic west of Portugal.

**ETO: The Battle of the Bulge.** General Eisenhower decides to split the Bulge in half to ease operational control of units in combat and those arriving as reinforcements. The northern half of the Bulge is placed under Field Marshal Montgomery's operational control. General Bradley has operational control of all forces in the south of the Bulge. The Ninth Army and the VII, V, and XVIII Corps pass to Montgomery, while the Third Army and VII Corps remain with Bradley. Montgomery also takes operational control of the American IX and XXIX Tactical Air Forces. The XIX Tactical Air Force is reinforced with fighters and bombers from Eighth Air Force and fighter-bombers from Ninth Air Force.

The V Corps (9th, 99th, 2nd, and 1st Infantry Divisions) holds from Monschau to Malmédy. The 30th Infantry Division, the 82nd Airborne Division, and the 3rd Armored Division hold from Malmédy to Hotton. The 7th Armored Division holds St-Vith with a collection of units including Combat Command B of 9th Armored Division, the 424th Infantry Regiment of 106th Infantry Division, and the 112th Infantry Regiment of the 28th Infantry Division. Brigadier General Robert Hasbrouck, commander of the 7th Armored Division, reports to Lieutenant General Courtney Hodges of First Army that he can hold St-Vith one more day.

The 84th Infantry Division from Ninth Army moves south to block the approaches to Marche. The VII Corps, formed from a collection of units not engaged (the 75th Infantry Division, no combat experience and just arrived from the United States; the 2nd Armored and 3rd Armored Divisions and the 84th Infantry Division), is ordered to be prepared to assemble near Hotton and attack on order. The 501st Parachute Infantry Regiment stops several attacks. Brigadier General Anthony McAuliffe takes command of all American forces in Bastogne, a total of about 18,000 men. Along with the 101st Airborne Division, McAuliffe now commands Combat Command B and Combat Command Reserve of the 10th Armored Division, the 333rd Field Artillery Group, and the 705th Tank Destroyer Battalion. Paratroopers and tanks, supported by artillery, stop German attacks from the north, south, and east.

Bad weather prevents any combat operations by Eighth Air Force and Ninth Air Force.

General Eisenhower notifies General Devers to halt offensive operations in the 6th Army Group and extend its defensive lines northwest, with the XV Corps to cover the impending departure of Third Army's XII Corps. In addition, Devers is ordered to withdraw to more defensible areas. This causes the XV and VI Corps to abandon their penetrations of the West Wall into Germany.

Corporal Henry F. Warner mans the 57 millimeter antitank gun supporting 2nd Battalion, 26th Infantry Regiment, 1st Infantry Division, defending near Dom Butgenbach, Belgium. Corporal Warner employs his gun with deadly accuracy as two tanks and infantry make an attack on his position. In the face of tank and small arms fire, Warner knocks out the two tanks and then engages in a pistol duel with a tank commander of a third tank as it moves to within five yards of his position. He kills the tank commander, and the tank withdraws. After nearly constant artillery and mortar fire on the American position, the Germans conduct a strong attack to dislodge the Americans. Again Corporal Warner employs his antitank gun, hitting a tank, but in the fight he is first wounded and then killed as he struggles to load and fire his gun. Corporal Warner's exceptional courage and skill play a crucial role in the delay of German forces and will win him the Medal of Honor.

**MEDITERRANEAN:** Fifteenth Air Force sends more than 450 B-17s and B-24 Liberators escorted by over 300 P-38 Lightnings and P-51 Mustangs to bomb oil refineries in Germany and Austria, and armaments production facilities in Czechoslovakia. Bombers also hit marshaling yards in Austria.

The 859th Bombardment Squadron (Heavy), 492nd Bombardment Group (Heavy), from Eighth Air Force arrives at Brindisi, Italy, from England. The squadron's B-24 Liberators and C-47s are attached to the 15th Special Group (Provisional) and will fly Carpetbagger missions in the Mediterranean theater of operations on December 31.

**ITALY:** Twelfth Air Force A-20 Havocs and P-47 Thunderbolts attack rail lines, locomotives, vehicles, bridges, and roads near Genoa and La Spezia.

**SOUTHWEST PACIFIC AREA:** In the central Philippines over 150 B-24 Liberators, B-25 Mitchells, and A-20 Havocs attack airfields.

The headquarters and the P-38s of the 8th Fighter Group (35th, 36th, and 80th Fighter Squadrons) redeploy from Morotai Island to Mindoro Island.

**CENTRAL PACIFIC:** Seventh Air Force B-24 Liberators from Saipan bomb Iwo Jima.

During the night six B-24s conduct five snooper (radar-assisted bomb release) missions on Iwo Jima.

**NEW GUINEA:** FEAF B-24 Liberators attack an airfield on Java, and B-25 Mitchells attack Haroekoe Island in the Netherlands East Indies.

## December 21
**CBI:** In Burma, Tenth Air Force B-25 Mitchells and P-47 Thunderbolts attack bridges, logistics storage sites, troop concentrations, and rail lines. Another 12 P-47s bomb and strafe targets near Lashio.

Fourteenth Air Force sends 145 P-40s and P-51 Mustangs to attack bridges, troop areas, gun emplacements, and ammunition storage sites in south China, French Indochina, and Burma. The C-47s of the 4th Combat Cargo Squadron, 1st Combat Cargo Group, redeploy from India to Chengkung, China.

In the South China Sea, U.S. submarine *Sealion* makes a second attack on the previously damaged Japanese supply ship and sinks it.

**ETO: The Battle of the Bulge.** German tanks and infantry attack the St-Vith defenses with 10,000 infantry and 200 tanks. The Germans must capture St-Vith or the entire offensive is in danger of stalling. As German forces push into the town during the night, the 7th Armored Division begins to pull back. It has lost over 3,000 casualties and 88 tanks destroyed. Patton's Third Army, advancing north on a 30-mile front, enters Luxembourg City. The 1st Infantry Division holds off tank attacks in front of Elsenborn Ridge at Bütgenbach, supported by tank destroyers. The 30th Infantry Division counterattacks at Stoumont. The American defenders at Bastogne are surrounded.

Bad weather cancels all combat missions for Eighth Air Force and Ninth Air Force. The Royal Air Force's Second Tactical Air Force takes operational control of the IX and XXIX Tactical Air Commands from Ninth Air Force to support the defense of the northern shoulder of the Bulge. The XIX Tactical Air Command flies armed weather and intruder reconnaissance in the Saarbrücken-Trier area.

Hitler lays out plans for an attack against the U.S. Seventh Army called *Nordwind,* intended to threaten the right flank of Third Army and slow its advance toward the Ardennes. As the 6th Army Group extends its lines to cover units of Third Army departing for the Ardennes, Lieutenant General Alexander M. Patch places two divisions in reserve to deal with any possible German attack.

**Mediterranean:** Fifteenth Air Force sends more than 80 B-24 Liberators escorted by 40 P-51 Mustangs to attack a marshaling yard in Germany.

**Italy:** Twelfth Air Force A-20 Havocs attack highways, roads, and targets of opportunity in the Po Valley. P-47 Thunderbolts attack road and rail traffic.

**Southwest Pacific Area:** On Leyte, the 12th Cavalry Regiment from 1st Cavalry Division, X Corps, meets patrols from the 360th Infantry Regiment of the 77th Infantry Division of the XXIV Corps. At the same time, elements of the 11th Airborne Division link up with the 2nd Battalion, 32nd Infantry Regiment, having spent several weeks clearing Japanese strongholds in the mountains.

FEAF B-24 Liberators, B-25 Mitchells, and A-20 Havocs attack airfields on Negros Island and in the central Philippines. B-24s bomb an airfield on Mindanao Island. P-47 Thunderbolts and P-38 Lightnings from Leyte support the missions.

The P-47s of the 311th Fighter Squadron, 58th Fighter Group, redeploy from Leyte Island to Mindoro Island.

Kamikazes damage two LSTs and a destroyer off Mindoro; kamikazes hit a freighter off Panay, killing two and wounding 16 crew and passengers.

**Central Pacific:** Seventh Air Force sends 23 B-24 Liberators from Guam to bomb Iwo Jima.

During the night four B-24s conduct a raid on Iwo Jima.

**New Guinea:** FEAF B-25 Mitchells bomb targets on Halmahera Island.

**December 22**

**CBI:** In Burma Tenth Air Force B-25 Mitchells and P-47 Thunderbolts attack bridges, troop locations, and roads.

Fourteenth Air Force B-25 Mitchells damage a bridge at Song Hoa in French Indochina. P-40s and P-51 Mustangs attack airfields at Heho, Burma, and at Canton and Hong Kong, China.

U.S. submarine *Flasher* attacks a Japanese convoy in the South China Sea, sinking a fleet tanker and two merchant tankers off French Indochina.

**ETO: The Battle of the Bulge.** In three days of attacks the Germans have lost over 100 tanks and taken over a thousand casualties in a vain attempt to break the 1st Infantry, 2nd Infantry, and 99th Infantry Divisions at Elsenborn Ridge. The 30th Infantry Division recaptures Stoumont. The VII Corps battles German forces between Hotton and Rochefort. Bradley orders the remainder of the 9th Armored Division and the 106th and the 28th Infantry Divisions out of St-Vith and to reform behind the 82nd Airborne Division now defending the Salm River line. Patton's III Corps, commanded by Major General John B. Millikin, begins its attack into the southern flank of the Bulge. The 4th Armored Division heads for Bastogne, the 26th Infantry Division advances toward Wiltz, and the 80th Infantry Division for St-Vith. The corps has conducted a 100-mile road movement in less than 48 hours. The advance is difficult as the German forces hold good defensive terrain. Low on ammunition, medical supplies, and food, the Bastogne defenders receive an offer to surrender from the German commander, who threatens annihilation if the Americans do not give up. Brigadier General Anthony McAuliffe responds with a one-word reply: "Nuts!" The reply confuses the four Germans who are to relay the message. An American officer from the 327th Glider Infantry of the 101st Airborne clarifies the statement. He tells them, "In plain English it's the same as 'Go to Hell.'"

Eighth Air Force and Ninth Air Force combat missions are cancelled due to bad weather. Tactical control of three fighter groups of the IX Tactical Air Command is temporarily transferred to the XIX Tactical Air Command to support Third Army's movement north to attack the southern portion of the Bulge and relieve Bastogne. After December 25, tactical control reverts to the IX Tactical Air Command.

**MEDITERRANEAN:** German shore battery fire damages U.S. destroyer *Gleaves* during a bombardment of German troop concentrations on the French-Italian border.

**ITALY:** Twelfth Air Force B-25 Mitchells and B-26 Marauders attack rail and road bridges. A-20 Havocs and P-47 Thunderbolts attack rail lines and bridges.

**SOUTHWEST PACIFIC AREA:** In the Philippines, FEAF B-24 Liberators, with P-47 Thunderbolts escorting, bomb Clark Field on Luzon Island. P-40s attack Lipa airfield. B-24s and B-25 Mitchells with P-47s bomb airfields on Negros Island. B-24s bomb logistics storage areas and troop locations on Mindanao Island.

The headquarters of the 417th Bombardment Group (Light) and the A-20 Havocs of its four bombardment squadrons (672nd, 673rd, 674th, and 675th) redeploy from Leyte to Mindoro Island. The P-47s of the 69th and 310th Fighter Squadrons, 58th Fighter Group, also redeploy from Leyte to Mindoro.

A kamikaze damages a destroyer off Mindoro.

**PACIFIC:** Twentieth Air Force sends 78 B-29 Superfortresses from the Marianas to bomb the Mitsubishi aircraft industrial complex in Nagoya, Japan. Cloud cover limits the effectiveness of the strike, and 48 bombers hit the primary target. Aircrews report nine confirmed kills, 17 probables, and 15 possibles. Three B-29s are lost.

U.S. submarine *Tilefish* torpedoes and sinks a Japanese torpedo boat off Honshu, Japan.

**CENTRAL PACIFIC:** During the night Seventh Air Force sends two B-24 Liberators from Guam and Saipan to conduct a raid on Iwo Jima Island.

**NEW GUINEA:** FEAF P-40s B-24 Liberators, and B-25 Mitchells, along with Royal Australian Air Force (RAAF) bombers, attack targets on Halmahera Island.

FEAF B-24 Liberators attack Japanese shipping off north Borneo and sink six small cargo vessels.

## December 23

**CBI:** In Burma, Tenth Air Force B-25 Mitchells and P-47 Thunderbolts attack troop concentrations, rail lines, logistics storage sites, bridges, and roads.

Fourteenth Air Force B-25 Mitchells attack targets in French Indochina and attack rail targets in southern China. P-51 Mustangs and P-38 Lightnings attack river transportation targets around Wuchang and Hankow.

**ATLANTIC:** The JCS, fearing future entanglements in the Balkans, refuses to authorize the CCS to approve any unilateral British military action in Greece.

**ETO: The Battle of the Bulge.** The Germans have expanded the Bulge 45 miles wide and penetrated about 60 miles into American lines, just four miles away from the Meuse River. The German advance has slowed, but the pressure on the defenders is heavy. American forces abandon St-Vith, retreating to reform behind the 82nd Airborne Division. The Germans have been delayed for five important days. A German attack on Bastogne from the southeast fails. Two German tanks actually drive into Bastogne but are destroyed.

The weather improves over the battle area. Eighth Air Force sends more than 400 B-17s and B-24 Liberators escorted by over 400 P-47 Thunderbolts and P-51 Mustangs to attack communication centers and marshaling yards in an attempt to stall the momentum of the German attack in the Ardennes. A total of 176 bombers are damaged. Aircrews report six confirmed kills and four probables. Aircrew casualties are one killed, five wounded, and seven missing. Fighter pilots report 23 confirmed kills and three possibles in the air. One P-51 is lost and one is damaged.

Six B-17s conduct a screening mission to jam German radio interception efforts and conduct countermeasures against German radar sites.

During the night a total of 10 B-17s and B-24s drop leaflets over Germany, France, and the Netherlands.

Another 163 P-47 Thunderbolts and P-51 Mustangs conduct a fighter sweep near Bonn, Germany. Pilots report 46 confirmed kills, one probable, and 15 possibles. Three P-47s and three P-51s are lost. The pilots are reported missing.

The 361st Fighter Group's three fighter squadrons (the 374th, 375th, and 376th) redeploy from England to France with P-51 Mustangs. The P-51s of the 486th and 487th Fighter Squadrons, 352nd Fighter Group, redeploy from England to Belgium.

Ninth Air Force sends 500 B-26 Marauders and A-20 Havocs to attack railroad bridges, communication targets, villages, and rail and road junctions in Germany near the Bulge. German fighters and antiaircraft fire claim 31 bombers. P-47s and P-38 Lightnings fly escort, bomb airfields, and support ground forces along the northern edge of the Bulge and also provide support to the III, VIII, and XII Corps as they fight on the southern edge of the Bulge. Fighter pilots report over 100 confirmed kills. American aircraft mistakenly bomb Malmédy, killing civilians and troops of the 30th Infantry Division. Incredibly, the same mistake will be repeated over the next two days—despite Major General Leland Hobbs, commander of the 30th Infantry Division, speaking directly to Ninth Air Force headquarters.

Over 250 C-47s of the IX Troop Carrier Command drop 334 tons of supplies for the surrounded defenders of Bastogne.

**ITALY:** Based on Ultra intelligence, Major General Lucien Truscott reinforces IV Corps with the 339th and 337th Infantry Regiments of the 85th Infantry Division, and brings forward the 2nd Brigade of the 8th Indian Division to support the 92nd Infantry Division.

Twelfth Air Force A-20 Havocs attack rail lines and an airfield near Milan. Aircrews report several aircraft destroyed on the ground.

**SOUTHWEST PACIFIC AREA:** The airfields on Mindoro are operational.

FEAF B-24 Liberators escorted by P-38 Lightnings and P-47 Thunderbolts bomb airfields on Negros Island. B-24s also bomb an airfield outside of Manila. B-25 Mitchells bomb airfields on Mindanao Island,

U.S. submarine *Blenny* torpedoes and sinks a Japanese merchant tanker west of Luzon.

**PACIFIC:** The V Amphibious Corps planning staff issues its plan for the invasion of Iwo Jima. The V Amphibious Corps commander, Major General Harry Schmidt, directs a two-division landing on the southeast side of the island. The 5th Marine Division, commanded by Major General Keller E. Rockney, will land on the left, and the 4th Marine Division, commanded by Major General Clifton B. Cates, will land on the right. The 3rd Marine Division, commanded by Major General Graves B. Erskine, will be in reserve. The two divisions will attack to capture the lower airfield, Mount Suribachi, and gain control of the lower western half of the island before pivoting north and east to capture the rest of the island. Expecting heavy counterattacks on the first night, the marines plan to land as much artillery as possible early to eliminate the threat.

Admiral Raymond A. Spruance commands Fifth Fleet. Vice Admiral Richmond Kelly Turner commands the expeditionary forces. Rear Admiral Harry W. Hill commands the Attack Force, and Rear Admiral William H. P. Blandy commands the Amphibious Support Forces (demolitions, prelanding air and naval bombardment). Lieutenant General Holland M. Smith, commander of Fleet Marine Forces Pacific, serves as the commander of expeditionary troops.

The headquarters of the 313th Bombardment Wing (Very Heavy) and 504th Bombardment Group (Very Heavy) and the B-29 Superfortresses of the 398th and 421st Bombardment Squadrons (Very Heavy) arrive at Tinian Island from the United States.

**Central Pacific:** Seventh Air Force sends 26 B-24 Liberators from Saipan Island and Guam to bomb Iwo Jima. Another three B-24s from Guam bomb Woleai Atoll. During the night two B-24s conduct a raid on Iwo Jima.

**New Guinea:** FEAF B-25 Mitchells, P-40s, and A-20 Havocs bomb targets on Halmahera Island.

### December 24

**CBI:** In Burma, Tenth Air Force sends P-47 Thunderbolts to attack Lashio airfield, troop concentrations, rail lines, logistics storage sites, bridges, and roads.

Fourteenth Air Force B-25 Mitchells bomb the Kunlong ferry area and shipping in the South China Sea. Aircrews report one tanker sunk. P-40s, P-51 Mustangs, and P-38 Lightnings attack river, road, and rail traffic, troops, and buildings around Hengyang, Lingling, Siangtan, and Changsha. Fighters also attack shipping near Hong Kong and report one tanker sunk and other cargo ships damaged. Pilots report over 30 Japanese aircraft destroyed at Tsinan airfield.

**ETO:** German aircraft bomb Bastogne. An isolated element of the 3rd Armored Division under the command of Lieutenant Colonel Sam Hogan at Marcouray receives a demand to surrender. Hogan refuses to surrender and tells the Germans that he will fight to the death. Elements of the XVIII Airborne Corps pull back from Manhay on order of Field Marshal Montgomery, who desires to neaten the lines. American commanders protest this order. Giving up territory means only that it will have to be retaken eventually, with more casualties. As the Americans pull back, they are attacked by German tanks and infantry, causing heavy casualties and threatening to open the way to the Allied supply base at Liège.

The weather over western Europe clears, and Eighth Air Force sends its largest air strike of the war against transportation and communications behind the Bulge in Germany. Over 2,000 B-17s and B-24 Liberators escorted by over 800 P-47 Thunderbolts and P-51 Mustangs. A total of 12 bombers are lost and 619 damaged. Aircrews report 18 confirmed kills, five probables, and one possible. Aircrew casualties are 37 killed, 49 wounded, and 114 missing. Fighter pilots report 70 confirmed kills, one probable kill, and 19 possibles in the air. Ten fighters are lost and two damaged. The pilots are reported missing.

B-24 Liberators bomb the La Pallice coastal battery in France.

Ninth Air Force sends 276 B-26 Marauders and A-20 Havocs to attack railroad bridges and communication centers in western Germany. P-38 and P-47 fighters escort the 9th Bombardment Division, fly armed reconnaissance, and support the III, VIII, and XII Corps along the southern edge of the Bulge. Fighters fly cover for the 4th Armored Division of General George S. Patton, Jr.'s Third Army as it approaches Bastogne.

The IX Troop Carrier Command sends 160 C-47s to drop 160 tons of supplies to American troops surrounded at Bastogne.

A U.S. freighter at Antwerp is damaged when a German V-1 rocket hits close by.

**Southwest Pacific Area:** In the Philippines, FEAF B-24 Liberators bomb Clark Field on Luzon. B-25 Mitchells bomb targets on Mindanao and shipping around the island.

**PACIFIC:** Twentieth Air Force sends 29 B-29 Superfortresses from the Marianas to attack airfields on Iwo Jima. A total of 23 hit the primary targets.

The B-29s of the 482nd, 483rd, and 484th Bombardment Squadrons (Very Heavy) of the 505th Bombardment Group (Very Heavy) arrive at Tinian from the United States. The squadrons' first missions are scheduled for December 30.

**CENTRAL PACIFIC:** Seventh Air Force sends 50 B-24 Liberators from Saipan and Guam to bomb Iwo Jima. P-38 Lightnings from Saipan make low-level strafing attacks. Another 23 B-24 Liberators from Saipan bomb Chichi Jima. During the night B-24s conduct a raid on Iwo Jima.

Naval Task Group 94.9, commanded by Rear Admiral Allan E. Smith, bombards Iwo Jima after Seventh Air Force bombers hit the island. Two destroyers sink a Japanese fast transport and a landing ship.

**NEW GUINEA:** FEAF B-24 Liberators bomb the airfield in Borneo, and B-25 Mitchells, P-40s, and A-20 Havocs attack targets in the Molucca Islands.

U.S. submarine *Barbero* torpedoes and sinks a Japanese submarine chaser and damages a transport southwest of Borneo.

## December 25

**CBI:** In Burma, Tenth Air Force P-47 Thunderbolts bomb and strafe troop concentrations and supplies at Mabein, conduct fighter sweeps on the Burma Road, and strafe Lashio airfield.

Fourteenth Air Force P-51 Mustangs attack a railroad ferry, shipping, and an airfield near Nanking, China. Pilots report damaging a tanker and destroying 13 aircraft.

**ETO: The Battle of the Bulge.** The Germans again attack Bastogne from the northwest. Paratroopers and tank destroyers knock out 18 German tanks. In the VII Corps area, 2nd Armored Division counterattacks at Celles, supported by Ninth Air Force fighters and bombers, and secures the left flank of First Army. The XVIII Airborne Corps reserve, the 75th Infantry Division, fights its first battle and stops German forces at Manhay, restoring the line. The 7th Armored Division, the 30th Infantry Division, and the 82nd Airborne Division are all committed to defending the northwest edge of the Bulge against strong German pressure. As the German defenses stiffen, Patton commits the XII Corps to attack Echternach with the 5th Infantry Division. Soon Major General Manton S. Eddy, XII Corps commander, will funnel the other divisions of his corps into the battle.

Eighth Air Force sends 132 B-17s and B-24 Liberators escorted by over 400 P-51 Mustangs to attack railroad bridges and communication centers behind the Bulge in western Germany. A total of five bombers are lost and 132 damaged. Aircrews report three confirmed kills, one probable, and four possibles. Aircrew casualties are two killed, four wounded, and 47 missing. Fighter pilots report 46 confirmed kills, six probables, and eight possibles in the air. Nine P-51 fighters are lost and three damaged. Nine pilots are reported missing.

Ninth Air Force sends nearly 650 B-26s, A-20 Havocs, and A-26 Invaders to attack rail and road bridges, communications centers, and German tanks and troops in the Bulge. Fighters support the III, VIII, and XII Corps on the southern edge of the Bulge.

When Private Paul J. Wiedorfer's infantry company of the 318th Infantry Regiment, 80th Infantry Division, comes under heavy machine-gun fire from two German positions dug in along a wood line near Chaumont, Belgium, Private Wiedorfer takes action. He stands up and charges across 40 yards of deep snow to reach the German positions. Untouched by enemy fire he destroys the first machine-gun position with a hand grenade and rifle fire, then immediately turns to assault the second position. He wounds one soldier and forces the remaining six to surrender. As the platoon resumes its advance, both the platoon leader and the platoon sergeant are wounded. Without hesitation, Private Wiedorfer takes command and moves the platoon to take its objective. For his inspiring acts of courage and leadership, Private Wiedorfer will receive the Medal of Honor.

**MEDITERRANEAN:** Fifteenth Air Force sends more than 250 B-17s and B-24 Liberators escorted by P-38 Lightnings and P-51 Mustangs to attack a synthetic oil plant in Czechoslovakia and a marshaling yard in Austria.

**ITALY:** Twelfth Air Force A-20 Havocs and P-47 Thunderbolts attack rail lines to the Brenner Pass and the eastern Po Valley. Pilots report several locomotives destroyed.

**SOUTHWEST PACIFIC AREA:** The 1st Battalion, 305th Infantry Regiment, 77th Infantry Division, supported by engineers and artillery, makes an amphibious landing at Palompon and captures the last coastal town occupied by Japanese forces. The Ormoc Valley is closed, completing the final phase of operations for Sixth Army on Leyte. General MacArthur declares Leyte secure even though units of the 1st Cavalry Division, the 24th Infantry Division, and the 32nd Infantry Division will continue to encounter resistance as the units clear the last defenders on December 31.

FEAF B-24 Liberators escorted by P-38 Lightnings and P-47 Thunderbolts bomb airfields on Luzon Island and Mindanao Island.

Carrier aircraft from Task Force 38 attack Japanese shipping west of Luzon and sink a landing ship.

A naval air station at Samar is established.

German submarine *U-862* torpedoes and sinks a U.S. freighter in the Tasman Sea south of Sidney, Australia.

Major Thomas B. McGuire of the Thirteenth Air Force is leading a squadron of 15 P-38 Lightnings over Luzon, providing cover for bombers, when 20 Japanese fighters attack. During the battle he shoots down three enemy aircraft. Even after his guns jam, McGuire flies to the rescue of his fellow pilots and maneuvers his aircraft to give his wingman a good shot at the Japanese fighters. The following day he escorts a bombing mission against Clark Field and rescues a crippled bomber by exposing himself to enemy fire. During the battle he shoots down four enemy aircraft. His determination to protect his squadron mates, his aggressive action to engage the enemy, and his willingness to put himself in danger to save others will win him the Medal of Honor.

**CENTRAL PACIFIC:** Seventh Air Force sends 12 B-24 Liberators from Saipan to bomb Iwo Jima. During the night B-24s from Guam and Saipan conduct raids on Iwo Jima.

**NEW GUINEA:** FEAF B-24 Liberators bomb airfields in Borneo. B-25 Mitchells, along with Royal Australian Air Force (RAAF) fighter-bombers, attack Halmahera Island.

U.S. submarine *Barbero* attacks a Japanese convoy and sinks a transport west of Borneo.

FEAF B-24 Liberators sink two small cargo vessels and damage two others off Borneo.

## December 26

**CBI:** In Burma, Tenth Air Force B-25 Mitchells and P-47 Thunderbolts attack rail lines, roads, troop concentrations, and bridges.

Fourteenth Air Force sends 12 P-51 Mustangs to attack the Tsinan airfield. B-25 Mitchells, P-51 Mustangs, and P-38 Lightnings attack bridges, railroads, troop concentrations, and rail and road traffic in China, Thailand, and Burma.

**ETO: The Battle of the Bulge.** The 4th Armored Division reaches Bastogne. The 318th Infantry Regiment of the 80th Infantry Division makes contact with Combat Command A of the 9th Armored Division. The battle to keep Bastogne has cost the Americans over 3,000 casualties. Task Force Hogan of the 3rd Armored Division, after being surrounded and cut off for seven days, reaches American lines on foot. The 2nd Armored Division completes the destruction of German forces at Celles. The Germans lose 3,700 men killed, wounded, or captured, 82 tanks, and more than 500 other vehicles captured or destroyed. The 2nd Armored loses 27 tanks and has 17 men killed and 227 wounded. With the relief of Bastogne and the VII Corps counterattack at Celles, the momentum of the German offensive is stopped.

Eighth Air Force sends more than 150 B-17s and B-24 Liberators escorted by 249 P-47 Thunderbolts and P-51 Mustangs to attack marshaling yards and railroad bridges behind the Bulge. A total of 30 bombers are damaged. Fighter pilots report 11 confirmed kills.

P-51 Mustangs support the bombers by making a sweep around Bonn. Of the 70 aircraft engaged, two are lost and one damaged. The pilots are reported missing. Pilots report three confirmed kills.

During the night three B-17s and six B-24s drop leaflets over Germany and the Netherlands.

Ninth Air Force sends A-20 Havocs, A-26 Invaders, and B-26 Marauders to attack railroad bridges, road junctions, and communication targets in the Bulge. P-47 and P-38 fighters support the III and VIII Corps and the 4th Armored Division as they break the siege of Bastogne.

Lieutenant Colonel Keith L. Ware commands the 1st Battalion, 15th Infantry Regiment, 3rd Infantry Division, conducting an attack on a hill near Sigolsheim, France. The attack falters as the first company comes under heavy fire from artillery, mortar, and machine-gun fire. Lieutenant Colonel Ware advances forward and spends more than two hours alone scouting the German defenses. He returns to the company position and takes a Browning Automatic Rifle and leads an assault team of two officers, nine enlisted men, and a tank. Lieutenant Colonel Ware fires on the

German positions and marks targets for the tank. Running out of ammunition, Ware uses an M-1 rifle to engage a machine-gun position and marks the target for the tank. As nearly half of his small assault group become casualties, Ware continues the attack. Although wounded, he refuses medical treatment until the objective is secured. For his extreme courage under fire and his exceptional leadership, Lieutenant Colonel Ware will receive the Medal of Honor.

**MEDITERRANEAN:** Fifteenth Air Force sends more than 380 B-17s and B-24 Liberators escorted by P-38 Lightnings and P-51 Mustangs to bomb oil refineries in Germany and at Auschwitz, Poland.

**ITALY:** The Germans launch operation *Wintergewitter* (Winter Thunderstorm). The Germans attack with eight battalions, including alpine infantry and regular infantry. The objective is to attack and destroy the 92nd Infantry Division, which has had a poor performance record in combat. The 92nd is shattered as it retreats from Barga, but some of its units fight quite effectively. General Crittenberger of IV Corps adds reinforcements from the 1st Armored Division, the 34th Infantry Division, and the 8th Indian Division, supported by the XXII Tactical Air Command, to repel the German attacks and limit the advance.

Twelfth Air Force B-25 Mitchells and B-26 Marauders attack rail and road bridges. A-20 Havocs and P-47 Thunderbolts attack rail lines, bridges, and roads and support Fifth Army ground forces south of Bologna and in the Serchio River Valley.

**SOUTHWEST PACIFIC AREA:** General MacArthur transfers operational control of Leyte and Samar to Eighth Army. American troops will continue to fight scattered groups of Japanese until May of 1945.

The campaign on Leyte has cost the Japanese heavily. The Japanese leadership had believed this was the decisive battle to be fought and this was where the Americans could be stopped. The commanders threw the bulk of the air, land, and seapower that was available into battle at Leyte and have lost. Japanese casualties on Leyte amount to 49,000 men, not including the losses of ship crews and pilots. Without air or naval support, the remaining Japanese forces on Luzon and other smaller islands in the Philippines are isolated and can fight only to delay and make the cost to the Americans as heavy as possible. American casualties number 15,584 with over 3,500 killed.

Leyte is not what MacArthur desired the island to be—an airbase for future operations against Luzon. The ground is unsuitable for airfields that can handle large aircraft. Tacloban airfield cannot be suitably expanded, and, although an airfield is constructed at Tanauan on the east side of the island by the end of the campaign, it is never heavily used. High winds and heavy rains that mark the weather on the island wash away roads and delay other important construction.

FEAF B-24 Liberators bomb Clark Field on Luzon Island. B-25 Mitchells bomb Mindanao Island.

A Japanese naval force, consisting of a heavy cruiser, a light cruiser, three destroyers, and three escort destroyers, intends to bombard American positions on Mindoro. The ships are attacked on the way by FEAF B-25 Mitchells, P-38 Lightnings, P-40s, and P-47 Thunderbolts, along with U.S. Navy PB4Y Privateers and PBM Mariners. The two cruisers, three destroyers, and two destroyer escorts are damaged.

The ships bombard Mindoro, but a motor torpedo boat sinks one destroyer south of Manila. This is the last time the Japanese fleet will attempt to challenge U.S. forces in the Philippines.

**PACIFIC:** U.S. destroyer sinks an auxiliary submarine chaser in the Bonins.

U.S. submarine *Swordfish* departs Midway for her 13th war patrol, but disappears after making contact on January 3, 1945.

**CENTRAL PACIFIC:** Seventh Air Force B-24 Liberators from Guam bomb Iwo Jima.

During the night two B-24s from Saipan conduct a raid on Iwo Jima.

**NEW GUINEA:** FEAF B-24 Liberators, B-25 Mitchells, P-40s, and A-20 Havocs attack targets on Halmahera Island.

FEAF B-24 Liberators sink a Japanese cargo vessel east of Celebes Island.

## December 27

**CBI:** In Burma, Tenth Air Force B-25 Mitchells attack bridges and P-47 Thunderbolts hit troop concentrations and logistics storage areas.

In China, Fourteenth Air Force P-51 Mustangs attack White Cloud, Whampoa, and Tien Ho airfields in Canton. Fighter pilots report 10 Japanese aircraft destroyed. Two P-51s are lost.

U.S. submarine *Baya* locates the heavy cruiser, light cruiser, and two destroyers of the Mindoro attack force as they approach Cam Ranh Bay off French Indochina. USS *Baya* makes an unsuccessful attack on the ships.

**ETO:** The III Corps of Third Army fights to expand the corridor to Bastogne and prepares to attack north to St-Vith. Eighth Air Force sends more than 600 B-17s and B-24 Liberators escorted by 178 P-51 Mustangs to attack marshaling yards, rail bridges, and rail junctions. Two bombers are lost and 295 damaged. Aircrew casualties are 36 killed, 17 wounded, and 15 missing. Fighter pilots report 29 confirmed kills and one probable in the air. Three P-51 fighters are lost. The pilots are reported missing.

Ninth Air Force sends A-20 Havocs, A-26 Invaders, and B-26 Marauders to attack railroad bridges and communication centers in the Bulge. P-47 and P-38 fighters support 3rd Armored and 82nd Airborne Divisions in the Manhay and Trois-Ponts area of Belgium, and the III, VIII, and XII Corps in Saint-Hubert-Bastogne-Martelange area.

First Lieutenant Eli Whiteley is a platoon leader in L Company, 15th Infantry Regiment, 3rd Infantry Division. He leads his platoon in an attack to capture the town of Sigolsheim, France. He is wounded as the infantrymen attempt to assault a building, but he charges into the house alone and kills two Germans. Then, using smoke and fragmentation grenades, Whiteley charges into the next house and kills two Germans and takes the surrender of 11 more. With his left arm now useless, he continues to lead his men. After blasting a hole in the wall of a strongly defended house, he again rushes into the building. Firing his Thompson submachine gun by clamping it under his uninjured arm, he kills five soldiers and takes the surrender of another 12. Wounded again, First Lieutenant Whiteley refuses to be stopped and again leads an attack on another building before being forcibly evacuated. For his exemplary courage and determination in leading his men, First Lieutenant Whiteley will receive the Medal of Honor.

**MEDITERRANEAN:** Fifteenth Air Force sends more than 500 B-17s and B-24 Liberators escorted by P-38 Lightnings and P-51 Mustangs to attack an oil refinery and marshaling yards in Austria and rail lines in northern Italy.

**ITALY:** Operation Wintergewitter has reached its objective of severely damaging the 92nd Infantry Division. German forces begin withdrawing from Barga. The Allies are able to restore the line to its original position by December 31.

The 10th Mountain Division arrives in Italy.

The 370th Infantry Regiment of the 92nd Division is reorganized behind two brigades of Indian infantry sent by IV Corps to shore up the line. General Clark moves operational control of the 85th Infantry Division from II Corps to IV Corps and prepares the 1st Armored Division for a counterattack.

Twelfth Air Force B-25 Mitchells and B-26 Marauders attack rail and road traffic from Austria and Yugoslavia. P-47 Thunderbolts attack logistics storage areas near Bologna and support Fifth Army ground forces.

**SOUTHWEST PACIFIC AREA:** In the Philippines FEAF B-24 Liberators bomb airfields on Negros Island and an airfield on Mindanao.

Japanese aircraft bomb American positions and shipping at Mindoro.

**PACIFIC:** Twentieth Air Force sends 72 B-29 Superfortresses from the Marianas to bomb the Nakajima and Musashino aircraft plants in Tokyo. A total of 39 hit the primary targets. Japanese fighters make over 250 individual attacks on the bombers. Aircrews report 21 confirmed kills, 10 probables, and seven possibles. Three B-29s are lost.

The 313th Bombardment Wing (Very Heavy) of the XXI Bomber Command arrives with B-29s on Tinian.

Cruisers and destroyers of Task Group 94.9 bombard Iwo Jima after Seventh Air Force hits the island. Japanese shore batteries damage a U.S. destroyer, which, however, continues the fight, sinking a fast transport with the assistance of two other destroyers.

**CENTRAL PACIFIC:** Seventh Air Force B-24 Liberators from Saipan and Guam bomb Iwo Jima. P-38 Lightnings also strafe the island. B-24s from Saipan bomb Chichi Jima.

During the night two B-24s conduct a snooper (radar-assisted bomb release) mission on Iwo Jima.

**NEW GUINEA:** U.S. submarine *Barbero* is damaged in an aerial attack off Java and is forced to return to base.

### December 28

**CBI:** In Burma, Tenth Air Force B-25 Mitchells and P-47 Thunderbolts bomb bridges, roads, troop concentrations, logistics storage areas, and artillery positions.

In China, Fourteenth Air Force sends B-25 Mitchells, P-40s, and P-51 Mustangs to attack town areas, railroad targets, and gun positions near Hengyang and Leiyang. P-51 Mustangs and P-38 Lightnings attack airfields and other targets in French Indochina.

U.S. submarine *Dace* attacks a Japanese convoy, sinking a supply ship off French Indochina.

**ETO:** First Army is ordered to attack south toward Houffalize, in the center of the Bulge. Third Army is to strike for Houffalize from the south. At the same time, Bastogne is the target of another strong German attack. The III Corps of Third Army (4th and 6th Armored Divisions, the 35th and 26th Infantry Divisions) holds southeast of Bastogne against German attacks. The VIII Corps receives the 87th Infantry Division from SHAEF reserve and the 11th Armored Division.

Eighth Air Force sends more than 1,200 B-17s and B-24 Liberators escorted by 541 P-51 Mustangs to attack rail bridges and marshaling yards. Two B-24s are lost and 130 bombers damaged. Aircrew casualties are 12 killed, four wounded, and 22 missing.

During the night two B-24 Liberators drop leaflets over Belgium.

**MEDITERRANEAN:** Fifteenth Air Force sends more than 480 B-17s and B-24 Liberators escorted by P-38 Lightnings and P-51 Mustangs to attack oil storage facilities and railyards in Germany, marshaling yards in Austria, and oil refineries and oil storage facilities in Czechoslovakia.

**ITALY:** Twelfth Air Force B-25 Mitchells and B-26 Marauders attack German troop concentrations, rail lines, and bridges. P-47 Thunderbolts of the XXII Tactical Air Command attack rail lines, vehicles, bridges, roads, and support Fifth Army ground forces.

**SOUTHWEST PACIFIC AREA:** Kamikazes attack Task Group 77.11 as it approaches Mindoro. An LST and two freighters are hit. One freighter, carrying ammunition, explodes in a huge fireball, damaging surrounding ships.

**PACIFIC:** The headquarters of the 6th Bombardment Group (Very Heavy) and the 24th and 39th Bombardment Squadrons (Very Heavy) arrives in Tinian from the United States with B-29 Superfortresses. The headquarters of the 9th Bombardment Group (Very Heavy) and the B-29s of the 1st, 5th, and 99th Bombardment Squadrons (Very Heavy) also arrive at Tinian. All the squadrons' first missions are scheduled for late January 1945.

**CENTRAL PACIFIC:** Seventh Air Force sends 13 B-24 Liberators from Saipan to bomb Iwo Jima.

During the night B-24s from Guam and Saipan conduct raids on Iwo Jima.

**NEW GUINEA:** FEAF B-25 Mitchells bomb the airfields on Ambon Island, Celebes Island, and Haroekoe Island. P-40s and A-30s attack the airfield on Buru Island.

## December 29

**CBI:** In Burma, Tenth Air Force B-25 Mitchells bomb troops and logistics bases and P-47 Thunderbolts attack logistics support areas and troop concentrations.

Fourteenth Air Force B-25 Mitchells attack targets of opportunity from Dong Hoa to Lang Son in French Indochina.

**ETO:** The XII Corps gains control of Echternach.

Eighth Air Force sends more than 780 B-17s and B-24 Liberators, escorted by 433 P-51 Mustangs, to attack marshaling yards, communication centers, and rail bridges. Four bombers are lost and 333 are damaged. Aircrew casualties are 22 killed, 28 wounded, and 15 missing. Three fighters are lost and one is damaged. The three pilots are reported missing.

The Ninth Air Force, XIX Tactical Air Command, flies armed reconnaissance over Belgium and Germany and supports the III, VIII, and XII Corps in the Neufchateau-Bastogne-Arlon areas of Belgium.

German submarine *U-772* attacks a convoy in the English Channel, damaging two U.S. freighters.

**MEDITERRANEAN:** Fifteenth Air Force sends more than 450 B-17s and B-24 Liberators escorted by 300 P-38 Lightnings and P-51 Mustangs to attack marshaling yards in Germany, Austria, and northern Italy.

**ITALY:** The 8th Indian Division recaptures Barga with heavy air support from XXII Tactical Air Command fighter aircraft. The 92nd Division restores the defensive line in the Serchio Valley with the support of air strikes. The surprise German offensive delays the intended Allied offensive against Bologna.

Twelfth Air Force B-25 Mitchells and B-26 Marauders attack rail and road bridges. A-20 Havocs and P-47 Thunderbolts of the XXII Tactical Air Command attack communication targets and rail targets in support of Fifth Army ground forces.

**SOUTHWEST PACIFIC AREA:** In the Philippines, FEAF B-24 Liberators bomb an airfield on Mindanao Island.

**CENTRAL PACIFIC:** Seventh Air Force sends 26 B-24 Liberators from Guam to attack Iwo Jima. Other B-24s continue harassment bombing throughout the night.

**NEW GUINEA:** FEAF B-25 Mitchells, P-40s, and P-38 Lightnings attack targets on Buru Island.

B-24 Liberators, P-47 Thunderbolts, and A-20 Havocs bomb Celebes Island targets.

U.S. submarine *Hawkbill* torpedoes and sinks a Japanese merchant in the Java Sea.

### December 30

**CBI:** In Burma, Tenth Air Force P-47 Thunderbolts and P-38 Lightnings attack roads, troop concentrations, and artillery positions.

Fourteenth Air Force B-24 Liberators bomb a bridge near Kengtung, China, and rail targets in French Indochina. P-51 Mustangs and P-40s attack troop concentrations, gun positions, rail lines, logistics storage sites, bridges, and highways in Burma and southern China.

**ETO:** Third Army begins its attack north from Bastogne toward Houffalize. The VIII Corps attacks from west of Bastogne with the 87th Infantry Division and the 11th Armored Division. The 11th has never been in combat, and the 87th has very little experience. Their advance is almost immediately stopped by a German attack intended to surround Bastogne. To the east of the town German forces attempting to close the ring around Bastogne are stopped by elements of the 35th Infantry Division at Villers. The 26th Infantry Division makes limited gains.

Eighth Air Force sends more than 1,300 B-17s and B-24 Liberators escorted by 508 P-51 Mustangs to attack rail bridges and marshaling yards. Four B-17s are lost and 63 bombers are damaged. Aircrew casualties are 12 killed and 30 missing. Two P-51 fighters are lost and the pilots are reported missing.

During the night three B-17s and eight B-24s drop leaflets over Germany, Luxembourg, and the Netherlands.

The Ninth Air Force, XIX Tactical Air Command, supports the III, VIII, and XII Corps near St-Hubert and Bastogne in Belgium and around Diekirch in Luxembourg.

**ITALY:** Twelfth Air Force B-25 Mitchells and B-26 Marauders attack rail and road bridges. A-20 Havocs and P-47 Thunderbolts attack bridges and roads and support Fifth Army ground forces.

**SOUTHWEST PACIFIC AREA:** FEAF P-47 Thunderbolts, P-38 Lightnings, and A-20 Havocs attack airfields in the central Philippines.

Kamikazes attack a convoy bound for Mindoro, damaging two destroyers. A U.S. freighter is sunk during an aerial bombing run on the convoy. U.S. submarine *Razorback* attacks a Japanese convoy southeast of Formosa, sinking a destroyer and damaging two cargo ships.

Fifth Air Force B-25 Mitchells, A-20 Havocs, and P-40s attack Japanese shipping near Lingayen Gulf, sinking a coastal patrol ship, a submarine chaser, and three cargo ships.

**CENTRAL PACIFIC:** Seventh Air Force sends 26 B-24 Liberators from Saipan to attack Iwo Jima. Other B-24s from Guam continue harassment bombing throughout the night.

Admiral William F. Halsey's Third Fleet leaves its anchorage at Ulithi to support the Luzon invasion.

**NEW GUINEA:** FEAF P-40s and P-38 Lightnings attack airfields in northern Borneo and Celebes Island, while B-25 Mitchells attack a barge and logistics storage facilities on Haroekoe Island.

The headquarters of the 322nd Troop Carrier Wing is activated at Hollandia.

## December 31

**CBI:** In Burma, Tenth Air Force P-47 Thunderbolts attack airfields and bridges. Other P-47s and P-38 Lightnings attack a Japanese division headquarters at Ongyaw as well as troop concentrations and logistics storage areas.

Fourteenth Air Force sends four B-24 Liberators to bomb shipping off Hainan Island. Aircrews report one cargo ship sunk and another damaged. The Fourteenth Air Force reports that during this year over 33,000 Japanese ground troops have been killed and 494 aircraft have been destroyed. In addition, 640,000 tons of shipping have been sunk, another 237,000 tons probably sunk, and 396,000 tons of shipping damaged.

In China, P-40s and P-51 Mustangs attack troops, horses, town areas, and railroad targets near Hankow, Hengyang, Lingling, and Kweilin.

**ETO:** The 6th Armored Division of III Corps attacks east of Bastogne. The Germans attempt 17 separate counterattacks on Bastogne. Each one is stopped.

Eighth Air Force sends more than 1,300 B-17s and B-24 Liberators escorted by 676 P-47 Thunderbolts and P-51 Mustangs to attack oil industry targets at Hamburg, marshaling yards, and Rhine River bridges. A total of 27 bombers are lost and 372 are damaged. Aircrews report 26 confirmed kills, eight probables, and 16 possibles. Aircrew casualties are five killed, 31 wounded, and 248 missing. Fighter pilots report 60 confirmed kills, two probables, and 16 possibles in the air and one confirmed kill on the ground. Ten fighters are lost and one is damaged. The 10 pilots are reported missing.

German submarine *U-906*, a minesweeper, and three cargo vessels are sunk in the air attack on Hamburg.

During the night two B-17s and eight B-24s from Eighth Air Force drop leaflets over Germany, France, and Belgium.

The Ninth Air Force, XIX Tactical Air Command, supports the III, VIII, and XX Corps around Bastogne.

During the night the Germans launch Nordwind, an offensive aimed at the XV and VI Corps of Seventh Army and the 6th Army Group. The German First Army attacks toward Bitche and the Wissembourg Gap, while the German Nineteenth Army attacks from the Colmar Pocket toward Strasbourg. The XV Corps, commanded by Major General Wade Haislip, defends a 35-mile-long front with the 100th, 104th, and 44th Infantry Divisions. The French 2nd Armored Division is in reserve. The VI Corps, commanded by Major General Edward H. Brooks, defends about a 40-mile front with the 45th and 79th Infantry Divisions. The 14th Armored Division is in reserve. Three separate task forces formed from newly arriving units are organized to support both corps. The 44th Infantry Division supported by Task Force Harris (formed from the 63rd Infantry Division) stops the German attack at Rimling. The 398th and 399th Infantry Regiment of the 100th Infantry Division fight in three directions for three days, holding off German attacks as the Germans drive a 10-mile salient into the XV Corps lines. Four German divisions attack near Bitche, advancing past weak cavalry units. Task Force Harris, along with the 14th Armored Division and the 100th Infantry Division, counterattacks from the north and VI Corps supports with Task Force Herren (formed from the 70th Infantry Division) and units of the 45th and 75th Infantry Divisions.

**ITALY:** Twelfth Air Force A-20 Havocs and P-47 Thunderbolts of the XXII Tactical Air Command report destroying five railroad bridges and damaging two others in the Po Valley and report destroying or damaging more than 200 railcars and several locomotives.

**SOUTHWEST PACIFIC AREA:** In the Philippines, FEAF B-24 Liberators and B-25 Mitchells bomb airfields on Luzon and Mindanao Islands.

Japanese torpedo planes hit a U.S. freighter off Mindoro.

**PACIFIC:** The Twentieth Air Force's Brigadier General Haywood S. Hansell, Jr., commander of the XXI Bomber Command forward echelon headquarters, and his staff redeploy from Saipan to Guam.

**CENTRAL PACIFIC:** Seventh Air Force sends 19 B-24 Liberators from Guam to attack Iwo Jima. Ten other B-24s continue harassment bombing throughout the night.

**NEW GUINEA:** FEAF B-24 Liberators and B-25 Mitchells bomb the airfield on Celebes Island, Dili on Timor Island, and airfields and logistics bases on Halmahera Island. P-40s and A-20 Havocs attack targets on Halmahera Island and on Celebes Island.

# 1945

### January 1
**ALEUTIANS:** Eleventh Air Force sends five B-24 Liberators to fly coverage for U.S. Navy ships after aborting a bomb mission against the Kurile Islands.

**CBI:** Major General George E. Stratemeyer's Eastern Air Command is flying 2,000 tons of supplies to Allied forces in Burma to sustain the offensive against the Japanese defending along the Akyab-Mandalay-Wanting line.

In China, Fourteenth Air Force sends P-51 Mustangs and P-40s to attack roads and rail lines, supply depots, troop positions, industrial targets, and gun positions from Yoyang to Puchi and between Siaokan and Hsuchang. P-51 Mustangs attack Suchow airfield. Fighter pilots report 25 aircraft destroyed. A P-51 detachment of the 16th Fighter Squadron, 51st Fighter Group, begins operating from Laohokow. In Burma, the Tenth Air Force sends 71 P-47 Thunderbolts and P-38 Lightnings to attack villages, general supply areas, fuel storage areas, tanks and troop concentrations.

**ETO:** First Army is organized into three corps: the V Corps (9th, 99th, 2nd, and 1st Infantry Divisions), the XVIII Airborne Corps (30th, 7th, and 106th Infantry Divisions, the 82nd Airborne, and the 7th Armored Division), and the VII Corps (83rd and 84th Infantry Divisions and the 2nd and 3rd Armored Divisions). Third Army is organized into four corps: VIII Corps (the 9th and 11th Armored Divisions, the 87th Infantry Division, and the 101st Airborne), III Corps (the 4th and 6th Armored Divisions and the 35th and 26th Infantry Divisions), XII Corps (the 80th, 5th, and 4th Infantry Divisions), and XX Corps (28th Infantry Division, the 10th Armored Division, and the 17th Airborne).

Nearly 1,000 German aircraft attack Allied airfields in Holland and Belgium. About 300 Allied aircraft are destroyed, limiting air support to the 12th Army Group for more than a week. About 90 German aircraft are shot down by antiaircraft fire. German forces attack in the VI Corps area, threatening Strasbourg.

Eighth Air Force sends 845 B-17s and B-24 Liberators escorted by 725 P-47 Thunderbolts and P-51 Mustangs to attack oil production facilities, marshaling yards, and railroad bridges in western Germany using both visual and radar-guided bomb release. Aircrews report 23 confirmed kills, one possible, and three probables, including one jet aircraft. Five B-17s are lost and 167 are damaged. One B-24 is lost and 67 are damaged. Two P-51 Mustangs are lost and one is damaged. Two pilots are reported missing. Aircrew losses are 40 killed, 16 wounded, and 28 missing. Fighter pilots report 17 confirmed kills, one probable, and one possible. A total of 12 B-17s fly a screening force mission, and aircrews report six confirmed kills. Five of the bombers are lost and one damaged. Casualties are 45 crewmen missing. Two B-17s fly an Aphrodite (see August 4, 1944 ETO entry) mission against Oldenburg without loss. During the night three B-17s and five B-24s drop leaflets over Belgium and Germany. The 1st, 2nd, and 3rd Bombardment Divisions are redesignated as air divisions.

The Germans attack Ninth Air Force airfields near Brussels, Belgium, Eindhoven, Holland, and Metz, France, with nearly 800 aircraft. The Allies lose 127 fighters on the ground. Allied fighters report 160 confirmed kills in the air, while antiaircraft units report 300 enemy aircraft shot down.

Ninth Air Force sends nearly 200 A-20 Havocs, A-26 Invaders, and B-26 Marauders attack rail bridges, communication centers, and command and control sites in Belgium and Germany. P-47 Thunderbolts escort 9th Bombardment Division and Eighth Air Force bombers, fly patrols, and conduct armed reconnaissance. Fighter pilots report 39 confirmed kills. Fighters also provide support to the III, VII, and XII Corps.

Sergeant Charles A. MacGillivary, a squad leader in I Company, 71st Infantry Regiment, 44th Infantry Division, is ordered to take his men forward to protect the platoon's left flank and block advancing German forces near Woelfling, France. As he moves his men forward in the darkness, he encounters German panzer-grenadiers digging in. As he reports their location, the Germans fire on the squad. MacGillivary circles around to the German machine gun, then attacks, eliminating the enemy position. Early in the afternoon Sergeant MacGillivary locates six German machine-gun positions. He again moves out alone to outflank the enemy, destroying one position with a hand grenade. Using a discarded submachine gun he attacks a second machine-gun position and eliminates it. He attacks a third position with hand grenades, then assaults it, and in the fight his left arm is shot away. He holds the position until his unit is able to attack through the remaining enemy defenders. For his exceptional courage and initiative in the face of a determined enemy Sergeant MacGillivary will receive the Medal of Honor.

**ITALY:** Twelfth Air Force B-25 Mitchells and B-26 Marauders attack bridges and an ammunition storage site. A-20 Havocs and P-47 Thunderbolts destroy a fuel storage depot at Parma and support Fifth Army ground forces south of Bologna. The headquarters of the 319th Bombardment Group (Medium) departs Corsica for the United States. The group will convert to A-26 Invaders in preparation for redeployment to the Pacific theater.

**SOUTHWEST PACIFIC AREA:** Eighth Army takes operational control of Mindoro Island from Sixth Army. Eighth Army is assigned a zone of operations covering all of the Philippine islands south of Luzon.

On Mindoro, infantry units move to the eastern shore of the island to draw Japanese attention away from the Lingayen Gulf area and focus on a possible landing from Mindoro to southern Luzon. Navy minesweepers begin operating in the Batangas area, followed by merchant cargo ships and airdrops of dummy parachutists to simulate landing operations.

In the Philippines, Far East Air Force B-25 Mitchells, P-47 Thunderbolts, and P-38 Lightnings attack Negros Island airfields. B-25s bomb a barracks on Luzon. B-24 Liberators escorted by P-38s attack targets near Manila and bomb Clark Field on Luzon and an airfield on Mindanao.

The headquarters of the 345th Bombardment Group (Medium) moves from Dulag to Tacloban on Leyte Island.

U.S. submarine *Stingray* lands supplies at Tawi Tawi in the Philippines.

**PACIFIC:** Seventh Air Force sends 19 B-24s from Saipan to bomb Iwo Jima. Another nine more conduct snooper (radar-assisted bomb release) missions during the night.

**NEW GUINEA:** B-24 Liberators and B-25 Mitchells attack troop concentrations and an ammunition storage area on Halmahera Island and airfields on Ceram Island in the Moluccas.

### January 2

**CBI:** In Burma, Fourteenth Air Force B-25 Mitchells bomb Kentung; P-40s and P-51 Mustangs attack railroad traffic. Tenth Air Force P-47 Thunderbolts and P-38 Lightnings attack troop concentrations and supplies in Burma.

**ETO:** Eighth Air Force sends nearly 1,700 B-17s and 296 B-24 Liberators to attack marshaling yards communication centers, rail bridges. The B-17s are escorted by 256 P-51 Mustangs; the B-24 Liberators are escorted by 215 P-47 Thunderbolts and P-51 Mustangs. The bombers use Gee-H (bombing through the clouds technique in which the lead bomber's navigator locates the bomb release point by sending a radio pulse signal to two ground station transponders). A total of four B-17s are lost and 65 B-24s and B-17s are damaged. Aircrew casualties are 10 killed, two wounded, and 37 missing. Three P-51s are lost and one is damaged. The two pilots are reported missing.

During the night two B-17s and six B-24s drop leaflets over Germany and France.

A total of six B-17s conduct screening missions to jam German radio interception efforts and conduct countermeasures against German radar sites.

Ninth Air Force sends more than 130 A-20 Havocs, A-26 Invaders, and B-26 Marauders to attack railroad bridges and communication centers. In Belgium and Germany, P-47 and P-38 fighters support ground forces of the III and VIII Corps near Bastogne and support XII Corps.

The P-47 Thunderbolts of the 314th, 315th, and 316th Fighter Squadrons, 324th Fighter Group of the First Tactical Air Force (Provisional), redeploy from Tavaux to Luneville, France.

Vice Admiral Sir Bertram H. Ramsay (RN), Allied Commander in Chief, Expeditionary Force, is killed in an airplane accident near Paris, France.

**ITALY:** Twelfth Air Force A-20 Havocs and P-47 Thunderbolts attack rail lines, trains, and vehicles in the Po River valley, support Fifth Army ground forces, and bomb the Milan marshaling yard.

**SOUTHWEST PACIFIC AREA:** In the Philippines, Far East Air Force P-38 Lightnings and A-20 Havocs attack shipping in San Fernando harbor on Negros Island. B-24 Liberators bomb Clark Field on Luzon Island and targets on Mindanao Island. B-25 Mitchells attack airfields in the central Philippine Islands, supported by A-20s.

The P-38 Lightnings of the 8th Fighter Squadron, 49th Fighter Group, redeploy from Tacloban on Leyte Island to Mindoro Island in the Philippines.

U.S. submarine *Aspro* torpedoes and damages a Japanese landing ship south of Formosa Strait.

**PACIFIC:** Twentieth Air Force sends 49 B-29 Superfortresses from Calcutta, India, to bomb the railroad bridge at Bangkok, Thailand. A total of 44 bombers hit the primary target and two hit an alternative and a target of opportunity. Crewmen report one probable and one possible kill.

**CENTRAL PACIFIC:** Seventh Air Force sends 12 B-24 Liberators from Guam to bomb Haha Jima Island, while 14 other B-24s bomb Iwo Jima Island. During the night 10 B-24s from Guam conduct a snooper (radar-assisted bomb release) mission on Iwo Jima.

**NEW GUINEA:** FEAF B-24 Liberators bomb targets on Celebes Island and Halmahera Island.

U.S. submarine *Becuna* torpedoes and sinks a Japanese ship in the Java Sea.

Fifth Air Force A-20 Havocs and P-38 Lightnings attack Japanese shipping off Luzon and sink a coastal patrol ship, a transport, and five cargo ships.

### January 3

**ALEUTIANS:** Eleventh Air Force sends B-25 Mitchells to fly coverage for naval forces over the Kurile Islands.

**CBI:** The British XV Corps captures Akyab.

In Burma, Tenth Air Force sends 10 B-25 Mitchells, supported by 12 P-47 Thunderbolts, to attack the airfield at Aungban and attack troop concentrations, logistics storage areas, and ammunition supply points.

In China, Fourteenth Air Force sends 10 P-51 Mustangs to attack the airfield at Tsinan. Fighter pilots report 13 Japanese aircraft destroyed. Six P-51s attacks river traffic, reporting several river steamers sunk in the Hankow-Chiuchiang area.

**ETO: The Battle of the Bulge.** First Army begins a counterattack toward Houffalize, attacking with VII Corps, employing the 2nd and 3rd Armored Divisions followed by the 83rd Infantry Division. The Germans have established strong defensive lines, and the weather makes the roads difficult for tanks to move.

In the Seventh Army area, German forces attacking as part of operation Nordwind hit the 179th Infantry Regiment of the 45th Infantry Division at Wingen-sur-Moder, forcing the regiment to retreat two miles. The line is restored by counterattacks by elements of the 313th Infantry Regiment (79th Infantry Division) and the 276th Infantry Regiment (70th Infantry Division) as well as the 180th Infantry Regiment from the 4th Infantry Division.

Eighth Air Force sends more than 1,260 B-17s and B-24 Liberators escorted by over 500 P-51 Mustangs to attack marshaling yards, communication centers, and rail junctions in Germany and Belgium. A total of 15 bombers are damaged. Aircrew casualties are two wounded. Fighter pilots report four confirmed kills. Four fighters are lost and four are damaged. The four pilots are reported missing.

**MEDITERRANEAN:** German submarine *U-870* torpedoes and damages a U.S. freighter in the Mediterranean near Gibraltar.

**ITALY:** Twelfth Air Force B-25 Mitchells and B-26 Marauders attack railroad bridges. A-20 Havocs and P-47 Thunderbolts attack rail lines and trains in the Po River valley.

**SOUTHWEST PACIFIC AREA:** Third Fleet begins strike operations aimed at neutralizing Japanese air capability from Formosa and other areas in preparation for the Luzon landings on January 9.

In the Philippines, Far East Air Force B-24 Liberators bomb Clark Field on Luzon Island and two airfields on Mindanao Island. B-25 Mitchells bomb airfields in the central Philippines.

Naval Task Force 38, commanded by Vice Admiral John S. McCain, begins attacks against Japanese airfields and shipping around Formosa. Carrier aircraft sink a landing ship, five cargo ships, and damage five others.

Leading elements of the Luzon invasion fleet are hit by kamikazes as they pass through Surigao Strait. An oiler is damaged.

Thirteenth Air Force B-25 Mitchells sink a Japanese auxiliary submarine chaser off Davao.

**PACIFIC:** Twentieth Air Force sends 97 B-29s from the Marianas to bomb docks and urban areas of Nagoya, Japan. Of the 97 sent, 57 hit the primary target and 21 bomb alternatives and targets of opportunity. Over 300 Japanese fighters attack the bombers. Five B-29s are lost. Aircrews repot 14 confirmed kills, 14 probables, and 20 possible kills.

U.S. submarine *Kingfish* attacks a Japanese convoy, sinking three cargo ships north of Chichi Jima.

**CENTRAL PACIFIC:** Seventh Air Force sends 22 B-24 Liberators from Saipan to bomb Iwo Jima. Three B-24s from Guam attack Marcus Island in the North Pacific. During the night 10 B-24s from Guam attack Iwo Jima.

**NEW GUINEA:** FEAF B-24 Liberators attack the Djailolo supply area on Halmahera Island. B-25 Mitchells bomb Namlea airfield on Buru Island in the Moluccas.

## January 4

**CBI:** In China, Fourteenth Air Force sends four B-24 Liberators to bomb the Fort Bayard area and the Samah Bay area on Hainan Island. In Burma, six B-25 Mitchells damage a bridge and a warehouse, and 21 P-40s on armed reconnaissance attack targets of opportunity near Wanling. P-51 Mustangs destroy a bridge at Huizan, Thailand.

In Burma, Tenth Air Force sends 13 B-25 Mitchells escorted by 12 P-47 Thunderbolts to bomb an airfield at Namsang. P-47s and P-38 Lightnings attack bridges, troops and logistics depots.

**ETO:** Eighth Air Force sends 10 B-24 Liberators, using radar-guidance to assist in accuracy, to bomb a coastal battery near Bordeaux, France. During the night one B-17 and two B-24s drop leaflets over Germany, Belgium, and the Netherlands. One B-24 is lost.

Staff Sergeant Isadore S. Jachman of B Company, 513th Parachute Infantry Regiment, 17th Airborne Division, faces an attack by two German tanks at Flamierge, Belgium. Without hesitation, Staff Sergeant Jachman runs across open ground through enemy fire to take a bazooka from a fallen paratrooper and attacks the tanks alone. As the tanks turn their weapons on him, Jachman fires and damages one tank; although mortally wounded, he forces the other tank to withdraw. Staff Sergeant Jachman's heroic action will be worthy of the nation's highest award for valor, the Medal of Honor.

**MEDITERRANEAN:** Fifteenth Air Force sends more than 370 B-17s and B-24 Liberators escorted by P-38 Lightnings and P-51 Mustangs to bomb marshaling yards and rail targets in northern Italy. Other B-24s drop supplies in Yugoslavia.

**ITALY:** Twelfth Air Force B-25 Mitchells and B-26 Marauders attack bridges. A-20 Havocs and P-47 Thunderbolts attack ammunition storage areas and transportation targets in the Po River valley.

**SOUTHWEST PACIFIC AREA:** As the Luzon invasion convoy approaches Lingayen Gulf, a kamikaze hits escort carrier USS *Ommaney Bay,* causing heavy damage. The ship is later scuttled.

In the Philippines, Far East Air Force B-24 Liberators bomb Palawan, Luzon, and Mindanao Islands. B-25 Mitchells attack road and rail lines on Luzon and Mindanao Islands.

Carrier aircraft from Naval Task Force 38 continue attacks on Japanese airfields and shipping around Formosa. Three auxiliary submarine chasers and an auxiliary netlayer are sunk. An escort vessel, a minesweeper, and an auxiliary submarine chaser are damaged.

A kamikaze hits a U.S. freighter carrying bombs south of Mindoro, causing a tremendous explosion. FEAF aircraft damage five Japanese submarine chasers off Luzon.

**CENTRAL PACIFIC:** Seventh Air Force sends 13 B-24 Liberators from Guam to bomb Iwo Jima.

During the night 13 B-24s conduct harassment raids on the island.

**NEW GUINEA:** FEAF B-24 Liberators and B-25 Mitchells bomb targets on Celebes Island and shipyards in north Borneo.

### January 5

**ALEUTIANS:** Eleventh Air Force sends four B-24 Liberators to provide air cover for a naval task force approaching Paramushiru Island in the Kuriles.

**CBI:** Fourteenth Air Force sends four B-25 Mitchells to attack logistics storage buildings at Kengtung, China. P-40s and P-51 Mustangs attack airfields at Hankow and Wuchang. Pilots report 50 aircraft destroyed in the air and on the ground. P-51 Mustangs and P-38 Lightnings attack the airfield on Hainan Island. Pilots report 11 aircraft destroyed. Other P-40s and P-38 Lightnings attack various targets of opportunity in China and Burma. B-25 Mitchells destroy a bridge at Dara, Thailand.

In Burma, Tenth Air Force sends 16 B-25 Mitchells to attack a number of airfields. P-47 Thunderbolts attack logistics storage areas, tanks, trucks, and troop concentrations.

Air Transport Command completes Operation Grubworm, which over the past 30 days has airlifted over 25,000 Chinese soldiers, 396 American soldiers, 1,596 animals, 42 jeeps, 48 howitzers, 48 heavy mortars, and 48 antitank guns to Chanyi, Kunming, Luliang, and Yunnani in China. A total of only three aircraft have been lost.

**ETO:** The German attack against the Seventh Army (Nordwind) reaches its limit at Wingen-sur-Moder. The combination of difficult terrain in the Vosges Mountains, weather, and the rapid response of American units to the threat leads to the failure of the offensive. At the same time a second offensive is aimed at VI Corps north of Strasbourg. The 274th Infantry Regiment of the 70th Infantry Division distinguishes itself in its first combat operation at Wingen.

Eighth Air Force sends more than 1,000 B-17s and B-24 Liberators escorted by 584 P-51 Mustangs to attack communication centers, marshaling yards, and airfields. The bombing mission involves a combination of visual, Pathfinder, H2X, and Gee-H (bombing through the clouds technique in which the lead bomber's navigator locates the bomb release point by sending a radio pulse signal to two ground station transponders). One B-17 is lost and 170 B-17s and B-24s damaged. Aircrew casualties are 19 killed, 10 wounded, and one missing. Fighter pilots report one confirmed kill in the air and four confirmed kills on the ground. One P-51 is lost and one damaged. One pilot is reported missing.

A total of 24 B-17s conduct screening missions to jam German radio interception efforts and conduct countermeasures against German radar sites.

During the night one B-17s and four B-24s drop leaflets over Belgium.

Ninth Air Force sends A-20 Havocs, A-26 Invaders, and B-26 Marauders to attack railroad bridges and communication centers in Belgium. P-47 and P-38 fighters attack road traffic, communication centers, and support III and VIII Corps near Bastogne and the 2nd and 3rd Armored Divisions.

The headquarters of the 368th Fighter Group and the P-47 Thunderbolts of the 395th, 396th, and 397th Fighter Squadrons redeploy from Juvincourt to Metz, France.

**MEDITERRANEAN:** Fifteenth Air Force P-38 Lightnings bomb the railroad bridge at Doboj in Yugoslavia.

**ITALY:** During the night Twelfth Air Force A-20 Havocs conduct bombing runs in the Po River valley near Modena.

**SOUTHWEST PACIFIC AREA:** Kamikazes continue their relentless attacks on the Luzon invasion fleet. A heavy cruiser, a destroyer, and a destroyer escort are damaged, along with escort carriers USS *Manila Bay* and USS *Savo Island*. Kamikazes also hit and damage an Australian heavy cruiser and a destroyer. Carrier aircraft from Naval Task Group 77.4 (escort carrier group) sink a Japanese destroyer near Manila Bay. Two other destroyers are damaged.

The USS *Boise* with General MacArthur aboard narrowly avoids two torpedoes fired from a Japanese midget submarine. A U.S. destroyer later sinks the submarine.

In the Philippines, Far East Air Force sends B-25 Mitchells to attack shore installations around Lingayen Gulf on Luzon Island. A-20 Havocs and P-47 Thunderbolts attack airfields on Luzon and Mindanao Islands.

The P-51 Mustangs of the 4th Fighter Squadron (Commando), 3rd Air Commando Group, arrive on Leyte Island from the United States. The 547th Night Fighter Squadron of the 86th Fighter Wing, under the operational control of the 310th Bombardment Wing (Medium), redeploys from Schouten Island to Mindoro Island with P-38 Lightnings and P-61 Black Widow night fighters.

**PACIFIC:** Naval Task Force 92, commanded by Rear Admiral John L. McCrea, with three light cruisers and nine destroyers, bombards Japanese installations on Paramushiru in the Kuriles.

**CENTRAL PACIFIC:** Seventh Air Force sends 22 B-24 Liberators from Saipan Island to bomb Iwo Jima. With three B-24 Liberators providing navigational escort, seven P-38 Lightnings strafe the island as well.

Naval Task Group 94.9, with three heavy cruisers and six destroyers under Rear Admiral Allan E. Smith, supported by FEAF B-24 Liberators with P-38 Lightnings, attacks Japanese shipping and installations on Chichi Jima, Haha Jima, and Iwo Jima. Three U.S. destroyers sink a landing ship. A U.S. destroyer is damaged by a mine, and another U.S. destroyer is also damaged by fire from shore. Three U.S. destroyers sink a landing ship off Iwo Jima.

Navy PB4Y-1 Privateers sink Japanese midget submarine *Ha.71* off Chichi Jima.

**NEW GUINEA:** Far East Air Force B-25 Mitchells and B-24 Liberators bomb Celebes Island, escorted by P-40s. B-24 Liberators attack Miri airfield in Borneo.

U.S. submarine *Cavalla* torpedoes and sinks two Japanese auxiliary netlayers in the Java Sea.

### January 6

**ALEUTIANS:** Eleventh Air Force sends 10 B-25 Mitchells to provide air cover for a naval task force. B-24 Liberators bomb the airfield and facilities at Suribachi Bay on Paramushiru Island.

**CBI:** In China, Fourteenth Air Force sends 40 P-40s, P-51 Mustangs, and P-47 Thunderbolts to bomb the Hankow-Wuchang area. Pilots report nine enemy aircraft destroyed.

**ETO:** Fifteenth Army is operational under 12th Army Group.

In the Seventh Army area, the 12th Armored Division is transferred to VI Corps in preparation for an attack to push back a German salient near Herrlisheim.

Eighth Air Force sends more than 800 B-17s and B-24 Liberators escorted by over 600 P-51 Mustangs to attack marshaling yards and communication targets in western Germany. Most of the bombing runs are made using Gee-H and H2X. Two bombers are lost and 92 are damaged. Aircrew casualties are five killed, three wounded, and 10 missing. Fighter pilots report 14 confirmed kills and one possible on the ground. Two fighters are lost and four damaged. Two pilots are reported missing, and two are killed.

During the night six B-17s drop leaflets over Belgium and the Netherlands.

Six B-17s conduct screening missions to jam German radio interception efforts and conduct countermeasures against German radar sites.

**ITALY:** Twelfth Air Force A-20 Havocs and P-47 Thunderbolts of the XXII Tactical Air Command attack rail lines, bridges, and roads and bomb ships in the harbors at Genoa and Imperia.

**SOUTHWEST PACIFIC AREA:** The heaviest kamikaze attacks to date hit Seventh Fleet's Bombardment and Fire Support Group in Lingayen Gulf. Two battleships and two cruisers are damaged. Third Fleet aircraft attack Japanese airfields on Luzon.

In the Philippines, Far East Air Force B-24 Liberators bomb Clark Field and Nichols Field, along with other airfield targets on Luzon Island, while B-25 Mitchells, A-20 Havocs, and P-47 Thunderbolts attack bridges and targets of opportunity. A-20s, with P-38 Lightnings flying cover, bomb Carolina airfield on Negros Island.

Kamikazes continue the attack on the Luzon invasion force as it approaches Lingayen Gulf. Battleships USS *New Mexico* and USS *California*, a heavy cruiser, a light cruiser, and four destroyers are damaged. Another destroyer is damaged by friendly fire.

Kamikazes attack minesweepers, sinking one and damaging another.

Destroyer USS *Walke*, covering minesweeping operations, is hit by four aircraft. One crashes into the bridge where Commander George F. Davis is standing. In the midst of the carnage and destruction, Commander Davis refuses to leave the bridge and fights to save his ship, directing efforts and encouraging his men. Although mortally wounded, Davis refuses treatment; only when assured that the ship and crew are safe, does he allow himself to be carried below. For his indomitable courage and dedication to duty Commander Davis will receive the Medal of Honor.

To limit the destructive kamikaze attacks, Vice Admiral John S. McCain orders Task Force 38 to attack airfields on Formosa and Japanese shipping headed to Luzon. Carrier aircraft sink a cargo ship and six merchant tankers off northern Luzon.

U.S. submarine *Besugo* torpedoes and sinks a Japanese fleet tanker in the Gulf of Thailand. U.S. submarine *Sea Robin* attacks a Japanese convoy and sinks a fleet tanker east of Hainan Island.

**PACIFIC:** Tenth Army completes its operational planning for Operation Iceberg, the invasion of Okinawa. After several delays, the date for execution (designated as L-day) is set for April 1 and approved by Admiral Nimitz.

The 77th Infantry Division is assigned the mission of seizing the Kerama Islands west of Okinawa prior to the main landings. The 2nd Marine Division will act as a diversionary landing force at the eastern end of Okinawa as the main landing will occur on the western coast in the center of the island. Prelanding fires and operations to destroy Japanese defenses on Okinawa and isolate the landing area from enemy sea and air forces will begin March 24. On April 1 the III Amphibious Corps will land the 6th and 1st Marine Divisions abreast on the beach landing site north of the town of Hagushi. The 6th Marine Division is to capture Yontan airfield and move to capture the Ishikawa Isthmus. The 1st Marine Division is to capture the Katchin Peninsula. The XIV Corps will land the 7th and the 96th Infantry Divisions abreast to the south of Hagushi. The 7th Infantry Division will capture Kadena airfield and move to the east coast to cut the island in two. The 96th Infantry Division will control the high ground south of the landing beaches, then move south on the eastern coastal road to capture the bridges at Chantan, then move to protect the corps's southern flank. Altogether the Americans will be landing about 116,000 men on L-day. The 27th Infantry Division will be available as a floating reserve one day after the initial landings (L+1).

The Twentieth Air Force's XX Bomber Command flies its last mission against targets in Japan. A total of 49 B-29s are sent from Chengtu, China, to bomb an aircraft production facility at Omura, on Kyushu Island in Japan. Only 28 bombers hit the primary target, and 13 hit a secondary target at Nanking, China. Six others bomb targets of opportunity. Aircrews report four confirmed kills, six probable kills, and 10 possible kills. One B-29 is lost.

**CENTRAL PACIFIC:** Seventh Air Force B-24 Liberators from Guam bomb Iwo Jima.

During the night nine B-24s conduct a snooper (radar-assisted bomb release) mission on the airfields at Iwo Jima.

**NEW GUINEA:** FEAF B-25 Mitchells and P-40s attack Mapanget airfield on Celebes Island.

## January 7

**CBI:** In China, Fourteenth Air Force sends five B-24 Liberators to bomb Fort Bayard and attack shipping in Samah Bay on Hainan Island. Aircrews report one ship sunk.

Fourteenth Air Force B-24 Liberators attack a Japanese convoy in the South China Sea and sink a stores ship in the Formosa Strait.

**ETO:** The VII Corps cuts the LaRoche-Vielsam road, intercepting the main supply line of the German forces in the north of the Bulge.

The Germans launch a second attack at VI Corps near Strasbourg called Sonnewende (Winter Solstice). German tanks and infantry open a 10-mile gap in the VI Corps lines. Other German units attack near Lauterbourg and are stopped by Seventh Army's reserve, the 14th Armored Division. The 157th Infantry Regiment of the 45th Infantry Division takes heavy casualties defending the Low Vosges against attacks by German mountain troops.

Eighth Air Force sends more than 1,000 B-17s and B-24 Liberators escorted by 700 P-51 Mustangs to attack marshaling yards, bridges, oil storage depots, and communication centers. The bombers use a combination of Pathfinder bombers, H2X radar, and Gee-H. A total of three bombers are lost and 28 damaged. Aircrew casualties are one killed, three wounded, and 28 missing. One P-51 is lost, and the pilot is reported missing.

During the night two B-17s and five B-24s drop leaflets over Belgium and France.

Six B-17s conduct screening missions to jam German radio interception efforts and conduct countermeasures against German radar sites.

Field Marshal Sir Bernard L Montgomery, commander of the 21st Army Group, gives a press conference and implies that he has made most of the major decisions that led to the Germans being halted before the Meuse River. This infuriates nearly all the American leadership and creates a rift between the Americans and British that will never fully be reconciled. General Eisenhower will later write, "I doubt Montgomery ever came to realize how deeply resentful some American commanders were."

**ITALY:** Twelfth Air Force A-20 Havocs and P-47 Thunderbolts of the XXII Tactical Air Command attack rail lines at Brenner and marshaling yards.

**SOUTHWEST PACIFIC AREA:** Vice Admiral Thomas C. Kinkaid, the Seventh Fleet commander, requests that Admiral William F. Halsey's Third Fleet carrier aircraft conduct intensified air attacks on Luzon airfields to forestall the kamikaze attacks. General MacArthur requests XX Bomber Command to shift targets on Formosa to airfields at the southern part of the island, also to limit kamikaze attacks.

In the Philippines, Far East Air Force B-25 Mitchells and A-20 Havocs, supported by P-38 Lightnings, attack Clark Field, while B-24 Liberators bomb Nichols Field. B-24s attack airfields on Mindanao Island.

Rear Admiral Jesse B. Oldendorf's bombardment and fire support group (Task Group 77.2) and escort carrier group aircraft of Task Group 77.4 commanded by Rear Admiral Calvin T. Durgin conduct pre-assault attacks on Japanese defenses at Lingayen Gulf. Japanese torpedo planes sink a minesweeper and bombs damage another minesweeper. Kamikazes damage an attack transport *Callaway* and an LST (landing ship, tank).

Four destroyers sink a Japanese destroyer west of Manila Bay. U.S. submarine *Picuda* torpedoes and damages a Japanese army tanker northwest of Formosa.

**PACIFIC:** U.S. submarine *Spot* torpedoes and sinks a Japanese guardboat west of Kyushu, Japan.

**CENTRAL PACIFIC:** Seventh Air Force sends 11 B-24 Liberators from Saipan to bomb airfields on Iwo Jima.

Ten B-24s conduct single-ship snooper (radar-assisted bomb release) missions on Iwo Jima throughout the night.

**NEW GUINEA:** FEAF B-25 Mitchells and P-40s attack targets on Celebes Island.

## January 8

**CBI:** In Burma, Tenth Air Force sends 21 B-25 Mitchells to attack troops and logistics storage areas, while 74 P-47 Thunderbolts and P-38 Lightnings attack troop concentrations and logistics stockpiles.

**ETO:** Hitler orders a retreat from the Ardennes to avoid the entrapment of thousands of troops in front of Houffalize.

The VI Corps commits the 56th Armored Infantry Battalion supported by the 714th Tank Battalion to attack Herrlisheim. The infantrymen take a portion of the town but are greatly outnumbered.

Eighth Air Force sends more than 700 B-17s and B-24 Liberators escorted by nearly 300 P-51 Mustangs to attack communication centers, road and rail bridges, and marshaling yards in Germany. The bombers use a combination of Pathfinder bombers, H2X radar, and Gee-H. Two bombers are lost and 77 are damaged. Aircrew casualties are one killed, eight wounded, and nine missing. During the night one B-17 and two B-24s drop leaflets over Belgium.

Technical Sergeant Russell E. Dunham of I Company, 30th Infantry Regiment, 3rd Infantry Division, is participating in an attack on Hill 616 near Kayserberg, France. Wearing winter camouflage made from a mattress cover and carrying 12 M-1 carbine magazines and a dozen hand grenades, Technical Sergeant Dunham moves up the snow-covered hill toward a German machine-gun position. Far ahead of his platoon, Dunham crawls to within 75 yards of the emplacement, then runs toward the enemy. Hit by a machine-gun bullet, he falls backward, but jumps to his feet again, dodging hand grenades and firing his carbine into the position, killing two soldiers. With his weapon now empty, Dunham drags out the remaining German soldier with his bare hands. He then moves to attack a second machine gun, ignoring the fire directed toward him and throwing hand grenades toward the position. He assaults the position, killing the machine-gun crew and firing his carbine into the foxholes of the supporting infantrymen, causing them to scatter. Staggering from his wound, Dunham continues to move uphill to another defensive position. As machine-gun bullets hit around him and grenades explode close by, Dunham eliminates the position with hand grenades, then shoots several Germans to take the position. Technical Sergeant Dunham's bravery under fire and indomitable fighting spirit will win him the nation's highest award for valor, the Medal of Honor.

Technical Sergeant Charles F. Carey commands an antitank platoon in the 379th Infantry Regiment, 100th Infantry Division. At Rimling, France, a German counterattack shatters part of the battalion defenses. Technical Sergeant Carey takes the initiative to organize a patrol to collect the members of his platoon trapped in the breakthrough area. He then organizes an attack on a house that the enemy had occupied. As members of the patrol provide covering fire, Carey moves toward the house alone. Entering the house after throwing a grenade, he returns with 16 prisoners. With another patrol he attacks a German tank, disabling it with bazooka fire, then eliminates the crew. Technical Sergeant Carey later goes to the rescue of one of his squads that has been trapped in a building during a German counterattack. Carey continues this pattern of aggressive leadership until killed by a sniper. For his fearless and consistently heroic actions during this bitter battle, Technical Sergeant Carey will receive the Medal of Honor.

A German V-1 or V-2 rocket damages a U.S. freighter at Antwerp, Belgium.

**MEDITERRANEAN:** Fifteenth Air Force sends more than 300 B-17s and B-24 Liberators escorted by over 200 P-38 Lightnings and P-51 Mustangs to attack marshaling yards in Austria.

**ITALY:** During the night Twelfth Air Force A-20 Havocs make bombing runs in the Po River valley.

The 437th Bombardment Squadron (Medium), 319th Bombardment Group (Medium), begins a redeployment from Corsica to the United States. The squadron will convert from B-25 Mitchells to A-26 Invaders and is scheduled to transfer to the Pacific theater in July of 1945.

**SOUTHWEST PACIFIC AREA:** In the Philippines, Far East Air Force P-51 Mustangs and P-40s strafe airfields in the Lingayen Gulf area. A-20 Havocs and P-47 Thunderbolts attack railyards and vehicle convoys and B-24 Liberators, and A-20s attack Nichols Field and other airfields on Luzon Island. B-25 Mitchells with P-47s providing cover bomb Fabrica airfield on Negros Island. B-24s bomb an airfield and oil storage facility on Mindanao Island.

Kamikazes damage escort carriers USS *Kitkun Bay* and USS *Kadashan Bay* and damage an Australian heavy cruiser in Lingayen Gulf.

Coordinated submarine attack group (Task Group 17.21, Commander Charles E. Loughlin) attacks a Japanese convoy off the northwest coast of Formosa. USS *Barb* torpedoes and sinks two cargo ships and damages another and sinks a merchant tanker. USS *Picuda* damages a cargo ship, and USS *Queenfish* damages a tanker.

**PACIFIC:** U.S. submarine *Balao* torpedoes and sinks a Japanese cargo ship southwest of Korea. USS *Piranha* damages an auxiliary netlayer south of Kyushu, Japan.

**CENTRAL PACIFIC:** Seventh Air Force B-24 Liberators from Guam bomb Iwo Jima.

During the night 10 B-24s conduct single-bomber snooper (radar-assisted bomb release) attacks on Iwo Jima.

**NEW GUINEA:** FEAF P-38 Lightnings attack airfields in Borneo.

## January 9

**ALEUTIANS:** Eleventh Air Force sends four B-24 Liberators to attack Suribachi Bay airfield on Paramushiru Island using H2X radar equipment.

**CBI:** The 124th Cavalry links with the 475th Infantry Regiment at Mong Hkak. The new mission of the Mars Task Force is to cut the Burma Road.

Fourteenth Air Force sends six B-25 Mitchells to bomb rail lines, road bridges, and buildings near Thanh Moi in French Indochina. P-40s, P-38 Lightnings, and P-51 Mustangs attack targets of opportunity near Wanling, Burma.

In Burma, Tenth Air Force P-47 Thunderbolts attack a Japanese division headquarters, provide support to ground forces, and attack logistics storage sites, tanks, antiaircraft positions, and troop concentrations.

**ATLANTIC:** German submarine *U-1055* torpedoes and damages a U.S. freighter as it leaves England for New York by the Bristol Channel. The ship is abandoned and later sinks.

**ETO:** The III Corps of Third Army attacks north with the 90th Infantry Division from XX Corps, now attached to III Corps.

Ninth Air Force sends 15 B-26 Marauders to bomb the Rinnthal rail bridge in Germany in an attempt to slow the movement of three German tank divisions into the Bulge.

**ITALY:** Twelfth Air Force B-25 Mitchells and B-26 Marauders attack bridges and assembly areas. A-20 Havocs and P-47 Thunderbolts attack rail lines, vehicles, ammunition and fuel storage sites, gun positions, and German defenses in the northern Apennines.

The 438th, 439th, and 440th Bombardment Squadrons (Medium), 319th Bombardment Group (Medium), begin to redeploy from Corsica to the United States. The group will convert from B-26 Marauders to A-26 Invaders and is scheduled to move to the Pacific theater in July 1945.

**SOUTHWEST PACIFIC AREA: The Invasion of Luzon.** Vice Admiral Thomas C. Kinkaid, commander of Task Force 77, lands the Sixth Army, commanded by Lieutenant General Walter Krueger, at Lingayen Gulf. The landing is supported by naval gunfire from Vice Admiral Jesse B. Oldendorf's bombardment force (TG 77.2) and aircraft from the escort carrier force (TG 77.4, commanded by Rear Admiral Calvin T. Durgin). Japanese air attacks, kamikazes, and assault demolition boats attack the invasion force. Kamikazes damage the battleship USS *Mississippi*, a light cruiser, and a destroyer escort. The Australian heavy cruiser is forced to retire for repairs. Battleship USS *Colorado* is damaged by friendly fire. Japanese assault demolition boats damage a transport and two LSTs. Vice Admiral John S. McCain's Task Force 38 supports the landings at Lingayen Gulf, attacking airfields and shipping on Formosa, the Ryukyus, and Pescadores. Carrier aircraft sink a coastal patrol ship, a submarine chaser, two tankers, two cargo ships, and a small cargo vessel off Formosa. Pilots report damaging an escort vessel, an oiler, an escort destroyer, and a cargo ship, three coastal patrol ships, three auxiliary submarine chasers, and a minesweeper off Formosa.

I Corps (Lieutenant General Innis P. Swift) lands the 6th and 43rd Infantry Divisions near San Fabian; XIV Corps (Lieutenant General Oscar W. Griswold) lands the 37th and 40th Infantry Divisions at Lingayen and Dagupan. There is almost no opposition. The 43rd Infantry Division, along with the 63rd RCT of the 6th Infantry Division, advances into the mountains north and east of the beachhead and encounters entrenched Japanese troops defending the passes and roads into the open valleys beyond. About 68,000 men have landed on Luzon and occupy a beachhead 15 miles wide and four miles deep.

In the Philippines, Far East Air Force B-24 Liberators, B-25 Mitchells, A-20 Havocs, P-47 Thunderbolts, and P-38 Lightnings attack bridges, vehicles, trains, roads, and airfields throughout Luzon Island in support of the Sixth Army landing at Lingayen Gulf.

**PACIFIC:** Twentieth Air Force sends 46 B-29s from Chengtu, China, to bomb the harbor at Kirun on the island of Formosa, in support of Sixth Army's invasion of

Luzon Island in the Philippines. A total of 39 hit the primary target, and six others hit targets of last resort along the China coast.

Another Twentieth Air Force bombing mission involves 72 B-29s from the Marianas in an attack on the Musashino aircraft production facility near Tokyo. Only 18 B-29s hit the primary target, while 34 others hit either alternatives or targets of opportunity. Aircrews report 13 confirmed kills, three probable kills, and 11 probables. Six B-29s are lost.

**CENTRAL PACIFIC:** Seventh Air Force B-24 Liberators from Saipan bomb Iwo Jima.

During the night eight B-24s conduct individual snooper (radar-assisted bomb release) missions on Iwo Jima.

**NEW GUINEA:** FEAF B-24 Liberators, A-20 Havocs, B-25 Mitchells, P-38 Lightnings, and P-40s attack barges, airfields, and targets of opportunity on Halmahera Island, the Ceram Island area, north Borneo, and Timor Island.

## January 10

**ALEUTIANS:** Eleventh Air Force sends three B-24 Liberators to bomb and photograph Kurabu airfield on Paramushiru Island in the Kuriles.

**CBI:** Fourteenth Air Force sends over 50 P-51 Mustangs, P-40s, and P-38 Lightnings to attack targets of opportunity near Wanling in Burma. Tenth Air Force P-47 Thunderbolts continue to attack Japanese troops, logistics distribution points, tanks, artillery, and buildings.

**ETO:** Eighth Air Force sends more than 1,100 B-17s and B-24 Liberators escorted by over 360 P-47 Thunderbolts and P-51 Mustangs to attack road and rail bridges, marshaling yards, and airfields. The bombers use a combination of Pathfinder bombers, H2X radar, and Gee-H. A total of 10 bombers are lost and 364 damaged. Aircrew casualties are 15 killed, 24 wounded, and 100 missing. Fighter pilots report one confirmed kill in the air and two confirmed kills on the ground. A total of eight fighters are lost, and five are damaged. One pilot is reported missing.

Ninth Air Force sends more than 30 B-26 Marauders to attack communication centers and road bridge targets, but the bombers are unable to finish the mission due to bad weather. P-47 and P-38 fighters support III, VIII, XII, and XX Corps.

Master Sergeant Vito R. Bertoldo of A Company, 242nd Infantry Regiment, 42nd Infantry Division, is guarding two command posts near Hatten, France. The headquarters area is threatened by a force of German tanks and infantry that has broken through the front lines. Moving from the protection of a building, Master Sergeant Bertoldo sets up his machine gun in the street and begins engaging German soldiers. He remains there for almost 12 hours, holding off the attack. Later he moves into a building and continues to fight from a place near a window, despite tank fire hitting all around him. As the command post retreats, Bertoldo covers their withdrawal and holds his advanced position throughout the night. He withstands several direct assaults against his position; though nearly killed several times by tank fire, he continues to fight and holds his position. For his skill and courage in nearly singlehandedly stopping a major assault in 48 hours of nonstop combat, Master Sergeant Bertoldo will receive the Medal of Honor.

**ITALY:** Twelfth Air Force A-20 Havocs and P-47 Thunderbolts attack rail lines, communication targets, vehicles, and fuel and ammunition storage areas in the Po River valley.

**SOUTHWEST PACIFIC AREA, LUZON:** The 43rd Infantry Division of I Corps supported by the 18th RCT fights to open the Damortis-Rosario road. The 6th Infantry Division on the right flank of I Corps is slowed near the Cabaruan Hills.

Far East Air Force B-24 Liberators bomb an airfield and warehouse area near Manila, while A-20 Havocs, P-47 Thunderbolts, and P-38 Lightnings attack airfields, trucks, highways, trains, railyards, and rail lines on Luzon.

Japanese assault demolition boats make a surprise attack in Lingayen Gulf, sinking infantry landing craft that are providing indirect fire support to the landing force, and damaging two destroyers, a transport, and an LST. Kamikazes damage a destroyer, destroyer escort, and a transport.

**PACIFIC:** U.S. submarine *Puffer* torpedoes and sinks a Japanese coastal patrol ship and damages another in the Ryukyus.

**CENTRAL PACIFIC:** Seventh Air Force sends 30 B-24 Liberators from Guam to bomb Iwo Jima.

During the night B-24s from Guam conduct individual snooper (radar-assisted bomb release) missions on Iwo Jima. B-24s attack the airfield on Woleai Atoll in the Carolines.

**NEW GUINEA:** About 60 FEAF P-40s bomb and strafe the Galela area on Halmahera Island. B-25 Mitchells and P-38 Lightnings attack Kendari airfield on Celebes Island.

The headquarters of XIII Fighter Command redeploys from Sansapor, New Guinea, to Leyte Island.

## January 11

**ALEUTIANS:** Eleventh Air Force sends three B-24 Liberators on an armed reconnaissance over Paramushiru Island. Five B-25 Mitchells attack Kotani Shima in the Kuriles.

**CBI:** In Burma, Fourteenth Air Force sends five B-25 Mitchells to attack a bridge. Aircrews report some damage. Other B-25s bomb storage buildings near Lashio. Tenth Air Force P-47 Thunderbolts support ground forces and strafe trucks, troop concentrations, artillery pieces, and logistics storage sites.

**ETO:** During the night Eighth Air Force sends two B-17s and six B-24s to drop leaflets over Belgium.

Ninth Air Force sends 120 A-20 Havocs, A-26 Invaders, and B-26 Marauders to attack communication centers and rail bridges in Belgium and Germany. P-47 and P-38 fighters escort the bombers and attack an ammunition storage facility.

Staff Sergeant Archer T. Gammon, A Company, 9th Armored Infantry Battalion, 6th Armored Division, charges 30 yards through hip-deep snow to knock out a machine gun with grenades near Bastogne, Belgium. As the platoon enters the woods, a machine gun with riflemen and a tank fire on the Americans. Staff Sergeant Gammon jumps forward and runs toward the enemy. Using hand grenades he destroys the machine gun emplacement, fires at German infantry, and advances toward the tank. The tank then fires a main gun round that kills Gammon. His exceptional courage and fighting skills are worthy of the nation's highest award for valor, the Medal of Honor.

**ITALY:** Twelfth Air Force A-20 Havocs and P-47 Thunderbolts attack targets of opportunity in the Po River valley and attack ammunition and fuel storage sites, rail lines, vehicles, and roads in support of Fifth Army operations.

**SOUTHWEST PACIFIC AREA, LUZON:** The 25th Infantry Division moves into the I Corps area between the 6th and 43rd Infantry Divisions as the 43rd stalls in the foothills of the mountains. The 158th RCT lands and advances to the left flank of the 43rd Infantry Division. The 25th Infantry Division, the 13th Armored Group, and 6th Ranger Battalion land in the I Corps zone. The Japanese in the Cabaruan Hills are fighting to the last man, occupying defensive positions that are extraordinarily strong and expertly camouflaged. Concrete pillboxes, trenches, and tunnels cover the hills.

The XIV Corps, advancing in parallel columns on well-paved highways, encounters no serious opposition.

Far East Air Force B-24 Liberators, B-25 Mitchells, A-20 Havocs, P-47 Thunderbolts, and P-38 Lightnings attack communication targets, airfields, and town areas on Luzon and Mindanao islands.

The headquarters of the 308th Bombardment Wing (Heavy) redeploys from Leyte to Luzon Island.

A kamikaze damages a high speed transport off Luzon. Shore batteries damage two LSTs. A U.S. destroyer sinks an auxiliary minesweeper south of Lingayen Gulf.

Major William A. Shomo of the 82nd Tactical Reconnaissance Squadron, Fifth Air Force, is lead pilot of a P-51D Mustang, with two other fighters, ordered to photograph and strafe Aparri and Laoag airfields on Luzon. While en route to the objective, Shomo discovers a Japanese twin-engine bomber, escorted by 12 fighters, flying in the opposite direction about 2,500 feet above him. Shomo orders an attack and quickly shoots down three enemy fighters. Diving below the bomber, he fires into it, causing it to crash. Pulling up from this pass, he encounters another fighter and shoots it down, then dives on another fighter and destroys it. For his extraordinary display of skill and courage against overwhelming odds, Major Shomo will receive the Medal of Honor.

**PACIFIC:** Twentieth Air Force sends 47 B-29 Superfortresses from Calcutta, India, to bomb the dry docks at Singapore. Only 25 hit the primary target, and others bomb targets of opportunity. Aircrews report six confirmed kills, one probable, and 17 possibles. Two B-29s are lost.

**CENTRAL PACIFIC:** Seventh Air Force sends 23 B-24 Liberators from Saipan to bomb Iwo Jima.

During the night three B-24s conduct individual snooper missions on Iwo Jima.

U.S. destroyer and destroyer escort bombard Japanese defenses on Yap.

Japanese submarines begin employing suicide torpedoes (*kaiten*). Japanese submarine *I-36* launches *kaiten* that damage a U.S. ammunition ship and an LCI (landing craft, infantry) at Ulithi.

**NEW GUINEA:** FEAF B-25 Mitchells and P-38 Lightnings attack Kendari airfield on Celebes Island.

**January 12**

**CBI:** Colonel Lewis A. Pick leads the first convoy of 113 vehicles, mostly cargo trucks, jeeps, and ambulances out of Ledo and bound for Kunming, China. The convoy has representation from every engineer unit that has worked on the road, as well as 65 members of the press.

Fourteenth Air Force sends six B-25 Mitchells to make a second attack on a bridge in Burma. P-51 Mustangs and P-47 Thunderbolts attack targets of opportunity near Wanting, China.

Tenth Air Force P-47 Thunderbolts attack Japanese troops, logistics storage sites, and vehicles.

**ETO:** The 90th Infantry Division advancing from the north and the 6th Armored Division and the 35th Infantry Division from Bastogne trap about 15,000 German soldiers between Bastogne and Wiltz. The Germans abandon any further efforts to capture the town.

**ITALY:** Twelfth Air Force A-20 Havocs and P-47 Thunderbolts attack rail lines and vehicles in the Po River valley.

**SOUTHWEST PACIFIC AREA:** Halsey's Third Fleet conducts air strikes on Japanese facilities and airfields from Saigon to Cam Ranh Bay in French Indochina.

In the Philippines, Far East Air Force B-24 Liberators bomb airfields and troop locations on Luzon. Other B-24s attack an airfield on Mindanao Island. B-25 Mitchells bomb warehouses on Negros Island.

Naval Task Force 38 operating in the South China Sea attacks Japanese shipping, airfields, and other shore installations in southeastern French Indochina. Carrier aircraft sink a training cruiser, an escort vessel, five coastal defense vessels, two submarine chasers, a minesweeper, a patrol boat, 10 tankers, a landing ship, a stores ship, an auxiliary minesweeper, three transports, and 13 cargo ships. TF 38 planes also damage two escort vessels, a coastal defense vessel, two fleet tankers, a submarine chaser, four cargo ships, three landing ships, a guardboat, and a merchant tanker. A Vichy French light cruiser is sunk, and a French surveying vessel is damaged.

Off Lingayen Gulf, kamikazes damage two destroyer escorts, an attack transport, an LST, and five freighters, one of which is carrying over 500 soldiers. More than a quarter are killed.

Staff Sergeant Robert E. Laws, G Company, 169th Infantry Regiment, 43rd Infantry Division, leads an assault squad when G Company attacks a Japanese reinforced infantry company defending a hill in Pangasinan Province, Luzon. The approach to the hill is a 70-yard-long narrow ridge covered by a pillbox and infantry foxholes. As his squad provides covering fire, Staff Sergeant Laws moves toward the pillbox under constant enemy fire. He eliminates the pillbox with grenades but is in turn wounded. Supported by his squad, Laws now attacks the rifle positions but is wounded twice more. He kills two Japanese soldiers with his Thompson submachine gun and kills another soldier in hand-to-hand combat. As his squad clears the remaining foxholes, Staff Sergeant Laws receives medical attention and is evacuated. For his leadership and exceptional courage in closing with the enemy, Staff Sergeant Laws will receive the Medal of Honor.

**CENTRAL PACIFIC:** Seventh Air Force sends 28 B-24 Liberators from Guam to bomb Iwo Jima.

During the night four B-24s from the Marianas conduct individual snooper missions on Iwo Jima. Three B-24s from Saipan bomb Marcus Island.

Japanese submarine *I-53* launches *kaiten* (suicide torpedoes) at Palau without effect.

Japanese submarine *I-58* also launches *kaiten* at Apra Harbor, Guam, without effect.

**NEW GUINEA:** Japanese submarine *I-47* launches *kaiten* (suicide torpedoes) that damage a U.S. freighter off Hollandia. Japanese submarine *I-56* launches *kaiten* at Manus in the Admiralties without effect.

## January 13

**CBI:** In China, Fourteenth Air Force sends six B-25 Mitchells to bomb six storage buildings at Kengtung, while P-51 Mustangs, P-38 Lightnings, and P-40s attack targets of opportunity near Wanting.

In Burma, Tenth Air Force sends P-47 Thunderbolts against an airfield, while four P-47s support ground forces and attack Japanese troops and vehicles.

**ETO:** The VIII Corps attacks toward Houffalize reinforced by the 4th Armored Division and the 17th Airborne Division. The XVIII Airborne Corps attacks toward Saint-Vith supported by V Corps. The Third Army's III Corps attacks toward Wiltz.

Eighth Air Force sends more than 900 B-17s and B-24 Liberators escorted by over 450 P-47 Thunderbolts and P-51 Mustangs to attack Rhine River rail bridges, highway bridges, and marshaling yards. The bombers use Pathfinder bombers, H2X radar, and Gee-H. A total of eight bombers are lost and 180 are damaged. Aircrew casualties are four killed, 13 wounded, and 61 missing. Fighter pilots report three confirmed kills in the air and three confirmed kills on the ground. Two fighters are lost and seven are damaged.

Ninth Air Force A-20 Havocs, A-26 Invaders, and B-26 Marauders attack road and rail bridges, and a marshaling yard. P-47 and P-38 fighters support VII Corps near Houffalize and III, VIII, XII, and XX Corps.

In the VI Corps area, the 12th Armored Division is ordered to destroy German forces west of the Rhine River near Herrlisheim.

**SOUTHWEST PACIFIC AREA:** In the Philippines, Far East Air Force B-24 Liberators attack airfields and Japanese barracks and logistics storage areas on Luzon, while P-47 Thunderbolts fly a sweep, destroying aircraft on the ground and vehicles. A-20 Havocs attack airfields, railroads, and highways.

Kamikaze attacks in Lingayen Gulf damage an escort carrier, USS *Salamaua*.

**CENTRAL PACIFIC:** Seventh Air Force sends 14 B-24 Liberators from Saipan to bomb Iwo Jima.

During the night two B-24s from Guam and Saipan conduct individual snooper missions on Iwo Jima.

A destroyer escort sinks Japanese submarine *I-362* off Truk.

During one of the coldest winters on record in Europe, men of the 347th Infantry Regiment, 87th Infantry Division, get some hot food near La Roche, Belgium, January 13, 1945.

**NEW GUINEA:** The headquarters of the 18th Fighter Group redeploys from Sansapor, New Guinea, to Lingayen on Luzon Island. The P-38 Lightnings of the 12th Fighter Squadron also redeploy from Morotai Island to Luzon.

## January 14

**CBI:** In China, Fourteenth Air Force sends 27 B-24 Liberators, supported by 45 P-51 Mustangs and P-40s, to attack Hankow. Fighter pilots report eight Japanese aircraft destroyed. Seven B-25 Mitchells attack targets near Kengtung, while 42 P-47 Thunderbolts, P-40s, and P-51 Mustangs attack airfields at Wuchang and Hankow. Fighter pilots report 17 Japanese aircraft destroyed. Over 20 P-40s and P-51 Mustangs attack targets of opportunity near Wanting.

In Burma, Tenth Air Force sends 12 B-25 Mitchells to attack troops, logistics storage areas, and bridges. P-47 Thunderbolts support ground forces and attack logistics storage areas and troop concentrations.

U.S. submarine *Cobia* torpedoes and sinks a Japanese minelayer off the east coast of Malaya. Fourteenth Air Force P-51 Mustangs sink a Japanese cargo ship in the Yangtze River.

**ATLANTIC:** German submarine *U-1232* torpedoes and damages a U.S. freighter off Nova Scotia.

**ETO:** In the Seventh Army area, the 157th Infantry Regiment of the 45th Infantry Division attacks to capture the hills north of Reipertswiller. The 3rd Battalion is trapped behind German lines and fights for more than a week.

Eighth Air Force sends 911 B-17s and B-24 Liberators escorted by 860 P-47 Thunderbolts and P-51 Mustangs to attack road and rail bridges, marshaling yards, oil refineries, and oil production facilities. The bombers are able to release bombs visually. The bombers are met by 250 German fighters. A total of seven bombers are lost and 298 damaged. Aircrews report three confirmed kills, nine probables, and seven possibles. Aircrew casualties are 12 killed, five wounded, and 59 missing. Fighter pilots report 13 confirmed kills and 19 possibles in the air and three confirmed kills and five possibles on the ground. A total of eight fighters are lost, and four are damaged. The pilots are reported missing, and one is wounded.

Over 100 P-47 Thunderbolts and P-51 Mustangs fly a sweep over northern Germany. The fighter pilots report 42 confirmed kills and six possibles. Two P-47s and a P-51 are lost, and one P-47 is damaged. The pilots are reported missing.

Six B-17s conduct screening missions to jam German radio interception efforts and conduct countermeasures against German radar sites.

During the night two B-17s and five B-24s drop leaflets over Germany and Belgium.

Ninth Air Force sends 280 A-20 Havocs and B-26 Marauders to attack bridges and communication sites. P-47 and P-38 fighters support ground forces.

A German V-2 rocket damages a U.S. freighter at Antwerp, Belgium.

Soldiers of the 158th Regimental Combat Team use an improvised litter to carry away wounded men after an unsuccessful attempt to clear the Japanese from the Rosario-Damortis road on Luzon, around January 14, 1945.

**SOUTHWEST PACIFIC AREA:** Far East Air Force B-25 Mitchells and P-51 Mustangs attack airfields on Luzon. A-20 Havocs bomb Clark Field and destroy a number of Japanese aircraft on the ground. B-24 Liberators attack troop concentrations at Cabanatuan. B-24s, B-25s, A-20s, P-38 Lightnings, and P-47 Thunderbolts attack vehicles, bridges, and airfields on Mindanao and Negros Islands. The B-24s of the 408th Bombardment Squadron (Heavy), 22nd Bombardment Group (Heavy), redeploy from Angaur Island in the Palau Islands to Samar in the Philippines.

**PACIFIC:** Twentieth Air Force sends 82 B-29 Superfortresses from Chengtu, China, to bomb air installations on Formosa. A total of 55 B-29s hit the primary target, while others bomb targets of opportunity.

Another 73 B-29s from the Marianas are sent to bomb the Mitsubishi aircraft production facility at Nagoya, Japan. A total of 40 B-29s hit the primary target while others bomb targets of opportunity. Aircrews report 16 confirmed kills, seven probables, and 26 possibles. Five B-29s are lost.

**CENTRAL PACIFIC:** Seventh Air Force sends 22 B-24 Liberators from Saipan escorted by P-38 Lightnings and 21 additional B-24s from Guam to bomb airfields on Moen Island at Truk.

B-24s from Guam bomb Iwo Jima.

During the night two B-24s from the Marianas conduct individual snooper missions on Iwo Jima.

**NEW GUINEA:** FEAF B-25 Mitchells bomb the Molucca Islands.

## January 15

**CBI:** Colonel Lewis A. Pick's Ledo Road convoy reaches Myitkyina and remains for about a week as Japanese forces are cleared from the area ahead.

Lieutenant General Albert C. Wedemeyer, commander of the China theater, Lieutenant General George E Stratemeyer, commander of Eastern Air Command, and Lieutenant General Daniel I. Sultan, commander of the India-Burma theater, meet at Myitkyina. They agree to establish a new headquarters in China to command both the Tenth and Fourteenth Air Forces.

Fourteenth Air Force sends 18 B-25 Mitchells, supported by 20 P-51 Mustangs and P-40s, to attack Hankow, China. Over 130 P-40s and P-51 Mustangs on armed reconnaissance attack numerous targets of opportunity throughout southern and southeast China.

In Burma, Tenth Air Force sends 12 B-24 Liberators to bomb a troop concentration and logistics storage area. P-47 Thunderbolts damage a bridge and support ground forces, attacking logistics storage sites, tanks, and targets of opportunity.

**ETO:** The 84th Infantry Division and the 2nd Armored Division reach the Ourthe River west of Houffalize.

SHAEF headquarters estimates that since the Normandy landings 1.5 million German soldiers have been killed, wounded, or captured.

Eighth Air Force sends more than 640 B-17s and B-24 Liberators escorted by 782 P-47 Thunderbolts and P-51 Mustangs to attack marshaling yards in Germany. The bombers use a combination of visual and H2X radar. No bombers are lost and 22 damaged. Aircrew casualties are one killed. Fighter pilots report 14 confirmed kills and 19 possibles in the air. Two P-51s are lost and one P-51 is damaged. Two pilots are reported missing.

During the night two B-17s and seven B-24s drop leaflets over Germany and the Netherlands.

Ninth Air Force sends B-26 Marauders to attack bridges. P-47 and P-38 fighters support ground forces of the III and VIII Corps near Houffalize and Bastogne.

Corporal Arthur O. Beyer is a tank destroyer gunner in C Company, 603rd Tank Destroyer Battalion, fighting German defenses near Arloncourt, Belgium. As the tank destroyers support the infantry with direct fire, Corporal Beyer spots a machine-gun position and advances toward it in full view of the enemy. Attacking the position with a hand grenade, he captures two soldiers. Now within the German lines, he attacks parallel, using grenades and rifle fire to eliminate the defenders, destroying two machine-gun positions, killing eight enemy soldiers and capturing 18 more. Corporal Beyer's act of courage and initiative will win him the Medal of Honor.

**MEDITERRANEAN:** Fifteenth Air Force sends more than 400 B-17s and B-24 Liberators escorted by nearly 300 P-38 Lightnings and P-51 Mustangs to attack marshaling yards and rail lines in Austria and Italy.

**ITALY:** Twelfth Air Force B-25 Mitchells and B-26 Marauders attack rail traffic near Brenner. A-20 Havocs and P-47 Thunderbolts of the XXII Tactical Air Command attack rail cars, bridges, and roads in the Po River valley.

**SOUTHWEST PACIFIC AREA, LUZON:** The XIV Corps crosses the Agno River without encountering any major Japanese forces.

In the Philippines, Far East Air Force B-24 Liberators, B-25 Mitchells, A-20 Havocs, P-38 Lightnings, and P-47 Thunderbolts attack vehicles on highways, railroads, airfields, tanks, and troops on Luzon and Palawan islands.

Naval Task Force 38 attacks Japanese shipping and aircraft off Formosa and the China coast. Carrier aircraft sink two destroyers, a fast transport, a fleet tanker, and a cargo ship. In addition an auxiliary minelayer and two cargo ships are damaged. TF 38 aircraft also sink a Japanese salvage ship off Luzon.

**PACIFIC:** Admiral Halsey's Third Fleet attacks Japanese airfields on Formosa, Hainan Island, and Hong Kong.

**CENTRAL PACIFIC:** Seventh Air Force sends 12 B-24 Liberators from Saipan to bomb Iwo Jima.

During the night two B-24s from Guam and Saipan conduct individual snooper (radar-assisted bomb release) missions on Iwo Jima airfields.

**NEW GUINEA:** FEAF B-24 Liberators bomb airfields in Borneo.

## January 16

**CBI:** In China, Fourteenth Air Force sends four B-25 Mitchells escorted by eight P-40s to attack rail targets near Hankow. Aircrews report a train is destroyed. Over 180 P-51 Mustangs, P-40s, and P-38 Lightnings fly armed reconnaissance over China below the Yangtze River, attacking targets of opportunity.

In Burma, Tenth Air Force sends 12 B-25 Mitchells to bomb a troop concentration and a logistics storage area. P-47 Thunderbolts support ground forces, attacking logistics storage sites, tanks, and targets of opportunity.

**ATLANTIC:** Four destroyer escorts sink German submarine *U-248* in the North Atlantic.

**ETO: The Battle of the Bulge.** Patrols from Third Army's 11th Armored Division meet the 41st Infantry Regiment of the 2nd Armored Division, First Army, at Houffalize. First Army and Third Army have trapped nearly 20,000 German soldiers. The divisions turn eastward toward the German border, closing the Bulge. SHAEF headquarters estimates that since the beginning of the battle on December 16 the Germans have lost 120,000 men, 600 tanks, and 1,600 aircraft.

Major General Leonard T. Gerow takes command of Fifteenth Army, leaving V Corps. Major General Clarence R. Heubner replaces Gerow at V Corps. Gerow establishes his headquarters at Rheims. The army's mission is to train, equip, and provide for the onward movement of all U.S. ground forces entering the ETO. His army is also responsible for resting and refitting units from the 12th Army Group. Its combat tasks are to defend the Meuse River line, conduct occupation of areas in the rear of the 12th Army Group, and assume command of American units containing German troops in the Brittany port cities. If required, Gerow's personnel are to be prepared to act as an operational headquarters.

In the VI Corps area, Major General Roderick Allen leads the 12th Armored Division against German forces at Herrlisheim. The 17th Armored Infantry captures part of the town but is forced to withdraw during the night after nearly being surrounded.

Eighth Air Force sends a total of 627 B-17s and B-24 Liberators escorted by nearly 700 P-47 Thunderbolts and P-51 Mustangs to attack marshaling yards, oil production facilities, and industrial targets. The bombers use H2X radar. Two bombers are lost and 10 are damaged. Aircrew casualties are four killed, 23 wounded, and 22 missing. Two P-51s are lost and one is damaged. Two pilots are reported missing.

During the night one B-24 drops leaflets over Belgium.

Ninth Air Force A-20 Havocs, A-26 Invaders, and B-26 Marauders attack communication centers, road and rail bridges, and a motor transport repair facility in Germany. P-47 and P-38 fighters support ground forces of the III Corps near Houffalize.

**ITALY:** Twelfth Air Force A-20 Havocs bomb motor transport around Genoa and Milan.

**SOUTHWEST PACIFIC AREA:** B-25 Mitchells, A-20 Havocs, P-38 Lightnings, and P-47s attack communication sites, vehicles, and targets of opportunity on Negros Island.

Naval Task Force 38 attacks Japanese shipping and installations at Hong Kong, Hainan Island, and along the China coast. Carrier aircraft sink a transport, four merchant tankers, and a cargo ship and damage an oiler, a destroyer, a fast transport, three escort destroyers, and a coastal defense vessel. TF 38 planes sink a guardboat east of Hainan and sink a tanker off the coast of southern China.

**SOUTHWEST PACIFIC AREA, LUZON:** The 43rd Infantry Division and the 18th RCT control the Damortis-Rosario road and continue to advance against strong enemy defenses.

Far East Air Force B-24 Liberators, A-20 Havocs, P-38 Lightnings and P-47 Thunderbolts attack Japanese troop concentrations, trains, trucks, and targets of opportunity on Luzon Island.

**PACIFIC:** Twentieth Air Force sends B-29s of the 313th Bombardment Wing (Very Heavy) on a shakedown mission against the airfield on Pagan Island in the Marianas. The headquarters of the 316th Bombardment Wing (Very Heavy), the headquarters of the 19th Bombardment Group (Very Heavy), and the B-29 Superfortresses of the 28th, 30th, and 93rd Bombardment Squadrons (Very Heavy) arrive on Guam from the United States. The squadrons' first missions are scheduled for mid-February.

**CENTRAL PACIFIC:** Seventh Air Force sends 10 B-24 Liberators from Guam to bomb Iwo Jima.

During the night three B-24s conduct snooper (radar-assisted bomb release) missions on Iwo Jima.

**NEW GUINEA:** FEAF B-24 Liberators attack airfields on north Borneo and on Halmahera Island.

The headquarters of the 86th Fighter Wing redeploys from Sansapor, New Guinea, to Luzon. The 70th Fighter Squadron, 18th Fighter Group, redeploys from Morotai Island to Luzon with P-38 Lightnings. The 547th Night Fighter Squadron, 86th Fighter Wing, under the operational control of the 308th Bombardment Wing, redeploys from Mindoro Island to Luzon with P-38s and P-61 Black Widow night fighters.

## January 17

**CBI:** The Mars Task Force (the 5332nd Brigade Provisional) reaches the Burma Road with the intention of forcing the Japanese out of their defenses south of Wantung. The Chinese 50th and British 36th Divisions attack south toward Lashio and Mandalay to cut the Burma Road between the two cities. The Chinese 38th and 30th Divisions begin the attack toward the Burma Road to drive Japanese forces south.

Fourteenth Air Force sends more than 180 P-40s, P-51 Mustangs, and P-38 Lightnings to attack targets of opportunity from Wanling, Burma, to Shanghai, China. The airfields near Shanghai, Wuchou, and Wuchang are primary targets.

In Burma, Tenth Air Force sends B-25 Mitchells to attack bridges. P-47 Thunderbolts support ground forces and attack logistics storage sites and targets of opportunity.

**ETO:** Field Marshal Sir Bernard L. Montgomery returns operational control of First Army to General Omar N. Bradley's 12th Army Group but retains operational control of Ninth Army. First Army attacks toward St-Vith, while Third Army attacks toward the northeast. VIII Corps of Third Army attacks through Houffalize and the XX Corps attacks northward.

The 43rd Tank Battalion of the 12th Armored Division is overrun by German forces at Herrlisheim.

Although there are 71 Allied divisions available, most of them are seriously understrength. Noncombat units have been stripped to provide riflemen. In violation of army policy and tradition, black soldiers are asked to volunteer to serve in all-black units as infantrymen. General Eisenhower now examines future operations in three phases. Destroying German forces west of the Rhine is the first phase; seizing a bridgehead over the Rhine is the second phase; and the destruction of German forces followed by an advance into central Germany is the third phase. The destruction of German forces will be accomplished by two axes of advance—one north of the Ruhr into the open space of the north German plain and the other attacking from Mainz through Frankfurt to Kassel. The goal is a double envelopment of the Ruhr. Eisenhower wants to push 35 divisions across the Rhine north of the Ruhr and get as many divisions as possible across in the south to draw German units away from the main effort in the north. SHAEF headquarters estimates that eight divisions will be available in March, including six airborne divisions and between five and eight French divisions.

Eighth Air Force sends more than 700 B-17s and B-24 Liberators escorted by over 350 P-47 Thunderbolts and P-51 Mustangs to attack oil refineries, a U-boat base, and rail targets in northern Germany. The bombers use H2X radar or Gee-H. A total of nine bombers are lost and 152 are damaged. Aircrew casualties are one killed, seven wounded, and 92 missing. Seven fighters are lost and one is damaged. Seven pilots are reported missing.

**ITALY:** Twelfth Air Force B-25 Mitchells and B-26 Marauders attack rail traffic near Brenner. A-20 Havocs and P-47 Thunderbolts attack rail lines, bridges, and roads.

**SOUTHWEST PACIFIC AREA:** The Fifth Air Force assumes responsibility for all air operations over Luzon.

In the Philippines, Far East Air Force B-24 Liberators bomb railyards at Legaspi, while B-25 Mitchells attack road and rail targets near Manila. Other B-24s bomb targets on Mindanao and Negros Island. A-20 Havocs, P-38 Lightnings, and P-47 Thunderbolts attack bridges, shipping, port facilities, airfields, vehicles, and targets of opportunity.

**PACIFIC:** Twentieth Air Force sends 92 B-29s from Chengtu, China, to bomb the airfield at Shinchiku on Formosa. Only 77 bombers hit the primary target, while others attack targets of opportunity in China. One B-29 is lost.

The headquarters of the 29th Bombardment Group (Very Heavy) and the B-29 Superfortresses of the 6th, 43rd, and 52nd Bombardment Squadrons (Very Heavy) arrive at Guam from the United States. The squadrons' first missions are scheduled for mid-February.

U.S. submarine *Tautog* torpedoes and sinks a Japanese fast transport off southern Kyushu, Japan.

**CENTRAL PACIFIC:** Seventh Air Force sends 14 B-24 Liberators from Saipan to bomb Iwo Jima. Three B-24s from Guam bomb Marcus Island.

During the night two B-24s from Guam and Saipan conduct individual snooper missions on Iwo Jima.

### January 18

**ALEUTIANS:** Eleventh Air Force sends three B-24 Liberators on a reconnaissance mission over Paramushiru Island. One B-24 is forced to land in Soviet territory as the aircraft are returning to base.

**CBI:** In China, Fourteenth Air Force sends 29 B-24 Liberators along with 25 P-40s to attack shipping and railroad targets at Hong Kong. Nearly 140 P-51 Mustangs, P-40s, and P-38 Lightnings conduct armed reconnaissance missions over southern China from the Burma boundary to Hong Kong and attack targets of opportunity.

In Burma, Tenth Air Force sends B-25 Mitchells, P-47 Thunderbolts, and P-38 Lightnings to attack airfields. Other P-47s support ground forces attacking troops, logistics storage areas, and targets of opportunity.

**ETO:** The XII Corps of Third Army attacks to clear German forces from the Sauer River. The Americans face only light resistance.

SHAEF informs the CCS of its operational plan to destroy German forces west of the Rhine River and seize bridgeheads over the river in preparation for the anticipated final campaign within Germany. There are 71 Allied divisions currently available, but Eisenhower anticipates the number of divisions available in spring to rise to a total of 85. Eisenhower proposes a three-phase campaign. The first phase is the elimination of German forces west of the Rhine by the 21st, 12th, and 6th Army Groups. The second phase is the establishment of bridgeheads over the Rhine in the 21st Army Group area and the 12th Army Group area. The third phase is the reduction of the Ruhr and the occupation of the Saar River basin. Montgomery's 21st Army Group with the Ninth Army (reinforced to a strength of 12 divisions) will cross the Rhine and attack the Ruhr from the north. Bradley's 12th Army Group will close on the Rhine north of the Moselle River and move north to cut off the Ruhr. With the capture of the Ruhr, German forces in the west are eliminated along with Germany's industrial capability to continue the war. Afterward, the 12th Army Group will attack either northeast to Berlin or east to Leipzig, with the 21st Army Group supporting from the north and the 6th Army Group providing support from the south. Eisenhower's concept is tempered by uncertainties as to whether the Germans have the capability to conduct another major counteroffensive. The SHAEF commander is extremely sensitive to threats that may emerge during the advance, thus slowing the tempo of offensive operations.

In the VI Corps area, 12th Armored Division withdraws from Herrlisheim and establishes defensive positions west of the Zorn River.

Eighth Air Force sends 114 B-17s escorted by over 100 P-51 Mustangs to bomb the marshaling yard at Kaiserslautern, Germany. No bombers are lost, but three fighters are lost. The pilots are reported missing. Six B-17s conduct screening missions to jam German radio interception efforts and conduct countermeasures against German radar sites.

The headquarters of the IX Tactical Air Command returns to the operational control of Ninth Air Force.

**MEDITERRANEAN:** Operational control of the British XIII Corps passes from Fifth Army to Eighth Army. Field Marshal Sir Harold R. L. G. Alexander, supreme Allied commander in the Mediterranean theater of operations, has decided to move to the "offensive defensive." In other words, his forces will take no more major-combat offensive actions until the weather improves, sufficient artillery ammunition is available, and replacements for combat losses have been integrated into units.

The 15th Special Group (Provisional) is organized and given operational control of the 859th (B-24) and 885th (B-17) Bombardment Squadrons (Heavy), which drop supplies in France, Italy, and Yugoslavia.

**ITALY:** Twelfth Air Force A-20 Havocs and P-47 Thunderbolts attack rail lines, bridges, trains, ammunition and fuel storage sites, and roads in the Po River valley.

**Southwest Pacific Area:** In the Philippines, Far East Air Force B-25 Mitchells bomb targets, and P-38 Lightnings strafe parked aircraft on Mindanao Island.

**Southwest Pacific Area, Luzon:** In the I Corps area the 25th Infantry Division attacks toward Binalonan to capture the road junction that opens into the Cagayan Valley. The 43rd Infantry Division captures Pozorrubio and advances up the Damortis-Rosario road after encountering strong Japanese defenses.

FEAF B-24 Liberators bomb targets on Luzon Island, while A-20 Havocs attack warehouses and highway traffic near Bataan.

**Central Pacific:** Seventh Air Force sends 19 B-24 Liberators from Saipan to bomb targets on Chichi Jima and Haha Jima islands. B-24 Liberators from Saipan bomb Iwo Jima.

During the night three B-24s conduct individual snooper missions on Iwo Jima.

A Japanese raiding force lands on Peleliu attempting to destroy aircraft at the airfield, but fails to inflict any damage.

**New Guinea:** FEAF B-24 Liberators bomb targets on Halmahera Island.

The 66th and 67th Troop Carrier Squadrons, 433rd Troop Carrier Group, redeploy from Biak Island to Mindoro Island and Leyte Island with C-46s and C-47s.

### January 19

**CBI:** The Mars Task Force attacks the Japanese at Nawhkam near the Burma Road, effectively cutting the main line of supply for the Japanese 56th Division.

Over 100 P-51 Mustangs, P-40s, and P-38 Lightnings from Fourteenth Air Force conduct armed reconnaissance over south China and the border with French Indochina, attacking targets of opportunity, many of them near Wanting, China.

In Burma, Tenth Air Force sends nine B-25 Mitchells to bomb troops and logistics storage sites while P-47 Thunderbolts support ground forces.

**ETO:** A winter blizzard hits the Ardennes, stopping all forward movement by the 12th Army Group.

In the VI Corps area, the 12th Armored Division stops a German attack and is later relieved in place by the 36th Infantry Division.

During the night Eighth Air Force sends two B-17s and nine B-24 Liberators to drop leaflets in the Netherlands, Belgium, and Germany.

Ninth Air Force P-47 Thunderbolts and P-38 Lightnings support elements of III and VIII Corps near Houffalize and support the 5th Infantry Division near Bettendorf, Germany.

**Mediterranean:** Fifteenth Air Force sends more than 400 B-17s and B-24 Liberators to attack road and rail bridges and marshaling yards in Yugoslavia. P-38 Lightnings and P-51 Mustangs fly sweeps. P-51 Mustangs shoot down five enemy aircraft over Zagreb, Yugoslavia.

**Italy:** Twelfth Air Force A-20 Havocs bomb rail lines, vehicles, bridges, and roads in the Po River valley.

**Southwest Pacific Area:** In the Philippines, Far East Air Force B-24 Liberators and B-25 Mitchells bomb airfields on Negros Island. A-20 Havocs attack shipping and B-25 Mitchells, P-38 Lightnings, and P-47 Thunderbolts attack airfields, vehicles, storage areas, and highways.

**SOUTHWEST PACIFIC AREA, LUZON:** The XIV Corps protects its flanks against Japanese defenders in the Cabaruan Hills by capturing Paniqui and Anao. The road to Manila is open, and the north-south lines of communication for the Japanese forces in Luzon are mostly cut off.

**PACIFIC:** U.S. submarine *Spot* torpedoes and sinks a Japanese cargo ship in the Yellow Sea.

Twentieth Air Force sends 80 B-29 Superfortresses to bomb the Kawasaki aircraft plant at Akashi, Japan. A total of 62 hit the primary target, while others hit alternative targets and targets of opportunity. Aircrews report four confirmed kills, four probables, and eight possibles.

**CENTRAL PACIFIC:** Seventh Air Force sends seven B-24 Liberators from Saipan to bomb harbor installations at Chichi Jima Island. Another nine B-24 Liberators from Saipan bomb Iwo Jima.

During the night three B-24s from the Marianas conduct individual snooper missions on Iwo Jima.

**NEW GUINEA:** The headquarters of the 433rd Troop Carrier Group redeploys from Biak Island to Leyte Island in the Philippines. The P-38 Lightnings of the 70th Fighter Squadron, 18th Fighter Group, redeploy from Sansapor, New Guinea, to Luzon.

## January 20

**ALEUTIANS:** Eleventh Air Force sends four B-24 Liberators to bomb Shimushu Island in the Kuriles.

**CBI:** Patrols of the 38th Chinese Division moving from the north meet elements of the Chinese Y Force (also known as the Chinese Expeditionary Force) advancing south at Mong Yu. Wantung falls to Chinese forces. Allied forces begin attacking south toward Leshio.

Fourteenth Air Force sends four B-25 Mitchells to bomb a bridge and railroad cars near Hanoi, in French Indochina. In China, B-25 Mitchells attack targets of opportunity, and aircrews report a small cargo ship damaged in the East China Sea. P-51 Mustangs attack airfields near Shanghai. Pilots report 22 Japanese aircraft destroyed on the ground. Over 200 P-40s, P-51 Mustangs, and P-38 Lightnings conduct armed reconnaissance over south China and the border with French Indochina.

In Burma, Tenth Air Force P-47 Thunderbolts support ground forces, attack ammunition storage areas and logistics bases, troop concentrations, and targets of opportunity.

**ETO:** Hungary surrenders to the Allies.

The 157th Infantry Regiment of the 45th Infantry Division holds at Reipertsweler against heavy German attacks, supported by a battalion of the 411th Infantry Regiment of the 103rd Infantry Division. The units suffer heavy losses, with 158 killed and over 1,000 wounded, captured, or evacuated for noncombat illness. Only two men of the 750 men from the 3rd Battalion of the 157th Infantry Regiment will escape after being surrounded by German forces.

The I Corps of the French First Army, 6th Army Group, initiates the attack to reduce the Colmar Pocket, a German bridgehead about 30 miles deep and 50 miles wide west of the Rhine River. The XXI Corps of Seventh Army becomes operational under the command of Major General Frank W. Milburn. General Patch orders a withdrawal to the Moder River during the night.

Eighth Air Force sends more than 700 B-17s escorted by over 450 P-51 Mustangs to attack synthetic oil plants, rail targets, and bridges in western Germany. The bombers use H2X radar to improve accuracy. A total of four bombers are lost and 122 damaged. Aircrew casualties are eight killed, 33 wounded, and six missing. Fighter pilots report one confirmed kill. Two fighters are lost and the pilots are reported missing.

P-51 Mustangs fly a fighter sweep in the Frankfurt area. One P-51 is lost, and the pilot is reported missing.

**MEDITERRANEAN:** Fifteenth Air Force sends more than 300 B-17s and B-24s to attack marshaling yards at Linz and Salzburg, Austria, and at Rosenheim, Germany, as well as oil storage facilities at Regensburg, Germany.

**ITALY:** Twelfth Air Force B-25 Mitchells and B-26 Marauders attack bridges. A-20 Havocs and P-47 Thunderbolts attack fuel and ammunition storage areas in the Po River valley.

**SOUTHWEST PACIFIC AREA:** In the Philippines, Far East Air Force B-24 Liberators attack an airfield on Negros Island and bomb underground storage areas on Luzon Island. A-20 Havocs and B-25 Mitchells attack rail lines, trains, airfields, and artillery positions on Luzon.

U.S. submarine *Nautilus* lands supplies on the south coast of Mindanao.

**PACIFIC:** In Twentieth Air Force, Brigadier General Roger M. Ramey becomes commander of XX Bomber Command; Major General Curtis Emerson LeMay takes command of XXI Bomber Command.

U.S. submarine *Spot* torpedoes and sinks a Japanese merchant fishing boat in the Yellow Sea. U.S. submarine *Tautog* torpedoes and sinks a Japanese vessel at southern end of Tsushima Strait.

**CENTRAL PACIFIC:** Seventh Air Force sends 12 B-24 Liberators from Guam to bomb Iwo Jima.

During the night 10 B-24s from Guam conduct individual snooper missions on Iwo Jima.

Japanese submarine *I-48* launches *kaiten* against U.S. shipping at Ulithi without success.

**NEW GUINEA:** The headquarters of the 35th Fighter Group redeploys from Morotai Island to Luzon. The B-24 Liberators of the 2nd Bombardment Squadron (Heavy), 22nd Bombardment Group (Heavy), redeploys from Angaur Island in the Palau Islands to Samar Island in the central Philippines. The 82nd Tactical Reconnaissance Squadron's F-6s (photo reconnaissance Lightnings) and P-40s redeploy from Morotai to Luzon; the 110th Tactical Reconnaissance Squadron's P-40s redeploy to Leyte. Both squadrons belong to the 71st Tactical Reconnaissance Group.

## January 21
**CBI:** Mars Task Force fights to clear Japanese defenders from the key hills overlooking the Burma Road.

In China, Fourteenth Air Force sends 30 B-24 Liberators to pound the Hong Kong area and P-51 Mustangs to attack Nanking airfield. Fighter pilots report 11 enemy aircraft destroyed on the ground. P-51s also attack targets of opportunity along the Yangtze River to Hankow.

In Burma, Tenth Air Force sends 10 B-25 Mitchells to bomb Heho airfield. P-38 Lightnings and P-47 Thunderbolts support ground forces and attack troop concentrations, supplies, and targets of opportunity.

Fourteenth Air Force B-24 Liberators sink a Japanese salvage vessel at Hong Kong.

U.S. submarine *Tautog* sinks Japanese merchant tanker in the Korea Strait.

**ETO:** The weather in the Ardennes clears, allowing First and Third Armies to advance toward St-Vith. Wiltz is retaken.

Major General Edward H. Brooks orders his VI Corps to withdraw and organizes a strong defensive line. The last German reserves on the western front have been committed and have accomplished no major objectives.

Eighth Air Force sends more than 900 B-17s and B-24 Liberators escorted by over 500 P-47 Thunderbolts and P-51 Mustangs to attack marshaling yards, military vehicle production facilities, oil production facilities, and bridges. The bombers use a combination of Pathfinder bombers, H2X radar, and Gee-H. A total of eight bombers are lost and 68 are damaged. Aircrew casualties are 21 killed, 15 wounded, and 57 missing. Fighter pilots report eight confirmed kills and one probable on the ground. No fighters are lost.

During the night two B-17s and nine B-24s drop leaflets over Germany, France, and the Netherlands.

Ninth Air Force sends 166 A-20 Havocs, A-26 Invaders, and B-26 Marauders to attack railroad bridges and a marshaling yard. P-47 and P-38 fighters back up ground forces flying in support of the 7th Armored Division.

German submarine *U-1199* torpedoes and damages a U.S. freighter off the Isle of Wight.

**MEDITERRANEAN:** Fifteenth Air Force sends 170 B-17s escorted by 131 P-38 Lightnings and P-51 Mustangs to attack oil refineries in Austria. Another 43 P-38s attack an oil refinery in Italy.

**ITALY:** Twelfth Air Force B-25 Mitchells attack bridges and logistics storage sites. A-20 Havocs and P-47 Thunderbolts attack rail lines, bridges, logistics storage sites, and ammunition storage areas.

**SOUTHWEST PACIFIC AREA:** In the Philippines, Far East Air Force B-24 Liberators bomb an airfield, a barracks, and coastal defense guns. B-25 Mitchells, A-20 Havocs, P-38 Lightnings, and P-47 Thunderbolts conduct armed reconnaissance and make attacks on airfields, road networks, bridges, gun positions, vehicles, and other targets of opportunity on Luzon.

The headquarters of the 22nd Bombardment Group (Heavy) and the B-24s of the 33rd Bombardment Squadron (Heavy) redeploy from Angaur Island in the Palau Islands to Samar in the Philippines.

**PACIFIC:** Task Force 38 attacks Japanese shipping and airfields on Formosa, the Pescadores, and Okinawa in the Ryukyus. Carrier aircraft sink two fleet tankers, five cargo ships, four army tankers, a merchant tanker, and two cargo vessels and damage three destroyers, two landing ships, a cargo ship, and a supply vessel off Formosa. Kamikazes attacking the task force damage the carrier USS *Ticonderoga*, the small carrier USS *Langley*, and a destroyer.

**CENTRAL PACIFIC:** Seventh Air Force sends 12 B-24 Liberators from Guam to bomb Iwo Jima.

During the night eight B-24s from Saipan conduct individual snooper missions on Iwo Jima.

## January 22

**CBI:** Elements of the Chinese 30th Division reach the Burma Road north of the Mars Task Force.

In China, Fourteenth Air Force sends 16 P-40s and P-51 Mustangs on armed reconnaissance attack against various targets near Wanting. Another 14 P-51 Mustangs and P-40s attack railroad yards, destroying locomotives and trucks.

In Burma, Tenth Air Force sends 46 P-47 Thunderbolts to support ground forces while 12 others attack roads, troop concentrations, fuel storage sites, ammunition storage areas, vehicles, and targets of opportunity.

**ETO:** The XIX Tactical Air Force attacks German forces crossing the Our River. Pilots report over 1,700 vehicles destroyed.

The French II Corps of 6th Army Group supports the French I Corps attacking the Colmar Pocket. The 3rd Infantry Division and a regiment of the 63rd Infantry Division clear the Colmar Forest. The U.S. 12th Armored Division is transferred from VI Corps to the First French Army. The division loses more than 1,100 men (nearly half of them missing in action) in the battle for Herrlisheim. It is now known as the "suicide division."

Eighth Air Force sends 206 B-17s escorted by 258 P-51 Mustangs to attack a synthetic oil plant, road and rail bridges, and marshaling yards. The bombers use H2X radar and visual release methods. A total of eight bombers are lost and 68 are damaged. Aircrew casualties are 13 wounded and 45 missing. Fighter pilots report three confirmed kills and one possible on the ground. P-51 Mustangs fly a sweep over St-Vith, Belgium, and over Karlsruhe, Darmstadt, and Koblenz in Germany. One P-51 is lost, and the pilot is reported missing.

During the night one B-17 and eight B-24s drop leaflets over France and the Netherlands.

Ninth Air Force sends 166 A-20 Havocs, A-26 Invaders, and B-26 Marauders to attack railroad bridges and a marshaling yard. P-47 and P-38 fighters support the 7th Armored Division near Montfort in the Netherlands and the III, VIII, and XII Corps from St-Vith to Luxembourg. Fighters also fly armed reconnaissance missions and support the 4th, 5th, 94th, and 95th Infantry Divisions from Luxembourg to Saarlautern, Germany.

**ITALY:** Twelfth Air Force B-25 Mitchells attack bridges. A-20 Havocs and P-47 Thunderbolts attack vehicles and rail lines, destroying rail cars and locomotives. Logistics storage sites and ammunition storage areas are also attacked.

**SOUTHWEST PACIFIC AREA:** Far East Air Force B-24 Liberators, escorted by P-38 Lightnings, bomb Heito airfield on Formosa, the first major Fifth Air Force attack on the island. In the Philippines, B-24s bomb an airfield, a barracks, and gun positions across Manila Bay on Luzon.

The headquarters of Fifth Air Force and the headquarters of V Bomber Command and V Fighter Command redeploy from Leyte Island to Mindoro Island.

**PACIFIC:** Admiral William F. Halsey's Third Fleet conducts air strikes on Okinawa. In 19 days of operations ranging all across the main sea lines of communication of the Japanese Empire, Halsey's fleet has claimed 586 enemy aircraft destroyed and nearly 700 others damaged. Over 130 ships have been sunk and another 167 reported damaged.

Task Force 38 attacks Japanese shipping, airfields, and installations in the Ryukyus. Carrier aircraft sink a cargo vessel, two merchant tankers, a cargo ship, and a guardboat.

**CENTRAL PACIFIC:** Seventh Air Force sends 20 B-24 Liberators from Guam to bomb Iwo Jima.

During the night eight B-24s from Guam bomb the island again.

**NEW GUINEA:** The P-47 Thunderbolts of the 39th Fighter Squadron, 35th Fighter Group, redeploy from Morotai Island to Luzon.

### January 23

**ALEUTIANS:** Eleventh Air Force sends four B-24 Liberators to attack targets on Paramushiru Island. The Japanese respond with 10 fighters to attack the bombers. Aircrews report two confirmed kills. One B-24 is lost.

**CBI:** In China, Fourteenth Air Force sends 40 P-51 Mustangs and P-40s on armed reconnaissance, attacking river, road, and rail traffic.

In Burma, Tenth Air Force sends 12 B-25 Mitchells to bomb airfields, while 34 P-47 Thunderbolts support ground forces, and 55 P-47 Thunderbolts and P-38 Lightnings attack troop concentrations, storage areas, and vehicles.

The 88th Fighter Squadron, 80th Fighter Group, redeploys its P-47s from Shingbwiyang to Myitkyina.

**ATLANTIC:** President Roosevelt arrives at Newport News, Virginia, to board the heavy cruiser USS *Quincy*, which will take him to Malta for a U.S.-British strategy meeting related to the Argonaut Conference at Yalta.

**ETO:** The 7th Armored Division's Combat Command A, led by Brigadier General Bruce C. Clarke, whose unit had been pushed out of St-Vith after a brilliant defense of the town during the Ardennes offensive, recaptures the town.

General Eisenhower estimates that the German Ardennes offensive has delayed Allied offensive operations by six weeks.

The 3rd and 28th Infantry Divisions support the French attack on the Colmar Pocket.

Eighth Air Force sends more than 200 B-17s escorted by over 70 P-51 Mustangs to attack marshaling yards at Neuss, Germany. The bombers use Gee-H. One B-17 is lost and 98 are damaged. Aircrew casualties are five killed, six wounded, and 10 missing. Fighter pilots report one confirmed kill. One P-51 is damaged.

During the night five B-24s drop leaflets over the Netherlands.

Ninth Air Force P-47 and P-38 fighters support ground forces of the III, VIII, and XII Corps and the 94th and 95th Infantry Divisions as well as fly armed reconnaissance missions.

**ITALY:** Twelfth Air Force A-20 Havocs and P-47 Thunderbolts attack rail lines, vehicles, logistics storage sites, and ammunition storage areas.

**SOUTHWEST PACIFIC AREA:** In the Philippines, Far East Air Force B-24 Liberators and A-20 Havocs attack Corregidor Island. B-24s bomb an airfield on Negros Island.

During the night B-24 Liberators bomb an aluminum factory at Takao on Formosa.

U.S. submarine *Barb* reports sinking three ships and damaging two more on the southern coast of China across from Formosa. But only one cargo ship is actually sunk.

U.S. submarine *Nautilus* delivers supplies to east coast of Mindanao.

U.S. submarine *Sennet* torpedoes and sinks a Japanese guardboat in Hangchow Bay, China.

**SOUTHWEST PACIFIC AREA, LUZON:** In the XIV Corps area the two RCTs of the 40th Infantry Division hold the Bamban River line, a possible threat to the corps' left flank. General Griswold is wary of exposing his flanks to possible attack and slows his advance toward Manila. FEAF A-20s attack an airfield, and P-38 Lightnings and P-47 Thunderbolts attack bridges and coastal guns on Grande Island at the mouth of Subic Bay.

**PACIFIC:** Twentieth Air Force sends 73 B-29 Superfortresses from the XXI Bomber Command to bomb the Mitsubishi engine production facility at Nagoya, Japan. A total of 28 hit the primary target and 27 attack the secondary target. Nine others bomb other alternatives and targets of opportunity. The bombers are met by over 600 Japanese fighters. Aircrews report 33 confirmed kills, 22 probable kills, and 40 possible kills. Two B-29s are lost.

**CENTRAL PACIFIC:** Seventh Air Force sends 12 B-24 Liberators from Saipan to bomb Iwo Jima.

B-24s from Guam conduct an armed reconnaissance mission over Woleai Atoll and bomb the main runway on the island.

During the night 10 B-24s from Saipan conduct harassment bombing on Iwo Jima.

Three destroyer escorts sink Japanese submarine *I-48* off Yap.

## January 24

**ALEUTIANS:** Eleventh Air Force sends eight B-25 Mitchells on a low-level bombing run on Torishima Island in the Kurile Islands, but four abort due to mechanical trouble. The other four bomb buildings. Two B-25s are damaged by Japanese antiaircraft fire.

**CBI:** The Mars Task Force harasses the Japanese 56th Division as it withdraws on the Burma Road.

In China, Fourteenth Air Force P-51 Mustangs on armed reconnaissance attack railroad targets. Pilots report 21 locomotives destroyed.

In Burma, Tenth Air Force sends 12 B-25 Mitchells to bomb an airfield. P-47 Thunderbolts support ground forces and attack bridges, troop concentrations, logistics storage sites, and targets of opportunity

The USS *Blackfin* (SS-322), a Balao-class submarine, had a crew of 66, carried 24 torpedoes, could patrol for 75 days and stay submerged for as long as 48 hours. The *Blackfin* conducted a total of five war patrols and sunk the Japanese destroyer *Shigure* on January 24, 1945.

U.S. submarine *Blackfin* torpedoes and sinks a Japanese destroyer in the Straits of Malacca and coordinates with USS *Besugo,* damaging a merchant tanker off the east coast of the Malay Peninsula.

**ATLANTIC:** The JCS reports to President Roosevelt that the Soviet Union is essential to the defeat of Japan. The JCS requests the president to ask the Soviet leadership to provide a date for their entry into the war and suggests that collaboration begin for planning as soon as possible.

**ETO: The End of the Battle of the Bulge.** The VII Corps goes to First Army reserve. Bradley orders the rest of First Army to attack northeast to break the West Wall defenses. Third Army is to guard the southern flank.

The Battle of the Bulge is the greatest combat action ever fought by the U.S. Army, involving 26 divisions and 600,000 men. A total of 81,000 men are killed, wounded, or missing throughout the entire operation. Over 70 tanks and tank destroyers are lost. The Germans suffer between 67,000 and 103,000 casualties and have lost 400 tanks. The German army in the west is shattered. American public morale is shaken by the German surprise attack and shocked at the cost of the battle. The American commanders of First Army are embarrassed and bitter that they have been caught by surprise. Nevertheless, commanders at all levels have fought intelligently and with great determination. Small units often made the difference between victory and disaster. The Americans have fought the best the German army can muster, in terrible weather and without air support for nearly a week, and disrupted the entire offensive. Then, in the following weeks, the massed power of the American air and ground forces became

Paratroopers of the 3rd Battalion, 504th Parachute Infantry Regiment, 82nd Airborne Division, move into the attack near Herresbach, Belgium, during the Battle of the Bulge, January 28, 1945.

overwhelming. The battle in the Ardennes in many ways marks the finest performance of the American combat soldier in World War II.

Eighth Air Force P-51 Mustangs from airfields in Belgium are sent to fly sweeps over western Germany. Fighter pilots report three confirmed kills in the air. One P-51 is lost, and the pilot is reported missing.

Ninth Air Force sends A-20 Havocs, A-26 Invaders, and B-26 Marauders to attack communication targets over Germany. P-47 and P-38 fighters fly armed reconnaissance missions and support ground forces of the III, VIII, XII, and XX Corps along the battlefront from St-Vith, Belgium, to Saarlautern, Germany.

German aircraft attack shipping at the port of Antwerp, damaging a U.S. freighter.

**SOUTHWEST PACIFIC AREA:** In the Philippines, Far East Air Force B-24 Liberators attack Corregidor Island, Cavite, and Grande Island at the mouth of Subic Bay. P-38 Lightnings and P-47 Thunderbolts conduct armed reconnaissance and sweeps, attacking vehicles, airfields, logistics storage sites, and Japanese positions throughout Luzon.

During the night B-24 Liberators conduct a snooper (radar-assisted bomb release) mission against Takao airfield on Formosa.

Navy aircraft from the Philippines bomb Japanese shipping at Formosa, sinking a cargo ship and damaging another.

**PACIFIC:** Twentieth Air Force sends more than 20 B-29 to bomb the airfields on Iwo Jima. They are preceded in their approach by Naval Task Group 94.9, with the battleship USS *Indiana,* three heavy cruisers, seven destroyers, and a light minelayer, under the command of Rear Admiral Oscar C. Badger, which bombards Iwo Jima. The task group's approach is protected by a barrier patrol of PB4Y Privateers. As the task group begins firing, B-24 Liberators, escorted by P-38 Lightnings, hit the island. Two destroyers sink a transport and two auxiliary minesweepers arriving at Iwo Jima.

U.S. submarine *Atule* torpedoes and sinks a Japanese cargo ship in the Yellow Sea.

**CENTRAL PACIFIC:** Seventh Air Force sends 33 B-24 Liberators from Guam and Saipan to bomb Iwo Jima, while other bombers act as spotters for naval gunfire.

During the night 10 B-24s conduct harassment bombing runs on the island.

The P-51 Mustangs of the 78th Fighter Squadron, 15th Fighter Group, begin redeployment from Hawaii, destined for Iwo Jima.

### January 25

**CBI:** Lieutenant General Albert C. Wedemeyer establishes the Chinese Combat Command under Major General Robert B. McClure and the Chinese Training Command under Brigadier General John W. Middleton. These organizations are to equip and train Chinese divisions as part of Plan Alpha.

Fourteenth Air Force sends 21 P-51 Mustangs to attack Lantienchang and Nanyuan airfields near Beijing (Peking). A total of 35 Japanese aircraft attack the U.S. fighters. Pilots report five confirmed kills. In China, Fourteenth Air Force P-51 Mustangs attack rail targets and airfields near Peking (Beijing). Fighter pilots report four locomotives and 40 aircraft destroyed. P-40s and P-51s attack railroad targets and report another 42 locomotives destroyed.

In Burma, Tenth Air Force sends 12 B-25 Mitchells to bomb an airfield. P-47 Thunderbolts support ground forces and attack bridges, troop concentrations, logistics storage sites, and targets of opportunity.

**ETO:** The last German attack on the Moder River defensive line is stopped near Hagenau. Operations Nordwind and Sonnewende (Winter Solstice) have failed, costing the German army 25,000 casualties. American losses in the Seventh Army are 15,600. In the Colmar Pocket, the XXI Corps commanded by Major General Frank W. Milburn takes operational control of the 3rd, 28th, and 75th Infantry Divisions and the 12th Armored Division and 5th French Armored Division. The Allied attacks split the German Nineteenth Army, forcing the Germans to conduct delaying actions.

Eighth Air Force sends more than 100 P-51 Mustangs from airfields in Belgium to fly a sweep over southwest Germany. Fighter pilots report two enemy confirmed kills. One P-51 is lost.

Ninth Air Force sends 170 A-20 Havocs, A-26 Invaders, and B-26 Marauders to attack communication centers, railroad bridges, and rail lines in an attempt to stop German troop movements. P-47 and P-38 fighters support the 5th Infantry Division near Echternach in Luxembourg.

Private First Class Jose F. Valdez of B Company, 7th Infantry Regiment, 3rd Infantry Division, occupies a forward position with five other soldiers about 500 yards from the main company position near Rosenkrantz, France. The Germans launch a major counterattack. Valdez engages a tank and forces it to withdraw; he then fires on a German machine-gun crew, killing all three men. It becomes clear that the Americans are faced with an attack of two infantry companies. As the Americans withdraw, Private Valdez volunteers to stay behind to delay the enemy. Firing on the enemy, Valdez is badly wounded but continues fighting and calls for artillery by using a field telephone, correcting fire until the shells are falling within 50 yards of his position. The German attack is broken. As the enemy retreats, Valdez crawls back to his own lines where he dies of his wounds. For his extraordinary courage and determination to save the lives of his comrades at the risk of his own life, Private First Class Valdez will receive the Medal of Honor.

**ITALY:** Twelfth Air Force A-20 Havocs and P-47 Thunderbolts of the XXII Tactical Air Command attack rail lines, ammunition storage areas, bridges, and roads.

**SOUTHWEST PACIFIC AREA:** In the Philippines, Far East Air Force B-24 Liberators bomb Corregidor Island. B-24s, B-25 Mitchells, A-20 Havocs, P-38 Lightnings, and P-47 Thunderbolts conduct sweeps, armed reconnaissance, and attack vehicles, Japanese positions, airfields, ammunition storage areas, logistics storage sites, barges, communication targets, and targets of opportunity over Luzon and Palawan Islands. During the night B-24s conduct a harassing raid on Takao, Formosa.

The A-20 Havocs of the 387th Bombardment Squadron (Light), 312th Bombardment Group (Light), redeploy from Leyte to Mindoro Island.

**PACIFIC:** U.S. submarine *Greenling* is damaged in a depth-charge attack off Kyushu, Japan, and is forced to end her patrol. U.S. submarine *Silversides* torpedoes and sinks a Japanese cargo ship off Kyushu.

**CENTRAL PACIFIC:** Seventh Air Force sends 14 B-24 Liberators from Saipan to bomb Iwo Jima. During the night 10 B-24s conduct harassment bombing runs on Iwo Jima.

## January 26

**CBI:** In China, Fourteenth Air Force sends 15 P-51 Mustangs and P-40s to attack Chenghsien airfield as well as locomotives, tracks, and vehicles at Nanking and Sinsiang.

In Burma, Tenth Air Force sends more than 140 P-47 Thunderbolts to support ground forces and attack bridges, troop concentrations, logistics storage sites, and targets of opportunity.

**ETO:** Ninth Air Force sends 27 B-26 Marauders to bomb the Euskirchen rail bridge to interdict rail traffic. P-47 and P-38 fighters of the XIX Tactical Air Command support Third Army operations from St-Vith in Belgium to Saarlautern in Germany.

Second Lieutenant Audie L. Murphy is commander of B Company, 15th Infantry Regiment, 3rd Infantry Division, advancing toward the Colmar Canal when German tanks and infantry counterattack near Holtzwihr, France. Deploying the company in a defensive position, Murphy begins calling artillery fire on the enemy. As German tanks approach his position Lieutenant Murphy climbs on a burning American tank destroyer and fires the .50-caliber machine gun against an enemy advancing on three sides and turns the infantry back. Although wounded in the leg, he holds this position for three hours as German infantry attempt to overwhelm him. When his ammunition is exhausted, he returns to his company and leads a counterattack, forcing the Germans to retreat. For his extraordinary courage and selfless dedication to duty, Second Lieutenant Murphy will receive the Medal of Honor.

**ITALY:** The 10th Mountain Division arrives in Italy and is placed under the operational control of IV Corps.

During the night Twelfth Air Force A-20 Havocs fly armed reconnaissance, bombing Po River crossings, an airfield, and vehicle movement throughout the Po River valley.

**SOUTHWEST PACIFIC AREA:** In the Philippines, the headquarters of the 3rd Air Commando Group, the 3rd and 4th Fighter Squadrons (Commando), and the 318th Troop Carrier Squadron (Commando) redeploy from Leyte Island to Luzon with P-51 Mustangs and C-47s. The A-20s of the 386th Bombardment Squadron (Light), 312th Bombardment Group (Light), redeploy from Leyte to Mindoro.

A Japanese cargo ship is sunk by a mine laid by U.S. submarine *Dace* off the southern coast of French Indochina.

**SOUTHWEST PACIFIC AREA, LUZON:** The XIV Corps has advanced 59 miles and occupies a 124-mile front with the 40th and 37th Infantry Divisions. No Japanese forces have put up any resistance. The commander of Japanese forces in the Philippines, General Tomoyuki Yamashita, has decided to hold northern Luzon, protecting the Cagayan Valley. Two other groups, the Kembu Group and the Shimbu Group, will defend other key areas. The Kembu Group will defend the area west of Clark Field. The Shimbu Group will defend the area east of Manila. Yamashita is limited by a lack of fuel and ammunition and has almost no air support.

Far East Air Force B-24 Liberators attack coastal guns on Corregidor Island. B-25 Mitchells bomb an airfield and coastal guns on Carabao Island, while A-20 Havocs attack Grande Island coastal defenses at the mouth of Subic Bay. P-47 Thunderbolts, A-20s, and B-24s attack communications, vehicles, and towns throughout Luzon Island. B-25 Mitchells and P-38 Lightnings attack targets on Mindanao Island.

**PACIFIC:** Admiral Richard A. Spruance assumes operational control of all forces assigned to Operation Detachment, the amphibious assault on Iwo Jima.

Twentieth Air Force sends 25 B-29 Superfortresses to mine harbors at Saigon, Cam Ranh Bay, and Phan Rang Bay in French Indochina. Another 41 B-29s mine the approaches to Singapore and Penang harbor and the Pakchan River and Koh Si Chang Channel in Thailand.

U.S. submarine *Tautog* torpedoes and sinks a Japanese merchant fishing boat southeast of Kyushu, Japan.

**CENTRAL PACIFIC:** Seventh Air Force sends 17 B-24 Liberators from Guam to bomb the airfields on Iwo Jima. During the night nine B-24s conduct harassment bombing runs on the airfields.

**NEW GUINEA:** The headquarters of the 90th Bombardment Group (Heavy) and the B-24s of the 321st and 400th Bombardment Squadrons (Heavy) redeploy from Biak Island to Mindoro Island. The C-47s of the 69th Troop Carrier Squadron, 433rd Troop Carrier Group, redeploy from Biak to Leyte.

## January 27

**CBI:** Chinese Y Force units link up with Allied units from Burma.

Company B of the 236th Engineers completes the junction of the Ledo and Burma Roads. The 71st Light Pontoon Company finishes a 450-foot pontoon bridge over the Shweli River at Wanting on the Chinese border. The Burma Road is opened to Allied traffic.

In China, Fourteenth Air Force sends 22 P-40s and P-51 Mustangs to attack locomotives, trucks, and shipping.

In Burma, Tenth Air Force P-47 Thunderbolts support ground forces and attack bridges, troop concentrations, logistics storage sites, and targets of opportunity.

A Japanese cargo ship is sunk by a mine dropped by Fourteenth Air Force B-24s in the Yangtze River.

**ATLANTIC:** German submarine *U-852* torpedoes and damages a U.S. freighter off the west coast of England.

**ITALY:** Twelfth Air Force A-20 Havocs and P-47 Thunderbolts of the XXII Tactical Air Command attack rail lines, logistics storage sites, bridges, and roads in the Po River valley. P-47 pilots report destroying an oil production facility.

**SOUTHWEST PACIFIC AREA, LUZON:** The XIV Corps launches a tank and infantry attack against Clark Field and Fort Stotsenburg led by the 37th Infantry Division. The 40th Infantry Division attacks west against the Japanese defenses in the Bamban Hills. The goal is to drive the Japanese back and allow XIV Corps to link with XI Corps advancing along Highway 7 from Bataan.

The 1st Cavalry Division, the 32nd Infantry Division, and the 112th Cavalry RCT land at Lingayen Gulf.

Far East Air Force B-24 Liberators attack targets around Subic Bay, and B-25 Mitchells, A-20 Havocs, P-38 Lightnings, and P47 Thunderbolts attack airfields, town areas, gun emplacements, harbors, communications, and transportation targets throughout Luzon.

The A-20 Havocs of the 388th and 389th Bombardment Squadrons (Light), of the 312th Bombardment Group (Light), redeploy from Leyte Island to Mindoro Island.

**PACIFIC:** Twentieth Air Force completes the redeployment of the four forward detachments of XX Bomber Command B-29 groups from Chengtu, China, to bases in India as part of a general redeployment of strategic bomber assets from the CBI theater to the Pacific Operations Area. Both the Japanese offensive in China that threatens the American airfields and the overwhelming logistics support requirements necessary to fly fuel and spare parts over the Hump to sustain the bombers in China lead to the redeployment. The XX Bomber Command sends 22 B-29s Superfortresses to bomb the navy yard and arsenal at Saigon in French Indochina. One B-29 bombs a bridge at Bangkok, Thailand. Bomber crews report negligible results.

Over 70 B-29s of the 73rd Bombardment Wing (Very Heavy) are sent from the Marianas to bomb the Musashiho and Nakajima aircraft production facilities near Tokyo. Cloud cover and high winds prevent the bombers from attacking the primary target, and most of the bombers divert to hit urban targets in Tokyo. Japanese fighters shoot down five B-29s, and four other bombers are forced down. Aircrews report 60 confirmed kills, 39 probables, and 39 possibles.

**CENTRAL PACIFIC:** Seventh Air Force sends 19 B-24 Liberators from Saipan to bomb Iwo Jima. During the night 10 B-24s from Saipan and Guam Island conduct individual harassment raids.

**NEW GUINEA:** The B-24 Liberators of the 19th Bombardment Squadron (Heavy), 22nd Bombardment Group (Heavy), redeploy from Angaur Island to Samar Island. The B-24 Liberators of the 320th Bombardment Squadron (Heavy), 90th Bombardment Group (Heavy), redeploy from Biak Island to Mindoro Island.

U.S. submarine *Bergall* torpedoes and sinks a Japanese auxiliary minesweeper in Lombok Strait, Java.

### January 28

**CBI:** Colonel Lewis A. Pick leads the first overland convoy into Wanting, China, where T. V. Soong, the Chinese minister of foreign affairs, is there to welcome the group.

In China, Fourteenth Air Force P-40s and P-51 Mustangs attack rail and river traffic.

In Burma, Tenth Air Force P-47 Thunderbolts support ground forces and attack logistics storage sites and troop concentrations.

**ETO:** The III Corps of Third Army reaches the Our River. The XII Corps closes on the Our and Sauer Rivers (4th Armored Division and the 5th, 76th, and 80th Infantry Divisions). First Army attacks toward Euskirchen east of Bonn with the XVIII Airborne Corps (1st, 30th, 84th Infantry Divisions and the 82nd Airborne Division).

Eighth Air Force sends more than 1,000 B-17s and B-24 Liberators escorted by 172 P-51 Mustangs to attack bridges, marshaling yards, and oil and chemical production facilities in western Germany. The bombers use a combination of radar and visual bomb release methods. A total of 12 bombers are lost and 466 damaged. Aircrew casualties are 16 killed, 31 wounded, and 106 missing.

During the night two B-17s and six B-24s drop leaflets over Germany, Luxembourg, and the Netherlands.

Ninth Air Force sends B-26 Marauders to attack communication centers, railroad bridges, and targets of opportunity. P-47 and P-38 fighters support ground forces near Monschau and Butgenbach in Germany.

**ITALY:** Twelfth Air Force B-25 Mitchells attack rail bridges. A-20 Havocs and P-47 Thunderbolts of the XXII Tactical Air Command attack rail lines, bridges, and roads.

**SOUTHWEST PACIFIC AREA, LUZON:** The 161st Infantry Regiment of the 25th Infantry Division captures San Manuel, a key strongpoint in the Japanese defenses, after repelling several fierce tank and infantry counterattacks. A total of 41 medium and four light Japanese tanks are destroyed in the battle. The Cabaruan Hills are cleared of the enemy. An estimated 1,400 have been killed and only two captured. American casualties total 279.

In the XIV Corps area, Major General Griswold decides to attack with most of his corps to clear his right flank before making an advance toward Manila. The 37th Infantry Division initiates the attack against Japanese strongpoints at Fort Stotsenburg, while the 40th Infantry Division attacks across the hills north of the Bamban River. Elements of the 37th Infantry Division advance as far as Calumpit on the Pampanga River without encountering any opposition. Manila is about 30 miles distant.

Far East Air Force B-24 Liberators, B-25 Mitchells, A-20 Havocs, P-47 Thunderbolts, and P-38 Lightnings attack targets on Luzon Island. Corregidor Island and targets between Subic Bay and Manila Bay are hardest hit.

**PACIFIC:** U.S. submarine *Spadefish* attacks a Japanese convoy in the Yellow Sea and sinks an escort vessel and a transport.

**CENTRAL PACIFIC:** Seventh Air Force sends 10 B-24 Liberators from Guam to bomb Iwo Jima. During the night 10 B-24s conduct harassment bombing runs on the Iwo Jima.

## January 29

**CBI:** The Chinese 30th and 38th Divisions block the Burma Road north of Ho-Si, but are driven back by strong counterattacks as the Japanese attempt to keep the road open for a retreat.

In China, Fourteenth Air Force P-40s and P-51 Mustangs attack airfields, rail, and river traffic.

In Burma, Tenth Air Force sends 13 B-25 Mitchells to bomb road bridges while P-47 Thunderbolts and P-38 Lightnings attack airfields, troop concentrations, and logistics storage sites.

**ETO:** The VIII Corps of Third Army (4th, 87th, and 90th Infantry Divisions) attacks on a 14-mile-wide front, crossing the Our and Prum Rivers.

Brigadier General Glenn O. Barcus takes command of the XII Tactical Air Command. Eighth Air Force sends more than 1,100 B-17s and B-24 Liberators, escorted by 700 P-47 Thunderbolts and P-51 Mustangs, to attack marshaling yards in western Germany, using H2X radar to locate the targets. One B-24 is lost and 59 bombers are damaged. Aircrew casualties are 18 killed, one wounded, and nine missing. Aircrews report six confirmed kills and two possibles. Fighter pilots report five confirmed kills and two possibles in the air and one confirmed kill on the ground. Two fighters are lost and two are damaged. One pilot is reported missing and one is killed.

During the night one B-17 and eight B-24s drop leaflets over Germany and the Netherlands.

Ninth Air Force sends 364 A-20 Havocs, A-26 Invaders, and B-26 Marauders to attack logistics storage sites and communication centers. P-47 and P-38 fighters support Third Army operations from St-Vith in Belgium to Saarlautern in Germany.

First Sergeant Leonard A. Funk, C Company, 508th Parachute Infantry Regiment, 82nd Airborne Division, takes over as company executive officer when that officer is wounded in an attack on a German defensive position near Holzheim, Belgium. Funk organizes men from the headquarters section into a combat unit and, with elements of an infantry platoon, attacks 15 houses, clears them of the enemy, and takes 30 prisoners without suffering a casualty. C Company moves through the town, leaving First Sergeant Funk with four men to guard about 80 prisoners. A German patrol enters the town, frees the prisoners, and prepares to attack Company C from the rear. At this time First Sergeant Funk discovers the Germans. A German officer orders him to surrender, jamming a weapon into his stomach. Funk slowly begins to unsling his Thompson submachine gun from his shoulder as though surrendering, but pulls it up and fires into the enemy. In the close-range gun battle that follows, 21 Germans are killed and many others are wounded. First Sergeant Funk's heroic actions to save his company from certain destruction will be recognized with the nation's highest award for valor, the Medal of Honor.

**ITALY:** During the night Twelfth Air Force A-20 Havocs attack rail lines, bridges, and vehicles in the Po River valley.

**SOUTHWEST PACIFIC AREA:** U.S. submarine *Picuda* attacks a Japanese convoy in Formosa Strait, sinking a cargo ship.

Far East Air Force B-24 Liberators attack the Heito airfield on Formosa.

**SOUTHWEST PACIFIC AREA, LUZON:** The 37th Infantry Division of XIV Corps succeeds in capturing Clark Field and Fort Stotsenburg, overcoming mines, obstacles, and heavy fire from strongly entrenched enemy positions.

The Eighth Army's XI Corps, commanded by Major General Charles P. Hall and composed of the 38th Infantry Division and the 34th RCT of the 24th Infantry Division, lands 35,000 men between San Antonio and San Felipe on the west coast of Luzon to capture the airfield at San Marcelino, occupy the naval base at Olongapo, and move to control the Bataan Peninsula and prevent Japanese forces from using the area as a defensive bastion, as General MacArthur did in 1942.

FEAF B-24s bomb Corregidor Island in Manila Bay. B-25 Mitchells, A-20 Havocs, P-47 Thunderbolts, and P-38 Lightnings attack targets of opportunity and support ground forces on Luzon Island.

Naval Task Group 78.3, commanded by Rear Admiral Arthur D. Struble, lands the 38th and 34th Infantry Regiments of the 24th Infantry Division near San Antonio, northwest of Subic Bay.

**PACIFIC:** Twentieth Air Force sends 28 B-29 Superfortresses from the Marianas to bomb the airfields on Iwo Jima.

B-25 Mitchells sink a Japanese auxiliary submarine chaser off Chichi Jima.

**CENTRAL PACIFIC:** Seventh Air Force sends 19 B-24 Liberators from Guam to bomb Iwo Jima.

During the night five B-24s from Saipan conduct harassment bombing runs on the island.

**NEW GUINEA:** The headquarters of the 38th Bombardment Group (Medium) and the 822nd Bombardment Squadron (Medium) redeploy from Morotai Island to Luzon with B-25 Mitchells. The B-24 Liberators of the 319th Bombardment Squadron (Heavy) of the 90th Bombardment Group (Heavy) redeploy from Biak Island to Mindoro Island.

## January 30

**CBI:** In China, Fourteenth Air Force sends 27 B-24 Liberators escorted by 32 P-40s and P-51 Mustangs to bomb Hankow.

In Burma, Tenth Air Force sends more than 100 P-47 Thunderbolts to support ground forces and attack troop concentrations, logistics storage sites, communication targets, and artillery positions.

**ETO:** The V Corps (2nd, 9th, 99th Infantry Divisions and the 7th Armored Division) attacks to capture the Roer River dams.

**ITALY:** Twelfth Air Force B-25 Mitchells attack rail lines. A-20 Havocs and P-47 Thunderbolts of the XXII Tactical Air Command attack rail lines, bridges, fuel storage areas, and production facilities in northeast Italy and the Po River valley.

**SOUTHWEST PACIFIC AREA, LUZON:** The American flag is raised over Clark Field. The XIV Corps takes operational control of XI Corps. The 34th RCT captures Olongapo and Subic Bay.

The 40th Infantry Division battles Japanese defenders in the ridges and valleys north and west of Fort Stotsenburg. The Japanese of the Kembu Group are isolated and becoming less of a threat to General Griswold's flank.

During the night five officers and 115 Rangers from the 6th Ranger Battalion, led by Lieutenant Colonel Henry A. Mucci and supported by the Alamo Scouts and Philippine guerrillas, attack the prisoner of war camp at Cabanatuan, killing the Japanese guards and freeing 513 Allied prisoners. Among those rescued are 486 Americans, most of them survivors of Bataan and Corregidor. The Rangers lose two killed and one wounded while inflicting over 200 casualties on the Japanese. The guerrillas destroy 12 tanks and add another 300 casualties to Japanese forces.

The 32nd Infantry Division arrives on Luzon from Leyte and links with the left flank of the 25th Infantry Division.

After visiting the 37th Infantry Division near Calumpit, MacArthur is impatient to get U.S. troops into Manila and notes that there is a lack of aggressive action. As a result, General Krueger issues his order for the assault on Manila. Japanese forces defending Manila are estimated at 18,000.

Far East Air Force A-20 Havocs, P-47 Thunderbolts, and P-38 Lightnings support ground forces and attack ammunition storage areas, artillery positions, and troop concentrations on Luzon.

Naval Task Group 78.3 with a light cruiser and two destroyers provides naval gunfire support as elements of the 38th Infantry Regiment land on Grande Island in Subic Bay. The island is unoccupied. Aircraft from Task Group 77.4, with six escort carriers and screening ships commanded by Rear Admiral William D. Sample, provide air cover.

Japanese submarine *RO-46* torpedoes and sinks an attack transport off Subic Bay.

**PACIFIC:** U.S. submarine *Threadfin* torpedoes and sinks a Japanese cargo ship off southern Honshu. The submarine is damaged in a depth-charge attack but remains on patrol.

**CENTRAL PACIFIC:** Seventh Air Force sends 17 B-24 Liberators from Saipan to bomb Iwo Jima.

During the night 10 B-24s conduct harassment bombing runs on the Iwo Jima.

B-24s bomb the airfield on Woleai Atoll in the Caroline Islands. Another five B-24s from Angaur Island hit targets in the Palaus. Ten B-24s from Saipan conduct individual snooper missions on Iwo Jima.

**NEW GUINEA:** The B-25 Mitchells of the 405th Bombardment Squadron (Medium), 38th Bombardment Group (Medium), redeploy from Morotai Island to Luzon.

U.S. submarine *Bergall* torpedoes and damages a Japanese storeship south of Java.

### January 31

**CBI:** The Japanese begin their retreat down the Burma Road.

The Fourteenth Air Force reports destroying over 300 Japanese aircraft during the month of January.

In China, Fourteenth Air Force P-51 Mustangs attack rail traffic.

In Burma, Tenth Air Force sends 12 B-25 Mitchells to bomb Japanese troop positions and logistics storage areas. P-47 Thunderbolts attack bridges, troop concentrations, and logistics storage sites.

**ETO:** Eighth Air Force sends more than 400 B-24 Liberators and B-17s escorted by 186 P-51 Mustangs to attack targets in Germany, but bad weather forces a recall to the bases in England. During the mission four bombers are damaged; six airmen are killed and eight are injured.

Staff Sergeant Jonah E. Kelley is a squad leader in E Company, 311th Infantry Regiment, 78th Infantry Division, clearing houses in Kesternich, Germany. Early on January 30, he leads his men through mortar and small arms fire and is wounded by mortar fragments that make his left hand useless, but he refuses to leave his men and continues to fight, firing his M-1 rifle with his right hand as he rests the rifle across his left forearm. Advancing from house to house, he kills enemy soldiers without regard for his own safety and clears the way for his squad to advance. As night falls, he organizes a defensive perimeter and refuses to seek aid for his wounds. The next day, the squad continues the attack but is stopped by automatic and small arms fire. Staff Sergeant Kelley walks out by himself to find the enemy, killing one hidden rifleman, then attacking a house that holds a machine-gun position. Hit by enemy fire, he falls to his knees, but stands up again and fires his last few rounds toward the Germans and eliminates the position. For his superb courage and inspirational leadership Staff Sergeant Kelly will win the Medal of Honor.

**MEDITERRANEAN:** Fifteenth Air Force sends more than 670 B-17s and B-24 Liberators escorted by P-38 Lightnings and P-51 Mustangs to attack an oil refinery and marshaling yard in Austria and a marshaling yard in Yugoslavia. P-38s drop supplies into Austria and B-24s drop supplies into northern Italy.

**ITALY:** Twelfth Air Force B-25 Mitchells and B-26 Marauders attack rail bridges and a marshaling yard. A-20 Havocs and P-47 Thunderbolts of the XXII Tactical Air Command attack rail lines, bridges, and roads in northern Italy. During the night A-20s attack rail targets in the Po River valley.

**SOUTHWEST PACIFIC AREA:** U.S. submarine *Boarfish* torpedoes and sinks a Japanese cargo ship and damages another off the southern coast of French Indochina. U.S. submarine *Pargo* torpedoes and damages a Japanese escort vessel in the South China Sea off the southern coast of French Indochina.

FEAF B-25 Mitchells sink a Japanese escort destroyer and damage a destroyer and another escort destroyer off Formosa.

**SOUTHWEST PACIFIC AREA, LUZON:** In the I Corps area the 6th Infantry Division defeats the Japanese 2nd Armored Division at Munoz in a battle to gain Highway 5, the last north-south line of communication for the Japanese in Luzon. The 25th Infantry Division advances to San Quintin.

In the XIV Corps area Major General Griswold orders the two RCTs of the 37th and the 1st Cavalry Division to press southeast to clear the northern approaches to Manila. The bridge over the Pampanga River at Cabanatuan is captured during the night by elements of the 1st Cavalry Division. One RCT of the 37th along with the 40th Infantry Division will continue to attack southwest to clear Japanese forces from the hills beyond Fort Stotsenburg.

The XI Corps begins isolating the Bataan Peninsula, moving to the east and encountering strong Japanese positions in the Zambales Mountains.

Two parachute infantry regiments of the 11th Airborne Division under command of Major General Joseph M. Swing make an amphibious landing near Nasugbu outside of Manila Bay and 50 miles south of the city of Manila. There is no opposition, and the paratroopers advance toward the main highway leading to Manila.

Since the campaign began, Japanese casualties are estimated at 15,000. A total of 586 soldiers have been captured. U.S. casualties total 5,754, including 1,297 killed.

Brigadier General Earl W. Barnes takes command of XIII Fighter Command.

Naval Task Group 78.2, commanded by Rear Admiral William M. Fechteler, lands two RCTs of the 11th Airborne Division at Nasugbu, south of the entrance to Manila Bay. Task Group 77.4 (Rear Admiral William D. Sample) provides air cover. Japanese assault demolition boats sink a submarine chaser.

**PACIFIC:** U.S. submarine *Spadefish* makes an unsuccessful torpedo attack on a Japanese ship in the Yellow Sea.

**CENTRAL PACIFIC:** Seventh Air Force sends 20 B-24 Liberators from Guam to bomb Iwo Jima.

During the night nine B-24s conduct harassment bombing runs on Iwo Jima.

The headquarters of the 419th Troop Carrier Group is activated on Guam.

## February 1

**CBI:** Fourteenth Air Force sends six B-24 Liberators to attack shipping off the coast of French Indochina. Aircrews report one cargo vessel sunk and one patrol boat damaged. In China, four P-40s attack a Japanese division headquarters near Yungning.

In Burma, Tenth Air Force sends 12 B-25 Mitchells to bomb a bridge. P-47 Thunderbolts support ground forces and attack bridges, airfields, troop concentrations, logistics storage sites, gun positions, and highways.

**ETO:** General Eisenhower halts the 12th Army Group offensive as it stalls before the West Wall. SHAEF conducts a reorganization of American forces in preparation for the upcoming offensive to close on the Rhine River. Ninth Army receives 10 additional divisions (75th, 79th, 30th, 83rd, 84th, 35th, and 95th Infantry Divisions and the 2nd, 5th, and 8th Armored Divisions) to create XVI Corps, commanded by Major General J. B. Anderson.

The 6th Army Group, on the defensive since January, forms the XXI Corps under Major General Frank W. Milburn composed of the 3rd, 28th, 7th, and 1st Infantry Divisions along with the 12th Armored Division to spearhead the main effort of the offensive to eliminate the Colmar Pocket. The French I and II Corps will support the main effort, and the XII Tactical Air Command will provide support to the ground forces.

Eighth Air Force sends nearly 1,400 B-17s escorted by over 500 P-51 Mustangs to attack rail and road bridges and marshaling yards in western Germany. The bombers use radar to hit the targets. A total of 26 bombers are damaged. Aircrew casualties are three wounded.

During the night six B-24s drop leaflets over Germany, France, and the Netherlands.

Ninth Air Force sends 146 A-20 Havocs, A-26 Invaders, and B-26 Marauders to attack railroad bridges and German defensive positions along the Rhine and Moselle Rivers. P-47 and P-38 fighters attack the Euskirchen marshaling yard.

**MEDITERRANEAN:** Fifteenth Air Force sends more than 300 B-17s and B-24 Liberators escorted by P-38 Lightnings and P-51 Mustangs to attack an oil refinery and marshaling yards in Austria.

**SOUTHWEST PACIFIC AREA:** In the Philippines, FEAF B-25 Mitchells attack targets on Palawan Island. Three destroyers and a destroyer escort sink Japanese submarine *RO-115* southwest of Manila. FEAF P-51 Mustangs sink a Japanese landing ship in Luzon Straits and damage a submarine chaser.

FEAF B-24 Liberators attack Okayama airfield on Formosa during the night.

**SOUTHWEST PACIFIC AREA, LUZON:** The 38th Infantry Division of XI Corps encounters Japanese defenses at Zig Zag Pass. The eight-mile pass, surrounded by rugged mountains, is thoroughly protected by a series of carefully camouflaged and heavily protected positions.

Far East Air Force B-24 Liberators bomb a shipyard, a seaplane base, communication centers, and logistics storage sites on Luzon.

**PACIFIC:** Twentieth Air Force sends 113 B-29 Superfortresses to bomb the naval base, a dry dock, and other targets at Singapore. Aircrews report three confirmed kills, four probables, and 14 possibles. Two B-29s are lost. An oiler is damaged.

**CENTRAL PACIFIC:** Seventh Air Force sends 21 B-24 Liberators from Saipan to bomb Iwo Jima.

During the night 10 B-24s conduct individual snooper missions on Iwo Jima. Another 20 B-24s from Angaur Island in the Palaus bomb Corregidor Island in the Philippines.

**NEW GUINEA:** The 71st and 823rd Bombardment Squadrons (Medium) of the 38th Bombardment Group (Medium) redeploy their B-25 Mitchells from Morotai Island to Luzon. The B-24 Liberators of the 529th Bombardment Squadron (Heavy), 380th Bombardment Group (Heavy), redeploy from Darwin, Australia, to Mindoro Island.

## February 2

**CBI:** The 2nd Squadron, 124th Cavalry attacks Japanese positions near Hpapen, where Japanese troops have entrenched themselves to protect the retreat route of their army. The Americans capture the position, losing 22 killed and 88 wounded.

In Burma, Tenth Air Force sends 11 B-25 Mitchells to bomb logistics storage areas and troop concentrations, while over 60 P-47 Thunderbolts support ground forces and attack troop concentrations, logistics storage sites, and vehicles.

First Lieutenant Jack L. Knight is a troop leader in the 124th Cavalry Regiment, Mars Task Force. He leads his company in capturing a hill near Loi-kang, Burma; while organizing the defense, he locates a number of Japanese pillboxes and foxholes to the right front of the troop's position. He leads the attack and destroys two pillboxes and kills Japanese in several foxholes. As he attacks another pillbox, he is blinded by a Japanese grenade. Nevertheless, he rallies his men and urges them to attack the other pillboxes. During the attack Knight is killed. For his courage and leadership in the face of a determined enemy, First Lieutenant Knight will receive the Medal of Honor.

**ATLANTIC:** A series of intelligence reports is completed for the JCS entitled "Estimate of Soviet Post-war Capabilities and Intentions." The assessments conclude that the USSR will seek to control eastern Europe and influence central Europe, China, and Japan. Soviet foreign policy will be characterized by fear and suspicion of American motives. The USSR will avoid a conflict with the United States and Great Britain until at least 1952, but the Soviets will go to war earlier if they perceive their vital interests are at stake.

The CCS approves SHAEF's January 18 plan for offensive operations into Germany. The CCS in its response emphasizes that the main effort remains in the north and that phase two of the campaign (crossing the Rhine River) can occur at any time during phase one (eliminating all German forces west of the Rhine).

**ETO:** The V Corps breaks the German defenses at Schleiden.

During the night Eighth Air Force sends one B-17 and eight B-24s to drop leaflets over western Germany.

Ninth Air Force sends more than 350 A-20 Havocs, A-26 Invaders, and B-26 Marauders to attack rail and road bridges. P-47 and P-38 fighters support ground forces in the Third Army area.

**MEDITERRANEAN:** The CCS notifies Field Marshal Sir Harold R. L. G. Alexander that five British and Canadian divisions and two fighter groups for the Twelfth Air Force will be removed from the Mediterranean theater to the European theater. Alexander is given three tasks in his area of responsibility. His forces are to contain German troops on the Italian front and prevent them from being withdrawn to other battlefronts; he is to hold the current frontline in Italy; and take any advantage of the weakening or withdrawal of German forces. Despite losing several divisions and being given rather bland requirements both Alexander and General Clark, as Fifteenth Army Group commander, believe something can be done to break the stalemate. Clark orders preparations to be made for an offensive by Fifth and Eighth Armies to begin on April 9. Instead of attacking directly toward Bologna, which has proven costly, the Allies decide to conduct simultaneous attacks to encircle Bologna. The objective is to destroy German forces south of the Po River.

The USS *Quincy,* with President Roosevelt on board, arrives in Valletta harbor, Malta. Meeting the warship at the dock is Prime Minister Churchill.

In the meeting that follows, both agree that they will not accept the Soviet-sponsored and supported Lublin government in Poland. The two leaders discuss the CCS report over strategic differences between the British and Americans in Germany. The British maintain that a main effort in the north should continue, with Berlin as the objective. The Americans believe that an attack through central Germany will be more decisive. The CCS recommends a dual thrust into Germany, but with priority of effort remaining in the north.

Churchill agrees to transfer three more Allied divisions from the Mediterranean theater to the ETO, even though he desires that the Allies drive north into Austria as quickly as possible to forestall any Soviet advances up the Danube River. That night, aircraft fly from Malta, taking 700 members of the British and American delegations to Yalta in the Soviet Crimea for the Argonaut conference with Stalin. Churchill is eager to foster British-American unity before meeting with Stalin. Roosevelt is wary of giving the appearance that the Americans and British are plotting behind Stalin's back. He intends to work with Stalin openly and build a partnership that he believes will guarantee future peace and security.

**ITALY:** Twelfth Air Force B-25 Mitchells and B-26 Marauders attack rail and road traffic and bridges.

**SOUTHWEST PACIFIC AREA:** FEAF B-24 Liberators bomb Okayama and Heito airfields and a seaplane base on Formosa.

Colonel Carl A. Brandt takes command of XIII Bomber Command.

U.S. submarine *Besugo* attacks a Japanese convoy east of the Malay Peninsula and sinks a coastal defense vessel. U.S. submarine *Hardhead* torpedoes and sinks a Japanese merchant tanker in the Straits of Malacca.

**SOUTHWEST PACIFIC AREA, LUZON:** In the XIV Corps area the 1st Cavalry Division makes contact with elements of the 37th Infantry Division northwest of Manila.

The 511th Parachute Infantry Regiment conducts an airborne landing to capture Tagaytay Ridge and link with the two other regiments of the 11th Airborne Division advancing from the coast.

Far East Air Force B-24 Liberators bomb Corregidor Island and Cavite. A-20 Havocs attack the targets in the Baler Bay area on Luzon. B-25 Mitchells bomb pillboxes, gun positions, and river barges on Mindanao Island.

**CENTRAL PACIFIC:** Seventh Air Force sends 20 B-24 Liberators from Guam to bomb Iwo Jima.

During the night 10 B-24s conduct harassment bombing runs on Iwo Jima.

A total of 22 B-24 Liberators from Angaur Island bomb Corregidor Island in the Philippines.

## February 3

**CBI:** The 1st and 2nd Battalions of the 475th Infantry Regiment attack Japanese defenses at Loi-kang ridge just west of the Burma Road. Supported by artillery and air strikes, the Americans overwhelm the enemy in heavy fighting at a key position named Knight's Hill. The Japanese are cleared out at a cost of two killed and 15 wounded. The Mars Task Force has lost 122 killed and 938 wounded since the beginning of the operation. Japanese casualties are estimated at over 670.

In Burma, Tenth Air Force sends 12 B-25 Mitchells to bomb troop concentrations and logistics storage sites. P-47 Thunderbolts support ground forces and attack bridges, troop concentrations, logistics storage sites, town areas, and Japanese tanks.

**ETO:** The XXI Corps and French forces eliminate the Colmar Pocket, opening the way to the Rhine River.

Eighth Air Force sends more than 1,400 B-17s and B-24 Liberators escorted by over 900 P-51 Mustangs to attack synthetic oil production facilities at Magdeburg and rail targets in Berlin. Over Berlin, 23 B-17s are lost and 345 damaged. Over Magdeburg, two B-24s are lost and 59 are damaged. Aircrews report 38 confirmed kills, one probable kill, and 18 possibles. Aircrew casualties are 18 killed, 11 wounded, and 208 missing. Fighter pilots report 12 confirmed kills and one probable in the air and 17 confirmed kills and 11 possibles on the ground. Seven P-51 fighters are lost, and two are damaged. Seven pilots are reported missing.

P-47 Thunderbolts fly an airfield sweep and report nine confirmed kills and six possible kills in the air. One P-47 is lost, and the pilot is reported missing.

During the night one B-17 and 10 B-24s drop leaflets over Germany and the Netherlands.

Ninth Air Force sends A-20 Havocs, A-26 Invaders, and B-26 Marauders to attack communication centers, railroad bridges, and repair depots in western Germany. P-47 and P-38 fighters support ground forces and fly armed reconnaissance missions.

Technician 5th Grade Forrest E. Peden is a forward artillery observer in C Battery, 10th Field Artillery Battalion, 3rd Infantry Division, moving with a group of about 45 infantrymen near Biesheim, France. The Americans walk into an ambush and take heavy casualties. Peden assists two wounded soldiers and, unable to use his radio, runs out of the kill zone to reach the battalion command post and bring two light tanks to the ambush site. He climbs on the lead tank and directs it into the fight as bullets and mortar fragments fly against the tank's hull. Peden is killed when the tank is destroyed by a direct hit. For his gallant sacrifice Technician 5th Grade Peden will receive the Medal of Honor.

**SOUTHWEST PACIFIC AREA, LUZON:** A squadron of the 8th Cavalry crosses the bridge over the Tuliahan River just moments before the Japanese are able to destroy it. Brigadier General William C. Chase, commander of the 1st Cavalry Brigade, leads two motorized cavalry squadrons reinforced with tanks and artillery as a rescue force to enter Manila and free about 3,700 American citizens and other Allied nationals who are being held at the University of Santo Thomas. The cavalrymen surprise the enemy in a night attack and free all but 300 of the civilians who are being held hostage by Japanese troops.

In the Philippines, Far East Air Force B-24 Liberators bomb Corregidor Island, and A-20 Havocs fly ground support missions on Luzon. B-24s bomb Cebu City on Cebu Island. B-25 Mitchells and P-38 Lightnings attack airfields on Mindanao Island.

**CENTRAL PACIFIC:** Seventh Air Force sends nine B-24 Liberators from Saipan to bomb Chichi Jima and another 10 B-24s attack Iwo Jima. During the night nine B-24s conduct harassment bombing runs on the island.

**NEW GUINEA:** U.S. submarine *Sea Robin* torpedoes and damages a Japanese transport off Bawean Island in the Java Sea.

## February 4

**CBI:** Colonel Lewis A. Pick's convoy reaches Kunming and receives a hero's welcome from the Chinese.

The Japanese 56th Division escapes mostly intact from the Chinese and American forces attempting to block the Burma Road. The division will reorganize near Lashio.

In China, Fourteenth Air Force sends 10 P-40s to bomb the airfield and the Japanese headquarters at Yungning and the railyards at Sinyang. Two P-40s are lost.

In Burma, Tenth Air Force sends 54 P-38 Lightnings and P-47 Thunderbolts to attack bridges. P-47 Thunderbolts support ground forces and attack bridges, logistics supply points, and vehicles.

**ATLANTIC: Argonaut—The Yalta Conference Begins.** President Roosevelt, Prime Minister Churchill, and Premier Stalin meet at Yalta in the USSR. They discuss Soviet entry into the war against Japan and postwar issues regarding the division of Germany, the extent of the Soviet sphere of influence in Europe, and the status of Poland.

**ETO:** The V Corps of First Army is ordered to capture the Roer River dams in support of Ninth Army's planned attack to the north. Bradley maintains a strongly held belief that the two Roer River dams, located about 15 miles from Düren, must be captured before any major advance can be made.

During the night Eighth Air Force sends seven B-24s to drop leaflets over Germany and the Netherlands.

Ninth Air Force sends A-20 Havocs, A-26 Invaders, and B-26 Marauders to attack a repair depot and rail and road bridges. P-47 and P-38 fighters fly armed reconnaissance missions.

**ITALY:** Operation Fourth Term begins. The 92nd Infantry Division attacks in the Serchio River valley. The 365th and 366th Infantry Regiments make progress initially but are slowed down and stopped by obstacles, mines, and strong German counterattacks.

Twelfth Air Force B-25 Mitchells and B-26 Marauders attack rail and road bridges. A-20 Havocs and P-47 Thunderbolts of the XXII Tactical Air Command attack rail lines, bridges, and roads.

**SOUTHWEST PACIFIC AREA:** U.S. submarine *Pargo* bombards Woody Island, French Indochina, destroying a weather station, communications, and facilities.

**SOUTHWEST PACIFIC AREA, LUZON:** Japanese troops give up the 300 hostages taken during the raid on Santo Tomas and are allowed to leave the city after turning the hostages over to U.S. forces.

The 37th Infantry Division enters Manila and frees the 800 American prisoners at Bilibid Prison, then advances into the city, encountering Japanese strongpoints amid fires set by retreating enemy units. Rumors of massacres of civilians reach the Americans.

The 40th Infantry Division, commanded by Major General Rapp Brush, continuing operations against the Kembu Group, makes contact with XI Corps near Dinalupihan.

In the Philippines, Far East Air Force B-24 Liberators bomb Corregidor Island and Cavite. B-25 Mitchells and A-20 Havocs attack targets throughout Luzon.

The headquarters of the 348th Fighter Group and the P-47 Thunderbolts of the 340th Fighter Squadron redeploy from Leyte to Luzon.

**PACIFIC:** Twentieth Air Force sends 110 B-29 Superfortresses of the 73rd and 313th Bombardment Wings (Very Heavy), XXI Bomber Command, to attack the Japanese home islands. About 200 Japanese fighters attack the bombers, downing one B-29 and damaging 35. Aircrews report four confirmed kills, 20 probables, and 39 possibles.

U.S. submarine *Spadefish* torpedoes and sinks a Japanese cargo ship in the Yellow Sea.

**CENTRAL PACIFIC:** Seventh Air Force sends nine B-24 Liberators from Guam to bomb antiaircraft positions on Iwo Jima and 10 other B-24s attack Haha Jima. A total of 23 B-24s from Angaur Island bomb Caballo Island in the Philippines. During the night eight B-24s from Guam conduct harassment bombing runs on Iwo Jima.

**NEW GUINEA:** U.S. submarine *Barbel* is sunk in the Balabac Strait by Japanese naval aircraft.

## February 5

**ALEUTIANS:** Eleventh Air Force sends five B-24 Liberators to bomb Kataoka on Shimushu Island in the Kuriles.

**CBI:** In China, Fourteenth Air Force sends 14 P-51 Mustangs and P-40s to attack rail and vehicle targets. Fighter pilots report at least nine locomotives and a number of trucks destroyed.

In Burma, Tenth Air Force sends 35 P-47 Thunderbolts to support ground forces, while P-38 Lightnings and P-47s attack troops and logistics storage areas.

**ETO:** The 78th Infantry Division of V Corps, supported by the 7th Armored Division and the 82nd Airborne Division, attacks into the Hürtgen Forest toward Schmidt to capture the Roer River dams and secure the right flank of Ninth Army.

The XXI Corps of Seventh Army meets the French I Corps at Rouffach, splitting the Colmar Pocket.

Ninth Air Force P-47 and P-38 fighters fly armed reconnaissance missions over the First Army area.

**MEDITERRANEAN:** Fifteenth Air Force sends more than 700 B-17s and B-24 Liberators escorted by P-38 Lightnings and P-51 Mustangs to attack oil storage facilities at Regensburg, Germany, marshaling yards in Austria and Germany, and a road bridge in Italy.

**ITALY:** Twelfth Air Force B-25 Mitchells and B-26 Marauders attack rail and road bridges. A-20 Havocs and P-47 Thunderbolts of the XXII Tactical Air Command attack communication targets and bomb a truck park with incendiaries. During the night A-20s attack roads and motor transport in the Po River valley.

**SOUTHWEST PACIFIC AREA, LUZON:** In the XI Corps area the 152nd Infantry Regiment of the 38th Infantry Division takes heavy casualties at Zig Zag Pass. Patrols of the 149th Infantry Regiment link with elements of the 40th Infantry Division after crossing over the mountains on an unguarded trail.

In the I Corps area the 6th Infantry Division captures San José and traps Japanese defenders at Munoz.

General MacArthur orders Eighth Army to begin clearing Japanese forces from around the Visayan Sea to open a more direct line of supply to Manila from Leyte. The operations are code-named Victor.

Far East Air Force sends 60 B-24 Liberators to bomb Corregidor. B-25 Mitchells conduct a shipping sweep and aircrew reports claim nine barges sunk and several more damaged.

The headquarters of the 475th Fighter Group redeploys from Leyte Island to Mindoro Island. P-38 Lightning detachments from the group's three subordinate fighter squadrons (the 431st, 432nd, and 433rd) will operate from Mindoro, but the squadrons remain on Leyte.

**PACIFIC:** The headquarters of the 15th Fighter Group prepares to redeploy from Hawaii to Iwo Jima.

**CENTRAL PACIFIC:** Seventh Air Force sends 21 B-24 Liberators from Saipan to bomb antiaircraft positions and a bivouac site on Iwo Jima. During the night 10 B-24s from Saipan conduct individual snooper (radar-assisted bomb release) missions on Iwo Jima.

**BORNEO:** FEAF B-24 Liberators with P-38 support attack airfields in Borneo.

### February 6

**CBI:** In China, Fourteenth Air Force sends 20 P-51 Mustangs to attack the Peking (Beijing) airfield. Fighter pilots report seven Japanese aircraft destroyed on the ground.

In Burma, Tenth Air Force sends 86 P-47 Thunderbolts and P-38 Lightnings along with 25 B-25 Mitchells to attack troop concentrations, logistics storage areas, and antiaircraft positions near Lashio.

U.S. submarine *Pampanito* attacks a Japanese convoy and sinks a merchant tanker northeast of Singapore.

**ETO:** Eighth Air Force sends nearly 1,400 B-17s and B-24 Liberators escorted by over 900 P-51 Mustangs to attack marshaling yards and targets of opportunity as weather conditions prevent bombing of the primary target, oil production facilities. The bombers use radar to identify targets. A total of five bombers are lost and 190 are damaged. Aircrews report four confirmed kills and one possible. Aircrew casualties are 41 killed, seven wounded, and 42 missing. Fighter pilots report one confirmed kill and one possible in the air and three confirmed kills on the ground. Four P-51s are lost and seven are damaged. The four pilots are reported missing.

Ninth Air Force sends 261 A-20 Havocs, A-26 Invaders, and B-26 Marauders to attack an ammunition storage area, communication centers, and a motor transport depot. P-47 and P-38 fighters fly armed reconnaissance missions and attack rail lines and bridges.

The 509th and 510th Fighter Squadrons (with P-47s) of the 405th Fighter Group and the 513th and 514th Fighter Squadrons (with P-47s) of the 406th Fighter Group redeploy from France to Belgium.

German submarine *U-245* torpedoes and sinks a U.S. freighter, part of a convoy headed for Antwerp in the English Channel.

**ITALY:** Twelfth Air Force B-25 Mitchells and B-26 Marauders attack rail bridges and marshaling yards. A-20 Havocs and P-47 Thunderbolts of the XXII Tactical Air Command attack rail bridges. Fighter pilots report three confirmed kills in the air. During the night A-20s attack roads and motor transport in the Po River valley.

**SOUTHWEST PACIFIC AREA:** In the Philippines, Far East Air Force B-24 Liberators bomb Corregidor Island gun positions. B-25 Mitchells, P-38 Lightnings, and A-20 Havocs attack targets and support ground forces on Luzon. B-24s and B-25s fly coastal sweeps. A-20s attack an airfield on Negros Island.

The P-47 Thunderbolts of the 342nd and 460th Fighter Squadrons of the 348th Fighter Group redeploy from Leyte to Luzon.

A Japanese tanker is sunk by a mine dropped by Twentieth Air Force B-29s on January 25 in Johore Strait off Singapore. A Japanese battleship-carrier, (a converted battleship) is damaged by a mine off Singapore.

German submarine *U-862* torpedoes and sinks a U.S. freighter off the southeast coast of Australia.

**PACIFIC:** U.S. submarine *Spadefish* torpedoes and sinks a Japanese merchant passenger-cargo ship off Port Arthur, Korea.

Navy PB4Y Privateers attack a Japanese convoy in the Ryukyus, sinking a small cargo ship.

**CENTRAL PACIFIC:** Seventh Air Force sends nine B-24 Liberators from Guam to bomb antiaircraft positions and radar sites on Iwo Jima. Other B-24s bomb Ototo Jima Island and attack a town on Kyushu Island, Japan. A total of 19 B-24s from Angaur Island bomb Corregidor.

During the night eight B-24s conduct harassment bombing runs on Iwo Jima.

**BORNEO:** FEAF B-24 Liberators with P-38 support attack airfields in Borneo.

### February 7

**CBI:** In China, Fourteenth Air Force sends 11 P-51 Mustangs to attack a bridge at Hengshan. Aircrews report the bridge is destroyed. P-40s attack river, road, and rail traffic.

In Burma, Tenth Air Force sends 11 B-25 Mitchells to attack tanks and troops, while 50 P-47 Thunderbolts support ground forces and P-40s attack troop concentrations and logistics sites.

**ETO:** The 78th Infantry Division captures Schmidt and Kommerscheidt in the Hürtgen Forest, opening the way to the Roer River dams.

The Third Army begins limited attacks along the West Wall to hold German forces in place while the Ninth and First Armies prepare for the main attack.

**MEDITERRANEAN:** Fifteenth Air Force sends more than 600 B-17s and B-24 Liberators escorted by 274 P-38 Lightnings and P-51 Mustangs to attack oil refineries in Austria, oil storage areas in Yugoslavia, and the harbor at Trieste, Italy. B-24s drop supplies in Yugoslavia.

**ITALY:** Twelfth Air Force B-25 Mitchells bomb bridges and rail lines. P-47 Thunderbolts attack rail lines, supply points, and bridges. A-20s attack roads and motor transport in the Po River valley.

**SOUTHWEST PACIFIC AREA:** U.S. submarine *Bergall* attacks a Japanese convoy off the east coast of French Indochina and sinks a coastal defense vessel and damages a merchant tanker. U.S. submarine *Guavina* attacks a Japanese convoy and sinks a merchant tanker south of Saigon, French Indochina. U.S. submarine *Parche* torpedoes and sinks a Japanese cargo ship in the Philippine Sea.

**SOUTHWEST PACIFIC AREA, LUZON:** General MacArthur arrives in Manila.

In the XI Corps area, the 149th Infantry Regiment of the 38th Infantry Division crosses by an unguarded trail into the rear of Japanese positions at Zig Zag Pass.

Far East Air Force B-24 Liberators with P-38 support attack targets of opportunity at Heito airfield on Formosa, and B-25 Mitchells, with P-51 Mustangs flying cover, make several sweeps over the island. Aircrews report one tanker damaged, one submarine and a motor launch sunk, and several vehicles and an airplane destroyed. In the Philippines, A-20 Havocs support ground forces, attacking Japanese forces in the hills west of Clark Field. B-24 Liberators attack targets on Negros Island. The 341st Fighter Squadron, 348th Fighter Group, redeploys its P-47 Thunderbolts from Leyte to Luzon.

A destroyer escort sinks Japanese submarine *RO-55* off Luzon.

During the night two motor torpedo boats enter Manila Bay to conduct reconnaissance. They are the first U.S. Navy vessels to return to Manila Bay since the fall of Corregidor in April 1942.

Master Sergeant Charles L. McGaha of G Company, 35th Infantry Regiment, 25th Infantry Division, is pinned down near Lubao, Luzon. His platoon and one other from Company G are pinned down in a roadside ditch by heavy fire from five tanks supported by 10 machine-guns and a platoon of Japanese infantry, When one of his soldiers is wounded 40 yards away, McGaha leaves cover to rescue him. Although wounded himself, he stays with his men. When the platoon leader is wounded, he assumes command and rallies his men. McGaha rescues another wounded man and deliberately draws enemy fire to allow another casualty to be rescued and taken to safety. Once he knows the platoon has pulled back safely, he returns to his men and collapses from his wounds. For his willingness to risk his life to save his soldiers, Master Sergeant McGaha will receive the Medal of Honor.

**PACIFIC:** Twentieth Air Force sends 67 B-29 Superfortresses to attack Saigon in French Indochina. Only 44 hit the primary target, although most miss the target area by dropping bombs prematurely. Others hit Phnom Penh and the marshaling yard at Martaban, Burma. Aircrews report one possible kill. One B-29 is lost. Another 64 B-29s are sent to bomb a bridge in Bangkok, Thailand. Most of the bombers hit the target, destroying the middle span of the bridge.

U.S. submarine *Ronquil* torpedoes and damages a Japanese cargo ship south of Kyushu, Japan.

**CENTRAL PACIFIC:** Seventh Air Force sends six B-24 Liberators from Saipan to bomb Haha Jima. Other B-24s bomb antiaircraft positions and radar positions on Iwo Jima. B-24s from Angaur Island bomb airfields on Negros Island in the Philippines. During the night nine B-24s conduct individual snooper missions on Iwo Jima.

**BORNEO:** FEAF B-24 Liberators bomb an airfield, an oil refinery pump station, and a power station house in Borneo.

## February 8

**ALEUTIANS:** Naval Task Force 92, commanded by Rear Admiral John F. McCrea, with three light cruisers and seven destroyers, departs from Attu to bombard Matsuwa Island in the Kuriles.

**CBI:** In China, 10 P-51 Mustangs of Fourteenth Air Force attack bridges, rail lines, and airfields.

In Burma, Tenth Air Force sends 72 P-47 Thunderbolts to support ground forces. Other P-47s and P-38 Lightnings attack troop concentrations, logistics support areas, ammunition storage facilities, and targets of opportunity.

**ATLANTIC: Argonaut—The Yalta Conference.** President Roosevelt and Joseph Stalin meet privately without Prime Minister Churchill attending. The leaders come to an agreement that the Soviet Union will enter the war against Japan within a month after Germany surrenders. In return, Roosevelt agrees to the Soviet Union occupying the southern half of Sakhalin Island and taking possession of the Kurile Islands. Roosevelt also accepts the USSR's preeminent interests in Port Arthur and Port Dairen in China, the Chinese Eastern Railway, and the South Manchurian Railway.

**ETO:** Operation Veritable, Montgomery's offensive to clear German forces west of the Rhine River, begins with a 500,000-shell artillery barrage.

Ninth Air Force sends more than 300 A-20 Havocs, A-26 Invaders, and B-26 Marauders to attack roads, communication centers, railroad bridges, and marshaling yards in Germany. P-47 and P-38 fighters support XII Corps.

**MEDITERRANEAN:** Fifteenth Air Force sends more than 500 B-17s and B-24 Liberators escorted by over 270 P-38 Lightnings and P-51 Mustangs to attack communication targets and marshaling yards in Austria. Another 12 B-24s drop supplies in Yugoslavia, and 11 P-51s sweep the Zagreb area.

**ITALY:** After losing 700 men, the 92nd Infantry Division stops its attack and returns to its original starting point.

Twelfth Air Force B-25 Mitchells and B-26 Marauders attack bridges. P-47 Thunderbolts attack rail bridges and oil storage areas and support Fifth Army ground forces. A-20s attack roads and motor transport in the Po River valley.

**SOUTHWEST PACIFIC AREA:** U.S. submarine *Pampanito* attacks a Japanese convoy in the Gulf of Siam, sinking a gunboat off the southern end of French Indochina.

FEAF B-24 Liberators bomb airfields in Borneo.

The headquarters of the 309th Bombardment Wing (Heavy) redeploys from Schouten Islands to Luzon Island.

**SOUTHWEST PACIFIC AREA, LUZON:** In the I Corps area, the 6th Infantry Division is dispatched to Manila to come under the operational control of XIV Corps. The 25th Infantry Division takes over and advances east past San José toward Balete Pass.

In the Philippines, Far East Air Force B-24 Liberators bomb the Bataan Peninsula, and B-25 Mitchells attack several small vessels along the east coast of Bataan and also bomb Legaspi airfield.

The 421st Night Fighter Squadron of the 86th Fighter Wing redeploys from Leyte to Luzon with P-38 Lightnings and P-61 Black Widow night fighters.

**PACIFIC:** Twentieth Air Force sends 30 B-29s from the Mariana Islands to bomb an airfield on Moen Island in the Truk Atoll of the Carolines.

**CENTRAL PACIFIC:** Seventh Air Force sends 20 B-24 Liberators from Guam to bomb antiaircraft positions and radar sites on Iwo Jima.

During the night 10 B-24s conduct individual snooper missions on Iwo Jima.

## February 9

**CBI:** The Chinese-American Composite Wing (CACW) P-40 fighters attack Tsingtao airfield. Fighter pilots report about 100 aircraft destroyed or damaged. Pilots also report several nearby locomotives destroyed in the raid.

In Burma, Tenth Air Force sends 10 B-25 Mitchells to bomb bridges. P-47 Thunderbolts support ground forces and attack bridges, troop concentrations, logistics storage sites, and communication targets.

**ETO:** SHAEF headquarters estimates that more than 22,000 German soldiers have become casualties in the battles to clear the west bank of the Rhine River.

The last remaining German forces in the Colmar Pocket escape across the Rhine. The operation to close the pocket has cost the Allies 18,000 casualties, including 8,000 from XXI Corps.

Eighth Air Force sends nearly 1,300 B-17s and B-24 Liberators escorted by over 800 P-47 Thunderbolts and P-51 Mustangs to attack oil production facilities, a munitions factory, and marshaling yards. The bombers use a combination of Pathfinder bombers, H2X radar, and Gee-H. A total of eight bombers are lost and 138 damaged. Aircrews report 61 confirmed kills, four probables, and 22 possibles. Aircrew casualties are 20 killed, nine wounded, and 74 missing. Fighter pilots report 19 confirmed kills, two probables, and one possible in the air and 37 confirmed kills and 13 possibles on the ground. Five fighters are lost, and two are damaged. Five pilots are reported missing.

A total of 33 P-51 Mustangs fly a scouting mission. Fighter pilots report five confirmed kills, one probable kill.

Ninth Air Force sends 347 A-20 Havocs, A-26 Invaders, and B-26 Marauders to attack railroad bridges and a marshaling yard. P-47 and P-38 fighters support XII Corps ground forces.

**MEDITERRANEAN:** Fifteenth Air Force sends one B-17 and 10 B-24 Liberators to drop supplies in northern Italy. A total of 11 B-24s drop supplies in Yugoslavia. P-38 Lightnings and P-51 Mustangs fly reconnaissance missions.

**ITALY:** During the night Twelfth Air Force A-20s and A-26 Invaders attack roads and motor transport in the Po River valley.

**SOUTHWEST PACIFIC AREA:** In the Philippines, Far East Air Force B-24 Liberators and A-20 Havocs bomb Corregidor Island. B-24 Liberators and A-20 Havocs bomb targets on the Bataan Peninsula. B-25 Mitchells and P-51 Mustangs attack shipping near Luzon and attack ground targets on Negros Island. A-24 Banshees and P-40s attack Japanese troops and attack bridges and roads in Luzon.

Private First Class John N. Reese, Jr., of B Company, 148th Infantry Regiment, 37th Infantry Division, is part of a platoon assigned to attack the Paco railroad station in Manila. The Japanese have 300 heavily armed infantrymen defending this critical location. The attack is halted 100 yards from the station by intense enemy fire. Reese and another soldier advance toward an enemy defensive position in a house 60 yards from the objective. Although under constant enemy observation, the two soldiers remain in this position for an hour, firing on the Japanese and killing more than 35. Advancing toward the station, they catch a group of Japanese soldiers unawares and kill more than 40, leaving some key emplacements unmanned. Reese purposely exposes himself to enemy fire while his comrade engages the enemy, killing another seven soldiers and destroying a 20 millimeter gun with hand grenades. As they begin to return to friendly lines to replenish their ammunition, Reese is killed. For his gallant determination in the face of tremendous odds, his aggressive fighting spirit, and extreme heroism at the cost of his life, Private First Class Reese will receive the nation's highest award for valor, the Medal of Honor.

**PACIFIC:** Twentieth Air Force sends 29 B-29 Superfortresses of the XXI Bomber Command to bomb the airfield at Moen Island on Truk Atoll, Carolines.

**CENTRAL PACIFIC:** Seventh Air Force sends 22 B-24 Liberators from Guam and Saipan to bomb antiaircraft positions, airfields, and radar sites on Iwo Jima.

During the night 11 B-24s from Saipan conduct harassment bombing runs on the island.

The headquarters of the 21st Fighter Group begins redeployment to Iwo Jima from Hawaii.

## February 10

**CBI:** Chinese forces link with the Mars Task Force. The Japanese have escaped, reorganizing near Lashio. Detachment 101 commanded by Colonel William R. Peers continues operations against the Japanese along the Burma Road. He has 1,500 Kachin guerrillas and another 1,500 Karen, Chinese, Ghurka, and Shan volunteers.

In Burma, Tenth Air Force sends five B-25 Mitchells and P-47 Thunderbolts to bomb bridges. Other P-47s support ground forces and attack bridges, troop concentrations, logistics storage sites, and targets of opportunity.

**ETO:** The last of the Roer River dams is captured, but water at Schwammenauel dam has been released, causing limited flooding and delaying the Ninth Army attack until February 23.

Eighth Air Force sends nine B-17s to carry out the first Disney mission, using a rocket bomb developed by the Royal Navy. It is a 14-foot-long, hard-case streamlined bomb weighing 4,500 pounds with a rocket motor in its tail. Because of its length and weight, the bombs are mounted on the wings of the B-17s. When dropped, the rocket motors ignite at 5,000 feet, accelerating the bombs to 2,400 feet per second on impact, allowing them to penetrate thick concrete before exploding. These bombs are used against the U-boat pens at Ijmuiden in the Netherlands, which are heavily fortified with concrete.

Another 140 B-17s attack the oil storage depot at Dulmen, Germany, using radar to identify the release point. Over 100 P-51 Mustangs escort the bombers. Five B-17s are damaged. Two P-51s are lost during a strafing mission.

During the night one B-17 and 11 B-24s drop leaflets over Germany and the Netherlands. One crewman is killed on the operation.

Five B-17s conduct screening missions to jam German radio interception efforts and conduct countermeasures against German radar sites.

Ninth Air Force sends more than 300 A-20 Havocs, A-26 Invaders, and B-26 Marauders to attack communication centers, rail bridges, and a vehicle depot. P-47 and P-38 fighters support VIII and XII Corps.

**MEDITERRANEAN:** Fifteenth Air Force sends 12 B-24 Liberators to drop supplies in Yugoslavia, while P-38 Lightnings fly reconnaissance and escort missions.

**ITALY:** Twelfth Air Force B-25 Mitchells bomb bridges. A-20 Havocs and P-47 Thunderbolts attack rail lines and vehicles. During the night A-20s and A-26 Invaders attack roads and motor transport in the Po River valley.

**SOUTHWEST PACIFIC AREA:** P-47 Thunderbolts conduct a fighter sweep over Formosa. Fighter pilots report 10 confirmed kills in the air. The headquarters of the 312th Bombardment Group (Light) and the 386th and 387th Bombardment Squadrons (Light) redeploy from Leyte Island to Luzon with A-20s.

Brigadier General Frederick H Smith, Jr., takes command of V Fighter Command.

**SOUTHWEST PACIFIC AREA, LUZON:** The 1st Cavalry Division crosses the Pasig River in Manila and links with the 37th Infantry Division.

Operational control of the 11th Airborne Division passes from Eighth Army to Sixth Army. The 11th Airborne encounters Japanese defensive positions south of Manila, known as the Genko Line, and attacks to capture Nichols Field.

Far East Air Force B-24 Liberators bomb Japanese gun positions, while P-51 Mustangs and P-38 Lightnings support ground forces on Luzon. B-24s, A-20 Havocs, P-38s, and P-47s attack targets on the Bataan Peninsula.

**PACIFIC:** Twentieth Air Force sends 118 B-29 Superfortresses from the Marianas to attack the Nakajima aircraft production facility at Ota, Japan. More than 80 bombers hit the primary target, and 14 attack other targets. Aircrews report 21 confirmed kills, 15 probables, and 26 possibles. American losses are 12 B-29s.

**CENTRAL PACIFIC:** Seventh Air Force sends 10 B-24 Liberators from Guam to bomb Haha Jima. Six P-39 Lightnings fly a sweep over Iwo Jima. Another 17 B-24s with P-38 escort hit Iwo Jima in the afternoon. During the night nine B-24s conduct harassment bombing runs on the island.

## February 11

**ALEUTIANS:** Eleventh Air Force sends seven B-24 Liberators to provide air cover for a naval task force, but only three reach the target.

Naval Task Force 92 arrives off Matsuwa Island in the Kuriles but weather prevents any offensive action. The ships begin the return to Attu.

**CBI:** In China, Fourteenth Air Force sends 17 B-25 Mitchells to attack railroad yards at Sinyang and Lohochai and a locomotive foundry at Hsuchang. P-47 Thunderbolts attack Hankow and Anyang airfields. B-24 Liberators attack shipping in the South China Sea. Aircrews report two cargo ships sunk.

In Burma, Tenth Air Force sends 11 B-25 Mitchells to bomb troops and logistics storage sites. P-47 Thunderbolts support ground forces and attack Japanese positions, logistics storage sites, ammunition storage areas, and targets of opportunity.

**ATLANTIC: Argonaut Conference Ends.** Roosevelt, Churchill, and Stalin, and their military advisers, reach agreements on the occupation of Germany and Austria, including the creation of a French zone in Germany. Roosevelt and Stalin make a secret agreement on Soviet territorial gains in the Far East in return for Soviet participation in the war against Japan. A Declaration on Liberated Europe is issued in which the Allies commit to free elections and democratic governments in the countries freed from the Nazis. President Roosevelt, Prime Minister Churchill, and Premier Stalin make agreements on a broad-based government in Poland that will hold free and democratic elections. The borders of Poland are to be restructured, with the Soviet Union keeping the territory it gained in 1939. The future Polish state will have its borders expanded westward into Germany.

**ETO:** The XVIII Airborne Corps and its divisions are taken out of the line to prepare for an airborne assault in support of the 21st Army Group's crossing of the Rhine River. It is replaced with III Corps from Third Army, commanded by Major General John B. Millikin, with the 78th, 1st, and 9th Infantry Divisions and the 9th Armored Division.

Eighth Air Force sends 124 B-24 Liberators escorted by 50 P-51 Mustangs to attack the Dulmen oil depot. The bombers use radar to locate the bomb release point. Over 180 P-51s make a sweep over northwest Germany. One P-51 is lost, and the pilot is reported missing.

Ninth Air Force sends 97 A-20 Havocs and B-26 Marauders to attack marshaling yards. P-47 and P-38 fighters support XII Corps.

**ITALY:** Operation Fourth Term is a failure. After suffering 700 casualties, the 92nd Infantry Division is spent and unable to conduct further combat operations.

Twelfth Air Force B-25 Mitchells and B-26 Marauders attack rail and road traffic and bridges. A-20 Havocs and P-47 Thunderbolts of the XXII Tactical Air Command attack rail lines and bridges.

During the night A-20s attack roads and motor transport in the Po River valley and German defensive positions in the northern Apennines.

**SOUTHWEST PACIFIC AREA:** In the Philippines, Far East Air Force B-24 Liberators bomb Corregidor Island. P-38 Lightnings and P-47 Thunderbolts support ground forces on Luzon. P-47s attack a train near Heito on Formosa. B-24 Liberators bomb targets on Negros Island.

The A-20 Havocs of the 388th and 389th Bombardment Squadrons (Light), 312th Bombardment Group (Light), redeploy from Mindoro Island to Luzon.

Japanese submarine *RO-50* torpedoes and sinks an LST in a convoy originating at Hollandia and headed for Leyte. The LST is hit off the west coast of Mindanao and is scuttled. The *RO-50* is damaged by gunfire.

U.S. submarine *Batfish* sinks Japanese submarine *RO-112* off northern Luzon.

**PACIFIC:** Twentieth Air Force sends 56 B-29s to bomb logistics storage areas around Rangoon, Burma. Aircrews report three possible kills. Twentieth Air Force sends nine B-29s from the Marianas to conduct reconnaissance for the U.S. Navy.

Twentieth Air Force B-29s from the Marianas and navy PB4Y Privateers conduct advance search missions to spot Japanese guardboats as Naval Task Force 58 (Vice Admiral Marc A. Mitscher) moves north toward Japan.

U.S. submarine *Burrfish* is damaged by depth charges and an air attack off the Bonins but remains on patrol.

**CENTRAL PACIFIC:** Seventh Air Force sends 21 B-24 Liberators from Saipan to bomb airfields and defenses on Iwo Jima Island. Three B-24s bomb Marcus Island. A total of 25 B-24s based at Angaur Island bomb Corregidor Island. During the night 10 B-24s from Saipan fly individual harassment raids on Iwo Jima.

### February 12

**CBI:** In China, Fourteenth Air Force P-51 Mustangs destroy locomotives and strafe airfields. P-40s bomb troops and attack trains.

Tenth Air Force P-47 Thunderbolts support ground forces and severely damage a bridge. P-47s and P-38 Lightnings attack logistics support areas, troops, tanks, and trucks.

**ETO:** During the night Eighth Air Force sends six B-24s to drop leaflets over Germany and the Netherlands.

The headquarters of the 434th Troop Carrier Group and the C-47s of the 71st, 72nd, 73rd, and 74th Troop Carrier Squadrons, IX Troop Carrier Command, redeploy from England to France.

**ITALY:** Twelfth Air Force P-47 Thunderbolts attack rail lines, bridges, gun positions, and roads in the Po River valley. During the night A-20s attack communication targets in the Po River Valley.

**SOUTHWEST PACIFIC AREA, LUZON:** The 11th Airborne Division fights through mines, obstacles, and heavy gun emplacements to reach Nichols Field, supported by artillery and air bombardment.

Far East Air Force B-24 Liberators bomb Corregidor Island. A-20 Havocs sweep the Bataan Peninsula. Pilots report sinking about 30 barges loaded with troops, ammunition, and supplies. B-25 Mitchells and P-38 Lightnings support ground forces on the Bataan Peninsula and from the Lingayen Gulf area to Nichols Field.

The B-25s of the 498th, 499th, 500th, and 501st Bombardment Squadron (Medium), 345th Bombardment Group (Medium), redeploy from Leyte to Luzon.

**PACIFIC:** Twentieth Air Force sends 21 B-29 Superfortresses from the Marianas to bomb antiaircraft positions on Iwo Jima. Another 10 B-29s fly a reconnaissance mission for the navy.

**CENTRAL PACIFIC:** Seventh Air Force sends nine B-24 Liberators from Guam to bomb Chichi Jima Island, while 19 other B-24s bomb airfields and antiaircraft positions on Iwo Jima. During the night eight B-24s from Guam fly individual harassment raids on Iwo Jima.

**NEW GUINEA:** The P-38 Lightnings of the 67th Fighter Squadron, 347th Fighter Group, begin operating from Morotai Island.

U.S. submarine *Hawkbill* torpedoes and sinks a small Japanese cargo vessel and two large landing barges in Lombok Strait, Java.

## February 13

**CARIBBEAN:** The B-24 Liberators of the 74th Bombardment Squadron (Heavy), VI Bomber Command, redeploy from the Galápagos Islands to Panama.

**CBI:** In China, Fourteenth Air Force P-51 Mustangs and P-40s conduct a sweep of airfields and bridges from Sinyang to Hsuchang.

In Burma, Tenth Air Force sends P-47 Thunderbolts to support ground forces and attack bridges, troop concentrations, logistics storage sites, and targets of opportunity.

**ETO:** During the night Eighth Air Force sends nine B-24s to drop leaflets over Germany and the Netherlands.

Ninth Air Force sends 320 A-20 Havocs, A-26 Invaders, and B-26 Marauders to attack railroad bridges, military transportation depots, and targets of opportunity. P-47 and P-38 fighters support troops in the Third Army area and fly armed reconnaissance missions.

The headquarters of the 435th Troop Carrier Group, IX Troop Carrier Command, redeploys from England to France.

**MEDITERRANEAN:** Fifteenth Air Force sends more than 600 B-17s and B-24 Liberators escorted by P-38 Lightnings and P-51 Mustangs to attack railyards and marshaling yards in Austria, Hungary, and Yugoslavia.

**ITALY:** Fifteenth Air Force fighters attack rail transportation, especially locomotives.

Twelfth Air Force B-25 Mitchells and B-26 Marauders attack bridges. A-20 Havocs and P-47 Thunderbolts of the XXII Tactical Air Command attack marshaling yards.

During the night A-20s attack roads and motor transport in the Po River valley.

**SOUTHWEST PACIFIC AREA:** In the Philippines, Far East Air Force B-24 Liberators bomb Corregidor Island and the Bataan Peninsula in conjunction with attacks by A-20 Havocs and P-47 Thunderbolts. B-25 Mitchells and P-38s conduct shipping sweeps on the north and east coasts of Luzon. B-25s, with P-47s in support, bomb Kagi airfield on Formosa.

The headquarters of the 345th Bombardment Group (Medium) redeploys from Leyte to Luzon.

U.S. submarine *Batfish* sinks Japanese submarine *RO-113* off the Babuyan Islands north of Luzon.

Private First Class Manuel Perez, Jr., is the lead scout for A Company, 511th Parachute Infantry, 11th Airborne Division, before Fort William McKinley on Luzon. Perez leads the company in destroying a series of fortified defensive positions covering the approach to the fort. During the attack Perez kills five Japanese soldiers and attacks pillboxes with grenades. As he approaches the largest pillbox in the defensive line, he moves toward the rear of the position, killing another four enemy soldiers in the process, then throws grenades into the pillbox. Firing his M-1 rifle at the retreating defenders, he eliminates four but fights with a Japanese rifle when he runs out of ammunition. He then fights the last remaining defenders in hand-to-hand combat. For his courageous actions and extraordinary fighting spirit, Private First Class Perez will be awarded the Medal of Honor

**PACIFIC:** South of Honshu, Japan, U.S. submarine *Sennet* is damaged by gunfire from a Japanese guardboat after damaging the guardboat with a torpedo attack in coordination with USS *Lagarto*. USS *Sennet* sinks another guardboat, which had been damaged by *Lagarto* and *Haddock*. USS *Haddock* then sinks the damaged guardboat first hit by *Sennet*.

**CENTRAL PACIFIC:** Seventh Air Force sends 25 B-24 Liberators from Saipan to bomb airfields, antiaircraft positions, and radar sites on Iwo Jima Island. Another 10 B-24s bomb Haha Jima. During the night five B-24s fly individual harassment raids on Iwo Jima.

**NEW GUINEA:** The P-38 Lightnings of the 339th Fighter Squadron, 347th Fighter Group, begin operating from Morotai Island.

## February 14

**ALEUTIANS:** Eleventh Air Force sends three B-24 Liberators to bomb and photograph Suribachi airfield on Paramushiru Island in the Kuriles.

**CBI:** Lieutenant General Albert C. Wedemeyer submits to Chiang Kai-shek his plan for a Chinese offensive based on Plan Alpha. The plan is intended to recapture Liuchow and Nanning, followed by an offensive to capture Hong Kong and Canton. Chiang approves the outlined concept.

In China, Fourteenth Air Force P-47 Thunderbolts and P-51 Mustangs attack airfields. Fighter pilots report several confirmed kills on the ground. P-51s attack 14 locomotives and report destroying a fuel storage site.

In Burma, Tenth Air Force sends 12 B-25 Mitchells to attack vehicles along roads from Lashio to Hopong.

**ATLANTIC:** German submarine *U-711* torpedoes and damages a U.S. freighter at the entrance to Kola Inlet in the Barents Sea.

**ETO:** Eighth Air Force sends more than 1,300 B-17s and B-24 Liberators escorted by over 900 P-51 Mustangs to attack oil production facilities, airfields, and marshaling yards in Germany and Czechoslovakia. One of the targets is the marshaling yards at Dresden, a city heavily damaged in a previous raid by RAF bombers. Most of the bombers use radar to identify the release point over their targets. A total of seven bombers are lost and 103 are damaged. Aircrews report 11 confirmed kills and three probables. Aircrew casualties are six killed, 19 wounded, and 72 missing. Fighter pilots report 10 confirmed kills and three possibles in the air. Seven P-51s are lost and two damaged. The seven pilots are reported missing.

During the night 10 B-24s drop leaflets over Germany and the Netherlands.

Ninth Air Force sends more than 600 A-20 Havocs, A-26 Invaders, and B-26 Marauders to attack communication centers, railroad bridges, an ammunition storage area, and a marshaling yard. P-47 and P-38 fighters support ground forces in the Third Army area and fly armed reconnaissance missions.

**MEDITERRANEAN:** Fifteenth Air Force sends more than 500 B-17s and B-24 Liberators escorted by P-38 Lightnings and P-51 Mustangs to attack oil refineries in Austria and marshaling yards in Yugoslavia.

**ITALY:** Twelfth Air Force B-25 Mitchells and B-26 Marauders attack bridges and gun positions. A-20 Havocs and P-47 Thunderbolts attacks communication targets in the Po River valley. During the night A-20s attack bridges and targets of opportunity in the Po River Valley.

**SOUTHWEST PACIFIC AREA, LUZON:** The 152nd Infantry Regiment of the 38th Infantry Division battles Japanese defenders in concrete emplacements and caves at Zig Zag Pass on Highway 7. Supported by napalm strikes, and a simultaneous attack from the rear of the Japanese defenses by the 149th Infantry Regiment, the infantrymen clear the pass and open the way to Manila Bay. More than 2,400 Japanese are killed and 25 taken prisoner. American losses are over 1,400 killed.

In Manila, the Japanese are trapped in a small pocket along the shore of Manila Bay. The 37th Infantry Division, reinforced with a brigade of the 1st Cavalry Division, is tasked with clearing Manila. The rest of the 1st Cavalry is to move east to capture Fort McKinley, reinforced by the 6th Infantry Division, which has passed from the operational control of I Corps to XIV Corps. The 11th Airborne Division is to support the attack on Fort McKinley, then clear Japanese forces south and east to Laguna de Bay.

The 40th Infantry Division has cleared the Kembu Group out of its defenses in the hills beyond Clark Field and Fort Stotsenburg and thus secures the XIV Corps line of supply. Over 4,400 Japanese soldiers have been killed.

Far East Air Force B-24 Liberators bomb Corregidor Island and B-24s, and A-20 Havocs bomb Bataan Peninsula. B-25 Mitchells and P-38 Lightnings bomb airfields and ground support forces. B-25s bomb barges on Mindanao Island, and P-38s bomb an airfield. P-38s and P-47 Thunderbolts flying armed reconnaissance missions strafe airfields on Negros and Cebu Islands. B-25 Mitchells bomb Kagi airfield and targets of opportunity on Formosa.

Two U.S. support landing craft are sunk by shore batteries off Luzon.

Mines damage two U.S. destroyers south of Manila Bay.

A Japanese hospital ship is damaged by a mine in Singapore Strait.

Japanese shore batteries sink a minesweeper and damage two destroyers (USS *Fletcher* and USS *Hopewell*) north of Corregidor. On board USS *Fletcher,* Watertender First Class Elmer C. Bigelow, without any protective gear, fights a fire in the number-one gun magazine that threatens to destroy the ship. Bigelow unselfishly sacrifices himself to save his ship and his shipmates. His act of courage will win him the Medal of Honor.

**PACIFIC:** Twentieth Air Force sends six B-29 Superfortresses from the Marianas on a reconnaissance mission for the navy.

U.S. submarine *Gato* torpedoes and sinks a Japanese coast defense vessel in the Yellow Sea. U.S. submarines *Haddock, Lagarto,* and *Sennet* damage a Japanese guardboat south of Honshu, Japan. A Japanese cargo ship is sunk by a mine west of Kyushu, Japan.

**CENTRAL PACIFIC:** Seventh Air Force sends 17 B-24 Liberators from Guam to bomb airfields, antiaircraft positions, and radar sites on Iwo Jima Island. During the night five B-24s conduct individual snooper missions on Iwo Jima.

**NEW GUINEA:** The headquarters of the 54th Troop Carrier Wing redeploys from Biak to Leyte Island. The 550th Night Fighter Squadron, XIII Fighter Command (under operational control of XIII Bomber Command), redeploys from Hollandia to Morotai Island with P-38 Lightnings, P-61 Black Widow night fighters, and P-70 Havocs (converted night fighters).

U.S. submarine *Hawkbill* torpedoes and sinks two Japanese auxiliary submarine chasers in the Java Sea.

## February 15

**CBI:** Fourteenth Air Force P-51 Mustangs attack Shihkiachuang airfield. The eight fighter pilots report four confirmed kills on the ground. This attack ends an offensive by P-51 Mustangs of the 530th Fighter Squadron operating from Sian airfield. The pilots report a total of 37 confirmed kills and 24 probables in the air and 130 confirmed kills and 22 probable kills on the ground as well as 517 locomotives destroyed since the offensive began on November 7, 1944. The squadron begins to redeploy to Kwanghan for rest and refitting.

In Burma, Tenth Air Force sends 12 B-25 Mitchells to attack buildings, troops, and other targets of opportunity.

**ETO:** Eighth Air Force sends more than 1,100 B-17s and B-24 Liberators escorted by over 500 P-47 Thunderbolts and P-51 Mustangs to attack oil production facilities and marshaling yards in Germany. The bombers use radar to find the release point for their targets. The city of Dresden is again bombed as a target of opportunity. German authorities report to Berlin that 500,000 people are without shelter. Tens of thousands have been killed. A total of two bombers are lost and 82 are damaged. Aircrews report two confirmed kills. Aircrew casualties are nine killed, 11 wounded, and 12 missing. Fighter pilots report two confirmed kills in the air. Four fighters are lost. The four pilots are reported missing.

Ninth Air Force sends 90 A-20 Havocs, A-26 Invaders, and B-26 Marauders to attack railroad bridges and targets of opportunity. P-47 and P-38 fighters support ground forces of the VII, VIII, XII, and XX Corps.

**MEDITERRANEAN:** Fifteenth Air Force sends more than 650 B-17s and B-24 Liberators escorted by P-38 Lightnings and P-51 Mustangs to attack oil refineries and marshaling yards in Austria and shipyards in Fiume, Italy.

**ITALY:** Twelfth Air Force B-25 Mitchells and B-26 Marauders attack an ammunition storage area. A-20 Havocs and P-47 Thunderbolts bomb rail lines.

**SOUTHWEST PACIFIC AREA:** Far East Air Force B-25 Mitchells attack bridges in southern Formosa.

**SOUTHWEST PACIFIC AREA, LUZON:** Naval Task Group 78.3, commanded by Rear Admiral Arthur D. Struble, lands the 151st Infantry Regiment of the 38th Infantry Division, reinforced by 3rd Battalion, 34th RCT, of the 24th Infantry Division, at Mariveles on Bataan to seal off the peninsula. The 1st RCT of the 6th Infantry Division, now attached to XI Corps, moves south along the east highway.

FEAF B-24 Liberators, A-20 Havocs, and P-47 Thunderbolts bomb Corregidor Island. B-25 Mitchells and A-20s attack the Bataan Peninsula, hit troops and gun positions near Fort William McKinley, and bomb airfields.

**PACIFIC:** The Japanese Imperial General Headquarters submits a report on the war situation to the Supreme War Council. Despite difficulties raised by the American offensives in the Marianas and the Philippines, Japan has the means to continue to fight as long as her people have the courage and determination to do so. It is apparent that the United States is planning for an invasion of the Japanese home islands. The estimate is that the Americans will land on Kyushu first. Defenses are prepared and reinforcements are sent that will build to a total of 900,000 troops defending the island.

After conducting final rehearsals, V Amphibious Corps landing forces leave the Mariana Islands for Iwo Jima.

Twentieth Air Force sends 117 B-29 Superfortresses from the Marianas to bomb the Mitsubishi aircraft engine production facility at Nagoya, Japan. Only 33 hit the primary target; 68 others bomb targets of opportunity. Aircrews report seven confirmed kills, eight probables, and 23 possibles. American losses are one B-29.

Carrier aircraft from Vice Admiral Marc A. Mitscher's Naval Task Force 58 sink two Japanese guardboats off eastern Honshu, Japan.

**CENTRAL PACIFIC:** Seventh Air Force sends 24 B-24 Liberators from Saipan to bomb Iwo Jima airfields and antiaircraft positions. Another 12 B-24s bomb the airfield on Chichi Jima. Four B-24s from Guam, escorting photo aircraft over Truk Atoll, bomb airfields on Param and Moen Islands. During the night five B-24s fly harassment raids against Iwo and Chichi Jima.

**NEW GUINEA:** The C-46s of the 68th Troop Carrier Squadron, 433rd Troop Carrier Group, redeploy from Biak to Leyte Island.

## February 16

**CBI:** In China, Fourteenth Air Force P-51s and P-40s attack airfields in the Nanking area, railyards, and rail and river traffic.

In Burma, Tenth Air Force sends 12 B-25 Mitchells to bomb troops, logistics storage sites, and vehicles. P-47 Thunderbolts and P-38 Lightnings support ground forces and attack town areas, troop concentrations, artillery positions, transportation targets, and targets of opportunity.

**ETO:** Eighth Air Force sends more than 1,000 B-17s and B-24 Liberators escorted by nearly 200 P-51 Mustangs to attack oil refineries, benzol production facilities, and marshaling yards in central Germany. The bombers use a combination of radar and visual means to locate the release points on the targets. A total of eight bombers are lost and 293 damaged. Aircrew casualties are 15 wounded, and 67 missing.

Six B-24 Liberators conduct screening missions to jam German radio interception efforts and conduct countermeasures against German radar sites.

Ninth Air Force sends 300 A-20 Havocs, A-26 Invaders, and B-26 Marauders to attack communication centers, an ordnance depot, a turbo-jet component production facility, and targets of opportunity. P-47 and P-38 fighters support the VIII, XII, and XX Corps.

The C-47s of the 77th Troop Carrier Squadron, 435th Troop Carrier Group, IX Troop Carrier Command, redeploy from England to France.

**MEDITERRANEAN:** Fifteenth Air Force sends more than 600 B-17s and B-24 Liberators escorted by P-38 Lightnings and P-51 Mustangs to attack airfields and marshaling yards in Germany, and marshaling yards in Austria and Italy. Over 260 B-24 Liberators bomb the jet airfield and aircraft production facility at Regensburg. Twenty German jet aircraft (Me-262s) are destroyed on the ground.

**ITALY:** Twelfth Air Force A-20 Havocs and P-47 Thunderbolts attack rail lines, fuel storage areas, and ammunition storage areas.

**SOUTHWEST PACIFIC AREA:** Far East Air Force P-47 Thunderbolts attack vehicles and trains in southern Formosa.

A PB4Y-1 Privateer sinks a Japanese cargo ship off French Indochina.

**SOUTHWEST PACIFIC AREA, LUZON:** After a heavy air and naval bombardment, over 2,000 men of the 503rd Parachute Regimental Combat Team conduct an airborne assault on Corregidor Island, jumping from 500 feet and dropping six to eight men each time in multiple passes. Motor torpedo boats rescue paratroopers who land in the water, and six destroyers provide naval gunfire support. The 3rd Battalion of the 34th Infantry Division conducts an amphibious landing at San José Bay and captures the top of Malinta Hill. The Japanese fight back fiercely, threatening to overwhelm the paratroopers' perimeter at Topside, but the American forces link and hold their positions. About 6,000 Japanese troops are on the island, far above the estimated strength of 850.

In the I Corps area the 33rd Infantry Division relieves the 43rd Infantry Division on the left flank of the corps and begins a series of night attacks against Japanese positions in the high ground overlooking the Rosario-Pozorrubio Road.

FEAF A-20 Havocs and B-24 Liberators bomb Corregidor prior to the amphibious and airborne landings. B-25 Mitchells support ground forces on Luzon. P-38 Lightnings attack airfields on Mindanao Island.

**PACIFIC:** Task Force 58 under command of Vice Admiral Marc A. Mitscher sends carrier aircraft to attack airfields and aircraft production facilities near Tokyo.

Carrier aircraft from Task Force 58 bomb airfields, aircraft production facilities, and shipping around Tokyo.

Rear Admiral John L. McCrea's Task Force 92 bombards Japanese installations at Paramushiru in the Kuriles.

U.S. submarine *Sennet* torpedoes and sinks a Japanese minelayer southeast of Honshu, Japan. USS *Sennet* is damaged by air attack.

**CENTRAL PACIFIC:** During the night Seventh Air Force sends four B-24 Liberators from Guam to bomb the airfield on Chichi Jima.

Fire support vessels and carrier aircraft begin a three-day prelanding bombardment of Iwo Jima.

**NEW GUINEA:** FEAF B-24 Liberators attack an airfield on Celebes Island.

## February 17

**ALEUTIANS:** Eleventh Air Force sends four B-25 Mitchells to provide air cover for a naval task force en route to Paramushiru Island in the Kuriles.

**CBI:** In China, Fourteenth Air Force sends 30 B-25 Mitchells to bomb Linfen and Yuncheng. P-40s and P-51 Mustangs attack animal transport, barracks, railroad targets, and the town area at Puchi. P-47 Thunderbolts attack railyards and road and river traffic.

In Burma, Tenth Air Force P-47 Thunderbolts support ground forces and attack troop concentrations, tanks, ammunition storage sites, and targets of opportunity.

**ATLANTIC:** German submarine *U-300* torpedoes and damages a U.S. freighter in convoy UGS-72 (United States to Mediterranean Slow) near Gibraltar. The freighter is able to continue with the convoy.

**SOUTHWEST PACIFIC AREA:** Fifth Air Force B-24 Liberators on an antishipping sweep over the South China Sea, sink a Japanese landing ship off the southern coast of Formosa.

**SOUTHWEST PACIFIC AREA, LUZON:** The 503rd Parachute Regimental Combat Team and the 3rd Battalion of the 34th Infantry Division split Corregidor in two. Additional paratroopers arrive by landing craft at San José Bay from Subic Bay. The Japanese make a determined resistance in the ruins of the old American fortress, as their positions are methodically destroyed one at a time.

On Bataan, the 151st Infantry Regiment of the 38th Infantry Division occupies the southern half of the peninsula.

Two light cruisers and three destroyers provide fire support for the battle to take Corregidor. A light cruiser and two destroyers bombard the south shore of Manila Bay.

**PACIFIC:** U.S. submarine *Bowfin* torpedoes and sinks a Japanese coastal defense vessel off central Honshu, Japan. Later, *Bowfin* and Navy aircraft sink a guardboat south of Honshu.

**CENTRAL PACIFIC, IWO JIMA:** Fire support ships, minesweeping units, and underwater demolition teams (UDT) arrive off Iwo Jima. Landing craft supporting navy and marine underwater demolition teams (UDT) fire rockets and guns at the beaches. The Japanese, believing this to be the main assault, open fire from previously hidden shore batteries. Shore batteries sink an infantry landing craft supporting UDT operations. U.S. battleships, destroyers, and cruisers destroy many of the guns. The UDT frogmen find no obstacles on the approaches to the beaches. The landing craft take heavy punishment from the Japanese guns as they work to collect the frogmen. U.S. casualties on the landing craft are 47 killed and 153 wounded. One destroyer is hit by enemy fire, resulting in seven sailors killed and 33 wounded.

The battleship USS *Tennessee,* a heavy cruiser, and a destroyer are damaged by gunfire. Eleven infantry landing craft (gunboats) intended to provide fire support are damaged.

**ETO:** Eighth Air Force sends nearly 900 B-17s and B-24 Liberators escorted by 183 P-51 Mustangs to bomb synthetic oil production facilities and marshaling yards. Most of the bombers abort the mission due to bad weather. The weather is so cold that aircraft controls freeze. Five bombers are lost and 108 are damaged. Aircrew casualties are 17 killed, two wounded, and 38 missing. One P-51 is lost and one is damaged. The pilot is reported missing.

Ninth Air Force sends 31 B-26 Marauders to attack a railroad bridge.

**MEDITERRANEAN:** Fifteenth Air Force sends more than 500 B-17s and B-24 Liberators escorted by P-38 Lightnings and P-51 Mustangs to attack a steel plant, a benzol production facility, a tank production facility, and a marshaling yard in Austria and the harbors at Trieste and Fiume in Italy.

**ITALY:** The 10th Mountain Division attacks on a four-mile front to clear Route 64 of enemy observers. Monte Belvedere and Monte Torracia are the objectives.

Twelfth Air Force B-25 Mitchells and B-26 Marauders bomb bridges. A-20 Havocs and P-47 Thunderbolts of the XXII Tactical Air Command attack bridges and communication targets in the Po River valley and bomb logistics storage areas and gun positions near Bologna.

**SOUTHWEST PACIFIC AREA:** Far East Air Force B-24 Liberators, with P-47 Thunderbolts providing support, attack the airfield, railyard, and aluminum plant at Takao, Formosa.

FEAF B-24 Liberators bomb an airfield in Borneo. The headquarters of the 375th Troop Carrier Group moves from Biak in New Guinea to Mindoro Island in the Philippines.

**SOUTHWEST PACIFIC AREA, LUZON:** The 149th and 151st Infantry Regiments of the 38th Infantry Division and the 1st RCT of the 6th Infantry Division link, eliminating all organized resistance on Bataan. The 1st RCT returns to the operational control of XIV Corps.

FEAF A-20 Havocs support ground forces and attack caves and dugouts in hills near Fort Stotsenburg. A-20s, B-25 Mitchells, and P-38 Lightnings attack targets throughout Luzon.

**PACIFIC:** Twentieth Air Force sends eight B-29 Superfortresses from Saipan to bomb the submarine pens on Dublon Island at Truk.

A U.S. destroyer rams a Japanese guardboat south of Kyushu, Japan. A destroyer sinks a Japanese auxiliary submarine chaser northwest of Iwo Jima, but sustains some damage from gunfire during the battle. A kamikaze damages a light minelayer south of Iwo Jima. Task Force 58 carrier aircraft sink a Japanese gunboat near Chichi Jima.

Three destroyers sink three Japanese guardboats south of Honshu, Japan.

**CENTRAL PACIFIC:** Seventh Air Force sends 42 B-24 Liberators from Saipan to bomb airfields and a bivouac site on Iwo Jima Island. Three B-24s from Guam bomb Truk. During the night five B-24s from Saipan fly individual snooper missions on Chichi Jima.

The P-61 Black Widow night fighters of the 548th Night Fighter Squadron, VII Fighter Command, begin operating from Saipan.

**CENTRAL PACIFIC, IWO JIMA:** Rear Admiral William H. P. Blandy decides to concentrate the pre-assault naval bombardment of the amphibious support force on the landing beaches. Over 200 targets are destroyed or heavily damaged. The marines will face over 21,000 well-trained and well-led Japanese soldiers sheltered in caves and tunnels nearly impervious to the bombardment.

## February 19

**ALEUTIANS:** Eleventh Air Force sends seven B-24 Liberators to fly cover sorties for a naval force during its approach to Kurabu Cape, Paramushiru Island, in the Kuriles.

**CBI:** In China, Fourteenth Air Force P-40s and P-51 Mustangs attack airfields, railroad yards, and targets of opportunity. Four B-24 Liberators bomb shipping in the South China Sea. Aircrews report two vessels damaged.

The B-24s of the 374th, 375th, and 425th Bombardment Squadrons (Heavy), 308th Bombardment Group (Heavy), redeploy from Chengkung and Kunming to Kwanghan.

In Burma, Tenth Air Force sends 12 B-25 Mitchells to bomb bridges. P-47 Thunderbolts support ground forces and attack bridges, troop concentrations, logistics storage sites, and targets of opportunity.

**ETO:** The XX Corps (the 26th and 94th Infantry Divisions and the 10th Armored Division) of Third Army attacks north between the Saar and Moselle Rivers, catching the Germans by surprise, and advances toward Saarbourg.

Ninth Air Force sends more than 60 B-26 Marauders to attack a railroad bridge and targets of opportunity in support of operations to isolate the Ruhr.

**MEDITERRANEAN:** Fifteenth Air Force sends 160 B-17s escorted by 20 P-38 Lightnings to bomb a benzol production facility and a marshaling yard in Austria. Other missions are aborted because of weather.

**ITALY:** Operation Encore begins. The Fifth Army attempts to open routes into the Po River valley. The 1st Battalion, 86th Infantry Regiment of the 10th Mountain Division drives the enemy off Riva Ridge.

Fifteenth Air Force fighters report 31 locomotives, 25 rail cars, and 17 vehicles destroyed.

Twelfth Air Force A-20 Havocs and P-47 Thunderbolts attack rail lines, ammunition storage areas, and bridges in the Po River valley. During the night A-20s attack towns and bridges in the Po River valley.

**SOUTHWEST PACIFIC AREA:** Far East Air Force B-24 Liberators and B-25 Mitchells bomb Takao, Okayama, and Toshien airfields on Formosa. P-38 Lightnings provide support.

FEAF B-24 Liberators bomb an airfield in Borneo.

**SOUTHWEST PACIFIC AREA, LUZON:** Elements of the 1st Cavalry Division capture Fort McKinley.

FEAF B-25 Mitchells, P-38 Lightnings, and P-47 Thunderbolts fly numerous missions in support of the ground forces on Luzon.

Private Lloyd G. McCarter, a paratrooper in the 503rd Parachute Infantry Regiment, landed on Corregidor on February 16 and, after getting out of his parachute harness, immediately attacked a Japanese machine-gun firing 30 yards away from where he landed. Over the next days and nights, he eliminates snipers and ambushes Japanese infiltrators trying to bypass his company. By the early morning of the 19th, relentless enemy attacks have reduced the paratroopers' position to only a few unwounded men. McCarter protects his comrades, shouting encouragement and attacking the enemy single-handedly, then returning to his own lines to replenish his ammunition. When his Thompson submachine gun fails him, he picks up a discarded Browning Automatic Rifle and continues the fight. When it ceases to operate, he picks up an M-1 rifle. By dawn McCarter is still fighting as the Japanese prepare to overwhelm the position he has defended. Locating the enemy, he is seriously wounded, but refuses to be evacuated until he can pass the information about the enemy location to other leaders. For his example of courage under fire, indomitable fighting spirit, and dedication to duty, Private McCarter will receive the nation's highest award for valor, the Medal of Honor.

**PACIFIC:** Twentieth Air Force sends 36 B-29 Superfortresses from the Marianas to bomb airfields on Moen Island in Truk Atoll. The headquarters of the 39th and 330th Bombardment Groups (Very Heavy) and the B-29s of the 457th, 458th, and 459th Bombardment Squadrons (Very Heavy) arrive at Guam from the United States. The squadrons' first missions are scheduled for mid-April.

The 5th Marine Division lands on Red Beach 1 on Iwo Jima under heavy Japanese fire, February 19, 1945. The marines will move with great difficulty through the deep and soft black sand.

**Central Pacific, Iwo Jima: Operation Detachment Begins.** In overall command of the operation is Admiral Raymond A. Spruance, Commander Fifth Fleet; Vice Admiral Richmond K. Turner is Joint Expeditionary Force Commander. Supported by naval and air bombardment that carpets the landing beaches, the 4th and 5th Marine Divisions land abreast simultaneously on Iwo Jima. Within several minutes over 6,000 marines are on the beach. Soft volcanic sand and heavy surf cause the rapid accumulation of men and equipment on the landing beaches. The 28th Marines of the 5th Marine Division advance rapidly 700 yards to the western edge of the island. The 27th Marines advance under heavy fire toward the airfield. Tanks are unable to move in the soft sand, leaving the infantry alone to advance against pillboxes and hidden firing positions. The 23rd and 25th Marines of the 4th Division encounter strong defenses. The 25th Marines advance only 300 yards against Japanese positions at the Rock Quarry. Japanese artillery now begins to hit the beach landing areas with a steady and devastating bombardment. The 26th Marines of the 5th Division and the 24th Marines of the 4th Division land shortly after noon as casualties from the landing force begin to mount. Unloading heavy artillery in the soft sand while under continuous bombardment consumes time and energy, slowing the pace of the landing. The beachhead becomes an enormous collection of human and materiel wreckage.

Shore battery fire damages a destroyer. Japanese mortar fire damages four medium landing ships.

The 3rd Battalion, 25th Marines, 4th Division, captures the cliffs before the Rock Quarry on the far right flank of the division. The battalion has lost over 500 men to capture the position. At the end of the first day, the marines have moved between 500 and 1,000 yards inland at the cost of over 2,400 men. There are now 30,000 marines on Iwo awaiting a night counterattack that does not come. Instead,

Mount Suribachi looms over marines on Iwo Jima, February 19, 1945.

there is a steady barrage of artillery fire and numerous infiltrators prowling around the marine positions.

Corporal Tony Stein of A Company, 1st Battalion, 28th Marine Regiment, 5th Marine Division, is one of the first men of his company on the beach at Iwo Jima. Corporal Stein has rigged a weapon from an aircraft, which he carries into battle. It proves to be very worthwhile because of its high volume of fire. He provides suppressive fire for his platoon, standing in full view of the enemy, and locates Japanese positions. He then charges forward toward the pillboxes and kills 20 Japanese soldiers. Maintaining the high rate of fire for his weapon causes him to run back to the beach and replenish his ammunition eight separate times; each time he returns to the beach, he brings a wounded marine with him. Throughout the day's brutal and confused fighting Corporal Stein and his special weapon provide support to the platoon. Corporal Stein's amazing performance, initiative, courage, and devotion to duty in the face of terrific odds will be recognized with the Medal of Honor.

**CENTRAL PACIFIC:** During the night Seventh Air Force sends nine B-24 Liberators from Guam to individual harassment raids on Chichi Jima.

### February 20

**CBI:** In China, Fourteenth Air Force P-40s and P-51 Mustangs attack locomotives, rail cars, and river traffic.

In Burma, Tenth Air Force P-47 Thunderbolts severely damage a bridge. P-38 Lightnings and P-47s support ground forces and attack troop concentrations, logistics storage sites, ammunition storage areas, and targets of opportunity.

**ETO:** Eighth Air Force sends nearly 1,300 B-17s and B-24 Liberators escorted by 726 P-51 Mustangs to bomb the marshaling yard at Nürnberg, Germany. The bombers use a combination of visual sighting and radar to locate the bomb release point. Five bombers are lost and 244 damaged. Aircrews report 49 confirmed kills, one probable kill, and 21 possibles. Aircrew casualties are 12 killed, 12 wounded, and 47 missing. Fighter pilots report 14 confirmed kills and one possible in the air and 43 confirmed kills, one probable, and 22 possibles on the ground. A total of 13 P-51s are lost. All the pilots are reported missing.

During the night 10 B-24s drop leaflets over Germany and the Netherlands. Another six B-24s fly a Carpetbagger mission.

Ninth Air Force P-47 and P-38 fighters support the VII, XII, and XX Corps.

The headquarters of the 53rd Troop Carrier Wing, IX Troop Carrier Command, redeploys from England to France.

**MEDITERRANEAN:** Fifteenth Air Force sends more than 500 B-17s and B-24 Liberators escorted by P-38 Lightnings and P-51 Mustangs to attack a steel plant, oil refineries, and marshaling yards in Austria, a harbor facility in Yugoslavia, and the shipyards at Trieste and Fiume in Italy.

**ITALY:** Twelfth Air Force B-25 Mitchells and B-26 Marauders bomb bridges. A-20 Havocs and P-47 Thunderbolts attack German positions near Monte Torraccia in support of Fifth Army. During the night A-20s attack marshaling yards in the Po River valley.

The First Tactical Air Force (Provisional) in France takes operational control of the 27th and 86th Fighter Groups from Twelfth Air Force. The headquarters of the 86th Fighter Group redeploys from Italy to France.

**SOUTHWEST PACIFIC AREA:** U.S. submarine *Guavina* attacks a Japanese convoy off the southern coast of French Indochina and damages a merchant tanker. U.S. submarine *Pargo* torpedoes and sinks a Japanese destroyer off the southern coast of French Indochina.

U.S. submarine *Hawkbill* attacks a Japanese convoy in the South China Sea northwest of Singapore and sinks a cargo ship. U.S. submarine *Pintado* is damaged in an aerial attack in the Gulf of Siam, but remains on patrol.

FEAF B-24 Liberators bomb runways and a warehouse at an airfield in Borneo.

The headquarters of the 380th Bombardment Group (Heavy) redeploys from Darwin, Australia, to Mindoro Island in the Philippines. The B-24s of the 23rd Bombardment Squadron (Heavy), 5th Bombardment Group (Heavy), redeploy from Morotai Island in New Guinea to Samar Island in the Philippines.

**SOUTHWEST PACIFIC AREA, LUZON:** Two of the 1st Cavalry Division's brigade combat teams cross the Marikina River, supported on their left flank by the 6th Infantry Division. The Shimbu Group holds the hills east of the river. The Shimbu positions occupy about 30 miles of the high ground overlooking the city of Manila and are defended by 30,000 troops. General Krueger assembles the 6th Infantry Division, the 43rd Infantry Division, elements of the 1st Cavalry Division, and the 112th Cavalry RCT for an offensive against the Japanese defenders. The objective of the offensive is to gain control of the water supply for the city of Manila, collected behind dams on the Angat and Marikina rivers. The Sixth Army planners believe that the Wawa Dam is one of the critical objectives. In reality most of Manila's water comes from the Ipo Dam in the Marikina River Valley. The 6th Infantry Division is to attack to capture the Wawa Dam. The 2nd Cavalry Brigade of the 1st Cavalry Division is to capture Antipolo. The 11th Airborne Division, reinforced by the 158th RCT, prepares to clear the area south of Manila.

Far East Air Force B-24 Liberators bomb Corregidor Island.

B-25 Mitchells and P-38 Lightnings attack the town of Choshu and railyards, vehicles, rail cars, and buildings on Formosa.

**CENTRAL PACIFIC:** During the night Seventh Air Force sends seven B-24 Liberators to fly individual harassment raids on Haha Jima.

The P-61 Black Widow night fighters of the 549th Night Fighter Squadron, VII Fighter Command, begin operating from Saipan.

**CENTRAL PACIFIC, IWO JIMA:** The 28th Marines of the 5th Division attack to seize Mount Suribachi, advancing 200 yards and destroying 40 enemy positions. The 26th and 27th Marines attack across the airfield, taking heavy casualties. The 25th Marines, reinforced by a battalion from the 24th Marines, fights the Japanese in the Rock Quarry on the 4th Division's right flank. The 23rd Marines advance 800 yards across the airfield. Major General Harry Schmidt attempts to commit the 21st Marines from the 3rd Division, but the seas are so rough that they are unable to land. Heavy surf destroys 34 LVTs, and 88 more sink in deep water.

An LST and a medium landing ship are damaged by Japanese mortar fire.

## February 21

**CBI:** Fourteenth Air Force P-40s and P-51 Mustangs attack troops and rail and river traffic in southern and eastern China.

In Burma, Tenth Air Force P-47 Thunderbolts and P-38 Lightnings support ground forces and attack bridges, troop concentrations, logistics storage sites, and roads.

**ETO:** Eighth Air Force sends more than 1,200 B-17s and B-24 Liberators escorted by nearly 800 P-47 Thunderbolts and P-51 Mustangs to bomb a tank production facility, marshaling yards, and locomotive repair shops at Nürnberg, Germany. The bombers use radar to locate the bomb release point. A total of 362 bombers are damaged. Aircrews report four confirmed kills and one possible on the ground. Aircrew casualties are two killed and nine wounded. Fighter pilots report four confirmed kills in the air. Five P-51s are lost, and the pilots are reported missing.

Over 40 P-51s make a sweep of the Nürnberg target area. One fighter is lost; another 23 P-51s fly a scouting mission and a fighter is lost. Both pilots are reported missing.

During the night 25 B-24 Liberators attack the Duisburg power and gas stations using a Pathfinder bomber. Two B-24s are lost.

Ninth Air Force A-20 Havocs, A-26 Invaders, and B-26 Marauders attack communications centers, an oil storage depot, railroad bridges, and a marshaling yard. P-47 and P-38 fighters attack rail targets and airfields, support ground forces of VII, XII, and XX Corps, and fly armed reconnaissance missions in the First Army area.

The C-47s of the 75th Troop Carrier Squadron, 435th Troop Carrier Group, and the 79th Troop Carrier Squadron, 436th Troop Carrier Group, IX Troop Carrier Command, redeploy from England to France.

**MEDITERRANEAN:** Fifteenth Air Force sends more than 500 B-17s and B-24 Liberators escorted by P-38 Lightnings and P-51 Mustangs to attack marshaling yards in Austria and Hungary and shipyards at Trieste and Fiume in Italy.

During the night one B-17 and 13 B-24s drop supplies in northern Italy.

**ITALY:** The 1st Brazilian Division of IV Corps captures Monte Castello. The 10th Mountain Division captures Monte Torracia.

Twelfth Air Force B-25 Mitchells and B-26 Marauders bomb bridges. A-20 Havocs and P-47 Thunderbolts support Fifth Army ground forces. During the night A-20s attack communication targets and logistics targets in the Po River valley.

The First Tactical Air Force (Provisional) takes operational control of the 522nd, 523rd, and 524th Fighter Squadrons, 27th Fighter Group. The P-47 Thunderbolts of the squadrons redeploy from Italy to France.

**SOUTHWEST PACIFIC AREA:** FEAF B-24 Liberators and A-20 Havocs bomb airfields and the town of Jesselton in Borneo. The 528th Bombardment Squadron (Heavy), 380th Bombardment Group (Heavy), redeploys from Darwin, Australia, to Mindoro Island in the Philippines, with B-24 Liberators.

**SOUTHWEST PACIFIC AREA, LUZON:** On Corregidor, the Japanese blow up the ammunition storage area near the Malinta Hill Tunnel, causing many casualties for 3rd Battalion, 34th Infantry Regiment.

Far East Air Force B-24 Liberators bomb Japanese positions in the hills west of Fort Stotsenburg. P-47 Thunderbolts bomb Corregidor. B-25 Mitchells, A-20 Havocs, P-40s, and P-38 Lightnings support ground forces on Luzon.

**PACIFIC:** U.S. submarine *Gato* torpedoes and sinks a Japanese cargo ship in the Yellow Sea.

**CENTRAL PACIFIC:** Seventh Air Force sends 24 B-24 Liberators from Saipan to make a bombing strike with napalm on Pagan Island in the northern Marianas. P-38 Lightnings from Guam escort photo aircraft over Truk Atoll and strafe aircraft on Moen Island. B-34s from Guam bomb Marcus Island. A total of 25 B-24s based at Angaur Island bomb Corregidor Island. During the night six B-24s from Guam conduct individual snooper missions on Chichi Jima.

**CENTRAL PACIFIC, IWO JIMA:** The 3rd Battalion of the 21st Marines lands and is assigned to the 4th Division. The 28th Marines of the 5th Division resume the attack on Mount Suribachi. The advance is measured in yards.

The Japanese launch 50 kamikazes against the American fleet. Kamikazes sink escort carrier USS *Bismarck Sea* and damage carrier USS *Saratoga*, escort carrier USS *Lunga Point*, two LSTs, and a net cargo ship. Small carrier USS *Langley* is damaged during an aerial bombing attack. Japanese mortar fire damages an LST.

Japanese submarine *RO-43* torpedoes destroyer USS *Renshaw* south of Iwo Jima.

Sergeant Ross F. Gray is a platoon sergeant attached to A Company, 1st Battalion, 25th Marine Regiment, 4th Marine Division on Iwo Jima. Advancing toward the high ground northeast of the airfield, Sergeant Gray conducts a quick reconnaissance to find Japanese positions. He discovers a minefield and a strong network of emplacements joined by covered trenches. He proceeds to clear the mined area and ignore the fire directed at him. Returning to the platoon, he takes an explosive charge and, supported with covering fire, he returns to the mined area to place the demolition in one of the covered trenches. As machine guns fire on him, he returns to the platoon to obtain another demolition charge and crawls back to demolish the enemy position. In this manner he attacks and destroys a total of six Japanese positions. His extraordinary personal courage, dedication to duty, and high combat skill will win Sergeant Gray the Medal of Honor.

Captain Joseph J. McCarthy commands a rifle company in 2nd Battalion, 24th Marine Regiment, 4th Marine Division, attacking near Motoyama airfield No. 2 on Iwo Jima. Organizing a demolition and flamethrower team to accompany him, McCarthy charges across 75 yards of open ground to attack a pillbox on the ridge. Using grenades, he destroys the position and eliminates the enemy defenders; he directs the next attack on an emplacement as the Japanese defenders now turn their fire on the small

The USS *Saratoga*, supporting night air patrols over Iwo Jima, is attacked by six Japanese planes and hit by five bombs on February 21, 1945. Fires rage in the hangar deck and 123 seamen will be killed or missing.

group of marines. After killing one enemy soldier in hand-to-hand combat, he brings his company forward to attack through the gap created in the Japanese defenses to sweep the ridge. For his cool courage and decisive leadership, Captain McCarthy will receive the Medal of Honor.

### February 22

**CBI:** In China, Fourteenth Air Force P-40s and P-51 Mustangs attack troops, tanks, trucks, and rail and river traffic. Fighter pilots report one cargo ship sunk in the Yangtze River between Hankow and Nanking.

In Burma, Tenth Air Force sends 12 B-25 Mitchells to bomb an airfield. P-47 Thunderbolts support ground forces and attack gun positions, troop concentrations, logistics storage sites, and trucks.

**ETO:** Operation Clarion begins with the intention of paralyzing the German national transportation structure by employing thousands of small aerial attacks over a one-million-square-mile area of what is left of the German Reich. Almost 9,000 aircraft are involved, dropping 8,500 tons of bombs.

Eighth Air Force sends more than 1,400 B-17s and B-24 Liberators escorted by over 800 P-47 Thunderbolts and P-51 Mustangs to begin a coordinated effort with the British Royal Air Force and the U.S. Ninth Air Force and Fifteenth Air Force to bomb the remainder of the German road and rail system and paralyze the enemy's capability to continue the war. To gain the best accuracy, the bombers will fly at 10,000 feet and visually identify the bomb release point. Marshaling yards are the main targets. Six bombers are lost and 97 damaged. Aircrews report 28 confirmed kills, two probables, and 43 possibles. Aircrew casualties are four wounded and 57 missing. Fighter pilots report four confirmed kills, two probables, and 18 possibles in the air and 22 confirmed kills and 21 possibles on the ground. A total of 12 P-51s are lost, and the pilots are reported missing.

Nearly 100 P-51s fly a freelance mission in support of the bombers. Fighter pilots report two confirmed kills in the air. One fighter is lost, and the pilot is reported missing. Another 28 P-51s fly a scouting mission and report two confirmed kills and three possibles on the ground.

Ninth Air Force sends more than 450 A-20 Havocs, A-26 Invaders, and B-26 Marauders to attack viaducts, railroad bridges, and marshaling yards. Over 1,000 P-47 and P-38 fighters escort the bombers as they make their low-level attacks. Fighters also support VII, XII, and XX Corps.

The headquarters of the 27th Fighter Group redeploys from Italy to France under the operational control of the First Tactical Air Force (Provisional).

**MEDITERRANEAN:** Fifteenth Air Force in support of Operation Clarion sends more than 350 B-17s and B-24 Liberators escorted by P-38 Lightnings and P-51 Mustangs to attack marshaling yards, rail lines, and bridges in Germany, Austria, and Italy.

**ITALY:** Twelfth Air Force B-25 Mitchells and B-26 Marauders attack bridges and marshaling yards. A-20 Havocs and P-47 Thunderbolts support Fifth Army ground forces and attack airfields, gun positions, and communication targets. During the night A-20s attack ammunition storage areas, rail lines, and bridges, and vehicles traveling on roads in the Po River Valley.

**SOUTHWEST PACIFIC AREA:** U.S. submarine *Becuna* torpedoes and sinks a Japanese merchant tanker off the south coast of French Indochina. A Japanese fleet tanker is damaged by a mine dropped by Twentieth Air Force B-29s. Fifth Air Force B-25 Mitchells locate the tanker after it has run aground and destroy it on the southern coast of French Indochina.

FEAF B-24 Liberators bomb airfields in Borneo.

**SOUTHWEST PACIFIC AREA, LUZON:** The 37th Infantry Division and the attached cavalrymen of the 1st Cavalry Division battle the Japanese in Manila, fighting house-to-house and employing direct artillery fire to destroy houses turned into small fortresses. The Japanese are holding their last position, the old walled city or Intramuros. The walls here are 16 feet high and 40 feet thick. Many noncombatants have come here for refuge from the fighting. Broadcasted appeals to the Japanese to surrender and allow the noncombatants to move into American lines are ignored. During the night Intramuros is subjected to intense artillery fire that creates breaches in the north and east sections of the walls.

On Luzon, Far East Air Force sends 100 B-24 Liberators to bomb Japanese troop concentrations near Fort Stotsenburg. P-47 Thunderbolts attack Corregidor Island and A-20 Havocs and P-51 Mustangs attack troop concentrations. B-24s bomb logistics storage areas.

**CENTRAL PACIFIC:** Seventh Air Force sends three B-24 Liberators to bomb Marcus Island. During the night six B-24s fly individual harassment raids on Haha Jima.

During the night B-24s from Guam and Saipan conduct individual snooper missions on Iwo Jima.

**CENTRAL PACIFIC, IWO JIMA:** Heavy rain on the island reduces movement. The 21st Marines of the 3rd Division relieve the 23rd Marines of the 4th Division and make an advance of 200 yards when they encounter the southeastern edge of the main Japanese defenses. The 3rd Battalion of the 25th Marines battles the Japanese at the Rock Quarry. Patrols from the 28th Marines link at Tobiishi Point on the southern tip of the island, isolating Mount Suribachi.

Admiral Raymond A. Spruance authorizes a carrier strike from Admiral Marc Mitscher's Task Force 58 against Honshu and Okinawa.

Lieutenant Colonel Justice M. Chambers is commander of the 3rd Assault Battalion Landing Team, 25th Marine Regiment, 4th Marine Division, and lands on Iwo Jima after the initial assault waves. His battalion faces a wall of fire from well-directed Japanese artillery, mortar rocket, machine-gun, and rifle fire. Chambers rallies his men and leads them in an attack on the critical high ground that has to be captured to protect the rest of the invasion force. Lieutenant Colonel Chambers holds his unit together during the day-long battle for the cliffs. Having lost most of his officers and suffered terrible losses, Chambers provides inspiration and leadership until wounded. For his extraordinary courage in the face of near impossible odds, accomplishing what was the most difficult mission on Iwo Jima, Lieutenant Colonel Chambers will receive the Medal of Honor.

**NEW GUINEA:** The headquarters of the 42nd Bombardment Group (Medium) redeploys to Morotai Island, while the 75th and 100th Bombardment Squadrons (Medium) remain at Sansapor. The squadrons' B-25 Mitchells will operate from

Morotai. The headquarters of the 347th Fighter Group redeploys from Middelburg Island to Mindoro Island, and the P-38 Lightnings of the 67th and 339th Fighter Squadrons will operate from Morotai.

## February 23

**PACIFIC:** A P-38 Lightning from Santa Rosa Army Airfield shoots down a Japanese balloon over Calistoga, California.

**CBI:** In China, Fourteenth Air Force P-51 Mustangs attack river traffic from Nanking to Hankow. Five B-24 Liberators sweep the Gulf of Tonkin and South China Sea. P-40s attack targets of opportunity near Kaifeng.

In Burma, Tenth Air Force sends 12 B-25 Mitchells and over 120 P-47 Thunderbolts and P-38 Lightnings to bomb troop concentrations, ammunition storage areas, and logistics storage sites.

**ETO:** Operation Grenade begins. The Ninth Army, under the operational control of Field Marshal Montgomery's 21st Army Group, sends units across the Roer River to establish a bridgehead. The XIX Corps (2nd Armored Division and the 30th and 29th Infantry Divisions) and XIII Corps (5th Armored Division and the 102nd and 84th Infantry Divisions) of Ninth Army cross the Roer River near Jülich. The attack is conducted in heavy rain. The melting snow and soft ground are quickly churned into deep mud by the advancing vehicles and the 45-minute pre-assault artillery bombardment. German forces are surprised and give ground quickly. Seven bridges are rapidly built and a bridgehead nearly four miles deep is established. American losses for this attack are 92 killed, 913 wounded, and 61 missing.

VII Corps (3rd Armored Division and the 8th and 99th Infantry Divisions) of First Army crosses the Roer River south of Düren.

The VIII Corps (4th Infantry Division and the 6th and 11th Armored Divisions) and XII Corps (4th Armored Division and the 5th, 76th, and 80th Infantry Divisions) of Third Army reach the Prüm River after fighting for nearly two weeks to break through the West Wall defenses.

Eighth Air Force sends more than 1,200 B-17s and B-24 Liberators escorted by over 700 P-47 Thunderbolts and P-51 Mustangs to bomb marshaling yards in Germany as part of Operation Clarion. One B-24 is lost and 62 bombers are damaged. Aircrews report 15 confirmed kills and 16 possibles. Aircrew casualties are 21 killed, four wounded, and four missing. Fighter pilots report one confirmed kill in the air and five confirmed kills and two possibles on the ground. Five P-51s are lost. One pilot is reported killed, and four pilots are reported missing.

Over 140 P-47 Thunderbolts and P-51 Mustangs make a sweep of Neuburg, Landsberg, and Leipheim airfields. Fighter pilots report nine confirmed kills and 14 possibles on the ground. One P-51 is lost and the pilot is reported missing. During the night 24 B-24s bomb the Neuss marshaling yard using a Pathfinder bomber to mark the bomb release point.

Ninth Air Force A-20 Havocs, A-26 Invaders, and B-26 Marauders attack communication centers near the Roer River as Ninth Army participates in Operation Grenade. P-47 and P-38 fighters support the 104th and 8th Infantry Divisions near Düren and support XIII and XIX Corps and VIII, XII, and XX Corps.

A V-2 rocket hits the port of Antwerp, damaging a U.S. freighter.

German aircraft attack and sink a U.S. freighter straggling from a convoy bound for Scotland in the Norwegian Sea.

**MEDITERRANEAN:** Fifteenth Air Force sends nearly 400 B-17s and B-24 Liberators escorted by over 140 P-38 Lightnings and P-51 Mustangs to attack marshaling yards and rail lines in Austria and marshaling yards in Italy.

**ITALY:** The 85th, 86th, and 87th Infantry Regiments of the 10th Mountain Division capture Monte Belvedere and Monte della Torraccia.

Twelfth Air Force B-25 Mitchells and B-26 Marauders bomb bridges. A-20 Havocs and P-47 Thunderbolts of the XXII Tactical Air Command attack rail lines, airfields, bridges, and troop movements in the central and northern Po River valley.

During the night A-20s attack marshaling yards and airfields throughout northern Italy.

The P-47 Thunderbolts of the 527th Fighter Squadron, 86th Fighter Group, redeploy from Italy to France to come under the operational control of the First Tactical Air Force (Provisional).

**SOUTHWEST PACIFIC AREA:** In French Indochina, FEAF B-25 Mitchells on shipping sweeps bomb vessels in Phan Rang harbor and attack a small convoy southwest of Cam Ranh Bay.

U.S. submarine *Hammerhead* intercepts a Japanese convoy and sinks an escort vessel off the southern coast of French Indochina and escapes a counterattack. Fifth Air Force B-25 Mitchells on a shipping sweep off French Indochina attack a Japanese convoy and sink a submarine chaser and damage another submarine chaser and a small tanker.

FEAF B-24 Liberators and P-47 Thunderbolts attack airfields in Borneo.

**SOUTHWEST PACIFIC AREA, LUZON:** The 37th Infantry Division assaults Intramuros, the last Japanese position in the city of Manila. A savage battle lasts for the next two days, as every area in the old city must be cleared.

A company of paratroopers from the 511th Parachute Infantry Regiment makes a jump at Los Baqos to free 2,147 Americans interred at the camp.

In the XI Corps area, two regiments of the 40th Infantry Division attack Japanese forces west of Fort Stotsenburg. The preceding bombing attacks from B-24 Liberators have eliminated all organized resistance.

Far East Air Force B-25 Mitchells, A-20 Havocs, P-47 Thunderbolts, and P-38 Lightnings support ground forces on Luzon Island.

**CENTRAL PACIFIC:** Seventh Air Force sends 26 B-24 Liberators from Angaur Island to bomb Mindanao Island in the Philippines. During the night seven B-24s from Guam conduct individual snooper missions on Chichi Jima and Haha Jima.

**CENTRAL PACIFIC, IWO JIMA:** A patrol of the 3rd Platoon of E Company 2nd Battalion, 28th Marines, reaches the top of Mount Suribachi and raises an American flag. A few hours later, a larger flag is raised. The moment is captured by Associated Press photographer Joe Rosenthal. It will become one of the most famous photographs ever taken. The capture of Mount Suribachi has cost the 28th marines 900 men in four days of fighting.

This iconic photo by Joe Rosenthal captures the spirit and determination of the marines who took Iwo Jima. It is one of the unforgettable moments of World War II.

Lieutenant General Holland Smith and Secretary of the Navy James V. Forrestal land on Iwo Jima and visit marines and stay for about two hours as artillery shells continue to land close by.

Japanese shore batteries damage two LSTs and two LSMs.

Corporal Hershel W. Williams is the demolition sergeant with the 21st Marine Regiment, 3rd Marine Division, and volunteers to assist tanks attempting to open a lane for the infantry through a network of reinforced concrete pillboxes, buried mines, and black volcanic sands. For the next four hours Williams carries on a single battle with the Japanese, moving forward under covering fire from four marines. He lays demolitions in the face of deadly fire from the enemy, then moves back to prepare additional demolition charges and flamethrowers, then struggles back through the soft black sand to destroy another position, often attacking them from the rear. Over and over he fights off Japanese infantry and moves in to blast and burn the enemy out of fortified positions. For his exceptional display of aggressive fighting spirit and valiant devotion to duty, Corporal Williams will receive the Medal of Honor.

**NEW GUINEA:** The P-38 Lightnings of the 68th Fighter Squadron, 347th Fighter Group, redeploy from Middelburg Island to Mindoro Island. The 69th Bombardment Squadron (Medium), 42nd Bombardment Group (Medium), begins operating from Morotai Island with B-25 Mitchells.

## February 24

**ALEUTIANS:** Eleventh Air Force sends four B-25 Mitchells on a shipping sweep in the Kurile Islands. On the return flight the B-25s encounter and photograph a Japanese balloon carrying a bomb and drifting toward the continental United States.

**CBI:** In China, Fourteenth Air Force sends five B-24 Liberators on individual sweeps over the South China Sea. Aircrews report four vessels sunk.

In Burma, Tenth Air Force sends 12 B-25 Mitchells and over 125 P-47 Thunderbolts and P-38 Lightnings to attack vehicles, bridges, troop concentrations, towns, and villages occupied by Japanese troops, logistics storage sites, and targets of opportunity.

**ETO:** Ninth Army captures Jülich.

Eighth Air Force sends nearly 1,200 B-17s and B-24 Liberators escorted by nearly 600 P-51 Mustangs to bomb oil refineries, U-boat yards, and marshaling yards in northern Germany. The bombers use radar to locate the bomb release point. One B-24 and one B-17 are lost, and 228 bombers are damaged. Aircrews report one confirmed kill and three possibles. Aircrew casualties are four killed, 12 wounded, and 21 missing. Fighter pilots report one confirmed kill and three possibles on the ground. A total of 11 P-51s are lost. The pilots are reported missing. German submarine *U-3007* is sunk at Bremen.

During the night 12 B-24s drop leaflets over Germany and the Netherlands.

Twelve B-17s conduct screening missions to jam German radio interception efforts and conduct countermeasures against German radar sites.

Ninth Air Force sends nearly 500 A-20 Havocs, A-26 Invaders, and B-26 Marauders to attack communication centers, railroad bridges, and marshaling yards to interdict German troop movements. P-47 and P-38 fighters support the 8th and 104th Infantry Divisions and XIII and XIX Corps at the Roer River bridgehead, and also the VIII, XII, and XX Corps.

**MEDITERRANEAN:** Fifteenth Air Force sends more than 500 B-17s and B-24 Liberators escorted by P-38 Lightnings and P-51 Mustangs to attack rail bridges and marshaling yards in Italy and marshaling yards in Austria.

**ITALY:** Twelfth Air Force B-25 Mitchells and B-26 Marauders attack rail lines, roads, and bridges. A-20 Havocs and P-47 Thunderbolts attack rail lines, bridges, airfields, and roads in the Po River valley and support the 10th Mountain Division at Monte Torraccia.

During the night A-20s attack marshaling yards and airfields.

**SOUTHWEST PACIFIC AREA:** FEAF B-25 Mitchells conduct a sweep off the China coast, bombing the naval base at Formosa.

FEAF B-24 Liberators bomb airfields in Borneo.

**SOUTHWEST PACIFIC AREA, LUZON:** The 2nd Battalion of the 151st Infantry Regiment of the 38th Infantry Division begins the relief of the 2nd Battalion of the 34th RCT on Corregidor.

In Manila, the 12th Cavalry Regiment captures the port facilities and the 129th and 145th Infantry Regiments of the 37th Infantry Division capture Fort Santiago.

Lieutenant General Robert L. Eichelberger's Eighth Army assumes responsibility for clearing Leyte and Samar of Japanese forces.

Far East Air Force B-25 Mitchells, A-20 Havocs, P-47 Thunderbolts, and P-38 Lightnings attack Corregidor Island and Japanese positions near Fort Stotsenburg on Luzon Island.

**PACIFIC:** Twentieth Air Force sends 105 B-29 Superfortresses all armed with incendiary bombs to attack the Empire Dock area at Singapore. Aircrews report heavy damage to the warehouse area. One B-29 is lost.

The XX Bomber Command begins its redeployment, sending the headquarters units of the 58th Bombardment Wing (Very Heavy) and the 468th Bombardment Group (Very Heavy) from India to the Marianas.

U.S. submarine *Lagarto* torpedoes and sinks Japanese submarine *I-371* and a cargo ship off Kyushu, Japan. U.S. submarine *Trepang* torpedoes and sinks a Japanese cargo ship off Kyushu.

**CENTRAL PACIFIC:** Seventh Air Force sends 28 B-24 Liberators from Angaur Island to bomb Mindanao Island in the Philippines. Three B-24s bomb Marcus Island. During the night five B-24s from Guam conduct individual snooper missions on Chichi Jima and Haha Jima.

**CENTRAL PACIFIC, IWO JIMA:** The marines begin an attack to the north with three regiments abreast—the 26th Marines on the left, the 21st Marines in the center, and the 24th Marines on the right. Major General Schmidt has consolidated all of the marine tanks into a single unit commanded by Lieutenant Colonel William Collins to support the infantry. The attack stalls almost immediately as the marines hit the main defensive line. Tanks hit mines and encounter anti-tank fire. The infantry is pinned by accurate machine-gun and mortar fire.

Major General Schmidt arrives ashore to establish his headquarters on Iwo. Although the 9th Marines land to support the 21st Marines in the center, Lieutenant General Holland Smith decides to keep the 3rd Marine Regiment of the 3rd Division out of the battle, looking ahead to future operations on Okinawa. Schmidt receives reports that casualties now number over 6,800.

**NEW GUINEA:** The B-25s of the 390th Bombardment Squadron (Medium), 42nd Bombardment Group (Medium), redeploy to Morotai Island.

### February 25

**CBI:** In China, Fourteenth Air Force B-25 Mitchells, P-40s, and P-51 Mustangs attack rail and river traffic. Four B-24 Liberators over the Gulf of Tonkin and South China Sea attack shipping targets. Aircrews report two vessels damaged.

In Burma, Tenth Air Force sends nine B-25 Mitchells and 85 P-47 Thunderbolts and P-38 Lightnings to attack bridges, troop concentrations, road traffic, logistics storage sites, and targets of opportunity. P-47s provide support to the British 36th Division and the Chinese 38th and 50th Divisions.

**ETO:** The VII Corps clears Düren, and bridgeheads are established over the Roer River as the rest of First Army pushes toward Cologne. The Ninth Army bridgehead has increased to 10 miles deep and 20 miles wide.

Eighth Air Force sends nearly 1,200 B-17s and B-24 Liberators escorted by 755 P-51 Mustangs to bomb oil storage areas, rail bridges, marshaling yards, tank production facilities, and airfields supporting jet aircraft. The bombers use radar to locate the bomb release point. A total of five bombers are lost and 366 are damaged. Aircrew casualties are five killed, 11 wounded, and 45 missing. Fighter pilots report three confirmed kills and five possibles on the ground. Two P-51s are lost and the pilots are reported missing. Over 260 P-47 Thunderbolts and P-51s fly close escort and area patrols. Fighter pilots report 21 confirmed kills and four possibles in the air and 10 confirmed kills and 12 possibles on the ground. Six P-51s are lost and the pilots are reported missing.

During the night 12 B-24s drop leaflets over France, Germany, and the Netherlands.

Ninth Air Force sends A-20 Havocs, A-26 Invaders, and B-26 Marauders to attack communication centers, railroad bridges, and a marshaling yard in support of Operation Clarion. P-47 and P-38 fighters support the 8th and 104th Infantry Divisions, XIII and XIX Corps, and VIII, XII, and XX Corps.

The headquarters of the 437th Troop Carrier Group and the C-47s of the 83rd, 84th, 85th, and 86th Troop Carrier Squadrons, IX Troop Carrier Command, redeploy from England to France.

**MEDITERRANEAN:** Fifteenth Air Force sends more than 600 B-17s and B-24 Liberators escorted by P-38 Lightnings and P-51 Mustangs to bomb marshaling yards and a benzol plant in Austria.

P-51s strafe rail lines in Germany.

**ITALY:** Twelfth Air Force B-25 Mitchells and B-26 Marauders attack bridges. A-20 Havocs and P-47 Thunderbolts of the XXII Tactical Air Command attack rail lines, marshaling yards, motor transport, and roads. During the night A-20s attack marshaling yards and airfields.

**SOUTHWEST PACIFIC AREA:** FEAF B-24 Liberators and P-51 Mustangs attack targets on Formosa.

U.S. submarine *Flasher* torpedoes and sinks a Japanese cargo vessel near Hainan Island and makes an unsuccessful attack on a submarine chaser rescuing survivors. U.S. submarine *Hoe* attacks a Japanese convoy and sinks an escort vessel south of Hainan Island. U.S. submarine *Piper* torpedoes and sinks a Japanese guardboat and cargo ship off Hainan Island.

FEAF B-24 Liberators bomb airfields in Borneo.

**SOUTHWEST PACIFIC AREA, LUZON:** In Manila the 37th Infantry Division captures Intramuros.

In the XI Corps area the 40th Infantry Division eliminates all Japanese resistance west of Fort Stotsenburg.

Far East Air Force B-24 Liberators bomb troop concentrations on Luzon. The headquarters of the 49th Fighter Group and the P-38 Lightnings of the 7th Fighter Squadron redeploy from Mindoro Island to Luzon.

**PACIFIC:** The C-87 transport aircraft carrying Lieutenant General Millard F. Harmon, commander of Army Air Forces, Pacific Operations Area, and deputy commander of Twentieth Air Force, disappears over the Marshalls. Harmon had departed Guam for Washington, D.C., via Kwajalein and Oahu, Hawaii.

Twentieth Air Force sends 172 B-29 Superfortresses of the 73rd, 313th, and 314th Bombardment Wings (Very Heavy) to bomb the urban area of Tokyo. Three B-29s are lost.

The XX Bomber Command redeploys the headquarters of the 40th Bombardment Group (Very Heavy) from India to the Marianas.

Carrier aircraft from Task Force 58 bomb aircraft production facilities and airfields near Tokyo.

Japanese shore battery fire damages an LCI off Iwo Jima.

Two U.S. destroyers sink three Japanese guardboats south of Honshu, Japan.

**CENTRAL PACIFIC:** Seventh Air Force sends nine B-24 Liberators from Guam to bomb Japanese mortar positions, fortifications, and rocket launchers on Iwo Jima. During the night eight B-24s conduct individual harassment raids on Chichi Jima.

**CENTRAL PACIFIC, IWO JIMA:** The 5th Marine Division attacks the high ground at Nishi Ridge and Hills 362-A and 362-B. The 4th Marine Division encounters a collection of nearly impregnable Japanese positions, which they call "The Meatgrinder." The 3rd Marine Division fights in an area named "Cushman's Pocket."

Shore battery fire damages two LSTs off Iwo Jima. Aircraft from escort carrier USS *Anzio* sink Japanese submarines *I-368* and *RO-43* off Iwo Jima. A U.S. destroyer escort sinks Japanese submarine *I-370* south of Iwo Jima.

### February 26

**CBI:** In China, Fourteenth Air Force sends B-25 Mitchells to bomb bridges, rail lines, and heavy port equipment in French Indochina. P-40s and P-51 Mustangs attack airfields, towns, and rail and river traffic.

In Burma, Tenth Air Force sends B-25 Mitchells to bomb bridges. P-47 Thunderbolts and P-38 Lightnings along with B-25s support ground forces and attack bridges, troop concentrations, logistics storage sites, and targets of opportunity. P-47s support the Mars Task Force near Lashio and the British 36th Division.

**ETO:** In the Ninth Army area, 2nd Armored Division of XIX Corps is pushed across the Roer River to support the attack, even though conditions are very difficult for tanks, due to the bad weather.

Eighth Air Force sends more than 1,200 B-17s and B-24 Liberators escorted by over 700 P-51 Mustangs to bomb rail stations in Berlin, Germany. The bombers use radar to mark the bomb release points. Three bombers are lost and 93 are damaged. Aircrews report six confirmed kills. Aircrew casualties are eight killed, six wounded, and 30 missing. Fighter pilots report four confirmed kills in the air and two confirmed kills on the ground. Three P-51s are lost and two pilots are reported missing.

Six B-24 Liberators and 17 B-17s conduct screening missions to jam German radio interception efforts and conduct countermeasures against German radar sites.

During the night 12 B-24s drop leaflets over Germany and the Netherlands. During the night five B-24s fly a Carpetbagger mission.

Ninth Air Force sends over 230 A-20 Havocs, A-26 Invaders, and B-26 Marauders to attack communication centers, rail and road junctions, and logistics and ammunition storage sites.

The headquarters of the 436th Troop Carrier Group and the C-47s of the 80th, 81st, and 82nd Troop Carrier Squadrons, IX Troop Carrier Command, redeploy from England to France.

**MEDITERRANEAN:** Fifteenth Air Force sends P-38 Lightnings to attack rail lines in Austria.

**ITALY:** Twelfth Air Force B-25 Mitchells and B-26 Marauders attack rail bridges. A-20 Havocs and P-47 Thunderbolts of the XXII Tactical Air Command support the Fifth Army south of Bologna and attack rail lines, bridges, airfields, and vehicles. During the night A-20s attack marshaling yards.

**SOUTHWEST PACIFIC AREA:** FEAF B-24s attack Takao airfield on Formosa while P-47s strafe railroad targets.

FEAF B-24 Liberators attack airfields in Borneo.

**SOUTHWEST PACIFIC AREA, LUZON:** On Corregidor, the Japanese blow up the ammunition storage area near Monkey Point, causing many casualties for the 1st Battalion of the 503rd Parachute Infantry.

In the I Corps area the 25th Infantry Division captures Carranglan in the Pampanga River Valley.

Far East Air Force B-24 Liberators bomb troop concentrations; A-20 Havocs, P-38 Lightnings, and P-47 Thunderbolts support ground forces and attack Japanese troops near Fort Stotsenburg on Luzon. A-20s, P-38s, and P-47s attack targets on Palawan Island and B-25 Mitchells bomb an airfield on Jolo Island.

The 9th Fighter Squadron, 49th Fighter Group, redeploys from Mindoro Island to Luzon with P-38 Lightnings. The P-38s of the 70th Fighter Squadron, 18th Fighter Group, redeploy from Luzon to Mindoro.

**PACIFIC:** The XX Bomber Command redeploys the headquarters of the 462nd Bombardment Group (Very Heavy) from India to the Marianas.

**CENTRAL PACIFIC:** During the night Seventh Air Force sends eight B-24s to fly individual harassment raids on Chichi Jima.

## February 27

**CBI:** In China, Fourteenth Air Force sends B-24 Liberators to attack shipping in the Gulf of Tonkin and South China Sea. Aircrews report four vessels sunk.

In Burma, Tenth Air Force P-47 Thunderbolts and P-38 Lightnings support ground forces and attack bridges, gun positions, road traffic, troop concentrations, logistics storage sites, elephant transport, and targets of opportunity

**ETO:** The VII Corps captures a bridgehead at Erft and organizes for an attack toward Cologne.

Eighth Air Force sends more than 1,100 B-17s and B-24 Liberators escorted by 745 P-51 Mustangs to bomb road and rail targets at Halle and Leipzig, Germany. The bombers use radar to locate the bomb release point. Two B-24s are lost and eight damaged. Aircrews report 83 confirmed kills and 19 possibles. Aircrew casualties are two killed, one wounded, and 18 missing. Fighter pilots report two confirmed kills in the air and 81 confirmed kills and 19 possibles on the ground. Two P-51s are lost, and the pilots are reported missing.

During the night one B-17 and 11 B-24s drop leaflets over Germany and the Netherlands. A total of 26 B-24 Liberators bomb Wilhelmshaven oil storage areas, using a Pathfinder bomber to locate the bomb release point.

Ninth Air Force sends 118 A-20 Havocs, A-26 Invaders, and B-26 Marauders to attack communication centers, railroad bridges, and a marshaling yard. P-47 and P-38 fighters support XIII and XIX Corps.

Navy PB4Y-1 Privateers along with British escort vessels sink German submarine *U-327* in the English Channel.

**MEDITERRANEAN:** Fifteenth Air Force sends more than 500 B-17s and B-24 Liberators, escorted by P-38 Lightnings and P-51 Mustangs, to attack marshaling yards in Germany and Austria.

**ITALY:** Twelfth Air Force B-25 Mitchells and B-26 Marauders attack rail bridges. A-20 Havocs and P-47 Thunderbolts of the XXII Tactical Air Command attack rail lines and rail cars in northeast Italy. During the night A-20s attack airfields, marshaling yards, motor transport, and roads in the Po River valley.

**SOUTHWEST PACIFIC AREA:** In the Philippines, Far East Air Force B-24 Liberators, A-20 Havocs, and P-38 Lightnings strike Puerto Princesa on Palawan Island in preparation for the amphibious landings. P-51 Mustangs support ground forces on Luzon; P-38 Lightnings and marine fighters attack airfields on Mindanao.

B-24 Liberators bomb Takao on Formosa, while P-47s sweep the west coast. B-25s sweeping the China coast attack a fleet of junks and sampans near Hong Kong. Aircrews report damaging or destroying more than 25.

U.S. submarine *Blenny* attacks a Japanese convoy off French Indochina and sinks a merchant tanker. U.S. submarine *Scabbardfish* torpedoes and sinks a Japanese guardboat off Formosa.

FEAF B-24 Liberators bomb airfields in Borneo.

**SOUTHWEST PACIFIC AREA, LUZON:** Corregidor is captured after the paratroopers of the 503rd Parachute Infantry Regiment eliminate the last Japanese positions on the extreme eastern tip of the island. The Japanese have lost nearly 4,000 men and 19 captured. The number of men buried alive in the tunnels is unknown. American casualties are 209 killed, 725 wounded, and 19 missing.

General MacArthur officially turns over the civil administration of the Philippines to President Sergio Osmeña.

The 8th Fighter Squadron, 49th Fighter Group, redeploys from Mindoro to Luzon with P-38 Lightnings; the P-38s of the 12th Fighter Squadron, 18th Fighter Group, redeploy from Luzon to Mindoro. The P-38s of the 432nd Fighter Squadron, 475th Fighter Group, redeploy from Leyte Island to Clark Field, Luzon.

**PACIFIC:** During the night Twentieth Air Force sends 10 B-29 Superfortresses to mine Johore Strait and Penang harbor. Personnel of the 58th Bombardment Wing (Very Heavy) begin redeployment from India to Tinian and Guam Islands.

**CENTRAL PACIFIC:** Seventh Air Force sends nine B-24 Liberators from Guam to bomb fortifications and artillery positions on Iwo Jima. A total of 22 B-24s from Angaur Island bomb airfields on Mindanao Island in the Philippines. During the night nine B-24s from Guam conduct individual snooper missions on Haha Jima.

**CENTRAL PACIFIC, IWO JIMA:** The 3rd Maine Division occupies the airfield and controls Hills Peter and 199-Oboe.

Japanese shore battery fire damages an attack cargo ship and an LST. Mortar fire damages an LSM (Landing Ship, Medium).

Private Wilson D. Watson, 2nd Battalion, 9th Marine Regiment, 3rd Marine Division, attacks a Japanese pillbox when his squad is hit by fire from fortifications in the high rocky ridges and crags near the line of advance. Watson's bold and swift attack allows the platoon to take its objective. When Japanese fire stops the platoon, Watson climbs a small hill while under constant enemy fire and charges the enemy, firing his Browning Automatic Rifle (BAR) from the hip. Standing on the hill in full view of the enemy, he rakes them with automatic fire, killing 60 Japanese troops before running out of ammunition. For his courageous initiative and valiant fighting spirit against devastating odds Private Watson will receive the Medal of Honor.

**NEW GUINEA:** The 65th and 66th Troop Carrier Squadrons of the 403rd Troop Carrier Group redeploy from Biak to Morotai Island with C-46s and C-47s

## February 28

**CBI:** Detachment 101 of the OSS (Office of Strategic Services) has 10,200 guerrillas under its control. The Americans that make up the detachment total 131 officers and 588 enlisted.

In Burma, Tenth Air Force sends P-47 Thunderbolts and P-38 Lightnings to support ground forces and attack bridges, troop concentrations, road traffic, logistics storage sites, and targets of opportunity.

**ETO:** Eighth Air Force sends more than 1,100 B-17s and B-24 Liberators escorted by 737 P-51 Mustangs to bomb viaducts, a tank production facility, road junctions, and marshaling yards in Germany. The bombers use a variety of radar techniques to mark the bomb release point. One B-17 is lost. Aircrews report 18 confirmed kills and 11 possibles. Aircrew casualties are three missing. Fighter pilots report one possible kill in the air and 18 confirmed kills and 10 possibles on the ground. Five P-51s are lost, and the pilots are reported missing.

During the night 11 B-24s drop leaflets over Germany and the Netherlands. During the night 22 B-24s bomb the Freiburg rail depot using a Pathfinder bomber to mark the bomb release point.

Ninth Air Force sends 340 A-20 Havocs, A-26 Invaders, and B-26 Marauders to attack communication centers, railroad bridges, and a marshaling yard. P-47 and P-38 fighters support the 3rd Armored Division at the Paffendorf bridgehead, the 2nd Armored Division advancing toward the Rhine River, and VIII, XII, and XX Corps.

The headquarters of the 313th and 314th Troop Carrier Groups and the C-47s of the 32nd and 61st Troop Carrier Squadrons, IX Troop Carrier Command, redeploy from England to France.

**MEDITERRANEAN:** Fifteenth Air Force sends nearly 700 B-17s and B-24 Liberators escorted by P-38 Lightnings and P-51 Mustangs to bomb marshaling yards in Austria and Italy. P-38s and P-51s attack marshaling yards and rail lines in Austria and rail lines in Yugoslavia.

A U.S. destroyer escort and French submarine chaser *L'Indiscret* sink German submarine *U-869* off Morocco.

**ITALY:** Twelfth Air Force B-25 Mitchells and B-26 Marauders attack rail lines and rail bridges. A-20 Havocs and P-47 Thunderbolts attack airfields and ammunition storage areas. During the night A-20s attack marshaling yards, bridges, and airfields.

**SOUTHWEST PACIFIC AREA:** FEAF B-24 Liberators and B-25 Mitchells bomb airfields in Borneo. The B-25s use napalm against their assigned target.

**SOUTHWEST PACIFIC AREA, LUZON:** Major General Verne D. Mudge, commander of the 1st Cavalry Division, is wounded. He is replaced by Brigadier General Hugh F. T. Hoffman.

In the Eighth Army area the 186th RCT of the 41st Infantry Division lands at Puerto Princesa on Palawan Island, in the Sulu Sea southwest of Mindoro. Rear Admiral William M. Fechteler is the commander of Naval Task Group 78.2. Naval Task Group 74.2 (Rear Admiral Ralph S. Riggs), with three light cruisers and four destroyers, provides naval gunfire support.

Far East Air Force B-24 Liberators and B-25 Mitchells attack an airfield on Mindanao. The P-38 Lightnings of the 431st and 433rd Fighter Squadrons, 475th Fighter Group, redeploy from Leyte to Clark Field on Luzon.

**CENTRAL PACIFIC:** Seventh Air Force sends eight B-24 Liberators from Guam to bomb Chichi Jima. A total of 23 B-24s based at Angaur Island bomb an airfield on Mindanao Island. During the night six B-24s from Guam fly individual harassment raids on Chichi Jima.

The ground echelon of the 548th Night Fighter Squadron, VII Fighter Command, arrives on Iwo Jima from Hawaii. The squadron's P-61 Black Widow night fighters continue to operate temporarily from Saipan.

**CENTRAL PACIFIC, IWO JIMA:** The 4th Marine Division captures Hill 382 in the Meatgrinder. The 28th Marines of the 5th Division capture Hill 362-A, losing 200 men. The 26th Marines capture Hill 362-B, losing 500 men. The 3rd Marine Division struggles forward against two positions named Peter and 199-Oboe. The marines have advanced 4,000 yards with about half the island under American control.

Major General James E. Chaney arrives on Iwo Jima with advance elements of the 145th Infantry Regiment of the army's 37th Infantry Division. Once the island is secured, General Chaney is to take control for the U.S. Army.

A U.S. destroyer is damaged in an air attack. Another destroyer is hit and damaged by shore battery fire. An LSM is hit by mortar fire.

Pharmacist's Mate First Class John H. Willis is the platoon corpsman serving with the 3rd Battalion, 27th Marine Regiment, 5th Marine Division, in the midst of artillery and mortar fire from Japanese pillboxes and caves covering Hill 362 on Iwo Jima. Willis administers first aid to wounded marines during the furious fighting. When he is wounded and evacuated, Willis leaves the aid station without authorization to return to his platoon. During an enemy counterattack, Willis moves far forward to assist a wounded marine and administers blood plasma. The Japanese throw grenades into the shell hole where he is, and Willis throws the grenades back out as quickly as he can until one explodes and kills him. For his great personal valor in saving others at the sacrifice of his own life, Pharmacist's Mate First Class Willis will receive the Medal of Honor.

**NEW GUINEA:** The B-24s of the 530th Bombardment Squadron (Heavy), 380th Bombardment Group (Heavy), redeploy from Darwin, Australia, to Mindoro. The 70th Troop Carrier Squadron, 433rd Troop Carrier Group, redeploys from Hollandia, New Guinea, to Leyte Island with C-46s and C-47s.

## March 1

**CBI:** In China, Fourteenth Air Force P-40s and P-51 Mustangs attack rail and river traffic.

In Burma, Tenth Air Force sends 12 B-25 Mitchells to bomb an airfield. P-47 Thunderbolts and P-38 Lightnings support ground forces and attack bridges, troop concentrations, logistics storage sites, and targets of opportunity.

Fourteenth Air Force B-24 Liberators sink a Japanese merchant tanker in Tonkin Gulf, French Indochina.

**ETO:** Ninth Army captures München-Gladbach, about 12 miles from the Rhine River. The attack is spearheaded by the 2nd, 5th, and 8th Armored Divisions.

Bradley's 12th Army Group launches Operation Lumberjack, the offensive intended to reach the Rhine River and link with Third Army attacking northeast. First Army, with 13 divisions, is to advance to the Rhine south of Düsseldorf, capture the high ground northeast of Cologne, and seize the road network at Euskirchen.

Eighth Air Force sends more than 1,200 B-17s and B-24 Liberators escorted by 488 P-51 Mustangs to bomb marshaling yards in central and southern Germany and jet aircraft production facilities. The bombers use radar to mark their bomb release point. A total of 33 bombers are damaged. Aircrews report 12 confirmed kills and eight possibles. Aircrew casualties are 16 killed and two wounded. Fighter pilots report two confirmed kills in the air and nine confirmed kills and seven probables on the ground. Seven P-51s are lost, and the pilots are reported missing.

During the night 11 B-24s drop leaflets over Germany and the Netherlands.

Six B-24 Liberators conduct screening missions to jam German radio interception efforts and employ countermeasures against German radar sites.

Ninth Air Force sends 340 A-20 Havocs, A-26 Invaders, and B-26 Marauders to attack an ordnance depot, railroad bridges, and marshaling yards. P-47 and P-38 fighters support the 3rd and 9th Armored Divisions, and the VIII, XIX, XII, XX, XVI, and XIII Corps.

**MEDITERRANEAN:** U.S. Army Forces in the Middle East (USAFIME) takes over northwest Africa from the Mediterranean theater of operations and is redesignated the Africa-Middle East Theater (AMET).

Fifteenth Air Force sends more than 600 B-17s and B-24 Liberators escorted by over 200 P-38 Lightnings and P-51 Mustangs to bomb oil refineries and marshaling yards in Austria and marshaling yards in Yugoslavia.

**ITALY:** During the night Twelfth Air Force A-20s attack bridges.

**SOUTHWEST PACIFIC AREA:** In the Philippines, Far East Air Force B-25 Mitchells attack an airfield on Jolo Island. Aircraft conduct napalm strikes on Japanese troops on Corregidor and Japanese defensive positions near Fort Stotsenburg on Luzon.

Over Formosa, B-24 Liberators bomb the Takao aluminum plant and airfields, while P-47 Thunderbolts attack buildings, oil storage tanks, railroad yards, and targets of opportunity.

The XIII Fighter Command redeploys from Leyte to Puerto Princesa on Palawan Island. The headquarters of the 18th Fighter Group moves from Luzon to Mindoro Island.

Fifth Air Force B-25 Mitchells sink a Japanese transport off the Pescadores in the South China Sea near Formosa.

FEAF B-24 Liberators bomb airfields in Borneo.

**PACIFIC:** The headquarters of the 444th Bombardment Group (Very Heavy) begins a redeployment from India to the Marianas.

Operational control of VII Fighter Command changes from Seventh Air Force to Army Air Forces Pacific Operational Area. The headquarters of VII Fighter Command will redeploy from Oahu, Hawaii, to Iwo Jima.

Carrier aircraft from Task Force 58 attack ground installations, airfields, and shipping around Okinawa. A torpedo boat and a minelayer and two cargo ships are sunk and an escort destroyer, an auxiliary minesweeper, a supply ship, six cargo ships, a gunboat, a transport, a torpedo boat, a minesweeper, and a submarine chaser are damaged.

Two destroyers are damaged by shore battery fire off Iwo Jima.

U.S. submarine *Sterlet* sinks a Japanese cargo ship east of Honshu, Japan.

U.S. submarine *Kete* departs Guam on her second war patrol. The submarine fails to report after March 20.

**CENTRAL PACIFIC:** Seventh Air Force sends seven B-24 Liberators from Guam to bomb the airfield on Chichi Jima. Three B-24s bomb Marcus Island. A total of 25 B-24s based at Angaur Island bomb Corregidor Island. During the night five B-24s fly individual harassment raids on Haha Jima.

**CENTRAL PACIFIC, IWO JIMA:** The 4th Marine Division fights in the Meatgrinder and consolidates its position on Hill 382; the 3rd Marine Division gains part of the second, unfinished airfield in the center of the island. The 5th Marine Division attacks to capture Hill 362-A near Nishi Ridge. Each and every yard of ground must be first bombed with artillery or air strikes, then tanks and flamethrowers, then finally marines must move in with hand grenades, explosive charges, and rifle fire to destroy the fanatical defenders in the cave and tunnel entrances.

**NEW GUINEA:** The headquarters of the Thirteenth Air Force redeploys from Morotai to Leyte. The B-24s of the 531st Bombardment Squadron (Heavy), 380th Bombardment Group (Heavy), redeploy from Darwin, Australia, to Mindoro.

## March 2

**CBI:** Fourteenth Air Force sends three B-24 Liberators on sweeps over the Gulf of Tonkin and the South China Sea. Aircrews report two vessels sunk and three damaged.

In Burma, Tenth Air Force sends P-47 Thunderbolts and P-38 Lightnings to support ground forces and attack bridges, gun positions, troop concentrations, logistics storage sites, and targets of opportunity.

**ETO:** The XIX Corps of Ninth Army reaches the Rhine River.

The 10th Armored Division of XX Corps of Third Army captures Trier and the important bridge across the Moselle. XII Corps secures a bridgehead east of Bitburg. Since the beginning of February the troops of Third Army are capturing about 1,000 German soldiers a day. A pervasive sense of defeat is shown in the attitude of the prisoners. Third Army has lost 12,000 men (including 1,500 killed) over the past 30 days of combat.

Eighth Air Force sends more than 1,200 B-17s and B-24 Liberators escorted by over 700 P-47 Thunderbolts and P-51 Mustangs to bomb synthetic oil production facilities in Germany. The city of Dresden is attacked again. The bombers use radar to locate bomb release points. A total of 14 bombers are lost and 167 are damaged. Aircrews report 110 confirmed kills, nine probables, and 60 possibles. Aircrew casualties are three killed, seven wounded, and 29 missing. Fighter pilots report 66 confirmed kills, six probables, and 30 possibles in the air and 36 confirmed kills and 29 possibles on the ground. A total of 13 fighters are lost and two are damaged. All the pilots are reported missing.

During the night 11 B-24s drop leaflets over Germany and the Netherlands. Four B-24s fly Carpetbagger missions.

Six B-24 Liberators conduct screening missions to jam German radio interception efforts and employ countermeasures against German radar sites.

Ninth Air Force sends A-20 Havocs, A-26 Invaders, and B-26 Marauders to attack communication centers, railroad bridges, ordnance depots, and a motor transport depot to slow down German forces attempting to withdraw before Third Army. Over 1,700 P-47 and P-38 fighters support ground forces, particularly the 3rd Armored Division at the Erft River, the XVI and XIX Corps and the VIII, XII, and XX Corps.

**MEDITERRANEAN:** Fifteenth Air Force sends more than 400 B-17s and B-24 Liberators escorted by P-38 Lightnings and P-51 Mustangs to attack marshaling yards in Austria and Italy. During the night B-24s drop supplies in northern Italy and Yugoslavia.

**ITALY:** Twelfth Air Force A-20 Havocs and P-47 Thunderbolts of the XXII Tactical Air Command attack logistics storage sites and ammunition storage areas in the Po River valley.

**SOUTHWEST PACIFIC AREA:** On Formosa, B-24 Liberators, B-25 Mitchells, A-20 Havocs, P-38 Lightnings, and P-47s attack airfields.

Fifth Air Force B-25 Mitchells sink a Japanese landing ship in the South China Sea near the Pescadores.

FEAF B-24 Liberators bomb airfields and the waterfront area of Sandakan in Borneo.

**SOUTHWEST PACIFIC AREA, LUZON:** General MacArthur arrives on Corregidor. He personally raises the American flag over the ruined parade ground at the location of the former U.S. Army barracks.

In the Philippines, the detachment of the 432nd Fighter Squadron, 475th Fighter Group, operating from Mindoro Island with P-38 Lightnings, returns to base at Clark Field on Luzon.

**PACIFIC:** Twentieth Air Force sends 50 of 64 B-29 Superfortresses to bomb support installations at the naval base in Singapore. Aircrews report one probable kill and four possibles. Two B-29s are lost.

Major General Willis H. Hale, the deputy commander for operations of Army Air Forces Pacific Operations Area (AAFPOA), takes command to replace Lieutenant General Millard F. Harmon, commanding general AAFPOA and deputy commander of the Twentieth Air Force, who was lost February 25 in an aircraft over the Pacific.

A naval task group under command of Rear Admiral Francis E. M. Whiting with three light cruisers and eight destroyers bombards Japanese positions on Okino Daito Jima, in the Ryukyus.

Shore battery fire damages a light cruiser off Iwo Jima.

U.S. submarine *Bowfin* torpedoes and sinks a Japanese transport east of Honshu, Japan.

A navy PB4Y-2 Privateer attacks a Japanese convoy, sinking a transport in the East China Sea.

**CENTRAL PACIFIC:** Seventh Air Force sends seven B-24 Liberators from Guam to bomb the airfield on Chichi Jima. During the night five B-24s fly individual harassment raids on Haha Jima and Chichi Jima.

The P-51 Mustangs of the 78th Fighter Squadron, 15th Fighter Group, arrive on Iwo Jima from Hawaii. The squadron's first mission will be in early March.

General MacArthur salutes while the American flag is raised over the devastated American barracks area on Corregidor, with parachutes from the 503rd Parachute Infantry Regiment dangling in the trees, March 2, 1945.

**Central Pacific, Iwo Jima:** The 2nd Battalion of the 4th Marines of the 4th Marine Division pushes past Hill 382 and advances 150 yards. A maze of underground tunnels allowing Japanese soldiers to appear anywhere at any point beyond Hill 382 stops the advance. The other areas of the Meatgrinder, Turkey Knob, the Amphitheater, and Minami Village Japanese troops continue to resist any American advance. The 3rd Marine Division gains 500 yards in approaching Hill 362-B. The 5th Marine Division moves from Hill 362-A toward Nishi Ridge.

**New Guinea:** B-24s of the 394th Bombardment Squadron (Heavy), 5th Bombardment Group (Heavy), redeploy from Morotai to Samar Island in the Philippines.

## March 3

**CBI:** Fourteenth Air Force sends four B-24 Liberators over the Gulf of Tonkin and the South China Sea to attack shipping targets of opportunity. Aircrews report one vessel sunk and three damaged.

In Burma, Tenth Air Force sends P-38 Lightnings and P-47 Thunderbolts to support elements of the Chinese 50th Division and British 36th Division.

B-25 Mitchells, P-38s, and P-47s join attacks on troops, logistics sites, tanks, and gun positions.

**ETO:** Canadian troops meet Americans near the Rhine at Geldern, marking the elimination of German forces west of the Rhine above Cologne. Third Army attacks with VIII Corps and XII Corps toward the Kyll River to break the German lines and attack to the Rhine.

Eighth Air Force sends more than 1,100 B-17s and B-24 Liberators escorted by over 700 P-51 Mustangs to bomb oil refineries, industrial facilities, and rail bridges in Germany. The bombers use radar to locate the bomb release point. A total of nine bombers are lost and 206 are damaged. Aircrews report 35 confirmed kills, two probables, and 37 possibles. Aircrew casualties are nine killed, nine wounded, and 80 missing. One hundred P-51 Mustangs fly a fighter sweep in the Leipzig-Magdeburg area. Fighter pilots report four confirmed kills and 10 possibles in the air and 19 confirmed kills and 25 possibles on the ground. A total of eight P-51s are lost, and one is damaged. All pilots are reported missing.

During the night 18 B-24s bomb the marshaling yard at Emden using a radar-equipped Pathfinder bomber to mark their bomb release point.

Ninth Air Force sends A-20 Havocs, A-26 Invaders, and B-26 Marauders to attack communication centers, ammunition storage sites, motor transport targets, and a marshaling yard. P-47 and P-38 fighters support the 9th Infantry Division and 3rd Armored Division and the VII, XIII, XVI, and XIX Corps.

**Italy:** Twelfth Air Force A-20 Havocs and P-47 Thunderbolts of the XXII Tactical Air Command attack vehicles, logistics storage sites, and ammunition storage areas.

During the night A-20s attack roads, ammunition storage areas, and motor transport in the Po River valley.

**Southwest Pacific Area:** FEAF B-24 Liberators and P-47 Thunderbolts bomb targets on Formosa.

In the Philippines, Far East Air Force B-25 Mitchells bomb an airfield on Mindanao Island. B-24 Liberators and B-25s attack an airfield on Jolo Island.

**SOUTHWEST PACIFIC AREA, LUZON:** In the I Corps area the 25th Infantry Division captures Digdig.

In the Eighth Army area the 186th RCT of the 41st Infantry Division on Palawan Island meets Japanese defenders. A five-day battle begins in which the Japanese withdraw into the mountains. American losses are light: 12 killed and six wounded. The Japanese lose over 900 men. The Japanese will continue to resist for another month. Airfield construction begins on the island.

FEAF A-20 Havocs and B-25s bomb targets on Samar and Luzon Islands and Caballo Island in Manila Bay.

**PACIFIC:** U.S. submarine *Trepang* torpedoes and sinks a Japanese gunboat off southern Honshu, Japan.

**CENTRAL PACIFIC:** Seventh Air Force sends 10 B-24 Liberators from Guam to bomb airfields, antiaircraft positions, and radar sites on Chichi Jima. During the night four B-24s fly individual harassment raids on Chichi Jima.

**CENTRAL PACIFIC, IWO JIMA:** The 4th Marine Division continues to battle Japanese positions in the Meatgrinder. The Amphitheater, Minami Village, and Turkey Knob defenders continue to resist despite near continuous air and artillery bombardment. The 5th Marine Division advances about 500 yards along the western coast of the island, but loses over 500 men. The 3rd Division makes little progress in the center at Cushman's Pocket. The Japanese, now reduced to less than 3,500 defenders with little food or water left, continue to hold about one-third of the island.

Aircraft from the Mariana Islands land on the rebuilt airfield, evacuating casualties and bringing in supplies. Shore battery fire damages an attack transport off Iwo Jima.

Corporal Charles J. Berry is a member of a machine-gun crew in the 1st Battalion, 26th Marines, 5th Marine Division. As night falls over Iwo Jima, Corporal Berry and his crew stay alert for signs of Japanese infiltrators. Locating the marine position, Japanese troops throw hand grenades. A furious effort to locate and toss the grenades safely away occurs in the darkness. When one grenade lands in his position, Corporal Berry covers the explosion with his own body to save his comrades. This unselfish act of heroism will win him the Congressional Medal of Honor.

Sergeant William G. Harrell of the 1st Battalion, 28th Marines, 5th Marine Division, is the leader of an assault group and is holding a position in a perimeter defense around the company command post. While standing watch alternately with another marine in terrain covered with caves and ravines, Japanese infiltrators attack at early dawn. Sergeant Harrell kills two with his M-1 carbine and faces a hail of gunfire that tears off his left hand and fractures his thigh. As a Japanese soldier hits him with a saber, Harrell kills him with his .45-caliber automatic pistol. With his wound now causing him to weaken, Harrell orders the other marine to safety while he battles on alone, killing two more enemy soldiers and losing his right hand. He is later discovered and evacuated, surrounded by the bodies of 12 enemy soldiers. For his indomitable courage and his fierce fighting spirit in the face of heavy odds, Sergeant Harrell will receive the Medal of Honor.

Pharmacist's Mate Second Class George E. Wahlen continues to serve with 2nd Battalion, 26th Marine Regiment, 5th Marine Division, on Iwo Jima even after suffering a painful wound on February 26. Wahlen often goes forward to rescue and treat wounded marines beyond friendly lines. He ignores mortar and rifle fire to care for the wounded, often working in an area under constant enemy fire. On March 2 he is wounded again and continues to stay with his company even as they make a desperate assault across 600 yards of open terrain. During the entire time Wahlen takes care of the wounded in the face of direct enemy fire. After suffering a third wound, he is unable to walk but does crawl 50 yards to provide first aid to a wounded marine. For his extraordinary dedication to duty, courage under fire, and selfless service, Pharmacist's Mate Second Class Wahlen will receive the Medal of Honor.

**NEW GUINEA:** U.S. submarine *Sea Robin* torpedoes and sinks a Japanese transport off Java.

U.S. submarine *Tuna* lands supplies on the northeast coast of Borneo.

## March 4

**CBI:** Fourteenth Air Force sends four B-24 Liberators on a sea sweep in the South China Sea. Aircrews report damage to a Japanese destroyer escort.

In Burma, Tenth Air Force sends 100 P-47 Thunderbolts and P-38 Lightnings to support ground forces and attack bridges, animal transport, troop concentrations, logistics storage sites, and targets of opportunity.

**ETO:** Eighth Air Force sends more than 1,000 B-17s and B-24 Liberators escorted by over 500 P-47 Thunderbolts and P-51 Mustangs to bomb the jet aircraft production facility, ordnance depots, and marshaling yards. The bombers use radar to locate bomb release points. One B-24 is lost and 39 damaged. Aircrew casualties are eight killed, three wounded, and 17 missing. One P-51 is lost and one damaged. The pilot is reported missing.

During the night one B-17 and 11 B-24s drop leaflets over Germany and the Netherlands.

Ninth Air Force sends 180 A-20 Havocs, A-26 Invaders, and B-26 Marauders to attack communication centers, rail junctions, and marshaling yards. P-47 and P-38 fighters support XX Corps.

**MEDITERRANEAN:** Fifteenth Air Force sends more than 600 B-17s and B-24 Liberators escorted by P-38 Lightnings and P-51 Mustangs to bomb marshaling yards in Austria, Hungary, and Yugoslavia.

B-24s, with P-51 escort, drop supplies in Yugoslavia.

**ITALY:** Twelfth Air Force B-25 Mitchells and B-26 Marauders attack rail bridges. A-20 Havocs and P-47 Thunderbolts of the XXII Tactical Air Command attack rail bridges and roads in the Po River valley. During the night A-20s attack bridges, a radar station, roads, and motor transport in the central Po River valley.

**SOUTHWEST PACIFIC AREA:** U.S. submarine *Baya* attacks a Japanese convoy, sinking a merchant tanker off the southern coast of French Indochina.

**SOUTHWEST PACIFIC AREA, LUZON:** The 1st Brigade Combat Team of the 1st Cavalry Division clears the last Japanese strongpoints in Manila after a nine-day battle to clear the government buildings outside of Intramuros. Japanese casualties are estimated at over 16,000. U.S. casualties are 1,010 dead and 5,565 wounded. At least 100,000 Filipinos have been deliberately killed by the Japanese.

The 6th Infantry Division of XIV Corps pushes the Japanese off the crest of Mount Pacawagan.

Far East Air Force B-24 Liberators bomb airfields on Mindanao and gun positions, ammunition storage areas, airfields, and targets of opportunity on Luzon. B-24 Liberators also hit fortifications on Caballo Island in Manila Bay.

The P-38 Lightning detachments of the 431st and 433rd Fighter Squadrons, 475th Fighter Group, redeploy from Mindoro Island and return to Clark Field on Luzon.

**PACIFIC:** During the night Twentieth Air Force sends 11 B-29s from China to mine the confluence of the Hwangpoo and Yangtze Rivers and the Tai-hsing Narrows at Shanghai.

Twentieth Air Force sends 192 B-29 Superfortresses from the Mariana Islands to bomb Musashi, Japan. Heavy clouds prevent bombing the primary target. A total of 159 B-29s bomb the secondary target, the urban areas of Tokyo, and 18 others attack alternative targets. One B-29 is lost.

Lieutenant General Barney McKinney Giles becomes the commander of Army Air Forces Pacific Operations Area and deputy commander of the Twentieth Air Force.

U.S. submarine *Tilefish* torpedoes and sinks a Japanese fishing vessel in the Ryukyus.

**CENTRAL PACIFIC:** Seventh Air Force sends 10 B-24 Liberators from Guam to bomb the airfield on Chichi Jima. A B-29 makes an emergency landing on Iwo Jima Island. This is the first of over 2,400 emergency landings on the island that will save the lives of thousands of crewmen who otherwise would have been lost at sea.

**CENTRAL PACIFIC, IWO JIMA:** A B-29 Superfortress, damaged and returning from a bombing run on the Japanese home islands, makes an emergency landing on the airfield at Iwo Jima. Lieutenant General Holland Smith refuses Major General Harry Schmidt's request to land the 3rd Marine Regiment to replace the heavy unit losses in the 4th and 5th Divisions. Smith maintains control of the veteran regiment and instead provides the divisions with untested individual replacements. Because of heavy officer casualties, the marine divisions have sergeants leading half-strength platoons. Multiple companies are merged into one unit commanded by whatever ranking officer is still alive.

## March 5

**CBI:** In China, Fourteenth Air Force B-25 Mitchells, escorted by P-47 Thunderbolts, attack bridges while P-51 Mustangs and P-40s on armed reconnaissance attack road, rail, and river traffic. In French Indochina, 30 B-25 Mitchells bomb bridges.

In Burma, Tenth Air Force sends P-47 Thunderbolts to support the British 36th Division and the Chinese 50th Division. P-47 Thunderbolts and B-25 Mitchells attack troop concentrations along the battle lines and attack logistics sites, road traffic, and targets of opportunity.

**ETO:** Elements of the VII Corps, First Army, enter Cologne and begin a fight for the city. The 4th Armored Division of XII Corps (plus the 5th, 76th, and 80th Infantry Divisions) of Third Army moves north of the Moselle River.

Since the beginning of Operation Grenade, Ninth Army has cleared the Rhine River from Düsseldorf to Moers. In the process, 36,000 German soldiers have been killed or captured. American casualties have been 7,300. First Army has secured all of its assigned objectives for Operation Lumberjack, controlling the Rhine River from Cologne northward to link with Ninth Army.

Eighth Air Force sends more than 400 B-17s and B-24 Liberators escorted by nearly 700 P-47 Thunderbolts and P-51 Mustangs to bomb synthetic oil production facilities and marshaling yards. The bombers use radar to mark the bomb release point. One B-17 is lost and 15 damaged. Aircrew casualties are nine missing. Four fighters are damaged. One pilot is reported killed.

During the night nine B-24s drop leaflets over Germany and the Netherlands, and 21 B-24 Liberators bomb the Wiesbaden rail station, using a Pathfinder bomber to mark the bomb release point.

Ninth Air Force sends 565 A-20 Havocs, A-26 Invaders, and B-26 Marauders to attack communication centers, ordnance depots, and marshaling yards. P-47 and P-38 fighters fly armed reconnaissance missions.

The headquarters of the 52nd Troop Carrier Wing, IX Troop Carrier Command, redeploys from England to France.

**ITALY:** The 10th Mountain Division secures the ridgelines along Highway 64 to support future offensive operations in the spring.

Twelfth Air Force A-20 Havocs and P-47 Thunderbolts attack rail bridges. During the night A-20s attack roads and motor transport in the Po River valley.

**SOUTHWEST PACIFIC AREA:** In the Philippines, Far East Air Force B-25 Mitchells attack an airfield on Mindanao Island. On Luzon, B-24 Liberators with P-38 Lightnings attack troops. P-47 Thunderbolts attack Fort Drum in Manila Bay, attack Japanese troops near Fort Stotsenburg, and support guerrilla forces northeast of Lingayen Gulf. B-25 Mitchells attack an airfield on Jolo Island.

B-24s and P-47s fly armed reconnaissance over Formosa. Fighters conduct sweeps against railroad targets.

U.S. submarine *Bashaw* attacks the Japanese convoy hit by USS *Baya* the previous day, sinking an oiler and an army tanker off the southern coast of French Indochina. U.S. submarine *Peto* is damaged in an air attack off Hainan but continues her patrol in the South China Sea.

Task Force 58 carrier aircraft sink a Japanese auxiliary submarine chaser off the Pescadores in the South China Sea. Fifth Air Force B-25 Mitchells attack a Japanese convoy, sinking two auxiliary submarine chasers and a cargo ship off the southern coast of French Indochina.

**PACIFIC:** U.S. submarine *Tilefish* torpedoes and damages a Japanese minesweeper south of Kyushu, Japan.

**CENTRAL PACIFIC:** Seventh Air Force sends 11 B-24 Liberators from Guam to bomb the airfield on Chichi Jima. Three B-24s bomb Marcus Island. A total of 22 B-24s based at Angaur Island bomb an airfield on Mindanao in the Philippines. During the night five B-24s conduct individual snooper (radar-assisted bomb release) missions on Chichi Jima.

**CENTRAL PACIFIC, IWO JIMA:** Lieutenant General Holland Smith orders the 3rd Regiment of the 3rd Marine Division to return to Guam. Major General Schmidt orders units on Iwo Jima to halt for rest, resupply, and to receive replacements.

**NEW GUINEA:** The headquarters of 5th Bombardment Group (Heavy) redeploys from Morotai Island to Samar Island.

U.S. submarine *Sea Robin* attacks a Japanese convoy in the Java Sea, sinking a gunboat, an auxiliary netlayer, and a cargo ship. Thirteenth Air Force B-24 Liberators sink a Japanese auxiliary submarine chaser southeast of Celebes Island.

## March 6

**CBI:** In China, Fourteenth Air Force P-40s and P-51 Mustangs attack troop concentrations, rail and river traffic, and logistics storage facilities.

In Burma, Tenth Air Force sends 12 B-25 Mitchells, P-47 Thunderbolts, and P-38 Lightnings to attack fuel storage areas, road traffic, troop concentrations, logistics storage sites, and targets of opportunity.

**ETO:** During the night Eighth Air Force sends 12 B-24s to drop leaflets over Germany and the Netherlands. Five B-24s fly a Capetbagger mission.

Ninth Air Force sends more than 260 A-20 Havocs, A-26 Invaders, and B-26 Marauders to attack communication centers, storage depots, and marshaling yards. P-47 and P-38 fighters support ground forces and fly armed reconnaissance missions.

**MEDITERRANEAN:** The 302nd Fighter Squadron (with P-51 Mustangs) of the 332nd Fighter Group is inactivated at Ramitelli airfield in Italy.

**ITALY:** Twelfth Air Force B-25 Mitchells and B-26 Marauders attack rail and road bridges. A-20 Havocs and P-47 Thunderbolts support Fifth Army ground forces south and southwest of Bologna. During the night A-20s attack targets of opportunity in the Po River valley.

**SOUTHWEST PACIFIC AREA:** In the Philippines, Far East Air Force B-24 Liberators bomb targets on Mindanao. On Luzon, B-24s, B-25 Mitchells, P-47 Thunderbolts, and P-38 Lightnings attack a number of targets in support of ground forces and Philippine guerrillas.

B-25s and P-38 Lightnings attack an airfield on Hainan Island, while fighters conduct a sweep over Formosa.

The headquarters of the 347th Fighter Group and the P-38 Lightnings of the 67th, 68th, and 339th Fighter Squadrons redeploy from Mindoro Island to Palawan Island. The 67th and 339th operate from Morotai Island.

**CENTRAL PACIFIC:** Seventh Air Force sends 11 B-24 Liberators from Guam to bomb the airfield on Chichi Jima. Three B-24s bomb Marcus Island. During the night five B-24s fly individual harassment raids on Chichi Jima.

The headquarters of the 15th Fighter Group arrives on Iwo Jima Island from Hawaii. The P-61 Black Widow night fighters of the 548th Night Fighter Squadron redeploy from Saipan to Iwo Jima.

**CENTRAL PACIFIC, IWO JIMA:** P-51 Mustangs of the 15th Fighter Group, VII Fighter Command, arrive on Iwo Jima. The pilots begin flying air support missions for the marines, delivering 1,000-pound bombs with delay fuses to destroy underground positions.

**NEW GUINEA:** The 419th Night Fighter Squadron from XIII Fighter Command redeploys from New Guinea to Palawan Island in the Philippines. The squadron operates from Morotai Island with P-38 Lightnings and P-61 Black Widow night fighters.

## March 7

**CBI:** British Fourteenth Army occupies Mandalay.

In China, Fourteenth Air Force sends four B-25 Mitchells and nine P-40s to bomb railroad targets. Over 130 P-40s and P-51 Mustangs attack rail and river traffic.

In Burma, Tenth Air Force sends nearly 50 P-47 Thunderbolts to support the British 36th Division and the Chinese 50th Division. Twelve B-25 Mitchells, supported by P-47 Thunderbolts and P-38 Lightnings, attack road traffic, troop concentrations, logistics storage sites, and targets of opportunity.

**ETO: The Remagen Bridge is Captured.** A task force commanded by Lieutenant Colonel Leonard Engeman composed of the 14th Tank Battalion and the 27th Armored Infantry Battalion, 9th Armored Division, captures the Ludendorff railroad bridge at Remagen, about 20 miles northwest of Koblenz, the only bridge still intact along the entire Rhine River. Lieutenant Karl H. Timmermann, commander of A Company, 27th Armored Infantry Battalion, leads a group of soldiers across the bridge even as German engineers attempt to blow it up. A few charges explode but do not bring the bridge down. Timmermann is the first American to set foot on German soil over the Rhine River. Engineers quickly disable other charges, and infantry and tanks cross the bridge. Upon hearing the news, General Eisenhower orders General Omar Bradley to put at least five divisions across as quickly as possible.

First Army occupies Cologne.

Curious soldiers of the 3rd Armored Division inspect a knocked out German Mark V Panther tank in front of the Cologne cathedral, March 1945.

The 4th Armored Division of XII Corps and the 11th Armored Division of VIII Corps of Third Army close on the Rhine River after a rapid advance of 60 miles in three days. The 4th Armored has captured 6,000 prisoners and destroyed nearly 900 vehicles at a cost of 29 men killed.

Eighth Air Force sends more than 900 B-17s and B-24 Liberators escorted by over 300 P-47 Thunderbolts and P-51 Mustangs to bomb oil production facilities, benzol plants, and marshaling yards. The bombers use radar to locate the bomb release point. A total of 81 bombers are damaged. Aircrew casualties are 11 killed. One P-51 is lost on a photo reconnaissance mission. The pilot is reported missing.

Six B-24 Liberators and six B-17s conduct screening missions to jam German radio interception efforts and employ countermeasures against German radar sites.

During the night 11 B-24s drop leaflets over Germany and the Netherlands. A total of 19 B-24s bomb Dortmund during the night using a Pathfinder radar-equipped bomber to mark their bomb release point. One B-24 is lost.

Ninth Air Force P-47 and P-38 fighters support XVI Corps.

American soldiers in the railroad tunnel across the Rhine River look back on the distinctive towers of the Ludendorff railroad bridge at Remagen, Germany. The capture of an intact bridge across the Rhine was one of the most fortuitous events of the war for General Omar Bradley's 12th Army Group.

**MEDITERRANEAN:** Naval Task Group 89.9, comprising an aviation supply ship and a fleet tug, departs Naples, Italy, for Odessa, on the Black Sea coast of the USSR, with supplies for American prisoners of war freed by Soviet troops.

**ITALY:** Twelfth Air Force B-25 Mitchells and B-26 Marauders attack rail and road bridges. A-20 Havocs and P-47 Thunderbolts attack fuel and ammunition storage areas.

During the night A-20s attack bridges and targets of opportunity.

**SOUTHWEST PACIFIC AREA:** On Luzon in the Philippines, Far East Air Force B-24 Liberators attack Japanese positions while A-20 Havocs, P-38 Lightnings, and P-40s attack troop concentrations and gun positions.

**CENTRAL PACIFIC:** Seventh Air Force sends 11 B-24 Liberators from Guam to bomb the airfield on Chichi Jima and a town on Haha Jima. During the night five B-24s fly individual harassment raids on Chichi Jima.

**CENTRAL PACIFIC, IWO JIMA:** At dawn the 3rd Battalion of the 9th Marines, 3rd Division, makes a surprise attack without any artillery preparation against Hill 362-C. Advancing 500 yards, the marines gain complete surprise and report capturing their objective. At first light the marines discover that the objective is still 250 yards away. Lieutenant Colonel Harold C. Boem orders an advance to capture the hill, even though the Japanese are fully aware a marine battalion has entered their lines. By the afternoon Hill 362-C is captured. Two other battalions of the 9th Marines are unsuccessful against Japanese positions in Cushman's Pocket.

The 5th Marine Division battles close to Kitano Point, the northernmost tip of the island. The 4th Marine Division continues to attack the Meatgrinder defenses, but Japanese strength is weakening.

Second Lieutenant John H. Leims is the commander of B Company, 1st Battalion, 9th Marine Regiment, 3rd Marine Division, leading an attack on a fortification located on a rocky hill. His marines blast the Japanese out of caves and pillboxes and occupy the objective, but Leims quickly realizes that he has advanced far beyond friendly lines and is ordered to fall back. During the reorganization after the withdrawal, Leims is notified that several marines have been left behind. Leims goes back into the area, as Japanese machine guns fire all around him. He locates one marine and brings him back to safety, then returns to locate and bring back a second marine. For his example of extraordinary courage and dedication to duty, Second Lieutenant Leims will receive the Medal of Honor.

## March 8

**CBI:** In China, Fourteenth Air Force B-24 Liberator aircrews report sinking a Japanese transport in the South China Sea. P-40s and P-51 Mustangs attack bridges, troops, gun positions, and rail and river traffic.

In Burma, Tenth Air Force sends P-47 Thunderbolts to support the British 36th Division. Other P-47s attack road traffic, gun positions, troop concentrations, and logistics storage sites.

Fourteenth Air Force B-24 Liberators sink a Japanese coast defense vessel southeast of Hainan Island. Tenth Air Force B-24s attack Japanese shipping in the Andaman Sea, sinking a cargo vessel. Fourteenth Air Force P-51 Mustangs attack Japanese shipping in the Yangtze River near Hankow, sinking a cargo vessel.

**ETO:** Eighth Air Force sends more than 1,300 B-17s and B-24 Liberators escorted by over 300 P-51 Mustangs to bomb oil production facilities, benzol plants, and marshaling yards. The bombers use radar to mark the bomb release point over the targets. No bombers are lost, but 27 are damaged. There are no aircrew casualties.

Four B-17s conduct screening missions to jam German radio interception efforts and employ countermeasures against German radar sites.

During the night 11 B-24s drop leaflets over Germany and the Netherlands. Four B-24s fly a Carpetbagger mission. A total of 19 B-24s bomb Dortmund during the night, using a Pathfinder radar-equipped bomber to mark bomb release points.

Ninth Air Force sends 328 A-20 Havocs, A-26 Invaders, and B-26 Marauders to attack a military transportation depot, railroad bridges, and marshaling yards. P-47 and P-38 fighters support ground forces and fly armed reconnaissance missions.

**MEDITERRANEAN:** Fifteenth Air Force sends more than 550 B-17s and B-24 Liberators escorted by P-38 Lightnings and P-51 Mustangs to bomb marshaling yards in Hungary and Italy and a locomotive works in Yugoslavia.

**ITALY:** Twelfth Air Force B-25 Mitchells and B-26 Marauders bomb marshaling yards and rail and road bridges. A-20 Havocs and P-47 Thunderbolts attack rail lines, road bridges, and roads. During the night A-20s attack roads and motor transport in the Po River valley.

**SOUTHWEST PACIFIC AREA, LUZON:** The 1st Cavalry Division attacks the Japanese Shimbu Group defenses near Antipolo behind a heavy artillery and air bombardment.

Far East Air Force B-24 Liberators bomb targets on Mindanao Island. On Luzon, B-24s, A-20 Havocs, P-47 Thunderbolts, and P-38 Lightnings attack Japanese defenses, gun positions, fuel storage sites, and support guerrilla forces.

**PACIFIC:** Fifth Air Force aircraft sink a Japanese cargo ship in the South China Sea near Hainan Island. Navy PBM Mariner patrol bombers bomb a Japanese convoy, sinking a cargo vessel west of Formosa.

**CENTRAL PACIFIC:** Seventh Air Force sends 14 B-24 Liberators from Guam to bomb the airfield on Chichi Jima. During the night five B-24s fly individual harassment raids on Chichi Jima.

**CENTRAL PACIFIC, IWO JIMA:** About 1,500 Japanese troops make a counterattack against the 4th Marine Division. The Japanese lose over 800 men before retreating. The marines suffer nearly 300 casualties in desperate and close fighting.

First Lieutenant Jack Lummus is a rifle platoon leader in the 2nd Battalion, 27th Marine Regiment, 5th Marine Division. He begins an attack on yet another Japanese defensive network after two days and nights of unrelenting combat. As his platoon is stopped by a high volume of accurate fire, Lieutenant Lummus goes forward by himself to locate the hidden positions. A Japanese grenade knocks him down, but he rises to his feet and attacks the emplacement. He is immediately fired on by the adjoining position and is wounded by another grenade but attacks the pillbox, eliminating the enemy. He returns to his platoon and leads them forward with supporting tanks until heavy fire from another network of defenses halts the advance. Lieutenant Lummus again goes forward alone and attacks a fortified installation, eliminating the defenders. Inspired by his actions, his marines move through the area, eliminating

Japanese defenders in foxholes and spider traps as Lummus leads the way, firing his M-1 carbine into the positions. He is killed when he steps on a land mine. For his extraordinary valor, exceptional combat skills, and dedicated leadership, First Lieutenant Lummus will receive the Congressional Medal of Honor.

## March 9

**CBI:** The Japanese seize complete control of French Indochina, claiming the French administration is covertly assisting the Allies.

In China, Fourteenth Air Force sends 32 B-24 Liberators, escorted by five P-51 Mustangs, to bomb railroad yards. Another 15 B-25 Mitchells and two P-40s destroy two bridges. P-40s and P-51 Mustangs attack gun positions, troops, and rail and river traffic.

In Burma, Tenth Air Force sends P-47 Thunderbolts to support the Chinese 50th Division. Over 80 P-47s and P-38 Lightnings attack road traffic, troop concentrations, logistics storage sites, artillery, and targets of opportunity.

**ETO:** At Remagen, General Omar N. Bradley's 12th Army Group has established a lodgment three miles deep across the Rhine. German reinforcements are rushed to the area but have neither the manpower nor the capability to stop the Americans. The 9th Armored Engineer Battalion repairs damage to the Ludendorff Bridge and lays timber planking across for rapid movement of tanks and infantry. About 8,000 troops have crossed the river.

Bonn, some 10 miles downriver from Remagen, is captured by V Corps (2nd, 28th, and 69th Infantry Divisions) of First Army.

Field Marshall Bernard L. Montgomery lays out the final plan for Operation Plunder, the 21st Army Group's crossing of the Rhine. The U.S. Ninth Army (XIII Corps, XVI Corps, and XIX Corps) is to cross south of Wesel. The XVI Corps will make the initial assault with two divisions; XIX Corps will be prepared to pass through the right of the British Second Army and attack toward Hamm-Münster. The XIII Corps will hold along the Rhine. The XVIII Airborne Corps (U.S. 17th Airborne and the British 6th Airborne Divisions) are to support the attack at Wesel and expand the bridgehead, capture crossing sites at the Issel River, and then link with Ninth Army. Ninth Army is well prepared. It has collected 138,000 tons of supplies to support the operation along with 14,000 tons of bridging equipment. Over 600 artillery pieces are in place to support the U.S. divisions. Most of the Allied air support in-theater will be dedicated to the 21st Army Group's crossing.

Eighth Air Force sends more than 1,000 B-17s and B-24 Liberators escorted by over 400 P-51 Mustangs to bomb industrial targets, a tank production facility, and marshaling yards. A total of seven bombers are lost and 425 are damaged. Aircrews report two possible kills. Aircrew casualties are 12 wounded and 68 missing. Fighter pilots report two possible kills in the air. Two P-51s are damaged.

Six B-17s conduct screening missions to jam German radio interception efforts and employ countermeasures against German radar sites.

During the night 11 B-24s drop leaflets over France, Germany, and the Netherlands. Two B-24s fly a Carpetbagger mission.

Ninth Air Force sends more than 600 A-20 Havocs, A-26 Invaders, and B-26 Marauders to attack depots and storage facilities, ammunition production facilities, and marshaling yards. P-47 and P-38 fighters support ground forces over the Remagen bridgehead and support the 9th Infantry Division and 9th Armored Division, the XX Corps, and XVI Corps.

**MEDITERRANEAN:** Fifteenth Air Force sends 372 B-17s and B-24 Liberators escorted by P-38 Lightnings and P-51 Mustangs to bomb marshaling yards in Austria and Yugoslavia.

**ITALY:** Twelfth Air Force B-25 Mitchells and B-26 Marauders bomb bridges and marshaling yards. A-20 Havocs and P-47 Thunderbolts attack rail lines, vehicles, logistics storage sites, bridges, and roads.

During the night A-20s attack river crossings in the Po River valley.

**SOUTHWEST PACIFIC AREA:** In the Philippines, Far East Air Force B-24 Liberators bomb Mindanao. B-25 Mitchells support a PT boat operation against targets on Basilan Island. On Luzon Island, B-24s, B-25s, A-20 Havocs, P-38 Lightnings, and P-47 Thunderbolts attack Japanese forces around Manila Bay, and airfields, bridges, and towns on Luzon.

B-24 Liberators bomb the docks at Takao on Formosa.

**CENTRAL PACIFIC:** Seventh Air Force sends 13 B-24 Liberators from Guam to bomb the airfield on Chichi Jima. During the night five B-24s fly individual harassment raids on Chichi Jima and a total of 24 B-24s based at Angaur Island bomb Mindanao Island in the Philippines.

**CENTRAL PACIFIC, IWO JIMA:** A patrol of the 3rd Marine Division reaches the northwest coast of the island. The remainder of the division continues to reduce Cushman's Pocket.

Platoon Sergeant Joseph R. Julian, with the 1st Battalion, 27th Marine Regiment, 5th Marine Division, sets his machine guns to support the platoon's attack on a series of Japanese trenches and fortified positions, then moves to attack the enemy alone, throwing demolition charges and white phosphorus grenades into the emplacements, then jumping into a trench in pursuit of fleeing enemy soldiers. Picking up a discarded rifle, he kills five of the enemy and then obtains more demolition charges to continue the attack. With the assistance of another marine, Julian attacks two cave positions and uses a bazooka to destroy another pillbox. He is mortally wounded in his final attack. For his extraordinary fighting skill, great courage, and inspiring leadership, Sergeant Julian will be awarded the Congressional Medal of Honor.

## March 10

**ALEUTIANS:** Eleventh Air Force sends five B-24 Liberators to bomb targets on Shimushu and Paramushiru Islands in the Kuriles. The bombers use radar to mark bomb release points.

**CBI:** In China, Fourteenth Air Force sends 32 B-24 Liberators to attack railyards while P-40s and P-51 Mustangs attack rail and river traffic, logistics storage facilities, troops, and airfields.

In Burma, Tenth Air Force sends P-47 Thunderbolts to support the British 36th Division. Other P-47s and P-38 Lightnings attack road traffic, troop concentrations, logistics storage sites, and a truck park.

**ETO:** First Army and Third Army link along the Rhine, accomplishing General Eisenhower's objective to clear German forces from the west bank of the Rhine River. Third Army collects another 12,000 prisoners. The 6th Army Group commander, Lieutenant General Jacob L. Devers, orders Seventh Army (VI Corps, XV Corps, and XXI Corps), commanded by Major General Alexander M. Patch, to attack toward Kaiserslautern and seize a bridgehead near Worms. The French First Army is ordered to cover the Rhine River from Strasbourg to the Swiss border.

The 51st and 291st Combat Engineer Battalions begin construction of two pontoon bridges at Remagen. Despite German artillery fire and heavy casualties, the engineers complete the heavy pontoon bridges in 29.5 hours.

Eighth Air Force sends more than 1,300 B-17s and B-24 Liberators escorted by over 600 P-47 Thunderbolts and P-51 Mustangs to bomb road and rail bridges, marshaling yards, and airfields. The bombers use radar to mark the bomb release point. A total of 81 bombers are damaged. Aircrews report two confirmed kills and one possible. Aircrew casualties are three wounded. Fighter pilots report two confirmed kills and one possible in the air. Two fighters are lost and one is damaged.

Twelve B-17s conduct screening missions to jam German radio interception efforts and employ countermeasures against German radar sites.

During the night 12 B-24s drop leaflets over France, Germany, and the Netherlands. A total of 13 B-24s bomb Munster during the night.

Ninth Air Force sends nearly 400 A-20 Havocs, A-26 Invaders, and B-26 Marauders to attack communication centers and marshaling yards. P-47 and P-38 fighters support the 9th Infantry Division, the 4th Armored Division, and XX and XVI Corps.

**MEDITERRANEAN:** Fifteenth Air Force sends nearly 200 B-17s and B-24 Liberators escorted by P-38 Lightnings and P-51 Mustangs to bomb a railroad bridge and marshaling yards in Italy.

**ITALY:** Twelfth Air Force B-25 Mitchells bomb bridges. A-20 Havocs and P-47 Thunderbolts attack bridges, vehicles, logistics storage sites, and ammunition storage areas in the Po River valley. During the night A-20s attack bridges in the Po River Valley.

**SOUTHWEST PACIFIC AREA:** In the Eighth Army area, Naval Task Group 78.1 (Rear Admiral Forrest B. Royal) lands the 162nd and 163rd Infantry Regiments of the 41st Infantry Division, near Zamboanga City on the island of Mindanao. Japanese shore batteries sink two LSTs and two LCIs.

In the Philippines, Far East Air Force B-24 Liberators and B-25 Mitchells bomb towns and airfields on Mindanao. On Luzon, B-24s bomb an airfield, while B-25s and A-20 Havocs support guerrillas and bomb enemy positions. P-38 Lightnings and P-47 Thunderbolts attack Japanese troop concentrations near Fort Stotsenburg and other locations on Luzon.

Fifth Air Force B-25 Mitchells attack and sink a Japanese army tanker off the southern coast of French Indochina.

FEAF B-24 Liberators bomb airfields in Borneo.

Private First Class Thomas E. Atkins is a member of a platoon in A Company, 127th Infantry Regiment, 32nd Infantry Division, occupying a defensive position on a high hill near Villa Verde Trail, Luzon. In the early morning hours the Japanese conduct a heavy counterattack. Private First Class Atkins is wounded but maintains his position and returns fire. He refuses medical attention and stays at his position, repelling a number of attacks over the next four hours. Firing over 400 rounds and using three rifles until they no longer function, he withdraws during a lull to pick up another rifle and ammunition. As unit medics begin first aid, he kills a Japanese soldier within the perimeter, then sees a group of Japanese moving to outflank the platoon's position. Lying on a litter, Private First Class Atkins picks up his rifle and drives the enemy off with well-aimed and accurate fire. His exceptional courage and skill in performing his duties in the face of overwhelming odds and painful wounds will win Atkins the Medal of Honor.

**PACIFIC:** Twentieth Air Force sends B-29s to bomb the marshaling yard at Kuala Lumpur in Malaya.

Another raid on Tokyo is conducted by 279 B-29 Superfortresses from the XXI Bomber Command's 73rd, 313th, and 314th Bombardment Wings (Very Heavy) based on Guam Island, Tinian, and Saipan. The bombers hit the urban area with incendiaries in the hours before dawn. This attack destroys over 267,000 buildings and kills or injures nearly 125,000 people (nearly 84,000 are reported killed)—the highest loss of life of any aerial bombardment of World War II. Fourteen B-29s are lost.

U.S. submarine *Kete* attacks a Japanese convoy north of Okinawa, sinking a transport and two cargo ships.

**CENTRAL PACIFIC:** Seventh Air Force sends 10 B-24 Liberators from Guam to bomb the airfield on Chichi Jima. Three B-24s bomb Marcus Island. A total of 23 B-24s from Angaur Island bomb an airfield on Mindanao Island in the Philippines. During the night nine B-24s fly individual snooper missions on Chichi Jima.

**CENTRAL PACIFIC, IWO JIMA:** The 4th Marine Division succeeds in clearing the Meatgrinder and capturing Turkey Knob and Minami Village. Units begin advancing with little enemy contact. The 5th Marine Division advancing along the coast reaches the Japanese defenses at Death Valley, a series of sharp ravines and ridges filled with tunnels, about 500 yards south of Kitano Point. This heavily defended position stops the marine advance. The 3rd Marine Division reduces Cushman's Pocket. Most of the marines are too battle weary to function effectively. A large number of the men in the division are now untrained replacements.

## March 11

**CBI:** Fourteenth Air Force B-24 Liberators attack shipping targets in the Gulf of Tonkin and the South China Sea. Aircrews report one cargo ship sunk and another damaged. P-40s and P-51 Mustangs attack rail and river traffic. In French Indochina, B-25 Mitchells attack bridges and rail cars.

In Burma, Tenth Air Force sends 14 B-25 Mitchells to bomb vehicles, logistics storage sites, ammunition storage areas, and troops. P-47 Thunderbolts and P-38 Lightnings attack road traffic and targets of opportunity.

**ETO:** Eighth Air Force sends more than 1,200 B-17s and B-24 Liberators escorted by over 800 P-47 Thunderbolts and P-51 Mustangs to bomb the U-boat yards at Kiel and Bremen and the shipyard and refinery area at Hamburg, Germany. The bombers use radar to mark bomb release points over the targets. One B-17 is lost and 52 are damaged. Four P-51s are lost. Six B-17s conduct screening missions to jam German radio interception efforts and employ countermeasures against German radar sites.

During the night 11 B-24s drop leaflets over Germany and the Netherlands.

Ninth Air Force sends nearly 700 A-20 Havocs, A-26 Invaders, and B-26 Marauders to attack communication centers, ammunition plants, airfields, and marshaling yards. P-47 and P-38 fighters support the 9th Infantry Division at the Remagen bridgehead and support XX Corps.

Navy LCVPs, part of Task Group 122.5.1, support army engineers in laying a pontoon bridge at the Remagen bridgehead.

Eighth Air Force bombers sink German submarines *U-2515* and *U-2530* during a raid on Hamburg. A Navy PB4Y-1 Privateer sinks German submarine *U-681* southwest of England in the Celtic Sea.

**ITALY:** Twelfth Air Force B-25 Mitchells and B-26 Marauders bomb bridges in Italy and Austria. A-20 Havocs and P-47 Thunderbolts of the XXII Tactical Air Command attack rail lines, logistics storage sites, and ammunition storage areas in the Po River valley. During the night A-20s attack river crossing sites, airfields, and roads in the Po River valley.

**SOUTHWEST PACIFIC AREA:** General MacArthur orders Eighth Army to capture the island of Mindanao, even as the 41st Infantry Division continues operations on the Zamboanga Peninsula. The island has 43,000 Japanese troops, most of which are near Davao City. They lack supplies and have been harried by a 24,000-man guerrilla force run by Colonel Wendell W. Fertig, an American who escaped from Bataan in 1942. Lieutenant General Eichelberger and his staff develop a plan to land at Illana Bay and advance eastward.

In the Philippines, Far East Air Force B-24 Liberators and B-25 Mitchells bomb airfields, Japanese positions, and support PT boat operations on Mindanao.

**SOUTHWEST PACIFIC AREA, LUZON:** The 2nd Cavalry Brigade of the 1st Cavalry Division captures Antipolo. The 1st Cavalry suffers nearly 400 casualties during the 19 days of combat to capture the position.

FEAF B-24 Liberators, A-20 Havocs, P-38 Lightnings, and P-47 Thunderbolts support ground forces, attack logistics storage sites, and hit targets of opportunity.

B-24s and P-47s attack towns on Formosa.

**PACIFIC:** Twentieth Air Force sends more than 300 B-29s to bomb the urban area of Nagoya, Japan, with incendiaries. One B-29 is lost.

U.S. submarine *Segundo* torpedoes and sinks a Japanese cargo ship off southern Korea.

**CENTRAL PACIFIC:** Seventh Air Force sends 11 B-24 Liberators from Guam to bomb the airfield on Chichi Jima. P-51 Mustangs from Iwo Jima attack the airfields on Chichi Jima and Haha Jima. During the night eight B-24s fly individual harassment raids on Chichi Jima.

Japanese aircraft from Kanoya, Japan, attack the U.S. fleet anchorage at Ulithi, damaging the carrier USS *Randolph*. American casualties are 25 killed and 106 wounded.

### March 12

**CBI:** Fourteenth Air Force sends four B-25 Mitchells to bomb the Song Rang bridge in French Indochina. Aircrews report the bridge is destroyed.

In Burma, Tenth Air Force sends 13 B-25 Mitchells and 35 P-47 Thunderbolts to attack troop concentrations, logistics sites, vehicles, and antiaircraft guns. P-47 Thunderbolts attack road traffic during several sweeps.

**ETO:** Eighth Air Force sends more than 1,300 B-17s and B-24 Liberators escorted by nearly 800 P-47 Thunderbolts and P-51 Mustangs to bomb marshaling yards in Germany. The bombers use radar-equipped Pathfinder bombers or radar signal intercepts to mark bomb release points over the targets. One B-17 is lost and 10 are damaged. Aircrews report four confirmed kills and one possible. Aircrew casualties are three wounded and 10 missing. Fighter pilots report four confirmed kills and one possible in the air. Four P-51s are lost. Three pilots are reported missing.

During the night 11 B-24s drop leaflets over Germany and the Netherlands. Ten B-24s fly a Carpetbagger mission.

Ninth Air Force sends A-20 Havocs, A-26 Invaders, and B-26 Marauders to attack ammunition production facilities and marshaling yards. P-47 and P-38 fighters support the 9th Infantry Division and the XX Corps.

**MEDITERRANEAN:** Fifteenth Air Force sends nearly 800 B-17s and B-24 Liberators escorted by P-38 Lightnings and P-51 Mustangs to bomb oil refineries and marshaling yards in Austria.

**ITALY:** Twelfth Air Force B-25 Mitchells bomb rail bridges. A-20 Havocs and P-47 Thunderbolts attack rail lines and bridges. During the night A-20s attack roads and motor transport in the Po River Valley.

**SOUTHWEST PACIFIC AREA:** FEAF B-24s, with P-38 escort, attack targets on Formosa. P-51s also attack power plants on Formosa. In the Philippines, Far East Air Force B-24 Liberators bomb Mindanao Island.

**SOUTHWEST PACIFIC AREA, LUZON:** The two RCTs of the 43rd Infantry Division relieve the 1st Cavalry Division. The 6th and the 43rd Infantry Divisions continue the attack eastward, clearing Japanese positions. A counterattack by several battalions of the Shimbu Group fails to stop the 6th Infantry Division's attack.

B-24 Liberators bomb Japanese troops; B-25 Mitchells attack logistics storage areas and Japa-

Sherman tanks support infantry on Luzon in the Philippines.

nese troops, and A-20 Havocs, P-38 Lightnings, and P-47 Thunderbolts support ground forces.

The B-24s of the 33rd Bombardment Squadron (Heavy), 22nd Bombardment Group (Heavy), redeploy from Samar Island to Clark Field, Luzon.

**PACIFIC:** Twentieth Air Force sends 49 B-29 Superfortresses to attack oil storage facilities in Malaya and Sumatra. Only 44 hit their primary targets. Aircrews report one possible kill. Aircrews report negligible results.

**CENTRAL PACIFIC:** Seventh Air Force sends 13 B-24 Liberators to bomb the airfield on Chichi Jima. A total of 16 P-51 Mustangs bomb Haha Jima. B-24s based at Angaur Island bomb a logistics storage area on Mindanao in the Philippines. During the night eight B-24s fly individual harassment raids on Chichi Jima.

**NEW GUINEA:** The C-47s of the 6th Troop Carrier Squadron, 374th Troop Carrier Group, redeploy from Biak to Leyte Island. The 69th Bombardment Squadron (Medium), 42nd Bombardment Group (Medium), redeploys its B-25s from Sansapor, New Guinea, to Palawan Island in the Philippines. The 69th Bombardment Squadron (Medium) operates from Morotai Island.

## March 13

**CBI:** Fourteenth Air Force sends seven B-24 Liberators over the Gulf of Tonkin and the South China Sea to attack shipping. Aircrews report a large junk and one cargo ship are sunk. P-40s, P-38 Lightnings, and P-51 Mustangs attack a logistics storage site.

In Burma, Tenth Air Force sends 12 B-25 Mitchells to attack troop concentrations, logistics sites, and gun positions. P-47 Thunderbolts support the Chinese 50th Division, P-38 Lightnings attack road targets, and P-47s support the British 36th Division.

**ETO:** General Eisenhower orders General Omar N. Bradley to limit his 12th Army Group's bridgehead over the Rhine to no more than 10 miles deep and 25 miles wide. He does this in order that Field Marshal Bernard L. Montgomery's 21st Army Group will remain the main effort as it prepares to cross the Rhine. Eisenhower's offensive plans, which have all centered on the assumption that Montgomery's 21st Army Group will make the Rhine crossing first, were thrown askew when an intact bridge was found over the Rhine. With 12th Army Group now in the lead, he decides to adhere to the broad-front approach. Rather than fully exploit the opportunity presented, he limits Bradley in order for Montgomery to catch up. Bradley controls the bridgehead with two divisions of VII Corps and three divisions of III Corps.

The XX Corps of Third Army attacks from its bridgehead at Trier with three infantry divisions.

Eighth Air Force sends 16 P-51 Mustangs to conduct an aircraft sweep in the area from Remagen to Koblenz in Germany. Fighter pilots report no activity.

Ninth Air Force sends more than 450 A-20 Havocs, A-26 Invaders, and B-26 Marauders to attack rail targets, airfields, and marshaling yards. P-47 and P-38 fighters support the 9th Infantry Division and the XX Corps.

The headquarters of the 61st Troop Carrier Group and the 14th and 15th Troop Carrier Squadrons, IX Troop Carrier Command, redeploy from England to France with C-47s.

**MEDITERRANEAN:** Fifteenth Air Force sends more than 500 B-17s and B-24 Liberators escorted by over 280 P-38 Lightnings and P-51 Mustangs to bomb marshaling yards in Germany. P-51s on a strafing mission attack rail traffic in Germany and Austria.

**ITALY:** Twelfth Air Force B-25 Mitchells bomb rail bridges. A-20 Havocs and P-47 Thunderbolts attack rail lines, bridges, antiaircraft positions, logistics storage sites, and support Fifth Army ground forces. During the night A-20s attack rail lines, ammunition storage sites, and motor transport in the Po River valley.

**SOUTHWEST PACIFIC AREA:** In the Eighth Army area the 162nd and 163rd Infantry Regiments of the 41st Infantry Division meet strong Japanese resistance outside of Zamboanga City. The enemy is dug in along a rugged line of hills overlooking the city.

On Mindanao, Far East Air Force B-24 Liberators attack targets, and B-25 Mitchells support ground operations. B-25s, A-20 Havocs, and P-38 Lightning fighters support ground forces in the Cagayan Valley on Luzon Island.

B-25 Mitchells and P-51s attack targets on Hainan Island, China. B-24s attack targets on Formosa. The 408th Bombardment Squadron (Heavy), 22nd Bombardment Group (Heavy), redeploys its B-24s from Samar Island to Clark Field, Luzon.

Fifth Air Force B-24 Liberators sink a Japanese coast defense vessel and a transport in the South China Sea.

**PACIFIC:** Twentieth Air Force sends 301 B-29 Superfortresses to conduct an incendiary attack on the urban area of Osaka, Japan, just after midnight. Of the 274 that hit the primary target, all use radar to identify the bomb release points. The raid destroys eight square miles of the city and kills nearly 4,000 people. Approximately 9,000 more are injured or missing. Aircrews report one confirmed kill and two B-29s lost.

**CENTRAL PACIFIC:** Seventh Air Force sends six B-24 Liberators from Guam Island to attack Woleai Atoll. Another 10 B-24s bomb the airfield on Chichi Jima. A total of 24 B-24s from Angaur Island bomb a logistics storage area on Mindanao Island in the Philippines. During the night eight B-24s fly individual harassment raids on Chichi Jima.

## March 14

**CBI:** The Mars Task Force is airlifted to China with a new mission to train Chinese troops.

In China, Fourteenth Air Force sends three B-24 Liberators to attack shipping in the South China Sea. Aircrews report one cargo ship sunk. P-40s and P-51 Mustangs attack rail and river traffic.

In Burma, Tenth Air Force sends 11 B-25 Mitchells to bomb troops and vehicles. P-47 Thunderbolts attack troop concentrations, vehicles, and logistics storage sites.

**ETO:** Eighth Air Force sends more than 1,200 B-17s and B-24 Liberators, escorted by more than 800 P-47 Thunderbolts and P-51 Mustangs, to bomb oil refineries, munitions production facilities, road and rail bridges, marshaling yards, and airfields. The bombers use visual means and radar to identify the bomb release points. A total of three bombers are lost and 249 damaged. Aircrew casualties are three killed, 12 wounded, and 28 missing. Fighter pilots report four confirmed kills and one possible in the air. One fighter is lost and two damaged. The pilot is reported missing.

P-51s fly a sweep and report 11 confirmed kills. Other P-51s fly a sweep over the Remagen bridgehead. One P-51 is lost and one damaged. The pilot is reported missing. P-51s on a scouting mission report one confirmed kill in the air.

Six B-17s conduct screening missions to jam German radio interception efforts and employ countermeasures against German radar sites.

A total of seven B-24s bomb the Wiesbaden marshaling yard during the night using a radar-equipped Pathfinder bomber to mark bomb release points.

Ninth Air Force sends more than 350 A-20 Havocs, A-26 Invaders, and B-26 Marauders to attack airfields, rail lines, and targets of opportunity. P-47 and P-38 fighters support XII Corps and XX Corps.

**MEDITERRANEAN:** Fifteenth Air Force sends more than 600 B-17s and B-24 Liberators escorted by P-38 Lightnings and P-51 Mustangs to bomb oil refineries and marshaling yards in Hungary, Austria, and Yugoslavia. P-38s attack bridges and rail traffic in Yugoslavia and rail traffic in Austria. B-17s and B-24s drop supplies to Partisans in northern Italy and Yugoslavia.

**ITALY:** Twelfth Air Force B-25 Mitchells bomb rail bridges. A-20 Havocs and P-47 Thunderbolts attack roads, vehicles, rail traffic, logistics storage sites, and ammunition storage areas in northern Italy. During the night A-20s attack river crossing sites and targets of opportunity in the Po River valley.

**SOUTHWEST PACIFIC AREA:** FEAF B-24s bomb a naval base on Formosa. B-25 Mitchells conduct armed reconnaissance and a shipping sweep along the China coast.

In the Philippines, Far East Air Force B-24 Liberators and B-25 Mitchells attack a number of targets, including antiaircraft positions, villages, and docks on Mindanao.

**SOUTHWEST PACIFIC AREA, LUZON:** Major General Edwin D. Patrick, commander of the 6th Infantry Division, is mortally wounded on the front lines along with one of his regimental commanders. The Shimbu defenses are shattered after attacks by the 43rd and 6th Infantry Divisions. Japanese casualties in this month-long battle are estimated at over 3,300. U.S. losses are over 1,300 killed and wounded.

The XI Corps takes over the mission to capture the dams and destroy the Shimbu Group.

A-20 Havocs, P-38 Lightnings, and P-47 Thunderbolts attack installations and defensive positions throughout Luzon.

The 2nd Bombardment Squadron (Heavy), 22nd Bombardment Group (Heavy), redeploys its B-24s from Samar Island to Clark Field on Luzon.

**PACIFIC:** U.S. submarine *Trepang* torpedoes and sinks a Japanese guardboat off eastern Honshu, Japan.

Two U.S. destroyers sink two Japanese guardboats off the Bonins.

**CENTRAL PACIFIC:** Seventh Air Force sends 11 B-24 Liberators from Guam to bomb the airfield on Chichi Jima. A total of 25 B-24s based at Angaur Island bomb a logistics storage area on Mindanao Island in the Philippines. P-51 Mustangs from Iwo

Jima attack targets on both Haha Jima and Chichi Jima. During the night five B-24s fly individual harassment raids on Chichi Jima.

**CENTRAL PACIFIC, IWO JIMA:** Major General Harry Schmidt, V Amphibious Corps commander, leads a formal flag raising ceremony on the island.

**NEW GUINEA:** U.S. submarine *Bream* torpedoes and sinks a Japanese auxiliary submarine chaser in the Java Sea. USS *Rock* lands supplies on Lombok Island, Netherlands East Indies.

### March 15

**ALEUTIANS:** Naval Task Force 92, commanded by Rear Admiral John L. McCrea, consisting of three light cruisers and seven destroyers, bombards Japanese installations on Matsuwa, Kuriles.

**CBI:** Fourteenth Air Force sends four B-24 Liberators to attack shipping in the South China Sea. Aircrews report one cargo ship sunk. P-51 Mustangs attack locomotives.

In Burma, Tenth Air Force sends 30 P-47 Thunderbolts to support elements of the Chinese 50th Division while 32 P-38 Lightnings conduct a sweep of roads.

**ETO:** Operation Undertone begins. The XX Corps of Third Army supports an attack by VI and XV Corps of Seventh Army to drive the last German defenders from the west bank of the Rhine River in the Saar area. The XXI Corps attacks to capture Saarbrücken.

The XII Corps of Third Army sends the 4th Armored Division across its bridgehead on the Moselle River.

German fighter aircraft conduct nearly continuous attacks against the Ludendorff Bridge at Remagen. Sixteen German fighters are lost to concentrated antiaircraft fire.

Eighth Air Force sends more than 1,350 B-17s and B-24 Liberators, escorted by over 800 P-47 Thunderbolts and P-51 Mustangs, to bomb a German army headquarters near Berlin and marshaling yards. A total of nine bombers are lost and 342 damaged. Aircrews report one confirmed kill. Aircrew casualties are four killed, 16 wounded, and 87 missing. Fighter pilots report one confirmed kill. Four fighters are lost, and the pilots are reported missing.

Six B-17s conduct screening missions to jam German radio interception efforts and employ countermeasures against German radar sites.

A total of 14 B-24s bomb the rail station at Munster during the night using a radar-equipped Pathfinder bomber to mark the bomb release point.

Ninth Air Force sends A-20 Havocs, A-26 Invaders, and B-26 Marauders to attack communication centers, railroad bridges, antiaircraft positions, and marshaling yards. P-47 and P-38 fighters support XII Corps and XX Corps.

**MEDITERRANEAN:** Fifteenth Air Force sends more than 600 B-17s and B-24 Liberators escorted by P-38 Lightnings and P-51 Mustangs to bomb oil refineries in Germany and Czechoslovakia and oil refineries and marshaling yards in Austria. Bombers airdrop supplies into northern Italy and Yugoslavia.

**ITALY:** Twelfth Air Force B-25 Mitchells bomb rail bridges. A-20 Havocs and P-47 Thunderbolts of the XXII Tactical Air Command attack rail lines, logistics storage sites, and ammunition storage areas. During the night A-20s attack river crossing sites.

**SOUTHWEST PACIFIC AREA:** On Mindanao Island, FEAF B-24 Liberators and B-25 Mitchells attack Japanese troops and gun positions. B-24s bomb Lahug on Cebu Island.

On Formosa, P-47s conduct dive-bomb attacks on power installations.

**SOUTHWEST PACIFIC AREA, LUZON:** In the XIV Corps area the 11th Airborne and the 158th RCT begin clearing Japanese forces from the Lake Taal area. Operational control of the 6th Infantry Division and the 112th RCT passes from XIV Corps to XI Corps. The 37th Infantry Division occupies Manila under the operational control of Sixth Army. The XIV Corps retains the 1st Cavalry Division and well as the 11th Airborne and the 158th RCT.

The XI Corps continues the attack on the Shimbu Group with the 38th and 43rd Infantry Divisions.

In the I Corps area the 33rd Infantry Division drives the Japanese from the high ground overlooking the Rosario-Pozorrubio Road and advances north toward Baguio and Bauang. I Corps covers the north of Luzon and has protected the flank of XIV Corps and kept the Japanese on the defensive. XI Corps has control of the center of Luzon and XIV Corps has the southern part of Luzon. The Japanese have been divided into two groups, one occupying the mountain in the northeast and the other in the mountains east of Manila. The number of Japanese killed is over 85,000 since the beginning of the campaign on January 9. During this same period Sixth Army has lost 18,579 casualties.

Far East Air Force B-24 Liberators, A-20 Havocs, and P-38 Lightnings attack a Japanese headquarters; P-47 Thunderbolts attack a bridge and enemy concentrations in the Balete Pass and Japanese defenses near Fort Stotsenburg; A-20s and P-47s attack gun positions and occupied areas.

The headquarters of the 22nd Bombardment Group (Heavy) and the B-24s of the 19th Bombardment Squadron (Heavy) redeploy from Samar Island to Clark Field, Luzon. The 403rd Bombardment Squadron (Heavy), 43rd Bombardment Group (Heavy), also redeploys B-24s from Leyte to Clark Field.

**CENTRAL PACIFIC:** Seventh Air Force sends eight B-24 Liberators from Guam to bomb the airfield on Chichi Jima. During the night three B-24s conduct individual snooper missions on Chichi Jima.

**NEW GUINEA:** The 100th Bombardment Squadron (Medium), 42nd Bombardment Group (Medium), redeploys its B-25 Mitchells from Sansapor, New Guinea, to Palawan Island in the Philippines.

U.S. submarine *Bream* is damaged by depth charges off North Borneo and is forced to terminate her patrol.

## March 16

**ALEUTIANS:** Eleventh Air Force sends two B-24 Liberators on a photo mission to Matsuwa Island in the Kuriles. A navigational error puts the bombers 130 miles south of the island. This represents the deepest penetration of the Japanese home islands up to this time. After conducting their photo mission, the bombers attack Shimushiru Island on the return flight.

**CBI:** In China, Fourteenth Air Force sends 32 B-24 Liberators, escorted by 10 P-51 Mustangs, to attack railroad yards.

In Burma, Tenth Air Force sends 12 B-25 Mitchells to bomb a fuel storage site and troops. P-47 Thunderbolts support the Chinese 50th Division, and P-38 Lightnings support the British 36th Division. Other P-38s also attack artillery positions and sweep roads.

**ETO:** During the night Eighth Air Force sends 12 B-24 Liberators to drop leaflets in Germany and the Netherlands, while 20 B-24s fly Carpetbagger missions.

Ninth Air Force sends more than 280 A-20 Havocs, A-26 Invaders, and B-26 Marauders to attack communication centers, rail junctions, and marshaling yards. P-47 and P-38 fighters support XII Corps, XX Corps, and VIII Corps.

**MEDITERRANEAN:** Fifteenth Air Force sends more than 700 B-17s and B-24 Liberators escorted by P-38 Lightnings and P-51 Mustangs to bomb oil refineries and marshaling yards in Austria and marshaling yards in Yugoslavia. P-51s strafe rail lines in Germany and Austria.

Bombers conduct supply drops in northern Italy and Yugoslavia.

**ITALY:** Twelfth Air Force B-25 Mitchells bomb a rail bridge in Austria. B-25s also attack a power plant and bridges in Italy. During the night A-20s attack bridges and targets of opportunity in the Po River valley.

**SOUTHWEST PACIFIC AREA:** On Luzon Island in the Philippines, Far East Air Force A-20s and B-24 Liberators bomb Japanese installations; P-51 Mustangs attack vehicles and logistics support sites. B-24s bomb airfields on Negros Island and bomb targets marked by Filipino guerrillas on Cebu Island. B-25 Mitchells bomb the airfield on Mindanao Island.

The headquarters of the 43rd Bombardment Group (Heavy) and the B-24s of the 65th Bombardment Squadron (Heavy) redeploy from Leyte to Clark Field, Luzon.

On Formosa, B-24s bomb towns, airfields, and the naval airbase.

FEAF B-25 Mitchells attack airfields in Borneo.

**PACIFIC:** Twentieth Air Force sends 331 B-29s of the XXI Bomber Command to conduct an incendiary bombing raid on Kobe, Japan. The 307 Superfortresses that hit the primary target in the hours just before dawn leave about 20 percent of the city destroyed. More than 242,000 people are without shelter and another 13,900 are dead or injured. Although aircrews report over 300 Japanese aircraft making attacks, only one enemy fighter is reported as a confirmed kill. Three B-29s are lost, but none to fighter attacks.

**CENTRAL PACIFIC:** Seventh Air Force sends 13 B-24 Liberators from Guam to bomb the airfield on Chichi Jima. A total of 16 P-51 Mustangs based at Iwo Jima bomb and strafe targets on Chichi Jima. During the night five B-24s fly individual harassment raids on Chichi Jima.

**CENTRAL PACIFIC, IWO JIMA:** The 3rd Marine Division captures Cushman's Pocket and advances against weakening resistance. The 4th Marine Division clears enemy positions in its area. The 5th Marine Division continues to be held up at Death Valley. About 90 percent of the island is under American control. Iwo Jima is declared secure.

Pharmacist's Mate First Class Francis J. Pierce is with 2nd Battalion, 24th Marine Regiment, 4th Marine Division, providing medical support to the marines. Repeatedly he risks his life to recover and evacuate wounded on Iwo Jima. He protects wounded men with his own body as he renders aid and carries wounded men on his back through deadly fire. Without hesitation, Pierce takes enormous risks to save others. While leading a combat patrol to locate a Japanese sniper position, he is wounded but refuses any assistance, as he concentrates on assisting a casualty. For his gallant and selfless conduct and extraordinary dedication to duty, Pharmacist's Mate First Class Pierce will receive the Medal of Honor.

## March 17

**ALEUTIANS:** Eleventh Air Force sends two B-24 Liberators to conduct bombing and photo missions over the airfield on Matsuwa Island in the Kuriles.

**CBI:** In China, a Fourteenth Air Force B-25 Mitchell and 12 P-51 Mustangs damage 21 locomotives and a river launch near Peking (Beijing).

In Burma, Tenth Air Force sends 12 B-25 Mitchells to bomb troops and logistics sites. P-47 Thunderbolts support the British 36th Division while other P-47s and P-38 Lightnings attack Japanese troops, logistics storage sites, tanks, and trucks.

**ETO:** General Eisenhower meets with Lieutenant General Jacob L. Devers, 6th Army Group commander, Lieutenant General George S. Patton, Jr., of Third Army, and Lieutenant General Alexander M. Patch, commander of Seventh Army. Operation Undertone is changed to an effort to trap German forces between the Third and Seventh Armies along the Rhine.

Major General James A. Van Fleet takes command of III Corps from Major General Millikin. The VII Corps of First Army attacks with one division to expand the Remagen bridgehead. The damaged Ludendorff railroad bridge collapses after days of constant traffic, killing 28 American engineers working on the bridge. Since March 12, two pontoon bridges have been supporting most of the river traffic. The Germans throw the equivalent of 10 divisions against the bridgehead and send everything, including V-2 rockets, jet fighter aircraft, swimmers with demolitions, artillery fire, and mines in an effort to destroy the bridge.

LCVPs of Naval Task Group 122.5.1 ferry 2,500 soldiers across the Rhine River at Remagen.

Eighth Air Force sends more than 1,300 B-17s and B-24 Liberators escorted by 800 P-51 Mustangs to bomb oil refineries, munitions and tank production facilities, and marshaling yards. The bombers use both radar-equipped Pathfinder bombers and radar signal intercepts to mark bomb release points over the targets. A total of five bombers are lost and 67 damaged. Aircrew casualties are one killed, one wounded, and 44 missing. Two fighters are lost, and the pilots are reported missing.

Six B-24s conduct screening missions to jam German radio interception efforts and employ countermeasures against German radar sites.

During the night nine B-24s drop leaflets over Germany, France, and the Netherlands.

Ninth Air Force sends more than 650 A-20 Havocs, A-26 Invaders, and B-26 Marauders to attack communication centers, an ordnance depot, and marshaling yards. P-47 and P-38 fighters support III Corps and XX Corps.

**MEDITERRANEAN:** Fifteenth Air Force B-24 Liberators airdrop supplies to Partisans in northern Italy.

**ITALY:** Twelfth Air Force B-25 Mitchells bomb rail bridges. A-20 Havocs and P-47 Thunderbolts attack rail lines, bridges, vehicles, logistics storage sites, and ammunition storage areas in the Po River valley. During the night A-20s and B-26 Marauders attack river crossing sites, bridges, and motor transport in the Po River Valley.

**SOUTHWEST PACIFIC AREA:** In the Philippines, Far East Air Force B-25 Mitchells, A-20 Havocs, P-47 Thunderbolts, and P-38 Lightnings support ground forces on Luzon. B-24s bomb Panay Island beaches, bomb Japanese troops on Mindanao Island, and hit airfields on Negros Island. B-24s also bomb airfields on Formosa.

The headquarters of the 317th Troop Carrier Group redeploys from Leyte to Clark Field on Luzon.

U.S. submarine *Sealion* torpedoes and sinks a Thai oiler in the Straits of Malacca.

**PACIFIC:** Twentieth Air Force sends 77 B-29 Superfortresses to attack a logistics storage area at Rangoon.

U.S. submarine *Spot* attacks a Japanese convoy, sinking a cargo vessel and damaging a cargo ship off Yushiyama Island in the East China Sea, near Formosa. USS *Spot* is damaged by gunfire.

**CENTRAL PACIFIC:** Seventh Air Force sends 11 B-24 Liberators from Guam to bomb the airfield on Chichi Jima. During the night five B-24s fly individual harassment raids on Chichi Jima.

The headquarters of the 30th Bombardment Group (Heavy) and B-24s of the 27th, 30th, and 819th Bombardment Squadrons (Heavy) redeploy from Saipan Island to Wheeler Field, Hawaii.

**NEW GUINEA:** The B-24 Liberators of the 31st Bombardment Squadron (Heavy), 7th Bombardment Group (Heavy), redeploy from Morotai Island to Samar Island in the Philippines.

## March 18

**CBI:** In China, Fourteenth Air Force sends six B-24 Liberators to conduct a sweep of the Gulf of Tonkin and South China Sea. Aircrews report one cargo ship sunk.

In Burma, Tenth Air Force sends 11 B-25 Mitchells and P-47 Thunderbolts to attack troop concentrations and logistics storage sites. Other P-47s support the British 50th Division.

**ATLANTIC:** In the northwest Atlantic three U.S. destroyer escorts sink German submarine *U-866*.

**ETO:** Eighth Air Force sends more than 1,300 B-17s and B-24 Liberators escorted by over 700 P-47 Thunderbolts and P-51 Mustangs to bomb rail targets and tank production facilities in Berlin. The bombers use visual methods or radar signal intercepts to mark bomb release points over the targets. A total of 13 bombers are lost and 729 damaged. Aircrews report 21 confirmed kills, one probable, and five possibles. The Germans attack the bomber formations with a large number of Me-262 jet aircraft. Aircrew casualties are three killed, 31 wounded, and 139 missing. Fighter pilots report 14 confirmed kills and four possibles. Six fighters are lost.

During the night 10 B-24s drop leaflets over France, Germany, and the Netherlands.

Ninth Air Force sends more than 660 A-20 Havocs, A-26 Invaders, and B-26 Marauders to attack communication centers and marshaling yards. P-47 and P-38 fighters support III Corps, XII Corps, and XX Corps.

First Lieutenant Jack L. Treadwell commands F Company, 180th Infantry Regiment, 45th Infantry Division, and has been stopped for several hours before a German defensive position on the Siegfried Line near Nieder-Wurzbach, Germany. All attacks have been unsuccessful until Lieutenant Treadwell, carrying a Thompson submachine gun and hand grenades, moves forward alone. With no cover to protect him, Treadwell runs toward the first pillbox and throws grenades, then, reaching a concrete emplacement, he fires into the firing port. Four Germans quickly surrender. Ignoring the enemy fire directed at him, he attacks a second emplacement in the same manner, eliminating it. He then runs across the crest of the hill to a third pillbox and attacks it and eliminates it. Again and again Treadwell moves along, taking out German pillboxes until the men of Company F rise and assault the remaining defenses and capture the hill. For his courage in facing nearly impossible odds and by his extraordinary example of leadership and initiative, First Lieutenant Treadwell will receive the nation's highest award for valor, the Medal of Honor.

**MEDITERRANEAN:** Fifteenth Air Force P-38 Lightnings attack railroad bridges and rail lines in Yugoslavia.

**ITALY:** Twelfth Air Force B-25 Mitchells bomb rail bridges. A-20 Havocs and P-47 Thunderbolts attack ammunition storage areas, rail lines, roads, and support Fifth Army ground forces south of Bologna. Fighter pilots report 14 locomotives destroyed during an attack on the Novara marshaling yard. During the night A-20s and A-26 Invaders attack river crossing sites in the Po River valley.

**SOUTHWEST PACIFIC AREA:** In the Eighth Army area Naval Task Group 78.3, commanded by Rear Admiral Arthur D. Struble, lands the 185th Infantry Regiment of the 40th Infantry Division on Panay Island in the Visayan Sea. A light cruiser and three destroyers of Task Unit 74.2.2 provide naval gunfire support. Supported by a heavy air and naval bombardment, the infantrymen are met upon landing by a large force of Filipino guerrillas. The Americans attack and clear the small garrison at Iloilo, leaving the 2nd Battalion of the 160th Infantry Regiment and the guerrillas to mop up the remaining troops. Base construction and an airfield are started in anticipation of using the island as a training and support base for troops arriving for the invasion of Japan.

In the Philippines, Far East Air Force B-24 Liberators, A-20 Havocs, P-38 Lightnings, and P-47 Thunderbolts support ground forces on Luzon. B-24s bomb Negros Island and attack several targets on Cebu Island.

B-24 Liberators bomb a seaplane base and airfields on Formosa,

B-24s bomb airfields on Borneo.

**PACIFIC:** Twentieth Air Force sends more than 300 B-29s from XXI Bomber Command to bomb the city of Nagoya, Japan, with incendiaries. About three square miles of the city are destroyed, but little damage is caused to aircraft engine production facilities or freight yards.

Carrier aircraft from Task Force 58 bomb airfields on southern Kyushu and shipping. One transport and a tanker are sunk and a cargo ship is damaged. Japanese aircraft attack carriers USS *Enterprise* and USS *Yorktown* south of Kyushu, Japan. Both carriers are damaged by bombs. A kamikaze hits carrier USS *Intrepid*, which is also hit by friendly fire. Carrier aircraft sink an auxiliary submarine chaser and a merchant vessel and damage two merchant ships.

U.S. submarine *Balao* torpedoes and sinks a Japanese merchant trawler in the Yellow Sea.

U.S. submarine *Springer* attacks a Japanese convoy and sinks a fast transport and damages a minesweeper in the Ryukyus. USS *Trigger* torpedoes and sinks a Japanese cargo ship northwest of Okinawa.

**CENTRAL PACIFIC:** Seventh Air Force sends 14 B-24 Liberators from Guam to bomb the airfield on Chichi Jima. During the night five B-24s fly individual harassment raids on Chichi Jima. A total of 16 P-51 Mustangs from Iwo Jima conduct a dive-bombing attack on radar and radar installations and barges on Chichi Jima.

The 392nd Bombardment Squadron (Heavy), 30th Bombardment Group (Heavy), redeploys its B-24s from Saipan Island to Hawaii.

## March 19

**ALEUTIANS:** Eleventh Air Force sends five B-24 Liberators and eight B-25 Mitchells to bomb and photograph the Kashiwabara naval base on Paramushiru Island in the Kuriles.

**CBI:** Fourteenth Air Force sends five B-24 Liberators on a sweep over the South China Sea and Gulf of Tonkin. Aircrews report one cargo ship sunk.

In Burma, Tenth Air Force sends 24 P-38 Lightnings to support the Chinese 50th Division, while other P-38s sweep roads. P-47 Thunderbolts attack troop concentrations and logistics storage sites.

U.S. submarine *Balao* attacks a Japanese convoy, sinking a troopship and damaging a transport near Shanghai.

A Japanese river gunboat and merchant ship in the Yangtze River are sunk by mines dropped by Fourteenth Air Force aircraft early in March.

**ETO:** Koblenz is captured by VIII Corps. The Third Army's armored divisions have covered 950 square miles in 24 hours. Infantry divisions follow behind the tanks, clearing out isolated pockets of resistance. Seventh Army's XXI Corps captures Saarbrücken.

General Eisenhower orders Bradley to have First Army ready to break out of the Remagen bridgehead anytime after March 22. Bradley gives Patton authorization to cross the Rhine as soon as possible.

Eighth Air Force sends more than 1,200 B-17s and B-24 Liberators escorted by over 600 P-51 Mustangs to bomb marshaling yards and airfields. The bombers use a combination of visual means and radar signal intercepts to mark the bomb release points over the targets. A total of six bombers are lost and six are damaged. Aircrews report 41 confirmed kills, three probables, and 19 possibles. Of the 36 Me-262 jet aircraft spotted during the raids, aircrews report three of the jets downed. Aircrew casualties are nine killed, three wounded, and 20 missing. Fighter pilots report seven confirmed kills and three possibles in the air. Four fighters are lost.

Another 98 P-51s fly a freelance sweep for the bombers. Fighter pilots report 33 confirmed kills, two probables, and 14 possibles in the air. Six fighters are lost.

During the night 11 B-24s drop leaflets over Germany and the Netherlands.

Ninth Air Force sends A-20 Havocs, A-26 Invaders, and B-26 Marauders to attack communication centers, railroad bridges, and marshaling yards. P-47 and P-38 fighters support III Corps and the 4th Armored Division.

Corporal Edward G. Wilkin, C Company, 157th Infantry Regiment, 45th Infantry Division, is part of an assault unit attacking the Siegfried Line in Germany. As German machine-gun and rifle fire stop the advance, Wilkin moves forward to observe the enemy and to look for a route of advance. He moves into an area with a number of concrete emplacements and attacks one after another using his Browning Automatic Rifle (BAR) and grenades. When barbed wire entanglements stop him, Wilkin uses demolitions to clear a path as grenades and mortar shells burst around him and bullets hit close by. He stands up often to fire a burst from his BAR and allow his comrades an opportunity to advance. In this manner he penetrates a full 200 yards into the German defenses. During the night he assists in distributing rations and supplies to his unit and assists another company by guiding litter bearers evacuating the wounded. For the next two days, Wilkin fearlessly ventures into enemy fire to rescue wounded soldiers. For his superb fighting skill, dauntless courage, and gallant, inspiring actions, Corporal Wilkin will receive the Medal of Honor.

**MEDITERRANEAN:** Fifteenth Air Force sends more than 800 B-17s and B-24 Liberators escorted by P-38 Lightnings and P-51 Mustangs to bomb marshaling yards in Germany. P-38s bomb a marshaling yard in Yugoslavia. B-24s airdrop supplies in Yugoslavia.

**ITALY:** Twelfth Air Force A-20 Havocs and P-47 Thunderbolts of the XXII Tactical Air Command attack rail bridges, logistics storage sites, ammunition storage areas, and roads in the Po River valley.

**SOUTHWEST PACIFIC AREA:** In the Philippines, Far East Air Force B-24 Liberators, A-20 Havocs, P-38 Lightnings, and P-47 Thunderbolts attack installations on Luzon. B-24s bomb targets on Cebu Island.

The 63rd Bombardment Squadron (Heavy), 43rd Bombardment Group (Heavy), redeploys its B-24s from Leyte to Clark Field on Luzon.

PV-1 Harpoon patrol bombers damage a Japanese midget submarine at Cebu.

**PACIFIC:** Carrier aircraft from Task Force 58 attack airfields on Kyushu and shipping on Honshu, Japan. Three battleships, four carriers, a small carrier, an escort carrier, a heavy cruiser, and a light cruiser are damaged, as well as two submarines, an auxiliary submarine chaser, and an escort destroyer.

Japanese aircraft attack USS *Wasp* and USS *Franklin* with bombs off Kyushu and damage both carriers. USS *Franklin* is seriously damaged, but the crew is able to keep the ship afloat; 724 sailors are killed.

U.S. submarine *Bluefish* torpedoes and damages a Japanese guardboat south of Kyushu, Japan.

Lieutenant (j.g.) Donald A. Gary is stationed on the third deck of the carrier USS *Franklin* off Honshu, Japan, near Kobe when it comes under air attack. The carrier's ordnance storage area is hit and explodes, trapping a number of sailors. Gary risks his life to assist several hundred men trapped in a compartment filled with smoke. As the explosions continue to shake the ship, Gary calms the group and leads them through the dark corridors until he finds a passageway that allows everyone to get out safely. He returns to the compartment three times, through flame and debris, to lead other groups of trapped sailors out. He organizes and leads fire-fighting parties on the flight deck and takes life-threatening risks to support damage control efforts. For his courageous performance in leading his shipmates from danger and for risking his life repeatedly to save his ship, Lieutenant (j.g.) Gary will receive the Medal of Honor.

**CENTRAL PACIFIC:** Seventh Air Force sends 12 B-24 Liberators from Guam to bomb the airfield on Chichi Jima. A total of 16 P-51 Mustangs from Iwo Jima strafe the airfield, logistics storage areas, and radio installation on Chichi Jima. During the night five B-24s fly individual harassment raids on Chichi Jima.

**CENTRAL PACIFIC, IWO JIMA:** The 4th Marine Division embarks on ships headed for Hawaii. The 5th Marine Division attacks Japanese positions in Death Valley with flamethrower tanks and demolition charges. Casualties within the division are reaching 100 percent.

**NEW GUINEA:** The C-46s of the 8th Combat Cargo Squadron, 2nd Combat Cargo Group, redeploy from Biak to Leyte Island in the Philippines.

## March 20

**ALEUTIANS:** Naval Task Force 92, commanded by Captain John M. Worthington and with six destroyers, departs Attu to bombard Japanese installations at Paramushiro. The operation will be cancelled after the ships encounter heavy ice.

**CBI:** British forces capture Mandalay.

In Burma, Tenth Air Force sends 20 P-47 Thunderbolts to sweep roads, while 16 other P-47s attack logistics storage areas.

**ATLANTIC:** German submarine *U-995* torpedoes and damages a U.S. freighter in the Barents Sea near Murmansk. German submarine *U-968* torpedoes and sinks a U.S. freighter in the same area.

**ETO:** Zweibrücken is captured. Seventh Army breaks the West Wall and drives north to meet Third Army.

Eighth Air Force sends more than 400 B-17s and B-24 Liberators escorted by over 350 P-51 Mustangs to bomb the shipyard and dock area at Hamburg, an airfield, and an oil refinery. A total of four bombers are lost and 64 are damaged. Aircrews report 14 confirmed kills, three probables, and 17 possibles. Aircrew casualties are one killed, two wounded, and 39 missing. Fighter pilots report two confirmed kills and five possibles in the air and one confirmed kill and two possibles on the ground. One P-51 is lost and the pilot is reported missing.

Seventy-eight P-51s fly a strafing mission in the Bremen-Hannover area. Pilots report two confirmed kills and three possibles in the air and three confirmed kills and two possibles on the ground. One P-51 is lost, and the pilot is reported missing. Six B-17s conduct screening missions to jam German radio interception efforts and employ countermeasures against German radar sites.

During the night 12 B-24s drop leaflets over Germany and the Netherlands. Two A-26 Invaders fly Carpetbagger missions one; one A-26 is lost.

Ninth Air Force sends more than 360 A-20 Havocs, A-26 Invaders, and B-26 Marauders to attack ammunition manufacturing sites, railroad bridges, and marshaling yards. P-47 and P-38 fighters support III and VII Corps and XI and XX Corps.

**MEDITERRANEAN:** Fifteenth Air Force sends more than 760 B-17s and B-24 Liberators escorted by P-38 Lightnings and P-51 Mustangs to bomb oil refineries and marshaling yards in Austria.

U.S. destroyer *Parker* bombards German positions, logistics storage sites, and facilities on the French-Italian border.

**ITALY:** Twelfth Air Force B-25 Mitchells bomb rail bridges. A-20 Havocs and P-47 Thunderbolts attack rail lines, bridges, and roads in the Po River valley

**SOUTHWEST PACIFIC AREA:** In the Eighth Army area elements of the 40th Infantry Division capture Guimaras Island between Panya and Negros Islands.

In the Philippines, Far East Air Force B-24 Liberators, A-20 Havocs, P-38 Lightnings, and P-47 Thunderbolts conduct ground support missions at Balete Pass and other areas on Luzon. B-24s bomb Japanese forces and logistics storage sites near Cebu City on Cebu Island. B-24s also bomb Japanese defensive positions and antiaircraft guns on Negros Island.

Other B-24s bomb targets on Formosa. B-25 Mitchells conduct a shipping sweep and aircrews report three small vessels sunk in the Gulf of Tonkin

U.S. submarine *Blenny* attacks a Japanese convoy off the coast of French Indochina, near Cam Ranh Bay, sinking two merchant tankers and a fishing boat.

**LUZON:** Staff Sergeant Ysmael R. Villegas is a squad leader with F Company, 127th Infantry Regiment, 32nd Infantry Division, attacking a strongly defended hill on the Villa Verde Trail. As the Japanese throw grenades and demolition charges, he encourages his men as they prepare to assault the position. As the Americans reach the crest of the hill and begin consolidating on the objective, hidden Japanese riflemen begin a deadly fire. Staff Sergeant Villegas charges a soldier in a hidden position and kills him. Soon Villegas is moving from position to position blasting the enemy in their foxholes. As he nears the sixth fighting position, he is killed. For his heroism and indomitable fighting spirit, and his inspiring leadership, Staff Sergeant Villegas will receive the Medal of Honor.

**PACIFIC:** Carrier USS *Enterprise* is damaged by friendly fire off Shikoku, Japan. A kamikaze hits a destroyer in the same area. Carrier aircraft sink a Japanese guardboat off Honshu.

A kamikaze hits and damages U.S. submarine *Devilfish* near the Volcano Islands, terminating her patrol.

**CENTRAL PACIFIC:** Seventh Air Force sends 12 B-24 Liberators from Guam to bomb the airfield on Chichi Jima. During the night four B-24s fly individual harassment raids on Chichi Jima.

The 549th Night Fighter Squadron redeploys its P-61 Black Widow night fighters from Saipan to Iwo Jima.

**CENTRAL PACIFIC, IWO JIMA:** The army's 147th Infantry Regiment joins the 3rd Marine Division on the island.

**NEW GUINEA:** The B-24 Liberators of the 72nd Bombardment Squadron (Heavy), 5th Bombardment Group (Heavy), redeploy from Morotai Island to Samar Island in the Philippines.

U.S. submarine *Perch* lands personnel on the east coast of Borneo.

## March 21

**CBI:** The Japanese launch a coordinated attack between the Yangtze and Yellow Rivers to capture the American air bases at Laohokow and Ankang.

Fourteenth Air Force sends six B-24 Liberators on a shipping sweep. Aircrews report one vessel damaged in South China Sea.

In Burma, Tenth Air Force sends 13 B-25 Mitchells and 18 P-47 Thunderbolts to attack troop concentrations and vehicles. Another 30 P-47 Thunderbolts support Chinese ground forces and 34 P-38 Lightnings sweep roads.

**ATLANTIC:** A Fourth Air Force P-63 Kingcobra (a fighter aircraft used for training) from Walla Walla Army Airfield, Washington, intercepts a Japanese balloon and eventually shoots it down near Reno, Nevada.

**ETO:** Seventh and Third armies link, meeting the goals of Operation Undertone. The German Seventh Army is demolished, and the German First Army is trapped along the Rhine River. Patton's divisions have covered 4,000 square miles and captured 63,000 prisoners. American casualties are about 1,700.

The Remagen bridgehead is 20 miles wide and eight miles deep, supported by six temporary bridges. Six divisions of First Army are east of the Rhine.

Eighth Air Force sends more than 1,400 B-17s and B-24 Liberators escorted by over 800 P-51 Mustangs to bomb marshaling yards and airfields in support of the anticipated crossing of the Rhine River. The bombers use mostly visual means to mark the bomb release points over the targets. A total of seven B-17s are lost and 250 are damaged. Aircrews report 58 confirmed kills, three probables, and 49 possibles. Aircrew casualties are one killed, 11 wounded, and 65 missing. Fighter pilots report nine confirmed kills and two possibles in the air and 46 confirmed kills and 44 possibles on the ground. Seven P-51s are lost and one is damaged. The pilots are reported missing.

Three B-17s, escorted by six P-51s, conduct a Disney operation, attacking the E-boat pens at Ijmuiden in the Netherlands with wing-mounted 4,500-pound concrete-penetrating rocket bombs. A single B-17, escorted by four P-51s, bombs Oberursel, Germany, as part of a radar test. During the night eight B-24s drop leaflets over Germany and the Netherlands.

Ninth Air Force sends more than 580 A-20 Havocs, A-26 Invaders, and B-26 Marauders to attack communication centers and marshaling yards. P-47 and P-38 fighters support VII Corps, XII Corps, and XX Corps.

**MEDITERRANEAN:** Fifteenth Air Force sends more than 660 B-17s and B-24 Liberators escorted by P-38 Lightnings and P-51 Mustangs to bomb an airfield in Germany and marshaling yards in Austria and Yugoslavia.

**ITALY:** Twelfth Air Force B-25 Mitchells bomb rail and road traffic and bridges. A-20 Havocs and P-47 Thunderbolts attack logistics storage sites, rail lines, bridges, and roads in the Po River valley and support Fifth Army ground forces.

During the night A-20s attack river crossing sites in the Po River valley.

**SOUTHWEST PACIFIC AREA:** In the Philippines, Far East Air Force B-25 Mitchells, A-20 Havocs, P-38s, and P-47 Thunderbolts attack Japanese defenses on Luzon Island. B-24 Liberators and A-20 Havocs attack targets on Cebu Island.

FEAF B-24s bomb an airfield on Hainan Island. B-25s conduct a shipping sweep and damage a freighter off Nanao Island, China.

U.S. submarine *Baya* torpedoes and sinks an auxiliary netlayer off Cam Ranh Bay, French Indochina. USS *Baya* is damaged by depth charges but remains on patrol. Fifth Air Force B-25 Mitchells sink a submarine chaser, a cable layer, and three cargo vessels and damages a submarine chaser off Nha Trang, French Indochina.

**PACIFIC:** The Japanese launch rocket-powered suicide bombs *(oka)* from aircraft against Task Force 58.

**CENTRAL PACIFIC:** Seventh Air Force sends 13 B-24 Liberators from Guam to bomb the airfield on Chichi Jima. A total of 16 P-51 Mustangs from Iwo Jima strafe the airfield, logistics storage areas, and radar installation on Chichi Jima. During the night five B-24s fly individual harassment raids on Chichi Jima.

**NEW GUINEA:** The headquarters of the 42nd Bombardment Group (Medium) and the B-25 Mitchells of the 390th Bombardment Squadron (Medium) redeploy from Morotai Island to Palawan Island in the Philippines.

## March 22

**CBI:** In China, Fourteenth Air Force P-40s and P-51 Mustangs attack rail and river traffic.

In Burma, Tenth Air Force sends 12 B-25 Mitchells and P-47 Thunderbolts to bomb troop concentrations and logistics storage sites. P-47 Thunderbolts and P-38 Lightnings support ground forces of the Chinese 50th Division.

**ETO:** Mainz is captured. The 5th Infantry Division of XII Corps of Third Army begins a night crossing of the Rhine River at Oppenheim, an operation planned six months in advance. Six battalions of infantrymen make the initial crossing in rafts. About 7,500 engineers support the operation, building a steel treadway bridge within 20 hours after the first troops cross.

Eighth Air Force sends more than 1,300 B-17s and B-24 Liberators, escorted by over 600 P-47 Thunderbolts and P-51 Mustangs, to bomb German positions across the Rhine River, marshaling yards, and airfields. One B-17 is lost and 147 damaged. Aircrews report 27 confirmed kills, one probable, and 12 possibles. Aircrew casualties are 10 killed, 11 wounded, and nine missing. Fighter pilots report three confirmed kills and one possible in the air and 13 confirmed kills and eight probables on the ground.

P-51 Mustangs escorting a photo reconnaissance mission over Germany report 11 confirmed kills, one probable kill, and three possible kills in the air.

Six B-17s conduct screening missions to jam German radio interception efforts and employ countermeasures against German radar sites.

During the night nine B-24s drop leaflets over Germany and the Netherlands. Ninth Air Force sends nearly 800 A-20 Havocs, A-26 Invaders, and B-26 Marauders to attack communication centers and a marshaling yard. P-47 and P-38 fighters support the 1st and 9th Infantry Divisions and XX Corps.

German submarine *U-399* torpedoes and sinks a U.S. freighter at the entrance to the English Channel; another submarine, possibly *U-1195*, torpedoes and damages another U.S. freighter in the same convoy. A U.S. freighter leaving Antwerp hits a mine.

**MEDITERRANEAN:** Fifteenth Air Force sends 136 B-17s to attack the synthetic oil production facility at Ruhland, Germany. Ruhland's facility is Germany's leading producer of fuel. As the bombers approach the target, 20 German fighter-jets attack and shoot down three bombers. P-51 Mustangs flying escort damage three jets and shoot down one.

B-17s and B-24 Liberators escorted by P-38 Lightnings and P-51 Mustangs bomb oil refineries in Austria and Czechoslovakia and railyards and marshaling yards in Austria and Czechoslovakia.

**ITALY:** Twelfth Air Force B-25 Mitchells bomb bridges in Austria and Italy. P-47 Thunderbolts attack rail lines, bridges, and roads in the Po River valley. During the night A-20s and A-26 Invaders attack river crossing sites in the Po River valley.

**SOUTHWEST PACIFIC AREA:** In the Philippines, Far East Air Force B-24 Liberators, B-25 Mitchells, A-20 Havocs, P-38 Lightnings, and P-47 Thunderbolts attack Balete Pass and other areas in support of ground forces on Luzon. B-24s and A-20s attack targets on Cebu Island.

On Formosa, B-24s attack airfields. Aircrews report hangars, antiaircraft gun positions, and aircraft destroyed.

The 64th Bombardment Squadron (Heavy), 43rd Bombardment Group (Heavy), redeploys B-24s from Leyte to Clark Field on Luzon.

Japanese aircraft attack American shipping in Lingayen Gulf, but the attack is ineffective.

**PACIFIC:** Twentieth Air Force sends 78 B-29 Superfortresses to bomb logistics storage areas at Rangoon, Burma.

**CENTRAL PACIFIC:** Seventh Air Force sends 13 B-24 Liberators from Guam to bomb the airfield on Chichi Jima. Sixteen P-51 Mustangs from Iwo Jima strafe logistics storage areas and a radar installation on Chichi Jima. During the night four B-24s fly individual harassment.

A total of 20 B-24s based at Angaur Island bomb Cebu Island in the Philippines.

**NEW GUINEA:** The 69th and 100th Bombardment Squadrons (Medium), 42nd Bombardment Group (Medium), redeploy B-25s from Morotai to Palawan Island in the Philippines. The 75th Bombardment Squadron (Medium), 42nd Bombardment Group (Medium), redeploys its B-25s from Sansapor to Palawan in the Philippines.

The 868th Bombardment Squadron (Heavy), Thirteenth Air Force, redeploys from Noemfoor to Morotai Island with radar-equipped B-24s.

U.S. submarine *Perch* torpedoes and sinks a Japanese vessel in the Makassar Strait.

## March 23

**CBI:** In China, Fourteenth Air Force sends 28 B-24 Liberators to bomb railroad facilities and a bridge.

In Burma, Tenth Air Force sends nine B-25 Mitchells to bomb lines of communication to block Japanese force movements. P-47 Thunderbolts support Chinese ground forces and attack targets of opportunity.

**ATLANTIC:** German submarine *U-532* torpedoes and sinks a U.S. freighter in the mid-Atlantic.

**ETO:** Third Army expands its bridgehead over the Rhine, adding a regiment from the 90th Infantry Division to the 5th Infantry Division's three regiments already across. Tanks and other vehicles are being ferried across. By midnight the bridgehead is five miles deep.

Eighth Air Force sends nearly 1,300 B-17s and B-24 Liberators escorted by nearly 500 P-51 Mustangs to bomb rail bridges, marshaling yards, and airfields. A total of seven bombers are lost and 275 damaged. Aircrews report one confirmed kill and one possible. Aircrew casualties are seven killed, 10 wounded, and 72 missing. More than 120 P-51s fly a fighter sweep of the Bremen-Kassel area. Pilots report one confirmed kill in the air and one possible kill on the ground. One B-17, escorted by four P-51s, bombs Ettinghausen airfield as part of a radar test.

During the night nine B-24s drop leaflets over Germany and the Netherlands. A total of 19 B-24s fly Carpetbagger missions to Denmark.

Ninth Air Force sends 800 A-20 Havocs, A-26 Invaders, and B-26 Marauders to attack communication centers and targets of opportunity. P-47 and P-38 fighters support III Corps, VII Corps, and XII and XX Corps.

**ETO: Operation Plunder.** Field Marshal Bernard L. Montgomery's 21st Army Group crosses the Rhine River in a set piece orchestration of land and air power. General Eisenhower and Prime Minister Churchill witness the attack, equal in size and complexity to the Normandy landings. Three Allied armies, including the XVI Corps (30th and 79th Infantry Divisions) of the U.S. Ninth Army, make a largely uneventful crossing after a heavy hour-long artillery bombardment followed by the laying of a smokescreen. Operation Varsity is the drop of the First Allied Airborne Army's XVIII Airborne Corps, under the command of Major General Matthew B. Ridgway and composed of the U.S. 17th Airborne Division (commanded by Major General William Miley) and the British 6th Airborne Division. The U.S. IX Troop Carrier Command employs 903 aircraft and 897 gliders on this operation. The drop zones and landing zones are only a few miles from the Rhine where the Allied ground forces will land and are within German artillery range. The 21,000 paratroopers and glider infantry take significant casualties from antiaircraft guns near the drop zones and landing zones. Paratroopers capture crossings over the Issel River and capture 3,500 prisoners. The 3rd Battalion of the 507th Parachute

Infantry Regiment captures Diersfordt Castle after a difficult fight that ends with five German tanks destroyed and 500 prisoners. The two divisions of Ninth Army occupy a bridgehead about nine miles wide and six miles deep and have captured 1,900 prisoners. Ninth Army casualties are 41 killed, 450 wounded, and seven missing. A total of 37,000 British and 22,000 American engineer troops support the crossing. Navy LCVPs (landing craft, vehicle personnel) from Task Group 122.5.1 ferry nearly 4,500 troops from Third Army across the Rhine River at Oppenheim.

**MEDITERRANEAN:** Fifteenth Air Force sends more than 600 B-17s and B-24 Liberators escorted by P-38 Lightnings and P-51 Mustangs to bomb oil refineries in Germany and Austria and marshaling yards in Czechoslovakia and Austria.

**ITALY:** Twelfth Air Force B-25 Mitchells bomb rail and road bridges. P-47 Thunderbolts attack rail lines, bridges, vehicles, logistics storage sites, ammunition storage areas, and roads. During the night A-20s attack river crossing points in the Po River valley.

**SOUTHWEST PACIFIC AREA:** In the Eighth Army area the 162nd and 163rd Infantry Regiments of the 41st Infantry Division capture the center of the Japanese position outside of Zamboanga City. The 186th Infantry Regiment from Palawan arrives to relieve the 162nd Infantry Regiment.

In the Philippines, Far East Air Force B-24 Liberators, B-25 Mitchells, A-20 Havocs, and P-47 Thunderbolts bomb Visayan Island and Cebu City on Cebu Island. On Luzon, P-38 Lightnings, A-20s, and B-25s bomb Balete Pass. B-24s attack targets on Mindanao Island. P-47s attack targets on Formosa.

Infantrymen of the 25th Infantry Division cautiously search for Japanese positions at Balete Pass on Luzon, March 23, 1945.

A U.S. destroyer rams and sinks Japanese submarine *RO-41* in the Philippine Sea.

**PACIFIC:** Task Force 58 attacks Japanese shipping and installations near Okinawa. Carrier aircraft sink two cargo ships and a midget submarine and damage another midget submarine, a coastal defense ship, and a submarine chaser.

U.S. submarine *Seahorse* is damaged in an air attack off the Ryukyus. U.S. submarine *Spadefish* attacks a Japanese convoy in the East China Sea, sinking a transport.

**CENTRAL PACIFIC:** Seventh Air Force sends 15 P-51 Mustangs from Iwo Jima to strafe the airfield, logistics storage areas, and a radio installation on Chichi Jima and attack targets on Haha Jima and Ani Jima. During the night five B-24s fly individual harassment raids on Chichi Jima.

## March 24

**CBI:** Fourteenth Air Force B-24 Liberators escorted by P-51 Mustangs bomb locomotives and a bridge. B-25 Mitchells and 100 P-40s and P-51s attack tanks, trucks, locomotives, troop concentrations, logistics storage areas, airfields, gun positions, and targets of opportunity throughout southern and eastern China.

In Burma, Tenth Air Force sends nine B-25 Mitchells to bomb troop concentrations, logistics storage sites, and targets of opportunity. P-47 Thunderbolts and P-38 Lightnings attack targets of opportunity along roads.

**ETO:** A bridgehead at Remagen extends 25 miles long and 10 miles deep and contains three corps.

Allied air attacks on German positions near Montgomery's 21st Army Group landing sites across the Rhine reach their highest point after a near-continuous bombardment of three days.

The XII Corps of Third Army establishes a bridgehead nine miles wide and six miles deep outside of Oppenheim. Engineers build a heavy pontoon bridge across the Rhine River. The 5th and 90th Infantry Divisions and the 4th Armored Division are across the river and advance toward the Main River. American troops capture 19,000 German prisoners.

Navy LCVPs of Task Group 122.5.1 support Third Army's crossing of the Rhine at Boppard. Task Group 122.5.1 also ferries troops of Ninth Army across the Rhine south of Wesel.

During the night 10 B-24s drop leaflets over Germany and the Netherlands. Twenty-four B-24s fly a Carpetbagger mission over Scandinavia.

Ninth Air Force sends nearly 700 A-20 Havocs, A-26 Invaders, and B-26 Marauders to attack communication centers, railroad bridges, antiaircraft positions, and marshaling yards. P-47 and P-38 fighters support the 30th and 79th Infantry Divisions, attacking antiaircraft positions, German defensive positions, and road and rail traffic.

**ETO: Operation Varsity.** Over 2,000 transports and gliders of the IX Troop Carrier Command deliver the British 6th Airborne and U.S. 17th Airborne Divisions to their designated drop zones and landing zones.

Eighth Air Force sends more than 1,000 B-17s and B-24 Liberators escorted by 1,158 P-47 Thunderbolts and P-51 Mustangs to bomb airfields. A total of 19 bombers are lost and 103 are damaged. Aircrews report 54 confirmed kills and six possibles. Aircrew casualties are nine killed, five wounded, and 37 missing. Fighter pilots report 53 confirmed kills and two probables in the air and four possible kills on the ground. Nine fighters are lost. Eight pilots are reported missing. A total of 240 B-24 Liberators are sent to drop supplies to support the American and British river crossing operations. They must fly at very low levels, between 300 and 400 feet. German small-arms fire destroys 14 bombers and damages 107 more. Five airmen are killed, 30 wounded, and 116 are missing. In the afternoon 448 B-17s and B-24s attack marshaling yards and an airfield. They are escorted by 95 P-47s and P-51s. There are 38 bombers damaged but no fighter or bomber losses. One P-51 is lost on a scouting mission.

Private George J. Peters is a platoon radio operator with G Company, 507th Parachute Infantry, 17th Airborne Division, jumping into a drop zone over the Rhine River near Fluren, Germany. He lands with 10 other paratroopers in a field about 75 yards away from a German machine gun supported by riflemen. As they struggle to free themselves from their parachute harnesses, the Germans begin firing on them. Peters stands up and charges the enemy firing his M-1 rifle. Although wounded and knocked down, Peters struggles to his feet and advances. He is quickly wounded again and, unable to stand, he crawls forward until close enough to throw hand grenades and eliminate the machine gun. For his dedication to duty, his aggressiveness, and his heroic sacrifice to save the lives of his comrades, Private Peters will win the Medal of Honor.

**MEDITERRANEAN:** Fifteenth Air Force sends 150 B-17s with an escort of P-51 Mustangs to attack the jet aircraft production facility at Neuburg near Berlin. German fighter jets attack the formation. Six B-17s are lost and six are damaged. Aircrews report six jets as confirmed kills and four as probables. Fighter pilots report five jet aircraft shot down.

Lieutenant General John K. Cannon takes command of Army Air Forces, Mediterranean Theater of Operations (AAFMTO) and is scheduled to take command of the Mediterranean Allied Air Force (MAAF).

Fifteenth Air Force sends more than 600 B-17s and B-24 Liberators escorted by P-38 Lightnings and P-51 Mustangs to bomb a tank production facility at Berlin and an airfield at Munich, a marshaling yard in Czechoslovakia, and airfields in Germany and Italy.

**ITALY:** Twelfth Air Force B-25 Mitchells bomb bridges. P-47 Thunderbolts attack rail lines and rail cars. During the night A-20s and A-26 Invaders attack marshaling yards, river crossings, bridges, and targets of opportunity.

**SOUTHWEST PACIFIC AREA:** On Luzon, in the XIV Corps area, the 158th RCT is detached from 11th Airborne Division and placed under Sixth Army operational control to prepare for an amphibious assault at Legaspi on the Bicol Peninsula.

In the Philippines, Far East Air Force B-24 Liberators and A-20 Havocs bomb Cebu City and defenses and installations on Cebu Island. On Luzon Island, B-24s, B-25 Mitchells, A-20 Havocs, and P-38 Lightnings attack Balete Pass and other targets.

On Formosa, B-24s bomb the harbor at Takao and industrial targets.

**PACIFIC:** During the night Twentieth Air Force sends more than 200 B-29 Superfortresses from the Marianas to bomb the Mitsubishi aircraft engine production facility at Nagoya, Japan. Five B-29s are lost.

Naval Task Force 59, commanded by Vice Admiral Willis A. Lee, bombards Okinawa. Carrier aircraft from TG 58.1 (carriers USS *Bennington* and USS *Hornet* and small carriers USS *Belleau Wood* and USS *San Jacinto*) eliminate a convoy, sinking a torpedo boat, a coastal defense ship, two auxiliary minesweepers, and four cargo ships northwest of Okinawa. Carrier aircraft from TF 58 sink three cargo ships in the northern Ryukyus.

**CENTRAL PACIFIC:** Seventh Air Force sends nine B-24 Liberators from Guam to bomb the torpedo storage facility on Marcus Island. P-51 Mustangs attack air, naval, and radar installations and targets of opportunity on Chichi Jima. A total of 24 B-24s based on Angaur Island bomb defensive positions and the town of Naga on Luzon Island in the Philippines.

During the night five B-24s from Guam fly individual harassment raids on Haha Jima.

**NEW GUINEA:** Thirteenth Air Force B-24 Liberators sink a Japanese cargo ship off Celebes Island.

## March 25

**CBI:** Fourteenth Air Force sends B-25 Mitchells and over 150 P-40s and P-51s to attack river, road, and rail traffic, airfields, troop concentrations, logistics storage areas, horses, and gun positions throughout southern and eastern China.

In Burma, Tenth Air Force P-47 Thunderbolts support forces of the Chinese 50th Division, while B-25 Mitchells, P-38 Lightnings, and P-47s attack troops, logistics support sites, and targets of opportunity along roads.

**ETO: The Rhine River Is Breached.** The 17th Airborne links with elements of the Ninth Army east of the Rhine River, marking the success of Operation Varsity and Operation Plunder. The Allied bridgehead is two miles wide and six miles deep, occupied by five British and four U.S. divisions. Major General Leland S. Hobbs, commander of the 30th Infantry Division, presses an aggressive attack to attempt a breakout but is held up by poor roads and heavily forested terrain.

The XII Corps of Third Army captures Darmstadt. The 87th Infantry Division of the VIII Corps of Third Army establishes a bridgehead over the Rhine River at Boppard, expanding it to eight miles wide and three miles deep. During the night, the 89th Infantry Division (now under the operational control of the VIII Corps) makes an assault crossing of the Rhine.

Bradley orders Patton's Third Army to attack from its bridgeheads to clear German forces out of its zone of action all the way to the area between Hanau and Giessen. Third Army should be ready to continue the attack toward Kassel. First Army will attack out of the Remagen bridgehead to clear German forces from the Giessen-Siegen line and assist the advance of Third Army. Fifteenth Army will take over the west bank of the Rhine River and be prepared to occupy, organize, and govern German municipalities along the Rhine River. Bradley intends to attack eastward then turn north to link with Ninth Army and encircle the Ruhr.

The V Corps, VII Corps, and III Corps of First Army attack out of the Remagen bridgehead, advancing toward Wiesbaden.

The Rhine is the last natural obstacle to SHAEF's campaign for the final battle in Germany. All three Allied army groups are now across the Rhine, and 24 bridges have been built.

Eighth Air Force sends more than 1,000 B-17s and B-24 Liberators escorted by 341 P-47 Thunderbolts and P-51 Mustangs to bomb a tank production facility and oil depots. A total of four bombers are lost and 24 are damaged. Aircrews report six confirmed kills, four probables, and 13 possibles. Aircrew casualties are 25 killed, two wounded, and 39 missing. Fighter pilots report four confirmed kills and three probables in the air. A total of 24 P-51s fly a fighter-bomber mission against an ammunition storage area. One P-51 is lost and the pilot is reported missing. P-51s flying a scouting mission report one possible kill in the air.

During the night 10 B-24s drop leaflets over Germany and the Netherlands. Ninth Air Force sends A-20 Havocs, A-26 Invaders, and B-26 Marauders to attack communications centers, antiaircraft positions, and marshaling yards. P-47 and P-38 fighters support the 79th Infantry Division and II Corps and VII Corps, as well as XII Corps.

**MEDITERRANEAN:** Fifteenth Air Force sends more than 650 B-17s and B-24 Liberators escorted by P-38 Lightnings and P-51 Mustangs to bomb airfields and a tank production facility in Czechoslovakia.

**ITALY:** Twelfth Air Force B-25 Mitchells bomb rail and road bridges. P-47 Thunderbolts attack rail lines, bridges, fuel storage sites, and roads. During the night A-20s and A-26 Invaders attack river crossing sites, roads, and motor transport in the Po River valley.

**SOUTHWEST PACIFIC AREA:** In the Philippines, Far East Air Force B-24 Liberators bomb Cebu City on Cebu Island. On Luzon Island, B-24 Liberators attack Legaspi, and B-25 Mitchells, P-47 Thunderbolts, and P-38 Lightnings provide support to ground forces. B-25s attack Pandanan Island.

The P-38s of the 339th Fighter Squadron, 347th Fighter Group, return to Palawan from Morotai Island.

Fifth Air Force B-24 Liberators sink a Japanese cargo ship near Shanghai.

**PACIFIC:** Battleships, cruisers, and destroyers of Naval Task Force 54 (Rear Admiral Morton L. Deyo) bombard Okinawa. Kamikazes damage a destroyer, a light minelayer, and a high-speed transport off Okinawa. A bomber damages a high-speed transport.

Carrier aircraft from TF 58 sink two cargo ships near Okinawa.

U.S. submarine *Tirante* torpedoes and sinks a Japanese auxiliary netlayer off Kyushu, Japan.

**PACIFIC, OKINAWA:** The Americans initiate a psychological warfare effort to induce the Japanese to surrender. About 8 million leaflets are dropped by aircraft during the campaign. This effort, plus loudspeaker broadcasts and other means, promises humane treatment to gain confidence among the civilian population and affect the morale of the defenders.

**CENTRAL PACIFIC:** Seventh Air Force sends 23 B-24s based at Angaur Island to bomb Cebu Island in the Philippines. A total of 32 P-51 Mustangs from Iwo Jima strafe the airfield, troops, logistics storage areas, and a radar installation on Chichi Jima. During the night five B-24s fly individual harassment raids on Chichi Jima.

**CENTRAL PACIFIC, IWO JIMA:** The 5th Marine Division captures Death Valley, ending the last pocket of resistance on the island.

**NEW GUINEA:** The C-46s of the 6th Combat Cargo Squadron, 2nd Combat Cargo Group, redeploy from Biak to Leyte Island.

## March 26

**ALEUTIANS:** Eleventh Air Force sends eight B-25 Mitchells to conduct two separate bombing runs with four bombers attacking each target in the Kuriles. Japanese fighters drive off one group, and the other is unable to locate the target due to weather. One group of four B-24s bombs the Kataoka naval base on Shimushu Island.

**CBI:** The American airfield at Laohokow is abandoned to advancing Japanese forces.

Fourteenth Air Force B-25 Mitchells, P-40s, and P-51s attack trucks, tanks, logistics sites, horses, troops, and artillery in southern and eastern China.

In Burma, Tenth Air Force P-47 Thunderbolts and B-25 Mitchells attack artillery positions, troop concentrations, road communications, and logistics sites.

**ETO:** The armored divisions of First Army's III Corps, VII Corps, and V Corps break out of the Remagen bridgehead.

The XV Corps of Seventh Army establishes a bridgehead over the Rhine River near Worms, with the 3rd and 45th Infantry Divisions occupying an area 15 miles wide and seven miles deep. The 3rd Infantry Division meets strong opposition during its crossing. The landing is supported by a 10,000-round artillery barrage that allows the division to establish a solid bridgehead.

The XII Corps of Third Army enters Frankfurt. Patton directs VIII and XII Corps to Giessen.

Navy medium landing craft from Task Group 122.5.1 ferry Third Army troops across the Rhine at Oberwesel.

Lieutenant General William H. Simpson orders the 8th Armored Division of XVI Corps forward to support the 30th and 79th Infantry Divisions as they fight against strong defenses and difficult terrain. Difficulties with bridging the Rhine in the British Second Army area lead to heavy competition for the existing bridges at Wesel, leaving Simpson unable to build his forces in sufficient strength to flank enemy defenses.

Eighth Air Force sends more than 330 B-17s escorted by 527 P-51 Mustangs to bomb tank production facilities and synthetic oil facilities. Thirty bombers are damaged. Aircrew casualties are 19 killed, five wounded.

Ninth Air Force sends 300 A-20 Havocs, A-26 Invaders, and B-26 Marauders to attack marshaling yards and targets of opportunity. P-47 and P-38 fighters support XII Corps and the 2nd, 3rd, 7th, and 9th Armored Divisions.

**MEDITERRANEAN:** Fifteenth Air Force sends more than 500 B-17s and B-24 Liberators escorted by P-38 Lightnings and P-51 Mustangs to bomb marshaling yards in Austria, Czechoslovakia, and Hungary. P-51s attack bridges and rail traffic in Austria.

**ITALY:** Twelfth Air Force P-47 Thunderbolts attack rail lines, bridges, and roads in the Po River valley. During the night A-20s attack bridges.

**SOUTHWEST PACIFIC AREA:** In the Eighth Army area, Naval Task Group 78.2 lands the Americal Division's 132nd and 182nd Infantry Regiments at Cebu City on Cebu Island in the Visayan Sea. Naval Task Group 74.3, commanded by Rear Admiral Russell S. Berkey with one Australian and two U.S. light cruisers and six destroyers, supports the landing.

The beach is heavily mined, and the landings are slowed considerably as 10 LVTs are destroyed in the first wave.

In the Philippines, Far East Air Force B-24 Liberators, B-25 Mitchells, A-20 Havocs, P-38 Lightnings, and P-47 Thunderbolts bomb Legaspi and a fuel storage site, while A-20 Havocs, P-38s, and P-47s support ground forces throughout Luzon. B-24s and A-20s attack Cebu City on Cebu Island.

Fifth Air Force B-24 Liberators bomb shipping in Takao harbor, Formosa, sinking two cargo vessels.

**PACIFIC:** A U.S. destroyer is sunk by a mine off Okinawa. Kamikazes damage battleship USS *Nevada,* a light cruiser, three destroyers, a destroyer escort, a high-speed minesweeper, and a minesweeper. One destroyer is damaged by a dive-bomber.

U.S. submarine *Balao* (SS-285) sinks a Japanese army stores ship in the Yellow Sea.

Carrier aircraft from TF 58 sink an auxiliary submarine chaser and a cargo ship in the Ryukyus.

**PACIFIC, OKINAWA:** Four battalions of infantry from the 305th Infantry Regiment of the 77th Infantry Division land on the Kerama Islands, about 30 miles southwest of the island of Okinawa. Most of the defenders are Japanese suicide boat pilots who are preparing for attacks on the American fleet. A U.S. destroyer hits a mine and sinks near the Kerama Islands.

Admiral Blandy's task force begins the prelanding bombardment of Okinawa.

The 3rd Battalion of the 305th Infantry Regiment, 77th Infantry Division, lands at Kerama Island.

**CENTRAL PACIFIC:** Thirty-seven Seventh Air Force P-51 Mustangs from Iwo Jima strafe the airfield, logistics storage areas, and radar installation on Chichi Jima. Nine B-24s bomb Marcus Island. During the night three B-24s from Guam conduct individual snooper missions on Chichi Jima.

The headquarters of the 21st Fighter Group arrives at Central Field, Iwo Jima, from Hawaii. The 72nd and 531st Fighter Squadrons, 21st Fighter Group, redeploy their P-51s from Hawaii to Iwo Jima.

**CENTRAL PACIFIC, IWO JIMA:** About 300 Japanese conduct a last counterattack on the airfield during the night. Marines, Seabees, shore party units, and P-51 pilots group together to form a hasty defense. The Japanese are thrown back, losing 250 killed and 18 captured. American losses in the surprise attack number 150.

The marines of the 5th and 3rd Divisions will depart the island over the next few days, leaving the army's 147th Infantry Regiment to complete clearing the island. In the following two months the 147th will kill or capture 2,400 Japanese soldiers.

Iwo Jima is the costliest battle in Marine Corps history, with 24,053 Marine casualties. A total of 6,140 men have been killed. Japanese losses are roughly 22,000 men. The marines have succeeded despite staggering casualties. The veterans of Guam, Bougainville, Saipan, Tinian, and members of the old Marine Raiders from Guadalcanal have made the difference. Their unshakable spirit has guaranteed the victory. Admiral Nimitz, referring to the formidable performance of the marines at Iwo Jima, will say, "uncommon valor was a common virtue."

For the duration of the war, 2,251 B-29 Superfortresses will make emergency landings on Iwo Jima, saving the lives of nearly 25,000 crewmen who otherwise would have been lost in the Pacific.

**NEW GUINEA:** The 6th Combat Cargo Squadron, 2nd Combat Cargo Group, redeploys from Biak to Leyte Island with C-46s.

## March 27

**CBI:** Fourteenth Air Force sends 25 B-25 Mitchells to bomb towns, rail, road, and river traffic, and targets of opportunity. P-51 Mustangs and P-40s attack trucks, trains, ammunition storage areas, sampans, and power generation facilities.

In Burma, Tenth Air Force P-47 Thunderbolts and P-38 Lightnings attack road traffic, troop concentrations, logistics storage sites, and targets of opportunity.

**ETO:** Seventh Army and Third Army link at Darmstadt. The 45th Infantry Division of XV Corps battles strong German resistance at Aschaffenburg.

The XX Corps of Third Army sends the 80th Infantry Division in an assault crossing of the Rhine and Main Rivers at Mainz. In the face of heavy fire, navy landing craft from Task Group 122.5.1 ferry troops across the Rhine at Mainz.

VIII Corps eliminates a large pocket of resistance near Wiesbaden and makes contact with First Army.

Eighth Air Force sends more than 100 P-47 Thunderbolts and P-51 Mustangs to escort 262 Royal Air Force Lancaster bombers attacking Paderborn, Germany. During the night nine B-24s drop leaflets over Germany and the Netherlands.

Ninth Air Force sends P-47 and P-38 fighters to support VIII Corps and XII Corps.

The headquarters of the XII Tactical Air Command redeploys from France to Germany.

**SOUTHWEST PACIFIC AREA:** In the Eighth Army area in the Philippines, the Americal Division's 132nd and 182nd Infantry Regiments capture Cebu City. FEAF B-24s bomb Negros Island airfields, while B-25s and P-38s attack the Cebu City area on Cebu Island.

B-25s bomb Formosa.

B-24 Liberators attack targets on Borneo.

**SOUTHWEST PACIFIC AREA, LUZON:** In the XI Corps area, the Shimbu Group's defensive line in the mountains northeast of Manila is threatened with destruction, forcing a withdrawal. Preceded by an air strike, the 2nd Battalion, 151st Infantry Regiment, 38th Infantry Division, supported by two destroyers and three rocket-equipped motor torpedo boats, lands on Caballo Island near Corregidor.

Far East Air Force B-24 Liberators, B-25 Mitchells, A-20 Havocs, P-38 Lightnings, and P-47 Thunderbolts bomb Legaspi and several other locations throughout Luzon. P-47s and P-38s support the amphibious landings on Caballo Island in Manila Bay.

**PACIFIC:** Twentieth Air Force sends more than 250 B-29 Superfortresses from the Marianas to bomb airfields and an aircraft production facility on Kyushu, Japan, and mine Shimonoseki Strait between Honshu and Kyushu islands in support of the Okinawa Island invasion. Aircrews report two confirmed kills, two probables, and four possibles. Three B-29s are lost.

Operation Starvation begins, intended to support operations on Okinawa through aerial mining of the Shimonoseki Strait of Japan. B-29s of the Twentieth Air Force conduct the missions.

Kamikazes damage a light minelayer off Okinawa.

U.S. submarine *Trigger* torpedoes and sinks a Japanese cable layer southwest of Kyushu, Japan.

Carrier aircraft from TF 58 sink two Japanese guardboats and a cargo ship south of Kyushu, Japan.

**PACIFIC, OKINAWA:** Two battalions of the 306th Infantry Regiment of the 77th Infantry Division lands on Tokashiki Island in the Keramas. Many Okinawan civilians are on the island, moved there by the Japanese. Many commit suicide, convinced by Japanese propaganda that the Americans will torture and kill them.

Japanese kamikaze attacks hit the battleship USS *Nevada*, a cruiser, two destroyers, and a minesweeper. U.S. losses are more than 60 sailors killed and 125 wounded.

**CENTRAL PACIFIC:** Seventh Air Force sends 16 P-51 Mustangs from Iwo Jima to strafe the ammunition storage area on Chichi Jima. During the night five B-24s fly individual harassment raids on Chichi Jima.

## March 28

**CBI:** Fourteenth Air Force sends six B-24 Liberators to bomb the Haiphong and Hanoi docks in French Indochina. P-40s and P-51s attack trucks, tanks, logistics sites, horses, troop concentrations, and artillery in southern and eastern China.

In Burma, Tenth Air Force P-47 Thunderbolts and P-38 Lightnings attack road traffic, troop concentrations, logistics storage sites, and targets of opportunity.

**ETO:** SHAEF issues orders for 12th Army Group to move to Leipzig in anticipation of meeting Soviet forces. The 21st Army Group and the 6th Army Group will protect the flanks of the 12th Army Group's advance. The purpose of the advance on Leipzig is to destroy German forces and capture a key industrial area in order to cut Germany in half. The axis of advance suits armored and mechanized forces and meets the military mission of Allied forces. The British are relegated to a secondary and vague mission. Without prior approval, General Eisenhower informs Stalin of his strategic intent.

The VII Corps of First Army (78th, 104th, and 1st Infantry Divisions and the 3rd Armored Division) occupies a front of 130 miles and reaches Marburg. The 7th Armored Division of III Corps clears Giessen. The 9th Armored Division of V Corps moves to attack Frankfurt from the rear in support of VIII Corps.

The 6th Army Group breaks out of its bridgehead at Worms with XV Corps, VI Corps, and XXI Corps.

Ninth Army's XVI Corps makes slow progress against strong German resistance, capturing Dorsten. The 17th Airborne Division, working with British tank units, outflanks Dorsten and creates a corridor for a XIX Corps breakout. Simpson brings the 2nd Armored Division of XIX Corps into the bridgehead.

Eighth Air Force sends 965 B-17s and 390 P-51 Mustangs to attack industrial targets, marshaling yards, and tank production facilities in Berlin and Hannover, Germany. The bombers use radar signal intercepts to mark the bomb release points over the targets. Two B-17s are lost and 204 are damaged. Aircrew casualties are one killed, 11 wounded, and 19 missing.

Ninth Air Force sends 215 A-20 Havocs, A-26 Invaders, and B-26 Marauders to attack oil storage depots and targets of opportunity. P-47 and P-38 fighters support XII Corps and the 2nd and 8th Armored Divisions.

**SOUTHWEST PACIFIC AREA:** In the Eighth Army area the Americal Division's 182nd Infantry Regiment battles Japanese forces north of Cebu City.

In the Philippines, Far East Air Force B-24 Liberators, P-38 Lightnings, and P-47 Thunderbolts attack Balete Pass and support ground forces on Luzon. B-25 Mitchells and A-20 Havocs also attack troop concentrations on Luzon. B-24s and B-25s bomb the Cebu City area on Cebu Island and hit airfields on Negros Island. B-24s bomb the airfield on Mindanao Island.

B-24s attack Formosa while B-25s attack shore targets along the French Indochina coast. The 39th Troop Carrier Squadron, 317th Troop Carrier Group, redeploys from Leyte Island to Clark Field with C-47s.

U.S. submarine *Blackfin* is damaged by depth charges off the southeast coast of French Indochina and is forced to terminate her patrol. Another submarine, USS *Bluegill,* attacks a Japanese convoy moving up the southern coast of French Indochina and damages a tanker.

Fifth Air Force B-24 Liberators sink a Japanese cargo ship off the north coast of Formosa.

**PACIFIC:** During the night Twentieth Air Force sends 10 B-29s to mine the mouth of the Hwangpoo River and the south channel of the Yangtze River at Shanghai, China. Another 17 B-29s mine the waters at Saigon and Cam Ranh Bay in French Indochina, and 32 B-29s mine an area near Singapore.

A U.S. minesweeper is sunk by mine; a kamikaze damages a medium landing ship off Okinawa.

U.S. submarine *Threadfin* torpedoes and sinks a Japanese escort vessel off Kyushu, Japan.

USS *Tirante* torpedoes and sinks a Japanese fishing boat off Kyushu. U.S. submarine *Trigger* is sunk by three Japanese vessels southeast of Kyushu. Aircraft from carrier USS *Hornet* sink a Japanese coastal defense vessel south of Kyushu that participated in the sinking of USS *Trigger.*

**PACIFIC, OKINAWA:** Japanese kamikaze planes from Okinawa make unsuccessful attacks on landing craft.

**CENTRAL PACIFIC:** Seventh Air Force sends 15 P-51 Mustangs from Iwo Jima to strafe the airfield and defenses on Chichi Jima. During the night five B-24s fly individual harassment raids on Chichi Jima, and 10 B-24s from Guam conduct individual snooper missions on Truk.

**NEW GUINEA:** Thirteenth Air Force B-24 Liberators attack Japanese shipping in the Celebes, sinking a minesweeper and a patrol boat.

### March 29

**ALEUTIANS:** Eleventh Air Force sends six B-24 Liberators to bomb Kataoka naval base on Shimushu Island in the Kuriles.

**CBI:** Fourteenth Air Force sends 11 B-24 Liberators to attack shipping in the South China Sea and at Haiphong, French Indochina. Aircrews report one destroyer and a cargo ship are heavily damaged. In China, 18 B-25 Mitchells, escorted by 12 P-40s, bomb railyards. P-40s and P-51s attack trucks, tanks, logistics sites, horses, troops, and artillery in southern and eastern China.

In Burma, Tenth Air Force sends six B-25 Mitchells to bomb troop concentrations.

**ETO:** Wiesbaden is captured, along with Frankfurt; Mannheim falls. Since the beginning of March, American forces are capturing 10,000 prisoners a day. First Army begins its turn northward toward Paderborn to link with Ninth Army for the encirclement of the Ruhr. A task force of the 3rd Armored Division and a regiment from the 104th Infantry Division lead the attack.

The 2nd Armored Division of XIX Corps, Ninth Army, breaks out of the bridgehead northeast of Dorsten.

Third Army attacks northeast toward Kassel, protecting the flank of First Army.

**ITALY:** Twelfth Air Force and P-47 Thunderbolts of the XXII Tactical Air Command attack rail lines, bridges, ammunition storage areas, and roads in the Po River valley. During the night A-20s attack vehicles, river crossing points, logistics storage sites, roads, bridges, and rail loading sites.

**SOUTHWEST PACIFIC AREA:** On Luzon, in the XIV Corps area, the 1st Cavalry Division and the 11th Airborne Division conduct a double envelopment, trapping about 1,300 Japanese troops at Lipa.

In the Eighth Army area, the 185th RCT of the 40th Infantry Division lands on Negros. American forces secure a key bridge on the way to Bacolod, allowing for a rapid advance.

In the Philippines, Far East Air Force B-24 Liberators and P-51 Mustangs attack Legaspi and the surrounding area on Luzon, while A-20 Havocs and P-38 Lightnings attack targets in support of ground forces. B-25s bomb Cebu Island, while A-20s support troops landing on Negros Island.

B-24 Liberators and B-25 Mitchells bomb Formosa.

U.S. submarine *Bluegill* attacks the same Japanese convoy as yesterday while it moves up the southern coast of French Indochina. The tanker torpedoed previously is hit again. U.S. Submarine *Hammerhead* damages a coastal defense vessel. Fifth Air Force B-25 Mitchells sink two coastal defense vessels and a cargo ship off French Indochina and sink three auxiliary submarine chasers and a merchant tanker in Takao harbor, Formosa.

FEAF B-24 Liberators bomb an airfield in Borneo.

**PACIFIC:** During the night Twentieth Air Force sends 29 B-29s to fly the last mission under XX Bomber Command, attacking oil storage facilities on Bukum Island in the Malay States. Two other B-29s bomb individual targets on the Malay Peninsula.

Naval Task Groups 58.1 (Rear Admiral Joseph J. Clark) and 58.3 (Rear Admiral Frederick C. Sherman) attack airfields and shipping around Kagoshima Bay, Kyushu, Japan. Carrier aircraft sink three auxiliary submarine chasers and nine cargo vessels. One merchant vessel is damaged.

Japanese submarine *I-47* carrying *kaiten* is damaged by Fifth Fleet surface ships off Okinawa and forced to return to Japan for repairs.

**PACIFIC, OKINAWA:** The 77th Infantry Division secures the islands of the Keramas. Over 500 Japanese are killed. Nearly 1,200 civilians are under American control. U.S. losses are 31 killed and 81 wounded. Over 290 boats, intended for attacks on the U.S. Fleet, are captured.

Task Force 58's carrier aircraft attack Kyushu Island.

Underwater demolition teams conduct a reconnaissance on the Hagushi landing beaches.

**CENTRAL PACIFIC:** Seventh Air Force sends nine B-24 Liberators from Guam Island to bomb Truk. A total of 31 P-51 Mustangs from Iwo Jima bomb and strafe Haha Jima.

The headquarters of Twentieth Air Force's 58th Bombardment Wing (Very Heavy) arrives at Tinian from India.

## March 30

**CBI:** Fourteenth Air Force B-24 Liberators bomb the Samah Bay area of Hainan Island. In China, B-25 Mitchells, supported by 24 P-40s, destroy a bridge and other B-25s bomb railyards. B-25 Mitchells, with 15 P-40s providing escort, bomb Hankow airfield. P-40s and P-51s attack troops, rail targets, trucks, tanks, logistics sites, airfields, and rivercraft in southern and eastern China.

In Burma, Tenth Air Force sends B-25 Mitchells to bomb road bridges, troop concentrations, logistics storage sites, and trucks. P-47 Thunderbolts and P-38 Lightnings attack Japanese troops and logistics sites.

**ETO:** General Eisenhower orders Field Marshal Bernard L. Montgomery's 21st Army Group and General Omar N. Bradley's 12th Army Group to link at Kassel-Paderborn to encircle the Ruhr and destroy the final organized elements of the German army in the west. The 6th Army Group is to advance to protect the flank of the 12th Army Group. Once the pocket in the Ruhr is cleared, the 12th Army Group is to advance to the east. The focus of effort is now shifted from the north to the center, with both army groups conducting a simultaneous envelopment, rather than a main effort from the north with a supporting attack in the center as was originally planned.

The U.S. Fifteenth Army is created under the command of Lieutenant General Leonard T. Gerow to hold the rear areas so combat operations into Germany can continue. Gerow's army is responsible for governing the parts of Germany already occupied by the Allies and is responsible for the territory west of the Rhine between Bonn and Homberg. Lieutenant General Gerow also has operational control of the 66th Infantry Division guarding the German garrisons at Lorient and St-Nazaire.

The British leadership presses the Americans for a rapid advance on Berlin to beat the Soviets, arguing that Berlin is an important strategic political objective.

During the month of March, the Allies have moved 1.8 million tons of supplies to the forward areas, most of it by rail but a significant amount by pipeline, barges, and trucks as well. About 40 percent of all these supplies are delivered through Antwerp and Ghent; about 30 percent through Le Havre, Cherbourg, and Rouen; and about 10 percent through Marseille. About 230,000 men in the rear areas have been retrained as infantrymen to replace combat losses. Draftees also flow into theater, providing enough of a manpower pool to bring the American divisions to full strength by late March.

The 4th Armored Division of XII Corps, Third Army, reaches Hersfeld. The 3rd Armored Division of VII Corps moves 90 miles and approaches Paderborn. Major General Maurice Rose, the division's commander, is killed when he encounters German troops outside the city.

Eighth Air Force sends more than 1,400 B-17s and B-24 Liberators escorted by nearly 900 P-51 Mustangs to bomb U-boat facilities, port areas, and oil depots. A total of five bombers are lost and 536 are damaged. Aircrews report eight confirmed kills, one probable, and 12 possibles. Aircrew casualties are 22 killed, 11 wounded, and 28 missing. Fighter pilots report one probable and three possibles in the air. Three P-51s are lost. Over 150 P-51s fly a freelance mission for the bombers. Pilots report one confirmed kill. Three submarines are sunk at Wilhelmshaven, six submarines are sunk at Bremen, and four at Hamburg.

A total of 32 B-17s fly a Disney mission, launching rocket-powered concrete-penetrating bombs against the U-boat yard at Farge. Fourteen B-17s are damaged.

Six B-17s conduct screening missions to jam German radio interception efforts and employ countermeasures against German radar sites.

During the night 13 B-24s drop leaflets over Germany and the Netherlands. Nineteen B-24 Liberators fly Carpetbagger missions to Norway. One B-24 is lost, and another crashes in the Orkney Islands.

Ninth Air Force sends 337 A-20 Havocs, A-26 Invaders, and B-26 Marauders to attack a tank production facility, an ordnance depot, and an oil depot. P-47 and P-38 fighters support the 3rd and 7th Armored Divisions, XII Corps, XX Corps, and XVI Corps.

The headquarters of the 349th Troop Carrier Group and the C-46s of the 312th Troop Carrier Squadron, IX Troop Carrier Command, arrive in England from the United States.

First Lieutenant Walter J. Will, K Company, 18th Infantry Regiment, 1st Infantry Division, rescues two wounded soldiers in the face of heavy enemy fire near Eisern, Germany, and even though he is wounded himself, risks his life again to rescue another soldier. Ignoring his injury, he leads his platoon forward until they are pinned down by flanking fire from two enemy machine guns. Will moves out alone and reaches the first machine-gun position and eliminates the enemy with grenades. He continues to crawl to the next position and charges it, capturing the gun and nine soldiers. He takes one of his squads on a flanking movement to attack another two machine-gun positions firing on another platoon. In the face of direct enemy fire, Will throws three grenades at the Germans, knocking out one machine gun. He then attacks the second position and destroys it with a grenade. The platoon then sweeps forward to clear the enemy off the objective, and during this last action Will is killed. For his heroic leadership, indomitable courage, and unflinching devotion to duty, First Lieutenant Will will receive the Medal of Honor.

**MEDITERRANEAN:** Fifteenth Air Force sends more than 60 B-17s and B-24 Liberators escorted by P-38 Lightnings and P-51 Mustangs to bomb marshaling yards in Austria. P-38s and P-51s fly sweeps over Yugoslavia and Austria.

**ITALY:** Twelfth Air Force B-25 Mitchells bomb rail bridges. P-47 Thunderbolts of the XXII Tactical Air Command attack rail lines, bridges, vehicles, fuel storage sites, and ammunition storage areas. During the night A-20s and A-26 Invaders attack roads, river crossing sites, and motor transport in the Po River valley.

**SOUTHWEST PACIFIC AREA:** In the Eighth Army area, the 186th and 163rd Infantry Regiments of the 41st Infantry Division eliminate the final Japanese defenders outside of Zamboanga City. American casualties are 220 killed. The Japanese have lost nearly 7,000 killed. Airfields in the area are improved and expanded.

The 185th RCT of the 40th Infantry Division captures Bacolod on Negros.

In the Philippines, Far East Air Force B-24 Liberators bomb Balete Pass, P-38 Lightnings attack artillery positions, and A-20 Havocs and P-47 Thunderbolts conduct ground support missions in the Laguna de Bay area and on Japanese positions near Fort Stotsenburg on Luzon. B-24s and A-20s support ground forces on Cebu Island. B-24s, B-25s, and P-38 Lightnings attack Bongao Island.

FEAF B-24 Liberators and B-25 Mitchells attack targets in Borneo.

**PACIFIC:** During the night Twentieth Air Force sends more than 90 B-29s to attack the Mitsubishi aircraft engine production facility at Nagoya, Japan. One B-29 is lost. Twentieth Air Force B-29s mine the Shimonoseki Strait and the waters off Kure, Hiroshima, and Sasebo, Japan.

A kamikaze damages heavy cruiser USS *Indianapolis* off Okinawa. U.S. submarine *Tirante* torpedoes and sinks a Japanese guardboat off Kagoshima, Kyushu, Japan,

**CENTRAL PACIFIC:** Seventh Air Force sends 10 B-24 Liberators from Guam to bomb the airfield on Marcus Island. During the night five B-24s fly individual harassment raids on Chichi Jima.

## March 31

**CBI:** In China, Fourteenth Air Force B-24 Liberators with nine P-51 Mustangs escorting, bomb railyards. B-25 Mitchells bomb a bridge and gun positions. B-25s, P-40s, and P-51s attack trucks, tanks, logistics sites, horses, troops, and artillery in southern and eastern China. Over 20 P-51s attack Ningpo airfield. Fighter pilots report a number of Japanese aircraft destroyed on the ground. Six P-51s are lost.

In Burma, Tenth Air Force sends 12 B-25 Mitchells to bomb a road bridge behind Japanese lines.

**ATLANTIC:** The United States and Britain bar a Soviet-supported provisional regime in Warsaw from entering the United Nations meeting in San Francisco.

**ETO:** The 9th Armored Division of V Corps reaches Warburg. The French First Army makes an assault crossing of the Rhine River at Speyer and Gemersheim. General de Lattre de Tassigny is under orders from General Charles de Gaulle to push

French forces into German territory. Fearing that the French will be marginalized in the postwar peace, de Gaulle wants to strengthen France's hand.

The 2nd Armored Division of the XIX Corps of Ninth Army advances 40 miles in two days to reach Beckum, cutting the main highway to Berlin and cutting the main rail lines to the Ruhr. One arm of the envisioned encirclement of the Ruhr is in place.

Eighth Air Force sends more than 1,300 B-17s and B-24 Liberators escorted by nearly 900 P-47 Thunderbolts and P-51 Mustangs to bomb synthetic oil production facilities, industrial targets, and marshaling yards. The bombers use radar signal intercepts to mark the bomb release points over the targets. A total of five bombers are lost and 153 damaged. Aircrews report nine confirmed kills, three probables, and nine possibles. Aircrew casualties are 11 killed, three wounded, and 59 missing. Fighter pilots report five confirmed kills and seven possibles in the air. Four P-51s are lost, and the pilots are reported missing. Over 25 P-51s fly scouting missions. Pilots report one confirmed kill and one possible.

Eight B-17s conduct screening missions to jam German radio interception efforts and employ countermeasures against German radar sites.

Ninth Air Force sends more than 550 A-20 Havocs, A-26 Invaders, and B-26 Marauders to attack storage depots and a marshaling yard. P-47 and P-38 fighters support the 3rd and 9th Armored Divisions, XII Corps, XX Corps, XVI and XIX Corps.

**MEDITERRANEAN:** Fifteenth Air Force reports that, in the first three months of 1945, fighters have destroyed 1,100 locomotives, 3,600 rail cars, and 132 vehicles. A total of 65 U.S. fighters have been lost during the same period.

Fifteenth Air Force sends more than 540 B-17s and B-24 Liberators escorted by P-38 Lightnings and P-51 Mustangs to bomb rail lines and marshaling yards in Austria and Italy.

**ITALY:** Twelfth Air Force B-25 Mitchells bomb bridges. P-47 Thunderbolts attack rail lines, logistics storage sites, and ammunition storage areas. During the night A-20s attack river crossing points, rail lines, and ammunition storage areas in the Po River valley.

**SOUTHWEST PACIFIC AREA:** On Luzon, Private First Class William R. Shockley, L Company, 128th Infantry Regiment, 32nd Infantry Division, faces a Japanese counterattack on the Villa Verde Trail. As artillery fire lands around the Americans, Shockley tells his comrades to fall back while he holds off the Japanese. With supreme bravery he stops one charge, even when his weapon malfunctions. He shifts fire to stop a flanking movement and fights on until overwhelmed by superior numbers. For his heroic sacrifice to save the lives of his comrades, Private First Class Shockley will receive the Medal of Honor.

In the Philippines, Far East Air Force P-47 Thunderbolts and P-38 Lightnings attack Japanese positions in the Cagayan Valley and bridges and gun positions throughout Luzon. B-25 Mitchells, A-20 Havocs, and P-38 Lightnings attack targets on Cebu Island.

On Formosa, A-20s attack an army camp, and P-51s conduct a sweep across the island. B-24s bomb harbors and shipping at Kirun and Yulin, China.

FEAF B-24 Liberators bomb targets on Borneo and fighters attack airfields in north Borneo. Thirteenth Air Force B-24 Liberators attack a Japanese convoy off Makassar, sinking four small cargo vessels and damaging another.

**PACIFIC:** Twentieth Air Force sends more than 130 B-29 Superfortresses to bomb the Tachiarai machine works and Omura airfield on Kyushu Island, Japan. This attack is intended to divert Japanese aircraft from the invasion of Okinawa. The machine works is completely destroyed. Aircrews report 11 confirmed kills, five probables, and three possibles. One B-29 is lost and 15 are damaged.

**PACIFIC, OKINAWA:** Kerama Islands are secured. American casualties are 31 killed and 81 wounded. Japanese casualties number over 600. Keise Shima Island is captured without resistance. The 420th Field Artillery Group will occupy the island to provide fire support for the invasion of Okinawa with 155 millimeter guns.

Intense air and naval bombardment of suspected Japanese positions near the landing beaches continues.

Japanese kamikaze aircraft hit Admiral Spruance's flagship, the cruiser USS *Indianapolis,* killing nine sailors and wounding 20. Spruance transfers to the battleship USS *New Mexico.*

Underwater demolition teams complete the destruction of underwater obstacles at the Hagushi landing beach sites.

Kamikazes damage a light minelayer, an attack transport, and two LSTs off Okinawa. Two U.S. destroyers sink Japanese submarine *I-8* southeast of Okinawa.

**CENTRAL PACIFIC:** Seventh Air Force sends 15 P-51 Mustangs from Iwo Jima to strafe the airfield, logistics storage areas, shipping, and radar installation on Chichi Jima. During the night five B-24s from Guam fly individual harassment raids on Chichi Jima.

## April 1

**CBI:** In China, seven Fourteenth Air Force B-24 Liberators bomb the Fort Bayard logistics storage area. B-25 Mitchells and P-51 Mustangs attack river shipping and warehouses.

In Burma, Tenth Air Force sends 10 B-25 Mitchells to attack roads and bridges behind enemy lines in central Burma as the British 36th Division begins to advance down the railroad from Mandalay to Rangoon.

**ETO:** A task force of the 3rd Armored Division, VII Corps, First Army, meets with elements of the 2nd Armored Division, XIX Corps, Ninth Army, at Lippstadt. The encirclement of the Ruhr is completed, thus accomplishing General Eisenhower's strategic design developed in 1944. A total of 21 divisions representing Germany's Army Group B and two corps of Army Group H are completely isolated in a 4,000-square-mile area.

The Fifteenth Army's XXII Corps, commanded by Major General Ernest N. Harmon, takes over a section of the pocket with the 94th Infantry Division and the 101st and 82nd Airborne Divisions. Fifteenth Army is placed under the operational control of Bradley's 12th Army Group. The First and Ninth Armies also hold the pocket. The Ninth Army's XVI Corps and two divisions of XIX Corps will hold the pocket from the north while the XIII Corps moves eastward. The XVIII Airborne

Corps (now under First Army operational control) and III Corps of First Army will hold the pocket from the south while V Corps and VII Corps advance eastward.

The French II Corps establishes a bridgehead at Philippsburg and prepares to attack toward Stuttgart.

During the night Eighth Air Force sends 12 B-24s to drop leaflets over Germany and the Netherlands.

Ninth Air Force P-47 and P-38 fighters support the 3rd and 9th Armored Divisions, XX Corps and XII Corps.

**MEDITERRANEAN:** Fifteenth Air Force sends more than 400 B-17s and B-24 Liberators escorted by P-38 Lightnings and P-51 Mustangs to bomb bridges in Yugoslavia and in Austria. P-51s strafe rail lines in Czechoslovakia.

**ITALY:** Twelfth Air Force B-25 Mitchells bomb rail and road traffic and bridges. P-47 Thunderbolts attack rail lines, bridges, marshaling yards, logistics storage sites, and roads in the Po River valley. During the night A-20 Havocs and A-26 Invaders attack road and rail bridges and motor transport in the Po River valley.

**SOUTHWEST PACIFIC AREA:** On Luzon, the 158th RCT conducts an amphibious landing on Legaspi on the southeast coast of the Bicol Peninsula, supported by naval gunfire and air bombardment. Japanese resistance is light and unorganized.

In the Philippines, Far East Air Force B-24 Liberators, A-20 Havocs, P-38 Lightnings, and P-47 Thunderbolts attack the Legaspi area in support of amphibious landing operations and attack Japanese positions near Balete Pass and other areas on Luzon. B-25 Mitchells and A-20 Havocs support ground forces near Cebu City on Cebu Island and on Negros Island.

B-24 Liberators bomb an airfield on Formosa, while B-25s and P-47s sweep across wide areas of the island.

The headquarters of Fifth Air Force prepares to redeploy from Mindoro Island to Clark Field on Luzon.

In the Formosa Straits, U.S. submarine *Queenfish* sinks a Japanese relief ship carrying Red Cross supplies for Allied prisoners of war at Singapore.

FEAF B-24 Liberators attack Oelin airfield in Borneo.

**PACIFIC:** The Japanese Imperial General Headquarters adopts Ketsu, a plan for the defense of the home islands and China. Most Japanese forces in China will be withdrawn to the home islands, while the remainder of Japanese forces in China will consolidate along the southern coast of China, primarily to preclude any Allied invasions.

Twentieth Air Force begins the redeployment of the B-29s of the 25th Bombardment Squadron (Very Heavy), 40th Bombardment Group (Very Heavy), the 676th, 677th, and 678th Bombardment Squadrons (Very Heavy), 444th Bombardment Group (Very Heavy), and the 768th, 769th, and 770th Bombardment Squadrons (Very Heavy) of the 462nd Bombardment Group (Very Heavy), from India to Tinian Island.

Six B-29s mine the waters off Kure, Japan. Mines dropped in the Shimonoseki Strait sink a cargo ship and damage an escort vessel and an auxiliary submarine chaser.

**PACIFIC: Operation Iceberg: the Invasion of Okinawa.** The operation is under the overall command of Admiral Raymond A. Spruance, Commander Fifth Fleet. Vice Admiral Richmond K. Turner commands the Joint Expeditionary Force. Lieutenant General Simon B. Buckner commands the ground forces. The invasion of Okinawa begins with the largest concentration of naval gunfire in World War II. Ten battleships, nine cruisers, 23 destroyers, and 117 rocket gunboats fire nearly 4,000 tons of shells onto the island. The 2nd Marine Division conducts a diversionary landing near Minatoga, off the southeast coast of the island.

The 96th and 7th Infantry Divisions land along with the 1st and 6th Marine Divisions—a total of 16,000 men—nearly simultaneously. It is one of the greatest spectacles of the war. The landing is unopposed, and the Americans move rapidly inland to their objectives. By the end of L-day, 60,000 men are ashore, along with vehicles and supplies.

There are no Japanese near the beaches. Enemy troops have pulled back into other prepared defensive positions on the island, waiting for the Americans to come to them. Within a few hours, the 6th Marine Division reaches Yomitan airfield, while the 17th Infantry Regiment of the 7th Infantry Division captures Kadena airfield, both objectives far ahead of the L+3 timeline. The 22nd and 4th Marine Regiments of the 6th Marine Division move north and east. On the left flank of the 6th Marines, the 1st Marine Division occupies the high ground after encountering only a few Japanese. The 7th Infantry Division's 17th and 32nd Infantry Regiments advance 4,700 yards and establish defensive positions. The 96th Infantry Division's 381st and 383rd Infantry Regiments, landing on the south edge of the beachhead, clear out a number of defensive positions.

U.S. casualties for the day are 28 killed, 104 wounded, and 27 missing.

Kamikazes damage battleship USS *West Virginia,* two attack transports, and an LST. Japanese dive-bombers damage a destroyer and a minesweeper. Bombers damage an attack transport. A kamikaze damages British fleet carrier HMS *Indefatigable.* A British destroyer is damaged by a bomb.

## April 2

**CBI:** In China, Fourteenth Air Force sends 25 B-25 Mitchells to attack trucks, tanks, rivercraft, and targets of opportunity. B-24 Liberators bomb the Kowloon docks in Hong Kong and attack shipping near Hainan Island. P-51 Mustangs bomb airfields near Shanghai, while B-25s, P-40s, and P-51s attack trucks, tanks, logistics sites, horses, troops, and artillery in southern and eastern China.

In French Indochina, 28 B-25 Mitchells knock out a bridge and attack shipping and other targets of opportunity along the coast of the Gulf of Tonkin.

**ETO:** The XVIII Corps takes control of part of the Ruhr Pocket, gaining two divisions from VII Corps (8th and 78th Infantry Divisions). The XVIII Corps now has the 97th, 78th, 8th, and 86th Infantry Divisions under its operational control.

Bad weather cancels a mission by over 600 B-17s and B-24 Liberators to bomb airfields in Denmark. One B-17 is lost, one P-51 is lost, and one fighter is damaged. During the night 10 B-24s drop leaflets over France, Germany, and the Netherlands, and 10 B-24 Liberators fly Carpetbagger missions to Denmark.

Ninth Air Force P-47 Thunderbolts and P-38 Lightnings support the 9th Armored Division.

**MEDITERRANEAN:** Fifteenth Air Force sends more than 600 B-17s and B-24 Liberators escorted by P-38 Lightnings and P-51 Mustangs to bomb marshaling yards and a rail bridge in Austria. P-38s and P-51s attack rail traffic in Germany, Austria, and Yugoslavia.

**ITALY:** Major General Benjamin W. Chidlaw takes command of Twelfth Air Force and is scheduled to take command of the Mediterranean Allied Tactical Air Force (MATAF). Twelfth Air Force B-25 Mitchells bomb rail bridges. P-47 Thunderbolt pilots report 13 German aircraft destroyed in the air during attacks on rail lines, bridges, and roads in the Po River valley. During the night A-20 Havocs and A-26 Invaders attack river crossing points, roads, and motor transport in the Po River valley.

**SOUTHWEST PACIFIC AREA:** Marine fighters and three destroyers support the 163rd RCT, 41st Infantry Division, as it lands on Sanga Sanga, in the Sulu Archipelago, Philippines. No enemy forces are found.

In the Philippines, Far East Air Force B-25 Mitchells, P-38 Lightnings, and P-47 Thunderbolts attack bridges and the Balete Pass area. B-25s bomb Japanese troops at Cebu City on Cebu Island. Japanese troops are also attacked by B-25s and P-38s on Negros Island. B-24 Liberators bomb Bongao Island and the Sarangani Bay area on Mindanao Island.

B-24 Liberators bomb the harbor at Hong Kong.

U.S. submarine *Hardhead* lays mines off the southern coast of French Indochina.

U.S. submarine *Sea Devil* attacks a Japanese convoy in the Yellow Sea, sinking an auxiliary vessel and two cargo ships and damaging another cargo ship.

FEAF B-24 Liberators attack the Sandakan shipyards and Tawau airfield on Borneo.

**PACIFIC:** Twentieth Air Force sends more than 100 B-29 Superfortresses to bomb the Nakajima aircraft production facility at Tokyo. Aircrews report one confirmed kill and one probable. Six B-29s are lost. During the night six B-29s mine the harbors at Kure and Hiroshima on Honshu Island, Japan.

Naval Task Group 58.4 carrier aircraft sink a Japanese coast defense vessel, a fast transport, and a landing ship and damage a submarine chaser and a landing ship in the Ryukyus.

**PACIFIC, OKINAWA:** The 2nd Marine Division repeats its diversionary landing near Minatoga off the southeast coast of the island. The 6th Marine Division advances three miles northward. The 22nd and 29th Marines encounter no opposition, but the 4th Marines fight through a number of strongpoints. The 1st Marine Division encounters no resistance as it advances across the island. The 7th Infantry Division reaches the eastern coast of Okinawa without encountering significant resistance. The 32nd and the 17th Infantry Regiments occupy ridges overlooking Nakagusuku Bay on the east edge of the island. The 96th Infantry Division advances 3,000 yards in difficult terrain, supported by tanks and aircraft. The American advance secures the 10th Army's beachhead.

A destroyer and a destroyer escort are hit by bombs. Kamikazes damage three attack transports, two attack cargo ships, and a high-speed transport off Okinawa.

**Central Pacific:** Seventh Air Force sends 12 B-24 Liberators to bomb Marcus Island.

## April 3

**CBI:** Fourteenth Air Force sends 17 B-25 Mitchells to bomb railyards and bridges in French Indochina.

**Atlantic:** The army chief of staff, General George C. Marshall, informs the JCS of reports indicating that the Soviets are becoming increasingly less cooperative in fulfilling their obligations under the Yalta agreement. Marshall is concerned that such actions will threaten Allied unity at a critical point in the war.

**ETO:** The Ninth Army is returned to Bradley's operational control. Ninth Army captures Recklinghausen in the Ruhr, while First Army captures Fulda and Kassel.

The III Corps of First Army (99th, 9th, and 5th Infantry Divisions and the 7th Armored Division) is directed to attack along the eastern edge of the Ruhr Pocket. This frees Lieutenant General Hodges to use two remaining corps of First Army for the attack to the east.

The 45th Infantry Division, XV Corps, Seventh Army, captures Aschaffenburg after a six-day battle for the city.

Eighth Air Force sends more than 750 B-17s and B-24 Liberators escorted by 569 P-51 Mustangs to bomb the U-boat yards at Kiel. Two bombers are lost and 121 are damaged. Aircrews report one confirmed kill. Aircrew casualties are one wounded and 20 missing. Fighter pilots report one confirmed kill in the air. Two fighters are lost and three are damaged. At the U-boat yards at Kiel, three submarines are destroyed by air attack. Seventeen P-51s fly a scouting mission and two fighters are lost.

During the night one B-17 and 10 B-24s drop leaflets over Germany, France, and the Netherlands. Ninth Air Force sends 230 A-20 Havocs, A-26 Invaders, and B-26 Marauders to attack marshaling yards. P-47 and P-38 fighters support 2nd, 8th, and 9th Armored Divisions, XX Corps and XII Corps.

The C-47s of the 23rd, 313th, and 314th Troop Carrier Squadrons, 349th Troop Carrier Group, IX Troop Carrier Command, arrive in England from the United States.

Private First Class Walter C. Wetzel is acting squad leader with the Antitank Company, 13th Infantry Regiment, 8th Infantry Division, guarding his platoon's command post in a house at Birken, Germany. Spotting German troops moving quickly into the town, Wetzel warns the command post and returns fire as the German infantry advances on the house. Taking up a firing position in the house, Wetzel reacts when the Germans throw grenades into the room. Shouting a warning to his fellow soldiers, Wetzel throws himself on the grenades and is killed, but saves the lives of his comrades. For his supreme sacrifice, Private First Class Wetzel will receive the Medal of Honor.

**Mediterranean:** Fifteenth Air Force sends 95 P-38 Lightnings to conduct dive-bombing on a railroad bridge in Austria.

**Italy:** Twelfth Air Force B-25 Mitchells bomb rail and road traffic and bridges. A-20 Havocs and P-47 Thunderbolts of the XXII Tactical Air Command attack vehicles, logistics storage sites, ammunition storage areas, rail lines, bridges, and roads in the Po River valley. During the night A-20s attack the marshaling yard at Mantua, river crossing sites, and roads and motor transport in the Po River valley.

**SOUTHWEST PACIFIC AREA:** Eighth Army plans to land X Corps, commanded by Major General Franklin C. Sibert, with the 24th and 31st Infantry Divisions, on the west side of Mindanao. The 24th will land and capture the airfield at Malabang; two days later the 31st Infantry Division will land at Parang to control Highway 1, the main road to Davao. Rear Admiral Albert G. Noble's task group will support the landings. Before the landing at Malabang takes place, the guerrillas notify the Americans that the airfield is already secured. Marine aviators from Dipolog land on the airfield and attack Japanese positions.

In the Philippines, Far East Air Force A-20 Havocs, P-38 Lightnings, and P-47 Thunderbolts attack the Balete Pass and the Cagayan Valley areas.

B-25 Mitchells attack north Hainan Island. B-24 Liberators bomb the docks at Hong Kong. Other B-24s and B-25 Mitchells attack the airfield, a butanol plant, and railroad yards at Kagi, on Formosa, while A-20s sweep other rail targets.

Far East Air Force B-24 Liberators bomb Japanese shipping in Hong Kong harbor, sinking two cargo vessels and damaging an escort vessel.

**PACIFIC:** Twentieth Air Force sends 48 B-29s to bomb the aircraft production facility at Shizuoka, Japan. Another 43 B-29s attack the Koizumi aircraft production facility and urban areas in Tokyo. Aircrews report one confirmed kill. A total of 61 B-29s hit the primary target, the aircraft production facility at Tachikawa, while 49 others hit the urban area of Kawasaki as a target of opportunity. One B-29 is lost. During the night nine B-29s mine the waters off Kure and the harbor at Hiroshima, Honshu, Japan. Escort carrier USS *Wake Island* and a high-speed minesweeper are damaged by near-misses of kamikazes. A kamikaze damages an LST.

Carrier aircraft from TF 58 sink a Japanese guardboat and damage a guardboat southeast of Honshu, Japan, and sink a cargo ship off southwestern Kyushu, Japan. A coastal defense vessel is also damaged.

**PACIFIC, OKINAWA:** Advancing south, the 96th Infantry Division ties in with the 7th Infantry Division as it captures the town of Kuba. General Buckner orders the 6th Marine Division to attack and seize the northern half of Okinawa to prevent enemy reinforcements from landing in the rear of 10th Army. The 1st Marine Division prepares to advance into the Katchin Peninsula. The beachhead now stretches across the middle of the island.

## April 4

**CBI:** In French Indochina, Fourteenth Air Force sends two B-25 Mitchells to attack shipping in the Gulf of Tonkin. Six P-38 Lightnings strafe trucks around Dien Bien Phu.

**ATLANTIC:** The Joint Chiefs of Staff designates General of the Army Douglas MacArthur as Commander in Chief, U.S. Army Forces, Pacific (CINCUSAFPAC) and Fleet Admiral Chester W. Nimitz as Commander in Chief, Pacific (CINCPOA).

**ETO:** General Eisenhower orders General Omar N. Bradley's 12th Army Group to attack from Kassel to Leipzig and establish a bridgehead over the Elbe River. Bradley will be the main effort in the final defeat of Germany. Field Marshal Bernard L. Montgomery's 21st Army Group is also to advance to the Elbe River and then north along the Baltic coast, but will primarily protect Bradley's left flank. Lieutenant General Jacob L. Devers's 6th Army Group is to protect Bradley's southern flank and advance to Bayreuth, then be prepared to advance to Nürnberg and Linz. The British Chiefs of Staff notify Eisenhower that his plan for the final offensive in Germany is inadequate. Having Montgomery's 21st Army Group advance to Bremen, then to the Elbe River, ignores Berlin as a critical objective that must be occupied before the Soviets get to the capital. Eisenhower believes Berlin is no longer a military objective. The Soviet advance and the heavy Allied bombing have rendered it useless as a military objective. Eisenhower believes that SHAEF's mission is to focus on German military forces and not on political issues.

The French First Army's II Corps, part of the 6th Army Group, captures Karlsruhe.

The Ninth Army's XIX Corps advances to link with First Army and attack toward the Ruhr Pocket. The 2nd Armored Division of XIX Corps and the 5th Armored Division of XIII Corps of Ninth Army reach the Weser River. The XVI Corps (95th, 75th, 35th, and 79th Infantry Divisions, the 8th Armored Division, and the 17th Airborne Division) battles German defenders north of the Ruhr River.

In the Third Army area, 4th Armored Division and elements of the 89th Infantry Division make the first Western encounter with a concentration camp, at Ohrdruf. This is a subcamp of the Buchenwald concentration camp and the first Nazi camp liberated by American forces. It was established in 1944 to supply forced labor for construction projects. In March it held nearly 12,000 prisoners, but by April most have been moved to Buchenwald by a series of forced marches. Those too weak to move have been killed. Bodies lie in heaps; most are victims of malnutrition. There are indications that the guards have made hasty attempts to cover up the evidence by burning the remains.

Eighth Air Force sends more than 1,400 B-17s and B-24 Liberators escorted by over 800 P-47 Thunderbolts and P-51 Mustangs to bomb airfields, shipyards, and U-boat facilities. The bombers use a combination of visual techniques and radar signal intercepts to mark the bomb release points over the targets. A total of 10 bombers are lost and 187 are damaged. Aircrews report six confirmed kills, four probables, and six possibles. Aircrew casualties are two killed, six wounded, and 90 missing. At the U-boat yards at Hamburg and Kiel three submarines are destroyed.

A total of 22 of 24 B-17s fly a Disney mission attacking the Finkenwarder U-boat yard at Hamburg with wing-mounted, 4,500-pound, concrete-penetrating rocket bombs.

Fighter pilots report 23 confirmed kills and five possibles in the air. Five fighters are lost. P-51 Mustangs flying a scouting mission and escorting photo and radar reconnaissance missions over Germany report one confirmed kill and one possible in the air.

Ninth Air Force sends 330 A-20 Havocs, A-26 Invaders, and B-26 Marauders to attack oil depots, road and rail junctions, and targets of opportunity. P-47 and P-38 fighters support the 104th Infantry Division, the 9th Armored Division, XX Corps, and the 8th, 2nd, and 5th Armored Divisions.

The headquarters of Ninth Air Force's XXIX Tactical Air Command (Provisional) returns to the operational control of Ninth Air Force from the RAF Second Tactical Air Force, as the U.S. Ninth Army reverts to control of General Omar Bradley's 12th Army Group from General Montgomery's 21st Army Group.

**MEDITERRANEAN:** Fifteenth Air Force sends 94 P-51 Mustangs to attack rail traffic near Munich and Regensburg, Germany, at Plzen in Czechoslovakia, and at two areas in Austria.

**ITALY:** Twelfth Air Force B-25 Mitchells bomb rail bridges. P-47 Thunderbolts of the XXII Tactical Air Command attack rail lines, logistics storage sites, and ammunition storage areas in the Po River valley.

**SOUTHWEST PACIFIC AREA:** On Luzon, in the XIV Corps area, the 1st Cavalry Division and the 11th Airborne Division conduct a double envelopment, trapping about 1,600 Japanese troops at Tiaong.

In the Philippines, Far East Air Force A-20 Havocs, P-38 Lightnings, and P-51 Mustangs bomb targets on Luzon. A-20s bomb Negros Island and B-24 Liberators bomb targets on Mindanao Island.

On Formosa, B-24s bomb airfields and harbor installations, while A-20s attack factories and railyards. B-24s bomb the harbor at Hong Kong.

Far East Air Force B-24 Liberators bomb Japanese shipping at Mako, Pescadores, sinking a merchant tanker and a cargo vessel.

**PACIFIC:** The headquarters of the 40th and 462nd Bombardment Groups (Very Heavy) arrive at Tinian from India.

A Japanese escort vessel and a cargo ship are sunk by mines dropped by Twentieth Air Force B-29s and two submarines are damaged.

**PACIFIC, OKINAWA:** Major General John R. Hodge, commander of XXIV Corps, orders the 96th Infantry Division to capture the Urasoe-Mura escarpment straddling Highways 1 and 5. He also orders the 7th Infantry Division to capture Hill 178, with the high ground controlling Highway 13, called Skyline Ridge. Hodge needs these roads clear to supply the advancing troops. Unknown to the Americans, the Japanese have prepared this area as the first line of their layered defenses.

The 6th Marine Division attacks northward into the Ishikawa Isthmus with three regiments. At Yae-Take, on the Motobu Peninsula, the marines meet the first serious Japanese opposition.

An LCI is sunk by an assault demolition boat. A kamikaze damages a destroyer, and another destroyer suffers bomb damage off Okinawa.

**CENTRAL PACIFIC:** The 147th Infantry Regiment assumes control of Iwo Jima, allowing the 9th Marine Regiment to prepare to depart.

Seventh Air Force sends 24 B-24 Liberators from Angaur Island to bomb targets on Mindanao Island in the Philippines.

## April 5

**CBI:** Fourteenth Air Force sends P-40s, P-38 Lightnings, and P-47 Thunderbolts on armed reconnaissance to attack troops, horses, and river, road, and rail traffic in French Indochina and southern China.

**ATLANTIC:** German submarine *U-857* damages a U.S. tanker off Cape Cod. The tanker is towed to Boston for repairs.

**ETO:** The III Corps of First Army (9th 28th, and 99th Infantry Divisions and the 7th Armored Division) attacks the Ruhr Pocket from the south in support of Ninth Army's attack.

The XXI Corps (12th Armored Division and the 42nd, 36th, and 4th Infantry Divisions) of Seventh Army captures Würzburg.

Eighth Air Force sends more than 1,300 B-17s and B-24 Liberators escorted by over 600 P-47 Thunderbolts and P-51 Mustangs to bomb ordnance depots, armament production facilities, marshaling yards, and airfields. The bombers use both visual methods and radar signal intercepts to mark the bomb release points over the targets. A total of 10 bombers are lost and 123 are damaged. Aircrews report eight confirmed kills and six possibles. Aircrew casualties are 19 killed, 10 wounded, and 83 missing. Fighter pilots report one confirmed kill and three possibles in the air and seven confirmed kills and three possibles on the ground. One P-51 is lost and the pilot is reported missing.

During the night 12 B-24s drop leaflets over France, Germany, and the Netherlands.

Ninth Air Force P-47 and P-38 fighters support XX Corps, and 8th, 2nd and 7th Armored Divisions.

Corporal Thomas J. Kelly is the aid man with the first platoon, C Company, 48th Armored Infantry Battalion, 7th Armored Division, when it is halted by heavy fire from German machine guns and tanks hidden in the woods of the town of Alemert, Germany. As the platoon retreats, Corporal Kelly returns to assist the wounded under direct machine-gun fire. To avoid being hit, he crawls 300 yards, dragging the wounded soldiers behind him to safety. He makes 10 separate trips bringing wounded men out, and assists seven more casualties to crawl out of the line of fire. Although completely exhausted by his efforts, Kelly refuses to rest, supporting his platoon throughout the rest of the battle. For his dedication to duty and exceptional bravery in saving the lives of his fellow soldiers, Corporal Kelly will receive the Medal of Honor.

**MEDITERRANEAN:** Fifteenth Air Force sends more than 450 B-17s and B-24 Liberators escorted by P-38 Lightnings and P-51 Mustangs to bomb a rail bridge in Yugoslavia and marshaling yards and locomotive depots in Italy. P-38s dive-bomb a rail bridge in Yugoslavia and P-51s attack rail targets in Germany and Austria.

**ITALY:** The 92nd Infantry Division conducts Operation Second Wind, a diversion intended to draw attention away from Eighth Army's main attack in the east. The division is to capture Massa on the Ligurian coast. The 370th Infantry Regiment leads the attack, supported by air and artillery bombardment. The unit is also shored up by the addition of the battle-hardened 442nd Regimental Combat Team (composed of Japanese-Americans) and the 473rd Regimental Combat Team, a unit composed of former antiaircraft artillerymen, now trained and organized as infantry. The 370th soon falters, but the 100th battalion of the 442nd RCT captures Monte Fragolita.

Twelfth Air Force B-25 Mitchells bomb bridges and gun positions. P-47 Thunderbolts attack gun positions, vehicles, logistics storage sites, ammunition storage areas, and support Fifth Army ground forces. During the night A-20 Havocs and A-26 Intruders attack bridges.

Private First Class Sadao S. Munemori of A Company, 100th Infantry Battalion, 442nd Regimental Combat Team, faces strong German defenses on the mountain approaches to Seravezza, Italy. As casualties mount, Munemori must take command of his squad. He chooses to attack the enemy alone rather than risk the lives of his comrades and moves up the hill to destroy two machine guns with grenades. Withdrawing to the squad's position, he is followed by a large number of hand grenades, which roll down the hill. One grenade hits Munemori's helmet and lands nearby. Without hesitation, Munemori covers the grenade with his body. For his courage under fire and his willingness to sacrifice himself so others may live, Private First Class Munemori will receive the Medal of Honor.

**SOUTHWEST PACIFIC AREA:** In the Philippines, Far East Air Force A-20 Havocs and P-61 Black Widow night fighters support ground forces on Cebu and Negros Islands.

The headquarters of the 58th Fighter Group redeploys from Mindoro Island to Luzon.

B-24s bomb the Kowloon Docks in Hong Kong and a nearby airfield, while other B-24s bomb Kiirun harbor in Formosa. Fifth Air Force B-24 Liberators, B-26 Marauders, and P-38 Lightnings attack a Japanese convoy, sinking a cargo ship, east of Hong Kong. Other B-24s bomb Japanese shipping at Hong Kong, damaging two coastal defense vessels, two submarine chasers, and a fleet oiler.

U.S. submarine *Hardhead* attacks a Japanese convoy, damaging a cargo ship in the Gulf of Siam.

FEAF P-38 Lightnings attack Tarakan Island and Tawau in Borneo.

U.S. submarine *Besugo* attacks a Japanese light cruiser in the Flores Sea.

**PACIFIC:** Twentieth Air Force receives the headquarters of the 315th Bombardment Wing (Very Heavy), which arrives on Guam Island from the United States.

Mines dropped by B-29s sink a cargo ship and damage another near Shimonoseki Strait.

**PACIFIC, OKINAWA:** In the south of the island XIV Corps moves the 382nd and 383rd Infantry Regiments of the 96th Infantry Division and the 184th and 32nd Infantry Regiments of the 7th Infantry Division forward. Japanese defenses at Cactus Ridge and the Pinnacle await the Americans. These heavily fortified positions block the advance.

The 383rd Infantry Regiment of the 96th Infantry Division encounters Japanese forces entrenched on Cactus Ridge behind anti-tank ditches and barbed wire.

The 184th Infantry Regiment of the 7th Infantry Division attacks Japanese defenders at the Pinnacle.

The battleship USS *Nevada* is damaged off Okinawa by shore battery fire. A U.S. destroyer sinks Japanese submarine *RO-41* west of Okinawa.

**CENTRAL PACIFIC:** The Naval Advanced Air Base at Iwo Jima is established.

## April 6

**ALEUTIANS:** Eleventh Air Force sends bombers against targets in the Kurile Islands. Eight B-24 Liberators attack and photograph the airfield on Paramushiru Island. Eight B-25 Mitchells attack radar installations on Hayakegawa, Kotani Island, and Minami Cape, dropping napalm on buildings and shipping. Another B-25 flies a weather reconnaissance mission.

**CBI:** In China, P-51 Mustangs attack railroad targets; P-38 Lightnings attack a bridge near Dien Bien Phu in French Indochina.

In Burma, Tenth Air Force P-47 Thunderbolts and P-38 Lightnings attack road traffic, troop concentrations, tanks, fuel storage sites, and targets of opportunity.

**ETO:** The XVIII Airborne Corps (78th, 8th, and 86th Infantry Divisions) of First Army attack northward into the Ruhr Pocket.

Eighth Air Force sends more than 600 B-17s and B-24 Liberators escorted by nearly 600 P-47 Thunderbolts and P-51 Mustangs to bomb marshaling yards. The bombers use radar signal intercepts to mark the bomb release points over the targets. A total of four B-17s are lost and two damaged. Aircrew casualties are 17 killed, one wounded, and 33 missing. One P-51 is lost, and the pilot is reported missing.

During the night, three B-24 Liberators fly Carpetbagger missions.

Ninth Air Force sends nearly 100 A-20 Havocs, A-26 Invaders, and B-26 Marauders to attack marshaling yards. P-47 and P-38 fighters support VIII Corps and XX Corps.

The headquarters of the 315th Troop Carrier Group and the C-47s of the 34th, 309th, and 310th Troop Carrier Squadrons, IX Troop Carrier Command, redeploy from England to France.

First Lieutenant Raymond O. Beaudoin is the platoon leader of second platoon, F Company, 119th Infantry, 30th Infantry Division, approaching Hamelin, Germany. German defenders open a heavy fire on his platoon as it crosses the flat, open terrain. The platoon is unable to move, so Lieutenant Beaudoin orders them to dig foxholes. He himself digs in where the enemy fire is heaviest and keeps up a steady return fire, accounting for six German casualties. As the Germans prepare to attack and destroy the isolated platoon, Lieutenant Beaudoin rises up to attack a sniper. Ignoring the constant fire directed at him, Beaudoin gets to within 10 yards of the sniper, then jumps up to assault the position, killing three Germans and driving off another soldier. He then moves to attack another position, firing his carbine toward a dugout, but there he is killed by machine-gun fire. By taking decisive action at the risk of his own life to save the lives of his men, First Lieutenant Raymond Beaudoin will receive the Medal of Honor.

**MEDITERRANEAN:** Fifteenth Air Force sends 387 B-17s and B-24 Liberators escorted by P-38 Lightnings and P-51 Mustangs to bomb antiaircraft positions near marshaling yards in northern Italy.

**ITALY:** Brigadier General Thomas C. Darcy takes command of the XXII Tactical Air Command. Twelfth Air Force B-25 Mitchells bomb bridges. P-47 Thunderbolts support Fifth Army ground forces. During the night A-20 Havocs and A-26 Invaders bomb bridges in the Po River valley.

**SOUTHWEST PACIFIC AREA:** In the Philippines, Far East Air Force A-20 Havocs, P-47 Thunderbolts, and P-38 Lightnings support ground forces in Luzon, attacking Japanese positions around Balete Pass and west of Fort Stotsenburg. B-24 Liberators bomb a town north of Cebu City, while P-47s support ground units on Cebu Island. A-20s support ground forces on Negros Island. B-25 Mitchells bomb Bunawan on Mindanao Island. B-24 Liberators bomb defensive positions, ammunition storage areas, and logistics sites on Jolo Island. The U.S. Army Forces, Pacific (AFPAC) headquarters is established under General of the Army Douglas MacArthur in Manila.

The P-47s of the 310th Fighter Squadron, 58th Fighter Group, redeploy from Mindoro Island to Luzon.

B-25 Mitchells bomb the town of Hokko on Formosa.

U.S. submarine *Hardhead* attacks the Japanese convoy it has been following, sinking a cargo ship in the Gulf of Siam.

**PACIFIC:** General MacArthur becomes commander of all army forces in Pacific. Admiral Nimitz takes command of all navy forces in the Pacific. This directive from the Joint Chiefs of Staff ends the conflicting theaters of war and unites American land, air, and naval power for the final attack on the Japanese homeland.

The headquarters of Twentieth Air Force's 468th Bombardment Group (Very Heavy) arrives at Tinian from India.

**PACIFIC, OKINAWA:** The 383rd Infantry Regiment of the 96th Infantry Division captures Cactus Ridge and holds it against a Japanese counterattack that night.

The 184th Infantry Regiment of the 7th Infantry Division captures the Pinnacle. The Japanese begin firing heavy and accurate artillery barrages on the American positions.

Nearly 300 Japanese aircraft from Formosa and Kyushu, half of them kamikazes, attack U.S. ships in Task Force 58. No carriers are hit, but three destroyers on early warning picket duty are sunk and another severely damaged. Four other destroyers are damaged near Ie Shima Island. One destroyer off the east coast of Okinawa is damaged. One LST is sunk and two ammunition ships are hit and burn out of control.

The battleship *Yamato,* escorted by a light cruiser and eight destroyers, sets sail from Tokuyama Bay in Japan on a suicide mission that attempts to draw away American carrier aircraft from Okinawa and so allow kamikazes to destroy transport ships near the landing beaches. Unknown to the Japanese, their encoded plan has already been intercepted and deciphered. Two U.S. submarines, USS *Threadfin* and USS *Hackleback,* track the progress of the force. Admiral Mitscher begins to deploy his carriers to intercept the Japanese.

Kamikazes sink destroyer USS *Bush* and damage seven destroyers, two destroyer escorts, two high-speed minesweepers, four minesweepers, two motor minesweepers, and an LST. The small carrier USS *San Jacinto* and a destroyer are damaged by near-misses from kamikazes. A destroyer is damaged by both a kamikaze and a torpedo. Bombs damage a destroyer and a high-speed minesweeper. A kamikaze damages a freighter carrying 7,000 tons of ammunition, which is abandoned and scuttled. Another freighter has to be abandoned after a kamikaze crashes into the ship.

**CENTRAL PACIFIC:** Seventh Air Force sends 11 B-24 Liberators from Guam Island to bomb the airfield on Marcus Island. A total of 23 B-24s from Angaur Island bomb barracks and a wharf at Mindanao Island in the Philippines.

**NEW GUINEA:** U.S. submarine *Besugo* torpedoes and sinks a Japanese minesweeper south of Java.

## April 7

**CBI:** In China, Fourteenth Air Force sends 14 B-25 Mitchells to attack town areas and targets of opportunity and 24 P-51 Mustangs to attack river, road, and rail traffic. P-38 Lightnings attack targets of opportunity around Dien Bien Phu in French Indochina.

In Burma, Tenth Air Force sends P-47 Thunderbolts and P-38 Lightnings to attack troop concentrations, trucks, and logistics support sites, and conduct sweeps along roads.

**ATLANTIC:** U.S. destroyer escort sinks German submarine *U-857* off Cape Cod, Massachusetts.

German submarine *U-1024* torpedoes and damages a U.S. freighter in the Irish Sea. The ship is repaired.

**ETO:** Ninth Army captures Hamelin and Eisenach on the road to Leipzig.

Eighth Air Force sends more than 1,300 B-17s and B-24 Liberators escorted by nearly 900 P-47 Thunderbolts and P-51 Mustangs to bomb oil depots, munition production facilities, marshaling yards, and airfields. The bombers use visual methods to mark the bomb release points over the targets. The German response is significant—over 100 fighters and more than 50 Me-262 jet fighters attack the bombers. A total of 15 bombers are lost and 189 are damaged. Aircrews report 40 confirmed kills, 12 probables, and 17 possibles. Aircrew casualties are eight killed, 15 wounded, and 142 missing. Fighter pilots report 61 confirmed kills, one probable, and 15 possibles. Five P-51s are lost and two are damaged. The pilots are reported missing.

Ninth Air Force sends 268 A-20 Havocs, A-26 Invaders, and B-26 Marauders to attack marshaling yards. P-47 and P-38 fighters support 7th Armored Division and the 3rd and 9th Armored Divisions, and VIII, XX, and XII Corps.

Private First Class Mike Colalillo of C Company, 398th Infantry Regiment, 100th Infantry Division, is pinned down by German fire near Untergriesheim, Germany. In the midst of artillery, mortar, and machine-gun fire, Colalillo stands up and runs forward following an American tank, urging his comrades to follow. When his weapon is broken, he climbs on the back of the tank and mans the machine gun of the turret, firing at the German defenders with great accuracy. As the tank advances he is completely exposed to enemy fire, but continues to engage the enemy by firing on three more defensive positions. When the machine gun on the turret jams, he obtains a Thompson submachine gun from the tank crew and continues forward on foot. As the tanks are called back, Colalillo remains behind to rescue a wounded comrade and brings him back to friendly lines, enduring heavy fire the entire way. For his inspiring acts of courage in the face of the enemy, Private First Class Colallilo will receive the Medal of Honor.

**MEDITERRANEAN:** Fifteenth Air Force sends more than120 B-17s and B-24 Liberators escorted by P-38 Lightnings and P-51 Mustangs to bomb rail bridges in Italy and marshaling yards in Austria. P-38s bomb a rail bridge in Austria.

**ITALY:** Twelfth Air Force B-25 Mitchells bomb rail and road traffic and bridges. P-47 Thunderbolts attack ammunition storage areas and communication centers and support ground forces near Monte Belvedere. During the night A-20 Havocs and A-26 Invaders bomb bridges and river crossing sites in the Po River valley.

Technical Sergeant Yukio Okutsu of the 100th Infantry Battalion, 442nd Regimental Combat Team, is stopped by a crossfire from two machine guns on Mount Belvedere, Italy. Technical Sergeant Okutsu crawls through heavy fire to within 30 yards of one of the positions and destroys it with two hand grenades. Crawling and moving forward, he reaches the other machine-gun position and destroys that one with grenades as well. A third machine gun opens fire and he attacks, firing his Thompson submachine gun and driving off several German riflemen, and then capturing the machine-gun crew. For his courageous attack against a formidable enemy at the risk of his life, Technical Sergeant Okutsu will receive the Congressional Medal of Honor.

**SOUTHWEST PACIFIC AREA:** In the Philippines, Far East Air Force A-20 Havocs, P-38 Lightnings, and P-47 Thunderbolts support ground forces on Luzon. B-24 Liberators bomb Bunawan on Mindanao Island. Other B-24s and P-38s attack Jolo Island and B-24s bomb an airfield on Sumbawa Island in the Lesser Sunda Islands. B-24s and P-38s attack various targets of opportunity over Formosa.

The 311th Fighter Squadron, 58th Fighter Group, redeploys its P-47s from Mindoro to Luzon.

**PACIFIC:** Twentieth Air Force sends more than 100 B-29 Superfortresses to bomb the Nakajima aircraft engine production facility at Tokyo. Aircrews report 80 confirmed kills, 23 probables, and 50 possibles. Three B-29s are lost. Over 150 B-29s bomb the Mitsubishi aircraft production facility at Nagoya. Aircrews report 21 confirmed kills, 11 probables, and 22 possibles. Two B-29s are lost. Seventh Air Force supports these raids with over 100 P-51 Mustangs escorting the bombers. Pilots report 21 confirmed kills, five probables, and seven possibles. Two P-51s are lost.

The headquarters of the Twentieth Air Force's 444th Bombardment Group (Very Heavy) arrives at Tinian from India.

U.S. submarine *Tirante* torpedoes and sinks a Japanese auxiliary submarine chaser in the Yellow Sea.

A mine dropped by B-29s sinks a cargo ship west of Nagasaki.

**PACIFIC, OKINAWA:** The 6th Marine Division captures Nago, the second-largest town on the island, and prepares to advance into the Motobu Peninsula.

A total of 386 F6F Hellcats, SB2C Helldivers, and TBM Avenger torpedo-bombers from the carriers USS *Hornet,* USS *Essex,* USS *Bunker Hill,* and USS *Bennington* and from the light carriers USS *Bataan,* USS *Belleau Wood,* and USS *San Jacinto,* swarm a Japanese attack force, formed around the *Yamato*—largest battleship ever built—and moving through the East China Sea toward Okinawa. *Yamato* and a light cruiser are sunk south of Kagoshima, Kyushu, Japan. Four destroyers are sunk and four others damaged in the East China Sea. Kamikazes damage carrier USS *Han-*

*cock,* the battleship USS *Maryland,* two destroyers, a destroyer escort, and a motor minesweeper off Okinawa. U.S. losses are 10 aircraft and 12 crewmen.

The carrier USS *Hancock* is damaged by a kamikaze, which drops a bomb on the flight deck before crashing onto the ship. The battleship USS *Maryland* and a destroyer and destroyer-escort are damaged in kamikaze attacks.

**CENTRAL PACIFIC:** Seventh Air Force sends 24 B-24 Liberators from Angaur Island to bomb the barracks area at Bunawan on Mindanao Island in the Philippines.

**NEW GUINEA:** The 550th Night Fighter Squadron, XIII Fighter Command, redeploys P-38 Lightnings, P-61 Black Widow night fighters, and P-70s (an A-20 Havoc converted into a night fighter) from Morotai Island to Leyte Island.

U.S. submarines *Gabilan* and *Charr* sink a Japanese light cruiser transporting troops in the Flores Sea.

## April 8

**CBI:** The Japanese Twentieth Army launches an offensive directed at capturing the Fourteenth Air Force airfield at Chihchiang. The American airfield at Laohokow is captured. Chinese forces are unable to stop the advance.

In China, Fourteenth Air Force sends B-24 Liberators to attack shipping targets of opportunity in the South China Sea, Bakli Bay on Hainan Island, and the Kowloon Docks in Hong Kong. P-51 Mustangs attack a bridge and a number of road and rail targets.

Tenth Air Force sends more than 50 P-38 Lightnings and P-47 Thunderbolts to attack troops, logistics sites, gun positions, and trucks.

**ETO:** Seventh Army captures Pforzheim near the Rhine River.

Eighth Air Force sends more than 1,100 B-17s and B-24 Liberators escorted by nearly 800 P-47 Thunderbolts and P-51 Mustangs to bomb oil depots, jet aircraft production facilities, marshaling yards, and ordnance depots. The bombers use a combination of visual methods and radar signal intercepts to mark the bomb release points over the targets. A total of nine bombers are lost and 153 damaged. Aircrew casualties are two killed, six wounded, and 78 missing. A group of 28 P-51s fly a scouting mission, and one fighter is damaged.

Ten B-17s conduct screening missions to jam German radio interception efforts and employ countermeasures against German radar sites.

During the night 11 B-24s drop leaflets over Germany and the Netherlands. A total of 12 B-24s bomb the port facilities at Travemunde during the night, using a Pathfinder radar-equipped bomber to mark bomb release points.

Ninth Air Force sends more than 600 A-20 Havocs, A-26 Invaders, and B-26 Marauders to attack communication centers, an oil storage depot, and marshaling yards. P-47 and P-38 fighters support VIII, XII, and XX Corps.

**MEDITERRANEAN:** Fifteenth Air Force sends more than 500 B-17s and B-24 Liberators escorted by P-38 Lightnings and P-51 Mustangs to bomb communication centers, bridges, and marshaling yards in northern Italy. P-38s attack rail bridges in Germany and Austria.

**ITALY:** Twelfth Air Force B-25 Mitchells bomb rail bridges. P-47 Thunderbolts attack bridges and roads. During the night A-20 Havocs and A-26 Invaders attack command and control centers and logistics support sites.

**SOUTHWEST PACIFIC AREA:** In the Philippines, Far East Air Force A-20 Havocs, P-38 Lightnings, and P-47 Thunderbolts support ground forces east of Manila. B-24 Liberators, A-20s, P-47s, and P-38s support ground forces on Cebu and Negros Islands. Other B-24s bomb Mindanao Island and Jolo Island.

B-24s and B-25 Mitchells attack airfields in the Pescadores Islands, and bomb a town and railyards on Formosa.

The 69th Fighter Squadron, 58th Fighter Group, redeploys from Mindoro to Luzon with P-47s.

**PACIFIC:** Twentieth Air Force sends more than 70 B-29 Superfortresses against airfields on Kyushu Island to disrupt and eliminate kamikaze attacks on the fleet off Okinawa. One B-29 is lost.

U.S. submarine *Snook* on her ninth war patrol makes contact with U.S. submarine *Tigrone,* but is never heard from again.

**PACIFIC, OKINAWA:** The Pinnacle and Cactus Ridge are cleared of enemy forces, but American casualties are heavy. More than 1,500 men have been killed or wounded. Japanese losses are estimated to be around 4,500. The mission of each Japanese soldier is to kill as many Americans as possible before sacrificing himself.

A kamikaze damages a destroyer, and another destroyer is damaged by an assault demolition boat off Okinawa.

**CENTRAL PACIFIC:** Seventh Air Force sends 25 B-24 Liberators from Angaur Island to bomb the Bunawan area on Mindanao Island in the Philippines.

During the night six P-61 Black Widow night fighters from Iwo Jima conduct single coordinated bombing attacks on Chichi Jima, Haha Jima, Ani Jima, and Ototo Jima islands.

**NEW GUINEA:** The 33rd Troop Carrier Squadron, 374th Troop Carrier Group, redeploys its C-47s from Hollandia to Luzon.

## April 9

**CBI:** In Burma, Tenth Air Force sends more than 70 P-38 Lightnings and P-47 Thunderbolts to attack troops, logistics sites, gun positions, and general targets of opportunity. The British Fourteenth Army attacks south down the Irrawaddy and Sittang Rivers toward Prome.

In China, Fourteenth Air Force sends nine B-24 Liberators to bomb docks at Canton and Kowloon in Hong Kong and attack targets of opportunity on Hainan Island. B-25 Mitchells bomb railyards. In French Indochina P-38 Lightnings attack vehicles near Dien Bien Phu.

**ETO:** The XVIII Corps attacks into the Ruhr Pocket.

First and Ninth Armies establish bridgeheads over the Leine River.

Eighth Air Force sends more than 1,200 B-17s and B-24 Liberators escorted by over 800 P-47 Thunderbolts and P-51 Mustangs to bomb oil storage areas, munitions production facilities, and airfields supporting Me-262 jet aircraft. A total of seven bombers are lost and 64 damaged. Aircrews report 85 confirmed kills, one probable, and 60 possibles. Aircrew casualties are four killed, seven wounded, and 65 missing. Fighter pilots report one confirmed kill and three possibles in the air and 84 confirmed kills and 56 possibles on the ground. Four fighters are lost, and the pilots are reported missing. A group of 24 P-51s fly a scouting mission. One fighter is lost, and the pilot is reported missing.

During the night 11 B-24s drop leaflets over France, Germany, and the Netherlands. A total of 14 B-24s bomb an airfield during the night, using a Pathfinder radar-equipped bomber to mark bomb release points.

Ninth Air Force sends over 700 A-20 Havocs, A-26 Invaders, and B-26 Marauders to attack oil production and storage targets, airfields, and marshaling yards. P-47 and P-38 fighters support III Corps, VIII Corps, XII and XX Corps, and 3rd Armored Division.

A German midget submarine torpedoes a U.S. freighter in a convoy headed to Cherbourg, France, at the entrance to the English Channel. The ship is towed and arrives safely.

**MEDITERRANEAN:** Fifteenth Air Force sends more than 800 B-17s and B-24 Liberators escorted by P-38 Lightnings and P-51 Mustangs to bomb German positions near Bologna in support of the British Eighth Army. Over 150 P-38s attack rail lines in Germany.

**ITALY:** Operation Craftsman, the 15th Army Group's main effort for the spring offensive in Italy, begins with an attack by Eighth Army, preceded by heavy air and artillery bombardment. Fifth Army is to follow two or three days later, focusing on breaking the German lines and moving into the southern Po River valley. The IV Corps, with the U.S. 10th Mountain Division, the 1st Brazilian Division, and the U.S. 1st Armored Division, is to attack toward Bazzano, generally down the Samoggia River valley. The II Corps, with the 34th, 88th, and 91st Infantry Divisions, the 6th South African Armored Division, and the Italian Legnano Combat Group, will attack generally along Route 64 to reach Bodeno and link with Eighth Army.

Twelfth Air Force B-25 Mitchells and the A-20 Havocs and P-47 Thunderbolts of the XXII Tactical Air Command attack German positions in support of the British Eighth Army offensive. During the night A-20 Havocs and A-26 Invaders attack bridges, vehicles, and targets of opportunity.

**SOUTHWEST PACIFIC AREA:** In the Eighth Army area, elements of the 163rd Infantry Regiment of the 41st Infantry Division attack Japanese positions on Jolo Island in the Sulu Archipelago, supported by three destroyers and marine fighters.

On Negros, the 185th and 160th Infantry Regiments of the 40th Infantry Division, plus the 503rd Parachute Infantry Regiment, attack into the mountains beyond Bacolod. The Japanese defenses are strong, with minefields, entrenchments, and pillboxes dominating the crests of the hills.

In the Philippines, Far East Air Force A-20 Havocs, P-38 Lightnings, and P-47 Thunderbolts support ground forces on Luzon Island. B-24 Liberators, P-38s, and P-47s support ground forces on Cebu and Negros Islands.

B-24s conduct armed reconnaissance missions, attacking coastal targets in China and French Indochina.

**PACIFIC:** During the night Twentieth Air Force sends 20 B-29s to mine Shimonoseki Strait between Kyushu and Honshu Islands.

U.S. submarine *Parche* torpedoes and sinks a Japanese minesweeper escorting a transport northeast of Sendai, Honshu, Japan. USS *Sunfish* makes an unsuccessful

Troops of the 370th Infantry Regiment, 92nd Infantry Division, advance into the mountains at Prato, Italy, April 9, 1945. Beyond the mountains are the German Gothic Line defenses.

attack on the transport. U.S. submarine *Spadefish* damages a cargo ship in the Yellow Sea. U.S. submarine *Tirante* attacks a Japanese convoy in the Yellow Sea, sinking an army tanker and damaging a coastal defense vessel.

**PACIFIC, OKINAWA:** The 383rd Infantry Regiment of the 96th Infantry Division attacks Kakazu Ridge. It is one of the strongest positions on the island. These defenses are expertly camouflaged and honeycombed with deep and well-protected caves, bunkers, observation posts, barracks, hospitals, and fighting positions. Most of the Japanese troops are positioned behind the ridge, not on it. American artillery fire explodes harmlessly against the face of the ridge. When the barrage stops, the Japanese emerge from behind the ridge and take up firing positions to rake attacking infantry with mortar shells, artillery, grenades, machine-gun, and rifle fire. Nearly every foot of ground to the front of the ridge is covered by some type of weapon.

The 381st Infantry Regiment also makes no progress at Kakazu. The two regiments will be stopped by Japanese mortar and artillery fire, rain, and counterattacks over the next three days.

The 27th Infantry Division, commanded by Major General George W. Griner, Jr., lands on Okinawa to reinforce the depleted 96th and 77th Infantry Divisions.

A kamikaze damages a destroyer off Okinawa. Two destroyers sink Japanese submarine *RO-56* east of Okinawa.

Private First Class Edward J. Moskala of C Company, 383rd Infantry Regiment, 96th Infantry Division, is part of the leading elements attacking Kakazu Ridge, one of the strongest positions on Okinawa. As Japanese rifle and machine-gun fire force the Americans to take cover, Moskala charges 40 yards and eliminates two machine-gun positions with grenades and his Browning Automatic Rifle (BAR). When a Japanese counterattack forces his company to withdraw, Moskala remains behind with eight other soldiers to cover the withdrawal. For over three hours Moskala engages in deadly combat with Japanese troops, killing scores of them until the order is given to fall back. Reaching relative safety, Moskala learns that one of the soldiers who stayed behind with him is left wounded. Moskala returns up the slope to provide covering fire, killing another four Japanese infiltrators as the wounded solder is recovered and evacuated. He is standing protective guard over the wounded man when he is killed while assisting another wounded soldier. For his determined combat skill, his courageous actions in fighting for his comrades and risking his life to save others, Private First Class Moskala will receive the Medal of Honor.

**CENTRAL PACIFIC:** Seventh Air Force sends 17 B-24 Liberators from Guam to bomb the airfield on Marcus Island. A total of 22 B-24s from Angaur Island attack Japanese troops at Kabacan, on Mindanao Island in the Philippines. P-51 Mustangs from Iwo Jima bomb and strafe military installations at Chichi Jima Island.

## April 10

**ALEUTIANS:** Eleventh Air Force sends seven B-24 Liberators to bomb Kataoka naval base on Shimushu Island in the Kuriles with napalm. Three B-25 Mitchells attack facilities on the island.

**CBI:** Chinese forces counterattack near Laohokow, stopping the Japanese advance and regaining lost territory.

Fourteenth Air Force sends 23 B-24 Liberators to bomb logistics storage areas, while B-25 Mitchells, P-40s, and P-51 Mustangs attack trucks, tanks, logistics sites, horses, troops, and artillery in southern and eastern China.

In Burma, Tenth Air Force sends P-47 Thunderbolts and P-38 Lightnings to attack troop concentrations.

In the Yangtze River, a cargo vessel is sunk by a mine dropped by B-29s in late March.

**ETO:** The XVI Corps of Ninth Army captures Essen in the Ruhr Pocket.

Ninth, Third, and First Armies attack on a 150-mile front with seven corps. Ninth Army has XIII Corps and XIX Corps, the Third Army has XX Corps, VIII Corps, and XII Corps. First Army has V Corps and VII Corps. Lieutenant General Hodges's First Army is the center force. It will advance 130 miles toward Leipzig and the Elbe River. Lieutenant General Simpson's Ninth Army is the northern force. It will attack toward Magdeburg and the Elbe River, 65 miles north of Leipzig. Lieutenant General Patton's Third Army is the southern force. It will advance to Chemnitz 40 miles south of Leipzig and turn south into Austria. Patton's attack supports General Devers's 6th Army Group, which is to attack into southern Germany to Austria and the Alps and forestall any possible rallying of German forces in that area.

Eighth Air Force sends more than 1,300 B-17s and B-24 Liberators escorted by over 900 P-47 Thunderbolts and P-51 Mustangs to bomb airfields supporting Me-262 jet aircraft, also munitions depots. About 60 Me-262 German fighters attack the bombers. A total of 19 bombers are lost and 258 damaged. Aircrews report 17 confirmed kills, 11 probables, and five possibles. Aircrew casualties are two killed, 95 wounded, and 91 missing. Fighter pilots report 18 confirmed kills and 11 possibles in the air and 288 confirmed kills and 190 possibles on the ground. Seven fighters are lost, and the pilots are reported missing. A group of 59 P-47s fly a freelance mission for the bombers. Pilots report two confirmed kills and two possibles in the air and 41 confirmed kills and 66 possibles on the ground. Thirty P-51s fly a scouting mission, and one fighter is lost. The pilot is reported missing.

During the night 12 B-24s drop leaflets over Germany, France, and the Netherlands. A total of 13 B-24s bomb the Dessau rail depot during the night, using a Pathfinder radar-equipped bomber to mark bomb release point.

Ninth Air Force sends more than 400 A-20 Havocs, A-26 Invaders, and B-26 Marauders to attack oil storage depots, ordnance depots, railroad bridges, and marshaling yards. P-47 and P-38 fighters support the 13th, 3rd, and 9th Armored Divisions, the XII and XX Corps, the 2nd and 5th Armored Divisions, and XVI Corps.

**MEDITERRANEAN:** Fifteenth Air Force sends more than 600 B-17s and B-24 Liberators escorted by P-38 Lightnings and P-51 Mustangs to attack German defensive positions along the Santerno River in Italy in support of the British Eighth Army offensive. Over 150 P-38s attack bridges, tunnels, and marshaling yards in Austria.

**ITALY:** The 473rd Infantry captures Massa with support of the 758th and 760th Tank Battalions. The 442nd RCT captures Monte Bruguana.

Twelfth Air Force B-25 Mitchells and P-47 Thunderbolts of the XXII Tactical Air Command attack German defenses in support of the British Eighth Army.

During the night A-20 Havocs and A-26 Invaders attack German positions.

**SOUTHWEST PACIFIC AREA:** In the I Corps area, on Luzon, the 37th Infantry Division comes under the operational control of I Corps and moves to the Bauang area in support of the 33rd Infantry Division's attempt to capture Baguio. Baguio is the former summer capital of the Philippines and the headquarters of General Yamashida, the commander of Japanese forces.

In the Philippines, Far East Air Force A-20 Havocs, P-38 Lightnings, and P-47 Thunderbolts support ground forces in Luzon. B-24 Liberators and P-47s support ground forces on Cebu Island.

B-24s bomb the town of Koshun on Formosa.

The headquarters of the 35th Fighter Group and the P-51s of the 39th Fighter Squadron redeploy from Mangaldan to Luzon.

**PACIFIC:** U.S. submarine *Crevalle* torpedoes and damages a Japanese escort destroyer west of Nagasaki.

**PACIFIC, OKINAWA:** The 3rd Battalion, 105th Infantry Regiment, 27th Infantry Division, lands on Tsugen Shima Island to destroy coastal defense guns guarding Nakagusuku Bay. The island is secured the following day. American losses are 11 killed and 80 wounded.

**CENTRAL PACIFIC:** During the night Seventh Air Force sends six P-61 Black Widow night fighters from Iwo Jima to fly individual strikes on Chichi Jima, Muko Jima, Ani Jima, and Haha Jima Islands.

**NEW GUINEA:** FEAF B-24 Liberators bomb Liang airfield on Ambon Island with Molucca Islands, and Bingkalapa airfield on Celebes Island.

## April 11

**ALEUTIANS:** Eleventh Air Force P-38 Lightnings and navy aircraft destroy a bomb-carrying paper balloon over Attu in the Aleutian Islands.

**CBI:** Fourteenth Air Force B-25 Mitchells, P-40s, and P-51s attack trucks, tanks, logistics sites, horses, troops, and artillery in southern and eastern China.

In Burma, Tenth Air Force sends P-47 Thunderbolts and P-38 Lightnings to attack trucks, troop concentrations, and targets of opportunity.

**ATLANTIC:** President Roosevelt sends what will be his last communication to Prime Minister Churchill: "I would minimize the general Soviet problem as much as possible because these problems in one form or another, seem to arise every day and most of them straighten out . . . we must be firm however, and our course thus far is correct."

**ETO:** The XX Corps (76th and 80th Infantry Divisions and the 4th and 6th Armored Divisions) of Third Army reach Weimar. The 6th Armored Division discovers the concentration camp at Buchenwald.

The Ninth Army's XIX Corps (the 83rd and 30th Infantry Divisions and the 2nd Armored Division) reach the Elbe River near Magdeburg.

The XXI Corps (the 36th, 42nd, and 4th Infantry Divisions) of the 6th Army Group occupies Schweinfurt. The VI Corps attacks German forces at the Neckar River. Heilbronn falls to the 100th Infantry Division of VI Corps after nine days of fighting.

Eighth Air Force sends more than 1,300 B-17s and B-24 Liberators escorted by over 900 P-47 Thunderbolts and P-51 Mustangs to bomb oil depots, munition storage facilities, marshaling yards, and airfields. One B-17 is lost and 23 bombers damaged. Aircrew casualties are 23 killed and 10 missing.

During the night nine B-24s drop leaflets over Germany and the Netherlands and 11 B-24s fly Carpetbagger missions in Denmark.

Ninth Air Force sends 689 A-20 Havocs, A-26 Invaders, and B-26 Marauders to attack industrial targets and an ordnance depot. P-47 and P-38 fighters conduct armed reconnaissance and report 43 German fighters shot down. The fighters also support 3rd and 9th Armored Divisions, the 2nd Armored Division, and XX, XVI, VIII, and XII Corps.

**MEDITERRANEAN:** Fifteenth Air Force sends more than 500 B-17s and B-24 Liberators escorted by P-38 Lightnings and P-51 Mustangs to bomb bridges and marshaling yards in northern Italy to isolate German forces. P-38s conduct dive-bombing runs on a rail bridge in Germany and P-51s attack rail lines in Germany, Czechoslovakia, and Austria.

**ITALY:** The 442nd RCT captures Carrara. The 92nd Infantry Division's advance is stopped beyond Carrara by strong German defenses along Carione Creek. This ends Operation Second Wind. German forces have been pulled eastward just as the main attack begins in the west.

Twelfth Air Force B-25 Mitchells bomb German defensive positions in support of the British Eighth Army. P-47 Thunderbolts of the XXII Tactical Air Command attack vehicles, logistics storage sites, and ammunition storage areas in northern Italy.

During the night A-20 Havocs and A-26 Invaders attack river crossing sites, bridges, roads, and motor transport in the Po River valley.

**SOUTHWEST PACIFIC AREA:** In the Eighth Army area a battalion of the 164th Infantry Regiment of the Americal Division lands on Bohol Island and moves inland with the support of Filipino guerrillas. The Americans will fight Japanese defenders for more than two weeks.

In the Philippines, Far East Air Force B-24 Liberators bomb Cotabato on Mindanao. On Negros Island, B-24s and A-20 Havocs attack Japanese positions. On Luzon Island B-24s, B-25 Mitchells, A-20s, P-38s, and P-47 Thunderbolts attack bridges, troop concentrations, and logistics support sites. Japanese defensive positions are hit with napalm.

B-24s and B-25s bomb targets on Formosa.

FEAF P-38 Lightnings attack gun positions at Tarakan, Borneo.

**PACIFIC:** U.S. submarine *Parche* torpedoes and sinks a Japanese auxiliary minesweeper off eastern Honshu, Japan. U.S. submarine *Spadefish* torpedoes and sinks a Japanese auxiliary minesweeper in the Yellow Sea.

**PACIFIC, OKINAWA:** The 32nd Infantry Regiment of the 7th Infantry Division occupies the town of Ouiki, but is forced to retreat after a Japanese counterattack. The 382nd Infantry Regiment of the 96th Infantry Division is forced to consolidate and go on the defensive after attacks on Tombstone Ridge fail.

Kamikaze attacks on Task Force 58 result in minor damage to the carriers USS *Essex* and USS *Enterprise*. The *Essex* has 33 men killed. The battleship USS *Missouri* is hit, but its massive hull is not damaged. The destroyer USS *Kidd* is hit and suffers 38 killed and 35 wounded. Another destroyer, USS *Mannert L. Able,* is sunk. Another destroyer and destroyer escort are damaged by strafing attacks.

**CENTRAL PACIFIC:** Seventh Air Force sends 24 B-24 Liberators from Angaur to attack logistics storage areas and troops on Mindanao Island in the Philippines. B-24s from Guam bomb Japanese positions on Eten Island at Truk.

### April 12

**ALEUTIANS:** Eleventh Air Force P-38 Lightnings shoot down bomb-carrying balloons over Attu Island.

**CBI:** Fourteenth Air Force B-25 Mitchells, P-40s, and P-51s attack trucks, tanks, logistics sites, horses, troops, and artillery in southern and eastern China.

B-24 Liberators attack railyards and airfields

In Burma, Tenth Air Force sends P-47 Thunderbolts and P-38 Lightnings to support ground forces and attack road traffic, troop concentrations, logistics storage sites, and targets of opportunity.

**ATLANTIC:** President Roosevelt dies at Warm Springs, Georgia. Vice President Harry S. Truman is sworn in as the new president.

German submarine *U-1024* torpedoes a U.S. freighter in a convoy in the Irish Sea. The ship is beached and later repaired.

**ETO:** The 2nd Armored Division of XIX Corps, Ninth Army, crosses the Elbe, awaiting the order to drive forward to Berlin, just 50 miles away. First Army reaches the Elbe River near Magdeburg.

Third Army is ordered to halt in front of Chemnitz and go no farther east. General Eisenhower plans to push Third Army south toward Linz.

Generals Eisenhower, Bradley, and Patton visit the Ohrdruf camp to see first-hand the Nazi atrocities. The same day Eisenhower writes a letter to General George C. Marshall, army chief of staff, describing his experience:

> The things I saw beggar description. While I was touring the camp I encountered three men who had been inmates and by one ruse or another had made their escape. I interviewed them through an interpreter. The visual evidence and the verbal testimony of starvation, cruelty and bestiality were so overpowering as to leave me a bit sick. In one room, where they were piled up twenty or thirty naked men, killed by starvation, George Patton would not even enter. He said that he would get sick if he did so. I made the visit deliberately, in order to be in a position to give firsthand evidence of these things if ever, in the future, there develops a tendency to charge these allegations merely to "propaganda."

During the night Eighth Air Force sends 10 B-24 Liberators to drop leaflets in the Netherlands and Germany, while six B-24 Liberators fly Carpetbagger missions in Denmark.

Ninth Air Force sends 167 A-20 Havocs, A-26 Invaders, and B-26 Marauders to attack railroad bridges, ordnance depots, and marshaling yards. P-47 and P-38 fighters support III, XVIII, and XVI Corps as well as the 9th Armored Division and XII, VIII, and XX Corps.

Private First Class Joe R. Hastings is a squad leader of a light machine-gun section in C Company, 386th Infantry Regiment, 97th Infantry Division, attacking a German strongpoint near Drabenderhohe, Germany. Here he moves completely exposed to enemy fire over a distance of 350 yards to put his machine gun into action to support the attack of two platoons. Firing on the Germans, he has an immediate effect, killing the gun crew of a 20 millimeter gun and a machine gun. He shifts the location of his gun to fire on another German position, suppressing a 40 millimeter gun and machine gun, then runs 150 yards, firing his weapon and killing the German gun crew. He now leads the platoon assault, firing his machine gun from the hip as the Americans capture the objective. For his courage and leadership, Private First Class Hastings will receive the Medal of Honor.

**MEDITERRANEAN:** Fifteenth Air Force sends more than 400 B-17s and B-24 Liberators escorted by P-51 Mustangs to bomb rail bridges in Italy and Austria and an ammunition storage site and logistics support area in Italy. P-38 Lightnings bomb rail bridges in Austria.

**ITALY:** Twelfth Air Force B-25 Mitchells bomb rail lines and support Eighth Army operations. P-47 Thunderbolts of the XXII Tactical Air Command attack rail lines, bridges, logistics storage sites, and ammunition storage areas. During the night A-20 Havocs and A-26 Invaders attack river crossing sites.

**SOUTHWEST PACIFIC AREA:** In the Philippines, Far East Air Force P-38 Lightnings and A-20 Havocs support ground troops on Cebu and Negros Islands. B-24 Liberators and P-38s attack targets on Mindanao Island. On Luzon Island, B-24s, B-25s, A-20s, and P-47 Thunderbolts attack targets in the Cagayan Valley and at Balete Pass.

B-24s attack Tainan and bomb Okayama airfield on Formosa.

**PACIFIC:** Twentieth Air Force sends 94 B-29s, escorted by 90 Seventh Air Force P-51 Mustangs, to bomb the Nakajima aircraft production facility at Tokyo. Aircrews report 16 Japanese fighters downed. Pilots report 15 confirmed kills, six probables, and three possibles. Four P-51s are lost. Another 66 B-29s attack a chemical plant at Koriyama and nine attack targets of opportunity. More than 70 B-29s attack a chemical plant at Koriyama and targets of opportunity. Two B-29s are lost.

U.S. submarine *Silversides* torpedoes and sinks a Japanese auxiliary submarine chaser south of Kyushu, Japan.

During the night five B-29s mine Shimonoseki Strait.

Staff Sergeant Henry E. Erwin is the radio operator of a B-29 Superfortress in the 52nd Bombardment Squadron, 29th Bombardment Group, Twentieth Air Force. The mission is to bomb Koriyama, Japan. As he drops phosphorus smoke bombs to mark the aircraft assembly area, Japanese fighters attack the bomber, causing an accident that brings a white phosphorus bomb back into the interior of the aircraft. Staff Sergeant Erwin is badly burned in the face and is blinded. As heavy white smoke fills the aircraft, threatening the lives of the entire crew, Erwin ignores certain death and, grasping the burning bomb between his forearm and body, struggles to reach the copilot's window to throw it out of the aircraft. With his body aflame, and grievously injured, Erwin succeeds in saving the bomber and crew. For his extraordinary sacrifice and willingness to give his life for his comrades, Staff Sergeant Erwin will receive the Medal of Honor.

**PACIFIC, OKINAWA:** XXIV Corps headquarters receives the casualty reports from the 7th and 96th Infantry Divisions for the past three days of fighting against the Japanese main defensive line. The total losses are 2,880; included in this number are 451 killed.

At dark, Japanese artillery hits the 381st and 383rd Infantry Regiments of the 96th Infantry Division and the 184th Infantry Regiment of the 7th Infantry Division in preparation for a major counterattack. During the night, preceded by a five-hour mortar and artillery barrage, four battalions of Japanese troops attack the 96th Infantry Division and are stopped with heavy losses.

Off Okinawa, destroyer USS *Mannert L. Abele* is sunk by an *oka*, a rocket-powered suicide bomb. Another destroyer is damaged by an *oka*. A high-speed minesweeper is damaged by an oka and a kamikaze. Kamikazes sink a support landing craft and damage battleships USS *Idaho* and USS *Tennessee,* a destroyer, and a destroyer escort. Two destroyers, three destroyer escorts, a light minelayer, and a minesweeper are also damaged by kamikaze near-misses.

**CENTRAL PACIFIC:** Seventh Air Force sends 24 B-24 Liberators from Angaur to attack a personnel area at Kabacan on Mindanao Island in the Philippines.

During the night six P-51 Mustangs from Iwo Jima conduct individual strikes at intervals on Kita Jima, Chichi Jima, Haha Jima, and Ani Jima Islands.

**NEW GUINEA:** U.S. submarine *Chub* is damaged in an air attack in the Java Sea but remains on patrol.

## April 13

**ALEUTIANS:** Eleventh Air Force sends 27 P-38 Lightnings and P-40s to intercept and destroy a group of Japanese bomb-carrying paper balloons. Nine of the 11 sighted are shot down over the western Aleutians.

**CBI:** The Japanese Twentieth Army attacks in southern China with 60,000 men to capture the American airfield at Chihchiang.

In China, Fourteenth Air Force B-25 Mitchells bomb railyards and warehouses. B-25s attack shipping in the South China Sea and Bakli Bay on Hainan Island. P-40s and P-51s attack trucks, tanks, logistics sites, horses, troops, and artillery in southern and eastern China.

In Burma, Tenth Air Force sends P-47 Thunderbolts and P-38 Lightnings to attack road traffic and targets of opportunity.

**ATLANTIC:** President Harry S. Truman calls a meeting of Roosevelt's cabinet members and asks the secretary of war, the secretary of the navy, and the chiefs of staff to remain in their positions. After the meeting, Secretary of War Henry Stimson tells the president about the existence of "a new explosive of almost unbelievable power."

**ETO:** The German forces in the Ruhr pocket are unable to sustain resistance, lacking food, fuel, and ammunition. The 8th Infantry Division of XVIII Airborne Corps reaches the south bank of the Ruhr River.

In the Third Army area, Jena is captured; the 4th Armored Division is near Chemnitz. The XII Corps and VIII Corps are advancing toward Bayreuth and Neustadt. The 5th Armored Division of XIX Corps crosses the Elbe.

Eighth Air Force sends more than 200 B-17s escorted by 256 P-51 Mustangs to bomb marshaling yards. Two B-17s are lost and four damaged. Fighter pilots report 137 confirmed kills and 83 possibles in the air. Six P-51s are lost, and the pilots are reported missing. A group of 97 P-47 Thunderbolts and P-51 Mustangs fly a freelance mission in support of the bombers. Pilots report 147 confirmed kills and 137 possibles on the ground. One P-47 and one P-51 are lost. The pilots are reported missing. Ten B-24s bomb the Beizenburg rail junction during the night, and 10 other B-24s drop leaflets over France and Germany. One of four B-24s completes a Carpetbagger mission to Denmark.

Ninth Air Force sends P-47 and P-38 fighters to attack the headquarters of Field Marshal Walter Model's Army Group B at Haus Waldesruh in the Ruhr Pocket.

Fighter pilots spot Soviet fighters in the skies over Germany. Fighters support 3rd and 5th Armored Divisions, III Corps, XX Corps, and XVI Corps.

**ITALY:** During the night Twelfth Air Force A-20 Havocs and A-26 Invaders attack river crossing sites in the Po River Valley.

**SOUTHWEST PACIFIC AREA:** In the Eighth Army area, the Americal Division on Cebu Island is reinforced by the 164th Infantry Regiment (minus one battalion). It has moved behind Japanese lines and supports a frontal attack by the 132nd and 182nd Infantry Regiments. Progress is slow, but the Japanese are forced to move northward to avoid destruction.

In the Philippines, Far East Air Force B-24 Liberators and B-25 Mitchells bomb targets on Mindanao and in the Sulu Archipelago.

B-24s attack docks on the Hong Kong waterfront and storage areas in Canton, China. B-24s attack airfields on Formosa, while B-25 Mitchells attack rail lines.

Private First Class Dexter J. Kerstetter, C Company, 130th Infantry Regiment, 33rd Infantry Division, participates in a dawn attack against hill positions near Galiano, Luzon. The narrow ridge they are on is paralleled on each side by steep cliffs that are strongly fortified and heavily defended. The Americans run into intense fire and are immediately pinned down. Kerstetter's squad moves to the front and then advances alone to attack the Japanese positions along the cliff. With well-aimed shots he takes out positions one by one. Out of ammunition and grenades, he returns to his squad and then helps guide a platoon into a position that allows the Americans to overrun the enemy and capture the hill. For his courage in facing an impossible task and saving the lives of many of his fellow soldiers, Private First Class Kerstetter will receive the Medal of Honor.

**PACIFIC:** Twentieth Air Force sends more than 300 B-29s to bomb the Tokyo arsenal area. Seven B-29s are lost.

U.S. submarine *Parche* torpedoes and sinks a Japanese auxiliary minesweeper and guardboat off eastern Honshu, Japan.

Mines dropped by B-29s sink two Japanese cargo ships and damage a coastal defense vessel near Shmonoseki Strait.

**PACIFIC, OKINAWA:** During the night, Japanese troops make a second attack on the 96th Infantry Division.

A kamikaze damages a U.S. destroyer off Okinawa.

When the Japanese conduct a strong counterattack against his position, Technical Sergeant Beauford T. Anderson of the 381st Infantry Regiment, 96th Infantry Division, orders his men to safety while he faces the enemy alone. Armed only with an M-1 carbine, he fires his weapon as rapidly as possible, killing a number of the enemy. In desperation, he seizes a mortar round, pulls the safety pin, and bangs the base of the round on the rocks to arm it. He then throws it at the enemy troops. As the round explodes in their midst, he fires his carbine again, then picks up another mortar round, arms it, and throws it at the Japanese. After single-handedly breaking up the assault, Technical Sergeant Anderson gives a full report to his company commander, even though he has suffered a dangerous wound. For his extraordinary courage Anderson will win the Medal of Honor.

**CENTRAL PACIFIC:** Seventh Air Force sends 18 B-24 Liberators from Guam to bomb Japanese positions on Marcus Island. B-24 Liberators from Angaur bomb personnel and storage areas at Kabacan on Mindanao Island in the Philippines. Two P-61 Black Widow night fighters from Saipan bomb and strafe Pagan Island in the Marianas.
**NEW GUINEA:** Thirteenth Air Force B-24 Liberators sink a Japanese merchant tanker off southeast Borneo.

## April 14

**CBI:** Fourteenth Air Force sends more than 30 B-25 Mitchells and 130 P-40s and P-51 Mustangs to attack bridges, river, road, and rail traffic, troops, logistics storage areas, towns, and general targets of opportunity over southern and eastern China.

In Burma, Tenth Air Force sends 41 P-47 Thunderbolts and P-38 Lightnings to attack troops, logistics support sites, and fuel storage areas.

Fourteenth Air Force B-24 Liberators bomb Japanese shipping at Shanghai, sinking a cargo vessel.
**ETO:** The Ruhr Pocket is split in two by Ninth Army's XVI Corps (75th and 79th Infantry Division and the 8th Armored Division) and XVIII Airborne Corps of First Army at Hagen.

German forces counterattack to reduce the Elbe bridgehead, forcing XIX Corps to withdraw. The 3rd Armored Division of VII Corps, First Army, reaches Dessau, encircling 10,000 German troops in the Harz Mountains.

The XII Corps of Third Army captures Bayreuth.

Eighth Air Force sends nearly 1,200 B-17s and B-24 Liberators to bomb German defensive positions, strongpoints, and antiaircraft positions in the area of Bordeaux to break the enemy's hold on critical port facilities. Two B-24s are lost and six damaged. Aircrew casualties are 18 killed, nine wounded, and 12 missing.

During the night 10 B-24s drop leaflets over Germany and the Netherlands. One of four B-24s completes a Carpetbagger mission to Denmark.

Ninth Air Force sends P-47 and P-38 fighters to support 3rd and 9th Armored Divisions, and XX, VIII, and XII Corps, and the 2nd and 5th Armored Divisions.
**MEDITERRANEAN:** Fifteenth Air Force sends more than 300 B-17s and B-24 Liberators escorted by P-38 Lightnings and P-51 Mustangs to bomb ammunition production facilities and a motor transport depot in Italy. P-38s attack rail targets in Germany and Austria.
**ITALY:** General Lucien K. Truscott attacks with Fifth Army in support of the British Eighth Army's attack as part of Operation Craftsman. The IV Corps (1st Brazilian Division, 10th Mountain Division, and 1st Armored Division) advances west of Route 64 supported by heavy air bombardment from Fifteenth Air Force and a 2,000-gun artillery barrage.

Twelfth Air Force B-25 Mitchells support the British Eighth Army and support Fifth Army ground forces. P-47 Thunderbolts attack German positions southwest of Bologna in support of Fifth Army. During the night A-20 Havocs and A-26 Invaders attack roads and motor transport in the Po River valley.

When G Company, 85th Infantry Regiment, 10th Mountain Division, is pinned down near Castel d'Aiano by German artillery, mortar, and small-arms fire, Private

First Class John D. Magrath volunteers to act as a scout to locate German positions. He moves forward and attacks a German machine-gun position. Taking the weapon with him, he crosses an open field and attacks two more machine-gun positions. Carrying the machine gun in his arms, he methodically engages a number of German positions. Under heavy mortar fire, Private Magrath is killed. His heroism and extraordinary actions in the face of certain death will win him the Medal of Honor.

**SOUTHWEST PACIFIC AREA:** In the Philippines, Far East Air Force B-24 Liberators, B-25 Mitchells, A-20 Havocs, P-38 Lightnings, and P-47 Thunderbolts support ground forces and attack airfields, gun positions, Japanese defenses, and troop concentrations throughout Luzon, Cebu, Negros, and Mindanao Islands.

B-25s sweep the Canton-Hong Kong, China, waterways, attacking shipping and other targets. B-24s bomb four airfields on Formosa.

**PACIFIC:** Twentieth Air Force takes operational control of the headquarters, 16th Bombardment Group (Very Heavy), and the B-29s of the 16th and 17th Bombardment Squadrons (Very Heavy), and the headquarters, 501st Bombardment Group (Very Heavy), and the B-29s of the 21st and 485th Bombardment Squadrons (Very Heavy). These units arrive on Guam from the United States.

U.S. submarine *Tirante* attacks a Japanese convoy in the approaches to the Yellow Sea, sinking a transport, an escort vessel, and a coastal defense vessel.

Lieutenant Commander George L. Street, III, commands the submarine USS *Tirante* during its first war patrol, conducting a reconnaissance of the harbor at Quelpart Island off the coast of Korea. With the crew at surface battle stations, Street approaches the island and penetrates the mine field to enter the harbor. Street sends two torpedoes into a Japanese transport *Jusan Maru* and sinks it. As the ship explodes, the *Tirante* comes under fire, and he orders two more torpedoes fired, sinking the escort vessel *Nomi* and Coast Defense Vessel *No. 31* as the submarine makes its escape and dives to avoid a depth charge attack. For his daring and skill, Lieutenant Commander Street will receive the Medal of Honor.

**PACIFIC, OKINAWA:** The 4th and 29th Marines of the 6th Marine Division attack into the Japanese defenses at Yae Take on the Motobu Peninsula, in the northern section of the island. The Japanese are well dug in and delay the advance with small ambush teams.

Kamikazes damage battleship USS *New York* and three destroyers off Okinawa.

**CENTRAL PACIFIC:** Seventh Air Force sends 24 B-24 Liberators from Angaur Island to bomb logistics support areas and troops on Mindanao in the Philippines.

**NEW GUINEA:** U.S. submarine *Gabilan* attacks a Japanese convoy, sinking a cargo vessel and an auxiliary submarine chaser in the Flores Sea.

## April 15

**CBI:** Fourteenth Air Force B-25 Mitchells and 200 P-40s and P-51s attack trucks, tanks, rail traffic, logistics sites, troops, and gun positions in southern China.

In Burma, Tenth Air Force sends 62 P-38 Lightnings and P-47 Thunderbolts to attack troop concentrations and logistics storage areas.

**ATLANTIC:** Two U.S. destroyer escorts sink German submarine *U-1235* in the North Atlantic.

**ETO:** The French First Army captures Kehl and Offenburg on the Rhine River.

General Eisenhower gives final orders to his commanders that Berlin is not a military objective. Eisenhower orders 6th Army Group to advance through Bavaria and western Austria to link with Allied forces in Italy.

Eighth Air Force sends more than 1,300 B-17s and B-24 Liberators to bomb strongpoints and antiaircraft positions on the French Atlantic coast. The bombers drop napalm on the targets with little or no effect. No bombers are lost and nine damaged. Two crewmen are killed. During the night 10 B-24s drop leaflets over France, Germany, and the Netherlands.

Ninth Air Force sends 258 A-20 Havocs, A-26 Invaders, and B-26 Marauders to attack marshaling yards. Over 100 Eighth Air Force P-51 Mustangs support Ninth Air Force B-26s. One P-51 is lost, and the pilot is reported missing.

P-47 and P-38 fighters support 3rd and 9th Armored Divisions, VIII and XX Corps, and 6th and 2nd Armored Divisions.

**MEDITERRANEAN:** Fifteenth Air Force sends more than 800 B-17s and B-24 Liberators escorted by 145 P-38 Lightnings to support Fifth Army, attacking gun positions, troop concentrations, logistics storage sites, ammunition storage areas, and German headquarters units. Another 312 B-17s and B-24s escorted by 191 P-51 Mustangs attack rail lines and bridges in Italy. P-38s and P-51s attack rail lines in Germany, Austria, and Czechoslovakia.

**ITALY:** The 1st Armored Division captures Vergato and pushes into Suzzano. The 1st Brazilian Division captures Montese, and the 10th Mountain Division captures Rocca di Roffeno, turning the flank of two divisions and splitting the boundary between two German corps. The attack costs the division over 550 casualties.

During the night II Corps begins its attack. The 6th South African Armored Division captures Monte Sole, after a devastating barrage of 35,000 rounds of artillery hit German positions. The 88th Infantry Division attacks toward Monterumici; the 91st attacks toward Monte Adone; the 34th Infantry Division attacks to seize the ridges beyond Monte Belmonte. Over 500 artillery pieces support the corps attack. The American divisions make no progress against the heavily defended positions.

Twelfth Air Force B-25 Mitchells and P-47 Thunderbolts support Fifth Army ground forces and the British Eighth Army attacking troop concentrations, guns, and strongpoints. During the night A-20 Havocs and A-26 Invaders attack roads and motor transport in the Po River valley.

**SOUTHWEST PACIFIC AREA:** In the Philippines, Far East Air Force B-24 Liberators, P-38 Lightnings, and P-47 Thunderbolts attack island fortifications in Manila Bay, bivouac sites, and other targets on Luzon. B-24s, P-38s, and P-47s support ground forces on Negros and Cebu Islands. B-24s and B-25s bomb the Davao area on Mindanao Island, along with Marine aircraft.

B-24s bomb airfields and B-25s attack railyards on Formosa.

U.S. submarine *Charr* lays mines off the Malay Peninsula.

**PACIFIC:** During the night Twentieth Air Force sends 194 B-29s to bomb the Kawasaki urban area. Twelve B-29s are lost. More than 100 B-29s attack the urban area of Tokyo. One B-29 is lost.

Carrier aircraft from TF 58 attack airfields and aircraft on the ground in southern Kyushu, Japan, to stop the kamikaze strikes on the fleet off Okinawa.

A cargo ship is sunk off Shimonoseki Strait by a mine dropped by B-29s.

**PACIFIC, OKINAWA:** The 4th and 29th Marines of the 6th Marine Division attack the Yae Take defenses on the Motobu Peninsula, supported by napalm strikes from aircraft, artillery, and naval gunfire. Hill 200 falls to the 4th Marines; the 29th Marines are halted before Green Hill.

The 27th Infantry Division moves into the front lines to the right of the 96th Infantry Division in preparation for a major attack.

Kamikazes damage two destroyers off Okinawa. A Japanese assault demolition boat damages a motor minesweeper.

Private First Class Harold Gonsalves is the acting scout sergeant with the 4th Battalion, 15th Marine Regiment, 6th Marine Division, fighting the Japanese at Mount Yaetake on the Motobu Peninsula. Gonsalves accompanies his battalion commander as he moves up to the front lines to assist the forward observation team in directing artillery fire on Japanese positions. When a Japanese grenade falls close within the group, PFC Gonsalves covers the grenade with his body, saving the lives of the other marines. For his distinct act of heroism and self-sacrifice, PFC Gonsalves will receive the Medal of Honor.

## April 16

**ALEUTIANS:** Eleventh Air Force sends six B-24 Liberators to bomb the Kataoka naval base on Shimushu Island in the Kuriles. The bombers use radar to mark the bomb release points over the target.

**CBI:** Fourteenth Air Force sends B-24 Liberators to bomb targets of opportunity in the Bakli Bay, Hainan Island, and Canton areas. About 120 P-40s and P-51 Mustangs attack river, road, and rail traffic, town areas, troops, and general targets of opportunity in southern and eastern China.

In Burma, Tenth Air Force P-47 Thunderbolts attack troop concentrations.

**ATLANTIC:** President Truman, addressing a joint session of Congress, reaffirms his commitment to the unconditional surrender of Germany and Japan.

Troubled by the Soviet machinations in Poland, Truman and Churchill send a letter to Stalin appealing to him to live up to the Yalta agreements.

Two destroyer escorts sink German submarine *U-880* in the North Atlantic.

**ETO:** The eastern half of the Ruhr Pocket is eliminated.

The 3rd and 45th Infantry Divisions of XV Corps of Seventh Army reach Nürnberg. German troops fight to defend the city. The Americans are capturing an average of 50,000 prisoners a day.

Eighth Air Force sends more than 1,200 B-17s and B-24 Liberators escorted by over 900 P-47 Thunderbolts and P-51 Mustangs to bomb rail bridges and marshaling yards. One B-24 is lost and 12 bombers are damaged. Aircrew casualties are seven missing. Fighter pilots report two confirmed kills in the air and 314 confirmed kills and 175 possibles on the ground. Twenty fighters are lost and the pilots are reported missing. Over 280 P-51s fly a free-lance mission in support of bombers attacking landing areas in Germany and Czechoslovakia. Pilots report one confirmed kill and one possible in the air and 410 confirmed kills and 198 possibles on the ground. Nine fighters are lost, and the pilots are reported missing. P-51 Mustangs escort a photo reconnaissance mission over Germany. Two fighters are lost, and the pilots are reported missing.

In an early morning strike, 485 B-17s bomb the tank ditch defense line near the Bordeaux area in support of ground forces. Fourteen B-17s are damaged. During the night 11 B-24s drop leaflets over France, Germany, and the Netherlands.

Ninth Air Force sends 450 A-20 Havocs, A-26 Invaders, and B-26 Marauders to attack communication centers and marshaling yards. P-47 and P-38 fighters support the 3rd and 9th Armored Divisions, XX and VIII Corps, XIX Corps and V Corps, and the 2nd Armored Division. Pilots report 25 German fighters downed. The P-51s of the 354th Fighter Group claims their 900th air victory.

**MEDITERRANEAN:** Fifteenth Air Force B-24 Liberators escorted by 102 P-51 Mustangs bomb German positions southwest of Bologna. P-51s attack airfields in Germany and sweep areas of Austria and Czechoslovakia.

**ITALY:** The 10th Mountain Division makes large gains. The 86th Mountain Infantry Regiment and the 751st Tank Battalion capture Montepastore. The 11th Armored Infantry Regiment of the 1st Armored Division captures Monte Mosca.

Fifteenth Air Force B-24 pilots of the 98th and 376th Bomber Groups prepare to return to the United States for B-29 training to support the anticipated invasion of Japan.

Twelfth Air Force B-25 Mitchells bomb bridges along the British Eighth Army battle lines. P-47 Thunderbolts support Fifth Army ground forces. During the night A-20 Havocs and A-26 Invaders attack river crossing sites in the Po River valley.

**SOUTHWEST PACIFIC AREA:** In the Philippines, Far East Air Force P-38 Lightnings and P-47 Thunderbolts support ground forces and conduct sweeps over Luzon, Negros, and Mindanao Islands. B-25 Mitchells bomb highways on Mindanao, while B-24 Liberators attack defenses on Carabao Island.

B-25s, B-24s, and P-51s bomb airfields on Formosa. During the night B-24s bomb Formosa.

FEAF P-38 Lightnings bomb a tank farm and other targets at Tarakan, Borneo.

**PACIFIC:** U.S. submarine *Sea Dog* torpedoes and sinks a cargo ship off eastern Honshu, Japan. U.S. submarine *Sunfish* attacks a Japanese convoy leaving Yamado harbor, Honshu, Japan, and sinks a coastal defense vessel and a transport.

A mine from Twentieth Air Force B-29s damages a Japanese cargo vessel off Shimonoseki.

**PACIFIC, OKINAWA:** Major General Lemuel C. Shepherd, commander of the 6th Marine Division, orders a renewed attack on the Yae Take defenses on the Motobu Peninsula, using the 22nd Marines to flank the Japanese positions. The 3rd Battalion of the 29th Marines captures Green Hill, while the 4th Marines battle to the top of Yae Take. After repeated counterattacks throughout the night, the Japanese withdraw into the jungle, headed for the northern section of Okinawa. The marines will

The USS *Intrepid* is hit by a kamikaze off Okinawa on April 16, 1945.

occupy Yae Take for another four days, clearing the last Japanese defenders. Marine casualties to secure the Motobu Peninsula are nearly 1,000 men.

The 305th and 306th Infantry Regiments of the 77th Infantry Division land on Ie Shima Island off the Motobu Peninsula to capture the airfield. The fierce Japanese resistance at Bloody Ridge before Iegusugu Mountain forces the Americans to land the 307th Infantry Regiment to reinforce the attack. Although slowed by minefields, the Americans capture the airfield and stop a Japanese counterattack during the night.

The carrier *Intrepid* is hit by a kamikaze. Ten sailors are killed and 87 are wounded. The damage is severe enough to take the carrier out of battle. The destroyer *Laffey* takes on 22 Japanese aircraft, some making suicide attacks, others dropping bombs. The *Laffey* takes four direct bomb hits and six kamikaze strike the ship. A total of 32 sailors are killed, and 21 are wounded. Although seriously damaged in the fight, the destroyer prevents the enemy from threatening the transports and cargo ships off Hagushi. The *Laffey* earns a Presidential Unit Citation.

Kamikazes sink destroyer USS *Pringle* and damage battleship USS *Missouri*, a destroyer, a destroyer escort, two high-speed minesweepers, and an oiler off Okinawa.

**CENTRAL PACIFIC:** Seventh Air Force sends 18 B-24 Liberators from Guam to bomb Marcus Island.

P-51 Mustangs from Iwo Jima, with Twentieth Air Force B-29s providing navigational escort, strafe and bomb targets at Kanoya airfield on Kyushu Island. Four P-51s are lost.

## April 17

**CBI:** In China, Fourteenth Air Force sends four B-25 Mitchells and four P-51 Mustangs to bomb river shipping. P-51 Mustangs and P-40s attack troops, town areas, road traffic, river shipping, and general targets of opportunity in southern and eastern China.

In Burma, Tenth Air Force sends P-47 Thunderbolts and P-38 Lightnings to attack road traffic, troop concentrations, logistics storage sites, and targets of opportunity.

**ATLANTIC:** Prime Minister Winston Churchill addresses the House of Commons a few days after President Roosevelt's death, describing Roosevelt as "the greatest champion of freedom who has ever brought help and comfort from the New World to the Old."

**ETO:** General Eisenhower's directive for the final operations in Germany is passed to subordinate commanders. With Germany now split in half, the Allied forces in the west will attack to the north and south to eliminate the last resistance. The Elbe River is the halt line for farther advances eastward. The 12th Army Group is to defend the Elbe-Mulde River line while Third Army is to attack southward toward Nürnberg and Regensburg and into the Danube River valley. The 6th Army Group is to occupy western Austria and the adjacent territory of Germany within its area of responsibility. The 21st Army Group is to cross the Elbe, secure Hamburg, and advance to the Baltic toward Kiel and be prepared to attack into Denmark.

Eighth Air Force sends more than 1,000 B-17s and B-24 Liberators escorted by over 800 P-47 Thunderbolts and P-51 Mustangs to bomb rail bridges, marshaling yards, and rail junctions in Germany and Czechoslovakia. The marshaling yards at Dresden are attacked again. About 50 German Me-262 jet fighters attack the bomber formations. A total of eight bombers are lost and 178 damaged. Aircrews report one confirmed kill and one possible. Aircrew casualties are seven wounded and 68 missing. Fighter pilots report 13 confirmed kills and five possibles in the air and 286 confirmed kills and 113 possibles on the ground. A total of 16 fighters are lost. Two pilots are wounded, and 16 pilots are reported missing.

During the night 10 B-24s drop leaflets over Germany, France, and the Netherlands. A total of 19 B-24s fly Carpetbagger missions.

Ninth Air Force sends A-20 Havocs, A-26 Invaders, and B-26 Marauders to attack ordnance depots and marshaling yards. P-47 and P-38 fighters support 3rd and 9th Armored Divisions, VIII and XX Corps, and 2nd and 5th Armored Divisions.

First Lieutenant Frank Burke is the battalion transportation officer of the 15th Infantry Regiment, 3rd Infantry Division, looking to select a motor pool site in Nürnberg, Germany, during the fighting for the city. He inadvertently passes beyond friendly lines and discovers 10 German infantrymen preparing to make a counterattack. Returning to friendly lines, Burke gets a light machine gun and ammunition and moves forward alone to attack the Germans. His accurate fire breaks up the attack and silences a machine-gun position not far away. He then picks up a rifle and runs to an abandoned tank to fire on the Germans from behind. He eliminates a sniper from a cellar window and withdraws to obtain a new rifle, ammunition, and grenades, then walks out into the street to continue the fight. Putting an armed grenade in each hand, Burke charges toward enemy troops in a building, throws the grenades, and eliminates the position even as he appears to be killed by a German hand grenade that explodes in front of him. Unhurt, Burke picks up his rifle to kill three German soldiers charging toward him. For the rest of the day Lieutenant Burke moves from street to street participating in the small but brutal battles that rage in the city. For his extraordinary bravery and superb fighting skill, First Lieutenant Frank Burke will receive the Medal of Honor.

**MEDITERRANEAN:** Fifteenth Air Force sends more than 700 B-17s and B-24 Liberators escorted by 143 P-51 Mustangs to bomb troop concentrations, logistics storage sites, and targets of opportunity in support of Fifth Army. P-51s attack targets of opportunity in Germany, Austria, and Czechoslovakia.

**ITALY:** The 88th, 91st, and 18th Infantry Divisions capture key mountain points overlooking Route 64 and the Reno River. The 92nd Infantry Division's 473rd Infantry Regiment attacks up the coastal road and approaches La Spezia. The 442nd RCT is halted by German defenses at Fosdinovo.

Twelfth Air Force B-25 Mitchells bomb bridges and support Eighth Army. A-20 Havocs and P-47 Thunderbolts of the XXII Tactical Air Command support Fifth Army ground forces. During the night A-20 Havocs and A-26 Invaders attack river crossing sites in the Po River valley.

**SOUTHWEST PACIFIC AREA:** In the Eighth Army area, the 24th Infantry Division lands at Parang and advances toward Davao on Highway 1. One battalion of the 21st Infantry Regiment lands at Malabang, already under control of Filipino guerrillas. The 533rd Engineer Boat and Shore Regiment provides support to the advance, traveling on the Mindanao River paralleling Highway 1. The river becomes the main line of supply for the 24th Infantry Division.

In the Philippines, Far East Air Force B-24 Liberators, B-25 Mitchells, A-20 Havocs, P-38 Lightnings, and P-47 Thunderbolts support ground forces over Luzon, Cebu, Negros, and Mindanao Islands. B-24s bomb targets on Mindanao.

B-24s and B-25s bomb airfields on Formosa.

**PACIFIC:** Twentieth Air Force sends more than 100 B-29s to bomb airfields at Tachiarai, Kokubu, Izumi, Nittagahara, and Kanoya, Japan, in an attempt to stop kamikaze attacks on navy ships off Okinawa.

A mine from Twentieth Air Force B-29s sinks a Japanese cargo ship off Shanghai. A mine from a 21st Bomber Command B-29 sinks a Japanese cargo ship off western Kyushu.

**PACIFIC, OKINAWA:** The 305th and 306th Infantry Regiments of the 77th Infantry Division are reinforced by the 307th Infantry as the Japanese hold Ie town and Bloody Ridge.

A kamikaze damages a destroyer off Okinawa.

**CENTRAL PACIFIC:** Seventh Air Force sends 18 P-51 Mustangs from Iwo Jima to fly two strikes against vessels at Futamiko in the Bonin Islands.

## April 18

**CBI:** Fourteenth Air Force B-25 Mitchells, P-40s, and P-51s attack trucks, tanks, logistics sites, horses, troops, and artillery in southern and eastern China.

In Burma, Tenth Air Force sends P-38 Lightnings to attack troop concentrations, tanks, artillery positions, and targets of opportunity.

**ATLANTIC:** German submarine *U-1107* torpedoes and sinks a U.S. freighter in convoy HX 348 southwest of Brest, France. German submarine *U-548* torpedoes a U.S. freighter off Cape Henry, Virginia. Although driven off by gunfire initially, the U-boat returns and finishes off the freighter.

**ETO:** The Ruhr Pocket is eliminated. About 325,000 German soldiers, including 30 general officers, surrender. There are no organized German formations within 100 miles. German prisoners are so numerous that they are kept in huge open fields enclosed in barbed wire. Taking care of prisoners, refugees, displaced people, and combat forces strains the Allied supply capability.

The Third Army enters Czechoslovakia. The XIX Corps of Ninth Army captures Magdeburg after a strong defense by German forces.

Eighth Air Force sends more than 700 B-17s and B-24 Liberators escorted by 700 P-47 Thunderbolts and P-51 Mustangs to bomb rail bridges and marshaling yards in southern Germany and Czechoslovakia. Two B-17s are lost and 18 damaged. Aircrews report 16 confirmed kills and 14 possibles. Aircrew casualties are 10 missing. Fighter pilots report three confirmed kills and four possibles in the air and 12 confirmed kills and eight possibles on the ground. Two P-51s are lost, and the pilots are reported missing.

During the night 11 B-24s drop leaflets over Germany, France, and the Netherlands. A total of 17 B-24s fly Carpetbagger missions to Denmark and Norway.

Ninth Air Force sends nearly 600 A-20 Havocs, A-26 Invaders, and B-26 Marauders to attack oil storage areas, rail junctions, and marshaling yards. Over 100 P-51 Mustangs escort Ninth Air Force B-26 Marauders. Pilots report one confirmed kill and two possibles in the air. P-47 and P-38 fighters support V and VII Corps, 2nd and 5th Armored Divisions, and XIX Corps.

The headquarters of the 349th Troop Carrier Group and the C-47s of the 23rd, 312th, 313th, and 314th Troop Carrier Squadrons, IX Troop Carrier Command, redeploy from England to France.

Private Joseph F. Merrell of I Company, 15th Infantry Regiment, 3rd Infantry Division, assaults a hill near Lohe, Germany, whose capture will open the way to Nürnberg. When the attack is stalled by heavy enemy fire, Private Merrell continues forward alone, running 100 yards and shooting down four German soldiers. His rifle damaged by a sniper bullet, he continues forward with the three grenades he has. Running another 200 yards, he reaches a machine-gun position, throws two grenades, and then jumps in ready to fight any survivors. Unarmed, he obtains a German pistol and eliminates the defenders. Crawling toward a second machine gun 30 yards away, he kills four Germans in camouflaged foxholes on the way, but is badly wounded. Staggering forward, he throws his last grenade into the machine-gun position and again jumps in to fight the enemy. He is shot and killed by the defenders. For his complete fearlessness, initiative, and willingness to sacrifice his own life so that his comrades can go on to victory, Private Merrell will receive the nation's highest award for valor, the Medal of Honor.

**MEDITERRANEAN:** Fifteenth Air Force sends more than 400 B-17s and B-24 Liberators escorted by 89 P-51 Mustangs to bomb defensive positions near Bologna in support of Fifth Army. P-38 Lightnings attack rail bridges in Austria.

**ITALY:** General Lucian K. Truscott commits the 85th Infantry Division to exploit the success west of Route 64 along the Reno River. The 91st Infantry Division of II Corps captures Pianoro. The 10th Mountain Division approaches Monte San Michele, the last major defensible position before the open plain that reaches to Route 9 west of Bologna. The 85th Infantry Division moves through disorganized German units to approach Pradura on Route 64 leading into Bologna.

Twelfth Air Force B-25 Mitchells bomb bridges. P-47 Thunderbolts of the XXII Tactical Air Command support Fifth Army ground forces. During the night A-20 Havocs and A-26 Invaders attack river crossing sites in the Po River valley.

**SOUTHWEST PACIFIC AREA:** In the Philippines, Far East Air Force A-20 Havocs, P-47 Thunderbolts, and P-38 Lightnings support ground forces on Luzon, Negros, and Cebu Islands. B-24s bomb Mindanao Island.

On Formosa, B-24s and B-25s bomb airfields, while P-38s conduct sweeps against rail and road transportation targets.

FEAF B-25 Mitchells and P-38 Lightnings attack Tarakan and Sandakan on Borneo.

**PACIFIC:** The last elements of the 3rd Marine Division leave Iwo Jima.

Twentieth Air Force sends more than 100 B-29s to attack Japanese airfields at Tachiarai, Izumi, Kokubu, Nittagahara, and Kanoya, while 13 other B-29s attack targets of opportunity. Two B-29s are lost.

U.S. submarine *Seahorse* is damaged in a depth charge attack in Tsushima Strait and is forced to terminate her patrol. U.S. submarine *Sea Owl* torpedoes and sinks Japanese submarine *RO-46* off Wake Island.

**PACIFIC, OKINAWA:** The 305th and 307th Infantry Regiments of the 77th Infantry Division attack into Ie town to capture Bloody Ridge. The Japanese have fortified the town, and throughout the day the Americans battle house by house. While driving in a jeep with the commander of the 305th Infantry Regiment, renowned correspondent Ernie Pyle, author of *Brave Men* and *Here Is Your War,* is killed by Japanese machine-gun fire.

Five destroyers and TBM Avengers from small carrier USS *Bataan* sink Japanese submarine *I-56* east of Okinawa.

**CENTRAL PACIFIC:** During the night Seventh Air Force sends three P-61 Black Widow night fighters from Iwo Jima to make individual attacks on Futamiko and the radio station on Chichi Jima.

## April 19

**CBI:** In China, Fourteenth Air Force sends B-25 Mitchells to attack bridges and rail and road traffic, while over 100 P-40s, P-51 Mustangs, and P-47 Thunderbolts attack town areas, troops, river, road, and rail traffic, and general targets of opportunity in southern and eastern China.

In Burma, Tenth Air Force P-38 Lightnings attack, logistics storage sites, bridges, and targets of opportunity.

**ATLANTIC:** President Truman agrees to changes in the U.S. approach to trusteeships at the upcoming San Francisco conference, at the strong urging of his military advisers. Any trusteeship given to another state would have to take into consideration American strategic and security interests. This will preclude giving away territories to states that could use them against American interests as the Japanese did with islands in the Pacific after World War I. The deteriorating situation with the Soviet Union makes the issue more urgent.

Two destroyer escorts sink German submarine *U-879* in the North Atlantic.

**ETO:** The 9th Infantry Division of V Corps clears the last German resistance from Leipzig.

Eighth Air Force sends more than 600 B-17s and B-24 Liberators escorted by 584 P-51 Mustangs to bomb rail lines and marshaling yards in Germany and Czechoslovakia. Five B-17s are lost and 13 are damaged. Aircrews report 18 confirmed kills, one probable, and five possibles. Aircrew casualties are 46 missing. Fighter pilots report 12 confirmed kills and three possibles in the air. One P-61 is lost, and the pilot is reported missing.

Six P-51s escort a photo reconnaissance mission over Germany. One P-51 is lost, and the pilot is reported missing.

During the night 11 B-24s fly Carpetbagger missions to Norway. Two B-24s are lost.

Ninth Air Force sends A-20 Havocs, A-26 Invaders, and B-26 Marauders to attack marshaling yards. P-47 and P-38 fighters support VII Corps, XII Corps, and XX and XIX Corps.

**MEDITERRANEAN:** Fifteenth Air Force sends more than 600 B-17s and B-24 Liberators escorted by P-38 Lightnings and P-51 Mustangs to bomb a rail bridge and marshaling yards in Austria, and marshaling yards in Germany and Italy.

**ITALY:** The 85th Mountain Infantry Regiment captures Monte San Michele and the 87th captures Monte San Pietro. The 1st Armored Division engages in a tank battle along the Samoggia River.

Twelfth Air Force B-25 Mitchells bomb bridges. P-47 Thunderbolts attack logistics storage sites, ammunition storage areas, and support Fifth Army ground forces. During the night A-20 Havocs and A-26 Invaders attack river crossing sites, roads, and vehicles in the Po River valley.

**SOUTHWEST PACIFIC AREA:** In the Philippines, Far East Air Force B-25 Mitchells, A-20 Havocs, P-47 Thunderbolts, and P-38 Lightnings support ground forces on Luzon, Cebu, and Negros Islands. B-24 Liberators bomb personnel areas on Mindanao Island.

B-24s bomb an airfield and a town on Formosa.

FEAF B-25s strike Borneo, while B-24s returning from a French Indochina coastal sweep bomb Sandakan in Borneo.

**PACIFIC:** U.S. submarine *Cero* torpedoes and sinks a Japanese guardboat southeast of Kyushu, Japan. U.S. submarine *Sennet* attacks a Japanese convoy off the south coast of Kyushu and sinks an auxiliary submarine chaser and a cargo ship. U.S. submarine *Silversides* torpedoes and sinks a Japanese guardboat east of Honshu. U.S.

Members of the 96th Infantry Division occupy fighting positions on Okinawa, April 1945.

submarine *Sunfish* attacks a Japanese convoy off Hokkaido, sinking a gunboat and a cargo ship. U.S. submarine *Trutta* torpedoes and sinks a Japanese merchant vessel and merchant fishing boats in the Yellow Sea.

**PACIFIC, OKINAWA:** The heaviest artillery bombardment of the Pacific war, over 300 artillery pieces firing for 20 minutes, initiates the XIV Corps assault on the Shuri defensive line. Three divisions (the 27th, the 7th, and the 96th) are massed across a four-and-a-half-mile front. The 27th Division on the west coast of the island is to capture Kakazu Ridge. The 96th Division in the center is to capture the town of Shuri, and the 7th Division in the east is to capture Hill 178. With 27 artillery battalions and six battleships, six cruisers, and six destroyers all firing in support, the infantry advances on the Japanese defenses. A total of 650 aircraft hit targets all along the defensive front. Protected in their underground shelters, the Japanese suffer few losses and are fully prepared to resist the attacks.

The 96th Infantry Division attacks to capture Tombstone Ridge, the 7th to capture Skyline Ridge and Hill 178. The 7th is stopped short of the Japanese positions, while the 96th makes minimal progress after taking heavy casualties. The 27th Infantry Division, advancing down Highway 5, bypasses enemy defenses but gains no advantage by nightfall. The American effort ends in failure with more than 700 casualties.

On Ie Shima, elements of the 307th Infantry Regiment of the 77th Infantry Division reach Bloody Ridge as the battle for Ie town continues.

**CENTRAL PACIFIC:** Seventh Air Force sends 17 B-24 Liberators from Guam to attack Truk. Another 25 B-24 Liberators from the Palaus bomb nearby Arakabesan and Koror Islands. P-51 Mustangs from Iwo Jima bomb and strafe Futamiko in the Bonin Islands. During the night six P-61 Black Widow night fighters from Iwo Jima conduct individual harassment raids on Chichi Jima, Haha Jima, and Muko Jima islands.

Over 100 P-51 Mustangs fly a fighter sweep to Atsugi and Yokosuka airfields in Japan. Pilots report 23 confirmed kills and seven possibles in the air and 14 confirmed kills and 23 possibles on the ground. Two P-51s are lost.

## April 20

**CBI:** Fourteenth Air Force B-25 Mitchells, P-40s, and P-51s attack rail targets, trucks, tanks, logistics sites, horses, troops, and artillery in southern and eastern China.

In Burma, Tenth Air Force P-38 Lightnings attack bridges, while P-47 Thunderbolts attack road traffic, troop concentrations, and land gun positions.

**ETO:** Organized resistance in Nürnberg ends. The Americans capture 10,000 prisoners and free about 13,000 British and American prisoners of war.

First Army captures Leipzig after strong resistance near the Mulde River.

Eighth Air Force sends more than 800 B-17s and B-24 Liberators escorted by nearly 900 P-47 Thunderbolts and P-51 Mustangs to bomb rail bridges, rail junctions, and marshaling yards in Germany and Czechoslovakia One B-17 is lost and 25 damaged. Aircrews report seven confirmed kills and four possibles. Aircrew casualties are one wounded and 10 missing. One P-51 is lost. A total of 100 P-51s fly a freelance fighter sweep for the bombers. Pilots report seven confirmed kills and four possibles in the air.

Six B-17s conduct screening missions to jam German radio interception efforts and employ countermeasures against German radar sites.

During the night 12 B-24s fly Carpetbagger missions to Norway. Two B-24 Liberators are lost.

Ninth Air Force sends 564 A-20 Havocs, A-26 Invaders, and B-26 Marauders to attack oil storage areas, ordnance depots, and marshaling yards. P-47 and P-38 fighters support VII and VIII Corps, XII and XX Corps, and XIX Corps.

**MEDITERRANEAN:** Fifteenth Air Force sends more than 700 B-17s and B-24 Liberators escorted by P-38 Lightnings and P-51 Mustangs to bomb road and rail lines to block the German withdrawal into northern Italy. Over 100 P-38s attack rail lines and marshaling yards in Germany and Austria.

**ITALY:** Elements of the 10th Mountain Division capture Ponte Samoggia on Route 9. The 88th and 85th Infantry Divisions cross the Lavino River and occupy positions just south of Route 9. The 6th South African Armored Division of II Corps captures Casalecchio at the base of the Reno River Valley on Route 64.

Twelfth Air Force B-25 Mitchells bomb rail bridges. P-47 Thunderbolts of the XXII Tactical Air Command support Fifth Army ground forces. During the night A-20 Havocs and A-26 Invaders attack river crossing sites and vehicles in the Po River valley.

**SOUTHWEST PACIFIC AREA:** In the Eighth Army area the Americal Division conducts a pursuit of defeated Japanese forces into the northern mountains of Cebu Island. Supported by Filipino guerrillas, the American infantrymen succeed in isolating over 8,500 enemy troops. The Americans have lost over 400 killed and 1,700 wounded in the fight for Cebu, not including another 8,000 casualties as a result of disease. The Japanese have lost nearly 6,000 men. Cebu City with its excellent harbor is intended to become a staging base for three infantry divisions preparing for the invasion of Japan.

In the Philippines, Far East Air Force B-25 Mitchells, A-20 Havocs, P-47 Thunderbolts, and P-38 Lightnings support ground forces on Luzon, Cebu, and Negros Islands. B-24 Liberators and P-51s bomb airfields on Formosa.

FEAF B-24 Liberators bomb airfields on Borneo, and P-38 Lightnings and B-25 Mitchells attack Tarakan Island.

U.S. submarine *Guitarro* lays mines in Berhala Strait off the northeast coast of Sumatra.

**PACIFIC:** Mines dropped by Twentieth Air Force B-29s sink two cargo vessels and damage another at the western entrance of Shimonoseki Strait.

**PACIFIC, OKINAWA:** XXIV Corps renews its attack on the Shuri defenses. Two battalions of the 165th Infantry Regiment of the 27th Infantry Division bypass Japanese defenses and reach the Machinato airfield. Japanese forces occupying a position named Item Pocket stop any farther advance; the position controls all approaches to Machinato and the nearby airfield.

On Ie Shima, the 306th Infantry Regiment gains control of the north side of Iegusugu Yama, the mountain that anchored the Japanese defenses. Japanese counterattacks during the night, on Bloody Ridge, fail.

**CENTRAL PACIFIC:** Seventh Air Force sends 11 P-51 Mustangs from Iwo Jima to bomb Haha Jima.

## April 21

**CBI:** In China, Fourteenth Air Force P-40s and P-51 Mustangs attack rail and river traffic.

**ETO:** First Army eliminates the Harz Mountain pocket. SHAEF headquarters estimates that 1 million German soldiers have been captured since the beginning of April.

The French First Army captures Stuttgart.

Eighth Air Force sends more than 500 B-17s and B-24 Liberators escorted by 444 P-51 Mustangs to attack airfields supporting Me-262 jet aircraft. Two bombers are lost and 12 are damaged. Aircrew casualties are eight killed, one wounded, and 19 missing. Two fighters are lost and one is damaged. The pilots are reported missing. During the night 10 B-24s drop leaflets over France, Germany, and the Netherlands.

Brigadier General Ralph F. Stearley takes command of IX Fighter Command and IX Tactical Air Command, Ninth Air Force. P-47 and P-38 fighters support VIII Corps, XII Corps, and XX Corps.

**MEDITERRANEAN:** Fifteenth Air Force sends more than 200 B-17s and B-24 Liberators escorted by P-51 Mustangs to bomb marshaling yards in Germany and in Austria. Over 130 P-38 Lightnings bomb rail lines in Germany and Austria.

**ITALY:** The 133rd Infantry Regiment of the 34th Infantry Division riding the tanks of the 752nd Tank Battalion enters Bologna.

The 10th Mountain Division forms a task force of the 85th and 86th Mountain Infantry Regiments and the 91st Cavalry Reconnaissance Squadron to seize the Bomporto Bridge over the Panaro River. The unit is called Task Force Duff after its commander, Brigadier General Robinson E. Duff.

Twelfth Air Force B-25 Mitchells bomb bridges. P-47 Thunderbolts support Fifth Army ground forces as they move into Bologna. During the night A-20 Havocs and A-26 Invaders attack river crossing sites in the Po River valley.

**SOUTHWEST PACIFIC AREA:** In the Philippines, Far East Air Force B-25 Mitchells, A-20 Havocs, P-47 Thunderbolts, and P-38 Lightnings support ground forces on Luzon, Cebu, Negros, and Jolo Islands. The 39th Fighter Squadron, 35th Fighter Group, redeploys its P-47s from Lingayen to Clark Field, Luzon.

FEAF B-24 Liberators bomb airfields on Borneo, and P-38 Lightnings attack Tarakan Island and airfields, oil storage areas, and, with B-24s, attack targets of opportunity along the southwest Celebes coast.

**PACIFIC:** Twentieth Air Force sends more than 200 B-29s to attack airfields at Oita, Kanoya, Usa, Kokubu, Kushira, Tachiarai, Izumi, and Nittagahara in Japan to forestall kamikaze attacks on naval forces off Okinawa. Another 21 B-29s attack targets of opportunity, including the city of Kagoshima.

**PACIFIC, OKINAWA:** The 32nd Infantry Regiment of the 7th Infantry Division captures Skyline Ridge, forcing the outflanked defenders of Hill 178 to withdraw the following night. The 3rd Battalion of the 382nd Infantry Regiment, 96th Infantry Division, holds off successive Japanese counterattacks near Tombstone Ridge.

On Ie Shima, Iegusugu Yama falls to the 77th Infantry Division. The American flag is raised on the summit. The island is secured several days later. The division's casualties to capture this small island are 1,120—nearly as many as the division lost during the battle for Guam.

A destroyer is damaged by a near-miss bomb off Okinawa.

Private First Class Martin O. May is a machine gunner in the 307th Infantry Regiment, 77th Infantry Division, battling Japanese defenders on the rugged slopes of Legusuku-Yama on Ie Shima. Placing his gun in an exposed position to support the infantry, he immediately comes under heavy fire but engages attacking Japanese infantry effectively, stopping the enemy. After reforming, the Japanese attack again, and May repulses this attack with hand grenades and accurate fire. May holds this position throughout the day and into the next day, risking constant fire from the enemy and continuing to support the infantry until he is severely wounded and his gun destroyed by a mortar explosion. Refusing to give up, May throws hand grenades at the Japanese infantry until he is killed. For his gallant action, dedication to duty, and indomitable fighting spirit, Private First Class Martin will receive the Medal of Honor.

Central Pacific: Seventh Air Force sends 18 B-24 Liberators from Guam to bomb Marcus Island.

## April 22

**CBI:** Fourteenth Air Force B-24 Liberators bomb targets of opportunity at Canton and in Bakli Bay on Hainan Island. P-40s and P-51s attack trucks, tanks, logistics sites, horses, troops, and artillery in southern and eastern China.

U.S. submarine *Hardhead* torpedoes and sinks a Japanese cargo vessel in the Andaman Sea.

**ATLANTIC:** Two destroyer escorts sink German submarine *U-518* in the North Atlantic.

**ETO:** Third Army sends XX Corps toward the Danube River to clear the area of enemy forces. Seventh Army's XV Corps is ordered to advance toward Munich. The XXI and VI Corps of Seventh Army cross the Danube River.

During the night Eighth Air Force sends 10 B-24 Liberators to drop leaflets in France, the Netherlands, and Germany. Four B-24 Liberators fly Carpetbagger missions to Norway.

**MEDITERRANEAN:** Fifteenth Air Force sends 258 P-51 Mustangs and P-38 Lightnings to fly armed reconnaissance over northeast Italy, bombing marshaling yards, bridges, railroads, highways, and strafing an airfield, rail and road traffic, and numerous other targets of opportunity.

**ITALY:** Task Force Duff reaches the Po River at San Benedetto. Brigadier General Duff is seriously wounded when his vehicle hits a mine. IV Corps engineers support the 1st Battalion of the 87th Mountain Infantry Regiment as it crosses the Po River.

Twelfth Air Force B-25 Mitchells, A-20 Havocs, A-26 Invaders, and P-47 Thunderbolts attack troops and vehicles throughout the day and into the night as German forces retreat north across the Po River.

Private Joe Hayashi of K Company, 442nd Regimental Combat Team, attacks a strongly defended hill near Tendola, Italy. Private Hayashi brings his squad to within 75 yards of enemy positions before they are fired on. Moving the wounded to safety, Hayashi directs mortar fire on the enemy even as bullets fly all around him. He then attacks with his squad to occupy the position. During the attack on the village of Tendola, Hayashi attacks a German position alone, destroying one position and forcing several other enemy soldiers to abandon their positions. As he is throwing grenades and moving forward to pursue the Germans, he is killed. For his extraordinary courage and superb leadership Private Hayashi will receive the Medal of Honor.

**SOUTHWEST PACIFIC AREA:** In the Eighth Army area elements of the 63rd Infantry Regiment of the 41st Infantry Division, supported by Philippine guerrillas, capture Japanese positions on Mount Daho on Jolo Island in the Sulu Archipelago. The battle to control the island continues for another three weeks. During that time American casualties will number 165. Japanese casualties will be over 2,000 killed. The airfield on Jolo is improved and expanded.

The 31st Infantry Division lands at Parang and follows the 24th Infantry Division before turning north as ordered by Major General Sibert to attack up the Sayre Highway to Macajalar Bay. The 24th is ordered to capture Digos and then advance to capture Davao City.

In the Philippines, Far East Air Force B-25 Mitchells, A-20 Havocs, P-47 Thunderbolts, and P-38 Lightnings support ground forces on Luzon, Cebu, and Negros Islands.

B-24 Liberators attack shipping and harbor installations at Saigon in French Indochina.

FEAF B-24 Liberators bomb airfields at Manggar and Jesselton and P-38 Lightnings attack Kuching.

**PACIFIC:** Twentieth Air Force sends 87 B-29s to bomb airfields at Izumi, Kushira, Miyazaki, Tomitaka, and Kanoya and targets of opportunity. One B-29 is lost. P-51 Mustangs from Iwo Jima attack Akenogahara and Suzuko airfields; they claim 10 Japanese aircraft shot down and 15 destroyed on the ground.

U.S. submarine *Cero* torpedoes and sinks a Japanese guardboat and damages a guardboat south of Honshu, Japan.

**PACIFIC, OKINAWA:** A support landing craft *LCS-15* is sunk in an air attack off Okinawa. Kamikazes sink a minesweeper and damage two destroyers. A destroyer, a minesweeper, and a light minelayer are damaged by near-misses of kamikazes. Another minesweeper is damaged by strafing and a near-miss.

## April 23

**CBI:** In China, Fourteenth Air Force B-25 Mitchells attack railyards. B-24 Liberators attack targets of opportunity in the South China Sea. P-47 Thunderbolts and P-51 Mustangs attack troops, horses, trains, and river craft.

In Burma, Tenth Air Force sends seven P-61 Black Widow night fighters that use napalm, rockets, and cannon to attack airfields, a bridge, trucks, and other targets. P-47 Thunderbolts attack troop concentrations.

**ATLANTIC:** President Truman has a meeting with Foreign Minister Vyacheslav Molotov in Washington. Molotov is told in direct, blunt language that the United States has pledged itself to adhere to all the Yalta agreements and expects the USSR to do the same.

**ETO:** During the night Eighth Air Force sends one B-17 and 12 B-24 Liberators to drop leaflets in France, the Netherlands, and Germany, and 14 B-24s to fly Carpetbagger missions to Denmark.

Ninth Air Force P-47 Thunderbolts and P-38 Lightnings operate in conjunction with XII Corps and fly armed reconnaissance over eastern Germany and western Czechoslovakia.

**MEDITERRANEAN:** Fifteenth Air Force sends more than 700 B-17s and B-24 Liberators to bomb bridges and logistics storage areas in Italy. P-38 Lightnings and P-51 Mustangs bomb and strafe rail and road bridges, highways, trains and vehicles, and other targets of opportunity.

**ITALY:** The 1st Armored Division, the 6th South African Armored Division, and the 88th Infantry Division reach the Po River. All organized resistance south of the Po River ends as Eighth Army arrives to link with Fifth Army.

Twelfth Air Force B-25 Mitchells bomb road bridges. A-20 Havocs and P-47 Thunderbolts support Fifth Army ground forces. During the night A-20 Havocs and A-26 Invaders attack river crossing sites, a marshaling yard, airfields, vehicles, trains, and targets of opportunity in the Po River valley.

**SOUTHWEST PACIFIC AREA:** In the Philippines, Far East Air Force P-47 Thunderbolts and P-38 Lightnings support ground forces on Luzon, attacking numerous artillery positions, logistics storage areas, and general targets of opportunity.

In China, B-24 Liberators bomb a military depot at Shanghai and shipping in Yulin harbor on Hainan Island.

B-24 Liberators bomb the naval base at Saigon, in French Indochina.

B-25 Mitchells attack railyards, P-51s attack an airfield, and P-38s attack targets of opportunity on Formosa.

FEAF B-24 Liberators bomb airfields at Sepinggang and Jesselton, and P-38 Lightnings drop napalm on Tarakan Island targets. Other B-24s fly a shipping sweep over the Makassar Strait and damage several small vessels.

U.S. submarine *Besugo* sinks German submarine *U-183* in the Java Sea. (In 1943, the Germans had begun deploying U-boats to the Far East to operate out of Japanese bases in Indonesia.)

Navy PB4Y Privateers launch automatic homing missiles at Japanese shipping off Balikpapan, Borneo. This is the first use of this type of missile in combat.

**PACIFIC, OKINAWA:** Elements of the 1st Battalion of the 105th Infantry Regiment of the 27th Infantry Division battle to the top of the Urasoe-Mura Escarpment.

**CENTRAL PACIFIC:** Seventh Air Force sends 13 B-24 Liberators from Guam to bomb Marcus Island.

## April 24

**CBI:** In China, Fourteenth Air Force B-24 Liberators damage a vessel at Bakli Bay on Hainan Island, and B-25 Mitchells attack railroad targets of opportunity and a bridge. P-51 Mustangs, P-61 Black Widow night fighters, and P-40s attack rivercraft, railroad targets, trucks, bridges, troops, horses, and other targets of opportunity.

In French Indochina, B-24s bomb railyards and attack targets of opportunity in the South China Sea.

In Burma, Tenth Air Force sends P-47 Thunderbolts and P-38 Lightnings to attack troop concentrations, storage areas, vehicles, and targets of opportunity.

**ATLANTIC:** Stalin replies to the Truman-Churchill letter, complaining that the USSR has every right to install a friendly government in a country that is vital to Soviet security. He points out that the USSR made no complaint when the pro-Western governments of Belgium and Greece were established.

German submarine *U-546* torpedoes and sinks destroyer escort USS *Frederick C. Davis* off Newfoundland. Eight other destroyer escorts converge to sink the U-boat.

**ETO:** Seventh Army crosses the Danube and captures Ulm.

The zones of occupation for Germany are allocated. The United States has southwest Germany. Berlin is in the Soviet Zone, but the city itself will be divided into occupation zones.

During the night Eighth Air Force sends 11 B-24 Liberators to drop leaflets in France, the Netherlands, and Germany.

Ninth Air Force P-47 Thunderbolts and P-38 Lightnings operate in conjunction with the XII Corps and XX Corps.

**MEDITERRANEAN:** Fifteenth Air Force sends more than 700 B-17s and B-24 Liberators to bomb road and rail bridges in Austria and Italy, motor transport and marshaling yards in Italy, and a logistics storage area.

**ITALY:** The 10th Mountain Division's Po River beachhead is expanded as the remainder of the division crosses on a pontoon bridge. There is no opposition.

General Truscott orders all divisions of Fifth Army to cross the river as soon as possible. Truscott wants to reach Verona and cut off the escape of German units in the west of Italy. Units of II and IV Corps begin to find expedient means to cross the river in response to Truscott's orders.

Twelfth Air Force B-25 Mitchells bomb rail lines and Po River crossings. A-20 Havocs and P-47 Thunderbolts attack roads, vehicles, and rail lines along the Po River.

During the night A-20 Havocs and A-26 Invaders attack airfields, marshaling yards, vehicles, and other targets of opportunity in the Po River valley and northern Italy.

**SOUTHWEST PACIFIC AREA:** In the Philippines, Far East Air Force A-20 Havocs, P-38 Lightnings, and P-47 Thunderbolts support ground forces on Luzon Island.

A-20 Havocs attack sugar refineries on Formosa, while B-24 Liberators bomb other targets on the island.

FEAF B-24 Liberators bomb Tabanio and Miri in Borneo.

**PACIFIC:** Twentieth Air Force sends 101 B-29s to bomb the aircraft production facility at Tachikawa. Aircrews report 16 Japanese aircraft kills; five B-29s are lost.

**PACIFIC, OKINAWA:** An attack by units of the 96th and 7th Infantry Divisions leads to advances of over 1,000 yards. The center and left flank of the main defensive line has been quietly and carefully abandoned.

**CENTRAL PACIFIC:** The headquarters of the 506th Fighter Group and the 457th, 458th, and 462nd Fighter Squadrons arrive at North Field, Iwo Jima, from the United States with P-51 Mustangs.

## April 25

**CBI:** In China, Fourteenth Air Force B-25 Mitchells and P-47 Thunderbolts damage a bridge and knock out an antiaircraft position, while over 50 P-47 Thunderbolts and P-51 Mustangs attack river, road, and rail targets, troops, horses, and buildings.

In French Indochina B-24s bomb railyards.

In Burma, Tenth Air Force sends 16 P-38 Lightnings to attack truck parks, fuel storage areas, and logistics support sites, while 20 other P-38s attack troops.

**ATLANTIC:** The San Francisco Conference opens to create a new international organization that will be called the United Nations.

**ETO:** A patrol led by First Lieutenant Albert L. Kotzebue from the 3rd Battalion, 273rd Infantry Regiment, 69th Infantry Division, V Corps, First U.S. Army, meets elements of the 175th Rifle Regiment of the Soviet 58th Guards Division, 34th Corps, at Torgau on the Elbe River, commanded by Lieutenant Colonel Alexander T. Gardiev. As a result of the linkup, the Elbe-Mulde rivers become the temporary operational boundary between Soviet and U.S. forces as agreed upon by the Soviet High Command and the CCS.

The XX Corps of Third Army establishes a bridgehead on the Danube River at Regensburg and attacks south. XII Corps attacks north.

Eighth Air Force sends nearly 600 B-17s and B-24 Liberators escorted by nearly 500 P-51 Mustangs to bomb airfields, industrial targets, rail bridges, and marshaling yards in southeast Germany and Czechoslovakia. A total of six bombers are lost and 204 damaged. Aircrews report one confirmed kill and one probable. Aircrew casualties are nine wounded and 42 missing. Fighter pilots report one confirmed kill in the air. A group of 19 P-51s fly a sweep of the Prague-Linz area. Pilots report one probable kill in the air. One P-51 is lost, and the pilot is reported missing.

During the night 11 B-24s drop leaflets over France, Germany, and the Netherlands. A total of 12 B-24s and one A-26 Invader fly a Carpetbagger mission to Norway. Seven aircraft complete the mission.

Ninth Air Force sends nearly 300 A-20 Havocs, A-26 Invaders, and B-26 Marauders to attack an ordnance depot and airfields. P-47 and P-38 fighters operate in conjunction with XII Corps and XX Corps.

Navy PB4Y Privateers based in England sink German submarine *U-1107* in the English Channel.

**MEDITERRANEAN:** Fifteenth Air Force sends more than 400 B-17s and B-24 Liberators escorted by P-38 Lightnings and P-51 Mustangs to bomb railyards and marshaling yards in Austria.

**ITALY:** General Truscott orders II Corps to advance to the Adige River between Verona and Legnano. The IV Corps is to advance north to Verona, destroy or capture German forces in northwest Italy, and use the 1st Brazilian Infantry Division and the 34th and 92nd Infantry Divisions to attack west toward the Italian-Swiss border. Two combat commands of the 1st Armored Division are to support the western attack. One combat command will support the 10th Mountain Division and the 85th Infantry Division toward Verona. The 1st Battalion of the 85th Mountain Infantry Regiment reaches the airfield near Mantua. Italian partisans control most of the area.

The 351st Infantry Regiment of the 88th Infantry Division crosses the Po River and moves rapidly to occupy Verona.

Twelfth Air Force B-25 Mitchells bomb rail and road traffic and bridges to block the German retreat in the northern Po Valley. P-47 Thunderbolts of the XXII Tactical Air Command attack rail lines, bridges, and roads in the Po River valley and support Fifth Army ground forces.

During the night A-20 Havocs and A-26 Invaders attack river crossing sites and vehicles in the Po River Valley and along the Adige River.

First Lieutenant Raymond L. Knight, 350th Fighter Group, Twelfth Air Force, volunteers to lead two other P-47 Thunderbolts against the strongly defended airfield at Ghedi in the northern Po Valley. Knight takes the first pass on the airfield, skimming low over the ground to locate targets as antiaircraft fire bursts around him. Informing his flight, he then leads the attack, destroying five aircraft himself while the other P-47s destroy two more on the ground. Returning to base, Knight volunteers to lead three other P-47s in an aerial reconnaissance of Bergamo airfield. Again Knight makes the first pass and locates a German squadron under camouflage. Although his fighter is damaged, he leads the attack and makes 10 deliberate passes to destroy lucrative targets, including six fully loaded enemy bombers and two fighters. His fellow pilots account for four other bombers and one fighter. The following morning, he again leads three other aircraft against the Bergamo airfield, destroying three bombers on the ground. Knight's P-47 is badly damaged by antiaircraft fire and, rather than abandon the plane, he attempts to bring it back to base. He crashes en route over the Apennines. For his exceptional bravery and skill, First Lieutenant Knight will receive the Medal of Honor.

**SOUTHWEST PACIFIC AREA:** In the Philippines, Far East Air Force B-24 Liberators bomb Balete Pass and bridges on Luzon. B-25 Mitchells, A-20 Havocs, P-47 Thunderbolts, and P-38 Lightnings attack Japanese troop positions and bridges in the Cagayan Valley.

B-24s bomb the harbor at Saigon, French Indochina.

U.S. submarine *Cod* torpedoes and sinks a Japanese minesweeper off Formosa.

FEAF B-24 Liberators on an anti-shipping sweep sink a Japanese vessel in the Makassar Strait.

Private First Class David M. Gonzales of A Company, 127th Infantry, 32nd Infantry Division, is pinned down by Japanese fire on the Villa Verde Trail in Luzon. A 500-pound bomb explodes, burying five men. With the volume of fire making it extremely dangerous to move, Gonzales nevertheless moves to the area where the men are buried. Enemy fire kills his company commander, who was also coming to the aid of the buried men. Gonzales reaches the spot and begins digging with his hands and an entrenching tool as Japanese bullets hit all around him. As he digs each man out, he stands to assist them, heedless of the enemy fire. As the third man is brought out, Gonzales is hit and mortally wounded. For his courage under fire and his willingness to risk his own life to save the lives of his comrades, Private First Class Gonzales will receive the Medal of Honor.

**PACIFIC:** Brigadier General Joseph Smith takes command of Headquarters, XX Bomber Command.

**PACIFIC, OKINAWA:** The 165th Infantry Regiment of the 27th Infantry Division gains control of a ridge at Item Pocket, allowing the Americans to seize the defenses along the seaside. The 27th will continue to clear the enemy from the position over the next week. The 96th and 7th Infantry Divisions are stopped before formidable positions at Conical Hill and Kochi Ridge.

High-speed transport sinks Japanese submarine *RO-109* south of Okinawa.

**NEW GUINEA:** FEAF B-24 Liberators bomb the airfields on Celebes Island.

## April 26

**CARIBBEAN:** Sixth Air Force sends the B-24 Liberators of the 29th Bombardment Squadron (Heavy), VI Bomber Command, from Rio Hato, Panama, to the Galápagos Islands.

**CBI:** In China, Fourteenth Air Force sends 10 B-25 Mitchells and four P-47 Thunderbolts to attack bridges near Wuchang. Over 80 P-40s and P-51 Mustangs attack troops, horses, road and rail transport, tanks, gun positions, and targets of opportunity in southern and eastern China.

In French Indochina, B-24s bomb the docks at Hongay.

In Burma, 30 P-38 Lightnings and P-47 Thunderbolts of Tenth Air Force attack troop concentrations.

**ETO:** During the night Eighth Air Force sends six B-24 Liberators to drop leaflets in France, the Netherlands, and Germany. Two B-24s fly Carpetbagger missions.

Ninth Air Force sends 125 A-20 Havocs, A-26 Invaders, and B-26 Marauders to attack an airfield and support XII Corps as it crosses into Austria and XX Corps as it crosses the Danube River at Regensburg. P-47 and P-38 fighters report 19 German fighters shot down.

**MEDITERRANEAN:** Fifteenth Air Force sends more than 100 B-17s and B-24 Liberators escorted by P-38 Lightnings and P-51 Mustangs to bomb marshaling yards in Austria and a motor transport depot in Italy. P-38s dive-bomb rail lines and road bridges.

**ITALY:** Twelfth Air Force B-25 Mitchells bomb rail and road bridges. A-20 Havocs and P-47 Thunderbolts attack vehicles, rail lines, bridges, and roads in the Po River valley and support Fifth Army ground forces.

**SOUTHWEST PACIFIC AREA:** On Luzon in the I Corps area the 33rd and 37th Infantry Divisions, supported by tanks and artillery and air support, capture Baguio.

In the Eighth Army area the 164th Infantry Regiment of the Americal Division (minus one battalion on Bohol Island) lands on Negros Island.

In the Philippines, Far East Air Force B-25 Mitchells, A-20 Havocs, P-38 Lightnings, and P-47 Thunderbolts support ground forces on Luzon. B-24 Liberators along with marine aircraft attack several targets on Cebu Island.

B-25s attack a sugar refinery and nearby targets of opportunity on Formosa. P-38 Lightnings on a sweep also attack targets of opportunity.

B-24s bomb Shanghai, China.

FEAF B-24 Liberators attack Miri airfield, and B-25 Mitchells and P-38 Lightnings attack targets on Tarakan Island.

U.S. submarine *Perch* is damaged by depth charges off North Borneo but remains on patrol.

**PACIFIC:** Twentieth Air Force sends nearly 200 B-29s, some escorted by P-51 Mustangs of VII Fighter Command, from Iwo Jima, to bomb airfields at Usa, Oita, Saeki, Tomitaka, Imabari, Nittagahara, Miyazaki, Kanoya, Kokubu, and Miyakonojo, Japan.

**PACIFIC, OKINAWA:** The 105th and 106th Infantry Regiments of the 27th Infantry Division attack into the Urasoe-Mura Escarpment, while the 165th Infantry Regiment continues to clear Item Pocket. The 17th and 32nd Infantry Regiments of the 7th Infantry Division are stopped at Kochi Ridge. The 383rd Infantry Regiment of the 96th Infantry Division gains some ground on the Maeda escarpment but is driven off by counterattacks.

**CENTRAL PACIFIC:** Seventh Air Force sends 13 B-24 Liberators from Guam Island to bomb Truk.

### April 27

**ALEUTIANS:** Eleventh Air Force sends six B-24 Liberators to drop fragmentation bombs on the Kataoka naval base on Shimushu Island in the Kuriles.

**CBI:** Fourteenth Air Force B-25 Mitchells and P-40 and P-51 Mustangs attack bridges, troop positions, villages and town areas, gun emplacements, and river, road, and rail traffic throughout southern and eastern China.

In Burma, 37 P-38 Lightnings and P-47 Thunderbolts of Tenth Air Force attack troop concentrations.

**ETO:** First Army captures Straubing and Kempten in Bavaria.

Eighth Air Force is notified it will no longer receive P-51, B-17, and B-24 replacement aircraft.

Ninth Air Force P-47s and P-38 Lightnings fly sweeps, conduct armed reconnaissance, attack airfields, and fly air cover for XII Corps as the 11th Armored Division reaches the German-Czech border. Fighters operate in conjunction with XX Corps as it takes the surrender of Regensburg and expands its bridgehead over the Danube River.

**ITALY:** The 473rd Infantry Regiment of the 92nd Infantry Division, Fifth Army, enters Genoa.

Twelfth Air Force B-25 Mitchells bomb rail and road traffic and bridges. A-20 Havocs and P-47 Thunderbolts attack rail lines, gun positions, vehicles, and rail cars in support of Fifth Army ground forces. Fighters also operate in support of the 1st Armored Division.

**SOUTHWEST PACIFIC AREA:** In the Eighth Army area, the 24th Infantry Division advances quickly along Highway 1 on Mindanao and captures Digos, surprising Japanese defenders who expected an attack from the sea at Davao Gulf. The 31st Infantry Division begins moving north toward Macajalar Bay, led by the 124th Infantry Regiment.

In the Philippines, Far East Air Force B-25 Mitchells attack Japanese installations, A-20 Havocs attack towns, and A-20s, P-38 Lightnings, and P-47 Thunderbolts attack targets near Manila and the Legaspi area.

**PACIFIC:** Twentieth Air Force sends 109 B-29s to hit airfields at Izumi, Miyazaki, Kokubu, Miyakonojo, Kanoya, and Kushira on Kyushu Island, Japan. Two B-29s are lost.

A mine dropped in late March by Twentieth Air Force B-29s sinks a cargo vessel west of Shimonoseki Strait.

**PACIFIC, OKINAWA:** Kamikazes damage a destroyer, a destroyer escort, and a high-speed transport off Okinawa. A heavy cruiser is damaged by shore battery fire. A kamikaze hits a U.S. freighter and sinks it.

**CENTRAL PACIFIC:** Seventh Air Force sends 11 B-24 Liberators from Guam to bomb Woleai Atoll.

**NEW GUINEA:** FEAF B-24 Liberators bomb Mandai airfield on Celebes Island and other B-24s attack Surabaya, Java.

B-24 Liberators attack Jesselton airfield and B-25 Mitchells bomb Tarakan Island in Borneo.

## April 28

**CBI:** In China, Fourteenth Air Force B-25 Mitchells bomb an airfield, a bridge, and railyards. Nearly 80 P-40s and P-51 Mustangs attack troops, airfields, logistics storage facilities, railroad targets, river craft, trucks, and defensive positions in southern and eastern China. One B-24 reports sinking a cargo ship in the South China Sea.

In Burma, Tenth Air Force P-38 Lightnings attack a cavalry regiment and logistics sites, while six other P-38s attack a bivouac area. P-47 Thunderbolts attack troops, artillery positions, trucks, elephants, and carts along and behind the enemy lines.

**ETO:** General Marshall sends the following message to General Eisenhower concerning whether United States forces should enter Czechoslovakia and capture

Prague ahead of the Soviets. "Personally and aside from all logistic, tactical or strategic implications, I would be loath to hazard American lives for purely political purposes."

The XXI Corps of Seventh Army captures Augsburg. The VI Corps crosses into Austria.

Seventh Army occupies Augsburg, Regensburg, and Ingolstadt.

Adolf Hitler marries his mistress, Eva Braun, and appoints Admiral Karl Dönitz as his successor.

**ITALY:** The 88th Infantry Division of II Corps occupies Vicenza, but like most areas at this time, Italian partisan forces control the towns and cities.

Tanks of the 1st Armored Division enter Milan. The 34th Infantry Division and the Italian Legnano Combat Group are ordered to advance to Brescia to block passes out of the Po Valley.

Task Force Darby meets strong resistance from German units along the eastern shore of Lake Garda. Task Force Darby, consisting of the 86th Mountain Infantry Regiment and the 13th Tank Battalion with detachments of artillery, engineers, tank destroyers, and a medical support, is under the command of Colonel William O. Darby, who previously commanded Rangers in Italy.

A-20 Havocs and P-47 Thunderbolts of the XXII Tactical Air Command attack roads and vehicles in support of Fifth Army ground forces.

**SOUTHWEST PACIFIC AREA:** In the Eighth Army area, the 164th Infantry Regiment of the Americal Division encounters Japanese defenders on Negros Island near Dumaguete. The Americans will fight the Japanese for a month.

In the Philippines, Far East Air Force B-25 Mitchells, A-20 Havocs, P-38 Lightnings, and P-47 Thunderbolts attack targets throughout Luzon.

B-24 Liberators bomb several targets on Formosa.

In French Indochina, FEAF B-25 Mitchells and P-38 Lightnings bomb Japanese shipping in Saigon harbor, sinking a tanker and six small ships.

FEAF B-24 Liberators bomb Masamba, Malimpoeng, and Mandai airfields on Celebes Island. B-24s attack Kuching, while B-25 Mitchells and P-38 Lightnings attack Tarakan Island and targets of opportunity along the Sarawak coast in Borneo.

**PACIFIC:** Twentieth Air Force sends 119 B-29s to attack airfields at Kushira, Kanoya, Miyakonojo, Kokubu, Miyazaki, and Izumi on Kyushu Island, Japan. Aircrews report 14 Japanese fighters shot down. Five B-29s are lost.

U.S. submarine *Sennet* torpedoes and sinks a Japanese cable layer off southern Honshu, Japan. U.S. submarine *Springer* torpedoes and sinks a Japanese submarine chaser escorting a landing ship west of Kyushu; U.S. submarine *Trepang* will later sink the landing ship.

A mine dropped by Twentieth Air Force B-29s sinks a cargo vessel at the west end of Shimonoseki Strait.

**PACIFIC, OKINAWA:** The 27th Infantry Division opens Highway 1 to traffic after clearing most of Item Pocket on the right flank of the American line.

The hospital ship *Comfort* is hit by a kamikaze, killing 30 and wounding 33. Kamikaze damage four destroyers and a high-speed minesweeper off Okinawa.

Tenth Army commander Lieutenant General Simon B. Buckner decides not to conduct an amphibious landing at Minatoga in southern Okinawa to outflank the Japanese defensive line. Instead, he decides to replace the 27th Infantry Division with the 1st Marine Division to maintain the 27th Division for garrison duties on the island and to clear Japanese troops from the northern section of the island. The 96th Infantry Division will be replaced by the 77th Infantry Division, and the 6th Marine Division will take the far left flank of the line. The marine divisions will be under the operational control of Major General Roy S. Geiger as commander of III Amphibious Corps.

**CENTRAL PACIFIC:** Seventh Air Force sends 12 B-24 Liberators from Guam to bomb Truk Atoll during the early morning hours, and 12 more B-24s attack again in the afternoon. A total of 20 P-47 Thunderbolts from Saipan sweep Truk, strafing small vessels and airfields on Param and Moen Islands.

## April 29

**ALEUTIANS:** Eleventh Air Force sends six B-24 Liberators to hit the Kataoka naval base on Shimushu Island in the Kuriles using radar to locate bomb release points.

**CBI:** In China, Fourteenth Air Force B-25 Mitchells and P-47 Thunderbolts bomb a railyard. P-40s and P-51 Mustangs attack troops, airfields, railroad targets, and trucks in southern and eastern China.

In Burma, Tenth Air Force P-47 Thunderbolts attack an airfield and strafe troops and horses.

**ETO:** The U.S. XVIII Airborne Corps, under the operational control of Montgomery's 21st Army Group, crosses the Elbe River.

Elements of the 157th Infantry Regiment of the 45th Infantry Division and elements of the 222nd Infantry Regiment of the 42nd Infantry Division arrive at Dachau concentration camp, where about 23,000 inmates await liberation. Another 2,300 inmates from Buchenwald are found in railroad cars outside the camp—all dead.

Eighth Air Force sends eight B-17s to drop leaflets in France, the Netherlands, and Germany.

Ninth Air Force P-47 Thunderbolts and P-38 Lightnings fly patrols and airfield cover, attack special targets, fly armed reconnaissance over eastern Germany and western Czechoslovakia, and support XII Corps and XX Corps.

**MEDITERRANEAN:** German officers representing General Heinrich von Vietinghoff's Army Group C, meet with Allied command representatives in Caserta and sign a document of surrender effective at 1200 on May 2.

Fifteenth Air Force P-51 Mustangs fly armed reconnaissance over northeast Italy. Fighters bomb and strafe various targets of opportunity, including vehicles, motor transport, and two aircraft on the ground.

**ITALY:** Task Force Darby, supported by elements of the 85th and 87th Mountain Infantry Regiments, clears German positions around Lake Garda. Colonel Darby is wounded by an artillery shell and dies later in the day.

Twelfth Air Force A-20 Havocs and P-47 Thunderbolts attack retreating German troops and vehicles and attack roads and airfields.

**SOUTHWEST PACIFIC AREA:** In the Philippines, Far East Air Force A-20 Havocs, P-38 Lightnings, and P-47 Thunderbolts attack troop concentrations, logistics storage areas, pillboxes, gun positions, vehicles, and other targets on Luzon.

P-38 Lightnings sweep French Indochina and strafe an airfield.

FEAF B-24 Liberators on an anti-shipping sweep sink a Japanese cargo vessel in Makassar Strait.

FEAF B-24 Liberators attack airfields on Celebes Island.

In Borneo, B-24s bomb an airfield, while B-25 Mitchells bomb Tarakan Island.

U.S. submarine *Besugo* torpedoes and sinks a Japanese guardboat southeast of Borneo.

U.S. submarine *Bream* torpedoes and sinks a German minesweeper depot ship off Borneo.

**PACIFIC:** Twentieth Air Force sends 111 B-29s to bomb Miyazaki, Miyakonojo, Kokubu, Kanoya, and Kushira airfields on Kyushu Island, Japan. Aircrews report 30 Japanese aircraft shot down. Two B-29s are lost.

U.S. submarine *Cero* torpedoes and sinks a Japanese cargo ship off eastern Honshu, Japan.

**PACIFIC, OKINAWA:** The 307th Infantry Regiment of the 77th Infantry Division attacks the Maeda Escarpment on the eastern end of the Urasoe-Mura Escarpment. The 381st Infantry Regiment of the 96th Division has failed to make any progress and has lost over 1,000 casualties before being relieved by the 77th Division.

Two destroyers are seriously damaged in kamikaze attacks. More than 100 sailors are killed and wounded.

Kamikazes damage two destroyers and two light minelayers off Okinawa. TBM Avengers from escort carrier USS *Tulagi* sink Japanese submarine *I-44* southeast of Okinawa.

**CENTRAL PACIFIC:** Seventh Air Force sends 20 P-47 Thunderbolts from Saipan on a sweep of Truk, hitting airfields, defenses, and gun positions. Some fighters use rockets against targets. A total of 24 B-24 Liberators from Guam conduct a follow-on attack on Truk. Another 20 B-24s, operating in two forces, bomb airfield installations on Marcus Island.

During the night Japanese aircraft from Truk attack the naval base at Manus, Admiralty Islands, dropping torpedoes on dock sections that they think are aircraft carriers.

## April 30

**CBI:** Fourteenth Air Force B-25 Mitchells and P-47 Thunderbolts attack railyards. P-47s, P-51 Mustangs, and P-40s attack troops, defensive positions, bridges, rail lines, and targets of opportunity in southern and eastern China.

**ATLANTIC:** Two destroyer escorts and a frigate sink German submarine *U-548* off Virginia. A PBY Catalina sinks German submarine *U-1055* west of France.

**ETO:** The XV Corps and XXI Corps of Seventh Army occupy Munich.

The 83rd Infantry Division of XIX Corps of Ninth Army encounters Soviet forces at Apollensdorf. At Torgau, Lieutenant General Courtney Hodges, commander of First Army, meets Colonel-General Zhadov, commander of the 1st Ukrainian Front.

Adolf Hitler, führer and chancellor of the German Reich and supreme commander of the German armed forces, commits suicide in his bunker in Berlin as Soviet troops close in.

Eighth Air Force sends six B-17s to drop leaflets over the Netherlands and France.

Ninth Air Force P-47 Thunderbolts and P-38 Lightnings fly in coordination with XII Corps and XX Corps.

**ITALY:** General Lucian K. Truscott transfers operational control of the 85th Infantry Division from IV Corps to II Corps. The 85th now moves north into the Alps to make a link up with Seventh Army. The 88th Infantry Division advances up the Brenta River, seeking the remnants of the German Fourteenth Army.

The 91st Infantry Division reaches Treviso, north of Venice. The 6th South African Armored Division begins moving west as a garrison force for the city of Milan.

Twelfth Air Force P-47 Thunderbolts attack guns, vehicles, and other targets of opportunity. During the night A-20 Havocs and A-26 Invaders attack motor transport.

**SOUTHWEST PACIFIC AREA:** In the Philippines, Far East Air Force B-25 Mitchells, A-20 Havocs, P-38 Lightnings, and P-47 Thunderbolts support ground forces on Luzon and Negros Islands. B-24 Liberators attack the Davao area on Mindanao Island.

On Formosa, B-24s attack fuel storage areas and airfields while B-25 Mitchells attack Taito. P-38 Lightnings provide escort and attack numerous targets of opportunity. P-51 Mustangs bomb Okayama airfield.

FEAF B-24 Liberators bomb Malimpoeng Airfield on Celebes Island. P-38 Lightnings attack Tarakan Island and B-24s bomb Manggar airfield on Borneo.

A U.S. destroyer is damaged by a mine off Borneo.

Thirteenth Air Force B-24 Liberators sink a Japanese transport in Balikpapan Bay in the Makassar Strait.

**PACIFIC:** Twentieth Air Force sends 69 B-29s escorted by 104 P-51 Mustangs to attack the Tachikawa air depot. Another 56 B-29s attack airfields at Kokubu, Oita, Tomitaka, Saeki, and Kanoya on Kyushu Island, and bomb the city of Hamamatsu. Aircrews report 10 Japanese aircraft shot down.

U.S. submarine *Trepang* attacks a Japanese convoy and sinks a transport in the Yellow Sea.

**PACIFIC, OKINAWA:** The 307th Infantry Regiment of the 77th Infantry Division gains a precarious foothold on the top of the Maeda Escarpment and battles fierce Japanese assaults to hold the ground and, yard by yard, gain control by attacking the caves on the back side of the escarpment with grenades and demolitions.

Kamikazes damage a destroyer and a minelayer off Okinawa. A kamikaze damages a U.S. freighter.

**CENTRAL PACIFIC:** Seventh Air Force sends 20 P-47 Thunderbolts from Saipan to attack the seaplane base, an airfield, a barracks, a radio station, and targets of opportunity on Truk. This is followed by 24 B-24 Liberators from Guam bombing airfields on Truk.

More than 20 B-24 Liberators operating in two separate waves bomb air installations on Marcus Island.

The headquarters of the 318th Fighter Group and the P-38 Lightnings of the 19th, 73rd, and 333rd Fighter Squadrons redeploy from Saipan to Ie Shima Island, Ryukyu Islands.

### May 1

**ALEUTIANS:** One Eleventh Air Force B-24 flies a weather reconnaissance mission over the Kurile Islands.

**CBI:** Lieutenant General Albert C. Wedemeyer, commanding general of U.S. forces in the China theater, names Lieutenant General George E. Stratemeyer as the commander of Army Air Forces, China theater, responsible for bringing the headquarters of both the Tenth and Fourteenth Air Forces under his command.

The Japanese offensive is curtailed to concentrate forces in the coastal cities of China in preparation for transfer to the home islands.

Fourteenth Air Force B-25 Mitchells and P-51s attack bridges, antiaircraft positions, and locomotives near the bridges, gun emplacements, and trucks in southern and eastern China.

**ETO:** The XX Corps of the Third Army arrives at Braunau.

Grand Admiral Karl Dönitz, commander in chief of the German navy, receives a message from Berlin notifying him of the death of Adolf Hitler and his appointment as president of Germany.

Eighth Air Force sends 396 B-17s to air-drop over 700 tons of food supplies in the area of The Hague and Rotterdam in the Netherlands. During the night four B-24 Liberators drop leaflets in Germany.

Ninth Air Force A-26 Invaders bomb an ammunition plant at Stod, Czechoslovakia. P-38 Lightnings and P-47 Thunderbolts of the IX Tactical Air Command escort the bombers and conduct patrols over Germany. P-47s of the XIX Tactical Air Command fly patrols and armed reconnaissance over eastern Germany, western Czechoslovakia, and Austria. Pilots conduct dive-bomb attacks on Berchtesgaden (a favorite assembly point of Nazi Party members and the location of the vacation home of Adolf Hitler) and support XII Corps and XX Corps.

**MEDITERRANEAN:** Fifteenth Air Force sends 27 B-17s to bomb the main station and marshaling yard at Salzburg, Austria. P-38 Lightnings and P-51 Mustangs fly reconnaissance and reconnaissance escort missions.

**ITALY:** The 442nd RCT occupies Turin, capturing 3,000 prisoners. Since the beginning of the Italian offensive on April 9, Allied units have captured 145,000 prisoners.

During the night Twelfth Air Force A-20 Havocs and A-26 Invaders bomb targets of opportunity in northern Italy. P-47 Thunderbolts attack motor and horse-drawn vehicles in northeast Italy as Fifth Army approaches the Brenner Pass.

**SOUTHWEST PACIFIC AREA:** In the Philippines, Far East Air Force B-25 Mitchells, A-20 Havocs, P-38 Lightnings, and P-47 Thunderbolts support ground forces on Luzon and Negros Islands.

B-25s bomb a sugar refinery and the town of Kagi on Formosa.

FEAF B-24 Liberators support Australian landings on Tarakan Island and bomb Tawau, and B-25 Mitchells attack airfields at Jesselton on Tarakan Island.

Vice Admiral Daniel E. Barbey, commanding a naval attack force, lands Australian troops on Tarakan Island, Borneo. Naval gunfire and aircraft provide support for the landing.

**PACIFIC:** U.S. submarine *Bowfin* torpedoes and sinks a Japanese gunboat southeast of Hokkaido, Japan. U.S. submarine *Sennet* torpedoes and damages a Japanese coastal defense vessel off southern Honshu, Japan.

Navy PBM Mariner patrol bombers sink a Japanese cargo vessel off western Korea.

**PACIFIC, OKINAWA:** The 1st Marine Division replaces the 27th Infantry Division on the right flank of the American line.

**CENTRAL PACIFIC:** Seventh Air Force sends 16 B-24 Liberators from Guam to bomb the airfield on Marcus Island, while another 10 B-24s attack air installations at Truk. During the night B-24s conduct individual snooper (radar-assisted bomb release) attacks on airfields on Param and Moen Islands of Truk.

## May 2

**CBI:** British paratroopers and elements of XVth Corps land at the mouth of the Rangoon River.

Fourteenth Air Force B-25 Mitchells, P-40s, and P-51s attack trucks, tanks, logistics sites, horses, troops, and artillery in southern and eastern China.

Five B-24 Liberators mine areas of the Yangtze River.

**ETO:** The XII Corps of Third Army reports that the Danube has been cleared of enemy forces to Passau. The III Corps reports it is at Wasserburg.

Grand Admiral Dönitz sends representatives to Field Marshal Montgomery's headquarters with an offer to surrender all German forces in northwestern Germany, Denmark, and occupied German islands.

Eighth Air Force sends 401 B-17s to airdrop 767 tons of food supplies in the Netherlands. Eight B-17s, escorted by nine P-51 Mustangs, drop leaflets in France, the Netherlands, and Germany.

Ninth Air Force P-38 Lightnings and P-47 Thunderbolts patrol the Third Army front in Austria and Czechoslovakia.

**ITALY:** Field Marshal Albert Kesselring, appointed by Dönitz as commander in chief of southern Germany, authorizes the cease-fire order for Army Group C. The Germans broadcast the order at 1400, the Allies at 1830.

**SOUTHWEST PACIFIC AREA:** On Luzon, elements of the 1st Cavalry Division link with the 158th RCT at Naga, completing the sweep of the Bicol Peninsula.

In the Philippines, Far East Air Force B-24 Liberators and P-51 Mustangs attack Japanese positions near Ipo Dam, and B-25 Mitchells, A-20 Havocs, and P-47 Thunderbolts attack targets in the Cagayan Valley on Luzon.

FEAF B-25 Mitchells continue support for Australian troops on Tarakan Island and bomb Kudat airfield along with navy aircraft.

Three motor minesweepers are sunk by shore batteries off Tarakan, Borneo. Another motor minesweeper is damaged by a mine.

**PACIFIC:** U.S. submarine *Raton* attacks a Japanese convoy, sinking a cargo ship southeast of the Shantung Peninsula in the Yellow Sea. U.S. submarine *Springer* torpedoes and sinks a Japanese escort vessel in the Yellow Sea.

**PACIFIC, OKINAWA:** Private First Class William A. Foster, a rifleman with the 3rd Battalion, 1st Marine Regiment, 1st Marine Division, is occupying a fighting position with another marine on Okinawa after a successful attack. Japanese infiltrators begin throwing hand grenades into the marine positions and one lands near Corporal Foster. He covers the grenade with his body to protect his fellow marine and, though mortally wounded, hands grenades to his comrade to help him defend the position. For his courage and self-sacrifice, Private First Class Foster will receive the Medal of Honor.

Hospital Apprentice Second Class Robert E. Bush, serving as a corpsman with a rifle company or the 2nd Battalion, 5th Marines, is administering blood plasma to a wounded marine when Japanese troops attack the marines' position. Staying by the wounded marine, Bush holds a plasma bottle in one hand and his .45-caliber pistol in the other, firing at the Japanese as they advance toward him. Out of ammunition, he picks up a discarded carbine and continues to protect his wounded patient, killing six enemy soldiers despite several wounds, including the loss of an eye. Bush refuses medical treatment until the marine he has treated is evacuated first. Bush's gallant actions and dedication to duty will win him the Medal of Honor.

**CENTRAL PACIFIC:** Seventh Air Force sends 12 B-24 Liberators from Guam to bomb the airfield on Param Island in Truk Atoll. A total of 21 B-24s, operating in two strike groups, attack airfields and gun positions on Marcus Island. During the night nine B-24s conduct individual harassment bombings on several islands in Truk Atoll. P-51 Mustangs of the VII Fighter Command from Iwo Jima attack a radio station on Chichi Jima.

### May 3

**CBI:** The Chinese-American staff of Alpha Force orders a counterattack against Japanese forces southeast of Chihchiang.

In China, Fourteenth Air Force sends nine B-25 Mitchells and P-40s to attack truck convoys in the Hsiang River valley and near Changsha and Hengyang, and rail lines, rail cars, and bridges. P-40s and P-51 Mustangs attack troops, town areas, ammunition storage sites, river shipping, and targets of opportunity over southern and eastern China.

Tenth Air Force's combat operations end with the capture of Rangoon on May 6. Several squadrons begin a redeployment to India. The P-47 Thunderbolts of the 88th Fighter Squadron, 80th Fighter Group, begin their redeployment from Myitkyina to India.

**ETO:** The U.S. XVIII Airborne Corps encounters Soviet troops at Wismar and Grabow. Innsbruck is captured. The 103rd Infantry Division of the VI Corps, Seventh Army, moves into the Brenner Pass.

The German High Command seeks to avoid surrendering to the Soviets and asks General Eisenhower for terms that allow German forces to pass into Allied lines in the West. Eisenhower replies that unconditional surrender is all he can offer.

Eighth Air Force sends 399 B-17s to air-drop 739 tons of food supplies in the Netherlands. Fourteen B-17s, escorted by 43 P-51 Mustangs, drop leaflets in Germany.

Ninth Air Force sends 132 A-26 Invaders to bomb the ammunition production facility at Stod, Czechoslovakia. P-38 Lightnings and P-47 Thunderbolts patrol the Third Army front, conduct armed reconnaissance over Germany, Austria, and Czechoslovakia, and escort the A-26 bombing run at Stod.

**MEDITERRANEAN:** Fifteenth Air Force B-25 Mitchells drop leaflets in northern Italy, escorted by P-38 Lightnings.

**ITALY:** The 85th and 88th Infantry Divisions collect German troops near the Austrian border and the Brenner Pass.

Twelfth Air Force P-47 Thunderbolts fly reconnaissance missions over northern Italy and southwest Austria to locate German forces and ensure compliance with surrender instructions. B-25 Mitchells drop leaflets in several areas where German units may not yet have received orders to surrender.

German officers representing General von Vietinghoff formally surrender the remaining Axis forces in Italy to General Mark Clark of 15th Army Group headquarters at Caserta.

**SOUTHWEST PACIFIC AREA:** In Eighth Army area, the 24th Infantry Division captures Davao City on Mindanao Island. The Japanese offer only limited resistance, but retreat into the abaca fields that cover the interior of the island. Here, in airless fields and among 20-foot-tall plants, the Americans will battle the Japanese in brutal close combat for more than 60 days.

Rear Admiral Albert G. Noble, commander of Naval Task Group 78.2, lands troops at Santa Cruz in Davao Gulf, Mindanao.

U.S. submarine *Lagarto* is sunk by a Japanese minelayer in the Gulf of Siam.

In the Philippines, Far East Air Force B-24 Liberators and P-51 Mustangs attack the area near Ipo Dam, while A-20 Havocs, P-38 Lightnings, and P-47 Thunderbolts support ground forces on Luzon. Saigon, French Indochina, is bombed by B-24 Liberators, which greatly damage a boatyard and oil storage areas.

FEAF B-25 Mitchells continue support of Australian ground forces on Tarakan Island in northeast Borneo. B-25s and B-24 Liberators attack other targets on Borneo and Celebes. B-24s and P-38 Lightnings bomb an airfield at Manggar and U.S. Navy aircraft attack warehouses in the Brunei Bay area.

The C-47s of the 63rd Troop Carrier Squadron, 403rd Troop Carrier Group, redeploy from Biak to Leyte Island.

**PACIFIC:** Twentieth Air Force sends 59 B-29s to bomb airfields at Tachiarai, Miyazaki, Miyakonojo, Kokubu, and Kanoya. Aircrews report 10 Japanese fighters shot down. One B-29 is lost. During the night 88 B-29s mine Shimonoseki Strait and the Inland Sea of Japan off Kobe and Osaka, Honshu, Japan.

U.S. submarine *Springer* torpedoes and sinks a Japanese coastal defense ship in the Yellow Sea.

**PACIFIC, OKINAWA:** Kamikazes sink destroyer USS *Little* and a medium landing ship off Okinawa. A destroyer and a high-speed minesweeper are damaged also. A Japanese assault demolition boat damages a light minelayer and a large support landing craft.

**CENTRAL PACIFIC:** Seventh Air Force sends 10 B-24 Liberators from Guam to bomb airfields and targets of opportunity on several islands of Truk. During the night eight B-24s fly individual harassment raids on Truk airfields.

## May 4

**ALEUTIANS:** Brigadier General Isaiah Davies takes temporary command of Eleventh Air Force from Major General Davenport Johnson.

**CBI:** Fourteenth Air Force sends 12 B-25 Mitchells and over 180 P-40s and P-51s to attack trucks, tanks, logistics sites, horses, troops, river shipping, airfields, artillery, and targets of opportunity in southern and eastern China.

**ETO:** The 3rd Infantry Division of XV Corps clears Hitler's compound at Berchtesgaden and occupies Salzburg. At Vipiteno, near near the south entrance of Brenner Pass, the 103rd Infantry Division makes contact with the 349th Infantry Regiment of the 88th Infantry Division of Fifth Army, linking the European and Mediterranean theaters. The 6th Army Group has captured 900,000 prisoners.

At Field Marshal Montgomery's headquarters on Lüneburg Heath, a German delegation led by Grossadmiral Hans Georg von Friedeburg, commander in chief of the Kriegsmarine, agrees to the unconditional surrender of all German land and sea forces in northwest Germany, Holland, and Denmark. A total of 1.5 million men come under control of British forces.

First Army headquarters is alerted to redeploy to the Pacific. Operational control of V Corps passes to Third Army; operational control of VII and VIII Corps passes to Ninth Army. Third Army's V Corps and XII Corps enter Czechoslovakia.

Field Marshal Montgomery at his headquarters near Lüneburg receives representatives of Grand Admiral Karl Dönitz and Field Marshal Busch, who surrender unconditionally all German forces in Holland, northwestern Germany, Schleswig-Holstein, and Denmark.

During the night Eighth Air Force sends one B-17 and eight B-24 Liberators to drop leaflets in France, the Netherlands, and Germany.

Ninth Air Force P-47 Thunderbolts and P-38 Lightnings conduct patrols and armed reconnaissance and operate in coordination with the movement of XII Corps to Linz, Austria, and support XX Corps.

**ITALY:** Twelfth Air Force P-47 Thunderbolts of the XXII Tactical Air Command continue flying visual reconnaissance missions in northern Italy as the 85th Infantry Division approaches the Brenner Pass.

**MEDITERRANEAN:** Fifth Army commander, General Mark Clark, meets with General von Senger, commander of the German XIV Panzer Corps, to work out the implementation of the surrender documents signed on April 29.

**SOUTHWEST PACIFIC AREA:** In the Philippines, Far East Air Force B-25 Mitchells, A-20 Havocs, P-38 Lightnings, and P-47 Thunderbolts support ground forces on Luzon and Negros Islands.

P-38 Lightnings attack Itu Aba Island, China. In French Indochina, B-24 Liberators bomb oil installations near Saigon.

Thirteenth Air Force B-24 Liberators attack Japanese shipping off the southern coast of French Indochina, sinking an auxiliary netlayer.

FEAF B-25 Mitchells and P-38 Lightnings support Australian ground forces on Tarakan Island in northeast Borneo and B-24 Liberators attack Sandakan and Kota Baru and bomb airfields on Celebes Island.

**PACIFIC:** Twentieth Air Force's 792nd, 793rd, and 794th Bombardment Squadrons (Very Heavy), 468th Bombardment Group (Very Heavy), begin redeploying their B-29s from India to Tinian.

Twentieth Air Force sends 47 B-29s to attack airfields at Oita, Omura, Saeki, and Matsuyama on Kyushu and Shikoku Islands, Japan. One B-29 is lost.

U.S. submarine *Cero* torpedoes and sinks a Japanese cargo ship off northeast Honshu, Japan. U.S. submarine *Trepang* torpedoes and sinks a Japanese minesweeper in the Yellow Sea. Navy PBM Mariner patrol bombers sink two Japanese merchant tankers off Pusan, Korea. Navy Mariners also damage a cargo vessel off the southern end of the Korean Peninsula. A Japanese tanker hits a mine dropped by 20th Bomber Command B-29s and sinks off Singapore.

**PACIFIC, OKINAWA:** The Japanese conduct a second major counterattack against the weakened American divisions battering against the Shuri defensive line. Tanks and infantry assault the center of XXIV Corps, supported by a massive artillery barrage against the 7th and 77th Infantry Divisions. The 306th Infantry Regiment of the 77th Infantry Division holds off the enemy in desperate fighting. The Japanese fail to break the American lines and lose more than 5,000 men.

Japanese aircraft attack Yontan airfield, Okinawa, and U.S. and British ships supporting the Okinawa operation. Kamikazes sink the destroyers USS *Luce* and USS *Morrison* and two medium landing craft. On board the *Luce,* nearly all of the crew is lost; the *Morrison* loses 153 crewmen. A light cruiser and an escort carrier are damaged as well. The British carrier HMS *Formidable* is damaged. A light minelayer is damaged by an oka and a minesweeper is damaged by near-misses of a kamikaze and an oka. Total losses are over 560 sailors.

**CENTRAL PACIFIC:** Seventh Air Force sends 22 B-24 Liberators from Angaur to bomb antiaircraft positions on Koror Island. B-24s from Guam attack the airfield on Marcus Island.

## May 5

**CBI:** Fourteenth Air Force B-25 Mitchells attack bridges and rail lines, while P-40s and P-51s attack trucks, tanks, logistics sites, troops, and artillery in southern and eastern China.

Tenth Air Force redeploys the headquarters of the 33rd Fighter Group and the P-47 Thunderbolts of the 90th Fighter Squadron, 80th Fighter Group, to India.

**ATLANTIC:** German submarine *U-853* torpedoes and sinks a U.S. freighter off Rhode Island. This will be the last U.S.-flagged merchant cargo ship sunk by a U-boat in World War II.

**ETO:** The 11th Armored Division of the XII Corps, Third Army, captures Linz.

Near Munich, German Army Group G surrenders to General Jacob L. Devers, commander of the 6th Army Group.

German representatives of Grand Admiral Dönitz arrive in Rheims, France, to seek an arrangement that would delay surrender and allow the greatest possible number of German soldiers and refugees to reach American and British lines instead of surrendering to the Soviets. The High Command also seeks to make a separate surrender arrangement with Eisenhower in order to buy more time. General Eisenhower threatens to seal his lines to prevent any further crossing and demands that all hostilities cease within 48 hours.

Eighth Air Force sends 403 B-17s to air-drop 744 tons of food in the Netherlands.

**MEDITERRANEAN:** Fifteenth Air Force sends 14 P-51 Mustangs to escort C-47s dropping supplies over Yugoslavia.

**ITALY:** Twelfth Air Force P-47 Thunderbolts of the XXII Tactical Air Command conduct reconnaissance flights over northern Italy, southwest Austria, and over Munich, Germany. Pilots report a number of German aircraft destroyed on the ground.

**SOUTHWEST PACIFIC AREA:** In the Philippines, Far East Air Force A-20 Havocs, P-38 Lightnings, and P-47 Thunderbolts attack Japanese positions in the Cagayan Valley and other targets on Luzon.

On Formosa, B-24 Liberators bomb an airfield, while B-25 Mitchells and P-47 Thunderbolts attack a sugar refinery, railyards, and airfields.

B-24s bomb an airfield and an oil storage plant at Amoy, China.

FEAF B-25 Mitchells and P-38 Lightnings support Australian forces on Tarakan Island.

P-38 Lightnings attack the waterfront on the west coast and an airfield in the north. B-24 Liberators bomb the waterfront on the west coast.

Thirteenth Air Force B-24 Liberators attack Japanese shipping and shore installations at Makassar, sinking a cargo vessel.

**PACIFIC:** Twentieth Air Force sends 55 B-29s to bomb airfields at Oita, Tachiarai, Kanoya, and Chiran on Kyushu Island, Japan. Three B-29s are lost. Over 140 B-29s attack a naval aircraft production facility and arsenal at Kure, Japan. Aircrews report 11 Japanese fighters shot down. Two B-29s are lost. During the night 86 B-29s drop mines in Tokyo Bay, Ise Bay, and at points in the Inland Sea of Japan.

Twentieth Air Force B-29s drop mines in the Inland Sea and off Kobe, Osaka, Tokyo, and Nagoya. A cargo ship is damaged by a mine in the Inland Sea.

Navy patrol bombers sink a Japanese cargo ship in the Yellow Sea.

**PACIFIC, OKINAWA:** In the early morning hours a second Japanese counterattack is aimed at the center of the American line. The 306th Infantry Regiment of the 77th Infantry Division stops the main attack, while a battalion of Japanese infantry is isolated behind American lines before the 17th Infantry Regiment of the 7th Infantry Division.

Off Okinawa, kamikazes damage a seaplane tender and surveying ship.

**CENTRAL PACIFIC:** Seventh Air Force sends 12 B-24 Liberators from Angaur Island to bomb Koror Island.

## May 6

**CBI:** Rangoon falls to British forces.

Fourteenth Air Force B-25 Mitchells and P-51 Mustangs destroy a bridge, while P-40s and P-51s attack targets of opportunity in southern and eastern China.

U.S. submarine *Hammerhead* torpedoes and sinks a Japanese fleet tanker in the Gulf of Thailand.

**ATLANTIC:** A destroyer escort and a frigate sink German submarine *U-853* near Rhode Island. A destroyer escort sinks German submarine *U-881* in the North Atlantic. This will be the last U-boat sunk in the Atlantic by American forces in World War II.

**ETO:** Pilsen, Czechoslovakia is captured. Third Army halts any farther advance as Soviet forces close on Prague.

Eighth Air Force sends 383 B-17s to air-drop 693 tons of food over the Netherlands. Fifteen B-17s, escorted by eight P-51 Mustangs, drop leaflets in France and Germany. During the night, 10 B-24 Liberators drop leaflets in France, the Netherlands, and the Channel Islands.

**MEDITERRANEAN:** Fifteenth Air Force P-38 Lightnings escort Royal Air Force cargo planes on a supply drop to Yugoslavia.

**ITALY:** Units of the 10th Mountain Division move north to establish contact with the U.S. Seventh Army.

Brigadier General Robert S. Israel, Jr., takes command of the XXII Tactical Air Command.

**SOUTHWEST PACIFIC AREA:** In Eighth Army area the 124th Infantry Regiment of the 31st Infantry Division fights Japanese defenders on the Sayre Highway near Maramag.

In the Philippines, Far East Air Force A-20 Havocs, P-38 Lightnings, and P-47 Thunderbolts support ground forces on Luzon.

In French Indochina, B-25 Mitchells bomb warehouses at Dong Hoi.

In Formosa, B-24 Liberators bomb an airfield and bomb town areas along with B-25s.

FEAF B-24 Liberators bomb Kudat and Keningau airfields, while Lightnings attack Ranau and the Labuan Island airfields off north side of Borneo. B-25 Mitchells support Australian troops on Tarakan Island. B-24 Liberators bomb an airfield on Celebes Island.

**PACIFIC:** Navy patrol bombers sink two cargo ships in the Yellow Sea.

**CENTRAL PACIFIC:** Seventh Air Force sends 18 P-47 Thunderbolts from Saipan to sweep Truk Atoll, strafing an airfield, a seaplane base, and shipping.

## May 7

**CBI:** Fourteenth Air Force B-24 Liberators, B-25 Mitchells, and P-47 Thunderbolts attack bridges. P-40s and P-51s attack targets of opportunity in southern and eastern China.

**ETO:** At Rheims, France, the chief of staff of the German Armed Forces, Colonel-General Alfred Jodl, signs the act of surrender on behalf of the German High Command. The surrender is official at midnight on May 8.

The Supreme Allied Commander, General Dwight D. Eisenhower, sends the following message to the Allied forces under his command:

> The route you have traveled through hundreds of miles is marked by the graves of former comrades. Each of the fallen died as a member of the team to which you

belong, bound together by a common love of liberty and a refusal to submit to enslavement. Our common problems of the immediate and distant future can be best solved in the same conceptions of co-operation and devotion to the cause of human freedom as have made this Expeditionary Force such a mighty engine of righteous destruction.

Eisenhower issues a statement: "The mission of this Allied force was fulfilled at 0241 local time, May 7, 1945."

Eighth Air Force sends 231 B-17s to air-drop 426 tons of food supplies over the Netherlands. Fifteen B-17s, with 30 P-51 Mustangs escorting, drop leaflets in Germany.

Ninth Air Force P-47 Thunderbolts and P-38 Lightnings of the XIX Tactical Air Command fly sweeps over eastern Germany and western Czechoslovakia and carry out demonstration flights over prisoner of war camps.

**MEDITERRANEAN:** Fifteenth Air Force sends 13 P-51 Mustangs to escort Royal Air Force cargo planes air-dropping supplies over Yugoslavia.

**ITALY:** Twelfth Air Force sends P-47 Thunderbolts to fly reconnaissance missions over the Austrian Alps.

**SOUTHWEST PACIFIC AREA:** In the Philippines, Far East Air Force B-25 Mitchells, A-20 Havocs, P-38 Lightnings, and P-47 Thunderbolts attack targets in the Cagayan Valley and support ground forces elsewhere on Luzon.

In French Indochina, B-25s attack railroad targets.

FEAF B-24 Liberators bomb Bingkalapa airfield, Celebes, and the harbor at Surabaya, Java.

Thirteenth Air Force B-24 Liberators bomb Japanese shipping and shore installations at Makassar, sinking a gunboat and a cargo ship.

**PACIFIC:** Twentieth Air Force sends 41 B-29s to bomb airfields at Usa, Oita, Ibusuki, and Kanoya on Kyushu Island. Aircrews report 34 Japanese aircraft shot down. Three B-29s are lost. The B-29s of the 792nd, 793rd, and 794th Bombardment Squadrons (Very Heavy), 468th Bombardment Group (Very Heavy), arrive at Tinian from India.

A Japanese minesweeper and a cargo vessel hit mines dropped by B-29s in Shimonoseki Strait.

Navy patrol bombers sink four Japanese cargo ships in the Yellow Sea off the coast of Korea.

**PACIFIC, OKINAWA:** The survivors of the Japanese counterattack force withdraw to their defensive lines, having lost over 5,000 men. American losses number nearly 700.

Corporal John P. Fardy, leading a squad in C Company, 1st Battalion, 1st Marine Regiment, 1st Marine Division, encounters a hail of Japanese fire from a strongly fortified position during an attack on Okinawa. Deploying his men along a drainage ditch, Corporal Fardy catches sight of a hand grenade falling in among his marines in the ditch. Fardy jumps on the grenade to save the lives of his men and sacrifices his own life. Corporal Fardy's gallant act of self-sacrifice will be recognized with the nation's highest award for valor, the Medal of Honor.

**CENTRAL PACIFIC:** Seventh Air Force sends 11 B-24 Liberators from Guam to bomb Marcus Island. P-47 Thunderbolts from Saipan strafe a radio station, airfield installations, and gun positions on islands at Truk.

## May 8

**CBI:** Japanese forces are stopped by a Chinese counterattack, supported by Fourteenth Air Force. The Chinese forces inflict over 11,000 casualties on the enemy in the first major victory for the Chinese in two years.

In China, Fourteenth Air Force P-40s and P-51 Mustangs attack rail and river traffic. In French Indochina B-25 Mitchells attack bridges and P-51 Mustangs attack rail and road traffic along the coast.

**ATLANTIC: VE Day.** President Truman announces the end of the war in Europe.

**ETO:** At 2301, hostilities cease in Europe. General of the Army Dwight D. Eisenhower, Supreme Allied Commander of the European theater of operations, has under his command 90 Allied divisions: 61 U.S., 13 British, five Canadian, 10 French, and one Polish.

Eighth Air Force sends 12 B-17s to drop leaflets over Germany.

Ninth Air Force P-47 Thunderbolts and P-38 Lightnings of the IX and XIX Tactical Air Commands patrol over the cities of Leipzig, Chemnitz, and Adorf, Germany, and Linz, Austria. Fighters also fly sweeps and demonstration missions.

**MEDITERRANEAN:** Fifteenth Air Force orders all aircraft to stand down and no further offensive operations will be conducted.

**SOUTHWEST PACIFIC AREA:** Eighth Army reports that the Leyte-Samar area has been cleared, and that over 24,000 Japanese troops have been killed and another 439 taken prisoner since February. American losses are reported as 432 killed, 1,852 wounded, and 22 missing.

In the Philippines, Far East Air Force B-24 Liberators, B-25 Mitchells, P-38 Lightnings, and P-47 Thunderbolts attack Japanese positions in Cagayan Valley on Luzon. B-24s attack Davao on Mindanao, while P-38 Lightnings attack the airfield area.

B-25s bomb railway installations in French Indochina.

U.S. submarine *Bream* lays mines off the coast of French Indochina.

FEAF P-38 Lightnings attack Jesselton, Sengkawang, and Kudat airfields, while B-25 Mitchells bomb the Kuching and Labuan Island airfield areas at Borneo. Other B-24 Liberators bomb an airfield on Celebes Island.

**PACIFIC:** Twentieth Air Force sends 40 B-29s to attack airfields at Kanoya, Miyakonojo, Oita, and Matsuyama on Kyushu and Shikoku Islands.

U.S. submarine *Bowfin* torpedoes and sinks a Japanese fishing boat off northeast Honshu, Japan.

A transport is damaged by a mine dropped by B-29s off southern Korea.

**PACIFIC, OKINAWA:** The 1st Marine Division fights for control of Hill 60 and Nan Hill, sealing every opening to keep the Japanese from moving underground to new locations.

**CENTRAL PACIFIC:** Seventh Air Force sends 12 B-24 Liberators from Guam to bomb the airfield on Marcus Island. Another 12 B-24s from Guam bomb a runway on Param Island at Truk.

### May 9

**ALEUTIANS:** Eleventh Air Force sends 12 B-24 Liberators to bomb shipping between Paramushiru and Shimushu Islands in the Kuriles.

**CBI:** Fourteenth Air Force sends B-24 Liberators, B-25 Mitchells, and P-51 Mustangs to attack targets of opportunity.

**ATLANTIC:** German submarine *U-249* surrenders to a Navy PB4Y Privateer off the Scilly Islands, at the western tip of England. This submarine is the first to surrender after cessation of hostilities was declared.

**ETO:** The chief of the German High Command and the commanders in chief of the army, navy, and air force sign a ratification document of unconditional surrender with the representatives of the Soviet High Command in Berlin.

Eighth Air Force begins the redeployment of the headquarters of the 453rd Bombardment Group (Heavy) and the 732nd, 733rd, 734th, and 735th Bombardment Squadrons (Heavy) from England to the United States. The group will move by ship.

Ninth Air Force fighters of the XIX Tactical Air Command patrol areas above Linz, Austria, and Klatovy, Czechoslovakia, and carry out demonstration flights.

**MEDITERRANEAN:** Fifteenth Air Force begins redeploying the B-24 Liberators of the 828th, 829th, 830th, and 831st Bombardment Squadrons (Heavy), 485th Bombardment Group (Heavy), to the United States. The headquarters of the 47th Bombardment Wing (Heavy) is scheduled to follow.

**SOUTHWEST PACIFIC AREA:** In the Philippines, Far East Air Force A-20 Havocs, P-38 Lightnings, and P-47 Thunderbolts fly offensive sweeps over the Cagayan Valley and support ground forces on Luzon. B-24 Liberators bomb targets on Mindanao in preparation for Allied landings in the Macajalar Bay area on May 10.

B-24 Liberators bomb airfields in the Canton, China, area.

FEAF P-38 Lightnings attack Tarakan Island in support of Australian ground forces.

**PACIFIC:** The Japanese government announces that regardless of the change in the situation in Europe, Japan will continue to fight.

**PACIFIC, OKINAWA:** The 7th Infantry Division's 17th Infantry Regiment gains control of Kochi Ridge. The division is relieved by the 96th Infantry Division.

Kamikazes damage two U.S. destroyer escorts and two British carriers, HMS *Formidable* and HMS *Victorious,* off Okinawa.

**CENTRAL PACIFIC:** Seventh Air Force sends 29 B-24 Liberators from Guam to bomb targets on the islands at Truk. Another 14 P-47 Thunderbolts from Saipan bomb a number of targets at Truk.

### May 10

**ALEUTIANS:** Eleventh Air Force and the navy's Fleet Air Wing Four attack targets in the Kurile Islands. B-24 Liberators bomb shipping targets at the Kataoka naval base on Shimushu Island and fly photo reconnaissance over the island on their return.

B-25s from Attu attack shipping between Kashiwabara on Paramushiru Island and Kataoka. One B-25 is shot down by antiaircraft fire. One B-24 and a B-25 make forced landings in the Soviet Union.

**CBI:** Fourteenth Air Force B-25 Mitchells and P-47 Thunderbolts attack bridges and P-40s and P-51s attack trucks, highways, logistics storage sites, rail lines, troops, and artillery in southern and eastern China.

**ETO:** Major General William E. Kepner takes command of Eighth Air Force, replacing Lieutenant General James H. Doolittle, who returns to Washington, D.C.

Ninth Air Force redesignates the 9th Bombardment Division as the 9th Air Division.

**SOUTHWEST PACIFIC AREA:** In the Eighth Army area Lieutenant General Eichelberger orders Colonel Maurice D. Stratta's 108th Infantry Regiment of the 40th Infantry Division to land at Macajalar Bay on Mindanao and move south on the Sayre Highway to link with the 31st Infantry Division advancing north. Naval Task Group 78.3, commanded by Rear Admiral Arthur D. Struble, lands the troops.

In the Philippines, Far East Air Force A-20 Havocs, P-38s, and P-47 Thunderbolts attack Japanese positions in the Cagayan Valley and support ground operations throughout Luzon. B-24 Liberators and B-25s support ground forces on Mindanao.

B-25s, with P-47s escorting, attack town areas and communication targets of opportunity on Formosa.

B-24s bomb an airfield in the Canton, China, area.

FEAF B-24 Liberators bomb Makassar ship basins and an airfield on Celebes Island and shore targets at Balikpapan on Borneo.

**PACIFIC:** Twentieth Air Force sends 42 B-29s to attack airfields at Matsuyama, Usa, Miyazaki, and Kanoya on Kyushu and Shikoku Islands. Aircrews report 10 Japanese aircraft shot down. One B-29 is lost. Over 40 B-29s attack airfields at Matsuyama, Usa, Miyazaki, and Kanoya on Kyushu and Shikoku Islands. More than 50 B-29s bomb the Tokuyama naval fuel station. A total of 56 B-29s bomb the Tokuyama coal yards; over 100 B-29s attack the Otake oil refinery. One B-29 is lost. Eighty B-29s bomb the Amami-O-Shima naval oil storage facilities.

Navy patrol bombers sink a Japanese merchant tanker and a cargo ship off the west coast of Korea.

**PACIFIC, OKINAWA:** Kamikazes damage a destroyer and a light minelayer off Okinawa.

Pharmacist's Mate Second Class William D. Halyburton, Jr., is serving with a marine rifle company in the 2nd Battalion, 5th Marines, 1st Marine Division, during an attack on a draw on Okinawa. As he moves forward to meet with the first squad, it is pinned down under a heavy volume of mortar, machine-gun, and sniper fire. As marines fall wounded, Halyburton comes to their aid and shields them with his body as he gives first aid. He continues in this manner, aiding each man in turn until he is mortally wounded. For his extraordinary dedication to duty and willingness to sacrifice his own life to save the lives of others, Pharmacist's Mate Second Class Halyburton will receive the Medal of Honor.

**CENTRAL PACIFIC:** Seventh Air Force sends 11 B-24 Liberators from Guam to bomb the airfield on Marcus Island. Another 19 B-24s from Guam bomb airfields on Param and Moen islands at Truk Atoll.

### May 11

**ALEUTIANS:** Eleventh Air Force B-24 Liberators sink a Japanese cargo ship and damage an escort destroyer in the Kuriles.

**CBI:** Fourteenth Air Force B-25 Mitchells and P-47 Thunderbolts attack bridges, while P-40s and P-51s attack trucks, highways, logistics storage sites, rail lines, troops, and artillery in southern and eastern China.

**SOUTHWEST PACIFIC AREA:** In the Eighth Army area, the 167th Infantry Regiment of the 31st Infantry Division begins a reconnaissance in force along a trail leading into the Japanese main defensive area on Mindanao. Before long it will take the effort of the entire regiment, battling not only Japanese troops but also constant rainfall and jungle, to advance 13 miles over the next 18 days.

In the Philippines, Far East Air Force B-25 Mitchells, A-20 Havocs, P-38 Lightnings, and P-47 Thunderbolts support ground forces on Luzon.

B-24 Liberators bomb an airfield and, with B-25s, bomb town areas on Formosa.

FEAF B-24 Liberators bomb an airfield, and B-25 Mitchells bomb the Brunei Bay area on Borneo. B-24 Liberators attack airfields on Celebes Island.

**PACIFIC:** Twentieth Air Force sends 50 B-29s to attack airfields at Oita, Saeki, Nittagahara, Miyazaki, and Miyakonojo on Kyushu Island, and 92 B-29s bomb the Kawanishi aircraft production facility at Kobe. Aircrews report nine Japanese fighters shot down. One B-29 is lost.

Navy PB4Y-2 Privateers sink two cargo ships off the west coast of Korea.

**PACIFIC, OKINAWA:** Believing the Japanese are near their breaking point, Lieutenant General Simon B. Buckner orders a Tenth Army offensive. The attack proceeds after 30 minutes of artillery fire, with the 6th and 1st Marine Divisions of the III Amphibious Corps on the right and the 77th and 96th Infantry Divisions of the XXIV Corps on the left. The 7th Infantry Division will be the reserve of Tenth Army. Buckner desires to press the flanks while maintaining pressure on the center. The attack gains about 600 yards, with many casualties, and quickly bogs down into positional warfare as small units fight dug-in Japanese forces along a line of small hills and ridgelines.

Two destroyers are heavily damaged by kamikaze attacks. The carrier *Bunker Hill*, Admiral Mitscher's flagship, is also hit, causing over 660 casualties. The damage is heavy, and the carrier is out of action. Mitscher moves his flag to the carrier *Enterprise.*

**CENTRAL PACIFIC:** Seventh Air Force sends 10 B-24 Liberators from Guam to bomb the airfield on Param Island at Truk and 13 other B-24s bomb Marcus Island. P-51 Mustangs from Iwo Jima attack the radio station on Chichi Jima.

### May 12

**CBI:** In China, Fourteenth Air Force sends 17 B-25 Mitchells and eight P-51 Mustangs to bomb the barracks and logistics storage area at Loyang and attack railroad

Deck-level view of the kamikaze strike on the aircraft carrier USS *Bunker Hill* (National Archives and Records Administration)

targets. P-40s and P-51 Mustangs attack rail and river traffic, vehicles, and logistics storage sites.

**ATLANTIC:** President Truman orders an immediate halt to all Lend-Lease shipments to the USSR. This brings immediate howls of protest from the Soviets.

**ETO:** Ninth Air Force P-38 Lightnings and P-47 Thunderbolts of the XIX Tactical Air Command fly demonstration missions.

**MEDITERRANEAN:** Fifteenth Air Force begins the redeployment of the headquarters, 450th Bombardment Group (Heavy), and the B-24 Liberators of the 723rd Bombardment Squadron (Heavy) from Italy to the United States.

**ITALY:** Twelfth Air Force begins redeploying 17 assigned units from the theater. Another 43 assigned service units will be disbanded to form 21 new service units, and nine assigned units will be transferred to other headquarters in the theater.

**SOUTHWEST PACIFIC AREA:** In the Philippines, Far East Air Force A-20 Havocs, P-38 Lightnings, and P-47 Thunderbolts support ground forces on Luzon and Negros Islands.

In French Indochina, B-24 Liberators bomb rail and road bridges and attack a railyard and other railroad targets.

FEAF B-24 Liberators, B-25 Mitchells, and P-38 Lightnings attack targets in the Brunei Bay area, including Labuan Island, Brooketon, and Jesselton airfields, and troops on Tarakan Island off Borneo. B-24s bomb Makassar shipyards and Limbo-eng airfield on Celebes Island.

**PACIFIC:** Twentieth Air Force receives the headquarters of the 331st Bombardment Group (Very Heavy) and the B-29s of the 355th, 356th, and 357th Bombardment Squadrons (Very Heavy), and the headquarters of the 502nd Bombardment Group (Very Heavy) and the B-29s of the 402nd, 411th, and 430th Bombardment Squadrons (Very Heavy) at Guam from the United States.

U.S. submarine *Raton* sinks a Japanese cargo ship in the Yellow Sea. Another cargo ship is sunk off Shimonoseki after hitting a mine dropped by B-29s.

**PACIFIC, OKINAWA:** Tenth Army runs into some of the toughest defenses on the island. The 96th Infantry Division faces Conical Hill; the 22nd Marines of the 6th Marine Division face Sugar Loaf. The 1st Marine Division fights on Dakeshi and Wana Ridges.

A kamikaze damages battleship USS *New Mexico* off Okinawa.

**CENTRAL PACIFIC:** Seventh Air Force sends nine B-24 Liberators from Guam to bomb the airfield on Marcus Island. Another 12 B-24s from Guam bomb a runway on Param Island at Truk Atoll.

### May 13

**CBI:** In China, Fourteenth Air Force B-24 Liberators lay mines in the Yangtze River and 10 B-25 Mitchells attack bridges. P-40s and P-51s attack trucks, highways, logistics storage sites, and rail lines in southern and eastern China.

**MEDITERRANEAN:** Fifteenth Air Force redeploys B-24 units from Italy to the United States, including the 717th Bombardment Squadron (Heavy) of the 449th Bombardment Group (Heavy) and the 720th Bombardment Squadron (Heavy) of the 450th Bombardment Group (Heavy).

**SOUTHWEST PACIFIC AREA:** On Luzon in the I Corps area the 25th Infantry Division captures Balete Pass after weeks of heavy fighting.

In the Eighth Army area, the 108th Infantry Regiment of the 40th Infantry Division encounters strong Japanese resistance along the Sayre Highway on Mindanao. The regiment will continue the fight for four days.

In the Philippines, Far East Air Force B-25 Mitchells, A-20 Havocs, P-38 Lightnings, and P-47 Thunderbolts support ground forces on Luzon.

B-24 Liberators again pound bridges along the coast of French Indochina.

FEAF B-24 Liberators bomb airfields, and B-25 Mitchells and P-38 Lightnings bomb Sandakan and support ground forces on Tarakan Island off Borneo.

U.S. submarine *Baya* attacks a Japanese convoy, sinking a tanker in the Java Sea.

**PACIFIC:** During the night Twentieth Air Force sends 12 B-29s to mine the Shimonoseki Strait and the waters off Niigata, Japan, in an attempt to blockade the Japanese home islands.

U.S. submarine *Cero* torpedoes and sinks a Japanese cargo ship off Honshu, Japan.

Carrier aircraft from Task Force 58 attack airfields on Kyushu. U.S. submarine *Plaice* attacks a Japanese guardboat in the Kuriles.

**PACIFIC, OKINAWA:** The 383rd Infantry Regiment of the 96th Infantry Division, supported by the 763rd Tank Battalion, assaults Conical Hill, a key position on the Shuri defensive line.

Off Okinawa, kamikazes damage a destroyer and a destroyer escort.

**CENTRAL PACIFIC:** Seventh Air Force sends 10 B-24 Liberators from Guam to bomb an underground hangar on Moen Island at Truk. Another nine B-24s bomb the airfield on Marcus Island.

## May 14

**CBI:** Mars Task Force begins training Chinese troops in China.

In China, Fourteenth Air Force B-24 Liberators mine the Yangtze River. B-25 Mitchells attack river shipping near Hengshan. P-40s and P-51s attack trucks, highways, logistics storage sites, rail lines, troops, and artillery in southern and eastern China.

**SOUTHWEST PACIFIC AREA:** In the Eighth Army area, the 124th Infantry Regiment of the 31st Infantry Division stops a Japanese attack during the night near Colgan Woods, named for Captain (Chaplain) Thomas A. Colgan, who was killed while attending to wounded soldiers. In the six-day battle for Maramag, the 124th has lost 69 killed and 177 wounded.

In the Philippines, Far East Air Force B-25 Mitchells, A-20 Havocs, P-38 Lightnings, and P-47 Thunderbolts support ground forces on Luzon and Negros Islands.

B-24 Liberators bomb the military and air supply center on Formosa.

U.S. submarine *Cobia* is damaged in a depth charge attack in the Gulf of Siam but remains on patrol.

FEAF B-24 Liberators and B-25 Mitchells attack airfields in Borneo and B-25s support ground forces on Tarakan Island. B-24s raid Makassar harbor, Sidate airfield, and Parepare warehouses on Celebes Island and bomb an airfield on Soembawa Island, in the Lesser Sunda Islands.

Private First Class James H. Diamond is a machine gunner in D Company, 21st Infantry Regiment, 24th Infantry Division, who displays an extraordinary fighting spirit. He fearlessly attacks Japanese positions at Mintal, Mindanao, with his Thompson submachine gun, then calls in artillery fire to eliminate them. He assists in evacuating casualties from a bridgehead, volunteering to take them to the rear through mortar and artillery fire while being wounded himself. He assists in repairing a bridge under heavy enemy fire. On May 14, he is leading a patrol to evacuate casualties from his battalion, as it fights to escape entrapment by the Japanese. When his patrol is attacked, Diamond locates a machine gun and, braving enemy fire, fires the machine gun to draw additional fire upon himself so that the members of the patrol can escape. Private First Class Diamond's indomitable spirit, his selflessness, and heroic sacrifice to save his comrades will be worthy of the nation's highest award for valor, the Medal of Honor.

**PACIFIC:** U.S. submarine *Sand Lance* torpedoes and sinks a Japanese auxiliary minesweeper off Hokkaido, Japan.

Mines dropped by Twentieth Air Force B-29s damage a Japanese merchant ship, a cargo ship, and a merchant tug east of Shikoku, Japan. Mines sink a Japanese transport off Shimonoseki.

**PACIFIC, OKINAWA:** A single kamikaze hits the carrier *Enterprise,* causing enough damage to take it out of action for repairs. Admiral Mitscher again transfers his flag, this time to the carrier *Randolph.*

**PACIFIC:** Twentieth Air Force sends 472 B-29s of the XXI Bomber Command to bomb the urban area of north Nagoya, Japan. Aircrews report 20 Japanese fighters shot down. Eleven B-29s are lost.

## May 15

**ALEUTIANS:** Eleventh Air Force sends 13 B-24 Liberators to bomb targets in the Kuriles. Aircrews report one cargo ship destroyed. Antiaircraft fire damages two B-24s; one makes a forced landing in the Soviet Union.

**CBI:** Fourteenth Air Force B-25 Mitchells, P-40s, and P-51s attack trucks, highways, logistics storage sites, rail lines, troops, and artillery in southern and eastern China.

**MEDITERRANEAN:** Fifteenth Air Force begins redeploying the headquarters of the 485th Bombardment Group (Heavy) and the B-24 Liberators of the 716th, 718th, and 719th Bombardment Squadrons (Heavy), of the 449th Bombardment Group (Heavy), to the United States.

**SOUTHWEST PACIFIC AREA:** In the Philippines, Far East Air Force P-38 Lightnings support ground forces and attack gun positions on Negros Island.

B-24 Liberators bomb targets on Formosa.

U.S. submarine *Hammerhead* torpedoes and sinks a Japanese transport in the Gulf of Siam.

FEAF B-24 Liberators and B-25 Mitchells attack airfields in Borneo and support Australian ground forces on Tarakan Island.

**PACIFIC:** U.S. submarine *Sea Poacher* torpedoes and sinks Japanese army vessels in the Kuriles.

U.S. submarine *Shad* torpedoes and damages a Japanese cargo ship in the Yellow Sea.

Navy patrol bombers sink a cargo ship in the East China Sea, a cargo ship off western Kyushu, Japan, and a cargo ship off the east coast of Korea.

**PACIFIC, OKINAWA:** Major Henry A. Courtney, Jr., is the executive officer of the 2nd Battalion, 22nd Marines, 6th Marine Division, holding a defensive line behind Sugar Loaf Hill, and decides to mount a night attack on the Japanese before the enemy has a chance to organize their own attack. Major Courtney then begins the attack, blasting cave positions and neutralizing enemy guns as he moves forward. The marines make a swift advance against the surprised Japanese, braving intense fire to occupy the ridge that Courtney had designated as their objective. Reinforced and resupplied, Courtney now decides to capture the crest of the hill. Without waiting to see who is following, Major Courtney moves forward, throwing grenades into cave openings and suspected enemy positions. Reaching the crest of the hill, he finds large numbers of Japanese troops forming for an attack. Without hesitation, he plunges forward, completely disorganizing the enemy and forcing them to retreat to the safety of the caves. Determined to hold his position, he reorganizes and deploys for the defense, ignoring the high volume of fire directed at him. Shortly afterward he is killed when a mortar shell explodes near him. For his initiative and personal display of courage in the face of a determined enemy, Major Courtney will receive the Medal of Honor.

## May 16

**CBI:** In China, Fourteenth Air Force B-24 Liberators lay mines in the Yangtze River. B-25 Mitchells, P-47 Thunderbolts, and P-51 Mustangs attack trucks, headquarters units, highways, logistics storage sites, rail lines, bridges, troops, town areas, and artillery in southern and eastern China.

**MEDITERRANEAN:** Fifteenth Air Force redeploys the headquarters of the 449th Bombardment Group (Heavy) and the 721st and 722nd Bombardment Squadrons (Heavy) of the 450th Bombardment Group (Heavy) to the United States.

**SOUTHWEST PACIFIC AREA:** On Luzon Island in the Philippines, Far East Air Force sends nearly 100 P-38 Lightnings to attack Japanese positions near the Ipo Dam with napalm.

B-24 Liberators bomb town areas and B-25 Mitchells attack alcohol plants and railroad yards on Formosa.

U.S. submarine *Hawkbill* torpedoes and sinks a Japanese minelayer off the east coast of Malaya.

FEAF B-24 Liberators attack Balikpapan and Manggar on Borneo, and Tondano on Celebes Island. B-25 Mitchells and P-38 Lightnings attack Miri, Brookton, Bintula, Fort Brook, and a floating antiaircraft platform near Labuan Island. P-38 Lightnings support Australian ground forces on Tarakan.

**PACIFIC:** Mines dropped by Twentieth Air Force B-29s sink a cargo ship near Shikoku, Japan.

U.S. submarine *Raton* torpedoes and sinks a Japanese cargo ship in the Yellow Sea off the west coast of Korea.

During the night Twentieth Air Force sends 25 B-29s to mine Shimonoseki Strait.

**CENTRAL PACIFIC:** Seventh Air Force sends 13 B-24 Liberators from Guam to bomb the airfield on Marcus Island.

## May 17

**CBI:** Fourteenth Air Force B-25 Mitchells, P-47 Thunderbolts, and P-51 Mustangs attack trucks, river traffic, highways, logistics storage sites, rail lines, bridges, troops, and town areas in southern and eastern China.

**SOUTHWEST PACIFIC AREA:** On Luzon, XI Corps captures the Ipo Dam, supported by the heaviest use of napalm against the enemy in the theater.

In the Eighth Army area, the 24th Infantry Division, supported by Filipino guerrillas, attacks into the Japanese defenses on Mindanao. Marine air and artillery support the division's attack.

In the Philippines, Far East Air Force P-38 Lightnings and P-47 Thunderbolts attack Japanese positions near the Ipo Dam on Luzon Island.

B-25 Mitchells and P-51 Mustangs attack railyards, bridges, and alcohol production facilities on Formosa. B-24 Liberators bomb airfields on Formosa.

FEAF B-24 Liberators bomb airfields on Borneo and Celebes Island.

Aircraft from U.S. carrier *Saratoga* and British carrier HMS *Illustrious* sink on auxiliary minesweeper near Surabaya, Java.

**PACIFIC:** Twentieth Air Force sends more than 500 B-29s to attack the Mitsubishi Aircraft Works and a number of other industrial production facilities located at Nagoya. Another 11 B-29s attack targets of opportunity. Three B-29s are lost. B-29s of the 21st Bomber Command attack airfields on Kyushu and Shikoku to limit their use for kamikaze attacks.

Mines dropped by Twentieth Air Force B-29s sink a Japanese transport and a cargo ship in the Inland Sea.

**PACIFIC, OKINAWA:** Admiral Nimitz begins replacing the navy staff at Okinawa as preparations for the invasion of the Japanese home islands begin. Vice Admiral Harry W. Hill takes command of Task Force 51 from Admiral Richmond Kelly Turner.

A kamikaze damages a destroyer off Okinawa.

Corporal James Day, a squad leader in the 2nd Battalion, 22nd Marine Regiment, 6th Marine Division, engaged in heavy fighting to seize the front lines of Sugar Loaf Hill. He rallies his squad and the remnants of another unit and leads them forward into heavy artillery and mortar fire. The Japanese infantry now counterattack. His unit is reduced to less than half-strength in a matter of minutes, Corporal Day refuses to retreat, encouraging his men, throwing hand grenades, and directing fire against the enemy to stop the counterattack. He receives six additional marines, but in the course of repelling night attacks, his small group is further reduced by casualties. Throughout the night Corporal Day locates four seriously wounded marines and, braving enemy fire each time, returns them one by one to a corpsman. Again and again he reorganizes his defense after each attack, often in hand-to-hand combat. As morning breaks over the embattled unit, the Japanese again attempt to overwhelm the marines, but fail each time. By the third day, the marines have repulsed another attack and have stayed firm. This extraordinary demonstration of will and courageous leadership in exceptionally difficult circumstances will win Corporal Day the Medal of Honor.

**CENTRAL PACIFIC:** P-51 Mustangs from Iwo Jima attack airfields at Atsugi, Japan. Pilots report 10 confirmed kills on the ground. During the night two P-47 Thunderbolts of the 318th Fighter Group located on Ie Shima conduct harassment strikes over Kyushu Island, Japan.

Carrier aircraft from Task Unit 77.4.3 (Rear Admiral Clifton A. F. Sprague) attack Japanese installations at Maloelap Atoll, Marshall Islands.

## May 18

**ALEUTIANS:** Eleventh Air Force sends eight B-24 Liberators to bomb naval, harbor, and airfield targets at Kataoka on Shimushu Island in the Kuriles.

**CBI:** Fourteenth Air Force B-25 Mitchells, P-47 Thunderbolts, and P-51 Mustangs attack logistics storage sites and rail lines, bridges, troops, and town areas in southern and eastern China.

**SOUTHWEST PACIFIC AREA:** In the Philippines, Far East Air Force A-20 Havocs, P-38 Lightnings, and P-47 Thunderbolts support ground forces on Luzon and Negros islands.

B-24 Liberators bomb airfields, and B-25 Mitchells and P-47s fly sweeps against targets on Formosa.

FEAF B-24 Liberators and B-25 Mitchells attack Fort Brook and Sarawak on Borneo, while B-24s and P-38 Lightnings attack Japanese defenses on Tarakan Island.

**PACIFIC:** During the night Twentieth Air Force sends 30 B-29s to mine Shimonoseki Strait and Tsuruga Harbor in Japan.

U.S. submarine *Shad* torpedoes and sinks a Japanese cargo ship in the Yellow Sea. Navy patrol bombers sink a Japanese cargo vessel off western Korea.

The advance air echelon of the 509th Composite Group arrives on Tinian Island. The 509th, commanded by an experienced and distinguished bomber pilot, Colonel Paul W. Tibbets, Jr., is tasked with conducting an atomic bomb attack on Japan.

**PACIFIC, OKINAWA:** The 6th Marine Division captures Sugar Loaf, a key defensive position. Losses have reached over 2,600 since the beginning of the attack on May 11.

Fire from a shore battery damages destroyer USS *Longshaw*. The ship then explodes off Naha, Okinawa. A kamikaze damages a high-speed transport, and an LST is hit and damaged by a torpedo dropped in an air attack.

**CENTRAL PACIFIC:** P-47 Thunderbolts from Ie Shima Island make bombing, strafing, and rocket attacks on radar and ground installations on Kume Jima Island. During the night other P-47s fly harassment attacks against targets on Kyushu Island, Japan.

## May 19

**ALEUTIANS:** Eleventh Air Force sends eight B-25 Mitchells to bomb the Minami Cape radar installation and cannery on the Naka River on Shimushu Island. Antiaircraft fire and enemy fighters drive off most of the bombers. One B-25 is shot down, another is reported missing, and a third makes a forced landing at Petropavlovsk in the Soviet Union.

U.S. destroyers bombard Japanese installations on Paramushiru, in the Kuriles.

**CBI:** The Japanese abandon Foochow.

Fourteenth Air Force B-25 Mitchells attack warehouses and rail lines. P-47 Thunderbolts and P-51 Mustangs attack trucks, river traffic, highways, logistics storage sites, rail lines, bridges, troops, and targets of opportunity in southern and eastern China.

**ETO:** Eighth Air Force redeploys the headquarters of the 93rd Bombardment Group (Heavy) to the United States.

**SOUTHWEST PACIFIC AREA:** In the Philippines, Far East Air Force B-25 Mitchells, A-20 Havocs, P-38 Lightnings, and P-47 Thunderbolts support ground forces on Luzon near Ipo Dam. P-38s support ground forces on Cebu Island.

On Formosa, B-24 Liberators attack Kiirun harbor; B-25 Mitchells sweep the west coast, attacking a rail yard, logistics storage facilities, and damaging an alcohol production facility. P-47s also conduct sweeps across the island.

FEAF B-24 Liberators bomb an airfield and, with P-38 Lightnings supporting, attack targets on Tarakan Island off northwest Borneo.

**PACIFIC:** Twentieth Air Force sends 272 B-29s to attack the Tachikawa Aircraft Company, but the bombers are forced to abort the mission and instead bomb the city of Hamamatsu. Fourteen B-29s attack targets of opportunity. Four B-29s are lost. Thirty B-29s mine Shimonoseki Strait and the waters off Shikoku and Kyushu, Japan.

**PACIFIC, OKINAWA:** The 7th Marines of the 1st Marine Division make slow, but steady progress against Japanese positions on Wana Ridge, supported by tanks.

**CENTRAL PACIFIC:** The headquarters of the 413th Fighter Group and the P-47 Thunderbolts of the 1st, 21st, and 34th Fighter Squadrons arrive on Ie Shima Island from the United States.

## May 20

**CBI:** Major General Lewis A. Pick announces the formal completion of the Ledo Road. He describes the feat as the toughest job ever given to U.S. Army engineers in wartime. Officially it is named the Stilwell Road, but among his engineers it is known only as Pick's Pike, much to the consternation of Major General Pick.

Fourteenth Air Force B-25 Mitchells, P-47 Thunderbolts, and P-51 Mustangs attack trucks, river traffic, highways, fuel storage areas, logistics storage sites, rail lines, bridges, troops, and targets of opportunity in southern and eastern China.

**SOUTHWEST PACIFIC AREA:** In the Philippines, Far East Air Force B-25 Mitchells, A-20 Havocs, P-38 Lightnings, and P-47 Thunderbolts attack Japanese positions in the Cagayan Valley. B-24 Liberators and P-38s support ground forces on Mindanao.

B-25 Mitchells bomb various communication targets and an alcohol production facility on Formosa.

Fifth Air Force B-24 Liberators sink a cargo vessel off Formosa.

In Borneo, FEAF P-38 Lightnings attack Sandakan, Keningau, and Tarakan Island, while B-25 Mitchells attack shipping at Balikpapan harbor and a nearby barracks area.

**PACIFIC:** During the night Twentieth Air Force sends 30 B-29s to mine Shimonoseki Strait and the waters off Shikoku and Kyushu, Japan. One B-29 is lost.

U.S. submarine *Cero* torpedoes and sinks a Japanese merchant whaler east of Honshu, Japan.

**PACIFIC, OKINAWA:** Kamikazes damage a destroyer, a destroyer escort, two high-speed transports, and an LST off Okinawa. TBF/TBM Avengers from Naval Task Group 58.3 provide close air support for ground forces near Shuri castle.

**CENTRAL PACIFIC:** Seventh Air Force sends 10 B-24 Liberators from Guam to bomb the airfield on Marcus Island. Sixteen P-47 Thunderbolts from Saipan attack airfields on Moen and Eten Islands and a seaplane base and barges off Dublon Island at Truk. P-47 Thunderbolts from Ie Shima attack a hangar and boats at Fukue-Shima. Another 32 P-47s attack airfields, railroads, buildings, and radar facilities on Kyushu Island.

The 396th and 820th Bombardment Squadrons (Medium) of the 41st Bombardment Group (Medium) begin deploying from Hawaii to Okinawa with B-25 Mitchells.

## May 21

**CBI:** Fourteenth Air Force B-25 Mitchells bomb bridges. P-47 Thunderbolts and P-51 Mustangs attack trucks, river traffic, highways, rail lines, bridges, and troops in southern and eastern China.

**ETO:** Eighth Air Force redeploys the headquarters of the 482nd Bombardment Group (Heavy) to the United States.

**SOUTHWEST PACIFIC AREA:** In the Eighth Army area, the 155th Infantry Regiment of the 31st Infantry Division continues the advance up the Sayre Highway on Mindanao and occupies Malaybalay.

In the Philippines, Far East Air Force B-25 Mitchells bomb targets in the Cagayan Valley, while A-20 Havocs and P-51 Mustangs support ground forces. P-38 Lightnings drop napalm on Japanese positions near Ipo Dam and attack positions throughout Negros Island.

In French Indochina, P-38s strafe rail cars near Saigon.

In Borneo, FEAF B-24 Liberators attack Brunei, an airfield, shipyards, and troop concentrations on Tarakan Island

U.S. submarine *Chub* torpedoes and sinks a Japanese minesweeper in the Java Sea.

**PACIFIC:** Mines dropped by Twentieth Air Force B-29s sink a Japanese cargo ship in the Inland Sea.

**PACIFIC, OKINAWA:** The 1st Marine Division gains control of Dakeshi and Wana Ridges, but at a cost of over 1,700 men in 11 days of combat.

The 306th and 307th Infantry Regiments of the 77th Infantry Division batter against hills named Chocolate Drop, Wart Hill, and Flattop. Defended by minefields and trenches, the ground covered by machine-gun and anti-tank gun positions, the infantry must fight without tank support. Casualties are very heavy. In 10 days of combat the division has lost nearly 1,500 casualties.

The 96th Infantry Division's 381st Infantry Regiment gains control of Conical Hill after days of continuous fighting. The division has lost over 1,100 men in 10 days.

Private First Class Desmond T. Doss is a company aid man with the 1st Battalion, 307th Infantry Regiment, 77th Infantry Division, as his unit attacks up a steep escarpment 400 feet high. As the infantrymen reach the summit, they are hit with a heavy concentration of artillery and mortar fire, which causes nearly 75 casualties and forces the survivors off the objective. Doss refuses to leave the wounded, moving as many as he can to the edge of the escarpment and there lowering each one down on a litter attached to a rope. Throughout the next few days, Private First Class Doss rescues wounded men, ignoring all danger and braving enemy fire as he provides treatment. During a night attack on May 21 near Shuri, he purposely exposes himself to enemy fire to treat wounded soldiers left ahead of the front lines. He is seriously wounded in the legs when a grenade explodes nearby. To avoid risking another medic's life, he treats his own wound and waits over five hours until litter bearers can assist him. As he is being carrier to the rear, he sees a far more seriously wounded soldier and gets off the litter to allow him to have treatment first. As the litter bearers move off, he is again wounded, this time in the arm. He calmly makes a field expedient splint for his arm, then crawls 300 yards to the aid station. For his extraordinary dedication to duty and exceptional courage in performing that duty, Private First Class Doss will receive the Medal of Honor.

**CENTRAL PACIFIC:** During the night P-47 Thunderbolts fly harassment raids against targets on Kyushu Island, Japan.

## May 22

**CBI:** Fourteenth Air Force B-25 Mitchells bomb road and rail bridges. P-51 Mustangs drop napalm on trucks, barracks, and storage areas. P-47 Thunderbolts and P-51s attack trucks, river traffic, highways, rail lines, and targets of opportunity in southern and eastern China.

**SOUTHWEST PACIFIC AREA:** In the Philippines, Far East Air Force B-25 Mitchells, A-20 Havocs, P-38 Lightnings, and P-47 Thunderbolts support ground forces on Luzon at Ipo Dam and elsewhere.

B-24 Liberators bomb town areas on Formosa, while B-25s attack an oil production facility and several targets of opportunity.

FEAF B-24 Liberators, B-25 Mitchells, and P-38 Lightnings attack Jesselton, Kudat, and Bintula on Borneo and support Australian ground forces on Tarakan Island.

**PACIFIC:** Aircraft from carriers USS *Bennington* and USS *Hornet* sink two Japanese submarine chasers and a landing ship southwest of Kyushu, Japan.

Mines dropped by Twentieth Air Force B-29s sink two Japanese cargo ships and damage an auxiliary submarine chaser in the Inland Sea.

During the night Twentieth Air Force sends 30 B-29s to mine Shimonoseki Strait and approaches. One B-29 is lost.

**PACIFIC, OKINAWA:** Heavy rain on the island slows all offensive operations as the roads turn to mud.

## May 23

**ALEUTIANS:** Eleventh Air Force sends seven B-24 Liberators to bomb the Kataoka naval base area on Shimushu Island, using radar signal intercepts to mark the bomb release points over the target.

**CBI:** Fourteenth Air Force B-25 Mitchells and P-51 Mustangs attack bridges and rail targets. P-47 Thunderbolts and P-51s attack convoys and targets of opportunity in southern and eastern China.

**ETO:** Major General Otto P. Weyland takes command of Ninth Air Force; Brigadier General Homer L. Sanders takes command of XIX Tactical Air Command.

Karl Dönitz's attempt to form a new German government at Flensburg is ended when he is placed under arrest by British troops.

**SOUTHWEST PACIFIC AREA:** In the I Corps area the 25th Infantry Division captures Santa Far East Air Force on Luzon.

In the Philippines, Far East Air Force B-25 Mitchells, A-20 Havocs, P-38 Lightnings, and P-51 Mustangs support ground forces on Luzon at Cagayan Valley, Ipo Dam, and Balete Pass.

FEAF B-24 Liberators and B-25 Mitchells attack targets on Borneo, and P-38 Lightnings attack targets on Tarakan Island.

Staff Sergeant John C. Sjogren of I Company, 160th Infantry Regiment, 40th Infantry Division, leads his squad on an attack against a high ridge near San Jose Hacienda, Negros Island, in the Philippines. Entrenched Japanese riflemen defend the ridge, and they are supported by pillboxes with machine guns covering the avenues of approach. As his squad moves forward, he sees a buddy go down badly wounded. He runs to provide aid to the soldier, ignoring the rifle and machine-gun fire. He then moves forward into the face of the enemy fire and attacks the infantry positions, killing eight of the enemy defending the approach to the pillbox. He uses grenades to eliminate the position, even though wounded by grenade fragments. He leads his squad through the enemy position with his men providing covering fire while he throws grenades into the pillboxes. He even pulls a light machine gun out through an embrasure as it is firing, then throws a grenade into the pillbox. For his acts of courage, his selfless acts of leadership, and his aggressive determination to overcome a determined enemy, Staff Sergeant Sjogren will receive the Medal of Honor.

**PACIFIC:** During the night Twentieth Air Force sends more than 500 B-29s against the urban-industrial area of Tokyo. This is the largest number of B-29s involved in a single mission during the war. A total of 17 B-29s are lost.

Mines dropped by Twentieth Air Force B-29s sink three Japanese cargo ships and damage another in the Inland Sea and the Shimonoseki Strait.

**PACIFIC, OKINAWA:** The 184th Infantry Regiment of the 7th Infantry Division conducts an attack supported by large numbers of tanks, including flamethrower tanks. The attacks gain 2,000 yards past the town of Yonbaru. The 6th Marine Division enters the town of Naha, the capital of the island. Heavy rains make movement extremely difficult and slow the pace of battle to a crawl.

Japanese forces begin a gradual withdrawal to the south, using the overcast skies to cover their movement from aerial reconnaissance.

**CENTRAL PACIFIC:** VII Fighter Command sends 32 P-47 Thunderbolts from Saipan to strafe Moen Island airfields, boats off Tol Island, buildings on Tarik Island, and the seaplane base, buildings, and small boats at Dublon Island at Truk.

## May 24

**CBI:** Fourteenth Air Force B-25 Mitchells, P-47 Thunderbolts, and P-51 Mustangs attack trucks, river traffic, highways, logistics storage sites, rail lines, bridges, troops, and targets of opportunity in southern and eastern China.

**ETO:** Brigadier General Richard C. Sanders takes command of the 9th Air Division.

**SOUTHWEST PACIFIC AREA:** In the Philippines, Far East Air Force B-24 Liberators bomb Cagayan Valley targets, supported by B-25 Mitchells, A-20 Havocs, and P-51 Mustangs. P-38 Lightnings support ground forces on Negros Island.

In Borneo, FEAF B-24 Liberators, B-25 Mitchells, and P-38 Lightnings attack Fort Brook, Bintula, Tawau, Beaufort, Jesselton, targets along the Lawas River, and Malinau.

**PACIFIC:** Carrier aircraft from TF 58 attack airfields in southern Kyushu, Japan.

Navy PBM Mariner patrol bombers sink a coastal defense ship in the South China Sea.

Mines dropped by Twentieth Air Force B-29s sink five Japanese cargo ships and a merchant tanker and damage a transport and three cargo ships in the Inland Sea and the Shimonoseki Strait.

During the night Twentieth Air Force sends 25 B-29s to mine Shimonoseki Strait.

**PACIFIC, OKINAWA:** Kamikazes damage a destroyer escort, a high-speed transport, and a large support landing craft off Okinawa.

**CENTRAL PACIFIC:** Seventh Air Force sends 26 B-24 Liberators from Guam to bomb the airfield on Marcus Island. VII Fighter Command sends 120 P-51 Mustangs from Iwo Jima to attack targets at Matsudo and Tokorozawa, Japan, but the mission is aborted due to bad weather. During the night P-47 Thunderbolts fly harassment strikes against Kyushu Island, Japan.

## May 25

**CBI:** Fourteenth Air Force B-25 Mitchells and P-51 Mustangs attack bridges. P-47 Thunderbolts and P-51s fly armed reconnaissance missions.

**ATLANTIC:** Concluding that air bombardment and naval blockade alone will not force Japan's unconditional surrender, the Joint Chiefs of Staff approves the directive to begin formal planning for Operation Downfall, the invasion of the Japanese home islands. Downfall has two subordinate plans, Operation Olympic, the invasion of Kyushu, scheduled for November 1, 1945, and Operation Coronet, the invasion of Honshu, scheduled for April 1, 1946.

**MEDITERRANEAN:** Fifteenth Air Force sends the headquarters of the 484th Bombardment Group (Heavy) and the B-24 Liberators of the 824th, 825th, 826th, and 827th Bombardment Squadrons (Heavy) from Torretto, Italy, to Casablanca, French Morocco, to begin transporting troops home to the United States.

**SOUTHWEST PACIFIC AREA:** In Luzon, elements of the 1st Cavalry Division capture Infanta on the east coast of Luzon and stand on the left flank of the perimeter of the remainder of the Shimbu Group. The 38th and 43rd Infantry Divisions of XI Corps continue pressure on the Japanese defenders, now with their backs to the sea.

In the Philippines, Far East Air Force B-25 Mitchells, A-20 Havocs, P-38 Lightnings, and P-51 Mustangs support ground forces on Luzon and Cebu Islands.

In Borneo, FEAF B-24 Liberators bomb Oelin, Fort Brook, and along with P-38 Lightnings, attack targets on Tarakan Island. B-25 Mitchells and P-38s attack Kudat.

U.S. submarine *Blenny* torpedoes and sinks a Japanese gunboat in the Java Sea.

**PACIFIC:** Admiral Nimitz approves the transfer of operational and administrative control of VII Fighter Command to Twentieth Air Force.

P-51 Mustangs from Iwo Jima attack Matsudo and Tokorozawa airfields in Japan. Pilots report eight confirmed kills and one possible in the air and 10 confirmed kills and 40 possibles on the ground. Three P-51s are lost. During the night 464 B-29s bomb the urban area of Tokyo. Six other B-29s bomb targets of opportunity. Aircrews report 19 Japanese fighters shot down. A total of 26 B-29s are lost, the highest single-day loss of B-29s in the war.

Mines dropped by Twentieth Air Force B-29s sink four cargo vessels, a merchant tanker, and a transport and damage two destroyers, three cargo ships, and a merchant tanker in the Inland Sea and the Shimonoseki Strait.

U.S. submarine *Ray* torpedoes and sinks a Japanese schooner in the Yellow Sea.

**PACIFIC, OKINAWA:** Kamikazes sink a high-speed transport and a medium landing ship and damage two destroyers, a destroyer escort, two high-speed transports, a high-speed minesweeper, and a minesweeper off Okinawa. A U.S. freighter is hit by an aerial torpedo.

## May 26

**CBI:** Fourteenth Air Force B-25 Mitchells and P-51 Mustangs bomb bridges and rail targets. P-47 Thunderbolts and P-51s attack trucks, road traffic, highways, rail lines, bridges, and troops in southern and eastern China. Japanese forces complete their withdrawal from Yungning and Chinese troops retake Nanning.

**ETO:** Eighth Air Force begins the redeployment of the headquarters, 398th Bombardment Group (Heavy), and the B-17s of the 600th, 601st, 602nd, and 603rd Bombardment Squadrons (Heavy) to the United States.

**MEDITERRANEAN:** Brigadier General James A. Mollison takes command of Fifteenth Air Force.

**SOUTHWEST PACIFIC AREA:** In the Philippines, Far East Air Force A-20 Havocs, P-38 Lightnings, and P-51 Mustangs support ground forces on Luzon and P-47 Thunderbolts attack targets on Cebu Island.

B-25s and P-38s sweep Formosa, hitting a number of communication and industrial targets.

FEAF B-24 Liberators, B-25 Mitchells, and P-38 Lightnings attack Tarakan Island and town areas on Borneo.

**PACIFIC:** Twentieth Air Force sends 16 P-47 Thunderbolts from Saipan to strafe airfields on Moen Island, the seaplane base on Dublon Island, and several targets of opportunity at Truk. Mines dropped by Twentieth Air Force B-29s sink an auxiliary submarine chaser and four cargo ships and damage a gunboat, a transport, and five cargo ships in the Inland Sea and the Shimonoseki Strait.

U.S. submarine *Billfish* torpedoes and sinks a Japanese cargo ship off Nagasaki, Japan.

During the night 29 B-29s mine waters in Shimonoseki Strait and waters off Shikoku and Kyushu, Japan.

**PACIFIC, OKINAWA:** Kamikazes damage a high-speed minesweeper and a submarine chaser off Okinawa.

**CENTRAL PACIFIC:** Seventh Air Force sends 10 B-24 Liberators from Guam to bomb the airfield on Marcus Island.

## May 27

**CBI:** Fourteenth Air Force B-25 Mitchells attack rail bridges and rail cars. P-47 Thunderbolts and P-51 Mustangs attack trucks, rail lines, bridges, and troops in southern and eastern China.

**SOUTHWEST PACIFIC AREA:** In the Philippines, Far East Air Force B-24 Liberators, A-20 Havocs, P-38 Lightnings, and P-51 Mustangs support ground forces on Luzon at Cagayan Valley, the Balete Pass, Baguio, and Ipo Dam.

In French Indochina, B-24s bomb the railyards and rail cars.

B-25 Mitchells and P-38 Lightnings attack targets of opportunity on Formosa.

FEAF B-24 Liberators, B-25 Mitchells, and P-38 Lightnings attack town areas on Borneo and attack targets on Tarakan Island.

**PACIFIC:** During the night Twentieth Air Force sends nine B-29s to lay mines in Shimonoseki Strait and the area of the Inland Sea off Kyushu, Japan. One B-29 is lost.

Mines dropped by Twentieth Air Force B-29s sink two cargo ships and a merchant tanker and damage a cargo ship in the Inland Sea and the Shimonoseki Strait.

**PACIFIC, OKINAWA:** Admiral William F. Halsey, Jr., Commander Third Fleet, takes operational control of Task Force 58 from Admiral Raymond A. Spruance, Commander Fifth Fleet. The Fifth Fleet is redesignated as Third Fleet. TF 58 is redesignated TF 38.

Kamikazes damage two destroyers, a high-speed minesweeper, two high-speed transports, a surveying ship, and a submarine chaser.

**CENTRAL PACIFIC:** P-47 Thunderbolts from Saipan sweep Truk, strafing the airfield and facilities, aircraft, and the radio tower on Moen Island. Other targets on and near Dublon Island seaplane base are also attacked.

U.S. submarine *Tigrone* torpedoes and sinks a Japanese guardboat north of the Bonin Islands.

## May 28

**CBI:** In China, Fourteenth Air Force P-51 Mustangs attack a bridge and military installations near Wuchang. P-51s attack bridges, troops, logistics storage sites, trucks, locomotives, river craft, and other targets near Yoyang.

In French Indochina, 19 B-25 Mitchells, along with eight P-51 Mustangs, attack rail, road, and river traffic.

**ETO:** Eighth Air Force redeploys the headquarters of the 445th Bombardment Group (Heavy) and the B-24 Liberators of the 564th, 565th, 566th, and 567th Bombardment Squadrons (Heavy) of the 389th Bombardment Group (Heavy).

**SOUTHWEST PACIFIC AREA:** In Luzon, the XI Corps captures the Wawa Dam. Japanese forces of the Shimbu Group are forced to withdraw into the Sierra Madre, where they will remain isolated until the end of the war.

In the Eighth Army area, the 164th Infantry Regiment of the Americal Division defeats the Japanese on Negros Island near Dumaguete. The Americans have lost 35 men killed and 180 wounded; Japanese casualties are 350 killed and 15 captured.

In the Philippines, Far East Air Force B-24 Liberators, B-25 Mitchells, A-20 Havocs, P-38 Lightnings, and P-47 Thunderbolts support ground forces on Luzon.

In French Indochina, B-24s bomb the railyards near Saigon.

On Formosa, B-25 Mitchells and P-38s attack industrial targets.

In Borneo, FEAF B-24 Liberators, B-25 Mitchells, and P-38 Lightnings attack gun positions and other targets at Balikpapan. P-38s conduct dive-bombing attacks on Keningau and Jesselton airfields.

U.S. submarines *Blueback* and *Lamprey* fight a surface engagement with a Japanese submarine chaser in the Java Sea.

**PACIFIC:** Twentieth Air Force sends P-51 Mustangs from Iwo Jima Island to attack the airfield at Kasumigaura. Pilots report six aircraft destroyed and over 40 damaged.

Mines dropped by Twentieth Air Force B-29s sink a transport and damage a coastal defense vessel, two cargo ships, and a fishing vessel in the Inland Sea and the Shimonoseki Strait.

U.S. submarine *Ray* torpedoes and sinks a Japanese cargo ship in the Yellow Sea.

During the night P-47 Thunderbolts fly harassment attacks against Kyushu.

**PACIFIC, OKINAWA:** Kamikazes sink destroyer USS *Drexler* and damage an attack transport and a large support landing craft. On *Drexler,* over 200 sailors are killed or injured. Kamikazes damage three U.S. freighters off Okinawa.

## May 29

**SOUTHWEST PACIFIC AREA:** In Luzon, in the I Corps area, the 32nd Infantry Division captures Imugan after more than 90 days of battle to advance 6,000 yards up the Villa Verde Trail. The infantrymen have sealed 214 caves and killed over 9,000 enemy soldiers. The 32nd has lost 900 killed and 2,500 other casualties. The division's agonizing effort opens the way for the 25th Infantry Division to advance to Santa Fe.

In the Philippines, Far East Air Force B-24 Liberators, B-25 Mitchells, A-20 Havocs, P-38 Lightnings, and P-51 Mustangs support ground forces on Luzon in the Cagayan Valley, and at Baguio, Balete, and Ipo.

On Formosa, over 100 B-24s bomb town areas, and B-25 Mitchells and P-38 Lightnings attack an alcohol production facility and targets of opportunity.

In Borneo, FEAF B-24 Liberators attack airfields at Oelin, Tabanio, and Fort Brook.

**PACIFIC:** Twentieth Air Force sends 454 B-29s, escorted by 101 VII Fighter Command P-51 Mustangs, to bomb Yokohama with incendiaries. About 150 Japanese fighters attack the bombers. Aircrews report six fighters shot down. Fighter pilots report 26 confirmed kills, nine probables, and 23 possibles. Seven B-29s and three P-51s are lost.

Mines dropped by Twentieth Air Force B-29s sink a cargo ship and damage another in the Inland Sea and the Shimonoseki Strait.

U.S. submarine *Sterlet* torpedoes and sinks two Japanese cargo ships north of the Kuriles.

The headquarters of the 509th Composite Group arrives on Tinian Island from the United States.

**PACIFIC, OKINAWA:** The 5th Marine Regiment of the 1st Marine Division occupies Shuri, one of the main objectives of the American offensive since the invasion began. It is nothing but rubble.

The Japanese withdrawal to their final defensive line is completed. About 30,000 troops reach the new defenses successfully. The loss of civilians, who joined the Japanese troops, is particularly heavy. Many are killed by shellfire and aerial strafing. About 15,000 Japanese troops are also killed or wounded during the retreat.

Kamikazes hit a destroyer and a high-speed transport off Okinawa.

## May 30

**CBI:** Fourteenth Air Force B-25 Mitchells attack railyards and rail bridges. P-47 Thunderbolts and P-51 Mustangs attack barracks, trucks, highways, rail lines, bridges, troops, and targets of opportunity in southern and eastern China.

**ETO:** Eighth Air Force begins redeploying the headquarters, 389th Bombardment Group (Heavy), and the B-24 Liberators of the 700th, 701st, 702nd, and 703rd Bombardment Squadron (Heavy) of the 445th Bombardment Group (Heavy).

**SOUTHWEST PACIFIC AREA:** In the Philippines, Far East Air Force A-20 Havocs support ground forces on Luzon in the Cagayan Valley.

On Formosa, over 100 B-24 Liberators bomb town areas. B-25 Mitchells hit town areas and P-38 Lightnings conduct sweeps.

FEAF B-24 Liberators and P-38 Lightning fighters attack personnel and logistics targets on Borneo.

U.S. submarine *Blenny* torpedoes and sinks a Japanese cargo ship in the Java Sea. U.S. submarine *Croaker* torpedoes and sinks two shuttle boats in the Java Sea.

**PACIFIC:** Twentieth Air Force sends 14 P-47 Thunderbolts to strafe barges at Truk Atoll. P-47 Thunderbolts from Ie Shima attack shipping and a lighthouse at Amami-O-Shima, Japan, and Okino Erabu in the Ryukyus.

Mines dropped by Twentieth Air Force B-29s sink a transport, three cargo ships, and damage two cargo ships in the Inland Sea and the Shimonoseki Strait.

The 320th Troop Carrier Squadron (C-47s and C-54s) and the B-29s of the 393rd Bombardment Squadron (Very Heavy) of the 509th Composite Group arrive at Tinian from the United States.

**PACIFIC, OKINAWA:** The 1st Marine Division links with the 96th Division south of Shuri, after the 96th advances 1,200 yards. Supported by tanks and self-propelled howitzers, the 7th Infantry Division advances against Japanese delaying forces at Mabel Hill. The 6th Marine Division moves past Naha and encounters a few strongpoints near the Kokuba River.

Aircraft from escort carrier USS *Anzio* sink Japanese submarine *I-361* southeast of Okinawa.

**CENTRAL PACIFIC:** Seventh Air Force sends 10 B-24 Liberators from Guam to attack the airfield on Marcus Island.

## May 31

**CBI:** In China, Fourteenth Air Force B-25 Mitchells and P-47 Thunderbolts attack rail lines and rail cars and attack bridges.

All Tenth Air Force units and U.S. components of the Eastern Air Command (EAC) are withdrawn from the Southeast Asia Command (SEAC) and returned to the operational control of Army Air Forces. The Eastern Air Command is inactivated, along with the Strategic Air Force and the Combat Cargo Task Force.

**ETO:** Eighth Air Force sends the headquarters of the 303rd Bombardment Group (Heavy) and the B-17s of the 358th, 359th, 360th, and 427th Bombardment Squadrons to Casablanca, French Morocco, from England to begin flying troops from Europe to North Africa for return to the United States.

**SOUTHWEST PACIFIC AREA:** In Luzon in the I Corps area, the 37th Infantry Division, which has been moved from Baguio to Santa Fe, advances past the 25th Infantry Division in pursuit of the retreating Japanese.

In the Philippines, Far East Air Force B-25 Mitchells, A-20 Havocs, P-38 Lightnings, and P-47 Thunderbolts support ground forces on Luzon in the Cagayan Valley, Balete Pass, and at Baguio and Ipo. P-38s also support ground forces on Cebu Island.

On Formosa, B-24 Liberators, B-25s, and P-47s attack transportation and communication targets.

In Borneo, FEAF B-25 Mitchells and P-38 Lightnings attack troop concentrations on Tarakan Island and buildings at Belait. P-38s also attack airfields on Borneo and on Labuan Island.

**PACIFIC:** Mines dropped by Twentieth Air Force B-29s sink a cargo ship and damage a gunboat, a transport, and three cargo ships in the Inland Sea and the Shimonoseki Strait.

**PACIFIC, OKINAWA:** Private First Class Clarence B. Craft is a rifleman in G Company, 382nd Infantry Regiment, 96th Infantry, making a platoon attack to capture Hen Hill. The Japanese defenders of Hen Hill have broken every American attack, and now Craft and five men are sent forward to conduct a reconnaissance. They come under rifle and machine-gun fire and are bombarded with hand grenades that wound three of the group. Craft stands in full view of the enemy and fires on the Japanese, then moves forward, hitting every enemy soldier he sees. He reaches the crest of the hill, throwing hand grenades into the enemy positions. This incredible act of bravery allows the assault units to move forward quickly and support his one-man battle by bringing more grenades to the hilltop. He then attacks the main trenchline, firing his rifle into the packed defenders, forcing them to flee. He then destroys a heavy machine-gun position. Moving down the central trench to the mouth of a cave, Craft employs a demolition charge to seal the entrance, but it fails to explode. Without hesitation, he retrieves the explosive and relights the fuse. For his extraordinary act of heroism and combat skill in the face of an overwhelmingly large enemy force, Private First Class Craft will receive the Medal of Honor.

**CENTRAL PACIFIC:** Seventh Air Force sends eight P-47 Thunderbolts from Ie Shima Island to strafe buildings, barracks, and seaplane ramps at Amami-O-Shima, Japan.

## June 1

**CBI:** Fourteenth Air Force B-25 Mitchells bomb railyards and bridges. P-51 Mustangs attack trucks, river traffic and logistics storage sites near Yoyang. P-47 Thunderbolts attack river shipping and bridges.

**ETO:** B-17s and B-24 Liberators of the 812th, 813th, and 814th Bombardment Squadrons (Heavy), 482nd Bombardment Group (Heavy), begin redeployment from England to the United States.

**MEDITERRANEAN:** The headquarters of the 465th Bombardment Group (Heavy) and the B-24 Liberators of the 780th, 781st, 782nd, and 783rd Bombardment Squadrons

(Heavy) begin redeployment from Italy to Trinidad, British West Indies. These aircraft will transport troops arriving from the European and Mediterranean theaters to the United States.

**SOUTHWEST PACIFIC AREA:** In Luzon, the XIV Corps commander, Major General Oscar W. Griswold, notifies Sixth Army commander, Lieutenant General Krueger, that all organized resistance in southern Luzon has been eliminated. The XIV Corps has killed over 14,000 enemy soldiers in southern Luzon.

In the Philippines, Far East Air Force B-25 Mitchells, A-20 Havocs, P-38 Lightnings, and P-47 Thunderbolts support ground forces on Luzon in the Cagayan Valley.

In Formosa, B-24 Liberators bomb town areas, while P-38s conduct sweeps along the coastline.

In Borneo, FEAF B-24 Liberators and P-38 Lightnings attack Tarakan Island troop concentrations, while B-24s, B-25s, and P-38s attack Kota Belud, Victoria, Jesselton, Langkon, and Labuan Island.

**PACIFIC:** Twentieth Air Force sends more than 450 B-29s to attack Osaka, escorted by 148 P-51 Mustangs of the VII Fighter Command. Severe weather prevents most of the fighters from making the rendezvous with the bombers. Conditions are so bad that 27 P-51s are lost. Aircrews report 16 Japanese fighters shot down. Fighter pilots report one confirmed kill in the air. Ten B-29s are lost. P-47 Thunderbolts from Ie Shima Island conduct strafing and rocket attacks against Kikaiga Island, Tokuno, and Amami Gunto, Japan.

B-29s bomb Osaka, damaging eight cargo ships, two army tankers, and two merchant tankers.

Mines dropped by Twentieth Air Force B-29s sink five cargo ships and a tanker and damage six cargo ships in the Inland Sea and the Shimonoseki Strait.

**PACIFIC, OKINAWA:** Tenth Army begins the final drive into the southern end of the island. The XXIV Corps on the left sends the 7th Infantry Division to cut off the Chinen Peninsula at the eastern end of the island to prevent the Japanese from using it as a stronghold. The 96th Infantry Division is to attack south toward the town of Iwa in the center. The III Amphibious Corps on the right sends the 6th Marine Division to clear the Oroku Peninsula below Naha to allow the port at Naha to be occupied and cleared for use.

**CENTRAL PACIFIC:** The naval air facility at Peleliu, Palau Islands, is established. The naval air base on Tarawa is shut down.

## June 2

**CBI:** Fourteenth Air Force B-25 Mitchells attack fuel storage sites and ammunition storage areas in Burma. P-47 Thunderbolts and P-51 Mustangs attack airfields, railyards, trucks, tanks, logistics storage sites, and bridges in southern and eastern China.

**SOUTHWEST PACIFIC AREA:** In the Philippines, Far East Air Force B-25 Mitchells, A-20 Havocs, P-38 Lightnings, and P-47 Thunderbolts support ground forces on Luzon in the Cagayan Valley, the Balete Pass, and Ipo Dam. P-47s and P-38s attack Japanese defenses on Negros and Cebu Islands.

On Formosa, B-24 Liberators bomb town areas and attack warehouses and dock facilities at Kiirun.

In Borneo, FEAF B-24 Liberators attack an airfield and bomb Tarakan and Labuan Islands, while B-25 Mitchells and P-38 Lightnings attack Kudat, Sandakan, and Miri.

**PACIFIC:** Naval Task Force 38, commanded by Vice Admiral John S. McCain, bombs airfields in southern Kyushu, Japan.

U.S. submarine *Tench* torpedoes and sinks a Japanese cargo ships south of Hokkaido, Japan.

Mines dropped by Twentieth Air Force B-29s damage five cargo ships in the Inland Sea and the Shimonoseki Strait.

**CENTRAL PACIFIC:** Seventh Air Force sends 11 B-24 Liberators from Guam to bomb the airfield on Moen Island at Truk.

## June 3

**ALEUTIANS:** Eleventh Air Force sends eight B-24 Liberators against the naval base on Shimushu Island in the Kuriles. The bombers use radar signal intercepts to mark the bomb release points over the target. Bombers also photograph targets. Three B-25 Mitchells conduct a low-level bomb run on a cannery near the Masugawa River.

**CBI:** Fourteenth Air Force B-25 Mitchells and P-47 Thunderbolts attack warehouses and river traffic. P-51 Mustangs attack bridges and trains.

**SOUTHWEST PACIFIC AREA:** In the Philippines, B-24 Liberators and P-38 Lightnings attack Japanese defenses on Negros Island. P-51 Mustangs attack coastal cargo vessels over the southeast China coast.

In Borneo, FEAF B-24 Liberators attack Kota Waringin and Muara Island and bomb Batavia, Java.

U.S. submarine *Blueback* torpedoes and sinks a merchant fishing boat near the Sunda Strait.

**PACIFIC:** Twentieth Air Force P-47 Thunderbolts from Ie Shima strafe targets of opportunity on Amami-O-Shima Island, Japan.

A naval task group commanded by Rear Admiral Lawrence F. Reifsnider lands marines on Iheya Jima in the Ryukyus.

Mines dropped by Twentieth Air Force B-29s sink four cargo ships and damage a minelayer and a cargo ship in the Inland Sea and Shimonoseki Strait.

U.S. submarine *Segundo* torpedoes and sinks a Japanese merchantman in the Yellow Sea.

**PACIFIC, OKINAWA:** The 4th Marine Regiment of the 6th Marine Division, supported by the 6th Tank Battalion, makes an amphibious landing on the Oroku Peninsula. The Naha airfield is quickly captured. The Japanese have strong defensive positions but not enough troops to man them adequately. The marines still have to fight yard by yard.

Task Group 38.4, commanded by Rear Admiral A. W. Radford, attacks Japanese airfields on Kyushu to eliminate the kamikaze menace.

Kamikazes damage a cargo ship and a large infantry landing craft off Okinawa.

## June 4

**ALEUTIANS:** Eleventh Air Force sends 11 B-24 Liberators to bomb Kataoka naval base on Shimushu Island in the Kuriles. The bombers use radar signal intercepts to mark the bomb release point over the target.

**CBI:** Fourteenth Air Force B-25 Mitchells bomb railyards and warehouses. P-47 Thunderbolts and P-51 Mustangs attack road and rail traffic, bridges, and vehicles in southern and eastern China.

**MEDITERRANEAN:** Fifteenth Air Force begins redeploying the headquarters of the 451st Bombardment Group (Heavy) and the B-24 Liberators of the 724th, 725th, 726th, and 727th Bombardment Squadrons (Heavy) from Italy to the United States.

**SOUTHWEST PACIFIC AREA:** In the Eighth Army area, the 40th Infantry Division clears the Japanese from the hills beyond Bacolod on Negros. The battle has taken nearly 45 days and has cost the Americans over 1,300 casualties. The Japanese have lost more than 4,000 killed, and the survivors have scattered into the mountains.

In the Philippines, Far East Air Force B-25 Mitchells, A-20 Havocs, P-38 Lightnings, and P-47 Thunderbolts support ground forces on Luzon.

B-24 Liberators bomb town areas on Formosa.

In Borneo, FEAF B-24 Liberators bomb Balikpapan and Manggar and support ground forces on Tarakan Island. B-25 Mitchells attack Manggar, Djembajan, and Kudat.

Thirteenth Air Force B-24 Liberators sink a Japanese auxiliary submarine chaser and motor torpedo boat and damage an auxiliary submarine chaser in the Java Sea.

**PACIFIC:** U.S. submarine *Billfish* torpedoes and sinks a Japanese cargo ship in the Yellow Sea.

U.S. submarine *Tench* torpedoes and sinks a Japanese transport off western Honshu in the Japan Sea.

Mines dropped by Twentieth Air Force B-29s sink five cargo ships and damage a transport and two cargo ships in the Inland Sea and the Shimonoseki Strait.

During the night P-47 Thunderbolts from Ie Shima conduct strikes against Kyushu Island, Japan.

**CENTRAL PACIFIC:** Seventh Air Force sends 13 B-24 Liberators from Guam to bomb the airfield on Marcus Island.

Twentieth Air Force sends eight P-51 Mustangs from Iwo Jima to bomb the radio station on Chichi Jima and strafe the town of Okimura on Haha Jima.

## June 5

**CBI:** Fourteenth Air Force P-47 Thunderbolts and P-51 Mustangs attack road and river traffic in southern and eastern China.

B-24 Liberators bomb town areas on Formosa.

**SOUTHWEST PACIFIC AREA:** In the Philippines, Far East Air Force B-25 Mitchells, A-20 Havocs, P-38 Lightnings, and P-47 Thunderbolts support ground forces on Luzon in the Cagayan Valley, at Balete Pass and at Ipo.

In Borneo, FEAF B-24 Liberators bomb airfields and Tarakan and Labuan Islands. B-25 Mitchells and P-38 Lightnings attack Tuaran, Mensalung, and Kudat.

Corporal Harry R. Harr of D Company, 124th Infantry Regiment, 31st Infantry Division, is manning a machine gun near Maglamin, Mindanao, as the Japanese launch a fierce counterattack on his company's position. The Japanese throw hand grenades toward Harr's machine gun and then move in quickly. As the crew struggles to put the gun into action after the grenade explosions, Harr sees another grenade land in the emplacement. He covers the grenade with his own body to save the lives of his comrades. For his supremely courageous act to save the lives of others, Corporal Harr will receive the Medal of Honor.

**PACIFIC:** Task Force 38 under command of Admiral William F. Halsey is caught in a typhoon after an incorrect weather estimate puts the task force in the path of the storm. The typhoon damages four battleships, two carriers, two small carriers, four escort carriers, three heavy cruisers, four light cruisers, 11 destroyers, three destroyer escorts, two oilers, and an ammunition ship.

Halsey is nearly relieved of duty, but Secretary of the Navy James V. Forrestal decides to keep the fighting admiral in place.

Twentieth Air Force sends more than 470 B-29s to bomb the city of Kobe, Japan, with incendiaries. Aircrews report 86 Japanese fighters shot down. A total of 11 B-29s are lost. About four square miles of the city are destroyed. P-47 Thunderbolts from Ie Shima Island patrol over Amami Gunto Island, Japan.

Mines dropped by Twentieth Air Force B-29s sink two cargo ships and damage a destroyer, an escort destroyer, and three cargo ships in the Inland Sea and the Shimonoseki Strait.

**PACIFIC, OKINAWA:** Kamikazes damage battleship USS *Mississippi* and a heavy cruiser off Okinawa.

## June 6

**CBI:** Fourteenth Air Force B-25 Mitchells and P-51 Mustangs attack railyards and bridges. P-47 Thunderbolts and P-51s attack bridges, trucks, troops, and targets of opportunity in southern and eastern China.

**ETO:** The headquarters of Ninth Air Force moves from Chantilly, France, to Bad Kissingen, Germany.

**MEDITERRANEAN:** Fifteenth Air Force begins redeployment of the headquarters of the 460th Bombardment Group (Heavy) and the B-24 Liberators of the 760th, 761st, 762nd, and 763rd Bombardment Squadrons (Heavy) from Italy to Trinidad, British West Indies. The headquarters of the 464th Bombardment Group (Heavy) and the B-24s of the 776th, 777th, 778th, and 779th Bombardment Squadrons (Heavy) also begin redeployment from Italy to Trinidad, British West Indies.

**SOUTHWEST PACIFIC AREA:** Far East Air Force A-20 Havocs, P-38 Lightnings, and P-47 Thunderbolts support ground forces on Luzon.

In Borneo, FEAF B-24 Liberators, B-25 Mitchells, and P-38 Lightnings attack logistics storage sites, airfields, and troops on Labuan Island and provide support to ground forces on Tarakan Island, attack targets around Brunei, and bomb town areas.

Staff Sergeant Howard E. Woodford, I Company, 130th Infantry Regiment, 33rd Infantry Division, arrives at the line of departure for a Filipino guerrilla battalion near Tabio, Luzon, to find out why the unit has not attacked as ordered. Japanese mortar, machine-gun, and rifle fire has stopped the first element of the battalion. Woodford takes command of the lead company, evacuates the wounded, and prepares the men for the attack. He repeatedly exposes himself to draw fire so that he can locate the Japanese strongpoints, and then move forward with a group of five men to locate the Japanese defenses. He takes the company forward and captures the objective and organizes a perimeter defense for the night. Before dawn the next morning, the Japanese attack the position with mortars, grenades, and rifle fire. Although wounded by a grenade, Staff Sergeant Woodford calls for mortar fire until bullets destroy his radio. He picks up an M-1 rifle and encourages the guerrillas and takes a position where two guerrillas have been killed. Here he fights off enemy attacks until killed. A total of 37 dead Japanese soldiers lie about his position. For his daring, skillful, and inspiring leadership and courage under fire against a determined enemy, Staff Sergeant Woodford will receive the Medal of Honor.

**PACIFIC:** Twentieth Air Force sends 36 P-47 Thunderbolts from Ie Shima to conduct a sweep of southern Kyushu Island, Japan. Fighter pilots both strafe targets of opportunity and use rockets. Pilots report nine Japanese aircraft downed. Other P-47s patrol over Amami Gunto Island, Japan, strafing a lighthouse and buildings.

Mines dropped by Twentieth Air Force B-29s sink an auxiliary submarine chaser, a guardboat, two cargo ships, a destroyer, and a destroyer escort in the Inland Sea and the Shimonoseki Strait.

**PACIFIC, OKINAWA:** The Tenth Army attack stalls amid steady rain and a lack of adequate supply. The final Japanese defensive line is as strong as any the Americans have encountered. Anchored on Hills 95, 89, 69, and 155, with ridges, plateaus, and valleys of coral rock, the defensive line uses the terrain to its best advantage. Although 30,000 troops defend the line, only about 6,000 are capable of any type of determined resistance.

Lieutenant General Simon B. Buckner will pause three days to ensure enough supplies are brought forward to support the attack on the Japanese defensive line.

Kamikazes damage two light minelayers off Okinawa.

**CENTRAL PACIFIC:** Seventh Air Force sends 12 B-24 Liberators from Guam to bomb oil storage areas on Eten Island at Truk.

## June 7

**CBI:** Japanese forces of the 20th Army are forced back by the Chinese divisions trained and supported by American advisers. The Japanese Imperial General Headquarters orders a general consolidation of Japanese forces into northern and central China to protect key ports and be available for movement to the home islands.

Fourteenth Air Force P-47 Thunderbolts and P-51 Mustangs attack trucks, river traffic, logistics storage sites, bridges, troops, and town areas in southern and eastern China.

**ETO:** Eighth Air Force begins redeployment of the B-24 Liberators of the 578th and 579th Bombardment Squadrons (Heavy) of the 392nd Bombardment Group (Heavy) from England to the United States.

**SOUTHWEST PACIFIC AREA:** In Luzon in the I Corps area the 37th Infantry Division captures Bayambong, dividing the Shobu Group in half.

In the Philippines, Far East Air Force A-20 Havocs, P-38 Lightnings, and P-47 Thunderbolts support ground forces on Luzon.

In Borneo, FEAF B-24 Liberators bomb Brooketon and Muara Island. B-25 Mitchells and P-38 Lightnings attack Kudat, Fort Brook, Belait, Jesselton, and Keningau.

Naval Task Group 74.3, commanded by Rear Admiral Russell S. Berkey, with three U.S. light cruisers, an Australian light cruiser, and seven destroyers, provides fire support for minesweepers and underwater demolition teams off Brunei Bay, Sarawak.

**PACIFIC:** Twentieth Air Force sends 409 B-29s, escorted by 138 P-51 Mustangs from VII Fighter Command, to bomb Osaka, Japan, with incendiary and high-explosive bombs. The bombers use radar to locate bomb release points. Over two square miles of the city are destroyed. Fighter pilots report two confirmed kills and one possible in the air. Two B-29s and a P-51 are lost.

During the night 26 B-29s mine Shimonoseki Strait and the waters off Fukuoka, Kyushu, Japan.

P-47 Thunderbolts from Ie Shima attack a radio station, warehouses, cargo ships, and motor launches on Kyushu Island, Japan. Pilots report five enemy aircraft downed.

U.S. submarine *Shad* torpedoes and sinks a Japanese army transport and a tanker in the East China Sea off Korea. U.S. submarine *Tench* torpedoes and sinks a Japanese guardboat in the Sea of Japan.

**PACIFIC, OKINAWA:** Kamikazes damage escort carrier USS *Natoma Bay* and a destroyer off Okinawa.

**CENTRAL PACIFIC:** Seventh Air Force sends 24 B-24 Liberators from Angaur Island to bomb the boat repair basin on Aurapushekaru Island in the Palaus.

The headquarters of the 41st Bombardment Group (Medium) and the B-25 Mitchells of the 396th and 820th Bombardment Squadrons (Medium) redeploy from Hawaii to Okinawa.

## June 8

**CBI:** Fourteenth Air Force P-51 Mustangs and P-40s attack bridges near Hankow. P-47 Thunderbolts and P-51 Mustangs attack trucks, river traffic, airfields, logistics storage sites, and town areas in southern and eastern China.

**SOUTHWEST PACIFIC AREA:** In the Philippines, Far East Air Force P-38 Lightnings and P-47 Thunderbolts attack targets in the Cagayan Valley.

U.S. submarine *Cobia* torpedoes and sinks a Japanese transport and tanker off the southern coast of French Indochina.

In Borneo, FEAF B-24 Liberators bomb an airfield, while other B-24s, B-25 Mitchells, and P-38 Lightnings attack gun positions at Balikpapan.

Naval Task Group 74.3, commanded by Rear Admiral Russell S. Berkey, conducts a bombardment of Japanese positions in preparation for landings at Brunei Bay. A U.S. minesweeper clearing Brunei Bay hits a mine and sinks.

**PACIFIC:** Twentieth Air Force sends 104 P-51 Mustangs from Iwo Jima to attack Kagamigahara airfield and Meiji in Nagoya, Japan. Bad weather forces the fighters to abort the mission. The P-61 Black Widow night fighters of 548th Night Fighter Squadron, VII Fighter Command, redeploy from Iwo Jima to Ie Island.

Carrier aircraft from Naval Task Force 38 attack Kanoya airfield, Kyushu, Japan.

**PACIFIC, OKINAWA:** Hospital Apprentice First Class Fred F. Lester is a medical corpsman with an assault rifle platoon, 1st Battalion, 22nd Marines, 6th Marine Division, conducting an attack on a fortified hill position on Okinawa. When a marine falls wounded, Lester crawls toward him as small-arms fire and grenades hit nearby. Seriously wounded, Lester pulls the wounded marine to cover but is unable to assist him. He instructs two other marines in providing first aid. Realizing his own wounds are fatal, Lester refuses treatment and continues to direct treatment for two other wounded marines as his life ebbs away. For his dedication to duty and willingness to sacrifice his life to save others, Hospital Apprentice First Class Lester will receive the Medal of Honor.

## June 9

**ALEUTIANS:** Eleventh Air Force sends B-24 Liberators and B-25 Mitchells in a coordinated attack with navy ships and aircraft to attack targets on Paramushiru Island in the Kuriles. Eight Japanese fighters attack the B-25s, forcing them to fly over Soviet airspace in Kamchatka. Soviet antiaircraft fire shoots down one B-25, and the entire aircrew is killed. Another B-25 crash-lands in Petropavlovsk.

**CBI:** Fourteenth Air Force P-47 Thunderbolts and P-51 Mustangs attack river traffic, bridges, and town areas in southern and eastern China.

**ETO:** Eighth Air Force begins redeploying the headquarters of the 351st Bombardment Group (Heavy) and its three B-17 squadrons and two of the B-24 squadrons of the 392nd Bombardment Group (Heavy) from England to the United States.

**SOUTHWEST PACIFIC AREA:** In the Philippines, Far East Air Force P-38 Lightnings and P-47 Thunderbolts support ground forces on Luzon in the Cagayan Valley.

In Borneo, FEAF B-24 Liberators bomb Labuan Island and drop napalm on Brooketon.

**PACIFIC:** Twentieth Air Force sends 44 B-29s to attack the Kawanishi Aircraft Company's production facility at Narao; another 24 B-29s use radar to locate bomb release points to attack the Kawasaki production facility at Akashi. More than 40 B-29s attack Aichi's Atsuta production facility.

During the night 26 B-29s mine Shimonoseki Strait.

A total of 20 P-47 Thunderbolts from Ie Shima strafe various targets of opportunity on Kyushu Island, Japan. P-51 Mustangs from Iwo Jima Island bomb Kagamigahara airfield and the surrounding area at Nagoya, Japan. Pilots report over 20 Japanese aircraft destroyed on the ground. Three P-51 Mustangs are lost.

A naval task group commanded by Rear Admiral Lawrence F. Reifsnider lands marines on Aguni Jima in the Ryukyus. Rear Admiral Arthur W. Radford's naval task group bombards Okino Daito Jima in the Ryukyus.

U.S. submarine *Sea Owl* torpedoes and sinks a Japanese coastal defense vessel in Tsushima Strait. U.S. submarine *Crevalle* torpedoes and sinks a Japanese cargo ship in the Japan Sea west of Honshu, Japan. U.S. submarine *Sea Dog* attacks Japanese shipping off the northwest coast of Honshu, sinking two cargo ships. U.S. submarine *Tench* torpedoes and sinks a Japanese transport off southern Hokkaido. U.S. submarine *Tinosa* torpedoes and sinks a Japanese cargo ship off the east coast of Korea.

Mines dropped by Twentieth Air Force B-29s sink two cargo ships in the Inland Sea and the Shimonoseki Strait.

Navy patrol bombers sink a Japanese cargo ship in the Japan Sea off the east coast of Korea.

**PACIFIC, OKINAWA:** The commander of the 7th Infantry Division, Major General Archibald V. Arnold, orders the 32nd and 17th Infantry Regiments to clear Japanese positions defending Hill 95. Japanese fire is accurate and effective against the exposed infantrymen.

## June 10

**ALEUTIANS:** Eleventh Air Force sends two B-24 Liberators to fly a shipping attack mission with navy bombers. Aircrews report one cargo ship sunk off the coast of Paramushiru Island in the Kuriles.

**CBI:** Fourteenth Air Force P-51 Mustangs attack trucks, river traffic, highways, fuel storage sites, bridges, and barracks in southern and eastern China.

**SOUTHWEST PACIFIC AREA:** In the Philippines, Far East Air Force P-38 Lightnings, and P-47 Thunderbolts support ground forces on Luzon in the Cagayan Valley.

In Borneo, FEAF B-24 Liberators bomb Labuan Island and Brooketon, in coordination with landings of the Australian 9th Division on the shore of Brunei Bay, and attack targets on Labuan and Muara Islands.

Naval Task Group 74.3 provides naval bombardment while American and Royal Australian Air Force aircraft attack Japanese positions as Australian troops land at Brunei Bay, Borneo.

**PACIFIC:** Twentieth Air Force sends 23 B-29s to bomb the seaplane base at Kasumigaura. Over 30 B-29s bomb the Japan Aircraft Company production facility at Tomioka; over 100 B-29s attack the Nakajima Aircraft production facility at Musashi, but cloud cover over the primary target brings the bombers to the Attackachi engineering works at Kaigan. A total of 26 B-29s attack the Attackachi production facility at Chiba. Over 50 B-29s attack the Nakajima production facilities at Ogikubu and Omiya. One B-29 is lost. Nearly 30 B-29s bomb the Tachikawa Army Air Arsenal. The bombers are escorted by 107 VII Fighter Command P-51 Mustangs. Fighter pilots report 27 confirmed kills, seven probables, and 10 possibles in the air.

P-47 Thunderbolts from Ie Shima conduct a sweep over Kyushu Island, Japan, strafing numerous ground targets of opportunity. Pilots report 17 enemy aircraft shot down.

A naval task group commanded by Rear Admiral Joseph J. Clark attacks the airfield and other installations on Minami Daito Jima in the Ryukyus.

U.S. submarine *Crevalle* torpedoes and sinks a Japanese cargo ship near Tsugaru Strait, between Honshu and Hokkaido Islands. U.S. submarine *Dace* attacks a Japanese convoy in Sea of Okhotsk, sinking a cargo ship. U.S. submarine *Flying Fish* torpedoes and sinks a Japanese cargo ship in the Yellow Sea. U.S. submarine *Skate* torpedoes and sinks Japanese submarine *I-122* in the Sea of Japan. U.S. submarine *Spadefish* attacks Japanese shipping off Hokkaido and sinks a cargo ship, a transport, and a cargo ship. U.S. submarine *Tench* torpedoes and sinks a Japanese merchant tanker off southern Hokkaido, Japan.

Navy PB4Y-2 Privateers from Okinawa conduct aerial mining around Korea to limit the range of Japanese shipping. The bombers encounter intense antiaircraft fire from Japanese warships in Tsushima Strait as they attempt to drop mines at Pusan harbor. Other Privateers sink a Japanese merchant tanker off the west coast of Korea.

**PACIFIC, OKINAWA:** Tenth Army commander Lieutenant General Simon B. Buckner sends a personal letter to Lieutenant General Mitsuru Ushijima, the commander of the Japanese 32nd Army, requesting that he surrender his troops to prevent further useless bloodshed. Ushijima, who receives the letter on June 17, cannot help but laugh at the American commander's lack of understanding of the Japanese military code of honor and sacrifice.

The 381st and 383rd Infantry Regiments of the 96th Infantry Division attack Japanese defenses at Yaeju Dake and Yuza Dake. The area is heavily mined, and the hills are well defended with veteran troops.

The 1st Marine Division attacks against the strongest and best defended position of the final Japanese defensive line, Kunishi Ridge. During the night Japanese soldiers attempt to enter the marine lines mixed among civilians. The Japanese soldiers are discovered and killed in a wild fight. Some women among the group are killed and are found to be carrying explosives and grenades for a suicide attack.

A kamikaze sinks destroyer USS *William D. Porter* off Okinawa. As the destroyer burns, Lieutenant Richard M. McCool, Jr., maneuvers his large support landing craft alongside to take on survivors. A destroyer escort is damaged by fire from a shore battery.

## June 11

**ALEUTIANS:** Eleventh Air Force sends eight B-24 Liberators on a shipping sweep over the Kurile Islands. Bad weather precludes finding any targets. The bombers then use radar to assist in locating and bombing installations on Kurabu Cape, Paramushiru Island, and around the Kataoka area of Shimushu Island.

**CBI:** Fourteenth Air Force B-25 Mitchells attack railyards. P-47 Thunderbolts and P-51 Mustangs attack river traffic, highways, rail lines, bridges, and targets of opportunity in southern and eastern China.

**SOUTHWEST PACIFIC AREA:** In the Philippines, Far East Air Force B-25 Mitchells, A-20 Havocs, P-38 Lightnings, and P-47 Thunderbolts support ground forces on Luzon in the Cagayan Valley and near Ipo.

In Borneo, FEAF B-24 Liberators support ground forces on Tarakan Island and bomb Kota Baru, Laoet Island, and Tawau. P-38 Lightnings attack Beaufort while B-25 Mitchells support ground forces in the Brunei Bay sector.

**PACIFIC:** During the night Twentieth Air Force sends 26 B-29s to mine Shimonoseki Strait and Tsuruga Bay. P-51 Mustangs from Iwo Jima attack Tokorozawa airfield, Japan. Fighter pilots report 18 aircraft destroyed on the ground and over 30 damaged. Combat crews and B-29s of the 509th Composite Group begin to arrive at Tinian.

U.S. cruisers and destroyers commanded by Rear Admiral John H. Brown, Jr., bombard Japanese installations on Matsuwa, in the Kuriles.

U.S. submarine *Bowfin* torpedoes and sinks a Japanese cargo ship off Korea. U.S. submarine *Crevalle* torpedoes and sinks a Japanese gunboat off Honshu, Japan. U.S. submarine *Flying Fish* torpedoes and sinks a Japanese cargo ship off Korea. U.S. submarine *Sea Dog* torpedoes and sinks a Japanese cargo ship off western Honshu, Japan. U.S. submarine *Segundo* torpedoes and sinks a Japanese cargo ship in the Yellow Sea. U.S. submarine *Tirante* torpedoes and sinks a Japanese cargo ship near southern Kyushu, Japan. A Navy PB4Y-2 Privateer sinks a Japanese auxiliary submarine chaser at the entrance to Ise Bay, Honshu, Japan, but the aircraft is damaged when the submarine chaser explodes.

Navy PB4Y-2 Privateers from Okinawa attempt a second aerial mining mission in Korean waters but abort due to bad weather.

**PACIFIC, OKINAWA:** The 32nd Infantry Regiment uses a flame tank from C Company, 713th Flame Tank Battalion, and a company of infantrymen to burn its way to the top of Hill 95.

When two kamikazes approach his large support landing craft off Okinawa, Lieutenant Richard M. McCool, Jr., orders his crew into action. One enemy plane is destroyed, but the other crashes into landing craft, hitting the conning tower where Lieutenant McCool is, and turning the entire area into an inferno. Although wounded and burned, he leads his men to fight the flames and turns to rescue sailors trapped in a burning compartment. Lieutenant McCool carries one sailor to safety and suffers additional burns. Ignoring his condition and the dangers around him, Lieutenant McCool stays at his post until other ships come to his aid. For his extraordinary leadership and demonstrated courage, in addition to his cool actions the previous day in rescuing survivors of the destroyer USS *William D. Porter,* Lieutenant Richard M. McCool, Jr., will receive the Medal of Honor.

## June 12

**ALEUTIANS:** Eleventh Air Force sends four B-25 Mitchells to strafe shipping off Paramushiru Island. Aircrews report four cargo ships and two barges damaged. One B-25 is lost.

**CBI:** Fourteenth Air Force B-25 Mitchells attack a bridge. P-51 Mustangs and P-61 Black Widow night fighters attach rail lines, logistics storage sites, highways, troops, and antiaircraft positions in southern and eastern China.

**ETO:** Eighth Air Force moves the headquarters of the 92nd Bombardment Group (Heavy) and two B-17 squadrons to Istres, France, where they will begin transporting troops from Marseille to Casablanca for return to the United States. The headquarters of the 379th Bombardment Group (Heavy) begins moving to Casablanca,

French Morocco. The headquarters of the 467th Bombardment Group (Heavy) and four squadrons of B-24s begin redeployment from England to the United States.

**SOUTHWEST PACIFIC AREA:** In Luzon, the two RCTs of the 6th Infantry Division move into the Bayambong area to support the 33rd Infantry Division in reducing the Kiangan Pocket, one of the isolated elements of the Shobu Group.

In the Philippines, Far East Air Force B-25 Mitchells, A-20 Havocs, P-38 Lightnings, and P-47 Thunderbolts support ground forces on Luzon at Cagayan Valley, Balete Pass, and east of Manila.

In French Indochina, B-24 Liberators bomb the railyards at Saigon. B-24s also attack the navy yard and dock area at Hong Kong. Aircrews report heavy damage to the facilities.

FEAF P-38 Lightnings attack targets on Tarakan Island, the Brunei Bay area, and coastal routes in north Borneo.

**PACIFIC:** U.S. submarine *Sea Dog* torpedoes and sinks two cargo ships in the Sea of Japan west of Honshu. U.S. submarine *Skate* torpedoes and sinks three Japanese cargo ships and damages a cargo ship in the Sea of Japan off northern Honshu. U.S. submarine *Spadefish* torpedoes and sinks a Japanese guardboat west of Hokkaido. U.S. submarine *Tinosa* torpedoes and sinks a Japanese cargo ship in the Sea of Japan off Korea.

Mines dropped by Twentieth Air Force B-29s sink three cargo ships and a liaison ship and damage an army tanker in the Inland Sea and the Shimonoseki Strait.

**PACIFIC, OKINAWA:** The 4th and 29th Marine Regiments of the 6th Marine Division break the final resistance on the Oroku Peninsula. Over 1,600 marines are casualties in nine days of fighting an understrength enemy in prepared positions. The marines find elaborate cave complexes and tunnels that are completely impervious to artillery bombardment.

Two battalions of the 17th Infantry Regiment of the 7th Infantry Division conduct a night attack on Yaeju Dake escarpment near Hill 95 and gain complete surprise, using flame tanks to destroy Japanese positions, preventing the Japanese from controlling a key position and stopping a counterattack.

The 96th Infantry Division also holds off Japanese counterattacks.

**CENTRAL PACIFIC:** Seventh Air Force sends 12 B-24 Liberators from Guam to bomb the airfield on Marcus Island.

### June 13

**CBI:** Fourteenth Air Force B-25 Mitchells and P-51 Mustangs attack railyards and communication centers near Puchou. P-51s attack rail lines and bridges.

U.S. submarine *Bergall* is damaged when it hits an Allied mine in the Gulf of Siam and is forced to terminate her patrol.

Mines dropped by Fourteenth Air Force B-24 Liberators sink a Japanese cargo ship off Macao.

**SOUTHWEST PACIFIC AREA:** In the Philippines, Far East Air Force B-25 Mitchells, A-20 Havocs, P-38 Lightnings, and P-47 Thunderbolts support ground forces on Luzon in the Cagayan Valley.

B-24 Liberators bomb a town area, a naval base, and airfields in Formosa.

FEAF B-24 Liberators bomb targets near Balikpapan-Sepinggang. B-25 Mitchells and P-38 Lightnings support ground forces in the Brunei Bay area and sweep north Borneo, attacking numerous targets of opportunity.

**PACIFIC:** During the night Twentieth Air Force sends 29 B-29s to drop mines in Shimonoseki Strait and in the waters at Niigata, west-central Honshu, Japan. Mines dropped by Twentieth Air Force B-29s sink four cargo ships and damage an escort destroyer and five cargo ships in the Inland Sea and the Shimonoseki Strait.

P-47 Thunderbolts from Ie Shima strafe and fire rockets at vessels, buildings, a radio station, barracks, and airfields at Amakusa Jima and Amami-O-Shima Islands, and Tokuno, Japan.

U.S. submarine *Bonefish* torpedoes and sinks a Japanese cargo ship in the Sea of Japan.

U.S. submarine *Bowfin* torpedoes and sinks a Japanese cargo ship in the Sea of Japan east of Korea. U.S. submarine *Skate* torpedoes and sinks a Japanese cargo ship in the Sea of Japan.

U.S. submarine *Spadefish* mistakenly sinks a Russian cargo ship west of Hokkaido, Japan.

**PACIFIC, OKINAWA:** The 7th Marines of the 1st Marine Division gain a foothold on Kunishi Ridge. Tanks support the marines, bringing supplies and reinforcements. The battle to control the ground will last for five more days as the 5th Marines support the 7th in clearing the caves and tunnels.

The destroyer USS *Twiggs* is sunk by a Japanese torpedo plane; over 150 sailors are lost.

**CENTRAL PACIFIC:** Seventh Air Force sends 13 B-24 Liberators from Guam to bomb the airfield on Moen Island at Truk.

## June 14

**CBI:** In China, Fourteenth Air Force sends 42 P-51 Mustangs to attack bridges, shipping, antiaircraft positions, rail lines, trucks, and communications around Hengyang, Hankow, Yoyang, Lingling, Puchou and other nearby areas.

**ATLANTIC:** The Joint Chiefs of Staff directs Generals of the Army Henry H. Arnold and Douglas MacArthur and Fleet Admiral Chester W. Nimitz to initiate planning for the immediate occupation of Japan in case the Japanese are unable to resist any longer or surrender.

**ETO:** Eighth Air Force prepares the headquarters of the 458th Bombardment Group (Heavy) for redeployment from England to the United States.

**SOUTHWEST PACIFIC AREA:** In the Philippines, Far East Air Force B-25 Mitchells, A-20 Havocs, P-38 Lightnings, and P-47 Thunderbolts support ground forces on Luzon in the Cagayan Valley and east of Manila.

FEAF B-24 Liberators bomb warehouses and troop assembly areas on Celebes Island. B-24s bomb antiaircraft positions at Balikpapan in Borneo.

**PACIFIC:** U.S. submarine *Sea Devil* torpedoes and sinks a Japanese transport in the northern Yellow Sea. U.S. submarine *Spadefish* torpedoes and sinks a Japanese cargo ship off western Sakhalin Island.

Navy PB4Y-2 Privateers from Okinawa conduct aerial mining of the waters of southern Korea.

## June 15

**CBI:** Fourteenth Air Force sends three B-25 Mitchells, as well as P-47 Thunderbolts, and P-51 Mustangs to attack trucks, river traffic, barracks, highways, gun positions, logistics storage sites, rail lines, bridges, and town areas in southern and eastern China.

Tenth Air Force B-24 Liberators attack a Japanese convoy in the Gulf of Siam, sinking a merchant tanker and damaging a destroyer and a minesweeper.

**ATLANTIC:** The Joint War Plans Committee submits a briefing paper to the Joint Chiefs of Staff reaffirming its recommendation that an invasion of the home islands is the only means for the decisive defeat of Japan. Planners estimate 193,000 American casualties. Although Soviet participation in the invasion is no longer essential to success, Soviet forces could be useful in holding Japanese troops in northern China and Manchuria and preventing them from reinforcing the home island defenses.

**ETO:** Eighth Air Force begins to redeploy the headquarters of the 44th Bombardment Group (Heavy) and the two B-24 squadrons to the United States. The headquarters of the 392nd Bombardment Group and its three B-24 squadrons are also returning to the United States.

**MEDITERRANEAN:** Eighth Air Force sends the headquarters of the 460th Bombardment Group (Heavy) from Italy to Trinidad, British West Indies, to support the transport of American troops returning to the United States.

**SOUTHWEST PACIFIC AREA:** In Luzon, the XIV Corps is relieved of responsibility for southern Luzon. The corps headquarters is transferred to San José to support offensive operations in northern Luzon.

In the Philippines, Far East Air Force B-25 Mitchells, A-20 Havocs, P-38 Lightnings, and P-47 Thunderbolts support ground forces on Luzon in the Cagayan Valley.

In Formosa, B-24 Liberators bomb an airfield and B-25 Mitchells attack town areas and an airfield.

In Borneo, FEAF B-24 Liberators bomb gun positions at Balikpapan and B-25 Mitchells and P-38 Lightnings attack Japanese positions between Brunei and Kudat.

**PACIFIC:** Twentieth Air Force sends 444 B-29s to bomb the Osaka-Amagasaki urban area in Japan with incendiaries. Over two square miles of the cities are burned out. Two B-29s are lost. The 123 P-51 Mustangs from Iwo Jima that were to escort the bombers are forced to abort due to weather. One fighter is lost.

Twentieth Air Force sends 30 B-29s to mine Shimonoseki Strait and the waters off Fukuoka, west Honshu, and Karatsu, west Kyushu, Japan.

U.S. submarine *Sea Dog* torpedoes and sinks a Japanese cargo ship in the Sea of Japan west of Honshu, Japan.

The B-29s of the 680th Bombardment Squadron (Very Heavy), under the operational control of 504th Bombardment Group (Very Heavy), arrives at Tinian Island from the United States.

**Pacific, Okinawa:** The 8th Marine Regiment of the 2nd Marine Division is placed under the operational control of the 1st Marine Division on Okinawa. The regiment has arrived from Guam and has been involved in capturing two small offshore islands. Observing the regiment's first offensive operation with III Amphibious Corps commander, Lieutenant General Roy S. Geiger, Lieutenant General Simon B. Buckner, commander of Tenth Army, is killed by Japanese artillery fire. Geiger takes command of Tenth Army.

## June 16

**Aleutians:** Eleventh Air Force sends four B-24 Liberators to bomb and strafe shipping off Suribachi Bay, Paramushiru Island, and a radar site on Minami Cape of Shimushu Island in the Kuriles. One B-24 crashes into the water. Four B-25 Mitchells on a shipping strike attack a cargo ship, and two of the B-25s are forced to land at Petropavlovsk in the Soviet Union because of mechanical trouble.

**CBI:** Fourteenth Air Force B-25 Mitchells attack road convoys, while P-51 Mustangs attack trucks, river traffic, highways, rail lines, bridges, power facilities, and targets of opportunity in southern and eastern China.

**Southwest Pacific Area:** In the Philippines, Far East Air Force B-25 Mitchells, A-20 Havocs, P-38 Lightnings, and P-47 Thunderbolts support ground forces on Luzon in the Cagayan Valley and east of Manila.

B-24 Liberators bomb Kiirun harbor and town areas on Formosa. The headquarters of the 308th Bombardment Wing (Heavy) redeploys from Luzon to Okinawa Island.

In Borneo, FEAF B-24 Liberators bomb Balikpapan gun emplacements, while B-25 Mitchells attack the Brunei Bay area and P-38 Lightnings attack airfields and targets of opportunity in north Borneo.

**Pacific:** Twentieth Air Force receives P-61 Black Widow night fighters on Ie Shima Island. Other P-61 Black Widow night fighters fly night intruder missions over Amami Gunto Island, Japan, bombing various targets of opportunity. P-47 Thunderbolts from Ie Shima Island dive-bomb boats, antiaircraft positions, runways, and buildings on Kikai Island, Japan.

U.S. destroyer *Twiggs* is sunk during an attack by an aerial torpedo off Okinawa.

U.S. submarine *Piranha* torpedoes and sinks a Japanese cargo ship in the Sea of Japan west of Honshu.

**Pacific, Okinawa:** The 382nd and 381st Infantry Regiments of the 96th Infantry Division clear the last Japanese defenders from Yuza Dake. The infantry often must clear the same position several times as the enemy will return to those positions through a maze of underground tunnels. Japanese troops and civilians are caught in the open near the town of Makabe and hit by 22 battalions of artillery firing at once.

## June 17

**Aleutians:** Eleventh Air Force sends four B-25 Mitchells to bomb shipping near Kataoka, Shimushu Island. Aircrews report one cargo ship destroyed, another damaged. Four other B-25s fly a shipping sweep.

**CBI:** General of the Army Henry H. Arnold, Commanding General U.S. Army Air Forces, requests that Lieutenant General Albert C. Wedemeyer, Commander of U.S. Forces in China, replace Major General Clare L. Chennault as commander of Fourteenth Air Force with Lieutenant General George E. Stratemeyer. Chennault has become increasingly unpopular and is seen as being too close to Generalissimo Chiang-Kai-shek.

Fourteenth Air Force B-25 Mitchells attack road and rail lines. P-47 Thunderbolts, P-61 Black Widow night fighters, and P-51 Mustangs attack trucks, river traffic, highways, logistics storage sites, rail lines, bridges, troops, and town areas in southern and eastern China.

The headquarters of XX Bomber Command begins redeployment from India to Okinawa.

**SOUTHWEST PACIFIC AREA:** In the Philippines, Far East Air Force B-25 Mitchells, A-20 Havocs, P-38 Lightnings, and P-47 Thunderbolts support ground forces on Luzon in the Cagayan Valley.

B-24 Liberators bomb industrial and railroad targets and P-38 Lightnings bomb a railroad bridge and trucks on Formosa.

In Borneo, FEAF B-24 Liberators bomb gun positions and oil targets in the Balikpapan area. B-25 Mitchells and P-38 Lightnings attack towns and conduct a sweep from Beaufort to Jesselton, attacking communication targets and troop concentrations on Labuan Island.

**PACIFIC:** During the night Twentieth Air Force sends 25 B-29s to mine Shimonoseki Strait and waters around Kobe, Honshu, Japan. Over 100 B-29s attack the Kagoshima urban area with incendiaries, destroying over two square miles of the city. One B-29 is lost. Over 100 B-29s attack the Omuta urban area. A total of 130 B-29s attack the Hamamatsu urban area with incendiaries, destroying over two square miles of the city. Nearly 90 B-29s attack the Yokkaichi urban area, destroying one square mile of the city. P-47 Thunderbolts from Ie Shima bomb and strafe shipping, the airfield, villages, a bridge, and radar and radio facilities on Amami Gunto Island and Tokuno, Japan. During the night P-61 Black Widow night fighters from Ie Shima attempt an intruder strike over Amami Gunto and Kyushu, Japan, but are turned back because of bad weather.

U.S. submarine *Spadefish* attacks a Japanese convoy, sinking an auxiliary minelayer off Hokkaido, Japan.

**PACIFIC, OKINAWA:** The 7th Infantry Division captures Hills 115 and 155 employing flame tanks to burn lanes for the infantry to advance.

### June 18

**ALEUTIANS:** Eleventh Air Force send six B-24 Liberators along with navy aircraft to attack Kataoka, Shimushu Island, and Tomari Cape, Paramushiru Island.

**CBI:** Fourteenth Air Force P-47 Thunderbolts, P-61 Black Widow night fighters, and P-51 Mustangs attack trucks, river traffic, highways, barracks, logistics storage sites, rail lines, bridges, troop concentrations, and town areas in southern and eastern China.

**ATLANTIC:** President Harry S. Truman approves Operation Olympic, the invasion of Kyushu. It involves three army and three marine divisions that will land near

Kagoshima Bay. Three more army divisions will land at Miyazaki on Kyushu's east coast. Truman delays authorizing Coronet and asks the JCS and the service secretaries for their views on whether the Soviet Union's assistance is still necessary to defeat Japan. General Marshall believes that a Soviet declaration of war may be enough to force the Japanese to surrender. All recommend that the president seek a way to modify the unconditional surrender terms for Japan so that Emperor Hirohito, the national leader, can stay in power. Truman also hears from his political advisers that the war must be ended soon before the British and the Soviets become too deeply involved in the postwar planning in the Pacific.

**SOUTHWEST PACIFIC AREA:** In the Philippines, Far East Air Force B-25 Mitchells, A-20 Havocs, P-38 Lightnings, and P-47 Thunderbolts support ground forces on Luzon in the Cagayan Valley, Balete Pass, and other areas.

In Formosa, B-24 Liberators bomb buildings, warehouses and small vessels at Kiirun. P-51 Mustangs attack airfields and targets of opportunity and P-38 Lightnings bomb a town area.

In Borneo, FEAF B-24 Liberators bomb troop concentrations in Balikpapan and near Miri, Manggar airfield, and defenses at Sepinggang. B-25 Mitchells support ground forces on Labuan Island.

U.S. submarine *Bullhead* torpedoes and sinks a Japanese auxiliary sailing vessel in the Sunda Strait off Sumatra.

**PACIFIC:** U.S. submarine *Apogon* attacks a Japanese convoy and sinks a transport and guardboat southwest of Paramushiro, Kuriles.

U.S. submarine *Tinosa* torpedoes and sinks a Japanese ship in the Yellow Sea.

U.S. submarine *Bonefish* in cooperation with USS *Tunny* sinks a cargo ship off Honshu.

An escort destroyer and several coastal defense vessels will later sink USS *Bonefish*.

U.S. submarine *Dentuda* torpedoes and sinks two Japanese guardboats in the East China Sea.

Navy PB4Y-2 Privateers continue aerial mining operations of Korean waters.

Mines dropped by Twentieth Air Force B-29s sink a transport, an auxiliary submarine chaser, and two cargo ships in the Inland Sea and the Shimonoseki Strait.

**PACIFIC, OKINAWA:** Reinforced by a battalion of the 22nd Marines from the 6th Marine Division, the 5th and 7th Marines of the 1st Marine Division break the Japanese defenses at Kunishi and Mezado Ridge. The Japanese left flank has been turned.

## June 19

**ALEUTIANS:** Eleventh Air Force sends a B-24 on the longest mission in theater, a 2,700-mile flight lasting over 15 hours and flying as far as Uruppu Island, Japan. The B-24 bombs a small convoy off Shimushu Bay, Shimushu Island. Aircrew reports one vessel sunk, one heavily damaged, and two set afire.

**CBI:** Fourteenth Air Force B-25 Mitchells and P-47 Thunderbolts attack a rail bridge. P-47s and P-51 Mustangs attack trucks, river traffic, highways, logistics storage sites, rail lines, bridges, troops, and targets of opportunity in southern and eastern China.

**ETO:** Eighth Air Force begins the redeployment of the headquarters of the 95th Bombardment Group (Heavy) to the United States.

**Southwest Pacific Area:** In the Philippines, Far East Air Force A-20 Havocs, P-38 Lightnings, and P-47 Thunderbolts support ground forces on Luzon in the Cagayan Valley and elsewhere.

In Formosa, B-24 Liberators bomb docks, warehouses, and rail yards at Kiirun, and B-25 Mitchells bomb railroad yards. P-51 Mustangs attack antiaircraft positions and bridges.

FEAF B-24 Liberators bomb fortifications and antiaircraft guns at Balikpapan while B-25 Mitchells attack airfields and other targets in north Borneo.

U.S. submarine *Bullhead* torpedoes and sinks a Japanese auxiliary sailing vessel in the Sunda Strait.

**Pacific:** Twentieth Air Force sends 136 B-29s to attack the Toyohashi urban area, destroying nearly two square miles of the city. Over 200 B-29s attack the Fukuoka urban area, destroying nearly 1.5 square miles of the city. Another 123 B-29s attack the Shizuoka urban area, destroying nearly 2.5 square miles of the city. One B-29 is lost. A total of 28 B-29s mine Shimonoseki Strait and the waters off Niigata, west-central Honshu, and Maizuru, south Honshu, Japan.

P-47 Thunderbolts from Ie Shima bomb the airfield on Tokuno Island, while 16 others patrol over Amami-O-Shima Island. Another 117 P-51 Mustangs from Iwo Jima sent against Kagamigahara airfield and Meiji, Japan, abort because of bad weather.

U.S. submarine *Cabezon* attacks a Japanese convoy and sinks a cargo ship southwest of Paramushiro, in the Kuriles.

U.S. submarine *Sea Dog* attacks a Japanese convoy off the northwest coast of Hokkaido, Japan, and sinks two cargo ships and damages a merchant vessel.

Navy PB4Y-2 Privateers continue aerial mining in Korean waters. Japanese antiaircraft fire damages all of the patrol bombers during the mission.

**Pacific, Okinawa:** The commander of the 96th Infantry Division, Major General Claudius M. Easley, is killed as he directs fire against Japanese positions. Large numbers of Japanese soldiers begin surrendering. The 305th Infantry Regiment of the 77th Infantry Division attacks into the Medeera pocket.

Technical Sergeant John Meagher, E Company, 305th Infantry Regiment, 77th Infantry Division, attacking Japanese defenses near Ozato, Okinawa, jumps on a tank supporting the infantry and points out targets to the tank crew even as bullets hit all around him. Spotting a Japanese soldier charging toward the tank with an explosive charge, Meagher jumps off the deck and meets the soldier head-on, killing him with his bayoneted rifle. He then takes a machine gun from the tank and moves forward to engage the enemy alone. Advancing while firing the machine gun from the hip, Meagher moves untouched through a deadly crossfire, shooting into a pillbox and eliminating the defenders. Attacking another pillbox, he runs out of ammunition, then uses the machine gun as a club to kill the six Japanese soldiers inside. His incredible courage and fearless attack against a determined enemy will win him the Medal of Honor.

**CENTRAL PACIFIC:** Seventh Air Force sends 22 B-24 Liberators from Guam to bomb the airfield on Marcus Island.

## June 20

**CBI:** The Mars Task Force is inactivated.

In China, 37 P-51 Mustangs attack rail, road, and river traffic, bridges, and general targets of opportunity around Liuchow, Kweilin, Hankow, Changsha, Hengshan, and Fort Bayard.

In French Indochina, B-25 Mitchells and P-51 Mustangs attack bridges and antiaircraft positions.

A mine laid by U.S. submarine *Ray* sinks a Japanese merchant tanker off the southern coast of French Indochina.

**ETO:** Eighth Air Force begins to redeploy the headquarters of the 401st Bombardment Group (Heavy) and its three subordinate B-17 squadrons to the United States.

**SOUTHWEST PACIFIC AREA:** In the Philippines, Far East Air Force A-20 Havocs, P-38 Lightnings, and P-47 Thunderbolts support ground forces on Luzon and support a guerrilla offensive in the central Cayagan Valley.

B-24 Liberators bomb an airfield on Formosa.

Fifth Air Force B-24 Liberators conduct a shipping sweep off the coast of Korea and sink a cargo ship off the southern coast of Korea.

In Borneo, FEAF B-24 Liberators bomb antiaircraft positions near Balikpapan.

U.S. submarine *Kraken* torpedoes and sinks a Japanese auxiliary sailing vessel in the Sunda Strait.

**PACIFIC:** Twentieth Air Force sends 14 P-47 Thunderbolts from Ie Shima to bomb and strafe vessels, buildings, a lighthouse, and a village on Amami Gunto Island and the airfield on Tokuno Island. Another 38 P-47s bomb the airfield at Omura and attack Tokuno as they return to base.

U.S. submarine *Tinosa* torpedoes and sinks two Japanese cargo ships in the Sea of Japan off Korea.

Mines dropped by Twentieth Air Force B-29s sink two cargo ships and a merchant tanker and damage three cargo ships in the Inland Sea, the west Honshu coast, and the Shimonoseki Strait.

Navy patrol bombers sink a Japanese cargo ship off Pusan, Korea.

Navy PB4Y-2 Privateers continue aerial mining of waters off Korea and receive heavy antiaircraft fire from Japanese warships.

Naval Task Group 12.4, commanded by Rear Admiral Ralph E. Jennings, sailing to Leyte from Pearl Harbor, attacks Wake Island. Aircraft from carriers USS *Hancock* and USS *Lexington* and from small carrier USS *Cowpens* bomb Japanese installations.

**PACIFIC, OKINAWA:** American troops capture 977 soldiers, the highest tally of Japanese surrenders during the war.

## June 21

**CBI:** Fourteenth Air Force P-51 Mustangs and P-38 Lightnings attack trucks, river traffic, highways, logistics storage sites, coastal shipping, rail lines, bridges, troops, and town areas in southern and eastern China and in French Indochina.

In French Indochina, 16 B-25 Mitchells bomb Japanese strongpoints, railyards and trains, damage a tunnel, and hit several barges.

**ETO:** Major General Westside T. Larson takes command of Eighth Air Force from Major General William E. Kepner.

**SOUTHWEST PACIFIC AREA:** A contingent of Rangers and Filipino guerrillas captures Aparri on the north coast of Luzon.

In the Philippines, Far East Air Force P-38 Lightnings and P-47 Thunderbolts support ground forces on Luzon in the Cagayan Valley and elsewhere.

On Formosa, P-38 Lightnings attack targets of opportunity along the west coast.

In Borneo, FEAF B-24 Liberators bomb the Balikpapan town area, airfields, and Japanese defenses at Sepinggang. B-25 Mitchells bomb the town of Keningau, while P-38 Lightnings attack the nearby airfield.

**PACIFIC:** During the night Twentieth Air Force sends 25 B-29s to mine the sea approaches off Nanao, west-central Honshu, and Osaka, Japan.

Navy PB4Y-2 Privateers from Okinawa continue aerial mining of waters off the Korea coast.

U.S. submarine *Parche* torpedoes and sinks a Japanese cargo ship off eastern Hokkaido, Japan. U.S. submarine *Piranha* torpedoes and damages a Japanese cargo ship off northeast Honshu, Japan.

**PACIFIC, OKINAWA:** The 32nd Infantry Regiment of the 7th Infantry Division captures Hill 89, the headquarters area of the Japanese Thirty-second Army, and the town of Mabuni, sealing off one of the three remaining pockets of resistance. The 5th Marines of the 1st Marine Division captures Hills 79 and 81, while the 96th Infantry Division breaks Japanese defenses around Medeera.

Kamikazes damage a destroyer escort and two seaplane tenders and sink a medium landing ship off Okinawa.

M4 Sherman tanks of the 769th Tank Battalion support the attack on Hill 89, the location of the Japanese Thirty-second Army headquarters during the final stages of the battle for Okinawa, June 21–22, 1945.

**Central Pacific:** Seventh Air Force sends 24 B-24 Liberators from Guam Island to bomb fuel oil storage and power plant buildings on Eten Island at Truk.

Japanese submarine *I-36* damages a landing craft repair ship north of Truk.

## June 22

**Aleutians:** Major General John B. Brooks takes command of Eleventh Air Force from Brigadier General Isaiah Davies.

**CBI:** Fourteenth Air Force B-25 Mitchells and P-47 Thunderbolts attack railyards, highways, river traffic, artillery, and other targets in southern and eastern China and French Indochina.

In French Indochina, 23 B-25 Mitchells and four P-47 Thunderbolts attack trucks, trains, and gun positions near Hanoi.

**ETO:** Eighth Air Force begins redeployment of the headquarters, 2nd Air Division, to the United States. The headquarters of the 384th Bombardment Group (Heavy) and 544th Bombardment Squadrons (Heavy) move from England to Istres, France, with their B-17s to move American soldiers to Casablanca, French Morocco, for return to the United States.

**Southwest Pacific Area:** In the Philippines, Far East Air Force A-20 Havocs, P-38 Lightnings, and P-47 Thunderbolts support ground forces on Luzon in the Cagayan Valley.

On Formosa, B-24 Liberators attack oil facilities. P-38 Lightnings attack town areas.

In Borneo, FEAF B-24 Liberators bomb gun positions and defenses near Balikpapan. B-25 Mitchells attack warehouses and buildings. P-38 Lightnings conduct dive-bomb runs on pillboxes.

**Pacific:** Twentieth Air Force sends 446 B-29s over targets on south Honshu Island, Japan, to attack the Kure Naval Arsenal, the Mitsubishi aircraft production facility, the Kawanishi aircraft production facility, the Mitsubishi and Kawasaki aircraft production facilities at Kagamigahara, and the Kawasaki aircraft production facility at Akashi. Five B-29s are lost. Two partially completed submarines are destroyed in the attack and an escort destroyer and submarine *RO-67* are damaged.

Over 40 P-47 Thunderbolts from Ie Shima fly combat patrols over Amami Gunto Island, Japan. Pilots report 11 Japanese aircraft destroyed.

U.S. submarine *Crevalle* torpedoes and damages a Japanese escort destroyer in the Sea of Japan. U.S. submarine *Parche* torpedoes and sinks a fishing boat in the Tsugaru Strait. U.S. submarine *Piranha* torpedoes and damages a coastal defense vessel off northeast Honshu, Japan.

Mines dropped by Twentieth Air Force B-29s sink four cargo ships and damage a transport in the Inland Sea, west Honshu, and the Shimonoseki Strait.

Navy PB4Y-2 Privateers from Okinawa continue aerial mining of waters off the Korean coast. PBM Mariner patrol bombers attack a lighthouse and shipping off the south coast of Korea.

**Pacific, Okinawa:** The 305th Infantry Regiment of the 96th Infantry Division gains control of Hill 85 near Medeera.

Kamikazes damage a high-speed minesweeper and a tank landing ship off Okinawa.

### June 23

**ALEUTIANS:** Eleventh Air Force sends two B-24 Liberators on a shipping sweep between Matsuwa and Paramushiru Islands in the Kuriles. Aircrews report one cargo ship sunk and one damaged. Aircrews also report one confirmed Japanese fighter kill in the air. Six other B-24s bomb Kataoka on Shimushu Island.

**CBI:** Fourteenth Air Force P-51 Mustangs strafe airfields near Canton.

In French Indochina, B-25 Mitchells bomb a bridge, and P-38 Lightnings bomb locomotives and a barracks area.

**ETO:** Eighth Air Force prepares to redeploy the headquarters of the 91st Bombardment Group (Heavy) and one of its B-17 squadrons to the United States.

**MEDITERRANEAN:** Twelfth Air Force prepares to redeploy the A-20 Havocs of the 85th and 86th Bombardment Squadrons (Light), 47th Bombardment Group (Light), to the United States.

**SOUTHWEST PACIFIC AREA:** In Luzon, paratroopers of the 11th Airborne Division land at Aparri and advance south to link with the 37th Infantry Division near Tuguegarao.

In the Philippines, Far East Air Force A-20 Havocs, P-38 Lightnings, and P-47 Thunderbolts support ground forces on Luzon in the Cagayan Valley.

FEAF sends over 150 B-24 Liberators, B-25 Mitchells, and P-38 Lightnings to attack gun emplacements and defensive positions near Balikpapan, Borneo.

U.S. submarine *Hardhead* torpedoes and sinks a Japanese auxiliary submarine chaser in the Java Sea, evades a counterattack by another auxiliary submarine chaser, then sinks it and another vessel.

**PACIFIC:** During the night Twentieth Air Force sends 26 B-29s to mine the waters off Karatsu and Fukuoka, west Kyushu, and Osaka and Niigata on west-central Honshu, Japan. One B-29 is lost.

A total of 38 P-47 Thunderbolts from Ie Shima bomb airfields at Hakata and Itazuke and attack two boats off Amami Gunto Island as they return to base. Other P-47s bomb Saitozaki airfield. One hundred P-51 Mustangs from Iwo Jima attack airfields at Kagamigahara and Hyakuri. Pilots report 19 confirmed kills, three probables, and 16 possibles in the air and 13 confirmed kills and 40 probables on the ground. Three P-51s are lost.

U.S. submarine *Tirante* torpedoes and sinks a Japanese sailing junk in the Yellow Sea near the coast of Korea.

Navy patrol bombers damage a Japanese cargo ship off Pusan, Korea.

**PACIFIC, OKINAWA:** General Joseph W. Stilwell takes command of Tenth Army. Japanese morale crumbles as unit cohesion is lost. Japanese soldiers begin purposely exposing themselves in order to be killed. American divisions begin a sweep to clear remaining positions, blast cave entrances, and collect prisoners.

**CENTRAL PACIFIC:** Major General Thomas D. Wattacke takes command of Seventh Air Force.

## June 24

**ALEUTIANS:** Eleventh Air Force sends two B-24 Liberators on a shipping sweep, but the bombers use radar to bomb Kurabu Cape on Paramushiru Island in the Kuriles.

**CBI:** Fourteenth Air Force B-25 Mitchells bomb bridges. P-47 Thunderbolts and P-51 Mustangs attack trucks, river traffic, highways, logistics storage sites, rail lines, and bridges in southern and eastern China.

**ETO:** Eighth Air Force begins to redeploy the headquarters of the 381st Bombardment Group (Heavy) and its three subordinate B-17 squadrons to the United States.

**SOUTHWEST PACIFIC AREA:** In the Eighth Army area, the 1st Battalion of the 155th Infantry Regiment, 31st Infantry Division, lands at the mouth of the Agusan River on Mindanao and moves to flank Japanese defenses from the east. They are resupplied entirely by air and attack Japanese units wherever they find them.

In the Philippines, Far East Air Force A-20 Havocs, P-38 Lightnings, and P-47 Thunderbolts support ground forces on Luzon.

In Borneo, FEAF B-24 Liberators bomb coastal guns and the town of Balikpapan and P-38 Lightnings also attack coastal guns. B-25 Mitchells bomb warehouses and an airfield.

**PACIFIC:** Twentieth Air Force sends 36 P-47 Thunderbolts from Ie Shima to attack boats and a village in the Sakishima Archipelago, a wharf on Kuro Island, Ishigaki Island, and buildings, villages, targets of opportunity, and several points in the Ryukyu Islands. The headquarters of the 507th Fighter Group and the P-47s of the 463rd, 464th, and 465th Fighter Squadrons arrive on Ie Shima from the United States.

U.S. submarine *Tirante* torpedoes and sinks a Japanese merchant sailing junk in the Yellow Sea off the coast of Korea.

Navy PB4Y-2 Privateers from Okinawa continue aerial mining of waters off the Korean coast. After completing the mining mission, the Privateers strafe rail lines, airports, and Japanese shipping. Pilots report a merchant ship a sunk.

**CENTRAL PACIFIC:** Seventh Air Force sends one B-24 from Guam Island to bomb buildings on Marcus Island; later another 18 B-24s bomb the airfield.

The headquarters of the 494th Bombardment Group (Heavy) and the B-24s of the 864th, 865th, 866th, and 867th Bombardment Squadrons (Heavy) redeploy from Angaur Island to Yontan on Okinawa.

## June 25

**CBI:** Fourteenth Air Force B-25 Mitchells attack bridges, railyards, and industrial targets. P-47 Thunderbolts and P-51 Mustangs attack road and rail lines, bridges, and troops in southern and eastern China.

**SOUTHWEST PACIFIC AREA:** In the Philippines, Far East Air Force B-25 Mitchells, A-20 Havocs, P-38 Lightnings, and P-47 Thunderbolts support ground forces on Luzon in the Cagayan Valley and elsewhere.

In Borneo, B-24 Liberators, B-25 Mitchells, and P-38 Lightnings attack oil facilities, shore defenses and an airfield near Balikpapan. B-24s bomb an airfield on Celebes Island.

**PACIFIC:** During the night Twentieth Air Force sends 26 B-29s to mine Shimonoseki Strait and the waters off Tsugaru Strait, Japan. Mines sink two Japanese cargo ships and damage an escort destroyer.

Navy PB4Y-2 Privateers from Okinawa, continue aerial mining of waters off the Korean coast. After completing the mining mission, the Privateers strafe lighthouses and Japanese shipping.

**CENTRAL PACIFIC:** Seventh Air Force sends three B-24 Liberators from Guam to bomb the airfield on Marcus Island.

### June 26

**CBI:** Chinese forces capture the airfield at Liuchow.

In China, Fourteenth Air Force sends 21 P-51 Mustangs to bomb and strafe road, river, and rail traffic, motor pools, gun positions, and buildings.

**ATLANTIC:** The United Nations conference ends in San Francisco. The UN Charter is signed by the 200 attending delegates.

**ETO:** Eighth Air Force begins to redeploy the headquarters of the 40th Bombardment Wing (Heavy) from England to Istres, France, to direct those units transporting troops from France to North Africa for return to the United States.

**SOUTHWEST PACIFIC AREA:** In the Philippines, Far East Air Force B-25 Mitchells, A-20 Havocs, P-38 Lightnings, and P-47 Thunderbolts support ground forces on Luzon in the Cagayan Valley and east of Manila.

During the night P-61 Black Widow night fighters hit a sugar refinery and B-24 Liberators follow up with a morning attack against the same target.

Japanese aircraft strafe a U.S. destroyer escort in Davao Gulf, Mindanao, Philippines.

In Borneo, FEAF B-24 Liberators and B-25 Mitchells attack oil targets and the airfield near Balikpapan. Other B-24s bomb the airfield at Limboeng, Celebes Island.

A U.S. motor minesweeper hits a mine off Balikpapan, Borneo, and is severely damaged. It is later scuttled.

**PACIFIC:** Twentieth Air Force sends 510 B-29s, escorted by 148 P-51 Mustangs, to attack aircraft production facilities, light-metals industries, and arsenals in southern Honshu and Shikoku. Six B-29s and one P-51 are lost. Aircrews report 20 Japanese fighters destroyed. P-51 pilots report two confirmed kills and five probables in the air. During the night 33 B-29s attack the Utsube Oil Refinery at Yokkaichi.

A naval task group, commanded by Captain Charles A. Buchanan, lands marines on Kume Jima in the Ryukyus.

Navy PB4Y-2 Privateers from Okinawa continue aerial mining of waters off the Korean coast.

Four U.S. destroyers sink three Japanese auxiliary submarine chasers and a guardboat and damage an auxiliary submarine chaser south of Onnekotan Island in the Kuriles.

U.S. submarine *Parche* attacks a Japanese convoy and sinks a gunboat and a cargo ship off southern Honshu, Japan. *Parche* survives a depth charge attack and, although damaged, remains on patrol.

**CENTRAL PACIFIC:** Seventh Air Force sends one B-24 from Guam to bomb the anti-aircraft positions on Marcus Island.

## June 27

**CBI:** Tenth Air Force begins to redeploy the headquarters of the 306th Bombardment Group (Heavy) and its three subordinate B-24 squadrons from China to India.

**SOUTHWEST PACIFIC AREA:** In the Philippines, Far East Air Force A-20 Havocs, P-38 Lightnings, and P-47 Thunderbolts support ground forces on Luzon and attack Japanese troop concentrations.

During the night FEAF B-24 Liberators bomb an airfield in Java. In Borneo, B-24s attack oil facilities and shore defenses near Balikpapan. B-25 Mitchells attack warehouses, other buildings, and the general waterfront area. B-24s bomb airfields on Celebes Island.

A U.S. destroyer hits a mine and suffers damage in Brunei Bay, Borneo. U.S. submarine *Blueback* torpedoes and sinks a Japanese submarine chaser in the Java Sea.

**PACIFIC:** During the night Twentieth Air Force sends 29 B-29s to mine the waters off Hagi, southwest Honshu, Niigata, west-central Honshu, Kobe and Osaka, southern Honshu, Japan.

Over 100 P-51 Mustangs from Iwo Jima are sent to attack the Kasumigaura, Imba, and Tsukuba airfields in the Tokyo area. Bad weather causes the mission to be aborted. P-47 Thunderbolts from Ie Shima attack shipping and a village on Kikai Island, Japan. Antiaircraft fire shoots down two P-47s. Other P-47s attack shipping off Kakeroma Island and vessels and targets of opportunity throughout the Sakishima Archipelago. During the night five P-61 Black Widow night fighters fly intruder attacks, hitting vessels off Amami Gunto Island and aircraft on Wan airfield.

Navy PB4Y-2 Privateers from Okinawa continue aerial mining of waters off the Korean coast.

Navy patrol bombers sink Japanese submarine *I-165* east of Saipan in the Marianas.

Navy patrol bombers damage a Japanese cargo vessel in the Sea of Japan near the Korea Straits.

**CENTRAL PACIFIC:** Seventh Air Force sends three B-24 Liberators from Guam Island to bomb the underground storage area and fortifications on Marcus Island. Another 18 B-24s attack the airfield on Moen Island at Truk.

## June 28

**CBI:** In China, Fourteenth Air Force B-25 Mitchells and P-51 Mustangs bomb the town of Changsha, troop concentrations and logistics storage areas, truck convoys and ammunition trains near Yoyang. Other P-51s attack gun emplacements, defensive positions, rail traffic, and a road bridge.

**SOUTHWEST PACIFIC AREA:** In the Philippines, Far East Air Force P-38 Lightnings and P-47 Thunderbolts support ground forces on Luzon.

B-24 Liberators bomb a butanol plant on Formosa.

In Borneo, FEAF B-24 Liberators bomb installations in the Manggar area and runways at Tabanio and Oelin. B-24s, B-25 Mitchells, and P-38 Lightnings attack Japanese defenses near Balikpapan. P-38s also make skip bombing attacks on oil storage areas. B-24s attack the airfields at Limboeng and Langoan on Celebes Island.

A U.S. motor minesweeper is damaged by a mine, and another motor minesweeper is hit by shore battery fire off Balikpapan.

**PACIFIC:** During the night Twentieth Air Force sends 487 B-29s to conduct incendiary bombing raids on Okayama (more than two square miles destroyed), Sasebo (less than one square mile destroyed), Moji (less than one square mile destroyed), Nobeoka (about a half square mile destroyed). P-47 Thunderbolts from Ie Shima attack shipping at Koniya, Japan, with rockets and bombs and attack Tokuno Island. Another 26 P-47s attack targets of opportunity on the Sakishima Archipelago.

Navy PB4Y-2 Privateers from Okinawa continue aerial mining of waters off the Korean coast.

**CENTRAL PACIFIC:** Seventh Air Force sends three B-24 Liberators from Guam Island to bomb a fuel storage area on Marcus Island.

U.S. destroyer attacks Japanese submarine *I-36* after it conducts an unsuccessful kaiten attack on a stores ship southeast of the Marianas. One *kaiten* is destroyed, and the submarine is damaged in the counterattack.

### June 29

**CBI:** Fourteenth Air Force B-25 Mitchells and P-47 Thunderbolts attack bridges. P-51 Mustangs attack gun emplacements, bridges, troops, and targets of opportunity in southern and eastern China.

**SOUTHWEST PACIFIC AREA:** In the Philippines, Far East Air Force B-25 Mitchells, A-20 Havocs, P-38 Lightnings, and P-47 Thunderbolts support ground forces on Luzon.

B-24 Liberators bomb an oil refinery on Formosa.

In Borneo, FEAF B-24 Liberators, B-25 Mitchells, and P-38 Lightnings bomb defensive positions and oil installations near Balikpapan. P-38s and B-24s bomb airfields.

**PACIFIC:** During the night Twentieth Air Force sends 32 B-29s to drop 209 tons of bombs on the Nippon Oil Company refinery at Kudamatsu, Japan. Another 25 B-29s mine the west Shimonoseki Strait and waters off Maizuru, southern Honshu, and Sakata, northwest Honshu, Japan. Mines dropped by Twentieth Air Force B-29s sink a cargo ship and damage a naval vessel and three cargo ships in the Inland Sea, the west coast of Honshu, and the Shimonoseki Strait.

P-47 Thunderbolts from Ie Shima attack airfields at Kanoya and Kushira on Kyushu Island, Japan, with rockets and machine-gun fire, and attack shipping. Pilots report seven small vessels sunk.

Navy PB4Y-2 Privateers from Okinawa continue aerial mining of waters off the Korean coast.

### June 30

**CBI:** The headquarters of Army Air Forces, China Theater is established. Lieutenant General George E. Stratemeyer is appointed as commander. The new command will consist of the subordinate elements: the Tenth and Fourteenth Air Forces, China Air Service Command, and the 8th Reconnaissance Group.

**ATLANTIC:** The navy's total personnel strength at this time is over 4 million (U.S. Navy: 3,383,196; Marine Corps: 476,709; Coast Guard: 171,192). The navy has 67,952 vessels of all types available for operations.

**SOUTHWEST PACIFIC AREA:** In the Eighth Army area, Lieutenant General Eichelberger reports to General MacArthur that organized resistance on Mindanao has ended, despite the fact that 22,000 Japanese soldiers are still actively resisting.

In the Philippines, Far East Air Force B-25 Mitchells, A-20 Havocs, P-38 Lightnings, and P-47 Thunderbolts support ground forces on Luzon in the Cagayan Valley and east of Manila.

During the night P-61 Black Widow night fighters hit a sugar refinery, and B-24 Liberators follow up with a morning attack against the same target.

FEAF B-24 Liberators attack targets near Balikpapan and B-25 Mitchells hit targets in northeast Borneo.

Fire from a shore battery damages a U.S. destroyer, and a U.S. minesweeper is damaged when it hits a mine off Balikpapan.

U.S. submarines *Baya* and *Capitaine* attack a Japanese convoy engaging a submarine chaser and sinking a cargo vessel in the Flores Sea.

**PACIFIC:** The 509th Composite Group begins combat flight training from Tinian as the aircrews prepare for an atomic bomb attack on Japan.

Navy PB4Y-2 Privateers from Okinawa continue aerial mining of waters off the Korean coast.

A Japanese escort destroyer is damaged when it hits a mine off Shimonoseki, Kyushu, Japan.

**CENTRAL PACIFIC:** Seventh Air Force sends two B-24 Liberators from Guam to bomb the boat basin on Marcus Island.

## July 1

**CBI:** In China, Fourteenth Air Force B-25 Mitchells bomb a bridge and ferry terminal, and P-47 Thunderbolts strafe an airfield, locomotives, and railyards. P-51 Mustangs attack a bridge. Chinese forces capture Liuchow.

Fifth Air Force aircraft sink a Japanese cargo ship at the mouth of the Yangtze River.

**ETO:** Eighth Air Force begins moving the B-17s of the 547th Bombardment Squadron (Heavy), 384th Bombardment Group (Heavy), from England to Istres, France, to move troops from the European theater to North Africa en route to the United States.

Over the vehement protests of Prime Minister Churchill, U.S. forces begin a withdrawal from central and southern Germany to their designated occupation zones. The territory abandoned will be part of the Soviet occupation zone. Churchill believes that no British or American troops should give up any territory to the Soviets until there is assurance that Stalin will abide by the Yalta agreements for free and open elections in the liberated areas of Europe. President Truman, still following Roosevelt's conciliatory policy toward the Soviets, argues that the Soviets will abide by their agreements if they see the United States living up to its obligations. Churchill worries that the Americans and British will arrive at the upcoming Potsdam conference with no bargaining position with the Soviets.

**MEDITERRANEAN:** Fifteenth Air Force begins to redeploy the headquarters of the 461st and 454th Bombardment Groups (Heavy) and each of their three subordinate B-24 squadrons to the United States. The headquarters of the 301st Bombardment Group (Heavy) and its three subordinate B-17 squadrons are also scheduled to return to the United States.

**SOUTHWEST PACIFIC AREA:** Eighth Army takes responsibility for the Philippines from Sixth Army. Eighth Army under Lieutenant General Eichelberger takes operational control of X Corps and XIV Corps and the 6th, 31st, 32nd, 38th, 24th, 37th, and 93rd Infantry Divisions. (The 93rd Infantry Division is at Morotai and New Guinea.) Sixth Army under Lieutenant General Krueger has operational control of I Corps and XI Corps and a new headquarters for IX Corps. Krueger takes operational control of the 11th Airborne and the 1st Cavalry Divisions and the 33rd, 41st, 40th, and 43rd Infantry Divisions. The 81st Infantry Division, which arrived in May, is added to Sixth Army, as is the 77th Infantry Division, which will return from Okinawa on July 15. Eighth Army takes over operations on Luzon, and Sixth Army prepares to undergo refitting and training for the invasion of Japan.

In the Philippines, Far East Air Force P-38 Lightnings and P-47 Thunderbolts support ground forces on Luzon, attacking troops and gun positions.

In Borneo, FEAF B-24 Liberators bomb defenses at Balikpapan as Australian forces conduct an amphibious landing in the area. B-24s, B-25 Mitchells, and P-38 Lightnings attack airfields. B-24 Liberators attack airfields on Celebes Island.

Naval Task Group 78.2, commanded by Rear Admiral Albert G. Noble, lands units of the 7th Australian Division at Balikpapan. The landing is supported by naval gunfire and air attack.

**PACIFIC:** Twentieth Air Force sends 152 B-29s to attack the Kure urban area, destroying over one square mile of the city. Another 154 B-29s attack the Kumamato urban area. Nearly three square miles of the city is destroyed. One B-29 is lost. A total of 100 B-29s bomb the Ube urban area, destroying less than one square mile of the city. Another 126 B-29s attack the Shimonoseki urban area, destroying about one-half square mile of the city. One B-29 is lost. B-29s mine Shimonoseki Strait and the waters off Nanao, west-central Honshu, Japan. Mines sink a Japanese cargo ship at the entrance of Niigata harbor, west-central Honshu, and damage two cargo ships in the Inland Sea, Japan.

Nearly 148 P-51 Mustangs from Iwo Jima attack airfields in the Nagoya area. Pilots report two confirmed kills in the air and three confirmed kills and seven probables on the ground. Two P-51s are lost.

Navy PB4Y-2 Privateers from Okinawa continue aerial mining of waters off the Korean coast.

U.S. submarine *Haddo* torpedoes and sinks a Japanese coastal defense vessel and three cargo ships in the Yellow Sea off the west coast of Korea.

**CENTRAL PACIFIC:** Seventh Air Force sends two B-24 Liberators from Guam to bomb buildings on Marcus Island. B-25 Mitchells, operating in two flights from Okinawa, bomb an airfield on Kyushu Island, Japan.

The headquarters of VII Bomber Command prepares to redeploy from Saipan to Okinawa.

## July 2

**CBI:** In China, Fourteenth Air Force sends 28 P-51 Mustangs to attack rail, river, and road traffic, bridges, and buildings around Hengyang, Hankow, and Yoyang. The fighters attack a Japanese headquarters near Changsha and bomb a troop concentration and buildings at Yangan.

**ATLANTIC:** Secretary of War Henry Stimson, concerned that the invasion of the Japanese home islands will result in far greater casualties than Okinawa, appeals to the president to make some adjustment of the Allied demand for Japan's unconditional surrender.

**ETO:** Eighth Air Force begins moving the B-17s of the 545th Bombardment Squadron (Heavy), 384th Bombardment Group (Heavy), from England to Istres, France, to transport troops from the European theater to North Africa en route to the United States.

Ninth Air Force begins to redeploy the headquarters of the 405th Fighter Group and its three P-47 fighter squadrons from Germany to the United States.

**SOUTHWEST PACIFIC AREA:** In the Philippines, Far East Air Force P-38 Lightnings and P-47 Thunderbolts attack Japanese positions on Luzon.

B-24 Liberators bomb an airfield on Formosa.

In Borneo, FEAF B-24 Liberators bomb defenses in the Balikpapan area, and P-38 Lightnings support Australian forces as they complete the capture of Balikpapan and its oil installations. B-25 Mitchells attack troops near Bintula.

**PACIFIC:** During the night Twentieth Air Force sends 39 B-29s to bomb an oil refinery at Minoshima.

U.S. submarine *Apogon* torpedoes and damages two Japanese auxiliary submarine chasers off the Kuriles.

U.S. submarine *Barb* conducts a rocket bombardment of Japanese shore installations at Kaihyo Island off the Kamchatka Peninsula. This is the first successful use of rockets against shore positions by an American submarine.

U.S. submarines *Haddo* and *Paddle* attack Japanese shipping in the Yellow Sea, sinking one cargo vessel and damaging another.

Mines sink a Japanese auxiliary submarine chaser northwest of Kyushu in the Tsushima Strait.

Navy patrol bombers sink a Japanese sailing vessel off the west coast of Korea and a cargo ship in the Yellow Sea south of Korea.

**PACIFIC, OKINAWA:** General Joseph Stilwell declares Okinawa secured. Japanese aircraft attack U.S. ships off Okinawa. No damage is reported.

The total American casualties for the Okinawa campaign are staggering—49,151, with over 12,000 Americans killed. This represents a loss rate of 35 percent of the forces engaged. Tenth Army losses are 7,374 killed and 32,000 wounded and missing. The navy has lost 36 ships sunk and 368 damaged. Nearly 5,000 sailors are lost, and another 4,800 are injured. Air losses number 763 aircraft. The Japanese losses are estimated at between 95,000 and 110,000, with 7,400 captured. Civilian casualties are unknown but are estimated between 42,000 and 60,000.

**CENTRAL PACIFIC:** Seventh Air Force sends three B-24 Liberators from Guam to bomb the radar installation on Marcus Island.

The headquarters 11th Bombardment Group (Heavy) and the B-24 Liberators of the 26th, 98th, and 431st Bombardment Squadrons (Heavy) redeploy from Guam to Okinawa along with the headquarters of the 319th Bombardment Group (Light) and the A-26 Invaders of the 437th, 439th, and 440th Bombardment Squadrons (Light) arriving at Kadena on Okinawa from the United States.

### July 3

**CBI:** Fourteenth Air Force B-25 Mitchells attack bridges. P-47 Thunderbolts and P-51 Mustangs attack trucks, highways, bridges, and troops as Japanese forces retreat to the east.

In French Indochina, P-47s and P-51s attack shipping, a cement plant, an airfield, and a barracks area near Haiphong.

**ETO:** Eighth Air Force begins to redeploy the three subordinate B-24 squadrons of the 458th Bombardment Group (Heavy) to the United States.

Vice Admiral Robert L. Ghormley, commander of U.S. Naval Forces, Germany, establishes headquarters at Frankfurt am Main, Germany.

**SOUTHWEST PACIFIC AREA:** In the Philippines, Far East Air Force P-38 Lightnings and P-47 Thunderbolts attack Japanese areas of resistance on Luzon.

Fifth Air Force P-51 Mustangs fly their first mission over Japan, destroying floatplanes in the Fukuoka harbor area on Kyushu.

In Borneo, FEAF B-24 Liberators bomb an airfield near Kuching and defensive positions near Balikpapan in support of Australian ground forces. On Celebes Island, B-24s bomb airfields.

The 868th Bombardment Squadron (Heavy), Thirteenth Air Force, redeploys from Morotai Island in New Guinea to Leyte Island with B-24 Liberators. This squadron is capable of conducting low-level night attacks and conducting Pathfinder missions, using radar to locate bomb release points for other bombers.

**PACIFIC:** Twentieth Air Force sends 509 B-29s to conduct incendiary strikes on urban areas of Japan and mining operations off the Japanese coast. Twentieth Air Force sends 31 B-29s to mine Shimonoseki Strait and the waters off Maizuru, southern Honshu, Japan.

Takamatsu, Kochi, Himeji, and Tokushima urban areas are bombed with incendiaries, destroying between 48 and 78 percent of the cities. A total of three B-29s are lost.

The remaining units of Twentieth Air Force's XX Bomber Command depart India by ship enroute to the Marianas.

**CENTRAL PACIFIC:** Seventh Air Force sends two B-24 Liberators from Guam to attack water storage buildings on Marcus Island. A total of 36 B-25 Mitchells from Okinawa, operating in two flights, attack Chiran airfield, Japan. The A-26 Invaders of 438th Bombardment Squadron (Light), 319th Bombardment Group (Light), arrive at Kadena, Okinawa, from the United States.

## July 4

**ALEUTIANS:** Eleventh Air Force sends eight B-24 Liberators using radar to locate bomb release points and conduct napalm strikes on the Kataoka naval base on Shimushu Island.

**CBI:** Fourteenth Air Force sends 30 P-51 Mustangs and P-38 Lightnings over French Indochina to attack docks and shipping at Haiphong and boat traffic on the Red River.

**ETO:** Eighth Air Force begins to redeploy the headquarters of the 446th Bombardment Group (Heavy) and its three subordinate B-24 squadrons to the United States.

**SOUTHWEST PACIFIC AREA:** In the Philippines, Far East Air Force P-38 Lightnings and P-47 Thunderbolts support ground forces on Luzon in the Cagayan Valley and attack Japanese positions on Bataan Island.

Fifth Air Force P-51 Mustangs fly a sweep along the west coast of Kyushu Island, Japan.

In Borneo, FEAF B-24 Liberators attack Japanese positions near Balikpapan. On Celebes Island, B-24 Liberators bomb a seaplane base and airfields.

**PACIFIC:** Twentieth Air Force sends 159 P-51 Mustangs from Iwo Jima to attack the Yokosuka naval base and airfields in the Tokyo area. Pilots report nine confirmed kills and 25 probables on the ground. One P-51 is lost.

Naval Task Force 32, commanded by Rear Admiral Jesse B. Oldendorf, with three battleships, two heavy cruisers, a light cruiser, four escort carriers, 11 destroyers, and four destroyer escorts, departs Buckner Bay, Okinawa, to provide cover for a minesweeping operation.

A U.S. destroyer intercepts a Japanese hospital ship evacuating sick and injured troops from Wake Island. The condition of the casualties indicates that the garrison is suffering greatly.

U.S. submarine *Tirante* torpedoes and sinks two Japanese guardboats in the Yellow Sea.

Mines damage a Japanese transport southeast of Shimonoseki, northwest Kyushu, and damage a cargo ship off Osaka.

**CENTRAL PACIFIC:** Seventh Air Force sends three B-24 Liberators from Guam to attack antiaircraft positions on Marcus Island.

## July 5

**CBI:** In China, Fourteenth Air Force P-51 Mustangs attack bridges, docks, and rail and river traffic.

In French Indochina, B-25 Mitchells sink small vessels and damage several larger vessels at Haiphong. P-51 Mustangs attack shipping.

**ETO:** Eighth Air Force begins to redeploy the headquarters of the 448th Bombardment Group (Heavy) and its three subordinate B-24 squadrons to the United States. The headquarters of the 491st Bombardment Group (Heavy) and its three subordinate B-24 squadrons are also scheduled to return to the United States, along with the B-24s of the 707th Bombardment Squadron (Heavy), 446th Bombardment Group (Heavy).

**SOUTHWEST PACIFIC AREA:** General of the Army Douglas MacArthur announces the liberation of the Philippines.

In the Philippines, Far East Air Force P-38 Lightnings and P-47 Thunderbolts support ground forces on Luzon.

B-24 Liberators bomb town areas, logistics storage areas, and airfields on Formosa.

Fifth Air Force P-51 Mustangs sweep Kyushu Island, Japan, and strafe targets of opportunity; pilots report several Japanese aircraft shot down.

In Borneo, FEAF B-24 Liberators bomb targets in support of Australian ground forces as they cross Balikpapan Bay.

U.S. submarines *Lizardfish* and *Puffer* bombard Japanese port facilities and shipping off the north coast of Bali. USS *Lizardfish* sinks an auxiliary submarine chaser and another vessel, as well as several barges and landing craft. USS *Puffer* destroys two cargo vessels south of Bali.

**PACIFIC:** Seventh Air Force sends 46 B-24 Liberators and 24 B-25 Mitchells from Okinawa to bomb an airfield and towns in the Omura-Nagasaki area of Japan.

Twentieth Air Force sends 100 P-51 Mustangs from Iwo Jima to attack airfields in the Tokyo area. Pilots report five confirmed kills and 11 probables on the ground.

Naval Task Force 39, commanded by Rear Admiral Alexander Sharp, with seven light minelayers, 52 minesweepers, six high-speed minesweepers, 49 motor minesweepers, and seven netlayers, begins minesweeping operations in the East China Sea.

U.S. submarine *Barb* torpedoes and sinks a Japanese cargo ship southwest of Sakhalin Island.

Mines sink a Japanese transport off western Kyushu and a merchant tanker off west-central Honshu and damage three cargo ships near Shimonoseki, Japan.

## July 6

**CBI:** Lieutenant General George E. Stratemeyer assumes command of Army Air Forces, China Theater.

**ETO:** Eighth Air Force begins to redeploy the headquarters of the 466th Bombardment Group (Heavy) and its four subordinate B-24 squadrons to the United States.

**SOUTHWEST PACIFIC AREA:** In the Philippines, Far East Air Force P-38 Lightnings and P-47 Thunderbolts support ground forces on Luzon.

Fifth Air Force P-51 Mustangs from Okinawa attack transportation targets in the Kagoshima Bay area of Japan.

B-24 Liberators bomb airfields, and A-26 Invaders attack railyards on Formosa.

In Borneo, FEAF B-24 Liberators bomb warehouses, buildings, shipyards, and areas near Balikpapan and Manggar.

**PACIFIC:** Twentieth Air Force sends 517 B-29s to attack urban areas of Japan with incendiaries and attack an oil refinery with high-explosive bombs. The cities of Chiba, Akashi, Shimizu, and Kofu are bombed and 43 to 65 percent of the urban areas are destroyed. One B-29 is lost. B-29s drop 500-pound bombs on the oil refinery at Wakayama. 110 P-51 Mustangs from Iwo Jima attack airfields in the Tokyo area. Pilots report one confirmed kill in the air and six confirmed kills and 25 probables on the ground. One P-51 is lost.

Mines sink two cargo ships near Shimonoseki and damage an auxiliary submarine chaser off Niigata harbor and damage three cargo ships off west-central Honshu, Japan.

## July 7

**CBI:** Fourteenth Air Force P-47 Thunderbolts and P-51 Mustangs attack trucks, highways, logistics storage sites, bridges, and troops in southern and eastern China.

**ATLANTIC:** President Harry S. Truman, Secretary of State James F. Byrnes, and Fleet Admiral William D. Leahy board the heavy cruiser USS *Augusta* for Antwerp, Belgium, en route to Potsdam, Germany.

**SOUTHWEST PACIFIC AREA:** In the Philippines, Far East Air Force B-25 Mitchells, P-38 Lightnings, and P-47 Thunderbolts support ground forces on Luzon, attacking troop concentrations.

B-24 Liberators bomb airfields on Formosa.

In Borneo, FEAF B-24 Liberators, B-25 Mitchells, and P-38 Lightnings support Australian ground forces near Balikpapan.

**PACIFIC:** Twentieth Air Force sends more than 100 P-51 Mustangs from Iwo Jima to attack airfields in the Tokyo area; they abort the mission due to bad weather.

U.S. submarine *Trepang* torpedoes and sinks a Japanese cargo ship off southern Hokkaido, Japan.

Mines sink two Japanese cargo ships off the coast of west-central Korea. Mines damage a merchant tanker in Osaka harbor.

The headquarters of XX Bomber Command arrives at Okinawa from India. The headquarters of the 414th Fighter Group and the P-47 Thunderbolts of the 413th, 437th, and 456th Fighter Squadrons arrive at Iwo Jima from the United States. The squadrons' first missions are scheduled for mid-July.

## July 8

**CBI:** Fourteenth Air Force B-25 Mitchells and P-47 Thunderbolts attack bridges. P-38 Lightnings, P-47s, and P-51 Mustangs attack river traffic, highways, logistics storage sites, and troops in southern and eastern China and in French Indochina.

**ETO:** Eighth Air Force begins to redeploy the headquarters of the 492nd Bombardment Group (Heavy) to the United States.

**SOUTHWEST PACIFIC AREA:** In the Philippines, Far East Air Force P-38 Lightnings and P-51 Mustangs support ground forces on Luzon and attack troops and logistics storage sites.

B-24 Liberators bomb an airfield and P-38 Lightnings attack an oil production area on Formosa.

The P-47s of the 69th and 311th Fighter Squadrons, 58th Fighter Group, Fifth Air Force, redeploy from Luzon to Okinawa.

In Borneo, FEAF B-24 Liberators and B-25 Mitchells, supporting Australian forces, attack Japanese defensive positions near Balikpapan and attack shipyards, road traffic, and warehouses. U.S. and Australian B-24s bomb warehouses on Celebes Island.

**PACIFIC:** Twentieth Air Force sends more than 100 P-51 Mustangs from Iwo Jima to attack airfields and other targets at Hyakuri, Chofu, Tokorozawa, and Yachimata, Japan. Pilots report five confirmed kills and 25 other aircraft destroyed on the ground. Eight P-51s are lost.

U.S. submarine *Sea Robin* torpedoes and sinks a Japanese auxiliary submarine chaser in the East China Sea. U.S. submarine *Tirante* torpedoes and sinks a Japanese passenger-cargo ship near Dairen, Korea.

## July 9

**CBI:** Fourteenth Air Force B-25 Mitchells attack bridges. P-38 Lightnings and P-51 Mustangs attack river traffic, rail lines, and bridges in southern and eastern China and in French Indochina.

**SOUTHWEST PACIFIC AREA:** In the Philippines, Far East Air Force P-51 Mustangs and P-38 Lightnings support ground forces on Luzon in the Cagayan Valley.

B-24 Liberators bomb airfields and A-26 Invaders attack a town on Formosa.

The headquarters of the 348th Fighter Group and the P-51s of the 340th Fighter Squadron redeploy from Luzon to Ie Shima. The P-47s of the 310th Fighter Squadron, 58th Fighter Group, redeploy from Luzon to Okinawa.

U.S. submarine *Bluefish* torpedoes and sinks a Japanese auxiliary submarine chaser off the east coast of Malaya.

In Borneo, FEAF B-24 Liberators and P-38 Lightnings support Australian forces, attacking Japanese defensive positions and troops near Balikpapan, Manggar, and Sepinggang as Australian and Dutch forces complete the encirclement of Balikpapan Bay. B-24s also bomb the Samarinda shipyards; and B-25 Mitchells, in support of operations in the Brunei Bay area, bomb Japanese troop concentrations.

A U.S. motor minesweeper is sunk by a mine off Balikpapan.

**PACIFIC:** Seventh Air Force sends 43 B-24 Liberators from Okinawa to bomb an airfield on Kyushu, Japan. Over 50 B-25 Mitchells from Okinawa attack an airfield on Tokuno Shima in the Amami Islands.

During the night 29 B-29s of Twentieth Air Force mine Shimonoseki Strait and the waters off Niigata and Nanao, west-central Honshu. One B-29 is lost. Mines sink a cargo ship off western Kyushu, Japan, and damage another cargo ship. Mines also damage a cargo ship off Shimonoseki and a merchant tanker in Kobe harbor.

A total of 475 B-29s attack Senai, Sakai, Wakayama, and Gifu urban areas, destroying 27 to 74 percent of the sites bombed with incendiaries. Two B-29s are lost. Over 60 B-29s attack the oil refinery at Yokkaichi. Over 100 P-51 Mustangs from Iwo Jima attack airfields at Itami, Hamamatsu, Aichi, and Washinomiya. Pilots report one confirmed kill in the air and 15 confirmed kills and five probables on the ground. Three P-51s are lost.

## July 10

**ALEUTIANS:** Eleventh Air Force sends four B-24 Liberators to bomb Shimushu Island, using radar to assist in identifying the bomb release points.

**CBI:** In China, Fourteenth Air Force P-51 Mustangs and P-38 Lightnings bomb warehouses and attack railroad targets of opportunity and bridges.

In French Indochina, B-25 Mitchells bomb the town areas and rail targets.

**ETO:** Ninth Air Force begins the redeployment of the headquarters of the 358th Fighter Group and two of its subordinate P-47 fighter squadrons from Rheims, France, to the United States.

**SOUTHWEST PACIFIC AREA:** In the Philippines, Far East Air Force B-25 Mitchells, A-20 Havocs, P-51 Mustangs, P-38 Lightnings, and P-47 Thunderbolts support ground forces on Luzon in the Cagayan Valley and attack Japanese defensive positions east of Manila.

B-24 Liberators bomb an airfield and warehouses on Formosa. Aircrews report several aircraft are destroyed on the ground.

The headquarters of the 58th Fighter Group moves from Luzon to Okinawa.

In Borneo, FEAF B-24 Liberators attack the town of Muarakaman and an airfield. P-38 Lightnings strafe numerous targets of opportunity. B-24s bomb the warehouse area on Celebes Island.

**PACIFIC:** During the night Seventh Air Force sends one B-24 from Okinawa to bomb Karasehara airfield, Japan. Another 43 B-24s from Okinawa bomb Wan and Sateku airfields on Kikaiga-shima, in the Amami Islands. Over 50 B-25 Mitchells bomb Wan airfield and Saha-Saki on Nakano Shima in the Ryukyus, and Kurume on Kyushu, Japan.

Twentieth Air Force sends 102 P-51 Mustangs from Iwo Jima to attack airfields in Japan. Three fighters are lost.

Carrier aircraft from Vice Admiral John S. McCain's Task Force 38 attack airfields in and around Tokyo.

U.S. submarine *Hammerhead* torpedoes and sinks a Japanese cargo ship and a merchant tanker in the Gulf of Siam. U.S. submarine *Lionfish* attacks Japanese submarine *I-162* east of Kyushu but fails to do any damage. U.S. submarine *Runner* torpedoes and sinks a Japanese minesweeper off northern Honshu, Japan. U.S. submarine *Sea Robin* torpedoes and sinks a Japanese cargo ship off the southwest coast of Korea.

Mines dropped by B-29s sink Japanese cargo ship west of Kyushu and damage a merchant vessel west of Osaka harbor.

## July 11

**ALEUTIANS:** Eleventh Air Force sends five B-24 Liberators using radar to locate bomb release points as they attack Kataoka on Shimushu Island. Four B-25 Mitchells fly a shipping sweep and bomb a fishery.

**CBI:** In China, Fourteenth Air Force sends 25 P-51 Mustangs and P-40s to attack bridges, troops, gun positions, rail and river traffic, and coastal shipping.

**ETO:** Eighth Air Force begins to redeploy the headquarters of the 93rd Bombardment Wing (Heavy) and its three subordinate B-17 squadrons to the United States.

Ninth Air Force redeploys the P-47s of the 366th Fighter Squadron, 358th Fighter Group, to begin a movement from France to the United States.

**SOUTHWEST PACIFIC AREA:** In the Philippines, Far East Air Force B-25 Mitchells, P-51 Mustangs, P-38 Lightnings, and P-47 Thunderbolts support ground forces on Luzon in the Cagayan Valley and B-24 Liberators bomb Japanese troop concentrations on Negros Island.

P-51s sweep Kyushu, Japan.

B-24s bomb an airfield on Formosa.

In Borneo, FEAF B-25 Mitchells and P-38 Lightnings attack targets on highways near Balikpapan.

**PACIFIC:** During the night Seventh Air Force sends two B-24 Liberators from Okinawa to attack airfields on Kyushu, Japan.

During the night Twentieth Air Force sends 25 B-29s to mine Shimonoseki Strait and Maizuru, southern Honshu, Japan, and the waters off Najin and Pusan, Korea. Mines sink Japanese escort destroyer *Sakura* off Osaka. Mines also sink a cargo ship and damage a merchant vessel off southwest Honshu, Japan. U.S. submarine *Barb* torpedoes and sinks a Japanese guardboat and another vessel off Hokkaido. U.S. submarine *Kingfish* torpedoes and sinks a Japanese fishing boat off east-central Honshu, Japan.

Two B-29s mine Pusan and Najin in Korea.

## July 12

**ALEUTIANS:** Eleventh Air Force sends four B-25 Mitchells on a shipping sweep. Aircrews report bombing and strafing a cargo ship. One B-25 is lost.

**CBI:** In China, Fourteenth Air Force B-25 Mitchells bomb supply convoys moving through the Siang Chiang Valley. P-51 Mustangs and P-38 Lightnings attack bridges, river and road traffic, barracks, and coastal shipping.

**ETO:** Eighth Air Force begins redeployment of the headquarters of the 95th Combat Bombardment Wing (Heavy) from England to the United States.

**MEDITERRANEAN:** Twelfth Air Force deactivates the headquarters of the XII Air Forces Service Command.

**SOUTHWEST PACIFIC AREA:** In the XIV Corps area, where the 6th, 32nd, 37th, and 38th Infantry Divisions have been given responsibility for eliminating Japanese forces from northern Luzon, the 6th Infantry Division captures Kiangan. The 37th Infantry Division, with support from Philippine guerrillas, patrols into the dense mountain forests of the Sierra Madre Mountains to locate Japanese defenders. Many are discovered sick or starving. The 32nd Infantry Division also attacks into the Kiangan Pocket, destroying isolated units. These small combat actions will continue until the Japanese surrender.

The capture of Luzon and Leyte and the other islands of the Philippines, occupied by 380,000 Japanese soldiers, will prevent them from having any opportunity to be redeployed for the defense of the home islands. On Luzon alone, over 180,000 Japanese soldiers are lost, representing some of the finest units of the empire. American casualties on Luzon total over 37,000 with over 8,000 killed. Nonbattle casualties total 93,400 men.

In the Eighth Army area, the 1st Battalion of the 21st Infantry Regiment, 24th Infantry Division, lands at Sarangani Bay to clear Japanese forces from the area. The fierce jungle battle will continue until the end of the war, with 14 Americans killed and 13 wounded. Japanese casualties number over 400 killed and 25 captured.

In the Philippines, Far East Air Force P-51 Mustangs, P-38 Lightnings, and P-47 Thunderbolts attack Japanese strongpoints, troop concentrations, and support ground forces east of Manila. The 6th Infantry Division captures Kiangan. B-24 Liberators bomb troop concentrations on Negros Island.

Fifth Air Force P-51 Mustangs sweep Kyushu, Japan. B-24s bomb Canton, China.

B-24s bomb town areas on Formosa, while A-26 Invaders and P-51 Mustangs attack other targets.

Fifth Air Force redeploys the P-51s of the 341st, 342nd, and 460th Fighter Squadrons, 348th Fighter Group, from Luzon to Ie Shima.

In Borneo, FEAF B-24 Liberators destroy a barracks. Other B-24s attack warehouses on Celebes Island.

**PACIFIC:** Seventh Air Force sends 47 B-24 Liberators from Okinawa to attack the airfield on Kikaiga-shima in the Amami Islands. During the night other B-24s bomb airfields on Kyushu. B-25 Mitchells and A-26 Invaders bomb an airfield and the town areas on Kyushu, and other B-25s bomb an airfield on Tokuno Shima in the Amami Islands. A-26 Invaders also attack the Ibusuki seaplane station.

During the night Twentieth Air Force sends 453 B-29s to conduct incendiary raids on Japanese cities. The Utsunomiya, Ichinomiya, Tsuruga, and Uwajima urban areas suffer heavy damage, destroying large sections of the cities. Three B-29s are lost. Another 53 B-29s attack the Kawasaki Petroleum Center, destroying about 25 percent of the target; two B-29s are lost.

A Japanese salvage ship and cargo ship are sunk by mines off west-central Honshu, Japan. A cargo vessel hits a mine and sinks off Osaka harbor. A cargo ship and tanker hit mines and sink off southeast Honshu, and two cargo ships are damaged off Niigata, west-central Honshu.

## July 13

**CBI:** Fourteenth Air Force sends 14 B-25 Mitchells and 12 P-51 Mustangs to attack bridges, railyards, antiaircraft guns, and targets of opportunity in China and French Indochina. P-51s and P-38 Lightnings attack river shipping, buildings, and road and rail targets in both China and French Indochina.

**ETO:** Eighth Air Force begins to redeploy the headquarters of the 92nd Bombardment Wing (Heavy) to the United States.

**SOUTHWEST PACIFIC AREA:** In the Philippines, Far East Air Force B-25 Mitchells, P-51 Mustangs, P-38 Lightnings, and P-47 Thunderbolts attack pillboxes, ammunition storage areas, and vehicles on Luzon. B-24 Liberators bomb troop concentrations on Negros Island.

B-24s bomb storage areas at Canton, China.

On Formosa, B-24s bomb boat yards and buildings and A-26 Invaders attack railyards.

In Borneo, FEAF P-38 Lightnings attack gun positions. Other P-38 Lightnings sweep Celebes Island and attack vehicles and communication targets.

**PACIFIC:** Naval Task Force 95, commanded by Rear Admiral Francis S. Low, with two cruisers, four light cruisers, and nine destroyers departs Leyte Gulf to conduct anti-shipping sweeps in the East China Sea northwest of Okinawa. Naval Task Force 93, commanded by Rear Admiral John H. Brown, Jr., with two light cruisers and five destroyers, begins an anti-shipping sweep down the Kurile Islands into the Sea of Okhotsk.

During the night Twentieth Air Force sends 30 B-29s to mine Shimonoseki Strait and the waters off western Korea, and Fukuoka, on west Kyushu, Japan. Mines from the B-29s sink two cargo ships off western Kyushu and damage two cargo ships near Shimonoseki Strait.

## July 14

**CBI:** Fourteenth Air Force P-38 Lightnings and P-51 Mustangs attack trucks, river traffic, highways, logistics storage sites, rail lines, and bridges in both China and French Indochina.

**MEDITERRANEAN:** Twelfth Air Force begins to redeploy the headquarters of the 350th Fighter Group and its three subordinate P-47 fighter squadrons from Italy to the United States.

**SOUTHWEST PACIFIC AREA:** In the Philippines, Far East Air Force P-51 Mustangs and P-38 Lightnings support ground forces and attack Japanese positions on Luzon. B-24 Liberators support ground forces on Negros Island.

A-26 Invaders attack a refinery and warehouse area; P-51 Mustangs attack rail targets on Formosa. P-47 Thunderbolts sweep the north China coast and attack coastal cargo vessels.

On Celebes Island, FEAF B-24 Liberators bomb airfields and a Japanese headquarters.

**PACIFIC:** The U.S. Navy bombards the home islands of Japan for the first time. Naval Task Unit 34.8.1, commanded by Rear Admiral John F. Shafroth, with three battleships, two heavy cruisers, and nine destroyers attacks the coastal city of Kamaishi, northeast Honshu, hitting the Japan Ironworks production facility.

Carrier aircraft from TF 38 bomb shipping, rail facilities, and ground installations in northern Honshu and Hokkaido, Japan. Aircraft sink an escort destroyer, two coastal defense vessels, a submarine chaser, four auxiliary minesweepers, five guardboats, a gunboat, a transport, and 11 cargo ships all around the Tsugaru Straits, Hakodate, and southern Hokkaido, Japan. A destroyer, two coastal defense vessels, two auxiliary minesweepers, an auxiliary submarine chaser, a guardboat, 11 cargo ships and two tankers are also damaged in the same area.

Mines sink two Japanese cargo ships near Shimonoseki.

The headquarters of Seventh Air Force begins redeployment from Saipan Island to Okinawa. Far East Air Force takes operational control of Seventh Air Force from the U.S. Navy and Army Air Forces Pacific Ocean Area.

## July 15

**CBI:** In China, Fourteenth Air Force sends three B-25 Mitchells to attack truck convoys moving through the Siang Chiang Valley. P-47 Thunderbolts and P-51

Mustangs attack trucks, gun positions, river traffic, logistics storage sites, railyards, bridges, and troops in southern and eastern China and in French Indochina.

**ETO:** The USS *Augusta* with President Truman on board arrives at Antwerp.

**MEDITERRANEAN:** Fifteenth Air Force prepares to redeploy the headquarters of the 306th Fighter Wing from Italy to the United States.

**SOUTHWEST PACIFIC AREA:** In the Philippines, Far East Air Force B-25 Mitchells, P-51 Mustangs, and P-38 Lightnings support ground forces and attack Japanese defenses on Luzon.

B-24 Liberators bomb an arms manufacturing facility at Canton, China. P-51 Mustangs sweep the west coast of Formosa, attacking a warehouse and other buildings.

Nearly 60 B-24s attack airfields on Kyushu Island, Japan. Another 25 B-24s bomb Kikaiga-shima in the Amami Islands, Miranoura on Yaku-shima in the Osumi Islands, and an airfield on Tamega Island.

U.S. submarine *Bluefish* sinks Japanese submarine *I-351* near Borneo.

**PACIFIC:** A total of 59 B-29s bomb the Nippon Oil Company at Kudamatsu. Over 100 P-51 Mustangs from Iwo Jima attack airfields and other tactical targets at Meiji, Kagamigahara, Kowa, Akenogahara, Nagoya, and Suzuko, Japan. Pilots report 13 confirmed kills, four probables, and 20 possibles. Three P-51s are lost.

Three battleships, two light cruisers, and eight destroyers of TU 34.8.2 (Rear Admiral Oscar C. Badger) bombard steel and iron production facilities at Muroran on the southern coast of Hokkaido.

During the night Twentieth Air Force sends 26 B-29s to mine the waters off western Korea and off west-central Honshu, Japan.

Task Force 38 carrier aircraft sink a Japanese minesweeper, a coastal defense vessel, an auxiliary submarine chaser, a guardboat, and six cargo ships off northern Honshu, southern Hokkaido, and Tsugaru Strait. Three escort destroyers, a cargo ship, three coastal defense vessels, two auxiliary submarine chasers, and a submarine chaser are damaged in the same area.

U.S. submarine *Skate* torpedoes and sinks a Japanese transport at South Sakhalin Island, Kuriles.

## July 16

**ALEUTIANS:** Eleventh Air Force sends four B-25 Mitchells on a shipping sweep. One cargo ship is hit.

**CBI:** Major General Stratemeyer takes command of all U.S. air forces in China.

In China, Fourteenth Air Force sends B-25 Mitchells to attack truck convoys moving supplies through the Siang Chiang Valley. P-38 Lightnings, P-47 Thunderbolts, and P-51 Mustangs attack trucks, river traffic, highways, logistics storage sites, rail lines, bridges, and troops in southern and eastern China and French Indochina.

**ATLANTIC: Terminal, the Potsdam Conference Begins.** President Truman, Prime Minister Churchill, and Premier Stalin meet at Potsdam, in the Soviet-controlled zone of occupied Germany. The agenda includes decisions on the Pacific war, especially Soviet participation, the status of eastern Europe, the disposition of Germany under occupation, and reparations.

The first atomic bomb is successfully tested at the Trinity site, Alamogordo, New Mexico. President Truman receives word in Potsdam that evening.

**ETO:** Headquarters Eighth Air Force passes operational control of all Eighth Air Force units in Great Britain to VIII Fighter Command, having redeployed over 90,000 of its assigned personnel. Headquarters Eighth Air Force, along with Twentieth Air Force, is to become part of U.S. Army Strategic Air Forces in the Pacific (USASTAF), on Okinawa and under the command of General Carl A. Spaatz.

**MEDITERRANEAN:** Fifteenth Air Force begins to redeploy the four subordinate B-25 squadrons of the 340th Bombardment Group to the United States.

**SOUTHWEST PACIFIC AREA:** In the Philippines, Far East Air Force B-25 Mitchells and P-51 Mustangs support ground forces on Luzon.

P-51 Mustang sweep Formosa, attacking communication targets, a railroad station, a bridge, and a locomotive shed. B-24 Liberators, A-26 Invaders, B-25 Mitchells, P-51s, and P-47 Thunderbolts from Okinawa and Ie Shima attack airfields, bridges, and harbor installations on Kyushu Island, Japan.

FEAF B-24 Liberators bomb warehouses on Celebes Island.

U.S. submarine *Baya* torpedoes and sinks a Japanese torpedo boat in the Java Sea. U.S. submarine *Blenny* torpedoes and sinks a Japanese gunboat in the Java Sea.

**PACIFIC:** P-47 Thunderbolts attack Yanagawa and 96 P-51 Mustangs from Iwo Jima attack airfields on Honshu, Japan. Pilots report 22 Japanese fighters shot down. One P-51 is lost.

A British fast carrier task force commanded by Vice Admiral Henry B. Rawlings, Royal Navy, with one battleship, four aircraft carriers, eight light cruisers, and 18 destroyers, joins Third Fleet and is designated as Task Force 37.

Carrier aircraft from escort carrier USS *Anzio* along with a destroyer escort sink Japanese submarine *I-13* east of Yokohama, Japan.

During the night 469 B-29s are sent to bomb Japanese cities. Namazu, Oita, Kuwana, and Hiratsuka urban areas are hit with incendiaries, inflicting major damage.

The headquarters of Twentieth Air Force, now under command of Major General Curtis E. LeMay, is established on Guam. The XX Bomber Command is inactivated, and the headquarters of the XXI Bomber Command is redesignated as headquarters squadron for Twentieth Air Force. Operational control of all bomber wings passes to headquarters, Twentieth Air Force.

### July 17

**ALEUTIANS:** Eleventh Air Force sends four B-25 Mitchells on a shipping sweep. Two of the bombers are forced to land in the Soviet Union. Two B-24 Liberators fly a shipping sweep over Shimushiru Island in the Kuriles.

**CBI:** In China, Fourteenth Air Force sends B-25 Mitchells to attack truck convoys moving supplies through the Siang Chiang Valley. P-47 Thunderbolts and P-51 Mustangs attack trucks, river traffic, airfields, highways, gun positions, rail lines, bridges, and troops in southern and eastern China and French Indochina.

Over 200 B-24 Liberators, B-25 Mitchells, A-26 Invaders, and P-47 Thunderbolts attack Kiangwan airfield near Shanghai.

**SOUTHWEST PACIFIC AREA:** Far East Air Force sends nearly 150 B-24 Liberators, B-25 Mitchells, and A-26 Invaders to attack Chiang Wan airfield in China. P-47 Thunderbolts attack shipping, warehouses, and the airfield on Taishan Island and B-25 Mitchells attack Itu Aba Island. P-51 Mustangs attack shipping, severely damaging a cargo ship in the harbor on Amami-O-Shima Island and P-47 Thunderbolts dive-bomb railroad tunnels near Kagoshima, on Kyushu Island, Japan.

FEAF B-24 Liberators bomb barracks on Celebes Island and strafe a schooner off the island. B-25 Mitchells bomb Jesselton airfield in Borneo.

**PACIFIC:** Carrier aircraft from U.S. Task Force 38 and British Task Force 37 attack airfields around Tokyo.

Naval Task Unit 34.8.2 (Rear Admiral Oscar C. Badger), with five battleships, two light cruisers, and 10 destroyers (including the British battleship HMS *King George V* and two British destroyers), bombards industrial facilities in the Mito-Hitachi area near Tokyo on the east coast of Honshu, Japan.

During the night Twentieth Air Force sends 27 B-29s to mine Shimonoseki Strait and the waters off Chongjin, Korea, and southwest Honshu, Japan.

## July 18

**CBI:** In French Indochina, Fourteenth Air Force B-25 Mitchells attack railyards. P-51 Mustangs and P-38 Lightnings attack trucks, coastal shipping, troops, and targets of opportunity in French Indochina.

**ATLANTIC:** At Potsdam President Truman receives the details of the Alamogordo atomic bomb test and is impressed with the results. He notifies Prime Minister Churchill.

**SOUTHWEST PACIFIC AREA:** In the Philippines, Far East Air Force P-38 Lightnings attack Japanese troop concentrations on Mindanao Island.

On Formosa, P-38 Lightnings attack communication and transportation targets and B-24 Liberators bomb an airfield.

About 150 B-24 Liberators, B-25 Mitchells, and A-26 Invaders, escorted by 54 P-47 Thunderbolts, attack airfields, shipping, and docks in the Shanghai area.

P-51 Mustangs and P-47s attack communication lines, bridges, shipping, town areas, and targets of opportunity on Kyushu Island, Japan.

U.S. submarine *Hawkbill* is damaged in a depth charge attack off Malaya and is forced to terminate her patrol.

In Borneo, FEAF B-25 Mitchells attack Jesselton, and P-38 Lightnings attack Langkon. B-24 Liberators bomb targets on Celebes Island.

**PACIFIC:** Carrier aircraft from Task Force 38 attack the Yokosuka naval base, targeting the battleship *Nagato* and bombing airfields near Tokyo. At the naval base, a training ship, a partially built escort destroyer, a submarine, a submarine chaser, a motor torpedo boat, and three auxiliary patrol vessels are sunk. British aircraft from Task Force 37 and U.S. aircraft from TF 38 damage the battleship *Nagato,* a motor torpedo boat, a landing ship, a target ship, and an auxiliary submarine chaser.

Naval Task Group 35.4 (Rear Admiral Carl F. Holden), with four light cruisers and destroyers, conducts an anti-shipping sweep and bombards radar installations off Honshu, Japan.

Aircraft from carrier USS *Wasp* attack Japanese installations on Wake Island.

Navy patrol bombers sink three Japanese cargo vessels in the Korea and Tsushima Straits.

U.S. submarine *Barb* torpedoes and sinks a Japanese coastal defense vessel south of Sakhalin. U.S. submarine *Cero* is damaged in an aerial attack off the Kuriles and is forced to terminate her patrol.

General Carl A. Spaatz establishes the headquarters of U.S. Army Strategic Air Forces in the Pacific (USASTAF) at Guam.

### July 19

**CBI:** In China, Fourteenth Air Force sends 20 B-25 Mitchells, 16 P-51 Mustangs, and four P-47 Thunderbolts to attack railyards and seven B-25s and two P-51s to attack bridges and bomb convoys in the Siang Chiang Valley.

**MEDITERRANEAN:** Fifteenth Air Force begins to redeploy the headquarters of the 456th Bombardment Group (Heavy) and its four subordinate B-24 squadrons to the United States.

**SOUTHWEST PACIFIC AREA:** In the Philippines, Far East Air Force P-38 Lightnings support ground forces, attacking Japanese defensive positions on Mindanao Island.

B-25 Mitchells attack Itu Aba Island, China.

Over 90 P-51 Mustangs sweep over the Nagoya area on Honshu Island, Japan, attacking airfields, production and power facilities, and gun positions.

U.S. submarine *Bumper,* attacking a Japanese convoy in the Gulf of Siam, sinks a fleet tanker.

In Borneo, FEAF P-38 Lightnings attack a suicide boat hideout at Sandakan and B-25 Mitchells bomb Jesselton airfield.

**PACIFIC:** During the night Twentieth Air Force sends 470 B-29s to bomb Japanese cities. The Fukui, Attackachi, Choshi, Okazaki urban areas are hit with incendiaries, causing heavy damage. Three B-29s are lost. Twentieth Air Force sends 29 B-29s to mine the waters off the Japanese ports of Niigata, west-central Honshu, Kobe and Osaka, on the Inland Sea, Maizuru, and Miyazu in southern Honshu, Japan, and the Korean ports of Wonsan and Hungnam.

Another 83 B-29s bomb the Nippon oil plant at Amagasaki.

P-51 Mustangs from Iwo Jima attack airfields, factories, railroads, power lines, and other targets on Honshu Island, Japan.

Task Force 38 aircraft damage two Japanese carriers (*Amagi* and *Katsuragi*) and the battleship *Haruna* at Kure, Inland Sea, Honshu, Japan.

**PACIFIC, OKINAWA:** A kamikaze damages a destroyer off Okinawa.

### July 20

**ALEUTIANS:** Eleventh Air Force sends eight B-24 Liberators to bomb facilities at the airfield on Matsuwa Island.

The detachment of P-38 Lightnings and P-40s of the 11th Fighter Squadron, 343rd Fighter Group, operating from Amchitka Island since March of 1944, returns to base on Adak Island.

**CBI:** Fourteenth Air Force sends 10 B-25 Mitchells and six P-51 Mustangs to attack truck convoys around Hengyang and Wuchang, and a logistics storage area on an island near Changsha, China, and rail targets in French Indochina. P-51 Mustangs, P-38 Lightnings, and P-61 Black Widow night fighters attack trucks, river traffic, highways, logistics storage sites, and rail lines in southern and eastern China and in French Indochina.

**SOUTHWEST PACIFIC AREA:** In the Philippines, Far East Air Force B-25 Mitchells, A-20 Havocs, P-51 Mustangs, P-38 Lightnings, and P-47 Thunderbolts support ground forces in the Cagayan Valley on Luzon. B-24 Liberators bomb Japanese positions on Negros Island.

B-25s attack Itu Aba Island in China.

U.S. submarine *Bumper* attacks a Japanese convoy in the Gulf of Siam, sinking a guardboat.

In Borneo, FEAF P-38 Lightnings attack the town of Langkon. On Celebes Island, B-24 Liberators bomb Togian Island and P-38 Lightnings attack targets of opportunity.

**PACIFIC:** Twentieth Air Force sends the B-29 crews of the 393rd Bombardment Squadron (Very Heavy), 509th Composite Group, on the first of a series of precision attacks over Japan for the purpose of target familiarization and to practice tactical maneuvers related to employing the atomic bomb. The targets are cities mostly already bombed, and the missions are flown in groups of two to six aircraft at high altitudes. Over 90 P-51 Mustangs from Iwo Jima attack airfields on Honshu Island, Japan. Pilots report one confirmed kill and 11 probables on the ground. Three P-51s are lost.

U.S. submarine *Threadfin* torpedoes and sinks a Japanese minesweeper off the southern coast of Korea.

A Japanese merchant cargo ship is sunk by a mine in Shimonoseki Strait.

## July 21

**CBI:** In China, Fourteenth Air Force sends 11 B-25 Mitchells and two P-51 Mustangs to attack truck convoys in the Siang Chiang Valley, bomb a Japanese headquarters near Wuchang, and attack a bridge, trains, warehouses, and antiaircraft positions. P-51 Mustangs, P-38 Lightnings, and P-61 Black Widow night fighters attack trucks, river traffic, highways, logistics storage sites, and rail lines in southern and eastern China and in French Indochina.

**SOUTHWEST PACIFIC AREA:** In the Philippines, Far East Air Force P-38 Lightnings support ground forces on Luzon.

B-25 Mitchells and A-26 Invaders bomb shipping at Naze-Ko, in the Ryukyu Islands.

The radar-equipped B-24 Liberators of the 373rd Bombardment Squadron (Heavy), of the 308th Bombardment Group, Fourteenth Air Force, from Luliang, China, are transferred to the 494th Bombardment Group (Heavy), Seventh Air Force, at Okinawa.

The B-25s of the 405th Bombardment Squadron (Medium), 38th Bombardment Group (Medium), redeploy from Luzon to Okinawa.

**PACIFIC:** During the night Twentieth Air Force sends 23 B-29s, staging through Iwo Jima, to mine Shimonoseki Strait and the Korea coast at Najin (the longest B-29 combat mission of the war) and in the Pusan-Masan, Korea, area. One B-29 is lost. Another 72 B-29s bomb the coal liquefaction company at Ube. Over 100 P-51 Mustangs from Iwo Jima attack airfields, rail facilities, and other targets on Shikoku and Honshu islands, Japan.

U.S. submarine *Sea Robin* torpedoes and sinks two Japanese cargo vessels west of Kyushu, Japan. Mines sink a Japanese merchant cargo ship and damage another along the southern Korean coast.

**CBI:** In China, Fourteenth Air Force sends 16 B-25 Mitchells to attack truck convoys in the Siang Chiang Valley and bomb railyards and bridges. P-51 Mustangs, P-38 Lightnings, and P-47 Thunderbolts attack trucks, coastal shipping, highways, logistics storage sites, and rail lines in southern and eastern China and in French Indochina.

**SOUTHWEST PACIFIC AREA:** In the Philippines, Far East Air Force B-25 Mitchells, P-51 Mustangs, and P-38 Lightnings support ground forces on Luzon.

In China, 22 B-24 Liberators from Okinawa attack airfields; 37 B-25 Mitchells bomb an oil plant at Shanghai and a Japanese destroyer on the Whangpoo River. P-47 Thunderbolts from Ie Shima attack a destroyer, a gunboat, and a cargo ship on the Whangpoo River, and bomb factories and railroad shops in and around Shanghai. P-51 Mustangs from Okinawa also attack Whangpoo River shipping and 37 A-26 Invaders attack a nearby airfield. B-24 Liberators on a night shipping search and weather mission bomb airfields at Tinghai and on Chusan Island, China, at Pusan, Korea, and at Yonago, Honshu Island, Japan.

The B-24s of the 403rd Bombardment Squadron (Heavy), 43rd Bombardment Group (Heavy), redeploy from Luzon to Ie Shima.

**PACIFIC:** Twentieth Air Force sends 26 B-29s to mine Shimonoseki Strait and the waters off Najin, Pusan, and Masan, Korea.

Mines sink a Japanese cargo ship and damage another cargo ship off Niigata, west-central Honshu, and damage an auxiliary submarine chaser off Kobe, a cargo ship at Hagi harbor, southwest Honshu, and a merchant tanker. Mines damage a cargo ship off Najin on the northeast coast of Korea.

Japanese cargo ship is sunk by an aerial mine dropped by Twentieth Air Force west of Funagawa, northwest Honshu, Japan.

Naval Task Force 93 (Rear Admiral John H. Brown, Jr.), with two light cruisers and five destroyers, bombards installations at Suribachi, Paramushiru, Kuriles.

## July 23

**ALEUTIANS:** Eleventh Air Force sends two B-24 Liberators, using radar to locate bomb release points, to attack the airfield on Paramushiru Island in the Kuriles.

**CBI:** The Tenth Air Force and the Fourteenth Air Force are consolidated to form the Army Air Forces, China Theater. The headquarters of Tenth Air Force is established at Kunming. The commander is Lieutenant General George E. Stratemeyer.

Fourteenth Air Force B-25 Mitchells and P-51 Mustangs bomb railyards. P-51 Mustangs, P-38 Lightnings, and P-40s attack river traffic, vehicles, logistics storage sites, and rail lines in southern and eastern China and in French Indochina.

**SOUTHWEST PACIFIC AREA:** In the Philippines, Far East Air Force P-51 Mustangs and P-38 Lightnings support ground forces on Luzon.

B-25 Mitchells bomb Itu Aba Island, China. B-24 Liberators attack Miho and Saeki, Japan.

In Borneo, FEAF B-25 Mitchells bomb Jesselton, while B-24 Liberators bomb Amboina on Ambon Island and the Tolonoeoe Islands in the Netherlands East Indies.

U.S. submarine *Hardhead* torpedoes and sinks a Japanese auxiliary submarine chaser off Java.

**PACIFIC:** U.S. destroyers attack a Japanese convoy, sinking a cargo ship off south-central Honshu, Japan.

U.S. submarine *Sea Poacher* torpedoes and sinks a Japanese guardboat off northeast Honshu, Japan.

Fifth Air Force B-24 Liberators on an antishipping sweep off the south coast of Korea sink a Japanese merchant tanker.

U.S. submarine *Barb* lands eight commandos to destroy a Japanese train on the east coast of Karafuto, Sakhalin Island.

## July 24

**CBI:** In China, Fourteenth Air Force B-25 Mitchells and P-51 Mustangs attack truck convoys in the Hengyang area. P-51 Mustangs, P-38 Lightnings, and P-47 Thunderbolts attack trucks, river traffic, highways, logistics storage sites, and rail lines in southern and eastern China and in French Indochina.

**ATLANTIC:** At Potsdam, President Truman casually mentions to Stalin that "we have a new weapon of unusual destructive force." Stalin appears not to understand, but he understands perfectly well. Soviet spies in the U.S. atomic bomb program have been providing critical technical information and have passed word that a test will be conducted soon. Truman's aside confirms that the weapon he knows all about actually works. He immediately orders Soviet scientists to redouble their efforts to develop a workable atomic bomb as soon as possible.

**ETO:** The VIII Fighter Command begins to redeploy the four subordinate B-17 squadrons of the 391st Bombardment Group (Heavy) to the United States.

**SOUTHWEST PACIFIC AREA:** In the Philippines, Fifth Air Force P-51 Mustangs and P-38 Lightnings support ground forces on Luzon.

Over 100 Fifth Air Force B-24 Liberators conduct their first bombing run from Okinawa, hitting the Chiang Wan airfield near Shanghai. Seventh Air Force B-25 Mitchells from Okinawa also attack airfields near the Shanghai area while A-26 Invaders and B-25 Mitchells attack the Tachang and Tinghai airfields. Other B-25 Mitchells attack Itu Aba Island, China.

The B-24 Liberators of the 65th Bombardment Squadron (Heavy), 43rd Bombardment Group (Heavy), redeploy from Luzon to Ie Shima. The 421st Night Fighter Squadron, V Fighter Command, redeploys from Luzon to Ie Shima with P-61 Black

Widow night fighters. The B-24s of the 822nd and 823rd Bombardment Squadrons (Heavy) of the 38th Bombardment Group (Heavy) redeploy from Luzon to Okinawa.

Kaitens from Japanese submarine *I-53* damage a destroyer escort off Luzon. The destroyer is later scuttled by submarine chasers.

Thirteenth Air Force B-25 Mitchells and B-24 Liberators bomb airfields on Borneo.

U.S. submarine *Chub* torpedoes and sinks a Japanese tug in the Java Sea.

**PACIFIC:** Twentieth Air Force sends 625 B-29s to bomb aircraft production facilities, an arsenal, and the city of Tsu, in the Nagoya and Osaka areas on Honshu Island, Japan. One B-29 is lost. Over 90 P-51 Mustangs from Iwo Jima attack airfields near Nagoya, Japan.

Carrier aircraft from Task Force 38 conduct a two-day attack on the Inland Sea area, hitting the Kure naval base and airfields. Battleship-carrier *Hyuga*, a heavy cruiser, a training ship, a target ship, and a guardboat are sunk. Carrier *Ryuho*, a battleship-carrier, battleship *Haruna*, a light cruiser, a heavy cruiser, three escort destroyers, a fast transport, a torpedo cruiser, two destroyers, two coastal defense vessels, and a transport are damaged.

A Japanese escort carrier is damaged by aircraft from British carriers HMS *Formidable,* HMS *Indefatigable,* and HMS *Victorious,* then suffers further damage when it hits a mine dropped by B-29s off Beppu in the Inland Sea. Two Japanese cargo ships hit mines dropped by B-29s off the west coast of Korea.

Naval Task Group 35.3 (Rear Admiral J. Cary Jones, Jr.), with four light cruisers and six destroyers (from Task Group 38.4) conducts a shipping sweep.

**CENTRAL PACIFIC:** Aircraft from escort carrier USS *Vella Gulf* carries out air strikes on Pagan, a Japanese base in the Marianas.

## July 25

**CBI:** Fourteenth Air Force B-25 Mitchells and P-38 Lightnings attack bridges in French Indochina. P-47 Thunderbolts and P-51 Mustangs attack road, rail, and river traffic, and railyards in southern and eastern China and French Indochina.

**ATLANTIC:** General Carl Spaatz, the commander of Army Strategic Air Forces, receives an authorization from Secretary of War Henry Stimson and the Chief of Staff George C. Marshall for the 509th Composite Group to deliver its first "special bomb" after August 3, 1945, as soon as weather allows for visual bombing, on one of four targets in Japan: Hiroshima, Kokura, Nagasaki, or Niigata.

**MEDITERRANEAN:** The headquarters of the 303rd Bombardment Group (Heavy) and its four subordinate squadrons, the headquarters of the 379th Bombardment Group (Heavy) and its four subordinate squadrons, and the headquarters of the 484th Bombardment Group (Heavy) and its four subordinate squadrons are inactivated at Casablanca, French Morocco.

**SOUTHWEST PACIFIC AREA:** In the Philippines, Far East Air Force B-24 Liberators bomb Japanese defenses on Negros Island. B-25 Mitchells bomb Itu Aba Island, China. B-24s bomb Kikaiga-shima in the Amami Islands, targets in the Ryukyu Islands, and the town of Tsuiki on Kyushu Island, Japan.

The headquarters of the 38th Bombardment Group (Medium) and 71st Bombardment Squadron (Medium) redeploy from Luzon to Okinawa with B-25 Mitchells, and the headquarters of the 345th Bombardment Group (Medium) redeploys from Clark Field, Luzon, to Ie Shima.

In Borneo, FEAF B-24 Liberators bomb airfields, while B-25 Mitchells and fighters attack a dispersal area at the Jesselton airfield area.

**PACIFIC:** Task Force 38 carrier aircraft attack targets of opportunity around the Inland Sea area, sinking three Japanese guardboats, an army tanker, a cargo ship, and two merchant tankers and damaging a heavy cruiser, a coastal defense vessel, three cargo ships, and a merchant tanker.

Naval Task Group 35.3 (Rear Admiral J. Cary Jones, Jr.) with four light cruisers (from TG 38.3) and six destroyers (from TG 38.4) bombards Kushimoto seaplane base, the airfield near Shio-no-Misaki on southwest Honshu, and adjacent facilities.

Twentieth Air Force sends 30 B-29s to mine the waters off Chongjin and Pusan, Korea, and Fushiki and Nanao, west-central Honshu, Ohama, east-central Honshu, and Tsuruga, Japan. Mines sink two cargo ships off Honshu.

During the night Twentieth Air Force sends 75 B-29s to bomb the Mitsubishi Oil Company and the Hayama Petroleum Company at Kawasaki. One B-29 is lost to antiaircraft fire.

U.S. submarine *Barb* bombards a lumber mill and sampan-building yard at Shibetoro, Kuriles, destroying 35 sampans under construction.

## July 26

**ALEUTIANS:** Eleventh Air Force sends seven B-24 Liberators to bomb the Kataoka naval base on Shimushu Island with incendiaries.

**CBI:** In China, Fourteenth Air Force sends eight B-25 Mitchells and four P-51 Mustangs to attack railyards, logistics storage areas, and transportation targets. P-51 Mustangs, P-38 Lightnings, and P-61 Black Widow night fighters attack trucks, coastal shipping, river traffic, highways, logistics storage sites, bridges, town areas, and rail lines in southern and eastern China and in French Indochina.

**ATLANTIC:** President Truman issues a statement from Potsdam, Germany. The Potsdam declaration orders the unconditional surrender of the Japanese armed forces and specifies that Japan will maintain sovereignty only over its four main home islands, and will be occupied under the direction of a supreme Allied commander until the time that a stable and peaceful postwar government can be established. The Japanese people will not be punished, although Japanese war criminals will be prosecuted. The role of the Japanese emperor in postwar Japan is left unsaid, although the language of the declaration refers to a government that will be "established, in accordance with the freely expressed will of the Japanese people." The declaration promises "the complete and utter destruction of Japan" if the declaration is rejected.

The JCS recommends to President Truman that the United States resist Soviet demands for concessions that would extend Soviet influence and control farther into Europe.

Winston Churchill is defeated in national elections, resulting in a new prime minister, Clement Attlee, who will form a new government.

**SOUTHWEST PACIFIC AREA:** In the Philippines, Thirteenth Air Force B-25 Mitchells and P-38 Lightnings support ground forces in Luzon. B-24 Liberators bomb Japanese positions in support of ground forces on Negros Island.

B-25 Mitchells bomb Itu Aba Island, China.

B-24 Liberators on snooper (radar-assisted bomb release) strikes hit targets in the Ryukyu Islands, airfields at Tinghai, China, and at Nakazu, Japan, and the docks at Pusan, Korea.

The headquarters of the 43rd Bombardment Group (Heavy) and the B-24s of the 64th Bombardment Squadron (Heavy) redeploy from Clark Field, Luzon, to Ie Shima.

In Borneo, FEAF B-24 Liberators attack airfields.

**PACIFIC:** During the night Twentieth Air Force sends 350 B-29s to bomb Japanese cities.

Matsuyama, Tokuyama, and Omuta urban areas are hit with incendiaries, causing major damage. One B-29 is lost.

## July 27

**CBI:** Chinese forces capture Kweilin.

In China, Fourteenth Air Force sends 13 B-25 Mitchells with P-51 Mustangs to attack truck convoys in the Siang Chiang Valley, bomb railyards, and attack coastal shipping. P-51 Mustangs and P-38 Lightnings attack trucks, river shipping, road and rail traffic, logistics storage sites, and bridges in southern and eastern China and in French Indochina.

**ETO:** Ninth Air Force begins to redeploy the headquarters of the 386th Bombardment Group (Light) and its four subordinate B-26 squadrons to the United States.

**MEDITERRANEAN:** Twelfth Air Force begins to redeploy the headquarters of the 340th Bombardment Group (Medium) from Italy to the United States.

**SOUTHWEST PACIFIC AREA:** Over 60 Fifth and Seventh Air Force B-24 Liberators, escorted by 50 P-51 Mustangs, attack a marshaling yard at Kagoshima, Kyushu. More than 150 P-47 Thunderbolts attack a tunnel, bridges, and industrial targets on Kyushu.

The 500th Bombardment Squadron (Medium) of the 345th Bombardment Group (Medium) redeploys from Clark Field, Luzon, to Ie Shima with B-25 Mitchells.

Thirteenth Air Force B-24 Liberators attack an airfield on Borneo. U.S. submarine *Pargo* is damaged by a depth charge and air attack off northern Celebes Island, but remains on patrol.

**PACIFIC:** During the night Twentieth Air Force sends 24 B-29s to drop mines in Shimonoseki Strait and in the waters off Niigata, west-central Honshu, Miyazu and Senzaki, southwest Honshu, and Maizuru, southern Honshu, Japan. Three B-29s are hit by antiaircraft fire. Two bombers make a landing in the ocean; 13 crewmen are rescued, and the third bomber crash lands on Iwo Jima.

Fifth Air Force aircraft sink a Japanese landing ship off southern Kyushu, Japan.

Mines sink six Japanese cargo ships off western Kyushu, Japan.

U.S. submarine *Pogy* torpedoes and sinks a Japanese cargo ship west of Honshu, Japan.

A Japanese aerial torpedo hits and damages a U.S. freighter in Naha harbor, Okinawa. Another freighter is hit with an aerial torpedo south of Ie Shima, sinking an LST moored alongside.

## July 28

**CBI:** In China, Fourteenth Air Force sends seven B-25 Mitchells and four P-51 Mustangs to attack truck convoys in the Siang Chiang Valley, bomb a cargo ship, and attack troop concentrations. P-51 Mustangs, P-38 Lightnings, and P-61 Black Widow night fighters attack trucks, river traffic, logistics storage sites, and rail lines in southern and eastern China and in French Indochina.

**ATLANTIC:** The new British prime minister, Clement Attlee, arrives at Potsdam.

**SOUTHWEST PACIFIC AREA:** In the Philippines, Thirteenth Air Force B-25 Mitchells and P-38 Lightnings in support of ground forces, attack enemy positions on Luzon and other P-38s attack troop concentrations on Jolo Island. B-24 Liberators support ground forces on Negros Island.

P-47 Thunderbolts from Ie Shima conduct rocket attacks and strafe airfields, oil stores, railyards, warehouses, industrial targets, and gun positions on Kyushu Island, Japan. Other P-47s attack shipping, and A-26 Invaders and B-25 Mitchells bomb airfields. P-51 Mustangs and B-25s conduct sweeps over the Inland Sea, destroying two small cargo vessels and a patrol boat. Over 70 B-24 Liberators bomb a battleship and an aircraft carrier at Kure. Aircrews report both ships damaged.

The B-25s of the 499th and 501st Bombardment Squadrons (Medium), 345th Bombardment Group (Medium), redeploy from Clark Field to Ie Shima.

U.S. submarine *Hardhead* torpedoes and damages a Japanese vessel south of Bali.

**PACIFIC:** Carrier aircraft from TF 38 attack the Kure naval base and other targets in the Inland Sea area, sinking a battleship, a battleship-carrier, a training ship, a heavy cruiser, a light cruiser, a submarine, an escort destroyer, four guardboats, a submarine depot ship, a stores ship, an auxiliary minesweeper, four cargo ships, and two merchant tankers. British carrier aircraft (Task Force 37) sink two coastal defense vessels. U.S. carrier aircraft damage carrier *Katsuragi* and a training carrier, a torpedo cruiser, a submarine in drydock, a destroyer, three coastal defense vessels, a submarine chaser, an escort destroyer, two guardboats, a motor torpedo boat, two auxiliary minesweepers, a merchant passenger ship, three cargo ships, and three merchant tankers.

Four escort carriers of TF 32 (Rear Admiral Jesse B. Oldendorf) provide cover for minesweeping operations in the East China Sea, directed by Rear Admiral Alexander Sharp's Naval Task Force 39.

U.S. submarine *Sennet* attacks a Japanese convoy off western Honshu and sinks three cargo ships.

General Walter Krueger's Sixth Army issues orders for Operation Olympic, the landing on Kyushu Island and the first step in the decisive defeat of Japan. The operation is scheduled for November 1, 1945. Sixth Army will land four corps: I Corps under Major General Innis P. Swift (33rd and 25th Infantry Divisions), XI Corps under Lieutenant General Charles P. Hall (43rd Infantry Division, 1st Cavalry Division, and 112th Cavalry RCT), IX Corps under Major General Charles W. Ryder (77th, 98th, and 81st Infantry Divisions), and the V Marine Amphibious Corps under Major General Harry Schmidt (2nd, 3rd, and 5th Marine Divisions). The 11th Airborne Division will be the army reserve. The 40th Infantry Division and the 158th RCT will attack islands off Kyushu. The total number of troops available is 650,000 men.

During the night Twentieth Air Force sends more than 470 B-29s to bomb Japanese cities. Tsu, Aomori, Ichinomiya, Ogaki, Uji-Yamada, and Uwajima urban areas are hit with incendiaries, causing great destruction. Another 76 B-29s bomb an oil refinery. Over 140 P-51 Mustangs from Iwo Jima attack airfields and military targets around Tokyo and attack and damage a destroyer escort along the Chiba Peninsula.

**PACIFIC, OKINAWA:** A kamikaze sinks U.S. destroyer *Callaghan* southwest of Okinawa. Another destroyer aiding *Callaghan* is damaged by near-miss of another kamikaze.

### July 29

**CBI:** In China, Fourteenth Air Force sends four B-25 Mitchells and two P-51 Mustangs to attack shipping off the Luichow Peninsula, oil storage areas, and barracks. Over 100 P-51 Mustangs, P-38 Lightnings, and P-61 Black Widow night fighters attack trucks, river traffic, highways, logistics storage sites, and rail lines in southern and eastern China and in French Indochina.

**SOUTHWEST PACIFIC AREA:** In the Philippines, Thirteenth Air Force B-24 Liberators bomb Japanese troops holding out at Negros Island. B-25 Mitchells and P-38 Lightnings attack Japanese positions and troop concentrations on Luzon.

P-47 Thunderbolts from Ie Shima and B-24 Liberators, B-25 Mitchells, and A-26 Invaders from Okinawa attack targets in the Japanese home islands. Over 70 B-24s attack shipping at Kure, 41 B-24s attack industrial targets and logistics storage areas, shipping and engine works in Nagasaki and town areas. B-25s attack a bridge, barracks, warehouses, a lighthouse, and navigation light. A-26s attack the naval base and engine works at Nagasaki. P-47s attack the harbor at Kure, shipping and seaplane station at Ibusuki, railroad station, docks, and town areas, airfields, and shipping at Kagoshima Bay. P-51 Mustangs attack numerous targets of opportunity on the south coast of Korea and Kyushu, attacking shipping, rail lines, and industrial targets.

The radar-equipped B-24s of the 868th Bombardment Squadron (Heavy), Thirteenth Air Force, redeploy from Leyte to Okinawa.

Japanese submarine *I-58* torpedoes and sinks heavy cruiser USS *Indianapolis* northeast of Leyte. The *Indianapolis* has just delivered the atomic weapons to Tinian.

FEAF B-24 Liberators attack an airfield and warehouses on Celebes Island.

Corporal Melvin Mayfield, D Company, 20th Infantry Regiment, 6th Infantry Division, comes to the rescue of two Filipino companies in the Cordillera Mountains, Luzon, moving from shell hole to shell hole until he reaches several caves where the enemy is located on top of a hill. With grenades and his M-1 carbine, he attacks each one of the cave positions. As he reaches the last cave, a machine-gun bullet destroys his carbine and wounds his left hand. He continues the attack with only hand grenades, charging directly into point-blank fire to destroy the position. For his selfless heroism and gallant leadership, Corporal Mayfield will receive the nation's highest award for valor, the Medal of Honor.

**PACIFIC:** Naval Task Unit 34.8.1 commanded by Rear Admiral John F. Shafroth, with three battleships, four heavy cruisers, and 10 destroyers, bombards an aircraft production facility and other production facilities at Hamamatsu, Honshu. British battleship HMS *King George V* and three destroyers, although operating independently, provide supporting fire on the targets.

Seventh Air Force P-47 Thunderbolts conduct a sweep for targets of opportunity over Nagasaki, Japan, and sink an auxiliary submarine chaser. Fifth Air Force B-25 Mitchells damage a Japanese escort carrier *Kaiyo* in the Inland Sea. B-25s and P-51 Mustangs on a shipping sweep off the southeast coast of Korea sink three cargo ships and a tanker. A-26 Invaders damage a Japanese merchant tanker off Nagasaki.

During the night Twentieth Air Force sends 24 B-29s to mine Shimonoseki Strait and the waters off Najin, Korea, and Fukuoka, west Kyushu, Japan.

**PACIFIC, OKINAWA:** Kamikazes damage a destroyer and high-speed transport off Okinawa.

## July 30

**CBI:** In China, Fourteenth Air Force sends two B-25 Mitchells to attack truck convoys in the Siang Chiang Valley. P-51 Mustangs, P-38 Lightnings, and P-61 Black Widow night fighters attack river and rail traffic, highways, and logistics storage sites in southern and eastern China and in French Indochina.

**SOUTHWEST PACIFIC AREA:** In the Philippines, Thirteenth Air Force B-25 Mitchells and P-38 Lightnings support ground forces east of Manila and in other areas on Luzon.

Over 60 B-25 Mitchells and A-26 Invaders bomb airfields and P-47 Thunderbolts support the strike and also attack numerous nearby targets of opportunity on Honshu Island, Japan. B-25 Mitchells make a shipping sweep over Korean waters, then attack targets on the Japanese mainland near Sendai. P-51 Mustangs escorting the bombers attack nearby targets of opportunity. P-47s bomb Sendai, causing widespread destruction. P-51s on photo reconnaissance along southern Kyushu destroy trains and small craft. Nearly 80 P-47s attack warehouses, barracks, and airfield facilities

FEAF B-24 Liberators bomb an airfield in Borneo.

**PACIFIC:** Premier Baron Kantoro Suzuki announces that Japan will respond to the Potsdam Declaration with "contemptuous silence."

Twentieth Air Force sends P-51 Mustangs from Iwo Jima to attack airfields, railroads, and other targets throughout the Kobe-Osaka, Japan, area.

Carrier aircraft from Task Force 38 bomb airfields and industrial targets in central Honshu, and fly sweeps against Japanese shipping in Maizuru Bay. Aircraft sink an escort vessel, a submarine chaser, a minelayer, four auxiliary submarine chasers, two guardboats, two auxiliary submarine chasers, and three cargo ships. Aircraft also damage an escort destroyer, a submarine depot ship, two submarines, two coastal defense vessels, a minelayer, an auxiliary submarine chaser, a guardboat, and two cargo ships. British carrier aircraft from Task Force 37 destroy a grounded transport.

U.S. submarine *Sennet* torpedoes and sinks a Japanese cargo ship off western Hokkaido.

Mines from B-29s sink a destroyer and damage another inside Miyazu Bay, western Honshu, and a passenger-cargo vessel in the Tsugaru Strait.

Rear Admiral Alexander Sharp's Naval Task Force 39 completes minesweeping operations in the East China Sea, having covered about 7,300 square miles and destroyed 404 mines without any losses.

## July 31

**CBI:** In China, Fourteenth Air Force sends three B-25 Mitchells to bomb truck convoys in the Siang Chiang Valley. P-51 Mustangs and P-61 Black Widow night fighters attack trucks, river traffic, highways, ammunition storage sites, and rail lines in southern and eastern China.

**SOUTHWEST PACIFIC AREA:** In the Philippines, Thirteenth Air Force B-25 Mitchells and P-38 Lightnings support ground forces on Luzon in the Cagayan Valley. B-24 Liberators bomb Japanese positions on Negros Island. The headquarters of Fifth Air Force redeploys from Clark Field, Luzon, to Okinawa.

Over 80 B-24s bomb railyards and several other targets, including the Sasebo naval base on Kyushu Island, Japan. A-26 Invaders and B-25 Mitchells bomb airfields and nearby targets, the Sasebo naval base, warehouses at Nagasaki, and a factory and power plant on Koyagi Island. P-51 Mustangs attack antiaircraft positions, coastal shipping off Kyushu, and bomb railroad targets and warehouses in the Izumi area. P-61 Black Widow night fighters continue harassing missions during the night. P-51s attack airfields on the Ryukyu Islands.

**PACIFIC:** Twentieth Air Force receives the headquarters of the 301st Fighter Wing arriving on Ie Shima from the United States.

U.S. destroyers conduct a shipping sweep and bombard railyards and an industrial area near Shimizu, southeast Honshu, Japan.

PB4Y Privateers from Okinawa destroy a span of the Seisen River bridge in Korea.

U.S. submarine *Thornback* torpedoes and damages a Japanese submarine chaser off east-central Honshu, Japan.

## August 1

**CBI:** Major General Albert F. Hegenberger takes command of Tenth Air Force, with headquarters at Kunming, China. Tenth Air Force will provide tactical support to Chinese ground forces.

The P-51 Mustangs of the 26th Fighter Squadron, 51st Fighter Group, redeploy from Kunming to Nanning. The P-51s of the 528th, 529th, and 530th Fighter Squadrons, 311th Fighter Group, Tenth Air Force, redeploy to Hsian.

**Southwest Pacific Area:** In the Philippines, P-38 Lightnings support ground forces in Luzon.

In French Indochina, B-24s bomb a marshaling yard, while escorting P-51 Mustangs strafe boxcars. Other B-24s hit logistics storage areas on Formosa.

B-24s, B-25 Mitchells, and P-47 Thunderbolts bomb the Nagasaki docks and harbor facilities, railyards, and shipping. Other B-24s bomb an airfield and attack Kakeroma Island. Over 80 P-47s attack rail bridges and other railroad targets at Sendai. P-47s flying from Iwo Jima for the first time join VII Fighter Command P-51s in a sweep over south Honshu Island, attacking airfields and rail targets near Okazaki, Itami, and Nagoya.

The headquarters of V Bomber Command and V Fighter Command prepare to redeploy from Clark Field, Luzon, to Okinawa.

Thirteenth Air Force B-24 Liberators bomb shipyards at Pontianak, Borneo. B-24s attack barracks and antiaircraft positions along Makassar Strait, Celebes Island. P-38 Lightnings strafe locomotives in the Surabaya, Java, area.

**Pacific:** During the night Twentieth Air Force sends more than 620 B-29s to bomb Japanese cities. The bombers drop incendiaries on the Toyama, Nagaoka, Mito, and Hachioji urban areas. The targets are heavily damaged. One B-29 is lost. Another 120 B-29s bomb the Mitsubishi Oil Company at Kawasaki, and 37 B-29s drop mines in the Shimonoseki Strait and in the waters off Najin and Chongjin, Korea, and Hamada, northwest Honshu, Japan.

P-51 Mustangs from Iwo Jima attack airfields and other targets in the Osaka-Nagoya area.

FEAF B-24 Liberators bomb the dockyard area at Nagasaki. B-25 Mitchells, P-38 Lightnings, and P-47 Thunderbolts bomb Japanese shipping in Nagasaki harbor. Pilots report a cargo ship and a tanker are damaged.

Naval Task Group 95.2, commanded by Rear Admiral Francis S. Low, with two cruisers, four light cruisers, and nine destroyers, departs Okinawa for the East China Sea to conduct shipping sweeps off Shanghai, China. Task Group 95.3 (Vice Admiral Jesse B. Oldendorf), with three battleships, a heavy cruiser, a light cruiser, three escort carriers, six destroyers, and three destroyer escorts, is in support of Low.

## August 2

**Aleutians:** Eleventh Air Force sends five B-24 Liberators to bomb the naval base on Shimushu Island in the Kuriles.

**CBI:** In China, Fourteenth Air Force sends 10 B-25 Mitchells, escorted by two P-47 Thunderbolts, to bomb bridges. B-25s bomb truck convoys in the Siang Chiang Valley. P-51 Mustangs and P-47 Thunderbolts attack trucks, river traffic, highways, fuel storage sites, and railyards in southern and eastern China.

**Atlantic: The Terminal Conference Ends.** President Truman, Prime Minister Clement Attlee (who has replaced Churchill as prime minister in the July general elections in Britain), and Premier Stalin issue a protocol statement, which, among other details, establishes a Council of Foreign Ministers from Britain, the United States, France, China, and the Soviet Union to address the conclusion of peace treaties with Italy, Romania, Bulgaria, Hungary, and Finland and to address the settlement of territorial questions. During the Allied occupation of Germany, the nation will be disarmed and demilitarized, and the German people will be convinced that they have suffered complete military defeat. The National Socialist (Nazi) Party organization will be destroyed, and German political life will be reorganized toward democracy. A Polish Provisional Government of National Unity is recognized by the United States and Great Britain with the understanding that "free and unfettered elections" will be held.

**SOUTHWEST PACIFIC AREA:** In the Philippines, Thirteenth Air Force P-38 Lightnings support ground forces on Luzon.

U.S. submarine *Bugara* operating against Japanese coastal shipping off the Malay Peninsula, sinks a schooner with gunfire and takes the crew on board. Later, USS *Bugara* encounters Malay pirates attacking a Japanese schooner en route to Singapore. The Chinese crew is taken on board, and the schooner is sunk. *Bugara* pursues the pirate vessel and sinks it.

A PV-1 Ventura patrol bomber en route from Saipan to the Philippines locates survivors of the USS *Indianapolis* east of Samar.

**PACIFIC:** Mines dropped by B-29s sink a Japanese cargo ship off Niigata, west-central Honshu, Japan, and damage a minesweeper on the eastern coast of Korea.

Lieutenant General Nathan F. Twining takes command of Twentieth Air Force. The previous commander, Lieutenant General Curtis E. LeMay, becomes chief of staff of U.S. Army Strategic Air Forces in the Pacific (USASTAF).

## August 3

**CBI:** Fourteenth Air Force B-25 Mitchells attack rail lines. P-47 Thunderbolts and P-51 Mustangs attack bridges, highways, railyards, logistics storage sites, rail lines, and troops in southern and eastern China.

**MEDITERRANEAN:** Brigadier General William L. Lee takes command of Fifteenth Air Force.

**SOUTHWEST PACIFIC AREA:** In the Philippines, P-38 Lightnings and B-25 Mitchells support ground forces attacking Japanese positions and buildings in Luzon.

FEAF B-24 Liberators bomb airfields on Celebes Island and bomb the seaplane base on Kangean Island in the Java Sea.

**PACIFIC:** Twentieth Air Force sends P-51 Mustangs from Iwo Jima to attack airfields, rail lines, and trains throughout the Tokyo area.

Mines dropped by B-29s sink Japanese cargo ships off the northeast coast of Korea, in Kobe harbor, and sink a transport off the southwest coast of Honshu, Japan. An army ship is damaged when it hits a mine from a B-29 off Tsuruga. Two cargo ships are damaged by B-29 mines off west-central Honshu.

## August 4

**CBI:** In China, Fourteenth Air Force B-25 Mitchells attack a rail bridge. Four B-25s and two P-51 Mustangs bomb an airfield and trucks, and other P-51s damage 12 locomotives and several trucks, and bomb a bridge.

**ETO:** Major General William E. Kepner takes command of Ninth Air Force.

**SOUTHWEST PACIFIC AREA:** In the Philippines, B-25 Mitchells and P-38 Lightnings support ground forces on Luzon. B-24 Liberators bomb Japanese positions on Negros Island.

P-38 Lightnings fly a sweep over Singapore. Pilots report two Japanese planes shot down.

FEAF B-24 Liberators bomb an airfield on Halmahera Island in New Guinea.

**PACIFIC:** A Japanese merchant tanker hits a mine in Osaka harbor and sinks. Mines damage a cargo ship in Najin harbor, northeast Korea.

Navy PBM Mariner patrol bombers sink a Japanese vessel off the China coast in the East China Sea.

FEAF B-25s attack warehouses, factories, a rail bridge, and a marshaling yard on Kyushu Island, Japan.

## August 5

**CBI:** In China, Fourteenth Air Force sends 20 P-51 Mustangs to attack bridges, railroad targets, and river traffic.

**SOUTHWEST PACIFIC AREA:** In the Philippines, P-38 Lightnings support ground forces on Luzon. B-24 Liberators bomb Japanese positions on Negros Island.

Over 330 B-24s, B-25 Mitchells, A-26 Invaders, P-47 Thunderbolts, and P-51 Mustangs attack town areas, industrial targets, and targets of opportunity on Kyushu and the Ryukyu Islands.

The 80th Fighter Squadron, 8th Fighter Group, Fifth Air Force, redeploys its P-38s from Mindoro to Ie Shima.

FEAF B-24 Liberators bomb logistics storage areas, troop concentrations, and antiaircraft positions in the Makassar area on Celebes Island. B-24s also bomb Miti on Halmahera Island in New Guinea.

**PACIFIC:** During the night Twentieth Air Force sends more than 460 B-29s to bomb Japanese cities. Saga, Maebashi, Imabari, and Nishinomiya-Mikage urban areas are hit with incendiaries and are heavily damaged. Two B-29s are lost. Another 27 B-29s mine the waters off Najin, Korea, and mine Tsuruga Strait, northern Honshu, and Oura and Hagi, southwest Honshu, Japan. Over 100 B-29s bomb the Ube Coal Liquefaction Company, destroying or damaging nearly all the facilities.

Over 100 P-51 Mustangs attack airfields and military installations in a large area around Tokyo.

A U.S. destroyer escort in the Philippine Sea is damaged by the near-miss of a *kaiten* fired by submarine *I-53*.

U.S. submarine *Aspro* rescues a downed P-51 pilot at the entrance to Tokyo Bay while PB4Y Privateer patrol bombers provide cover. Aircrews report 12 Japanese aircraft attempted to intercept the bombers and four were shot down.

U.S. submarine *Billfish* attacks a Japanese convoy in the Yellow Sea and sinks a cargo ship. U.S. submarine *Pogy* torpedoes and sinks a Japanese cargo ship in the Japan Sea west of Akita, Honshu, Japan.

Headquarters of Twentieth Air Force takes operational control of VII Fighter Command. Eighth Air Force receives the headquarters of the 333rd Bombardment Group (Very Heavy) and B-29s of the 435th, 460th, and 507th Bombardment Squadrons (Very Heavy), arriving at Okinawa from the United States.

## August 6

**CBI:** Representatives of the China and Pacific theaters meet to review a plan called Carbonado for capturing the Liuchow Peninsula beginning September 1 and initiating offensive operations against Canton on November 1.

In China, Fourteenth Air Force sends 10 P-51 Mustangs and P-47 Thunderbolts to attack locomotives and bridges.

**ATLANTIC:** A press release from Washington, released after the news of the successful bombing of Hiroshima, promises "a rain of ruin from the sky, the like of which has never been seen on this earth" if Japan refuses to surrender.

**SOUTHWEST PACIFIC AREA:** B-24 Liberators, B-25 Mitchells, P-47 Thunderbolts, and A-26 Invaders attack targets on Kyushu Island, Japan. B-25s and P-51 Mustangs attack shipping and ground targets of opportunity in the Tsushima Strait area and in the north Ryukyu Islands. P-51 Mustangs bomb an airfield and strafe numerous targets of opportunity on Saishu Island.

U.S. submarine *Bugara* supports British submarine HMS *Sleuth* in sinking two Japanese junks by gunfire off the Malay Peninsula.

U.S. submarine *Bullhead* is sunk, probably by air attack off Bali.

FEAF B-25 Mitchells and P-51 Mustangs attack Japanese shipping in Tsushima Strait, sinking two cargo ships.

**PACIFIC: The First Atomic Bomb.** At 0245 hours, Colonel Paul W. Tibbets, Jr., pilots the B-29 *Enola Gay* (509th Composite Group) off the runway at North Field, Tinian Island, for Hiroshima, the location of the Japanese 2nd Army, now preparing for the expected Allied invasion of Honshu. Two observation B-29s follow. Navy Captain William S. Parsons is the weaponeer on the mission. He arms the bomb in flight, having just learned the procedure the day before. At 0915 hours (0815 hours Japan time—1145 hours, August 5, Washington time) the atomic bomb is released over the city of Hiroshima at 31,600 feet, detonating 50 seconds later. The *Enola Gay* lands on Tinian at 1458 hours, followed later by the two observation B-29s. The bomb's destructive power is equal to 12,500 tons of TNT. Initial estimates are that about 80 percent of the city's buildings are destroyed and between 70,000 and 80,000 people are killed and 68,000 injured.

Mines dropped by B-29s sink Japanese cargo ships, one off west-central Honshu, one west of Kyushu, and one off Shikoku, Japan. Almost 100 P-51 Mustangs from Iwo Jima attack airfields and military installations around Tokyo.

Aircraft from escort carriers USS *Lunga Point*, USS *Makin Island*, and USS *Cape Gloucester* (Vice Admiral Jesse B. Oldendorf's Naval Task Group 95.3) attack Japanese shipping in Tinghai harbor, China.

Colonel Paul Tibbets about to take off for Hiroshima *(National Archives and Records Administration)*

Aircraft from the carrier USS *Intrepid* bomb Japanese installations on Wake Island as the ship passes to join Task Force 38 in the western Pacific.

Task Force 58 aircraft damage a Japanese coastal defense vessel and a small minelayer-netlayer off northwest Honshu, Japan.

## August 7

**ALEUTIANS:** Eleventh Air Forces ends five B-24 Liberators to bomb Kataoka airfield on Shimushu Island in the Kuriles. Two bombers are damaged by antiaircraft fire.

**CBI:** The headquarters of Fourteenth Air Force redeploys from Kunming to Paishiyi, China.

**SOUTHWEST PACIFIC AREA:** The U.S. First Army headquarters arrives in Manila from the ETO as part of the redeployment of forces to participate in the invasion of Japan.

In the Philippines, B-25 Mitchells and P-38 Lightnings support ground forces on Luzon.

B-24 Liberators bomb an airfield on Formosa.

Over Kyushu Island, Japan, B-24s and A-26 Invaders attack airfields and B-25s attack bridges and other targets and bomb a convoy off Pusan, Korea. Other B-25s attack airfields. P-51 Mustangs and P-47 Thunderbolts attack communication and transportation facilities.

The A-26s of the 8th and 13th Bombardment Squadrons (Light), 3rd Bombardment Group (Light), redeploy from Mindoro to Okinawa.

In the Netherlands East Indies, FEAF B-24 Liberators bomb an area near Bandjermasin, Borneo, and P-51 Mustangs attack the harbor at Surabaya, Java.

**PACIFIC:** Eighth Air Force receives the headquarters of the 346th Bombardment Group (Very Heavy) at Okinawa from the United States.

Twentieth Air Force sends 154 B-29s, escorted by VII Fighter Command P-51 Mustangs, to bomb the naval arsenal at Toyokawa. One B-29 is lost. The P-51s attack rail targets and shipping. During the night 29 B-29s, escorted by FEAF P-47 Thunderbolts, drop mines in Shimonoseki Strait and in the waters off southern Honshu and Osaka, Japan, and Najin, Korea.

Fifth Air Force B-25 Mitchells attack a Japanese convoy off Pusan, Korea, sinking a coastal defense vessel and two merchant tankers.

U.S. submarine *Pargo* attacks a Japanese convoy off northeastern Korea and sinks a cargo ship.

## August 8

**CBI:** In China, Fourteenth Air Force P-51 Mustangs attack buildings, trucks, river traffic, and other targets of opportunity.

**SOUTHWEST PACIFIC AREA:** In the Philippines, Far East Air Force B-24 Liberators and P-38 Lightnings support ground forces on Luzon.

B-24 Liberators bomb an airfield on Formosa.

B-24s, B-25 Mitchells, A-26 Invaders, P-51 Mustangs, and P-47 Thunderbolts from Okinawa attack airfields, communications, and transport targets on Kyushu Island, Japan. Shipping between Kyushu and Korea, and targets of opportunity in the Ryukyu Islands, on the China coast, and on Formosa are also hit.

The headquarters of the 475th Fighter Group and 431st, 432nd, and 433rd Fighter Squadrons redeploy from Luzon to Ie Shima with P-38 Lightnings. The B-24s of the 528th Bombardment Squadron (Heavy), 380th Bombardment Group (Heavy), redeploy from Mindoro to Okinawa.

FEAF B-24 Liberators on a shipping search attack an airfield on Halmahera Island in New Guinea.

**PACIFIC:** FEAF B-24 Liberators, B-25 Mitchells, A-26 Invaders, P-51 Mustangs, and P-47 Thunderbolts attack a number of targets on Kyushu and shipping in the Korea and Tsushima Straits, sinking two cargo ships and damaging another.

PB4Y Privateer patrol bombers attack Japanese shipping off Pusan, Korea, sinking two cargo ships and a guardboat.

U.S. submarine *Muskallunge* is damaged by machine-gun fire in an engagement off the Kuriles, but remains on patrol.

Twentieth Air Force sends 221 B-29s to bomb the Japanese city of Yawata with incendiaries. One B-29 is shot down by Japanese fighters, and three are lost due to mechanical reasons. A total of 60 B-29s bomb an aircraft production facility and arsenal complex at Tokyo. Two B-29s are lost to antiaircraft fire and one to mechanical failure. During the night 91 B-29s attack Fukiyama with incendiaries. P-47 Thunderbolts escort the B-29s and report 10 Japanese planes shot down. Over 100 P-51 Mustangs from Iwo Jima attack airfields, factory buildings, barracks, and rail installations around Osaka, Japan.

Over 5 million leaflets are airdropped over Japan explaining the destruction of Hiroshima and warning of similar attacks until the Japanese government accepts the Potsdam Declaration.

The Japanese Supreme War Direction Council meets to discuss options following the atomic attack on Hiroshima. The Air Defense General Headquarters reports that 44 major cities have been largely destroyed; another 37 cities, including Tokyo, have suffered over 30 percent destruction. Civilian and military casualties are approaching 2 million and another 8 million Japanese are injured or without shelter. Despite these facts, the Japanese leadership cannot come to a decision.

## August 9

**CBI:** In China, Fourteenth Air Force B-25 Mitchells, with P-51 escorts, bomb a rail bridge and rail traffic. P-51s strafe antiaircraft positions and targets of opportunity. Other B-25s attack truck convoys and targets of opportunity in the Siang Chiang Valley.

Headquarters Tenth Air Force redeploys from Kunming to Liuchow, China.

U.S. submarine *Hawkbill* shells Tambelan Island, 230 miles east of Singapore, destroying a Japanese radio station.

**SOUTHWEST PACIFIC AREA:** In the Philippines, Far East Air Force B-25 Mitchells and P-38 Lightnings support ground forces on Luzon.

B-24 Liberators bomb military storage areas on Formosa.

Over Kyushu Island, Japan, B-25s bomb airfields, town areas, shipping, bridges, factories, oil storage, coastal villages, and communication targets in the Tsushima

Strait area. A-26 Invaders and A-20 Havocs attack an airfield and industrial areas in Kyushu. B-24 Liberators bomb the airfield on Honshu Island, Japan, and over 200 P-47 Thunderbolts and P-51 Mustangs attack airfields, barracks, harbor installations, bridges, shipping, vehicles, industrial targets, and logistics storage facilities on Shikoku and Kyushu Islands, and the Ryukyu Islands.

The headquarters of the 380th Bombardment Group (Heavy) redeploy from Mindoro to Okinawa. The P-38s of the 35th Fighter Squadron, 8th Fighter Group, redeploy from Mindoro to Ie Shima.

In Borneo, FEAF B-24 Liberators fly over Ambon and Ceram Islands and bomb barracks on Ambon.

**PACIFIC: The Second Atomic Bomb.** Major Charles W. Sweeney pilots a B-29, *Bock's Car* (509th Composite Group), off the runway at Tinian at 0230 hours, followed by two observation B-29s. Commander Frederick W. Ashworth (USN) is the weaponeer on the mission. The primary target, Kokura, is obscured by bad weather. Sweeney flies to the secondary target, Nagasaki. The bomb is released from 28,900 feet at 1158 hours (1058 hours Nagasaki time), detonating about one minute after release. At least 40,000 people are killed and 60,000 injured. After refueling on Okinawa, the B-29s return to Tinian by 2339 hours.

The Soviet Union declares war on Japan and ground forces begin an invasion of Manchuria.

Spurred by Emperor Hirohito, the Japanese Cabinet and the Supreme Council vote to accept the Potsdam Declaration with the condition that the imperial prerogatives are preserved. The Japanese government's message to the Allies asks for surrender "without prejudice to the Emperor's position."

During the night 95 B-29s bomb the Nippon Oil Refinery at Amagasaki.

Carrier aircraft from Task Force 58 (Admiral William F. Halsey) attack Japanese shipping and airfields from northern Honshu and Hokkaido to the coast of Korea. Aircraft sink three auxiliary submarine chasers, two minesweepers, a fleet tanker, and a cargo ship. U.S. (TF 38) and British carrier aircraft (TF 37) sink two escort vessels. A kamikaze damages a U.S. destroyer off Honshu.

Naval Task Unit 34.8.1, with battleships and cruisers under the command of Rear Admiral John F. Shafroth, bombards industrial targets at Kamaishi, Honshu. Two British light cruisers support the American task unit.

Soviet forces enter Korea. Soviet aircraft sink a Japanese coastal defense vessel off the northeast coast of Korea and sink two cargo ships off Kamchatka in the Sea of Okhotsk.

B-25 Mitchells on a shipping sweep off the southern coast of Korea sink an auxiliary submarine chaser and two cargo ships. Fifth Air Force B-25s damage a Japanese fast transport in the Inland Sea.

Mines damage two Japanese cargo ships off west-central Honshu and damage a vessel near Sumoto in the Inland Sea.

Naval Task Unit 12.5.6, composed of battleship USS *New Jersey,* a light cruiser, and four destroyers, bombards Wake Island as the ships pass en route to Eniwetok.

## August 10

**CBI:** In China, B-25 Mitchells and P-51 Mustangs bomb convoys in the Siang Chiang Valley, attack a logistics storage area, tucks, and antiaircraft positions. P-47 Thunderbolts and P-51s attack river and rail traffic, troops, trucks, and bridges at several points in southern and eastern China.

Major General Charles B. Stone III assumes command of the Fourteenth Air Force, replacing Major General Claire L. Chennault.

**SOUTHWEST PACIFIC AREA:** In the Philippines, Far East Air Force P-38 Lightnings attack troop concentrations.

B-24 Liberators bomb Formosa.

Another 100 B-24s, 118 B-25 Mitchells, and over 220 P-47 Thunderbolts and P-38 Lightnings bomb targets on Kyushu. P-51 Mustangs provide cover. B-25s attack destroyers, cargo ships, and small vessels on a shipping sweep between Kyushu Island and Korea. P-47 Thunderbolts bomb Sasebo harbor on Kyushu, and P-51s attack various targets of opportunity on Honshu and Kyushu. B-25s bomb targets of opportunity in the Ryukyu Islands.

The headquarters of the 90th Bombardment Group (Heavy) and the B-24s of the 320th Bombardment Squadron (Heavy) redeploy to Ie Shima from Mindanao. The 530th Bombardment Squadron (Heavy), 380th Bombardment Group (Heavy), redeploys its B-24s to Okinawa.

**PACIFIC:** The Unites States receives the Japanese surrender offer. The question of the emperor's status causes delays in accepting the offer. Accepting the reservation would mean that the Japanese would not be surrendering unconditionally as the Potsdam Declaration stipulated.

Twentieth Air Force sends 70 B-29s, escorted by P-51 Mustangs, to bomb the arsenal complex at Tokyo.

Carrier aircraft from U.S. Task Force 58 and British Task Force 37 attack Japanese shipping, airfields, and a rail line in northern Honshu. A submarine chaser, a minesweeper, and an auxiliary minesweeper are sunk off northeast Honshu. Two cargo ships and a tanker are sunk off northeast Honshu. A cargo ship is sunk off the east coast of Korea. Mines sink a cargo ship and damage a coastal defense vessel off west-central Honshu, two cargo ships in the Inland Sea, and a merchant tanker in Maizuru harbor, southern Honshu, Japan.

Soviet aircraft sink a Japanese coastal defense vessel north of Joshin, Korea, and two merchant vessels off the Kamchatka Peninsula in the Sea of Okhotsk.

U.S. submarine *Hawkbill* shells Djemadja Island 150 miles northeast of Singapore, destroying a Japanese radio station.

During the night 31 B-29s mine Shimonoseki Strait and the waters off Hagi, southwest Honshu, Japan, and Wonsan, Korea.

**PACIFIC, OKINAWA:** A Japanese aircraft torpedoes a U.S. freighter off Naha, Okinawa.

## August 11

**ALEUTIANS:** The Eleventh Air Force redeploys the P-38 Lightnings of the 11th Fighter Squadron, 343rd Fighter Group, from Adak Island to Shemya Island.

**CBI:** In China, Fourteenth Air Force sends nine P-51 Mustangs to attack troops, trains, and river traffic around Chenhsien, Tehsien, and Hengyang.

**SOUTHWEST PACIFIC AREA:** In the Philippines, Far East Air Force P-38 Lightnings attack buildings and artillery on Luzon.

B-24 Liberators bomb an airfield on Formosa.

Over Japan, B-24 Liberators, B-25 Mitchells, A-26 Invaders, A-20 Havocs, P-47 Thunderbolts, and P-51 Mustangs from Okinawa attack targets in the Inland Sea, in the Tsushima area, and communication, transportation, and other targets throughout Kyushu Island.

The B-24s of the 400th Bombardment Squadron (Heavy), 90th Bombardment Group (Heavy), redeploy from Mindoro to Ie Shima.

In New Guinea, FEAF B-24 Liberators bomb a barracks on Ambon Island.

U.S. submarine *Chub* torpedoes and sinks a Japanese army auxiliary sailing vessel off southern Borneo. U.S. submarine *Hawkbill* lands Australian commandos ashore at Matak Island, Anambas Islands, in the South China Sea northeast of Singapore. The raid destroys a gasoline storage site and rescues an Indian prisoner of war.

**PACIFIC:** Carrier aircraft from Task Force 38 damage a Japanese destroyer and submarines *I-36*, *I-159*, and *I-402* at Kure, Japan.

A U.S. destroyer is damaged by naval gunfire in the Kuriles.

U.S. submarine *Jallao* torpedoes and sinks a Japanese cargo ship in the Sea of Japan.

Mines dropped by B-29s sink a Japanese cargo ship west of Kyushu and damage a landing ship.

**PACIFIC, OKINAWA:** Naval Task Group 95.4 (Captain Henry J. Armstrong, Jr.), comprising four light minelayers, 40 minesweepers, and 10 motor minesweepers, along with supporting vessels, departs Buckner Bay, Okinawa, for the East China Sea to conduct minesweeping operations.

## August 12

**ALEUTIANS:** Eleventh Air Force sends four B-24 Liberators to make a combined visual and radar bomb run over Kataoka on Shimushu Island in the Kuriles. Three other B-24s bomb the airfield and facilities on Paramushiru Island.

**SOUTHWEST PACIFIC AREA:** In the Philippines, Far East Air Force P-38 Lightnings support ground forces on Luzon.

B-24 Liberators bomb airfields and a marshaling yard on Formosa.

B-25 Mitchells and A-26 Invaders attack airfields, and P-47 Thunderbolts, A-26s, and A-20s attack town areas on Kyushu. B-25s, P-47s, and P-51 Mustangs attack shipping and bridges, rail lines, production facilities, and other targets of opportunity on Kyushu, the Ryukyu Islands, and the Tsushima Straits between Japan and Korea. Pilots report several small cargo ships sunk and damaged.

The 319th Bombardment Squadron (Heavy), 90th Bombardment Group (Heavy), redeploys its B-24s from Mindoro to Ie Shima. The 387th Bombardment Squadron (Heavy), 312th Bombardment Group (Heavy), redeploys its A-20s from Luzon to Okinawa. The 529th Bombardment Squadron (Heavy), 380th Bombardment Group (Heavy), redeploys from Mindoro to Okinawa with B-24s.

**PACIFIC:** The Japanese government receives the U.S. reply to its surrender offer, which states that no modification to the surrender terms are acceptable. The language of the reply is such that the status of the emperor falls under the interpretation of the Potsdam Declaration language of a government "established, in accordance with the freely expressed will of the Japanese people."

Naval Task Force 92, Rear Admiral John H. Brown, Jr., with two light cruisers and 12 destroyers, bombards Japanese installations in the Kuriles. Ten trawlers are sunk in the Sea of Okhotsk.

Mines sink a Japanese cargo ship north of Kyushu and damage two cargo ships off west-central Honshu, Japan.

**PACIFIC, OKINAWA:** Japanese submarine *I-58* conducts an unsuccessful kaiten attack on a dock landing ship en route to Leyte Gulf from Okinawa. Battleship USS *Pennsylvania* suffers damage from an aerial torpedo attack in Buckner Bay, Okinawa.

## August 13

**ALEUTIANS:** Eleventh Air Force sends six B-24 Liberators to bomb the Kashiwahara staging area on Paramushiru Island in the Kuriles. The bombers use radar to locate the bomb release points and drop incendiaries on the target.

**SOUTHWEST PACIFIC AREA:** In the Philippines, Far East Air Force B-25 Mitchells attack Japanese forces on Luzon.

B-24 Liberators and B-25s from Okinawa attack shipping in the waters off Korea and Kyushu Island and in the Inland Sea. Aircrews report several vessels sunk and damaged. P-47 Thunderbolts over Keijo (Seoul, Korea) encounter 20 Japanese aircraft. Pilots report at least 16 are shot down.

P-38 Lightnings attack shipping near Singapore, Malaysia.

**PACIFIC:** Aircraft from Vice Admiral John S. McCain's Task Force 38 attack targets around Tokyo.

An Army Air Force Catalina flying boat (OA-10A) rescues the crew of a downed TBM Avenger) from USS *Ticonderoga* inside Tokyo Bay.

U.S. submarine *Atule* torpedoes and sinks a Japanese coast defense vessel and damages another off southern Hokkaido. U.S. submarine *Torsk* torpedoes and sinks a Japanese cargo ship off west-central Honshu, Japan.

A Japanese army tanker is damaged when it hits a mine off north Kyushu.

**PACIFIC, OKINAWA:** A kamikaze hits an attack transport in Buckner Bay, Okinawa.

**CENTRAL PACIFIC:** Eighth Air Force receives the B-29s of the 461st, 462nd, and 463rd Bombardment Squadrons (Very Heavy) of the 346th Bombardment Group (Very Heavy) on Okinawa from the United States.

## August 14

**SOUTHWEST PACIFIC AREA:** B-25 Mitchells, P-47 Thunderbolts, and P-51 Mustangs attack shipping in Korea and Kyushu waters, claiming several vessels destroyed and damaged. P-47 Thunderbolts over the Osaka-Nagoya area on Honshu, Japan, report several Japanese aircraft shot down.

Upon the announcement of the president that Japan has surrendered, the 11th Airborne Division leaves the Philippine Islands by air for Okinawa, where it is prepared to deploy as the initial occupation force for Japan.

**Pacific:** Emperor Hirohito of Japan instructs the cabinet and the Supreme War Council to endorse the American implied acceptance of Japan's request to maintain the emperor as the titular, but not actual, ruler of Japan. The full cabinet meets, debates the issue, and comes to the conclusion that the members must approve the emperor's decision. Japan sends word that it will accept the provisions of the Potsdam Declaration and agrees to surrender. A coup by military officers to stop Japan's acceptance of the surrender terms fails.

Twentieth Air Force sends more than 300 B-29s escorted by over 160 P-51 Mustangs, to bomb the naval arsenal at Hikari and the Osaka army arsenal on Honshu Island, Japan. The P-51s attack airfields in the Nagoya area. One P-51 is lost. Over 100 B-29s bomb the railyards at Marifu.

U.S. submarine *Spikefish* sinks Japanese submarine *I-373* in the East China Sea off Shanghai, China.

U.S. submarine *Torsk* torpedoes and sinks two coastal defense vessels in the Sea of Japan.

Mines dropped by B-29s sink a Japanese gunboat west of Kyushu, a cargo ship in the Yellow Sea, a cargo ship in Osaka harbor, and another cargo ship off the east coast of Korea.

During the night 132 B-29s from the Marianas fly 3,650 miles to bomb the Nippon Oil Company near Akita on Honshu. Over 160 B-29s drop incendiaries on the cities of Kumagaya and Isezaki. Over 39 B-29s mine Shimonoseki Strait and the waters off Nanao, west-central Honshu, Maizuru, southern Honshu, and Hamada on northwest Honshu, Japan.

As the bombers are returning from their mission, they get word of Japan's surrender.

## August 15

**CBI:** Chinese Communist forces under Mao Tse-tung (Mao Zedong) begin occupying large areas of northern and central China.

**Atlantic: VJ Day.** The message that Japan accepts the Allied surrender terms reaches President Harry S. Truman in mid-afternoon. The president announces the unconditional surrender of Japan at 1900 hours Washington time, proclaiming a two-day holiday. The news is followed by tremendous celebrations throughout America.

Truman orders a cease-fire message to be issued to all U.S. commands in the Pacific.

**Southwest Pacific Area:** All offensive action against Japan ends. General of the Army Douglas MacArthur is notified that he is appointed Supreme Commander for Allied powers. MacArthur passes a message to the Japanese via the Army Airways Communications System, using a frequency that has been sending uncoded weather information.

From Supreme Commander for the Allied Powers To The Japanese Emperor, the Japanese Imperial Government, the Japanese Imperial General Headquarters

Message Number Z-500

> I have been designated as the Supreme Commander for the Allied Powers (the United States, the Republic of China, the United Kingdom and the Union of Soviet Socialist Republics) and empowered to arrange directly with the Japanese authorities for the cessation of hostilities at the earliest practicable date.
>
> It is desired that a radio station in the Tokyo area be officially designated for continuous use in handling radio communications between this headquarters and your headquarters. Your reply to this message should give the call signs, frequencies and station designation. It is desired that the radio communication with my headquarters in Manila be handled in English text. . . .
>
> Upon receipt of this message, acknowledge.
>
> Signed
> MacArthur.

The Japanese reply about two hours later, representing the first direct communication between the Allies and Japan.

At noon, Tokyo time, the Japanese people hear the voice of the emperor of Japan for the first time, over Radio Tokyo. They bow in reverent silence as they hear his words:

> We have ordered our government to communicate to the governments of the United States, Great Britain, and the Soviet Union that Our Empire accepts the provisions of the Joint Declaration [Potsdam]. . . . Cultivate the ways of rectitude; foster nobility of spirit; and work with resolution. . . .

Carrier aircraft from Vice Admiral John S. McCain's Task Force 38 attack airfields near Tokyo and are met by a large number of Japanese aircraft. A second strike is cancelled while the aircraft are approaching their targets as confirmation of Japan's surrender is received.

Soviet aircraft sink a Japanese escort vessel off Wonsan, Korea.

Naval Task Group 30.6, under Commodore Rodger W. Simpson, is formed to liberate, evacuate, and care for Allied prisoners of war in Japan.

## August 17

**PACIFIC:** General Prince Higashikuni becomes prime minister of Japan and forms a new cabinet.

A Japanese coastal defense vessel hits a mine off the southwest coast of Korea and sinks.

The Third Fleet maneuvers off Tokyo Bay.

## August 18

**PACIFIC:** Soviet forces land on Shimushu Island in the Kuriles and meet heavy resistance from Japanese forces. The Soviets suffer a large number of casualties.

## August 19

**CBI:** Two Chinese junks commanded by Lieutenant Livingston Swentzel, Jr. (USN), with a total of seven Americans (one army captain, two marine officers, one navy lieutenant, and four navy enlisted men) and 20 Chinese guerrillas on board engage in a close battle with a Japanese junk with 83 men on board, off the coast of China near Hainan. Swentzel directs the fight, hitting the Japanese junk with bazookas, machine guns, and grenades and then maneuvering to board the enemy vessel. The Japanese junk is boarded, and the assault party finds the decks littered with dead and wounded. Lieutenant Swentzel has fought the U.S. Navy's first battle under sail since the Civil War and the last surface action of World War II.

**SOUTHWEST PACIFIC AREA:** Two B-25Js of the 345th Bombardment Group (Medium) intercept two Japanese Mitsubishi G4M-1 bombers north of Ie Shima, painted white with green crosses. The aircraft from Tokyo are en route to Manila to meet General MacArthur's staff to work out details of the surrender and occupation. The 16-man delegation, led by Lieutenant General Kawabe Torashiro, the deputy chief of the Japanese army general staff, land on Ie Shima, and the delegation transfer to C-54s for the flight to Manila. On the return flight from Ie Shima to Japan, the Japanese aircraft run out of fuel and crash-land in Tokyo Bay. The delegation is rescued and returns safely to Tokyo.

**PACIFIC:** A Japanese escort vessel is damaged when it hits a mine off Pusan, Korea.
  Soviet forces begin landing on Sakhalin Island.

## August 20
**PACIFIC:** Naval Task Force 31, commanded by Rear Admiral Oscar C. Badger, is formed to assume responsibility for the occupation of Yokosuka naval base at the mouth of Tokyo Bay.

## August 21
**ALEUTIANS:** Eleventh Air Force sends B-24 Liberators to photograph Soviet activities in the Kurile Islands. Cloud cover forces the bombers to abort.
**PACIFIC:** A cease-fire is arranged between Soviet and Japanese forces in the Kuriles.

## August 22
**CBI:** The China theater command suspends all training and support for the Chinese Nationalist Army.
**PACIFIC:** A Japanese destroyer is damaged when it hits a mine in the Shimonoseki Strait.
**CENTRAL PACIFIC:** Captain Harold B. Grow, commander of Majuro Atoll, accepts the surrender of Japanese troops on Mille Atoll, Marshalls, on board destroyer escort USS *Levy*. Mille Atoll is the first overseas Japanese post to surrender.

## August 23
**ALEUTIANS:** Eleventh Air Force sends four B-24 Liberators to fly a photo reconnaissance mission over Paramushiru and Shimushu Islands to observe Soviet occupation activities in the Kuriles.
**PACIFIC:** Soviet forces begin the occupation of the southern Kuriles.

## August 24
**PACIFIC:** The Soviets calls off plans to occupy Hokkaido and drop their demands for a Soviet zone of occupation in Tokyo.

### August 25

**PACIFIC:** Aircraft from the carrier task groups begin daily flights over the Japanese home islands, monitoring airfields and shipping and locating prisoner of war camps.

TG 95.4 (Captain Henry J. Armstrong, Jr.) returns to Buckner Bay, having destroyed 578 mines in the East China Sea.

Carrier USS *Wasp* and a destroyer are damaged in a typhoon.

### August 27

**PACIFIC:** Twentieth Air Force B-29s begin supplying prisoners of war and internee camps in Japan, China, and Korea with medical supplies, food, and clothing. The first supply drop is to Weihsien Camp near Peking (Beijing), China.

Japanese submarine *I-14* and submarine *I-400* surrender to U.S. destroyers east of northern Honshu.

Commander Third Fleet, Admiral William F. Halsey, Jr., stands into Sagami Wan, the outer bay to Tokyo, Japan. The Japanese destroyer *Hatsuzakura* carries Japanese officers to meet with Admiral Halsey's staff for a piloting conference to work out details of the entry of American and British warships into Sagami Wan and Tokyo Bay for the Japanese surrender ceremonies.

### August 28

**PACIFIC:** The occupation of Japan officially begins as an advance party arrives in the Home Islands. Colonel Gordon Blake and five men of the 68th Army Airways Communications System (AACS) Group, 7th AACS Wing, arrive at Atsugi airfield near Tokyo to set up the communications equipment, air traffic control, and navigation aids for occupation troops arriving by air. They are part of a 150-man task force with 24 C-47 aircraft. They are the first American troops to land in Japan and are met by an honor guard from the Japanese navy.

Administrative and operational control of the Seventh Fleet under Admiral Thomas C. Kinkaid passes from General of the Army Douglas MacArthur, Commander in Chief, Southwest Pacific Area, to Fleet Admiral Chester W. Nimitz, Commander in Chief, Pacific Fleet.

### August 29

**PACIFIC:** U.S. submarine *Segundo* accepts surrender of Japanese submarine *I-401* off the northeast coast of Honshu.

Commodore Rodger W. Simpson, commander of Task Group 30.6, arrives in Tokyo Bay to evacuate Allied prisoners of war. Guided by TBM Avengers from small carrier USS *Cowpens,* he is taken by LCVPs to the camp at Omori. Prisoners are severely malnourished and suffering from a host of maladies.

Fleet Admiral Chester W. Nimitz, Commander in Chief, Pacific Fleet, arrives in Tokyo Bay on board a PB2Y Coronado and establishes battleship USS *South Dakota* as his flagship.

**NEW GUINEA:** Japanese garrisons on Halmahera and Morotai surrender.

### August 30

**PACIFIC:** The occupation of Japan begins with the 11th Airborne Division arriving at Atsugi airfield, while the 6th Marine Division lands at Yokosuka naval base. The

Third Fleet is prominently arrayed offshore, and navy and army aircraft fly patrols overhead.

Rear Admiral Robert B. Carney and Rear Admiral Oscar C. Badger accept the surrender of Yokosuka naval base. The naval base will serve as the headquarters for the commander of Third Fleet. General MacArthur arrives at Atsugi to set up temporary Supreme Allied headquarters at Yokohama.

**CENTRAL PACIFIC:** Aboard the destroyer USS *Stack,* Brigadier General Leo D. Hermle (USMC) leads the American side in discussions with the Japanese concerning the surrender of Truk.

## August 31

**MEDITERRANEAN:** Twelfth Air Force is inactivated in Italy.

**PACIFIC:** U.S. Marines land at Tateyama naval base on the northeast shore of Sagami Wan to take the Japanese surrender. They will conduct a beach reconnaissance and cover the landing of the 112th Cavalry Regiment.

Japanese submarine *I-401* surrenders to submarine USS *Segundo* at the entrance to Tokyo Bay.

The Soviet Union completes its occupation of the Kurile Islands.

**CENTRAL PACIFIC:** Aboard the destroyer USS *Bagley,* Rear Admiral Francis E. M. Whiting accepts the surrender of Marcus Island from the Japanese.

## September 1

**PACIFIC:** Soviet forces occupy Kunashiri and Shikotan Islands.

## September 2

**PACIFIC: Japan Surrenders.** Hostilities with Japan end officially with Japanese military and government representatives signing the instrument of surrender aboard the USS *Missouri* in Tokyo Bay. A framed flag is mounted on the forward 16-inch gun turret overlooking the table where the surrender documents have been placed. It is the American flag flown by Commodore Matthew C. Perry's flagship as he entered Tokyo Bay in 1853. General of the Army Douglas MacArthur signs for the Allied Powers. Fleet Admiral Chester W. Nimitz signs for the United States. He is followed by representatives of the USSR, China, Great Britain, Australia, Canada, France, the Netherlands, and New Zealand. The ceremony ends at 0925 hours Tokyo time.

Naval Task Force 33, commanded by Rear Admiral John L. Hall, lands army occupation troops at Yokohama.

**CENTRAL PACIFIC:** On board the destroyer escort USS *Amick,* the Japanese surrender forces in the Palau Islands. On board the heavy cruiser USS *Portland,* the Japanese surrender forces on Truk. On board the destroyer USS *Rhind,* the Japanese

General of the Army Douglas MacArthur, supreme commander for the Allied Powers, closes the surrender proceedings aboard the USS *Missouri* in Tokyo Bay, Japan, on September 2, 1945.

surrender forces on Pagan Island, Marianas. On board the destroyer escort USS *Heyliger*, the Japanese surrender forces on Rota in the Marianas.

### September 3

**SOUTHWEST PACIFIC AREA:** The formal surrender of Japanese forces in the Philippines takes place at Baguio. General Yamashita surrenders 50,500 men from the original 350,000 defenders.

In the Eighth Army area, the campaign for the southern Philippines is completed. American losses for this campaign are 2,100 killed and nearly 7,000 wounded.

**PACIFIC:** The Japanese garrison of the Bonin Islands surrenders on board the destroyer USS *Dunlap* off Chichi Jima. Lieutenant General Tachibana Yoshio, the local commander, makes the formal surrender. He is later convicted and executed for atrocities committed against American aviators who had been captured in the area between 1944 and 1945.

Soviet troops occupy Shibotsu and Taraku Islands in the Habomai Island group.

### September 4

**PACIFIC:** Rear Admiral Sakaibara Shigematsu, commander of the Wake Island garrison, surrenders to American forces. The American flag, which had been taken down in defiant anger on December 23, 1941, again waves over the island.

**CENTRAL PACIFIC:** On board The Coast Guard cutter USCG 83425, the Japanese surrender the garrison of Aguijan Island in the Marianas.

The American flag flies again over Wake Island in a formal ceremony after the final Japanese surrender, September 4, 1945.

### September 5

**PACIFIC:** Soviet troops complete the occupation of the Habomai group of islands.

**CENTRAL PACIFIC:** On board the destroyer USS *Tillman*, the Japanese surrender Yap Island.

### September 6

**CENTRAL PACIFIC:** On board the destroyer escort USS *Wingfield* the Japanese surrender Maloelap Atoll.

Vice Admiral Frederick C. Sherman, commander of Task Force 11, departs Tokyo Bay for the United States, carrying the first few of the tens of thousands of combat veterans who are coming home.

The Rabaul garrison surrenders to the Australians.

### September 7

**PACIFIC:** Japanese forces in the Ryukyu Islands surrender to the Tenth Army commander, Lieutenant General Joseph W. Stilwell, on Okinawa.

**September 8**
**PACIFIC:** Allied forces land at Inchon to begin the occupation of southern Korea.

**September 9**
**CBI:** Japanese forces in China formally surrender at Nanking.
**PACIFIC:** Admiral Thomas C. Kinkaid and Lieutenant General John R. Hodge sign surrender documents, during ceremonies in the government building at Keijo (Seoul), Korea.

**September 11**
**PACIFIC:** Operation Magic Carpet begins as navy ships begin transporting ground troops back to the United States.

**September 12**
**CBI:** Japanese forces in Southeast Asia formally surrender to Allied forces in Singapore.

**September 22**
**PACIFIC:** The evacuation of 16,000 Allied prisoners of war from the Japanese islands of Honshu and Kyushu is completed.

**September 28**
**ATLANTIC:** The navy transport USS *General Greeley* arrives in New York Harbor bringing home the first shipload of American units from the China and India-Burma theaters. Among those returning are men who served in the Flying Tigers, the Kachin Rangers, Merrill's Marauders, and the Mars Task Force.

**October 10**
**ATLANTIC:** Fleet Admiral Ernest J. King, Commander in Chief, U. S. Fleet, orders his headquarters to stand down.

**November 1**
**CBI:** The Stilwell Road is abandoned.

**November 19**
**ATLANTIC:** General Eisenhower replaces General Marshall as chief of staff of the army. The JCS initiates contingency planning for nuclear war with the Soviet Union.

# AMERICAN SERVICEMEN AWARDED THE MEDAL OF HONOR IN WORLD WAR II*

*Note: A "(P)" denotes that the honor was received posthumously.

## 1941

**Bennion, Mervyn S. (P)**
Captain, U.S. Navy. Commanding Officer of USS *West Virginia*, Pearl Harbor, 7 December 1941.

**Bulkeley, John D.**
Lieutenant Commander, U.S. Navy. Commander of Motor Torpedo Boat Squadron 3, Philippine waters, 7 December 1941 to 10 April 1942.

**Cannon, George H. (P)**
First Lieutenant, U.S. Marine Corps. Sand Island, Midway Islands, 7 December 1941.

**Elrod, Henry T. (P)**
Captain, U.S. Marine Corps. Marine Fighting Squadron 211, Wake Island, 8 to 23 December 1941.

**Finn, John W.**
Lieutenant, U.S. Navy. Naval Air Station, Kaneohe Bay, Territory of Hawaii, 7 December 1941.

**Flaherty, Francis C. (P)**
Ensign, U.S. Naval Reserve. Pearl Harbor, 7 December 1941.

**Fuqua, Samuel G.**
Lieutenant Commander, U.S. Navy. USS *Arizona*, Pearl Harbor, 7 December 1941.

**Hill, Edwin J. (P)**
Chief Boatswain, U.S. Navy. Pearl Harbor, 7 December 1941.

**Jones, Herbert C. (P)**
Ensign, U.S. Naval Reserve. USS *Oklahoma*, Pearl Harbor, 7 December 1941.

**Kidd, Isaac C. (P)**
Rear Admiral, U.S. Navy. Pearl Harbor, 7 December 1941.

**Pharris, Jackson C.**
Lieutenant, U.S. Navy. USS *California*, Pearl Harbor, 7 December 1941.

**Reeves, Thomas J. (P)**
Radio Electrician (Warrant Officer), U.S. Navy. Pearl Harbor, 7 December 1941.

**Ross, Donald K.**
Machinist, U.S. Navy. USS *Nevada*, Pearl Harbor, 7 December 1941.

**Scott, Robert R. (P)**
Machinist's Mate First Class, U.S. Navy. Pearl Harbor, 7 December 1941.

**Tomich, Peter (P)**
Chief Watertender, U.S. Navy. Pearl Harbor, 7 December 1941.

**Van Valkenburgh, Franklin (P)**
Captain, U.S. Navy. Commander aboard USS *Arizona*, Pearl Harbor, 7 December 1941.

**Ward, James R. (P)**
Seaman First Class, U.S. Navy. Pearl Harbor, 7 December 1941.

**Young, Cassin**
Commander, U.S. Navy. Captain of USS *Vestal*, Pearl Harbor, 7 December 1941.

## 1942

**Antrim, Richard N.**
Commander, U.S. Navy. Makassar, Celebes, Netherlands East Indies, April 1942.

**Bailey, Kenneth D. (P)**
Major, U.S. Marine Corps. Commander of Company C, 1st Marine Raider Battalion, Henderson Field, Guadalcanal, Solomon Islands, 12–13 September 1942.

**Basilone, John**
Sergeant, U.S. Marine Corps. 1st Battalion, 7th Marines, 1st Marine Division, in the Lunga Area, Guadalcanal, Solomon Islands, 24 and 25 October 1942.

**Bauer, Harold W. (P)**
Lieutenant Colonel, U.S. Marine Corps. Commander of Marine Fighting Squadron 212 in the South Pacific Area, 10 May to 14 November 1942.

**Bianchi, Willibald C. (P)**

First Lieutenant, U.S. Army. 45th Infantry, Philippine Scouts, near Bagac, Bataan Province, Philippine Islands, 3 February 1942.

**Burr, Elmer J. (P)**

First Sergeant, U.S. Army. Company I, 127th Infantry, 32nd Infantry Division, Buna, New Guinea, 24 December 1942.

**Callaghan, Daniel J. (P)**

Rear Admiral, U.S. Navy. Off Savo Island, Solomon Islands, on the night of 12–13 November 1942.

**Calugas, Jose**

Sergeant, U.S. Army. Battery B, 88th Field Artillery, Philippine Scouts, at Culis, Bataan Province, Philippine Islands, 16 January 1942.

**Casamento, Anthony**

Corporal, U.S. Marine Corps. Company D, 1st Battalion, 5th Marines, 1st Marine Division, Guadalcanal, Solomon Islands, 1 November 1942.

**Craw, Demas T. (P)**

Colonel, U.S. Army Air Corps. Near Port Lyautey, French Morocco, 8 November 1942.

**Doolittle, James H. (Air Mission)**

Brigadier General, U.S. Army Air Corps. Over Japan, 9 June 1942.

**Edson, Merritt A.**

Colonel, U.S. Marine Corps. Commander of the 1st Marine Raider Battalion, Solomon Islands, on the night of 13–14 September 1942.

**Fleming, Richard E. (P)**

Captain, U.S. Marine Corps Reserve. Flight Officer, Marine Scout-Bombing Squadron 241, Midway Island, 4–5 June 1942.

**Galer, Robert E.**

Major, U.S. Marine Corps. Commander, Marine Fighter Squadron 224, Solomon Islands area, August–September 1942.

**Gruennert, Kenneth E. (P)**

Sergeant, U.S. Army. Company L, 127th Infantry, 32nd Infantry Division, near Buna, New Guinea, 24 December 1942.

**Hall, William E.**

Lieutenant, Junior Grade, U.S. Naval Reserve. Coral Sea, 7 and 8 May 1942.

**Hamilton, Pierpont M.**

Major, U.S. Army Air Corps. Near Port Lyautey, French Morocco, 8 November 1942.

**Keppler, Reinhardt J. (P)**
Boatswain's Mate First Class, U.S. Navy. USS *San Francisco*, Solomon Islands, 12–13 November 1942.

**MacArthur, Douglas**
General, U.S. Army. Commanding U.S. Army Forces in the Far East, Bataan Peninsula, Philippine Islands, 1942.

**McCandless, Bruce**
Commander, U.S. Navy. USS *San Francisco*, off Savo Island, Solomon Islands, 12–13 November 1942.

**Munro, Douglas A. (P)**
Signalman First Class, U.S. Coast Guard. Petty Officer in charge of a group of 24 Higgins boats, Point Cruz, Guadalcanal, 27 September 1942.

**Nininger, Alexander R., Jr. (P)**
Second Lieutenant, U.S. Army. 57th Infantry, Philippine Scouts, near Abucay, Bataan, Philippine Islands, 12 January 1942.

**O'Hare, Edward H.**
Lieutenant, U.S. Navy. Fighting Squadron Three, 20 February 1942.

**Paige, Mitchell**
Platoon Sergeant, U.S. Marine Corps. Guadalcanal, Solomon Islands, 26 October 1942.

**Pease, Harl, Jr. (Air Mission) (P)**
Captain, U.S. Army Air Corps. Heavy Bombardment Squadron, near Rabaul, New Britain, 6–7 August 1942.

**Peterson, Oscar V. (P)**
Chief Watertender, U.S. Navy. USS *Neosho*, 7 May 1942.

**Powers, John J. (P)**
Lieutenant, U.S. Navy. Bombing Squadron 5, Coral Sea area and adjacent waters 4–8 May 1942.

**Ricketts, Milton E. (P)**
Lieutenant, U.S. Navy. Officer-in-Charge of Engineering Repair Party aboard USS *Yorktown*, Coral Sea, 8 May 1942.

**Rooks, Albert H. (P)**
Captain, U.S. Navy. Captain of USS *Houston*, 4–27 February 1942.

**Schonland, Herbert E.**
Commander, U.S. Navy. USS *San Francisco*, Savo Island, Solomon Islands, 12–13 November 1942.

**Scott, Norman (P)**
Rear Admiral, U.S. Navy. Savo Island, Solomon Islands, 11–12 October and 12–13 November 1942.

**Smith, John L.**
Major, U.S. Marine Corps. Marine Fighter Squadron 223, Solomon Islands area, August–September 1942.

**Thomason, Clyde (P)**
Sergeant, U.S. Marine Corps Reserve. Makin Island, 17–18 August 1942.

**Vandegrift, Alexander A.**
Major General, U.S. Marine Corps. Commander of 1st Marine Division, Guadalcanal, Solomon Islands, 7 August to 9 December 1942.

**Wainwright, Jonathan M.**
Lieutenant General, U.S. Army. Commander of U.S. Army Forces in the Philippines, 12 March to 7 May 1942.

**Wilbur, William H.**
Colonel, U.S. Army. Western Task Force, Fedala, North Africa, 8 November 1942.

## 1943

**Baker, Addison E. (P)**
Lieutenant Colonel, U.S. Army Air Corps. 93rd Heavy Bombardment Group, Raid on Ploeşti, Romania, 1 August 1943.

**Bjorklund, Arnold L.**
First Lieutenant, U.S. Army. 36th Infantry Division, near Altavilla, Italy, 13 September 1943.

**Bonnyman, Alexander, Jr. (P)**
First Lieutenant, U.S. Marine Corps Reserve. Executive Officer of 2nd Battalion Shore Party, 8th Marines, 2nd Marine Division, Tarawa, 20–22 November 1943.

**Booker, Robert D. (P)**
Private, U.S. Army. 34th Infantry Division, near Fondouk, Tunisia, 9 April 1943.

**Bordelon, William J. (P)**
Staff Sergeant, U.S. Marine Corps. Assault engineer platoon of 1st Battalion, 18th Marines, attached to 2nd Marine Division, Tarawa, 20 November 1943.

**Boyington, Gregory**
Major, U.S. Marine Corps Reserve. Commander of Marine Fighter Squadron 214, Central Solomons area, 12 September 1943 to 3 January 1944.

**Britt, Maurice L.**
Lieutenant, U.S. Army. 3rd Infantry Division, north of Mignano, Italy, 10 November 1943.

**Cheli, Ralph (Air Mission) (P)**
Major, U.S. Army Air Corps. Near Wewak, New Guinea, 18 August 1943.

**Childers, Ernest**

Second Lieutenant, U.S. Army. 45th Infantry Division, Oliveto, Italy, 22 September 1943.

**Craig, Robert (P)**

Second Lieutenant, U.S. Army. 15th Infantry, 3rd Infantry Division, near Favoratta, Sicily, 11 July 1943.

**Crawford, William J.**

Private, U.S. Army. 36th Infantry Division, near Altavilla, Italy, 13 September 1943.

**Cromwell, John P. (P)**

Captain, U.S. Navy. Commander of a Submarine Coordinated Attack Group with Flag aboard USS *Sculpin,* Truk Island, 19 November 1943.

**Davis, Charles W.**

Major, U.S. Army. 25th Infantry Division, Guadalcanal, 12 January 1943.

**Deblanc, Jefferson J.**

First Lieutenant, U.S. Marine Corps Reserve. Marine Fighter Squadron 112, off Kolombangara Island in the Solomons, 31 January 1943.

**Foss, Joseph J.**

Captain, U.S. Marine Corps Reserve. Marine Fighter Squadron #121, Guadalcanal, 9 October–19 November 1942 and 15 and 23 January 1943.

**Fournier, William G. (P)**

Sergeant, U.S. Army. Company M, 35th Infantry, 25th Infantry Division, Mount Austen, Guadalcanal, Solomon Islands, 10 January 1943.

**Gilmore, Howard W. (P)**

Commander, U.S. Navy. Captain of submarine USS *Growler* during her fourth war patrol in the Southwest Pacific, from 10 January to 7 February 1943.

**Gurke, Henry (P)**

Private First Class, U.S. Marine Corps. 3rd Marine Raider Battalion, Solomon Islands area, 9 November 1943.

**Hall, Lewis (P)**

Technician Fifth Grade, U.S. Army. Company M, 35th Infantry, 25th Infantry Division, Mount Austen, Guadalcanal, Solomon Islands, 10 January 1943.

**Hanson, Robert M. (P)**

First Lieutenant, U.S. Marine Corps Reserve. Marine Fighter Squadron 215, Bougainville Island, 1 November 1943; New Britain Island, 24 January 1944.

**Hasemoto, Mikio, (P)**

Private, U.S. Army. Vicinity of Cerasuolo, Italy, 29 November 1943.

**Hawkins, William D. (P)**
First Lieutenant, U.S. Marine Corps. Scout sniper platoon attached to assault regiment, Tarawa, 20 and 21 November 1943.

**Hayashi, Shizuya (P)**
Private, U.S. Army. Near Cerasuolo, Italy, 29 November 1943.

**Hughes, Lloyd H. (Air Mission) (P)**
Second Lieutenant, U.S. Army Air Corps. 564th Bomber Squadron, 389th Bomber Group, Ninth Air Force, Raid on Ploeşti, Romania, 1 August 1943.

**Hutchins, Johnnie D. (P)**
Seaman First Class, U.S. Naval Reserve. Lae, New Guinea, 4 September 1943.

**Jerstad, John L. (Air Mission) (P)**
Major, U.S. Army Air Corps. Ninth Air Force, Raid on Ploeşti, Romania, 1 August 1943.

**Johnson, Leon W. (Air Mission)**
Colonel, U.S. Army Air Corps. 44th Bomber Group, Ninth Air Force, Raid on Ploeşti, Romania, 1 August 1943.

**Kane, John R. (Air Mission)**
Colonel, U.S. Army Air Corps. Ninth Air Force, Raid on Ploeşti, Romania, 1 August 1943.

**Kearby, Neel E. (Air Mission)**
Colonel, U.S. Army Air Corps. Near Wewak, New Guinea, 11 October 1943.

**Kelly, Charles E.**
Corporal, U.S. Army. Company L, 143rd Infantry, 36th Infantry Division, near Altavilla, Italy, 13 September 1943.

**Kisters, Gerry H.**
Sergeant, U.S. Army. 2nd Armored Division, near Gagliano, Sicily, 31 July 1943.

**Lindstrom, Floyd K. (P)**
Private First Class, U.S. Army. 3rd Infantry Division, near Mignano, Italy, 11 November 1943.

**Logan, James M.**
Sergeant, U.S. Army. 26th Infantry Division, Salerno, Italy, 9 September 1943.

**Martinez, Joe P. (P)**
Private, U.S. Army. Company K, 32nd Infantry, 7th Infantry Division, Attu, Aleutians, 26 May 1943.

**Mathis, Jack W. (Air Mission) (P)**
First Lieutenant, U.S. Army Air Corps. 359th Bomber Squadron, 303rd Bomber Group, over Vegesack, Germany, 18 March 1943.

**Minue, Nicholas (P)**
Private, U.S. Army. Company A, 6th Armored Infantry, 1st Armored Division, near Medjez-el-Bab, Tunisia, 28 April 1943.

**Morgan, John C. (Air Mission)**
Second Lieutenant, U.S. Army Air Corps. 326th Bomber Squadron, 92nd Bomber Group, over Europe, 28 July 1943.

**Nelson, William L. (P)**
Sergeant, U.S. Army. 60th Infantry, 9th Infantry Division, Djebel Dardys, northwest of Sedjenane, Tunisia, 24 April 1943.

**Ohata, Allan M. (P)**
Sergeant, U.S. Army. Near Cerasuolo, Italy, 30 November 1943.

**Olson, Arlo L. (P)**
Captain, U.S. Army. 15th Infantry, 3rd Infantry Division, crossing the Volturno River, Italy, 13 October 1943.

**Owens, Robert A. (P)**
Sergeant, U.S. Marine Corps. Cape Torokina, Bougainville, Solomon Islands, 1 November 1943.

**Parle, John J. (P)**
Ensign, U.S. Naval Reserve. Officer-in-Charge of Small Boats aboard USS *LST-375*, Sicily, 9–10 July 1943.

**Petrarca, Frank J. (P)**
Private First Class, U.S. Army. Medical Detachment, 145th Infantry, 37th Infantry Division, at Horseshoe Hill, New Georgia, Solomon Islands, 27 July 1943.

**Reese, James W. (P)**
Private, U.S. Army. 26th Infantry, 1st Infantry Division, Monte Vassillio, Sicily, 5 August 1943.

**Sarnoski, Joseph R. (Air Mission) (P)**
Second Lieutenant, U.S. Army Air Corps. 43rd Bomber Group, over Buka area, Solomon Islands, 16 June 1943.

**Scott, Robert S.**
Lieutenant, U.S. Army. 172nd Infantry, 43rd Infantry Division, near Munda airfield, New Georgia, Solomon Islands, 29 July 1943.

**Shoup, David M.**
Colonel, U.S. Marine Corps. Commanding officer of marines on Betio Island, Tarawa Atoll, 20–22 November 1943.

**Slaton, James D.**
Corporal, U.S. Army. 157th Infantry, 45th Infantry Division, near Oliveto, Italy, 23 September 1943.

### Smith, Maynard H. (Air Mission)
Sergeant, U.S. Army Air Corps. 423rd Bombardment Squadron, 306th Bomber Group, over Europe, 1 May 1943.

### Swett, James E.
First Lieutenant, U.S. Marine Corps Reserve. Marine Fighter Squadron 221, with Marine Aircraft Group 12, 1st Marine Aircraft Wing, Solomon Islands area, 7 April 1943.

### Thomas, Herbert J. (P)
Sergeant, U.S. Marine Corps Reserve. 3rd Marines, 3rd Marine Division, Koromokina River, Bougainville Island, Solomon Islands, 7 November 1943.

### Van Noy, Nathan Jr. (P)
Private, U.S. Army. Headquarters Company, Shore Battalion, Engineer Boat and Shore Regiment, near Finschhafen, New Guinea, 17 October 1943.

### Van Voorhis, Bruce A. (P)
Lieutenant Commander, U.S. Navy. Commander of Bombing Squadron 102 and Plane Commander of a PB4Y-I patrol bomber, Greenwich Island, during the battle of the Solomon Islands, 6 July 1943.

### Vosler, Forrest T. (Air Mission)
Technical Sergeant, U.S. Army Air Corps. 358th Bomber Squadron, 303rd Bomber Group, over Bremen, Germany, 20 December 1943.

### Walker, Kenneth N. (Air Mission) (P)
Brigadier General, U.S. Army Air Corps. Commander of V Bomber Command, Rabaul, New Britain, 5 January 1943.

### Walsh, Kenneth A.
First Lieutenant, U.S. Marine Corps. Marine Fighter Squadron 124, Solomon Islands area, 15 and 30 August 1943.

### Watson, George (P)
Private, U.S. Army. 2nd Battalion, 29th Quartermaster Regiment near Porloch Harbor, New Guinea, 8 March 1943.

### Waybur, David C.
First Lieutenant, U.S. Army. 3rd Reconnaissance Troop, 3rd Infantry Division, near Agrigento, Sicily, 17 July 1943.

### Wilkins, Raymond H. (Air Mission) (P)
Major, U.S. Army Air Corps. Near Rabaul, New Britain, 2 November 1943.

### Young, Rodger W. (P)
Private, U.S. Army. 148th Infantry, 37th Infantry Division, New Georgia, Solomon Islands, 31 July 1943.

### Zeamer, Jay, Jr. (Air Mission)
Major, U.S. Army Air Corps. Over Buka area, Solomon Islands, 16 June 1943.

# 1944

**Adams, Lucian**
Staff Sergeant, U.S. Army. 30th Infantry, 3rd Infantry Division, near St. Die, France, 28 October 1944.

**Agerholm, Harold C. (P)**
Private First Class, U.S. Marine Corps Reserve. 4th Battalion, 10th Marines, 2nd Marine Division, Saipan, 7 July 1944.

**Anderson, Richard B. (P)**
Private First Class, U.S. Marine Corps. 4th Marine Division, Roi Island, Kwajalein Atoll, 1 February 1944.

**Antolak, Sylvester (P)**
Sergeant, U.S. Army. Company B, 15th Infantry, 3rd Infantry Division, near Cisterna di Littoria, Italy, 24 May 1944.

**Baker, Thomas A. (P)**
Sergeant, U.S. Army. Company A, 105th Infantry, 27th Infantry Division, Saipan, 19 June to 7 July 1944.

**Barfoot, Van T.**
Second Lieutenant, U.S. Army. 157th Infantry, 45th Infantry Division, near Carano, Italy, 23 May 1944.

**Barrett, Carlton W.**
Private, U.S. Army. 18th Infantry, 1st Infantry Division, near St-Laurent-sur-Mer, France, 6 June 1944.

**Bausell, Lewis K. (P)**
Corporal, U.S. Marine Corps. 1st Battalion, 5th Marines, 1st Marine Division, Peleliu, 15 September 1944.

**Bell, Bernard P.**
Technical Sergeant, U.S. Army. Company I, 142nd Infantry, 36th Infantry Division, Mittelwihr, France, 18 December 1944.

**Bender, Stanley**
Staff Sergeant, U.S. Army. Company E, 7th Infantry, 3rd Infantry Division, near La Lande, France, 17 August 1944.

**Benjamin, George, Jr. (P)**
Private First Class, U.S. Army. Company A, 306th Infantry, 77th Infantry Division, Leyte, Philippine Islands, 21 December 1944.

**Biddle, Melvin E.**
Private First Class, U.S. Army. Company B, 517th Parachute Infantry Regiment, near Soy, Belgium, 23–24 December 1944.

### Bloch, Orville E.
First Lieutenant, U.S. Army. Company E, 338th Infantry, 85th Infantry Division, near Firenzuola, Italy, 22 September 1944.

### Bolden, Paul L.
Staff Sergeant, U.S. Army. Company 1, 120th Infantry, 30th Infantry Division, Petit-Coo, Belgium, 23 December 1944.

### Bolton, Cecil H.
First Lieutenant, U.S. Army. Company E, 413th Infantry, 104th Infantry Division, Mark River, Holland, 2 November 1944.

### Bong, Richard I. (Air Mission)
Major, U.S. Army Air Corps. Over Borneo and Leyte, Philippines, 10 October to 15 November 1944.

### Boyce, George W. G., Jr. (P)
Second Lieutenant, U.S. Army. 112th Cavalry Regimental Combat Team, near Afua, New Guinea, 23 July 1944.

### Briles, Herschel F.
Staff Sergeant, U.S. Army. Company C, 899th Tank Destroyer Battalion, near Scherpenseel, Germany, 20 November 1944.

### Brostrom, Leonard C. (P)
Private First Class, U.S. Army. Company F, 17th Infantry, 7th Infantry Division, near Dagami, Leyte, Philippine Islands, 28 October 1944.

### Brown, Bobbie E.
Captain, U.S. Army. Company C, 18th Infantry, 1st Infantry Division, Crucifix Hill, Aachen, Germany, 8 October 1944.

### Burt, James M.
Captain, U.S. Army. Company B, 66th Armored Regiment, 2nd Armored Division, near Wurselen, Germany, 13 October 1944.

### Butts, John E. (P)
Second Lieutenant, U.S. Army. Company E, 60th Infantry, 9th Infantry Division, Normandy, France, 14, 16, and 23 June 1944.

### Carey, Alvin P. (P)
Staff Sergeant, U.S. Army. 38th Infantry, 2nd Infantry Division, near Plougastel, Brittany, France, 23 August 1944.

### Carr, Chris
Sergeant, U.S. Army. Company L, 337th Infantry, 85th Infantry Division, near Guignola, Italy, 1–2 October 1944.

### Carswell, Horace S., Jr. (Air Mission) (P)
Major, U.S. Army Air Corps. 308th Bombardment Group, over the South China Sea, 26 October 1944.

## Castle, Frederick W. (Air Mission) (P)

Brigadier General, U.S. Army Air Corps. Assistant Commander, 4th Bomber Wing, over Germany, 24 December 1944.

## Choate, Clyde L.

Staff Sergeant, U.S. Army. Company C, 601st Tank Destroyer Battalion, near Bruyeres, France, 25 October 1944.

## Christensen, Dale E. (P)

Second Lieutenant, U.S. Army. Troop E, 112th Cavalry Regiment, Driniumor River, New Guinea, 16–19 July 1944.

## Christian, Herbert F. (P)

Private, U.S. Army. 15th Infantry, 3rd Infantry Division, near Valmontone, Italy, 2–3 June 1944.

## Clark, Francis J.

Technical Sergeant, U.S. Army. Company K, 109th Infantry, 28th Infantry Division, near Kalborn, Luxembourg, 12 September 1944 and near Sevenig, Germany, 17 September 1944.

## Cole, Robert G. (P)

Lieutenant Colonel, U.S. Army. 101st Airborne Division, near Carentan, France, 11 June 1944.

## Connor, James P.

Sergeant, U.S. Army. 7th Infantry, 3rd Infantry Division, Cape Cavalaire, southern France, 15 August 1944.

## Coolidge, Charles H.

Technical Sergeant, U.S. Army. Company M, 141st Infantry, 36th Infantry Division, east of Belmont sur Buttant, France, 24–27 October 1944.

## Cowan, Richard E. (P)

Private First Class, U.S. Army. Company M, 23rd Infantry, 2nd Infantry Division, near Krinkelter Wald, Belgium, 17 December 1944.

## Currey, Francis S.

Sergeant, U.S. Army. Company K, 120th Infantry, 30th Infantry Division, Malmedy, Belgium, 21 December 1944.

## Dalessondro, Peter J.

Technical Sergeant, U.S. Army. Company E, 39th Infantry, 9th Infantry Division, near Kalterherberg, Germany, 22 December 1944.

## Damato, Anthony P. (P)

Corporal, U.S. Marine Corps. Engebi Island, Eniwetok Atoll, on the night of 19–20 February 1944.

## David, Albert L. (P)

Lieutenant, Junior Grade, U.S. Navy. USS *Pillsbury,* French West Africa, 4 June 1944.

### Davila, Rudolph B.
Staff Sergeant, U.S. Army. Near Artena, Italy, 28 May 1944.

### Dealey, Samuel D. (P)
Commander, U.S. Navy. Captain of submarine USS *Harder* during her fifth war patrol, 26 May–3 July 1944.

### Defranzo, Arthur F. (P)
Staff Sergeant, U.S. Army. 1st Infantry Division, near Vaubadon, France, 10 June 1944.

### Deglopper, Charles N. (P)
Private First Class, U.S. Army. Company C, 325th Glider Infantry, 82nd Airborne Division, Merderet River at la Fiere, France, 9 June 1944.

### Dervishian, Ernest H.
Second Lieutenant, U.S. Army. 34th Infantry Division, near Cisterna, Italy, 23 May 1944.

### Drowley, Jesse R.
Staff Sergeant, U.S. Army. Americal Division, Bougainville, Solomon Islands, 30 January 1944.

### Dutko, John W. (P)
Private First Class, U.S. Army. 3rd Infantry Division, near Ponte Rotto, Italy, 23 May 1944.

### Dyess, Aquilla J. (P)
Lieutenant Colonel, U.S. Marine Corps Reserve. Commander of 1st Battalion, 24th Marines (Rein), 4th Marine Division, Namur Island, Kwajalein Atoll, 1 and 2 February 1944.

### Ehlers, Walter D.
Staff Sergeant, U.S. Army. 18th Infantry, 1st Infantry Division, near Goville, France, 9–10 June 1944.

### Endl, Gerald L. (P)
Staff Sergeant, U.S. Army. 32nd Infantry Division, near Anamo, New Guinea, 11 July 1944.

### Epperson, Harold G. (P)
Private First Class, U.S. Marine Corps Reserve. 1st Battalion, 6th Marines, 2nd Marine Division, Saipan, 25 June 1944.

### Eubanks, Ray E. (P)
Sergeant, U.S. Army. Company D, 503rd Parachute Infantry, Noemfoor Island, New Guinea, 23 July 1944.

### Evans, Ernest E. (P)
Commander, U.S. Navy. Captain of USS *Johnston,* Samar, Philippines, 25 October 1944.

**Everhart, Forrest E.**
Technical Sergeant, U.S. Army. Company H, 359th Infantry, 90th Infantry Division, near Kerling, France, 12 November 1944.

**Femoyer, Robert E. (Air Mission) (P)**
Second Lieutenant, U.S. Army Air Corps. 711th Bombing Squadron, 447th Bomber Group, over Merseburg, Germany, 2 November 1944.

**Fields, James H.**
First Lieutenant, U.S. Army. 10th Armored Infantry, 4th Armored Division, Rechicourt, France, 27 September 1944.

**Fisher, Almond E.**
Second Lieutenant, U.S. Army. Company E, 157th Infantry, 45th Infantry Division, near Grammont, France, 12–13 September 1944.

**Fluckey, Eugene B.**
Commander, U.S. Navy. Captain of USS *Barb,* along coast of China, 19 December 1944–15 February 1945.

**Fowler, Thomas W. (P)**
Second Lieutenant, U.S. Army. 1st Armored Division, near Carano, Italy, 23 May 1944.

**Fox, John R. (P)**
Second Lieutenant, U.S. Army. Cannon Company, 366th Infantry Regiment, 92nd Infantry Division, near Sommocolonia, Italy, 26 December 1944.

**Fryar, Elmer E. (P)**
Private, U.S. Army. Company E, 511th Parachute Infantry, 11th Airborne Division, Leyte, Philippine Islands, 8 December 1944.

**Galt, William W. (P)**
Captain, U.S. Army. 168th Infantry, 34th Infantry Division, Villa Crocetta, Italy, 29 May 1944.

**Garcia, Marcario**
Staff Sergeant, U.S. Army. Company B, 22nd Infantry, 4th Infantry Division, near Grosshau, Germany, 27 November 1944.

**Garman, Harold A.**
Private, U.S. Army. Company B, 5th Medical Battalion, 5th Infantry Division, near Montereau, France, 25 August 1944.

**Gerstung, Robert E.**
Technical Sergeant, U.S. Army. Company H, 313th Infantry, 79th Infantry Division, Siegfried Line near Berg, Germany, 19 December 1944.

**Gibson, Eric G. (P)**
Technician Fifth Grade, U.S. Army. 3rd Infantry Division, near Isola Bella, Italy, 28 January 1944.

### Gordon, Nathan G.

Lieutenant, U.S. Navy. Commander of Catalina patrol plane. Bismarck Sea, 15 February 1944.

### Gott, Donald J. (Air Mission) (P)

First Lieutenant, U.S. Army Air Corps. 729th Bomber Squadron, 452nd Bombardment Group, Saarbrücken, Germany, 9 November 1944.

### Gregg, Stephen R.

Second Lieutenant, U.S. Army. 143rd Infantry, 36th Infantry Division, near Montelimar, France, 27 August 1944.

### Hajiro, Barney, F.

Private, U.S. Army. In the vicinity of Bruyeres and Biffontaine, eastern France, 19, 22, and 29 October 1944.

### Hall, George J.

Staff Sergeant, U.S. Army. 135th Infantry, 34th Infantry Division, near Anzio, Italy, 23 May 1944.

### Hallman, Sherwood H. (P)

Staff Sergeant, U.S. Army. 175th Infantry, 29th Infantry Division, Brest, France, 13 September 1944.

### Harmon, Roy W. (P)

Sergeant, U.S. Army. Company C, 362nd Infantry, 91st Infantry Division, near Casaglia, Italy, 12 July 1944.

### Harris, James L. (P)

Second Lieutenant, U.S. Army. 756th Tank Battalion, Vagney, France, 7 October 1944.

### Hawk, John D.

Sergeant, U.S. Army. Company E, 359th Infantry, 90th Infantry Division, near Chambois, France, 20 August 1944.

### Hawks, Lloyd C.

Private First Class, U.S. Army. Medical Detachment, 30th Infantry, 3rd Infantry Division, near Carano, Italy, 30 January 1944.

### Hendrix, James R.

Private, U.S. Army. Company C, 53rd Armored Infantry Battalion, 4th Armored Division, near Assenois, Belgium, 26 December 1944.

### Henry, Robert T. (P)

Private, U.S. Army. 16th Infantry, 1st Infantry Division, Luchem, Germany, 3 December 1944.

### Horner, Freeman V.

Staff Sergeant, U.S. Army. Company K, 119th Infantry, 30th Infantry Division, Wurselen, Germany, 16 November 1944.

**Howard, James H. (Air Mission)**
Lieutenant Colonel, U.S. Army Air Corps. Over Oschersleben, Germany, 11 January 1944.

**Huff, Paul B.**
Corporal, U.S. Army. 509th Parachute Infantry Battalion, near Carano, Italy, 8 February 1944.

**Jackson, Arthur J.**
Private First Class, U.S. Marine Corps. 3rd Battalion, 7th Marines, 1st Marine Division, Peleliu, 18 September 1944.

**Johnson, Elden H. (P)**
Private, U.S. Army. 15th Infantry, 3rd Infantry Division, near Valmontone, Italy, 3 June 1944.

**Johnson, Leroy (P)**
Sergeant, U.S. Army. Company K, 126th Infantry, 32nd Infantry Division, near Limon, Leyte, Philippine Islands, 15 December 1944.

**Johnson, Oscar G.**
Sergeant, U.S. Army. Company B, 363rd Infantry, 91st Infantry Division, near Scarperia, Italy, 16–18 September 1944.

**Johnston, William J.**
Private First Class, U.S. Army. Company G, 180th Infantry, 45th Infantry Division, near Padiglione, Italy, 17–19 February 1944.

**Kandle, Victor L. (P)**
First Lieutenant, U.S. Army. 15th Infantry, 3rd Infantry Division, near La Forge, France, 9 October 1944.

**Keathley, George D. (P)**
Staff Sergeant, U.S. Army. 85th Infantry Division, Monte Altuzzo, Italy, 14 September 1944.

**Kefurt, Gus (P)**
Staff Sergeant, U.S. Army. Company K, 15th Infantry, 3rd Infantry Division, near Bennwihr, France, 23–24 December 1944.

**Kelley, Ova A. (P)**
Private, U.S. Army. Company A, 382nd Infantry, 96th Infantry Division, Leyte, Philippine Islands, 8 December 1944.

**Kelly, John D. (P)**
Corporal, U.S. Army. Company E, 314th Infantry, 79th Infantry Division, Fort du Roule, Cherbourg, France, 25 June 1944.

**Kessler, Patrick L. (P)**
Private First Class, U.S. Army. Company K, 30th Infantry, 3rd Infantry Division, near Ponte Rotto, Italy, 23 May 1944.

### Kimbro, Truman (P)

Technician Fourth Grade, U.S. Army. Company C, 2nd Engineer Combat Battalion, 2nd Infantry Division, near Rocherath, Belgium, 19 December 1944.

### Kiner, Harold G. (P)

Private, U.S. Army. Company F, 117th Infantry, 30th Infantry Division, near Palenberg, Germany, 2 October 1944.

### Kingsley, David R. (Air Mission) (P)

Second Lieutenant, U.S. Army Air Corps. 97th Bombardment Group, Fifteenth Air Force, Raid on Ploeşti, Romania, 23 June 1944.

### Knappenberger, Alton W.

Private First Class, U.S. Army. 3rd Infantry Division, near Cisterna di Littoria, Italy, 1 February 1944.

### Kobashigawa, Yeiki

Technical Sergeant, U.S. Army. In the vicinity of Lanuvio, Italy, 2 June 1944.

### Kraus, Richard E. (P)

Private First Class, U.S. Marine Corps Reserve. 8th Amphibious Tractor Battalion, Fleet Marine Force, Peleliu, 5 October 1944.

### Kuroda, Robert T. (P)

Staff Sergeant, U.S. Army. Near Bruyeres, France, 20 October 1944.

### Lawley, William R., Jr. (Air Mission)

First Lieutenant, U.S. Army Air Corps. 364th Bomber Squadron, 305th Bomber Group, over Europe, 20 February 1944.

### Lee, Daniel W.

First Lieutenant, U.S. Army. Troop A, 117th Cavalry Reconnaissance Squadron, Montreval, France, 2 September 1944.

### Leonard, Turney W.

First Lieutenant, U.S. Army. Company C, 893rd Tank Destroyer Battalion, Kommerscheidt, Germany, 4–6 November 1944.

### Lindsey, Darrell R. (Air Mission) (P)

Captain, U.S. Army Air Corps. L'Isle Adam railroad bridge over the Seine, France, 9 August 1944.

### Lindsey, Jake W.

Technical Sergeant, U.S. Army. 16th Infantry, 1st Infantry Division, near Hamich, Germany, 16 November 1944.

### Lloyd, Edgar H. (P)

First Lieutenant, U.S. Army. Company E, 319th Infantry, 80th Infantry Division, near Pompey, France, 14 September 1944.

## Lobaugh, Donald R. (P)

Private, U.S. Army. 127th Infantry, 23rd Infantry Division, near Afua, New Guinea, 22 July 1944.

## Lopez, Jose M.

Sergeant, U.S. Army. 23rd Infantry, 2nd Infantry Division, near Krinkelt, Belgium, 17 December 1944.

## Mabry, George L., Jr.

Lieutenant Colonel, U.S. Army. 2nd Battalion, 8th Infantry, 4th Infantry Division, Hürtgen Forest near Schevenhutte, Germany, 20 November 1944.

## Mann, Joe E. (P)

Private First Class, U.S. Army. Company H, 502nd Parachute Infantry, 101st Airborne Division, Best, Holland, 18 September 1944.

## Mason, Leonard F. (P)

Private First Class, U.S. Marine Corps. 2nd Battalion, 3rd Marines, 3rd Marine Division, Asan-Adelup Beachhead, Guam, 22 July 1944.

## Mathies, Archibald (Air Mission) (P)

Sergeant, U.S. Army Air Corps. 510th Bomber Squadron, 351st Bomber Group, over Europe, 20 February 1944.

## Maxwell, Robert D.

Technician Fifth Grade, U.S. Army. 7th Infantry, 3rd Infantry Division, near Besançon, France, 7 September 1944.

## McCall, Thomas E.

Staff Sergeant, U.S. Army. Company F, 143rd Infantry, 36th Infantry Division, near San Angelo, Italy, 22 January 1944.

## McCampbell, David

Commander, U.S. Navy. Air Group 15, first and second battles of the Philippine Sea, 19 June 1944.

## McCard, Robert H. (P)

Gunnery Sergeant, U.S. Marine Corps. Company A, 4th Tank Battalion, 4th Marine Division, Saipan, 16 June 1944.

## McGarity, Vernon

Technical Sergeant, U.S. Army. Company L, 393rd Infantry, 99th Infantry Division, near Krinkelt, Belgium, 16 December 1944.

## McGill, Troy A. (P)

Sergeant, U.S. Army. Troop G, 5th Cavalry Regiment, 1st Cavalry Division, Los Negros Islands, Admiralty Group, 4 March 1944.

## McGraw, Francis X. (P)

Private First Class, U.S. Army. Company H, 26th Infantry, 1st Infantry Division, near Schevenhutte, Germany, 19 November 1944.

**McGuire, Thomas B., Jr. (Air Mission) (P)**

Major, U.S. Army Air Corps. Thirteenth Air Force, over Luzon, Philippine Islands, 25–26 December 1944.

**McVeigh, John J. (P)**

Sergeant, U.S. Army. Company H, 23rd Infantry, 2nd Infantry Division, near Brest, France, 29 August 1944.

**McWhorter, William A. (P)**

Private First Class, U.S. Army. Company M, 126th Infantry, 32nd Infantry Division, Leyte, Philippine Islands, 5 December 1944.

**Merli, Gino J.**

Private First Class, U.S. Army. 18th Infantry, 1st Infantry Division, near Sars la Bruyere, Belgium, 4–5 September 1944.

**Messerschmidt, Harold O. (P)**

Sergeant, U.S. Army. Company L, 30th Infantry, 3rd Infantry Division, near Radden, France, 17 September 1944.

**Metzger, William E., Jr. (Air Mission) (P)**

Second Lieutenant, U.S. Army Air Corps. 729th Bomber Squadron 452nd Bombardment Group, Saarbrücken, Germany, 9 November 1944.

**Michael, Edward S. (Air Mission)**

First Lieutenant, U.S. Army Air Corps. 364th Bomber Squadron, 305th Bomber Group, over Germany, 11 April 1944.

**Miller, Andrew (P)**

Staff Sergeant, U.S. Army. Company G, 377th Infantry, 95th Infantry Division, from Woippy, France, through Metz to Kerprich Hemmersdorf, Germany, 16–29 November 1944.

**Mills, James H.**

Private, U.S. Army. Company F, 15th Infantry, 3rd Infantry Division, near Cisterna di Littoria, Italy, 24 May 1944.

**Minick, John W. (P)**

Staff Sergeant, U.S. Army. Company I, 121st Infantry, 8th Infantry Division, near Hürtgen, Germany, 21 November 1944.

**Monteith, Jimmie W., Jr. (P)**

First Lieutenant, U.S. Army. 16th Infantry, 1st Infantry Division, near Colleville-sur-Mer, France, 6 June 1944.

**Montgomery, Jack C.**

First Lieutenant, U.S. Army. 45th Infantry Division, near Padiglione, Italy, 22 February 1944.

**Moon, Harold H., Jr. (P)**
Private, U.S. Army. Company G, 34th Infantry, 24th Infantry Division, Pawig, Leyte, Philippine Islands, 21 October 1944.

**Moto, Kaoru (P)**
Private First Class, U.S. Army. 100th Infantry Battalion. Near Castellina, Italy, 7 July 1944.

**Mower, Charles E. (P)**
Sergeant, U.S. Army. Company A, 34th Infantry, 24th Infantry Division, near Capoocan, Leyte, Philippine Islands, 3 November 1944.

**Muranaga, Kiyoshi K. (P)**
Private First Class, U.S. Army. Near Suvereto, Italy, 26 June 1944.

**Murray, Charles P., Jr.**
First Lieutenant, U.S. Army. Company C, 30th Infantry, 3rd Infantry Division, near Kaysersberg, France, 16 December 1944.

**Nakae, Masato (P)**
Private, U.S. Army. Near Pisa, Italy, 19 August 1944.

**Nakamine, Shinyei (P)**
Private, U.S. Army. Near La Torreto, Italy, 2 June 1944.

**Nakamura, William K. (P)**
Private First Class, U.S. Army. Near Castellina, Italy, 4 July 1944.

**Neppel, Ralph G.**
Sergeant, U.S. Army. Company M, 329th Infantry, 83rd Infantry Division, Birgel, Germany, 14 December 1944.

**Nett, Robert P.**
Lieutenant, U.S. Army. Company E, 305th Infantry, 77th Infantry Division, near Cognon, Leyte, Philippine Islands, 14 December 1944.

**New, John D. (P)**
Private First Class, U.S. Marine Corps. 2nd Battalion, 7th Marines, 1st Marine Division, Peleliu, 25 September 1944.

**Newman, Beryl R.**
First Lieutenant, U.S. Army. 133rd Infantry, 34th Infantry Division, near Cisterna, Italy, 26 May 1944.

**Nishimoto, Joe M. (P)**
Private First Class, U.S. Army. Near La Houssiere, France, 7 November 1944.

**O'Brien, William J. (P)**
Lieutenant Colonel, U.S. Army. 1st Battalion, 105th Infantry, 27th Infantry Division, Saipan, 20 June–7 July 1944.

**Ogden, Carlos C.**
First Lieutenant, U.S. Army. Company K, 314th Infantry, 79th Infantry Division, near Fort du Roule, France, 25 June 1944.

**O'Kane, Richard H.**
Commander, U.S. Navy. Captain of USS *Tang,* vicinity Philippine Islands, 23–24 October 1944.

**Okubo, James K. (P)**
Technician Fifth Grade, U.S. Army. In the Fôret Domaniale de Champ, near Biffontaine, eastern France, 28 and 29 October and 4 November 1944.

**Olson, Truman O. (P)**
Sergeant, U.S. Army. Company B, 7th Infantry, 3rd Infantry Division, near Cisterna di Littoria, Italy, 30–31 January 1944.

**Ono, Frank H. (P)**
Private First Class, U.S. Army. Near Castellina, Italy, 4 July 1944.

**Otani, Kazuo (P)**
Staff Sergeant, U.S. Army. Near Pieve Di S. Luce, Italy, 15 July 1944.

**Ozbourn, Joseph W. (P)**
Private, U.S. Marine Corps. 1st Battalion, 23rd Marines, 4th Marine Division, Tinian, 30 July 1944.

**Pendleton, Jack J. (P)**
Staff Sergeant, U.S. Army. Company I, 120th Infantry, 30th Infantry Division, Bardenberg, Germany, 12 October 1944.

**Peregory, Frank D. (P)**
Technical Sergeant, U.S. Army. Company K, 116th Infantry, 29th Infantry Division, Grandcampe France, 8 June 1944.

**Phelps, Wesley (P)**
Private, U.S. Marine Corps. 3rd Battalion, 7th Marines, 1st Marine Division Peleliu Island, Palan Group, 4 October 1944.

**Pinder, John J., Jr. (P)**
Technician Fifth Grade, U.S. Army. 16th Infantry, 1st Infantry Division, near Colleville-sur-Mer, France, 6 June 1944.

**Pope, Everett P.**
Captain, U.S. Marine Corps. Company C, 1st Battalion, 1st Marines, 1st Marine Division, Peleliu Island, Palau group, 19–20 September 1944.

**Power, John V. (P)**
First Lieutenant, U.S. Marine Corps. 4th Marine Division, Namur Island, Kwajalein Atoll, 1 February 1944.

**Powers, Leo J.**
Private First Class, U.S. Army. 133rd Infantry, 34th Infantry Division, northwest of Cassino, Italy, 3 February 1944.

**Preston, Arthur M.**
Lieutenant, U.S. Navy Reserve. Torpedo Boat Squadron 33, Wasile Bay, Halmahera Island, 16 September 1944.

**Prussman, Ernest W. (P)**
Private First Class, U.S. Army. 13th Infantry, 8th Infantry Division, near Les Coates, Brittany, France, 8 September 1944.

**Pucket, Donald D. (Air Mission)**
First Lieutenant, U.S. Army Air Corps. 98th Bombardment Group, Raid on Ploeşti, Romania, 9 July 1944.

**Ramage, Lawson P.**
Commander, U.S. Navy. Captain of USS *Parche*, Pacific, 31 July 1944.

**Ray, Bernard J. (P)**
First Lieutenant, U.S. Army. Company F, 8th Infantry, 4th Infantry Division, Hürtgen Forest near Schevenhutte, Germany, 17 November 1944.

**Riordan, Paul F. (P)**
Second Lieutenant, U.S. Army. 34th Infantry Division, near Cassino, Italy, 3–8 February 1944.

**Rivers, Ruben (P)**
Sergeant, U.S. Army. Guebling, France, 15–19 November 1944.

**Roan, Charles H. (P)**
Private First Class, U.S. Marine Corps Reserve. 2nd Battalion, 7th Marines, 1st Marine Division, Peleliu, 18 September 1944.

**Roeder, Robert E. (P)**
Captain, U.S. Army. Company G, 350th Infantry, 88th Infantry Division, Monte Battaglia, Italy, 27–28 September 1944.

**Roosevelt, Theodore, Jr.**
Brigadier General, U.S. Army. Omaha Beach, Normandy, France, 6 June 1944.

**Ross, Wilburn K.**
Private, U.S. Army. Company G, 350th Infantry, 3rd Infantry Division, near St. Jacques, France, 30 October 1944.

**Rouh, Carlton R.**
First Lieutenant, U.S. Marine Corps Reserve. 1st Battalion, 5th Marines, 1st Marine Division, Peleliu, 15 September 1944.

### Sadowski, Joseph J. (P)
Sergeant, U.S. Army. 37th Tank Battalion, 4th Armored Division, Valhey, France, 14 September 1944.

### Sakato, George T.
Private, U.S. Army. Hill 617 near Biffontaine, France, 29 October 1944.

### Salomon, Ben L. (P)
Captain, U.S. Army. Surgeon for the 2nd Battalion, 105th Infantry, 27th Infantry Division, Saipan, 7 July 1944.

### Sayers, Foster J. (P)
Private First Class, U.S. Army. Company L, 357th Infantry, 90th Infantry Division, near Thionville, France, 12 November 1944.

### Schaefer, Joseph E.
Staff Sergeant, U.S. Army. Company I, 18th Infantry, 1st Infantry Division, near Stolberg, Germany, 24 September 1944.

### Schauer, Henry
Private First Class, U.S. Army. 3rd Infantry Division, near Cisterna di Littoria, Italy, 23–24 May 1944.

### Shea, Charles W.
Second Lieutenant, U.S. Army. Company F, 350th Infantry, 88th Infantry Division, near Mount Damiano, Italy, 12 May 1944.

### Sheridan, Carl V. (P)
Private First Class, U.S. Army. Company K, 47th Infantry, 9th Infantry Division, Frenzenberg Castle, Weisweiler, Germany, 26 November 1944.

### Silk, Edward A.
First Lieutenant, U.S. Army. Company E, 398th Infantry, 100th Infantry Division, near St. Pravel, France, 23 November 1944.

### Skaggs, Luther, Jr.
Private First Class, U.S. Marine Corps Reserve. 3rd Battalion, 3rd Marines, 3rd Marine Division, Asan-Adelup beachhead, Guam, 21–22 July 1944.

### Smith, Furman L. (P)
Private, U.S. Army. 135th Infantry, 34th Infantry Division, near Lanuvio, Italy, 31 May 1944.

### Soderman, William A.
Private First Class, U.S. Army. Company K, 9th Infantry, 2nd Infantry Division, near Rocherath, Belgium, 17 December 1944.

### Sorenson, Richard K.
Private, U.S. Marine Corps Reserve. 4th Marine Division, Namur Island, Kwajalein Atoll, 1–2 February 1944.

**Specker, Joe C. (P)**
Sergeant, U.S. Army. 48th Engineer Combat Battalion, Monte Porchia, Italy, 7 January 1944.

**Spurrier, Junior J.**
Staff Sergeant, U.S. Army. Company G, 134th Infantry, 35th Infantry Division, Achain, France, 13 November 1944.

**Squires, John C. (P)**
Private First Class, U.S. Army. Company A, 30th Infantry, 3rd Infantry Division, near Padiglione, Italy, 23–24 April 1944.

**Tanouye, Ted T. (P)**
Technical Sergeant, U.S. Army. Near Moilno a Ventoabbto, Italy, 7 July 1944.

**Thomas, Charles L. (P)**
First Lieutenant, U.S. Army. Near Climbach, France, 14 December 1944.

**Thompson, Max**
Sergeant, U.S. Army. Company K, 18th Infantry, 1st Infantry Division, near Haaren, Germany, 18 October 1944.

**Thorne, Horace M. (P)**
Corporal, U.S. Army. Troop D, 89th Cavalry Reconnaissance Squadron, 9th Armored Division, near Grufflingen, Belgium, 21 December 1944.

**Thorson, John F. (P)**
Private First Class, U.S. Army. Company G, 17th Infantry, 7th Infantry Division, Dagami, Leyte, Philippine Islands, 28 October 1944.

**Timmerman, Grant F. (P)**
Sergeant, U.S. Marine Corps. 2nd Battalion, 6th Marines, 2nd Marine Division, Saipan, 8 July 1944.

**Tominac, John J.**
First Lieutenant, U.S. Army. Company I, 15th Infantry, 3rd Infantry Division, Saulx de Vesoul, France, 12 September 1944.

**Towle, John R. (P)**
Private, U.S. Army. Company C, 504th Parachute Infantry, 82nd Airborne Division. Near Oosterhout, Holland, 21 September 1944.

**Truemper, Walter E. (Air Mission) (P)**
Second Lieutenant, U.S. Army Air Corps. 510th Bomber Squadron, 351st Bomber Group, over Europe, 20 February 1944.

**Urban, Matt**
Captain, U.S. Army. 2nd Battalion, 60th Infantry Regiment, 9th Infantry Division, Renouf, France, 14 June to 3 September 1944.

**Vance, Leon R., Jr. (Air Mission) (P)**

Lieutenant Colonel, U.S. Army Air Corps. 489th Bomber Group, over Wimereaux, France, 5 June 1944.

**Vlug, Dirk J.**

Private First Class, U.S. Army. 126th Infantry, 32nd Infantry Division, near Limon, Leyte, Philippine Islands, 15 December 1944.

**Wai, Francis B. (P)**

Captain, U.S. Army. Red Beach, Leyte, Philippines, 20 October 1944.

**Ware, Keith L.**

Lieutenant Colonel, U.S. Army. 1st Battalion, 15th Infantry, 3rd Infantry Division, near Sigolsheim, France, 26 December 1944.

**Warner, Henry F. (P)**

Corporal, U.S. Army. Antitank Company, 2nd Battalion, 26th Infantry, 1st Infantry Division, near Dom Butgenbach, Belgium, 20–21 December 1944.

**Waugh, Robert T. (P)**

First Lieutenant, U.S. Army. 339th Infantry, 85th Infantry Division, near Tremensucli, Italy, 11–14 May 1944.

**Weicht, Ellis R. (P)**

Sergeant, U.S. Army. Company F, 142nd Infantry, 36th Infantry Division, St. Hippolyte, France, 3 December 1944.

**Whiteley, Eli**

First Lieutenant, U.S. Army. Company L, 15th Infantry, 3rd Infantry Division, Sigolsheim, France, 27 December 1944.

**Whittington, Hulon B.**

Sergeant, U.S. Army. 41st Armored Infantry, 2nd Armored Division, near Grimesnil, France, 29 July 1944.

**Wiedorfer, Paul J.**

Private, U.S. Army. Company G, 318th Infantry, 80th Infantry Division, near Chaumont, Belgium, 25 December 1944.

**Wigle, Thomas W. (P)**

Second Lieutenant, U.S. Army. Company K, 135th Infantry, 34th Infantry Division, Monte Frassino, Italy, 14 September 1944.

**Wilson, Alfred L. (P)**

Technician Fifth Grade, U.S. Army. Medical Detachment, 328th Infantry, 26th Infantry Division, near Bezange la Petite, France, 8 November 1944.

**Wilson, Louis H., Jr.**

Captain, U.S. Marine Corps. Rifle Company Commander, 2nd Battalion, 9th Marines, 3rd Marine Division, Fonte Hill, Guam, 25–26 July 1944.

**Wilson, Robert L. (P)**

Private First Class, U.S. Marine Corps. 2nd Battalion, 6th Marines, 2nd Marine Division, Tinian, 4 August 1944.

**Wise, Homer L.**

Staff Sergeant, U.S. Army. Company L, 142nd Infantry, 36th Infantry Division, Magliano, Italy, 14 June 1944.

**Witek, Frank Peter (P)**

Private First Class, U.S. Marine Corps Reserve. 1st Battalion, 9th Marines, 3rd Marine Division, Finegayen, Guam, 3 August 1944.

**Zussman, Raymond (P)**

Second Lieutenant, U.S. Army. 756th Tank Battalion, Noroy le Bourg, France, 12 September 1944.

# 1945

**Anderson, Beauford T.**

Technical Sergeant, U.S. Army. 381st Infantry, 96th Infantry Division, Okinawa, 13 April 1945.

**Atkins, Thomas E.**

Private First Class, U.S. Army. Company A, 127th Infantry, 32nd Infantry Division, Villa Verde Trail, Luzon, Philippine Islands, 10 March 1945.

**Baker, Vernon**

Second Lieutenant, U.S. Army. Near Viareggio Italy, 5–6 April 1945.

**Beaudoin, Raymond O. (P)**

First Lieutenant, U.S. Army. Company F, 119th Infantry, 30th Infantry Division, Hamelin, Germany, 6 April 1945.

**Bennett, Edward A.**

Corporal, U.S. Army, Company B, 358th Infantry, 90th Infantry Division, Heckhuscheid, Germany, February 1945.

**Berry, Charles J. (P)**

Corporal, U.S. Marine Corps. 1st Battalion, 26th Marines, 5th Marine Division, Iwo Jima, 3 March 1945.

**Bertoldo, Vito R.**

Master Sergeant, U.S. Army. Company A, 242nd Infantry, 42nd Infantry Division, Hatten, France, 9–10 January 1945.

**Beyer, Arthur O.**

Corporal, U.S. Army. Company C, 603rd Tank Destroyer Battalion, near Arloncourt, Belgium, 15 January 1945.

**Bigelow, Elmer C. (P)**
Watertender First Class, U.S. Naval Reserve. USS *Fletcher,* Corregidor Island, Philippines, 14 February 1945.

**Burke, Frank**
First Lieutenant, U.S. Army. 15th Infantry, 3rd Infantry Division, Nürnberg, Germany, 17 April 1945.

**Burr, Herbert H.**
Staff Sergeant, U.S. Army. Company C, 41st Tank Battalion, 11th Armored Division, near Dorrmoschel, Germany, 19 March 1945.

**Bush, Richard E.**
Corporal, U.S. Marine Corps Reserve. 1st Battalion, 4th Marines, 6th Marine Division, Mount Yaetake, Okinawa, 16 April 1945.

**Bush, Robert E.**
Hospital Apprentice First Class, U.S. Naval Reserve. Serving as medical corpsman with a rifle company, 2nd Battalion, 5th Marines, 1st Marine Division, Okinawa, 2 May 1945.

**Caddy, William R. (P)**
Private First Class, U.S. Marine Corps Reserve. Company I, 3rd Battalion, 26th Marines, 5th Marine Division, Iwo Jima, 3 March 1945.

**Carey, Charles F., Jr. (P)**
Technical Sergeant, U.S. Army. 379th Infantry, 100th Infantry Division, Rimling, France, 8–9 January 1945.

**Carter, Edward A., Jr. (P)**
Sergeant, U.S. Army. Near Speyer, Germany, 23 March 1945.

**Chambers, Justice M.**
Colonel, U.S. Marine Corps Reserve. 3rd Assault Battalion Landing Team, 25th Marines, 4th Marine Division, Iwo Jima, 19–22 February 1945.

**Cicchetti, Joseph J. (P)**
Private First Class, U.S. Army. Company A, 148th Infantry, 37th Infantry Division, south Manila, Luzon, Philippine Islands, 9 February 1945.

**Colalillo, Mike**
Private First Class, U.S. Army. Company C, 398th Infantry, 100th Infantry Division, near Untergriesheim, Germany, 7 April 1945.

**Cole, Darrell S. (P)**
Sergeant, U.S. Marine Corps Reserve. Company B, 1st Battalion, 23rd Marines, 4th Marine Division, Iwo Jima, 19 February 1945.

**Cooley, Raymond H.**
Staff Sergeant, U.S. Army. Company B, 27th Infantry, 25th Infantry Division, near Lumboy, Luzon, Philippine Islands, 24 February 1945.

## Courtney, Henry A., Jr. (P)

Major, U.S. Marine Corps Reserve. Executive Officer of 2nd Battalion, 22nd Marines, 6th Marine Division, Okinawa, 14–15 May 1945.

## Craft, Clarence B.

Private First Class, U.S. Army. Company G, 382nd Infantry, 96th Infantry Division, Hen Hill, Okinawa, 31 May 1945.

## Crain, Morris E. (P)

Technical Sergeant, U.S. Army. Company E, 141st Infantry, 36th Infantry Division, Haguenau, France, 13 March 1945.

## Crews, John R.

Staff Sergeant, U.S. Army. Company F, 253rd Infantry, 63rd Infantry Division, near Lobenbacherhof, Germany, 8 April 1945.

## Dahlgren, Edward C.

Sergeant, U.S. Army. Company E, 142nd Infantry, 36th Infantry Division, Oberhoffen, France, 11 February 1945.

## Daly, Michael J.

Lieutenant, U.S. Army. Company A, 15th Infantry, 3rd Infantry Division, Nürnberg, Germany, 18 April 1945.

## Davis, George F. (P)

Commander, U.S. Navy. Captain of USS *Walke*, Lingayen Gulf, Luzon, Philippine Islands, 6 January 1945.

## Day, James

Corporal, U.S. Marine Corps. 2nd Battalion, 22nd Marines, 6th Marine Division, Okinawa, 14–17 May 1945.

## Deleau, Emile, Jr. (P)

Sergeant, U.S. Army. Company A, 142nd Infantry, 36th Infantry Division, Oberhoffen, France, 12 February 1945.

## Diamond, James H. (P)

Private First Class, U.S. Army, Company D, 21st Infantry, 24th Infantry Division, Mintal, Mindanao, Philippine Islands, 8–14 May 1945.

## Dietz, Robert H. (P)

Staff Sergeant, U.S. Army. Company A, 38th Armored Infantry Battalion, 7th Armored Division, Kirchain, Germany, 29 March 1945.

## Doss, Desmond T.

Private First Class, U.S. Army. Medical Detachment, 307th Infantry, 77th Infantry Division, near Urasoe Mura, Okinawa, 29 April–21 May 1945.

**Dunham, Russell E.**
Technical Sergeant, U.S. Army. Company I, 30th Infantry, 3rd Infantry Division, near Kayserberg, France, 8 January 1945.

**Dunlap, Robert H.**
Captain, U.S. Marine Corps Reserve. Company C, 1st Battalion, 26th Marines, 5th Marine Division, Iwo Jima, 20 and 21 February 1945.

**Erwin, Henry E. (Air Mission)**
Staff Sergeant, U.S. Army Air Corps. 52nd Bombardment Squadron, 29th Bombardment Group, Twentieth Air Force, Koriyama, Japan, 12 April 1945.

**Fardy, John Peter (P)**
Corporal, U.S. Marine Corps. Company C, 1st Battalion, 1st Marines, 1st Marine Division, Okinawa, 7 May 1945.

**Foster, William A. (P)**
Private First Class, U.S. Marine Corps Reserve. 3rd Battalion, 1st Marines, 1st Marine Division, Okinawa, 2 May 1945.

**Funk, Leonard A., Jr.**
First Sergeant, U.S. Army. Company C, 508th Parachute Infantry, 82nd Airborne Division, Holzheim, Belgium, 29 January 1945.

**Gammon, Archer T. (P)**
Staff Sergeant, U.S. Army. Company A, 9th Armored Infantry Battalion, 6th Armored Division, near Bastogne, Belgium, 11 January 1945.

**Gary, Donald A. (P)**
Lieutenant, Junior Grade, U.S. Navy. USS *Franklin*, off the Japanese home islands near Kobe, Japan, 19 March 1945.

**Gonsalves, Harold (P)**
Private First Class, U.S. Marine Corps Reserve. Acting Scout Sergeant with the 4th Battalion, 15th Marines, 6th Marine Division, Okinawa, 15 April 1945.

**Gonzales, David M. (P)**
Private First Class, U.S. Army. Company A, 127th Infantry, 32nd Infantry Division, Villa Verde Trail, Luzon, Philippine Islands, 25 April 1945.

**Grabiarz, William J. (P)**
Private First Class, U.S. Army. Troop E, 5th Cavalry, 1st Cavalry Division, Manila, Luzon, Philippine Islands, 23 February 1945.

**Gray, Ross F. (P)**
Sergeant, U.S. Marine Corps Reserve. Company A, 1st Battalion, 25th Marines, 4th Marine Division, Iwo Jima, 21 February 1945.

**Halyburton, William D., Jr. (P)**
Pharmacist's Mate Second Class, U.S. Naval Reserve. Attached to the 2nd Battalion, 5th Marines, 1st Marine Division, Okinawa, 10 May 1945.

**Hammerberg, Owen F. P. (P)**
Boatswain's Mate Second Class, U.S. Navy. Rescue operations at West Loch, Pearl Harbor, 17 February 1945.

**Hansen, Dale M. (P)**
Private, U.S. Marine Corps. Company E, 2nd Battalion, 1st Marines, 1st Marine Division, Okinawa, 7 May 1945.

**Harr, Harry R. (P)**
Corporal, U.S. Army. Company D, 124th Infantry, 31st Infantry Division, near Maglamin, Mindanao, Philippine Islands, 5 June 1945.

**Harrell, William G. (P)**
Sergeant, U.S. Marine Corps. 1st Battalion, 28th Marines, 5th Marine Division, Iwo Jima, 3 March 1945.

**Hastings, Joe R. (P)**
Private First Class, U.S. Army. Company C, 386th Infantry, 97th Infantry Division, Drabenderhohe, Germany, 12 April 1945.

**Hauge, Louis J., Jr. (P)**
Corporal, U.S. Marine Corps Reserve. Company C, 1st Battalion, 1st Marines, 1st Marine Division, Okinawa, 14 May 1945.

**Hayashi, Joe (P)**
Private, U.S. Army. Near Tendola, Italy, 20 and 22 April 1945.

**Hedrick, Clinton M. (P)**
Technical Sergeant, U.S. Army. Company I, 194th Glider Infantry, 17th Airborne Division, near Lembeck, Germany, 27–28 March 1945.

**Herrera, Silvestre S.**
Private First Class, U.S. Army. Company E, 142nd Infantry, 36th Infantry Division, near Mertzwiller, France, 15 March 1945.

**Herring, Rufus G.**
Lieutenant, U.S. Naval Reserve. *LCI (G) 449*, Iwo Jima, 17 February 1945.

**Inouye, Daniel K.**
Second Lieutenant, U.S. Army. Vicinity of San Terenzo, Italy, 21 April 1945.

**Jachman, Isadore S. (P)**
Staff Sergeant, U.S. Army. Company B, 513th Parachute Infantry Regiment, Flamierge, Belgium, 4 January 1945.

**Jacobson, Douglas T.**
Private First Class, U.S. Marine Corps Reserve. 3rd Battalion, 23rd Marines, 4th Marine Division, Iwo Jima, 26 February 1945.

**James, Willy F. (P)**
Private First Class, U.S. Army. Near Lippoldsberg, Germany, 7 April 1945.

**Julian, Joseph R. (P)**
Platoon Sergeant, U.S. Marine Corps Reserve. 1st Battalion, 27th Marines, 5th Marine Division, Iwo Jima, 9 March 1945.

**Kelley, Jonah E. (P)**
Staff Sergeant, U.S. Army. 311th Infantry, 78th Infantry Division, Kesternich, Germany, 30–31 January 1945.

**Kelly, Thomas J.**
Corporal, U.S. Army. Medical Detachment, 48th Armored Infantry Battalion, 7th Armored Division, Alemert, Germany, 5 April 1945.

**Kerstetter, Dexter J.**
Private First Class, U.S. Army. Company C, 130th Infantry, 33rd Infantry Division, near Galiano, Luzon, Philippine Islands, 13 April 1945.

**Kinser, Elbert L. (P)**
Sergeant, U.S. Marine Corps Reserve. Company I, 3rd Battalion, 1st Marines, 1st Marine Division, Okinawa, 4 May 1945.

**Knight, Jack L. (P)**
First Lieutenant, U.S. Army. 124th Cavalry Regiment, Mars Task Force, near Loi-kang, Burma, 2 February 1945.

**Knight, Raymond L. (Air Mission) (P)**
First Lieutenant, U.S. Army Air Corps. Northern Po Valley, Italy, 24–25 April 1945.

**Krotiak, Anthony L. (P)**
Private First Class, U.S. Army. Company I, 148th Infantry, 37th Infantry Division, Balete Pass, Luzon, Philippine Islands, 8 May 1945.

**La Belle, James D. (P)**
Private First Class, U.S. Marine Corps Reserve. 27th Marines, 5th Marine Division, Iwo Jima, 8 March 1945.

**Laws, Robert E.**
Staff Sergeant, U.S. Army. Company G, 169th Infantry, 43rd Infantry Division, Pangasinan Province, Luzon, Philippine Islands, 12 January 1945.

**Leims, John H.**
Second Lieutenant, U.S. Marine Corps Reserve. Company B, 1st Battalion, 9th Marines, 3rd Marine Division, Iwo Jima, 7 March 1945.

**Lester, Fred F. (P)**
Hospital Apprentice First Class, U.S. Navy. Medical Corpsman attached to 1st Battalion, 22nd Marines, 6th Marine Division, Okinawa, 8 June 1945.

**Lucas, Jacklyn H.**
Private First Class, U.S. Marine Corps Reserve. 1st Battalion, 26th Marines, 5th Marine Division, Iwo Jima, 20 February 1945.

**Lummus, Jack (P)**
First Lieutenant, U.S. Marine Corps Reserve. 2nd Battalion, 27th Marines, 5th Marine Division, Iwo Jima, 8 March 1945.

**MacGillivary, Charles A.**
Sergeant, U.S. Army. Company I, 71st Infantry, 44th Infantry Division, near Woelfling, France, 1 January 1945.

**Magrath, John D. (P)**
Private First Class, U.S. Army. Company G, 85th Infantry, 10th Mountain Division, near Castel d'Aiano, Italy, 14 April 1945.

**Martin, Harry L. (P)**
First Lieutenant, U.S. Marine Corps Reserve. Company C, 5th Pioneer Battalion, 5th Marine Division, Iwo Jima, 26 March 1945.

**May, Martin O. (P)**
Private First Class, U.S. Army. 307th Infantry, 77th Infantry Division, Legusuku-Yama, Ie Shima, Ryukyu Islands, 19–21 April 1945.

**Mayfield, Melvin**
Corporal, U.S. Army. Company D, 20th Infantry, 6th Infantry Division, Cordillera Mountains, Luzon, Philippine Islands, 29 July 1945.

**McCarter, Lloyd G.**
Private, U.S. Army. 503rd Parachute Infantry Regiment, Corregidor, Philippine Islands, 16–19 February 1945.

**McCarthy, Joseph J.**
Captain, U.S. Marine Corps Reserve. 2nd Battalion, 24th Marines, 4th Marine Division, Iwo Jima, 21 February 1945.

**McCool, Richard M.**
Lieutenant, U.S. Navy. USS *LSC(L)(3) 122* off Okinawa, 10–11 June 1945.

**McGaha, Charles L.**
Master Sergeant, U.S. Army. Company G, 35th Infantry, 25th Infantry Division, near Lupao, Luzon, Philippine Islands, 7 February 1945.

**McGee, William D. (P)**
Private, U.S. Army. Medical Detachment, 304th Infantry, 76th Infantry Division, near Mulheim, Germany, 18 March 1945.

### McKinney, John R.
Private, U.S. Army. Company A, 123rd Infantry, 33rd Infantry Division, Tayabas Province, Luzon, Philippine Islands, 11 May 1945.

### McTureous, Robert M., Jr. (P)
Private, U.S. Marine Corps. 3rd Battalion, 29th Marines, 6th Marine Division, Okinawa, 7 June 1945.

### Meagher, John
Technical Sergeant, U.S. Army. Company E, 305th Infantry, 77th Infantry Division, near Ozato, Okinawa, 19 June 1945.

### Merrell, Joseph F. (P)
Private, U.S. Army. Company I, 15th Infantry, 3rd Infantry Division, near Lohe, Germany, 18 April 1945.

### Michael, Harry J. (P)
Second Lieutenant, U.S. Army. Company L, 318th Infantry, 80th Infantry Division, near Neiderzerf, Germany, 14 March 1945.

### Moskala, Edward J. (P)
Private First Class, U.S. Army. Company C, 383rd Infantry, 96th Infantry Division, Kakazu Ridge, Okinawa, 9 April 1945.

### Muller, Joseph E. (P)
Sergeant, U.S. Army. Company B, 305th Infantry, 77th Infantry Division, near Ishimmi, Okinawa, 15–16 May 1945.

### Munemori, Sadao S. (P)
Private First Class, U.S. Army. Company A, 100th Infantry Battalion, 442nd Combat Team, near Seravezza, Italy, 5 April 1945.

### Murphy, Audie L.
Second Lieutenant, U.S. Army. Company B, 15th Infantry, 3rd Infantry Division, near Holtzwihr, France, 26 January 1945.

### Murphy, Frederick C. (P)
Private First Class, U.S. Army. Medical Detachment, 259th Infantry, 65th Infantry Division, Siegfried Line at Saarlautern, Germany, 18 March 1945.

### O'Callahan, Joseph T. (P)
Commander (Chaplain Corps), U.S. Naval Reserve. USS *Franklin,* near Kobe, Japan, 19 March 1945.

### Okutsu, Yukio
Technical Sergeant, U.S. Army. Mount Belvedere, Italy, 7 April 1945.

### Oresko, Nicholas
Master Sergeant, U.S. Army. Company C, 302nd Infantry, 94th Infantry Division, near Tettington, Germany, 23 January 1945.

**Parrish, Laverne (P)**
Technician 4th Grade, U.S. Army. Medical Detachment, 161st Infantry, 25th Infantry Division, Binalonan, Luzon, Philippines, 18–24 January 1945.

**Peden, Forrest E. (P)**
Technician 5th Grade, U.S. Army. Battery C, 10th Field Artillery Battalion, 3rd Infantry Division, near Biesheim, France, 3 February 1945.

**Perez, Manuel, Jr. (P)**
Private First Class, U.S. Army. Company A, 511th Parachute Infantry, 11th Airborne Division, Fort William McKinley, Luzon, Philippines, 13 February 1945.

**Peters, George J. (P)**
Private, U.S. Army. Company G, 507th Parachute Infantry, 17th Airborne Division, near Fluren, Germany, 24 March 1945.

**Peterson, George (P)**
Staff Sergeant, U.S. Army. Company K, 18th Infantry, 1st Infantry Division, near Eisern, Germany, 30 March 1945.

**Phillips, George (P)**
Private, U.S. Marine Corps Reserve. 2nd Battalion, 28th Marines, 5th Marine Division, Iwo Jima, 14 March 1945.

**Pierce, Francis J.**
Pharmacist's Mate First Class, U.S. Navy. Serving with 2nd Battalion, 24th Marines, 4th Marine Division, Iwo Jima, 15–16 March 1945.

**Reese, John N., Jr. (P)**
Private First Class, U.S. Army. Company B, 148th Infantry, 37th Infantry Division. Paco Railroad Station, Manila, Philippine Islands, 9 February 1945.

**Robinson, James E., Jr. (P)**
First Lieutenant, U.S. Army. Battery A, 861st Field Artillery Battalion, 63rd Infantry Division, near Untergriesheim, Germany, 6 April 1945.

**Rodriguez, Cleto**
Private, U.S. Army. Company B, 148th Infantry, 37th Infantry Division, Paco Railroad Station, Manila, Luzon, Philippines, 9 February 1945.

**Rudolph, Donald E.**
Second Lieutenant, U.S. Army. Company E, 20th Infantry, 6th Infantry Division, Munoz, Luzon, Philippine Islands, 5 February 1945.

**Ruhl, Donald J. (P)**
Private First Class, U.S. Marine Corps Reserve. Company E, 28th Marines, 5th Marine Division, Iwo Jima, 19–21 February 1945.

**Ruiz, Alejandro R. R.**
Private First Class, U.S. Army. 165th Infantry, 27th Infantry Division, Okinawa, 28 April 1945.

**Schwab, Albert E. (P)**
Private First Class, U.S. Marine Corps Reserve, Okinawa, 7 May 1945.

**Shockley, William R. (P)**
Private First Class, U.S. Army. Company L, 128th Infantry, 32nd Infantry Division, Villa Verde Trail, Luzon, Philippine Islands, 31 March 1945.

**Shomo, William A. (Air Mission)**
Major, U.S. Army Air Corps. 82nd Tactical Reconnaissance Squadron, over Luzon, Philippine Islands, 11 January 1945.

**Shoup, Curtis F. (P)**
Staff Sergeant, U.S. Army. Company I, 346th Infantry, 8th Infantry Division, near Tillet, Belgium, 7 January 1945.

**Sigler, Franklin E.**
Private, U.S. Marine Corps Reserve. 2nd Battalion, 26th Marines, 5th Marine Division, Iwo Jima, 14 March 1945.

**Sjogren, John C.**
Staff Sergeant, U.S. Army. Company I, 160th Infantry, 40th Infantry Division, near San Jose Hacienda, Negros, Philippine Islands, 23 May 1945.

**Stein, Tony (P)**
Corporal, U.S. Marine Corps Reserve. Company A, 1st Battalion, 28th Marines, 5th Marine Division, Iwo Jima, 19 February 1945.

**Street, George L., III**
Commander, U.S. Navy. Captain of USS *Tiranle,* harbor of Quelpart Island, off the coast of Korea, 14 April 1945.

**Stryker, Stuart S. (P)**
Private First Class, U.S. Army. Company E, 513th Parachute Infantry, 17th Airborne Division, near Wesel, Germany, 24 March 1945.

**Terry, Seymour W. (P)**
Captain, U.S. Army. Company B, 382nd Infantry, 96th Infantry Division, Zebra Hill, Okinawa, 11 May 1945.

**Thomas, William H. (P)**
Private First Class, U.S. Army. 149th Infantry, 38th Infantry Division, Zambales Mountains, Luzon, Philippine Islands, 22 April 1945.

**Treadwell, Jack L.**
Captain, U.S. Army. Company F, 180th Infantry, 45th Infantry Division, near Nieder-Wurzbach, Germany, 18 March 1945.

**Turner, Day G. (P)**
Sergeant, U.S. Army. Company B, 319th Infantry, 80th Infantry Division, at Dahl, Luxembourg, 8 January 1945.

**Turner, George B.**
Private First Class, U.S. Army. Battery C, 499th Armored Field Artillery Battalion, 14th Armored Division, Philippsbourg, France, 3 January 1945.

**Valdez, Jose F. (P)**
Private First Class, U.S. Army. Company B, 7th Infantry, 3rd Infantry Division, near Rosenkrantz, France, 25 January 1945.

**Viale, Robert M. (P)**
Second Lieutenant, U.S. Army. Company K, 148th Infantry, 37th Infantry Division, Manila, Luzon, Philippine Islands, 5 February 1945.

**Villegas, Ysmael R. (P)**
Staff Sergeant, U.S. Army. Company F, 127th Infantry, 32nd Infantry Division, Villa Verde Trail, Luzon, Philippine Islands, 20 March 1945.

**Wahlen, George E.**
Pharmacist's Mate Second Class, U.S. Navy. Serving with 2nd Battalion, 26th Marines, 5th Marine Division, Iwo Jima, 3 March 1945.

**Wallace, Herman C. (P)**
Private First Class, U.S. Army. Company B, 301st Engineer Combat Battalion, 76th Infantry Division, near Prumzurley, Germany, 27 February 1945.

**Walsh, William G. (P)**
Gunnery Sergeant, U.S. Marine Corps Reserve. Company G, 3rd Battalion, 27th Marines, 5th Marine Division, Iwo Jima, 27 February 1945.

**Watson, Wilson D.**
Private, U.S. Marine Corps Reserve. 2nd Battalion, 9th Marines, 3rd Marine Division, Iwo Jima, 26–27 February 1945.

**Wetzel, Walter C. (P)**
Private First Class, U.S. Army. 13th Infantry, 8th Infantry Division, Birken, Germany, 3 April 1945.

**Wilkin, Edward G. (P)**
Corporal, U.S. Army. Company C, 157th Infantry, 45th Infantry Division, Siegfried Line in Germany, 18 March 1945.

**Will, Walter J. (P)**
First Lieutenant, U.S. Army. Company K, 18th Infantry, 1st Infantry Division, near Eisern, Germany, 30 March 1945.

**Williams, Hershel W.**
Corporal, U.S. Marine Corps Reserve. 21st Marines, 3rd Marine Division, Iwo Jima, 23 February 1945.

**Williams, Jack (P)**
Pharmacist's Mate Third Class, U.S. Naval Reserve. 3rd Battalion, 28th Marines, 5th Marine Division, Iwo Jima, 3 March 1945.

**Willis, John H.**

Pharmacist's Mate First Class, U.S. Navy. 3rd Battalion, 27th Marines, 5th Marine Division, Iwo Jima, 28 February 1945

**Woodford, Howard E. (P)**

Staff Sergeant, U.S. Army. Company I, 130th Infantry, 33rd Infantry Division, near Tabio, Luzon, Philippine Islands, 6 June 1945.

# Biographies of Key Leaders

The purpose of this section is to support the chronology and acquaint the reader with a brief summary of the education and significant prewar experiences of general and flag officers who held major command positions during the war.

## U.S. Army

### Bradley, Omar N. (1893–1981)

Graduated from West Point in 1915 and served as an instructor there from 1920 to 1924. He was an instructor at the Infantry School from 1929 to 1933. He graduated from the Army War College in 1934. He served in the War Department on the General Staff from 1938 to 1941. In February 1941 he was promoted to brigadier general. He was then appointed as commandant of the Infantry School, where he served from 1941 to 1942. Promoted to major general, he took command of the 82nd Infantry Division in February 1942 and then the 28th Infantry Division in June of 1942. He was promoted to lieutenant general in 1943 and took command of I Corps from April to September 1943, then the First Army Group from October 1943 to August 1944. He became commander of the 12th Army Group in August 1944 and led it until July 1945. He was promoted to general in March of 1945. Bradley commanded more American soldiers than any other general in American history.

### Buckner, Simon B. (1886–1945)

Son of General Simon Bolivar Buckner (CSA), he graduated from West Point in 1908 and served as an instructor there from 1918 to 1919 and from 1932 to 1936. He was also an instructor at the Command and General Staff College from 1925 to 1928. He graduated from the Army War College in 1929 and served as an instructor there from 1929 to 1932. He was commandant of cadets at West Point from 1933 to 1936. From August 1936 until May 1937, he served with the 23rd Infantry Regiment and was the commander of the 66th Infantry Regiment from 1937 to 1938. In 1939 he oversaw the Civilian Conservation Corps camps in Alabama. He was chief of staff of the 6th Infantry Division from 1939 to 1940. He was promoted to brigadier general in 1940 and commanded the Alaska Defense Force from July 1940 to March 1944. He was promoted to major general in August 1941 and to lieutenant general in 1943. He organized and commanded the U.S. Tenth Army from June 1944 until his death on Okinawa June 18, 1945, from a Japanese artillery explosion as he directed the final assaults on the island.

### Clark, Mark W. (1896–1984)

Graduated from West Point in 1917 and rose to battalion command in World War I. Served in the War Department on the General Staff from 1921 to 1924 and graduated from the Army War College

Lieutenant General Mark Clark aboard USS *Ancon*, during the Sicily Campaign *(National Archives and Records Administration)*

in 1937. Served in the 3rd Infantry Division from 1937 to 1940, then became an instructor at the Army War College. Promoted to brigadier general in August 1941, then to major general in April 1942, he served as I Corps commander from July to October 1942 and was promoted to lieutenant general in November 1942. He served as the deputy commander for Allied Forces in North Africa from November 1942 to January 1943. He took command of Fifth Army in January 1943 and served in that position until December 1944. He then became commander of the 5th Army Group and directed the last campaigns in Italy. Leaving the 5th Army Group in June 1945, he became an Allied commissioner for Austria from 1945 to 1947.

### Collins, Joseph Lawton (1896–1987)

Graduated from West Point in 1917 and served as an instructor there from 1921 to 1925. He was an instructor at the Infantry School from 1927 to 1931 and graduated from the Army War College in 1938. He also served as an instructor there from 1938 to 1941. He was appointed chief of staff of the Hawaii Department from 1941 to 1942 and during that time was promoted to brigadier general. He became a major general in May 1942 and took command of the 25th Infantry Division and took it to combat at Guadalcanal. He took over VI Corps in Europe in 1944 and commanded it throughout the final campaigns in France and Germany. He was promoted to lieutenant general in April 1945.

### Devers, Jacob L. (1887–1979)

Graduated from West Point in 1909 and served as an instructor there from 1912 to 1916 and again from 1919 to 1924. He graduated from the Army War College in 1933. He took a third assignment as an instructor at West Point from 1936 to 1939. He was promoted to brigadier general in May of 1940 and to major general in October of the same year. He was the 9th Infantry Division commander from October 1940 to July 1941, then took command of Armored Forces from May 1942 to January 1944. He was named the deputy supreme Allied commander for the Mediterranean theater of operations in January 1944 and served in that position until October 1944. He took command of 6th Army Group in October and served until May of 1945. He was promoted to general in March 1945.

### Eichelberger, Robert L. (1886–1961)

Graduated from West Point in 1909. He was the deputy chief of staff for the American Expeditionary Force in Siberia in 1918. He served in the War Department on the General Staff from 1935 to 1938. Served as the commander of the 30th Infantry Division from 1938 to 1940 and was promoted to brigadier general in 1940. Afterward he served as superintendent of West Point from 1940 to 1942. He was promoted to major general in March 1942 and took command of the 77th Infantry

Division, then took command of XI Corps until September 1942. He took command of I Corps, serving in the Southwest Pacific from September 1942 to September 1944. He was named commander of Eighth Army in September 1944 and served in that position until September 1948.

### Eisenhower, Dwight D. (1890–1969)

Graduated from West Point in 1915, then supported unit training for troops going to Europe in World War I. Graduated from the Army War College in 1928, he served as assistant executive to the assistant secretary of war from 1929 to 1932. He then became the special assistant to General Douglas MacArthur from 1933 to 1939, serving in both Washington, D.C., and the Philippines. He was executive officer of the 15th Infantry Regiment in 1940, then the chief of staff of the 3rd Infantry Division. In March 1941 he was chief of staff of IX Corps, then Third Army until September 1941. He was promoted to brigadier general in September, then moved to the war plans division of the General Staff, serving from December 1941 to May 1942. He was promoted to major general in April of 1942 and in June took command of U.S. Forces Europe. He was promoted to lieutenant general in July 1942 and then general in February 1943. In December 1943 he became Supreme Commander Allied Expeditionary Force with the responsibility for Operation Torch, the Allied invasion of North Africa. He oversaw the plans for the invasion of Europe (Overlord), and then led the Allied forces to victory as the supreme commander. He left the command in November 1945.

### Gerow, Leonard T. (1888–1972)

Graduated from the Virginia Military Institute in 1911 and graduated from the Army War College in 1931. He served in the war plans division of the General Staff from 1935 to 1942. He was promoted to brigadier general in 1940 and to major general in February 1942. He took command of the 29th Infantry Division in 1942, serving until 1943, when he took command of V Corps and fought

the final campaigns in Europe. He was the first American general to enter Paris, France, after the liberation of the city in 1944. He was promoted to lieutenant general in January 1945, and then took command of the 15th Army Group, serving until July 1945.

### Hodges, Courtney H. (1887–1966)

Cadet at West Point from 1904 to 1905, when he left and enlisted in the army from 1906 to 1909. He took a commission in the infantry in 1909 and fought in the great battles of World War I at St. Mihiel and the Argonne Forest. After the war he served on the Infantry Board at Fort Benning, Georgia, from 1929 to 1933. He graduated from the Army War College in 1934. He was the assistant commandant of the Infantry School from 1938 to 1941. In May of 1940 he was promoted to brigadier general and in May of 1941 was promoted to major general. He was the chief of infantry from 1941 to 1942, then took command of X Corps from 1942 to 1943. He was promoted to lieutenant general in February of 1943 and took command of Third Army. He served in that position until 1944, when he became deputy commander, then commander of the First Army. He commanded First Army throughout the campaigns in Europe, completing his time as commander in 1949.

### Krueger, Walter (1881–1967)

Enlisted in the U.S. Army in 1898 and was commissioned a lieutenant in the infantry in 1901. He attended the Army War College in 1921 and served as an instructor there from 1921 to 1922. He graduated from the National War College in 1926 and served as an instructor there from 1928 to 1932. He was the chief, War Plans Division, on the General Staff from 1936 to June 1938. He was promoted to brigadier general and served as commander of the 6th Infantry Brigade from June 1938 to February 1939. He was promoted to major general, then took command of the 2nd Infantry Division, where he served until October 1940. He served with VIII Corps from October until May

1941. Promoted to lieutenant general in May 1941, he took command of Third Army and held that position until February 1943, when he became commander of Sixth Army. Promoted to general in March 1945, he continued as commander of Sixth Army until September 1945.

### Lucas, John P. (1890–1949)

Graduated from West Point in 1911, then served in France and was wounded in 1918. He was an instructor at the Field Artillery School from 1921 to 1923. He served in the Personnel Division of the General Staff at the War Department from 1932 to 1936. He was promoted to brigadier general in October 1940, then took command of the 2nd Infantry Division artillery from 1940 to 1941. Promoted to major general in August of 1941, he took command of the 3rd Infantry Division and served in that position until 1942. In April 1942 he became commander of III Corps, serving until May 1943. He took command of VI Corps during the Sicily and Anzio operations. Relieved of command at Anzio, he returned to the United States and took the deputy commander's position in Fourth Army.

### MacArthur, Douglas (1880–1964)

The son of a Medal of Honor winner and lieutenant colonel in the Union Army, MacArthur graduated from West Point in 1903 and served as an aide to Theodore Roosevelt from 1906 to 1907. He was chief of staff, then commander of the 42nd Infantry Division in World War I. He was superintendent of West Point from 1919 to 1922. He was promoted to brigadier general in January of 1920, major general in January 1925, then general in 1930. He was chief of staff of the U.S. Army from 1930 to 1935. He served in the Philippines from 1935 to 1941, retiring from the army and taking a position as field marshal of the Philippine army in 1936. He was recalled to active duty in July 1941, given the rank of lieutenant general, and designated the commander of U.S. Army forces in the Far East. After the Japanese attack on the Philip-

General MacArthur, Commander in Chief of Southwest Pacific Area, wades ashore on Leyte on October 20, 1944, keeping the promise he made to the Philippine people in 1942 that he would return.

pines, he escaped from Corregidor and arrived in Australia. Winning both the Medal of Honor and a promotion to general in 1941, he took command of U.S. forces in the Southwest Pacific Area. He was promoted to general of the army (five-star) in December of 1944. In August 1945 he was named supreme commander Allied Forces Pacific and took the surrender of Japan in Tokyo Bay aboard the battleship USS *Missouri*. He supervised the occupation of Japan from 1945 to 1950.

### Marshall, George C. (1880–1959)

Graduated from the Virginia Military Institute in 1901 and served as a staff officer with the VIII Corps in France during the major offensives of the American Expeditionary Force. From 1919 to 1924, he was an aide to General John J. Pershing. In 1924 he took command of the 15th Infantry Regiment in China, serving there until 1927. He became the assistant commandant of the Infantry School in 1927, and in 1932 he left that position to take command of the 8th Infantry Regiment, a position he held until 1933. He became the senior instructor for the Illinois National Guard from 1933 to 1936. In July of 1936 he was promoted to brigadier general. He served in the War Department on the General Staff from 1938 to 1939. He was promoted to major general in July 1939, became the deputy chief of staff, then the acting chief of staff of the army from July through September 1939. He was appointed chief of staff of the U.S. Army in September 1939 and promoted to general. He served in this position throughout the war, directing the army's global effort to defeat Germany, Italy, and Japan. In this position he served as a member of the Joint Chiefs of Staff. He was promoted to general of the army (five-star) in December 1944, and in November of 1945 he resigned from the army.

### Merrill, Frank D. (1903–1955)

Graduated from West Point in 1929. He was an instructor in the Cavalry School from 1935 to 1938. He was the attaché in Tokyo, Japan, from 1938 to 1940. He became the deputy chief of staff for operations in the China, Burma, India theater, serving from 1942 to 1943. He was promoted to brigadier general in November 1943. In 1944 he organized and led the unit of American volunteers, the 5307th Composite Unit (Provisional) that eventually came to be known as Merrill's Marauders. He was promoted to major general in September 1944, and then served as chief of staff of Tenth Army from 1945 to 1948.

### Patch, Alexander M. (1889–1945)

Graduated from West Point in 1913 and commanded a machine-gun battalion in France in World War I. He was a professor of military science at Staunton Military Academy in Virginia from 1920 to 1924, and then again from 1925 to 1928. He graduated from the Army War College in 1932. Promoted to brigadier general in December 1940, then promoted to major general in March 1942. He organized and trained the Americal Division, the served with the division on Guadalcanal from October 1942 to February 1943. In 1943 he took

command of the III Corps Area, serving in that position until 1944. He was named commander of Seventh Army in March of 1944 and served until June 1945. He was promoted to general in August of 1944. He took command of Fourth Army in June of 1945, serving there until his death a few months later.

### Patton, George S., Jr. (1885–1945)

Graduated from West Point in 1909. He was commander of the 304th tank Brigade at the Battle of St. Mihiel and in the Meuse-Argonne, where he was wounded. He graduated from the Army War College in 1932 and took command of the 3rd Cavalry Regiment in 1938, serving until 1940. In 1940 he took command of the 2nd Armored Division and held that position until 1942. He was promoted to brigadier general in October 1940 and major

George S. Patton, Jr., strikes a well-deserved pose as conqueror of Sicily, August 1943. *(Virginia Military Institute Archives)*

general in April of 1941. He took command of the I Armored Corps, then the II Armored Corps between 1942 and 1943 in Tunisia. He was promoted to lieutenant general in April 1943. He was the commander of Seventh Army at Sicily and was the target of intense public scrutiny for slapping a soldier. He took command of Third Army in 1944 and held the position until the end of the war in Europe in May 1945. He was promoted to general in April of 1945. After the war, he took command of U.S. Forces Europe, when he was injured in a car accident and died of complications.

## Pick, Lewis A. (1890–1956)

Graduated from Virginia Polytechnic Institute in 1914. He was commissioned in the Corps of Engineers in 1917 and served as an instructor at the Army Command and General Staff College from 1934 to 1938. He graduated from the Army War College in 1939. He was a division engineer with the Ohio and Missouri River Division, U.S. Corps of Engineers, from 1939 to 1941. From 1942 to 1943 he was the division engineer for the Missouri River Division. From 1943 to 1945 he was the commander of the advance section, China, Burma, India theater and supervised the building of the Burma Road. He was promoted to brigadier general in February 1944, then major general in March of 1945.

## Ridgway, Matthew B. (1895–1993)

Graduated from West Point in 1917. Graduated from the Army War College in 1937. He served in the War Plans Division of the General Staff from September 1939 to January 1942. He was promoted to brigadier general in January 1942 and became the assistant division commander of the 82nd Infantry Division, later the 82nd Airborne Division. He was promoted to major general in August of 1942 and took command of the division. He led the division in combat, parachuting into Normandy, until August 1944. He then became commander of the XVIII Airborne Corps until September 1945. He was promoted to lieutenant general in June 1945.

## Stilwell, Joseph W. (1883–1946)

Graduated from West Point in 1904 and served in the Philippines from 1904 to 1906, then again from 1911 to 1912. He was the deputy chief of staff for intelligence, IV Corps, with the American Expeditionary Force in France in 1918. He served in the 15th Infantry Regiment in China from 1926 to 1928. He then became the chief of staff for U.S. forces in China from 1928 to 1929. He was an instructor in the Infantry School under George C. Marshall from 1929 to 1933. He was the attaché to China and Thailand from 1935 to 1939. He was promoted to brigadier general in May of 1939, then took command of the 3rd Infantry Brigade and then the 7th Infantry Division from 1939 to 1941. He was promoted to major general in October 1940. He took command of the II Corps from July 1941 to February 1942, when he was promoted to lieutenant general. He took command of all U.S. forces in the China-Burma-India theater and served simultaneously as the chief of staff to Chinese Generalissimo Chiang-Kai-shek as well as the deputy supreme Allied commander in-theater. He served in these multiple roles from March of 1942 to October 1944. In August 1944 he was pro-

"Vinegar Joe" Stilwell (right) with Marauder commander Frank Merrill *(National Archives and Records Administration)*

moted to general. He was relieved of command in October 1944 and became chief of Army ground forces from January to May of 1945. He took command of Tenth Army in June 1945 after the death of General Buckner on Okinawa and served as commander until October 1945.

### Truscott, Lucian K. (1895–1965)
Enlisted in the U.S. Army in 1917 and commissioned in the cavalry. He served in Hawaii from March 1919 to October 1921. He was an instructor at the Cavalry School from 1927 to 1931. From September 1940 to July 1941, he was the executive officer of the 2nd Battalion, 13th Armored Regiment. Afterward he served on the IX Corps staff from July 1941 to May 1942. He was promoted to brigadier general in May 1942 and served on the Combined Operations Staff under Britains Admiral Lord Louis Mountbatten. Truscott formed the first U.S. Army Ranger unit in 1942 and was promoted to major general in November 1942. He was the field deputy to Supreme Allied Commander Lieutenant General Dwight Eisenhower during the Tunisia campaign from 1942 to 1943. He took command of the 3rd Infantry Division in 1943 until he became the deputy commander, then commander of VI Army Corps, serving from January to December 1944. He was promoted to lieutenant general in September 1944. In December 1944 he took command of Fifth Army and served in that position until October 1945.

### Wainwright, Jonathan M. (1883–1953)
Graduated from West Point in 1906 and served as the assistant chief of staff with the 82nd Infantry Division at St. Mihiel and the Meuse-Argonne battles in France in 1918. He graduated from the Army War College in 1934. In 1938 he was promoted to brigadier general and took command of the 1st Cavalry Brigade in 1938. He served in that position until 1940. He was promoted to major general in September 1940 and took command of the Philippine Division. He defended Luzon and Bataan against the Japanese invasion and was promoted to major general in March 1942. He then took command of U.S. Forces in the Far East on Corregidor, surrendering his command to the Japanese in April 1942. He was a prisoner of war until his release in 1945 and stood behind General MacArthur on the USS *Missouri* as he signed the surrender documents ending the war with Japan. He was promoted to general in September of 1945 and awarded the Congressional Medal of Honor.

### Wedemeyer, Albert C. (1897–1989)
Graduated from West Point in 1919. He studied the Chinese language at Tientsin from 1930 to 1932 and attended the German Kriegsakademie (staff college) from 1936 to 1938. He served on the General Staff in the War Plans Division from May 1941 to October 1943. He was promoted to brigadier general in July 1942, then to major general in September 1943. He was the deputy chief of staff to Britain's Admiral Lord Louis Mountbatten, the Supreme Allied Commander, Southeast Asia, from October 1943 to October 1944. He became the commander of the China theater of operations after General Stilwell's dismissal and the commander of China-Burma-India theater until October 1945. He was promoted to lieutenant general in January of 1945.

# U.S. Army Air Forces

### Arnold, Henry H. (1886–1950)
Graduated from West Point in 1907. Orville Wright taught him to fly in 1911. He flew as a U.S. air mail pilot in September 1911. He was commander of March Field from 1931 to 1935 and was promoted to brigadier general in February 1935. In September 1938, he was promoted to major general, then became chief of the Air Corps (later the U.S. Army Air Forces). He was promoted to lieutenant general in December 1941, general in March 1943, and General of the Army (five stars) in December 1944. As chief of U.S. Army Air Forces, he served on the Joint Chiefs of Staff and directed all air operations during the war.

Henry Harley "Hap" Arnold  *(United States Air Force History Center)*

Lieutenant General Lewis H. Brereton had a number of commands throughout the war, beginning with the Far East Air Force in the Philippines in 1941, Tenth Air Force in Burma in 1942, U.S. Army Forces in the Middle East in 1943, and commander of Ninth Air Force in the European theater of operations. In 1944 and until the end of the war, he was commander of the First Allied Airborne Army

## Brereton, Lewis H. (1890–1967)

Commissioned an ensign in the U.S. Navy after graduating from Annapolis in 1911. He transferred to the army, eventually moving from coastal artillery to the aviation section of the Signal Corps. He was the commander of the 2nd and 12th Aero Squadrons and chief of aviation for the I Army Corps from October 1917 to 1919. He was an instructor at the Command and General Staff College from 1935 to 1939, then took command of the 17th Bomber Wing, serving in that position until 1941. He was promoted to brigadier general in October 1940, then to major general in July 1941. In July he took command of the Third Air Force and served there until December 1941. He then took command of the Far East Air Force, and from December 1941 to March 1942 he was commander in chief of Allied Air Forces Far East, then the commander of Tenth Air Force. He was transferred to take command of the Middle East Air Force, later U.S. Army Air Forces, Middle East, serving from March 1942 to October 1943. He became commander of the Ninth Air Force in October 1943 and was promoted to lieutenant general in April 1944. He then took command of the First Allied Airborne Army, playing a major role in Operation Market Garden. He remained in the position until May 1945.

## Chennault, Claire Lee (1890–1958)

He attended officer training camp at Fort Harrison, Indiana, in 1917 and was commissioned a reserve officer in the infantry. He later transferred to the aviation section of the Signal Corps. He retired in 1937 and was recruited by Chinese Generalissimo Chiang-Kai-shek to organize Chinese air defenses. He trained American volunteers as combat pilots between August and December 1941; a group officially known as the American Volunteer Group, they became famous as the Flying Tigers. Chennault was recalled to active duty in April 1942 and promoted to brigadier general. In July 1942 he was named the commander of Army Air Forces in China. In March 1943 he was promoted to major general and became the commander of Tenth Air Force. He served in this position until August of 1945.

## Doolittle, James H. (1896–1993)

He enlisted in the Army Reserve in October 1917 and was later commissioned in the aviation section of the Signal Corps in 1920. In September 1920, he was the first pilot to make a transcontinental flight in less than 24 hours. In 1930 he resigned his commission, but reentered active duty in July of 1940. As a lieutenant colonel, he led the raid on Tokyo, 18 April 1942. Promoted to brigadier general the next day and awarded the Medal of Honor, he organized and served as commander of Twelfth Air Force from September 1942 to March 1943. He was promoted to major general in November 1942, then between 1942 and 1945 took succeeding command positions with the Northwest Africa Air Force, the Fifteenth Air Force, and Eighth Air Force. He was promoted to lieutenant general in March 1944.

## Eaker, Ira C. (1896–1987)

Commissioned a reserve officer in 1917, then transferred to aviation, qualifying as a pilot in 1918. In 1936 he was the first pilot to make a

James H. "Jimmy" Doolittle *(National Archives and records Administrations)*

Ira Eaker *(United States Air Force History Center)*

transcontinental flight using only instruments. From 1941 to 1942 he was commander of the 30th Pursuit Group. He was promoted to brigadier general in January 1942. He then commanded the 8th Bomber Command until December 1942. In September 1942 he was promoted to major general. From December 1942 to January 1944 he commanded Eighth Air Force. He was promoted to lieutenant general in September 1943. In January 1944 he took command of the Mediterranean Allied Air Force and served in that position until May 1945.

### Harmon, M. F. (1889–1945)

Graduated from West Point in 1912 and qualified as a pilot in 1916. He flew with a French squadron in combat during World War I. He graduated from the Army War College in 1925. In October 1940 he was promoted to brigadier general and took command of the 7th Pursuit Wing and the 11th Wing. From January to June 1941 he was in England as an air warfare observer. He was promoted to major general in July 1941 and took command of Interceptor Command, Fourth Air Force, from January to June of 1942. He was the commander of U.S. Army Air Forces, Pacific Ocean Areas from July 1942 to February 1945. He was promoted to lieutenant general in February 1943. He was lost at sea on 26 February 1945.

### Kenney, George C. (1889–1977)

Commissioned in the Air Service in 1917 and served in the 91st Aero Squadron during World War I. He graduated from the Army War College in 1933 and became a brigadier general in January 1941. He commanded the Air Corps Experimental Depot from January 1941 to April 1942. Promoted to major general that month, he took command of Fourth Air Force, serving in that position until July 1942. He was promoted to lieutenant general in September 1942, then took command of Fifth Air Force. He served as its commander until June of 1944, when he became the Southwest Pacific Area Allied Air Forces commander. He served in this command until March 1945. After March 1945 he was commander of Allied Air Forces Pacific until September 1945.

### LeMay, Curtis E. (1906–1990)

Commissioned in the Air Corps in 1929, he was commander of the 305th Bomb Group, Eighth Air Force, and then the Third Bomb Division from 1942 to 1943. He was promoted to brigadier general in October 1943, then to major general in March of 1944. He took command of the 20th Bomber Command in the China-Burma-India theater from August 1944 to July 1945 and conducted a number of devastating raids on Japan.

### Quesada, Elwood R. (1904–1993)

Commissioned in the Air Reserve in 1925 and entered active duty in 1927. He served as an aide to the assistant secretary of war from 1932 to 1933. He was the commander of the 33rd Pursuit Group from 1941 to 1942. He was promoted to brigadier general in December 1942 and took command of the 1st Air Defense Wing until 1943. He then became commander of the 9th Fighter Command from 1943 to 1944. He was promoted to major general in April 1944 and took command of the 9th Tactical Air Command until the end of the war.

### Spaatz, Carl (1891–1974)

Graduated from West Point in 1914 and served in the 2nd Pursuit Group in France in 1918, where he had three confirmed kills in air combat. In 1939 he was the executive officer of the 2nd Wing, then became the executive officer and assistant to the chief of the Air Corps from 1939 to 1940. He was promoted to brigadier general in October 1940 and served as head of the Plans Division, then chief of the Air Staff from 1940 to 1942. He was promoted to major general in January of 1942, then became the chief of Army Air Force Combat Command from January to June of 1942. He commanded the Eighth Air Force from July to December 1942, then from 1942 to March 1943 took command of Twelfth Air Force, the North Africa Air Force, then

General Carl Spaatz (right) with Hoyt Vandenberg *(Dwight D. Eisenhower Presidential Library)*

became the deputy commanding general for the Mediterranean Allied Air Forces. In March 1943 he was promoted to lieutenant general, became the commander of the U.S. Strategic Air Force in Europe and then in the Pacific theater of operations from January 1944 to October 1945.

## Stratemeyer, George E. (1890–1969)

Graduated from West Point in 1915 and transferred to the aviation section of the Signal Corps

in 1916. He was an instructor at West Point from 1924 to 1929. He graduated from the Army War College in 1939. He was appointed head of the Training and Operations Division, Headquarters, Army Air Force, from 1940 to 1941. He was promoted to brigadier general in August 1941 and became the executive officer to General Henry H. Arnold from 1941 to 1942. He was promoted to major general in June 1942 and served as chief of staff of the Air Staff from 1942 to 1943. He was appointed the commanding general of Army Air Forces, China-Burma-India theater in 1943 and served in that position until 1946.

## Twining, Nathan F. (1897–1982)

Enlisted in the Oregon National Guard in 1916 and graduated from West Point in 1919. Between 1940 and 1942 he served in the Office of the Chief of the Air Corps. He was promoted to brigadier general in 1942 and served as the chief of staff for Allied Forces, Southern Pacific from 1942 to 1943. He was the commander of the Thirteenth Air Force and the air commander of the Solomon Islands. From 1943 to 1944 he was the commander of Fifteenth Air Force and was promoted to major general in February 1943. Between 1944 and 1945 he was commander of Mediterranean Allied Air Strategic Air Forces. He was promoted to lieutenant general in June of 1945. He took command of Twentieth Air Force in August 1945 and served in that position until October 1945.

## Vandenberg, Hoyt S. (1899–1954)

Graduated from West Point in 1923 and commissioned in the Air Corps. Graduated from the Army War College in 1939, served first in the Plans Division, then in the Operations and Training Office in the Office of the Chief of the Air Corps from 1939 to 1942. He was promoted to brigadier general in December of 1942 then served as the chief of staff of Twelfth Air Force and the Northwest Africa Strategic Air Force from 1942 to 1943. He was the deputy chief of the Air Staff, Headquarters, Army Air Force from 1943 to 1944. Promoted to major general in March of 1944, he served as the deputy commander for the Allied Expeditionary Air Force, then commander of Ninth Air Force from 1944 to the end of the war in Europe in 1945. From 1945 to 1946 he was the assistant chief of staff for operations, Army Air Force.

# U.S. NAVY

### Burke, Arleigh A. (1901–1996)
Graduated from Annapolis in 1923. Commanded the destroyer USS *Mugford* from 1939 to 1940. He served in the Bureau of Naval Ordnance from 1940 to 1943, then moved to the South Pacific to command Destroyer Squadron 23. His destroyers covered the initial landings at Bougainville in November 1943 and fought the Japanese in over 20 battles in four months. Destroyer Squadron 23 received credit for sinking a Japanese cruiser, nine destroyers, one submarine, several other vessels, and about 30 aircraft. He was promoted to commodore in October of 1944 and became Vice Admiral Marc Mitscher's chief of staff. He served in this position until the end of the war.

### Fletcher, Frank Jack (1885–1973)
Graduated from Annapolis in 1906, won the Medal of Honor at Vera Cruz, Mexico, in 1914, and commanded a destroyer in World War I. He graduated from the Naval War College in 1930 then the Army War College in 1931. From 1933 to 1936 he served as an aide to the secretary of the navy. In 1939 he was promoted to rear admiral. He commanded Cruiser Division Three with the Atlantic Fleet from 1939 to 1941. He commanded a task force during the Battle of the Coral Sea, 7–8 May 1942 and was the senior officer at the Battle of Midway. He was promoted to vice admiral in June 1942 and in 1943 took command of Naval Forces, North Pacific until the end of the war.

### Ghormley, Robert L. (1883–1958)
Graduated from the University of Idaho in 1902, then from Annapolis in 1906. He served with the Atlantic Fleet, then in the Office of the Chief of Naval Operations during World War I. He graduated from the Navy War College in 1938 and was promoted to rear admiral in October 1938. From 1938 to 1940 he served as the director of the War Plans Division in the Navy Department and was assistant to the chief of naval operations. He was a naval observer in England from 1940 to 1942 and was promoted to vice admiral in September 1941. From April to October 1942 he served as the commander of South Pacific Forces responsible for the offensive against the Japanese in the Solomons. He took command of the Fourteenth Naval District from 1943 to 1944 and then served on the staff of Admiral Harold R. Stark, commander of U.S. Naval Forces in Europe, from 1944 to May 1945, when he became commander of U.S. Naval Forces, German Waters, at the end of the war.

### Halsey, William F., Jr. (1882–1959)
Graduated from Annapolis in 1904 and commanded two destroyers during World War I. Between 1922 and 1934, he was a naval attaché with postings in Denmark, Sweden, Norway, and Berlin, Germany. He graduated from the Naval War College in 1933 and the Army War College in 1934. In March 1935 he qualified as a naval aviator. He commanded the carrier USS *Saratoga* from 1935 to 1937 and then took command of the Pensacola Naval Air Station from 1937 to 1938. He was promoted to rear admiral in March of 1938. Between 1938 and 1940 he served as commander of two different carrier divisions and was promoted to vice admiral in June of 1940. He was the battle force aircraft commander and was out at sea aboard the carrier USS *Enterprise* on December 7, 1941, during the attack on Pearl Harbor. He led the task force that raided Kwajalein in February 1942 and commanded the task force that launched the Doolittle raid on Tokyo, April 18, 1942. He took command of South Pacific Forces from vice admiral Ghormley in October 1942 and directed operations against the Japanese in the Solomons. He was promoted to admiral in November of

Admiral William F. Halsey, Jr., commander of the South Pacific Area during the Solomons offensive, 1942–43. He would later command the U.S. Third Fleet in 1944 and 1945

November 1933, then was commander of aircraft, battle force for the Atlantic Fleet from 1938 to 1939 and promoted to vice admiral. He served on the General Board, which advised the president of the United States on naval matters, from 1939 to 1940. He was promoted to admiral in February 1941 and took command of the Atlantic Fleet. After Pearl Harbor, he became Commander in Chief, U.S. Fleet (CominCh). In March he replaced Admiral Harold R. Stark as the chief of naval operations and combined the two positions. He directed all naval operations during the war and served as a member of the Joint Chiefs of Staff. In December 1944 he became a fleet admiral (five-star) and gave up the position of chief of naval operations to Admiral Chester W. Nimitz in November 1945.

### Kinkaid, Thomas C. (1888–1972)

Graduated from Annapolis in 1908 and served aboard the battleship USS *Arizona* during World War I. He graduated from the Naval War College in 1930 and from 1937 to 1938 commanded the heavy cruiser USS *Indianapolis*. From 1938 to 1941 he was the naval attaché in Rome and Belgrade. In

1942. From June 1944 to December 1945 he commanded Third Fleet, conducting operations in support of the American invasion of the Philippines. The USS *Missouri* served as Halsey's flagship when the Japanese surrendered on board in Tokyo Bay on September 2, 1945. In December 1945 he was promoted to fleet admiral (five-star).

### King, Ernest J. (1878–1956)

Graduated from Annapolis in 1901 and commanded the destroyer USS *Terry* during operations off Veracruz, Mexico, in 1914. From 1916 to 1922 he served on the staff of the commander of the Atlantic Fleet. In 1928 he qualified as a naval aviator, commanded the carrier USS *Lexington* in 1930, and graduated from the Navy War College in 1933. He was promoted to rear admiral in

MacArthur observes Philippine operations with Vice Admiral Thomas Kinkaid, February 1944. *(National Archives and Records Administration)*

November 1941 he was promoted to rear admiral. From 1941 to 1943 he commanded Cruiser Division Six, then took command of the task force centered on the carrier USS *Enterprise* and directed operations during the Solomons offensive and fought the Japanese in the naval battles of the Coral Sea, Midway, and Santa Cruz. From January to November 1943 he served as the commander of naval forces, North Pacific. In June of 1943 he became a vice admiral and was assigned to command the Seventh Fleet, subordinate to General MacArthur. He directed naval operations in support of amphibious operations in New Guinea and the Philippines. In April 1945 he was promoted to admiral and served as Seventh Fleet commander until November 1945.

### Leahy, William D. (1875–1959)

Graduated from Annapolis in 1897 and served aboard the battleship USS *Oregon* during the Spanish-American War. He commanded the battleship USS *Nevada* in World War I. Promoted to rear admiral, he then served as chief of the Bureau of Ordnance from 1927 to 1931. In March 1935 he became a vice admiral and commanded battleships of the Battle Force from 1935 to 1936. In April 1936 he was promoted to admiral and commanded the entire Battle Force. From January 1937 to July 1939 he served as chief of naval operations. He retired in 1939, serving as governor of Puerto Rico until 1940. From 1940 to 1942 he served as the U.S. ambassador to Vichy France. He was recalled to active duty in 1942 by President Roosevelt and served as chief of staff for the president. He was the senior member of the Joint Chiefs of Staff and provided the important interface between the president as commander in chief and the military leadership for all matters concerning strategy and policy. In December 1944 he was promoted to fleet admiral (five-star). After President Roosevelt's death in April 1945, he continued in his position under President Harry S. Truman.

Admiral William Leahy in 1935 *(U.S. Navy History Center)*

### Mitscher, Marc A. (1887–1947)

Graduated from Annapolis in 1910 and served on a number of ships, including cruisers, gunboats, and destroyers. He qualified as a naval aviator in 1916, and served at Pensacola, Florida, until 1917. He was then assigned to conduct experiments with shipboard catapults. From 1929 to 1930 he was the executive officer on the carrier USS *Langley* and also on the carrier USS *Saratoga* from 1934 to 1935. In 1941 he commanded the carrier USS *Hornet* and launched Doolittle's bombers off its decks in April 1942. He commanded the carrier in the Battle of Midway. Promoted to rear admiral he then commanded air units in the Southern Pacific during the Solomons campaign. In November 1944 he commanded Carrier Division Three during the Marshall Islands operations and was promoted to vice admiral. His command, redesignated as Fast Carrier Task Force 58, fought the Battles of Philippine Sea and Leyte Gulf, attacked Japanese forces across the Pacific, sup-

Admiral Marc Mitscher, commander of carrier Task Force 58 aboard USS *Lexington* in June of 1944

ported the assaults on Iwo Jima and Okinawa, and conducted strikes on the Japanese home islands. In July 1945 he became the deputy chief of naval operations for air.

### Nimitz, Chester W. (1885–1966)

Graduated from Annapolis in 1905 and served as chief of staff to the commander of submarines. He served with the Atlantic Fleet during World War I on submarine duty and graduated from the Naval War College in 1923. From 1929 to 1931 he commanded Submarine Division 20. From 1933 to 1935 he commanded the heavy cruiser USS *Augusta*. In June of 1938 he was promoted to rear admiral and commanded first a cruiser division, then a battleship division between 1938 and 1939. He was the chief of the Bureau of Navigation from June 1939 to December 1941. After Pearl Harbor he was promoted to admiral and took command of the Pacific Fleet. As the commander in chief of Pacific Ocean Areas throughout the war, Nimitz directed land and naval operations to stop the Japanese advance and establish bases for the eventual invasion of the Japanese home islands. He was promoted to fleet admiral (five-star) in December 1944. In November 1945 he became chief of naval operations.

Admiral Chester W. Nimitz, Commander in Chief, Pacific Ocean Areas

### Oldendorf, Jesse B. (1887–1974)

Graduated from Annapolis in 1909. Commanded the destroyer USS *Decatur* from 1925 to 1927. He graduated from the Naval War College in 1929 and the Army War College in 1930. He commanded the light cruiser USS *Houston* from 1939 to 1941, then served on the staff of the Naval War College from August 1941 to February 1942. Between February and July 1942 he was commander, U.S. Naval Forces, Aruba-Curaçao Area. He was promoted to rear admiral in June 1942, then commanded the U.S. naval base at Trinidad from 1942 to May 1943, when he took command of an Atlantic Fleet task force until November, then commanded Cruiser Division Four from January to December 1944. He was promoted to vice admiral and took command of Battleship Squadron One. In this command, he provided naval gunfire support for marine landings throughout the Central Pacific and army forces at Lingayen Gulf. He fought the Battle of Surigao Strait at Leyte, October 24, 1944, destroying a Japanese battle force in a classic employment of battleships.

### Sprague, Clifton A. F. (1896–1955)

Graduated from Annapolis in 1918 and served aboard the cruiser USS *Wheeling* during World War I. In 1921 he qualified as a naval aviator. He graduated from the Naval War College in 1939. From November 1939 to June 1942 he commanded the seaplane tender USS *Tangier* and was aboard during the Japanese attack on Pearl Harbor. *Tangier* was one of the few ships to get underway during the attack. He served as air officer on the staff of the commander, Gulf Sea Frontier, in Miami, Florida, until 1943. He commanded the carrier USS *Wasp* from 1943 to 1944, then took command of Carrier Division Twenty-Five from August 1944 to August 1945.

### Spruance, Raymond A. (1886–1969)

Graduated from Annapolis in 1907. From 1924 to 1925 he served on the staff of U.S. Naval Forces, Europe. He graduated from the Naval War College in 1927 and served as an instructor there from 1931 to 1932, and again from 1935 to 1938. He was promoted to rear admiral in 1939. From 1941 to 1942 he commanded Cruiser Division Five, Pacific Fleet. From June 1942 to September 1943 he was chief of staff to the commander in chief, U.S. Pacific Fleet. He then became the deputy commander in chief of the Pacific Fleet. In May 1943 he was promoted to vice admiral, and from 1943 to 1944 he served as commander, Central Pacific Area. On April 29, 1944, this was redesignated, and Spruance became commander, Fifth Fleet. He was in overall command of the occupation of the Gilbert Islands, the invasion of the Marshalls, and operations seizing Saipan, Tinian, and Guam in the Marianas. He also directed naval forces during the Battle of the Philippine Sea, June 19–20, 1944. He also directed operations for the assaults on Iwo Jima and Okinawa. In February 1944 he was promoted to admiral and in November 1945 took command of the Pacific Fleet from Fleet Admiral Nimitz.

Admiral Raymond A. Spruance led task force 16 during the Battle of Midway. He commanded the U.S. Fifth Fleet from 1943 to 1945. The fleet had over 300 fighting ships and more than 1,100 auxiliary ships and fought in all the major campaigns of the Pacific.

### Turner, Richmond Kelly (1885–1961)

Graduated from Annapolis in 1908, serving on battleships in World War I. He qualified as a naval aviator in 1927 and served on the staff of the Naval War College from 1935 to 1938. He commanded the heavy cruiser USS *Astoria* from 1938 to 1940. From 1940 to 1942 he served in the war plans division of the Navy Department. In December 1941 he was promoted to rear admiral and became the assistant chief of staff to the commander in chief, U.S. Fleet, until June 1942. He then took command of the Amphibious Force, South Pacific Force. From 1943 to 1945 he commanded the Fifth Amphibious Force, Central Pacific Area. He planned and directed the landings at Tarawa, Kwajalein, Guam, Iwo Jima, and Okinawa. In February

Rear Admiral Richmond Turner confers with General Alexander Vandegrift (USUC). *(National Archives and Records Administration)*

1944 he was promoted to vice admiral and in May 1945 was promoted to admiral and designated as commander of Amphibious Forces, Pacific. In this role he was to oversee the landings on Kyushu and Honshu, Japan.

# U.S. MARINE CORPS

### Geiger, Roy S. (1885–1947)
Commissioned in the Marine Corps in 1909 and served in Nicaragua and the Philippines from 1912 to 1913, then in Peking (Beijing) from 1913 to 1916. In June of 1917 he qualified as a naval aviator and commanded a squadron in the 1st Marine Aviation Force in France in 1918. He served in Haiti from 1919 to 1921 and again from 1925 to 1927. In 1929 he graduated from the Army War College. From 1931 to 1935 he was head of Marine Corps Aviation. In 1941 he was promoted to brigadier general and served as the assistant naval attaché in London. In August 1941 he became commanding general, 1st Marine Aircraft Wing, Fleet Marine Force. On Guadalcanal, he served as director of air operations. In August 1942 he was promoted to major general. In November 1943, he became the commanding general of the I Amphib-

Roy S. Geiger  *(United States Marine Corps)*

ious Corps during the Bougainville campaign. In April of 1944 his command was redesignated as the III Amphibious Corps. He led marine forces capturing Guam and the Palau Islands and was the commander of marine forces as part of Tenth Army landing on Okinawa. He temporarily commanded Tenth Army after the death of General Buckner. In July 1945 he became the commanding general of the Fleet Marine Force, Pacific, and served in that position until November 1946.

### Rupertus, William H. (1889–1945)
Enlisted in the District of Columbia National Guard in 1907 and served until 1910. Commissioned in the Marine Corps in 1913. Served in Haiti from 1920 to 1923 and served in the American Legation in Peking (Beijing) from 1929 to 1933. He remained in China, serving with the Fourth Marines in Shanghai from 1937 to 1938. In 1941 he was the assistant division commander

of the 1st Marine Division. In January 1942 he was promoted to brigadier general and promoted to major general in 1943. He then took command of the 1st Marine Division for the assaults on Cape Gloucester and Peleliu. He left the division in November 1944 and was commandant of Marine Corps Schools until his death in March of 1945.

### Schmidt, Harry (1886–1968)

Commissioned in the Marine Corps in 1909. He served on Guam from 1911 to 1912 and in the Philippines from 1912 to 1913. He was an instructor at Marine Corps Schools from 1923 to 1926. From 1927 to 1929 he served in China, then in Nicaragua. He was chief of staff of the 2nd Marine Brigade at Shanghai, China, from 1937 to 1938. From 1938 to 1942 he was a personnel officer at headquarters, Marine Corps. He was promoted to brigadier general in October 1941 and to major general in 1942. After serving as the assistant to the commandant of the Marine Corps from January 1942 to August 1943, he took command of the 4th Marine Division. He led the division in the capture of Roi and Namur Islands and at Saipan. In July 1944 he became the commanding general of the V Amphibious Corps for the landings on Tinian and Iwo Jima. He continued to serve in this position with occupation duties in Japan until February 1946.

### Smith, Holland M. (1882–1967)

Commissioned in the Marine Corps in 1905 and served in the Philippines from 1906 to 1908, in Panama from 1909 to 1910, and in the Philippines again from 1912 to 1914. He was in the Dominican Republic from 1916 to 1917, then served in France, where he participated in the Aisne-Marne offensive, St-Mihiel, and the Meuse-Argonne in World War I. He graduated from the Naval War College in 1921. He was promoted to brigadier general in 1939. From April to September 1939 he served as the assistant to the commandant, Marine Corps; he then took command of the 1st Marine Brigade at Quantico, Virginia. In February 1941 he was pro-

Holland M. "Howlin' Mad" Smith. *(United States Marine Corps)*

moted to major general. From June 1941 to August 1942 he served as the commander of Amphibious Forces, Atlantic Fleet, then took the same position as commander, Amphibious Corps, Pacific Fleet. From September 1943 to August 1944 he commanded the redesignated V Amphibious Corps. In February 1944 he was promoted to lieutenant general. In July 1944 he became the commanding general of Fleet Marine Force Pacific, until July 1945. He was reassigned to Camp Pendleton until his retirement.

### Vandegrift, Alexander A. (1887–1973)

Enlisted in the Marine Corps in 1908 and commissioned as an officer in 1909. Between 1912 and 1923 he served in Cuba, Nicaragua, Haiti, Panama, and at Veracruz, Mexico. From 1927 to 1929 and again from 1935 to 1937 he served in China. He was assistant to the commandant, Marine Corps, from 1937 to 1941. In 1940 he was promoted to brigadier general. In March 1942 he was promoted to major general and served as the assistant commander, then commander of the 1st Marine Division. He led the division in the battle for Guadalcanal and was awarded the Congressional Medal of Honor. In July 1943 he was promoted to lieutenant general and took command of the I Marines' Amphibious Corps and commanded the landing force at Empress Augusta Bay at Bougainville in November 1943. He served as commander until November 1943. In January 1944 he became the 18th commandant of the Marine Corps, serving in that position until January 1948. He was promoted to general in April 1945, the first marine to achieve four-star rank while on active duty.

# GLOSSARY OF TERMS

This glossary covers military terms and definitions found in the chronology.

**administrative control**   Command authority related to matters not directly related to combat, such as personnel management and services.

**airborne**   Airborne forces in World War II were light infantry highly trained to conduct parachute landings, usually behind enemy lines. Paratroopers would jump from transport aircraft onto a designated landing area called a Drop Zone. Because all of their supplies and heavy equipment must also be transported and landed by parachute or glider, the troops themselves were lightly armed. The troops would land on the Drop Zone, pick up their equipment (machine guns, mortars, radio sets, ammunition, medical supplies) from containers dropped by parachute. Heavier equipment (vehicles, anti-tank guns, artillery) would come later, delivered by gliders. Because they were lightly armed and had limited supplies, paratroopers were expected to use initiative and take aggressive action to achieve their designated mission.

**aircraft carrier**   A warship designed to launch, recover, and maintain combat aircraft. The ship is designed as a large floating flight deck with space below to arm, maintain, and store the aircraft. The ship is controlled from a superstructure called an island on the starboard (right) side of the ship. In World War II there were two classes of carriers: Fleet Carriers (CV) and Light Carriers (CVL). Fleet carriers were the decisive weapons of naval warfare and carried 70 to 90 aircraft. Light carriers had 35 to 45 aircraft. Many cargo ships and tanker hulls were converted into Escort Carriers (CVE) with 10 to 20 aircraft. These ships were primarily used for antisubmarine operations or close air support missions. Carriers, while powerful, are vulnerable to attack because of their limited armament. A certain number of aircraft launched from a carrier must always fly a protective screen to prevent enemy aircraft from attacking the ship. Other smaller ships also protect the carrier, providing antiaircraft fire and patrolling for submarines. Naval battles in the Pacific focused on locating and destroying the enemy's aircraft carriers.

**air interdiction**   An attack from aircraft by bombardment or gunfire against ground targets to destroy or disrupt them.

**air superiority**   The condition established during combat operations that allows the free air movement of supplies and reinforcements without any interference from enemy aircraft. This involves both the destruction of enemy aircraft as well as the destruction of airfields, supplies, logistics bases, and facilities. Air superiority is a requirement for the success of ground operations. Gaining air superiority over western France and the Channel coastline was essential for success of the Normandy landings in 1944. Air superiority was a primary factor in MacArthur's New Guinea campaign of 1943–44, and it was essential before any major landings at Guam, Saipan, Kwajalein, or Okinawa. Most campaigns began with air operations that lasted for months to achieve air superiority before any amphibious landings took place.

**amphibious operations** Amphibious operations place a friendly force on an enemy-held shore. Good beaches that can support large numbers of men and equipment are essential as well as tides that do not interfere with the steady flow of reinforcements and supplies after the initial landings have succeeded. Landing beaches should be within range of friendly aircraft, either carrier-based or land based. Naval forces are essential in both protecting the landing force and to provide the bombardment to suppress enemy defenses. Usually cruisers, destroyers, and battleships provide support. Landing areas are divided and designated for specific forces (Omaha and Utah beaches at Normandy, Red 1, Red 2, Red 3, and Green Beach at Tarawa), each with its own separate command. The amphibious assaults are designated as waves. The first wave clears the beach of obstacles and eliminates the strongpoints on the beach not already eliminated by air and naval bombardment. The successive waves push inland to capture objectives and broaden the penetration into the enemy's defenses as deeply as possible. Because amphibious forces carry a limited amount of equipment and supplies, they are vulnerable to counterattack until a sufficient buildup of forces can be achieved (Guadalcanal in 1942, Bougainville in 1943). Therefore speed and aggressive action are essential in achieving success.

**antiaircraft guns** High-angle, high-velocity guns either ground-based or mounted on ships that fire high-explosive shells intended to damage or destroy attacking aircraft. The intent is to put up a curtain or wall of exploding shells into which the attacking aircraft must fly. The fragmentation produced by the explosions would tear through engine components, fuel and hydraulic lines, and puncture the skin of the aircraft itself to kill or wound the pilot or crew.

**antisubmarine operations** Techniques used to prevent submarines from attacking targets or to locate and destroy submarines before they are able to attack. One main technique used to defend ships against submarine attack was to conduct convoys. Convoys were harder to detect in the open ocean. If detected, the submarines would be able to attack the convoy, but risked being detected themselves and overwhelmed by large numbers of warships or aircraft operating together. Radio direction-finding equipment was very successful in antisubmarine operations to pinpoint German submarines transmitting information. High-frequency direction-finding equipment also had a significant effect on locating and destroying German submarines in the latter stages of the Battle of the Atlantic. Once located, enemy submarines were often subjected to depth charges or air attack.

**army** A command organization of ground force units, designated by a number, composed of two or more corps. Armies can operate independently (Tenth Army at Okinawa) or can be subordinate to an Army Group (Patton's Third Army was subordinate to the 12th Army Group).

**army group** A command organization composed of two or more ground force armies. In the ETO, General Bradley commanded the 12th Army Group, composed of the First, Third, Ninth, and Fifteenth Armies.

**battalion** A ground force unit, usually part of a regiment or a brigade. Infantry battalions (marine or army) have three or more companies of riflemen with attached heavy weapons, such as mortars, machine guns, anti-tank guns. Tank battalions consisted or three or more companies, each with about 10 tanks. Artillery battalions are organized into batteries of six to eight cannons each.

**bazooka** An anti-tank rocket launcher, the word is often used to describe any anti-tank weapon during World War II. The 1942 bazooka fired a 2.36-inch projectile that could penetrate up to seven inches of armor. The optimum range was 40 to 50 meters, making it quite dangerous for an infantryman to use. It was used not only against tanks and other vehicles, it was also employed with great effect on fortifications.

**battleship**    A heavily armored warship with large-caliber guns used primarily to defeat other battleships but also to provide gunfire support to ground forces. Prior to World War II and in the first two years of the war, most navy leaders believed the battleship was the decisive weapon of naval warfare. All American naval plans were based on a decisive fleet engagement led by battleships. The employment of the aircraft carrier and submarine, however, showed the limitations of the battleship; by 1943, battleships in the U.S. Navy were used as antiaircraft platforms and assembled into groups for shore bombardment preceding amphibious landings. The Japanese built the largest and most powerful battleships ever made, but they were completely ineffective and were sunk during the Okinawa campaign by carrier-based aircraft. The engagement at Surigao Strait at Leyte was the last surface engagement of battleships.

**beachhead**    A section of enemy shoreline that is seized and occupied by friendly forces after an amphibious assault. The beachhead marks the area of friendly control and its expansion is critical to the sustainment and reinforcement of the initial landing force. The beachhead serves as the base for future offensive operations and is the launching point for further attacks. The failure to expand the beachhead at Anzio in January 1944 had dire consequences for Allied forces. Nevertheless, the successful defense of the beachhead allowed for sufficient reinforcements to arrive and eventually made possible the breakout that led to the capture of Rome.

**bomber**    A large multi-engine combat aircraft designed to deliver high-explosive bombs over long distances. In World War II, bombers were designated as light (A-20 Havoc, A-26 Invader), medium (B-25 Mitchell, B-26 Marauder), heavy (B-17 and B-24 Liberator), and very heavy (B-29), based on range and the number of bombs carried.

**bombardment**    The process of firing a large number of shells from naval ships at fixed targets, or aircraft dropping numerous bombs on fixed targets. Often bombardments consisted of both naval gunfire and aircraft attacks.

**bridgehead**    Ground on the opposite side of a river held by the enemy, then seized and defended by friendly forces. The bridgehead serves as a launching point for further offensive operations.

**brigade**    A ground force unit, usually composed of three battalions, which can operate independently or as part of a division. Brigades are the smallest ground force units that have the capability to operate independently. Brigades can be organized as only infantry or only tank or can be mixed. Many U.S. armored divisions in the ETO formed combat commands. The combat command was the equivalent of a brigade, a mixture of tank and mechanized infantry battalions to create a more powerful, flexible, and fast moving force.

**breakout or breakthrough**    When a ground force is able to disrupt the defensive lines of the enemy and move into weakly defended rear areas with little interference. Operation Cobra is an example of a plan to break out of the Normandy area and drive deep into France.

**campaign**    A planned series of battles or engagements within a specific theater of war or other designated area to achieve an operational or strategic objective. Examples are MacArthur's seizure of bases in New Guinea 1943–44, and the Solomons offensive in 1942–43.

**close air support**    The use of combat aircraft, primarily fighters, as flying artillery to support the maneuver of ground forces by suppressing or destroying enemy defenses. Close air support missions are usually conducted in close coordination with ground units.

**combined**    A term in World War II that described the involvement of committees, forces, units, or operations from the United States and Great Britain. The Combined Chiefs of Staff is an example of the committee formed by the U.S Joint Chiefs of Staff and the Imperial General Staff to provide a unified strategic direction for the war.

**commander in chief**   The commander of a major military force. It can also refer to army and navy forces under a single commander in a theater of war.

**company**   A ground forces unit that is part of a battalion. Three or four companies form a battalion. The equivalent unit in the artillery is called a battery.

**convoy**   A collection of merchant ships escorted by warships (and sometimes with aircraft as well). The warships and aircraft protected the vulnerable merchant ships against surface or subsurface attack. Ground convoys consist of a collection of vehicles traveling together with or without an armed escort.

**cruiser**   A fast warship designed for independent operations, it was more heavily armored than a destroyer but smaller and more lightly armored than a battleship. A light cruiser (CL) had five- or six-inch guns and was employed in antisubmarine operations, antiaircraft defense, surface battles, or naval gunfire support in amphibious operations. A heavy cruiser (CA) had eight-inch guns and was designed to fight surface threats and provide antiaircraft defense for carriers.

**depth charge**   A weapon used against submarines. It is a canister filled with high explosives and set by a hydrostatic fuse, which detonates the explosive at a specific depth. If a depth charge is detonated near a submarine, the force of the explosion can rupture the hull of the boat, sinking it or forcing it to the surface. To be effective the depth charge must be set for the proper depth, but this was often difficult due to the ability of the submarine to move up, down, or laterally to avoid being pinpointed. Successful depth charge attacks often involve several ships operating together to track and provide accurate information on the submarine and then maneuver the submarine into a position where another ship could drop the depth charges accurately.

**destroyer**   A fast, lightly armored, heavily armed warship designed to operate defensively (convoy escort or escorting larger ships) or offensively (amphibious operations, antisubmarine operations). Destroyers were used for scouting (locating an enemy fleet early) or picket duty (screening larger ships by providing early warning of air attack). The Fletcher-class destroyer of World War II was armed with 10 torpedo tubes, five 5-inch guns, antiaircraft weapons, and depth charges. Admiral Arleigh Burke became famous for his aggressive tactics as commander of Destroyer Squadron 23. American destroyers on picket duty off Okinawa in 1945 took heavy casualties from kamikazes.

**destroyer escort**   A small, slow, and lightly armed warship intended primarily for antisubmarine warfare, usually defending convoys or protecting larger ships.

**fighter aircraft**   Combat aircraft that has a crew of one or two, is highly maneuverable, and is primarily used for air-to-air combat against other enemy fighters. A fighter-bomber is an aircraft designed to engage enemy fighters but also to provide close support to ground units.

**fighter sweep**   An attack by fighter aircraft to locate and attack enemy aircraft or attack targets of opportunity in a specified area.

**flamethrower**   A man-portable weapon that projects an ignitable liquid in a steady stream. A soldier or marine carried the flamethrower on his back. Weighing about 40 pounds, it consisted of two fuel tanks, a pressure tank, and a hose with a nozzle that can project flame up to 30 meters away. Flamethrowers were especially effective against fortifications. Flamethrowers were also mounted on tanks.

**fleet**   A collection of ships, aircraft, and sometimes marine forces under the command of a naval officer who usually exercises both operational and tactical control of the subordinate elements.

**foxhole**   A hole dug by an infantryman or marine to shield him from enemy fire and effectively engage attacking enemy troops.

**grenade**   A small bomb weighing about a pound, thrown either by hand or launched from a rifle. The small charge has a delay fuse that allows it to explode without injuring the thrower. The casing of the grenade is designed to fragment over a 10 to 20 meter area. It is used to suppress or destroy enemy personnel, especially in confined areas.

**group**    An air force unit consisting of several squadrons.

**infantry**    Ground troops that fight primarily on foot to control ground. Light infantry is primarily foot mobile and lightly equipped. They can be highly versatile and, with proper support from aircraft or naval forces, can be a significant combat force. They have a limited capability against tanks. Mechanized infantry (also known as armored infantry in World War II) move to battle in carriers (half-tracks) in order to keep pace with tanks and artillery. Once dismounted, they have largely the same capabilities as light infantry, except for the capability of tank support and the ability to bring heavier weapons (anti-tank guns, mortars, and heavy machine guns) into battle quickly using their vehicles for supporting fire. No other force can control ground except the infantry. In forests, coral outcroppings, or jungle, the infantry is the only force capable of defeating the enemy.

**kamikaze**    A Japanese word meaning "divine wind." The kamikaze described both the pilot and his aircraft. The pilots had minimal training and were given a ceremony before departing on their mission. The pilot was directed toward a target area, then intentionally attempted to guide his explosive-laden aircraft into an enemy warship.

**landing craft**    A flat-bottom boat with a ramp in the front to disembark troops or vehicles directly on a beach during amphibious landings. Because of their ungainliness, landing craft (Landing Craft, Vehicle and Personnel, or LCVP, for example) must be launched in relatively calm seas and at a short distance from the beach. Mines, underwater obstacles, and artillery or mortar fire are particularly dangerous to landing craft. Landing craft are launched from larger ships. Larger landing ships (Landing Ship,

This landing craft, mechanized (LCM) belonged to the 533rd Engineer Boat and Shore Regiment of the 3rd Engineer Special Brigade. These units were essential to the success of the New Guinea-Philippines campaigns between 1944 and 1945. The LCM had a crew of four and brought troops and supplies ashore, carrying one tank, or 60 troops, or 60,000 pounds of cargo.

Tank, or LST, for example) have the capability to land troops, vehicles, and cargo directly onto the beach through large doors that open at the bow of the ship. They can do this only after the beach has been secured.

**lines of communication**    Air, land, or sea routes that connect combat forces with their source of supply, usually a local depot, but also the routes that connect far-flung forces with support from their home country. Without secure lines of communication, forces become ineffective over time because they cannot be resupplied with food, ammunition, or fuel to continue fighting. After the Japanese cut the American line of communication to the United States, the troops at Bataan and Corregidor became ineffective and were forced to surrender. In the same way, the United States used submarines to threaten Japan's lines of communication to its sources of supply in the southwest Pacific by sinking cargo ships. General MacArthur bypassed the Japanese base at Rabaul, effectively cutting off its lines of communication and leaving tens of thousands of troops stranded and ineffective. In military operations, commanders always seek to protect their own lines of communication while threatening the enemy's. Air or ground attacks to destroy bridges, road junctions, trails, or rail lines were critical to limit the enemy's ability to resupply its own forces; these lines of communication often became the focus of military operations.

**logistics**    All activities that supply and sustain combat forces. Logistics involves the acquisition, storage, transportation, distribution, maintenance, and repair of every single item used in war. Logistics planning is crucial to the success of combat operations. Sufficient stockpiles are needed to support the initial action; then forces must be resupplied and sustained sufficiently to maintain the level of action required to defeat the enemy. The heroic logistics effort to provide support to both Chinese forces as well as to maintain Fourteenth Air Force operations in China by using cargo aircraft to fly every item required over the Himalaya Mountains ("the Hump") is legendary. Logistics storage sites and depots and the means of transportation (rail, air, water, vehicle, or animal) were considered critical targets for air attack. Damaging or destroying these limited the effectiveness of the enemy. Much of the effort of Ninth Air Force in December and January of 1945 was the attack on supply depots and lines of communication deep in Germany to limit the effectiveness of German forces fighting in the Bulge.

**LST (Landing Ship, Tank)**    A large flat-bottomed assault vessel used in amphibious operations. The LST was over 300 feet long, had a large open deck and two large doors at the bow, which opened to allow a ramp to be dropped on the beach. This allowed the vehicles, troops, or cargo to be landed directly onto the beach. An LST could carry 17 tanks or 100 troops. Over 1,000 were built during the war and were an essential factor in both the ETO and the Pacific in achieving victory.

**machine gun**    A weapon that loads, chambers, fires, extracts, and reloads a cartridge automatically. Machine guns provide a sustained rate of high-volume fire to suppress or destroy enemy personnel, vehicles, or aircraft. Heavy machine guns fire a large-caliber cartridge (.50-caliber) with heavy barrels to maintain a high volume of fire. They have a crew of two or three and require the use of a tripod or must be mounted on a vehicle or boat. Light machine guns can be carried by one man and fired from a variety of positions. These guns had magazines holding 20 or more rounds of ammunition. They were used to support the movement of infantry in close combat. Other machine guns were supported by a crew of two or three, were fired from a bipod, and fed by a linked belt of ammunition. German forces especially employed these types of machine gun quite effectively.

**mine**    An explosive device buried in or placed on the ground that is detonated by pressure or by a tripwire. Mines are designated as anti-tank or anti-personnel. Anti-tank mines are intended to damage or destroy armored vehicles, while anti-personnel mines are employed to kill or wound enemy troops. Mines are used to block approaches to vulnerable points, limit the use of roads, or to channel enemy forces into vulnerable open areas where they can be engaged with machine gun or artillery fire. Naval mines, like land mines, were intended to delay an attacking force and put enemy forces in a vulnerable position for attack. Naval mines were usually contact type, anchored to the sea floor at a certain depth so that ships or landing craft would run into them. Other naval mines were acoustic and detonated when the sound of a ship's engine or propeller reached a certain level, marking the ship as close enough to cause damage.

**marines**    Naval infantry forces trained, organized, and equipped for amphibious warfare. The United States Marines fought as light infantry upon landing on a beachhead.

**mulberry**    The codeword for an artificial port established off the Normandy beaches to allow the rapid unloading of cargo from ships to the beaches.

**motor torpedo boats**    Known as PT (patrol torpedo) boats in the U.S. Navy and E-boats in Germany Navy (Kriegsmarine). These were fast, light boats armed with two or four torpedoes, machine guns, and antiaircraft guns. They were used for raids, night attacks on shipping, and patrolling.

**mortar**   A weapon designed to launch a high-explosive projectile at a high angle. Mortars are classified as light or heavy and each is composed of a smooth barrel, a base plate that provides stability for the barrel, a bipod, and an aiming sight. Light mortars (60 millimeter) are man portable and require a crew of two or three men. Like machine guns, these mortars provide fire support during close combat and are found at the company level. Mortars of higher caliber (81 millimeter or larger) are also crew served, but are transported by vehicle (or by pack animal as used by Merrill's Marauders and the Mars Task Force in Burma). These heavy mortars are found in infantry battalions. Mortars are easy to operate, have a high rate of fire, and are quickly put into action. They provide infantry companies and battalions with their own light artillery to suppress enemy troops in the attack or defense.

**napalm**   A jellied incendiary developed in the United States and used in bombs and as fuel for flamethrowers. Napalm was used effectively against troops, light vehicles, and concrete defensive positions.

*oka*   Japanese rocket missile piloted by one man and launched from an aircraft. Used in kamikaze attacks on U.S. ships during the Okinawa campaign.

**operational/operations**   This term describes the level of warfare between the strategic and tactical level. At the operational level of war, commanders are concerned with campaigns and the movement and actions of fleets, squadrons, corps, and divisions. For example, the Reno series of plans developed by General MacArthur's staff or the Granite plans developed by Admiral Nimitz's staff are all operational-level plans. At the strategic level, army groups or strategic air forces are the focus. In the ETO, Eisenhower directed the 12th and 21st Army Groups as Supreme Allied Commander. General Arnold directed the actions of the Twentieth Air Force in attacking strategic-level targets in Japan.

**operational control**   The command authority to organize and to employ subordinate forces as the commander deems necessary to accomplish assigned tasks.

**psychological warfare**   The use of information and ideas (either true or false) to influence the emotions, behaviors, or attitudes of a target audience to further the objectives of the sponsor. During the war, especially in the ETO, Eighth Air Force aircraft regularly dropped leaflets, small pieces of paper containing messages, often with information about Allied progress, directed at civilian populations in occupied France, Belgium, and the Netherlands to counter the false information broadcast by the Germans. Other leaflets were targeted at German soldiers to encourage surrender. In the last stages of the war with Japan, bombers dropped leaflets warning the civilian population to leave the cities or face destruction. Other leaflets were dropped informing the Japanese population about the effect of the atomic bombs dropped on Hiroshima and Nagasaki.

**radar**   A term formed from the words *radio detection and ranging*. Developed in the 1930s, this is a system that transmits electromagnetic energy and absorbs the reflection of that energy to determine range and position of objects either on the ground, on the sea, or in the air. During World War II it was used to locate ships and aircraft, locate targets for bombers, and as an aid in navigation.

**Rangers**   American light infantry trained, organized, and equipped for raids and attacks. These elite forces eventually grew to six battalions and served in Sicily, Italy, and in the ETO. One of the most famous Ranger operations was the attack on Pointe-du-Hoc at the Normandy beachhead on June 6, 1944.

**reconnaissance**   A specific mission tasked to ground or air forces to gain information about the enemy or to collect specific geographical, hydrological, or meteorological information about an area of interest.

**regiment**   A ground force unit, usually subordinate to a division (and the equivalent to a brigade), consisting of three or four battalions. U.S. Army units were often identified as regiments, even if they were not often employed as regiments in combat. Sometimes units fought as regimental combat teams (RCT), three infantry battalions combined with artillery, engineers, and other support units and tailored to a specific mission. RCTs were common in the Pacific. U.S. cavalry units (the 1st Cavalry Division in the Pacific, for example) fought as regiments.

**squadron**    A designation for air force units subordinate to a group. They were classified as bomber, fighter, or reconnaissance squadrons.

**strategy**    The art and science of employing a nation's political, economic, psychological, diplomatic, and military capabilities to achieve long-term goals during peace and war.

**submarine**    A boat designed for operations underwater. In World War II, submarines used diesel engines for propulsion and could operate on electric power, but battery capacity forced submarines to surface and run their diesel engines to recharge the batteries. This made them vulnerable to attack. Most submarines attacked targets on the surface during darkness and at short ranges. They were armed with deck guns to support surface attacks, and usually submerged to approach targets and escape pursuit.

**tactical**    Applies to actions of units at the brigade level or lower for ground forces, squadron level and below for air forces, and at the detachment, squadron, or individual ship level for naval forces.

**tactical control**    The command authority allowing detailed and local direction of a force to accomplish a specific task.

**tank**    A tracked armored fighting vehicle used as the principal assault weapon for armored or infantry forces. Tanks are classified as light, medium, and heavy depending on armor protection, weight, and size of their main gun. Light tanks were fast and lightly armored and had small-caliber guns. They were used mainly for reconnaissance and jungle fighting. Medium tanks had mobility, moderate armor protection, and medium-caliber guns. Most American tanks in World War II were medium tanks, and the M4 Sherman was the dominant medium tank. Heavy tanks carried thick armor, had limited mobility but powerful, large-caliber main guns.

**tank destroyer**    An armored fighting vehicle used to defeat enemy armor. American tank destroyers were lightly armored with high-velocity guns and had open turrets, making them vulnerable to artillery fire. Their light armor also limited their ability to engage enemy tanks in the open.

**target of opportunity**    A target not previously identified that is within range and engaged.

**task force**    A temporary grouping of units under one commander for a specific task. In the U.S. Navy, this most often involved grouping components of a fleet into task forces to accomplish specific missions. Admiral Marc Mitscher's carrier task force, Task Force 58, is one of the best known. A task group or task unit is a further subdivision of a task force used for independent operations from the task force and designated by an additional numeral added after the parent task force's number.

**theater of war or theater of operations**    A designated area of air, land, and water that allows the conduct of operational or strategic level military activities to accomplish a specified strategic task. The Southwest Pacific Area and European theater of operations are examples. In 1940 the U.S. War Department described the term theater of operations as "the land and sea areas to be invaded or defended, including areas necessary for administrative activities incident to the military operations."

**torpedo**    A self-propelled, cylindrical, underwater steel projectile with a high-explosive warhead, used against surface ships and submarines. Torpedoes could be launched by aircraft or submarines.

**troop**    A small unit of cavalry or tanks equivalent to a company. Even though they no longer had horses, units of the 1st Cavalry Division in the Pacific maintained their original designations for company-level units as troops.

**U-boat**　From the German word *Unterseeboot*. A German submarine.

**unconditional surrender**　A capitulation of the enemy in which all resistance ceases and the nation submits to the victor without any terms or conditions.

**V-1 and V-2**　The V-1 was a pilotless flying bomb launched from a ramp or by aircraft. It carried a 1,875-pound warhead and used a pulse-jet engine guided by a gyroscope on automatic pilot. The entire missile weighed 4,800 pounds and traveled at speeds near 400 miles per hour. At a predetermined time of flight, the fuel would be expended (usually between 10 and 125 miles) and the bomb would drop. Targeted at London, they were intended to cause terror and weaken civilian morale. About 10,000 of these bombs were fired at England; about 7,400 reached the coast. Of these, nearly 4,000 were shot down before causing any damage. The 3,500 that did hit London, Manchester, Southampton, and Portsmouth caused a total of 24,000 casualties.

The V-2 was a ballistic rocket over 46 feet long, carrying a 2,150-pound warhead and powered by alcohol and liquid oxygen. It had a preset guidance system and was able to travel at speeds reaching 3,600 miles per hour; it had a maximum range of 200 miles. It was first tested in 1942 and its first actual use was in September 1944. About 900 V-2 rockets were directed at Antwerp, and over 1,000 were fired at England, about half of these landing on London. Over 2,700 people were killed between September 1944 and the end of March 1945.

# GLOSSARY OF ABBREVIATIONS

**AAF** Army Air Forces

**AAI** Allied Armies in Italy

**ABDA** Australian-British-Dutch-American

**AEAF** Allied Expeditionary Air Force (ETO)

**AFHQ** Allied Forces Headquarters (Mediterranean)

**AFPAC** U.S. Army Forces in the Pacific

**AMET** Africa-Middle East Theater

**AMMISCA** American Military Mission to China

**Amtrac** Amphibious Tractor

**Aus** Australian

**AVG** American Volunteer Group (Flying Tigers, China)

**CACW** Chinese-American Composite Wing

**CAI** Chinese Army in India

**CAM** Composite Army-Marine

**CATF** Chinese Air Task Force

**CBI** China-Burma-India

**CCA** Combat Command A

**CCB** Combat Command B

**CCC** Combat Command C

**CCS** Combined Chiefs of Staff

**CG** Commanding General

**CinC** Commander in Chief

**CINCPAC** Commander in Chief, U.S. Pacific Fleet

**CINCPOA** Commander in Chief, Pacific Ocean Areas

**COMAIRSOLS** Commander, Air Forces Solomons

**COMCENPAC** Commander, Central Pacific

**COMINCH/CominCh** Commander in Chief

**COMSOPAC** Commander South Pacific

**COSSAC** Chief of Staff to the Supreme Allied Commander

**CTF** Commander Task Force

**EAC** Eastern Air Command (CBI)

**ETOUSA** European Theater of Operations, U.S. Army

**FEAF** Far East Air Force

**FF** Free French

**FMF** Fleet Marine Force

**JCS** Joint Chiefs of Staff

**MAAF** Mediterranean Allied Air Forces

**MAC** Marine Amphibious Corps

**MATAF** Mediterranean Allied Tactical Air Force

**ME** Middle East

**MTOUSA** Mediterranean Theater of Operations U.S. Army

**NAAF** Northwest African Air Force

**NATO** North African Theater of Operations

**NCAC** Northern Combat Area Command (Burma)

**NEI** Netherlands East Indies

**NZ** New Zealand

**PA** Philippine Army

**PGC** Persian Gulf Command

**PGSC** Persian Gulf Service Command

**POA** Pacific Ocean Areas

**RAAF** Royal Australian Air Force

**RAF** Royal Air Force

**RCT**   Regimental Combat Team

**SACMED**   Supreme Allied Commander Mediterranean

**SAF**   Strategic Air Force

**SEAC**   Southeast Asia Command

**SHAEF**   Supreme Headquarters, Allied Expeditionary Force

**SOPAC**   Southern Pacific

**SSF**   Special Service Force

**SWPA**   Southwest Pacific Area

**TAF**   Tactical Air Force

**TF**   Task Force

**U.K.**   United Kingdom

**U.S./US**   United States

**USA**   United States Army

**USAAF**   United States Army Air Force

**USAFFE**   United States Army Forces Far East

**USAFICPA**   United States Army Forces in the Central Pacific Area

**USAFIME**   United States Army Forces in the Middle East

**USAFISPA**   United States Army Forces in the South Pacific Area

**USFIP**   United States Army Forces in the Philippines

**USMC**   United States Marine Corps

**USN**   United States Navy

**USSAFE**   United States Strategic Air Forces in Europe

**USSR**   Union of Soviet Socialist Republics

**USSTAF**   United States Strategic Air Forces

**VAC**   V Amphibious Corps

**WDAF**   Western Desert Air Force

# WEAPONS

## AIRCRAFT

### Brewster F2A-3 Buffalo

**Type:** fighter
**Crew:** one
**Armament:** four .50-caliber machine guns
**Performance**
    **Range:** 965 miles (1,553 km)
    **Cruise Speed:** 161 MPH (259 km/hr.)
    **Max Speed:** 321 MPH (516 km/hr.)
    **Climb:** 2,290 ft./min. (697.96 m/min.)
    **Ceiling:** 33,200 ft. (10,119 m)

### Grumman F4F-4 Wildcat

**Type:** fighter
**Crew:** one
**Armament:** six .50-caliber machine guns
**Performance**
    **Range:** 770 miles (1,239 km)
    **Cruise Speed:** 155 MPH (249 km/hr.)
    **Max Speed:** 318 MPH (512 km/hr.)
    **Climb:** 1,950 ft./min. (594.33 m/min.)
    **Ceiling:** 34,800 ft. (10,607 m)

### Vought F4U Corsair

**Type:** fighter
**Crew:** one
**Armament:** six .50-caliber machine guns
**Performance**
    **Range:** 1,005 miles (1,618 km)
    **Max Speed:** 446 MPH (718 km/hr.)
    **Climb:** 3,870 ft./min. (1,179.52 m/min.)
    **Ceiling:** 41,500 ft. (12,649 m)

An F4U corsair supporting marines on Okinawa. The fighter had a top speed of 481 miles per hour and was armed with six .50-caliber machine guns and four 20 millimeter cannon. It had a range of 1,015 miles. This was the first American fighter plane that could match the Japanese Zero fighter.

### Grumman F6F-3 Hellcat

**Type:** fighter
**Crew:** one
**Armament:** six .50-caliber machine guns

**Performance**
Range: 945 miles (1,521 km)
Cruise Speed: 168 MPH (270 km/hr.)
Max Speed: 380 MPH (611 km/hr.)
Climb: 2,980 ft./min. (908.26 m/min.)
Ceiling: 37,300 ft. (11,368 m)

## General Motors FM-2 Wildcat

Type: single-seat carrier-based fighter
Crew: one
Armament: four .50-caliber machine guns; optional, two 250-lb. bombs or six/five-inch rockets
**Performance**
Range: 900 miles (1,448 km)
Cruise Speed: 164 MPH (264 km/hr.)
Max Speed: 332 MPH (534 km/hr.) at 28,800 ft.
Ceiling: 34,700 ft. (10,575 m)

## Lockheed P-38 D Lightning

Type: fighter
Crew: one
Armament: one 20 mm cannon, four .50-caliber machine guns
**Performance**
Range: 500 miles (805 km)
Cruise Speed: 300 MPH (483 km/hr.)
Max Speed: 390 MPH (628 km/hr.)
Climb: 2,500 ft./min. (761.96 m/min.)
Ceiling: 39,000 ft. (11,887 m)

## Bell P-39 Airacobra

Type: fighter
Crew: one
Armament: one 37 mm T9 cannon two .50-caliber machine guns four .30-caliber machine guns
**Performance**
Range: 350 miles (563 km)
Max Speed: 360 MPH (579 km/hr.)
Climb: 2,550 ft./min. (777.2 m/min.)
Ceiling: 31,900 ft. (9,722.6 m)

The P-39 Airacobra fighter was armed with a 37-millimeter cannon, two .50-caliber machine guns, and four 7.62-millimeter machine guns. It had a maximum range of 650 miles and a top speed of 386 miles per hour.

## Curtiss P-40 E Kittyhawk

Type: fighter
Crew: one
Armament: six .50-caliber machine guns
**Performance**
Range: 850 miles (1,368 km)
Cruise Speed: 235 MPH (378 km/hr.)
Max Speed: 362 MPH (582 km/hr.)
Ceiling: 30,000 ft. (9,143.6 m)

## Republic P-47 Thunderbolt

Type: fighter
Crew: one
Armament: six or eight .50-caliber machine guns
**Performance**
Range: 800 miles (1,297 km)
Cruise Speed: 300 MPH (483 km/hr.)
Max Speed: 467 MPH (762 km/hr.)
Ceiling: 43,000 ft. (13,105 m)

## North American P-51 D Mustang

Type: fighter
Crew: one
Armament: six .50-caliber machine guns

Ground support personnel rearm a P-47 Thunderbolt fighter with .50-caliber ammunition. The P-47 mounted eight .50-caliber machine guns.

The B-17 heavy bomber carried a crew of 10 and a maximum of 7,983 pounds of bombs. It had a maximum range of 2,000 miles with a 6,000-pound bomb load.

**Performance**
 **Range:** 1,000 miles (1,610 km)
 **Cruise Speed:** 275 MPH (442 km/hr.)
 **Max Speed:** 437 MPH (703 km/hr.)
 **Ceiling:** 41,900 ft. (12,770 m)

### Northrop P-61 Black Widow

**Type:** fighter
**Crew:** three
**Armament:** four 20 mm cannon, four .50-caliber machine guns in a dorsal turret
**Performance**
 **Range:** 1,200 miles (1,932 km)
 **Cruise Speed:** 275 MPH (442 km/hr.)
 **Max Speed:** 425 MPH (684 km/hr.)
 **Ceiling:** 46,200 ft. (14,081 m)

### Boeing B-17 Flying Fortress

**Type:** heavy bomber
**Crew:** 10: pilot, copilot, engineer, bombardier, radioman, five gunners
**Armament:** 13 .50-caliber machine guns (G model) up to 17,600 lbs. of bombs
**Performance**
 **Range:** 1,850 miles with 4,000 lb. bomb load
 **Cruise Speed:** 170 MPH (273 km/hr.)

 **Max Speed:** 300 MPH (483 km/hr.)
 **Ceiling:** 35,000 ft. (10,667 m)

### Consolidated B-24 Liberator

**Type:** heavy Bomber
**Crew:** eight to 10
**Armament:** 10 .50-caliber machine guns up to 12,800 lbs. of bombs
**D Model Performance**
 **Range:** 2,300 miles with 5,000 pound bomb load
 **Cruise Speed:** 175 MPH (281.00 km/hr.)
 **Max Speed:** 303 MPH (487.00 km/hr.)
 **Ceiling:** 28,000 ft. (8,534.00 m)
**L Model Performance**
 **Cruise Speed:** 214.00 MPH (346 km/hr.)
 **Max Speed:** 299.00 MPH (483 km/hr.)
 **Ceiling:** 27,978.0 ft. (8,530 m)

### North American B-25 Mitchell

**Type:** five-seat medium bomber
**Crew:** five
**Armament:** two to 18 .50-caliber machine guns up to 3,000 lbs. of bombs
**B Model Performance**
 **Range:** 1,200 miles (1,932 km)
 **Cruise Speed:** 230 MPH (370 km/hr.)

**Max Speed:** 275 MPH (442 km/hr.)
**Ceiling:** 25,000 ft. (7,619.6 m)
**D Model Performance**
　**Range:** 1,350 miles (2,173 km)
　**Max Speed:** 272 MPH (438 km/hr.)
　**Ceiling:** 24,200 ft. (7,375.80 m)

## Martin B-26 G Marauder

**Type:** seven-seat medium bomber
**Crew:** seven
**Armament:** 11 .50-caliber machine guns up to 4,000 lbs. of bombs
**Performance**
　**Range:** 1,100 miles (1,771.00 km)
　**Cruise Speed:** 216 MPH (348 km/hr.)
　**Max Speed:** 285 MPH (458.00 km/hr.)
　**Ceiling:** 19,800 ft. (6,034.7 m)

## Boeing B-29 Superfortress

**Type:** long-range strategic heavy bomber
**Crew:** 10: pilot, copilot, engineer, bombardier, radioman, five gunners
**Armament:** eight .50-caliber machine guns (two in each of four power turrets)
　three .50-caliber machine guns (or two .50-caliber and one 20 mm cannon) in the tail turret
　up to 20,000 lbs. of bombs
**Performance**
　**Range:** 3,250 miles (5,230 km)
　**Cruise Speed:** 230 MPH (370 km/hr.)

The B-26 Marauder was a medium bomber with a crew of seven and carried a 5,200-pound bomb load. It had a range of 675 miles.

The U.S. Navy's long-range patrol bomber, the Consolidated PB4Y-2, had a crew of 11 men and carried a maximum bomb load of 8,800 pounds. It had a maximum range of 2,800 miles.

**Max Speed:** 358 MPH (576 km/hr.)
**Ceiling:** 31,850 ft. (9,710 m)

## Consolidated PB4Y-2 Privateer

**Type:** land-based maritime patrol bomber
**Crew:** four to five
**Armament:** 12 .50-caliber machine guns up to 12,800 lbs. of bombs
**Performance**
　**Range:** 2,800 miles (4,506 km)
　**Cruise Speed:** 140 MPH (225 km/hr.)
　**Max Speed:** 237 MPH (381 km/hr.) at 13,750 ft.
　**Ceiling:** 20,700 ft. (6,310 m)

## Lockheed PV-1 Ventura

**Type:** patrol bomber
**Crew:** four to five
**Armament:** two forward firing .50-caliber machine guns
　two .50-caliber machine guns in dorsal turret
　two .30-caliber ventral machine guns
　six 500-lb. bombs or one torpedo in internal bomb bay
　up to two 1,000-lb. bombs external

The PV-1 Ventura navy patrol bomber was equipped with radar and had a 1,360-mile range and carried a bomb load of 3,000 pounds.

**Performance**
    **Range:** 1,360 miles
    **Cruise Speed:** 164 MPH
    **Max Speed:** 312 MPH at 13,800 ft.
    **Ceiling:** 26,300 ft.

## Lockheed PV-2 Harpoon

**Type:** patrol bomber
**Crew:** four to five
**Armament:** five fixed forward firing .50-caliber machine guns
    two flexible .50-caliber machine guns in dorsal turret
    two flexible .50-caliber machine guns in ventral mount
    six .30-caliber machine guns on flex mounts
    up to four 1,000-lb. bombs in internal bomb bay
    up to two 1,000-lb. bombs external
**Performance**
    **Range:** 1,790 miles
    **Cruise Speed:** 171 MPH
    **Max Speed:** 282 MPH at 13,700 ft.
    **Ceiling:** 23,900 ft.

## Douglas A-20 Havoc

**Type:** light bomber
**Crew:** three

The A-20 Havoc light bomber carried a crew of three, a bomb load of 4,000 pounds, and had a range of over 1,000 miles.

**Armament:** seven .50-caliber machine guns
    up to 4,000 lbs. of bombs
**Performance**
    **Range:** over 1,000 miles (1,521 km)
    **Cruise Speed:** 256 MPH (412 km/hr.)
    **Max Speed:** 317 MPH (510 km/hr.)
    **Ceiling:** 23,700 ft. (7,223.40 m)

## Douglas A-26 C Invader

**Type:** attack/medium bomber
**Crew:** three
**Armament:** six .50-caliber machine guns, optionally eight more
    up to 4,000 lbs. of bombs
**Performance**
    **Range:** 1,400 miles (2,255 km)
    **Cruise Speed:** 284 MPH (457 km/hr.)
    **Max Speed:** 355 MPH (571 km/hr.)
    **Ceiling:** 22,100 ft. (6,735 m)

## Curtiss SB2C Helldiver

**Type:** two-seat carrier-based scout bomber
**Crew:** two (pilot and gunner)
**Armament:** two 20 mm cannon in wings, two .30-caliber machine guns in rear cockpit
**Performance**
    **Range:** 1,165 miles (1,876 km)

**Cruise Speed:** 158 MPH (254 km/hr.)
**Max Speed:** 295 MPH (475 km/hr.)
**Ceiling:** 29,100 ft. (8,869 m)

## Douglas SBD-4 Dauntless

**Type:** dive bomber/scout bomber
**Crew:** two (pilot and observer/rear gunner)
**Armament:** two .50-caliber machine guns firing forward, two .30-caliber machine guns in rear cockpit, up to 1,600 lbs. of bombs centerline, 650 lbs. more under wings
**Performance**
   **Range:** 950 miles (1,530 km)
   **Cruise Speed:** 173 MPH (278 km/hr.)
   **Max Speed:** 250 MPH (402 km/hr.)
   **Climb:** 1,700 ft./min. (518 m/min.)
   **Ceiling:** 26,000 ft. (7,780 m)

## Douglas TBD-1 Devastator

**Type:** torpedo bomber
**Crew:** two (pilot and observer/rear gunner)
**Armament:** one .30-caliber machine gun firing forward, one .30-caliber machine gun in rear cockpit, one torpedo or one 1,000-lb. bomb
**Performance**
   **Range:** 716 miles (1,152 km)
   **Cruise Speed:** 128 MPH (206 km/hr.)
   **Max Speed:** 206 MPH (331 km/hr.)

The TBD-1 Devastator torpedo bomber carried one Mk 13 torpedo and a crew of two. Although the main torpedo bomber of its time prior to the war, it was slow, lightly armed, and had a limited range. Nevertheless, it played a major role in the Battle of the Coral Sea and the Battle of Midway.

**Climb:** 720 ft./min. (219.45 m/min.)
**Ceiling:** 19,500 ft. (5,943.3 m)

## Grumman TBF-1 Avenger

**Type:** torpedo bomber
**Crew:** three (pilot, bombardier, radio operator/gunner)
**Armament:** two wing-mounted .50-caliber machine guns, one .50-caliber machine gun in dorsal turret, one .30-caliber machine gun in ventral position, up to 2,000 lbs. of weapons (bombs/torpedo)
**Performance**
   **Range:** 1,010 miles (1,626 km)
   **Cruise Speed:** 147 MPH (236 km/hr.)
   **Max Speed:** 276 MPH (444 km/hr.)
   **Climb:** 2,060 ft./min. (627.86 m/min.)
   **Ceiling:** 30,100 ft. (9,174.00 m)

## Consolidated PBY-5A Catalina

**Type:** amphibious patrol bomber (flying boat)
**Crew:** seven
**Armament:** two .50-caliber machine guns
   three .30-caliber machine guns
   up to 4,000 lbs. of bombs or depth charges
**Performance**
   **Range:** 2,545 miles (4,096 km)
   **Cruise Speed:** 117 MPH (188 km/hr.) long-range cruise speed
   **Max Speed:** 179 MPH (288 km/hr.)
   **Ceiling:** 14,700 ft. (4,480 m)

## Curtiss C-46 Commando

**Type:** 54-seat military transport and troop carrier
**Crew:** three (pilot, copilot, radio operator)
**Armament:** none
**Performance**
   **Range:** 1,200 miles (1,931 km)
   **Cruise Speed:** 183 MPH (295 km/hr.)
   **Max Speed:** 269 MPH (433 km/hr.) at 15,000 ft.
   **Ceiling:** 27,600 ft. (8,410 m)

## Douglas C-47A Skytrain

**Type:** military transport and glider tug
**Crew:** three (pilot, copilot, radio operator)

The C-47 (a.k.a. C-47A) transport had a crew of three and a maximum range of 1,513 miles. It carried a maximum load of 7,000 pounds (paratroopers or cargo), although that limit was often exceeded.

**Armament:** none
**Performance**
  **Range:** 1,500 miles (2,414 km)
  **Cruise Speed:** 185 MPH (298 km/hr.) at 10,000 ft.
  **Max Speed:** 229 MPH (369 km/hr.) at 7,500 ft.
  **Climb:** 1,130 ft./min. (345 m/min.)
  **Ceiling:** 23,200 ft. (7,070 m)

### Douglas C-54 Skymaster

**Type:** cargo and passenger transport
**Crew:** six
**Armament:** none
**Performance**
  **Range:** 3,900 miles (6,276 km)
  **Cruise Speed:** 239 MPH (385 km/hr.)
  **Max Speed:** 274 MPH (441 km/hr.) at 14,000 ft.
  **Ceiling:** 22,000 ft. (6,705 m)

# GROUND FORCES

## Tanks and Armored Vehicles

### M3 General Stuart

**Type:** light tank
**Crew:** four
**Armament:** 37 mm gun, three .30-caliber machine guns
**Performance**
  **Range:** 70 miles (112 km)
  **Max Speed:** 36 MPH (58 km/hr.)

### M4A3 Sherman

**Type:** medium tank
**Crew:** five
**Armament:** 75 mm gun (by 1944, 76 mm gun), two .30-caliber machine guns, one .50-caliber machine gun
**Performance**
  **Range:** 100 miles (160 km)
  **Max Speed:** 25 MPH (40 km/hr.)

### M26 Pershing

**Type:** heavy tank
**Crew:** five
**Armament:** 90 mm gun, two .30-caliber machine guns, one .50-caliber machine gun
**Performance**
  **Range:** 110 miles (173 km)
  **Max Speed:** 30 MPH (48 km/hr.)

### Halftrack M3

**Type:** personnel carrier
**Crew:** three
**Armament:** one .50-caliber machine gun
**Capacity:** 10 (seven infantrymen plus the crew)
**Performance**
  **Range:** 200 miles (321 km)
  **Max Speed:** 45 MPH (72 km/hr.)

## Artillery

### 75 Millimeter Howitzer M1A1

**Type:** light or pack howitzer
**Weight:** 2,160 lbs.
**Max Range:** 9,760 yds. (8,925 km)

### 105 Millimeter Howitzer M2A1

**Type:** field howitzer
**Weight:** 4,260 lbs.
**Max Range:** 12,500 yds. (11,430 km)

## 155 Millimeter Howitzer M1917 and M1918A1

**Type:** medium howitzer
**Weight:** 22,550 lbs.
**Max Range:** 20,100 yds. (18,380 km)

### Infantry Weapons

### Automatic Pistol M1911A1

**Caliber:** .45
**Weight:** 2 lbs., 7 oz.
**Feed System:** seven-round magazine
**System of Operation:** feed system
**Performance**
    **Effective Range:** 82 feet (25 m)

### Rifle M1 Garand

**Caliber:** .30
**Weight:** 9 lbs., 8 oz.
**Feed System:** eight-round clip-fed
**System of Operation:** semi-automatic, gas operated
**Performance**
    **Effective Range:** 500 yds. (457 m)
    **Average Rate of Fire:** 10–12 rounds per minute

### Carbine M1/M2 (Selective fire: automatic or semiautomatic)

**Caliber:** .30
**Weight:** 5 lbs.
**Feed System:** 15-round detachable magazine
**System of Operation:** semi-automatic, gas operated
**Performance**
    **Effective Range:** 300 yds. (274 m)
    **Average Rate of Fire:** 30 rounds per minute (M2 on automatic: 650–700 rounds per minute)

### Browning Automatic Rifle M1918A1 (semiautomatic)/M1918A2 (fully automatic)

**Caliber:** .30
**Weight:** 22 lbs.
**Feed System:** 20-round detachable magazine

**System of Operation:** air-cooled, gas-operated, shoulder-fired
**Performance**
    **Effective Range:** 600 yds. (548 m)
    **Average Rate of Fire:** 200 rounds per minute for the semiautomatic M1918A1. The M1918A2 could be fired in two automatic modes, the slow rate (300 to 450 rounds per minute) or fast rate (500 to 650 rounds per minute). Marines favored the semiautomatic M1918A1.

### Thompson Submachine Gun M1/M1A1

**Caliber:** .45
**Weight:** 10 lbs., 2 oz.
**Feed System:** 20- or 30-round detachable magazine
**System of Operation:** selective fire (semi-automatic or automatic) blow-back system
**Performance**
    **Effective Range:** 50 yds. (45 m)
    **Average Rate of Fire:** 600 to 725 rounds per minute

### Submachine Gun M3

**Caliber:** .45
**Weight:** 8 lbs., 15 oz.
**Feed System:** 30-round detachable magazine
**System of Operation:** automatic, blow-back system
**Performance**
    **Effective Range:** 50 yds. (45 m)
    **Average Rate of Fire:** 450 rounds per minute

### Machine Guns

### Browning Machine Gun M1917A1/ M1919A4/M1919A6

**Caliber:** .30
**Weight:** M1917A1: 93 lbs. M1919A4: 41 lbs. with tripod; M1919A6: 32.5 pounds with tripod
**Feed System:** all models: belt-fed, 250 rounds
**System of Operation:** Automatic, recoil system; M1917A1 was water-cooled. The M1919A4 and A6 models were air-cooled

**Performance**

    **Effective Range:** M1917A1 and M1919A4: 1,100 yds.; M1919A6: 800 yds. (731 m)

    **Average Rate of Fire:** M1917A1: 400–600 rounds per minute; M1919A4: 400–550 rounds per minute; M1919A6: 400–550 rounds per minute

## Browning Machine Gun M2

**Caliber:** .50

**Weight:** 128 lbs. with tripod

**Feed System:** 110-round metallic linked belt

**System of Operation:** automatic, recoil system, air-cooled

**Performance**

    **Effective Range:** 2,500 yds. (2,286 m)

    **Average Rate of Fire:** 450–575 rounds per minute

## Mortars

### Mortar M2

**Caliber:** 60

**Weight in Action:** 42 lbs.

**System of Operation:** drop, fixed striker

**Performance**

    **Effective Range:** 100 yds. (91 m) (minimum); 1,985 yds. (1,815 m) (maximum)

    **Average Rate of Fire:** 18 rounds per minute (high-explosive only)

### Mortar M1

**Caliber:** 81

**Weight in Action:** 136 lbs.

**System of Operation:** drop, fixed striker

**Performance**

    **Effective Range:** 100 yds. (91 m); (minimum) to 3,290 yds. (3,008 m) (HE) or 2,470 yds. (smoke)

    **Average Rate of Fire:** 18 rounds per minute (high-explosive, smoke)

## Bazooka

### Launcher, Rocket, Anti-tank M1

**Caliber:** 2.36 in.

**Weight in Action:** 13.25 lbs.

**System of Operation:** electric

**Performance**

    **Effective Range:** 400 yds. (365 m) (maximum); 120 yds. (107 m) maximum effective range

    **Armor Penetration:** up to five inches of armor

## Grenades

### MarkIIA1 Fragmentation Grenade

**Length:** 4.5 in.

**Weight:** 1.3 lbs.

**Filling:** smokeless powder flakes

**Body:** serrated cast iron

**Fuse:** 4–5-second delay. The grenade could be thrown or launched by a rifle using an adapter.

### MarkIIIA2 Fragmentation Grenade

**Length:** 5.35 in.

**Weight:** 14 oz.

**Filling:** TNT

**Body:** fiberboard

**Fuse:** 4.5-second delay. The grenade relies on blast rather than fragmentation for effect. Used for clearing buildings and fortified positions.

# APPENDIX I

## SHIP AND LANDING CRAFT CLASSIFICATIONS

### U.S. NAVY SHIP CLASSIFICATION SYMBOLS

| | |
|---|---|
| BB | Battleship |
| BBc | Coastal Battleship |
| BC | Battle Cruiser |
| CA | Heavy Cruiser |
| CL | Light Cruiser |
| CL(AA) | Light Cruiser (Antiaircraft) |
| CM | Minelayer |
| CMc | Coastal Minelayer |
| CV | Aircraft Carrier (Fleet) |
| CVE | Aircraft Carrier (Escort) |
| CVL | Aircraft Carrier (Light) |
| CVS | Aircraft Carrier (Seaplane) |
| CX | Armed Merchant Cruiser |
| DD | Destroyer |
| DE | Destroyer Escort |
| DM | Light Minelayer |
| DMS | Fast Minesweeper (Destroyer) |
| SM | Submarine (Mine Laying) |
| SS | Submarine |

### LANDING CRAFT CLASSIFICATIONS

| | |
|---|---|
| LCC | Landing Craft, Control |
| LCI | Landing Craft, Infantry |
| LCI(G) | Landing Craft, Infantry (Gunboat) |
| LCI(L) | Landing Craft, Infantry (Large) |
| LCI(M) | Landing Craft, Infantry (Mortar) |
| LCI(R) | Landing Craft, Infantry (Rocket) |
| LCM | Landing Craft, Mechanized |
| LCP(L) | Landing Craft, Personnel (Large) |
| LCP(R) | Landing Craft, Personnel (Ramp) |
| LCR(L) | Landing Craft, Rubber (Large) |
| LCS(L) | Landing Craft, Support (Large) |
| LCS(S) | Landing Craft, Support (Small) |
| LCT | Landing Craft, Tank |
| LCV | Landing Craft, Vehicle |
| LCVP | Landing Craft, Vehicle & Personnel |
| LSV | Landing Ship, Vehicle |
| LSD | Landing Ship, Dock |
| LSM | Landing Ship, Medium |
| LSM(R) | Landing Ship, Medium (Rocket) |
| LST | Landing Ship, Tank |
| LVT | Landing Vehicle, Tracked |
| LVT(A) | Landing Vehicle, Tracked (Armored) |
| LVT(G) | Landing Vehicle, Tracked (Gunboat) |
| LVT(L) | Landing Vehicle, Tracked (Large) |
| LVT(M) | Landing Vehicle, Tracked (Mortar) |
| LVT(R) | Landing Vehicle, Tracked (Rocket) |

# Appendix II

## Commands

### Theater Commands

#### China-Burma-India Theater of Operations

Established in March 1942

Commander: March 1942–October 1944: General Joseph W. Stilwell

October 1944 to 1945: Major General Albert C. Wedemeyer

CBI was not a true theater of operations. Stilwell had operational control of the Northern Combat Area Command, a combined American and Chinese combat unit, but his role as commander in CBI was mostly in the administrative control of all U.S. forces in-theater. Operational control of forces nominally remained with Britain's Admiral Louis Mountbatten as commander of Southeast Asia Command. Stilwell, in his role as deputy commander of Southeast Asia Command, was often able to slip command boundaries. After Stilwell departed in October 1944, the China-Burma-India theater of operations was separated into the U.S. Forces, China theater, and U.S. Forces, India-Burman theater, commanded by Lieutenant General Daniel I. Sultan. General Wedemeyer took command of U.S. Forces, China theater. Wedemeyer also took over Stilwell's position as chief of staff to Generalissimo Chiang Kai-shek.

### European Theater of Operations

Established in England in June 1942

Commanded by Major General Eisenhower as the European theater of operations U.S. Army (ETOUSA). He gave up command of ETOUSA in February 1943 to command Operation Torch, the invasion of North Africa. In January 1944 he resumed command of ETOUSA, and in February he became the Supreme Allied Commander of the Allied Expeditionary Force (SHAEF). SHAEF was an operational command and ETOUSA the administrative command, and both were under Eisenhower until the end of the war. Under SHAEF, Eisenhower commanded the U.S. 12th Army Group (General Omar N. Bradley) and the British 21st Army Group (Field Marshal Bernard Montgomery), and after September 1944, the U.S. 6th Army Group (General Jacob L. Devers).

### Mediterranean Theater of Operations

The Mediterranean theater of operations evolved from the North African theater command structure. It had been established for Operation Torch, the invasion of North Africa, and when the decision was made by Roosevelt and Churchill to extend Allied operations into Italy, a new command was established under British authority with American armies and air force units subordinate.

### Southwest Pacific Area

Established April 1942
Commander 1942–1945: General Douglas MacArthur

### Pacific Ocean Areas

Established April 1942
Commander 1942–1945: Admiral Chester W. Nimitz.

### Central Pacific Ocean Area

Established April 1942
Commander 1942–1945: Admiral Chester W. Nimitz.

There were two commands subordinate to Nimitz:

### South Pacific Area

Established April 1942
Commander June 1942–October 1942: Vice Admiral Robert L. Ghormley
Commander October 1942–June 1944: Admiral William F. Halsey

### North Pacific Area

Established April 1942
Commander January 1943–October 1943: Vice Admiral Thomas C. Kinkaid
Commander October 1943–1945: Vice Admiral Frank Jack Fletcher

## Navy Fleets Prior to the War

Atlantic Fleet
Pacific Fleet
Asiatic Fleet (dissolved in June 1942)

## Numbered Fleets

### Third Fleet

Established March 1943 and under operational control of Commander, Central Pacific, September 1944 to January 1945, and from May 1945 to September 1945.
Commander 1943–1945: Admiral William F. Halsey

### Fourth Fleet

Established March 1943 and subordinate to Atlantic Fleet

### Fifth Fleet

Established April 1944 and under operational control of Commander, Central Pacific, April to September 1944 and January to May 1945.
Commander 1943–1945: Admiral Raymond A. Spruance

### Seventh Fleet

Established February 1943 and under command of General MacArthur
Commander November 1943–1945: Vice Admiral Thomas C. Kinkaid

### Tenth Fleet

Established in March 1943 as a shore-based headquarters to direct antisubmarine operations along the Atlantic coast.
Commanded by Admiral Ernest J. King, 1943–1945.

## Theater Air Force Commanders

### Commander in Chief Far East Air Forces

Established in June 1944 to coordinate the operations of the Fifth and the Thirteenth Air Forces (later the Seventh Air Force as well)
Commander: Lieutenant General George C. Kenney

## Commander in Chief Army Air Forces Pacific Ocean Areas

Established in August 1944 under command of Lieutenant General M. F. Harmon

## Commander in Chief U.S. Strategic Air Forces Pacific

Established in June 1945 to oversee the operations of the Twentieth Air Force and the Eighth Air Force arriving from Europe.
Commander: Lieutenant General Carl Spaatz

## Numbered Air Forces

### Fifth Air Force

Established in February 1942 from the Philippine Department Air Force and supported General MacArthur in Southwest Pacific Area.

### Sixth Air Force

Established February 1942 to defend the Panama Canal

### Seventh Air Force

Established February 1942 to defend Hawaii, then redeployed its forces to conduct combat operations in the Central Pacific.

### Eighth Air Force

Formed in January 1942 and deployed to England. Conducted strategic bombing of Germany and occupied Europe. Eighth Air Force grew to contain 40 heavy bomber groups, 15 fighter groups, and four specialized support groups. In February 1944, strategic bombers of the VIII Bomber Command were redesignated Eighth Air Force, while Eighth Air Force headquarters was redesignated U.S. Strategic Air Forces in Europe and combined with Fifteenth Air Force to coordinate strategic bombing efforts throughout Europe.

### Ninth Air Force

The U.S. Army Middle East Air Force was redesignated as Ninth Air Force in November 1942 and supported operations in North Africa and the Mediterranean until October 1943, when it became part of the European theater of operations to support the Allied invasion of Europe. It supported the advance of the American armies until the end of the war.

### Tenth Air Force

Formed in February 1942 and operated in China, Burma, and India until March 1943. With the activation of the Fourteenth Air Force, Tenth Air Force remained responsible for Burma and India. In July 1945 it became part of Fourteenth Air Force to support operations in China.

### Eleventh Air Force

Formed in February 1942 to defend Alaska but also conducted offensive operations against Japanese positions in the Aleutian and the Kurile Islands.

### Thirteenth Air Force

Established in December 1942 and served in the South Pacific and Southwest Pacific area in support of MacArthur and Halsey.

### Fourteenth Air Force

Established in March of 1943 and supported operations in China throughout the war.

### Fifteenth Air Force

Established in November of 1943 and subordinate to the Mediterranean Strategic Air Force under Mediterranean Allied Air Forces. It conducted bombing operations from southern Italy to destroy gasoline production and aircraft production facilities in southern Europe.

### Twentieth Air Force

Established in April 1944 to conduct strategic bombing of Japan from China. Because of limitations in logistics support, the Twentieth redeployed to the Mariana Islands in July

1945 and conducted attacks on the Japanese home islands, ending in the use of atomic bombs in August.

## Army Groups ETO

12th Army Group (General Omar N. Bradley)
First Army (attached to Montgomery's 21st Army Group temporarily during Battle of the Bulge, December 1944 to January 1945)
Third Army
Ninth Army (attached to Montgomery's 21st Army Group from October 1944 until April 1945)
Fifteenth Army

6th Army Group (General Jacob L. Devers)
Seventh Army
French First Army

## Army Group–MTO

15th Army Group
U.S. Fifth Army
British Eighth Army
In December 1944, Lieutenant General Mark W. Clark became commander 15th Army Group. Up to that time, the Army Group had been under British command.

## Armies

### First Army

In existence since 1933. Deployed to England in October 1943 under General Omar N. Bradley to prepare for the Normandy invasion. In August 1944 General Courtney H. Hodges took command of the army until the end of the war.

### Third Army

In existence since 1932. Deployed to England in January 1944. Operational in July 1944 and commanded by General George S. Patton until the end of the war.

### Fifth Army

Activated in Algiers in January 1943 for administrative support and training of U.S. Army troops in North Africa. In September 1943 it landed at Salerno and served in Italy as part of 15th Army Group until the end of the war. Under command of General Mark W. Clark to November 1944, then under General Lucian K. Truscott until the end of the war.

### Sixth Army

Activated in January 1943 and arrived in the Pacific in April 1943 under command of Lieutenant General Walter Krueger. From April 1943 to September 1944 it was known as the Alamo Task Force and conducted most of the offensive operations in MacArthur's New Guinea campaign.

### Seventh Army

Activated in July 1943 for the invasion of Sicily. It was subordinate to 15th Army Group until September 1944. In August it landed in southern France (Operation Dragoon) and came under the operational control of 6th Army Group. General George S. Patton commanded the army from July 1943 to January 1944; General Mark W. Clark commanded until March 1944 (while simultaneously serving as Fifth Army commander); it was under the command of General Alexander M. Patch until the end of the war.

### Eighth Army

Activated in June 1944 and arrived in September in the Southwest Pacific area. It was commanded by General Robert L. Eichelberger throughout its wartime service.

### Ninth Army

Activated in April 1944 and arrived in England in June. It became operational in France in October 1944 and was commanded by Lieutenant General William H. Simpson until the end of the war.

## Tenth Army

Activated in the Pacific in June 1944 and landed on Okinawa in April 1945. It was commanded by General Simon B. Buckner until he was killed on Okinawa; then under temporary command of General Roy S. Geiger (USMC) until July, when General Joseph W. Stilwell took command.

## Fifteenth Army

Activated in January 1945 to support rear area security and transition operations in occupied German territory. Under command of General Leonard T. Gerow.

## Marine Corps

### III Amphibious Corps

Established in October 1942 as I Amphibious Corps, then redesignated in April 1944.

Responsible for operations in the South Pacific.

### V Amphibious Corps

Established in September 1943 from Amphibious Corps Pacific Fleet. Responsible for operations in the Central Pacific.

## Commander in Chief Aircraft, Fleet Marine Forces Pacific

In September 1944 Marine Aircraft Wing Pacific was redesignated as Fleet Marine Forces Pacific with the responsibility for all marine aircraft in-theater.

# APPENDIX III

## COMPOSITION OF DIVISIONS

### Composition of a U.S. Infantry Division in 1943 (also Marine Corps)

14,253 officers and men
243 Browning Automatic Rifles
157 medium machine guns
236 heavy machine guns
144 mortars (60 and 81 millimeter)
557 bazookas
2,012 vehicles

#### Division Units

Reconnaissance Troop
Three Infantry Regiments (each with three infantry battalions)
Anti-tank Company
Cannon Company (six 105 millimeter howitzers)
Three Artillery Battalions (each with 12 105 millimeter howitzers)
Medium Artillery battalion (12 155 millimeter howitzers)
Engineer Battalion
Signal Company

### Composition of a U.S. Armored Division in 1943

10,937 officers and men
465 medium machine guns
404 heavy machine guns
93 mortars (60 and 81 millimeter)
77 light tanks
186 medium tanks
501 halftracks
2,653 vehicles

#### Division Units

Reconnaissance Battalion
Three Tank Battalions (53 medium tanks and 17 light tanks)
Three Armored Infantry Battalions (71 halftracks)
Three Artillery Battalions (18 105 millimeter self-propelled howitzers)
Engineer Battalion
Signal Company

### Composition of a U.S. Airborne Division in 1942

8,505 officers and men
54 Browning Automatic Rifles
187 medium machine guns
105 heavy machine guns
111 mortars (60 and 81 millimeter)
182 bazookas
27 flamethrowers
36 75 millimeter pack howitzers
385 trucks

#### Division Units

One Parachute Regiment (three parachute infantry battalions)

Two Glider Infantry Regiments (three battalions each of infantry)
Airborne Antiaircraft Battalion (24 37 millimeter guns)
Airborne Engineer Battalion
Airborne Signal Company

## Composition of a U.S. Marine Corps Division in 1944

17,465 officers and men
853 Browning Automatic Rifles
464 medium machine guns
161 heavy machine guns
153 Mortars (60 and 81 millimeter)
267 flamethrowers
172 bazookas
24 75 millimeter pack howitzers
36 105 millimeter howitzers
46 medium tanks
1,056 vehicles

### Division Units

Tank Battalion
Three Infantry Regiments (each with three infantry battalions and a weapons company)
Artillery Regiment (two battalions of 105 millimeter howitzers and one battalion of 75 millimeter howitzers)
Engineer Battalion
Pioneer Company
Amphibious Tractor Battalions (three or four battalions attached for amphibious landings)

# APPENDIX IV

## U.S. GROUND COMBAT UNITS BY DIVISION AND REGIMENT

No marking by division number—the division served only in the ETO.
# Division served in Italy.
+ Division served in North Africa.
× Division participated in the invasion of Sicily.
* Division served in the Pacific.
~ Division landed in southern France (Operation Dragoon) and joined the ETO.

| INFANTRY DIVISION | INFANTRY REGIMENT | INFANTRY REGIMENT | INFANTRY REGIMENT |
|---|---|---|---|
| 1+× To ETO in June 1944 | 16 | 18 | 26 |
| 2 | 9 | 23 | 38 |
| 3+×#~ | 7 | 15 | 30 |
| 4 | 8 | 12 | 22 |
| 5 | 2 | 10 | 11 |
| 6* | 1 | 20 | 63 |
| 7* | 17 | 32 | 184 |
| 8 | 13 | 28 | 121 |
| 9+× To ETO in June 1944 | 39 | 47 | 60 |
| 10 Mtn# | 85 | 86 | 87 |
| 24* | 19 | 21 | 34 |
| 25* | 27 | 35 | 161 |
| 26 | 101 | 104 | 328 |
| 27* | 105 | 106 | 165 |
| 28 | 109 | 110 | 112 |
| 29 | 115 | 116 | 175 |
| 30 | 117 | 119 | 120 |
| 31* | 124 | 155 | 167 |
| 32* | 126 | 127 | 128 |
| 33* | 123 | 130 | 136 |

| INFANTRY DIVISION | INFANTRY REGIMENT | INFANTRY REGIMENT | INFANTRY REGIMENT |
|---|---|---|---|
| 34+# | 133 | 135 | 168 |
| 35 | 134 | 137 | 320 |
| 36+#~ | 141 | 142 | 143 |
| 37* | 129 | 145 | 148 |
| 38* | 149 | 151 | 152 |
| 40* | 108 | 160 | 185 |
| 41* | 162 | 163 | 186 |
| 42 | 22 | 232 | 242 |
| 43* | 103 | 169 | 172 |
| 44 | 71 | 114 | 324 |
| 45x#~ | 157 | 179 | 180 |
| 63 | 253 | 254 | 255 |
| 65 | 259 | 260 | 261 |
| 66 | 262 | 263 | 264 |
| 69 | 271 | 272 | 273 |
| 70 | 274 | 275 | 276 |
| 71 | 5 | 14 | 66 |
| 75 | 289 | 290 | 291 |
| 76 | 304 | 385 | 417 |
| 77* | 305 | 306 | 307 |
| 78 | 309 | 310 | 311 |
| 79 | 313 | 314 | 315 |
| 80 | 317 | 318 | 319 |
| 81* | 321 | 322 | 323 |
| 83 | 329 | 330 | 331 |
| 84 | 333 | 334 | 335 |
| 85# | 337 | 338 | 339 |
| 86 | 341 | 342 | 343 |
| 87 | 345 | 346 | 347 |
| 88# | 349 | 350 | 351 |
| 89 | 353 | 354 | 355 |
| 90 | 357 | 358 | 359 |
| 91# | 361 | 362 | 363 |
| 92# | 365 | 370 | 371 |
| 93* | 25 | 368 | 369 |
| 94 | 301 | 302 | 376 |
| 95 | 377 | 378 | 379 |
| 96* | 381 | 382 | 383 |
| 97 | 303 | 386 | 387 |
| 99 | 393 | 394 | 395 |
| 100 | 397 | 398 | 399 |
| 102 | 405 | 406 | 407 |
| 103 | 409 | 410 | 411 |
| 104 | 413 | 414 | 415 |
| 106 | 422 | 423 | 424 |
| American* | 132 | 164 | 182 |

| ARMORED DIVISION | ARMORED REGIMENT | ARMORED REGIMENT | ARMORED INFANTRY REGIMENT |
|---|---|---|---|
| 2+× To ETO in 1943 | 66 | 67 | 41 |
| 3 | 32 | 33 | 36 |

These divisions remained under the 1942 organization throughout the war, with two armored regiments and one armored infantry regiment

| ARMORED DIVISION | TANK BATTALION | TANK BATTALION | TANK BATTALION | ARMORED INFANTRY BATTALION | ARMORED INFANTRY BATTALION | ARMORED INFANTRY BATTALION |
|---|---|---|---|---|---|---|
| 1+# | 1 | 4 | 3 | 6 | 11 | 14 |
| 4 | 8 | 35 | 37 | 10 | 51 | 53 |
| 5 | 10 | 34 | 81 | 15 | 46 | 47 |
| 6 | 15 | 68 | 69 | 9 | 44 | 50 |
| 7 | 17 | 31 | 40 | 23 | 38 | 48 |
| 8 | 18 | 36 | 80 | 7 | 49 | 58 |
| 9 | 2 | 14 | 19 | 27 | 52 | 60 |
| 10 | 3 | 11 | 21 | 20 | 54 | 61 |
| 11 | 22 | 41 | 42 | 21 | 55 | 63 |
| 12 | 23 | 43 | 714 | 17 | 56 | 66 |
| 13 | 24 | 45 | 46 | 16 | 59 | 67 |
| 14 | 25 | 47 | 48 | 19 | 62 | 68 |
| 16 | 5 | 16 | 26 | 18 | 64 | 69 |
| 20 | 9 | 20 | 27 | 8 | 65 | 70 |

| CAVALRY DIVISION | 1ST CAVALRY BRIGADE REGIMENTS | 2ND CAVALRY BRIGADE REGIMENTS |
|---|---|---|
| 1* | 5 and 12 | 7 and 8 |

Total strength: 12,724

| AIRBORNE DIVISION | GLIDER INFANTRY REGIMENT | GLIDER INFANTRY REGIMENT | PARACHUTE INFANTRY REGIMENT | PARACHUTE INFANTRY REGIMENT |
|---|---|---|---|---|
| 11a* | 187 | 188 | 511 | |
| 11b | 187 | | 511 | 588 |
| 17 a | 193 | 194 | | 513 |
| 17 b | | 194 | 507 | 513 |
| 82 a x# To ETO in March 1944 | 325 | | 504 | 505 |
| 82 b | 325 | | 504 | 505 |
| 101 a | 327 | 401 | 502 | |
| 101 b | 327 | | 502 | 506 |

a. This is the organization prior to March 1, 1945.
b. This is the unit organization after March 1, 1945. All units omitted were inactivated or disbanded on March 1, and all additional units listed were activated or assigned on that date.

| MARINE CORPS DIVISION | MARINE REGIMENT | MARINE REGIMENT | MARINE REGIMENT |
|---|---|---|---|
| 1 | 1 | 5 | 7 |
| 2 | 2 | 6 | 8 |
| 3 | 3 | 9 | 21 |
| 4 | 23 | 24 | 25 |
| 5 | 26 | 27 | 28 |
| 6 | 4 | 22 | 29 |

All marine divisions were assigned to the Pacific. Marine regiments are often designated by the regimental number and the title "Marines." Thus, the 1st Marines always refers to the 1st Marine Regiment. A marine division is always referred to as such, along with its division number: 1st Marine Division.

# APPENDIX V

## LOSSES: THE BATTLE OF THE ATLANTIC

### 1941

Allied shipping sunk (thousands of tons): 4,398
U.S. and British new ship construction: 1,984
Net tonnage loss or gain: -2,414
U-boats sunk: 35

### 1942

Allied shipping sunk (thousands of tons): 8,245
U.S. and British new ship construction: 7,182
Net tonnage loss or gain: -1,063
U-boats sunk: 85

### 1943

Allied shipping sunk (thousands of tons): 3,661
U.S. and British new ship construction: 14,585
Net tonnage loss or gain: +10,974
U-boats sunk: 237

### 1944

Allied shipping sunk (thousands of tons): 1,422
U.S. and British new ship construction: 13,349
Net tonnage loss or gain: +11,927
U-boats sunk: 241

### 1945 (January to May)

Allied shipping sunk (thousands of tons): 458
U.S. and British new ship construction: 3,834
Net tonnage loss or gain: +3,378
U-boats sunk: 153

### Totals for the war (1941–1945)

Allied shipping sunk (thousands of tons): 18,134
U.S. and British new ship construction: 40,934
Net tonnage loss or gain: +15,468
U-boats sunk: 751

# APPENDIX VI

## ENEMY AIRCRAFT DESTROYED BY THE ARMY AIR FORCE DURING WORLD WAR II

### 1942 (February to December)

Total enemy aircraft losses: 935
ETO kills: 327
MTO kills: 158
FEAF kills: 518
POA kills: 0
CBI kills: 53
Aleutian kills: 37

### 1943

Total enemy aircraft losses: 10,837
ETO kills: 3,865
MTO kills: 3,740
FEAF kills: 2,466
POA kills: 96
CBI kills: 636
Aleutian kills: 34

### 1944

Total enemy aircraft losses: 19,442
ETO kills: 10,425
MTO kills: 5,239
FEAF kills: 2,518
POA kills: 226
CBI kills: 772
Aleutian kills: 8
Twentieth Air Force kills: 254

### 1945 (January to August)

Total enemy aircraft losses: 8,477
ETO kills: 5,960
MTO kills: 291
FEAF kills: 416
POA kills: 472
CBI kills: 361
Aleutian kills: 6
Twentieth Air Force kills: 971

### Totals for the war

Total enemy aircraft losses: 39,691
ETO kills: 20,577
MTO kills: 9,428
FEAF kills: 5,918
POA kills: 794
CBI kills: 1,822
Aleutian kills: 85
Twentieth Air Force kills: 1,225

# APPENDIX VII

## CASUALTIES

Total number of Americans serving worldwide during World War II: 16,112,566

Total serving in the U.S. Army and Army Air Force: 11,260,000

Total serving in the U.S. Navy: 4,183,466

Total serving in the U.S. Marine Corps: 669,100

Total American deaths: 405,399

Total American battle deaths: 291,557

Total American deaths from other causes: 113,842

Total American wounds (not mortal): 671,846

Total Army deaths: 318,274*

Total Army battle deaths: 234,874

Total Army deaths other causes: 83,400

Total Army wounds (not mortal): 565,861

Total Navy deaths: 62,614**

Total Navy battle deaths: 36,958

Total Navy deaths other causes: 25,664

Total Navy wounds (not mortal): 37,778

Total Marine deaths: 24,511

Total Marine battle deaths: 19,733

Total Marine deaths other causes: 4,778

Total Marine wounds (not mortal): 68,207

*Includes Army Air Force
**Includes U.S. Navy casualties from October 1941
From *Historical Statistics of the United States*

# APPENDIX VIII

## MAPS

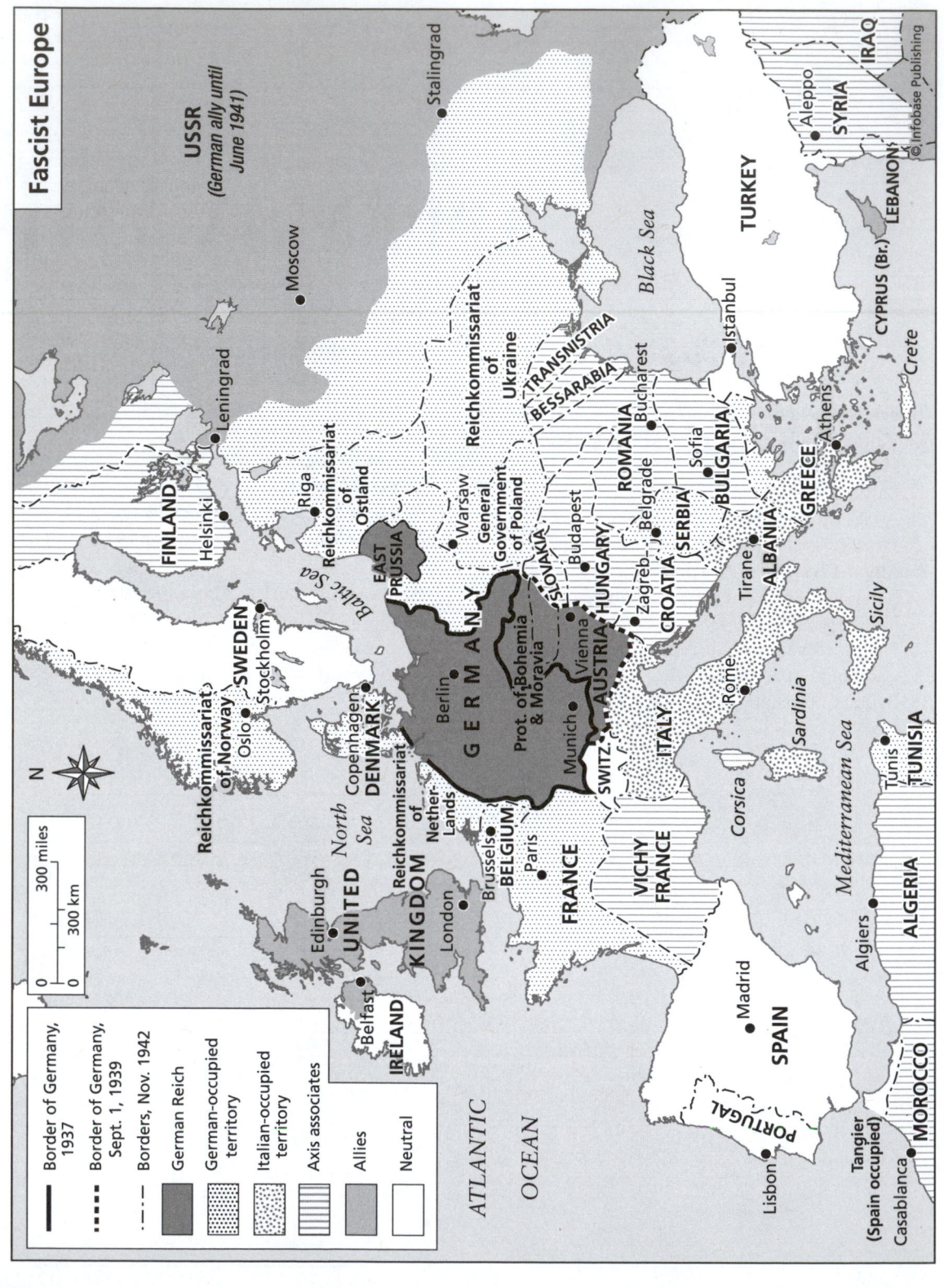

Fascist Europe

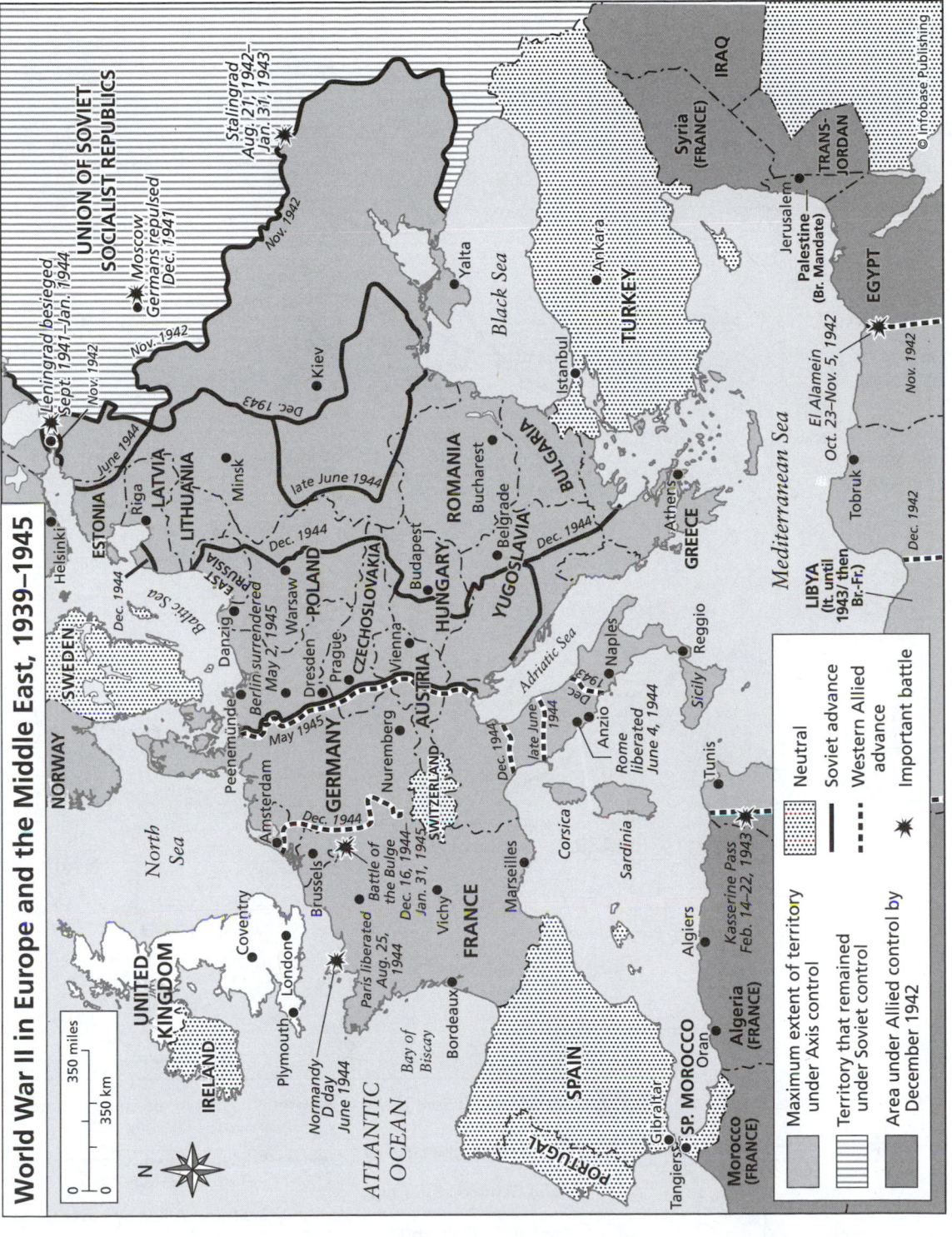

World War II in Europe and the Middle East, 1939–1945

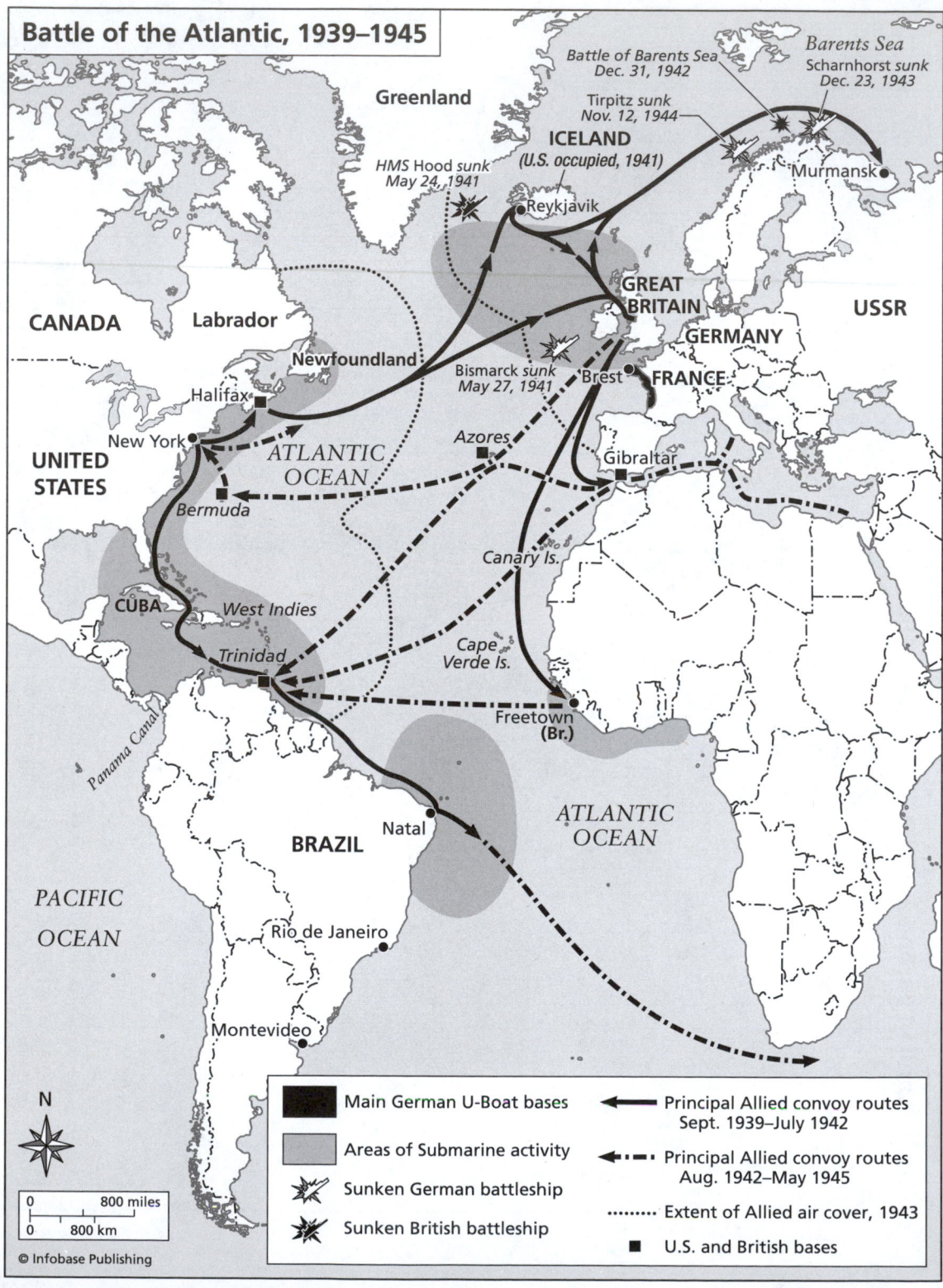

## Battle of the Atlantic, 1939–1945

**Greenland**

Battle of Barents Sea
Dec. 31, 1942

*Barents Sea*

Scharnhorst *sunk*
Dec. 23, 1943

*Tirpitz sunk*
Nov. 12, 1944

**ICELAND**
(U.S. occupied, 1941)

Murmansk

HMS *Hood sunk*
May 24, 1941

Reykjavik

**GREAT
BRITAIN**

**USSR**

**CANADA**   Labrador

**GERMANY**

**Newfoundland**

Bismarck *sunk*
May 27, 1941

Brest

**FRANCE**

Halifax

**UNITED
STATES**

New York

*ATLANTIC
OCEAN*

Azores

Gibraltar

Bermuda

Canary Is.

**CUBA**   *West Indies*

Trinidad

Cape
Verde Is.

*Panama Canal*

Freetown
(Br.)

*ATLANTIC
OCEAN*

**BRAZIL**   Natal

*PACIFIC
OCEAN*

Rio de Janeiro

Montevideo

**N**

0        800 miles
0        800 km

© Infobase Publishing

**Legend:**

- Main German U-Boat bases
- Areas of Submarine activity
- Sunken German battleship
- Sunken British battleship
- Principal Allied convoy routes Sept. 1939–July 1942
- Principal Allied convoy routes Aug. 1942–May 1945
- Extent of Allied air cover, 1943
- ■ U.S. and British bases

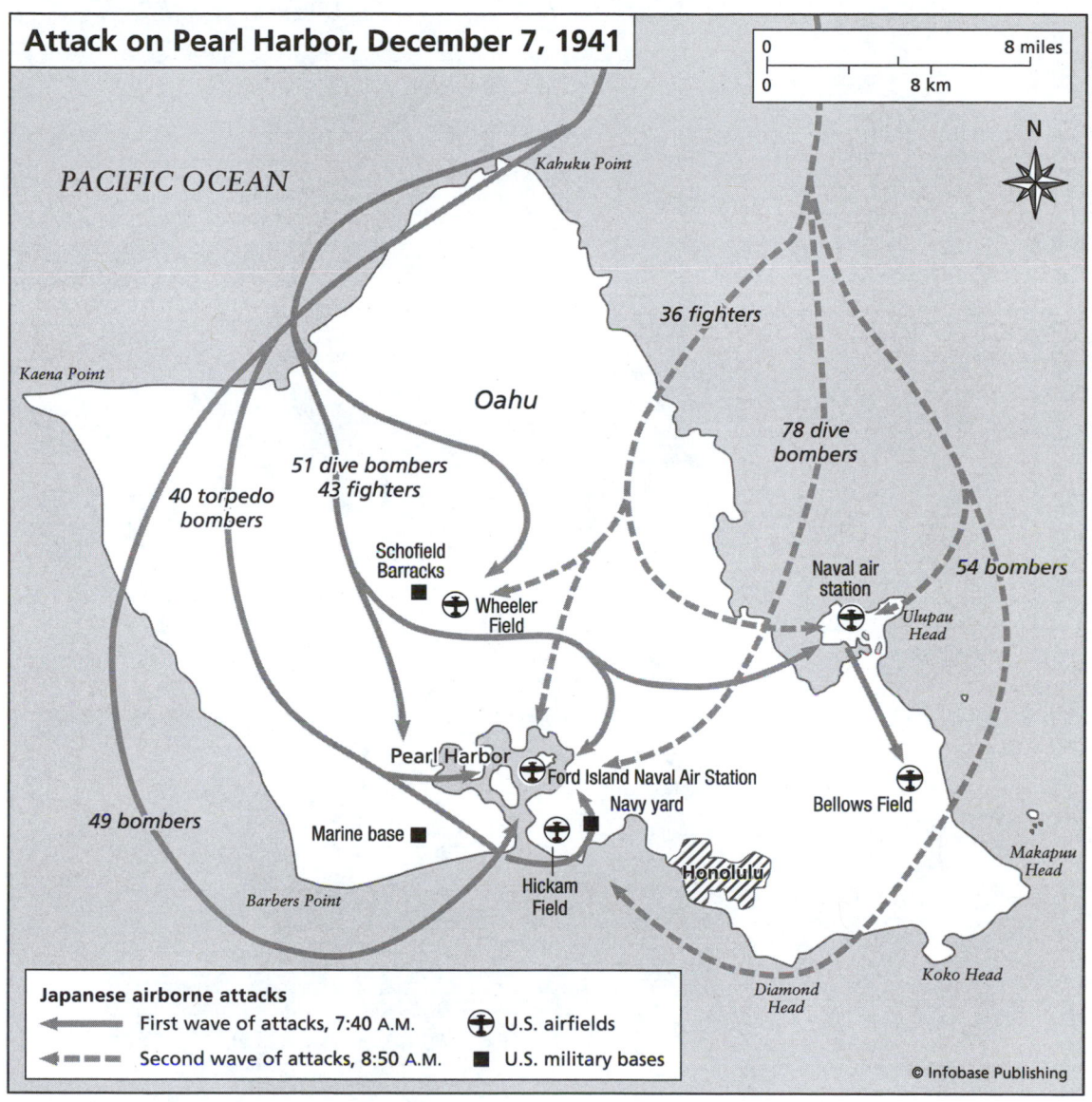

**Attack on Pearl Harbor, December 7, 1941**

PACIFIC OCEAN

Kahuku Point

0   8 miles
0   8 km

N

36 fighters

Kaena Point

Oahu

78 dive bombers

51 dive bombers
43 fighters

40 torpedo bombers

Naval air station

54 bombers

Schofield Barracks

Wheeler Field

Ulupau Head

Pearl Harbor

Ford Island Naval Air Station

Navy yard

Bellows Field

49 bombers

Marine base

Hickam Field

Honolulu

Makapuu Head

Barbers Point

Koko Head

Diamond Head

**Japanese airborne attacks**

← First wave of attacks, 7:40 A.M.   ✛ U.S. airfields

◄--- Second wave of attacks, 8:50 A.M.   ■ U.S. military bases

© Infobase Publishing

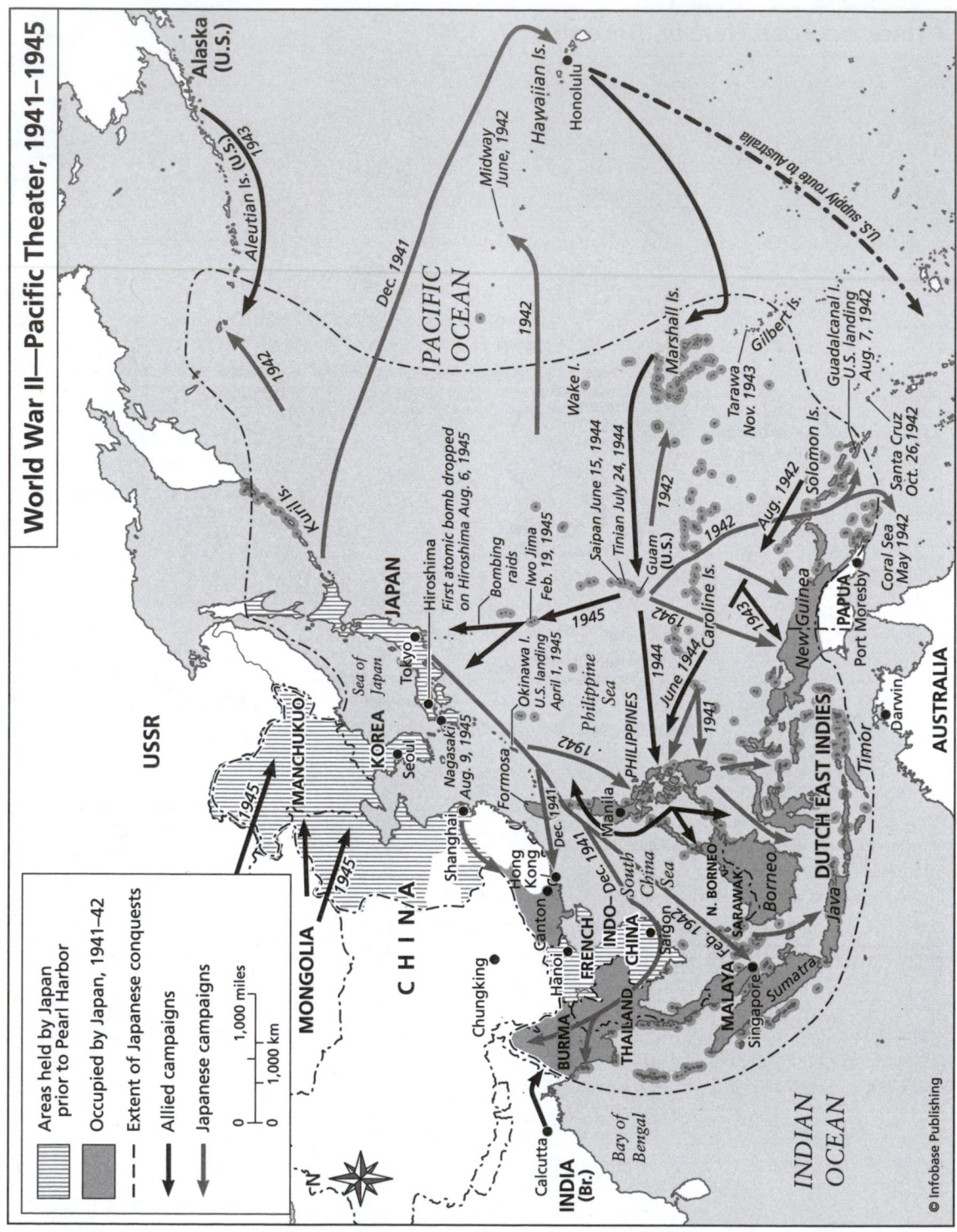

## World War II—Pacific Theater, 1941–1945

**Legend:**
- Areas held by Japan prior to Pearl Harbor
- Occupied by Japan, 1941–42
- Extent of Japanese conquests
- Allied campaigns
- Japanese campaigns

0 — 1,000 miles
0 — 1,000 km

© Infobase Publishing

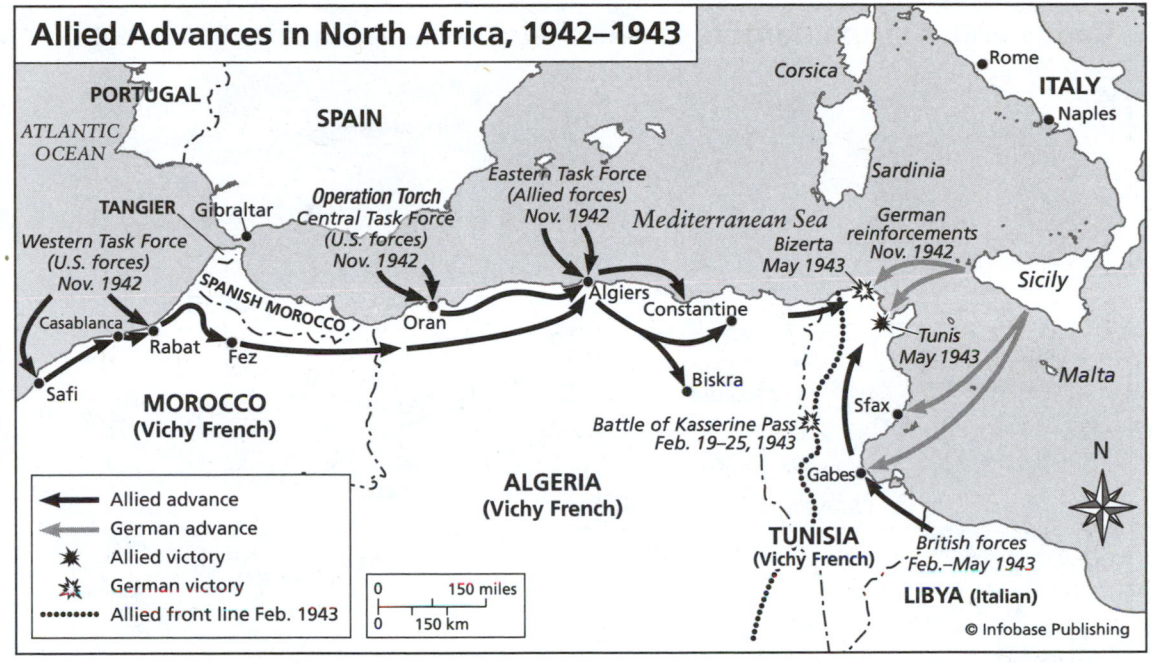

Allied Advances in North Africa, 1942–1943

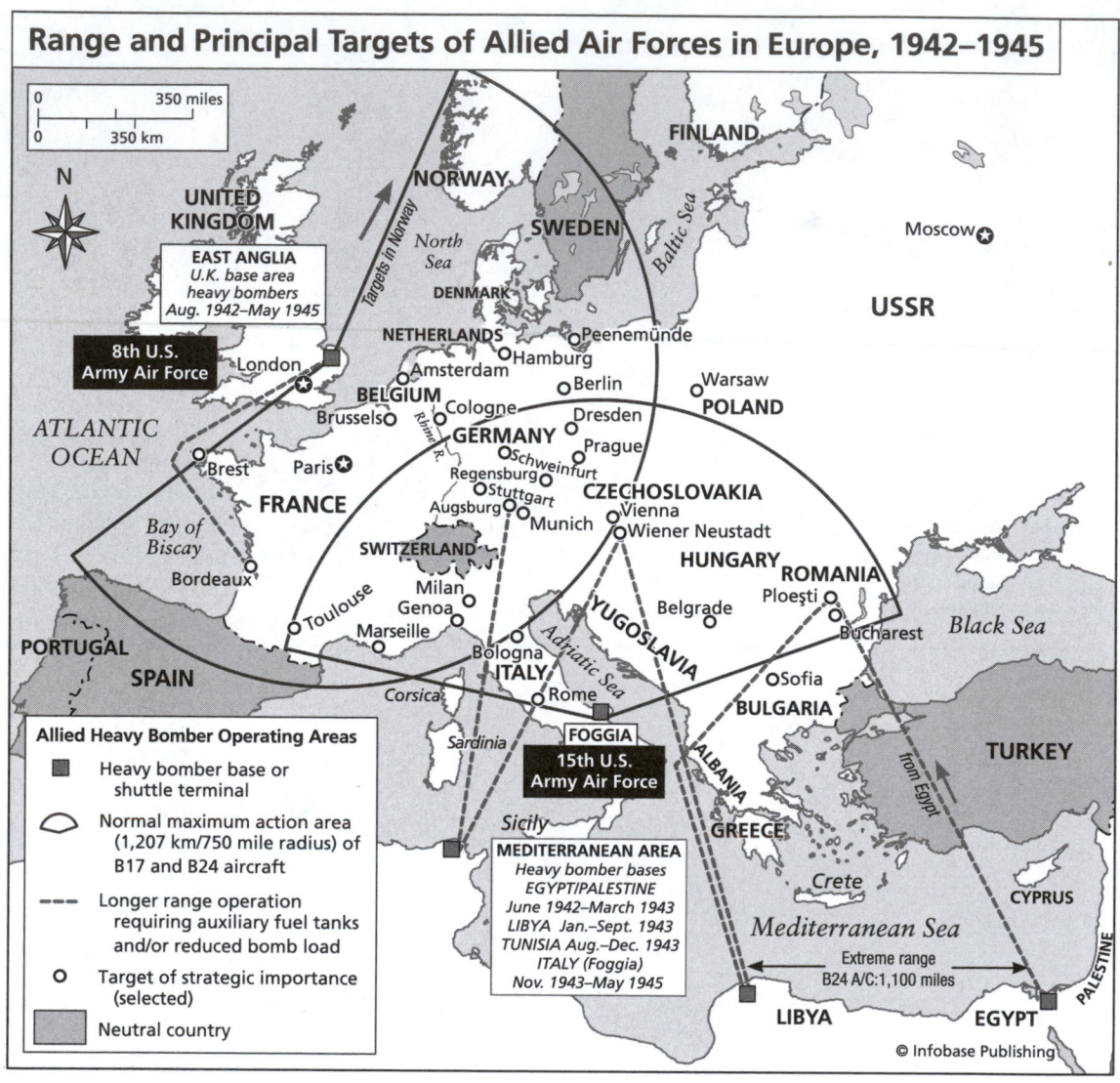

## Range and Principal Targets of Allied Air Forces in Europe, 1942–1945

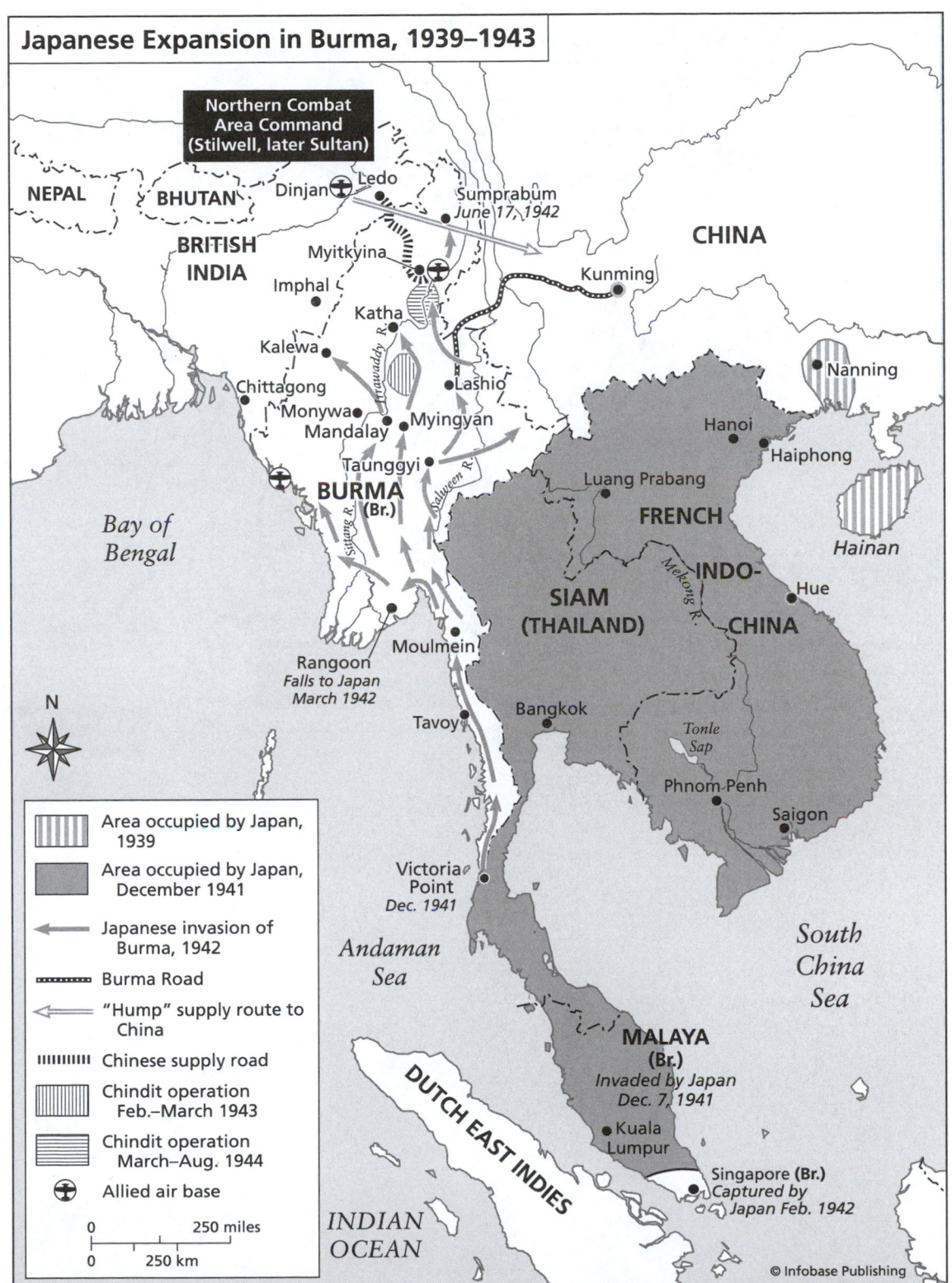

## Japanese Expansion in Burma, 1939–1943

Northern Combat Area Command (Stilwell, later Sultan)

NEPAL

BHUTAN

BRITISH INDIA

CHINA

Dinjan    Ledo

Sumprabum
June 17, 1942

Myitkyina

Imphal

Kunming

Katha

Kalewa

Nanning

Chittagong

Lashio

Monywa

Hanoi

Mandalay    Myingyan

Haiphong

Taunggyi

Luang Prabang

BURMA
(Br.)

FRENCH

*Irrawaddy R.*

*Salween R.*

*Sittang R.*

INDO-

Hue

*Mekong R.*

*Bay of Bengal*

SIAM
(THAILAND)

CHINA

*Hainan*

Moulmein

Rangoon
*Falls to Japan
March 1942*

Tavoy

Bangkok

*Tonle Sap*

Phnom Penh

Saigon

N

Victoria Point
*Dec. 1941*

*Andaman Sea*

*South China Sea*

*Area occupied by Japan, 1939*

*Area occupied by Japan, December 1941*

Japanese invasion of Burma, 1942

Burma Road

"Hump" supply route to China

Chinese supply road

Chindit operation Feb.–March 1943

Chindit operation March–Aug. 1944

Allied air base

*DUTCH EAST INDIES*

MALAYA
(Br.)
*Invaded by Japan
Dec. 7, 1941*

Kuala Lumpur

Singapore (Br.)
*Captured by
Japan Feb. 1942*

*INDIAN OCEAN*

0    250 miles

0    250 km

© Infobase Publishing

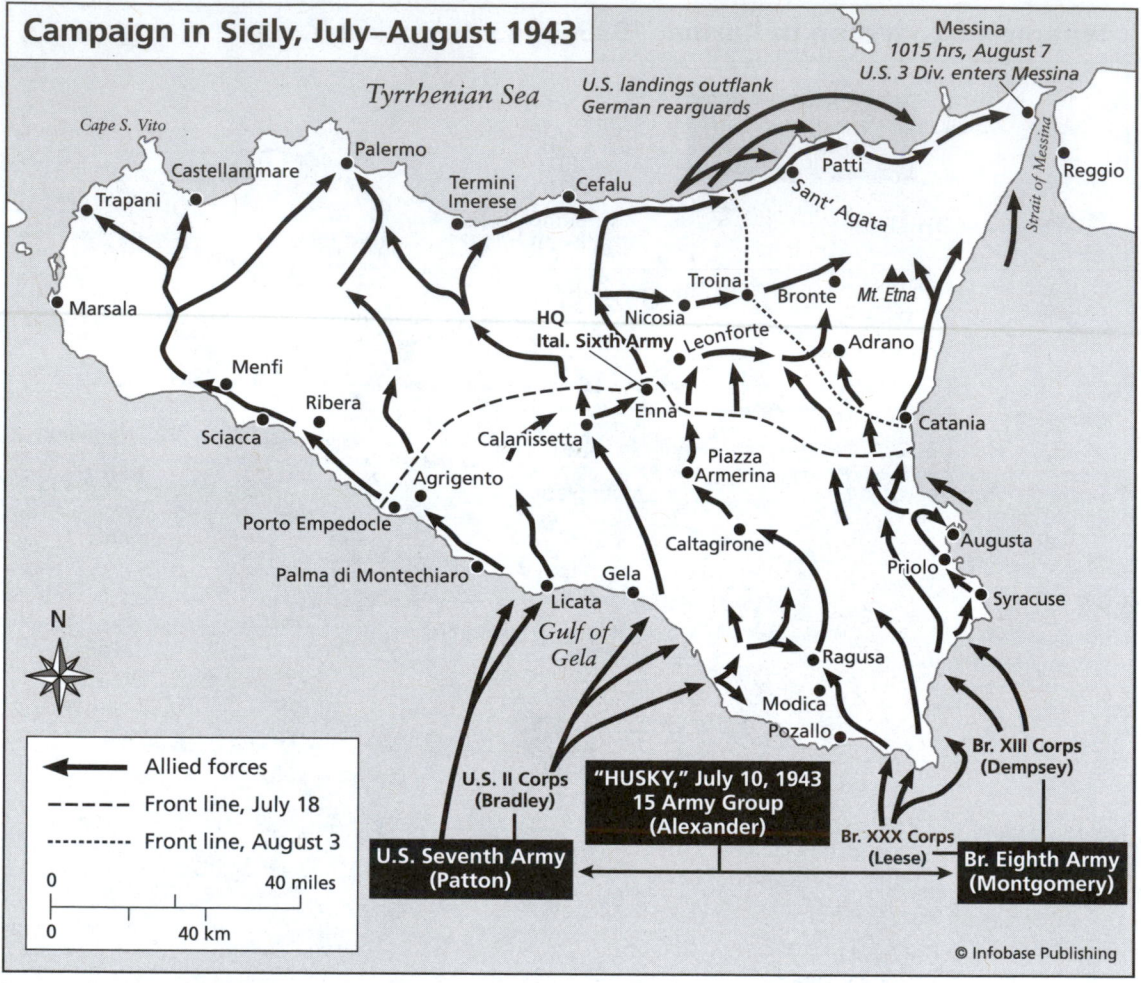

## Campaign in Sicily, July–August 1943

Messina
1015 hrs, August 7
U.S. 3 Div. enters Messina

Tyrrhenian Sea

U.S. landings outflank
German rearguards

Cape S. Vito

Palermo
Castellammare
Trapani
Termini Imerese
Cefalu
Patti
Sant' Agata
Reggio
Strait of Messina

Marsala

Troina
Bronte
Mt. Etna
Adrano
HQ Ital. Sixth Army
Nicosia
Leonforte

Menfi
Ribera
Sciacca
Calanissetta
Enna
Catania

Agrigento
Piazza Armerina

Porto Empedocle

Palma di Montechiaro
Gela
Caltagirone
Augusta
Priolo
Syracuse

Licata
Gulf of Gela
Ragusa
Modica
Pozallo

N

**Legend:**

— Allied forces
- - - Front line, July 18
······ Front line, August 3

0 ————— 40 miles
0 ————— 40 km

U.S. II Corps (Bradley)

"HUSKY," July 10, 1943
15 Army Group (Alexander)

U.S. Seventh Army (Patton)

Br. XXX Corps (Leese)

Br. XIII Corps (Dempsey)

Br. Eighth Army (Montgomery)

© Infobase Publishing

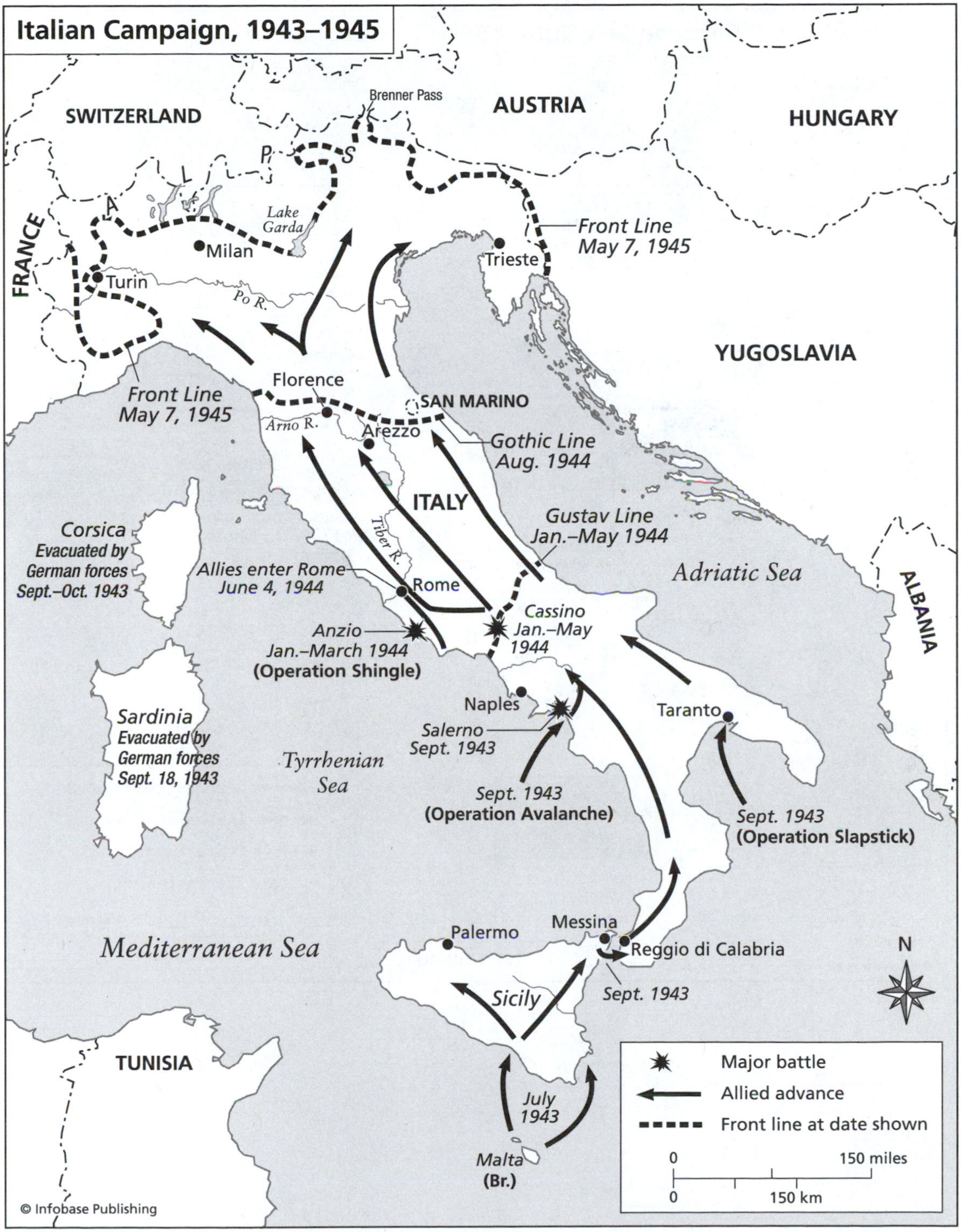

## Italian Campaign, 1943–1945

SWITZERLAND

Brenner Pass

AUSTRIA

HUNGARY

A L P S

Lake Garda

Milan

Turin

Po R.

FRANCE

Trieste

*Front Line May 7, 1945*

YUGOSLAVIA

Florence

SAN MARINO

*Front Line May 7, 1945*

Arno R.

Arezzo

*Gothic Line Aug. 1944*

ITALY

*Corsica Evacuated by German forces Sept.–Oct. 1943*

Tiber R.

*Gustav Line Jan.–May 1944*

*Adriatic Sea*

ALBANIA

*Allies enter Rome June 4, 1944*

Rome

*Anzio Jan.–March 1944* (Operation Shingle)

Cassino *Jan.–May 1944*

*Sardinia Evacuated by German forces Sept. 18, 1943*

*Tyrrhenian Sea*

Naples

*Salerno Sept. 1943*

Taranto

*Sept. 1943* (Operation Avalanche)

*Sept. 1943* (Operation Slapstick)

*Mediterranean Sea*

Palermo

Messina

Reggio di Calabria

N

*Sicily*

*Sept. 1943*

TUNISIA

July 1943

| | | Major battle |
| --- | --- | --- |
| | | Allied advance |
| | | Front line at date shown |

*Malta* (Br.)

0 — 150 miles

0 — 150 km

© Infobase Publishing

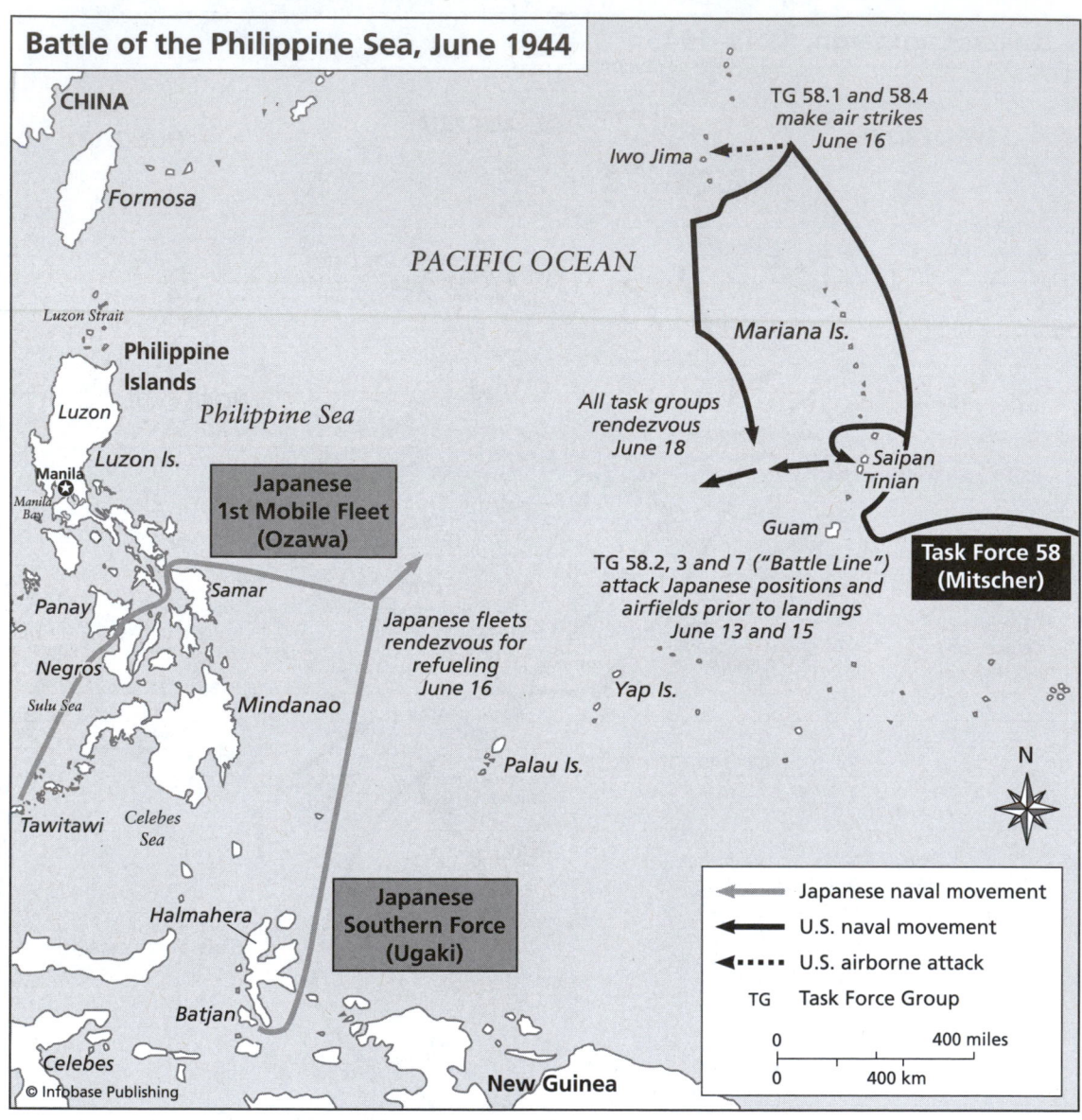

**Battle of the Philippine Sea, June 1944**

CHINA

Formosa

PACIFIC OCEAN

Iwo Jima

TG 58.1 and 58.4
make air strikes
June 16

Luzon Strait

Philippine
Islands

Luzon

Philippine Sea

Mariana Is.

Manila
Manila Bay

Luzon Is.

**Japanese
1st Mobile Fleet
(Ozawa)**

Samar

Japanese fleets
rendezvous for
refueling
June 16

All task groups
rendezvous
June 18

Saipan
Tinian

Guam

**Task Force 58
(Mitscher)**

TG 58.2, 3 and 7 ("Battle Line")
attack Japanese positions and
airfields prior to landings
June 13 and 15

Panay

Negros

Sulu Sea

Mindanao

Yap Is.

Palau Is.

Tawitawi

Celebes
Sea

N

Halmahera

**Japanese
Southern Force
(Ugaki)**

Batjan

Celebes

© Infobase Publishing

New Guinea

→ Japanese naval movement
→ U.S. naval movement
◀┈┈ U.S. airborne attack
TG  Task Force Group

0 —————— 400 miles
0 —————— 400 km

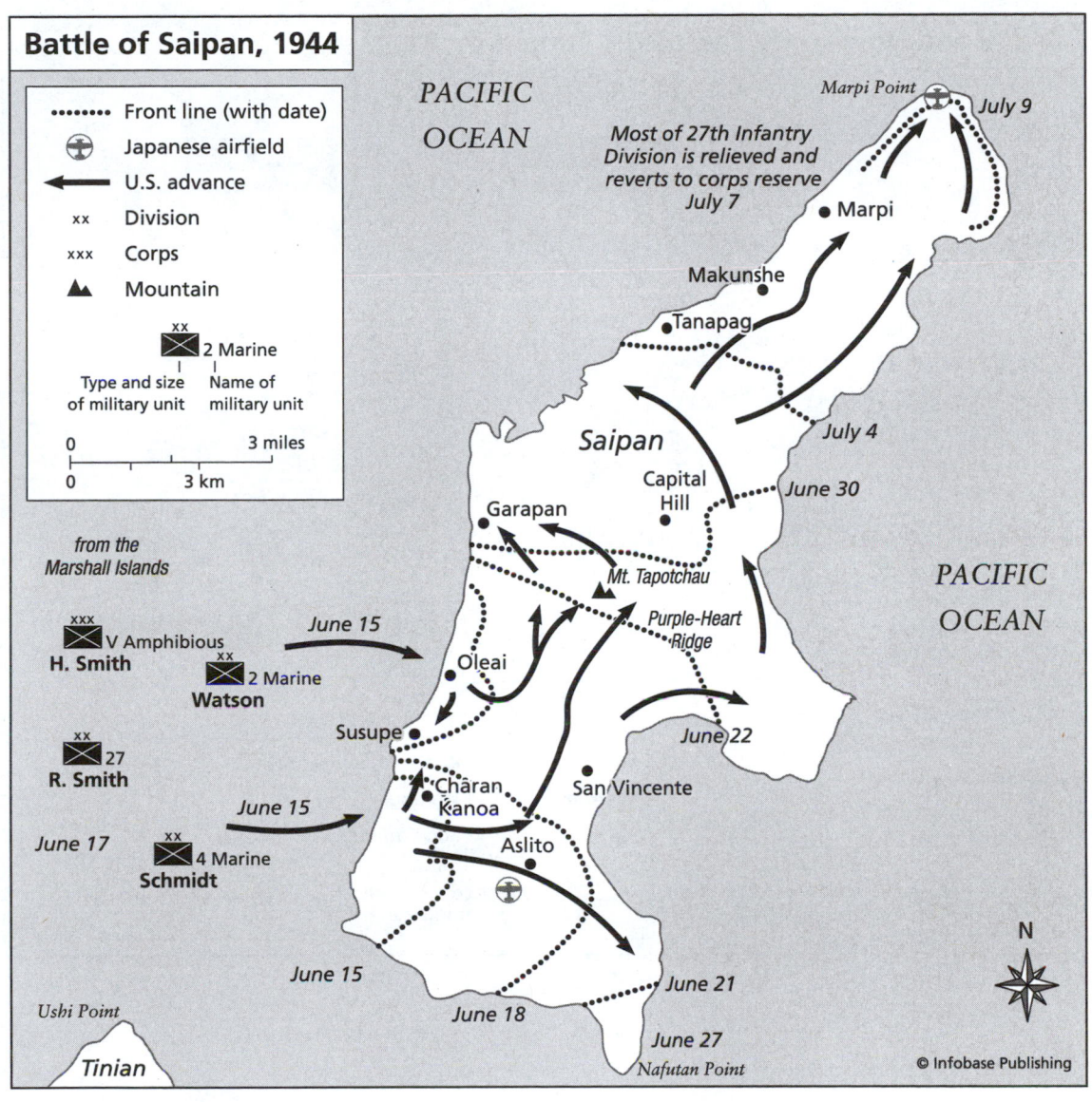

**Battle of Saipan, 1944**

Legend:
- Front line (with date)
- Japanese airfield
- U.S. advance
- xx  Division
- xxx  Corps
- ▲▲  Mountain

xx
2 Marine

Type and size of military unit | Name of military unit

0 — 3 miles
0 — 3 km

PACIFIC OCEAN

Marpi Point — July 9

Most of 27th Infantry Division is relieved and reverts to corps reserve July 7

Marpi

Makunshe

Tanapag

July 4

Saipan

Capital Hill

June 30

Garapan

PACIFIC OCEAN

Mt. Tapotchau

Purple-Heart Ridge

from the Marshall Islands

xxx
V Amphibious
**H. Smith**

June 15

xx
2 Marine
**Watson**

Oleai

Susupe

June 22

xx
27
**R. Smith**

June 17

xx
4 Marine
**Schmidt**

June 15

Charan Kanoa

San Vincente

Aslito

June 15

June 18

June 21

June 27

Ushi Point

Nafutan Point

Tinian

N

© Infobase Publishing

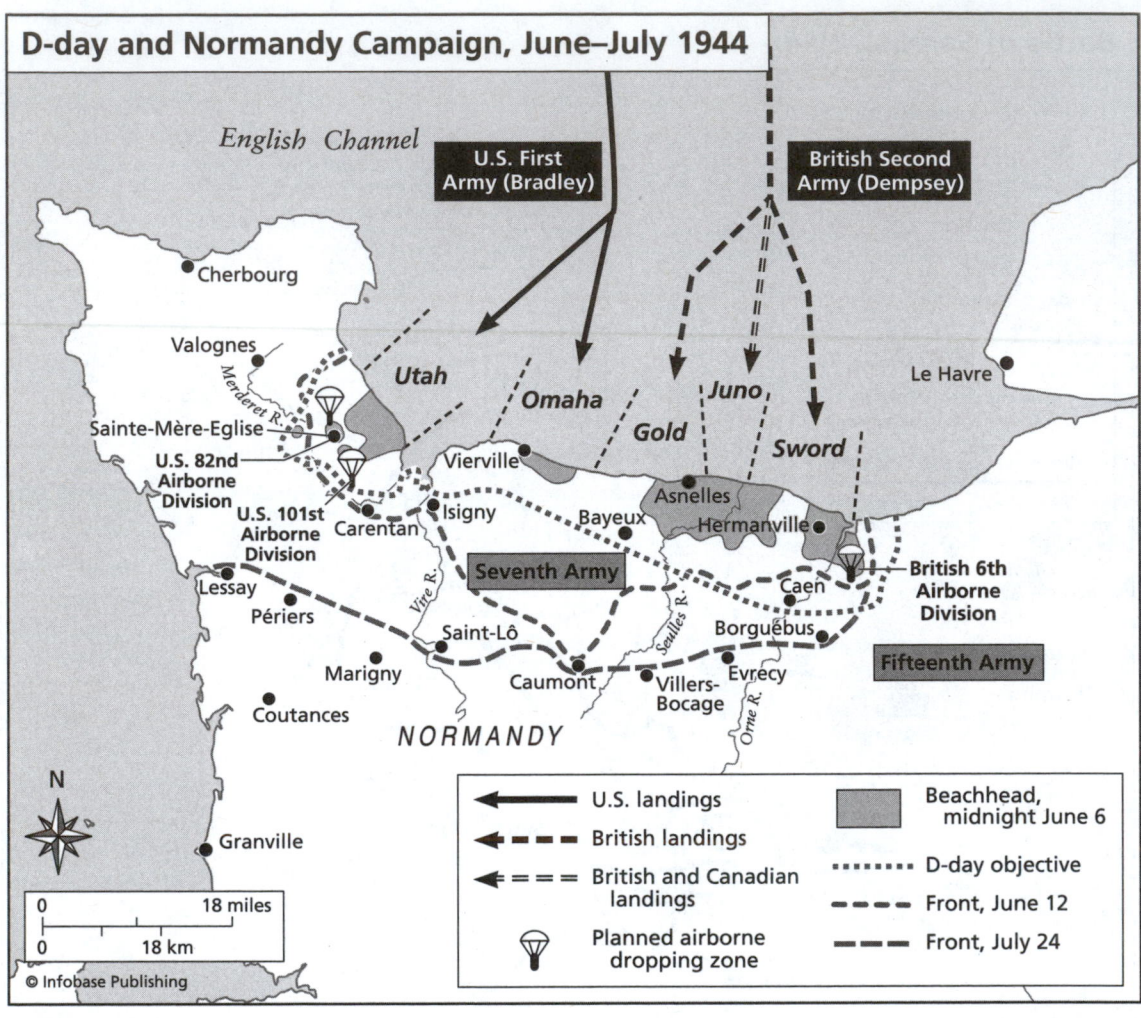

**D-day and Normandy Campaign, June–July 1944**

English Channel

U.S. First Army (Bradley)

British Second Army (Dempsey)

Cherbourg

Valognes

Le Havre

Merderet R.

Utah

Omaha

Juno

Gold

Sword

Sainte-Mère-Eglise

U.S. 82nd Airborne Division

Vierville

Asnelles

Hermanville

U.S. 101st Airborne Division

Isigny

Bayeux

Carentan

British 6th Airborne Division

Vire R.

Seventh Army

Caen

Lessay

Seulles R.

Fifteenth Army

Périers

Saint-Lô

Borguébus

Marigny

Caumont

Evrecy

Coutances

Villers-Bocage

Orne R.

NORMANDY

N

Granville

| | |
|---|---|
| ← U.S. landings | Beachhead, midnight June 6 |
| ← - - British landings | ···· D-day objective |
| ← = = British and Canadian landings | – – Front, June 12 |
| Planned airborne dropping zone | — — Front, July 24 |

0            18 miles

0            18 km

© Infobase Publishing

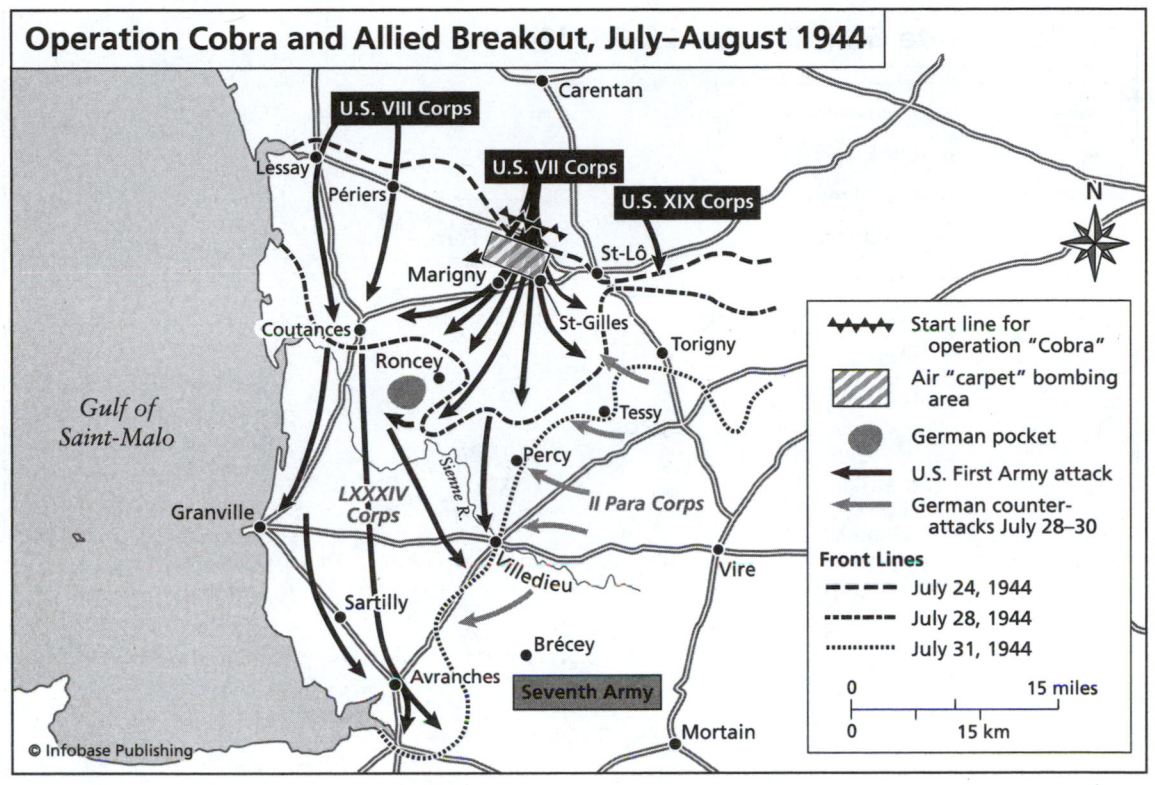

# Operation Cobra and Allied Breakout, July–August 1944

Carentan
U.S. VIII Corps
Lessay
U.S. VII Corps
Périers
U.S. XIX Corps
St-Lô
Marigny
St-Gilles
Coutances
Torigny
Roncey
Tessy
Gulf of Saint-Malo
Percy
LXXXIV Corps
Sienne R.
II Para Corps
Granville
Villedieu
Vire
Sartilly
Brécey
Avranches
Seventh Army
Mortain

© Infobase Publishing

N

**Legend:**
- Start line for operation "Cobra"
- Air "carpet" bombing area
- German pocket
- U.S. First Army attack
- German counter-attacks July 28–30

**Front Lines**
- July 24, 1944
- July 28, 1944
- July 31, 1944

0 — 15 miles
0 — 15 km

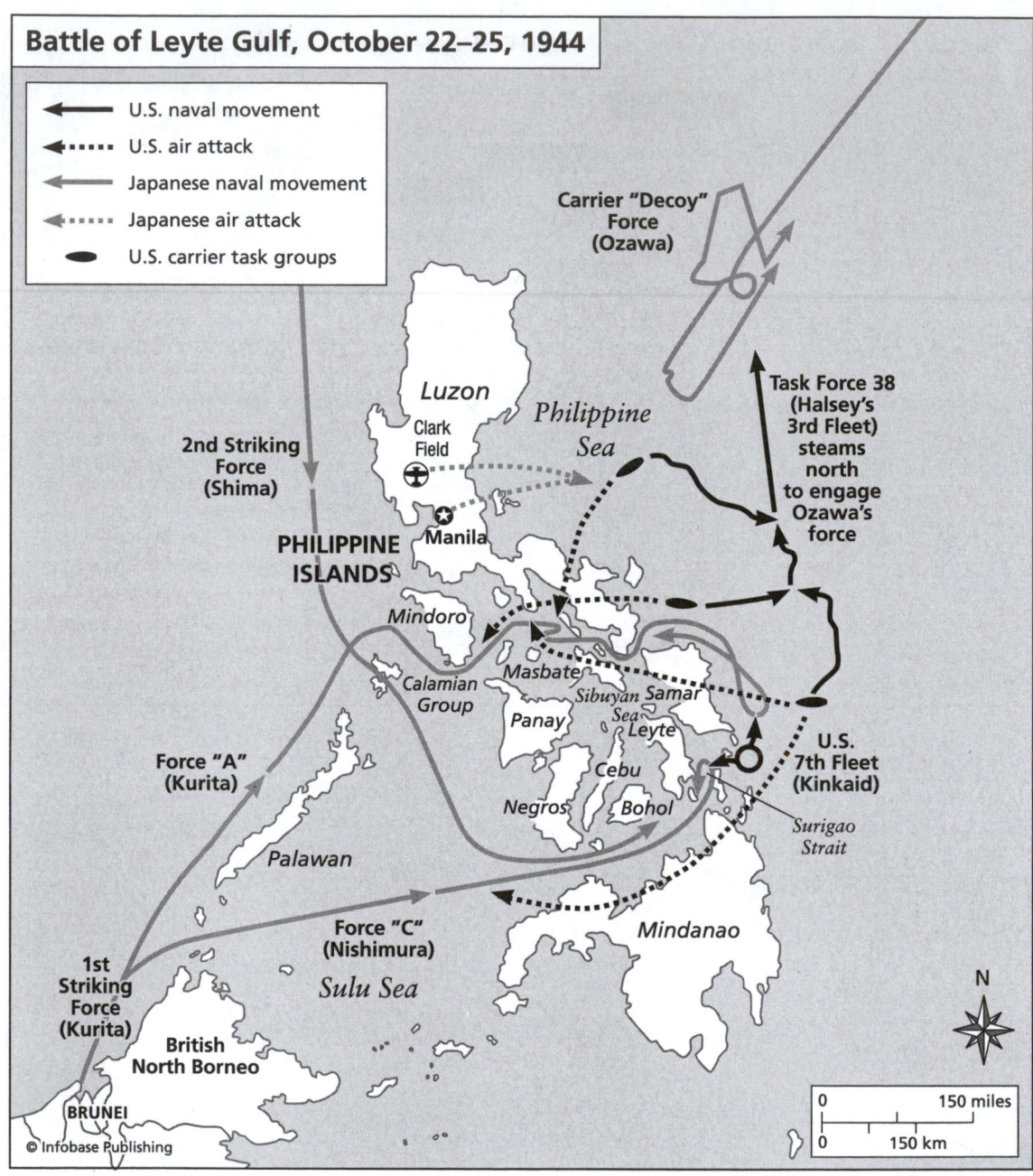

## Battle of Leyte Gulf, October 22–25, 1944

**Legend:**
- ← U.S. naval movement
- ◄···· U.S. air attack
- → Japanese naval movement
- ◄···· Japanese air attack
- ⬭ U.S. carrier task groups

Carrier "Decoy" Force (Ozawa)

Task Force 38 (Halsey's 3rd Fleet) steams north to engage Ozawa's force

Luzon

Clark Field

*Philippine Sea*

2nd Striking Force (Shima)

PHILIPPINE ISLANDS

Manila

*Mindoro*

*Calamian Group*

*Masbate*

*Panay*

*Sibuyan Sea*

*Samar*

*Leyte*

*Cebu*

U.S. 7th Fleet (Kinkaid)

Force "A" (Kurita)

*Negros*

*Bohol*

*Surigao Strait*

*Palawan*

Force "C" (Nishimura)

*Mindanao*

1st Striking Force (Kurita)

*Sulu Sea*

**British North Borneo**

**BRUNEI**

N

© Infobase Publishing

0 — 150 miles
0 — 150 km

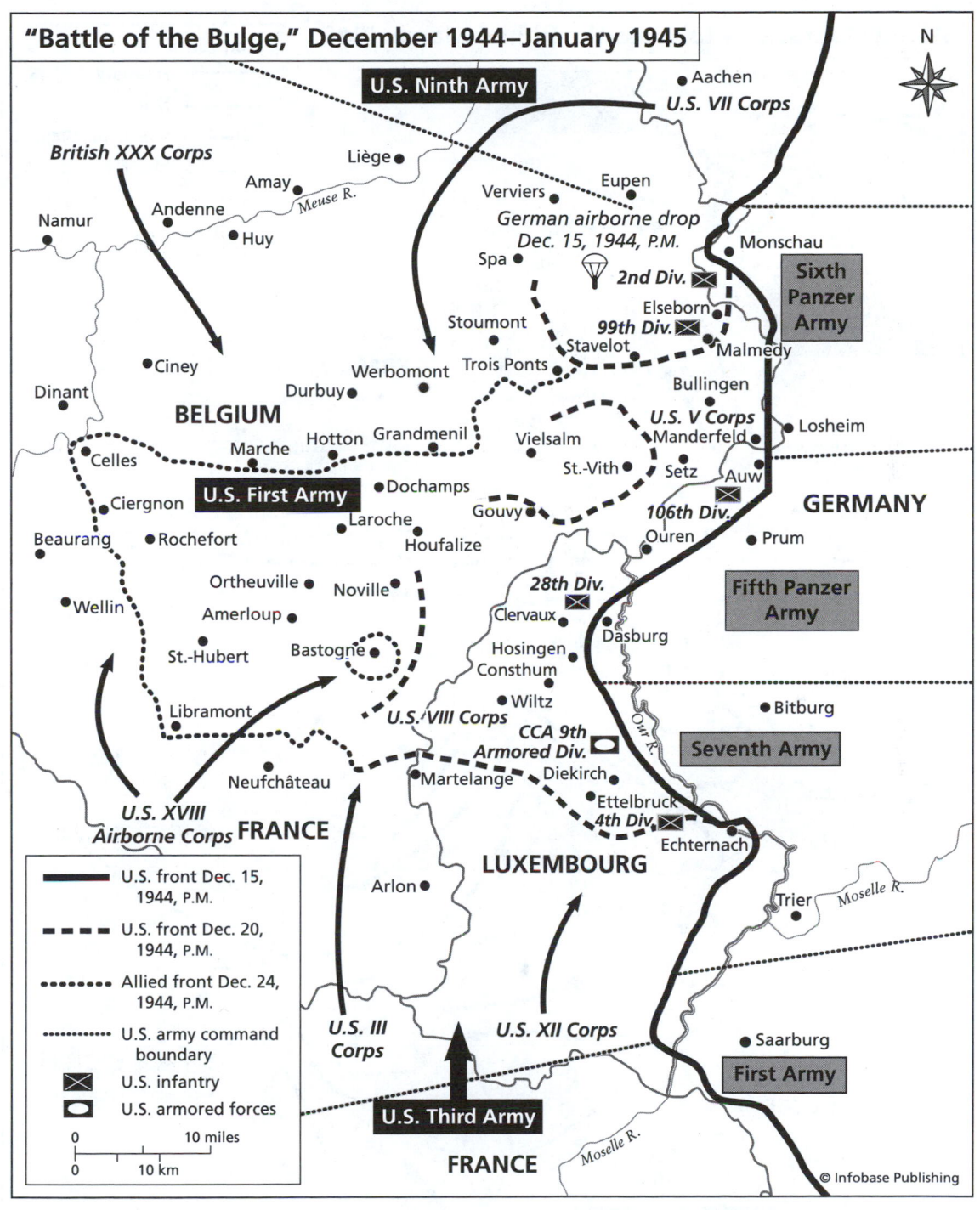

**"Battle of the Bulge," December 1944–January 1945**

N

U.S. Ninth Army

Aachen

U.S. VII Corps

British XXX Corps

Liège

Amay

Eupen

Andenne

Meuse R.

Verviers

Monschau

Namur

Huy

German airborne drop
Dec. 15, 1944, P.M.

Sixth
Panzer
Army

Spa

2nd Div.

Stoumont

Elseborn

99th Div.

Ciney

Werbomont

Trois Ponts

Stavelot

Malmedy

Durbuy

Dinant

BELGIUM

Bullingen

Celles

Hotton

Grandmenil

Vielsalm

U.S. V Corps

Manderfeld

Losheim

Marche

St.-Vith

Setz

Auw

Ciergnon

U.S. First Army

Dochamps

Gouvy

GERMANY

Beaurang

Laroche

Houfalize

106th Div.

Ouren

Prum

Rochefort

Ortheuville

Noville

28th Div.

Fifth Panzer
Army

Wellin

Amerloup

Clervaux

Dasburg

St.-Hubert

Bastogne

Hosingen
Consthum

Libramont

Wiltz

Bitburg

U.S. VIII Corps

CCA 9th
Armored Div.

Seventh Army

Neufchâteau

Martelange

Diekirch

U.S. XVIII
Airborne Corps   FRANCE

Ettelbruck

4th Div.

Our R.

LUXEMBOURG

Echternach

Arlon

Trier

Moselle R.

| | |
|---|---|
| ▬▬▬ | U.S. front Dec. 15, 1944, P.M. |
| ▬ ▬ ▬ | U.S. front Dec. 20, 1944, P.M. |
| ••••••• | Allied front Dec. 24, 1944, P.M. |
| ············· | U.S. army command boundary |
| ⊠ | U.S. infantry |
| ⬭ | U.S. armored forces |

U.S. III
Corps

U.S. XII Corps

Saarburg

First Army

0        10 miles
0      10 km

U.S. Third Army

FRANCE

Moselle R.

© Infobase Publishing

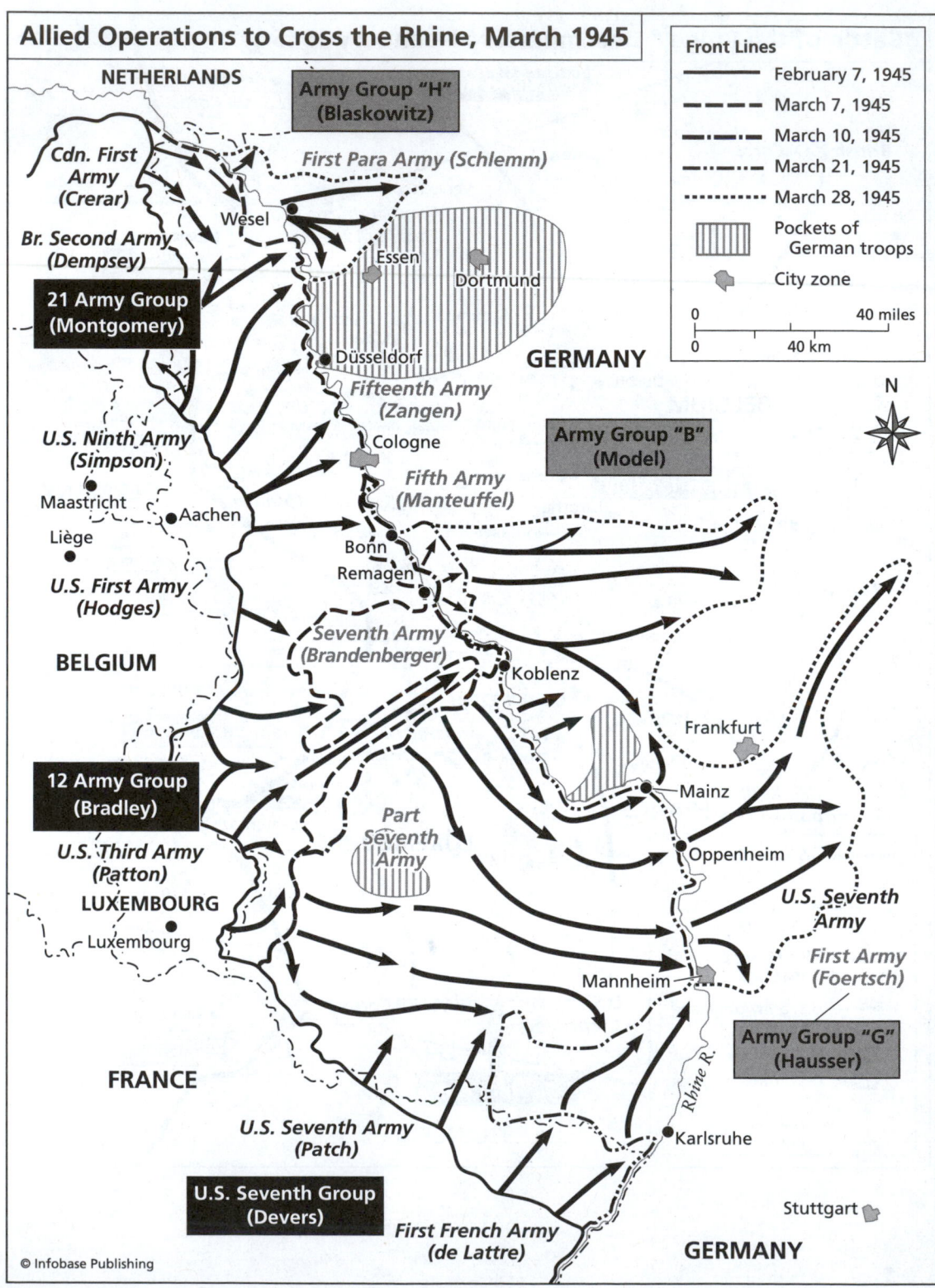

**Allied Operations to Cross the Rhine, March 1945**

Front Lines
- February 7, 1945
- March 7, 1945
- March 10, 1945
- March 21, 1945
- March 28, 1945

Pockets of German troops

City zone

0 — 40 miles
0 — 40 km

N

NETHERLANDS

Army Group "H" (Blaskowitz)

First Para Army (Schlemm)

Cdn. First Army (Crerar)

Wesel

Br. Second Army (Dempsey)

21 Army Group (Montgomery)

Essen

Dortmund

Düsseldorf

GERMANY

Fifteenth Army (Zangen)

Cologne

Army Group "B" (Model)

U.S. Ninth Army (Simpson)

Maastricht

Aachen

Liège

Fifth Army (Manteuffel)

Bonn

Remagen

U.S. First Army (Hodges)

BELGIUM

Seventh Army (Brandenberger)

Koblenz

Frankfurt

Mainz

12 Army Group (Bradley)

Part Seventh Army

Oppenheim

U.S. Third Army (Patton)

LUXEMBOURG

Luxembourg

U.S. Seventh Army

First Army (Foertsch)

Mannheim

Army Group "G" (Hausser)

FRANCE

Rhine R.

U.S. Seventh Army (Patch)

U.S. Seventh Group (Devers)

Karlsruhe

Stuttgart

First French Army (de Lattre)

GERMANY

© Infobase Publishing

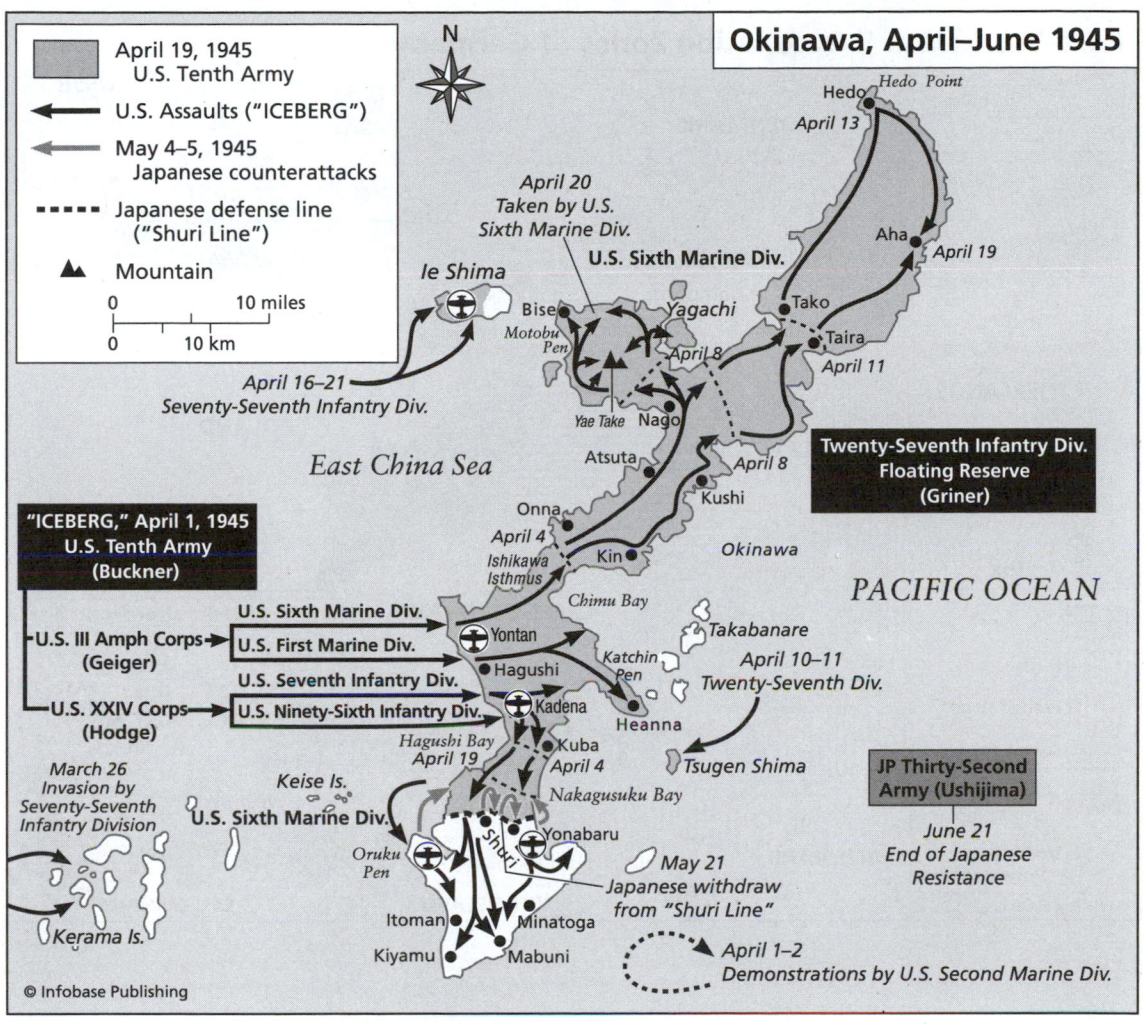

Okinawa, April–June 1945

**Post–World War II Occupation Zones of Germany**

# BIBLIOGRAPHY

## ESSENTIAL REFERENCES

Craven, Wesley F., and James L. Cate, eds. *The Army Air Forces in World War II*. 7 vols. Chicago: University of Chicago Press, 1948–58.

Headquarters, U.S. Air Force. *Air Force Combat Units of World War II*. Washington, D.C.: Office of Air Force History, 1961.

———. *Combat Squadrons of the Air Force, World War II*. Washington, D.C.: Office of Air Force History, 1982.

Historical Branch, G3 Division, Headquarters, United States Marine Corps. *History of U.S. Marine Corps Operations in World War II*. 5 vols. Washington, D.C.: U.S. Government Printing Office, 1959–68.

Office of the Chief of Military History. *The U.S. Army in World War II*. Washington, D.C.: Department of the Army, 1947–2004.

## CHRONOLOGIES

Carter, Kit C., and Robert Mueller. *Army Air Forces in World War II: Combat Chronology, 1941–1945*. Washington, D.C.: Center for Air Force History, 1991.

Cressman, Robert. *The Official Chronology of the U.S. Navy in World War II*. Annapolis, Md.: Naval Institute Press, 2000.

Headquarters, U.S. Air Force. *The Army Air Forces in World War II: Combat Chronology, 1941–1945*. Washington, D.C.: Office of Air Force History, 1973.

Kimble, David L. *Chronology of U.S. Navy Submarine Operations in the Pacific, 1939–1942*. Bennington, Vt.: World War II Historical Society, 1997.

Office of Naval History. *The Chronology of the Navy's War in the Pacific, World War II*. Washington, D.C., 1947.

Williams, Mary H. *Chronology 1941–45*. U.S. Army in World War II Series, Special Studies. Washington, D.C.: Office of the Chief of Military History, Department of the Army, 1960.

## BIOGRAPHIES AND COMMANDERS' ACCOUNTS

Ambrose, Stephen E. *The Supreme Commander: The War Years of General Dwight D. Eisenhower*. Garden City, N.Y.: Doubleday, 1970.

Blumenson, Martin. *Eisenhower*. New York: Ballantine Books, 1972.

Bradley, Omar N. *A Soldier's Story*. New York: Modern Library, 1999.

Brink, Randall. *Nimitz: The Man and His Wars*. New York: Penguin, 2000.

Buell, Thomas B. *The Quiet Warrior: A Biography of Admiral Raymond A. Spruance*. Boston: Little, Brown, 1974.

———. *Master of Sea Power: A Biography of Fleet Admiral Ernest J. King*. Boston: Little, Brown, 1980.

Blumenson, Martin. *Mark Clark*. New York: Congdon and Weed: 1984.

Coletta, Paolo E. *Admiral Marc A. Mitscher and U.S. Naval Aviation: Bald Eagle*. Lewiston, N.Y.: Edwin Mellen Press, 1997.

Daso, Dik A. *Hap Arnold and the Evolution of American Airpower*. Washington, D.C.: Smithsonian Institution Press, 2000.

Davis, Richard G. *Carl A. Spaatz and the Air War in Europe*. Washington, D.C.: Center for Air Force History, 1993.

D'Este, Carlo. *Patton: A Genius for War*. New York: HarperCollins, 1996.

———. *Eisenhower: A Soldier's Life.* New York: Henry Holt, 2002.

Hirshson, Stanley P. *General Patton: A Soldier's Life.* New York: HarperCollins, 2002.

James, D. Clayton. *The Years of MacArthur.* Vol. 2, *1941–1945.* Boston: Houghton Mifflin, 1970.

King, Michael J. *William Orlando Darby, a Military Biography.* Hamden, Conn.: Archon Books, 1981.

Larrabee, Eric. *Commander in Chief: Franklin Delano Roosevelt, His Lieutenants, and Their War.* New York: Harper and Row, 1987

Long, Gavin M. *MacArthur as Military Commander.* London: Van Nostrand, 1969.

Perret, Geoffrey. *Eisenhower.* New York: Random House, 1999.

———. *Old Soldiers Never Die: The Life of Douglas MacArthur.* New York: Random House, 1996.

Pogue, Forrest C. *George C. Marshall: Organizer of Victory, 1943–45.* New York: Viking Press, 1973.

———. *George C. Marshall: Ordeal and Hope, 1939–1942.* New York: Viking Press, 1963.

Schaller, Michael. *Douglas MacArthur: The Far Eastern General.* New York: Oxford University Press, 1989.

Schultz, Duane P. *Hero of Bataan: The Story of General Jonathan M. Wainwright.* New York: St. Martin's Press, 1981.

Sixsmith, E. K. G. *Eisenhower as Military Commander.* New York: Stein and Day, 1973.

Smith, Holland M., and Percy Finch. *Coral and Brass.* New York: Scribner, 1949.

Stilwell, Joseph W. *The Stilwell Papers.* New York: William Sloane Associates, 1948.

Truscott, Lucian K. *Command Missions: A Personal Story.* Novato, Calif.: Presidio Press, 1990.

Wheeler, Gerald E. *Kinkaid of the Seventh Fleet: A Biography of Admiral Thomas C. Kinkaid, U.S. Navy.* Annapolis, Md.: Naval Institute Press, 1996.

Whiting, Charles. *Bradley.* New York: Ballantine Books, 1971.

# General Histories

Adamczyk, Richard D., and Morris J. MacGregor. *The United States Army in World War II: A Reader's Guide.* Washington, D.C.: U.S. Army Center of Military History, 1992.

Anzuoni, Robert P. *I'm the 82nd Airborne Division!: A History of the All American Division in World War II After Action Reports.* Atglen, Pa.: Schiffer Military History, 2005.

Blair, Clay. *Ridgway's Paratroopers: The American Airborne in World War II.* Garden City, N.Y.: Dial Press, 1985.

Bradley, John H., Jack W. Dice, and Thomas E. Griess. *The Second World War: Asia and the Pacific.* Wayne, N.J.: Avery Publishing Group, 1984.

Bradley, John H., and Jack W. Dice. *The Second World War: Asia and the Pacific.* West Point, N.Y: Department of the Army, 1981.

Bradley, John N. *The Second World War.* Garden City, N.Y.: Square One, 2002.

Buell, Thomas B. *The Second World War: Europe and the Mediterranean.* Wayne, N.J.: Avery Publishing Group, 1989.

Congdon, Don, ed. *Combat WW II: Pacific Theater of Operations.* New York: Arbor House, 1983.

Dodson, Kenneth. *Away All Boats.* Annapolis, Md.: Naval Institute Press, 1996.

Ellis, John. *On the Front Lines: The Experience of War Through the Eyes of the Allied Soldiers in World War II.* New York: Wiley, 1991.

Eisenhower, Dwight D. *Crusade in Europe.* Garden City, N.Y.: Doubleday, 1948.

Franks, Clifton R. *The Second World War: Europe and the Mediterranean.* West Point, N.Y.: United States Military Academy Department of History, 1981.

Gailey, Harry A. *The War in the Pacific: From Pearl Harbor to Tokyo Bay.* Novato, Calif.: Presidio Press, 1995.

Hoyt, Edwin P. *Japan's War, the Great Pacific Conflict, 1853 to 1952.* New York: McGraw-Hill, 1986.

Morison, Samuel Eliot. *The Two Ocean War. A Short History of the United States Navy in the Second World War.* Boston: Little Brown, 1963.

Patton, George S. *War as I Knew It.* Boston: Houghton Mifflin, 1947.

Roehrs, Mark D., and William A. Renzi. *World War II in the Pacific.* Armonk, N.Y.: M.E. Sharpe, 2004.

Rottman, Gordon L. *U.S. Marine Corps World War II Order of Battle: Ground and Air Units in the Pacific War.* Westport, Conn.: Greenwood Press, 2001.

Schom, Alan. *The Eagle and the Rising Sun: the Japanese-American War, 1941–1943, Pearl Harbor through Guadalcanal.* New York: W.W. Norton, 2004.

Smith, Stanley E. *The United States Marine Corps in World War II*. New York: Random House, 1969.

Spector, Ronald H. *Eagle Against the Sun: The American War with Japan*. New York: Free Press, 1985.

Stamps, Thomas Dodson, and Vincent J. Esposito, eds. *A Military History of World War II with Atlas*. West Point, N.Y.: U.S. Military Academy, 1956.

United States Army Center of Military History. *A Brief History of the U.S. Army in World War II*. Washington, D.C., 1992.

———. *The War Against Japan*. Washington, D.C., 2001.

United States Military Academy Department of Military Art and Engineering. *Campaign Summaries of the Second World War*. West Point, N.Y.: U.S. Military Academy, 1945.

United States War Department, General Staff. *Biennial Reports of the Chief of Staff of the United States Army to the Secretary of War*. Washington, D.C.: Center of Military History, U.S. Army, 1996.

———. *Biennial Report of the Chief of Staff of the United States Army, July 1, 1943, to June 30, 1945*. Washington, D.C.: U.S. Government Printing Office, 1945.

Weinberg, Gerhard L. *A World at Arms: A Global History of World War II*. New York: Cambridge University Press, 1994.

White, William L. *They Were Expendable*. New York: Harcourt, Brace, 1942.

Willmott, H. P. *The Second World War in the Far East*. Washington, D.C.: Smithsonian Books, 2004.

## STRATEGY

Beschloss, Michael. *The Conquerors: Roosevelt, Truman, and the Destruction of Hitler's Germany, 1941–1945*. New York: Simon & Schuster, 2002.

Dupuy, Trevor N. *Options of Command*. New York: Hippocrene Books, 1984.

Ellis, John. *Brute Force: Allied Strategy and Tactics in the Second World War*. New York: Viking Press, 1990.

Greenfield, Kent R., ed. *Command Decisions*. Washington, D.C.: Center of Military History, U.S. Army, 1984.

Higgins, Trumbull. *Winston Churchill and the Second Front, 1940–1943*. New York: Oxford University Press, 1957.

Howard, Michael E. *Grand Strategy*. Vol. 4, *August 1942–August 1943*. London: HMSO, 1972.

———. *The Mediterranean Strategy in the Second World War*. New York: Praeger, 1968.

Irving, David J. C. *The War Between the Generals*. New York: Congdon, 1981.

Matloff, Maurice. *Strategic Planning for Coalition Warfare, 1943–1944*. United States Army in World War II Series. Washington, D.C.: Department of the Army, 1959.

Matloff, Maurice, and Edwin S. Snell. *Strategic Planning for Coalition Warfare 1941–1942*. United States Army in World War II Series. Washington, D.C.: Department of the Army, 1986.

Miller, Edward S. *War Plan Orange: The U.S. Strategy to Defeat Japan, 1897–1945*. Annapolis, Md.: Naval Institute Press, 1991.

Morton, Louis. *Germany First: the Basic Concept of Allied Strategy in World War II*. Washington, D.C.: Center of Military History, U.S. Army, 1990.

———. *Strategy and Command: The First Two Years*. Washington, D.C.: Center of Military History, 2000.

Pogue, Forrest C. *The Supreme Command*. United States Army in World War II Series. Washington, D.C.: Department of the Army, 1954.

Schnabel, James, F. *Policy and Direction: The First Year*. Washington, D.C.: Office of the Chief of Military History, 1972.

Smith, Robert Ross. *Luzon Versus Formosa*. Washington, D.C.: Center of Military History, U.S. Army, 1990.

Stoler, Mark A. *Allies and Adversaries: The Joint Chiefs of Staff, The Grand Alliance, and U.S. Strategy in World War II*. Chapel Hill: University of North Carolina Press, 2000.

Thorne, Christopher. *Allies of a Kind*. New York: Oxford University Press, 1978.

## EUROPEAN THEATER OF OPERATIONS—GROUND

Allen, Peter. *One More River: The Rhine Crossings of 1945*. New York: Scribner, 1980.

Allen, Robert S. *Lucky Forward: The History of Patton's Third U.S. Army*. New York: Vanguard Press, 1947.

Allied Forces, 12th Army Group G-3. *Report of Operations*. Bad Homburg, Germany, 1945.

Allied Forces, 21st Army Group. *Notes on the Operations of 21st Army Group, 6 June 1944–5 May 1945*. N.p., 1945.

Allied Forces, Supreme Headquarters. *Report by the Supreme Commander to the Combined Chiefs of Staff on the Operations in Europe of the Allied Expeditionary Force, 6 June 1944 to 8 May 1945*. Washington, D.C.: U.S. Government Printing Office, 1946.

Ambrose, Stephen E. *D-Day, June 6, 1944: the Climactic Battle of World War II*. New York: Simon & Schuster, 1994.

———. *Eisenhower and Berlin, 1945: the Decision to Halt at the Elbe*. New York: W. W. Norton, 1967.

———. *The Victors: Eisenhower and His Boys, the Men of World War II*. New York: Simon & Schuster, 1998.

Astor, Gerald. *A Blood-Dimmed Tide: The Battle of the Bulge by the Men Who Fought It*. New York: Donald I. Fine, 1992.

Balkoski, Joseph. *Beyond the Beachhead: the 29th Infantry Division in Normandy*. Harrisburg, Pa.: Stackpole Books, 1989.

———. *Utah Beach: The Amphibious Landing and Airborne Operations on D-Day, June 6, 1944*. Mechanicsburg, Pa.: Stackpole Books, 2005.

Ballard, Ted. *Rhineland*. Washington, D.C.: U.S. Army Center of Military History, 1995.

Blumenson, Martin. *Breakout and Pursuit*. The United States Army in World War II Series. Washington, D.C.: Department of the Army, 1961.

Bonn, Keith E. *When the Odds Were Even: The Vosges Mountains Campaign, October 1944–January 1945*. Novato, Calif.: Presidio Press, 1994.

Bowden, Mark. *Our Finest Day: D-Day, June 6, 1944*. San Francisco, Calif.: Chronicle Books, 2002.

Branton, Harold M. *The 103rd Infantry Division: The Trail of the Cactus*. Paducah, Ky.: Turner Publishing, 1993.

Breuer, William B. *Operation Dragoon: The Allied Invasion of the South of France*. Novato, Calif.: Presidio Press, 1987.

Burgett, Donald R. *Seven Roads to Hell: A Screaming Eagle at Bastogne*. Novato, Calif.: Presidio Press, 1999.

Byrnes, Lawrence G., ed. *History of the 94th Infantry Division in World War II*. Washington, D.C.: Infantry Journal Press, 1948.

Carafano, James J. *After D-Day: Operation Cobra and the Normandy Breakout*. Boulder, Colo.: Lynne Rienner, 2000.

Cirillo, Roger. *Ardennes—Alsace*. Washington, D.C.: U.S. Army Center of Military History, 1995.

Clarke, Jeffrey J. *Riviera to the Rhine: the European Theater of Operations*. Washington, D.C.: Center of Military History, 1993.

Clinger, Fred, Arthur Johnston, and Vincent Masel. *The History of the 71st Infantry Division*. Augsburg, Germany, 1946.

Cole, Hugh M. *The Ardennes: The Battle of the Bulge*. Washington, D.C.: Center of Military History, 1994.

Congdon, Don, ed. *Combat WW II: European Theater of Operations*. New York: Arbor House, 1983.

Crookenden, Napier. *Battle of the Bulge, 1944*. New York: Scribner, 1980.

———. *Dropzone Normandy: The Story of the American and British Airborne Assault on D-Day 1944*. New York: Scribner, 1976.

D'Este, Carlo. *Decision in Normandy*. New York: Dutton, 1983.

Department of the Army Historical Division. *Utah Beach to Cherbourg*. Washington, D.C., 1948.

Devlin, Gerard M. *Paratrooper!: The Saga of U.S. Army and Marine Parachute and Glider Combat Troops During World War II*. New York: St. Martin's Press, 1979.

Deyer, George. *XII Corps: Spearhead of Patton's Third Army*. Baton Rouge, La.: Military Press of Louisiana, 1947.

Doubler, Michael D. *Closing With the Enemy: How GIs Fought the War in Europe, 1944–1945*. Lawrence: University Press of Kansas, 1994.

Draper, Theodore. *The 84th Infantry Division in the Battle of Germany, November 1944–May 1945*. New York: Viking Press, 1946.

Dupuy, Trevor N. *Hitler's Last Gamble: the Battle of the Bulge, December 1944–January 1945*. New York: HarperCollins, 1994.

Eisenhower, John S. D. *The Bitter Woods: the Dramatic Story, Told at all Echelons, from Supreme Command to Squad Leader, of the Crisis that Shook the Western Coalition: Hitler's Surprise Ardennes Offensive*. New York: Putnam, 1969.

Elstob, Peter. *Bastogne: The Road Block*. New York: Ballantine Books, 1968.

Essame, Hubert. *The Battle for Germany*. New York: Scribner, 1969.

Ewing, Joseph H. *29, Let's Go!: A History of the 29th Infantry Division in World War II*. Washington, D.C.: Infantry Journal Press, 1948.

Farrar-Hockley, Anthony H. *Airborne Carpet: Operation Market Garden.* New York: Ballantine Books, 1969.

Featherston, Alwyn. *Battle for Mortain: The 30th Infantry Division Saves the Breakout, August 7–12, 1944.* Novato, Calif.: Presidio Press, 1998.

Fifth Armored Division Association. *Paths of Armor: The Fifth Armored Division in World War II.* Nashville, Tenn.: Battery Press, 1985.

Forty, George. *Patton's Third Army at War.* New York: Scribner, 1978.

———. *Road to Berlin: the Allied Drive from Normandy.* London: Cassell, 1999.

Fox, Don M. *Patton's Vanguard: The United States Army Fourth Armored Division.* Jefferson, N.C.: McFarland, 2003.

Fussell, Paul. *The Boys' Crusade: the American Infantry in Northwestern Europe, 1944–1945.* New York: Modern Library, 2003.

Gabel, Christopher R. *The Lorraine Campaign: An Overview, September–December 1944.* Fort Leavenworth, Kans.: Combat Studies Institute, 1985.

Gilbert, Martin. *D-Day.* Hoboken, N.J.: J. Wiley & Sons, 2004.

———. *The Day the War Ended: May 8, 1945 Victory in Europe.* New York: Henry Holt, 1995.

Hammond, William M. *Normandy.* Washington, D.C.: U.S. Army Center of Military History, 1994.

Harrison, Gordon A. *Cross-Channel Attack.* Washington, D.C.: Center of Military History, 2002.

Hastings, Max. *Armageddon: the Battle for Germany, 1944–45.* New York: Knopf, 2004.

———. *Overlord: D-Day and the Battle for Normandy.* New York: Simon & Schuster, 1984.

Headquarters, First Allied Airborne Army. *Airborne Operations in Holland, September–November 1944.* N.p., 1944.

Hewitt, H. K. *Invasion of Southern France: Report of Naval Commander, Western Task Force.* Washington, D.C.: United States Navy Eighth Fleet, 1944.

Hechler, Ken. *The Bridge at Remagen.* New York: Ballantine Books, 1957.

Hewitt, Robert L. *Work Horse of the Western Front: The Story of the 30th Infantry Division.* Washington, D.C.: Infantry Journal Press, 1946.

Historical Board 89th Infantry Division. *The 89th Infantry Division, 1942–1945.* Washington, D.C.: Infantry Journal Press, 1947.

Hoegh, Leo A. *Timberwolf Tracks: The History of the 104th Infantry Division, 1942–1945.* Washington, D.C.: Infantry Journal Press, 1946.

Hogan, David W. *A Command Post at War: First Army Headquarters in Europe, 1943–1945.* Washington, D.C.: U.S. Army Center of Military History, 2000.

———. *Northern France.* Washington, D.C.: U.S. Army Center of Military History, 1995.

Holmes, Richard. *The D-Day Experience: From Operation Overlord to the Liberation of Paris.* London: Carlton, 2004.

Houston, Donald E. *Hell on Wheels: The 2nd Armored Division.* San Rafael, Calif.: Presidio Press, 1977.

Keegan, John. *Six Armies in Normandy: From D-Day to the Liberation of Paris, June 6th–August 25th, 1944.* New York: Viking Press, 1982.

Kershaw, Alex. *The Longest Winter: the Battle of the Bulge and the Epic Story of WWII's Most Decorated Platoon.* Cambridge, Mass.: Da Capo Press, 2004.

Koyen, Kenneth A. *The Fourth Armored Division: From the Beach to Bavaria.* Munich, Germany: Herderdruck, 1946.

Lauer, Walter E. *Battle Babies: The Story of the 99th Infantry Division in World War II.* Baton Rouge, La.: Military Press of Louisiana, 1951.

Lewis, Adrian R. *Omaha Beach: A Flawed Victory.* Chapel Hill: University of North Carolina Press, 2001.

MacDonald, Charles B. *The Last Offensive.* Washington, D.C.: Office of the Chief of Military History, 1973.

———. *The Mighty Endeavor: American Armed Forces in the European Theater in World War II.* New York: Oxford University Press, 1969.

———. *The Operations of VII Corps in September 1944.* Washington, D.C.: Office of the Chief of Military History, Department of the Army, 1953.

———. *The Siegfried Line Campaign.* Washington, D.C.: Office of the Chief of Military History, 1963.

———. *A Time for Trumpets: The Untold Story of the Battle of the Bulge.* New York: Morrow, 1984.

Marshall, S. L. A. *Night Drop: The American Airborne Invasion of Normandy.* Boston: Little, Brown, 1962.

Maule, Henry. *Normandy Breakout.* New York: Quadrangle, 1977.

Messenger, Charles. *The Second World War in Europe.* Washington, D.C.: Smithsonian Books, 2004.

McKee, Alexander. *The Race for the Rhine Bridges: 1940, 1944, 1945.* New York: Stein and Day, 1971.

McManus, John C. *The Americans at D-day: the American Experience at the Normandy Invasion.* New York: Forge, 2004.

———. *The Americans at Normandy: The Summer of 1944—the American War from the Normandy Beaches to Falaise.* New York: Forge, 2004.

Miller, Robert A. *August 1944: The Campaign for France.* Novato, Calif.: Presidio Press, 1988.

Millis, Walter. *The Last Phase: The Allied Victory in Western Europe.* Boston: Houghton Mifflin, 1946.

Morison, Samuel Eliot. *The Invasion of France and Germany, 1944–1945.* Boston: Little, Brown, 1957.

Mueller, Ralph, and Jerry Turk. *Report After Action: The Story of the 103rd Infantry Division.* Innsbruck, Austria: Headquarters, 103rd Infantry Division, 1945.

Nichols, Lester M. *Impact: The Battle Story of the Tenth Armored Division.* New York: Bradbury, Sayles, 1954.

Pogue, Forrest C. *The Decision to Halt at the Elbe.* Washington, D.C.: Center of Military History, U.S. Army, 1990.

Quarrie, Bruce. *The Ardennes Offensive U.S. III & XII Corps: Southern Sector.* Oxford: Osprey, 2000.

Reardon, Mark J. *Victory at Mortain: Stopping Hitler's Panzer Counteroffensive.* Lawrence: University Press of Kansas, 2002.

Rickard, John N. *Patton at Bay: The Lorraine Campaign, September to December, 1944.* Westport, Conn.: Praeger, 1999.

Ruggero, Ed. *Combat Jump: The Young Men Who Led the Assault into Fortress Europe, July, 1943.* New York: HarperCollins, 2003.

———. *The First Men In: U.S. Paratroopers and the Fight to Save D-day.* New York: HarperCollins, 2006.

Ryan, Cornelius. *The Longest Day, June 6, 1944.* New York: Simon & Schuster, 1959.

Saunders, Tim. *Hell's Highway.* Barnsley, South Yorkshire, England: Leo Cooper, 2001.

Smith, Steven. *2nd Armored Division: "Hell on Wheels."* Surrey, England: Military Book Club, 2003.

Smith, Walter B. *Eisenhower's Six Great Decisions: Europe, 1944–1945.* New York: Longmans, Green, 1956.

Steidl, Franz. *Lost Battalions: Going for Broke in the Vosges, Autumn 1944.* Novato, Calif.: Presidio Press, 1997.

Stock, James W. *Rhine Crossing.* New York: Ballantine Books, 1973.

Sullivan, John J. *Overlord's Eagles: Operations of the United States Army Air Forces in the Invasion of Normandy in World War II.* Jefferson, N.C.: McFarland, 1997.

Third Armored Division. *Spearhead in the West, 1941–45: The Third Armored Division.* Frankfurt am Main, Germany: F.J. Henrich, 1945.

Thompson, Reginald William. *D-Day: Spearhead of Invasion.* New York: Ballantine Books, 1968.

Tolhurst, Michael. *Saint Vith: 106th US Infantry Division.* London: Leo Cooper, 1999.

United States Army VII Corps. *Mission Accomplished: The Story of the Campaigns of the VII Corps, United States Army in the War.* Leipzig, Germany: J. J. Weber, 1945.

United States Army XI Corps. *History of XI Corps, 15 June 1942–15 March 1946.* XI Corps Historical Section, 1946.

United States Army XVI Corps. *History of the XVI Corps From Its Activation to the End of the War in Europe.* Washington, D.C.: Infantry Journal Press, 1947.

United States Army, 82nd Airborne Division G-3. *The Eighty Second Airborne Division: Operation "Neptune": Normandy 6 June–8 July 1944.* N.p., 1944.

United States Army, 101st Airborne Division G-3. *Field Order No. 1.* N.p., 1944.

United States First Army. *Report of Operations, Oct. 20, 1943–Aug. 1, 1944–Feb. 23–May 8, 1945.* N.p., 1945.

United States Military Academy Department of Military Art and Engineering. *The Invasion of Western Europe: Part 2 (January to May 1945).* West Point, N.Y.: U.S. Military Academy, 1946.

———. *The War in Western Europe.* West Point, N.Y.: U.S. Military Academy, 1952.

———. *The Invasion of Western Europe: (6 June to 31 December 1944).* West Point, N.Y.: U.S. Military Academy, 1945.

United States Seventh Army. *Report of Operations: The Seventh United States Army in France and Germany 1944–1945.* Heidelberg, Germany: Aloys Gräf, 1946.

United States Seventh Army G-2. *Seventh Army Operations in Europe, 15 August 1944–8 May 1945.* N.p., 1945.

United States War Department, General Staff. *Omaha Beachhead.* Washington, D.C.: War Department Historical Division, 1945.

———. *St-Lô.* Washington, D.C.: War Department Historical Division, 1946.

United States War Department, Historical Division. *Omaha Beachhead.* Washington, D.C.: Center of Military History, 1994.

Von Luettichau, Charles V. *The Ardennes Offensive: Germany's Situation in the Fall of 1944.* Washington, D.C.: Research Section, Office of Military History, Department of the Army, 1953.

Weigley, Russell F. *Eisenhower's Lieutenants: The Campaign of France and Germany, 1944–1945.* Bloomington: Indiana University Press, 1981.

Whitaker, W. Denis. *Rhineland: The Battle to End the War.* New York: St. Martin's Press, 1989.

Whiting, Charles. *America's Forgotten Army: The Story of the U.S. Seventh.* Rockville Centre, N.Y.: Sarpedon, 1999.

———. *The End of the War, Europe: April 15–May 23, 1945.* New York: Stein and Day, 1973.

———. *The Other Battle of the Bulge: Operation Northwind.* Chelsea, Mich.: Scarborough House, 1990.

Wilmot, Chester. *The Struggle for Europe.* New York: Harper, 1952.

# European Theater of Operations—Air

Astor, Gerald. *The Mighty Eighth: The Air War in Europe As Told by the Men Who Fought It.* New York: D.I. Fine Books, 1997.

Comer, John. *Combat Crew: A True Story of Flying and Fighting in World War II.* New York: W. Morrow, 1988.

Conversino, Mark J. *Fighting With the Soviets: The Failure of Operation Frantic 1944–45.* Lawrence: University Press of Kansas, 1997.

Copp, DeWitt S. *Forged in Fire: Strategy and Decisions in the Air War Over Europe, 1940–45.* Garden City, N.Y.: Doubleday, 1982.

Crane, Conrad. *Bombs, Cities, and Civilians, American Airpower Strategy in World War II.* Lawrence: University Press of Kansas, 1993.

Hallion, Richard. *D-Day 1944: Air Power Over the Normandy Beaches and Beyond.* Washington, D.C.: Air Force Marine Corps Historical Center Program, 1994.

Hughes, Thomas A. *Overlord: General Pete Quesada and the Triumph of Tactical Air Power in World War II.* New York: Free Press, 1995.

Infield, Glenn B. *Big Week: The Classic Story of the Crucial Air Battle of WW II.* Washington, D.C.: Brassey's, 1993.

Middlebrook, Martin. *The Schweinfurt-Regensburg Mission.* New York: Scribner, 1983.

Miller, Donald L. *Masters of the Air: America's Bomber Boys Who Fought the Air War Against Nazi Germany.* New York: Simon & Schuster, 2006.

Morrison, Wilbur H. *Fortress Without a Roof: The Allied Bombing of the Third Reich.* New York: St. Martin's Press, 1982.

Office of Air Force History. *Condensed Analysis of the Ninth Air Force in the European Theater of Operations.* Washington, D.C., 1984.

Parker, Danny S. *To Win the Winter Sky: The Air War over the Ardennes, 1944–1945.* Conshohocken, Pa.: Combined Books, 1994.

Perret, Geoffrey. *Winged Victory: The Army Air Forces in World War II.* New York: Random House, 1993.

Ramsey, John. *Ninth Air Force in the ETO, 16 October 1943 to 16 April 1944.* Washington, D.C.: Assistant Chief of Intelligence, Historical Division, 1945.

United States Army Air Forces. *Sunday Punch in Normandy: The Tactical Use of Heavy Bombardment in the Normandy Invasion.* Washington, D.C.: Headquarters, Army Air Forces, 1945.

United States Army Air Forces Historical Office. *Ninth Air Force, April to November 1944.* N.p., Headquarters, Ninth Air Force, 1944.

IX Troop Carrier Command Headquarters. *Air invasion of Holland: Report on Operation Market.* N.p., 1945.

# European Theater of Operations—Naval

Office of the Chief of Naval Operations. *Amphibious Operations: Invasion of Northern France.* Washington, D.C.: United States Fleet, Headquarters of the Commander in Chief, 1944.

———. *Battle Experience: Supporting Operations for the Invasion of Northern France, June, 1944.* Washington, D.C.: United States Fleet, Headquarters of the Commander in Chief, 1944.

United States Naval Forces, Europe. *Operation Normandy Invasion: Report of Naval Commander Western Task Force (CTF 122).* London, 1944.

# NORTH AFRICA AND MEDITERRANEAN—GROUND OPERATIONS

Adleman, Robert H., and George Walton. *Rome Fell Today.* Boston: Little, Brown, 1968.

Alexander, Harold R. L. G. *Report by the Supreme Allied Commander, Mediterranean Field-Marshall the Viscount Alexander of Tunis, to the Combined Chiefs of Staff on the Italian Campaign, 12th December 1944 to 2nd May 1945.* London: H.M.S.O., 1951.

Allied Forces Mediterranean Theater. *Report by the Supreme Allied Commander, Mediterranean, to the Combined Chiefs of Staff on the Italian Campaign.* London: H.M.S.O., 1946.

Allied Forces Supreme Commander Mediterranean. *Report by the Supreme Allied Commander, Mediterranean, to the Combined Chiefs of Staff on the Operations in Southern France, August 1944.* London: H.M.S.O., 1946.

Allied Forces, Supreme Headquarters. *Lessons from the Tunisian Campaign.* Washington, D.C.: U.S. Government Printing Office, 1943.

Anderson, Charles R. *Tunisia.* Washington, D.C.: U.S. Army Center of Military History, 1993.

Birtle, Andrew J. *Sicily.* Washington, D.C.: Center of Military History, 1993.

Blumenson, Martin. *General Lucas at Anzio.* Washington, D.C.: Center of Military History, U.S. Army, 1990.

———. *Salerno to Cassino.* Washington, D.C.: Office of the Chief of Military History, 1969.

———. *Sicily: Whose Victory?* New York: Ballantine Books, 1969.

Bond, Harold L. *Return to Cassino: A Memoir of the Fight for Rome.* Garden City, N.Y.: Doubleday, 1964.

Breuer, William B. *Drop Zone, Sicily: Allied Airborne Strike, July 1943.* Novato, Calif.: Presidio Press, 1983.

Clark, Mark W. *Calculated Risk.* New York: Harper, 1950.

Clarke, Jeffrey J. *Southern France.* Washington, D.C.: U.S. Army Center of Military History, 1994.

D'Este, Carlo. *Fatal Decision: Anzio and the Battle for Rome.* New York: HarperCollins, 1991.

———. *World War II in the Mediterranean, 1942–1945.* Chapel Hill, N.C.: Algonquin Books, 1990.

Department of the Army, Office of Military History. *Anzio Beachhead, 22 January–25 May 1944.* Washington, D.C.: Historical Division, War Department, 1947.

Fisher, Ernest F. *Cassino to the Alps.* Washington, D.C.: Center of Military History, 1977.

Forty, George. *Fifth Army at War.* New York: Scribner, 1980.

Garland, Albert N., and Howard M. Smyth. *Sicily and the Surrender of Italy.* Washington, D.C.: United States Army in World War II. Government Printing Office, 1965.

Gibran, Daniel K. *The 92nd Infantry Division and the Italian Campaign in World War II.* Jefferson, N.C.: McFarland, 2001.

Graham, Dominick, and Shelford Bidwell. *Tug of War: The Battle for Italy, 1943–1945.* New York: St. Martin's Press, 1986.

Hammel, Eric M. *Air War Europa: America's Air War Against Germany in Europe and North Africa, 1942–1945.* Pacifica, Calif.: Pacifica Press, 1994.

Hargrove, Hondon B. *Buffalo Soldiers in Italy: Black Americans in World War II.* Jefferson, N.C.: McFarland, 1985.

Harpur, Brian. *The Impossible Victory: A Personal Account of the Battle for the River Po.* New York: Hippocrene Books, 1981.

Headquarters, Allied Forces Mediterranean Theatre. *Operation ANVIL.* N.p., 1944.

———. *The Report of the Commander-in-Chief, Mediterranean on the Invasion of Sicily.* N.p., 1945.

Headquarters, Fifteenth Army Group. *Finito: The Po Valley Campaign, 1945.* Milan, Italy: N.p., 1945.

Higgins, Trumbull. *Soft Underbelly: The Anglo-American Controversy Over the Italian Campaign, 1939–1945.* New York: Macmillan, 1968.

Historical Section, United States Fifth Army. *Fifth Army History.* N.p., 1945.

Hoyt, Edwin P. *Backwater War: The Allied Campaign in Italy, 1943–1945.* Westport, Conn.: Praeger, 2002.

Huff, Richard A. *A Pictorial History of the 36th "Texas" Infantry Division.* Austin, Tex.: 36th Division Association, n.d.

Jackson, W. G. F. *The Battle for Italy.* New York: Harper and Row, 1967.

Jenkins, McKay. *The Last Ridge: The Epic Story of the U.S. Army's 10th Mountain Division and the Assault on Hitler's Europe.* New York: Random House, 2003.

Lamb, Richard. *The War in Italy, 1943–1945: A Brutal Story.* New York: St. Martin's Press, 1996.

Laurie, Clayton D. *Anzio.* Washington, D.C.: U.S. Army Center of Military History, 1994.

Mason, David. *Salerno: Foothold in Europe.* New York: Ballantine Books, 1972.

Mathews, Sidney T. *General Clark's Decision to Drive on Rome.* Washington, D.C.: Center of Military History, U.S. Army, 1990.

Matloff, Maurice. *The Anvil Decision: Crossroads of Strategy.* Washington, D.C.: Center of Military History, U.S. Army, 1990.

Moorehead, Alan. *The March to Tunis: The North African War, 1940–1943.* New York: Harper and Row, 1967.

Morris, Eric. *Circles of Hell: The War in Italy, 1943–1945.* New York: Crown, 1993.

Newell, Clayton R. *Egypt-Libya.* Washington, D.C.: U.S. Army Center of Military History, 1993.

Oland, Dwight D. *North Apennines.* Washington, D.C.: U.S. Army Center of Military History, 1996.

Orgill, Douglas. *The Gothic Line: The Italian Campaign, Autumn, 1944.* New York: Norton, 1967.

Pack, S. W. C. *Operation Husky: The Allied Invasion of Sicily.* New York: Hippocrene Books, 1977.

Popa, Thomas A. *Po Valley.* Washington, D.C.: U.S. Army Center of Military History, 1996.

Porch, Douglas. *The Path to Victory: The Mediterranean Theater in World War II.* New York: Farrar, Straus, and Giroux, 2004.

Robbins, Robert A. *The 91st Infantry Division of World War II.* Washington, D.C.: Infantry Journal Press, 1947.

Shelton, Peter. *Climb to Conquer: The Untold Story of World War II's 10th Mountain Division Ski Troops.* New York: Scribner, 2003

Shepperd, G. A. The *Italian Campaign, 1943–45: A Political and Military Reassessment.* New York: Praeger, 1968.

Shirey, Orville C. *Americans: The Story of the 442nd Combat Team.* Washington, D.C.: Infantry Journal Press, 1947.

Smith, Kenneth V. *Naples-Foggia.* Washington, D.C.: U.S. Army Center of Military History, 1994.

Starr, Chester G. *From Salerno to the Alps: A History of the Fifth Army, 1943–1945.* Washington, D.C.: Infantry Journal Press, 1948.

Strawson, John. *The Italian Campaign.* New York: Carroll and Graf, 1988.

United States Fifth Army G-3. *The Advance on Rome of the Fifth Army: Under the Command of Lieutenant General Mark W. Clark.* N.p., 1944.

———. *Road to Rome: Salerno, Naples, Volturno, Cassino, Anzio, Rome.* N.p., 1944.

United States Fifteenth Army. *History of the Fifteenth United States Army, 21 August 1944 to 11 July 1945.* N.p., 1946.

United States Military Academy Department of Military Art and Engineering. *Operations in Sicily and Italy (July 1943 to December 1944).* West Point, N.Y.: U.S. Military Academy, 1945.

———. *Operations in Sicily and Italy (July 1943 to May 1945).* West Point, N.Y.: U.S. Military Academy, 1945.

United States Seventh Army G-3. *Dragoon: Field Order Number 1.* N.p., 1944.

United States War Department, General Staff. *Fifth Army at the Winter Line (15 November 1943–15 January 1944).* Washington, D.C.: Military Historical Division, War Department, 1945.

———. *From the Volturno to the Winter Line (6 October–15 November 1943).* Washington, D.C.: Military Historical Division, War Department, 1945.

———. *Salerno: American Operations from the Beaches to the Volturno (9 September–6 October 1943).* Washington, D.C.: Military Historical Division, War Department, 1945.

U.S. Army Center of Military History. *To Bizerte With the II Corps, 23 April–13 May 1943.* Washington, D.C., 1990.

———. *Fifth Army at the Winter Line, 15 November 1943–15 January 1944.* Washington, D.C., N.p., 1990.

# North Africa and Mediterranean—Air and Naval Operations

Allied Forces, Western Naval Task Force. *Operation Plan No. 7–43.* Algiers, Algeria: Allied Forces Headquarters, 1943.

———. *Operation Plan No. 4–44.* Algiers, Algeria: Headquarters, Allied Forces Mediterranean: 1944.

———. *The Sicilian Campaign: Operation "Husky" July–August, 1943.* N.p., 1943.

Clifford, Robert L., and William J. Maddocks. *Naval Gunfire Support of the Landing in Sicily.* Oklahoma City, Okla.: 45th Infantry Division Museum, 1984.

Coles, Harry L. *Participation of the Ninth and Twelfth Air Forces in the Sicilian Campaign.* Washington, D.C.: Army Air Force Historical Office, 1945.

Dugan, James, and Carroll Stewart. *Ploeşti: The Great Ground-Air Battle of 1 August 1943.* Washington, D.C.: Brassey's, 1998.

Koburger, Charles W. *Naval Warfare in the Eastern Mediterranean, 1940–1945.* Westport, Conn.: Praeger, 1993.

McCarthy, Michael C. *Air-to-Ground Battle for Italy.* Maxwell Air Force Base, Ala.: Air University Press, 2004.

Morison, Samuel Eliot. *Operations in North African Waters, October 1942–June 1943.* Boston: Little, Brown, 1947.

Office of Naval Intelligence. *The Sicilian Campaign, 10 July–17 August 1943.* Washington, D.C., 1945.

Russell, Edward T. *The U.S. Army Air Forces in World War II: Africa to the Alps. The Army Air Forces in the Mediterranean Theater.* Washington, D.C.: Air Force History and Museums Program, 1999.

United States Army Air Forces. *Air Phase of the Italian Campaign to 1 January 1944.* Washington, D.C.: Headquarters, Army Air Force, 1946.

United States Navy, Eighth Fleet. *Operation Plan 147–43 "Shingle."* N.p., 1944.

# Pacific–Army Ground and Air Forces (Southwest Pacific Area)

Abington, Juliette. *Summary of Air Action in the Philippines and Netherlands East Indies, 7 December 1941 to 26 March 1942.* Washington, D.C.: Historical Division, War Department, 1945.

Allied Forces South West Pacific Area. *Reno V: Outline Plan for Operations of the Southwest Pacific Area to Include the Reoccupation of the Philippines.* N.p., 1944.

———. *Reno IV: Outline Plan for Operations of the Southwest Pacific Area to Include the Reoccupation of the Philippines.* N.p., 1944.

Anderson, Charles R. *Papua.* Washington, D.C.: U.S. Army Center of Military History, 1992.

———. *Western Pacific.* Washington, D.C.: U.S. Army Center of Military History, 1994.

Andradé, Dale. *Luzon.* Washington, D.C.: U.S. Army Center of Military History, 1996.

Astor, Gerald. *Crisis in the Pacific: The Battles for the Philippine Islands by the Men Who Fought Them.* New York: Donald I. Fine, 1996.

Bailey, Jennifer L. *Philippine Islands.* Washington, D.C.: U.S. Army Center of Military History, 1992.

Beck, John J. *MacArthur and Wainwright: Sacrifice of the Philippines.* Albuquerque: University of New Mexico Press, 1974.

Belote, James H., and William M. Belote. *Corregidor: The Saga of a Fortress.* New York: Harper & Row, 1967.

Boggs, Charles W., Jr. *Marine Aviation in the Philippines.* Washington, D.C.: United States Marine Corps Historical Center, 1951.

Breuer, William B. *Retaking the Philippines: America's Return to Corregidor and Bataan, October 1944–March 1945.* New York: St. Martin's Press, 1986.

Cannon, M. Hamlin. *Leyte: The Return to the Philippines.* Washington, D.C.: Office of the Chief of Military History, 1954.

Commander in Chief, United States Navy Pacific Fleet and Pacific Ocean Areas. *Joint Staff Study: Olympic Naval and Amphibious Operations.* N.p., 1945.

Connaughton, R. M., John Pimlott, and Duncan Anderson. *The Battle for Manila.* Novato, Calif.: Presidio Press, 1995.

———. *MacArthur and Defeat in the Philippines.* Woodstock, N.Y.: Overlook Press, 2001.

Conroy, Robert. *The Battle of Bataan: America's Greatest Defeat.* New York: Macmillan, 1969.

Devlin, Gerard M. *Back to Corregidor: America Retakes the Rock.* New York: St. Martin's Press, 1992.

Drea, Edward J. *New Guinea.* Washington, D.C.: U.S. Army Center of Military History, 1993.

Falk, Stanley L. *Decision at Leyte.* New York: W. W. Norton, 1966.

———. *Liberation of the Philippines.* New York: Ballantine Books, 1971.

Far East Command Military History Section. *Eastern New Guinea Invasion Operations.* Washington, D.C.: Office of the Chief of Military History, 1953.

Flanagan, E. M. *Corregidor: The Rock Force Assault, 1945.* Novato, Calif.: Presidio Press, 1988.

Frank, Richard B. *Downfall: The End of the Imperial Japanese Empire.* New York: Random House, 1999.

Gailey, Harry A. *MacArthur Strikes Back: Decision at Buna, New Guinea, 1942–1943.* Novato, Calif.: Presidio Press, 2000.

———. *MacArthur's Victory: The War in New Guinea, 1943–1944.* New York: Presidio Press, 2004.

Greene, Jack. *The Midway Campaign, December 7, 1941–June 6, 1942.* Conshohocken, Pa.: Combined Books, 1995.

Griffith, Thomas E. *MacArthur's Airman: General George C. Kenney and the War in the Southwest Pacific.* Lawrence: University Press of Kansas, 1998.

Headquarters United States Army Forces, Middle Pacific. *Participation in the Western Carolines and Central Philippines Operations by the United States Army Forces Pacific Ocean Areas, September–November 1944.* Edited by Robert C. Richardson, N.p., 1945.

Hirrel, Leo. *Bismarck Archipelago.* Washington, D.C.: U.S. Army Center of Military History, 1994.

Hoyt, Edwin P. *MacArthur's Navy.* New York: Orion, 1989.

Kenney, George C. *General Kenney Reports: A Personal History of the Pacific War.* Washington, D.C.: Office of Air Force History, 1987.

Leary, William M. *We Shall Return!: MacArthur's Commanders and the Defeat of Japan, 1942–1945.* Lexington: University Press of Kentucky, 1988.

Lofgren, Stephen J. *Southern Philippines.* Washington, D.C.: U.S. Army Center of Military History, 1996.

MacArthur, Douglas. *Reports of General MacArthur, Supreme Commander for the Allied Powers.* Washington, D.C.: U.S. Army Center of Military History, 1994.

Mayo, Lida. *Bloody Buna.* Garden City, N.Y.: Doubleday, 1974.

McAulay, Lex. *MacArthur's Eagles: The U.S. Air War Over New Guinea, 1943–1944.* Annapolis, Md.: Naval Institute Press, 2005.

Miller, J. Michael. *From Shanghai to Corregidor: Marines in the Defense of the Philippines.* Washington, D.C.: Marine Corps Historical Center, 1997.

Miller, John. *Cartwheel: The Reduction of Rabaul.* Washington, D.C.: Office of the Chief of Military History, 1959.

Miller, John, Jr. *MacArthur and the Admiralties.* Washington, D.C.: U.S. Army, Center of Military History, 1990.

Milner, Samuel. *Victory in Papua.* Washington, D.C.: U.S. Army Center of Military History, 2003.

Morison, Samuel Eliot. *The Liberation of the Philippines: Luzon, Mindanao, the Visayans, 1944–1945.* Boston: Little, Brown, 1959.

———. *Leyte, June 1944–January 1945.* Boston: Little, Brown, 1958.

———. *Breaking the Bismarcks Barrier: 22 July 1942–1 May 1944.* Boston: Little, Brown, 1950.

Morris, Eric. *Corregidor: The End of the Line.* New York: Stein and Day, 1981.

Morton, Louis. *The Decision to Withdraw to Bataan.* Washington, D.C.: Center of Military History, U.S. Army, 1990.

———. *The Fall of the Philippines.* Washington, D.C.: Office of the Chief of Military History, 1953.

Office of the Chief of Naval Operations. *Amphibious Operations: Invasion of the Philippines, October 1944 to January 1945.* Washington, D.C.: United States Fleet, Headquarters of the Commander in Chief, 1945.

Prefer, Nathan. *MacArthur's New Guinea Campaign.* Conshohocken, Pa.: Combined Books, 1995.

Rees, David. *The Defeat of Japan.* Westport, Conn.: Praeger, 1997.

Rodman, Matthew K. *A War of Their Own: Bombers Over the Southwest Pacific.* Maxwell Air Force Base, Ala.: Air University Press, 2005.

Sakaida, Henry. *The Siege of Rabaul.* St. Paul, Minn.: Phalanx Press, 1996.

Smith, Robert R. *The Approach to the Philippines.* Washington, D.C.: Center of Military History, 1996.

———. *Triumph in the Philippines.* Washington, D.C.: U.S. Army Center of Military History, 1991.

Taaffe, Stephen R. *MacArthur's Jungle War: The 1944 New Guinea Campaign.* Lawrence: University Press of Kansas, 1998.

Templeman, Harold. *The Return to Corregidor.* New York: Strand Press, 1945.

United States Army Far East Command. *Jolo Island Invasion Operations Record.* Tokyo, 1952.

———. *Philippine Area Naval Operations, Part IV. Jan 45–Aug 45.* Tokyo, 1952.

———. *Philippine Operations Record: Phase Three, Vol. IV: General Outline of Mindoro Operations.* Tokyo, 1952.

———. *Tarakan Invasion Operations Record.* Tokyo, 1952.

United States Army Forces, Pacific. *Staff Study Operations: Olympic.* General Headquarters, U.S. Army Forces, Pacific, 1945.

United States Army, Headquarters, 37th Infantry Regiment. *After Action Report: Operations of the 37th Infantry Division, Luzon P.I., 1 November 1944 to 30 June 1945.* N.p., 1945.

United States Army I Corps. *History of the Hollandia Operation: Reckless Task Force.* N.p., 1944.

United States Army X Corps. *History of X Corps on Mindanao, 17 April 45–30 June 45.* N.p., 1945.

United States Eighth Army. *Report of the Commanding General, Eighth Army: On the Luzon Mop-Up.* N.p., 1945.

———. *Report of the Commanding General, Eighth Army: On the Mindanao Operation.* N.p., 1946.

———. *Report of the Commanding General, Eighth Army: On the Nasugbu and Bataan Operations.* N.p., 1946.

———. *Report of the Commanding General, Eighth Army: On the Palawan and Zamboanga Operations.* N.p., 1946.

———. *Report of the Commanding General, Eighth Army: On the Panay-Negros and Cebu Operations.* N.p., 1946.

United States Navy. *Report of Luzon Operation (Lingayen Gulf), Philippine Islands.* 3rd Amphibious Force, N.p., 1945.

———. *Seizure of Leyte: Report of Participation of Task Force Seventy-Nine.* 3rd Amphibious Force, N.p., 1944.

United States Sixth Army. *Report of the Leyte Operation, 17 October 1944–25 December 1944.* N.p., 1945.

———. *Report of the Luzon Campaign, 9 January 1945–30 June 1945.* N.p., 1945.

United States War Department, General Staff. *Papuan Campaign: The Buna-Sanananda Operation, 16 November 1942–23 January 1943.* Washington, D.C.: Military Intelligence Division, U.S. War Department, 1944.

U.S. Army Center of Military History. *The Admiralties, Operations of the 1st Cavalry Division, 29 February–18 May 1944.* Washington, D.C.: N.p., 1990.

———. *Papuan Campaign: The Buna–Sanananda Operation, 16 November 1942–23 January 1943.* Washington, D.C.: N.p., 1990.

Vader, John. *New Guinea: The Tide Is Stemmed.* New York: Ballantine Books, 1971.

Vego, Milan N. *The Battle for Leyte, 1944: Allied and Japanese Plans, Preparations, and Execution.* Annapolis, Md.: Naval Institute Press, 2006.

Whitman, John W. *Bataan, Our Last Ditch: The Bataan Campaign, 1942.* New York: Hippocrene Books, 1990.

# PACIFIC–NAVAL FORCES, MARINE, AND AIR FORCES (NORTHERN, CENTRAL, AND SOUTHERN PACIFIC)

*A History of the Tornado Task Force in the Wakde Islands—Sarmi Area, Dutch New Guinea, 12 June–18 July 1944.* N.p., 1944.

Alexander, Joseph H. *Across the Reef: The Marine Assault of Tarawa.* Washington, D.C.: Marine Corps Historical Center, 1993.

———. *The Final Campaign: Marines in the Victory on Okinawa.* Washington, D.C.: Marine Corps Historical Center, 1996.

Appleman, Roy E. *Okinawa: The Last Battle.* Washington, D.C.: Historical Division, Department of the Army, 1948.

Astor, Gerald. *Operation Iceberg: The Invasion and Conquest of Okinawa in World War II.* New York: D.I. Fine, 1995.

———. *Semper Fi in the Sky: Marine Air Battles of World War II.* New York: Ballantine, 2005.

———. *Wings of Gold: The U.S. Naval Air Campaign in World War II.* New York: Presidio Press, 2004.

Belote, James H., and William Belote. *Typhoon of Steel: The Battle for Okinawa.* New York: Harper & Row, 1970.

Bergerud, Eric M. *Fire in the Sky: The Air War in the South Pacific.* Boulder, Colo.: Westview Press, 2000.

———. *Touched With Fire: The Land War in the South Pacific.* New York: Viking Press, 1996.

Blair, Clay. *Silent Victory: The U.S. Submarine War Against Japan.* Philadelphia: J. B. Lippincott, 1975.

Chapin, John C. *Breaching the Marianas: The Battle for Saipan.* Washington, D.C.: Marine Corps Historical Center, 1994.

Chun, Clayton K. S. *The Doolittle Raid 1942: America's First Strike at Japan.* New York: Osprey Publishers, 2006.

Commander in Chief, Pacific Ocean Areas. *Campaign Plan Granite.* Pearl Harbor, Hawaii: N.p., 1944.

———. *Operation Plan No. 29–42 (Defense of Midway).* Pearl Harbor: 27 May 1942.

Cressman, Robert J. *A Magnificent Fight: Marines in the Battle for Wake Island.* Washington, D.C.: Marine Corps Historical Center, 1992.

Cronin, Francis D. *Under the Southern Cross: The Saga of the Americal Division.* Washington, D.C.: Combat Forces Press, 1951.

Crowl, Philip A. *Campaign in the Marianas.* Washington, D.C.: Office of the Chief of Military History, 1960.

———. and Edmund G. Love. *Seizure of the Gilberts and Marshalls.* Washington, D.C.: Office of the Chief of Military History, 1955.

DeRose, James F. *Unrestricted Warfare: How a New Breed of Officers Led the Submarine Force to Victory in World War II.* New York: J. Wiley, 2000.

Feifer, George. *Tennozan: The Battle of Okinawa and the Atomic Bomb.* New York: Ticknor and Fields, 1992.

———. *The Battle of Okinawa: The Blood and the Bomb.* Guilford, Conn.: Lyons Press, 2001.

Fisch, Arnold G. *Ryukyus.* Washington, D.C.: U.S. Army Center of Military History, 1995.

Frank, Benis M. *Okinawa: Capstone to Victory.* New York: Ballantine Books, 1970.

———. *Okinawa: The Great Island Battle.* New York: Elsevier-Dutton, 1978.

Gayle, Gordon D. *Bloody Beaches: The Marines at Peleliu.* Washington, D.C.: Marine Corps Historical Center, 1996.

Gorman, G. Scott. *Endgame in the Pacific: Complexity, Strategy, and the B-29.* Maxwell Air Force Base, Ala.: Air University Press, 2000.

Grace, James W. *The Naval Battle of Guadalcanal: Night Action, 13 November 1942.* Annapolis, Md.: Naval Institute Press, 1999.

Graham, Michael B. *Mantle of Heroism: Tarawa and the Struggle for the Gilberts, November 1943.* Novato, Calif.: Presidio Press, 1993.

Hallas, James H. *Killing Ground on Okinawa: The Battle for Sugar Loaf Hill.* Westport, Conn.: Praeger, 1996.

Hammel, Eric M. *Munda Trail: The New Georgia Campaign.* New York: Orion Books, 1989.

Harwood, Richard. *A Close Encounter: The Marine Landing on Tinian.* Washington, D.C.: Marine Corps Historical Center, 1994.

Haulman, Daniel L. *The U.S. Army Air Forces in World War II: The High Road to Tokyo Bay: The AAF in the Asiatic-Pacific Theater.* Washington, D.C.: Center for Air Force History, 1993.

———. *The U.S. Army Air Forces in World War II: Hitting Home: The Air Offensive Against Japan.* Washington, D.C.: Air Force History and Museums Program, 1999.

Headquarters Tenth Army. *Report of Operations in the Ryukyus Campaign.* N.p., 1945.

Heinl, R.D., Jr. *The Defense of Wake.* Washington, D.C.: Historical Section, United States Marine Corps, 1947.

Herbert, Kevin. *Maximum Effort: The B-29s Against Japan.* Manhattan, Kans.: Sunflower University Press, 1983.

Historical Office, Headquarters, Army Air Forces. *Operational History of the Seventh Air Force, 7 December 1941 to 6 November 1943.* Washington, D.C.: Headquarters, Army Air Forces, 1945.

———. *Operational History of the Seventh Air Force, 6 November 1943 to 31 July 1944.* Washington, D.C.: Headquarters, Army Air Forces, 1945.

Historical Section, 81st Infantry Division. *The 81st Infantry Wildcat Division in World War II.* Washington. D.C.: Infantry Journal Press, 1948.

Hoffman, Carl W. *Saipan: The Beginning of the End.* Washington, D.C.: Historical Division, United States Marine Corps, 1950.

———. *The Seizure of Tinian.* Washington, D.C.: Historical Division, United States Marine Corps, 1951.

Hoffman, Jon T. *From Makin to Bougainville: Marine Raiders in the Pacific War.* Washington, D.C.: Marine Corps Historical Center, 1993.

———. *Silk Chutes and Hard Fighting: U.S. Marine Corps Parachute Units in World War II.* Washington, D.C.: Marine Corps Historical Center, 1999.

Hough, Frank O. *The Assault on Peleliu.* Washington, D.C.: Historical Division, United States Marine Corps, 1950.

Hough, Frank O., and John A. Crown. *The Campaign on New Britain.* Washington, D.C.: Historical Division, United States Marine Corps, 1952.

Hoyt, Edwin P. *Storm over the Gilberts: War in the Central Pacific, 1943.* New York: Van Nostrand, 1978.

Isely, Jeter, and Philip A. Crowl. *The U.S. Marines and Amphibious War*. Princeton, N.J.: Princeton University Press, 1951.

Kilpatrick, C. W. *The Naval Night Battles in the Solomons*. Pompano Beach: Exposition Press of Florida, 1987.

Leckie, Robert. *Okinawa: The Last Battle of World War II*. New York: Viking Press, 1995.

MacGarrigle, George L. *Aleutian Islands*. Washington, D.C.: U.S. Army Center of Military History, 1992.

McGee, William L. *Amphibious Operations in the South Pacific in World War II*. Santa Barbara, Calif.: BMC Publications, 2000.

Miller, John. *Guadalcanal: The First Offensive*. Washington, D.C.: Historical Division, War Department, 1949.

Morison, Samuel Eliot. *Coral Sea, Midway and Submarine Actions: May 1942–August 1942*. Boston: Little, Brown, 1949.

———. *The Rising Sun in the Pacific: 1931–April 1942*. Boston: Little, Brown, 1948.

———. *The Struggle for Guadalcanal, August 1942–February 1943*. Boston: Little, Brown, 1949.

———. *Victory in the Pacific, 1945*. Boston: Little, Brown, 1960.

Newell, Clayton R. *Central Pacific*. Washington, D.C.: U.S. Army Center of Military History, 1992.

Nichols, Charles S., Jr., and Henry I. Shaw, Jr. *Okinawa: Victory in the Pacific*. Washington: D.C.: Historical Branch, United States Marine Corps, 1955.

O'Brien, Cyril J. *Liberation: Marines in the Capture of Guam*. Washington, D.C.: Marine Corps Historical Center, 1992.

Office of the Chief of Naval Operations. *Battle Experience: Assault and Occupation of Attu Island, May 1943*. Washington, D.C.: United States Fleet, Headquarters of the Commander in Chief, 1943.

———. *Battle Experience: Battleship, Cruiser and Destroyer Sweep around Truk, 16–17 February 1944*. Washington, D.C.: United States Fleet, Headquarters of the Commander in Chief, 1944.

———. *Battle Experience: Bombardments of Iwo Jima, November 1944–January 1945, Third Fleet Operations*. Washington, D.C.: United States Fleet, Headquarters of the Commander in Chief, 1945.

———. *Amphibious Operations: Excluding Marshall Islands: January–March 1944*. Washington, D.C.: United States Fleet, Headquarters of the Commander in Chief, 1944.

———. *Amphibious Operations During the Period August to December 1943*. Washington, D.C.: United States Fleet, Headquarters of the Commander in Chief, 1944.

Office of Naval Intelligence. *The Aleutians Campaign, June 1942–August 1943*. Washington, D.C.: Department of the Navy, 1945.

———. *The Java Sea Campaign*. Washington, D.C.: Department of the Navy, 1945.

Prange, Gordon W., Donald M. Goldstein, and Katherine V. Dillon. *Miracle at Midway*. New York: McGraw-Hill, 1982.

Renzi, William A., and Mark D. Roehrs. *Never Look Back: A History of World War II in the Pacific*. New York: M. E. Sharpe, 1991.

Rohfleisch, Kramer J. *Guadalcanal and the Origins of the Thirteenth Air Force*. Washington, D.C.: Assistant Chief of Staff, Intelligence, Historical Division, 1945.

———. *The Thirteenth Air Force, March–October 1943*. Washington, D.C.: Army Air Forces Historical Office Headquarters, 1946.

Shaw, Henry I. *Tarawa: A Legend Is Born*. New York: Ballantine Books, 1969.

Sledge, E. B. *With the Old Breed, at Peleliu and Okinawa*. Novato, Calif.: Presidio Press, 1981.

Sloan, Bill. *Brotherhood of Heroes: The Marines at Peleliu, 1944, the Bloodiest Battle of the Pacific War*. New York: Simon & Schuster, 2005.

———. *Given Up for Dead: America's Heroic Stand at Wake Island*. New York: Bantam Books, 2003.

Smith, Steven T. *Wolfpack: The American Submarine Strategy that Helped Defeat Japan*. Hoboken, N.J.: Wiley, 2003.

Stockman, James R. *The Sixth Marine Division*. Washington, D.C.: Historical Division, United States Marine Corps, 1946.

Thomas, David A. *Japan's War at Sea: Pearl Harbor to the Coral Sea*. London: A. Deutsch, 1978.

Thomas, Evan. *Sea of Thunder: Four Commanders and the Last Great Naval Campaign, 1941–1945*. New York: Simon & Schuster, 2006.

Tillman, Barrett. *Clash of the Carriers: The True Story of the Marianas Turkey Shoot of World War II*. New York: New American Library, 2005.

United States Army Far East Command. *Central Pacific Air Operations Record*. Tokyo: N.p., 1953.

United States Army XXIV Corps. *Ryukyus: XXIV Corps Action Report, 1 April 1945–30 June 1945*. N.p., 1945.

Urwin, Gregory J. W. *Facing Fearful Odds: The Siege of Wake Island*. Lincoln: University of Nebraska Press, 1997.

U.S. Army Center of Military History. *The Capture of Makin, 20–24 November 1943*. Washington, D.C., 1990.

———. *Guam, Operations of the 77th Division, 21 July–10 August 1944*. Washington, D.C., 1990.

Van der Vat, Dan. *The Pacific Campaign: World War II, the U.S.-Japanese Naval War, 1941–1945*. New York: Simon & Schuster, 1991.

War Department Historical Division. *The Capture of Attu*. Washington, D.C.: Infantry Journal, 1944.

———. *The Capture of Makin, 20–24 November 1943*. Washington, D.C.: U.S. Army Center of Military History, 1990.

Werstein, Irving. *Okinawa: The Last Ordeal*. New York: Crowell, 1968.

Wheeler, Richard. *A Special Valor: The U.S. Marines and the Pacific War*. New York: Harper & Row, 1983.

Wilmott, H. P. *The Battle of Leyte Gulf: The Last Fleet Action*. Bloomington: Indiana University Press, 2005.

Wright, Burton, III. *Eastern Mandates*. Washington, D.C.: U.S. Army Center of Military History, 1993.

Wukovits, John F. *One Square Mile of Hell: The Battle for Tarawa*. 2006.

———. *Pacific Alamo: The Battle for Wake Island*. New York: New American Library, 2003.

# CBI (China-Burma-India)

Callahan, Raymond. *Burma, 1942–1945*. Newark: University of Delaware Press, 1978.

Dunlop, Richard. *Behind Japanese Lines, with the OSS in Burma*. Chicago: Rand McNally, 1979.

Feis, Herbert. *China Tangle: The American Effort in China from Pearl Harbor to the Marshall Mission*. Princeton, N.J.: Princeton University Press, 1953.

Hogan, David W. *India–Burma*. Washington, D.C.: U.S. Army Center of Military History, 1992.

Kraus, Theresa, L. *China Offensive*. Washington, D.C.: U.S. Army Center for Military History, 1996.

Newell, Clayton R. *Burma 1942*. Washington, D.C.: U.S. Army Center for Military History, 1994.

Ogburn, Charlton, Jr. *The Marauders*. New York: Harper and Brothers, 1956.

Schaller, Michael. *The U.S. Crusade in China, 1938–1945*. New York: Columbia University Press, 1979.

Sherry, Mark D. *China Defensive*. Washington, D.C.: U.S. Army Center for Military History, 1996.

Tuchman, Barbara. *Stilwell and the American Experience in China. 1911–1945*. New York: Macmillan, 1970.

U.S. Army Center of Military History. *Merrill's Marauders, February–May 1944*. Washington, D.C., 1990.

# Battle of the Atlantic

Hickam, Homer H. *Torpedo Junction: U-boat War off America's East Coast, 1942*. Annapolis, Md.: Naval Institute Press, 1989.

Middlebrook, Martin. *Convoy*. New York: William Morrow, 1976.

Monsarrat, Nicholas. *The Cruel Sea*. Short Hills, N.J.: Burford Books, 2000.

# Deception and Intelligence

Bennett, Ralph F. *Ultra and Mediterranean Strategy*. New York: Morrow, 1989.

Breuer, William B. *Hoodwinking Hitler: the Normandy Deception*. Westport, Conn.: Praeger, 1993.

Cruickshank, Charles G. *Deception in World War II*. New York: Oxford University Press, 1979.

Drea, Edward J. *MacArthur's ULTRA: Codebreaking and the War Against Japan, 1942–1945*. Lawrence: University Press of Kansas, 1991.

Gannon, Michael. *Operation Drumbeat: The Dramatic True Story of Germany's First U-boat Attacks Along the American Coast in World War II*. New York: Harper and Row, 1990.

Handel, Michael I., ed. *Strategic and Operational Deception in the Second World War*. London: F. Cass, 1987.

Hartcup, Guy. *Code Name Mulberry: The Planning, Building, and Operation of the Normandy Harbours*. New York: Hippocrene Books, 1977.

Haswell, Jock. *The Intelligence and Deception of the D-Day Landings*. London: Batsford, 1979.

Whiting, Charles. *Ardennes: The Secret War*. New York: Stein and Day, 1985.

Winterbotham, F. W. *The Ultra Secret.* New York: Harper and Row, 1974.

Winton, John. *Ultra in the Pacific.* Annapolis, Md.: Naval Institute Press, 1993.

# INTERNET RESOURCES

U.S. Army Center of Military History    www.army.mil/cmh-pg/

World War II Documents—The Avalon Project at Yale Law School    www.yale.edu/lawweb/avalon/wwii/wwii.htm

American Memory Project, Library of Congress (World War II maps)    www.memory.loc.gov.ammem/collections/maps/wwii

U.S. Army Air Forces in World War II    www.USAAF.net

Naval Historical Center    www.history.navy.mil

The Pacific War: U.S. Navy    www.microworks.net.pacific/

Hyperwar: World War II History and Recommended World War II Web sites    www.ibiblio.org/hyperwar

# INDEX

**Note:** All numbered military units appear in an initial section in numeric order; those numbered in Roman numerals (Corps) appear at the end of the section. In subheads, all military units are arranged in numeric order. *Italic* page numbers indicate illustrations. Page numbers followed by *b* denote biographies.